THE OXFORD HANDBOOK OF THE SOCIAL SCIENCE OF OBESITY

THE OXFORD HANDBOOK OF THE SOCIAL SCIENCE OF OBESITY

Edited by
John Cawley

OXFORD
UNIVERSITY PRESS

OXFORD
UNIVERSITY PRESS

Oxford University Press, Inc., publishes works that further
Oxford University's objective of excellence
in research, scholarship, and education.

Oxford New York
Auckland   Cape Town   Dar es Salaam   Hong Kong   Karachi
Kuala Lumpur   Madrid   Melbourne   Mexico City   Nairobi
New Delhi   Shanghai   Taipei   Toronto

With offices in
Argentina   Austria   Brazil   Chile   Czech Republic   France   Greece
Guatemala   Hungary   Italy   Japan   Poland   Portugal   Singapore
South Korea   Switzerland   Thailand   Turkey   Ukraine   Vietnam

Copyright © 2011 by Oxford University Press, Inc.

Published by Oxford University Press, Inc.
198 Madison Avenue, New York, New York 10016
www.oup.com

Oxford is a registered trademark of Oxford University Press

Library of Congress Cataloging-in-Publication Data

The Oxford handbook of the social science of obesity / edited by John Cawley.
    p. ; cm.
  Other title: Handbook of the social science of obesity
  Includes bibliographical references and index.
  ISBN 978-0-19-973636-2
  1. Obesity—Social aspects. 2. Social sciences. I. Cawley, John H. (John Horan) II. Title:
Handbook of the social science of obesity.
  [DNLM: 1. Obesity. 2. Social Sciences. 3. Socioeconomic Factors. WD 210]
  RA645.O23O96 2011
  362.196'398—dc22

                                                                    2010029662

ISBN-13: 9780195398625

1 3 5 7 9 8 6 4 2

Printed in the United States of America
on acid-free paper

Contents

PREFACE

Thank you for reading the *Handbook of the Social Science of Obesity*. The purpose of this Handbook is to provide an accurate and convenient summary of the findings and insights of obesity research from the full range of social sciences, including anthropology, economics, government, psychology, and sociology. This volume offers something that has never before existed: primers and crash courses on the study of obesity from a wide variety of disciplinary perspectives, written by the most accomplished and distinguished researchers.

I was delighted that Terry Vaughn of Oxford University Press immediately grasped the importance of this Handbook and, as editor, shepherded the proposal through external review and internal approval. I particularly appreciate that Terry was willing to make the case within Oxford University Press that this Handbook needed to be multidisciplinary, and managed to secure the necessary approval of five disciplinary delegates at OUP in order for the title of this volume to include the words "Social Science." Catherine Rae of Oxford University Press was unfailingly helpful in answering the scores of questions that arise in producing a volume such as this, and shepherded the volume through Oxford's internal editing and formatting process. Jenny Wolkowicki and Theresa Stockton were the expert production editors, and Kiran Kumar the project manager.

I thank Angelica Hammer for her careful and diligent work formatting the chapters. She took 47 chapters, written by 87 authors, which had been composed in different word processing programs and in a multitude of styles, and formatted them all to ensure that the Handbook looks like a single work instead of a patchwork quilt. I am grateful for the assistance of Sara Catterall of SMC Indexing, who read every page of this Handbook to create the index.

I thank John Lathrop for the creative and thoughtful cover art. He did an exceptional job depicting global disparities in weight while adhering to the style of cover art in the Oxford University Press Handbooks series.

I am grateful to Simone French, John Komlos, Shiriki Kumanyika, Jeff Sobal, and Mary Story, who suggested possible authors for some chapters.

I thank my coauthors on research on the economics of obesity, from whom I have learned so much: Rosemary Avery, Richard Burkhauser, Julie Carmalt,

Sheldon Danziger, Matt Eisenberg, Markus Grabka, Euna Han, Kara Joyner, Don Kenkel, Barrett Kirwan, Dean Lillard, Feng Liu, J. Catherine Maclean, Sara Markowitz, Chad Meyerhoefer, John Moran, David Newhouse, Edward Norton, Joshua Price, John Rizzo, Larissa Roux, Chris Ruhm, Max Schmeiser, Kosali Simon, Jeff Sobal, Katharina Spiess, Matt Sweeney, John Tauras, Jay Variyam and Stephanie von Hinke Kessler Scholder. A great joy of academic life is working with your friends, and I hope we collaborate on research again.

I will always be grateful to the Robert Wood Johnson Foundation's Scholars in Health Policy Research Program for its generous support, at an early stage of my career, of my research on the economics of obesity. The "Scholars Program" is committed to multidisciplinary and interdisciplinary research on health, and it is no coincidence that Program alumni (Rogan Kersh and Abigail Saguy) are represented among the authors of this Handbook.

I am fortunate to work in a multidisciplinary academic department that values cross-disciplinary communication. I sincerely appreciate the encouragement and support of my Dean, Alan Mathios, and my department chair, Rosemary Avery. Don Kenkel has been the ideal senior mentor, always ready to provide valuable insights and advice even while on sabbatical, and Richard Burkhauser has been an invaluable informal mentor as well as research collaborator.

On a personal note, I am always grateful for the love and support of my wife, Rachel Dunifon, and my sons Jimmy and Will. This Handbook is dedicated to you.

John Cawley

Contributors

Marc A. Adams is an Adjunct Professor in the Department of Psychology at San Diego State University and a Postdoctoral Fellow in the Department of Family and Preventive Medicine at the University of California, San Diego.

Patricia M. Anderson is a Professor in the Department of Economics at Dartmouth College in Hanover, New Hampshire, and a Research Associate at the National Bureau of Economic Research.

M. Christopher Auld is an Associate Professor in the Department of Economics at the University of Calgary in Calgary, Canada.

Susan L. Averett is the Charles A. Dana Professor of Economics in the Department of Economics at Lafayette College in Easton, Pennsylvania.

Didem Bernard is a Senior Economist at the Agency for Healthcare Research and Quality in the US Department of Health and Human Services in Rockville, Maryland.

Tamara Brown is a Research Fellow in Liverpool Reviews and Implementation Group, in the Department of Health Services Research at the University of Liverpool in Liverpool, England.

Kelly D. Brownell is a Professor in the Department of Psychology and Director of the Rudd Center for Food Policy & Obesity at Yale University in New Haven, Connecticut.

Sahara Byrne is an Assistant Professor in the Department of Communication at Cornell University in Ithaca, New York.

Paul Campos is a Professor of Law at the University of Colorado Law School in Boulder, Colorado.

Scott Alan Carson is a Professor of Economics at the University of Texas of the Permian Basin in Odessa, Texas.

Victoria A. Catenacci is an Assistant Professor in the Division of Endocrinology, Metabolism, and Diabetes and a Clinical Researcher in the Center for Human Nutrition at the University of Colorado, Denver, Colorado.

John Cawley is a Professor in the Department of Policy Analysis and Management at Cornell University in Ithaca, New York, and a Research Associate at the National Bureau of Economic Research.

Frank J. Chaloupka is a Distinguished Professor of Economics at the University of Illinois at Chicago in Chicago, Illinois.

Virginia W. Chang is an Assistant Professor of Medicine in the Division of General Internal Medicine at the University of Pennsylvania School of Medicine and Assistant Professor of Sociology at the University of Pennsylvania in Philadelphia, Pennsylvania.

Jamie F. Chriqui is a Senior Research Scientist at the Institute for Health Research and Policy and a Research Associate Professor in the Department of Political Science at the University of Illinois at Chicago in Chicago, Illinois.

Steven Cummins is a Senior Lecturer and a National Institute for Health Research Fellow in the Department of Geography at Queen Mary, University of London in London, England.

Ding Ding is a doctoral student in the Joint Doctoral Program in Public Health at San Diego State University and University of California San Diego.

Julie S. Downs is an Assistant Research Professor and the Director of the Center for Risk Perception and Communication at Carnegie Mellon University in Pittsburgh, Pennsylvania.

Dongyi (Tony) Du is a Food and Drug Administration Commissioner's Fellow in Silver Spring, Maryland.

Christina D. Economos is an Associate Professor in the Friedman School of Nutrition Science and Policy and the Associate Director of the John Hancock Research Center on Physical Activity, Nutrition, and Obesity Prevention (JHRC) at Tufts University in Boston, Massachusetts.

William Encinosa is a Researcher at the Agency for Healthcare Research and Quality in Rockville, Maryland and he is an Adjunct Associate Professor at the Georgetown University Public Policy Institute in Washington, District of Columbia.

E. Whitney Evans is a doctoral student in the Nutritional Epidemiology Program at Tufts University in Boston, Massachusetts.

Diane T. Finegood is a Professor in the Department of Biomedical Physiology and Kinesiology at Simon Fraser University in Burnaby, British Columbia, Canada.

Eric Finkelstein is an Associate Professor and the Deputy Director for the Health Services and Systems Research Program at the Duke-NUS Graduate Medical School in Singapore, Singapore.

Jason M. Fletcher is an Assistant Professor at the Yale School of Public Health in New Haven, Connecticut.

Ellen Granberg is an Associate Professor of Sociology at Clemson University in Clemson, South Carolina.

Ron Z. Goetzel is the Director of the Emory University Institute for Health and Productivity Studies in Washington, District of Columbia and Vice President of Consulting and Applied Research for Thomson Reuters in Washington, District of Columbia.

Penny Gordon-Larsen is an Associate Professor of Nutrition in the Gillings School of Global Public Health and the School of Medicine, and a Fellow of the Carolina Population Center at the University of North Carolina at Chapel Hill, North Carolina.

Paul Grootendorst is an Associate Professor and the Director of the Division of Clinical, Social and Administrative Pharmacy at the University of Toronto, Canada.

James O. Hill is a Professor of Pediatrics and Medicine and the Director of the Center for Human Nutrition at the University of Colorado in Denver, Colorado.

Christine L. Himes is the Maxwell Professor of Sociology and the Director of the Center for Policy Research at Syracuse University in Syracuse, New York.

Jeffrey M. Hunger is a graduate student in Experimental Psychology at the California State University in Fullerton, California.

Pauline M. Ippolito is the Deputy Director of the Bureau of Economics at the Federal Trade Commission in Washington, District of Columbia.

LaShanda R. Jones-Corneille is a Psychologist and Instructor in the Department of Psychiatry at the University of Pennsylvania in Philadelphia, Pennsylvania.

Ichiro Kawachi is a Professor and Chair in the Department of Society, Human Development and Health at the Harvard School of Public Health in Boston, Massachusetts.

Inas Rashad Kelly is an Assistant Professor in the Economics Department at Queens College of the City University of New York, in New York City, New York.

Rogan Kersh is an Associate Professor of Public Policy and the Associate Dean for Academic Affairs at the New York University Wagner in New York City, New York.

Barrett Kirwan is an Assistant Professor in the Department of Agricultural and Consumer Economics at the University of Illinois in Urbana-Champaign, Illinois.

Niranjana Kowlessar is a Researcher at Thomson Reuters, in Evanston, Illinois.

Tanja V. E. Kral is a Research Assistant Professor of Nutrition in Psychiatry at the University of Pennsylvania School of Medicine in Philadelphia, Pennsylvania.

Darius N. Lakdawalla is an Associate Professor in the School of Policy, Planning, and Development and the Director of Research at the Schaeffer Center for Health Policy and Economics at the University of Southern California in Los Angeles, California.

Rivka C. Liss-Levinson is a Research Project Coordinator in the Department of Health Policy and Management at Emory University in Washington, District of Columbia.

George Loewenstein is the Herbert A. Simon Professor of Economics and Psychology at Carnegie Mellon University in Pittsburgh, Pennsylvania.

Paul S. MacLean is an Associate Professor of Medicine in the Division of Endocrinology, Metabolism, and Diabetes and a Researcher in the Center for Human Nutrition at the University of Colorado in Denver, Colorado.

Traci Mann is an Associate Professor in the Department of Psychology at the University of Minnesota in Minneapolis, Minnesota.

Lindsay McLaren is an Assistant Professor in the Department of Community Health Sciences at the University of Calgary in Calgary, Canada.

Neil K. Metha is a Health and Society Scholar sponsored by the Robert Wood Johnson Foundation at the University of Michigan in Ann Arbor, Michigan.

James Morone is Professor and Chair of Political Science at Brown University in Providence, Rhode Island.

Ashley Moskovich is a graduate student in the Department of Psychology and Neuroscience at Duke University in Durham, North Carolina.

Aviva Must is the Morton A. Madoff Professor and Chair of Public Health and Community Medicine, as well as the Dean of the Public Health and Professional Degree Programs at Tufts University in Boston, Massachusetts.

Jeff Niederdeppe is an Assistant Professor in the Department of Communication at Cornell University in Ithaca, New York.

Lorri G. Ogden is an Associate Professor in the Department of Biostatistics and Informatics at the Colorado School of Public Health in Aurora, Colorado.

Xiaofei Pei is an Economist with Thomson Reuters in Washington, District of Columbia.

Tomas J. Philipson is the Daniel Levin Professor of Public Policy Studies at The Irving B. Harris Graduate School of Public Policy Studies at The University of Chicago in Chicago, Illinois.

Sarit Polsky is an Endocrine Fellow in the Division of Endocrinology, Metabolism, and Diabetes and a Clinical Researcher in the Center for Human Nutrition at the University of Colorado in Denver, Colorado.

Barry M. Popkin is the Carla Smith Chamblee Distinguished Professor of Global Nutrition and Director of the Interdisciplinary Center for Obesity at the University of North Carolina in Chapel Hill, North Carolina.

Richard A. Posner is a Judge in the United States Court of Appeals for the Seventh Circuit and a Senior Lecturer at the University of Chicago Law School in Chicago, Illinois.

Lisa M. Powell is a Research Professor in the Department of Economics and a Senior Research Scientist at the Institute for Health Research and Policy at the University of Illinois at Chicago in Chicago, Illinois.

Rebecca M. Puhl is a Research Scientist and Director of Research and Weight Stigma Initiatives at the Rudd Center for Food Policy & Obesity at Yale University in New Haven, Connecticut.

Christina A. Roberto is a graduate student in Clinical Psychology and Epidemiology and Public Health at Yale University in New Haven, Connecticut.

Enid Chung Roemer is an Assistant Research Professor at the Emory University Institute for Health and Productivity Studies in Washington, District of Columbia.

Barbara J. Rolls is the Helen A. Guthrie Chair and Professor in the Department of Nutritional Sciences at the Pennsylvania State University in University Park, Pennsylvania.

Esther D. Rothblum is a Professor of Women's Studies at San Diego State University in San Diego, California.

Larissa Roux is a Primary Care Sport Medicine Physician and Health Economist in Vancouver, British Columbia, Canada and a Consultant to the Division of Nutrition and Physical Activity at the United States Centers for Disease Control and Prevention in Atlanta, Georgia.

Abigail C. Saguy is an Associate Professor in the Department of Sociology at the University of California in Los Angeles, California.

James F. Sallis is a Professor in the Department of Psychology and the Director of Active Living Research at San Diego State University in San Diego, California.

Daniel Samoly is an Assistant Program Coordinator at the Emory University Institute for Health and Productivity Studies in Washington, District of Columbia.

Sarah A. Sliwa is a doctoral student in the John Hancock Research Center on Physical Activity, Nutrition, and Obesity Prevention (JHRC) at the Friedman School of Nutrition Science and Policy at Tufts University in Boston, Massachusetts.

Dianna Smith is a Medical Research Council Fellow in the Department of Geography at Queen Mary, University of London in London, England.

Jeffery Sobal is a Professor in the Division of Nutritional Sciences at Cornell University in Ithaca, New York.

Rebecca M. Stack, MPH, is a Dietetic Intern for ARAMARK Corporation.

Roland Sturm is a Senior Economist at the RAND Corporation in Santa Monica, California.

Maryam Tabrizi is a Researcher at Thomson Reuters in Washington, District of Columbia.

Amanda L. Thompson is an Assistant Professor in the Department of Anthropology and a Fellow of the Carolina Population Center at the University of North Carolina at Chapel Hill, North Carolina.

Khoa Truong is an Assistant Professor in the Department of Public Health Sciences at Clemson University in Clemson, South Carolina.

Elizabeth A. Vandewater is an Associate Professor in Health Promotion and Behavioral Sciences at the University of Texas School of Public Health in Austin, Texas.

Michele Ver Ploeg is an Economist in the Economic Research Service at the United States Department of Agriculture in Washington, District of Columbia.

Jessica Waddell is a Senior Analyst with Thomson Reuters in Washington, District of Columbia.

Thomas A. Wadden is a Professor of Psychology in Psychiatry at the University of Pennsylvania School of Medicine and Director of the Center for Weight and Eating Disorders in Philadelphia, Pennsylvania.

Renee E. Walker is a Kellogg Health Scholar and Yerby Postdoctoral Fellow in the Department of Society, Human Development and Health at the Harvard School of Public Health in Boston, Massachusetts.

Brian Wansink is the John S. Dyson Professor of Marketing and the Director of the Cornell Food and Brand Lab in the Charles H. Dyson School of Applied Economics and Management at Cornell University in Ithaca, New York.

Ellen A. Wartella is the Al-Thani Professor of Communication, Professor of Psychology and Human Development and Social Policy at Northwestern University in Evanston, Illinois.

Holly R. Wyatt is an Associate Professor in the Division of Endocrinology, Metabolism, and Diabetes and a Clinical Researcher in the Center for Human Nutrition at the University of Colorado in Denver, Colorado.

Hae Kyung Yang is an Assistant Professor in the College of Commerce and Economics at Konkuk University in Seoul, Korea.

Yuhui Zheng is a Research Fellow, Harvard Center for Population and Development Studies, Harvard University, Cambridge, MA.

CHAPTER 1

....

INTRODUCTION

....

JOHN CAWLEY

OVER the past several decades the prevalence of obesity has risen dramatically worldwide (see the chapters on the epidemiology and demography of obesity in this volume). This increase is of great public policy and public health significance because obesity is a major risk factor for early mortality as well as stroke, coronary heart disease, and diabetes, with roughly $147 billion spent annually treating obesity-related illness in the United States alone (see chapter 29 on obesity and medical costs in this volume). In addition to suffering physical health consequences, obese individuals are also at greater risk of low self-esteem and depression as well as stigma and discrimination (see chapter 33 on bias, stigma, and discrimination in this volume). There is an urgent need to better understand the causes and consequences of obesity, and to learn what works to prevent or reduce obesity.

Social scientists have responded to these research needs by studying a large number of potential causes and consequences of obesity as well as evaluating possible methods of prevention and treatment and policies to counter obesity. The number of articles published on the topic of obesity in each social science discipline has risen dramatically in the past decade. Figure 1.1 plots the number of publications with the keyword "obese," "obesity," or "overweight," by year (1998 through 2009) and discipline (economics, sociology, public affairs, and psychology). Between 1998 and 2009, the number of published articles on obesity rose 6,750 percent in economics, 642 percent in sociology, 1,700 percent in public affairs, and 693 percent in psychology. This growth in obesity research has yielded tremendously important insights into obesity, but its sheer volume has made it challenging for current researchers to stay up to date, and made it harder for younger researchers, or researchers coming to obesity from another field, to get up to speed on the current literature.

The chapters in this Handbook rationalize and synthesize these vast research literatures. The chapters also identify the most important things about obesity that

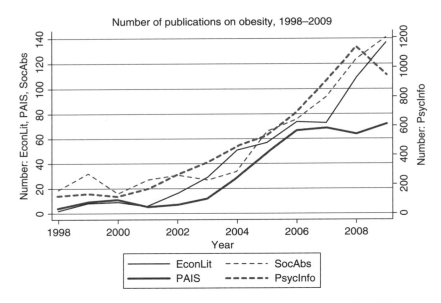

Figure 1.1. Number of publications on obesity, by year and discipline.
Notes: This graph shows the number of articles per year in which "overweight",
"obese", or "obesity" appeared as a keyword in the following types of journals:
economics (EconLit), sociology (Soc Abstracts), public affairs (PAIS), and psychology
(PsycInfo). The left-hand vertical axis corresponds to economics, sociology, and
public affairs, while the right-hand vertical axis corresponds to psychology.

we do not yet know; despite the large research literature, many important questions
remain unanswered. These gaps in research represent terrific directions for future
research. This Handbook is intended for researchers in every social science discipline, and serves to both bring them up to date on the relevant research in their own
discipline and allow them to quickly and easily understand the cutting-edge research
being produced by other disciplines. The research summaries in this Handbook are
also valuable for public health officials, policy makers, and medical practitioners.

Obesity is inherently a multidisciplinary problem, involving issues that are traditionally the subject of study by psychologists, sociologists, and economists, among
others. No one discipline has a monopoly on the answers. Each discipline interprets
the world using specific paradigms and is trained to use a specific set of tools. This
has some advantages; for example, specialization can lead to significant advances in
specific directions. However, it also has disadvantages; disciplines may unknowingly be working on complementary topics but fail to communicate and share
information. Cooperative opportunities that could lead to research breakthroughs
may be left unexploited as researchers fail to realize that they have complementary
pieces of the same puzzle. A goal of this Handbook is to provide a Rosetta Stone—
a single work that explains how different disciplines are approaching the same
topic—with the ultimate objective of facilitating discussion and collaboration
across disciplines in order to achieve research breakthroughs.

This Handbook is divided into five parts. Part I, Disciplinary Perspectives on Obesity, explains how each social science models human behavior (in particular, diet and physical activity), and summarizes the major strains of obesity research in that discipline. The section opens with chapters on epidemiology, demography, and cliometrics, as these provide readers with valuable information on the definition and prevalence of obesity, and how the prevalence of obesity has changed over time. All readers new to the study of obesity should begin with these chapters. Subsequent chapters summarize the perspectives and research findings in anthropology, psychology, sociology, economics, behavioral economics, politics, and the new field of fat studies.

Part II, Data and Methods, provides important practical information for researchers, including a guide to publicly available social science data on obesity, an introduction to the use of complex systems models to study obesity, and an overview of the challenges to causal inference in obesity research. It was difficult to decide which section of the book was most appropriate for the chapter on complex systems. It involves methods, certainly, but also represents a way of viewing the world, so in a sense it is similar to a disciplinary perspective. Ultimately I placed the complex systems chapter in the Methods section because I wanted it to be clear that one could take a complex systems approach informed by any or all of the disciplinary perspectives. It does not replace, but complements, the disciplinary perspectives described in Part I of the Handbook.

Part III, The Causes and Correlates of Diet, Physical Activity, and Obesity, synthesizes social science research on obesity and race and ethnicity, socioeconomic status, the nutrition transition, peer effects, maternal employment, depression and mental health, television and video games, portion sizes, mindless eating, food assistance programs, the built environment, food prices, income, food deserts, and agricultural policy.

Part IV, The Consequences of Obesity, summarizes social science research on the impact of obesity on medical costs, mortality, schooling, labor market outcomes, and discrimination and stigma. It also includes a chapter that offers a more skeptical viewpoint and challenges conventional wisdom on the harms of obesity.

Part V, Social Science Insights into Prevention, Treatment, and Policy, offers overviews of policy; for example, from the perspective of economics and drawing lessons from the public health campaign against smoking and the legal battle against cigarette companies. It also includes chapters that offer insights into policies and treatments such as food taxes and subsidies, school-based interventions, worksite interventions, community interventions, regulation of food advertising, public service messages, behavioral treatments, anti-obesity drugs, and bariatric surgery. It also summarizes the findings regarding the correlates of successful long-term weight loss and reviews the cost effectiveness of various anti-obesity interventions.

Some chapters overlap. Naturally, some of the disciplinary chapters discuss the causes and consequences that are explored in greater detail (and from multiple disciplinary perspectives) in later chapters. This is both intentional and desirable, as it allows one to both see obesity through a variety of disciplinary lenses, then examine the broader literatures on specific contributors to, and correlates of, obesity. Some chapters that are especially complementary and thus should be read in close succession include:

- anthropology (Thompson and Gordon-Larsen) and the nutrition transition (Popkin)
- race and ethnicity (Walker and Kawachi) and socioeconomic status (McLaren)
- food marketing, television, and video games (Vandewater and Wartella) and regulation of food advertising (Ippolito)
- mindless eating (Wansink) and portion sizes (Kral and Rolls)
- obesity politics and policy (Kersh and Morone), agricultural policy and childhood obesity (Cawley and Kirwan), and the imperative of changing public policy to address obesity (Roberto and Brownell)
- economics (Cawley), behavioral economics (Downs and Loewenstein), and economic perspectives on policy (Philipson and Posner)
- food prices (Lakdawalla and Zheng) and food taxes (Powell and Chriqui)
- psychology (Moskovich, Hunger, and Mann) and behavioral economics (Downs and Loewenstein)
- peer effects (Fletcher) and identification (Auld and Grootendorst)
- food deserts (Smith and Cummins), socioeconomic status (McLaren), and the built environment (Sallis, Adams, and Ding)
- medical costs (Finkelstein and Yang) and mortality (Mehta and Chang)
- labor market consequences (Averett) and bias, stigma, and discrimination (Puhl)
- fat studies (Rothblum) and debates over body weight (Saguy and Campos)
- community interventions (Economos and Sliwa) and complex systems models of obesity (Finegood)

I am delighted by the high quality of the chapters. This volume offers something that has never before existed: primers and crash courses on the study of obesity from a wide variety of disciplinary perspectives, written by the most accomplished and distinguished researchers. Specific chapters that to my knowledge do not exist in other forms include: Byrne and Niederdeppe's chapter on unintended consequences of public health messaging on obesity, Ippolito's chapter on the challenges in regulating food advertising, Finegood's chapter on complex systems models of obesity, Kelly's chapter that summarizes the publicly available data on obesity, and the chapter by Auld and Grootendorst on challenges to identification in the study of obesity.

The research syntheses contained here include findings that I suspect will surprise many people. Mehta and Chang point out that the mortality penalty associated with obesity has been falling in recent decades, a fact rarely mentioned in the discussion of obesity as a public health crisis. They also discuss how in current data the relationship between obesity and mortality is complex; although class II and III obesity are associated with elevated mortality risk, overweight and class I obesity are generally not associated with higher mortality. Moreover, the associations that do exist decrease with age to the point that weight becomes protective in the elderly. Another finding that may surprise some people is that, as Ippolito points out, American children's exposure to television advertisements for food declined between 1977 and 2004.

Another theme in this Handbook is that research findings can vary widely based on geography, age, race, and socioeconomic status. For example: although it is conventional wisdom that the poor are more likely to be obese, McLaren points out that the evidence is quite mixed, and that overall an association between poverty and obesity exists for women, but not men, in developed countries. The association of socioeconomic status (SES) and obesity varies by measure of SES (e.g., income and education) and between developed and developing countries. Smith and Cummins describe widely varying findings regarding food deserts (areas with few grocery stores or other sources of healthy foods), with disagreement over whether British inner cities are food deserts, whether food is more expensive there, and what impact food availability has on diet. Sallis and colleagues point out that street connectivity is positively correlated with physical activity for adults (e.g., the elderly walk to their local market) but negatively correlated with physical activity for children (e.g., youths are more likely to ride bikes in cul-de-sacs where there is no through traffic). Granberg describes how the relationship between obesity and depression is complex; it differs by age, gender, socioeconomic status, race, degree of obesity, and nation.

In some cases, findings are remarkably consistent and robust. Puhl discusses the evidence that men find obese women unattractive. For example, surveys indicate that obese women are considered less attractive sex partners than women who are in wheelchairs, are missing an arm, have a history of mental illness or sexually transmitted diseases. Also, men are more likely to respond to a dating ad from women with a history of drug problems than to an ad from a woman who is obese. Truong and Sturm present evidence on another consistent finding: that obese children score significantly lower on academic tests than healthy-weight children. This finding is robust for both genders, in different grades (kindergarten, first, third, and fifth), and for each subject (science, math, and reading). Encinosa, Du, and Bernard discuss the startlingly good outcomes associated with bariatric surgery, such as rapid improvement or even resolution of high blood pressure and Type II diabetes in almost all patients, and decreased mortality relative to a control group that is morbidly obese but did not get surgery.

It is my hope as editor that this Handbook will be a valuable reference for a wide variety of researchers. In particular, I would be delighted if this work encouraged communication and collaboration across disciplines, and provided guidance and research ideas for graduate students, the next generation of scholars.

PART I

DISCIPLINARY PERSPECTIVES ON OBESITY

CHAPTER 2

THE EPIDEMIOLOGY OF OBESITY

AVIVA MUST AND E. WHITNEY EVANS

EPIDEMIOLOGY: A PUBLIC HEALTH DISCIPLINE

ONE contemporary definition states that epidemiology is "the study of the distribution and determinants of disease frequency in human populations and the application of this study to control health problems" (Last 1995). To study the distribution and determinants of disease, epidemiology is considered one of two basic tools of public health (biostatistics is the other). Epidemiology is employed in public health settings for disease prevention and health promotion at the population level. With the emergence of chronic disease and a wave of newly characterized infectious disease in human populations, research using epidemiologic approaches has exploded over the last 50 years.

In many ways, however, epidemiology is an old discipline, one that can be traced back more than 2,000 years. In 400 B.C.E., Hippocrates laid the groundwork for epidemiology in his text *On Ancient Medicine*, when he acknowledged that environmental exposures, particularly diet, contributed to disease (Hippocrates 400 B.C.E.). In the mid-1600s, John Graunt, a London tradesman considered to be the first epidemiologist, published *Natural and Political Observations Mentioned in a*

Following Index, and Made upon the Bills of Mortality, in which he tabulated the Bills of Mortality and drew inferences about the patterns of morbidity and death in London. Graunt was the first person to track birth and death statistics, making observations on new diseases and causes of death (Aschengrau and Seage 2003). Other early contributors to the field of epidemiology include James Lind, who identified the cause of scurvy; William Farr, who first used mathematics to describe disease occurrence; and John Snow, who discovered that contaminated water was the cause of cholera in London in the mid-1800s (Aschengrau and Seage 2003). Epidemiology expanded from a discipline focused on infectious disease to include chronic disease through the work of Richard Doll and A. Bradford Hill, whose landmark study on smoking and lung cancer was among the first to suggest that chronic disease could result from environmental exposures and not simply due to aging—an important observation in that it implied that chronic disease was potentially preventable (Doll and Hill 1950).

Throughout the evolution of their field, epidemiologists have remained focused on the study of disease patterns in natural populations such as communities or nations. To do so, they rely on three branches of epidemiologic study: descriptive, analytical, and experimental. Descriptive epidemiology examines disease patterns in an effort to identify the person, place, and time patterns of disease, with methodology that heavily borrows from demography. Descriptive epidemiology can be used to answer such questions as: Who is getting disease?, Where is the disease most prevalent?, and, What is the time course of the disease? (Aschengrau and Seage 2003). Analytical epidemiology is used to study associations between exposures and disease in order to identify causes of and treatments for disease. Descriptive epidemiology and analytical epidemiology are commonly described as "observational" because researchers passively observe free-living individuals (Friedman 1994). In contrast, the key identifying characteristic of experimental epidemiology is that exposures are allocated by the researcher to test specific prevention or treatment strategies. Typically, an epidemiologic approach to disease begins with descriptive epidemiology, which informs analytic observational epidemiologic studies, and culminates in the development of preventive and therapeutic interventions (experimental epidemiology), which in turn inform public health policy.

As obesity rates have increased over the last three decades, activity in the area of "obesity epidemiology" has grown in parallel (Hu 2008). Obesity epidemiology uses descriptive, analytical, and experimental epidemiologic approaches to examine the distribution and determinants of and outcomes from obesity. Using the classic "person, place, and time" framework, descriptive epidemiology examines whom obesity affects, where it occurs, and how it is changing over time, in an effort to characterize the distribution of obesity using methods similar to those utilized by the founders of epidemiology. Identifying the determinants or causes of obesity is the focus of analytic epidemiology. This work, while still largely incomplete, is used to develop public health and clinical interventions aimed at reducing the occurrence of obesity.

BASIC EPIDEMIOLOGIC MEASURES OF OBESITY

Definitions of Obesity in Adults and Children

In order to characterize the descriptive epidemiology of obesity, a widely accepted, standardized obesity definition is needed in order to make valid comparisons between groups and over time. At present, all criteria recommended by national bodies (Cole, Bellizzi, et al. 2000) and the World Health Organization (2007) are based on body mass index (BMI), which is calculated as weight in kilograms divided by height in meters squared, as the primary measure used to identify obesity in both adults and children. BMI is an imperfect measure of excess adiposity, in that it does not distinguish between excess body fat and lean mass. Despite the likelihood of misclassification of a small percentage of individuals whose high BMI is due to lean muscle mass, the great majority of individuals with high BMI have excess body fat. Further, given the strong link between elevated BMI and adverse health consequences (Must, Spadano, et al. 1999), it is the most commonly used measure for assessing weight status in epidemiologic studies. BMI is a highly practical measure, as height and weight are routinely collected in health-related studies, and other more accurate measures have limited use in large population studies due to their invasiveness, expense, and availability (Clasey, Kanaley, et al. 1999). In large epidemiologic studies, height and weight are often self-reported, which can be a source of misclassification, as adults often underreport their weight and overreport their height (Chang and Christakis 2001). Yet, for the purposes of large epidemiological studies, BMI's advantages outweigh its limitations.

Diagnostic criteria for obesity differ according to age and, to a lesser extent, by race/ethnicity. The World Health Organization (WHO) defines overweight in adults as a BMI of 25.0 to 29.9, and obesity at a BMI > 30 kg/m². These measures are used worldwide, except in Asia, where the Working Group on Obesity in China recommended lower cutoff points (BMI of 24.0 to 27.9 as overweight, > 28.0 as obese) (Zhou 2002), based on a review of evidence suggesting increased disease risk at lower BMI. For children, establishing criteria is more complicated due to the natural variation in BMI with growth. The International Obesity Task Force (IOTF), established in 1994 to address the worldwide obesity epidemic, concluded that BMI offers a reasonable measure of body fatness in children and adolescents as well (Dietz and Bellizzi 1999). Several countries, such as the United States and United Kingdom, have developed population-specific reference standards, and they are under development elsewhere (Cole, Bellizzi, et al. 2000; Barlow 2007). To aid in international comparisons, the IOTF used population-based data on children in the United States, United Kingdom, Hong Kong, the Netherlands, Singapore, and Brazil to develop an international BMI reference that links childhood and adolescent BMI centiles to adult cutoffs of BMI > 30 kg/m² (Cole, Bellizzi, et al. 2000).

The WHO has also developed a set of international reference standards for boys and girls ages 5–19 years (World Health Organization 2007). These international standards are not generally recommended to define obesity at the individual level, but provide a useful metric for international comparisons (Must and Anderson 2006).

Occurrence Measures of Obesity

To monitor disease trends, a third element, disease frequency or occurrence, is considered in concert with determinants and distribution. Measures of occurrence are used by epidemiologists to study the distribution of obesity. The most commonly used measures of occurrence are prevalence and incidence, where prevalence is the proportion of individuals with disease at a particular point in time, and incidence measures the number of new cases that have developed within a population over a specific time period. With respect to obesity, prevalence data provide an epidemiological snapshot of what proportion of the population is obese at a single point in time. National cross-sectional surveys, such as National Health and Nutrition Examination Survey (NHANES) in the United States or the Health Survey for England in the United Kingdom, among many others, provide periodic data on the prevalence of obesity. Incidence, as measured by cumulative incidence (sometimes called simply incidence) or incidence density, is considered the purest measure of disease occurrence because it is unaffected by duration of disease. In the context of obesity, incidence measures an individual's risk of becoming obese by following non-obese individuals and counting who becomes obese over a specific period of time. Cumulative incidence, then, represents the proportion of an initially non-obese study population that develops obesity over a given period of time. Incidence density measures the instantaneous rate at which obesity develops by observing who becomes obese over a specific period of time and accounts for the number of disease-free years each individual contributes. Because obesity incidence must be assessed over time, estimates of obesity incidence most often derive from prospective cohort studies, such as the Framingham Heart Study in the United States or the Avon Longitudinal Study of Pregnancy and Childhood (ALSPAC) in the United Kingdom.

The prevalence of obesity is the measure commonly reported in the epidemiologic literature because these data are readily collected through surveys or cross-sectional studies. However, because prevalence reflects the obesity burden within a specific population at one point in time, it provides no information about how the disease develops. Both cumulative incidence and incidence density data can be interpreted in the context of risk, that is, who is at risk for becoming obese? Estimates of obesity risk based on incidence data can be especially valuable because they are easily understood by the public and may be more powerful in public health messages because they estimate an individual's probability of becoming obese over the remainder of his or her life or over another specific time period. Incidence measures are less common in the descriptive epidemiologic literature, however, because they are expensive to obtain given the nature of prospective longitudinal studies. Furthermore, unlike other disease states, individuals can move in and out of the obese state, which complicates interpretation of incidence.

Prevalence of Obesity in Adults

According to the WHO, approximately 400 million adults (age 15 and older) were obese worldwide in 2005 (World Health Organization 2006). Using the WHO definition for adult obesity of BMI ≥ 30 kg/m², the prevalence of obesity in countries around the world is listed in table 2.1 (World Health Organization 2009).

Table 2.1. Prevalence of Obesity in Adults (aged >15 years) in the WHO Member Nations (2000–2007)

Country	Obesity Prevalence (%)		Country	Obesity Prevalence (%)	
	Males	Females		Males	Females
Australia	20.6	25.5	Jordan	21.1	20.1
Azerbijan	4.9	17.9	Malaysia	10.1	18.8
Belgium	11.9	13.4	Mexico	24.2	34.5
Brazil	8.9	13.1	Morocco	8.2	11
Bulgaria	11.3	23.1	Netherlands	10.2	11.9
Canada	22.9	23.2	Peru	11.5	12.5
Chile	19	25	Poland	15.7	19.9
China	2.4	3.4	Portugal	15	13.4
Colombia	8.8	16.6	Romania	7.7	9.5
Czech Republic	13.7	16.3	Russian Federation	11.8	20.1
Denmark	11.8	11	Saudi Arabia	26.4	44
Finland	16	14	Slovakia	13.5	15
France	16.1	17.6	South Africa	8.8	27.4
Germany	20.5	21.1	Spain	13	13.5
Greece	26	18.2	Sweden	11	14
Hungary	17.1	18.2	Switzerland	7.9	7.5
India	1.3	2.8	Syria	15.5	27.7
Indonesia	1.1	3.6	Thailand	3.3	10.2
Iran	9.1	19.2	United Kingdom	22.3	23
Israel	19.8	25.4	USA	31.1	33.2
Italy	7.4	8.9	Uzbekistan	5.4	7.1
Japan	2.9	3.3			

Source: Data from World Health Organization 2009.

These data are not directly comparable across countries due to differences in sampling methods, age ranges (some countries define adulthood at age 15, while others use age 18) and because the years of data collection differ; nonetheless, they illustrate, albeit crudely, the extent and severity of the global obesity epidemic. One-third of the countries listed in table 2.1 have obesity rates greater than 20 percent. This level of obesity is especially concerning when considered in the context of secular trends in obesity prevalence, which is discussed further below.

Prevalence of Pediatric Obesity

The IOTF estimates suggest that 10 percent of the world's school-age children are overweight and that at least a quarter of these children are obese (Lobstein, Baur, et al. 2004). The 2005–2006 Health Behaviour in School-Aged Children (HBSC) study, an international study conducted in collaboration with the WHO, reported obesity prevalence in school-age youth in 41 countries around the world using a standardized obesity definition across all populations (BMI > 30 kg/m^2) (Haug, Rasmussen, et al. 2009). The maps of Europe and North America, shown in figure 2.1, suggest that obesity prevalence is highest in the United States, Great Britain, and the countries of southwestern Europe. These data suggest that obesity is a significant public health problem for much of the Western world (Haug, Rasmussen, et al. 2009).

Data from other parts of the world suggest that obesity is not just a problem in the West. Estimates from Beijing and Shanghai, China, suggest that the prevalence of overweight and obesity in 7- to 12-year-old boys was 29 percent and 15–17 percent in girls of the same age in the year 2000 (Chen 2008). A cross-sectional study of 2008 Indian schoolchildren aged 9–15 years suggested that the overall prevalence of obesity and overweight was 11.1 percent and 14.2 percent, respectively (Chhatwal, Verma, et al. 2004). A review of published studies in child overweight and obesity between 1980 and 2005 suggests that pediatric overweight and obesity have increased in almost all countries for which data are available (Wang and Lobstein 2006).

Incidence of Obesity in Adults and Children

Despite the difficulty of collecting and interpreting them, incidence data across different age groups are needed to determine when over the life-course public health or clinical intervention may have the most impact. Data from 4,117 non-obese, white participants enrolled in the Framingham Heart Study suggest that the long-term (10 to 30 years) obesity risk for both men and women exceeds 25 percent for a BMI ≥ 30 kg/m^2 and is approximately 10 percent for a BMI ≥ 35 kg/m^2 (Vasan, Pencina, et al. 2005). In a cohort study of individuals born in Helsinki, Finland, researchers followed 4,515 subjects from birth (1934–1944) to year 2000 and estimated a cumulative incidence of obesity of approximately one-third of men and of women (Eriksson, Forsen, et al. 2003). In a population of African origin conducted in the West Indies (The Barbados Eye Studies), the nine-year incidence of obesity for adult men and women was 10 percent (Nemesure, Wu, et al. 2008).

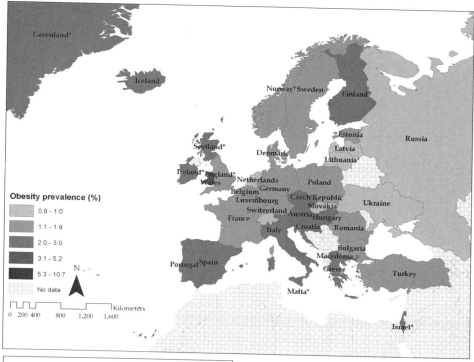

Figure 2.1. Geographic Prevalence of Pediatric Obesity in Europe and North America.
Source: Data adapted from (Haug, Rasmussen, et al. 2009).

Taken together, these three studies suggest that adults may have a risk of becoming obese during adulthood between 10–25 percent and greater than 30 percent risk of becoming obese over their lifetime.

Incidence data for the pediatric period are sparse as well. In a cohort of adolescents in the United States, the National Longitudinal Study of Adolescent Health, the five-year obesity incidence was 12.7 percent using the IOTF reference standards to define obesity (Gordon-Larsen, Adair, et al. 2004). These data, when considered along with the finding that fewer than 2 percent of the total sample who were obese as adolescents shifted to become non-obese as young adults, suggest that the probability of adolescents remaining obese into early adulthood is high. Although studies suggest that up to 70 percent of obese adolescents become obese adults, it should be noted that obesity is more likely to persist into adulthood for older children, severely obese children, and for children with at least one obese parent (Guo, Roche, et al. 1994; Whitlock, Williams, et al. 2005). Nonetheless, age-specific prevalence data do not suggest that the prevalence of obesity increases with age across childhood, which indicates the rate of remission is also high.

DESCRIPTIVE EPIDEMIOLOGY

In an effort to characterize the person, place, and time distribution of a disease such as obesity, epidemiologists primarily employ two study designs: ecological and cross-sectional. Both study designs examine the relationship between diseases or outcomes and other variables of interest at a specific point in time, but in an ecological study, the unit of observation is the population or whole community, whereas in a cross-sectional study, the unit of observation is the individual (Aschengrau and Seage 2003). Thus, in an ecological study, rates of exposure and disease are known for a whole population, whereas in a cross-sectional or prevalence study, exposure and disease status are known at the individual level. Both study designs allow researchers to screen for associations and generate hypotheses for subsequent studies.

Pattern of Obesity by Person, Place, and Time

Much of the descriptive epidemiology literature suggests that obesity affects individuals differentially with respect to age, gender, socioeconomic status (SES), and race/ethnicity. Research from the United States and Latin America suggests that women are more likely to be obese than men, whereas a study of 19 European countries found that the average prevalence of obesity was 11 percent in both women and men (Kain, Vio, et al. 2003; Roskam, Kunst, et al. 2009; Ogden, Flegal, et al. 2002). This difference may be attributable to differing effects of socioeconomic status (SES). A recent review of the relationship between SES and obesity found that for women in highly developed societies, lower SES was associated with obesity, whereas for women in less developed countries, high SES was associated with overweight and obesity (McLaren 2007). For example, in the United Kingdom, obesity is more prevalent in low-income populations, where as in Brazil, obesity tends to increase with income level (Roskam, Kunst, et al. 2009; Monteiro, Conde, et al. 2001). In men, the relationship between SES and obesity is rarely demonstrated, which may reflect gender differences in how body habitus is valued, especially in higher SES populations. For men, a larger body size may be valued as a sign of power and privilege (McLaren 2007).

In the United States, obesity prevalence varies by race, and this variation is most pronounced in women and children. Data from NHANES (1999–2008) suggest that almost 50 percent of non-Hispanic black women were obese, compared with about 33 percent of non-Hispanic white women of the same age (Flegal, Carroll, et al. 2010). In men, the racial differences were less pronounced, but obesity rates still varied from 37 percent in non-Hispanic black men to 32 percent among non-Hispanic white men (Flegal, Carroll, et al. 2010). Although disentangling SES differences from racial/ethnic differences is challenging, it is clear that obesity affects individuals of all ages, race/ethnicities, incomes, and both males and females to differing degrees.

With respect to "place," the descriptive epidemiology suggests that obesity affects people all over the world, as seen in table 2.1 and figure 2.1, and those living in rural and urban areas. Given the lifestyle differences of an urban versus rural life, one would assume that obesity would be more prevalent in urban populations. However, a recent study of adults aged 50–79 years in ten European countries found no differences in the prevalence of overweight and obesity between urban and rural areas (Peytremann-Bridevaux, Faeh, et al. 2007). Further, in a study of children living in urban and rural settings in Greece, no significant differences in BMI or body fat were observed (Tsimeas, Tsiokanos, et al. 2005). Results from a comprehensive study of women aged 15–49 years from 38 developing countries suggest that a country's overall economy may impact the relationship between place of residence and obesity. Obesity levels were found to be concentrated in urban areas as compared with rural areas in poorer countries in Sub-Saharan Africa and Southern Asia, whereas in more developed countries such as the United States, Mexico, Egypt, and Brazil no significant differences in obesity prevalence were found between urban and rural areas (Martorell, Kahn, et al. 2000).

Urbanization and modernization are associated with reduced physical activity and greater access to low-cost, energy-dense foods, so it follows that obesity was initially considered a condition of the developed world. Over the last few decades, however, obesity has become prevalent in the developing world as well (Hossain, Kawar, et al. 2007). The rise of obesity in developing countries is attributed to the documented dietary shift toward characteristically higher dietary fat and refined carbohydrate content and concomitant reductions in physical activity that are associated with advanced technology and mechanized transportation (Kim and Popkin 2000; Bell, Ge, et al. 2002). Although these factors explain the energy imbalance at the core of obesity development, understanding the mechanisms underlying the emergence of obesity in countries where protein-energy malnutrition is still prevalent is complicated by the link between under-nutrition early in life and obesity in adulthood (Popkin and Bisgrove 1988). In an apparent paradox, in some developing countries, such as Brazil and Mexico, it is not uncommon to find families in which children are underweight while the adults are overweight or obese (de Menezes Toledo Florencio, da Silva Ferreira, et al. 2001; Barquera, Peterson, et al. 2007). Given the existing data from developing and developed countries as well as that from urban and rural areas, it appears that populations worldwide are vulnerable to obesity.

Trend data, where they exist, suggest that obesity prevalence has increased dramatically in recent decades worldwide. In the United States, obesity rates among adults aged 18 and older have more than doubled since 1980, as data from the 1976–1980 NHANES estimated that 15 percent of the population were obese, while the most recent data from 2007–2008 NHANES show that 32 percent of men and 35.5 percent of women in the United States were obese (Flegal, Carroll, et al. 2002, 2010). In the United Kingdom, 24 percent of all adults (aged 16 and older) were obese in 2007, whereas only 15 percent were obese in 1993 (The Health and Social Care Information Centre 2009). Similarly, in Mexico, 9.4 percent of women (aged 18–49 years) were obese in 1988, and by 1999, only 11 years later, the percentage of obese women more than doubled to 24.4 percent (Arroyo, Loria, et al. 2000). In China, using the cutoff of BMI > 28 kg/m² as criteria for obesity, it is estimated that prevalence of obesity increased by 80.6 percent from 1992 to 2002 (Ma, Li, et al. 2005).

The prevalence of pediatric obesity has increased in both industrialized and non-industrialized nations over the last two decades as well (Deckelbaum and Williams 2001). In the United States, comparing NHANES data from 2003–2006 to those of the 1960s suggests that the prevalence of pediatric obesity in children ages 2 to 19 has tripled from 4–5 percent to 16.9 percent (Ogden, Flegal, et al. 2002; Ogden, Carroll, et al. 2008). In the United Kingdom, obesity has increased from 11 percent in 1995 to 17 percent in 2007 in boys and from 12 percent in 1995 to 16 percent in 2007 in girls (The Health and Social Care Information Centre 2007). A similar trend has been seen in China, where national surveys from 1985 and 1995 suggest that in the most developed Chinese cities, the prevalence of obesity has increased from 0.2 percent to 6–8 percent in boys and from 0.1 percent to 4–6 percent in girls ages 7–18 years (Ji, Sun, et al. 2004). While the prevalence of pediatric obesity differs between the United States or United Kingdom and China, all three countries have experienced prevalence trends indicative of a pandemic.

ANALYTIC EPIDEMIOLOGY

Analytical epidemiology studies associations between exposures and outcomes in an effort to establish the etiology of a given disease. Thus, while descriptive epidemiology characterizes the frequency and distribution (who, where, when?) of disease, analytical epidemiology is concerned with identifying the disease determinants (why, how?) (Friis and Sellers 1996). This is accomplished through the observational study of free-living individuals where exposure status is considered

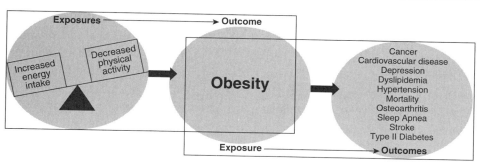

Figure 2.2. Antecedents and Outcomes of Obesity.

"self-selected," and is in contrast to experimental study designs, discussed in the following section.

A unique aspect of obesity is that in studying its etiology, one must also consider that a distinguishing characteristic of obesity is that it can be viewed both as an outcome (like other disease states) or as an exposure (risk factor) for other diseases. As shown in figure 2.2, obesity itself is a disease or outcome, and it can also increase one's risk for other diseases.

Where obesity is considered an outcome, analytic epidemiology seeks to answer questions such as, "What factors account for the high or low prevalence of obesity in a given group?" In situations where obesity is considered as an exposure (or risk/ protective factor), one might ask, "Does the presence of obesity increase the risk of disease X?" Several different study designs can be used to answer these questions, including cross-sectional, case-control, and cohort. Cross-sectional studies can be descriptive or analytic, depending on whether they are designed to test a specific a priori hypothesis (Gehlbach 1988). Cohort studies are commonly used in analytic obesity epidemiology. The incidence of obesity is compared across groups defined by levels of exposure, such as a dietary factor, or rates of disease are compared across groups defined by their weight status. Measures of disease frequency, such as prevalence, cumulative incidence, or incidence density, are compared through estimation of risk or rate differences, risk ratios, rate ratios, or odds ratios. These comparisons are referred to as measures of association or effect (Aschengrau and Seage 2003).

To establish valid associations between exposures and outcomes based on observational studies, the epidemiologist must minimize bias and confounding, either of which would distort study findings. Bias is used to describe any systematic error present in a study that results in an incorrect or invalid estimate of the measure of association. Bias typically results from the way subjects are selected, the manner in which study variables are measured or assessed, or from an uncontrolled confounding factor(s) (Rothman 2002). Confounding occurs when an association between an exposure and an outcome is influenced, wholly or in part, by a third factor (the confounder) that is both an independent risk factor for the outcome and associated with the exposure under study. Confounding is a particular problem in observational studies because risk factors, such as lifestyle factors, tend to co-occur within subjects. For example, in the relationship between obesity and coronary heart disease (CHD) mortality, smoking is considered a potential confounder because it is itself a risk factor for CHD mortality, and associated (negatively, in this case) with obesity (smokers tend to be thinner than non-smokers). Failure to account for smoking would underestimate the effect of obesity on CHD mortality because some of the deaths ascribed to low weight status would in fact be due to smoking. Confounding can be addressed in the design of the study (by restricting the study to non-smokers, for example), or at the analysis stage (by statistical adjustment for smoking or stratification by smoking status groups). Of course, in order to address confounding, one must know what factors could be confounding the exposure-outcome relationship and, if the plan is to adjust for them at the analysis stage, to collect valid data on them. Confounding factors bias or distort the association between the exposure and outcome within a study and represent a major threat to validity in observational studies.

Establishing Causation: The Determinants of Obesity

As a multifactorial condition, apart from a few rare genetic mutations, obesity is usually the result of several co-occurring metabolic, lifestyle, diet, environmental, and psychosocial factors. Inasmuch as a central goal of epidemiology is to identify which exposures cause and prevent disease, epidemiologists have offered various frameworks and guidelines to assess causation. In one such framework, three types of causes are distinguished: necessary, contributing, and sufficient. A necessary cause is one that must be present in order for an outcome to develop in a causal manner. A contributing cause is one that increases the risk of development of a given outcome, but is not required for its development. The level of sufficient cause is reached when all necessary and contributory causes, which are referred to as component causes, are present to bring about that outcome in a given individual. From one perspective, the only necessary cause for obesity is an energy imbalance: consuming more calories than are expended. Accordingly, some of the rare genetic mutations that cause obesity, such as mutations in the melanocortin receptors or the *ob* mutation on the *LEP* gene that block leptin production, are examples of sufficient causes, as they lead to an energy imbalance by promoting hyperphagia (Loos and Bouchard 2003). That obesity is a complex, multifactorial disease reflects the existence of many sufficient causes, each comprised of non-unique component causes. Additional considerations include the timing of action, sequencing, and "dose" of component causes.

The challenges of establishing causation in the absence of a controlled experiment have been appreciated since the science of epidemiology was young. In 1965, Sir Austin Bradford Hill published nine criteria for establishing causation from studies of association. They include strength of association, consistency of observed evidence, a temporal relationship between exposure and outcome, and biological plausibility, among others. Controversial from the time of their introduction, many epidemiologists argue that the only essential criterion is temporality—that the exposure must precede an outcome to be a cause (Rothman 2002). Others argue that, in his original work, Hill promoted the application of his criteria to emphasize that practical significance is not ensured by statistical significance (Phillips and Goodman 2004). Instead, Hill and other epidemiologists challenge researchers to critically evaluate associations found in observational research and consider that associations may be due to chance or bias, and, even if real, may not represent a cause-effect relationship (Newman, Browner, et al. 1988). Thus, in studying a complex disease like obesity, studies are often repeated several times before findings are used to inform intervention strategies.

Family studies, including those of twins, provide strong support that genetics plays a role in obesity development (Flier 2004). Given that the human genome has not changed substantially over the last three decades during which obesity prevalence has increased, one can reasonably conclude that obesity is the result of the interaction of genetic and environmental exposures. In a causal model, the genetic factors would be necessary, but not sufficient, to produce obesity in the absence of specific environmental characteristics. Environmental shifts over the last three decades, such as global modernization, appear to provide the contributing factors needed to interact with genetics to produce obesity and the observed rise in prevalence.

Diet, physical activity, and sedentary behaviors have emerged as the primary proximal behaviors (contributing factors) that give rise to the energy imbalance necessary to cause obesity in genetically susceptible individuals. Studying the relationship between nutrient and food intake, dietary patterns, and obesity in epidemiologic studies is hampered by the challenges of dietary measurement. The field of nutritional epidemiology, which concerns itself with the relations between dietary factors and occurrence of specific diseases, has evolved a battery of dietary assessment tools to attempt to address these challenges (Willett 1998). Commonly used dietary assessment tools include food frequency questionnaires, 24-hour recalls diet histories, and diet records, all of which are subject to error, particularly as implemented in large epidemiologic studies (Barrett-Connor 1991). When exposure groups are defined based on characteristics measured with error, the resulting misclassification biases estimates of relative risk toward the null. The myriad challenges in the measurement of diet (as well as physical activity and sedentary behavior) likely dampen effect estimates observed, and result in the null findings seen in many epidemiologic studies of obesity (Kipnis, Subar, et al. 2003). Nonetheless, the first law of thermodynamics, that increased energy intake in the presence of constant or decreased energy expenditure is required for obesity to develop, is unquestionable. Key dietary factors that appear to contribute to weight gain include increased total energy, total fat, added sugars and sugar-sweetened beverages, most of which can be attributed to eating more meals outside the home, choosing more convenience or processed foods, and lower dietary intake of fiber, milk, fruits, and non-starchy vegetables (Must, Hollander, et al. 2006).

Similarly, advances in technology and transportation, which have led to decreased physical activity for work or transport and have increased sedentary behavior, have also contributed to the development of obesity (Hill and Peters 1998). For example, increased use of computers, video games, and television (collectively referred to as screen time) have been associated with obesity development, particularly in children (Gortmaker, Must, et al. 1996). Screen time may contribute to obesity through decreased energy expenditure, or through increased energy intake due to snacking while viewing or through the effects on intake of increased exposure to advertisements for high-calorie foods (Crespo, Smit, et al. 2001; Matheson, Killen, et al. 2004). Like dietary assessment, misclassification is also common in epidemiologic studies that measure activity levels, as the tools used to measure physical activity, including accelerometers, pedometers, heart rate monitors, and direct observation, all have limitations as well. The measurement of sedentary behavior is complicated by the blending of media, the presence of televisions in fitness clubs, as well as video game systems that encourage and even require movement, and the portability of computers (Must and Tybor 2005).

The energy imbalance underlying obesity may also be the result of psychosocial factors, prenatal exposures, and short sleep duration. Psychosocial factors such as stress, depression, and social support appear to promote weight gain and obesity development (Korkeila, Kaprio, et al. 1998). Observations made on the weight status of children born during the Dutch Famine of 1944–1945 was among the first to suggest that programming during embryonic development can cause metabolic changes that predispose individuals to obesity later in life (Ravelli, Stein, et al. 1976). Further, studies of children of mothers with uncontrolled diabetes during the third trimester suggest that exposure to over-nutrition *in utero* may also increase an individual's risk for obesity (Pettit, Baird, et al. 1983). Lack of sleep or short sleep duration is also associated with excess body weight and metabolic disturbances across all age groups and in many race/ethnicities (Taheri 2006). The mechanisms by which these factors influence obesity development represent active areas of analytic epidemiologic research.

Obesity as an Exposure

Epidemiologists have long focused on obesity as an exposure or risk factor for other health conditions. Excess weight has been shown to increase insulin resistance, increase blood pressure, and elevate LDL cholesterol and triglycerides, lower HDL cholesterol, and cause a pro-inflammatory state (Bray 2004). It follows then that obesity is associated with increased incidence of type II diabetes mellitus, cardiovascular disease, hypertension, stroke, dyslipidemia, osteoarthritis, and some cancers. Additionally, there is a large body of research devoted to examining the level of excess weight associated with all-cause or cause-specific mortality outcomes.

Of all of the cardiovascular or metabolic diseases associated with obesity, the strongest association identified to date is with diabetes, where adult weight gain and duration of obesity are independent risk factors for type II diabetes (Wannamethee and Shaper 1999). An estimated 60 percent of all cases of diabetes can be directly attributed to excess weight gain (James, Jackson-Leach, et al. 2004). The WHO estimates that the prevalence of diabetes will double in the three decades from 2000 to 2030 as a result of the worldwide obesity epidemic (Wild, Roglic, et al. 2004). Obesity is also a risk factor for several abnormalities in cardiac function that can lead to cardiovascular disease, hypertension, and stroke (Alpert 2001). In a study of overweight and obese adults in the United States, obese men and women were found to have elevated prevalence ratios for coronary heart disease independent of age. Similar results were found for both high blood pressure and high blood cholesterol (Must, Spadano, et al. 1999). Because obesity affects so many metabolic pathways, its associated diseases are likely interrelated. In fact, the constellation of metabolic symptoms, characterized by increased waist circumference, elevated blood glucose levels, high blood pressure, dyslipidemia, and elevated serum triglyceride levels has been named metabolic syndrome (Grundy 2004).

A large epidemiologic study that began in the 1970s was among the first to provide evidence that increased adiposity is associated with cancer of the colon, breast, endometrium, pancreas, gallbladder, and liver; yet, in contrast to type II diabetes and cardiovascular disease, obesity receives less attention for its role in cancer development (Lew and Garfinkel 1979). In the United States, an estimate based on a prospective study of 900,000 adults suggests that as much as 15–20 percent of cancer deaths can be attributed to overweight and obesity (Calle, Rodriguez, et al. 2003). Similarly, data from a prospective study in Sweden suggests that obese persons have a 33 percent excess incidence of cancer, with significant risk increases for cancer of the small intestine, colon, gallbladder, and pancreas, among others (Wolk, Gridley, et al. 2001). Most epidemiologic studies suggest that cancer risk at individual sites differs by gender, yet in many cases, the reasons for this sex difference is unclear. Central adiposity, which is more common in men, may be responsible for the increased risk for cancers of the colon, stomach, and liver among men, whereas the known relationship between excess adiposity and endogenous sex steroid hormones may be the explanation for overweight and obese women experiencing greater risk for cancer of the breast, endometrium, cervix, and uterus (Kaaks, Lukanova, et al. 2002; Calle, Rodriguez, et al. 2003; Reeves, Pirie, et al. 2007).

Both clinical observations and epidemiological studies have long suggested a relationship between body weight and mental health outcomes. Interestingly, cross-sectionally, the relationship between BMI and major depression (as defined by the DSM-IV) appears to be best described by a U-shaped curve, whereby both high and low BMI values are associated with a significantly increased risk for depression (Carpenter, Hasin, et al. 2000). Several prospective studies suggest that obese individuals have elevated risk of becoming depressed, when controlling for confounding characteristics, such as marital status, social support, life events, and physical health problems (Roberts, Deleger, et al. 2003; Anderson, Cohen, et al. 2007). The development of depression in obese individuals (particularly in females) may be due, in part, to the social stigma of obesity as well as the association between obesity and low self-esteem (Eisenberg, Neumark-Sztainer, et al. 2003; Puhl and Brownell 2003).

Obesity is an established independent risk factor for several diseases, but the relationship between obesity and overall mortality is more controversial. In the

United States, estimates of the number of deaths attributable to obesity in the year 2000 vary from 112,000 (Flegal, Graubard, et al. 2005) to 350,000 (Mokdad, Marks, et al. 2005). This discrepancy may be due to methodological flaws in calculating these estimates, such as failure to control for smoking, over-control for co-morbidities in the causal pathway between obesity and mortality, and failure to eliminate early mortality from analyses. Some researchers question whether, given the complexities of weight status and illness, estimates of deaths attributable to obesity should be made at all (Manson, Stampfer, et al. 1987; Hu, Willett, et al. 2005; Mark 2005). While the debate over proper epidemiological methods for estimating the number of deaths attributable to obesity continues, few question that people worldwide die from obesity-related illness. A recent analysis of over 500,000 healthy, non-smoking men and women suggests an elevated risk of death of 20–40 percent in overweight persons and two to three times in obese individuals (Adams, Schatzkin, et al. 2006). Further, results from the Physicians' Health Study, a large prospective cohort of male physicians in the US, suggest a 70 percent increased risk of death for never smokers with a BMI > 30 kg/m^2 compared with the referent population (BMI 22.5–24.9) (Ajani, Lotufo, et al. 2004). Given these and similar findings, it is clear that obesity increases mortality risk.

In elucidating the role of obesity in the etiology of disease, an additional consideration is the presence of effect modification. Effect modification occurs when the strength of the association between the exposure and the outcome differs according to a third variable (Aschengrau and Seage 2003). In contrast to confounding, which is a nuisance to be "controlled," effect modification is an inherent attribute of a given relationship and should be described. For example, obesity status has been shown to modify the association between physical activity and risk of endometrial cancer: among normal weight women (BMI < 25); physical activity does not impact cancer risk, whereas among the most active overweight women (BMI ≥ 25) risk is 41 percent lower than among the least active overweight women (AL Patel, Int J Cancer 2008). The possibility that physical activity also modifies the obesity-related risk of mortality from cardiovascular disease has been a source of controversy in the obesity epidemiology literature (Stevens, Cai, et al. 2002; Fogelholm 2009), with the preponderance of evidence to date suggesting that physical inactivity and obesity are independent risk factors for cardiovascular disease mortality, as illustrated in figure 2.3 (Stevens, Cai, et al. 2002).

Effect modification can also provide insight into biological mechanisms and influence public health messages. As illustrated by figure 2.3, for obese individuals who have trouble losing weight and maintaining weight loss, a public health message suggesting that cardiovascular disease mortality risk may be reduced through increased physical activity may be effective (Fogelholm 2009).

Pediatric obesity was initially considered foremost a psychological problem, one that led to low self-esteem and teasing; however, childhood obesity is associated with several adverse physical health outcomes during childhood as well. Similar to adults, obesity in children gives rise to metabolic complications (Ebbeling, Pawlack, et al. 2002) that increase risk for high blood pressure (Faulkner,

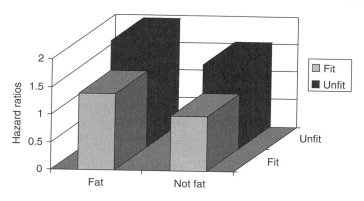

Figure 2.3. CVD Mortality in Women in the Lipid Research Clinics Study.

Gidding, et al. 2005), type II diabetes (Fagot-Campagna, Pettitt, et al. 2000), sleep apnea (Wing, Hui, et al. 2003), asthma (Ford 2005), polycystic ovarian syndrome (Guttmann-Bauman 2005), and other cardiovascular disease risk factors (Institute of Medicine [IOM] 2004), among others. A study that examined the social and economic consequences of being overweight or obese in adolescence and young adulthood found that both men and women who were overweight as adolescents were less likely to be married, and that women had completed fewer years of school, had lower household incomes, and had higher rates of household poverty (Gortmaker, Must, et al. 1993).

With increasing appreciation of the importance of the role of prenatal and childhood antecedents of adult obesity, life-course approaches seek to elucidate the long-term biologic, behavioral, and socioeconomic processes that link exposures to disease outcomes over a lifetime. At present, two competing models of chronic disease are posited: one that emphasizes the existence of critical periods in development and another that posits the accumulation of exposures over the life course. For obesity, the critical periods hypothesis has dominated the literature (Dietz 1994; Gillman 2004), although for socioeconomic position, there is evidence for accumulation (Power, Graham et al. 2005).

EXPERIMENTAL EPIDEMIOLOGY

In comparison with observational epidemiology, experimental epidemiology is characterized by the researcher's ability to allocate the exposure status to study participants (Friis and Sellers 1996). Experimental epidemiology uses the findings of observational studies to test the efficacy of preventive and therapeutic measures. The primary study design of experimental epidemiology is a randomized controlled trial (RCT); however, with respect to obesity, community interventions are also commonly employed. In an RCT, participants are randomized to one of two or more groups of varying exposures, one of which is typically a "placebo" or control condition. By randomizing participants, researchers minimize the risks of confounding, making RCTs the gold standard in evaluating causal relationships (Rothman 2002).

Testing the Efficacy of Preventive and Therapeutic Measures for Obesity

Weight loss of 5–15 percent of body weight in obese individuals reduces the risk for many outcomes associated with obesity (National Heart Lung and Blood Institute [NHLBI] 1998). Accordingly, RCTs have been done to test the efficacy of weight loss interventions such as diet, exercise, behavioral therapy, and pharmaceutical therapy. The Women's Health Initiative is an RCT in the United States in which 48,835 women aged 50–79 participated in a dietary modification trial of a low-fat dietary regimen for weight loss and subsequent cardiovascular disease prevention (Women's Health Initiative). While obesity was not the primary outcome, after 7.5 years, women in the study who followed a low-fat diet lost, on average, only 1.9 kilograms more than those in the control group (Howard, Manson, et al. 2006). In a randomized trial of 132 obese adults designed to evaluate the efficacy of a low-carbohydrate diet versus a conventional weight-loss diet (500 calorie reduction) over one year, researchers found both groups only achieved modest weight loss (−3.1 to −5.1 kg) and no significant differences in weight loss between those who followed the low-carbohydrate versus conventional diet (Stern, Iqbal, et al. 2004). Taken together, these findings suggest that with dietary modification alone, only modest weight loss is achievable. This conclusion is supported by a review of 33 trials evaluating diet, exercise, or diet and exercise, which found that diet combined with exercise produced 20 percent greater initial weight loss and 20 percent greater sustained weight loss after one year (Curioni and Lourenco 2005). Pharmacoepidemiolgy, or drug epidemiology, involves the use of RCTs to test the efficacy and safety of a drug. Several drugs, such as orlistat, sibutramine, and rimonabant, have been tested as pharmaceutical interventions aimed at reducing obesity, and both the efficacy and safety of these drugs are continuously being evaluated via post-marketing surveillance.

Both RCTs and community interventions have been effectively used to inform public health recommendations with respect to obesity treatment and prevention. School-based intervention designs demonstrate that obesity remission and prevention is achievable in children and adolescents through diet and lifestyle modification. In the United States, Planet Health, an intervention designed to reduce television viewing and dietary fat intake and to increase physical activity and fruit and vegetable intake, resulted in decreased obesity prevalence from 23.6 percent to 20.3 percent in female adolescents (Gortmaker, Peterson, et al. 1999). A similar intervention in Dutch secondary schools, the Dutch Obesity Intervention in

Teenagers (DOiT), aimed at preventing excessive weight gain resulted in significantly lower skinfold thickness measurements in females and a significant reduction in consumption of sugar-sweetened beverages in both males and females (Singh, Chin A Paw, et al. 2009). In the United Kingdom, the Christchurch obesity prevention project in schools (CHOPPS), a school-based educational program aimed at discouraging consumption of carbonated beverages, was found to be effective in reducing not only the number of carbonated beverages consumed, but also the number of overweight and obese children after one year (James, Thomas, et al. 2004). The magnitude of results from community-based studies tends to be quite modest, likely due to multiple factors, including measurement error, intervention dose, uptake of intervention elements, and treatment fidelity (Caballero 2004). Nonetheless, successful interventions like these provide the evidence base needed for policy approaches. Some public health departments across the United States and the National Health Service (NHS) in the United Kingdom, among others, have proposed and enacted school-based policies to remove vending machines from schools, increase physical activity during school hours, and improve school-based meal programs in an effort to treat and/or prevent obesity in children and adolescents (Arkansas Center for Health Improvement 2008; Department of Health 2008).

Conclusions

As the prevalence of obesity has reached epidemic proportions worldwide, epidemiologic studies aimed at identifying the distribution and determinants of obesity have increased concurrently. Descriptive epidemiologic studies have shed light on how obesity rates vary by person, by place, and over time. Elucidation of these patterns has helped to establish obesity as a worldwide epidemic and has also contributed importantly to hypothesis generation for further analytic study. Analytical epidemiologic studies of obesity illuminate both the causes and consequences of obesity, and thereby provide researchers and clinicians with insight into how obesity and its sequelae may be prevented and effectively treated. As more prevention and treatment methods are tested through experimental studies in community settings, the complex and multifactorial nature of obesity emerges as a major challenge. For example, as a condition of caloric imbalance, it is increasingly appreciated that the dietary choices and physical activity opportunities that contribute to weight gain are largely reflected by an individual's socioeconomic resources and environment, given that associations have been found between obesity development and access to supermarkets, access to fast food restaurants, neighborhood safety, and urban sprawl (Hu 2008). Key challenges to the epidemiologic methods with respect to obesity research include the following: measurement issues of the key dietary, physical activity, and behavioral risk factors, control of confounding variables, accounting for the presence of bidirectionality, and the need for experimental study designs that account for multiple levels of influence.

Other disciplines, particularly sociology, provide the multilevel statistical methods needed to tease out proximal from distal causes. The need for new designs to address these complexities in experimental studies is also pressing (Stevens, Taber, et al. 2007). While the principles of epidemiology are essential to obesity research, epidemiology alone lacks the full range of tools needed to fully elucidate the determinants of obesity and or to evaluate the effects of treatment and prevention paradigms. The future of obesity research, therefore, will depend on multidisciplinary approaches, wherein theories from the behavioral and social sciences, among others, are employed in concert with epidemiologic tools to fully examine obesity and all of its complexities.

REFERENCES

Adams, K. F., A. Schatzkin, et al. 2006. "Overweight, Obesity and Mortality in a Large Prospective Cohort of Persons 50 to 71 years old." *New England Journal of Medicine* 355: 763–778.

Ajani, U. A., P. A. Lotufo, et al. 2004. "Body Mass Index and Mortality among US Male Physicians." *Annals of Epidemiology* 14(10): 731–739.

Alpert, M. A. 2001. "Obesity Cardiomyopathy: Pathophysiology and Evolution of the Clinical Syndrome." *American Journal of Medical Science* 321: 225–236.

Anderson, S. E., P. Cohen, et al. 2007. "Adolescent Obesity and Risk for Subsequent Major Depressive Disorder and Anxiety Disorder: Prospective Evidence." *Psychosomatic Medicine* 69: 740–747.

Arkansas Center for Health Improvement. 2008. *Year Five Assessment of Childhood and Adolescent Obesity in Arkansas (Fall 2007-Spring 2008)*. Little Rock, AK: ACHI.

Arroyo, P., A. Loria, et al. 2000. "Prevalence of Pre-obesity and Obesity in Urban Adult Mexicans in Comparisons with Other Large Surveys." *Obesity Research* 32: 179–185.

Aschengrau, A., and G. R. Seage. 2003. *Essentials of Epidemiology in Public Health*. Sudbury, MA: Jones and Bartlett Publishers.

Barlow, S. E. 2007. "Expert Committee Recommendations Regarding the Prevention, Assessment and Treatment of Child and Adolescent Overweight and Obesity: Summary Report." *Pediatrics* 120(Supp.): S164–S192.

Barquera, S., K. E. Peterson, et al. 2007. "Coexistence of Maternal Central Adiposity and Child Stunting in Mexico." *International Journal of Obesity* 31: 601–607.

Barrett-Connor, E. 1991. "Nutritional Epidemiology: How Do We Know What They Ate?" *American Journal of Clinical Nutrition* 54(Supp.): 182S–187S.

Bell, A. C., K. Ge, et al. 2002. "The Road to Obesity or the Path to Prevention: Motorized Transportation and Obesity in China." *Obesity Research* 10(4): 277–283.

Bray, G. A. 2004. "Medical Consequences of Obesity." *Journal of Clinical Endocrinology and Metabolism* 89: 2583–2589.

Caballero, B. 2004. "Obesity Prevention in Children: Opportunities and Challenges." *International Journal of Obesity and Related Metabolic Disorders* 28(S3): S90–S95.

Calle, E. E., C. Rodriguez, et al. 2003. "Overweight, Obesity, and Mortality from Cancer in a Prospectively Studied Cohort of U. S. Adults." *New England Journal of Medicine* **348**: 1625–1638.

Carpenter, L. M., D. S. Hasin, et al. 2000. "Relationships between Obesity and DSM-IV Major Depressive Disorder, Suicidal Ideation, and Suicide Attempts: Results from a General Population Study." *American Journal of Public Health* **90**: 251–257.

Chang, V. A., and N. A. Christakis. 2001. "Extent and Determinants of Discrepancy between Self-evaluations of Weight Status and Clinical Standards." *Journal of General Internal Medicine* **16**(8): 538–543.

Chen, C. M. 2008. "Overview of Obesity in Mainland China." *Obesity Reviews* **9**(Supp. 1): 14–21.

Chhatwal, J., M. Verma, et al. 2004. "Obesity among Pre-adolescent and Adolescents of a Developing Country (India)." *Asia Pacific Journal of Clinical Nutrition* **13**(3): 231–235.

Clasey, J. L., J. A. Kanaley, et al. 1999. "Validity of Methods of Body Composition Assessment in Young and Older Men and Women." *Journal of Applied Physiology* **86**: 1728–1738.

Cole, T. J., M. C. Bellizzi, et al. 2000. "Establishing a Standard Definition for Childhood Overweight and Obesity Worldwide: International Survey." *British Medical Journal* **320**: 1240–1243.

Crespo, C., E. Smit, et al. 2001. "Television Watching, Energy Intake and Obesity in US Children." *Archives of Pediatrics and Adolescent Medicine* **155**: 360–365.

Curioni, C. C., and P. M. Lourenco 2005. "Long-term Weight Loss after Diet and Exercise: A Systematic Review." *International Journal of Obesity and Related Metabolic Disorders* **29**(10): 1168–1174.

Deckelbaum, R. J., and C. L. Williams. 2001. "Childhood Obesity: The Health Issue." *Obesity Research* **9**: 239S–243S.

de Menezes Toledo Florencio, T. M., H. da Silva Ferreira, et al. 2001. "Obesity and Undernutrition in a Very-Low-Income Population in the City of Maceió, Northeastern Brazil." *British Journal of Nutrition* **86**: 277–283.

Department of Health. 2008. "Healthy Weight, Healthy Lives: A Cross-Government Strategy for England." Retrieved November 16, 2009, from http://www.dh.gov.uk/en/Publicationsandstatistics/Publications/PublicationsPolicyAndGuidance/DH_082378.

Dietz, W. H. 1994. "Critical Periods in Childhood for the Development of Obesity." *American Journal of Clinical Nutrition* **59**: 955–959.

Dietz, W. H., and M. C. Bellizzi. 1999. "Introduction: The Use of Body Mass Index to Assess Obesity in Children." *American Journal of Clinical Nutrition* **70**(Supp.): 123S–125S.

Doll, R., and A. B. Hill. 1950. "Smoking and Carcinoma of the Lung." *British Medical Journal* **2**: 739–748.

Ebbeling, C. B., D. B. Pawlack, et al. 2002. "Childhood Obesity: Public-Health Crisis, Common Sense Cure." *Lancet* **360**: 473–482.

Eisenberg, M., D. Neumark-Sztainer, et al. 2003. "Associations of Weight-Based Teasing and Emotional Well-Being among Adolescents." *Archives of Pediatrics and Adolescent Medicine* **157**: 733–738.

Eriksson, J., T. Forsen, et al. 2003. "Obesity from Cradle to Grave." *International Journal of Obesity* **27**: 722–727.

Fagot-Campagna, A., D. J. Pettitt, et al. 2000. "Type 2 Diabetes among North American Children and Adolescents: An Epidemiologic Review and a Public Health Perspective." *Journal of Pediatrics* **136**: 664–672.

Faulkner, B., S. S. Gidding, et al. 2005. "The Relationship of Body Mass Index and Blood Pressure in Primary Care Pediatric Patients." *Journal of Pediatrics* **148**: 195–200.

Flegal, K. M., M. D. Carroll, et al. 2002. "Prevalence Trends in Obesity among US Adults, 1999–2000." *Journal of the American Medical Association* **288**(14): 1723–1727.

Flegal, K. M., M. D. Carroll, et al. 2010. "Prevalence and Trends in Obesity among US Adults, 1999–2008." *Journal of the American Medical Association* **303**(3): 235–241.

Flegal, K. M., B. I. Graubard, et al. 2005. "Excess Deaths Associated with Underweight, Overweight and Obesity." *Journal of the American Medical Association* **293**: 1861–1867.

Flier, J. S. 2004. "Obesity Wars: Molecular Progress Confronts an Expanding Epidemic." *Cell* **116**: 337–350.

Fogelholm, M. 2009. "Physical Activity, Fitness and Fatness: Relations to Mortality, Morbidity and Disease Risk Factors. A Systematic Review." *Obesity Reviews* Vol. 11, 3, 2010, 202–221

Ford, E. S. 2005. "The Epidemiology of Asthma." *Journal of Allergy and Clinical Immunology* **115**: 897–909.

Friedman, G. D. 1994. *Primer of Epidemiology*. New York: McGraw-Hill.

Friis, R. H., and T. A. Sellers. 1996. *Epidemiology for Public Health Practice*. Gaithersburg, MD: Aspen Publishers.

Gehlbach, S. H. 1988. *Interpreting the Medical Literature: Practical Epidemiology for Clinicians*. New York: Macmillan.

Gillman, M. W. 2004. A Life Course Approach To Obesity. In *A Life Course Approach to Chronic Disesae Epidemology,* eds. D. Kuh and Ben-Shlomo. New York: Oxford University Press, 189–217.

Gordon-Larsen, P., L. S. Adair, et al. 2004. "Five-year Obesity Incidence in the Transition Period between Adolescence and Adulthood: The National Longitudinal Study of Adolescent Health." *American Journal of Clinical Nutrition* **80**: 569–575.

Gortmaker, S., A. Must, et al. 1993. "Social and Economic Consequences of Overweight in Adolescence and Young Adulthood." *New England Journal of Medicine* **329**: 1008–1012.

Gortmaker, S., A. Must, et al. 1996. "Television Viewing as a Cause of Increasing Obesity among Children in the United States, 1986–1990." *Archives of Pediatrics and Adolescent Medicine* **150**(4): 356–362.

Gortmaker, S., K. E. Peterson, et al. 1999. "Reducing Obesity via a School-based Interdisciplinary Intervention among Youth." *Archives of Pediatrics and Adolescent Medicine* **153**: 409–418.

Grundy, S. M. 2004. "Obesity, Metabolic Syndrome and Cardiovascular Disease." *Journal of Clinical Endocrinology and Metabolism* **98**(6): 2595–2600.

Guo, S. S., A. F. Roche, et al. 1994. "The Predictive Value of Childhood Body Mass Index Values for Overweight at Age 35 Y." *American Journal of Clinical Nutrition* **59**: 810–819.

Guttmann-Bauman, I. 2005. "Approach to Adolescent Polycystic Ovary Syndrome in the Pediatric Endocrine Community in the USA." *Journal of Pediatric Endocrinology and Metabolism* **18**: 499–506.

Haug, E., M. Rasmussen, et al. 2009. "Overweight in School-Aged Children and Its Relationship with Demographic and Lifestyle Factors: Results from the WHO-Collaborative Health Behaviour in School-aged Children (HBSC) Study." *International Journal of Public Health* **54**: S167–S179.

Hill, J. O., and J. C. Peters. 1998. "Environmental Contributions to the Obesity Epidemic." *Science* **280**: 1371–1374.

Hippocrates. 400 B.C.E. "On Ancient Medicine." Retrieved December 4, 2009, from http://classics.mit.edu/Hippocrates/ancimed.html.

Hossain, P., B. Kawar, et al. 2007. "Obesity and Diabetes in the Developing World: A Growing Challenge." *New England Journal of Medicine* **356**: 213–215.

Howard, B. V., J. E. Manson, et al. 2006. "Low-fat Dietary Pattern and Weight Change over 7 Years." *Journal of the American Medical Association* **295**: 39–49.

Hu, F. 2008. *Obesity Epidemiology*. Oxford: Oxford University Press.

Hu, F., W. C. Willett, et al. 2005. "Calculating Deaths Attributable to Obesity." *American Journal of Public Health* **95**: 932.

Institute of Medicine (IOM). 2004. *Childhood Obesity in the United States: Facts and Figures*. Washington, D.C.: IOM.

James, J., P. Thomas, et al. 2004. "Preventing Childhood Obesity by Reducing Consumption of Carbonated Drinks: Cluster Randomised Controlled Trial." *British Medical Journal*. **328** : 1237.

James, W. P. T., R. Jackson-Leach, et al. 2004. "Overweight and Obesity." In *Comparative Quantification of Health Risks*, eds. M. Ezzati, A. D. Lopez, A. Rodgers, and C. J. L. Murray. Geneva: World Health Organization 497–596.

Ji, C., J. Sun, et al. 2004. "Dynamic Analysis on the Prevalence of Obesity and Overweight School-Aged Children and Adolescents in Recent 15 Years in China." *Chinese Journal of Epidemiology* **25**: 103–108.

Kaaks, R., A. Lukanova, et al. 2002. "Obesity, Endogenous Hormones, and Endometrial Cancer Risk: A Synthetic Review." *Cancer Epidemiology* **11**: 1531–1543.

Kain, J., F. Vio, et al. 2003. "Obesity Trends and Determinant Factors in Latin America." *Cadernos de Saúde Pública* **19**(Supp. 1): S77–S86.

Kim, S., and B. M. Popkin. 2000. "The Nutrition Transition in South Korea." *American Journal of Clinical Nutrition* **72**: 44–53.

Kipnis, V., A. F. Subar, et al. 2003. "Structure of dietary measurement error: results of the OPEN biomarker study." *Am J Epidemiol* **158**: 14–21.

Korkeila, M., J. Kaprio, et al. 1998. "Predictors of Major Weight Gain in Adult Finns: Stress, Life Satisfaction and Personality Traits." *International Journal of Obesity and Related Metabolic Disorders* **22**: 949–957.

Last, J. M. 1995. *A Dictionary of Epidemiology*. New York: Oxford University Press.

Lew, E. A., and L. Garfinkel. 1979. "Variations in Mortality by Weight among 750,000 Men and Women." *Journal of Chronic Disease* **32**: 563–576.

Lobstein, T., L. Baur, et al. 2004. "Obesity in Children and Young People: A Crisis in Public Health." *Obesity Reviews* **5**(S1): 4–85.

Loos, R. J. F., and C. Bouchard. 2003. "Obesity: Is It A Genetic Disorder?" *Journal of Internal Medicine* **254**: 401–425.

Ma, G. S., Y. P. Li, et al. 2005. "The Prevalence of Overweight and Obesity and Its Changes in Chinese People during 1992–2002." *Chinese Journal of Preventive Medicine* **39**: 311–316.

Manson, J. E., M. J. Stampfer, et al. 1987. "Body Weight and Longevity: A Reassessment." *Journal of the American Medical Association* **257**: 353–358.

Mark, D. H. 2005. "Deaths Attributable to Obesity." *Journal of the American Medical Association* **293**: 1918–1919.

Martorell, R., L. K. Kahn, et al. 2000. "Obesity in Women from Developing Countries." *European Journal of Clinical Nutrition* **54**: 247–252.

Matheson, D. M., J. D. Killen, et al. 2004. "Children's Food Consumption during Television Viewing." *American Journal of Clinical Nutrition* **79**: 1088–1094.

McLaren, L. 2007. "Socioeconomic Status and Obesity." *Epidemiologic Reviews* **29**: 29–48.

Mokdad, A. H., J. S. Marks, et al. 2005. "Correction: Actual Causes of Death in the United States, 2000." *Journal of the American Medical Association* **293**: 293–294.

Monteiro, C. A., W. L. Conde, et al. 2001. "Independent Effects of Income and Education on the Risk of Obesity in the Brazilian Adult Population." *Journal of Nutrition* **131**: 881S–886S.

Must, A., and S. E. Anderson. 2006. "Body Mass Index in Children and Adolescents: Consideration for Population-Based Applications." *International Journal of Obesity* **30**: 590–594.

Must, A., S. A. Hollander, et al. 2006. "Childhood Obesity: A Growing Public Health Concern." *Expert Review of Endocrinology and Metabolism* **1**(2): 233–254.

Must, A., J. Spadano, et al. 1999. "The Disease Burden Associated with Overweight and Obesity." *Journal of the American Medical Association* **282**(16): 1523–1529.

Must, A., and D. Tybor. 2005. "Physical Activity and Sedentary Behavior: A Review of Longitudinal Studies of Weight and Adiposity in Youth." *International Journal of Epidemiology* **29**(Supp.): S84–S96.

National Heart Lung and Blood Institute (NHLBI). 1998. "Clinical Guidelines on the Identification, Evaluation, and Treatment of Overweight and Obesity in Adults: The Evidence Report." *Obesity Research* **6**: 51S–209S.

Nemesure, B., S. Y. Wu, et al. 2008. "Nine-year Incidence of Obesity and Overweight in an African-origin Population." *International Journal of Obesity* **32**: 329–335.

Newman, T. B., W. S. Browner, et al. 1988. Enhancing Causal Inference in Observational Studies. In *Designing Clinical Research,* eds. S. B. Hulley and S. R. Cummings. Baltimore, MD: Williams and Wilkins 127–146.

Ogden, C. L., M. D. Carroll, et al. 2008. "High Body Mass Index for Age among US Children and Adolescents, 2003–2006." *Journal of the American Medical Association* **299**(20): 2401–2405.

Ogden, C. L., K. M. Flegal, et al. 2002. "Prevalence and Trends in Overweight among US Children and Adolescents, 1999–2000." *Journal of the American Medical Association* **288**(14): 1728–1732.

Patel, A. V., H. S. Feigelson, et al. 2008. "The role of body weight in the relationship between physical activity and endometrial cancer: Results from a large cohort of US women." *International Journal of Cancer* **123**(8): 1877–1882.

Pettit, D. J., H. R. Baird, et al. 1983. "Excessive Obesity in Offspring of Pima Women with Diabetes during Pregnancy." *New England Journal of Medicine* **308**: 242–245.

Peytremann-Bridevaux, I., D. Faeh, et al. 2007. "Prevalence of Overweight and Obesity in Rural and Urban Settings of 10 European Countries." *Preventative Medicine* **44**: 442–446.

Phillips, C. V., and K. J. Goodman. 2004. "The Missed Lessons of Sir Austin Bradford Hill." *Epidemiologic Perspectives & Innovations* **1**: 3.

Popkin, B. M., and E. Z. Bisgrove. 1988. "Urbanization and Nutrition in Low-Income Countries." *Food and Nutrition Bulletin* **19**(2–23).

Power, C., H. Graham, et al. 2005. "The Contribution of Childhood and Adult Socioeconomic Position to Adult Obesity and Smoking Behaviour: An International Comparison." *International Journal of Epidemiology* **34**(2): 335–344.

Puhl, R., and K. D. Brownell. 2003. "Psychosocial Origins of Obesity Stigma: Toward Changing a Powerful and Pervasive Bias." *Obesity Reviews* **4**: 213–227.

Ravelli, G. P., Z. A. Stein, et al. 1976. "Obesity in Young Men after Famine Exposure in Utero and Early Infancy." *New England Journal of Medicine* **7**: 349–354.

Reeves, G. K., K. Pirie, et al. 2007. "Cancer Incidence and Mortality in Relation to Body Mass Index in the Million Women Study: Cohort Study." *British Medical Journal* **335**: 1134–1145.

Roberts, R. E., S. Deleger, et al. 2003. "Prospective Association between Obesity and Depression: Evidence for the Alameda County Study." *International Journal of Obesity* **27**: 514–521.

Roskam, A. R., A. E. Kunst, et al. 2009. "Comparative Appraisal of Educational Inequalities in Overweight and Obesity among Adults in 19 European Countries." *International Journal of Epidemiology*: 1–13.

Rothman, K. J. 2002. *Epidemiology: An Introduction.* Oxford: Oxford University Press.

Singh, A. S., M. J. M. Chin A Paw, et al. 2009. "Dutch Obesity Intervention in Teenagers." *Archives of Pediatrics and Adolescent Medicine* **163**: 309–317.

Stern, L., N. Iqbal, et al. (2004). "The Effects of Low-Carbohydrate versus Conventional Weight Loss Diets in Severely Obese Adults: One-Year Follow-Up of a Randomized Trial." *Annals of Internal Medicine* **140**: 778–785.

Stevens, J., J. Cai, et al. 2002. "Fitness and Fatness as Predictors of Mortality from All Causes and from Cardiovascular Disease in Men and Women in the Lipid Research Clinics Study." *American Journal of Epidemiology* **156**(9): 832–841.

Stevens, J., D. R. Taber, et al. 2007. "Advances and Controversies in the Design of Obesity Prevention Trials[ast]." *Obesity* **15**(9): 2163–2170.

Taheri, S. 2006. "The Link between Short Sleep Duration and Obesity: We Should Recommend More Sleep to Prevent Obesity." *Archives of Disease in Childhood* **91**: 881–884.

The Health and Social Care Information Centre. 2007. "Health Survey for England." Retrieved November 18, 2009, from http://www.ic.nhs.uk/webfiles/publications/HSE07/Health percent20Survey percent20for percent20England percent202007 percent20Latest percent20Trends.pdf.

The Health and Social Care Information Centre. 2009. "Statisics on Obesity, Physical Activity and Diet: England, February 2009." Retrieved November 18, 2009, from http://www.ic.nhs.uk/webfiles/publications/opan09/OPAD percent20Feb percent202009 percent20final.pdf.

Tsimeas, P. D., A. L. Tsiokanos, et al. 2005. "Does Living in Urban or Rural Settings Affect Aspects of Physical Fitness in Children? An Allometric Approach." *British Journal of Sports Medicine* **39**: 671–674.

Vasan, R. S., M. J. Pencina, et al. 2005. "Estimated Risks for Developing Obesity in the Framingham Heart Study." *Annals of Internal Medicine* **143**: 473–480.

Wang, Y., and T. Lobstein. 2006. "Worldwide Trends in Childhood Overweight and Obesity." *International Journal of Pediatric Obesity* **1**: 11–25.

Wannamethee, S. G., and A. G. Shaper. 1999. "Weight Change and Duration of Overweight and Obesity in the Incidence of Type 2 Diabetes." *Diabetes Care* **22**: 1266–1272.

Whitlock, E. P., S. B. Williams, et al. 2005. "Screening and Interventions for Childhood Overweight: A Summary of Evidence for the US Preventive Services Task Force." *Pediatrics* **116**: e125–e144.

Wild, S., G. Roglic, et al. 2004. "Global Prevalence of Obesity: Estimates for the Year 2000 and Projections for 2030." *Diabetes Care* **27**: 1047–1053.

Willett, W. C. 1998. Nutritional Epidemiology. In *Modern Epidemiology*, eds. K. J. Rothman and S. Greenland. Philadelphia: Lippincott-Raven.

Wing, Y. K., S. H. Hui, et al. 2003. "A Controlled Study of Sleep Related Disordered Breathing in Obese Children." *Archives of Disease in Childhood* 88: 1043–1047.

Wolk, A., G. Gridley, et al. 2001. "A Prospective Study of Obesity and Cancer Risk." *Cancer Causes and Controls* 12: 13–21.

Women's Health Initiative. "Dietary Modification Fact Sheet." Retrieved January 6, 2010, from http://www.nhlbi.nih.gov/whi/diet.htm

World Health Organization. 2006. "Obesity and Overweight." Retrieved November 16, 2009, from http://www.who.int/mediacentre/factsheets/fs311/en/print.html.

World Health Organization. 2007. "BMI for Age (5–19 years)." Retrieved January 12, 2010, from http://www.who.int/growthref/who2007_bmi_for_age/en/index.html.

World Health Organization. 2009. *World Health Statistics, 2009.* Geneva: World Health Organization.

Zhou, B. F. 2002. "Predictive Value of Body Mass Index and Waist Circumference for Risk Factors of Certain Related Disease in Chinese Adults: Study on Optimal Cut-Off Points of Body Mass Index and Waist Circumference in Chinese Adults." *Biomedical Environmental Science* 15: 245–252.

CHAPTER 3

THE DEMOGRAPHY OF OBESITY

CHRISTINE L. HIMES

FIELD OF DEMOGRAPHY

DEMOGRAPHY is an interdisciplinary field drawing primarily on insights from sociology, economics, geography, public health, and anthropology. The field is characterized by its focus on the study of populations and aggregate groups. Demographers are concerned with the size, age structure, characteristics, and geographic distribution of populations. They may look at global, national, regional, state, or local groups. Often demographers examine the changes in a population over time, or the differences across space. In its purest form, demography focuses on the three forces that influence population size: fertility, mortality, and migration. The classic balancing equation of demography notes that a population changes in size due to the net differences in births compared to deaths and in immigrants compared to emigrants.

A few methodological techniques are characteristic of demography studies. One is the construction of life tables and the estimation of their underlying transition rates. Life tables simulate the effects of a particular set of rates on the likelihood that a person will experience an event, how long they will stay at risk of the event, or the average length of time spent in some state of risk. Life tables usually model the effects of mortality rates on life expectancy, but any life transition, for instance, marriage, divorce, or employment, can be simulated. Another technique of demography is standardization. Standardization allows a researcher to determine the extent to which differences in the rates of events between populations are due to differences in population characteristics, particularly the age structures of the populations. Demographers may also focus on the joint and individual effects of age, period, and cohort effects on the changing prevalence of a characteristic in the population over time. Because of the interest in change and rates of change, demographers often use longitudinal panel data or repeated cross-sectional data in their analyses.

Over time the field has broadened its focus beyond fertility, mortality, and migration to look at marriage and divorce (due to their relationship with fertility) and diseases and health behaviors (due to their relationship with mortality). With the aging of the population, increased focus has been put on the health conditions of the older population. Such studies are important for projecting both the future size of the population and its health care needs. For instance, demographers may be interested in the prevalence of a particular disease condition in the population; how the prevalence of that condition has changed over time, whom the condition affects, and how that condition affects other aspects of life such as functioning, independence, and economic status.

Obesity is of interest to demographers primarily because of its potential effects on mortality and its relationship to chronic health problems and disability, although obesity may also have implications for socioeconomic status, marriage, and fertility. Obesity's relationship to mortality is complex and dependent upon the extent of obesity, age, gender, and race. Extreme obesity is related to higher rates of death, particularly among those in middle adulthood (Mehta and Chang 2009). Obesity also is considered a risk factor for the development of several chronic diseases, primarily diabetes and heart disease. Obesity can complicate the effects of arthritis and is related to higher rates of functional limitations in later life (Himes 2000). Because the prevalence of obesity has increased rapidly in the population, many of the potential effects on health and quality of life are yet to be realized. Demography contributes to the study of obesity by outlining the trends in obesity prevalence, the differences in prevalence by characteristic, and projecting the effects of obesity into the future.

OBESITY MEASUREMENT

Obesity, an excess of body fat, results from an increased size and, in extreme cases, an increased number, of fat cells. At the most basic level, obesity results from an imbalance between energy intake and energy expenditure. This imbalance may result from excess caloric intake, decreased physical activity, or metabolic disorders, individually or in combination (National Institutes of Health [NIH] 1998). Increases in caloric intake combined with decreases in physical activity have resulted in high rates of obesity in the populations of the developed world. The most widely used measure of obesity is the body mass index (BMI), calculated as weight in kilograms divided by height in meters squared (kg/m^2). In the first federal guidelines on the evaluation and treatment of obesity (NIH 1998), the National Heart, Lung, and Blood Institute (NHLBI) adopted definitions of overweight as a BMI of 25 to 29.9 kg/m^2, and obesity as a BMI of 30 kg/m^2 or greater. Within the category of obesity, further distinctions are made between class I obesity, BMI of 30 up to 35; class II obesity, BMI of 35 up to 40; and class III obesity, BMI of 40 or above. These guidelines are consistent with those adopted by the WHO (2000) and used in international studies.

Body size among children and adolescents is characterized slightly differently. Rather than using a specific BMI cut-off, children ages 2 through 19 are considered obese if their BMI is at or above the 95th percentile for their age (Krebs et al 2007). Prior to 2005, a BMI at or above the 95th percentile was considered "overweight" and children between the 85th and 95th percentiles were considered "at risk for overweight" (Barlow and Deitz 1998). Those categories are now labeled as obese and overweight, respectively. Recently, a new category, children with a BMI at or above the 97th percentile, has been identified as of particular interest (Ogden et al. 2010).

In the United States, data on height and weight are routinely collected in four national surveys, all under the auspices of the Centers for Disease Control (CDC): the National Health and Examination Survey (NHANES), the National Health Interview Survey (NHIS), the Behavioral Risk Factor Surveillance System (BRFSS), and the Youth Risk Behavior Surveillance System (YRBSS). NHANES has the advantage of using direct measurement by trained health professionals to gather data. However, this limits the number of respondents and the frequency of data collection. In contrast, the NHIS is conducted annually, has a larger sample, but relies upon self-reports of height and weight. The BRFSS of adults and the YRBSS of youths are relatively new studies that collect self-reported height and weight. Their primary advantage is the ability to examine patterns and trends at the state level.

The use of a standard measure of obesity is useful for screening patients, for public health interests, and for comparison across time and countries. Because of its ease of collection (primarily from self-reports), BMI has become the standard measure of obesity. However, the limitations of this measure are well-known (Burkhauser and Cawley 2008). Other measures of adiposity, such as skin-fold thickness, waist-to-hip ratio, and direct measures of adiposity through bioelectrical impedance, bone density (DEXA) scan, or hydrostatic weighing provide more accurate measures of body composition but require special equipment and training (Brodie, Moscrip, and Hutcheon 1998). The distribution of body fat—in particular, abdominal obesity, as measured by waist circumference or waist-to-hip ratio—has repeatedly been shown to be a more important predictor of health than BMI alone (Pischon et al. 2008). Therefore, BMI, particularly at an individual level, must be considered as just one indicator of adiposity.

OVERALL TREND

The prevalence of obesity among American adults, defined by a BMI of 30.0 or more, has increased steadily since the mid-1970s. Using data from the NHANES and its predecessor, the National Health Examination Survey (NHES), the prevalence of class 1 obesity (BMI 30.0–34.9) showed very little change between the 1960–1962 study (NHES I) and the 1976–1980 study (NHANES II). About 10 percent of adults were found to have BMI scores in the range considered obese, and 4 percent had BMI measures exceeding 35.0 (Flegal et al. 1998). However, between the 1976–1980 survey and the 1988–1994 survey (NHANES III), obesity prevalence increased significantly. Those with a BMI in the range of 30.0 to 34.9 increased from an age-adjusted 10.1 percent to 14.4 percent. More dramatically, those with BMIs in the range of class II and class III obesity nearly doubled from 4.4 percent to 8.1 percent (Flegal et al. 1998). Looking at all classes of obesity, the prevalence of those with a BMI of 30.0 or higher increased from 13.4 percent in 1960–1962 to 23.3 percent by the 1988–1994 (Flegal et al. 2002).

If birth cohorts in the NHANES are examined, rather than a comparison of ages across time, an earlier increase in BMI is detected (Komlos, Breitfelder, and Sunder 2009). These researchers observe that the increase in body size can be traced back at least until the 1950s and may have been underway as early as the 1920s. Other studies, using skin-fold thickness rather than BMI as a marker of adiposity, also find an earlier increase in the obesity trend (Burkhauser, Cawley, and Schmeiser 2009). These findings highlight the importance of using diverse measures and methods for identifying the obesity prevalence and trend.

The timing of the beginning of the trend may be difficult to locate, but there was a clear change in prevalence during the 1980s continuing into the 1990s. The next round of NHANES data were collected in 1999–2000 and revealed that over 30 percent of the adult population were now in the obese range as measured by BMI (Flegal et al. 2002). This increase was observed for both men and women and for all ages. The obesity prevalence remained at about 30 percent in the next NHANES, 2001–2002 and increased slightly in 2003–2004 to 32.2 percent (Ogden et al. 2006). In 2007–2008 there was no further statistically significant increase (Ogden et al. 2007a). The most recent results, including data from the 2008 NHANES, continue to show a stabilization in obesity prevalence rates (Flegal et al. 2010), perhaps indicating an end to the upward trajectory.

In contrast to the trend in obesity, the trend for those considered overweight, having BMIs between 25.0 and 29.9, has been relatively flat over the same time period, 1960–2006. The proportion of the population considered overweight, but not obese, increased from 31.5 in 1960–1962 to 32.7 in 2005–2006 (Ogden et al. 2007b). At the other end of the spectrum, those considered extremely obese (BMI 40.0 or more) increased from less than one percent in the 1960–1962 study to over 5 percent in the 2003–2004 period (Ogden et al. 2007b). Together these patterns indicate that, overall, average BMI in the population has increased with the greatest increases coming at the upper percentiles of the distribution. The population as a whole is heavier and the heaviest have gained the most (Ogden et al. 2007a). Using data from the BRFSS, Sturm (2007) finds a similar trend in the prevalence of very high BMI. The percentage of the population with a BMI of 40 or more was 52 percent higher in 2005 compared to 2000, an increase from 2.02 to 3.07.

Among children and adolescents, an increase in the prevalence of obesity was also observed from the 1960s to the present. In the 1960s, the prevalence of children at or above the 95th percentile of BMI for age was around 4 percent, varying from a low of 3.4 percent for boys aged 6 to 8 to a high of 5.1 percent for girls aged 15 to 17 (Flegal and Troiano 2000). Between 1963 and 1994, the mean BMI for children aged 6 to 17 increased by 1 to 2 percent and the prevalence of those at or above the 95th percentile of BMI for age increased by 4 to 8 percent (Troiano and Flegal 1998). The largest increases in this time period were seen among boys 9 to 17. In 2007–2008, 11.9 percent of children aged 2 through 19 were at or above the 97th percentile, 16.9 percent were at or above the 95th percentile, and 31.7 percent were at or above the 85th percentile of BMI for age (Ogden et al. 2010).

AGE

Weight gain is steady through early adulthood (Baum and Ruhm 2009). After adjusting for the secular trend in obesity, average BMI rose from 24.3 to 27.3 between the ages of 18 and 40 in the National Longitudinal Survey of Youth (NLSY) cohort. This increase is somewhat greater for men than women. Similarly, the prevalence of obesity generally increases with age through adulthood (Cook and Daponte 2008). People between the ages of 18 and 32 have the lowest average BMI (Cook and Daponte 2008), and BMI increases steadily until about age 75, when there is a small drop (Flegal et al. 1998). For both men and women, the prevalence of obesity is highest for the age group 60 to 69; 38.1 percent of men in that age group were obese in NHANES 1999–2000 and 42.5 percent of women (Flegal et al. 2002). At the very oldest ages, 80 and older, more women are obese than men, 19.5 percent compared to 9.6 percent (Flegal et al. 2002). Ages below 60 show a decline in obesity prevalence for the most recent time period (2007–2008), while among those age 60 and older the prevalence of obesity continues to increase (Flegal et al. 2010).

Obesity in childhood is associated with obesity in adulthood: about one-third of obese preschoolers and half of obese school-age children are obese as adults (Serdula et al. 1993). Children who are obese at older ages and who have higher BMIs are more likely to be obese as adults. As a result, there is great interest in understanding the patterns of obesity prevalence in children and adolescents. About 10 percent of children aged 2 to 5 are at or above the 95th percentile BMI for age. This nearly doubles to 19.6 percent of children aged 6 to 11. Among adolescents aged

12 to 19, the proportion considered obese is 18.1 percent (Ogden et al. 2010). Below age 6, girls are slightly more likely to be obese, but from age 6 upward, boys have higher levels of obesity, measured by BMI.

Gender

Women are more likely to be obese than men. Currently 35.5 percent of adult women in the United States are considered obese, compared to 32.2 percent of adult men (Flegal et al. 2010). The largest gender difference is seen in younger ages; 27.5 percent of men ages 20 to 39 have BMI of 30.0 or higher, compared to 34.0 percent of women the same age. In the oldest age group, those 60 and older, however, the prevalence of obesity is higher for men than women, 37.1 percent versus 33.6 percent.

Looking at higher BMI levels, a slightly different picture is seen. Class II obesity, defined by a BMI of 35 or higher, is more common among women of all ages compared to men. Nearly 18 percent of women are in this category, compared to about 11 percent of men (Flegal et al. 2010). The same is true for class III obesity, a BMI of 40 or higher; 7.2 percent of women versus 4.2 percent for men are in this group. Unlike class I obesity, this gender difference, with women having higher rates than men, is found at all ages.

The only group of children to show an increase in obesity prevalence in recent years is boys aged 6 to 19 (Ogden et al. 2010). This gender difference is unexplained. One explanation could be biases in the BMI-for-age growth charts used to measure obesity. Understanding the factors affecting the trend among children may shed light on the future rate of obesity growth among the adult population.

Race and Ethnicity

Rates of overweight and obesity for women vary starkly by race and ethnicity but differences are not as apparent for men. Men across racial and ethnic groups have a similar prevalence of overweight and obesity (Flegal et al. 1998; Hedley et al. 2004). Black and Hispanic women, however, are much more likely to be overweight and obese than white women. According to the analysis of NHANES data (Hedley et al. 2004), 77.5 percent of black women are overweight, compared to 71.4 percent of Mexican women and 57 percent of white women. The prevalence of obesity is similarly skewed with the rates for black, Mexican, and white women at 49.6 percent, 38.9 percent, and 31.3 percent, respectively. Fully 10 percent of middle-aged black women are morbidly obese, with BMIs greater than 40 (Flegal et al. 1998).

In the 2007–2008 NHANES data, obesity prevalence rates are highest for non-Hispanic blacks (44.1 percent), followed by Hispanics (38.7 percent) and then non-Hispanic Whites (32.4 percent) (Flegal et al. 2010). As in the earlier data, the prevalence rate differences are much stronger for women than for men. The prevalence of obesity in men ranges from 37.3 percent (for non-Hispanic blacks) to 31.9 percent (for non-Hispanic whites), while for women the range is 49.6 percent (for non-Hispanic blacks) to 33.0 percent (for non-Hispanic whites) (Flegal et al. 2010).

A similar pattern in racial prevalence of obesity is observed at younger ages. Nearly 21 percent of both non-Hispanic black and Mexican American children are considered obese, compared to 14.6 percent of non-Hispanic white children (Ogden et al. 2010). Hispanic boys are more likely than either non-Hispanic white or non-Hispanic black boys to be obese at any level. Among girls, non-Hispanic black girls are more likely to be obese than Hispanic or non-Hispanic white girls.

GEOGRAPHY

Our information on state-level variation in the prevalence of obesity comes from the BRFSS. This state-level survey, established by the Centers for Disease Control, began in 1984 and is conducted monthly by telephone in all 50 states. The survey collects information on health risk behaviors and health practices, including self-reported height and weight, diet and nutrition, and participation in physical activity. The data are published annually by the CDC and available on their web site (www.cdc.gov/brfss).

Obesity is more common in the central and southern parts of the United States while, in general, the northeastern and western states have lower prevalence rates. The highest prevalence rates are found in Alabama, Mississippi, Oklahoma, South Carolina, Tennessee, and West Virginia, all with state-level obesity prevalence exceeding 30 percent in 2008 (because weight is self-reported in the BRFSS, state-wide prevalence of obesity is underestimated). Colorado is the only state with obesity levels below 20 percent in 2008 (http://www.cdc.gov/obesity/data/trends. html#State). Obesity levels at the local level also can be estimated with the BRFSS state level data. Results of the modeling indicate that high levels of obesity are found in the Mississippi Delta region, the Appalachian counties of Tennessee, Kentucky, and West Virginia, and the coastal regions of the Carolinas. Other areas with high levels of obesity include tribal lands in the western United States. The county-level map in figure 3.1 shows the wide variation in obesity by geographic region. These geographic patterns may be the result of differential geographic distribution of the population by race and ethnicity or socioeconomic status. To date, analyses have not disaggregated the effects of geography from these other sociodemographic characteristics.

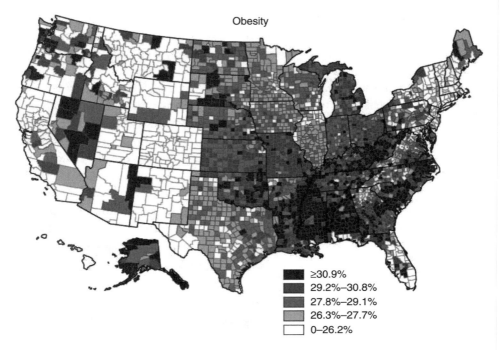

Figure 3.1. Age adjusted percentages of persons aged ≥ 20 years with obesity, by county—United States, 2007.

SOCIOECONOMIC STATUS

Body size is associated with socioeconomic status (SES). Cross-sectional descriptive statistics indicate that in the United States, low SES, measured either by educational level or income, is associated with higher levels of obesity for women (Chang and Lauderdale 2005; Mujahid et al. 2005; Zhang and Wang 2004). Untangling the effects of social class, education, and income from race and gender, however, can be difficult. In addition, obesity in young adulthood may influence the attainment of socioeconomic status, creating a bidirectional relationship (Gortmaker et al. 1993). The cross-sectional evidence supports the argument that social disadvantage is a fundamental cause of obesity. People with more money, power, and prestige may be better able to control their weight gain. Greater resources in terms of money and information may lead to better food choices through an increased awareness of and access to healthy foods (Morland et al. 2002). In addition, those with more resources have greater opportunities for and access to safe physical activity options (Powell, Slater, and Chaloupka 2004).

The effects of SES on body size seem to vary by race and ethnicity (Zhang and Wang 2004). As with race, obesity prevalence varies little by SES status for men, but for women there are strong effects of SES (Sobal and Stunkard 1989). Lower socioeconomic status is inversely associated with BMI for both white and black women

(Mujahid et al. 2005). The relationship between BMI and SES, however, may not be linear. Zhang and Wang (2004) find that SES is inversely associated with obesity (BMI ≥ 30) for women, but not men. However, when the measurement is over-weight (BMI ≥ 25), men of high SES are significantly more likely to be considered overweight than men of lower SES. On the other hand, women of higher SES were less likely to be overweight than their lower SES counterparts.

Several studies have examined the effects of SES on BMI trajectories using aggregate data (Clarke et al. 2009; Cook and Daponte 2008; Truong and Sturm 2005). These studies differ in the age groups and time periods examined, but reach many similar conclusions. The SES disparity in obesity prevalence seems to be declining over time; the "advantage" of higher SES is diminishing as those groups experience faster rates of increase in obesity prevalence. Individual-level data show that early life conditions may influence the trajectory of weight gain in adult-hood; weight gain is greater among those with lower SES in childhood (Baum and Ruhm 2009).

APPLICATIONS OF DEMOGRAPHIC METHODS TO OBESITY ISSUES

Demographers have contributed to our understanding of obesity differentials through the use of their specific techniques. In particular, standardization, age-period-cohort analyses, and estimates of life expectancy change have all been applied to the preva-lence of obesity or its consequences. In this section, I will briefly review some of the studies that highlight a demographic approach to the study of obesity.

Standardization helps explain the importance of changing characteristics of the population on obesity prevalence. Because obesity varies by race, gender, and edu-cational status, one explanation for the increases observed could be that the com-position of the population has changed over time. More women, more individuals of minority status, or lower levels of educational attainment might explain the observed aggregate trend. In fact, an analysis by Himes and Reynolds (2005) shows that the prevalence of obesity among those with more than a high school education increased at a faster rate than it had among those with less than a high school educa-tion between 1984 and 1994 (76 percent versus 41 percent among whites and 77 percent versus 27 percent among blacks). If the prevalence of obesity by educa-tional level had stayed the same, the increased educational attainment of the popu-lation would have led to a decline in overall obesity prevalence. If the educational differentials in obesity had not changed, obesity would have been expected to increase from 11.77 percent to 15.62 percent of the population between 1984 and 1994, compared to the 18.21 percent observed. In contrast to expectations, the increased educational level of the adult population has not resulted in a decline in obesity.

Three separate studies, one by Reither, Hauser, and Yang (2009), another by Cook and Daponte (2008), and an earlier analysis by Reynolds and Himes (2007) use age-period-cohort analyses to examine the reasons for the observed increase. Age-period-cohort analyses are useful for determining if an observed trend in the population is the result of a particular cohort's experience, of changes in one age group, or if the observed trend is seen across ages and cohorts at a particular time. All three studies use data from the NHIS for various time periods spanning about three decades. The overwhelming conclusion is that the observed increase in obesity prevalence occurred at all ages and for all cohorts. That is, period effects are principally responsible for the increased obesity prevalence. The increase may not have been uniform across population subgroups, however. Cook and Daponte (2008) note that the increases are fastest at youngest adult ages, indicating that more adolescents are reaching adulthood already obese. In addition, Reither and colleagues (2009) find that the increases in obesity prevalence are steepest for recent cohorts of Black women.

Finally, life table analyses have been used to look at the consequences of obesity for life expectancy (Olshansky et al. 2005). Olshansky and his colleagues estimated the extent to which the number of deaths in the United States might be reduced if obesity were eliminated. By using obesity-adjusted probabilities of death to create a life table, they are able to estimate the effects of this reduction in deaths on life expectancy. They estimate that the increase in life expectancy would range from about .3 of a year to nearly a year, depending on gender and race. Therefore, the current levels of obesity can be said to reduce life expectancy by one-third to three-fourths of a year, an amount equivalent to the elimination of deaths from accidents, homicide, and suicide. Not all researchers agree with this forecast, pointing out that there are many factors at work, for instance, better medical treatment, higher levels of education, and the experience of other nations, that may help maintain the steady increases in life expectancy experienced over the past several decades in the United States (Preston 2005).

Conclusions

The field of demography has contributed to our understanding obesity by explicating the trends in obesity prevalence and the correlates to those trends. Some groups are more likely to be obese than others, particularly women and members of minority groups. At the same time, demographic methods show that the obesity increase was seen across all ages and cohorts. Furthermore, rates of obesity among children have increased at the same time as those seen among adults. Knowledge of the scope of the problem underscores the need for a broad public health approach to addressing the issue.

Reasons for the increase in obesity range across economic, social, and cultural domains. Some attribute the rise of obesity to changes in food prices (Lakdawalla and Philipson 2009) or changes in labor force characteristics (Anderson et al. 2003; Chou et al. 2004). Others look at the influence of social networks (Christakis and Fowler 2007). Still other explanations focus on the availability of healthy food (Finkelstein, Ruhm, and Kosa 2005) or the use of particular food products, like high fructose corn syrup (Forshee et al. 2007). A demographic analysis of the obesity increase indicates that explanations, and consequently approaches to slowing or reversing the trend, are unlikely to be found in one factor. A multi-factor and multidisciplinary approach will be needed to curb the trend.

REFERENCES

Anderson, P. M., K. F. Butcher, and P. B. Levine. 2003. "Maternal Employment and Overweight Children." *Journal of Health Economics* 22: 477–504.

Barlow, S. E., and W. H. Dietz. 1998. "Obesity Evaluation and Treatment: Expert Committee Recommendations." *Pediatrics* 102: E29.

Baum, C. L., and C. J. Ruhm. 2009. "Age, Socioeconomic Status and Obesity Growth." *Journal of Health Economics* 28: 635–648.

Brodie, D., V. Moscrip, and R. Hutcheon. 1998. "Body Composition Measurement: A Review of Hydrodensity, Anthropometry, and Impedance Methods." *Nutrition* 14: 296–310.

Burkhauser, R. V. and J. Cawley. 2008. "Beyond BMI: The Value of More Accurate Measures of Fatness and Obesity in Social Science Research." *Journal of Health Economics* 27: 519–529.

Burkhauser, R. V., J. Cawley, and M. D. Schmeiser. 2009. "The Timing of the Rise in U.S. Obesity Varies with Measures of Fatness." *Economics and Human Biology* 7: 307–318.

Centers for Disease Control. 2009. "Estimated County-Level Prevalence of Diabetes and Obesity—United States, 2007." *Morbidity and Mortality Weekly Report* 58: 1259–1263.

Chang, V. W., and D. S. Lauderdale. 2005. "Income Disparities in Body Mass Index and Obesity in the United States, 1971–2002." *Archives of Internal Medicine* 165: 2122–2128.

Chou, S. Y., M. Grossman, H. Saffer. 2004. "An Economic Analysis of Adult Obesity: Results from the Behavioral Risk Factor Surveillance System." *Journal of Health Economics* 23: 565–587.

Christakis, N. A., and J. H. Fowler. 2007. "The Spread of Obesity in a Large Social Network over 32 Years." *New England Journal of Medicine* 357: 370–379.

Clarke, P., P. M. O'Malley, L. D. Johnston, and J. E. Schulenberg. 2009. "Social Disparities in BMI Trajectories across Adulthood by Gender, Race/Ethnicity and Lifetime Socioeconomic Position: 1986–2004." *International Journal of Epidemiology* 38: 499–509.

Cook, A., and B. Daponte. 2008. "A Demographic Analysis of the Rise in the Prevalence of the US Population Overweight and/or Obese." *Population Research and Policy Review* 27: 403–426.

Finkelstein, E. A., C. Ruhm, K. Kosa. 2005. "Economic Causes and Consequences of Obesity." *Annual Review of Public Health* 26: 239–257.

Flegal, K. M., M. D Carroll, R. J. Kuczmarski, and C. L. Johnson. 1998. "Overweight and Obesity in the United States: Prevalence and Trends, 1960–1994." *International Journal of Obesity and Related Metabolic Disorders* 22: 39–47.

Flegal, K. M., M. D. Carroll, C. L. Ogden, and C. L. Johnson. 2002. "Prevalence and Trends in Obesity among US Adults, 1999–2000." *JAMA* 288: 1723–1727.

Flegal, K. M., M. D. Carroll, C. L. Ogden, and L. R. Curtin. 2010. "Prevalence and Trends in Obesity among US Adults, 1999–2008." *JAMA*, published online January 13, 2010.

Flegal, K. M., and R. P. Troiano. 2000. "Changes in the Distribution of Body Mass Index of Adults and Children in the US Population." *International Journal of Obesity* 24: 807–818.

Forshee, R. A., et al. 2007. "A Critical Examination of the Evidence Relating High Fructose Corn Syrup and Weight Gain." *Critical Reviews in Food Science and Nutrition* 47: 561–582.

Gortmaker, S. L., A. Must, J. M. Perrin, A. M. Sobol, and W. H. Dietz. 1993. "Social and Economic Consequences of Overweight in Adolescence and Young Adulthood." *New England Journal of Medicine* 329: 1008–1012.

Hedley, A. A., C. L. Ogden, C. L. Johnson, M. D. Carroll, L. R. Curtin, and K. M. Flegal. 2004. "Prevalence of Overweight and Obesity among US Children, Adolescents, and Adults, 1999–2002." *JAMA* 291: 2847–2850.

Himes, C. L. 2000. "Obesity, Disease, and Functional Limitation in Later Life." *Demography* 37: 73–82.

Himes, C. L., and S.L. Reynolds. 2005. "The Changing Relationship between Obesity and Educational Status." *Gender Issues* 22: 45–57.

Komlos, J., A. Breitfelder, and M. Sunder. 2009. "The Transition to Post-Industrial BMI Values among US Children." *American Journal of Human Biology* 21: 151–160.

Krebs, N. F., J. H. Himes, D. Jacobson, T. A. Nicklas, P. Guilday, D. Styne. 2007. "Assessment of Child and Adolescent Overweight and Obesity." *Pediatrics* 120 (Supp. 4): S193–S228.

Lakdawalla, D. N., and T. J. Philipson. 2009. "The Growth of Obesity and Technological Change." *Economics and Human Biology* 7: 283–293.

Mehta, N. K., and V. W. Chang. 2009. "Mortality Attributable to Obesity among U.S. Middle-Aged Adults." *Demography* 46: 851–872.

Morland, K., S. Wing, A. and A. V. Diez Roux. 2002. "The Contextual Effect of the Local Food Environment on Residents' Diets." *American Journal of Public Health* 82: 1761–1767.

Mujahid, M. S., A. V. Diez Roux, L. N. Borrell, and F. J. Nieto. 2005. "Cross-sectional and Longitudinal Associations of BMI with Socioeconomic Characteristics." *Obesity Research* 13: 1412–1421.

National Institutes of Health. 1998. *Clinical Guidelines on the Identification, Evaluation and Treatment of Overweight and Obesity in Adults*. Bethesda, MD: National Institutes of Health.

Ogden, C. L., M. D. Carroll, L. R. Curtin, M. A. McDowell, C. J. Tabak, and K. M. Flegal. 2006. "Prevalence of Overweight and Obesity in the United States, 1999–2004." *JAMA* 295: 1549–1555.

Ogden, C. L., M. D. Carroll, M. A. McDowell, and K. M. Flegal. 2007a. "Obesity among Adults in the United States—No Change since 2003–2004." *NCHS Data Brief, No. 1.* Hyattsville, MD: National Center for Health Statistics.

Ogden, C. L., S. Z. Yanovski, M. D. Carroll, and K. M. Flegal. 2007b. "The Epidemiology of Obesity." *Gastroenterology* 132: 2087–2102.

Ogden, C., M. D. Carroll, and K. M. Flegal. 2008. "High Body Mass Index for Age among US Children and Adolescents, 2003–2006." *JAMA* 299: 2401–2405.

Ogden, C. L., M. D. Carroll, L. R. Curtin, M. M. Lamb, and K. M. Flegal. 2010. "Prevalence of High Body Mass Index in US Children and Adolescents, 2007–2008." *JAMA*, published online January 13, 2010.

Olshansky, S. J., D. J. Passaro, R. C. Hershow, J. Layden, B. A. Carnes, J. Brody, L. Hayflick, R. N. Butler, D. B. Allison, and D. S. Ludwig. 2005. "A Potential Decline in Life Expectancy in the United States in the 21st Century." *New England Journal of Medicine* 352: 1138–1145.

Pischon, T., H. Boeing, K. Hoffmann, et al. 2008. "General and Abdominal Adiposity and Risk of Death in Europe." *New England Journal of Medicine* 359: 2105–2120.

Powell, L. M., S. Slater, and F. J. Chaloupka. 2004. "The Relationship between Physical Activity Settings and Race, Ethnicity, and Socioeconomic Status." *Evidence Based Preventative Medicine* 1: 135–144.

Preston, S. H. 2005. "Deadweight? The Influence of Obesity on Longevity." *New England Journal of Medicine* 352: 1135–1137.

Reither, E. N., R. M. Hauser, and Y. Yang. 2009. "Do Birth Cohorts Matter? Age-Period-Cohort Analyses of the Obesity Epidemic in the United States." *Social Science and Medicine* 69: 1439–1448.

Reynolds, Sandra L., and Christine L. Himes. 2007. "Cohort Differences in Adult Obesity in the U.S.: 1982–1996." *Journal of Aging and Health* 19: 831–850.

Serdula, M. K., D. Ivery, R. J. Coates, D. S. Freedman, D. F. Williamson, and T. Byers. 1993. "Do Obese Children Become Obese Adults? A Review of the Literature." *Preventive Medicine* 22: 167–177.

Sobal, J., and A. J. Stunkard. 1989. "Socioeconomic Status and Obesity: A Review of the Literature." *Psychology Bulletin* 105: 260–275.

Sturm. R. 2007. "Increases in Morbid Obesity in the USA: 2000–2005." *Public Health* 121: 492–496.

Troiano, R. P. and K. M. Flegal. 1998. "Overweight Children and Adolescents: Description, Epidemiology, and Demographics." *Pediatrics* 101(Supp.): 497–504.

Truong, K. D., and R. Sturm. 2005. "Weight Gain Trends across Socioeconomic Groups in the United States." *American Journal of Public Health* 95: 1602–1606.

World Health Organization. 2000. *Obesity: Preventing and Managing the Global Epidemic.* Geneva: World Health Organization.

Zhang, Q., and Y. Wang. 2004. "Socioeconomic Inequality of Obesity in the United States: Do Gender, Age, and Ethnicity Matter?" *Social Science and Medicine* 58: 1171–1180.

CHAPTER 4

....

THE CLIOMETRICS
OF BMI AND
OBESITY

....

SCOTT ALAN CARSON

INTRODUCTION

....

CLIOMETRICS is the application of economic theory and statistics to the study of history and originated with Alfred Conrad and John Mayer's *The Economics of Slavery*. The field, however, was slow to take root because incumbent scholars were not trained in both economics and history. The field grew significantly when Robert Fogel and Stanley Engerman re-examined American slavery in *Time on the Cross*. Faced with limited slave diet, nutrition, and medical records, Fogel and Engerman turned to alternative metrics, such as housing and stature data. These data allowed Fogel and Engerman to consider slave biological conditions in depth, and Fogel's graduate students—Richard Steckel, John Komlos, and others—used stature data to study a broad set of historical and contemporary economic issues in what has come to be known as anthropometric history.

The use of the body mass index (BMI) became prominent in economic history as economists sought to better understand the social and economic forces contributing to the nineteenth century's widespread increase in life expectancy. Waaler (1984) offers a predictable biological explanation that corresponds with the emerging evidence for the relationship between relative mortality risk, stature, and BMI, and therefore longevity. Stature is a measure for a population's net cumulative biological conditions, and average stature is greater for well-fed populations and lower for poorly nourished populations. The BMI reflects net current health conditions and is, similarly, greater for well-fed populations and lower for poorly nourished populations.

When individuals fail to reach their genetically predetermined stature, their net cumulative biological conditions are substandard, and their statures may be stunted. When BMI values are low, net current biological-living conditions are also substandard, and weight-to-height ratios may be wasted. Low BMI values during industrialization focused economic historians' attention on BMI trends, characteristics associated with BMI variation, and calorie accounting. Moreover, biological conditions varied with labor market participation, and if workers were not healthy or were denied access to economic opportunity, their biological welfare suffered. For example, the bottom 10 percent of the eighteenth-century French labor force may have lacked the calories required to perform basic work (Fogel 1994, p. 373). While an improvement over the French experience, the bottom 3 percent of the eighteenth-century British labor force may have lacked the calories required to perform work (Ibid., p. 373). The missing element in explaining the human body's ability to survive in its physical environment is its response to the physical environment. Nineteenth-century statures and BMIs declined in order for the human body to have sufficient calories to sustain work and maintain health. This adaptability also applies to in-utero development, and it is hypothesized that poor fetal conditions modify fetal development as the fetus adapts to insufficient in-utero nutrition. However, poor in-utero conditions may contribute to later-life health conditions, such as coronary heart disease, stroke, diabetes, and hypertension (Barker 1992).

It is against this backdrop that this chapter outlines several key historical BMI findings. Several important BMI studies are reviewed, and a historical BMI composite is constructed for U.S. BMIs between the Civil War and World War I. Three questions are considered. First, how were nineteenth-century black and white BMIs distributed? Modern health studies demonstrate that twentieth-century BMI values have increased and become left-skewed (Sturm and Wells 2001, p. 230; Calle et al. 1999, p. 1103; Komlos et al. 2009; Cutler, Glaeser, and Shapiro 2003, p. 96). Evidence presented here, however, indicates that nineteenth-century BMIs were symmetric and neither wasting nor obesity was prominent among the working class. Second, how did black and white BMIs compare by race? Both nineteenth- and early-twentieth-century blacks had higher BMIs and obesity rates than whites (Flegal et al. 2010; Barondess, Nelson, and Schlaen 1997, p. 968; Nelson et al. 1993, pp. 18–20; Godoy et al. 2005, pp. 472–473; Flegal et al. 2002), nineteenth-century blacks had greater BMI values than whites. Third, how did black and white BMI values vary between 1873 and 1919, and how did they compare by socioeconomic status? While modern U.S. BMIs increased in the late twentieth century, I find no evidence for significantly increased black and white BMI values before 1920, and elevated obesity rates do not extend back into the late nineteenth century. Farmers also had consistently higher BMI values than non-farmers.

NINETEENTH-CENTURY BMIS
AND HEALTH

During the twentieth century, a nutritional pattern emerged in which increasing incomes in developed economies were associated with a substitution away from diets abundant in protein and complex carbohydrates and toward diets plentiful in saturated fats and simple sugars (Popkin 1993, pp. 145 and 148). Nineteenth-century BMIs were lower than modern BMIs, and by modern standards, historical obesity rates were limited. Modern populations in developing countries enjoy an abundance of nutritional allocations and encounter milder disease environments, unheard of in historical populations. This nutritional transition may subsequently be associated with changes in current biological conditions that are associated with changing health outcomes and BMI (Fogel 1994; Costa 2004; Cutler, Glaeser, and Shapiro 2003).

BMI serves as a reasonable approximation for health, especially in historical populations for whom medical records do not exist or are not well preserved. Waaler (1984) uncovers a U-shaped relationship between mortality risk and BMIs in a modern European sample, with the lowest mortality risk corresponding with a BMI of approximately 25. When BMIs are less than 19, health conditions related to undernutrition, infectious diseases, and respiratory conditions are prominent (Jee et al. 2006 p. 783; Calle et al. 1999, p. 1001), and if a population's average BMI is greater than 30, health conditions related to diabetes mellitus, cardiovascular disease, stroke, and cancer are prominent (Calle et al. 1999, p. 1101). Life-threatening conditions associated with high BMI values include cardiovascular disease, type 2 diabetes, and large bowel cancers (Pi-Sunyer, 1991). Obesity also elevates the risk of esophagus, colorectal, and breast cancers, as well as endometriosis and kidney disease (Calle et al. 2003, pp. 1628–1631). Costa (1993) and Murray (1997) demonstrate that the Waaler relationship is stable over time, and Jee et al. (2006, pp. 780, 784–785), Adams et al. (2006, p. 765), and Calle et al. (1999, p. 1101) demonstrate that the relationship is robust across racial groups, indicating that valid warrants and inferences may be drawn for past populations by using modern BMI-health relationships. Consequently, historical populations may have suffered more from infectious diseases, tuberculosis, and chronic diseases relative to the modern incidence of cardiovascular disease, type 2 diabetes, gall bladder disease, and large bowel cancer (Crimmins and Condran 1983, p. 33; Livi-Bacci 1983, p. 294).

These health conditions are also ethnically sensitive. Today, African Americans are more likely than whites to die from diabetes mellitus, stroke, and heart disease (Valanis 1999, p. 123), which are related to physical dimensions, diet, and exercise. Modern studies indicate the prevalence of obesity is greater in blacks than whites (Flegal et al. 2010; Barondess, Nelson, and Schlaen 1997, p. 968; CDC 2004, 1066–1067; Nelson et al. 1993, pp. 18–20; Godoy et al. 2005, pp. 472–473; Flegal et al. 2002), suggesting that racial differences in height and BMI may be, in part, attributable to differences in the environment. While we have few direct weight measures for slaves in the American South, a relevant period is between 1870 and 1920, a period when freed blacks were acclimating to conditions and hardships of life beyond the slave system. During the Reconstruction period, black incomes probably increased, and blacks devoted a higher share of their incomes to the acquisition of food, which may have increased black BMIs (Higgs 1977, p. 107). However, beyond stature studies, data to corroborate the historical relationship between nineteenth-century U.S. physical compositions and mortality risk are sparse. The BMI is an alternative source to highlight nineteenth-century health status.

HISTORICAL BMI STUDIES

Because more historical height data survives, stature studies have received more attention than BMI studies as a measure for historical health studies. Nonetheless, an increasing number of weight-to-height ratio studies are contributing to the historical record. Many early historical BMI studies tested the Waaler relationship and support the hypothesis that there is a stable, predictable relationship between stature, weight, and mortality risk (Costa 1993; Murray 1997).

Historical BMI studies also provide important perspectives on the evolution of health conditions. Cuff (1993) finds that mid-nineteenth-century West Point Cadets had BMI that were sufficiently low to place a large percentage of young nineteenth-century Northern white males into a high relative mortality risk category. Forty percent of 20- and 21-year-old cadets had values below 19, that which marks an increase in relative mortality risk. Coclanis and Komlos also find that late nineteenth-century BMI values at The Citadel military academy were comparable to those of West Point Cadets (Coclanis and Komlos 1995, pp. 102–103). Costa (2004, pp. 8–10) demonstrates that there were considerable differences between nineteenth-century black and white BMI values; specifically, blacks had higher average BMI than whites, and both increased between 1860 and 1950.

Carson (2009) considers nineteenth-century Middle Atlantic BMIs and finds that blacks had higher average BMI than whites, and although modern black and white BMIs have increased, neither malnutrition nor obesity were common among nineteenth-century Middle Atlantic working-class males. Moreover, nineteenth-century Middle Atlantic working-class BMIs were distributed symmetrically, and farmer BMIs were consistently greater than non-farmer BMIs; urban BMIs were lower than rural BMIs. Among nineteenth-century black and white prisoners aged 20 and 21, only 1.5 percent of blacks and 3.0 percent of whites had BMIs less than 19, indicating that the working class was ironically less likely than soldiers to be underweight. Nineteenth century BMIs also varied by nativity, and Southerners had low BMI values compared to Northerners.[1] The BMIs of nineteenth-century males who

---

1 However, BMIs are sensitive to height, and taller statures are associated with lower BMI values (Herbert 1993, pp. 1438). Early-nineteenth-century Southeastern males were taller than Northerners, which explains part of lower Southeastern BMI values.

lived in close proximity to major waterways and residence within urban centers had lower BMI values, indicating that nineteenth-century BMI patterns are similar to nineteenth-century stature patterns. Bodenhorn (forthcoming) uses nineteenth-century New York State legislator records to show that BMIs among an elite class of New Yorkers were also distributed symmetrically and neither malnutrition nor obesity was common. Therefore, existing historical BMI studies indicate that BMI values were related to mortality risk, symmetrically distributed, blacks had greater BMI values than whites, and rural farmers had greater BMI values than other nineteenth-century workers.

Factors associated with Nineteenth-Century U.S. BMIs

Here I use existing historical BMI studies to make a broad comparison of nineteenth-century BMI variation. The shape of the BMI distribution tells us much about the current biological conditions facing a population. If the BMI distribution is positively skewed, there is a disproportionate number of underweight individuals, and if the BMI distribution is negatively skewed, there is a disproportionate number of overweight individuals.[2] There are differing views about how nineteenth-century BMIs were distributed. On the one hand, BMIs may have been low because meagre seventeenth- and eighteenth-century diets relative to work expenditures continued into the nineteenth century (Fogel 1994, p. 373). On the other hand, nineteenth-century BMIs may have increased as US agricultural settlements produced more nutritious diets relative to calories devoted to work and to fend off disease. The overwhelming percentage of nineteenth-century black BMIs fell within the normal category; whites were even more likely than blacks to fall within the normal category (Costa 2004; Carson 2008, 2009). In both the North and South, there were remarkably few underweight individuals. There was also a sizeable percentage of nineteenth-century U.S. males in the overweight category and nearly no cases of nineteenth-century obesity.

Morbid obesity is defined as a BMI greater than 40, and is linked to elevated risks of diabetes mellitus, cardiovascular disease, and cancer (Pi-Sunyer 1991, p. 1599s; Kenchaiah 2002, pp. 306–312; Calle et al. 2003, pp. 1628–1630). Cases of nineteenth-century black and white morbid obesity were nearly nonexistent. Only .03 percent of blacks and .02 percent of whites were morbidly obese (Carson 2009). This contrasts with 2.9 percent in modern samples (Steinbrook 2004, p. 1077), which indicates that modern Americans are 100 times more likely to be morbidly

---

2 Using the World Health Organization BMI classification coding system for modern standards, blacks and whites with BMIs less than 18.5 are defined as underweight; BMIs between 18.5 and 24.9 are normal; BMIs between 24.9 and 29.9 are overweight; BMIs greater than 29.9 and less than 39.9 are obese.

obese than inmates in the nineteenth century. Therefore, compared to a developed modern economy, nineteenth-century blacks and whites in lower socio-economic status were in moderate weight ranges, and morbid obesity was nearly unheard of.

Other patterns emerge when examining nineteenth-century U.S. BMI variation. Farmers had higher BMI values than workers in other occupations and were less likely to be in the underweight category (Carson 2008, 2009). Greater farmer BMIs were due to close proximity to nutritious diets, and physical activity (Wardlaw, Hampl, and DiSilvestro 2004, pp. 457–460). BMIs represent an individual's composition between muscle and fat and are related to physical activity, therefore, occupations. Occupations requiring greater physical activity increased muscle and decreased fat. Modern agricultural workers use between 2.5 and 6.8 energy multiples of basal metabolic rate (FAQ/WHO, 195) indicating that nineteenth-century U.S. farmers had sufficient calories to maintain body weight because they were more physically active than workers in other occupations and closer to nutritious diets. On the other hand, modern skilled workers only use between 1.5 and 2.5 energy multiples of basal metabolic rate, and because of their physical inactivity, white skilled workers experienced excess weight gain.

HISTORICAL COMPARISON WITH MODERN BMIS

Considerable attention is currently devoted to modern BMI studies and their relationship with health outcomes and economic variables. For example, Helmchen and Henderson (2004) find that average U.S. male BMIs increased between 1890 and 2000 by 5.7 units among certain age groups, and the standard deviation nearly doubled. Costa (2004, pp. 8–10) demonstrates that BMI values increased

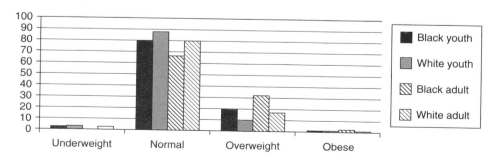

Figure 4.1 Nineteenth-Century U.S. Black and White BMI Classifications.
Source: See table 1. Includes black and white inmates in the Pennsylvania and Texas prisons (Carson 2008, 2009).

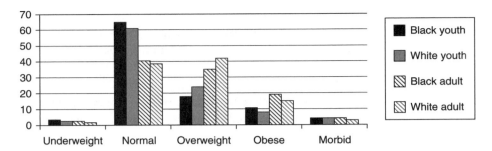

Figure 4.2. Modern Adult U.S. Black and White BMI Classifications.
Source: NHANES III.

between 1860 and 1950, and Komlos et al. (2009) find that U.S. BMI increases likely began in the 1920s. Cutler, Glaeser, and Shapiro (2003) also find that U.S. BMIs have increased since the early twentieth century; however, they find that the majority of increased BMI values occurred during the last 25 years because people consume more calories, not because they are physically inactive. Modern BMIs are also related to economic outcomes. Cawley (2004) finds that modern wages and occupational opportunity are inversely related with BMIs (Cawley, Grabka, Lillard 2005; Cawley and Danziger 2005; Cawley, Han, and Norton 2009).

A primary data source for modern U.S. BMI studies is the National Health and Nutritional Examination Survey (NHANES), which is periodically collected and sponsored by the National Center for Health Statistics to assess the health and nutritional status of U.S. children and adults. I use NHANES III for adult males observed between 1960 and 2000 to compare historic to modern BMIs.[3] According to modern standards, approximately 36 percent of adult men are overweight and an additional 23 percent are obese (Sturm and Wells 2001, p. 231; Calle et al. 1999, p. 1103; Cutler, Glaeser, and Shapiro 2003, p. 95). Figures 4.1 and 4.2 present the modern and historical BMI underweight, normal, overweight, and obese percentages by race. Three patterns are clear. First, only a small percentage of historic or modern males fell into the underweight category, indicating that wasting was not common in either historical or modern populations. In neither samples did the percentage in the underweight category exceed 4 percent. Second, compared to the percentage of historic BMIs, modern BMIs have shifted right (Cutler, Glaeser, and Shapiro 2003, pp. 96–98). Historically, nearly 73 percent of blacks and 84 percent of whites were in the normal category. During the nineteenth century, 19.6 and 33.3 percent of black youths and adults were overweight or obese; only 9.8 and 17.83 percent of historic white youths and adults were overweight or obese. The difference was the rise in the proportion of males in the overweight and obese categories (Costa 2004, pp. 8–10; Komlos et al. 2009; Cutler, Glaezer, and Shapiro 2003).

---

3 Ages are between 18 and 90, born between 1888 and 1980.

Third, compared to the nineteenth century, there was a sharp rise in the percentage of males classified as morbidly obese. Nineteenth century morbid obesity was virtually nonexistent; however, modern black and white morbid obesity rates are nearly 4 percent of the modern population, a larger percentage than the nineteenth-century share in the underweight or obese categories. This rise in morbid obesity is also accompanied by a rise in diseases associated with morbid obesity (Pi-Sunyer 1991, p. 1599s; Kenchaiah 2002, pp. 306–312; Calle et al. 2003, pp. 1628–1630).

BMI values vary over the course of the life cycle, and nineteenth-century BMI classification by age produces a clearer depiction for how historical BMIs compared to contemporary BMIs (see table 4.1). Compared to modern black BMIs by age, nineteenth-century blacks were historically less likely to be underweight, more likely to be in the normal category, and had about the same likelihood of being overweight. Moreover, blacks were historically less likely to be obese. Compared to modern white BMIs by age, nineteenth-century whites had the same likelihood of being underweight, were more likely to be in the normal category, and were less likely to be overweight or obese. Therefore, throughout the life cycle, historical working classes were less likely to be underweight or obese and were in healthier BMI ranges throughout life.

Table 4.1. Nineteenth-Century to Modern BMI Classification by Age

| | Blacks | | | | | | | | |
| | Prisoners | | | | Modern | | | | |
	Under	Normal	Over	Obese	Under	Normal	Over	Obese	Morbid
Teens	2.5	84.0	12.9	.6	3.6	60.9	18.7	12.0	4.9
20s	.6	70.4	27.9	1.1	2.0	53.9	25.5	14.5	4.0
30s	.6	64.5	33.2	1.7	1.5	40.4	34.5	18.6	5.1
40s	.7	62.7	33.5	3.2	1.3	37.6	36.4	21.5	3.1
50s	.7	60.6	36.3	2.4	2.5	35.0	37.7	20.4	4.3
60s	1.2	64.5	32.8	1.5	4.3	37.1	34.3	21.5	2.6

| | Whites | | | | | | | | |
| | Prisoners | | | | Modern | | | | |
	Under	Normal	Over	Obese	Under	Normal	Over	Obese	Morbid
Teens	3.52	88.4	7.59	.460	3.8	62.9	19.1	8.2	6.0
20s	2.03	84.1	13.5	.402	2.3	53.4	31.7	10.1	2.6
30s	2.50	79.1	16.8	1.57	1.2	40.9	41.6	13.0	3.4
40s	2.14	74.9	20.1	2.43	.8	34.0	44.2	17.1	4.0
50s	3.00	72.6	21.6	2.80	1.6	33.0	43.3	18.9	3.2
60s	5.33	72.8	18.3	3.55	2.2	34.8	43.3	16.3	3.4

Source: Carson 2008 and 2009.

DISCUSSION AND FUTURE DIRECTIONS

Diets in developed economies have undergone a nutritional transition, and nineteenth-century diets, abundant in protein and complex carbohydrates, have yielded to diets high in saturated fats and simple sugars. Physical dimensions, as measured by BMI, have correspondingly increased. This nutritional transition and BMI variation fell under the purview of economic historians as they sought to better understand the secular increase in life expectancy. Compared to modern BMIs, nineteenth-century black and white BMI values fell primarily into the normal category, and historical BMIs were in healthier ranges compared to the modern U.S. population. The proportion of black and white BMIs in the overweight and obese categories have increased and a striking comparison between nineteenth-century and modern BMIs is the rise in morbid obesity. Nineteenth-century blacks also had greater BMI values than whites, and mulatto BMIs were lower than darker pigmented blacks. Moreover, morbid obesity in modern populations is more common than the historical likelihood of being underweight. During the nineteenth century, health conditions associated with obesity were remote. However, the modern incidence of morbidities and mortalities related to obesity, including heart disease, diabetes mellitus, and certain cancers are now common.

BMIs are related with several economic variables, and nineteenth-century farmers consistently had higher BMI values than workers in other occupations. Heavier farmer BMI values also reflect the type of physical labor they performed, and physically active occupational regimens likely contributed to greater farmer muscle mass relative to fat compared to workers in other occupations.

While these nineteenth-century patterns and trends for African American and white BMIs shed light on historical health and socioeconomic patterns, the record is not complete. Future BMI studies will continue to explore the relationship between BMIs, ethnicity, and the historical relationship across economies. It is now well established that blacks were physically shorter than whites and had higher BMI values. However, future studies will clarify the observed pattern that darker complexioned blacks had greater BMI values than lighter complexioned blacks. This question is not without merit, because nineteenth-century mulattos were consistently taller than darker pigmented blacks and their BMI values lower than darker blacks, which may be inconsistent with a mulatto stature advantage. More can also be done in the use of calorie accounting, basal metabolic rate, and BMI. Other research directions will consider regional BMI variation by socioeconomic status and how BMIs varied over time. Little is also known about the relationship between stature, BMI, and historical labor force participation, which is a vital link between labor and health economics. Lastly, historical BMI research will also continue to explore promising data sources for female height and weight relationships to establish a more complete record of nineteenth-century U.S. BMI variation.

ACKNOWLEDGEMENTS

I appreciate comments from John Komlos, Marco Sunder, Marshalla Hutson, and Kelly Manning.

REFERENCES

Adams, Kenneth, Arthur Schatzkin, Tamara Harris, Victor Kipnis, Traci Mouw, Rachel Ballard-Barbash, Albert Hollenbeck, and Michael Leitzman 2006. "Overweight, Obesity and Mortality in a Large Prospective Cohort of Persons 50 to 71 Years Old." *New England Journal of Medicine* 335(8): 763–778.

Barker, David J. P. 1992. *Fetal and Infant Origins of Adult Disease*. London: British Medical Journal 301: 1111.

Barondess, David A., Dorothy A. Nelson, and Sandra E. Schlaen. 1997. "Whole Body Bone, Fat and Lean Mass in Black and White Men." *Journal of Bone and Mineral Research* 12(6): 967–971.

Bodenhorn, Howard. 1999. "A Troublesome Caste: Height and Nutrition of Antebellum Virginia's Rural Free Blacks." *Journal of Economic History* 59(4): 972–996.

Bodenhorn, Howard. 2002. "Mulatto Advantage: The Biological Consequences of Complexion in Rural Antebellum Virginia." *Journal of Interdisciplinary History* 33(1): 21–46.

Bogin, Barry. 1991. "Measurement of Growth Variability and Environmental Quality in Guatemalan Children." *Annals of Human Biology* 18(4): 285–294.

Calle, Eugenia, Carmen Rodriguez, Kimberly Walker-Thurmond, and Michael Thun. 2003. "Overweight, Obesity and Mortality from Cancer in a Prospectively Studied Cohort of U.S. Adults." *New England Journal of Medicine* 348(17): 1625–1638.

Calle, Eugenia, Michael Thun, Jennifer Petrelli, Carmen Roriguez, and Clark Meath. 1999. "Body-Mass Index and Mortality in a Prospective Cohort of U.S. Adults." *New England Journal of Medicine* 341(15): 1097–1104.

Carson, Scott Alan. 2007. "Mexican Body Mass Index Values in the 19th Century American West," *Economics and Human Biology* 5(1): 37–47.

Carson, Scott Alan. 2008. "The Stature and Body Mass of Mexicans and Hispanics in the nineteenth Century Southwestern United States." *Journal of Interdisciplinary History* 39(2) (Autumn): 211–232.

Carson, Scott Alan. 2009a. "Racial Differences in Body-Mass Indices for Male Convicts in nineteenth Century Pennsylvania." *Journal of BioSocial Science* 41(2): 231–248.

Carson, Scott Alan. 2009b. "The Effects of Demographics, Residence, and Socioeconomic Status on the Distributions of 19th Century Mexican Biological Living Conditions," *Social Science Journal* 46(3): 411–426.

Carson, Scott Alan. 2009c. "Racial Differences in Body-Mass Indices of Men Imprisoned in nineteenth Century Texas." *Economics and Human Biology* 7, no. 1 (2009): 121–127.

Cawley, John. 2004. "The Impact of Obesity on Wages." *Journal of Human Resources* 39(2): 451–474.

Cawley, John, and S. Danzinger. 2005. "Morbid Obesity and the Transition from Welfare to Work." *Journal of Policy Analysis and Management* 24(4): 1–17.

Cawley, John, Markus Grabka, and Dean Lillard. 2005. "A Comparison of the Relationship between Obesity and Earnings in the US and Germany." *Journal of Applied Social Science* 125(1): 119–129.

Centers for Disease Control. 2005. "Prevalence of Overweight and Obesity Among Adults with Diagnosed Diabetes—United States, 1988–1994 and 1999–2002." *Morbidity and Mortality Weekly Report* 53(45): 1066–1068.

Coclanis, Peter, and John Komlos. 1995. "The Nutrition and Economic Development in Post-Reconstruction South Carolina: an Anthropometric Approach." *Social Science History* 19: 91–115.

Conrad, Alfred, and John Meyer. 1964. *The Economics of Slavery and Other Studies in Econometric History.* Chicago: Aldine Publishing.

Costa, Dora. 1993. "Height, Weight, Wartime Stress, and Older Age Mortality: Evidence from the Union Army Records." *Explorations in Economic History* 30(4): 424–449.

Costa, Dora. 1998. *The Evolution of Retirement: An American Economic History* 1880–1990. Chicago: University of Chicago Press.

Costa, Dora. 2004. "The Measure of Man and Older Age Mortality: Evidence from the Gould Sample." *The Journal of Economic History* 64(4): 1–23.

Crimmins, Eileen M., and Gretchen Condran. 1983. "Mortality Variation in U. S. Cities in 1900: A Two-Level Explanation by Cause of Death and Underlying Factors." *Social Science History* 7(1): 31–58.

Cuff, Tim. 1993. "The Body Mass Index Values of Mid-19th Century West Point Cadets." *Historical Methods* 26: 171–183.

Cutler, David M., Edward L. Glaeser, and Jesse Shapiro. 2003. "Why Have Americans Become More Obese?" *Journal of Economic Perspectives* 17(3): 93–118.

Flegal, Katherine M., Margaret Carroll, Cynthia Ogden, and Clifford Johnson. 2002. "Prevalence and Trends in Obesity Among US Adults, 1999–2000." *Journal of the American Medical Association* 288(14): 1723–1727.

Flegal, Katherine, Margaret Carroll, and Cynthia Ogden, 2010. "Prevalence and Trends in Obesity Among US Adults, 1999–2008." *Journal of the American Medical Society* 303(3): 235–241.

Fogel, Robert. 1974. *Time on the Cross: The Economics of American Negro Slavery.* New York: W.W. Norton.

Fogel, Robert. 1994. "Economic Growth, Population Theory, and Physiology: The Bearing of Long-Term Processes on the Making of Economic Policy." *American Economic Review* 84(3): 369–395.

Godoy, Ricardo, E. Goodman, R. Levins, and W.R. Leonard. 2005. "Anthropometric Variability in the USA." *Annals of Human Biology* 32(4): 469–485.

Helmchen, Lorens, and R. Max Henderson. 2004. "Changes in the Distribution of Body Mass Index of White US Men." *Annals of Human Biology* 31(2): 174–181.

Henderson, R. Max. 2005. "The Bigger the Healthier: Are the Limits of BMI Risk Changing over Time?" *Economics and Human Biology* 3(3): 339–366.

Herbert, Patricia, Janet Richards-Edwards, Jo-Ann Manson, Paul Ridker, Nancy Cook, Gerald O'Conner, Julie Buring, and Charles Hennekens. 1993. "Height and Incidence of Cardiovascular Disease in Male Physicians." *Circulation* 88(4): 1437–1443.

Higgs, Robert. 1977. *Competition and Coercion.* Chicago: University of Chicago Press.

Jee, Ha Jee, Jae Woong Sull, Jengyoung Park, Sang-Yi Lee, Heechoul Ohrr, Eliseo Guallar, and Jonathan Samet. 2006. "Body-Mass Index and Mortality in Korean Men and Women." *New England Journal of Medicine* 355(8): 779–787.

Kenchaiah, Satish, Jane Evans, Daniel Levy, Peter Wilson, Emelia Benjamin, Martin Larson, William Kannel, and Ramachandran Vasan, 2002. "Obesity and the Risk of Heart Failure." *New England Journal of Medicine* 347(5): 305–313.

Komlos, John, Ariane Breitfelder, and Marco Sunder. 2009. "The Transition to Post-Industrial BMI values among US Children." *American Journal of Human Biology* 21(2): 151–160.

Livi-Bacci, Massimo. 1983. "The Nutritional-Mortality Link in Past Times: A Comment." *Journal of Interdisciplinary History* 14: 293–298.

Logan, Trevon. 2006a. "Nutrition and Well-Being in the Late Nineteenth Century." *The Journal of Economic History* 66(2): 313–341.

Logan, Trevon. 2006b. "Food, Nutrition, and Substitution in the late Nineteenth Century." *Explorations in Economic History* 43(3): 527–545.

Logan, Trevon. 2009a. "Health, Human Capital and African American Migration before 1910." *Explorations in Economic History* 46(2): 169–185.

Logan, Trevon. 2009b. "The Transformation of Hunger: The Demand for Calories Past and Present." *The Journal of Economic History* 69(2): 388–408.

Murray, John. 1997. "Standards of the Present for People of the Past: Height, Weight and Mortality Among Men of Amherst College, 1834–1949." *Journal of Economic History* 57(3): 585–606.

Nelson, Dorothy, M. Kleerekoper, E. Peterson and A. M. Parfitt. 1993. "Skin Color and Body Size as Risk Factors for Osteoporosis." *Osteoporosis International* 3(1): 18–23.

Pi-Sunyer, F. Xavier. 1991. "Health Implications of Obesity." *American Journal of Clinical Nutrition* 53(6): 1595s–1603s.

Popkin Barry, M. 1993. "Nutritional Patterns and Transitions." *Population Development Review* 19: 138–157.

Riggs, Paul. 1994. "The Standard of Living in Scotland, 1800-1850," in *Stature, Living Standards and Economic Development: Essays in Anthropometric History,* ed. John Komlos, Chicago: University of Chicago Press, 60–75.

Steinbrook, Robert. 2004. "Surgery for Severe Obesity." *New England Journal of Medicine* 350(1): 1075–1079.

Sturm, Roland, and Kenneth B. Wells. 2001. "Does Obesity Contribute as Much to Morbidity as Poverty or Smoking?" *Public Health* 115(3): 229–236.

Sunder, Marco. 2004. "The Height of Tennessee Convicts: Another Piece of the Antebellum Puzzle." *Economics and Human Biology* 2: 75–86.

Valanis, Barbara. 1999. *Epidemiology in Health Care*, 3rd ed. Stamford, CT: Prentice Hall.

Waaler, Hans T. 1984. "Height, Weight and Mortality: the Norwegian Experience," *Acta Medica Scandinavia,* supp. 679: 1–51.

Walker, Donald. R. 1988. *Penology for Profit: A History of the Texas Prison System,* 1867–1912, College Station: Texas A & M University Press.

Wardlaw, Gordon M., Jeffrey Hampl, and Robert A. DiSilvestro. 2004. *Perspectives in Nutrition*, 6th ed. New York: McGraw-Hill.

World Health Organization and United Nations University Food and Agricultural Organization of the United Nations. 1985. "Energy and Protein Requirements FAO/WHO/UNU Expert Consultation, Technical Report Series," No. 724. Geneva: WHO.

CHAPTER 5

THE ANTHROPOLOGY OF OBESITY

AMANDA L. THOMPSON AND PENNY GORDON-LARSEN

"THE health of a population is very accurately reflected in the rate of growth of its children."

Eveleth and Tanner 1976

INTRODUCTION

The domain of anthropology lies in the study of the biology and culture of human beings over space and time. The evolutionary perspective is a central theme, with much of the literature focused on variation in the form and function of human biology and culture in relation to context. Anthropology is generally broken into four interlinked fields: biological anthropology, cultural anthropology, archaeology, and anthropological linguistics. Given the primary interest in the integration of biology and culture, another major theme that sets the anthropological perspective apart from other approaches is its focus on the whole organism and its placement into wider societal, environmental, and cultural contexts. Obesity is a natural subject of interest, due to the central role of the human form and its relationship to the environment and society in which people live.

Obesity is essentially a simple issue of energy imbalance (higher energy intake relative to expenditure), resulting in excess storage of adipose tissue. Yet, obesity is far more complex than the simple law of thermodynamics. On the dietary side, food acquisition and preparation have shaped the health and survival of humans over time from hunting and gathering, to the storage and domestication of plants and animals, to the massive agricultural systems of today. On the energy expenditure side, there have also been major shifts in the types of activities in which humans engage, from transporting food and water to the use of modern, labor-saving devices. Energy intake is shaped by evolved food preferences and physiological needs as well as by cultural traditions that influence the types and amounts of food consumed, the symbolic meanings of food, and the social interactions shaping consumption. Similarly, evolutionary pressures and cultural and social forces that promote or reduce physical activity and fitness have molded the energy expenditure side of the equation. Consequently, both intake and expenditure have resulted from and have had substantial impact on societies and cultures across the globe and over time, shaping both human biology and culture.

In this chapter, we provide an explanation of how anthropological approaches tackle obesity, its determinants and consequences. Given the issue of energy balance and the fundamental role of biology in obesity, we focus this review on human biology (a subset of anthropology, which falls in the subfield of biological anthropology, while incorporating elements of the other three fields of anthropology) as a central unifying theme in the anthropology of obesity. First we provide a description of anthropological approaches to the study of obesity. Second, we present several theoretical models used to study obesity, with key examples of each type of model. Third, we discuss some of the essential methodologies used to model obesity. Fourth, we present a few examples of topical areas and current trends in the anthropology of obesity. We conclude with suggestions for future directions in obesity research.

ANTHROPOLOGICAL APPROACHES TO THE BIOCULTURAL STUDY OF OBESITY

Evolutionary Perspectives

An anthropological approach to obesity requires an understanding of how the human predisposition to obesity may have been determined during our species' evolutionary history, as well as the factors contributing to modern variation in obesity prevalence in different societies, social classes, or ethnic groups (Brown and Konner 1987; Ulijaszek 2007). The long human concern with fatness is evidenced by numerous figurines from the Paleolithic (dated to approximately 24,000–22,000 B.C.E.) that depict females with considerable excess fat, the most famous of which is the Willendorf Venus (Gamble 1986). The appearance of such figures at a time in our evolutionary history that predates the obesity epidemic of today suggests the value or symbolism of corpulence. For most of our evolutionary history, humans survived on subsistence agriculture or hunting and gathering, with a generally nutrient-dense diet of wild game, nuts, fruits, and vegetables. With the change from the Paleolithic to the Neolithic around 12,000 years ago, domestication and food production resulted in population pressure, agricultural centers, and stratified societies. This transition led to major changes in body shape and morphology and disease profiles (Omran 1983, 2001), carried further into the modern nutrition transition of chronic nutrition-related disease (Popkin 1996, 2004).

James Neel (1962) presented the idea of the thrifty genotype, increased efficiency in the intake and/or utilization of food leading to increased diabetes risk, which has been extended to metabolic efficiency and fat storage selected to sustain survival over cycles of feast and famine (Prentice et al. 2005). Most recently there has been debate related to the evolution of human fatness as proposed by the thrifty genotype hypothesis (Prentice et al. 2008; Speakman 2008). Prentice argues that women able to reproduce during periods of seasonal weight loss due to famine had a selective advantage (Prentice 2005). Conversely, Speakman argues that famines played less of a significant role in evolution, while other body size regulation mechanisms kept early humans from being too thin (to avoid starvation) and too fat (to avoid predation), resulting in upper and lower intervention levels for compensatory regulation of body mass (Speakman 2004, 2007). The importance of thrifty genes and a persistent cycle of feast and famine in shaping human obesity have also come under criticism from anthropologists who have argued that both approaches place too strong an emphasis on the extent of food shortages prior to the development of agriculture (Benyshek and Watson 2006; Wells 2009), and further that the human propensity to obesity arose much earlier in our evolutionary past (Ulijaszek 2007; Ulijaszek and Lofink 2006; Wells 2005, 2006, 2009).

Paleoanthropological investigations of the origins of obesity have attributed the human propensity to store excess fat to two unique, linked aspects of human biology: large body size with its concomitant increases in brain size and the greater fatness of adult females in comparison to males (Aiello and Wells 2002; Leonard 2008; Ulijaszek 2007). As Leonard and colleagues have argued (Leonard 2008; Leonard and Robertson 1992; Leonard et al. 2003), many of the important turning points in human evolution, such as the rapid expansion of brain size 1.6–1.8 million years ago, the initial migration of hominids out of Africa and the colonization of higher latitudes with their associated seasonality, are linked to improvements in energy efficiency and increased diet quality and are considered important selective pressures in the evolution of increased body fatness (Lieberman 2003). Human ancestors may have been at increased risk of starvation in these novel seasonal environments, and this stress is thought to have been critical in the evolution of the unique human profile of fatness (Wells 2005, 2006).

Exacerbating the risks of a seasonal environment were the large body and brains of human ancestors; the human brain is an energetically costly tissue, particularly in early life when the contribution of brain to energetic needs is at its highest (Foley and Lee 1991). Unlike some other tissues, the brain cannot respond to inadequate energy by reducing its size and, consequently, its energy requirements are both high and obligatory (Kuzawa 1998). This expense, particularly in early life, is also thought to contribute to the other characteristic of human adiposity, the systematically greater adiposity seen in human females (Ulijaszek and Lofink 2006; Wells 2006). Women's greater fat storage may buffer the development of the fetal brain during pregnancy and lactation from environmental energy constraints (Norgan 1997). This allows for larger brain size and higher body fat at birth (Ulijaszek 2002), which may help promote infant survival soon after birth and at weaning (Kuzawa 1998). The greater fatness of human females compared to males supports the hypothesis that reproductive energetics were particularly important in the evolution of our genus (Wells 2006), a role supported by the putative links between energy availability and fecundity in human females (Ellison 2003; Frisch and McArthur 1974).

Throughout most of evolutionary history, the human lifestyle was characterized by seasonal fluctuations in food availability, frequent periods of marginal or negative energy balance and high levels of physical activity and energy expenditure (Leonard 2008). These conditions may have selected for improvements in energy efficiency of human foraging strategies, with adaptations in food choice, subsistence strategies, and technological changes in food processing increasing the amount of energy available and contributing to a positive energy balance (Lieberman 2003). Accompanying these improvements in food quality and availability has been a reduction in the amount of daily physical activity. The lifestyle of foragers required a mixture of continuous and intermittent physical activity, ranging from mild exertion to intense, vigorous activity (Malina and Little 2008). While much lower than those of past foraging populations, the daily energy demands of modern subsistence-level societies are nonetheless considerably higher than those observed in the industrialized world. Comparisons between contemporary populations engaged in foraging, pastoralist and agricultural subsistence strategies suggest that the transition from these traditional lifestyles to a modern industrial one is associated with a 15–30 percent reduction in maintenance energy needs (Leonard 2008). Such evidence suggests that changes in energy balance, both improvements in energy availability and reductions in energy expenditure over the course of human history, are central to the development of obesity.

The link between human variability within and between individuals in fat storage and the development of a large brain suggests that the relatively high fat of human infants at birth and the tendency for the sexes to differ in body composition may have characterized the early evolution of the genus *Homo* (Wells 2006). This evolutionary propensity may have been further intensified with the development of agriculture and the more recent development of "obesogenic environments" with low levels of energy expenditure and abundant food supplies now contributing to strong positive energy balances and growing rates of obesity and chronic metabolic disorders (Leonard 2008; Ulijaszek 2007).

Cultural Approaches

Like human biology, human culture, the learned patterns of behaviors and beliefs that characterize particular societies, has also been shaped by both our history as hunter-gatherers and modern epidemiological, economic, and environmental transitions. Culture has been an important consideration in the study of human biology since at least the turn of the twentieth century with the writings of Boas (Little and Haas 1989). Boas's interest in human variation and biometry in particular was grounded in an exploration of biological variation in the context of cultural behavior (Boas 1892, 1912). More recently, biocultural anthropologists have reaffirmed the critical importance of culture as an important part of the human environment and have called for specific consideration of the impact of political and economic factors and social relations on human health and disease (Armelagos et al. 1992; Goodman and Leatherman 1998; McElroy 1990). Within the anthropological study of obesity, cultural context is understood to shape the epidemiological distribution of obesity, acting as an important determinant of energy intake and expenditure. Cultural beliefs that are particularly salient in the etiology of obesity include eating patterns, attitudes toward physical activity, the symbolic meaning of fatness, and the perceived risks of food shortages (Brown 1991; Sobal 2001).

On a larger scale, characteristics of social organization may also influence the predisposition to obesity. In highly stratified and culturally heterogeneous societies, the distribution of obesity is associated with ethnicity, age, and social class (Brown 1991). Within the United States, for example, obesity prevalence is higher among African American and Mexican American adults and children compared to non-Hispanic whites, and these differences are particularly pronounced among women (Ogden et al. 2006). The relationship between SES and obesity is not the same across all ethnic and age groups; an inverse association between SES and obesity prevalence is seen only among white girls, while obesity prevalence has been observed to increase with increasing SES in African American girls (Kumanyika 2008).

Gender, industrialization, and degree of acculturation all influence the magnitude and direction of the association between SES and obesity (Spring et al. 1994). Cultural values may be a particularly important component since these values help define what is "normal" and provide a basis for how people interpret their own body weights and the weights of others (Brown 1991). Cultural norms about body weight vary considerably, likely reflecting societal differences in the prevalence of food shortages, the potential for obesity in the given ecological context, and culturally defined standards of beauty (Kulick and Meneley 2005). Such norms may be an important factor linking obesity and social class. For many cultures, fatness is viewed positively as a sign of wealth and health, while for other cultures, like that of the United States, fat is increasingly stigmatized (Brown 1991; Kulick and

Meneley 2005). As described by Brown and Konner (1987) in their cross-cultural comparison of body preferences, even within countries like the United States, where obesity is culturally stigmatized, ethnic variation in accepted meanings of obesity is apparent. Among Mexican Americans, for example, increasing levels of acculturation have been associated with decreased obesity prevalence and have been shown to have a greater effect on decreasing prevalence than SES, suggesting that cultural values may play an important role in the etiology of obesity (Hazuda et al. 1988). While fatness is symbolically linked to psychological dimensions such as self-worth and sexuality in many cultures, the nature of the symbolic association is not constant (Brown 1991; Brown and Konner 1987), and it has been suggested that the most favored phenotype is the one most difficult to obtain within a given sociocultural context (Spring et al. 1994). Such variability in meaning highlights the need to investigate human obesity in not only a cultural context, but in the context of the community, the family, and individual behavior (Garn et al. 1977).

THEORETICAL MODELS

The Ecological Model

The ecological model derives from biology and refers to the interrelationship between organisms and their environments. For humans, the ecological model uses a broad definition of environment, to include physical, social, and cultural factors. A key factor in the ecological approach is the integration of social and biological factors and attention to the mechanisms and pathways that link social determinants to biological outcomes. A central feature of these recent models is the systems approach to obesity and the recognition that all of the environmental-level influences on obesity must operate through diet and physical activity, the primary proximate determinants of obesity. Although this orientation has been a part of anthropological approaches for a long time, such approaches have been advocated in recent calls from expert panels and committees (e.g., Pelto et al. 2003).

In the obesity literature, researchers have turned to ecological approaches to confronting obesity given lack of success in individual-level approaches (Egger and Swinburn 1997; Sallis et al. 1998; Sallis and Owen 1997). Chief in these approaches is the focus on multiple levels of social, cultural, and physical environmental influences that can be used to change health behaviors. For example, policy choices of governments at state and federal levels may affect the prices of food, the location and types of food markets or away-from-home eateries, which may become targets for taxation and other policy efforts to increase access to healthy foods and ultimately prevent and reduce obesity and its co-morbidities (Brownell and Frieden 2009; Brownell and Warner 2009; Chaloupka et al. 2002; Grossman and Chaloupka 1997; Warner 2005). Other examples of approaches incorporating the ecological approach address inequitable access to healthy foods and recreational opportunities by neighborhood and individual SES (Drewnowski and Darmon 2005; Drewnowski and Specter 2004; Gordon-Larsen et al. 2006; Maillot et al. 2007). Using ecological approaches, it is possible to model and identify factors such as food environments that exert influence on eating behaviors independent of individual SES factors (Dubowitz et al. 2008; Ellen et al. 2001). A critical element of ecological model-based research is the incorporation of biological factors; investigations of the broader environmental context that disregard human biology gloss over important issues in biological determinants and susceptibility to environmental contexts.

This element is particularly evident in ecological models of the role of developmental niches (the physical and social settings of a child's everyday life) in the etiology of obesity and the various social, ecological, and secular processes that may interact to place individuals at particular risk. While less attention has been paid to the local ecological and behavioral contexts associated with larger child size (Dufour 1997), several exemplary studies have recently explored the factors contributing to child obesity. Key among these studies has been a focus on parents' ethnotheories (culture-specific beliefs and norms) about appropriate child body size, eating behaviors, and diet quality (Bentley et al. 1999; Brewis and Gartin 2006). These ethnotheories have the potential to shape parental behavior and may link broader social changes, such as nutrition transition and modernization, to individual child growth. For example, Brewis (2003) has described the home and school environments associated with high prevalence of overweight in affluent Mexican schoolchildren. This research documented the aspects of children's developmental niches that predicted obesity risk most strongly: being a male only child or living in a home with parents who had permissive feeding styles. These risk factors were linked to cultural values: chubby children are considered healthier in this transitional economy, where under-nutrition among children is still common, and parents tend to show love through treats, sweets and snacks.

Gender-specific developmental niches preferentially placing boys at risk for obesity have also been seen among children in Appalachia (Crooks 2000), where boys were more likely to spend leisure time watching television or playing computer games, and among rural children in Ontario (Galloway 2007), where gender differences in obesity prevalence were linked to greater dietary energy intake from meat and grains among boys. Such studies highlight the need to explore the cultural values and behaviors that may influence pediatric obesity, as well as the important role of gender and gender-specific behaviors that may place children at risk.

Human Adaptability

Understanding the patterning of variation in health and disease within and between populations is one of the long-standing goals of human biology (Huss-Ashmore 2000). From this theoretical perspective, human biology and culture are considered the product of adaptation to environmental constraints. Historically, this interest has focused on the relationship between genetics and environment in producing variation in stature, body proportion, and body composition among ethnic or geographical groups (Baker 1969; Bindon and Baker 1985; Lasker 1969). Research focused on human adaptability in the context of environmental stress, and the goal was both to assess the ability of such stressors as heat, cold, and hypoxia to disrupt human biological function and to document the behavioral, developmental, physiological, and genetic responses of individuals and populations to these stressors (Huss-Ashmore 2000).

Studies, such as that of the International Biological Program (IBP) of the 1960s and 1970s, integrated the multidisciplinary perspectives of ecology, demography, epidemiology, nutrition, and auxology (the study of human growth) to study the health and biology of single populations such as the Peruvian Quechua (Baker 1969; Baker and Little 1976) and Arctic Eskimos (Jamison et al. 1978; Milan 1980) in extreme environments. These projects contributed to early understandings of the effects of the environment on human biology and health through a focus on "natural experiments," such as populations of different genetic ancestry living in the same environments or migration of individuals from a single gene pool into distinct environments (Garruto et al. 1989; Leslie and Gage 1989).

Central to human adaptability research was a developmental perspective and an interest in understanding how variation in human growth is shaped by environmental context (Cameron 2007; Eveleth and Tanner 1976). Early work in this area focused on under-nutrition (Habicht et al. 1974; Johnston et al. 1973), with studies such as the Institute of Nutrition of Central America and Panama (INCAP) longitudinal study of growth and development, which clarified the short- and long-term impact of high-energy, high-protein supplementation versus low-energy, no-protein supplementation on growth and development (Martorell et al. 1979). Such studies also focused on ethnic differences and the importance of environmental conditions supporting growth and development, honing in on the variation in human growth across socioeconomic status and urbanicity (Grantham-McGregor et al. 1991; Himes et al. 1975; Johnston and Martorell 1977; Malina et al. 1981; Martorell 1981; Martorell et al. 1977).

While most attention was initially paid to the consequences of small size and its relationship with long-term consequences for productivity, cognitive function, and reproduction (Grantham-McGregor et al. 1991; Martorell et al. 1977), human biologists have more recently turned their attention to the social and environmental factors underlying larger body size and adiposity (Bindon et al. 2007; Frisancho 2003; McGarvey 1991). Long-term research among Samoan populations, for example, has focused on the effects of discordance between past and rapidly changing present environments on the development of obesity and related metabolic disorders (Bindon and Baker 1985; McGarvey 1991; McGarvey et al. 1989).

Methodologies and Measures

Given the wide-ranging approaches and theoretical perspectives of anthropologists studying obesity, it should be of no surprise that the methodological approaches to understanding the causes and consequences of obesity are wide-ranging as well. Human biologists have incorporated a "whole body, whole organism" perspective (Morbeck et al. 1997) with methods ranging from anthropometric measurement to field-based metabolic assessment to qualitative analysis. We briefly describe several of these key methodologies below.

Auxology

Auxology, the study of human morphological and physiological growth, has been a central theme of human biology. One of the seminal leaders in the study of auxology is James M. Tanner, whose classic work in the mid-1950s set the stage for understanding the shape and body composition changes that occur over the life cycle (Tanner 1952, 1955). Tanner clarified growth as a sensitive, but non-specific measure of the overall health status of an infant or child; height-for-age reflects cumulative linear growth and long-term nutritional status, while weight-for-height reflects acute under-nutrition or chronic over-nutrition. Thus, growth must be viewed in terms of cumulative distance, providing a snapshot measure, or growth velocity over time, providing a more informative and dynamic view of the growth process. Early work in auxology led to major advances in several critical areas: statistical modeling of longitudinal growth data, sophisticated methodologies for assessment of body composition and understanding how variation in human growth is shaped by environmental context.

Early longitudinal studies, such as the Aberdeen Growth Study (Healy et al. 1956), the Harpenden Growth Study (Tanner 1955), the Fels Longitudinal Study (Roche 1992), and the Harvard Growth Study (Dearborn et al. 1938), paved the way for current understanding of longitudinal growth and the serial measures necessary to model growth trajectories. Statistical modeling to develop centiles and references ranges (e.g., Healy et al. 1988; Tanner 1952) led to standard deviation scores (e.g., Waterlow et al. 1977) and extrapolation of the lamda-mu-sigma (LMS) parameter method (Cole 1988; Cole and Green 1992), which forms the basis for the CDC and NCHS growth curves for the United States. This body of research has shaped current understanding of the normal growth curve, and consequently definitions of obesity in the pediatric population.

Early research focused on documenting variation in morphology, with techniques such as somatotyping, or describing human physique in three components: endomorphy (high adiposity), mesomorphy (high muscularity), and ectomorphy (high linearity) (Sheldon 1950), moving later to more detailed anthropometric measures (Garn 1957; Johnston et al. 1974; Lohman et al. 1988; Tanner and Whitehouse 1962), and most recently to advanced methodologies for body composition (Heymsfield 2008; Kelly et al. 2009; Wang et al. 1989). Human biologists have played a particularly important role in determining the validity and appropriateness of anthropometric measures of obesity (Cameron 1993; Himes and Bouchard 1985). This work was central in development of growth reference data (Tanner 1951; Tanner et al. 1966a, 1966b), with attention to the need for ethnic-specific growth curves (Goldstein and Tanner 1980; Johnston et al. 1984).

Genetics

The potential genetic contribution to obesity has also long been of interest to human biologists. Garn and colleagues in the Ten-State Nutrition Survey (TSNS) of 1968–1970 traced familial similarities in obesity and adiposity, attempting to distinguish between genetic and environmental components of obesity by comparing biological and adopted parents, offspring and siblings (Garn 1976; Garn et al. 1976; Garn and Clark 1976). Since this time, several lines of evidence support the role of genetics in body mass regulation (Coleman and Hummel 1973; Tartaglia et al. 1995; Zhang et al. 1994). In humans, family studies suggest that BMI and BMI changes are heritable (Austin et al. 1997; Fabsitz et al. 1994; Fox et al. 2005; Golla et al. 2003; Hunt et al. 2002; Strug et al. 2003). However, with rare exceptions, obesity does not follow a simple Mendelian mode of inheritance, with single gene defects being the exception rather than the rule (Farooqi and O'Rahilly 2005). The most recent Obesity Gene Map (Rankinen et al. 2006) includes 426 reports of positive association between an obesity-related trait and variants in 127 candidate genes. Genotype may influence sensitivity of individuals to environmental stressors (Chakravarti and Little 2003; Kendler 2001; Plomin et al. 1977; Rutter and Silberg 2002). Examples include inherited disease resistance or mutations that moderate disease expression. Body mass regulation may be best understood in the framework of gene-environment interaction because weight gain occurs when certain environments and certain genotypes combine. For example, in a large French cohort, significant associations were noted between body weight, BMI, and waist and hip circumferences and the *ADRB2* Gln27Glu polymorphism, but the associations were limited to sedentary subjects and were not present in the physically active (Meirhaeghe et al. 1999). Another example is the interaction between the *PPARG* Pro12Ala variant and both total dietary fat and the ratio of polyunsaturated to saturated dietary fat in relation to BMI (Luan et al. 2001; Memisoglu et al. 2003; Robitaille et al. 2003).

The findings from a study of Pima Indians provide another example of gene-environment interaction in the pathogenesis of obesity (Ravussin et al. 1994). The Pima Indians who now reside in Arizona in the United States and a remote area of Mexico, separated between 700–1,000 years ago. Despite a similar genetic heritage, the Mexican Indians have a much lower BMI (an average of 24.9 kg/m^2) than the U.S. Indians (33.4 kg/m^2). It has been suggested that the Mexican Pima have much lower levels of obesity because they live a traditional lifestyle, eating a diet with much less animal fat and caloric density, and having a far greater energy expenditure from physical labor.

Field Methods for the Measurement of Diet and Physical Activity

Many of the methodologies used by human biologists to measure the contributions of energy intake and expenditure to obesity are shared with other fields such as epidemiology, nutrition, public health and exercise science. Like these other scientists, human biologists tend to rely on food frequency questionnaires, dietary recalls, food weighing, and biomarker assessment to analyze energy intake and macro/micronutrient status (Haas and Pelletier 1989; Ulijaszek and Strickland 1993).

Similarly, they employ doubly-labeled water -isotopically-altered water that includes the elements deuterium and oxygen-18, which are traceable with metabolism. Using this isotopically altered water, it is possible to estimate metabolism through the individual's rate of uptake and elimination of deuterium and oxygen-18 over a period of days. Using doubly-labeled water in combination with activity records, heart-rate monitoring, and direct/indirect calorimetry, it is possible to assess energy expenditure and its components(Ainslie et al. 2003; Nydon and Thomas 1989). Each of these methods has its benefits and limitations and have been discussed extensively (Gibson 2005; Ulijaszek and Strickland 1993).

Where human biology differs from these other fields, however, is in the field-based application of these methods, which presents additional challenges and limitations based on the nature of the population and research setting. The traditional focus on "natural experiments" described above has meant that human biological research has tended to rely on long-term observations of populations in the natural settings (Garruto et al. 1989). Such settings may limit the methodologies used due to small sample sizes, lack of access to equipment or laboratory facilities, or the cultural appropriateness of research methodologies. The study of the effects of physical activity on health, for example, has been hampered by methodological limitations in the measurement of physical activity in naturalistic settings because of the competing problems of needing to record normal activity without interfering in that activity (Davies 1996; Dufour 1997). Similarly, nutritional anthropological researchers have stressed the need to supplement dietary data collection with ethnographic data on cultural factors that may facilitate or impede different collection methods, such as selection of a sampling frame that generates a representative dietary record for an individual or household (Pelto 1989).

The potential of field-based research for linking sociocultural factors, diet and activity of human populations to obesity is evidenced in a long-term study of metabolism among indigenous Siberian populations conducted by Leonard and colleagues (Leonard 2008; Leonard et al. 1999; Leonard et al. 2005; Snodgrass et al. 2006a; Snodgrass et al. 2005; Snodgrass et al. 2006b; Sorensen et al. 2005). This research has traced the rise in obesity in indigenous populations related to lifestyle changes brought about by economic development (Snodgrass et al. 2006a) through anthropometric assessment, calculation of metabolic rate, and laboratory analysis of serum lipids and thyroid hormones (Leonard et al. 2005). These wide-ranging methodologies have allowed researchers to document associations between total energy expenditure, excess body fatness and levels of acculturation.

Qualitative and Mixed Methods Approaches

In addition to field-based approaches, techniques that combine quantitative and qualitative methods are common in the field of anthropology. For example, ethnographic data collected via first-hand observation or interviews can provide contextual information that is an essential component of formative research. For example, anthropologists often use formative research to inform efforts for obtaining informed consent for clinical trials (Corneli et al. 2006) for designing clinical trial protocols (Corneli et al. 2007) or community-based interventions (Gordon-Larsen et al. 2004; Katz et al. 2004). Mixed methods have also been used to explore the contribution of parental feeding practices and beliefs to the intergenerational transmission of obesity (Birch and Fisher 2000; Faith et al. 2004; Parsons et al. 1999; Powers et al. 2006). Qualitative studies of infant and child feeding indicate that ethnotheories may be an important influence on customary infant feeding styles in African Americans and other groups and may influence over-feeding or the development of other inappropriate feeding behaviors (Bentley et al. 1999; Bronner et al. 1999; Corbett 2000). Studies, such as the Infant Care and Risk of Obesity Study (Lederman et al. 2004), an observational cohort study examining risk factors for the development of obesity in the first 18 months of life among low-income, African American children in North Carolina, have combined these qualitative observations with dietary, physical activity, and anthropometric measures to explore how early environments may influence the development of obesity in high-risk groups (Sacco et al. 2007; Slining et al. 2009; Thompson et al. 2009).

While anthropology has a long tradition of participant observation, new efforts in anthropology have focused on participatory action research. A strong example is that of the Agaston Urban Nutrition Initiative (AUNI) (Johnston 2009), a comprehensive program to promote nutritional health and community well-being through partnerships with university-assisted community schools. AUNI is based in West Philadelphia, an urban environment with low median family income and high unemployment rate, with obesity rates that have increased over threefold from the 1970s to the 1990s (Gordon-Larsen et al. 1997). Through academically-based partnerships between University of Pennsylvania faculty and students with local public schools, several AUNI programs address obesity. For example, University of Pennsylvania students enrolled in nutrition-related service learning courses through the anthropology department work with public school students to address nutrition-related issues in the community, incorporating hands-on community activities such as monthly healthy food tastings and comprehensive nutrition education. Other projects include partnerships to improve lunchroom choices, operate after-school fruit stands, and partner with neighborhood food stores to create convenient healthy food stations and to operate community farmers' markets as well as school day, after-school, and summer programs to improve exercise opportunities for schoolchildren and their families.

TOPICAL AREAS

Developmental Origins

The central point of life-cycle research is to explore the temporal sequencing of associations between exposures and outcomes (Lynch and Smith 2005).

Biomedical researchers now call for a life-cycle approach, viewing disease as the result of age-specific exposures at sensitive developmental periods as well as the temporal accumulation of exposures (Ben-Shlomo and Kuh 2002; Darnton-Hill et al. 2004; Demerath et al. 2004; Forrest and Riley 2004). Surprisingly little is known about the trajectory of obesity from childhood to early adulthood, when the major precursors of adult disease are developing (Adair et al. 2009; Smith 2007a, 2007b). However, mounting evidence suggests that early life under-nutrition, followed by nutritional excess during childhood and adulthood, is associated with increased adipose tissue relative to lean body mass and elevated chronic disease risk (Forsen et al. 2000; Law et al. 1992).

The importance of early life under-nutrition for the development of obesity was first documented among survivors of the Dutch Hunger Winter of 1944–1945, where men and women exposed to the famine in early gestation were more likely to be obese as adults (Ravelli et al. 1999; Ravelli et al. 1976). These results were supported by evidence from the United Kingdom, where low birth weight was found to be associated with higher BMI in adulthood (Phillips and Young 2000). More recently, low birth weight has also been related to adiposity in adulthood, measured by whole body energy X-ray absorptiometry (DEXA), indicating that low birth weight is related specifically to increased fat mass and not just "heaviness" (Kensara et al. 2005). Similar associations between birthweight and central adiposity have been found among UK and American adolescents and adults (Barker et al. 1997; Law et al. 1992; Malina et al. 1996), and it has been argued that this altered fat distribution may contribute to the risk of later metabolic complications, including insulin resistance (Eriksson et al. 2002). Furthermore, these observations have been used to support the idea that *in utero* exposure to maternal under-nutrition programs a "thrifty phenotype," (Hales and Barker 1992), whereby a developing fetus alters its metabolism to use energy more efficiently and ensure survival. This altered physiology may then be deleterious later in life if the individual grows up in conditions favoring over-nutrition and low energy expenditure, potentially leading to obesity and the metabolic syndrome (Gluckman et al. 2008).

Rapid weight gain in infancy is also associated with later adiposity and overweight, regardless of birth weight (Cameron et al. 2003; Monteiro et al. 2003; Stettler et al. 2003; Stettler et al. 2002; Toschke et al. 2004). Epidemiological evidence suggests that both excess early weight gain in infants of normal birth weight and rapid "catch-up" growth in infants with low birth weight may predispose individuals to obesity in childhood and adolescence (Ong et al. 2000; Singhal et al. 2003). Several recent reviews have suggested that breast-feeding may be protective against the development of later obesity (Dewey 2003; Dietz 2001; Gillman et al. 2001; Owen et al. 2005). This protective effect is thought to be due to the lower energy density of human breast milk compared with cows' milk formulas (Gluckman et al. 2008) and/or the greater infant control of feeding associated with breast-feeding (Taveras et al. 2004). The association between formula feeding and early excess weight gain has been observed in several settings and ethnic groups, including African Americans

(Stettler et al. 2003), and may contribute behaviorally to the intergenerational transmission of obesity.

Modernization and Migration

Modernization, the complex set of social changes that occur as societies shift from "traditional" to "modern" economies, involve shifts in economic production, diet and physical activity that substantially impact obesity risk for large segments of the population (Popkin 2004; Sobal 2001). Modernizing populations offer the opportunity to explore potential gene and environment interactions in obesity (McGarvey 1991), as modernization provides a natural experiment for exploring the role of new environments on relatively homogenous populations, such as those of Samoa. For Samoan young adults, modernization is associated with rapid accumulation of adiposity and increases in obesity. Body weights of similarly aged Samoans living in more traditional settings are much lower, however, indicating that this body morphology is not completely due to genetic factors (McGarvey 1991). In a classic study by Prior (1971), the diet and obesity of Polynesian islanders at different stages of acculturation were compared, with the results that the most traditional island had an obesity prevalence of 15.4 percent, a rapidly modernizing island had 29.3 percent and, for urban Maoris, the prevalence was 35.4 percent.

Migration between cultures places migrants, particularly those moving from developing to developed nations, into new food systems and new environments with potentially dramatic consequences for their health and well-being (Kasl and Berkman 1983). The process of acculturation into these new societies is often accompanied by changes in energy intake and expenditure with an impact on body weight. Among Puerto Rican migrants to Hartford, Connecticut, Himmelgreen and colleagues (2004) found higher BMI and rates of obesity with increasing length of residence in the United States. They attributed this effect to the abundance of food, labor-saving devices, and limited time for food preparation in the United States, along with the high value placed on convenience, assimilation, and acculturation. The specific mechanisms that put migrants at risk for the development of obesity likely vary among groups from distinctive origins and to unique destinations. However, migrants who gain weight in the new societies may be at increased risk of subsequent illness due to the loss of what Janes and Pawson (1986) have called "the buffering effects of traditional culture."

Body Image

Ethnographically, the thin body ideal and stigmatization of fatness that characterizes many Western societies has not been found to be universal; rather, plumpness is considered more attractive, more marriageable, higher status, or healthier in many traditional cultures (Anderson et al. 1992; Brown and Konner 1987). In their examination of the cross-cultural standards of ideal body type based on the Human Relation Area Files (HRAF), Brown and Konner (1987) found that in the majority

(81 percent) of the 38 societies with available data, a plump to moderately fat body was preferred, with only 19 percent preferring thinness. While none of the societies favored an extremely obese body type, available evidence suggested that a moderately fat body type was associated with health, wealth, and fecundity. In a famous ethnographic example, elite pubescent girls of the Efik of Nigeria spent up to two years before marriage in fattening huts, putting on weight as one of the symbols of womanhood and marriageability (Brown and Konner 1987). Similarly, Fellahin Arabs of Egypt were said to describe the proper woman as fat because fatness was associated with maternity and nurturance (Brown 1991).

However, as the prevalence of obesity has risen globally, the preference for thinner bodies has increased, even in societies that once preferred plumper figures (Anderson et al. 1992; Madrigal et al. 2000). The desire for thinner body sizes has been observed in European children and adolescents across all socioeconomic strata (Story et al. 1995), as well as Native American children (Bindon et al. 2007) and Pacific Islanders (Brewis and McGarvey 2000). Among Samoan women, who display some of the greatest adiposity of any human group and have traditionally venerated large body size, Brewis and McGarvey (2000) found that modernization was associated with preferences for a slimmer body ideal, with Samoan women living in Auckland preferring slimmer bodies than Samoan women living in less modernized areas of Samoa. However, idealism of slimmer bodies was apparent even among women living in the most traditional settings. They conclude that one of the effects of both modernization and acculturation is the increasing preference for smaller body size ideals at the same time that body size is generally increasing (Brewis and McGarvey 2000). This incongruity between actual body sizes and ideals suggests that not only is the most valued body shape the one associated with health and prosperity (Spring et al. 1994) but also that, under modern conditions of abundance, the tendency toward body weight above the ideal cannot be easily controlled, even with a reversal of widespread cultural ideals (Brown 1991).

CONCLUSION AND FUTURE DIRECTIONS

The global increase in obesity has been attributed to a mismatch between our modern obesogenic environment and our evolutionary heritage (Ulijaszek 2006). Consequently, efforts to address obesity must consider the integration of human biology and culture in relation to present and past environmental contexts. With modernization, relatively recent changes in diet and physical activity behaviors (and thus energy balance) have shaped current trends in body size, resulting in obesity as a critical, global issue. Since obesity is fundamentally linked to biology, culture, and environment, anthropological approaches have the potential to uniquely inform understanding of the biocultural determinants underlying susceptibility to the obesogenic environment.

ACKNOWLEDGEMENTS

The authors thank Margaret Bentley for her valued comments on a draft of this chapter and Noel Cameron for his advice regarding the field of auxology.

REFERENCES

Adair, L. S., R. Martorell, A. D. Stein, P. C. Hallal, H. S. Sachdev, D. Prabhakaran, A. K. Wills, S. A. Norris, D. L. Dahly, N. R, Lee, and others. 2009. "Size at Birth, Weight Gain in Infancy and Childhood, and Adult Blood Pressure in 5 Low- and Middle-Income-Country Cohorts: When Does Weight Gain Matter?" *American Journal of Clinical Nutrition* 89(5): 1383–1392.

Aiello, L. C., J. C. Wells. 2002. "Energetics and the Evolution of the Genus Homo." *Annual Review of Anthropology* 31: 323–338.

Ainslie, P., T. Reilly, K. Westerterp. 2003. "Estimating Human Energy Expenditure: A Review of Techniques with Particular Reference to Doubly Labelled Water." *Sports Medicine* 33(9): 683–698.

Anderson, J., C. Crawford, J. Nadeau, T. Lindberg. 1992. "Was the Duchess of Windsor Right? A Cross-Cultural Review of the Socioecology of Ideals of Female Body Shape." *Ethology and Sociobiology* 13: 197–227.

Armelagos, G. J., T. Leatherman, M. Ryan, L. Sibley. 1992. "Biocultural Synthesis in Medical Anthropology." *Medical Anthropology* 14(1): 35–52.

Austin, M. A., Y. Friedlander, B. Newman, K. Edwards, E. J. Mayer-Davis, M. C. King. 1997. "Genetic Influences on Changes in Body Mass Index: A Longitudinal Analysis of Women Twins." *Obesity Research* 5(4): 326–331.

Baker, P. T. 1969. "Human Adaptation to Altitude." *Science* 163: 1149–1156.

Baker, P. T., M. A. Little, eds. 1976. *Man in the Andes: A Multidisciplinary Study of Highland Quechua.* Stroudsburg, PA: Dowden, Hutchinson and Ross.

Barker, M., S. Robinson, C. Osmond, D. J. Barker. 1997. "Birth Weight and Body Fat Distribution in Adolescent Girls." *Archives of Disease in Childhood* 77(5): 381–383.

Ben-Shlomo, Y., and D. Kuh. 2002. "A Life Course Approach to Chronic Disease Epidemiology: Conceptual Models, Empirical Challenges and Interdisciplinary Perspectives." *International Journal of Epidemiology* 31(2): 285–293.

Bentley, M., L. Gavin, M. M. Black, and L. Teti. 1999. "Infant Feeding Practices of Low-Income, African-American, Adolescent Mothers: An Ecological, Multigenerational Perspective." *Social Science and Medicine* 49(8): 1085–100.

Benyshek, D. C., and J. T. Watson. 2006. "Exploring the Thrifty Genotype's Food-Shortage Assumptions: A Cross-Cultural Comparison of Ethnographic Accounts of Food Security among Foraging and Agricultural Societies." *American Journal of Physical Anthropology* 131(1): 120–126.

Bindon, J. R., and P. T. Baker. 1985. "Modernization, Migration and Obesity among Samoan Adults." *Annals of Human Biology* 12(1): 67–76.

Bindon, J. R., W. W. Dressler, M. J. Gilliland, and D. E. Crews. 2007. "A Cross-Cultural Perspective on Obesity and Health in Three Groups of Women: The Mississippi Choctaw, American Samoans, and African Americans." *Collegium. Antropologicum* 31(1): 47–54.

Birch, L. L., and J. O. Fisher. 2000. "Mothers' Child-Feeding Practices Influence Daughters' Eating and Weight." *American Journal of Clinical Nutrition* 71(5): 1054–1061.

Boas, F. 1892. "The Growth of Children." *Science* 19: 256–257, 281–282.

Boas, F. 1912. "Changes in the Bodily Form of Immigrants." *American Anthropologist* 14(3): 530–562.

Brewis, A. 2003. "Biocultural Aspects of Obesity in Young Mexican Schoolchildren." *American Journal of Human Biology* 15(3): 446–460.

Brewis, A., and M. Gartin. 2006. "Biocultural Construction of Obesogenic Ecologies of Childhood: Parent-Feeding versus Child-Eating Strategies." *American Journal of Human Biology* 18(2): 203–213.

Brewis, A., S. T. McGarvey. 2000. "Body Image, Body Size and Samoan Ecological and Individual Modernization." *Ecology of Food and Nutrition* 39(2): 105–120.

Bronner, Y. L., S. M. Gross, L. Caulfield, M. E. Bentley, L. Kessler, J. Jensen, B. Weathers, and D. M. Paige. 1999. "Early Introduction of Solid Foods among Urban African-American Participants in WIC. *Journal of the American Dietetic Association* 99(4): 457–461.

Brown, P. J. 1991. "Culture and the Evolution of Obesity." *Human Nature* 2(1): 31–57.

Brown, P. J., and M. Konner. 1987. "An Anthropological Perspective on Obesity." Annals of the New York Academy of Sciences 499: 29–46.

Brownell, K. D., and T. R. Frieden. 2009. "Ounces of Prevention—The Public Policy Case for Taxes on Sugared Beverages." *New England Journal of Medicine* 360:1805–1808.

Brownell, K. D., and K. E. Warner. 2009. "The Perils of Ignoring History: Big Tobacco Played Dirty and Millions Died. How Similar Is Big Food? *Milbank Quarterly* 87(1): 259–294.

Cameron, N. 1993. "Assessment of Growth and Maturation during Adolescence." *Hormone Research* 39 Suppl 3: 9–17.

Cameron, N. 2007. "Growth Patterns in Adverse Environments. *American Journal of Human Biology* 19(5): 615–621.

Cameron, N., J. Pettifor, T. De Wet, and S. Norris. 2003. "The Relationship of Rapid Weight Gain in Infancy to Obesity and Skeletal Maturity in Childhood." *Obesity Research* 11(3): 457–460.

Cawley, John, Euna Han, and Edward C.Norton. 2009. "Obesity and Labor Market Outcomes Among Immigrants to the United States From Developing Countries." *Economics and Human Biology* 7(2): 153–164.

Chakravarti, A., and P. Little. 2003. "Nature, Nurture and Human Disease." *Nature* 421(6921): 412–414.

Chaloupka, F. J., K. M. Cummings, C. P. Morley, and J. K. Horan. 2002. "Tax, Price and Cigarette Smoking: Evidence from the Tobacco Documents and Implications for Tobacco Company Marketing Strategies." *Tobacco Control* 11(Supp. 1): I62–172.

Cole, T. J. 1988. "Fitting Smoothed Centile Curves to Reference Data." *Journal of the Royal Statistical Society,* Series A(151): 385–418.

Cole, T. J., and P. J. Green. 1992. "Smoothing Reference Centile Curves: The LMS Method and Penalized Likelihood." *Statistics in Medicine* 11(10): 1305–1319.

Coleman, D. L., and K. P. Hummel. 1973. "The Influence of Genetic Background on the Expression of the Obese (Ob) Gene in the Mouse." *Diabetologia* 9(4): 287–293.

Corbett, K. S. 2000. "Explaining Infant Feeding Style of Low-Income Black Women." *Journal of Pediatric Nursing* 15(2): 73–81.

Corneli, A. L., M. E. Bentley, J. R. Sorenson, G. E. Henderson, C. van der Horst, A. Moses, J. Nkhoma, L. Tenthani, Y. Ahmed, C. M. Heilig, and others. 2006. "Using Formative Research to Develop a Context-Specific Approach to Informed Consent for Clinical Trials." *Journal of Empirical Research on Human Research Ethics* 1(4): 45–60.

Corneli, A. L., E. G. Piwoz, M. E. Bentley, A. Moses, J. R. Nkhoma, B. C. Tohill, L. Adair, B. Mtimuni, Y. Ahmed, A. Duerr, and others. 2007. "Involving Communities in the Design of Clinical Trial Protocols: The BAN Study in Lilongwe, Malawi." *Contemporary Clinical Trials* 28(1): 59–67.

Crooks, D. L. 2000. "Food Consumption, Activity, and Overweight among Elementary School Children In an Appalachian Kentucky Community." *American Journal of Physical Anthropology* 112(2): 159–170.

Darnton-Hill, I., C. Nishida, W. P. James. 2004. "A Life Course Approach to Diet, Nutrition and the Prevention of Chronic Diseases." *Public Health and Nutrition* 7(1A): 101–121.

Davies, P. S. W. 1996. "Total Energy Expenditure in Young Children." *American Journal of Human Biology* 8: 183–188.

Dearborn, W. F., J. W. M. Rothney, and F. K. Shuttleworth. 1938. *Data on the Growth of Public School Children From the Materials of the Harvard Growth Study*. Washington, DC: National Research Council.

Demerath, E. W., N. Cameron, M. W. Gillman, B. Towne, R. M. Siervogel. 2004. "Telomeres and Telomerase in the Fetal Origins of Cardiovascular Disease: A Review." *Human Biology* 76(1): 127–146.

Dewey, K. G. 2003. "Is Breastfeeding Protective against Child Obesity?" *Journal of Human Lactation* 19(1): 9–18.

Dietz, W. H. 2001. "Breastfeeding May Help Prevent Childhood Overweight." *Journal of the American Medical Association* 285(19): 2506–2507.

Drewnowski, A., and N. Darmon. 2005. "Food Choices and Diet Costs: an Economic Analysis." *Journal of Nutrition* 135(4): 900–904.

Drewnowski, A., and S. E. Specter. 2004. "Poverty and Obesity: The Role of Energy Density and Energy Costs." *American Journal of Clinical Nutrition* 79(1): 6–16.

Dubowitz, T., M. Heron, C. E. Bird, N. Lurie, B. K. Finch, R. Basurto-Davila, L. Hale, and J. J. Escarce. 2008. "Neighborhood Socioeconomic Status and Fruit and Vegetable Intake among Whites, Blacks, and Mexican Americans in the United States." *American Journal of Clinical Nutrition* 87(6): 1883–1891.

Dufour, D. L. 1997." Nutrition, Activity and Health in Children." *Annual Review of Anthropology* 26: 541–565.

Egger, G., and B. Swinburn. 1997. "An 'Ecological' Approach to the Obesity Pandemic. *British Medical Journalj* 315(7106): 477–480.

Ellen, I. G., T. Mijanovich, and K.N. Dillman. 2001. "Neighborhood Effects on Health: Exploring the Links and Assessing the Evidence." *Journal of Urban Affairs* 23: 391–408.

Ellison, P. T. 2003. "Energetics and Reproductive Effort." *American Journal of Human Biology* 15(3): 342–351.

Eriksson, J. G., T. Forsen, J. Tuomilehto, V. W. Jaddoe, C. Osmond, and D. J. Barker. 2002. "Effects of Size at Birth and Childhood Growth on the Insulin Resistance Syndrome in Elderly Individuals." *Diabetologia* 45(3): 342–348.

Eveleth, P. B., and J. M. Tanner. 1976. *Worldwide Variation in Human Growth*. Cambridge: Cambridge University Press.

Fabsitz, R. R., P. Sholinsky, and D. Carmelli. 1994. "Genetic Influences on Adult Weight Gain and Maximum Body Mass Index in Male Twins." *American Journal of Epidemiology* 140(8): 711–720.

Faith, M. S., K. S. Scanlon, L. L Birch, L. A. Francis, and B. Sherry. 2004. "Parent-Child Feeding Strategies and Their Relationships to Child Eating and Weight Status." *Obesity Research* 12(11): 1711–1722.

Farooqi, I. S., and S. O'Rahilly. 2005. "Monogenic Obesity in Humans." *Annual Review of Medicine* 56: 443–458.

Foley, R. A., and P. C. Lee. 1991. "Ecology and Energetics of Encephalization in Hominid Evolution." *Philosophical Transactions of the Royal Society of London: B Biological Sciences* 334(1270): 223–231; discussion 232.

Forrest, C. B., and A. W. Riley. 2004. "Childhood Origins of Adult Health: A Basis for Life-Course Health Policy." *Health Affairs (Millwood)* 23(5): 155–164.

Forsen, T., J. Eriksson, J. Tuomilehto, A. Reunanen, C. Osmond, and D. Barker. 2000. The Fetal and Childhood Growth of Persons Who Develop Type 2 Diabetes." *Annals of Internal Medicine* 133(3): 176–182.

Fox, C.S., N. L. Heard-Costa, R. S. Vasan, J. M. Murabito, R. B. D'Agostino, Sr., and L. D. Atwood. 2005. "Genomewide Linkage Analysis of Weight Change in the Framingham Heart Study." *Journal of Clinical Endocrinology and Metabolism* 90(6): 3197–3201.

Frisancho, A. R. 2003. "Reduced Rate of Fat Oxidation: A Metabolic Pathway to Obesity in the Developing Nations." *American Journal of Human Biology* 15(4): 522–532.

Frisch, R. E., and J. W. McArthur. 1974. "Menstrual Cycles: Fatness as a Determinant of Minimum Weight for Height Necessary for Their Maintenance or Onset." *Science* 185(4155): 949–951.

Galloway, T. 2007. "Gender Differences in Growth and Nutrition in a Sample of Rural Ontario Schoolchildren." *American Journal of Human Biology* 19(6): 774–788.

Gamble, C. 1986. *The Paleolithic Settlement of Europe.* Cambridge: Cambridge University Press.

Garn, S. M. 1957. "Selection of Body Sites for Fat Measurement." *Science* 125(3247): 550–551.

Garn, S. M. 1976. "The Origins of Obesity." *American Journal of Diseases of Children* 130(5): 465–467.

Garn, S. M., S. M. Bailey, P. E. Cole, and I. T. Higgins. 1977. "Level of Education, Level of Income, and Level of Fatness in Adults." *American Journal of Clinical Nutrition* 30(5): 721–725.

Garn, S. M., S. M. Bailey, and I. T. Higgins. 1976. "Fatness Similarities in Adopted Pairs." *American Journal of Clinical Nutrition* 29(10): 1067–1068.

Garn, S. M., and D. C. Clark. 1976. "Trends in Fatness and the Origins of Obesity Ad Hoc Committee to Review the Ten-State Nutrition Survey." *Pediatrics* 57(4): 443–456.

Garruto, R. M., A. B. Way, S. Zansky, and C. Hoff. 1989. "Natural Experimental Models in Human Biology, Epidemiology, and Clinical Medicine." In*Human Population Biology: A Transdisciplinary Approach*, eds. M. A. Little and J. D. Hass. New York: Oxford University Press, 82–113.

Gibson, R. S. 2005. *Principles of Nutritional Assessment.* New York: Oxford University Press.

Gillman, M. W., S. L. Rifas-Shiman, C. A. Camargo, Jr., C. S. Berkey, A. L. Frazier, H. R. Rockett, A. E. Field, and G. A. Colditz. 2001. "Risk of Overweight among Adolescents Who Were Breastfed as Infants." *Journal of the American Medical Association* 285(19): 2461–2467.

Gluckman, P. D., M. A. Hanson, A. S. Beedle, and D. Raubenheimer. 2008. "Fetal and Neonatal Pathways to Obesity." *Frontiers in Hormone Research* 36: 61–72.

Goldstein, H., and J. M. Tanner. 1980. "Ecological Considerations in the Creation and the Use of Child Growth Standards." *Lancet* 1(8168 Pt 1): 582–585.

Golla, A., K. Strauch, J. Dietter, and M. P. Baur. 2003. "Quantitative Trait Linkage Analysis of Longitudinal Change in Body Weight." *BioMed Central Genetics* 4 (Supp. 1): S7.

Goodman, A. H., and T. L. Leatherman, eds. 1998. *Building a New Biocultural Synthesis: Political-Economic Perspectives on Human Biology.* Ann Arbor: University of Michigan Press.

Gordon-Larsen, P., P. Griffiths, M. E. Bentley, D. S. Ward, K. Kelsey, K. Shields, and A. Ammerman. 2004. "Barriers to Physical Activity: Qualitative Data on Caregiver-Daughter Perceptions and Practices." *American Journal of Preventive Medicine* 27(3): 218–223.

Gordon-Larsen, P., M. C. Nelson, P. Page, and B. M. Popkin. 2006. "Inequality in the Built Environment Underlies Key Health Disparities in Physical Activity and Obesity." *Pediatrics* 117(2): 417–424.

Gordon-Larsen, P., B. S. Zemel, and F. E. Johnston. 1997. "Secular Changes in Stature, Weight, Fatness, Overweight, and Obesity in Urban African American Adolescents from the Mid-1950's to the Mid-1990's." *American Journal of Human Biology.* 9: 675–688.

Grantham-McGregor, S. M., C. A. Powell, S. P. Walker, and J. H. Himes. 1991. "Nutritional Supplementation, Psychosocial Stimulation, and Mental Development of Stunted Children: The Jamaican Study." *Lancet* 338(8758): 1–5.

Grossman, M., and F. J. Chaloupka. 1997. "Cigarette Taxes: The Straw to Break the Camel's Back." *Public Health Report* 112(4): 290–297.

Haas, J. D., and D. L. Pelletier. 1989. "Nutrition and Human Population Biology." In *Human Population Biology: A Transdisciplinary Science,* eds. M. A. Little and J. D. Haas. New York: Oxford University Press, 171–188.

Habicht, J. P., R. Martorell, C. Yarbrough, R. M. Malina, and R. E. Klein. 1974. "Height and Weight Standards for Preschool Children. How Relevant Are Ethnic Differences in Growth Potential?" *Lancet* 1(7858): 611–614.

Hales, C. N., and D. J. Barker. 1992. "Type 2 (Non-Insulin-Dependent) Diabetes Mellitus: The Thrifty Phenotype Hypothesis." *Diabetologia* 35(7): 595–601.

Hazuda, H. P., S. M. Haffner, M. P. Stern, and C. W. Eifler. 1988. "Effects of Acculturation and Socioeconomic Status on Obesity and Diabetes in Mexican Americans." *American Journal of Epidemiology* 128: 1289–1301.

Healy, M. J., R. D. Lockhart, J. D. Mackenzie, J. M. Tanner, and R. H. Whitehouse. 1956. "Aberdeen Growth Study. I. The Prediction of Adult Body Measurements from Measurements Taken Each Year from Birth to 5 Years. *Archives of Diseases in Childhood* 31(159): 372–381.

Healy, M. J., J. Rasbash, and M. Yang. 1988. "Distribution-free Estimation of Age-related Centiles." *Annals of Human Biology* 15(1): 17–22.

Heymsfield, S. B. 2008. "Development of Imaging Methods to Assess Adiposity and Metabolism. *International Journal of Obesity (London)* 32(Supp. 7): S76–S82.

Himes, J. H., and C. Bouchard. 1985. "Do the New Metropolitan Life Insurance Weight-Height Tables Correctly Assess Body Frame and Body Fat Relationships?" *American Journal of Public Health* 75(9): 1076–1079.

Himes, J. H., R. Martorell, J. P. Habicht, C. Yarbrough, R. M. Malina, and R. E. Klein. 1975. "Patterns of Cortical Bone Growth in Moderately Malnourished Preschool Children." *Human Biology* 47(3): 337–350.

Himmelgreen, D. A., R. Perez-Escamilla, D. Martinez, A. Bretnall, B. Eells, Y. Peng, and A. Bermudez. 2004. "The Longer You Stay, the Bigger You Get: Length of Time and Language Use in the U.S. Are Associated with Obesity in Puerto Rican Women." *American Journal of Physical Anthropology* 125(1): 90–96.

Hunt, M. S., P. T. Katzmarzyk, L. Perusse, T. Rice, D. C. Rao, and C. Bouchard. 2002. "Familial Resemblance of 7-Year Changes in Body Mass and Adiposity". *Obesity Research* 10(6): 507–517.

Huss-Ashmore, R. 2000. "Theory in Human Biology: Evolution, Ecology, Adaptability and Variation." In *Human Biology: An Evolutionary and Biocultural Perspective*, eds. S. Stinson, B. Bogin, R. Huss-Ashmore, and D. O'Rourke. New York: Wiley-Liss, 1–25.

Jamison, P. L., S. L. Zegura, and F. A. Milan, eds. 1978. *Eskimos of Northwestern Alaska: A Biological Perspective*. Stroudsburg: Dowden, Hutchinson, and Ross.

Janes, C. R., and I. G. Pawson. 1986. "Migration and Biocultural Adaptation: Samoans in California." *Social Science and Medicine* 22(8): 821–834.

Johnston, B. F., and R. Martorell. 1977. "Interrelationships among Nutrition, Health, Population, and Development." *Food Research Institute Studies in Agricultural Economics, Trade, and Development* 16(2): 1–9.

Johnston, F. E. 2009. "The Agatston Urban Nutrition Initiative: Working to Reverse the Obesity Epidemic through Academically Based Community Service." *New Directions for Youth Development* 122: 61–79.

Johnston, F. E., B. Bogin, R. B. MacVean, and B. C. Newman. 1984. "A Comparison of International Standards versus Local Reference Data for the Triceps and Subscapular Skinfolds of Guatemalan Children and Youth." *Human Biology* 56(1): 157–171.

Johnston, F. E., M. Borden, and R. B. MacVean. 1973. "Height, Weight, and Their Growth Velocities in Guatemalan Private School Children of High Socioeconomic Class." *Human Biology* 45(4): 627–641.

Johnston, F. E., P. V. Hamill, and S. Lemeshow. 1974. "Skinfold Thickness in a National Probability Sample of U.S. Males and Females Aged 6 through 17 Years." *American Journal of Physical Anthropology* 40(3): 321–324.

Kasl, S. V., and L. Berkman. 1983. "Health Consequences of the Experience of Migration." *Annual Review of Public Health* 4(1): 69–90.

Katz, M. L., P. Gordon-Larsen, M. E. Bentley, K. Kelsey, K. Shields, and A. Ammerman. 2004. "'Does Skinny Mean Healthy?' Perceived Ideal, Current, and Healthy Body Sizes among African-American Girls and Their Female Caregivers." *Ethnicity and Disease* 14(4): 533–541.

Kelly, T. L., K. E. Wilson, and S. B. Heymsfield. 2009. "Dual Energy X-Ray Absorptiometry Body Composition Reference Values from NHANES. *PLoS One* 4(9): e7038.

Kendler, K. S. 2001. "Twin Studies of Psychiatric Illness: An Update." *Archives of General Psychiatry* 58(11): 1005–1014.

Kensara, O. A., S. A. Wootton, D. I. Phillips, M. Patel, A. A. Jackson, M. Elia, Hertfordshire Study G. 2005. "Fetal Programming of Body Composition: Relation between Birth Weight and Body Composition Measured with Dual-Energy X-Ray Absorptiometry and Anthropometric Methods in Older Englishmen." American Journal of Clinical Nutrition 82(5): 980–987.

Kulick, D., and A. Meneley, eds. 2005. *Fat: The Anthropology of an Obsession*. New York: Jeremy P. Tarcher/Penguin.

Kumanyika, S. K. 2008. "Environmental Influences on Childhood Obesity: Ethnic and Cultural Influences in Context." *Physiology and Behavior* 94(1): 61–70.

Kuzawa, C. W. 1998. "Adipose Tissue in Human Infancy and Childhood: An Evolutionary Perspective." *American Journal of Physical Anthropology Supp.* 27: 177–209.

Lasker, G. W. 1969. "Human Biological Adaptability: The Ecological Approach in Physical Anthropology." *Science* 166(3912): 1480–1486.

Law, C. M., D. J. Barker, C. Osmond, C. H. Fall, and S. J. Simmonds. 1992. "Early Growth and Abdominal Fatness in Adult Life." *Journal of Epidemiology and Community Health* 46(3): 184–186.

Lederman, S., S. Akabas, B. Moore, M. E. Bentley, B. Devaney, M. W. Gillman, M. Kramer, J. Mennella, A. Ness, and J. Wardle. 2004. "Summary of the Presentations at the Conference on Preventing Childhood Obesity, December 8, 2003." *Pediatrics* 114(4): 1146–1173.

Leonard, W. R. 2008. "Lifestyle, Diet and Disease: Comparative Perspectives on the Determinants of Chronic Disease Risk." In *Evolution in Health and Disease*, eds. S. C. Stearns and J. C. Koella. New York: Oxford University Press, 265–276.

Leonard, W. R., V. A. Galloway, E. Ivakine, L. Osipova, and M. Kazakovtseva. 1999. "Nutrition, Thyroid Function and Basal Metabolism of the Evenki of Central Siberia." *International Journal of Circumpolar Health* 58(4): 281–295.

Leonard, W. R., and M. L. Robertson. 1992. "Nutritional Requirements and Human Evolution: A Bioenergetics Model." *American Journal of Human Biology* 4: 179–195.

Leonard, W. R., M. L. Robertson, J. J. Snodgrass, and C. W. Kuzawa. 2003. "Metabolic Correlates of Hominid Brain Evolution." *Comparative Biochemistry and Physiology Part A: Molecular and Integrative Physiology* 136(1): 5–15.

Leonard, W. R., J. J. Snodgrass, and M. V. Sorensen. 2005. "Metabolic Adaptation in Indigenous Siberian Populations." *Annual Review of Anthropology* 34: 451–471.

Leslie, P. W., and T. B. Gage. 1989. "Demography and Human Population Biology: Problems and Progress." In *Human Population Biology: A Transdisciplinary Science*, eds. M. A. Little and J. D. Haas. New York: Oxford University Press, 15–44.

Lieberman, L. S. 2003. "Dietary, Evolutionary, and Modernizing Influences on the Prevalence of Type 2 Diabetes." *Annual Review of Nutrition* 23: 345–377.

Little, M. A., and J. D. Haas, eds. 1989. *Human Population Biology: A Transdisciplinary Science*. New York: Oxford University Press.

Lohman, T. G., A. F. Roche, and R. Martorell. 1988. *Anthropometric Standardization Reference Manual*. Champaign, IL: Human Kinetics.

Luan, J., P. O. Browne, A. H. Harding, D. J. Halsall, S. O'Rahilly, V. K. Chatterjee, and N. J. Wareham. 2001. "Evidence for Gene-Nutrient Interaction at the PPARgamma Locus." *Diabetes* 50(3): 686–689.

Lynch, J., and G. D. Smith. 2005. "A Life Course Approach to Chronic Disease Epidemiology." *Annual Review of Public Health* 26: 1–35.

Madrigal, H., A. Sanchez-Villegas, M. A. Martinez-Gonzalez, J. Kearney, M. J. Gibney, J. Irala, J. A. Martinez. 2000. "Underestimation of Body Mass Index through Perceived Body Image as Compared to Self-Reported Body Mass Index in the European Union." *Public Health* 114(6): 468–473.

Maillot, M., N. Darmon, M. Darmon, L. Lafay, and A. Drewnowski. 2007. "Nutrient-Dense Food Groups Have High Energy Costs: An Econometric Approach to Nutrient Profiling." *Journal of Nutrition* 137(7): 1815–1820.

Malina, R. M., J. H. Himes, C. D. Stepick, F. G. Lopez, and P. H. Buschang. 1981. "Growth of Rural and Urban Children in the Valley of Oaxaca, Mexico." *American Journal of Physical Anthropology* 55(2): 269–280.

Malina, R. M., P. T. Katzmarzyk, and G. Beunen. 1996. "Birth Weight and Its Relationship to Size Attained and Relative Fat Distribution at 7 to 12 Years of Age." *Obesity Research* 4(4): 385–390.

Malina, R. M., and B. B. Little. 2008. "Physical Activity: The Present in the Context of the Past." *American Journal of Human Biology* 20(4): 373–391.

Martorell, R. 1981. "Notes on the History of Nutritional Anthropometry." *Federation Proceedings* 40(11): 2572–2576.

Martorell, R., C. Yarbrough, R. E. Klein, and A. Lechtig. 1979. "Malnutrition, Body Size, and Skeletal Maturation: Interrelationships and Implications for Catch-Up Growth." *Human Biology* 51(3): 371–389.

Martorell, R., C. Yarbrough, A. Lechtig, H. Delgado, and R. E. Klein. 1977. "Genetic-Environmental Interactions in Physical Growth." *Acta Paediatrica Scandinavia* 66(5): 579–584.

McElroy, A. 1990. "Biocultural Models in Studies of Human Health and Adaptation." *Medical Anthropology Quarterly* 4(3): 243–265.

McGarvey, S. T. 1991." Obesity in Samoans and a Perspective on Its Etiology in Polynesians." *American Journal of Clinical Nutrition* 53(6 Suppl): 1586S–1594S.

McGarvey, S. T., J. R. Bindon, D. E. Crews, and D. E. Schendel. 1989. "Modernization and Adiposity: Causes and Consequences." In *Human Population Biology: A Transdiciplinary Science*, eds. M. A. Little and J. D. Haas. New York: Oxford University Press, 263–279.

Meirhaeghe, A., N. Helbecque, D. Cottel, and P. Amouyel. 1999. "Beta2-Adrenoceptor Gene Polymorphism, Body Weight, and Physical Activity." *Lancet* 353(9156): 896.

Memisoglu, A., F. B. Hu, S. E. Hankinson, J. E. Manson, I. De Vivo, W. C. Willett, and D. J. Hunter. 2003. "Interaction between a Peroxisome Proliferator-Activated Receptor Gamma Gene Polymorphism and Dietary Fat Intake in Relation to Body Mass." *Human Molecular Genetics* 12(22): 2923–2929.

Milan, F. A, ed. 1980. *The Human Biology of Circumpolar Populations*. Cambridge: Cambridge University Press.

Monteiro, P. O., C. G. Victora, F. C. Barros, and L. M. Monteiro. 2003. "Birth Size, Early Childhood Growth, and Adolescent Obesity in a Brazilian Birth Cohort." *International Journal of Obesity and Related Metabolic Disorders* 27(10): 1274–1282.

Morbeck, M. E., A. Galloway, and A. L. Zihlman, eds. 1997. *The Evolving Female: A Life-History Perspective*. Princeton: Princeton University Press.

Neel, J.V. 1992. "Diabetes mellitus: a "thrifty" genotype rendered detrimental by "progress"?" *American Journal of Human Genetics* 14: 353–362.

Norgan, N. G. 1997. "The Beneficial Effects of Body Fat and Adipose Tissue in Humans." *International Journal of Obesity and Related Metabolic Disorders* 21(9): 738–746.

Nydon, J., and R. B. Thomas. 1989. "Methodological Procedures for Analysing Energy Expenditure." In *Research Methods in Nutritional Anthropology*, eds. G. H. Pelto, P. J. Pelto, and E. Messer. Tokyo: The United Nations University, 57–81.

Ogden, C. L., M. D. Carroll, L. R. Curtin, M. A. McDowell, C. J. Tabak, and K. M. Flegal. 2006. "Prevalence of Overweight and Obesity in the United States, 1999–2004." *Journal of the American Medical Association* 295(13): 1549–1555.

Omran, A. R. 1983. "The Epidemiologic Transition Theory. A Preliminary Update." *Journal of Tropical Pediatrics* 29(6): 305–316.

Omran, A. R. 2001. "The Epidemiologic Transition: A Theory of the Epidemiology of Population Change. 1971." *Bulletin of the World Health Organization* 79(2): 161–170.

Ong, K. K., M. L. Ahmed, P. M. Emmett, M. A. Preece, and D. B. Dunger. 2000. "Association between Postnatal Catch-Up Growth and Obesity in Childhood: Prospective Cohort Study." *British Medical Journal* 320(7240): 967–971.

Owen, C. G., R. M. Martin, P. H. Whincup, G. D. Smith, and D. G. Cook. 2005. "Effect of Infant Feeding on the Risk of Obesity across the Life Course: A Quantitative Review of Published Evidence." *Pediatrics* 115(5): 1367–1377.

Parsons, T. J., C. Power, S. Logan, and C. D. Summerbell. 1999. "Childhood Predictors of Adult Obesity: A Systematic Review." *International Journal of Obesity and Related Metabolic Disorders* 23(Supp. 8): S1–S107.

Pelto, G. H. 1989. "Introduction: Methodological Directions in Nutritional Anthropology." In *Research Methods in Nutritional Anthropology*, eds. G. H. Pelto, P. J. Pelto, and E. Messer. Tokyo: The United Nations University, ix–xvi.

Pelto, G. H., H. C. Freake, Committee ALRP. 2003. "Social research in an integrated science of nutrition: future directions." *Journal of Nutrition* 133(4): 1231–1234.

Phillips, D. I., and J. B. Young. 2000. "Birth Weight, Climate at Birth and the Risk of Obesity in Adult Life." *International Journal of Obesity and Related Metabolic Disorders* 24(3): 281–287.

Plomin, R., J. C. DeFries, and J. C. Loehlin. 1977. "Genotype-Environment Interaction and Correlation in the Analysis of Human Behavior." *Psychology Bulletin* 84(2): 309–322.

Popkin, B. M. 1996. "Understanding the Nutrition Transition." *Urban Health News* l (30): 3–19.

Popkin, B. M. 2004. "The Nutrition Transition: An Overview of World Patterns of Change." *Nutrition Reviews* 62(7 Pt 2): S140–S143.

Powers, S. W., L. A. Chamberlin, K. B. van Schaick, S. N. Sherman, and R. C. Whitaker. 2006. "Maternal Feeding Strategies, Child Eating Behaviors, and Child BMI in Low-Income African-American Preschoolers." *Obesity (Silver Spring)* 14(11): 2026–2033.

Prentice, A. M. 2005. "Starvation in Humans: Evolutionary Background and Contemporary Implications." *Mechanisms of Ageing and Development* 126(9): 976–981.

Prentice, A. M., B. J. Hennig, and A. J. Fulford. 2008. "Evolutionary Origins of the Obesity Epidemic: Natural Selection of Thrifty Genes or Genetic Drift Following Predation Release?" *International Journal of Obesity (London)* 32(11): 1607–1610.

Prentice, A. M., P. Rayco-Solon, and S. E. Moore. 2005. "Insights from The Developing World: Thrifty Genotypes and Thrifty Phenotypes." *Proceedings of the Nutrition Society* 64(2): 153–161.

Prior, I. A. 1971. "The Price of Civilization." *Nutrition Today* 6(4): 2–11.

Rankinen, T., A. Zuberi, Y. C. Chagnon, S. J. Weisnagel, G. Argyropoulos, B. Walts, L. Perusse, and C. Bouchard. 2006. "The Human Obesity Gene Map: The 2005 Update." *Obesity (Silver Spring)* 14(4): 529–644.

Ravelli, A. C., J. H. van Der Meulen, C. Osmond, D. J. Barker, and O. P. Bleker. 1999. "Obesity at the Age of 50 Y in Men and Women Exposed to Famine Prenatally." *American Journal of Clinical Nutrition* 70(5): 811–816.

Ravelli, G. P., Z. A. Stein, and M. W. Susser. 1976. "Obesity in Young Men after Famine Exposure in Utero and Early Infancy." *New England Journal of Medicine* 295(7): 349–353.

Ravussin, E., M. E. Valencia, J. Esparza, P. H. Bennett, and L. O. Schulz. 1994. "Effects of a Traditional Lifestyle on Obesity in Pima Indians." *Diabetes Care* 17(9): 1067–1074.

Robitaille, J., J. P. Despres, L. Perusse, and M. C. Vohl. 2003. "The PPAR-gamma P12A Polymorphism Modulates the Relationship between Dietary Fat Intake and Components of the Metabolic Syndrome: Results from the Quebec Family Study." *Clinical Genetics* 63(2): 109–116.

Roche, A. F. 1992. *Growth, Maturation, and Body Composition: The Fels Longitudinal Study 1929–1991*. Cambridge: Cambridge University Press.

Rutter, M., and J. Silberg. 2002. "Gene-environment Interplay in Relation to Emotional and Behavioral Disturbance." *Annual Review of Psychology* 53: 463–490.

Sacco, L. M., M. E. Bentley, K. Carby-Shields, J. B. Borja, and B. D. Goldman. 2007. "Assessment of Infant Feeding Styles among Low-Income African-American Mothers: Comparing Reported and Observed Behaviors." *Appetite* 49(1): 131–140.

Sallis, J., A. Bauman, and M. Pratt. 1998. "Environmental and Policy Interventions to Promote Physical Activity." *American Journal of Preventive Medicine* 15(4): 379–397.

Sallis, J., and N. Owen. 1997. "Ecological models." In *Health Behavior and Health Education*, eds. K. Glanz, F. Lewis, and B. Rimer. San Francisco: Jossey-Bass Publishers, 403–424.

Sheldon, W. H. 1950. "The Somatotype, the Morphophenotype and the Morphogenotype." *Cold Spring Harbor Symposia on Quantitative Biology* 15: 373–382.

Singhal, A., M. Fewtrell, T. J. Cole, and A. Lucas. 2003. "Low Nutrient Intake and Early Growth for Later Insulin Resistance in Adolescents Born Preterm." *Lancet* 361(9363): 1089–1097.

Slining, M. M., L. Adair, B. D. Goldman, J. Borja, and M. Bentley. 2009. "Infant Temperament Contributes to Early Infant Growth: A Prospective Cohort of African American Infants." *International Journal of Behavioral Nutrition and Physical Activity* 6: 51

Smith, G. D. 2007a. "Life-course Approaches to Inequalities in Adult Chronic Disease Risk." *Proceedings of the Nutrition Society* 66(2): 216–36

Smith, G. D. 2007b. "Lifecourse Epidemiology of Disease: A Tractable Problem?" *International Journal of Epidemiology* 36(3): 479–480.

Snodgrass, J. J., W. R. Leonard, M. V. Sorensen, L. A. Tarskaia,V. P. Alekseev, and V. Krivoshapkin. 2006a. "The Emergence of Obesity among Indigenous Siberians." *Journal of Physiological Anthropology* 25(1): 75–84.

Snodgrass, J. J., W. R. Leonard, L. A. Tarskaia, V. P. Alekseev, V. G. Krivoshapkin. 2005. "Basal Metabolic Rate in the Yakut (Sakha) of Siberia." *American Journal of Human Biology* 17(2): 155–172.

Snodgrass, J. J., W. R. Leonard, L. A. Tarskaia, and D. A. Schoeller. 2006b. "Total Energy Expenditure in the Yakut (Sakha) of Siberia as Measured by the Doubly Labeled Water Method." *American Journal of Clinical Nutrition* 84(4): 798–806.

Sobal, J. 2001. "Social and Cultural Influences on Obesity." In *International Textbook of Obesity*, ed. P. Bjorntorp. New York: Wiley and Sons, 305–433.

Sorensen, M. V., J. J. Snodgrass,W. R. Leonard, A. Tarskaia, K. I. Ivanov, V. G. Krivoshapkin, and V. A. Spitsyn. 2005. "Health Consequences of Postsocialist Transition: Dietary and Lifestyle Determinants of Plasma Lipids in Yakutia." *American Journal of Human Biology* 17(5): 576–592.

Speakman, J. R. 2004. "Obesity: The Integrated Roles of Environment and Genetics." *Journal of Nutrition* 134(8 Suppl): 2090S–2105S.

Speakman, J. R. 2007. "A Nonadaptive Scenario Explaining the Genetic Predisposition to Obesity: The 'Predation Release' Hypothesis." *Cell Metabolism* 6(1): 5–12.

Speakman, J. R. 2008. "Thrifty Genes for Obesity, An Attractive but Flawed Idea, and an Alternative Perspective: The 'Drifty Gene' Hypothesis." *International Journal of Obesity (London)* 32(11): 1611–1617.

Spring, B., R. Pingitore, E. Bruckner, and S. Penava. 1994. "Obesity: Idealized or Stigmatized? Sociocultural Influences on the Meaning and Prevalence of Obesity." In *Exercise and Obesity*, eds. A. P. Hills ad M. L. Wahlqvist. London: Smith-Gordon, 49–60.

Stettler, N., S. K. Kumanyika, S. H. Katz, B. S. Zemel, and V. A. Stallings. 2003. "Rapid Weight Gain during Infancy and Obesity in Young Adulthood in a Cohort of African Americans." *American Journal of Clinical Nutrition* 77(6): 1374–1378.

Stettler, N., B. S. Zemel, S. Kumanyika, and V. A. Stallings. 2002. "Infant Weight Gain and Childhood Overweight Status in a Multicenter, Cohort Study." *Pediatrics* 109(2): 194–199.

Story, M., S. A. French, M. D. Resnick, and R. W. Blum. 1995. "Ethnic/racial and Socioeconomic Differences in Dieting Behaviors and Body Image Perceptions in Adolescents." *International Journal of Eating Disorders* 18(2): 173–179.

Strug, L., L. Sun, and M. Corey. 2003. "The Genetics of Cross-Sectional and Longitudinal Body Mass Index." *Biomed Central Genetics* 4 Suppl 1: S14.

Tanner, J. M. 1951. "Some Notes on the Reporting of Growth Data." *Human Biology* 23(2): 93–159.

Tanner, J. M. 1952. "The Assessment of Growth and Development in Children." *Archives of Diseases of Childhood* 27(131): 10–33.

Tanner, J. M. 1955. *Growth at Adolescence: With a General Consideration of the Effects of Hereditary and Environmental Factors upon Growth and Maturation from Birth to Maturity.* Oxford: Blackwell Scientific.

Tanner, J. M., and R. H. Whitehouse. 1962. "Standards for Subcutaneous Fat in British children: Percentiles for Thickness of Skinfolds over Triceps and below Scapula." *British Medical Journal* 1(5276): 446–450.

Tanner, J. M, R. H. Whitehouse, and M. Takaishi. 1966a. "Standards from Birth to Maturity for Height, Weight, Height Velocity, and Weight Velocity: British Children, 1965. I." *Archives of Disease of Childhood* 41(219): 454–471.

Tanner, J. M., R. H. Whitehouse, and M. Takaishi. 1966b. "Standards from Birth to Maturity for Height, Weight, Height Velocity, and Weight Velocity: British Children, 1965. II." *Archives of Disease of Childhood* 41(220): 613–635.

Tartaglia, L. A., M. Dembski, X. Weng, N. Deng, J. Culpepper, R. Devos, G. J. Richards, L. A. Campfield, F. T. Clark, J. Deeds, and others. 1995. "Identification and Expression Cloning of a Leptin Receptor, OB-R." *Cell* 83(7): 1263–1271.

Taveras, E. M., K. S. Scanlon, L. Birch, S. L. Rifas-Shiman, J. W. Rich-Edwards, and M. W. Gillman. 2004. "Association of Breastfeeding with Maternal Control of Infant Feeding at Age 1 Year." *Pediatrics* 114(5): e577–583.

Thompson, A. L., M. A. Mendez, J. B. Borja, L. S. Adair, C. R. Zimmer, and M. E. Bentley. 2009. "Development and Validation of the Infant Feeding Style Questionnaire." *Appetite* 53(2): 210–221.

Toschke, A. M., V. Grote, B. Koletzko, and R. von Kries. 2004. "c." *Archives of Pediatriacs and Adolescent Medicine* 158(5): 449–452.

Ulijaszek, S. J. 2002. "Human Eating Behaviour in an Evolutionary Ecological Context." *Proceedings of the Nutrition Society* 61(4): 517–526.

Ulijaszek, S. J. 2007. "Obesity: A Disorder of Convenience." *Obesity Reviews* 8 Suppl 1: 183–187.

Ulijaszek, S. J., and H. Lofink. 2006. "Obesity in Biocultural Perspective." *Annual Review of Anthropology* 35: 337–360.

Ulijaszek, S. J., and S. S. Strickland. 1993. "Nutritional Studies in Biological Anthropology." In *Research Strategies in Human Biology: Field and Survey Studies*, eds. G. W. Lasker and C. G. N. Mascie-Taylor. Cambridge: Cambridge University Press, 108–139.

Wang, J., S. B. Heymsfield, M. Aulet, J. C. Thornton, and R. N. Pierson, Jr. 1989. "Body Fat from Body Density: Underwater Weighing vs. Dual-Photon Absorptiometry." *American Journal of Physiology* 256(6 Pt 1): E829–834.

Warner, K. E. 2005. "Tobacco Policy in the United States: Lessons for the Obesity Epidemic" In *Policy Challenges in Modern Health Care*, eds. D. Mechanic,

L. B. Rogut, D. C. Colby, and J. R. Knickman. New Brunswick, NJ: Rutgers University Press, 99–114.

Waterlow, J. C., R. Buzina, W. Keller, J. M. Lane, M. Z. Nichaman, and J. M. Tanner. 1977. "The Presentation and Use of Height and Weight Data for Comparing the Nutritional Status of Groups of Children under the Age of 10 Years." *Bulletin of the World Health Organization* 55(4): 489–498.

Wells, J. C. 2005. "Evolution of the Human Profile of Fatness." *Human Ecology* Special Issue 13: 17–22.

Wells, J. C. 2006. "The Evolution of Human Fatness and Susceptibility to Obesity: An Ethological Approach." *Biology Reviews* 81: 183–205.

Wells, J. C. 2009. "Thrift: A Guide to Thrifty Genes, Thrifty Phenotypes and Thrifty Norms." *International Journal of Obesity (London)* 33: 1331–1338.

Zhang, Y., R. Proenca, M. Maffei, M. Barone, L. Leopold, and J. M. Friedman. 1994. "Positional Cloning of the Mouse Obese Gene and Its Human Homologue." *Nature* 372(6505): 425–432.

CHAPTER 6

THE PSYCHOLOGY
OF OBESITY

ASHLEY MOSKOVICH, JEFFREY
HUNGER, AND TRACI MANN

THE field of psychology traditionally focuses on the study of individuals, their internal mental processes, and their behavior; as such, it has adopted this approach in the study of obesity. Rather than examining larger groups, such as communities, or distal factors, such as laws, policies, or environmental barriers, psychologists have explored people's emotions, beliefs, goals, and behaviors as causes and consequences of obesity. In recent years, however, and paralleling the direction of the field as a whole, psychologists have broadened their focus to include the influence of relationships and social networks on obesity, as well as the role of genetic and neurological factors in the development of obesity. With regard to treatment, psychologists have focused primarily on behavioral rather than medical interventions, and recently have begun to explore whether weight loss is a reasonable or even necessary goal in treatments for obesity.

CAUSES OF OBESITY

A substantial body of work in psychology has been dedicated to exploring the causes of obesity. Psychology originally viewed obesity as a result of psychopathology or as a response to a significant trauma in a person's past (Kolata 2007). However, support for these assumptions has been mixed, and these explanations are not thought to account for most cases of obesity (Stunkard and Wadden 1992). Rather, the focus has been on individual factors such as thoughts, behaviors, and biology, as well as aspects of the individual's social environment such as familial and peer influences. Many early theories of obesity continue to be refined and incorporated into current etiological models.

The Individual

In 1957 it was proposed that obesity was the result of overeating—a behavioral factor—and was not exclusively due to impaired metabolic functioning (Kaplan and Kaplan 1957). Much of the work within the field has since focused on behavioral, rather than biological, causes of obesity, and on overeating in particular. Early research focused on differences in eating between obese and non-obese individuals, but over time it became clear that many of the factors that promote overeating in obese individuals also promote overeating in some non-obese individuals. Interest has not only focused on determining *who* overeats, but also *when* and *why* overeating occurs. Four major individual factors have been explored as causes of overeating: interoceptive awareness (i.e., sensitivity to internal bodily states), response to emotional experience, cognition, and biology.

Schacter's internal-external theory of eating holds that different factors guide eating for obese individuals than those that guide eating for non-obese individuals (Schacter 1968; Schacter, Goldman, and Gordon 1968). According to this theory, non-obese individuals use the internal sensations of hunger and satiety to guide their eating, whereas obese individuals are less interoceptively aware and instead rely on external cues such as the time of day or the presence of appetizing foods to regulate eating. Although this theory is intuitive and parsimonious, original support for it was mixed and its basic premises have since been questioned (Rodin 1981). In particular, some have challenged the assertion that an overreliance on external cues by obese individuals necessarily indicates that they are less interoceptively aware than non-obese individuals (Rodin 1981; Herman and Polivy 2008). Furthermore, it has also been argued that non-obese individuals are not better than obese people at using internal cues to regulate their eating, and that they are also influenced by external cues (Rodin 1981; Herman and Polivy 2008).

Although it has been challenged, the internal-external hypothesis has not been abandoned; rather, recent work has instead been expanding upon it. For example, Herman and Polivy (2008) posit that the conflicting findings from past research actually demonstrate a clear pattern of eating behavior. They argue that some types of external cues (e.g., portion size), which the authors refer to as *normative* cues, influence everyone, whereas other cues (e.g., palatability), called *sensory cues*, only impact the eating of obese and dieting individuals. Thus the internal-external hypothesis is still present in the way in which we view the causes of obesity.

Differences in the way individuals respond to emotional experience is another factor that is thought to play a role in the development of obesity. According to the psychosomatic hypothesis (Kaplan and Kaplan 1957), obese people overeat as a way of coping with emotional distress. Obese individuals are thought to have learned that eating reduces feelings of anxiety and therefore overeat as a way to self-soothe. This results in a continuous cycle in which overeating aimed at reducing distress actually promotes further distress and subsequent overeating (Kaplan and Kaplan 1957). Similarly, and foreshadowing the internal-external hypothesis, Bruch theorized that obese individuals have difficulties with interoceptive awareness and therefore misinterpret emotional states as hunger (Bruch 1961).

Although these early theories have received only mixed support (Greeno and Wing 1994), eating in response to emotional experience is still viewed as an important contributor to overeating and obesity (Canetti, Bachar, and Berry 2002). Research shows that some individuals, not exclusively obese individuals, exhibit a tendency to overeat when in the presence of strong emotion, particularly negative affect (e.g., Van Strien and Ouwens 2003; Polivy, Herman, and McFarlane 1994). While emotional eating is well documented, it is still unclear *why* such behavior occurs. Many studies have been unable to demonstrate that emotional eating attenuates negative affect (i.e., negative emotion states such as anxiety) (e.g., Herman and Polivy 1975). Recent work, however, found that eating palatable food improved mood among individuals classified as emotional eaters (Macht and Mueller 2007). Replication of this effect and clarification of moderators and mechanisms will be essential to this growing body of work.

The third individual factor thought to contribute to overeating, cognitive control, was introduced in a study by Herman and Mack (1975). This study highlighted what has been termed the *disinhibition effect*—the phenomenon that restrained eaters, or dieters, engage in overeating after a perceived diet violation. This phenomenon is considered a cognitive one (as opposed to a physiological one, for example) because what matters is not whether restrained eaters actually violated their diets, but whether they *think* that they did. Research supporting the role of cognition shows that restrained eaters will overeat if they believe they have violated their diet when in fact they did not, but they will not overeat after an actual diet violation if they are led to believe that the food they consumed did not actually violate their diet (Polivy and Herman 1985).

An individual's self-imposed restraint essentially functions as a form of self-control and is therefore susceptible to a broad range of factors known to contribute to regulatory failures. These factors, such as ego threats (Heatherton, Herman, and Polivy 1991), stress (Greeno and Wing 1994), and distraction (Mann and Ward 2000), have been shown to lead to overeating among restrained eaters, but not among non-restrained individuals. Although restraint status has proven to be a reliable indicator of overeating and has generated a considerable amount of research, there is controversy over how it is best conceptualized and measured (Ruderman 1986); many believe that restraint only leads to self-regulation failure among individuals who are also disinhibited eaters.

The fourth factor that has been explored as a source of overeating is individual differences in biology. In an effort to explain discrepant results of externally based eating behavior among obese individuals, Nisbett proposed a biological explanation known as set-point theory (Nisbett 1972). According to Nisbett, everyone has a biologically determined and physiologically defended weight set-point that ultimately guides eating behavior. Regardless of current weight status, obese and non-obese individuals may at times be below their actual set-point, causing them to be in a state of deprivation that promotes externally guided eating. When individuals are at their set-point, deprivation ceases and externally guided eating diminishes. Set-point theories suggest that biology is a key predictor of obesity, but they are impossible to prove or disprove and cannot account for a variety of eating phenomenon, ultimately limiting their utility (Pinel, Assanand, and Lehman 2000).

Current research is examining how underlying differences in neurobiology guide eating behavior. For example, there are promising results in neuroimaging research on impulsivity, craving, binge eating, and restraint (Lowe et al. 2009). Such work may help explain conflicting results found in behavioral research and may provide necessary insight into the transactional relationship between internal and external variables.

The Environment

In addition to individual variables that contribute to overeating and the development of obesity, psychologists also focus on environmental causes, including familial and social influences.

Because obese children are likely to become obese adults (Epstein, Wing, and Valoski 1985), factors associated with the development of pediatric obesity, including the family environment, are the focus of much research. Parents affect the eating of their children both directly and indirectly. Parental influence, whether by modeling eating behavior, directly controlling their children's eating behavior, or providing feedback regarding the child's weight and shape, has been shown to foster restrained and disinhibited eating in children (e.g., Cutting et al. 1999; Pike and Rodin 1991; Carper, Fisher, and Birch 2000; Francis and Birch 2005). A restrained eating style, as mentioned above, promotes vulnerability to disinhibition and overeating, increasing the likelihood that obesity will result.

Preliminary evidence suggests that chronic levels of psychological stress in the family are related to obesity in children (Koch, Sepa, and Ludvigsson 2008). Psychological stress encountered in childhood may lead to the development of an emotional eating style. A recent study conducted by Greenfield and Marks (2009) found that individuals who reported experiencing physical and psychological violence from their parents when they were children had a greater risk for adult obesity than those who had not experienced such violence. Moreover, the association between a past history of physical and psychological violence and obesity was partially mediated by the use of food as a coping response to stress. Family stress levels, like parental influences over eating, appear to contribute to obesity by fostering individual behaviors that are associated with overeating.

In addition to familial influences on overeating and obesity, researchers have also looked at other social influences. A recent study by Christakis and Fowler (2007) investigated the "social spread" of obesity; that is, they examined whether weight gain in one individual was correlated with weight gain in members of their social networks. Their results suggest that obesity can spread through social ties. While the findings are not able to speak to mechanisms through which this may occur, the authors suggest that social influences may promote obesity by changing norms for acceptability of being overweight and also by directly influencing individual behaviors such as eating. A study exploring social influences of obesity in adolescents found similar results as overweight adolescents were more likely to have overweight friends than their normal weight peers (Valente et al. 2009). Recent work, however, has critiqued the methodology used to investigate social network effects and has argued that the studies should be interpreted with caution (Cohen-Cole and Fletcher 2008).

The past 50 years of research on the psychological causes of obesity have helped to isolate many important predictive factors and to clarify that obesity results from a variety of intra- and inter-individual factors. We hope that these factors (and other newly isolated factors) can ultimately be combined into an integrated model that can predict who will become obese and why.

Correlates or Consequences of Obesity

Because research on the causes and consequences of obesity is correlational by nature, any variable that is found to be associated with obesity can technically only be considered a correlate, as opposed to a predictor or a consequence. However, the literature does divide the correlates of obesity into those that have been shown to precede obesity in time and are thought to be causes, and those that follow obesity and are thus considered to be consequences. In this section, we focus on factors that may be consequences of obesity, or perhaps only correlates, but that we are reasonably certain are not causes.

Stigma and Discrimination

Overweight and obese individuals face stigmatization and unfair treatment simply because of their weight. It is often assumed that denigration and derision of overweight individuals can only serve to help motivate weight loss, justifying prejudice and discrimination as "for their own good" (Brownell 2005). In actuality, perceived weight discrimination and stigmatization likely have negative effects on an individuals' psychological well-being (Hatzenbuehler, Keyes, and Hasin 2009) and may contribute to the physical health problems (Maclean et al. 2009) that are usually directly attributed to obesity.

Implicit bias against overweight is particularly strong (Teachman et al. 2003), equivalent—if not greater than—bias due to age, race, and gender (Nosek, Banaji, and Greenwald 2002). Moreover, Puhl, Andreyeva, and Brownell (2008) demonstrated that approximately 5 percent of overweight (BMI between 25 and 30) men and 10 percent of overweight women experienced weight discrimination on a daily basis. For individuals with a BMI greater than 35, these numbers jumped to 28 percent and 45 percent for men and women, respectively. Among this segment of society, daily interpersonal discrimination—through decreased civility and increased harassment and rejection—is the agonizing norm.

Physicians and other health care professionals routinely endorse negative stereotypes about their overweight and obese patients. In a recent survey involving primary care physicians, more than half of the physicians in the sample believed that their obese patients were awkward, unattractive, and non-compliant, and a third believed that they were weak-willed, lazy, and sloppy (Foster et al. 2003). Given the sensitive nature of explicitly admitting such beliefs, this number is undoubtedly an underestimation. Similar stigmatizing attitudes are also expressed by the next generation of doctors, medical students (Wear et al. 2006). Particularly concerning is how this biased perception translates into diminished care for overweight patients. Nearly 70 percent of overweight and obese women reported weight stigmatization from their physician (e.g., inappropriate comments about their weight), and 46 percent reported similar experiences from nurses (Puhl and Brownell 2006). Given how likely it is for obese patients to view the medical setting as stigmatizing or threatening, it is not surprising that many patients avoid or delay treatment (Drury and Louis 2002). This under-utilization of health care services may lead to some of the physical health problems that are attributed to obesity.

Overweight individuals also face noticeable discrimination in employment settings, where they tend to be stereotyped as less conscientious and agreeable than non-overweight employees (Polinko and Popovich 2001). A meta-analytic review of weight discrimination in employment concluded that overweight applicants were at a particular disadvantage when applying for jobs with considerable contact with the public, and that they were rated less favorably when being evaluated as a potential coworker (Roehling et al. 2008). In a survey of over 2,000 overweight employees, 54 percent reported experiences of weight stigma by their fellow employees, and 43 percent reported such experiences by their employer (Puhl and Brownell 2006). This type of workplace discrimination ranges from inappropriate comments and abusive joking to denied promotions and termination (Puhl and Heuer 2009).

Weight bias can also have a negative effect on romantic relationships (Chen and Brown 2005), customer service interactions (King et al. 2006), and the educational environment (e.g., Puhl and Latner 2007). Given the unmistakably harmful impact that weight bias has on the lives of millions of overweight and obese individuals, and the lack of success in reducing obesity itself, social and behavioral scientists should consider it a priority to develop and test effective strategies for eliminating this pervasive bias. Attempts to reduce weight bias have involved providing information about the etiology of obesity or trying to create empathy for the daily struggles of obese people, but these efforts have had mixed results (e.g., Teachman et al. 2003). It may be the case that using multiple stigma-reduction approaches in concert will be necessary to combat such a strong bias.

Mental Health Consequences

Given the myriad ways in which obese people are discriminated against and stigmatized in our society, it would not be surprising if mental health problems resulted. And because it was thought that obesity was *caused by* psychopathology, many studies explored whether obesity and a variety of mental disorders co-occurred. Thus resulted several decades of cross-sectional studies that were similar in that they included a measure of obesity and a measure of at least one emotional problem, but that varied according to how they defined obesity, and how they defined and measured emotional problems (Friedman and Brownell 1995). In that generation of studies, individuals usually self-reported their weights, and trained clinicians almost never used diagnostic criteria to assess mental disorders, which were often measured with a single self-reported item. Findings from these studies rarely found evidence for the relationship between obesity and psychopathology, but because of the overall inconsistency of the results, it was possible to use them to support whatever conclusion one desired. The majority of reports concluded that obesity was not related to mental illness (see Stunkard and Wadden 1992 for a review), but some suggested that obesity was associated with increases in the prevalence of mental illness, while still others argued, in what became known (rather condescendingly, in our view) as the "jolly fat hypothesis," that obesity was actually related to improvements in emotional health (Crisp and McGuinness 1976).

In more recent years, a number of studies (Hasler et al. 2004; Mather et al. 2009; Onyike et al. 2003; Pickering et al. 2007; Scott et al. 2007; Simon et al. 2006) have addressed this question with carefully attained nationally representative samples and clinical measurement of mental illness. Like the prior generation of research, the results of these studies were inconsistent, with some finding evidence for associations between obesity and increased risk for depression or anxiety, and others finding no significant relationships (or in one case, the opposite: that obesity was associated with a lower risk of anxiety; Hasler et al. 2004). Even when significant associations are found, they tend to be small effects, with odds ratios around 1.3.

The most rigorous tests of the link between obesity and mental illness come from prospective longitudinal studies, and these have focused primarily on depression (Bjerkeset et al. 2008; Herva et al. 2006; Roberts et al. 2000, 2003). These studies measured BMI at baseline and then depression from one to 17 years later. All three found a significant relationship between baseline obesity and increased depression at follow-up, although in the study with the 17-year follow-up, the relationship was found for men, but not women. Importantly, the one prospective study that controlled for baseline depression still found a significant relationship between obesity and later depression (Roberts et al. 2003). In addition, that study also tested the reverse path, and found that baseline depression did not predict later obesity (controlling for baseline obesity), suggesting, in what appears to be the most rigorous test to date, that the causal direction of the relationship may be obesity preceding depression rather than the reverse.

Considering the findings from the nationally representative cross-sectional studies and the prospective longitudinal studies, it seems that a reasonable conclusion is that obesity does seem associated with later depression, but that this relationship is not particularly strong. Only one prospective study looked at anxiety, and it did not find evidence for a link between obesity and anxiety (Bjerkeset et al. 2008). In general, the evidence for a link between obesity and anxiety seems weaker and more tenuous than that between obesity and depression.

What does seem clear, however, is that regardless of whether obesity causes diagnosable mental disorders, it does have psychological consequences. Research with children and adolescents generally finds that obesity is related to body dissatisfaction (Ricciardelli and McCabe 2001; Wardle and Cooke 2005) and low self-esteem (French, Story, and Perry 1995; Wardle and Cooke 2005). When individuals of all ages and genders are studied, it appears that the relationship between obesity and low self-esteem is stronger in women than in men, gets stronger from childhood through college age, and then starts to weaken (but remains significant) among adults (Miller and Downey 1999).

The relationship between obesity and self-esteem may be mediated by the stigmatizing behaviors of others, such as, among children, weight-related teasing (Davison and Birch 2002; Thompson et al. 1995). It may also be mediated by individuals' own internalization of stigma, such as believing their obesity is entirely under their control (Pierce and Wardle 1997), or by the emotional toll of chronic and repeated diet failures (Miller and Downey 1999).

Physical Health Consequences

It has long been thought that obesity leads to physical health consequences, and the particular ailments attributed to obesity have included cardiovascular disease, strokes, hypertension, many cancers, diabetes, gallstones, chronic renal failure, fatty liver disease, gout, osteoarthritis, migraines, dementia, carpal tunnel syndrome, asthma, infertility, pregnancy complications, polycystic ovaries, erectile dysfunction, hirsutism, sleep apnea, and incontinence (NHLBI Expert Panel 1998). It has not been shown, however, that obesity per se actually causes these ailments, because the primary type of study that can show such causal links cannot be conducted for obesity. That type of study, the randomized controlled trial, is not possible because it requires randomly assigning individuals to either be obese or not obese, and then watching those individuals over the next several decades to see which diseases they contract.

Researchers must settle for the next best form of evidence, prospective longitudinal studies, in which individuals who happen to be obese (or not obese) are observed over many decades. Health differences found between obese and nonobese people in these studies may appear to have been *caused* by obesity, but in fact may have actually been caused by some additional factor that also varies between obese and non-obese people. It is all too easy for people not versed in research methods to mistakenly assume that such studies are convincing evidence of obesity's causal role in many diseases.

In the last 20 years, scientists (as well as activists and journalists) have begun to explore a variety of confounding factors that may account for the relationship between obesity and physical health problems (Campos et al. 2005). This has led to a contentious and politicized debate (described in Kolata 2007) that is unlikely to be easily resolved. The confounding factors that may play an important role in this relationship are obese people's greater likelihood (than non-obese people) of leading sedentary lifestyles, repeatedly gaining and losing weight (known as "weight cycling"), avoiding health care, and being in lower socioeconomic groups (Campos 2004; Ernsberger and Koletsky 1999). These factors have been shown to be associated with poor health and, to the extent that they are more likely to occur among obese people than non-obese people, may account for the relationship between obesity and disease.

Another factor that muddies the evidence for obesity as a cause of health problems is data suggesting that obesity does not shorten an individual's lifespan, or at least not until extremely high levels of obesity are reached (Flegal et al. 2005). It is difficult (although not impossible) to convincingly argue that obesity causes such a long list of ailments but somehow does not shorten one's life. The evidence is also called into question because studies supporting the relationship between obesity and health outcomes tend to be conducted by researchers with significant conflicts of interest (Fraser 1998).

As researchers with no vested interests on either side of this debate (as we study psychological outcomes of diets and obesity rather than physical ones), we have observed this debate from the outside. It is our conclusion that the links between obesity and some diseases are quite convincing, such as that between obesity and type 2 diabetes (Colditz et al. 1995; Ford, Williamson, and Liu 1997) and osteoarthritis (Hochberg et al. 1995). However, it is equally clear to us that the strength of the links between obesity and many other ailments has been overstated (Olshansky et al. 2005). Even if these relationships cannot be entirely explained away by confounding variables, they do not seem strong enough to warrant the amount of alarm they receive from the media, scientists, and the government.

TREATMENT OF OBESITY

Despite imperfect models regarding its etiology, strong beliefs in the physical health consequences of obesity have led researchers to develop treatment interventions. Most of these interventions have been diets designed to promote weight loss. More recent efforts, however, have included interventions aimed at treating the self-esteem and body dissatisfaction that result from obesity, without necessarily focusing on weight loss.

Treating the Physical Health Consequences of Obesity

Given the field of psychology's long history of research on behavior change, it is not surprising that its approach to the treatment of obesity is to try to alter people's eating habits by teaching them diet strategies. Over the past 60 years, psychologists have studied dozens of behavioral weight loss techniques to see which are effective (Leon 1976; Ayyad and Andersen 2000). They have taught dieters how to select appropriate foods to eat, count calories, resist temptation, monitor how much food they eat, and to reward (or punish) themselves for eating the right (or wrong) amount of food (see Leon 1976 for a review). In some treatments they gave the dieters all the food that they were allowed to eat, and in some cases the dieters were required to do all their eating in a researcher's laboratory or clinic (e.g., Wing and Jeffrey 2001; Musante 1976). Psychologists have also explored the effectiveness of having dieters give some of their own money to researchers and then trying to earn it back by losing certain amounts of weight (e.g., Harris and Bruner 1971). They also tested whether using social pressure could get obese people to reduce their consumption (e.g., Wollersheim 1970). Finally, in efforts to create negative associations with desired foods, researchers have paired dieters' favorite foods with horrible odors, and in other cases have actually jolted obese patients with electric shock whenever they tried to eat a food they craved (e.g., Foreyt and Kennedy 1971; Meyer and Crisp 1964).

As silly (or cruel) as some of these treatments may sound, by and large, whatever psychologists attempted generally led to at least *some* weight loss during the early months of the diet (Jeffery et al. 2000; Perri and Fuller 1995). Across over 200 diet studies conducted from 1966 up until 2000, participants lost from 8 to 22 pounds in as many weeks—about a pound a week (Wing 2002). For a diet to truly be considered successful, however, individuals must not just lose weight in the short term, but they also must keep it off. The majority of diet studies do not follow participants long enough to see if that happened. In fact, only 6 percent of over 800 diet studies found by researchers in the year 2000 had follow-ups of three years or more, and two-thirds of those had such serious flaws that they offered little useful information (Ayyad and Andersen 2000).

Across 14 studies with long-term follow-ups, participants initially lost an average of 30 pounds, but by four or five years later, they had gained back all but 7 of those pounds (Mann et al. 2007). These results likely *inflate* the success of these diets because the studies have multiple sources of systematic bias—all of which make the diets look more successful than they were. For example, most of the people who start these diet studies do not finish them, and the people who do finish are the ones who do the best on the diets. In addition, many of the people in these studies are not actually weighed by the researchers, but rather just tell the researchers their weight over the phone or by mail. Since most people lie about their weight—and say they weigh less than they actually do—this flaw causes the diets to look like they led to more weight loss than they really did. Another source of systematic bias in these studies is that many of the participants went on additional diets during the long follow-up period. This makes it appear as if the original diet had led to sustained weight loss, when, in fact, these dieters likely gained back a lot—if not all—of the weight before they started a new diet.

If the goal of obesity treatment is to have obese people lose enough weight to make them non-obese, and to maintain that weight loss in the long term, then it seems clear to us that behavioral treatments for obesity are unsuccessful. However, it is the association between obesity and physical health problems that makes effective obesity treatment a high priority in our country's research agenda. Given that, we suggest that it doesn't make sense to use weight loss—an indirect and imperfect measure of health—as a marker of successful obesity treatment when we could be measuring improvements in physical health more directly (Ernsberger and Koletsky 1999). The next generation of obesity treatment research should focus on physical health outcomes such as heart rate, blood pressure, and cholesterol levels, rather than weight change. Indeed, research on exercise interventions show positive health benefits on all of these outcomes, even in the absence of weight loss (Caudwell et al. 2009).

Treating the Mental Health Consequences of Obesity

Early psychological interventions focused on altering eating behavior to the neglect of mental health sequelae. It has even been argued that some mental health consequences of obesity, especially body distress, are important motivators for behavior change and that addressing them would be detrimental to weight-loss efforts. While there has been some support for this, the negative social and psychological effects of body distress and obesity are important areas of concern (Heinberg, Thompson, and Matzon 2001; Schwartz and Brownell 2004; Wilson 1996). Body image and self-acceptance themselves became primary aims of treatment due to the combination of these negative consequences and ineffective long-term weight loss treatments (Wilson 1996; Schwartz and Brownell 2004; Rosen et al. 1995).

It has been assumed that weight loss is a necessary prerequisite for improvement in body image. However, research findings have produced mixed results (see Schwartz and Brownell 2004). A randomized control trial comparing a cognitive behavioral body image therapy (CBT) or a no-treatment condition found that although weight status remained unchanged, individuals who received CBT showed significant improvement in body image as well as improvement in psychological symptoms, self-esteem, overeating, and eating guilt (Rosen et al. 1995). Another study found that the promotion of body and self-acceptance in a non-diet wellness intervention improved not only body image, but also physical health parameters, without changes in weight (Bacon et al. 2002). These positive psychological and health outcomes were sustained at a two-year follow-up, whereas initial improvements in the diet group were generally not maintained (Bacon et al. 2005). In contrast, a study comparing a combined body image treatment and weight control program to a weight control program alone did not find any additional improvement in body image (Ramirez and Rosen 2001).

In addition to being targets of treatment, body image and weight acceptance may also promote successful weight maintenance after weight loss occurs. A cognitive behavioral therapy intervention for obesity created by Cooper and Fairburn (2001) encourages a shift from weight loss to acceptance of weight stability following a pre-set period of time. Such promotion of weight- and self-acceptance is thought to prevent psychological barriers, including focusing on unattainable weight loss, from interfering with weight maintenance. In support of this, satisfaction with body weight has been associated with improved maintenance of weight loss, but findings have been inconsistent and more research is needed (Foster et al. 2004; Byrne, Cooper, and Fairburn 2004; Ames et al. 2005; Gorin et al. 2007).

Targeting body image dissatisfaction and self-acceptance either in isolation or in conjunction with behavior change therapy aimed at weight loss appears to be a promising component of treatment. While continued research is needed to explore the effects of these treatments, it is clear that the mental health consequences of obesity should not take a back seat to treatments aimed solely at the physical health consequences.

CONCLUSION

In 1999, psychologists, nutritionists, and other experts proposed a paradigm shift in research and policy on dieting and obesity (Cogan and Ernsberger 1999). They suggested a health-centered, rather than a weight-centered approach to obesity. This approach would encourage obesity researchers to design their interventions with the goal of promoting fitness rather than weight loss, and to use health markers as their outcome variables, rather than relying on weight as the primary and critical measure of success. Work consistent with this approach is accumulating, and although the proposed shift has not occurred, we believe that it would be a positive direction for the field. It seems to us that even though interventions based on this new paradigm may not reduce the prevalence of obesity, they are likely to improve the nation's health, and by helping to unlink the association between obesity and illness, may even reduce the stigma of obesity.

REFERENCES

Ames, G. E., M. G. Perri, L. D. Fox, E. A. Fallon, N. De Braganza, M. E. Murawski, et al. 2005. "Changing Weight-Loss Expectations: A Randomized Pilot Study." *Eating Behaviors* 6: 259–269.

Ayyad, C., and T. Andersen. 2000. "Long-term Efficacy of Dietary Treatment of Obesity: A Systematic Review of Studies Published between 1931 and 1999." *Obesity Reviews* 1: 113–119.

Bacon, L., N. L. Keim, M. D. Van Loan, M. Derricote, B. Gale, A. Kazaks, and J. S. Stern. 2002. "Evaluating a 'Non-Diet' Wellness Intervention for Improvement of Metabolic Fitness, Psychological Well-Being and Eating and Activity Behaviors." *International Journal of Obesity* 26: 854–865.

Bacon, L., J. S. Stern, M. D. Van Loan, and N. L. Keim. 2005. "Size Acceptance and Intuitive Eating Improve Health for Obese, Female Chronic Dieters." *Journal of the American Dietetic Association* 105: 929–936.

Bjerkeset, O., P. Romundstad, J. Evans, and D. Gunnell. 2008. "Association of Adult Body Mass Index and Height with Anxiety, Depression, and Suicide in the General Population." *American Journal of Epidemiology* 167: 193–202.

Brownell, Kelly. 2005. "The Social, Scientific, and Human Context of Prejudice and Discrimination Based on Weight." In *Weight bias: Nature, Consequences, and Remedies*, ed. Kelly Brownell, Rebecca Puhl, Marlene Schwartz, and Leslie Rudd, 1–11. New York: Guilford Press.

Bruch, H. 1961. "The Transformation of Oral Impulses in Eating Disorders: A Conceptual Approach." *Psychiatric Quarterly* 35: 458–481.

Byrne, S. M., Z. Cooper, and C. G. Fairburn. 2004. "Psychological Predictors of Weight Regain in Obesity." *Behaviour Research and Therapy* 42: 1341–1356.

Campos, P. 2004. *The Obesity Myth*. New York: Gotham.

Campos, P., A. Saguy, P. Ernsberger, E. Oliver, and G. Gaesser. 2005. "The Epidemiology of Overweight and Obesity: Public Health Crisis or Moral Panic?" *International Journal of Epidemiology* 35: 55–60.

Canetti, L., E. Bachar, and E. M. Berry. 2002. "Food and Emotion." *Behavioural Processes* 60: 157–164.

Carper, J. L., J. O. Fisher, and L. L. Birch. 2000. "Young Girls' Emerging Dietary Restraint and Disinhibition Are Related to Parental Control in Child Feeding." *Appetite* 35: 121–129.

Caudwell, P., M. Hopkins, N. A. King, R. J. Stubbs, and J. E. Blundell. 2009. "Exercise Alone Is Not Enough: Weight Loss Also Needs a Healthy (Mediterranean) Diet?" *Public Health Nutrition* 12: 1663–1666.

Chen, E., and M. Brown. 2005. "Obesity Stigma in Sexual Relationships." *Obesity Research* 13: 1393–1397.

Christakis, N. A., and J. H. Fowler. 2007. "The Spread of Obesity in a Large Social Network over 32 Years." *The New England Journal of Medicine* 357: 370–379.

Cogan, J. C., and P. Ernsberger. 1999. "Dieting, Weight, and Health: Reconceptualizing Research and Policy." *Journal of Social Issues* 55: 187–205.

Cohen-Cole, E., and J. M. Fletcher. 2008. "Detecting Implausible Social Network Effects in Acne, Height, and Headaches: Longitudinal Analysis." *British Medical Journal* 337: a2533.

Colditz G. A., W. C. Willett, A. Rotnitzky, and J. E. Manson. 1995. "Weight Gain as a Risk Factor for Clinical Diabetes Mellitus in Women." *Annals of Internal Medicine* 122: 481–486.

Cooper, Z., and C. G. Fairburn. 2001. "A New Cognitive Behavioural Approach to the Treatment of Obesity." *Behaviour Research and Therapy* 39: 499–511.

Crisp, A. H., and B. McGuinness. 1976. "Jolly Fat: Relation between Obesity and Psychoneurosis in the General Population." *British Medical Journal* 1: 7–9.

Cutting, T.M., J.O Fisher, K. Grimm-Thomas, and L.L. Birch. 1999. "Like Mother, Like Daughter: Familial Patterns of Overweight Are Mediated by Mothers' Dietary Disinhibtion." *American Journal of Clinical Nutrition* 69: 608–613.

Davison, K. K., and L. L. Birch. 2002. "Processes Linking Weight Status and Self-Concept among Girls from Ages 5 To 7 Years." *Developmental Psychology* 38: 735–748.

Drury, C., and M. Louis, M. 2002. "Exploring the Association between Body Weight, Stigma of Obesity, and Health Care Avoidance." *Journal of American Academy of Nurse Practitioners* 14: 554–560.

Epstein, L. H., R. R. Wing, and A. Valoski. 1985. "Childhood Obesity." *Pediatric Clinics of North America* 32(2): 363–379.

Ernsberger, P., and R. J. Koletsky. 1999. "Biomedical Rationale for a Wellness Approach to Obesity: An Alternative to a Focus on Weight Loss." *Journal of Social Issues* 55: 221–259.

Flegal, K., B. I. Graubard, D. F. Williamson, and M. H. Gail. 2005. "Excess Deaths Associated with Underweight, Overweight, and Obesity." *Journal of the American Medical Association* 293: 1861–1867.

Ford, E. S., D. F. Williamson, and S. Liu. 1997. "Weight Change and Diabetes Incidence: Findings from a National Cohort of US Adults." *American Journal of Epidemiology* 146: 214–222.

Foreyt, J. P., and W. A. Kennedy. 1971. "Treatment of Overweight by Aversion Therapy." *Behaviour Research and Therapy*, 9: 29–34.

Foster, G. D., S. Phelan, T. A. Wadden, D. Gill, J. Ermold, and E. Didie. 2004. "Promoting More Modest Weight Losses: A Pilot Study." *Obesity* 12: 1271–1277.

Foster, G. D., T. A.Wadden, A. P. Makris, D. Davidson, R. S. Sanderson, D. B. Allison, and A. Kessler. 2003. "Primary Care Physicians' Attitudes about Obesity and Its Treatment." *Obesity Research* 11: 1168–1177.

Francis, L. A., and L. L. Birch. 2005. "Maternal Influences on Daughters' Restrained Eating Behavior." *Health Psychology* 24: 548–554.

Fraser, L. 1998. *Losing It: False Hopes and Fat Profits in the Diet Industry*. New York: Plume.

French, S. A., M. Story, and C. L. Perry. 1995. "Self-esteem and Obesity in Children and Adolescents: A Literature Review." *Obesity Research* 3: 479–490.

Friedman, M. A., and K. D. Brownell. 1995. "Psychological Correlates of Obesity: Moving to the Next Research Generation." *Psychological Bulletin* 117: 3–20.

Gorin, A. A., A. Marinilli Pinto, D. F. Tate, H. A. Raynor, J. L. Fava, and R. R.Wing. 2007. "Failure to Meet Weight Loss Expectations Does Not Impact Maintenance in Successful Weight Losers." *Obesity* 15: 3086–3090.

Greenfield, E. A., and N. F. Marks. 2009. "Violence from Parents in Childhood and Obesity in Adulthood: Using Food in Response to Stress as a Mediator of Risk." *Social Science and Medicine* 68: 791–798.

Greeno, C. G., and R. R. Wing. 1994. "Stress-induced Eating." *Psychological Bulletin* 115: 444–464.

Harris, M. B., and C. G. Bruner. 1971. "A Comparison of a Self-Control and a Contract Procedure for Weight Control." *Behavior Research and Therapy* 9: 347–354.

Hasler, G., D. S. Pine, A. Gamma, G. Milos, V. Ajdacic, D. Eich, W. Rossler, and J. Angst. 2004. "The Associations between Psychopathology and Being Overweight: A 20-Year Prospective Study." *Psychological Medicine* 34: 1047–1057.

Hatzenbuehler, M. L., K. M. Keyes, and D. S. Hasin. 2009. "Associations between Perceived Weight Discrimination and the Prevalence of Psychiatric Disorders in the General Population." *Obesity* 17: 2033–2039.

Heatherton, T. F., C. P. Herman, and J. Polivy. 1991. "Effects of Physical Threat and Ego Threat on Eating Behavior." *Journal of Personality and Social Psychology* 60: 138–143.

Heinberg, L. J., J. K. Thompson, and J. L. Matzon. 2001. "Body Image Dissatisfaction as a Motivator for Healthy Lifestyle Change: Is Some Distress Beneficial?" In *Eating Disorders: Innovative Directions in Research and Practice*, eds. R. H. Striegel-Moore and L. Smolak. Washington, DC: American Psychological Association.

Herman, C. P., and D. Mack. 1975. "Restrained and Unrestrained Eating." *Journal of Personality* 43(4): 647–660.

Herman, C. P., and J. Polivy. 1975. "Anxiety, Restraint, and Eating Behavior." *Journal of Abnormal Psychology* 84: 666–672.

Herman, C. P., and J. Polivy. 2008. "External Cues in the Control of Food Intake in Humans: The Sensory-Normative Distinction." *Physiology and Behavior* 94: 722–728.

Herva, A., J. Laitinen, J. Miettunen, J. Veijola, J. T. Karvonen, K. Lasky, et al. 2006. "Obesity and Depression: Results from the Longitudinal Northern Finland 1966 Birth Cohort Study." *International Journal of Obesity (London)* 30: 520–527.

Hochberg, M. C., M. Lethbridge-Cejku, W. W. Scott, R. Reichle, C. C. Plato, and J. D. Tobin. 1995. "The Association of Body Weight, Body Fatness and Body Fat Distribution with Osteoarthritis of the Knee: Data from the Baltimore Longitudinal Study of Aging." *Journal of Rheumatology* 22: 488–493.

Jeffery, R. W., A. Drewnowski, L. H. Epstein, A. J. Stunkard, G. T. Wilson, R. R. Wing, et al. 2000. "Long-term Maintenance of Weight Loss: Current Status." *Heath Psychology* 19(Supp.): 5–6.

Kaplan, H. I., and H. S. Kaplan. 1957. "The Psychosomatic Concept of Obesity." *Journal of Nervous and Mental Disease* 125: 181–201.

King, E. B., J. R. Shapiro, M. R. Hebl, S. L. Singletary, and S. Turner. 2006. "The Stigma of Obesity in Customer Service: A Mechanism for Remediation and Bottom-Line Consequences of Interpersonal Discrimination." *Journal of Applied Psychology* 91: 579–593.

Koch, F. S., A. Sepa, and J. Ludvigsson. 2008. "Psychological Stress and Obesity." *The Journal of Pediatrics* 153: 839–844.

Kolata, Gina. 2007. *Rethinking Thin*. New York: Farrar Straus and Giroux.

Leon, Gloria R. 1976. "Current Directions in the Treatment of Obesity." *Psychological Bulletin* 83: 557–578.

Lowe, M. R., J. van Steenburgh, C. Ochner,, and M. Coletta. 2009. "Neural Correlates of Individual Differences Related to Appetite." *Physiology and Behavior* 97: 561–571.

Macht, M., and J. Mueller. 2007. "Immediate Effects of Chocolate on Experimentally Induced Mood States." *Appetite* 49: 667–674.

Maclean, L., N. Edwards, M. Garrard, N. Sims-Jones, K. Clinton, and L. Ashley. 2009. "Obesity, Stigma and Public Health Planning." *Health Promotion International* 24: 88–93.

Mann, T., A. J. Tomiyama, E. Westling, A. Lew, B. Samuels, and J. Chatman. 2007. "Medicare's Search for Effective Obesity Treatments: Diets Are Not the Answer." *American Psychologist* 62: 220–233.

Mann, T., and A. Ward. 2000. "Don't Mind If I Do: Disinhibited Eating under Cognitive Load." *Journal of Personality and Social Psychology* 78(4): 753–763.

Mather, A. A., B. J. Cox, W. E. Murray, and J. Sareen. 2009. "Associations of Obesity with Psychiatric Disorders and Suicidal Behaviors in a Nationally Representative Sample." *Journal of Psychosomatic Research* 66: 277–285.

Meyer, V., and A. H. Crisp. 1964. "Aversion Therapy in Two Cases of Obesity." *Behaviour Research and Therapy* 2: 143–147.

Miller, C. T., and K. T. Downey. 1999. "A Meta-Analysis of Heavyweight and Self-Esteem." *Personality and Social Psychology Review* 3: 68–84.

Musante, G. J. 1976. "The Dietary Rehabilitation Clinic: Evaluative Report of a Behavioral and Dietary Treatment of Obesity." *Behavior Therapy* 7: 198–204.

NHLBI Expert Panel. 1998. *Clinical Guidelines on the Identification, Evaluation, and Treatment of Overweight and Obesity in Adults: The Evidence Report.* NIH Publication Number 98–4083.

Nisbett, R. E. 1972. "Hunger, Obesity, and the Ventromedial Hypothalamus." *Psychological Review* 79(6): 433–453.

Nosek, B. A., Banaji, M., and A. G. Greenwald. 2002. "Harvesting Implicit Group Attitudes and Beliefs from a Demonstration Web Site." *Group Dynamics: Theory, Research, and Practice*, 6: 101–115.

Onyike, C. U., R. M. Crum, H. B. Lee, C. G. Lyketsos, and W. W. Eaton. 2003. "Is Obesity Associated with Major Depression? Results from the Third National Health and Nutrition Examination Survey." *American Journal of Epidemiology* 158: 1139–1147.

Olshansky, S. J., D. J. Passaro, R. C. Hershow, et al. 2005. "A Potential Decline in Life Expectancy in the United States in the 21st Century." *New England Journal of Medicine* 352: 1138–1145.

Perri, M. G., and P. R. Fuller. 1995. "Success and Failure in the Treatment Of Obesity: Where Do We Go from Here?" *Medicine, Exercise, Nutrition, and Health* 4: 255–272.

Pickering, R. P., B. F. Grant, S. P. Chou, et al. 2007. "Are Overweight, Obesity, and Extreme Obesity Associated with Psychopathology? Results from the National Epidemiologic Survey on Alcohol and Related Conditions." *Journal of Clinical Psychology* 68: 998–1009.

Pierce, J. W., and J. Wardle. 1997. "Cause and Effect Beliefs and Self-Esteem of Overweight Children." *Journal of Child Psychology and Psychiatry* 38: 645–650.

Pike, K. M., and J. Rodin. 1991. "Mothers, Daughters, and Disordered Eating." *Journal of Abnormal Psychology* 100: 198–204.

Pinel, J. P. J., S. Assanand, and D. R. Lehman. 2000. "Hunger, Eating and Ill Health." *American Psychologist* 55(10): 1105–1116.

Polinko, N. K., and P. M. Popovich. 2001. "Evil Thoughts but Angelic Actions: Responses to Overweight Job Applicants." *Journal of Applied Social Psychology* 31: 905–924.

Polivy, J., and C. P. Herman. 1985. "Dieting and Binging: A Causal Analysis." *American Psychologist* 40: 193–201.

Polivy, J., C. P. Herman, and T. McFarlane. (1994). "Effects of Anxiety on Eating: Does Palatability Moderate Distress-Induced Overeating in Dieters?" *Journal of Abnormal Psychology* 103: 505–510.

Puhl, R. M., T. Andreyeva, and K. D.Brownell. 2008. "Perceptions of Weight Discrimination: Prevalence and Comparison to Race and Gender Discrimination in America." *International Journal of Obesity* 32: 992–1000.

Puhl, R. M., and K. D.Brownell. 2006. "Confronting and Coping with Weight Stigma: An Investigation of Overweight and Obese Individuals." *Obesity* 14: 1802–1815.

Puhl, R. M., and C. A. Heuer. 2009. "The Stigma of Obesity: A Review and Update." *Obesity* 17: 941–964.

Puhl, R. M., and J. D. Latner. 2007. "Obesity, Stigma, and the Health of the Nation's Children." *Psychological Bulletin* 133: 557–580.

Ramirez, E. M., and J. C. Rosen. 2001. "A Comparison of Weight Control and Weight Control Plus Body Image Therapy for Obese Men and Women." *Journal of Consulting and Clinical Psychology* 69: 440–446.

Ricciardelli, L. A., and M. P. McCabe. 2001. "Children's Body Image Concerns and Eating Disturbance: A Review of the Literature." *Clinical Psychology Review* 21: 325–344.

Roberts, R. E., G. A. Kaplan, S. J. Shema, and W. J. Strawbridge. 2000. "Are the Obese at Greater Risk for Depression?" *American Journal of Epidemiology* 152: 163–170.

Roberts, R. E., S. Deleger, W. J. Strawbridge, and G. A. Kaplan. 2003. "Prospective Association between Obesity and Depression: Evidence from the Alameda County Study." *International Journal of Obesity and Related Metabolic Disorders* 27: 514–521.

Rodin, J. 1981. "Current Status of the Internal-External Hypothesis for Obesity: What Went Wrong?" *American Psychologist* 36: 361–372.

Roehling, Mark V., Shawn Pilcher, Fred Oswald, and Tamara A. Bruce. (2008). "The Effects of Weight Bias on Job-Related Outcomes: A Meta-Analysis of Experimental Studies." Paper presented at the annual meeting of the Academy of Management in Anaheim, CA, 2008.

Rosen, J. C., P. Orosan, and J. Reiter. 1995. "Cognitive Behavior Therapy for Negative Body Image in Obese Women." *Behavior Therapy* 26: 25–42.

Ruderman, A. J. 1986. "Dietary Restraint: A Theoretical and Empirical Review." *Psychological Bulletin* 99: 247–262.

Schacter, S. 1968. "Obesity and Eating." *Science* 16: 751–756.

Schacter, S., R. Goldman, and A. Gordon. 1968. "Effects of Fear, Food Deprivation, and Obesity on Eating." *Journal of Personality and Social Psychology* 10:96–106.

Schwartz, M. B., and K. D. Brownell. 2004. "Obesity and Body Image." *Body Image* 1: 43–56.

Scott, K. M., R. Bruffaerts, G. E. Simon, J. Alonso, M. Angermeyer, G. de Girolamo, et al. 2007. "Obesity and Mental Disorders in the General Population: Results from the World Mental Health Surveys." *International Journal of Obesity* 32: 192–200.

Simon, G. E., M. Von Korff, K. Saunders, D. L. Miglioretti, P. K. Crane, G. van Belle, et al. 2006. "Association between Obesity and Psychiatric Disorders in the US Adult Population." *Archives of General Psychiatry* 63: 824–830.

Stunkard, A. J., and T. A. Wadden. 1992. "Psychological Aspects of Severe Obesity." *American Journal of Clinical Nutrition* 55: 524S–532S.

Teachman, B. A., K. D. Gapinski, K. D. Brownell, M. Rawlins, and S. Jeyaram. 2003. "Demonstrations of Implicit Anti-Fat Bias: The Impact of Providing Causal Information and Evoking Empathy." *Health Psychology* 22: 68–78.

Thompson, J. K., M. Coovert, K .J. Richards, S. Johnson, and J. Cattarin. 1995. "Development of Body Image and Eating Disturbance in Young Females: Covariance Structure Modeling and Longitudinal Analyses." *International Journal of Eating Disorders* 18: 221–236.

Valente, T. W., K. Fujimoto, C. Chou, and D. Spruijt-Metz. 2009. "Adolescent Affiliations and Adiposity: A Social Network Analysis of Friendships and Obesity." *Journal of Adolescent Health* 45: 202–204.

Van Strien, T., and M. A. Ouwens. 2003. "Counterregulation in Female Obese Eaters: Schacter, Goldman and Gordons (1968) Test of Psychosomatic Theory Revisited." *Eating Behaviors* 3: 329–340.

Wardle, J., and L. Cooke. 2005. "The Impact of Obesity on Psychological Well-Being." *Best Practice and Research Clinical Endocrinology and Metabolism* 19: 421–440.

Wear, D., J. M. Aultman, J. D. Varley, and J. Zarconi. 2006. "Making Fun of Patients:
    Medical Students' Perceptions and Use of Derogatory and Cynical Humor in Clinical
    Settings." *Academy of Medicine* 81: 454–462.
Wilson, T. G. 1996. "Acceptance and Change in the Treatment of Eating Disorders and
    Obesity." *Behavior Therapy* 27: 417–439.
Wing, Rena R. 2002. "Behavioral Weight Control." In *Handbook of Obesity Treatment*, ed.
    Thomas A. Wadden and Albert J. Stunkard, 301–316. New York: The Guilford Press.
Wing, R. R., and R. W. Jeffery. 2001. "Food Provision as a Strategy to Promote Weight
    Loss." *Obesity Research* 9: s271–s275.
Wollersheim, J. P. 1970. "Effectiveness of Group Therapy Based upon Learning Principles
    in the Treatment of Overweight Women." *Journal of Abnormal Psychology*
    76: 462–474.

CHAPTER 7

THE SOCIOLOGY
OF OBESITY

JEFFERY SOBAL

INTRODUCTION

SOCIOLOGY is a core social science discipline that studies all aspects of societies (Ritzer 2007). Sociology is broad in scope, examining social units that range from macro-scale to micro-scale (Ritzer 2007), such as global systems, populations, classes, communities, organizations, groups, relationships, roles, identities, and others. Sociologists use a variety of theoretical perspectives that range in focus from taking an objective to taking a subjective approach to analyzing societies (Ritzer 2008).

It is challenging to characterize the work of a large and diverse discipline like sociology about a specific topic like obesity. Classification of components of the discipline can be accomplished by identifying major schools of thought within the discipline and then specific topics that have been dealt with within each approach. One way of conceptualizing the multiple facets of sociology is Ritzer's (1975) delineation of metatheories. Extending Kuhn's concept of paradigms, Ritzer (1975, 2008) identified three metatheories that represent major ontological and epistemiological orientations in sociology. Social definition metatheories take a constructionist perspective that assumes that individuals actively interpret the world and construct joint meanings about reality, typically using qualitative methods like in-depth interviews and participant observation. Social facts metatheories take a structurist perspective that assumes social structures are the primary forces shaping the social world and establish the facts of social life, typically using quantitative methods like surveys or analysis of existing records. Social behavior metatheories take a rationalist perspective that assumes individuals make deliberate choices based on utilitarian weighing of costs and benefits, typically using quantitative methods like experiments or simulations. Sociological analyses of obesity have employed all three of these metatheories, and this review will use these metatheories to classify some of the wide range of sociological analyses that have examined obesity.

Social Definitions of Obesity

Some sociological work examines how people actively and interactively perceive, experience, interpret, define, symbolize, negotiate, manage, and enact obesity, focusing on their social, cultural, and cognitive constructions of their own fatness or thinness as well as the body weights of others. Several themes in the sociological literature examine social definitions of obesity, including stigmatization of obesity, obese identities, dieting group dynamics, obesity as a social problem, and social movements and obesity.

Stigmatization of Obesity

The concept of stigma emerged in social science thinking with the pioneering work of Erving Goffman (1963) who defined a stigma as an "attribute that is deeply discrediting." Goffman (1963) mentioned obesity as an example of a stigmatized condition but did not focus on the topic. However, soon after Goffman's classic work, sociologists like Cahnman (1968), Maddox et al. (1968), Allon (1973), DeJong (1980), and others examined the stigmatization of obesity in greater depth by describing processes involved in the prejudice, bias, and discrimination associated with body weight.

Sociologists have focused on how obese people socially construct their weight (Sobal and Maurer 1999a), in contrast to the more individualistic approach to the stigmatization of obesity by psychologists and many other analysts of obesity. A review of sociological work about obesity found that stigmatization was highly prevalent, that obesity was stigmatized as severely as many other conditions, was perpetuated by many types of sources, occurred in several arenas of life, and was dealt with using several coping strategies including denial, concealment, avoidance, redefinition, and mutual assistance (Sobal 2008). For example, Carr and Friedman (2005, 2006) analyzed U.S. national data to reveal that obese individuals reported that they experienced pervasive discrimination in both their institutional and interpersonal lives and had low levels of self-acceptance and poor quality social relationships.

Obese Identities

Identities are the conceptualizations that people hold of themselves, including interpretation of their body weights as "spoiled identities" (Goffman 1963).

Sociological analyses have focused on dealing with the processes involved in identity development and management rather than treating identity as a static entity, describing how people recognize and interpret cues about their weight status and place themselves in a "fat" identity (Degher and Hughes 1999).

Sociologists have often examined how people construct and manage their weight identities when changes occur in their body weight and shape, often finding disjunctures between their expectations and actual experiences. For example, English (1993) described how obese dieters were often disappointed by the reactions of significant others in their lives to their new thin identities after they lost weight, which led many dieters to return to their former obesity. Similarly, Granberg (2006) also found that the personal transformation associated with weight loss did not fulfill obese people's expectations about possible selves after weight loss, and the gap between potential and actual thin selves required considerable negotiation of interpretations with others and management of ways to interpret their weight.

Obesity surgery often involves substantial identity change dilemmas as individuals deal with seeing and experiencing their newly sized bodies in new ways. The extreme weight loss accomplished through obesity surgery leads many women to struggle with conceptualizing their conversion from fat to thin (Rubin et al. 1993); studies offer accounts of how they became obese (Throsby 2007), explanations of their "re-birth" through surgery (Throsby 2008), and reconceptualizations of themselves after surgery (Joanisse 2005). Obesity surgery patients also negotiated their identities with respect to the medical conceptions of an "ideal patient" for weight loss surgery, with Drew (2008) reporting that patients followed several paths: embracing a medical ideal, mixed responses to a medical ideal, and strategic compliance with medical ideals.

Dieting Group Dynamics

Dieting to attempt to lose weight is a prevalent practice, and dieting groups have emerged as an important social institution in contemporary societies. Since the middle of the twentieth century (Sussman 1956), sociologists have analyzed organized weight loss groups to seek social insights about how dieting functions in social groups. Participant observation, where a researcher engages in a setting while also studying its social dynamics, has been an important method used to study dieting groups. For example, Allon (1975) revealed how dieting groups offered important social services beyond weight loss, including sociability, venting, expression of worries, exchanging knowledge, and support. Laslett and Warren (1975) described organizational strategies used by dieting organizations, including emphasizing in-group (fat) versus out-group (thin) differences and using those who have been successful in weight loss as change agents to foster weight normalization. Millman (1980) described how weight-loss camps for children used group pressures to encourage weight loss, and Gimlin (2007) described how older women interpret weight-loss groups differently from their younger counterparts. Stinson (2001) identified ways that weight loss groups emphasize broader social values about thinness using moral and religious rhetoric and an emphasis upon individual discipline. Most dieting group participants are women, and weight-loss activities and discourse use feminized weight-loss strategies (Broom and Dixon 2008; Germov and Williams 1996, 1999), but Monaghan (2008) described how organized dieting groups also use masculine and military metaphors to promote thinness for men. These sociological analyses of group dieting move beyond individualized psychological and health perspectives for group engineering of weight loss, and provide greater understanding of group dynamics, strategies employed by dieting organizations, and ways in which dieting groups are situated within larger social values and structures.

Obesity as a Social Problem

As social scientists, sociologists have often moved beyond conceptualizing obesity primarily as a personal issue of individuals to examining how obesity is broadly treated as a social problem in the larger society (Sobal and Maurer 1999b). Sociological analyses of obesity as a social problem often use constructionist approaches that identify how obesity is defined and interpreted as a broader societal issue and how vested social interests make claims about body weight to gather attention and promote their definition.

Framing is an important concept in the sociological analysis of obesity. Frames are cognitive understandings that focus attention and provide meaning, and framing is the active process of using frames to construct interpretations (Benford and Snow 2000). A number of sociological analyses examine framing of obesity. For example, Martin (2002) describes how different obesity groups maintain frame alignment (congruency between frames of groups and of individual) among their members, with health-based dieting groups using rationality frames based on biomedical logic, spiritual weight loss groups using redemptive frames based on spiritual logic, and size acceptance groups using justice frames based on ethical logic. Saguy and Riley (2005) explain how anti-obesity researchers and practitioners are engaged in framing contests with fat-acceptance advocates and activists as they compete between different ways of framing obesity. Kwan (2009a, 2009b) maps broader cultural frames for obesity that compete for societal attention as a medical frame, social justice frame, and market choice frame. Julier (2008) described how framing obesity as a problem serves social functions.

Sociological analysis has often examined changes in social problems as a process of medicalization, where definitions and solutions for the problem shift from being seen as "sickness," under the purview of medical authority, rather than as "badness," under the purview of moral evaluations (Conrad 2007). Obesity is a classic example of medicalization, where contested "ownership" of obesity as a problem has shifted from a moral perspective to a medical perspective (Sobal 1995). Weight-loss surgery promoted the commercialization of thin identities as a medical product (Hesse-Biber 1996), despite mixed acceptance of obesity surgery among the medical establishment (Drew 2008). Analyses of web site marketing for obesity surgery suggest that Internet advertisements seek to legitimize that form of weight loss intervention to advance economic and professional motivations in the process of medicalizing obesity (Salant and Santry 2006).

Social Movements and Obesity

Some sociologists suggest that medicalization has produced opposition as it creates a "moral panic" about obesity (Ben-Yehuda and Goode 1994), where the intensity of feeling about obesity among the broader population appears to threaten the existing social order (Boero 2007). In reaction, alternative perspectives about fatness and thinness have emerged to challenge medical models (Sobal 1999).

While individual reactions to the stigmatization and discrimination of obesity take many forms (Cordell and Ronai 1999; Joanisse and Synnott 1999), collective reactions to obesity have also emerged as individuals organized into groups (Sobal 1999). Sociological thinking provides conceptual tools for analyzing social movements. The size acceptance movement has often been contrasted with other organized interests like governmental and industry (e.g., Kwan 2009; Honeycutt 1999; Martin 2002; Saguy and Riley 2005), revealing different movement structures, ideologies, strategies, and tactics in promoting their perspectives.

Mobilization of obese individuals and their supporters has led to the development of social movement organizations that represent what has come to be known as the size acceptance movement. As with other social movements, the size acceptance movement includes subgroups based on political and personal orientations (Goode and Preissler 1983; Sobal 1999; Textor 1999).

Overall, much of the earliest sociological thinking about obesity used social definition perspectives, and that orientation continues to produce some of the most sociologically unique work about obesity that stands apart from research in other disciplines and fields. Various forms of definitionist, interpretivisit, and constructionist theories will continue to provide new sociological insights about obesity that can be applied in research and practice.

SOCIAL FACTS AND OBESITY

Social facts perspectives take a holistic, structurist stance, which assumes that structures such as institutions and environments shape individual behaviors and bodies. Social facts analyses assume that macro-level social entities exist and are important, with micro-level individual actors embedded within these structures. Much sociological analysis identifies social facts about institutions and the location of individuals in society, and is used to predict behaviors, like eating and physical activity, and attributes like body weight (Ross and Mirowsky 1983). For example, sociologists have examined predictors of obesity, like religion (Cline and Ferraro 2006) and marriage (Umberson et al. 2009; Sobal et al. 2003), and consequences or impacts of obesity, like health (Zajacova and Burgard 2010) and depression (Ross 1994) using quantitative analyses. These studies of which, where, when, and how individuals are obese are often used to suggest ways to engineer society to prevent and treat obesity (Peralta 2003). Social facts perspectives have received special consideration by sociologists in relationship to several aspects of obesity, including social stratification, historical materialism, social networks, and life course perspectives.

Social Stratification and Obesity

Social stratification is the structured social inequality between individuals and groups in society, and is a fundamental sociological topic. Sociologists have used a variety of concepts and methods to examine how socioeconomic status (SES) is associated with obesity. Sobal and Stunkard (1989) reviewed existing literature and found a direct association between SES and obesity in developing societies, an inverse association for women in developed societies, and mixed findings among men in developed societies. However, most studies of SES and body weight use cross-sectional data, which does not resolve questions about the extent to which SES causes obesity, obesity causes SES, or both, or neither (Sobal 1991).

Socioeconomic status as a cause of obesity is supported by individual-level sociological research that linked childhood poverty with obesity among young adults for women, but not men (Lee et al. 2009). Furthermore, income inequality at the community level is inversely associated with higher body weights among white women, but not other sociodemographic categories (Chang and Christakis 2005). Socioeconomic status and social inequality appear to influence both diet and physical activity, which in turn shape body weight and obesity (Peralta 2003).

Obesity as a cause of socioeconomic status is supported by the literature about stigmatization of obesity (Sobal 2008). Particularly among girls, obesity is a clear predictor of entry into college (Crosnoe 2007), although the relationship of education with obesity may be declining (Himes and Reynolds 2005). Obesity presents a barrier to upward mobility, and appears to be a crucial constraint in attaining higher socioeconomic status.

Social stratification is intertwined with many other factors, particularly ethnicity and community. Sociologists have examined ethnic and residential patterns in body weight to consider how racial and spatial segregation are involved with obesity. Individuals living in U.S. neighborhoods with a high proportion of black residents were more likely to have higher body weights (Boardman et al. 2005; Chang 2006), even when controlling for personal SES characteristics, with such neighborhood racial isolation focused primarily upon women (Chang et al. 2009). The community disadvantage of living in segregated places was related to higher weights among women, both concurrently (Robert and Reither 2004) and as rising weight trajectories over time (Ruel et al. 2010). These sociological analyses show how predictors of obesity involving socioeconomic status are complex and multifaceted, and require multivariate, multilevel, and dynamic analyses to be more fully understood.

Historical Materialism and Obesity

The theories of Karl Marx provided explanations of social structures and social changes based on economic modes of production that lead to social inequalities inherent in the economic base of society, including contemporary corporate food systems that focus upon economic efficiency rather than the health of individuals and populations (McIntosh 1996). Historical materialist perspectives have been invoked by sociologists to explain obesity. For example, Winson (2004) discusses supermarket marketing of unhealthy foods that contribute to individual obesity, and Sobal and McIntosh (2009) consider the role of transnational corporations in the globalization of obesity. However, some quantitative analyses of class position reveal that role in the productive system of the economy is not associated with body weight (Veenstra 2006). Guthman and DuPuis (2006) suggest that political economy critiques of corporate food systems oversimplify contemporary obesity and need to be tempered with cultural analyses.

Social Networks and Obesity

Social network analysis has been a special focus of sociologists, and sociological analyses of social networks and obesity have examined both how network relationships predict obesity, as well as how obesity predicts network relationships. For example, network relationships as a predictor of obesity were examined in a longitudinal network analysis by Christakis and Fowler (2007), who found that when a person became obese predicted the development of obesity among others in that person's network, extending to three degrees of separation, with development of obesity predicting future obesity among a person's friends, siblings, or spouse. Obesity as a predictor of network relationships was examined by Crosnoe, Frank, and Mueller (2008), who found that students who were heavier were less likely to be chosen by other students as friends, assumedly due to stigmatization, and that friends tended to have similar body weights, assumedly due to homophily in friendship formation. These studies suggest that the structure and dynamics of social networks in which individuals are embedded offer unique perspectives about obesity.

Life Course Analysis and Obesity

Sociologists developed the concept of the life course as a way of conceptualizing how individuals experience a developmental series of role transitions within broader contexts that together form life course trajectories (Mayer 2009). Some of the earliest explicit life course analysis about obesity by sociologists described how the progression through childhood, adolescence, and pregnancy were shaped by contextual factors like medical and popular interpretations of obesity (Gordon and Tobias 1984). Another contextual life course concept is that individuals are embedded in age cohorts that pass through historical time together. Sociologists have reported mixed findings about cohort effects and obesity as Reither et al. (2009) identified cohorts born between 1955 and 1975 at particular risk of becoming obese, while Reynolds and Himes (2007) found no cohort-specific obesity changes.

The concept of cumulative disadvantage suggests that risk factors of particular conditions, such as obesity, accumulate as individuals move through the life course. For example, the duration of exposure to obesity over the life course provides a cumulative disadvantage that leads to more hospital admissions and greater length of hospitalizations (Schafer and Ferraro 2007). Cumulative disadvantage may be reduced by compensatory mechanisms, however, with early obesity leading to later disability that may be attenuated by exercise (Ferraro and Kelly-Moore 2003). Being overweight in childhood increases risk of severe obesity later in life, although if overweight children did not become severely overweight they were not at additional mortality risk (Ferraro et al. 2003).

Social facts perspectives are often used to identify the prevalence, patterns, and impacts of obesity by sociologists and those in other disciplines and fields. While some non-sociologists have used the title "sociology of obesity" to describe epidemiological findings about body weight (e.g., Rosengren and Lissner 2008), sociological analyses in a social facts theoretical tradition bring a greater disciplinary depth to the topic and are growing rapidly within the discipline of sociology.

Social Behaviors and Obesity

Social behavior perspectives assume that individuals make rational choices in decisions about their personal activities and their body weight that optimize benefits and minimize costs. Rationalist approaches have been used by sociologists to examine obesity, including social exchange and rational choice perspectives.

Social Exchange Theories and Obesity

Exchange theories analyze the dynamics of interpersonal transactions in social relationships, considering how people deal with rewards, costs, and reciprocity in exchanges. Exchange thinking has been used by sociologists to examine romantic relationships and obesity. For example, Goode and Preissler (1983) described the bargaining problems of obese women who are devalued because of their weight in exchange relationships with romantic partners. Carmalt et al. (2008) reported that overall physical attractiveness, higher education, and good grooming may be exchanged in matching with romantic partners to compensate for the lower exchange value of having high body weight. These studies suggest that especially in romantic relationships, and probably in other types of relationships, the stigmatization of obesity may be overcome by trading of other personal attributes in exchanges between obese individuals and others.

Rational Choices and Obesity

Rational choice theories explain the actions of individuals as self-interested, forward-looking, volitional agents who make reasoned decisions about choices among a range of possible alternatives. Rational choice theories are widely used in many social science disciplines and fields, and sociologists are beginning to explicitly apply rational choice thinking to examining obesity. For example, Sobal et al. (1995) found that obese women reported higher marital quality than thinner women, suggesting that obese married women are more likely to accept their current relationship because they recognize their lower value in the marriage market. Cawley et al. (2006) found that thinness offered valuable human capital for adolescent boys and girls that was associated with the likelihood of beginning to engage in dating romantic partners, but that body weight was not a consistent predictor of engaging in sexual behavior. Social psychological analyses by Sturmer et al. (2003) revealed that individuals used rational choice thinking to consider costs and benefits of joining obesity organizations.

Other disciplines, especially economics and psychology, use social behavior perspectives to examine obesity in different ways than sociology. Various forms of exchange, rational choice, institutional choice, social choice, and related theories offer potential for future sociological analyses and cross-disciplinary analyses of food intake, physical activity, and obesity.

CONCLUSION

In addition to the unique body of sociological work specifically about obesity reviewed here, several disciplinary specialties including the sociology of food and nutrition (McIntosh 1996), sociology of sports and physical activity (Coakley and Dunning 2000), and sociology of health and medicine (Bird, Conrad, and Fremont 2000) offer useful perspectives relevant to obesity. For example, health problems from food risks are linked by the media to obesity (Lupton 2004), problematic relationships exist between sports participation and obesity (Smith et al. 2004), and the viewpoints of medicine about causes of body weight are shifting over time (Chang and Christakis 2002).

While much sociological analysis of obesity has an academic focus (Crossley 2004; Qvortrup 2007), sociologists also engage in a variety of activities they label as applied, public, or clinical sociological practice (Sobal 1992). Much sociological analysis is relevant to obesity and describes potential interventions or management strategies, such as identification and explication of socio-demographic predictors of body weight (Lee et al. 2009), examination of how institutions such as schools contribute to body weight (Downey and Boughton 2007; Poppendieck 2010; Von Hippel et al. 2007), or the development of strategies for people to cope with their body weight (Sobal 1991). Sociologists have been active in dealing with obesity through their work in medical and public health settings (Gortmaker et al. 1993), actions to influence public debate and policy about body weight (Hilbert et al. 2007), and other roles such as testimony in hearings and courtrooms about the stigmatization of obesity.

The multifaceted sociologies of obesity have produced unique insights about obesity. Sociological concepts and theories have been widely adopted by others seeking new ways to think about the causes and consequences of obesity. Sociological methods offer innovative ways to examine the influences upon and outcomes of obesity. Sociology is situated at the crossroads between many other disciplines, fields, and professions and can offer integrated insights about obesity and generate new ways to think about body weight. Overall, the study of obesity is growing rapidly within the discipline of sociology, and offers many insights that can be applied in diverse ways to predict, explain, prevent, and manage body weight. This chapter reveals that as social scientists have focused attention on obesity, sociologists have contributed important concepts, theories, methods, and findings and will continue to offer unique perspectives about obesity in the future.

REFERENCES

Allon, Natalie. 1973. "The Stigma of Obesity in Everyday Life." In *Obesity in Perspective*, ed. George A. Bray. Washington, DC: U.S. Government Printing Office, 83–102.

Allon, Natalie. 1975. "Latent Social Services in Group Dieting." *Social Problems* 23(1): 56–69.

Benford, Robert D., and David A. Snow. 2000. "Framing Processes and Social Movements: An Overview and Assessment." *Annual Review of Sociology* 26: 611–639.

Ben-Yehuda, Nachman, and Erich Goode. 1994. *Moral Panics: The Social Construction of Deviance*. Oxford: Blackwell.

Bird, Chloe E., Peter Conrad, and Allen Fremont. 2000. *Handbook of Medical Sociology*. 5th ed. New York: Prentice-Hall.

Boardman, Jason D., Jarron M. Saint Onge, Richard G. Rogers, and Justin T. Denney. 2005. "Race Differentials in Obesity: The Impact of Place." *Journal of Health and Social Behavior* 3: 229–243.

Boreo, Natalie. 2007. "All the News That's Fat to Print: The American 'Obesity Epidemic' and the Media." *Qualitative Sociology* 30(1): 41–60.

Broom, Dorothy H., and Jane Dixon. 2008. "The Sex of Slimming: Mobilizing Gender in Weight-Loss Programmes and Fat Acceptance." *Social Theory and Health* 6(2): 148–166.

Cahnman, Werner J. 1968. "The Stigma of Obesity." *Sociological Quarterly* 9: 283–299.

Carmalt, Julie H., John Cawley, Kara Joyner, and Jeffery Sobal. 2008. "Body Weight and Matching with a Physically Attractive Partner." *Journal of Marriage and Family* 70: 1287–1296.

Carr, Deborah, and Michael A. Friedman. 2005. "Is obesity stigmatizing? Body weight, perceived discrimination, and psychological well-being in the United States." *Journal of Health and Social Behavior* 3:244–259.

Carr, Deborah, and Michael A. Friedman. 2006. "Body Weight and the Quality of Interpersonal Relationships." *Social Psychology Quarterly* 69(2): 127–149.

Cawley, John, Kara Joyner, and Jeffery Sobal. 2006. "Size Matters: The Influence of adolescents' Weight and Height on Dating and Sex." *Rationality and Society* 18(1): 67–94.

Chang, Virginia W. 2006. "Racial Residential Segregation and Weight Status among US Adults." *Social Science and Medicine* 63(5): 1289–1303.

Chang, Virginia W., Amy E. Hillier, and Neill K. Mehta. 2009. "Neighborhood Racial Isolation, Disorder and Obesity." *Social Forces* 87(4): 2063–2092.

Chang, Virginia W., and Nicholas A. Christakis. 2002. "Medical Modelling of Obesity: A Transition from Action to Experience in a 20th Century American Medical Textbook." *Sociology of Health and Illness* 24(2): 151–177.

Chang, Virginia W., and Nicholas A. Christakis. 2005. "Income Inequality and Weight Status in US Metropolitan Areas." *Social Science and Medicine* 61(1): 83–96.

Christakis, Nicholas A., and James H. Fowler. 2007. "The Spread of Obesity in a Large Social Network over 32 Years." *New England Journal of Medicine* 357: 370–379.

Cline, Krista M. C., and Kenneth F. Ferraro. 2006. "Does Religion Predict the Prevalence and Incidence of Obesity? *Journal for the Scientific Study of Religion* 45(2): 269–281.

Coakley, Jay, and Eric Dunning. 2000. *Handbook of Sports Studies*. Thousand Oaks, CA: Sage.

Conrad, Peter. 2007. *The Medicalization of Society: On the Transformation of Human Conditions into Treatable Disorders*. Baltimore, MD: Johns Hopkins University Press.

Cordell, Gina, and Carol R. Ronai. 1999. "Identity Management among Overweight Women: Narrative Resistance to Stigma." In *Interpreting Weight: The Social Management of Fatness and Thinness*, eds. Jeffery Sobal and Donna Maurer, 29–47. Hawthorne, NY: Aldine de Gruyter.

Crosnoe, Robert. 2007. "Gender, Obesity, and Education." *Sociology of Education* 80(3): 241–260.

Crosnoe, Robert, Kenneth Frank, and Anna Strassmann Mueller. 2008. "Gender, Body Size and Social Relations in American High Schools." *Social Forces* 86(3): 1189–1216.

Crossley, Nick. 2004. "Fat Is a Sociological Issue: Obesity Rates in Late Modern, 'Body-Conscious' Societies." *Social Theory and Health* 2(3): 222–253.

Degher, Douglas, and Gerald Hughes. 1999. "The Adoption and Management of a "Fat" Identity." In *Interpreting Weight: The Social Management of Fatness and Thinness*, eds. Jeffery Sobal and Donna Maurer, 11–27. Hawthorne, NY: Aldeine de Gruyter.

DeJong, William. 1980. "The Stigma of Obesity: The Consequences of Naïve Assumptions Concerning the Causes of Physical Deviance." *Journal of Health and Social Behavior* 21: 75–87.

Downey, Douglas B., and Heather Boughton. 2007. "Childhood Obesity in America: Do Schools Make It Better or Worse?" *New Directions in Youth Development* 114: 33–43.

Drew, Patricia. 2008. "Weight Loss Surgery Patients' Negotiations of Medicine's Institutional Logic." *Research in the Sociology of Health Care* 26: 65–92.

English, Cliff. 1993. "Gaining and Losing Weight: Identity Transformations." *Deviant Behavior* 14(3): 227–241.

Ferraro, Kenneth F., and Jessica Kelly-Moore. 2003. "Cumulative Disadvantage and Health: Long-Term Consequences of Obesity?" *American Sociological Review* 68(5): 707–729.

Ferraro, Kenneth F., Roland J. Thorpe, and Jody A. Wilkinson. 2003. "The Life Course of Severe Obesity: Does Childhood Overweight Matter? *Journals of Gerontology* 58B(2): S110–S119.

Germov, John, and Lauren Williams. 1996. "The Sexual Division of Dieting: Women's Voices." *Sociological Review* 44(4): 630–647.

Germov, John, and Lauren Williams. 1999. "Dieting Women: Self-surveillance and the Body Panopticon." In *Weighty Issues: Fatness and Thinness as Social Problems*, eds. Jeffery Sobal and Donna Maurer, 117–132. Hawthorne, NY: Aldine de Gruyter.

Gimlin, Debra. 2007. "Constructions of Ageing and Narrative Resistance in a Commercial Slimming Group." *Ageing and Society* 27(3): 407–424.

Goffman, Erving. 1963. *Stigma: Notes on the Management of Spoiled Identity*. Englewood Cliffs, NJ: Prentice-Hall.

Goode, Erich, and Joan Preissler. 1983. "The Fat Admirer." *Deviant Behavior* 4(2): 175–202.

Gordon, Judith B., and Alice Tobias. 1984. "Fat, Female and the Life Course: The Developmental Years." *Marriage and Family Review* 7(1–2): 65–92.

Gortmaker, Steven L., Aviva Must, J. M. Perrin, A. M. Sobol, and William H. Dietz. 1993. "Social and Economic Consequences of Overweight among Young Adults." *New England Journal of Medicine* 329:1008–1012.

Granberg, Ellen. 2006. "'Is That All There Is?' Possible Selves, Self-Change, and Weight Loss." *Social Psychology Quarterly* 69(2): 109–126.

Guthman, Julie, and Melanie DuPuis. 2006. "Embodying Neoliberalism: Economy, Culture, and the Politics of Fat." *Environment and Planning D: Society and Space*. 24: 427–448.

Hesse-Biber, S. 1996. *Am I Thin Enough Yet? The Cult of Thinness and the Commercialization of Identity*. New York: Oxford University Press.

Hilbert, Anja, Winfried Rief, and Elmar Braehler. 2007. "What Determines Public Support for Obesity Prevention?" *Journal of Epidemiology and Community Health* 61: 585–590.

Himes, Christine L., and Sandra L. Reynolds. 2005. "The Changing Relationship between Obesity and Educational Status." *Gender Issues* 22(2): 45–57.

Honeycutt, Karen. 1999. "Fat World/Thin World: 'Fat Busters,' 'Equivocators,' 'Fat Boosters,' and the Social Construction of Obesity." In *Interpreting Weight: The Social Management of Fatness and Thinness*, eds. Jeffery Sobal and Donna Maurer, 165–181. Hawthorne, NY: Aldine de Gruyter.

Joanisse, Leanne. 2005. "'This Is Who I Really Am': Obese Women's Conceptions of Self Following Weight Loss Surgery." In *Doing Ethnography: Researching Everyday Life*, eds. Dorothy Pawlich, William Shaffir, and Charlene Miall, 248–259. Toronto: CSPI/Women's Press.

Joanisse, Leanne, and Anthony Synnott. 1999. "Fighting Back: Reactions and Resistance to the Stigma of Obesity." In *Interpreting Weight: The Social Management of Fatness and Thinness*, eds. Jeffery Sobal and Donna Maurer,. 49–70. Hawthorne, NY: Aldine de Gruyter.

Julier, Alice. 2008. "The Political Economy of Obesity: The Fat Pay All. In: *Food and Culture: A Reader*, eds. Carole Counihan and Penny Van Esterik, 482-499. New York: Routledge.

Kwan, Samantha. 2009a. "Framing the Fat Body: Contested Meanings between Government, Activists, and Industry." *Sociological Inquiry* 79(1): 25–50.

Kwan, Samantha. 2009b. "Individual versus Corporate Responsibility: Market Choice, the Food Industry, and the Pervasiveness of Moral Models of Fatness." *Food, Culture and Society* 12(4): 477–495.

Laslett, Barbara, and Carol A. B. Warren. 1975. "Losing Weight: The Organizational Promotion of Behavior Change." *Social Problems* 23: 69–80.

Lee, Hedwig, Kathleen M. Harris, and Penny Gordon-Larsen. 2009. "Life Course Perspectives on the Links between Poverty and Obesity during the Transition to Young Adulthood." *Population Research and Policy Review* 28(4): 505–532.

Lupton, Deborah. 2004. "A Grim Health Future': Food Risks in the Sydney Press." *Health, Risk and Society* 6(2): 187–200.

Maddox, G. L., K. W. Back, and V. R. Liederman. 1968. "Overweight as Social Deviance and Disability." *Journal of Health and Social Behavior* 9(4): 287–298.

Martin, Daniel D. 2002. "From Appearance Tales to Oppression Tales: Frame Alignment and Organizational Identity." *Journal of Contemporary Ethnography* 31(2): 158–206.

McIntosh, Wm. Alex. 1996. *Sociologies of Food and Nutrition.* New York: Plenum.

Mayer, Karl U. 2009. "New Directions in Life Course Research." *Annual Review of Sociology* 35: 413–433.

Millman, Marcia. 1980. *Such a Pretty Face: Being Fat in America.* New York: W.W. Norton.

Monaghan, Lee F. 2008. *Men and the War on Obesity: A Sociological Study.* New York: Routledge.

Peralta, Robert L. 2003. "Thinking Sociologically about Sources of Obesity in the United States." *Gender Issues* 21(3): 5–16.

Poppendieck, Janet. 2010. *Free for All: Fixing School Food in America.* Berkeley: University of California Press.

Qvortrup, Matt. 2007. "Obesity." In *Blackwell Encyclopedia of Sociology,* ed. George Ritzer. Blackwell References Online, August 03, 2009, <http://www.blackwellreference.com/ subscriber/tocnote? id=g9781405124331_chunk-g978140512433121_ss1-38>

Reither, Eric N., Robert M. Hauser, and Yang Yang. 2009. "Do Birth Cohorts Matter? Age-Period-Cohort Analyses of the Obesity Epidemic in the United States." *Social Science and Medicine* 69: 1439–1448.

Reynolds, Sandra L., and Christine L. Himes. 2007. "Cohort Differences in Adult Obesity in the United States: 1982–2002." *Journal of Aging and Health* 19(5): 831–850.

Ritzer, George. 1975. *Sociology: A Multi-Paradigm Science.* Boston: Allyn and Bacon.

Ritzer, George. (ed). 2007. *The Blackwell Encyclopedia of Sociology.* New York: Wiley-Blackwell.

Ritzer, George. 2008. *Sociological Theory.* 7th ed. New York: McGraw-Hill.

Robert, Stephanie A., and Eric Reither. 2004. "A Multilevel Analysis of Race, Community Disadvantage, and Body Mass Index in the US." *Social Science and Medicine* 59(12): 2421–2434.

Rosengren, Annika, and Lauren Lissner. 2008. "The Sociology of Obesity." In *Obesity and Metabolism,* Vol. 36, 260–270. Basel: Karger.

Ross, Catherine E. 1994. "Overweight and Depression." *Journal of Health and Social Behavior* 35(1): 63–75.

Ross, Catherine E., and John Mirowsky. 1983. "The Social Epidemiology of Overweight: A Substantive and Methodological Investigation." *Journal of Health and Social Behavior* 24(3): 288–298.

Rubin, Nissan, Carmella Shmilovitz, and Meira Weiss. 1993. "From Fat to Thin: Informal Rites Affirming Identity Change." *Symbolic Interaction* 16(1): 1–17.

Ruel, Erin, Eric N. Reigher, Stephanie A. Robert, and Paula M. Lantz. 2010. "Neighborhood Effects on BMI Trends: Examining BMI Trajectories for Black and White Women." *Health and Place* 16(2): 191–198.

Saguy, Abigail C., and Kjerstin Gruys. 2010. "Morality and Health: News Media Constructions of Overweight and Eating Disorders." *Social Problems* 57(2): 231–250.

Saguy, Abigail C., and Kevin Riley. 2005. "Weighing Both Sides: Morality, Mortality, and Framing Contests over Obesity." *Journal of Health Politics, Policy, and Law* 30(5): 869–921.

Salant, Talya, and Heena P. Santry. 2006. "Internet Marketing of Bariatric Surgery: Contemporary Trends in the Medicalization of Obesity." *Social Science and Medicine* 62(10): 2445–2457.

Schafer, Markus H., and Kenneth F. Ferraro. 2007. "Obesity and Hospitalization over the Adult Life Course: Does Duration of Exposure Increase Use?" *Journal of Health and Social Behavior* 48(4): 434–449.

Smith, Andrew, Ken Green, and Ken Roberts. 2004. "Sports Participation and the 'Obesity/Health Crisis': Reflections on the Case of Young People in England." *International Review for the Sociology of Sport* 39(4): 457–464.

Sobal, Jeffery. 1991. "Obesity and Nutritional Sociology: A Model for Coping with the Stigma of Obesity." *Clinical Sociology Review* 9: 125–141.

Sobal, Jeffery. 1991. "Obesity and Socioeconomic Status: A Framework for Examining Relationships between Physical And Social Variables." *Medical Anthropology* 13(3): 231–247.

Sobal, Jeffery. 1992. "The Practice of Nutritional Sociology." *Sociological Practice Review* 3(1): 23–31.

Sobal, Jeffery. 1995. "The Medicalization and Demedicalization of Obesity." In *Eating Agendas: Food and Nutrition as Social Problems*, eds. D. Maurer and J. Sobal, 79–90. Hawthorne, NY: Aldine De Gruyter.

Sobal, Jeffery. 2008. "Sociological Analysis of the Stigmatisation of Obesity."In. *A Sociology of Food and Nutrition: Introducing the Social Appetite*, eds. J. Germov and L. Williams, 381–400. Melbourne: Oxford University Press. 3rd ed.

Sobal, Jeffery, and Donna Maurer (eds). 1999a. *Interpreting Weight: Social Management of Fatness and Thinness*. Hawthorne, NY: Aldine De Gruyter.

Sobal, Jeffery, and Donna Maurer (eds). 1999b. *Weighty Issues: Fatness and Thinness as Social Problems*. Hawthorne, NY: Aldine De Gruyter.

Sobal, Jeffery, and Wm. Alex Mcintosh. 2009. "Globalization and Obesity." In *The Globalization of Food* eds. D. Gimlin and D. Inglis, 255–271. Oxford, UK: Berg.

Sobal, Jeffery, Barbara S. Rauschenbach, and Edward A. Frongillo. 1995. "Obesity and Marital Quality: Analysis of Weight, Marital Unhappiness, and Marital Problems in a U.S. National Sample." *Journal of Family Issues* 16(6): 746–764.

Sobal, Jeffery, Barbara S. Rauschenbach, and Edward A. Frongillo. 2003. "Marital Status Changes and Body Weight Changes: A U.S. Longitudinal Analysis." *Social Science and Medicine* 56(7): 1543–1555.

Sobal, Jeffery, and Albert J. Stunkard. 1989. "Socioeconomic Status and Obesity: A Review of the Literature." *Psychological Bulletin* 105(2): 260–275.

Stinson, Kandi M. 2001. *Women and Dieting Culture: Inside a Commercial Weight Loss Group*. New Brunswick, NJ: Rutgers University Press.

Sturmer, Stefan, Simon Bernd, Loewy Michael, and Jorger Heike. 2003. "The Dual-Pathway Model of Social Movement Participation: The Case of the Fat Acceptance Movement." *Social Psychology Quarterly* 66(1): 71–82.

Sussman, Marvin B. 1956. "The Calorie Collectors: A Study of Spontaneous Group Formation, Collapse, and Re-Construction." *Social Forces* 34: 351–356.

Textor, Alex R. 1999. "Organization, Specialization, and Desires in the Big Men's Movement: Preliminary Research in the Study of Subculture-Formation." *Journal of Gay, Lesbian, and Bisexual Identity* 4(3): 217–239.

Throsby, Karen. 2007. "'How Could You Let Yourself Get Like That?': Stories of the Origins of Obesity in Accounts of Weight Loss Surgery." *Social Science and Medicine* 65(8): 1561–1571.

Throsby, Karen. 2008. "Happy Re-Birthday: Weight Loss Surgery and the 'New Me." *Body and Society* 14(1): 117–133.

Umberson, Debra, Hui Liu, and Daniel Powers. 2009. "Marital Status, Marital Transitions, and Body Weight." *Journal of Health and Social Behavior* 50(3): 327–343.

Veenstra, Gerry. 2006. "Neo-Marxist Class Position and Socioeconomic Status: Distinct or Complementary Determinants of Health?" *Critical Public Health* 16(2): 111–129.

Von Hippel, Paul, Brian Powell, Douglas B. Downey, and Nicholas Rowland. 2007. "Changes in Children's Body Mass Index (BMI) during School and Summer." *American Journal of Public Health* 97: 696–702.

Winson, Anthony. 2004. "Bringing Political Economy into the Debate on the Obesity Epidemic." *Agriculture and Human Values* 21:299–312.

Zajacova, Anna, and Sarah A. Burgard. 2010. "Body Weight and Health from Early to Mid-Adulthood: A Longitudinal Analysis." *Journal of Health and Social Behavior* 51(1): 92–107.

CHAPTER 8

THE ECONOMICS OF OBESITY

JOHN CAWLEY

THIS chapter explains the economic approach to studying obesity-related behaviors such as diet and physical activity, and summarizes the research on the economic causes and consequences of obesity. It also describes the economic rationale for government intervention, and summarizes economic insights into obesity treatment and prevention, and the design of government policies concerning obesity. This chapter does not cover the topic of cost-effectiveness analysis, which is an economic method for comparing interventions on the basis of their benefits per dollar spent, because that is the subject of chapter 47 by Roux.

Although some may mistakenly believe that economics concerns the study of money, economics is a *social* science, devoted to the study of human behavior. In particular, it is the study of how people make decisions given that all resources are scarce and therefore decisions imply trade-offs.

For complex issues such as obesity, no single discipline has all of the answers to important questions. If one wishes to understand obesity, there is much to learn from many disciplines, including sociology, epidemiology, and psychology (that is, in fact, the motivation for this multidisciplinary Handbook). The advantages that economics brings to the study of obesity are that it offers a widely accepted framework for human behavior, is unusual in its focus on the role of incentives and trade-offs in influencing behavior (as a result, economics yields novel predictions concerning the causes of obesity and innovative policies to reduce it), and it offers clearly defined rationales for policy intervention.

Relative to other social sciences such as sociology and psychology, there is widespread agreement about theory in microeconomics (which is the study of individual consumers and firms). Still, there exist some important differences in how economists model human behavior. This chapter focuses on the "neoclassical" economic approach, which is based on a rational choice model. Chapter 9 in this Handbook, by Downs and Loewenstein, explains the "behavioral" economic approach, which departs from the rational choice model and incorporates concepts from psychology.

THE ECONOMIC FRAMEWORK FOR UNDERSTANDING OBESITY AND OBESITY-RELATED BEHAVIORS

This section describes the economic framework for studying obesity-related behaviors such as diet and physical activity. It is a summary of more technical and mathematical economic models of diet, physical activity, and body weight available elsewhere (Cawley 1999; Lakdawalla and Philipson, 2002; Cawley 2004a; Lakdawalla, Philipson, and Bhattacharya 2005).

In the economic framework, individuals are assumed to maximize their happiness (also called utility or welfare) subject to the constraints of time, budget, and biology. (Thus, consumers are said to solve a "constrained maximization" problem.) Happiness is assumed to be a function of weight, health, the quantity and quality of foods eaten, the amount and type of physical activity, how time is spent, and other factors. Individuals differ in their preferences, which may be influenced by genetics (e.g., people may be predisposed to think that fats and sugars taste good, and this may vary across individuals). People cannot directly choose their weight and health, but they can indirectly alter them through physical activity and diet.

If time and money were infinite, people could do anything and everything: eat whatever they want, sleep and work as long as they like, and exercise to their heart's content. However, people face constraints on their time and budgets. The time constraint is that there are only 24 hours in the day; if one wishes to exercise more, that time must come from somewhere: for example, one must reduce the amount of time spent working for pay or playing with one's children. The budget constraint reflects the fact that people have a limited amount of money at their disposal to allocate to competing ends such as buying vegetables or fast food, or paying rent.

These constraints on time and money imply trade-offs. Consumers must decide whether to buy relatively expensive healthy foods and less of everything else, or to buy relatively cheap energy-dense foods and more of other things. A healthy diet may cost more not only in terms of money, but also in terms of time spent preparing meals. Parents face the trade-off of cooking a healthy dinner and having less time to play with their children, or buying fast food and having more time to play with their children.

We also face biological constraints: the calories we consume that are not burned for energy or excreted will be stored as fat. When caloric intake is high relative to calorie expenditure, weight will rise. If calorie intake is less than calorie expenditure, weight will fall.

People allocate their scarce resources of time and money in order to maximize their utility. Put another way, people's decisions about diet and physical activity are determined by their preferences and the trade-offs that they face. Decisions about eating and time allocation will reflect both immediate and future costs and benefits. For fast food consumption, for example, the benefits include the instantaneous pleasure of eating, and the costs include the monetary cost of buying the food, the utility loss from higher future weight, and the utility loss from any future adverse health consequences. People value their health, but health is only one of many things that people value. People routinely engage in behaviors that entail risk of sickness, injury, or death (for example, driving to work) because the behaviors yield benefits (such as income from employment) and people judge the benefits to exceed the costs. In the present context, this implies the possibility that people who derive great enjoyment from consuming calories or being sedentary may rationally choose to consume many calories and be relatively inactive (and thus to be overweight), even if they have full information about the consequences of these actions. As Philipson (2001) points out, "overweight" is relative to a medical benchmark, not to the weight that maximizes happiness. A person who is clinically overweight may be perfectly satisfied with both his weight and the decisions that resulted in that weight. In other words, the fact that someone is clinically overweight is not proof that the person is irrational. (Although there are enormous differences between economics and the field of fat studies, this is one point upon which they agree; see chapter 11 on fat studies by Rothblum.)

Although we do not know exactly how each individual's happiness varies with weight, health, calorie intake, or exercise, it is possible to make a few generalizations about the trade-offs that each person faces.

When an individual has optimally allocated his resources of time and money, he will satisfy what is called the "last dollar" rule. The optimal allocation of money will be such that the individual will receive an equal increment of utility for the last dollar spent on each type of food and on all other goods. To see why this is true, consider a case in which the "last dollar" rule is violated. If a person received more utility from the last dollar he spent on candy bars than from the last dollar he spent on vegetables, he could increase his utility by spending less money on vegetables and more money on candy bars until the "last dollar" rule is satisfied. When the "last dollar" rule is satisfied, there is no way to make yourself happier by rearranging spending—money has been optimally allocated and utility has been maximized. The "last dollar" rule is useful for considering causes of the recent rise in obesity. For example, if the price of fast food fell relative to the prices of all other foods, then the "last dollar" rule implies that individuals will re-allocate their budgets in order to buy more fast food and less of other goods until the "last dollar" rule is again satisfied.

When a person has optimally allocated her resources, she will also receive an equal increment of utility for the last hour spent in each activity; this is called the "last hour" rule, which is for time what the "last dollar" rule is for money. To see why this rule is true, consider a case in which the "last hour" rule is violated. If a person received a larger increment of utility from the last hour of sedentary leisure than for the last hour spent at all other activities, then the individual could increase her utility by spending more time at sedentary leisure and less time at all other activities until the "last hour" rule is satisfied. When the last hour rule is satisfied, there is no way to make yourself happier by re-allocating your time—time has been optimally allocated and utility has been maximized. Like the "last dollar" rule, the "last hour" rule is useful for considering causes of the recent rise in obesity. For example, if the utility provided by an extra hour of sedentary entertainment rose (e.g., because of an increase in the quality and quantity of television channels and video games) while the marginal utility of all other activities remained constant, then the "last hour" rule implies that individuals will re-allocate their time in order to spend more time in sedentary pursuits until the "last hour" rule is again satisfied.

When considering how to extend the economic framework to children, one must consider how parents intervene and impose solutions for children, and the constrained maximization problem faced by the child's parents. Parents have some power to compel their children to allocate time in certain ways. For example, a parent can insist that a child go outside and play instead of sitting and watching television. Parents can deny children certain foods (although in my experience parents have limited ability to compel children to eat specific foods). Parents can attempt to impose on children the solution that they think is best.

Children are faced with what economists call the principal-agent problem: the utility of children (the principals) is affected by the decisions of the parents (the agents), so children employ various strategies to influence the behavior of the parents (e.g., nagging, tantrums). Children are also affected by how their parents choose to allocate their time. If parents choose to feed the family at fast food outlets because they would rather spend less time cooking and more time at work, the health and weight of the children may be affected. Just as people value their health but are willing to accept worse health in exchange for other things that they value, parents value the health of their children but may be willing to accept a higher probability of child obesity in exchange for other things that the parent values, such as a respite from the child nagging or more money available for things that the family needs (e.g., to pay rent or utilities).

The economic and public health views of obesity differ in important ways. First, they differ in their approach. Public health has a normative approach; it is concerned with what *should* be done to improve health outcomes. In contrast, economics avoids normative statements about what should be; instead, it offers a positive description of what is. Second, economics and public health differ in what they assume people are trying to maximize. Economists assume that people are maximizing their happiness, and for that reason people are sometimes willing to accept worse health in exchange for other things that they value (such as money or pleasure). In contrast, public health seems to assume that people want to maximize their health or longevity. As a result of this difference, the two fields view health behaviors differently. The public health view seems to be that the optimal prevalence of overweight is zero—that for the good of society, overweight should be completely eradicated. The economic view is that people weigh the costs and benefits of their actions, and that some people may find that the enjoyment of eating or being sedentary exceeds its costs; thus it is not clear that the socially optimal prevalence of overweight (meaning, the amount that would maximize social welfare) is zero.

Like all frameworks or models, the economic framework of obesity has limitations. Economics offers little guidance on the origin of consumers' preferences or how easily they may be changed. Some claim that the neoclassical model assumes that consumer behavior is too rational; partly in response to such critiques, behavioral economic models such as those described in the chapter by Downs and Lowenstein relax the assumptions of the neoclassical model and incorporate findings from psychology.

The Economic Causes and Correlates of Obesity

The economic framework implies that changes in obesity are the result of changes in dietary patterns and physical activity that are, in turn, driven by changes in the constraints and incentives that people face (such as income and prices). This section focuses on the contribution to obesity of the most important and obvious economic factors: food prices, income, maternal employment, and technological change.

Food Prices

One important change in incentives is that the real price of food (that is, the price of food adjusted for inflation across all goods and services) has declined since the 1970s (Cawley 1999). For example, just between 1990 and 2007, the real price of a 2-liter bottle of Coca Cola fell 34.9 percent, the real price of a 12-inch pizza at Pizza Hut fell 17.2 percent, and the real price of a McDonald's Quarter-Pounder with cheese fell 5.4 percent (Christian and Rashad 2009).

The "last dollar" rule implies that when the real price of energy-dense food falls, people will consume more of it. Chou et al. (2004) calculate that falling food prices explain roughly 12 percent of the rise in adult weight between 1984 and 1999. Lakdawalla and Philipson (2002) attribute 41–43 percent of the rise in young adult body mass index (BMI) between 1981 and 1994 to falling food prices.

The BMI of youths are higher where and when the price of fast food is low; a 10 percent increase in the price of a fast food meal is associated with a 0.4 percent decrease in BMI and a 5.9 percent decrease in the probability of overweight (Powell et al. 2007). Evidence from experiments indicates that even schoolchildren are sensitive to changes in the relative prices of high-fat and low-fat foods (French et al. 1997; French et al. 2001; Hannan et al. 2002).

In addition to a decrease in the real price of energy-dense foods, there has been an increase in the real price of less energy-dense, nutritious foods. For example, between 1997 and 2003 the real price of fruits and vegetables rose 17 percent (Auld and Powell 2009). Several studies have found that higher prices of fruits and vegetables are associated with higher BMI for children and adolescents (Sturm and Datar 2005; Powell and Bao 2009), presumably because when fruits and vegetables are expensive, people substitute away from them and toward cheaper, more energy-dense foods.

Income

Another economic variable that may be related to obesity is income. However, within an economically developed country, it is not obvious how obesity will vary with income (Lakdawalla, Philipson, and Bhattacharya 2005). Additional income could lead to weight loss by enabling consumers to substitute expensive healthier food for cheaper energy-dense foods, or by increasing demand for good health or an attractive appearance. On the other hand, additional income could promote weight gain by allowing people to consume more calories and spend more time in sedentary pursuits. Two studies have used natural experiments to measure the impact of income on weight in the United States. Schmeiser (2009) exploits variation across states and over time in the generosity of the Earned Income Tax Credit (EITC) program, and finds that an additional $1,000 of family income was associated with an increase in weight of roughly one to two pounds. He concludes that between 1990 and 2002, the increase in real family income explains 10–21 percent of the increase in women's BMI, and 23–29 percent of their increased prevalence of obesity. There was no detectable effect of income on the weight of men. Cawley, Moran, and Simon (2010) exploit variation in Social Security income due to a legislative accident that gives higher benefits to certain birth-year cohorts of retirees, and find that an extra $1,000 per year had no detectable impact on weight or the probability of obesity. The differences between these two studies may be due to the populations examined: Schmeiser (2009) studied low-income EITC recipients, and Cawley et al. (2010) examine elderly retirees.

Clearly, the level of economic development in an economy is relevant for the direction and size of any effect of income on weight. Specifically, in lesser developed countries it is expected that additional income will lead to weight gain, as poorer families may be severely constrained financially and even malnourished. For example, in a conditional income transfer program in Mexico, families spent an average of 70 percent of the cash transfer on what researchers called higher-quality calories: meat, fruits, and vegetables (Fernald, Gertler, and Hou 2008). The impact of higher cash payments on weight varied by age. For adults, higher payments raised BMI and increased the risk of overweight and obesity in adults (Fernald, Gertler, and Hou 2008), whereas for children aged 24–68 months, higher payments were associated with a lower prevalence of overweight (Fernald, Gertler, and Neufeld 2008).

Conversely, loss of income in poorer countries is expected to result in declines in weight. A dramatic example of this is provided by Cuba's "Special Period," the period of economic decline (1991–1995) that followed the collapse of the Soviet Union, which had been a major trade partner for Cuba. The economic crisis resulted in a dramatic decline in daily consumption of calories (from 2,899 in 1988 to 1,863 in 1993) and increases in energy expenditure (as people walked rather than used public transportation). As a result, average weight fell 5.6 percent (4.5 kg or roughly 10 pounds) and the prevalence of obesity was cut in half from 14.3 percent in 1991 to 7.2 percent in 1995 (Franco et al. 2007).

Maternal Employment

Another important economic change in the last three decades is the increase in maternal employment; between 1975 and 2005, the labor force participation rate of mothers with children under age 18 rose from 47 to 71 percent (Cawley and Liu 2007). Anderson, Butcher and Levine (2003) calculate that the increase in mothers' average weekly work hours explains 12–35 percent of the increase in the prevalence of childhood obesity in high-socioeconomic-status American families between 1975 and 1994. Courtemanche (2009) examines a longer time period and estimates that rising maternal work hours accounts for 10.4 percent of the increase in overweight children between 1968 and 2001. In British data, an association between maternal employment and childhood obesity was found only for employment that is full-time and during mid-childhood, not for full-time work at other child ages or for part-time work at any child age (von Hinke Kessler Scholder 2008).

There are several mechanisms by which maternal employment may affect child weight. Time use data for children indicate that children with working mothers watch more hours of TV and are more likely to skip breakfast (Fertig et al. 2009). Other research, however, finds no evidence that the amount of time a child spends watching television mediates the relationship between maternal employment and childhood obesity (Morrissey et al., forthcoming). Time use data on adults indicate that maternal employment reduces the amount of time mothers spend grocery shopping, cooking, and eating with their children, and increases the probability that the family purchases prepared foods; these decreases in time spent by mothers are only slightly offset by increases in time spent by fathers (Cawley and Liu 2007).

Technological Change

Another possible economic contributor to rising obesity is technological change that has made it possible to do more work while burning fewer calories (Philipson and Posner 1999). Cutler, Glaeser, and Shapiro (2003) argue that the recent rise in obesity is due to technological innovations that made it possible for food to be mass prepared far from the place of consumption and consumed with lower time costs of preparation. They support their argument with a variety of data that show that consumption of mass-produced foods increased the most, that people with the greatest ability to take advantage of these technological changes had the greatest increase in weight, and that obesity across countries is correlated with access to processed food. The "last hour" rule implies that when technological changes increase the enjoyment associated with sedentary leisure, people will spend more time in sedentary leisure. Sturm (2004) documents increases in sales of devices that make sedentary leisure more enjoyable, such as big-screen televisions.

Note that some of the trends that may have contributed to the rise in obesity are ones that we do not want to reverse, for example, the trends toward women in the labor force and technological innovation in general. It is not practical or desirable to lower childhood obesity by turning back the clock or reversing these trends; instead, society must find ways of addressing the deleterious side effects of technological change (Philipson 2001; Rashad and Grossman 2004).

In summary, differences across people in the economic trade-offs that they face partly explain differences in obesity, and changes over time in the relative costs or benefits of certain foods or activities partly explain the recent rise in obesity.

The Economic Consequences
of Obesity

The costs of obesity can be classified as direct (medical costs) or indirect (such as job absenteeism). The direct medical costs are substantial. The estimated annual cost of treating obesity-related illness in adults was $147 billion in 2008 (Finkelstein et al. 2009). In addition, childhood obesity is associated with annual prescription drug, emergency room, and outpatient costs of $14.1 billion (Trasande and Chatterjee 2009), plus inpatient costs of $237.6 million (Trasande, Liu et al. 2009). Obesity-related illness is now responsible for almost 10 percent of all medical spending in the United States (Finkelstein et al. 2009), and the rise in the prevalence of obesity explains 27 percent of the increase in overall health care spending between 1987 and 2001 (Thorpe et al. 2004).

The indirect costs of obesity include labor market costs to the obese individual and potentially the employer. Obesity-related job absenteeism totals $4.3 billion annually, with three-quarters of those costs attributable to female workers (Cawley, Rizzo, and Haas 2007). In addition, obesity is associated with lower productivity while at work (presenteeism) totaling $506 per obese worker per year (Gates et al. 2008).

Obesity is associated with delayed skill acquisition and worse educational outcomes in children. Cawley and Spiess (2008) find that, among 2- to 3-year-old boys, obesity is associated with reduced verbal skills, social skills, motor skills, and ability to perform activities of daily living. Among 2- to 3-year-old girls, obesity is associated with reduced verbal skills. These correlations exist even for preschool children who spend no time in day care, which implies that the correlations cannot be due solely to discrimination by teachers, classmates, or day care providers. Many studies have documented an association between obesity and poorer academic performance in school-age children. For example, among youths aged 14–17 years, there is a negative relationship between BMI and grade point average for white girls, but not non-white girls or males (Sabia 2007). In chapter 31 of this Handbook, Truong and Sturm present evidence that obese schoolchildren score significantly lower on academic tests than healthy-weight schoolchildren, a result that is robust for both genders, different grades (kindergarten, first, third, and fifth), and different subjects (science, math, and reading).

Even controlling for education and cognitive ability, adult obesity is associated with lower wages, especially for white females. Among white females, a difference in weight of two standard deviations (roughly 65 pounds) is associated with a difference in wages of 9 percent, which in absolute magnitude is equivalent to the wage effect of roughly 1.5 years of education or 3 years of work experience (Cawley 2004b). Among white females, overweight is associated with 4.4 percent lower wages, and obesity is associated with 11.2 percent lower wages, after controlling for a host of factors such as intelligence test score and education (Cawley 2004b).

There are several possible explanations for why the obese might earn less. Higher job absenteeism, and lower productivity while on the job, are possibilities. However, there is abundant evidence of workplace discrimination against the obese. A recent review of the literature on discrimination against the obese included the findings that obese respondents were 37 times more likely, and severely obese respondents were 100 times more likely, than normal-weight respondents to report suffering employment discrimination, and that women were 16 times more likely than men to report weight-related employment discrimination (Puhl and Heuer 2009). In a field experiment (Rooth 2009), fictitious job applications were sent to real job openings in Sweden; in otherwise identical applications, those that were accompanied by a facial photo that had been manipulated to show the applicant as obese were significantly less likely to receive a call for an initial interview: 6 percentage points less likely for men and 8 percentage points less likely for women. This apparent discrimination varied by the type of job the fictitious applicant applied for: there seemed to be discrimination against obese females who applied to be salespeople, accountants, and preschool teachers, but not against those who applied to be computer professionals or nurses.

Economic Rationales for Government Intervention

In the absence of market failures, the operation of free markets maximizes social welfare (Mas-Colell, Whinston, and Green 1995). Thus, if there are no market failures, government intervention can only decrease social welfare. However, market failure is not uncommon, and in such cases free markets do not maximize social welfare. In such situations, economists recommend policy interventions to reduce the inefficiency caused by the market failures. This section discusses several market failures that may be relevant to diet and physical activity: a lack of information, externalities, and failures of consumer rationality.

The economic rationale for government intervention—to correct market failure—respects consumer sovereignty, makes clear when government intervention is justified, and implies an easy method of measuring the success of such interventions. It respects consumer sovereignty because, in the absence of any market failure, consumers are allowed to make their own decisions. It makes clear when government intervention is justified because there are specific market failures one can look for—for example, lack of information, externalities, and failures of rationality—each of which will be addressed below.

The rule also implies an easy method of measuring the success of interventions: measure the extent to which the market failure has been corrected. For example, suppose that the market failure is a lack of information, and to fix that market failure, policy makers pass a law requiring that restaurants provide information on the nutritional and caloric content of their food. One can evaluate the success of this intervention by how well it supplies consumers with the information they previously lacked. Note that the success of the intervention is not judged by whether it led consumers to change their diets or their weight. It is possible that even after being provided full information, consumers might choose to engage in unhealthy behaviors.

Lack of Information

Consumers are often forced to make decisions about their calorie intake and expenditure with imperfect information. For example, consumers often have imperfect information about the calorie content of the foods they eat in restaurants. There is an economic rationale for government intervention to require food providers to publicize the nutritional and caloric content of the foods they sell, and to ensure that information is accurate.

The Nutrition Labeling and Education Act of 1990 (NLEA) required significant changes in the information about calories that manufacturers of packaged foods must provide to consumers in the form of the Nutrition Facts panel. Some research concludes that the Nutrition Facts panel increased the consumption of iron and fiber but did not affect consumption of total fat, saturated fat, or cholesterol (Variyam 2008), while other research suggests that the Nutrition Facts panel resulted in a larger fraction of consumers choosing low-fat options (Mathios 2000). It is estimated that the NLEA lowered the prevalence of obesity among white females by 2.36 percentage points relative to what it would have been without the new labels (Variyam and Cawley 2006).

One recent policy innovation is to require calorie labeling on menus and menu boards in restaurant chains. This policy was implemented in New York City in 2008, and was passed as part of the U.S. health care reform bill in 2010. Elbel et al. (2009) evaluate the impact of the New York City labeling law using before-and-after data collected at fast food chains in both New York City and a control city. They find that the menu labeling law raised the percentage of customers who reported seeing calorie labels, and the percentage who said that calorie information influenced their food choices. However, the receipts of consumer purchases showed no significant change in calories, saturated fat, sodium, or sugar purchased. Bollinger et al. (2010) also study the impact of the New York City law requiring calorie labels on restaurant menus, but focus on outcomes for the coffee chain Starbucks. They observe a 6 percent (15 calorie) decrease in the number of calories per transaction, which is almost entirely due to food purchases (there is no detectable effect on calories purchased through beverages). At present, research has not detected large impacts on calorie consumption from the New York City menu labeling law, but as the national law takes effect and additional data are collected, more precise estimates of the impact of menu labeling will become available.

External Costs

Economists classify the costs of production and consumption that are borne by consumers and producers as "internal" costs, while those imposed on other people in society are classified as "external" costs. When there exist external costs, decision makers are not taking into account the full consequences of their actions, and free markets may not maximize social welfare. There is an economic rationale for government action to ensure that decision makers face the full costs of their actions; in effect, to ensure that decisionmakers "internalize" all external costs.

Obesity imposes external costs through health insurance programs. Finkelstein et al. (2009) calculates that, in 2008, obesity-related illness cost Medicare $19.7 billion and Medicaid $8 billion. These costs are borne by the general population whose tax dollars fund these programs. In addition, private health insurance plans paid $49 billion to treat obesity-related illness in 2008 (Finkelstein et al. 2009). Because group health insurance premia are not based on obesity status, these costs of treating obesity-related illness are borne by others in the private insurance pool in the form of higher premiums. On the other side of the ledger, because obese individuals tend to die younger than healthy-weight individuals, they draw fewer pension benefits and receive less in retirement income from the Social Security system.

Broadly speaking, two strategies can "internalize" the external costs of obesity. The government can tax the problem, or it can subsidize the solution.

In theory, government could tax obesity itself, but I set this aside as politically unacceptable. Instead, the government could tax the behaviors that contribute to obesity. A challenge for food taxes is defining the scope of what should be taxed and what should be subsidized; for example, should apple juice be taxed because it is energy dense, subsidized because it is 100 percent fruit and sometimes contains added vitamins, or neither taxed nor subsidized? Prominent public health advocates have recently called for taxes on full-calorie soda. The mean published estimate is that a 1 percent increase in soda price would reduce the quantity of soda demanded by 0.79 percent (Andreyeva et al. 2010). Fletcher et al. (2009) estimate that a one-percentage point increase in soft drink tax reduces youth soda consumption by 8 calories per day (6 percent) but increases consumption of whole milk by 8 calories per day (14 percent). Their estimates suggest that, on net, soda taxes have no effect on weight, and they conclude that, as currently practiced, soda taxes are an ineffective anti-obesity policy. Chouinard et al. (2007) estimate that a 10 percent tax on the fat content of dairy products (the largest source of fat in the American diet) would reduce fat consumption by less than one percentage point. They estimate that it would take a 50 percent tax to reduce fat intake by just 3 percent. Schroeter et al. (2008) simulate a 10 percent tax on food away from home and conclude that it would lead to a decrease in consumption of food away from home but a more than off-setting increase in food consumption at home, with a net effect of increasing the body weight of the average person by one-third of a pound. More generally, Powell and Chaloupka (2009) survey the literature on the responsiveness of weight to food prices and conclude that small food taxes are unlikely to produce significant changes in BMI but that nontrivial taxes might have a measurable impact on weight. In general, a challenge for estimating the impact of a substantial tax on energy-dense foods is that none currently exists. One can extrapolate the effect of a large tax based on the effects of existing small taxes, but this requires projecting out of sample. If tax effects are nonlinear—for example, rise dramatically with the magnitude of the tax—then such extrapolations may be highly inaccurate.

The government can and does subsidize physical activity by funding physical education in public schools. However, additional years of physical education in high school have no detectable effect on youth weight or the probability of over-weight (Cawley, Meyerhoefer, and Newhouse 2007). Still, improvements in the *quality* of physical education might have an effect. The government also subsidizes physical activity by building and maintaining parks and playgrounds. It is difficult to measure the impact of such facilities, as they have not been the subject of randomized experiments. Research to date has been associational and there is not yet proof that providing such facilities increases physical activity or prevents overweight (Transportation Research Board 2005).

Some employers are acting on their own initiative to decrease external costs. For example, some are offering voluntary programs in which overweight employees receive financial rewards for weight loss. The logic is that the program could be "win-win": workers win by getting paid to do what they want to do anyway (lose weight) and employers win by decreasing health care costs. To date, the experience with such programs is mixed. Cawley and Price (forthcoming) examine a worksite intervention in which workers were paid financial rewards based on percentage of baseline weight lost. By the end of 12 months, those in one treatment group lost an average of just 1.4 pounds, which is less than the average of 1.7 pounds lost in the control group that were offered no financial rewards for weight loss. This is consistent with another study that found no significant weight loss after six months of a program of financial rewards (Finkelstein et al. 2007). Small experiments conducted in academic centers have found more promising results (e.g., Volpp et al. 2008). There is little doubt that if incentives are large enough, people will lose weight, so the frontier of this research is determining the optimal amount and structure of the incentives.

Failures of Rationality

Another economic rationale for government intervention in markets is to protect consumers who are acting irrationally. This is a criterion that should be used cautiously, because irrationality is in the eye of the beholder. One does not judge whether an individual is rational based on his weight or whether one agrees with his choices, but by whether the individual is capable of acting in his own interest (in economics jargon, maximizing his utility).

While society may trust adults to accurately weigh the costs and benefits of a high-calorie diet or a sedentary lifestyle, we may wish to intervene for paternalistic reasons to influence the decisions of children.

Some have advocated that, because children are vulnerable to marketing, advertising to children should be regulated (Nestle 2002; Schlosser 2001). For example, children as old as 11 years may fail to appreciate the difference between television advertisements and television programming; as a result, some European countries have banned food companies from advertising to children (IOM 2006a). It is estimated that a ban on television fast food advertising to children in the United States would reduce the prevalence of overweight by 18 percent among children aged 3–11 years and by 14 percent among youths aged 12–18 years (Chou et al. 2008).

However, Congress has historically tolerated very little regulation of commercial speech. In 1979 the Federal Trade Commission sought to regulate the television advertising of sweetened breakfast cereals to children under age 13 (not because of obesity but because of tooth decay). Congress interceded to defend commercial speech and limit the FTC's power; as a result, the FTC had to struggle just for reauthorization (Engle 2003).

In public schools, the government acts *in loco parentis*—in the place of parents. For this reason, schools can and do regulate children's choices as regard calorie intake and physical activity. States could mandate that all schools remove vending machines for caloric drinks and sweet and salty snacks. It is somewhat arbitrary where the line should be drawn as to what foods should be allowed in schools and which should be banned. Because children are unlikely to be able to choose foods to achieve energy balance, energy-dense foods such as candy and non-diet soda pop may be the most likely to lead to energy imbalance and subsequent obesity. School meals could be reconfigured to consist of low-energy dense foods that facilitate energy balance, and the portions served should take into account the portion size effect (see chapter 22 on portion size by Kral and Rolls in this volume).

By this same logic, schools can mandate certain levels of physical activity. Schools could seek to improve the quality of their physical education classes in order to increase youth physical activity and instill habits of active living.

They could also design and offer nutrition classes that train students to become educated consumers, in order to instill habits of healthy eating.

The food stamp program, recently renamed the Supplemental Nutrition Assistance Program (SNAP), allows a very broad set of foods to be purchased, including such energy-dense foods as soda, candy, cookies, potato chips, and donuts. If one believed that consumers are imperfectly rational, disallowing purchases of energy-dense foods and restricting use of SNAP to nutritious, less-energy-dense foods, may be justified. A precedent is the Women, Infants and Children (WIC) program, which is a U.S. Department of Agriculture food assistance program that provides specific food items that are carefully chosen in order to maximize the nutrient intake of the target populations (IOM 2006b). Limitations of this strategy are that recipients could still use their own money to purchase energy-dense foods, and that to the extent that energy-dense foods are cheaper, allowing recipients to purchase them with SNAP may allow them to stretch their scarce resources to feed more people.

Summary

This paper describes the economic approach to studying obesity and obesity-related behaviors such as diet and physical activity. The implications of the economic approach are summarized below in a set of "take away" points:

1. Individuals may rationally decide to accept a higher body weight in exchange for other things that they value, such as the enjoyment of eating, leisure, and time devoted to things other than cooking and exercise (such as playing with their children). The fact that a person is clinically "overweight" is not proof that the person is making irrational decisions.
2. To understand obesity, we need to understand why some people find it *optimal* to engage in the health behaviors that lead to obesity. This requires better understanding of their income, the demands on their time, and the costs and benefits of the options that are available to them regarding diet and physical activity.
3. Economic changes that altered the relative costs or benefits of certain foods or activities contributed to the recent rise in obesity in the United States.
4. Telling people they "should" behave differently is unlikely to have any effect; if you want to change people's behavior, you need to incentivize that change by altering the trade-offs that they face (e.g., by changing prices).
5. The economic rationale for government intervention is to fix market failures. The success of government programs can be measured by how well they fix the market failure they were designed to repair, not by how much they decrease obesity.

Obesity is a major public health problem facing the United States, with significant consequences for health care costs and productivity. Incorporating the economic perspective into obesity research and policy can help identify contributors to obesity, calculate the consequences of obesity, and design policies to prevent and treat obesity.

REFERENCES

Anderson, P. M., K. F. Butcher, and P. B. Levine. 2003. "Maternal Employment and Overweight Children." *Journal of Health Economics* 22: 477–504.

Andreyeva, T., M. W. Long, and K. D. Brownell. 2010. "The Impact of Food Prices on Consumption: A Systematic Review of Research on Price Elasticity of Demand for Food." *American Journal of Public Health* 100(2): 216–222.

Auld, M. C., and L. M. Powell. 2009. "Economics of Food Energy Density and Adolescent Body Weight." *Economica* 76: 719–740.

Bollinger, Bryan, Phillip Leslie, and Alan Sorensen. 2010. "Calorie Posting in Chain Restaurants." NBER Working Paper 15648.

Cawley, John. 1999. "Rational Addiction, the Consumption of Calories, and Body Weight." Ph.D. dissertation, Department of Economics, University of Chicago.

Cawley, John. 2004a. "An Economic Framework for Understanding Physical Activity and Eating Behaviors." *American Journal of Preventive Medicine* 27(3S): 117–125.

Cawley, John. 2004b. "The Impact of Obesity on Wages." *Journal of Human Resources* 39: 451–474.

Cawley, John, Chad Meyerhoefer, and David Newhouse. 2007. "The Impact of State Physical Education Requirements on Youth Physical Activity and Overweight." *Health Economics* 16(12): 1287–1301.

Cawley, John, and Joshua A. Price. Forthcoming. "Outcomes in a Program That Offers Financial Rewards for Weight Loss." In *Economic Aspects of Obesity*, eds. Michael Grossman and Naci Mocan. Chicago: NBER and University of Chicago Press.

Cawley, J., J. A. Rizzo, and K. Haas. 2007. "Occupation-Specific Absenteeism Costs Associated with Obesity and Morbid Obesity." *Journal of Occupational and Environmental Medicine* 49(12): 1317–1324.

Cawley, J., and C .K. Spiess. 2008. "Obesity and Skill Attainment in Early Childhood." *Economics and Human Biology* 6(3): 388–397.

Cawley, John, and Feng Liu. 2007. "Mechanisms for the Association between Maternal Employment and Child Cognitive Development." NBER Working Paper 13609.

Cawley, J., J. Moran, and K. Simon. 2010. "The Impact of Income on the Weight of Elderly Americans." *Health Economics.* 19(8): 979–993.

Chou, Shin-Yi, Michael Grossman, and Henry Saffer. 2004. "An Economic Analysis of Adult Obesity: Results from the Behavioral Risk Factor Surveillance System," *Journal of Health Economics* 23(3): 565–587.

Chou, S. Y., I. Rashad, and M. Grossman. 2008. "Fast-food Restaurant Advertising on Television and Its Influence on Childhood Obesity." *Journal of Law and Economics* 51: 599–618.

Chouinard, H. H., D. E. Davis, J. T. LaFrance, and J. M. Perloff. 2007. "Fat Taxes: Big Money for Small Change." *Forum for Health Economics and Policy* 10(2): Article 2.

Christian, T., and I. Rashad. 2009. "Trends in US food prices, 1950–2007." *Economics and Human Biology* 7: 113–120.

Courtemanche, Charles. 2009. "Longer Hours and Larger Waistlines? The Relationship between Work Hours and Obesity." *Forum for Health Economics and Policy*. 12(2): Article 2.

Cutler, D. M., E. L. Glaeser, and J. M. Shapiro. 2003. "Why Have Americans Become More Obese?" *Journal of Economic Perspectives* 17(3): 93–118.

Datar, A., R. Sturm, and J. Magnabosco., 2004. "Childhood Overweight and Academic Performance: National Study of Kindergarteners and First-Graders." *Obesity Research* 12: 58–68.

Elbel, Brian, Rogan Kersh, Victoria L. Brescoll, and L. Beth Dixon. 2010. "Calorie Labeling and Food Choices: A First Look at the Effects on Low-Income People in New York City." *Health Affairs* 28(6): w1110–w1121.

Engle, Mary. 2003. Testimony before the Institute of Medicine Committee on prevention of obesity in children and youth, December 9.

Fernald, Lia C. H., Paul J. Gertler, and Xiaohui Hou. 2008. "Cash Component of Conditional Cash Transfer Program Is Associated with Higher Body Mass Index and Blood Pressure in Adults." *Journal of Nutrition* 138: 2250–2257.

Fernald, Lia C. H., Paul J. Gertler, and Lynnette M. Neufeld. 2008. "Role of Cash in Conditional Cash Transfer Programmes for Child Health, Growth, and Development: An Analysis of Mexico's Oportunidades. *Lancet* 371: 828–837.

Fertig, A., G. Glomm, and R. Tchernis. 2009. "The Connection between Maternal Employment and Childhood Obesity: Inspecting the Mechanisms." *Review of Economics of the Household* 7: 227–255.

Finkelstein, E. A., J. G. Trogdon, J. W. Cohen, and W. Dietz. 2009. "Annual Medical Spending Attributable to Obesity: Payer- and Service-Specific Estimates." *Health Affairs* Web Exclusive. July 27.

Finkelstein, E. A., L. A. Linnan, D. F. Tate, and B. E. Birken. 2007. "A Pilot Study Testing the Effect of Different Levels of Financial Incentives on Weight Loss among Overweight Employees." *Journal of Occupational and Environmental Medicine* 49(9): 981–989.

Fletcher, Jason M., David Frisvold, and Nathan Tefft. 2009. "The Effects of Soft Drink Taxes on Child and Adolescent Consumption and Weight Outcomes." RWJF Scholars in Health Policy Research Program Working Papers Series. WP-44.

Franco, M., P. Ordúñez, B. Caballero, J. A. T. Granados, M. Lazo, J. L. Bernal, E. Guallar, and R. S. Cooper. 2007. "Impact of Energy Intake, Physical Activity, and Population-wide Weight Loss on Cardiovascular Disease and Diabetes Mortality in Cuba, 1980–2005." *American Journal of Epidemiology* 166: 1374–1380.

French, Simone A., Robert W. Jeffery, Mary Story, Kyle K. Breitlow, Judith S. Baxter, Peter Hannan, and M. Patricia Snyder. 2001. "Pricing and Promotion Effects on Low-Fat Vending Snack Purchases: The CHIPS Study." *American Journal of Public Health* 91:112–117.

French, Simone A., Robert W. Jeffery, Mary Story, Peter Hannan, and M. Patricia Snyder. 1997. "A Pricing Strategy to Promote Low-Fat Snack Choices Through Vending Machines," *American Journal of Public Health* 87(5): 849–851.

Gates, D., P. Succop, B. Brehm, G. Gillespie, and B. Sommers. 2008. "Obesity and Presenteeism: The Impact of Body Mass Index on Workplace Productivity." *Journal of Occupational and Environmental Medicine* 50(1): 39–45.

Hannan, Peter, Simone A. French, Mary Story, and Jayne A. Fulkerson. 2002. "A Pricing Strategy to Promote Sales of Lower Fat Foods in High School Cafeterias: Acceptability and Sensitivity Analysis." *American Journal of Health Promotion* 17(1): 1–6.

Institute of Medicine. 2006a. *Food Marketing to Children and Youth: Threat or Opportunity?* Washington, DC: National Academies Press.

Institute of Medicine. 2006b. *WIC Food Packages: Time for a Change.* National Academies Press: Washington DC.

Lakdawalla, D., and T. Philipson. 2002. "The Growth of Obesity and Technological Change: A Theoretical and Empirical Examination." NBER working paper 8946.

Lakdawalla, Darius, Tomas Philipson, and Jay Bhattacharya. 2005. "Welfare-Enhancing Technological Change and the Growth of Obesity." *American Economic Review* 95(2): 253–257.

Lundborg, Petter, Kristian Bolin, Soren Hojgard and Bjorn Lindgren. 2007. "Obesity and Occupational Attainment among the 50+ of Europe." *Advances in Health Economics and Health Services Research* 17: 219–251.

Mas-Colell, Andreu, Michael D. Whinston, and Jerry R. Green. 1995. *Microeconomic Theory.* New York: Oxford University Press.

Mathios, Alan. 2000. "The Impact of Mandatory Disclosure Laws on Product Choices: An Analysis of the Salad Dressing Market." *Journal of Law and Economics* 43(2): 651–677.

Morrissey, Taryn W., Rachel E. Dunifon, and Ariel Kalil. Forthcoming. "Maternal Employment, Work Schedules, and Children's Body Mass Index." *Child Development.*

Nestle, Marion. 2002. *Food Politics: How the Food Industry Influences Nutrition and Health.* Berkeley: University of California Press.

Philipson, T. 2001. "The World-Wide Growth in Obesity: An Economic Research Agenda." *Health Economics* 10: 1–7.

Philipson, T. J., and R. A. Posner. 1999. "The Long-Run Growth in Obesity as a Function of Technological Change." NBER Working Paper 7423.

Powell, L. M., and Y. Bao. 2009. "Food Prices, Access to Food Outlets and Child Weight." *Economics and Human Biology* 7: 64–72.

Powell, Lisa M., and Frank J. Chaloupka. 2009. "Food Prices and Obesity: Evidence and Policy Implications for Taxes and Subsidies." *Milbank Quarterly* 87(1): 229–257.

Powell, Lisa M., M. Christopher Auld, Frank J. Chaloupka, Patrick M. O'Malley, and Lloyd D. Johnston. 2007. "Access to Fast Food and Food Prices: Relationship with Fruit and Vegetable Consumption and Overweight among Adolescents." *Advances in Health Economics and Health Services Research* 17: 23–48.

Puhl, Rebecca M., and Chelsea A. Heuer. 2009. "The Stigma of Obesity: A Review and Update." *Obesity* 17: 941–964.

Rashad, I., and M. Grossman. 2004. "The Economics of Obesity." *Public Interest* 156: 104–112.

Rooth, Dan-Olof. 2009. "Obesity, Attractiveness, and Differential Treatment in Hiring: A Field Experiment." *Journal of Human Resources* 44(3): 710–735.

Sabia, J. 2007. "The Effect of Body Weight on Adolescent Academic Performance." *Southern Economic Journal* 73: 871–900.

Schlosser, Eric. 2001. *Fast Food Nation: The Dark Side of the All-American Meal.* New York: Houghton Mifflin.

Schmeiser, M. D. 2009. "Expanding Wallets and Waistlines: The Impact of Family Income on the BMI of Women and Men Eligible for the Earned Income Tax Credit." *Health Economics* 18: 1277–1294.

Schroeter, C., J. Lusk, and W. Tyner. 2008. "Determining the Impact of Food Price and Income Changes on Body Weight." *Journal of Health Economics* 27(1): 45–68.

Sturm, Roland. 2004. "The Economics of Physical Activity: Societal Trends and Rationales for Interventions." *American Journal of Preventive Medicine* 27(3S): 126–135.

Sturm, R., and A. Datar. 2005. "Body Mass Index in Elementary School Children, Metropolitan Area Food Prices and Food Outlet Density." *Public Health* 119: 1059–1068.

Thorpe, K. E., C. S. Florence, D. H. Howard, and P. Joski. 2004. "The Impact of Obesity on Rising Medical Spending." *Health Affairs* 23: w480–486.

Transportation Research Board. 2005. *Does the Built Environment Influence Physical Activity? Examining the Evidence.* National Academies Press: Washington DC.

Trasande, L., and S. Chatterjee. 2009. "The Impact of Obesity on Health Service Utilization and Costs in Childhood." *Obesity* 17: 1749–1754.

Trasande, L., Y. Liu, G. Fryer, and M. Weitzman. 2009. "Effects of Childhood Obesity on Hospital Care and Costs, 1999–2005." *Health Affairs* 28(4): w751–760.

Variyam, J. N. 2008. "Do Nutrition Labels Improve Dietary Outcomes?" *Health Economics* 17: 695–708.

Variyam, J. N., and J. Cawley. 2006. "Nutrition Labels and Obesity." NBER Working Paper 11956.

Volpp, K. G., L. K. John, A. B. Troxel, et al. 2008. "Financial Incentive Based Approaches for Weight Loss: A Randomized Trial." *Journal of the American Medical Association.* 300(22): 2631–2637.

von Hinke Kessler Scholder, S. 2008. "Maternal Employment and Overweight Children: Does Timing Matter?" *Health Economics* 17(8): 889–906.

....

CHAPTER 9

BEHAVIORAL ECONOMICS AND OBESITY

....

JULIE S. DOWNS AND GEORGE LOEWENSTEIN

INTRODUCTION

....

IN the last 30 years, under the undisputed leadership of Gary Becker, economists have extended the application of the rational choice perspective of economics to an ever-widening range of behaviors, including those that are commonly seen as self-destructive, such as suicide, addiction and, most recently, obesity—the focus of this handbook. The rational choice perspective provides potentially useful insights, particularly in its focus on the role of prices in determining behavior. Indeed, changes in prices seem to have played a role in the "obesity epidemic" that emerged in the 1980s and has been growing in recent decades (Cutler, Glaeser, and Shapiro 2003). The price of energy-dense food has decreased overall and especially relative to less energy-dense foods such as fruits and vegetables (Finkelstein et al. 2005; Monsivais and Drewnowski 2007). Other cultural and institutional changes that might have contributed to growing waistlines include increases in television viewing and in female labor force participation, although these trends began long before rates of obesity began their ascent.

Although the rational choice perspective sheds light on important aspects of obesity, it falls short of explaining many dimensions of the phenomenon. Most obviously, the rational choice perspective fails to explain the large amount of time, effort and money that people invest, often in vain, to lose weight. Whether for good reasons or bad, Americans want to be thinner but have difficulty achieving this goal, an observation supported not only by representative surveys, but also by the large amounts that Americans collectively spend on weight loss products and programs ($55 billion in 2007, according to one study).[1] The rational choice perspective also fails to account for a wide range of situational factors that have been shown to affect eating, from emotional influences (surprisingly, both positive and negative emotions seem to encourage eating among dieters) to the presence of food or of other people who are eating.

In part due to its failure to take account of the less rational side of obesity, we argue in this chapter, the rational choice perspective also falls short when it comes to offering policies to deal with the obesity epidemic. The conventional economic approach assumes that obese people are obese by choice; they have made a deliberate decision favoring the pleasures of eating over the advantages of lower body weight.[2] An important implication of such a perspective is that, barring externalities (costs that obese people impose on others), there is no reason for policy makers to intervene.

Of course, obese people do impose externalities on others, with high health care costs being a primary consideration (Wang et al. 2008), but these are probably not the primary reasons that policy intervention makes sense. The main rationale for intervention is that, beyond the externalities that it produces, obesity also generates what have been called *internalities* (Herrnstein et al. 1993; Gruber and Koszegi 2001)—costs that people impose on *themselves* but fail to fully internalize. Why people fail to internalize such costs and what can be done about it are the central topics of this chapter.

We begin by discussing different phenomena identified by behavioral economists that can shed light on the problem of obesity. Not everyone has a problem with excessive weight; some people can eat as much as they like without becoming obese, and some even have trouble maintaining adequate body weight. However, for those prone to becoming obese, there are several concepts from behavioral economics that help to explain why people would fail to adequately internalize the costs that they impose on themselves—that is, why weight loss is more difficult than the standard economic perspective recognizes. We then discuss limitations of the information-based approach to combating obesity offered by conventional economics, and review empirical research suggesting that the benefits of information provision for the population at large are minimal, at best. Finally, we discuss research examining two categories of alternative approaches to policies aimed at obesity, both of them inspired by ideas from behavioral economists: (1) environmental "nudges" to tip the balance of small decisions against weight-gaining behaviors; and (2) ways of "supercharging" incentive programs for weight loss.

---

1 Marketdata Enterprises, Inc. has released a new 393-page study entitled: "The U.S. Weight Loss and Diet Control Market (9th edition)."

2 Kevin Murphy, for example, argued that obesity could be viewed as a matter of rational choice, by which he meant that people who are obese have made a deliberate decision that the costs of cutting back on eating or increasing exercise would not justify the benefits of any resulting weight loss (Murphy, 2006).

Why Obesity Is Such an Intractable Problem; Insights from Behavioral Economics

Whatever one's metabolism, there is a simple formula for preventing or reversing obesity: burn more calories or take in fewer calories.[3] Both of these are difficult for the same reason: they require, at least for those who don't find exercise enjoyable, exposing oneself to immediate misery. Eating involves an additional complexity. For many other activities that are associated with problems of self-control, such as smoking and sex with unsuitable partners, it is possible to desist from the activity altogether, which constitutes a natural "bright line" to avoid crossing in attempts to exert self-control. Eating, in contrast, is a biological imperative. One has to eat; the only question is what and how much.

As we show in this section, there are many decision phenomena that encourage overeating or, perhaps more importantly, stand in the way of attempts to cut back by those prone to overeat. Indeed, given the length of the list, it is remarkable that anyone who is vulnerable to weight gain manages to avoid it.

Present-Biased Preferences

People tend to put disproportionate weight on immediate costs and benefits relative to those that are even slightly delayed. However, they also tend to be relatively even-handed toward costs and benefits occurring at different points in the future. The combination of such impatience in the present and patience toward the future has been dubbed "present-biased preferences" (see Ainslie 1975 and Strotz 1955, for seminal discussions). Present-biased preferences (also known as "hyperbolic time discounting") contribute to obesity because the benefits of eating (and the costs of exercising) are immediate, but the consequences of overeating and failing to exercise are delayed. Present-biased preferences help to explain not only why people fail to diet or exercise, but also why they are quite willing to resolve to do so in the future: because future benefits and costs are evaluated in a much more evenhanded fashion. When the future becomes the present, however, people often end up not going through with their resolutions, a pattern known as "impulsivity" or "dynamic inconsistency."

An important innovation in research and theorizing about present-bias is the observation, by O'Donoghue and Rabin (e.g., 1999, 2008), that people's self-awareness of their own patterns of time discounting are critical for understanding patterns of behavior. O'Donoghue and Rabin draw a continuum between complete "naivete"—where people fail to appreciate that their current evenhanded treatment

---

3 Actually, the problem is somewhat more complicated due to homeostatic and feedback processes (see, e.g., Katan & Ludwig, 2010).

of different future times will vanish when the future becomes the present, and they will come to overvalue that present—and "sophistication"—in which people recognize that they will overvalue the future when it becomes the present. The distinction between naivete and sophistication matters because, for example, if people are naive and so fail to anticipate that they will be impatient in the future, they may be perfectly willing to commit to going on a diet or exercising in the future, but they will see no need to do so at the moment because they will assume that they are not going to be impatient in the future. In contrast, someone who is sophisticated will both be willing to, and recognize the need to, commit to a plan for future diet or exercise.

Although the application of present-biased preferences to eating seems obvious, and diet is the paradigmatic domain of behavior used to illustrate present-biased preferences, the evidence supporting a link between the rise in obesity and either steep time discounting or present-biased preferences is mixed. Between individuals, there is correlational evidence that obesity is related to a higher discounting rate, especially among men (Smith et al. 2005; Zhang and Rashad 2008). Time series analyses of national data likewise show weak connections between changes in obesity over time and changes in some proxies for time discounting, such as private debt and savings rates, suggesting the possibility of a causal link (Komlos et al. 2004). However, in a careful analysis of a rich data set, the two proxies of discount rates that were most closely related to BMI (managing income and controlling expenditures), both remained unchanged during a decade of skyrocketing rates of obesity. Interestingly, these increases in obesity were concentrated among individuals with high discount rates as assessed by these measures, suggesting that a changing discount rate is not responsible for the obesity epidemic, but that high discounters are the ones gaining weight (Borghans and Golsteyn 2006).

Visceral Factors

Present-biased preferences predict that things become especially tempting when they are immediately available, but they fail to explain why food is especially prone to such effects, or to shed light on a wide range of other situational factors that lead to (over)eating, including various forms of sensory contact with food. As dieting researchers Herman and Polivy (2004, 462) note, "physical proximity is likely to be more powerful than is temporal proximity in inflaming desire. Knowing that it's 'time for dessert' is nowhere near as powerful an influence on desire (and eating) as is the actual presence of the dessert." An alternative account of impatience, proposed by Loewenstein (1996) holds that it is not immediacy, per se, that leads to a shortened time perspective, in which the pleasure from eating comes to dominate considerations of long-term well-being, but rather the action of "visceral factors"—emotions and drives (including hunger)—that are designed by evolution to make us attend to immediate needs.

According to this perspective, temporal immediacy is only one of many factors that activate the visceral drive to eat. Others include the sight or smell of a food item, or, unsurprisingly, hunger resulting from not having eaten in the recent past.

There is diverse empirical support for such a perspective. For example, when people are hungry, they show a particular impatience for consumption of a liked food (chocolate), relative to their impatience for money (Reuben, Sapienza, and Zingales 2010). Likewise, research by Mischel and his colleagues (e.g., Mischel and Ebbesen 1970) found that children given a choice between smaller snacks earlier and larger snacks later were less able to wait when put in the presence of the snacks. However, when the same children were shown photographs of the snacks, they were more able to wait; apparently the photographs helped them keep in mind what they were waiting for without activating visceral drives. Finally, in a recent study (McClure et al. 2007), people were given intertemporal choices between earlier smaller or larger later money amounts, while their brains were scanned with fMRI. Supporting the idea that immediacy leads to extreme time discounting because it activates emotions, emotional systems of the brain were only activated when one of the two choice options was available immediately; in those cases, activation of emotion systems predicted choice of the immediate reward.

Willpower

When economists use a term differently from the way it is used in popular language, it is often a clue to deficiencies in economic theory. One of the best examples of this is the term "impatience," which, to an economist, means a tendency to discount—that is, care less about—the future. Random House, in contrast, defines impatience as "eager desire for relief or change; restlessness;" or as "intolerance of anything that thwarts, delays, or hinders." Impatience, as the term is employed in popular language, is an aversive feeling. Modern research in psychology supports the popular interpretation of the construct. This research shows that resisting the motivational impetus of impatience requires the exertion of willpower, which is a scarce resource that—much like a muscle—is used up in the short run when exerted, but replenishes (and may even strengthen from use) in the long run. The notion of willpower can help to explain a wide range of phenomena, such as the greater difficulty of resisting eating when food is continuously available (e.g., when working at home instead of at the office) as well as the common failure of excessively ambitious diets (which leave one with severely depleted willpower). Indeed, sheer complexity of a diet can discourage adherence, if the dieter perceives the rules to be complex (Mata et al. 2010).

The "Peanuts Effect" and Intangibility

If one examines the most common situations in which people exhibit self-control problems, many have in common another property: in many situations, the costs are not only delayed but also intangible (Rick and Loewenstein 2008). This is true of smoking; it is extremely unlikely that any one cigarette will have a marked effect on one's health. It is also true of eating. Any one act of eating—even a huge meal—will not have much of an impact on one's weight.

Marketers seem to be aware of, and even play on, this effect. People who are trying to reduce their consumption (restrained eaters) seem to be susceptible to the allure of small packaging; they eat more when snacks are offered in "snack" packages. Unrestrained eaters succumb to the typical effect of eating more when packages are larger; but restrained eaters seem to be more vulnerable to a lapse in self-control when the temptation is small, but then they succumb repeatedly, leading to greater overall consumption (Scott et al. 2008). In effect, people who are more sensitive to overall gains and losses (those keeping track of what they eat) appear to be more susceptible to the "peanuts effect" of discounting very small single losses, and neglecting the cumulative effect of multiple losses.

Projection Bias

When people are in one visceral state, they have difficulty imagining how they would feel—and mispredict how they would behave—in a different visceral state. For hunger, as for other states, this bias can work in both directions. When not hungry, people have difficulty imagining how it would feel to be hungry or what they might do to procure food. When hungry, people find it difficult to imagine not being hungry. Both of these types of biases have implications for eating behavior.

The tendency, when not hungry, to underestimate the motivational force of hunger leads to a greater willingness to commit to diets, and a greater confidence that one will be able to stick with them, by people who are not—at the moment they commit—hungry. This can be beneficial if people are able to truly commit in a binding fashion, but it can lead to wasted resources, as evidenced by the many subscription to diets that aren't ultimately followed, as well as health club memberships and exercise equipment that go unused.

The tendency for those who are hungry to exaggerate the extent to which their hunger will persist leads to the opposite type of problem—over-ordering food at a restaurant (because one generally orders when in a state of hunger), and over-buying when shopping on an empty stomach (e.g., Gilbert et al. 2002; Read and van Leeuwen 1998). If we didn't end up eating all that food because it turned out that we weren't as hungry as anticipated, then overshopping on an empty stomach wouldn't be that much of a problem. However, consistent with points discussed above, once we have the food, it is difficult to resist (Rowland et al. 2008).

Narrow Decision Bracketing

Ideal rational decision makers make each individual decision while taking account of its interactions with all other decisions, both past and future. However, the reality is that people tend to make decisions largely one at a time, or in very thin slices. When it comes to dieting (as well as other activities; see, e.g., Camerer et al. 1997), people seem to "bracket" their decisions at the one-day level. Lowe (1982) has proposed, and Urbszat, Herman, and Polivy (2002) provided support for, the contention that anticipating a diet tomorrow disinhibits eating today. Khan and Dhar (2007) have shown a similar pattern not only for diet, but a wide range of self-control problems; informing people that they will have additional opportunities for exerting self-control in the future tends to disinhibit control in the present.

Note, however, that this effect could easily go in either direction. On the one hand, people might feel freer to indulge in the present, relying on the (typically mistaken) belief that they will have an opportunity to atone in the future. On the other hand, as argued by Ainslie (2009) and Elster (1989), if people believe that slipping today will inevitably lead to similar behavior in the future, then the knowledge that they will face similar future decisions could aid rather than impede self-control. Indeed, Khan and Dhar (2007) found that when dieters were explicitly informed that current behavior was a strong predictor of future behavior, the effect of learning about future, similar, opportunities to exert self-control was attenuated.

Extending the time over which weight loss is planned decreases the probability that it will occur at all, suggesting that behavior on each day is exempted from the overall plan to change behavior; in a study of people betting on their own weight loss (some with very high stakes), the more days they had to achieve the same daily planned weight loss, the less likely they were to achieve their planned loss and win their bet (Burger and Lynham 2008).

Diminishing Sensitivity

People don't judge the magnitude of things at an absolute level, but almost always relative to some relevant point(s) of comparison (Kahneman and Miller 1986). Thus one can refer to a giant mouse and a tiny elephant without anyone mistaking the correct ranking of their sizes. However, although people make appropriate adjustments for conversational norms, the tendency to judge relative rather than absolute magnitudes can influence decision making, sometimes in non-normative ways. Thus, for example, people will report that they would be willing to travel across town to get a $5 discount on a $20 calculator, but not on a $100 jacket, even though both would involve a certain expenditure of time in exchange for a saving of $5. This tendency toward "diminishing sensitivity" can explain a wide range of decision phenomena, from the widespread tendency to avoid risks for gains but seek them for losses, to the tendency for people to "throw good money after bad"— investing in a losing proposition in a desperate attempt to recoup a loss.

One consequence of diminishing sensitivity is that losing a particular amount of weight is likely to be far less motivating for those at higher levels of weight. Losing 10 pounds is likely to seem very desirable to a 130-pound woman who by doing so could achieve the weight she optimally desires, but a decline from 270 pounds to 260 pounds is likely to be much less inspiring, and hence not worth the effort. Diminishing sensitivity can also interact with narrow bracketing in producing a "what the heck" effect, whereby incremental increases are seen as less threatening once an initial cost is incurred. Believing that a diet is blown on a particular day leads to more subsequent eating for the remainder of that day (Knight and Boland 1989).

Motivated Information Processing

The mind is not a neutral information processor; desires exert a powerful influence on beliefs. Dieting researchers have observed myriad instances of desire-distorted beliefs, such as the many exceptions that dieters permit themselves—food from another person's plate, on holidays, while traveling, and so on. The influence of desires on beliefs is especially important for diet because, as already noted, not eating is not an option. A successful diet requires consumers to track their food intake over the course of days, weeks, and longer, which is a cognitively taxing, and inevitably unreliable, process. Thus, it is not surprising that researchers have observed systematic biases in the recording and recall of food consumption. For instance, people tend to underreport dietary consumption throughout the day, particularly of snacks (Poppitt et al. 1998). Even the task of ascertaining what research participants have eaten in a 24-hour period is difficult, requiring trained personnel to lead people to recall what they ate using a multiple-pass method to ensure that they mention such details as sauces, extra helpings, and details that may seem trivial to the eater but add a considerable number of extra calories throughout the course of the day. If such a high degree of training and care is required for professionals to ascertain how much someone has eaten, imagine how difficult it is for the eater to make such an assessment accurately, without expert help. Dieters and overeaters are particularly vulnerable to this underreporting, especially regarding their fat consumption (Ard et al. 2006; Lissner et al. 2000), perhaps in part due to the guilt associated with thoughts of dietary indiscretions.

POLICY LIMITATIONS OF CONVENTIONAL APPROACHES

The rational choice perspective offers two generic types of policy interventions: provide people with better information, or change relative prices (e.g., through taxes) in a fashion that changes eating patterns or encourages exercise. The former can be justified even in the absence of externalities; if people have imperfect information, then giving them more information should improve their welfare. The latter can only be justified on the basis of externalities; in the absence of externalities, changing relative prices will only decrease economic welfare.

Providing Information

If lack of information were the only problem contributing to obesity, one could expect that providing better information would improve the quality of decision making. In a situation in which many factors contribute to overeating, however, the problem is somewhat more complicated. Inevitably, some people will overestimate the caloric content of the food they consume and some will underestimate. The former group would theoretically respond to better information by increasing their food intake, the latter by decreasing it; thus, the overall impact of accurate information on obesity is ambiguous, and depends on the size of the groups and the magnitude of impacts. Moreover, if there is a systematic tendency among those who are trying to lose weight to overestimate the caloric content of food, as might be the case if people who want to lose weight exaggerate calories as a strategy for motivating themselves, then providing better information would be especially likely to backfire.

In light of these observations, it is perhaps not surprising that research examining the impact of providing diners with calorie information has generally found small or even null effects. For example, perhaps the best-known and most carefully studied effort at improving nutritional (including calorie) information was the Nutrition Labeling and Education Act (NLEA) of 1994, which required consistent nutritional information for packaged foods (USDA 1994). Empirical investigations of the NLEA's impact found that it helped consumers avoid food with high sodium, fat, and cholesterol, and even helped some groups lose weight (Kim et al. 2000; Mathios 2000; Neuhouser et al. 1999; Variyam and Cawley 2006). However, these beneficial effects were generally small in magnitude and limited to narrow segments of the population (Cole and Gaeth 1990; Finkelstein et al. 2005; Moorman 1996). Certainly, the NLEA did not lead a widespread, or even measurable, reduction in population obesity. Generally, availability of nutrition information has been linked to better knowledge, but much less strongly to better diet quality or health (Drichoutis et al. 2009).

Despite the small impact of the NLEA, recently there has been a new wave of enthusiasm about food labeling. New York City led the way, with regulations that mandated posting of calorie information at fast food restaurants, in the same size font as the food items themselves. The NYC regulations were met with optimism, based in part on a study conducted at Subway, a restaurant chain that, before the regulations were passed, started posting calorie information on the display case housing the sandwich ingredients. The research found that those leaving the restaurant who reported having noticed the calorie information consumed, on average, 50 fewer calories than those who did not (Bassett et al. 2008). Despite the fact that one cannot infer from this result that the calorie posting *led* to the difference in calorie consumption (it is equally, or possibly more, likely that those interested in cutting calories paid attention to the information), in a classic case of confusing correlation with causation, or perhaps wishful thinking, the study was widely interpreted in such a fashion.

More rigorous before-after comparisons of the New York City experience have generally tended to vindicate the more pessimistic interpretation of the Subway study. A study examining 14 different fast food chain restaurants in low-income New York neighborhoods before and after menu labeling went into effect found that patrons reported noticing and responding to the labels, but that there were no apparent effects on purchases compared to the period before labeling or to data from a comparison city (Elbel et al. 2009). Another study used internal register data from over 100 million transactions at Starbucks to examine purchases over time, allowing for a very sensitive evaluation, powered to find extremely small effects. This study found that customers purchased lower-calorie foods after labeling, about 14 fewer calories per transaction, but not lower-calorie drinks (Bollinger et al. 2010). Data from the same study examining individual cardholders suggest that those who had made larger purchases prior to menu labeling were more affected by labeling, and that individual consumers' changed purchasing behavior within New York City maintained when they ate at locations outside the city, relative to consumers in a control city. These findings reveal systematic—but very small—desirable effects of menu labeling among customers purchasing drinks and snacks, but these finding cannot necessarily be generalized to meals. In our own research (Downs et al. 2009), which involved a before-after comparison at two branches of McDonalds, one in Brooklyn and one in Manhattan, we not only measured the impact of calorie posting, but also gave diners information to help them make sense of the information. This study was powered to detect a difference of approximately 50 calories before versus after menu labeling, collapsing across locations, corresponding to one meal's worth of the 150 extra daily calories estimated to be responsible for the increase in obesity in recent decades (Cutler et al. 2003). We randomly selected some diners to receive information about how many calories it is recommended to eat per day, others how many calories it is recommended to eat at lunch (which is when the data were collected), and also collected a control condition in which diners did not receive calorie recommendations. Similar to the other studies, we did not observe a systematic reduction in calories following posting (calories increased at one branch and declined at the other); nor did we observe any impact of providing the calorie recommendations.

Experimental studies of calorie posting have been more likely to find promising results than field studies. Likewise, measures of intentions have tended to show stronger effects than actual behaviors, possibly reflecting that intentions correspond to high-level preferences to lose weight that may be activated by the presence of calorie information but undermined by lower-level visceral motivations that come into play in actual choice. For example, consumers who were informed that their existing food choices were a lot higher in calories and fat than they had believed reported willingness to switch to more healthful options (Burton et al. 2006). But in a review of six studies experimentally manipulating menu labeling, Harnack and French (2008) found the effects of labeling on actual food choices to be weak or inconsistent. The lack of impact of food labeling may be due, in part, to a, perhaps justifiable, lack of confidence in the nutritional information being provided; a recent analysis of restaurant meals revealed that healthier meal options averaged 18 percent more calories than reported on labels (Urban et al. 2010).

Other studies have more rigorously manipulated both specific information about how many calories each menu item contains, and whether a recommendation of overall caloric consumptions was provided, both of which, in laboratory studies, tend to reliably decrease consumption. For example, Roberto and her colleagues (2010) found that providing calorie information on menu items reduced consumption at that meal, but that consumption later in the day completely compensated for the earlier benefits, whereas adding a recommendation wiped out the compensation. Wisdom and the authors of this review (2010) manipulated calorie information and recommendations orthogonally and found additive effects of these two types of information on meal purchases with no interactions, suggesting that providing calorie recommendations may act more as a cue to eat less rather than a true information source.

Changing Prices

As noted earlier, there have been some studies by economists that have at least suggested a link between changes in relative food prices and changes in diet. However, given the long-term nature of both trends, and the multiplicity of other changes that occurred over the same interval, it is difficult to draw confident conclusions about causality. In laboratory studies, increasing the prices of energy-dense foods decreased their sales relative to less energy dense foods (Epstein et al. 2006), though, unfortunately, the impact of such price changes is smaller for overweight and obese consumers (Epstein et al. 2007).

In contrast to the case of calorie labeling, where there have been large-scale abrupt changes (nationwide for packaged foods and in several cities and states across the country thus far for restaurant menus), there have not been any comparable policies to shift food choice through changes in prices. There has been extensive discussion of the potential effects of taxing high calorie foods (Dodd et al. 2008), and proposals are currently under consideration across the country, but we have much less information about the likely impact of such policies. Price decreases in low-fat foods have been found to lead consumers to switch their choices (e.g., French et al. 1997), suggesting that moderate subsidization of more healthful foods may increase their consumption. But whether positively taxing less healthful options would have an equivalent effect is unclear, as controlled studies have generally subsidized "better" choices (e.g., lower-calorie, lower-fat items) rather than taxing worse ones (Faith et al. 2007).

In sum, available studies of food labeling and changes in relative prices have produced mixed results. Field studies have not generally documented large, or even reliable, effects of food labeling. More controlled randomized experiments have found such effects, but these studies have left important questions unanswered. One important question is whether observed effects will persist, weaken, or strengthen over time. Any of these patterns are possible. For example, once people get used to seeing the calorie information, they might begin to ignore it, in which case the impact on calorie intake would decline over time. Alternatively, it is possible that eating habits might take time to change, or that restaurants will eventually change their offerings once the information is posted, either of which could lead to larger long-term than short-term effects. A second important question is whether any changes in the food consumption that are observed in studies might be offset by changes in consumption occurring at other times. For example, someone induced by calorie labeling to eat a lower-calorie lunch might be more likely to snack later in the day, or might eat more, or higher-calorie, food for dinner.

BEHAVIORAL ECONOMICS: USING DECISION ERRORS TO HELP PEOPLE

By recognizing that people make systematic errors in decision making and suffer from self-control problems, behavioral economics opens the door to a wider range of interventions than those that naturally stem from the rational choice perspective of conventional economics. Many of these interventions use the same decision errors that usually hurt people to, instead, help them (see Loewenstein et al. 2007, 2010).

The "theory of the second best" (Lipsey and Lancaster 1956) states that when one of the conditions for economic optimality is not met, it may not be optimal to adhere to other optimality conditions. This theory applies to decision making: if decision makers make one type of error, it is not necessarily in their interest to avoid all others, because errors can in some cases at least partially cancel out. Thus, for example, if people smoke cigarettes in part because they tend to choose immediate gratification over their long-term health, it might benefit them to exaggerate the health risks of smoking (though we would, nonetheless, strongly oppose such a policy). If people were smoking at the optimal level, however, then exaggerating the risks to them would not make sense.

Behavioral economists have been using decision errors to help people in two ways. The first approach plays on people's natural laziness when it comes to either physical or mental effort. Thaler and Sunstein (2008), in a book so titled, refer to such interventions as "nudges."

Behavioral "Nudges"

One potential trick to shifting behaviors in healthier directions is to structure choices in such a way that people make more optimal choices for reasons unrelated to obesity concerns. One approach is to play on the natural human proclivity toward laziness—to take the path of least resistance when one is available. Many of the most successful policy interventions by behavioral economists have involved such an approach. For example, in the modern world of defined contribution retirement plans, one of the most important decisions that employees make is the amount of money to put aside into tax-protected retirement accounts. Until recently, the default at most companies was to not put aside such funds unless it was requested by employees (typically through a phone call or other trivial communication); despite the importance of the decision, many employees failed to put money aside, even with generous matches from their employer. Simply changing the default to a positive fraction of salary led to a very substantial change in retirement savings (Madrian and Shea 2001), and the success of field demonstrations of this effect led to national legislation efforts such as the Pension Protection Act of 2006, allowing employers to enroll workers automatically into default investment plans.

A similar approach that plays on people's laziness could be used to lead people toward lower-calorie meal options, by structuring menus, cookbooks, or buffet lines to make lower-calorie options more convenient. The portion size served onto people's plates is a great predictor of how much they'll end up eating (Wansink and Kim 2005; Wansink 1996, 2004). Even subtle environmental cues such as smaller plates and smaller serving spoons have been show to lead people to take less food and eat smaller meals (Wansink 2006; this volume). Historically, however, the opposite of these trends have generally occurred; food portions in restaurants have been growing larger and more energy-dense over time (Patrick and Nicklas 2005; Popkin et al. 2005), exemplified by the ubiquity of the option of "supersizing" combination meals in fast food restaurants. Indeed, the steady increase in restaurant portion sizes over recent decades has closely paralleled the rise in obesity (Young and Nestle 2002). Even portion sizes in the iconic *Joy of Cooking* cookbooks have been following a trend of increasing calories (Wansink and Payne 2009). Nevertheless, the food industry has shown some interest in these findings, with a very recent, but perhaps ineffective, trend toward marketing snacks in 100-calorie "snack pack" sizes.

To examine the potential impact of convenience on food choice, we conducted a pair of studies at a Subway sandwich shop, which we have already mentioned in connection with calorie labeling (Wisdom et al. 2010). We approached people entering Subway and asked them if they would complete a short survey in exchange for receiving a free "meal deal" consisting of a submarine sandwich, a side order, and a drink. We gave all diners an "express menu" on the front page of the materials that they used to order their free meal. For one-third of diners, the convenience menu contained only low-calorie subs; for one-third it contained a mix; and for the remaining third it contained only higher calorie subs.

In both of the studies we conducted, diners had the option of ordering from the full menu if they chose to, at a trivial extra effort. In one study, they had to open the full menu, which meant breaking a tiny seal (that allowed us to record whether they had done so); in the other, they simply had to turn the page. In both studies, the express menu had a significant impact on sandwich calories, but only in the study with the more difficult-to-access full menu did this translate into reduced total meal calories (77 fewer, on average). In the other study, diners did order lower-calorie subs when confronted with the low-calorie express menu, but they had to pass by their forgone (higher-calorie) options before making the rest of their selections. Perhaps seeing the options that they had forgone made them feel virtuous and entitled to reward themselves. In any case, in this study, they fully compensated for this reduction of calories in their choice of sides and drinks. Although we only examined diners' choices of a single meal (their lunch at Subway), this compensatory effect within the meal reinforces the important need for research that examines the consumption choices that follow—for example, snacks and at dinner.

Another example of using biases to nudge people toward healthier behavior involves the use of pre-commitment devices to disarm the ability of short-term urges to undermine long-term goals—for example, by asking consumers to make decisions in advance about what they want to eat later (Lynch and Zauberman 2006). As predicted by present-biased preferences, people are more likely to choose healthier foods when they select them in advance than when they select them at the moment when they will be consumed (Read and van Leeuwen 1998). Although their efficacy has yet to be evaluated systematically, web sites such as StickK.com give individuals the ability to make such commitments and the tools to make them "stick."

In sum, attempts to "nudge" consumers to make healthier food choices have shown some potential, but the true success of such measures will remain unclear until researchers are able to measure an individual's total food intake—not only calories at a single meal or in a single episode of snacking.

Supercharging Economic Incentives

One of the major trends in health care in recent years has been the use of economic incentives to improve health behaviors. The logic of such programs is compelling. A very large fraction of health problems result from "lifestyle" diseases caused by poor health behaviors such as smoking, lack of exercise, and poor diet. Policy makers, insurance companies, and employers have all begun to ask themselves whether, for example, it does not make more sense to spend money incentivizing a smoker to quit than to spend large amounts of money on ineffective treatments after the smoker has been diagnosed with lung cancer or heart disease. Incentives have been found to be effective for promoting healthier behavior in some cases and among some people (Charness and Gneezy 2009), but a better understanding of how people understand these incentives is needed.

Behavioral economists have been part of this new trend. A central insight of behavioral economics is that, contrary to the standard view that a dollar equals a dollar regardless of how it is delivered, the manner in which incentives are delivered can make a huge difference in whether, and to what degree, they alter behavior. The same dollar values of incentives that are often delivered in a fashion that is so ineffective that one might as well burn the money (e.g., by lumping small incentive payments with other large money amounts in year-end pay checks), could instead be delivered in ways that maximize their effectiveness.

In a variety of research projects conducted with Kevin Volpp and others, the second author of this chapter has been using ideas from behavioral economics to "supercharge" economic incentives in programs designed to improve health behaviors, including weight loss. In one study, Volpp, Loewenstein, and coauthors (Volpp et al. 2008) provided economic incentives for overweight veterans to lose one pound per week for 16 weeks. Some participants were randomly assigned to a "deposit contract" condition in which they deposited their own money (from $.01 to $3.00 a day), which was matched 1:1 by the experimenters. Those who remained under the target weight goal implied by losing one pound per week, and called in their weight by phone each day, received the money they had deposited back, plus the match (and a fixed payment of $3.00 per day); those who exceeded the target lost the money they had deposited and received no other payments. Like the nudge interventions, which play on natural laziness, the deposit contract plays on two decision errors: overconfidence (which leads people to be overly optimistic about their chances of losing weight, and hence to be willing to deposit substantial sums) and loss aversion (which makes them highly averse to losing the money once they have deposited it).

Other participants were assigned to a "regret lottery" condition in which they were given a two-digit number (e.g., 27), and each night experimenters drew a random two-digit number. If either of the two digits matched (e.g., the experimenters drew a 25 or a 57), then the participant was eligible for a $10 reward, and if both digits matched, the participant was eligible for a $100 reward. Participants were informed if they had matched each day, but only received payment if they had called in their weight earlier during the day and had been under the target weight. If they matched but were above their target weight, they were informed of the money they could have won but did not. The regret lottery again plays on decision errors, including the tendency to overvalue small probabilities, which contributes to the popularity of lotteries and, although arguably not an "error," the aversion most people have toward experiencing regret.

The program was highly successful, when measured by its success in achieving its goals. Forty-seven percent of those in the deposit contract condition achieved the target of losing 16 pounds (mean weight loss of 14 pounds in this condition), and 53 percent of those in the lottery condition achieved the goal (mean loss of 13 pounds). However, by three months after the termination of the study, participants in the two incentive conditions had gained back most of the weight they had lost. A subsequent study involving only deposit contracts (with no $3 fixed payment) was similarly successful in inducing participants to lose weight over an eight-month (as opposed to four-month) period, but again, after incentives were removed, participants regained most of the weight they had lost.

These findings, and others in domains other than weight loss, suggest that ideas from behavioral economics can, indeed, be used to enhance the effectiveness of economic incentives. However, many questions remain to be resolved by future research, and there is a pressing need for interventions that help people achieve lasting change that extends after the cessation of incentives.

CONCLUSIONS

In sum, behavioral economics can contribute to solutions to the problem of obesity both by providing a better understanding of the phenomenon than is offered by conventional economics and by suggesting new approaches to policies designed to combat the problem. Much research is still needed on both of these dimensions. For example, while it seems likely that some combination of "peanuts effects" and present-biased preferences plays a role in obesity, the relative importance of each of these factors, and of other decision errors, is unclear. Research is also needed to further fine-tune the effectiveness of behavior change programs that incorporate ideas from behavioral economics. Figuring out ways to develop habits that persist when rewards are withdrawn is an especially pressing priority.

REFERENCES

Ainslie, G. 2009. "Recursive Self-Prediction in Self-Control and Its Failure." In *Preference Change: Approaches from Philosophy, Economics and Psychology*, eds. T. Grüne-Yanoff and S. O. Hansson, 139–158. Dordrecht: Springer.

Ard, J., R. Desmond, D. Allison, and J. Conway. 2006. "Dietary Restraint and Disinhibition Do Not Affect Accuracy of 24-Hour Recall in a Multiethnic Population." *Journal of the American Dietetic Association* 106(3): 434–437.

Bassett, M. T., T. Dumanovsky, C. Huang, L. D. Silver, C. Young, C. Nonas, T. D. Matte, S. Chideya, and T. R. Frieden.2008. "Purchasing Behavior and Calorie Information at Fast-Food Chains in New York City, 2007." *American Journal of Public Health* 98(8): 1457–1459.

Bollinger, B., P. Leslie, and A. Sorensen. 2009. *Calorie Posting in Chain Restaurants*. Mimeo, Stanford GSB.

Borghans, L., and B. H. H. Golsteyn. 2006. "Time Discounting and Body Mass Index, Evidence from the Netherlands." *Economics of Human Biology* 4: 39–61.

Burger, Nicholas, and John Lynham. 2009. "Betting on Weight Loss. . . and Losing: Personal Gambles as Commitment Mechanisms." *Applied Economics Letters*. 17, 12, 2010, p. 1161.

Burton, S., E. Creyer, J. Kees, and K. Huggins. 2006. "Attacking the Obesity Epidemic: The Potential Health Benefits of Providing Nutrition Information in Restaurants." *American Journal of Public Health* 96(9): 1669–1675.

Camerer, C., L. Babcock, G. Loewenstein, and R. Thaler. 1997. "Labor Supply of New York City Cab Drivers: One Day at a Time." *Quarterly Journal of Economics* 111: 408–441.

Charness, G., and U. Gneezy. 2009. "Incentives and Exercise." *Econometrica* 77: 909–931.

Cole, C. A., and Gaeth, G. J. 1990. "Cognitive and Age-Related Differences in the Ability to Use Nutritional Information in a Complex Environment." *Journal of Marketing Research* 27(2): 175–184.

Cutler, D. M., E. L. Glaeser, and J. M. Shapiro. 2003. "Why Have Americans Become More Obese?" *The Journal of Economic Perspectives* 17(3): 93–118.

Dodd, M. 2008. "Obesity and Time-Inconsistent Preferences." *Obesity Research and Clinical Practice* 2: 83–89.

Downs, J. S., G. Loewenstein, and J. Wisdom. 2009. "Strategies for Promoting Healthier Food Choices." *American Economic Review* 99: 1–164.

Drichoutis, A., P. Lazaridis, and R. M. Nayga, Jr. 2009. "A Model of Nutrition Information Search with an Application to Food Labels." *Food Economics* 5: 138–151.

Elbel, B., R. Kersh, V. L. Brescoll, and L. B. Dixon. 2009. "Calorie Labeling and Food Choices: A First Look at the Effects on Low-Income People in New York City." *Health Affairs* 28(6): w1110–1121.

Elster, J. 1989. "Social Norms and Economic Theory." *The Journal of Economic Perspectives* 3: 99–117.

Epstein, L. H., K. K. Dearing, R. A. Paluch, J. N. Roemmich, and D. Cho. 2007. "Price and Maternal Obesity Influence Purchasing of Low- and High-Energy-Dense Foods." *American Journal of Clinical Nutrition* 86: 914–922.

Epstein, L. H., E. A. Handley, K. K. Dearing, D. D. Cho, J. N. Roemmich, R. A. Paluch, S. Raja, Y. Pak, and B. Spring. 2006. "Purchases of Food in Youth: Influence of Price and Income." *Psychological Science* 17: 82–89.

Faith, M. S., K. R. Fontaine, M. L. Baskin, and D. B. Allison. 2007. "Toward the Reduction of Population Obesity: Macrolevel Environmental Approaches to the Problems of Food, Eating, and Obesity." *Psychological Bulletin* 133(2): 205–226.

Finkelstein, E. A., C. J. Ruhm, and K. M. Kosa. 2005. "Economic Causes and Consequences of Obesity." *Annual Review of Public Health* 26: 239–257.

French, S. A. 2003. "Pricing Effects on Food Choices." *The Journal of Nutrtion* 133: 841S–843S.

French, S. A., R. W. Jeffery, M. Story, P. Hannan, and P. Snyder. 1997. "A Pricing Strategy to Promote Low-Fat Snack Choices Through Vending Machines." *American Journal of Public Health* 87: 849–851.

Gilbert, D. T., M. J. Gill, and T. D. Wilson. 2002. "The Future Is Now: Temporal Correction in Affective Forecasting." *Organizational Behavior and Human Decision Processes* 88: 430–444.

Gruber, J., and B. Koszegi. 2001. "Is Addiction Rational? Theory and Evidence." *Quarterly Journal of Economics* 116(4): 1261–1303.

Harnack, L. J., and S. A. French. 2008. "Effect of Point-of-Purchase Calorie Labeling on Restaurant and Cafeteria Food Choices: A Review of the Literature." *International Journal of Behavioral Nutrition and Physical Activity* 5(51): 54–55.

Herman, C. P., and J. Polivy. 2004. "The Self-regulation of Eating." In *The Handbook of Self-Regulation: Research, Theory, and Applications,* eds. R. F. Baumeister and K. D. Vohs, 492–508. New York: Guilford.

Herrnstein, R. J., G. F. Loewenstein, D. Prelec, and W. Vaughan, Jr. 1993. "Utility Maximization and Melioration: Internalities in Individual Choice." *Journal of Behavioral Decision Making* 6(3): 149–185.

Kahneman, D., and D. T. Miller. 1986. "Norm Theory: Comparing Reality to Its Alternatives." *Psychological Review* 93: 136–153.

Katan, M. B., and D. S. Ludwig. 2010. "Extra Calories Cause Weight Gain—But How Much?" *Journal of the American Medical Association* 303: 65–66.

Khan, U., and R. Dhar. 2007. "Where There Is a Way, Is There a Will? The Effect of Future Choices on Self-Control." *Journal of Experimental Psychology: General* 136(2): 277–288.

Kim, S., R. M. Nayga, and O. Capps. 2000. "The Effect of Food Label Use on Nutrient Intakes: An Endogenous Switching Regression Analysis." *Journal of Agricultural and Resource Economics* 25(1): 215–231.

Knight, L., and F. Boland. 1989. "Restrained Eating: An Experimental Disentanglement of the Disinhibiting Variables of Calories and Food Type." *Journal of Abnormal Psychology* 98: 412–420.

Komlos, J., P. K. Smith, and B. Bogin. 2004. "Obesity and the Rate of Time Preference: Is There a Connection?" *Journal of Biosocial Science* 36(2): 209–219.

Lipsey, R. G., and K. Lancaster. 1956. "The General Theory of Second Best." *The Review of Economic Studies* 24(1): 11–32.

Lissner, L., B. L. Heitmann, and C. Bengtsson. 2000. "Population Studies of Diet and Obesity." *British Journal of Nutrition* 83: S21–S24.

Loewenstein, G. 1996. "Out of Control: Visceral Influences on Behavior." *Organizational Behavior and Human Decision Processes* 65: 272–292.

Loewenstein, G., T. Brennan, and K. G. Volpp. 2007. "Asymmetric Paternalism to Improve Health Behaviors." *Journal of the American Medical Association* 298(20): 2415–2417.

Loewenstein, G., L. K. John, and K. G. Volpp. 2010. "Using Decision Errors to Help People Help Themselves." In *Behavioral Foundations of Policy,* eds. Eldar Shafir. New York: Russell Sage Foundation Press.

Lowe, M. G. 1982. "The Role of Anticipated Deprivation in Overeating." *Addictive Behaviors* 7: 103–112.

Lynch, J. G., Jr., and G. Zauberman. 2006. "When Do You Want It? Time, Decisions, and Public Policy." *Journal of Public Policy and Marketing* 25: 67–78.

Madrian, B. C., and D. F. Shea. 2001. "The Power of Suggestion: Inertia in 401(k) Participation and Savings Behavior." *The Quarterly Journal of Economics* 116(4): 1149–1187.

Mata, J., P. M. Todd, and S. Lippke. 2010. "When Weight Management Lasts: Lower Perceived Rule Complexity Increases Adherence." *Appetite* 54: 37–43.

Mathios, A. D. 2000. "The Impact of Mandatory Disclosure Laws on Product Choices: An Analysis of the Salad Dressing Market." *Journal of Law and Economics* 43: 651–677.

McClure, S. M., K. M. Ericson, D. L. Laibson, G. Loewenstein, and J. D. Cohen. 2007. "Time Discounting for Primary Rewards." *The Journal of Neuroscience* 27(21): 5796–5804.

Mischel, W., and E. B. Ebbesen. 1970. "Attention in Delay of Gratification." *Journal of Personality and Social Psychology* 16: 329–337.

Monsivais, P., and A. Drewnowski. 2007. "The Rising Cost of Low-Energy-Density Foods." *Journal of the American Dietetic Association* 107: 2071–2076.

Moorman, C. 1996. "A Quasi Experiment to Assess the Consumer and Informational Determinants of Nutrition Labeling Processing Activities: The Case of the Nutrition Labeling and Education Act." *Journal of Public Policy and Marketing* 15(1): 28–44.

Murphy, K. 2006. *Obesity Economics*, Plenary session at the McGill Health Challenge, October 26, 2006. Video presentation available at: http://www.mcgill.ca/healthchallenge/2006/presentations/module2/

Neuhouser, M. L., A. R. Kristal, and R. E. Patterson. 1999. "Use of Food Nutrition Labels is Associated with Lower Fat Intake." *Journal of the American Dietetic Association* 99(1): 45–53.

O'Donoghue, T., and M. Rabin. 1999. "Doing It Now or Later." *American Economic Review* 89: 103–124.

O'Donoghue, T., and M. Rabin. 2008. "Procrastination on Long-Term Projects." *Journal of Economic Behavior and Organization* 66: 161–175.

Patrick, H., and T. A. Nicklas. 2005. "A Review of Family and Social Determinants of Children's Eating Patterns and Diet Quality." *Journal of the American College of Nutrition* 24(2): 83–92.

Popkin, B. M., K. Duffey, and P. Gordon-Larsen. 2005. "Environmental influences on Food Choice, Physical Activity and Energy Balance." *Physiology and Behavior* 86(5): 603–613.

Poppitt, S. D., D. Swann, A. E. Black, and A. M. Prentice. 1998. "Assessment of Selective Under-Reporting of Food Intake by Both Obese and Non-Obese Women in a Metabolic Facility." *International Journal Of Obesity And Related Metabolic Disorders* 22: 303–311.

Read, D., and B. van Leeuwen. 1998. "Predicting Hunger: The Effects of Appetite and Delay on Choice." *Organizational Behavior and Human Decision Processes* 76: 189–205.

Reuben, E., Sapienza, P., and Zingales, L. 2010. "Time discounting for primary and monetary rewards." *Economics Letters* 106(2): 125–127.

Rick, S., and G. Loewenstein. 2008. "Hypermotivation (Commentary on 'Mazar et al., The Dishonesty of Honest People')." *Journal of Marketing Research* 45(6): 645–653.

Roberto, C. A., P. D. Larsen, H. Agnew, J. Baik, and K. D. Brownell. 2010. "Evaluating the Impact of Menu Labeling on Food Choices and Intake." *American Journal of Public Health* 100(2): 312–318.

Rowland, N. E., C. H. Vaughan, C. M. Mathes, and A. Mitra. 2008. "Feeding Behavior, Obesity, and Neuroeconomics." *Physiology and Behavior* 93: 97–109.

Scott, M. L., S. M. Nowlis, N. Mandel, and A. C. Morales. 2008. "The Effects of Reduced Food Size and Package Size on the Consumption Behavior of Restrained and Unrestrained Eaters." *Journal of Consumer Research* 35: 391–405.

Smith, P. K., B. Bogin, and D. Bishai 2005. "Are Time Preference and Body Mass Index Associated? Evidence from the National Longitudinal Survey of Youth." *Economics and Human Biology* 3: 259–270.

Strotz, R. H. 1955. "Myopia and Inconsistency in Dynamic Utility Maximization." *Review of Economic Studies*, 23(3): 165–180.

Thaler, R. H., and C. R. Sunstein. 2008. *Nudge: Improving Decisions about Health, Wealth, and Happiness.* New Haven, CT: Yale University Press.

Urban, L. E., G. E. Dallal, L. M. Robinson, L. M. Ausman, E. Saltzman, and S. B. Roberts. 2010. "The Accuracy of Stated Energy Contents of Reduced-Engergy, Commercially Prepared Foods." *Journal of the American Dietetic Association* 110: 116–123.

Urbszat, D., C. P. Herman, and J. Polivy. 2002. "Eat, Drink, and Be Merry, for Tomorrow We Diet: Effects of Anticipated Deprivation on Food Intake in Restrained and Unrestrained Eaters." *Journal of Abnormal Psychology* 111: 396–401.

United States Food and Drug Administration. 1994. *Nutrition Labeling.* Washington, DC: USFDA.

Variyam, J. N., and J. Cawley. 2006. "Nutrition Labels and Obesity." NBER Working Paper W11956.

Volpp, K. G., L.K. John, A. B. Troxel, L. Norton, J. Fassbender, and G. Loewenstein. 2008. "Financial Incentive-Based Approaches for Weight Loss: A Randomized Trial." *Journal of the American Medical Association* 300(22): 2631–2637.

Wang, Y., M. A. Beydoun, L. Liang, B. Caballero, and S. K. Kumanyika. 2008. "Will All Americans Become Overweight or Obese? Estimating the Progression and Cost of the US Obesity Epidemic." *Obesity* 16(10): 2323–2330.

Wansink, B. 1996. "Can Package Size Accelerate Usage Volume?" *Journal of Marketing* 60: 1–13.

Wansink, B. 2004. "Environmental Factors That Increase the Food Intake and Consumption Volume of Unknowing Consumers." *Annual Review of Nutrition* 24: 455–79.

Wansink, B. 2006. *Mindless Eating: Why We Eat More Than We Think.* New York: Bantam-Dell.

Wansink, B. and J. Kim. 2005. "Bad Popcorn in Big Buckets: Portion Size Can Influence Intake as Much as Taste." *Journal of Nutrition Education and Behavior* 37: 242–245.

Wansink, B., and C. R. Payne. 2009. "The Joy of Cooking Too Much: 70 Years of Calorie Increases in Classic Recipes." *Annals of Internal Medicine* 150(4): 291–292.

Wisdom, J., J. S. Downs, and G. Loewenstein. 2010. "Promoting Healthy Choices: Information vs. Convenience." *American Economic Review: Applied Economics* 2(2): 164–78.

Young, L. R., and M. Nestle. 2002. "The Contribution of Expanding Portion Sizes to the US Obesity Epidemic." *American Journal of Public Health* 92: 246–249.

Zhang, L., and I. Rashad. 2008. "Obesity and Time Preference: The Health Consequences of Discounting the Future." *Journal of Biosocial Science* 40: 97–113.

CHAPTER 10

OBESITY POLITICS AND POLICY

ROGAN KERSH AND JAMES MORONE

THIS chapter explores U.S. public-policy responses to the obesity crisis, along with the complicated political debates swirling around the topic. The politics of obesity are particularly muddled; perhaps no other issue in public health has such a wide gap between scientific findings and policy response. Obesity burst onto the American political agenda a decade ago, following a Surgeon General's report labeling obesity an "epidemic" and the wide publication of a set of Centers for Disease Control (CDC) maps graphically illustrating rising obesity rates across the United States. A number of prominent public officials have targeted obesity, most recently including Michelle Obama, the nation's First Lady, who has made the reduction of child obesity her signature issue. Yet few significant policies have been enacted in response. Some states and muncipalities have passed measures targeting obesity, but these are scattershot, episodic, and minimally effective. Until the 2010 health-reform bill included a mandate to feature calorie labels on fast food restaurant menu boards, no major anti-obesity measure had passed the U.S. Congress.

Evidence from European studies suggests that successful policy approaches to stemming the tide of child obesity involve several concentrated interventions, implemented simultaneously. The American polity, dominated by interest groups and featuring a system of elaborately separated powers, may not permit such a comprehensive approach to policy change. The U.S. public-health research enterprise exacerbates this concern. Researchers remain divided about which (if any) policy approaches could help reverse rising obesity rates. Moreover, the gold standard of scientific evaluation—studies that test a single intervention, often during the formative stage of implementation—may communicate to policy makers and the wider public misleading signals about the possibility of achieving sustainable reform.

CONTEXT: HEALTH EFFECTS AND MEDICAL TREATMENT

As this Handbook amply details, obesity is associated with a wide range of health problems at every stage of life. Obese adults suffer higher rates of heart disease, diabetes, hypertension, and other ailments. Of particular concern is the high rate of obesity and overweight among young people. Overweight adolescents have a 70 percent chance of becoming overweight or obese adults. This increases to 80 percent if one or more parent is overweight or obese (Office of the Surgeon General 2001). For children born in the United States in 2000, the lifetime risk of being diagnosed with Type 2 diabetes at some point in their lives is estimated at around 30 percent for boys and 40 percent for girls (Institute of Medicine 2005). Other well-documented health effects directly or indirectly caused by child obesity include, in a particularly distressing example, heart attacks in children as young as age 5 (Brownell and Horgan 2004). Psychological effects are significant: one well-specified study found that severely obese children aged 5 to 18 described their quality of life in terms similar to those of young cancer patients undergoing chemotherapy (Schwimmer et al. 2003).

Early-stage research suggests, to cap a long roster of discouraging health effects, that the current under-18 generation of Americans may be the first in the nation's history to live shorter average life spans than their parents (Olshansky et al. 2005; Stewart et al. 2009). While multiple factors contribute to this actuarial claim, an especially significant one is the prevalence of obesity among U.S. youth.

Medical Treatment: Costs and Efficacy

American policymakers' attention to obesity has been further aroused as the economic effects of medical treatment become clearer. Obesity accounts for an estimated 12 percent of the growth in spending on U.S. health care in the past 10 years. Based on current trends in obesity rates, the United States will spend an estimated $343 billion annually on health costs directly attributable to obesity by 2018 (Ginsburg 2010; Thorpe 2009). Most of this care was and remains palliative: illnesses exacerbated by obesity, like diabetes and asthma, will likely be chronic conditions lasting a lifetime. The global costs of obesity-related health conditions are difficult to ascertain with any precision, but appear to be rising sharply as well. The World Health Organization in 2000 estimated the cost of obesity at up to

7 percent of countries' total health care costs around the globe (World Health Organization 2000).

Chronic health problems accompanying obesity are exacerbated among lower-income Americans—a group with higher rates of uninsurance. Completing this vicious cycle, individuals without insurance coverage are more likely to be overweight or obese than those with private insurance or Medicaid coverage (Haas et al. 2003).

Despite rising attention to—and spending on—obesity, no reliable medical treatment to arrest or reverse this condition has been identified. Medical journals are replete with uncharacteristically plaintive titles like "Is New Hope on the Horizon for Obesity?" (The author's answer: probably not.) Another journal article's title summarizes: "Childhood Obesity: Public-Health Crisis, Common Sense Cure" (Bray 2008; Ebbeling, Pawlak, and Ludwig 2002). Lacking a reliable means of addressing obesity through pharmaceutical or even surgical intervention, medical authorities continue to recommend preventive measures where possible. This turns our attention to the *causal* factors affecting overweight and obesity.

ENTER THE POLICY MAKERS

Since the U.S. rise in obesity became a source of widespread public concern early in the present century, a fierce debate has centered around *causes*. What are the principal elements contributing to this "epidemic"?

Americans' increasingly inactive lifestyle is the primary culprit, according to one well-publicized perspective. Such a view also motivates one predominant response to rising obesity rates: encourage exercise. However, a wealth of research suggests that altering sedentary lives—for example, through school-based physical activity programs—has limited benefits without simultaneous and dedicated attention to caloric overconsumption (Harris et al. 2009). A prospective study involving middle-school students over the course of two academic years showed that both BMI and the risk of becoming obese increased for every additional serving of sugar-sweetened beverages per day—an effect that remained significant across different levels of exercise (Ludwig, Peterson, and Gortmaker 2001).

Thus, explanations for the rise of obesity must extend also to food and dietary practices—both *what* people are consuming, and *how much*. Ultimately, the effort to pin down causes and solutions boils down to age-old verities: improve diet and expand exercise. But achieving this grail has eluded public-health experts, physicians, school officials, and other advocates striving to reverse rising obesity rates. Enter, if reluctantly, public policy makers.

Political discussions in the United States about obesity broadly follow two primary frames. The first and, until quite recently, dominant perspective emphasizes *personal responsibility* (Brownell et al. 2010). Food consumption is, on this view, a deeply private matter best left up to each individual. More recently, with obesity rates rising despite efforts to appeal to personal choices, a competing frame has gained traction in policy debates: the *obesogenic environment* in which individuals, especially children, find their food choices conditioned and even manipulated by availability, price, and advertising. Although researchers have demonstrated that a more nuanced set of views exists among the general public than these two broad frames allow (Barry et al. 2009), much of the policy debate has been organized around these broad poles.

Personal Responsibility

The personal-responsibility frame holds that individuals or parents ought to make their own consumption decisions. This classic liberty-maximizing perspective has been advanced by conservative politicians and food/beverage industry representatives (Kersh and Morone 2005). Efforts to depart from this individualist view often provoke great protests about the loss of freedom or the rise of the "nanny state." Food choices—even unhealthy choices—can seem to be a fundamental component of personal freedom, just as an earlier generation of libertarians fought for the right to smoke.

The roster for policy action suggested by personal-responsibility views is very thin. It implies that legislative action to affect consumption and thereby reduce rising obesity rates should be off limits. This perspective also suggests that it is fine to applaud exercise and healthy diets—but do not encourage these too strenuously, lest we risk too much interference with the core value of individual liberty.

Obesogenic Environment

A leading alternative frame rests on descriptions of America's "obesogenic environment." A great tide of high-fat, low-nutrition, processed foods engulf consumers from an early age. Such food is available everywhere, including schools and other places where children congregate—and is reinforced by incessant advertising. A recent *Pediatrics* study shows that Philadelphia public schoolchildren who shopped at corner stores before or after school purchased more than 350 calories of foods and beverages per average visit (Borradaile et al. 2009). Chips, candy, and sugar-sweetened beverages were most frequently purchased, affirming one researcher's description of the "toxic food environment" that surrounds American children (Brownell and Horgan 2004).

The environmental frame offers a much stronger collection of potential policy responses. This perspective encourages public officials to actively attempt to reduce the availability of high-calorie, low-nutrition foods, and to shift consumption to healthier alternatives. Around the globe, policy makers have pursued these options by *controlling the conditions of sale*—for example, by limiting the foods that schools offer; *taxing unhealthy options* like sugary sodas; or *restricting advertising* of high-fat, low-nutrition foods that targets young children (see Hawkes 2007).

Policy makers also turn to "softer" alternatives like *restricting or banning certain ingredients*, like trans fats; *expanding information* by, for example, requiring calorie labels on menus; or *subsidizing healthier alternatives*, such as fruits and vegetables.

Even the simplest (or softest) alternatives have complications. For instance, subsidizing healthy alternatives may seem like common sense, but these choices typically have much higher per-calorie costs; the expense of providing subsidies to bring down the relative expense of fruits and vegetables is unlikely to be appealing during a time of budget difficulties for the U.S. government and most states (Fields 2004). At the same time, less healthy items often feature ingredients like high-fructose corn syrup that are heavily subsidized under current U.S. farm policies; withdrawing financial support from well-organized agriculture interests is never easy. Asking schools to offer healthier, more expensive lunches (often over the protests of the children who like their fries and pizzas) means, ultimately, raising taxes or cutting back on other programs.

The effort to frame obesity policy remains a contested struggle in every polity, across U.S. municipalities and states, and around the globe. The relative success of personal-responsibility views among the American public and policy makers helps explain the dearth of implemented policies, especially at the national level. But even the slow spread of the "obesogenic environment" frame among the public and policy makers (Barry et al. 2009) has not meaningfully altered obesity politics. Numerous political obstacles block the road to public health reform.

U.S. Solutions in Practice

What policies might be most effective in responding to the current prevalence of obesity in the United States? One group of researchers attempted to narrow the sprawling field of proposed policies by undertaking a novel "impact-feasibility" study. The authors compiled a list of 70 programs under consideration at the U.S. national level, then asked a varied set of obesity and nutrition researchers to rate each policy based on the *impact* it would have if enacted, using a standard 7-point impact scale. Separately and simultaneously, a similarly sized set of policy makers—varying by party, elective branch, and national/state level of government—were asked to rate each of the 70 policies' *feasibility*: how likely it was to pass their jurisdiction, again based on a 7-point scale. The researchers analyzed the results via simple cross-tabulation, yielding a 2 x 2 matrix comprising more and less promising (higher/lower impact *and* feasibility) policies (Brescoll, Kersh, and Brownell 2008).

Below we examine in detail three policies in the high-impact/high-feasibility category, all of which actually have been implemented in at least one U.S. jurisdiction. We report as well on public-health researchers' *evaluations* of such policies. The results in each case are mixed at best, inevitably leading some respondents—especially those in the "personal responsibility" camp—to conclude that the policy in question has limited or no efficacy in practice. Our conclusion is rather different, and draws on other findings in the health care arena: multiple solutions, implemented in tandem, are generally more effective than single interventions carried out in a vacuum.

Calorie Labeling on Menus

At the beginning of 2008, no town, city, or state in the United States required fast food restaurants to publicly post calorie labels on their menu. Two years later, more than 50 jurisdictions—including the nation's three largest cities, New York, Los Angeles, and Chicago, as well as the largest state, California—had enacted menu labeling laws, with dozens of other state and local legislatures debating doing so. As implementation began to spread, after New York City inaugurated its policy in July 2008, Congress included a national labeling mandate in the massive health-reform bill that passed in March 2010.

Labeling's prominent place in the health-reform package testifies to the rising profile of obesity concerns among policy makers. Yet few scientific studies have evaluated the influence of menu labeling on fast-food choices or calorie consumption. Those that have been carried out are typically laboratory-based or otherwise experimental. One ethnographic research project surveyed adolescents aged 11–18 who ordered meals from one of three fast food chains, McDonald's, Denny's, or Panda Express. Utilizing sample variation and with the cooperation of the chains, some respondents were exposed to calorie menu labels. The surveys indicated that calorie information was not a major consideration for the young respondents' meal choices; instead, taste and hunger were each more important (Yamamoto et al. 2005; cf. Larson et al. 2008).

New York City's implementation of calorie labeling opens the way to evaluating the policy, not as a controlled experiment but in actual practice. One study was conducted in the field in 2008, examining calorie labeling soon after it went into effect. Researchers surveyed fast food consumers in New York and in a control city—Newark, New Jersey—which had not introduced calorie labeling. The study was carried out in low-income neighborhoods; poverty is an established risk factor for obesity, and minority populations bear a greater burden of obesity and related health problems in the United States—a status exacerbated among lower-income children and youth (Ogden et al. 2002).

The researchers focused on the influence of city-wide calorie labeling on food choices at fast food restaurants, especially in low-income areas. The bottom line: the study found no statistically significant differences in caloric intake before and after labeling was implemented. While many respondents reported noticing the labels and considering the calorie information in making their meal selection, that awareness did not translate into reduced purchase or consumption of calories (Elbel et al. 2009).

With implementation of calorie labeling spreading in jurisdictions across the United States—a development that will be greatly sped by the national health-reform labeling mandate—other evaluation studies are underway, including across neighborhoods of differing income levels. New York City's Department of Health and Mental Hygiene (DOHMH) also carried out evaluation research before and after menu labeling was implemented; as with the abovementioned study, they found that calorie labels had minimal effects in practice.

Public health advocates have been disappointed by these results. Both studies, it should be noted, examine New York City's introduction of calorie labeling—a policy implemented in something of a vacuum. Calorie labels were not accompanied by other strong policy measures to combat obesity. There were no targeted efforts to educate consumers about calorie consumption: many did not know how to put into context the posted calorie counts they saw. We return to this important caveat in the conclusion.

Soft-Drink Tax

Forty states and several cities currently levy small taxes on one or more categories of less healthy foods, such as soft drinks, potato chips, candy, and chewing gum. In controlled experimental settings, price manipulations have yielded substantial changes in consumption practices: participants shifted from unhealthy, calorie-dense foods to healthy foods. For example, one experiment in a high school cafeteria slashed fruit and salad prices in half; fruit sales quadrupled and carrot sales doubled as a result, though salad sales did not change (French et al. 1997). Extending research from these laboratory-style settings to the "real world"—where participants may consume more calories outside the experimental location to compensate—has been difficult. One extensive review of international articles investigating food prices and obesity found only a handful of empirical studies, with inconclusive results (Powell and Chaloupka 2009).

The primary U.S. policy efforts in this vein are focused on enacting soft-drink taxes—or, in many places, reenacting them: the number of American jurisdictions featuring soda taxes actually dropped between 1990 and 2000, owing primarily to successful lobbying efforts by the food and beverage industries (Jacobson and Brownell 2000). Because adolescents and young children, as well as many obese adults, consume sodas and other "junk foods" at high rates, this approach to addressing high obesity rates has been embraced by nutrition and health professionals.

What would be the effect of a penny or half-penny levy per serving of soda? Two nutrition and obesity experts summarize the case as follows: "a tax on sugar-sweetened beverages would have strong positive effects on reducing consumption. In addition, the tax has the potential to generate substantial revenue to prevent obesity and address other external costs resulting from the consumption of sugar-sweetened beverages, as well as to fund other health related programs." (Brownell et al. 2009) Advocates often compare the proposals to tobacco taxes, which generate revenues while reducing consumption.

In actual practice, the benefits of a soda tax—again, considered as a stand-alone intervention—are less clear. One scientific study utilized multivariate analysis to assess the effect of soda taxes on adolescents' body mass, drawing body mass index (BMI) data from the long-running Monitoring the Future surveys. The results indicated no statistically significant connection between grocery store soda taxes and adolescent BMI, and only a weak causal relationship between vending machine soda tax rates and BMI among teens at risk for overweight. Taxes would have to be raised "substantially," the authors conclude, for a significant effect to be shown on BMI. (This evaluation did not measure revenue effects; other studies have affirmed the expectation that even small taxes on soda bring in significant revenue.) A more recent evaluation examined the impact of *changes* in state soft-drink taxes on obesity and overweight, again using BMI as the primary measure. The results again find a weak causal effect of soft-drink taxes on BMI, suggesting that only a fairly hefty tax would meaningfully shift consumption behavior (Fletcher, Frisvold, and Tefft 2009).

Competitive Foods: School-Based Policies

School meals and snacks are a major source of nutrition for U.S. children and adolescents. The federally subsidized National School Lunch Program (NSLP), launched in 1969, now serves over 30 million school children each day—nearly 60 percent of the children in participating schools (Musiker 2009). Students in the NSLP consume more milk, fruit, and vegetables, drink less sweetened beverages, and eat less candy than students outside or only occasionally in the program; at the same time, however, they also consume more sodium, fat, and saturated fat—and their calorie intake is on average higher (Cullen, Watson, and Zakeri 2001). In short, NSLP lunches and breakfasts provide too many calories from fat, according to nutritional experts, and too few from fresh fruits and vegetables.

Of greater concern to advocates of healthier food in schools is the practice of many U.S. school districts to contract with private beverage and food companies to sell "competitive foods" in cafeterias and vending machines. Soft-drink companies vigorously compete for "pouring rights" in school districts—contractual agreements that commit districts to selling only their brand in the schools. As Brownell and Horgan summarize: "Schools need money and the soft drink companies offer a way to get it" (*idem.*, 2004, p. 161). The conclusion, primarily from anecdotal and qualitative studies, is that competitive foods are a significant source of unhealthy food and drink consumed at school, contributing directly to the child obesity problem (Story, Kaphingst, and French 2006).

Given this dim view of competitive foods in schools, a host of policy initiatives to regulate or eliminate competitive foods' availability have been introduced at all levels of government. As with menu labeling and soda taxes, researchers are increasingly investigating the practical effects of these policies.

One evaluation assesses the causal effect of competitive food availability on a large national sample of U.S. fifth graders' BMI. Unsurprisingly, the authors found, the ready availability of competitive foods does boost in-school purchases of junk foods. Yet, contrary to widely held assumptions, no increase in BMI attributable to competitive foods was registered among the fifth graders in the study. The evaluation also assessed information beyond BMI, finding that the presence of competitive foods did not lead to substantial changes in overall consumption of healthy and unhealthy foods, or even in levels of physical activity. The authors conclude that there may *not* be "broader effects of junk foods in school on social/behavioral and academic outcomes," although a wide range of experimental and ethnographic studies have suggested otherwise (Datar and Nicosia 2009).

The Need for Multiple Approaches

Public policies such as menu labels, soft-drink taxes, and reducing competitive foods in schools each have been promoted by health advocates as a promising means of addressing the obesity crisis among children. Yet initial evaluations suggest that, at least in isolation, each policy falls short of the hoped-for benefits. Are public-health officials promoting the wrong policies? Or, even worse, are there no interventions on the horizon that are likely to be successful in reversing the rising rates of childhood obesity?

Our cautious conclusion is more optimistic. Medical experts know that single types of treatment often fail to address health problems, and that several simultaneous interventions are often preferable. Such a "multiple solutions" approach has become conventional practice in treating diseases from asthma to zoster. The same method also may be the most promising means of addressing obesity. One recent study, for example, combined calorie labels *and* nutrition education information; calorie counts were "anchored" to a reminder that 2,000 calories is the FDA's average recommended daily allowance. The combination of labels and informational anchor made a significant difference in consumption practices while, as we saw above, labels alone did not (Roberto et al. 2010). European health officials have found that a combination of banning junk-food television advertising to children, taxing unhealthful foods, and substituting healthier foods at school together help to reduce child obesity rates (1 er Symposium EEN 2009). Studies of broad interventions, involving several different alterations in food environments, at U.S. schools have seen at least modest declines in obesity rates (Gortmaker et al. 1999).

If multiple approaches prove to be a conceptual breakthrough in combating obesity, public advocates will inevitably have to face up to the next hurdle. American politics traditionally resists large-scale, multiple-approach policy interventions. The fragmented U.S. government, full of checks, balances, and "veto points" across different branches and levels (national, state, local), stand as a formidable barrier to large-scale policy innovation. Interest-group resistance makes it difficult to enact regulation of food or beverage markets, let alone a roster of concerted national approaches to childhood obesity.

Exacerbating this difficulty may be the very nature of quantitative evaluation research. By focusing on a single intervention in isolation, holding all other factors constant, any individual policy change is likely to appear ineffective. More sophisticated multivariate studies, investigating the effects of several policy shifts undertaken simultaneously, would seem preferable—but very difficult to perform. To fully explore this notion would require a revised approach to evaluation studies; suffice it to say that concerned inquiries into the nature and impact of evaluation research have recently been raised in the relevant literature (Johnson et al. 2009).

As obesity continues to move from a private matter to a subject of public policy attention, a separate but important set of concerns arises: the *stigma* associated with official expressions of concern about overweight and obesity. Negative weight-based discrimination is pervasive, extending from professional settings to schools to social situations (Puhl and Heuer 2009).

STIGMATIZING EFFECT OF
PUBLIC POLICIES

Extensive research has charted the negative effects that media reports on obesity can have on individuals' (especially children's) body images, exacerbating eating disorders and unhealthy weight-loss practices (Derenne and Beresin 2006). Policy makers debating obesity—calling attention to rising BMI, critiquing behavior, focusing on communities where obesity rates are highest—only exacerbate the problem of stigma. A sort of "Catch-22" characterizes policy makers' response to such a concern. Promoting solutions to obesity may heighten stigma and discrimination, but failing to address rising obesity rates means ignoring a public health crisis, permitting the problem to grow worse. The challenge for public health advocates is to find sensitive ways to address the problem, avoiding discourse that exacerbates stigma and victim blaming.

One particularly *in*sensitive response springs from a deeply rooted tendency in U.S. health policy making. American reformers eager to spread their healthy message—about the dangers of smoking or drinking or drug use—have traditionally turned to "demonization" of the purveyors of undesirable substances (think "Demon Rum" during the battle for prohibition, "Big Tobacco," and the like). Enthusiastic advocates have demonized, as well, those who behave in unhealthy or unsavory ways. These crusades for policy change often end up targeting members of dispossessed communities: immigrants, minorities, the urban poor. As the present authors have noted previously, "There is nothing quite like the fear of sinister 'others' to overcome the stalemate of American policy making" (Kersh and Morone 2002). Lawmakers, along with policy advocates, journalists, and academic researchers addressing this issue, must remain aware of—and deliberately avoid—the myriad ways in which promoting public-policy efforts can stigmatize obese people, including those who appear to resist the benefits of regulatory changes.

Policy makers can also focus their attention on stigmatization. Research on weight bias suggests that statutory attention to weight discrimination is desirable, even necessary, alongside nutrition and food policies designed to alleviate obesity. Legal scholar Jennifer Pomerantz concludes that "the public health community should be advocating for both obesity and food policy, and also antidiscrimination legislation. This could alleviate some of the institutionalized bias and result in making obesity policy more likely" (Pomerantz 2008). In such other arenas as civil rights for women and homosexuals, the promotion of antidiscrimination policies has demonstrably shifted cultural norms and reduced stigma, as well as rewritten statute books (Koppelman 1996). Hence, at least by analogy, there exists the possibility that efforts to legally address stigma surrounding obesity could diminish the undesirable side effects of aggressive obesity reduction policies.

Obesity issues have long been separated, both in analytic studies and medical or psychological treatment, from eating disorders and unhealthy weight-loss practices. Some clinicians and public-health researchers now call for integration of these traditionally disconnected realms, especially given that both have trended upward in recent years. Such an integrated approach builds on the "obesogenic environment" frame discussed above. On this view, contemporary (mainstream) American society "exults thinness, stigmatizes fatness, encourages unregulated consumption of energy-dense foods, and promotes 'quick fix' approaches to weight loss" (Irving and Neumark-Sztainer 2002). Responses to such an environment that maintain awareness of, and devise related interventions for, obesity and eating disorders, would seem to mitigate at least partly the potentially harmful effect of public policies designed to address obesity alone.

One related ethical concern arises from the broad thrust of health policy making in the United States over the past three or four decades. This realm has increasingly moved from efforts to achieve *collective* solutions to public issues—such as Medicare, or the Davis-Bacon Act establishing public hospitals around the United States—to a focus on *individual* issues like patients' bills of rights or sweeping efforts to address personal behaviors like smoking or drug use (Kersh and Morone 2005). The recently passed health reform measure is a welcome—if partial—exception. The shift from the single-payer approach (in Medicare) to the individual mandate (in the Obama plan), along with the familiar observation that this is the most ambitious social-policy legislation to pass since Medicare 45 years ago, suggests how the landscape has changed.

This shift from collective to individual has deeply affected the making of health policy—helping determine which issues are legitimately under consideration, for example, or how policy makers will respond to a particular topic. As managed-care organizations spread across the health system in the early 1990s, arousing popular ire due to denials of coverage and commodification of care, the public-health response was to call for a "patients' bill of rights": individual protections, enforceable in court. An earlier generation, still in the shadow of the New Deal, would more likely have called for a collective response.

Ethical concerns are spurred by the extensive—sometimes, it can appear, exclusive—debate on individual rights and protections in health policy making. Considerably less attention has been paid by legislators, public advocates, or even most academics to shared concerns or collective ethical principles. The strong individualist turn also drives everything from policy solutions to public-health research.

CONCLUSION

The state of childhood obesity, in the United States and worldwide, is widely described in terms like "alarming" and "devastating." Unless and until medical responses are devised, the public-policy arena appears to hold the most promising response. Yet policy tools to address this epidemic are underemployed in nearly every American jurisdiction.

The public health community faces two great challenges. First, it must discover effective treatments to combat the obesity epidemic. We have suggested that multiple policy solutions, implemented simultaneously or in tight sequence, are more likely to prove successful than single interventions. Other recent research embraces an approach suggested by behavioral social science: emphasize policies that promise to "modify social norms and create optimal defaults where the default option is the healthy choice, thus facilitating and reinforcing individual behavior change" (McKinnon et al. 2009).

Once effective interventions have been identified and tested, health policy advocates face an even larger challenge: the long-standing American policy-making practices of incrementalism and "muddling through" (Lindblom 1959). These characteristics of the U.S. system—rooted in the checks and balances accompanying our Madisonian separation of powers—empower well-organized groups (like the food industry) while deflecting the large-scale mobilization of community resources. Overcoming these obstacles will require sustained and committed advocacy efforts.

REFERENCES

Barry, Colleen L., Victoria L. Brescoll, Kelly D. Brownell, and Mark Schlesinger, 2009. "Obesity Metaphors: How Beliefs about the Causes of Obesity Affect Support for Public Policy." *Milbank Quarterly* 87: 1.

Borradaile, Kelley E., et al. 2009. "Snacking in Children: The Role of Urban Corner Stores." *Pediatrics* 10: 1542/peds. 1292–1298.

Bray, George A. 2008. "Is New Hope on the Horizon for Obesity?" *The Lancet* 372(9653): 1859–1860.

Brescoll, Victoria L., Rogan Kersh, and Kelly D. Brownell. 2008. "Assessing the Impact and Feasibility of Federal Childhood Obesity Policies." *Annals of the American Academy of Political and Social Science* 615: 178–194.

Brownell, Kelly D., and Katherine Battle Horgan. 2004. *Food Fight*. New York: McGraw-Hill.

Brownell, Kelly D., Rogan Kersh, David S. Ludwig, Robert C. Post, Rebecca M. Puhl, Marlene B. Schwartz, and Walter C. Willett. 2010. "Personal Responsibility and Obesity: A Constructive Approach to a Controversial Issue." *Health Affairs* 29(3): 379–387.

Brownell, Kelly D., et al. 2009. "The Public Health and Economic Benefits of Taxing Sugar-Sweetened Beverages." *New England Journal of Medicine* 361: 16.

Cullen, Karen Weber, Kathy Watson, and Issa Zakeri. 2007. "Middle School Student Lunch Consumption: Impact of National School Lunch Program Meal and Competitive Foods." USDA/ERS Contractor and Cooperator Report No. 30.

Datar, Ashlesha, and Nancy Nicosia. 2009. "Junk Food in Schools and Childhood Obesity: Much Ado about Nothing?" RAND Working Paper WR-672.

Derenne, Jennifer L., and Eugene V. Beresin. 2006. "Body Image, Media, and Eating Disorders." *Academic Psychiatry* 30: 257–261.

Ebbeling, Cara B., Dorota B. Pawlak, and David S. Ludwig. 2002. "Childhood Obesity: Public-Health Crisis, Common Sense Cure." *The Lancet* 360(9331): 473–482.

Elbel, Brian, Rogan Kersh, Victoria L. Brescoll, and L. Beth Dixon. 2009. "Calorie Labeling and Food Choices: A First Look at the Effects on Low-Income People in New York City." *Health Affairs* 28(6): w1110–1121.

Fields, Scott. 2004. "Do Agricultural Subsidies Foster Poor Health?" *Environmental Health Perspectives* 112: 14.

Fletcher, Jason M., David Frisvold, and Nathan Tefft. 2009. "Can Soft Drink Taxes Reduce Population Weight?" *Contemporary Economic Policy* 10: 1–13.

French, Simone A., et al. 1997. "Pricing Strategy to Promote Fruit and Vegetable Purchase in High School Cafeterias." *Journal of the American Dietetic Association* 97(9): 1008–1010.

Ginsburg, Paul. 2010. "Reforms in Health Insurance and Health Care Infrastructure May Reduce Health Costs." *Oncology Times* 32: 3.

Gortmaker, Steven L., et al. 1999. "Reducing Obesity via a School-Based Interdisciplinary Intervention Among Youth." *Archives of Pediatric and Adolescent Medicine* 153: 409–418.

Haas, Jennifer S., Lisa B. Lee, Celia P. Kaplan, Dean Sonneborn, Kathryn A. Phillips, and Su-Ying Liang. 2003. "The Association of Race, Socioeconomic Status, and Health Insurance Status with the Prevalence of Overweight among Children and Adolescents." *American Journal of Public Health* 93(12): 2105–2110.

Harris, K.T., et al. 2009. "Effect of School-based Physical Activity on Children's BMI." *AAP Grand Rounds* 22: 17.

Hawkes, Corinna. 2007. *Marketing Food to Children: Changes in the Global Regulatory Environment, 2004–2006*. Geneva: World Health Organization.

Institute of Medicine. 2005. "*Preventing Childhood Obesity: Health in the Balance*." Washington, DC: Institute of Medicine.

Irving, Lori M., and Dianne Neumark-Sztainer. 2002. "Integrating the Prevention of Eating Disorders and Obesity: Feasible or Futile?" *Preventive Medicine* 34: 299–309.

Jacobson, Michael F., and Kelly D. Brownell. 2000. "Small Taxes on Soft Drinks and Snack Foods to Promote Health." *American Journal of Public Health* 90(6): 854–857.

Johnson, Kelli, Lija O. Greenseid, Stacie A. Toal, Jean A. King, Frances Lawrenz, and Boris Volkov. 2009. "Research on Evaluation Use: A Review of the Empirical Literature From 1986 to 2005." *American Journal of Evaluation* 30(3): 377–410.

Kersh, Rogan, and James A. Morone. 2005. "Obesity, Courts, and the New Politics of Public Health." *Journal of Health Politics, Policy, and Law* 30: 5.

Kersh, Rogan, and James A. Morone. 2002. "The Politics of Obesity: Seven Steps to Government Action." *Health Affairs* 21(6): 142–153.

Koppelman, Andrew. 1996. *Antidiscrimination Law and Social Equality*. New Haven: Yale University Press.

Larson, N., et al. 2008. "Fast Food Intake: Longitudinal Trends during the Transition to Young Adulthood and Correlates of Intake." *Journal of Adolescent Health* 43: 79–86.

Lindblom, Charles E., 1959. "The Science of 'Muddling Through.'" *Public Administration Review* 19(2): 79–88.

Ludwig, D. S., K. E. Peterson, and S. L. Gortmaker. 2001. "Relation between Consumption of Sugar-Sweetened Drinks and Childhood Obesity: A Prospective, Observational Analysis." *The Lancet* 357: 505–508.

McKinnon, Robin A., C. Tracy Orleans, Shiriki K. Kumanyika, Debra Haire-Joshu, Susan M. Krebs-Smith, Eric A. Finkelstein, Kelly D. Brownell, Joseph W. Thompson, and Rachel Ballard-Barbash. 2009. "Considerations for an Obesity Policy Research Agenda." *American Journal of Preventative Medicine* 36: 4.

Musiker, Melissa. 2009. "National School Lunch Program Particpation Up 57 Percent since 1969." *Amber Waves* (U.S. Department of Agriculture) 7: 1.

Office of the Surgeon General. 2001. "*Call to Action to Prevent an Increase in Overweight and Obesity.*" Washington, DC: Government Printing Office.

Ogden, C. L., K. M. Flegal, M. D. Carroll, and C. L. Johnson. 2002. "Prevalence and Trends in Overweight Among US Children and Adolescents, 1999–2000." *Journal of the American Medical Association* 288: 1728–1732.

Olshansky, S. Jay, et al. 2005. "A Potential Decline in Life Expectancy in the United States in the 21st Century." *New England Journal of Medicine* 352: 1138–1145.

Pomeranz, Jennifer L. 2008. "A Historical Analysis of Public Health, the Law, and Stigmatized Social Groups: The Need for Both Obesity and Weight Bias Legislation." *Obesity* 16: S93–S103.

Powell, Lisa M., and Frank J. Chaloupka. 2009. "Food Prices and Obesity: Evidence and Policy Implications for Taxes and Subsidies." *Milbank Quarterly* 87(1): 229–257.

Powell, Lisa M., Michael H. Criqui, and Frank J. Chaloupka. 2009. "Associations between State-Level Soda Taxes and Adolescent Body Mass Index." *Journal of Adolescent Health* 45: S57–S63.

1er Symposium EEN. 2009. "*EPODE Community-Based Interventions Aimed at Preventing Childhood Obesity.*" Brussels: EPODE European Network.

Puhl, Rebecca M., and Chelsea A. Heuer. 2009. "The Stigma of Obesity: A Review and Update." *Obesity* 17: 5.

Roberto, Christina A., Peter D. Larsen, Henry Agnew, Jenny Baik, and Kelly D. Brownell. 2010. "Evaluating the Effect of Menu Labeling on Food Choices and Intake." *American Journal of Public Health* 100(2): 312–318.

Schwimmer, Jeffrey B., Tasha M. Burwinkle, and James W. Varni. 2003. "Health-Related Quality of Life of Severely Obese Children and Adolescents." *Journal of the American Medical Association* 289: 1813–1819.

Stewart, Susan T., David M. Cutler, and Allison B. Rosen. 2009. "Forecasting the Effects of Obesity and Smoking on U.S. Life Expectancy." *New England Journal of Medicine* 361:2252–2260.

Story, Mary, Karen M. Kaphingst, and Simone French. 2006. "The Role of Child Care Settings in Obesity Prevention." *Childhood Obesity* 16(1): 109–142.

Thorpe, Kenneth E. 2009. *"The Future Costs of Obesity: National and State Estimates of the Impact of Obesity on Direct Health Care Expenses."* Washington, DC: United Health Foundation.

World Health Organization, 2000. *Obesity: Preventing and Managing the Global Epidemic.* WHO TRS-894.

Yamamoto, J. A., et al. 2005. "Adolescent Fast Food and Restaurant Ordering Behavior With and Without Calorie and Fat Content Menu Information." *Journal of Adolescent Health* 37: 397–402.

CHAPTER 11

FAT STUDIES

ESTHER D. ROTHBLUM

IT has taken us a lifetime but today we draw the line
No one is going to fault us for our needs, our loves, our size
For we are shattering that mirror, and silencing that voice
And claiming our own beauty as a right, a gift, a choice
Song "Beauty" by Estelle Freedman (2007)

WHAT IS FAT STUDIES?

Fat studies is a field of scholarship that critically examines societal attitudes about body weight and appearance, and that advocates equality for all people with respect to body size. Fat studies seeks to remove the negative associations that society has about fat and the fat body. It regards weight, like height, as a human characteristic that varies widely across any population. Marilyn Wann, one of the first activists to use the term "fat studies," stated (2009, p. x): "Unlike traditional approaches to weight, a fat studies approach offers no opposition to the simple fact of human weight diversity, but instead looks at what people and societies make of this reality." Fat studies scholars ask why we oppress people who are fat and who benefits from that oppression. In that regard, fat studies is similar to academic disciplines that focus on race, ethnicity, gender, or age.

The size acceptance movement began in 1969 when William Fabrey founded NAAFA, the National Association to Advance Fat Acceptance (initially the National Association to Aid Fat Americans). NAAFA has remained the major U.S. organization advocating for an end to size discrimination (see naafa.org). It has established a Declaration of Health Rights for Fat People, holds an annual conference, publishes a newsletter, and works to eradicate fat discrimination in education, the workplace, and the media.

In the 1970s in Los Angeles, a group of fat women formed the Fat Underground (Fishman 2008) as a way to organize against discrimination of fat people by the medical profession via diets and medical practices. Two of their members, Judy Freespirit and Aldebaran, wrote the Fat Liberation Manifesto (1983). The Manifesto demanded respect and equal rights for fat people, singled out the false claims of the dieting industries, and, paraphrasing Karl Marx, ended with the statement "Fat people of the world, unite! You have nothing to lose" (p. 53).

NAAFA and the Fat Underground both used the word "fat" instead of "obese" or "overweight." In English, medical terms (such as "obese") tend to be based on Greek or Latin terms, and as oppressed groups organize they often replace the former medical or clinical diagnosis (e.g., "homosexual") with more descriptive or catchier terms (e.g., "gay"), sometimes reclaiming words that have been used against them or that had derogatory meanings (e.g., "queer"). Similarly, fat activists felt that the terms "overweight," "underweight," and "normal weight" all imply that there is an attainable "ideal" weight when in fact there is great diversity in weight.

THE CURRENT OBSESSION
WITH THINNESS

Fat studies scholars examine why Western cultures are currently preoccupied with weight. People in the United States, regardless of their own weight, have strong negative attitudes about fat people, and the stigma of weight is particularly apparent for women. Women are more concerned with their own weight than are men, and women of average weight who perceive themselves as fat are more likely than men to state that their weight has interfered with obtaining a job and with their sexual attractiveness (Tiggemann and Rothblum 1988). Women's self-confidence is more tied to their bodies than is men's self-confidence (Thompson 1986).

In a capitalist society that ranks people according to their financial value to society, women's appearance is often considered the most precious asset for marital and professional success (see Rothblum 1994 for a review). It is difficult to be female in the United States and not be aware of one's physical appearance. When asked to describe themselves, most women (even those who are professionally successful) begin by describing their appearance (Freeman 1986). *Looksism*, prejudice or discrimination based on appearance, disproportionally affects women who are not white, middle-class, heterosexual, young, thin, and able-bodied. Increasingly, diet products and services are also aimed at men, children, and even household pets.

There is a huge economic market that depends on people wanting to lose weight, feeling dissatisfied with their bodies, and buying diet products. Billions of dollars are at stake and these industries would lose revenue or go bankrupt if people became satisfied with their bodies.

WHEN DID FAT BECOME BAD?

As old paintings, photographs, and written descriptions will attest, women's fashions in appearance and dress have changed drastically across time and geographic region. Brownmiller (1984) described commonalities that exist among women's appearance norms throughout history and across cultures. First, women are expected to look and dress in ways that immobilize them. Second, this constricting appearance is thought by people of each time period to be invented and practiced by women. Nevertheless, without conformity to these appearance norms, women are considered ugly or immoral by men. Often the specific fashion focuses on physical characteristics (e.g., size of feet, body weight) that are already smaller in women and attempts to curtail its size even more. Finally, the medical profession endorses the practice as health-promoting, while simultaneously treating large numbers of women for medical complications (e.g., eating disorders, complications of weight-loss surgery) as a result of the practice.

Fat studies scholars have described how views about fatness in the United States changed from healthy and attractive to ugly and unhealthy between the 1880s and 1920s (see Fraser 2009). During that period the U.S. economy was changing from primarily agricultural to industrial. Food was more available, and when most people could afford enough to eat, plumpness was no longer a sign of prestige. A huge wave of immigrants entered the country, and Fraser stated that "well-to-do Americans of Northern European extraction wanted to be able to distinguish themselves, physically and racially, from stockier immigrants" (p. 12). Physicians followed this trend by providing scales, calorie counts, and weight-loss treatments.

By the 1990s, the medical and pharmaceutical corporations were playing a large role in the U.S. public health debate, a phenomenon that Lyons (2009, p. 79) has termed "Obesity, Inc." When U.S. Surgeon General C. Everett Koop declared "War on Obesity" in 1995, his Shape Up America Campaign was funded by Weight Watchers, Slimfast, and Jenny Craig (Lyons 2009). The *Wall Street Journal* (Johannes and Stecklow 1998; McKay 2002) and the *New York Times* (Kolata 2005) have investigated the conflicts of interest by weight researchers and clinicians who hold leadership positions in the Centers for Disease Control and the National Institutes of Health while also consulting to pharmaceutical companies and commercial diet products. Mundy (2001) described the relative powerlessness of the Food and Drug Administration against the powerful pharmaceutical lobbies who want to get new medications approved quickly.

Weapons of Mass Distraction:
Health and Dieting

> Weight loss treatments provide patients with failure experiences, expose them
> to professionals who hold them in low regard, cause them to see themselves as
> deviant and flawed, confuse their perceptions of hunger and satiety, and divert
> their attention away from other problems.
>
> (Wooley and Garner 1991, p. 1250)

Fat studies focuses on weight-based oppression and who benefits from that oppression, not on dieting. Yet it is impossible to talk about fat oppression without being asked about the health risks of fat and why fat people can't just lose weight. These two questions are so often the focus of talks about weight that I have termed them "weapons of mass distraction."

It is important to emphasize that weight and income are negatively correlated in the United States, and that this correlation is especially pronounced for women (Ernsberger 2009). When studies compare fat and thin people on health, they are also comparing poor and rich people. In a country with great discrepancies in access to health care and health insurance, this means that fat (i.e., poor) people are going to have more health problems. Low income is also related to illness and earlier death (Ernsberger 2009). It is thus vital that studies of weight and health control for income.

Most people believe that poor people are fat because of their inability to afford nutritious food or memberships in health clubs—in other words, they assume that poverty causes fatness. In fact, Ernsberger (2009) has shown that the opposite direction of causality has more evidence—fatness leads to poverty due to discrimination and downward social mobility. He stated: "While there is evidence that poverty is fattening, a stronger case can be made for the converse: fatness is impoverishing" (p. 26). A number of studies have shown the relationship between fatness and employment discrimination. This literature, which represents multiple disciplines, has shown that fat people are less likely to be hired, are perceived as having numerous undesirable traits related to job performance, are more harshly disciplined on the job, are assigned to inferior professional assignments, are paid less than their non-fat coworkers, and are even terminated for failure to lose weight at the employer's request (see Fikkan and Rothblum 2005; Puhl and Brownell 2001; Roehling 1999, 2002; Solovay 2000 for reviews). The self-report of fat men and women themselves have also revealed a high frequency of employment-related discrimination (Rothblum, Brand, Miller, and Oetjen 1990). In addition to these barriers, fat people have been perceived by employers as a liability when it comes to providing health care insurance (Paul and Townsend 1995; Roehling 2002) and even penalized through some companies' benefits programs for their weight status (Reese 2000). Women are more affected by employment discrimination because they tend to have service-related jobs, such as waitressing, clerical work, and receptionists, where they may be hired based on their appearance. Fat women are also less likely to marry wealthier men (Ernsberger 2009).

An additional factor that increases health risks is that fat people report negative experiences in medical settings (see Rothblum et al. 1990) and are more likely to avoid medical care such as routine gynecologic exams (Amy, Aalborg, Lyons, and Keranen 2005). Research has shown that medical students and physicians hold negative attitudes toward fat people (Blumberg and Mellis 1985; Maddox and Liederman 1969) and rate videotaped "patients" more negatively when they are made up to appear fat (Breytspraak, McGee, Conger, Whatly, and Moore 1977). Finally, the negative stigma of weight and the stress of living as a member of an oppressed group both contribute to health risks (Ernsberger 2009).

In 1998, 28 percent of men and 44 percent of women in the United States were trying to lose weight (Serdula et al. 1999), and fatter people are much more likely to be dieting than thin ones (Gaesser 2009). Most weight-loss studies have considerable attrition, as participants drop out of treatment, particularly if they are in the waiting list control group, don't like the treatment condition to which they are randomly assigned, or are not losing weight (see Rothblum 1999 for a review). This means that the post-treatment and follow-up data are based on those participants who stuck with it, who were willing to attend the treatment sessions regularly and engage in the activities associated with the treatment, and who were able to lose weight (Rothblum 1999). Commercial weight-loss programs typically do not publish long-term follow-up data, but among research studies, the long-term (five years or more) failure rate of diets is 90–95 percent (Gaesser 2009). Even then, "success" is defined in number of pounds lost and not in achieving and maintaining so-called "normal" weight, which is rarely the case.

Interestingly, media preoccupation with the health risks of fatness ignores that life expectancy has been increasing (Lyons 2009). We may be fatter than our grandparents, but we are outliving them by an average of twenty years.

INTERSECTION OF FATNESS WITH RACE, CLASS, AND SEXUAL ORIENTATION

Fat studies scholars realize that weight needs to be examined within the context of gender, race/ethnicity, socioeconomic class, and sexual orientation. Because weight is so strongly correlated with income for women (Ernsberger 2009), being fat is often synonymous with being poor (e.g., "fat people don't join health clubs" can be understood as "poor people don't join health clubs"). Although it is illegal to discriminate based on gender, race, and ethnicity in most institutions, only a handful of places—the state of Michigan and the cities of Washington, D.C.; San Francisco and Santa Cruz, California; Madison, Wisconsin; and Binghamton, New York—have legislation prohibiting discrimination based on weight. Consequently, Campos (2004) has argued that fat prejudice is a subtle way to discriminate against poor people (and thus also people of color) without being overtly racist and classist.

Boero (2009) described the connection between gender, race, socioeconomic class, and mother blame, because mothers are often held responsible for their children's weight and in fact have been charged with felonies and have lost custody when fat children did not lose weight (see Solovay 2000 for a review). When the media portray fat children as coming home to an "empty house" (Boero, p. 115), this description does not mention mothers specifically, but the implication here is that mothers, not fathers, should be home to monitor children's snacks after school. Similarly, media accounts of fat children mention ethnic foods ("pan dulce," or "collard greens smothered in fatback") so that readers can infer that the mothers are Latina or African American (Boero, p. 116).

How does weight and preoccupation with weight differ among lesbian, gay, bisexual or transgender people? Given men's socialization to focus on physical appearance of sexual partners, it has been hypothesized that people sexually involved with men (heterosexual women and gay men) are more focused on their own appearance than are people sexually involved with women (heterosexual men and lesbians; see Rothblum, 2002, for a review) and some research has confirmed this interaction for weight and dieting (Brand, Rothblum, and Solomon 1992; Siever 1994).

There is relatively little research on bisexual women and men, and this is an important area for future study. It is possible that bisexuals fall somewhere in between the continuum of body image concerns facing gay men, heterosexual women, lesbians, and heterosexual men. On the other hand, as bisexuals increasingly form their own communities and organizations, this group may have body image issues of its own. Bisexuals may also be sexually attracted to or involved with both male and female partners (either simultaneously or sequentially). This could permit study of how body and appearance issues differ for the same person when the sexual partner is male versus female. Taub's (1999) qualitative study of bisexual women indicates that bisexual women feel more pressure to conform to heterosexual beauty norms (e.g., dieting, shaving body hair, looking more feminine) when involved with men than with women.

Bergman (2009) described what happens when transgender people are perceived as female versus male:

Whether I'm fat or not depends on whether the person or people looking at me believe me to be a man or a woman. . . . As a man, I'm a big dude, but not outside the norm for such things. . . . As a big guy, I'm big enough to make miscreants or troublemakers decide to take their hostility elsewhere, big enough to walk calmly through the streets because I'm safe unless there's no easier target. As a woman, I am revolting. I am not only unattractively mannish but also grossly fat. The clothes I can fit into at the local big-girl stores tend to fit around the neck and then get bigger as they go downward, which results in a festive butch-in-a-bag look (pp. 140–141).

As this section illustrates, body weight, and even women's body weight, cannot be understood without reference to race, ethnicity, social class, and sexual orientation.

THE HEALTH AT EVERY SIZE MOVEMENT

If fat studies scholars and clinicians do not focus on weight loss as a desirable goal, what is their attitude about weight and health? The Health at Every Size (HAES) movement is a public health initiative that focuses on health for all people, regardless of body weight (see Bacon 2008; Burgard 2009, for overviews). HAES emphasizes improving nutrition and enjoying food, and also on the joy of movement instead of adherence to a structured exercise program. HAES clinicians strive to end bias against fat people, and underscore the fact that we cannot tell people's health or fitness level just from looking at them. Health is defined as physical, emotional, and spiritual well-being, and HAES clinicians focus on everyone appreciating their body and its appearance. Burgard (2009) describes how regimens that are prescribed for fat people would be defined as eating disorders if thin people engaged in them. In this way, HAES practitioners de-emphasize weight and dieting, and argue that if diets don't work in the long run, we are doing people a disservice by promoting such failure experiences. Burgard (2009) states:

If people have to do things in their day-to-day life in order to achieve a particular weight that a study says would be healthier, and the things they have to do (like stomach surgery, starving, or exercising 4 hours a day) are not compatible with loving self-care, then by definition, that is not a 'healthy' weight for that individual. It would be like starving a St. Bernard because a study of dogs shows that greyhounds live longer. We are genetically like different breeds of dogs, but we can't tell what breed we are by looking (p. 44).

FAT STUDIES AS AN ACADEMIC DISCIPLINE

In the 1980s and 1990s, researchers from the size-acceptance movement tended to be trained in health-related disciplines such as medicine, public health, nutrition, and exercise physiology. Their research examined and critiqued the health risks of fatness and the effectiveness of dieting. In the twenty-first century, fat studies has become more interdisciplinary. The Popular Culture Association and the National Women's Studies Association have fat studies tracks. The Smith College conference Fat and the Academy in 2006 focused on fat studies as an academic discipline, and the *New York Times* focused on fat studies in academia later that year (Ellin 2006). Fat studies became the focus of research in literature, cultural studies, theater, film and media studies, and the fine arts (see Rothblum and Solovay 2009). Scholars have examined fat characters in short stories, novels, television sitcoms, films, and plays.

A major focus on fat studies as social inequality needs to come from the social sciences, such as psychology, sociology, political science, and economics. There has been a significant body of research focusing on the stigma of weight (see Brownell, Puhl, Schwartz, and Rudd 2005). Social scientists have examined weight bias among children, adolescents, and adults, and the consequences of negative attitudes for social relationships (Sobal 2005) and self-esteem (Crocker and Garcia 2005). Schools have become alarmed about the rise of bullying and its association with psychological and physical problems; fat children are often the victims of bullying (Weinstock and Krehbiel 2009). Despite the large literature on violence against women, there is little attention on physical and sexual violence toward women because of their weight or appearance (Royce 2009). Prohaska and Gailey (2009) have described "hogging," the practice of men preying on fat women who are viewed as easy targets for sexual satisfaction. There has also been focus on weight bias by medical and mental health professionals, landlords, employers, and the media (see Rothblum 1992 for a review).

There has also been a surge of fat-positive movement and exercise programs. Lyons and Burgard (1990) published the book *Great Shape: The First Fitness Guide for Large Women*. As Ellison states:

> Despite cultural limitations faced by fat women who wanted to exercise, an independent fat women's only aerobics culture was thriving in Canada and the United States by 1990. What happened? Working against the notion that fatness was emblematic of a moral failing (laziness, overeating or ignorance), self-identified fat women developed aerobics classes for other fat women. Often driven by the politics of the fat liberation and fat acceptance movements, these classes offered a space where fat women could explore their physicality with women they perceived to be like themselves.
>
> (2009, p. 313)

Movement groups for large women, such as fat women's dance, fat women's yoga, fat women's scuba diving, and fat burlesque, began in some areas in North America and scholars wrote about these initiatives (e.g., Asbill 2009; Schuster and Tealer 2009).

The "fatosphere"—Internet sites on fat studies—proliferated in the past decade, with over twenty sites such as *BigFatBlog.com*, *FatStudies.com*, and *ShowMeTheData.com*, the latter for fat studies researchers. Fatshionista (www. fatshionista.com/cms/) focuses on fat fashion. The web site www.fatso.com is "For people who don't apologize for their size." *BodyImageHealth.org* is described as "Building health body esteem in a body toxic world," *AdiosBarbie.com* is for "A body lovin' site for every body," and *BodyPositive.com* is about "Boosting body image at any weight."

At a time when people in the United States are preoccupied with weight but also living longer, fat studies activists are working to ensure that people get on with their lives and accept their bodies. There are far more serious issues to worry about than weight. Just as other oppressed groups have fought for their rights, fat activists and the emerging scholarly discipline of fat studies need to continue examining the impact of weight-based prejudice and how to overcome it.

ACKNOWLEDGEMENTS

The author would like to thank Nanette Gartrell, Marny Hall, Marcia Hill, and Penny Sablove for their helpful reading of this chapter and their comments.

REFERENCES

Amy, N., A. Aalborg, P. Lyons, and L. Keranen. 2005. "Barriers to Routine Gynecological Cancer Screening for Obese White and African American Obese Women." *International Journal of Obesity (London)* 30(1): 147–155.

Asbill, D. L. 2009. "'I'm allowed to be a sexual being': The Distinctive Social Conditions of the Fat Burlesque Stage," In *The Fat Studies Reader*, eds. E. D. Rothblum and S. Solovay, 299–304. New York: New York University Press.

Bacon, L. 2008. *Health at Every Size: The Surprising Truth about Your Weight.* Dallas, TX: Benbella Books.

Bergman, S. B. 2009. "Part-time Fatso." In *The Fat Studies Reader*, eds. E. D. Rothblum and S. Solovay, 139–142. New York: New York University Press.

Blumberg, P., and L. P. Mellis. 1985. "Medical Students' Attitudes toward the Obese and the Morbidly Obese." *International Journal of Eating Disorders* 4: 169–175.

Boero, N. 2009. "Fat Kids, Working Moms, and the 'Epidemic Of Obesity': Race, Class and Mother Blame." In *The Fat Studies Reader*, eds. E. D. Rothblum and S. Solovay, 113–119. New York: New York University Press.

Brand, P. A., E. D. Rothblum, and L. J. Solomon. 1992. "A Comparison of Lesbians, Gay Men, and Heterosexuals on Weight and Restrained Eating." *International Journal of Eating Disorders* 11: 253–259.

Breytspraak, L. M., J. McGee, J. C. Conger, J. L. Whatly, and J. T. Moore. 1977. "Sensitizing Medical Students to Impression Formation Processes in the Patient Interview." *Journal of Medical Education* 52: 47–54.

Brownell, K. D., R. M. Puhl, M. B. Schwartz, and L. Rudd. 2005. *Weight Bias: Nature, Consequences, and Remedies.* New York: Guilford.

Brownmiller, S. 1984. *Femininity.* New York: Fawcett Columbine.

Burgard, D. 2009. "What Is 'Health at Every Size'?" In *The Fat Studies Reader*, eds. E. D. Rothblum and S. Solovay, 42–53. New York: New York University Press.

Campos, P. 2004. *The Obesity Myth: Why America's Obsession with Weight Is Hazardous to Your Health.* New York: Gotham.

Crocker, J., and J. A. Garcia. 2005. "Self-esteem and the Stigma of Obesity." In *Weight Bias: Nature, Consequences, and Remedies*, eds. K. D. Brownell, R. M. Puhl, M. B. Schwartz, and L. Rudd, 165–174. New York: Guilford.

Ellin, Abby. November 26, 2006. "Big People on Campus." *New York Times.*

Ellison, J. 2009. "Not Jane Fonda: Aerobics for Fat Women Only". In *The Fat Studies Reader,* eds. E. D. Rothblum and S. Solovay, 312–319. New York: New York University Press.

Ernsberger, P. 2009. "Does Social Class Explain the Connection between Weight and Health?" In *The Fat Studies Reader*, eds. E. D. Rothblum and S. Solovay, 25–36. New York: New York University Press.

Fikkan, J., and E. D. Rothblum. 2005. "Weight Bias in Employment." In *Bias, Stigma, Discrimination, and Obesity* , eds. K. D. Brownell, R. M. Puhl, M. B. Schwartz, and L. Rudd, 13–28. New York: Guilford Publications.

Fishman, S. Accessed June 30, 2008. "Life in the Fat Underground." http://www.largesse. net/Archives/FU/Life%20In%20The%20Fat%20Underground%20by%20Sara%20Fis hman.html.

Fraser, L. 2009. "The Inner Corset: A Brief History of Fat in the U.S." In *The Fat Studies Reader*, eds. E. D. Rothblum and S. Solovay, 11–14. New York: New York University Press.

Freedman, E. 2007. Compact disc: *Someday Has Come.*

Freeman, R. 1986. *Beauty Bound: Why We Pursue the Myth in the Mirror.* Lexington, MA: D.C. Heath.

Freespirit, J., and Aldebaran. 1983. "Fat Liberation Manifesto." In *Shadow on a Tightrope: Writings by Women on Fat Oppression*, eds. L. Schoenfielder and B. Wieser, 52–53. San Francisco: Spinsters/Aunt Lute.

Gaesser, G. 2009. "Is 'Permanent Weight Loss' an Oxymoron? The Statistics on Weight Loss and the National Weight Control Registry." In *The Fat Studies Reader*, eds. E. D. Rothblum and S. Solovay, 37–41. New York: New York University Press.

Johannes, L., and S. Stecklow. February 9, 1998. "Dire Warnings about Obesity Rely on a Slippery Statistic." *Wall Street Journal.* B1.

Kolata, G. April 29. 2005. "Still Counting on Calorie Counting." *New York Times*, C1.

Lyons, P. 2009. "Prescription for Harm: Diet Industry Influence, Public Health Policy and the 'Obesity Epidemic.'" In *The Fat Studies Reader*, eds. E. D. Rothblum and S. Solovay, 75–87. New York: New York University Press.

Lyons, P., and D. Burgard. 1990. *Great Shape: The First Fitness Guide for Large Women.* Palo Alto: Bull Publishing.

Maddox, G. L., and V. Liederman. 1969. "Overweight as Social Desirability with Medical Implications." *Journal of Medical Education* 44: 214–220.

McKay, B. July 23, 2002. "Who You Calling Fat?" *Wall Street Journal*, B1.

Mundy, A. 2001. *Dispensing with the Truth: The Victims, the Drug Companies, and the Dramatic Story behind the Battle over Fen-Phen.* New York: St. Martin's Press.

Paul, R. J., and J. B. Townsend. 1995. "Shape Up or Ship Out? Employment Discrimination against the Overweight." *Employee Responsibilities and Rights Journal* 8(2): 133–145.

Prohaska, A., and J. Gailey. 2009. "Fat Women as "Easy Targets": Achieving Masculinity through Hogging." In *The Fat Studies Reader*, eds. E. D. Rothblum and S. Solovay, 158–166. New York: New York University Press.

Puhl, R., and K. D. Brownell. 2001. "Bias, Discrimination, and Obesity." *Obesity Research* 9(12): 788–805.

Reese, S. 2000. "New Concepts In Health Benefits: Employee Incentives." *Business and Health,* 18(5): 21.

Roehling, M. V. 1999. "Weight-based Discrimination in Employment: Psychological And Legal Aspects." *Personnel Psychology* 52(4): 969–1016.

Roehling, M. V. 2002. "Weight Discrimination in the American Workplace: Ethical Issues and Analysis." *Journal of Business Ethics* 40: 177–189.

Rothblum, E. D. 1992. "The Stigma of Women's Weight: Social and Economic Realities." *Feminism and Psychology* 2(1): 61–73.

Rothblum, E. D. 1994. "I'll Die for the Revolution but Don't Ask Me Not to Diet: Feminism and the Continuing Stigmatization of Obesity." In *Feminist Perspectives on Eating Disorders*, eds. P. Fallon, M. Katzman, and S. Wooley, 53–76. New York: Guilford Press.

Rothblum, E. D. 1999. "Contradictions and Confounds in Coverage of Obesity: Psychology Journals, Textbooks, and Media." *Journal of Social Issues* 55: 355–369.

Rothblum, E. D. 2002. "Gay and Lesbian Body Images." In *Body Images: A Handbook of Theory, Research, and Clinical Practice*, eds. T. F. Cash and T. Pruzinsky, 257–265. New York: Guilford Press.

Rothblum, E. D., P. A. Brand, C. T. Miller, and H. A. Oetjen. 1990. "The Relationship between Obesity, Employment Discrimination, and Employment-Related Victimization." *Journal of Vocational Behavior* 37: 251–266.

Rothblum, E. D. and S. Solovay (eds.). 2009. *The Fat Studies Reader*. New York: New York University Press.

Royce, T. 2009. "The Shape of Abuse: Fat Oppression as a Form of Violence against Women." In *The Fat Studies Reader*, eds. E. D. Rothblum and S. Solovay, 151–157. New York: New York University Press.

Schuster, D., and L. Tealer. 2009. "Exorcising the Exercise Myth: Creating Women of Substance." In *The Fat Studies Reader*, eds. E. D. Rothblum and S. Solovay, 320–324. New York: New York University Press.

Serdula, M. K., A.H. Mokdad, D. F. Williamson, D. A. Galuska, J. M. Mendlein, and G. W. Heath 1999. "Prevalence of Attempting Weight Loss and Strategies for Controlling Weight." *Journal of the American Medical Association* 282: 1353–1358.

Siever, M. D. 1994. "Sexual Orientation and Gender as Factors in Socioculturally Acquired Vulnerability to Body Dissatisfaction and Eating Disorders." *Journal of Consulting and Clinical Psychology* 62: 252–260.

Sobal, J. 2005. "Social Consequences of Weight Bias by Partners, Friends, and Strangers." In *Weight Bias: Nature, Consequences, and Remedies*, eds. K. D. Brownell, R. M. Puhl, M. B. Schwartz, and L. Rudd,.150–164. New York: Guilford.

Solovay, S. 2000. *Tipping the Scales of Justice: Fighting Weight-Based Discrimination*. New York: Prometheus Books.

Taub, J. 1999. "Bisexual Women and Beauty Norms: A Qualitative Examination." *Journal of Lesbian Studies* 3: 27–36.

Thompson, J. K. April, 1986. "Larger than Life." *Psychology Today*, 41–44. Vol. 20, 4, 1986, p. 38.

Tiggemann, M., and E. D, Rothblum. 1988. "Gender Differences in Social Consequences of Perceived Overweight in the United States and Australia." *Sex Roles* 18: 75–86.

Wann, M. 2009. "Fat Studies: An Invitation to Revolution." In *The Fat Studies Reader*, eds. E. D. Rothblum and S. Solovay, ix–xxv. New York: New York University Press.

Weinstock, J., and M. Krehbiel. 2009. "Fat Youth as Common Targets for Bullying." In *The Fat Studies Reader*, eds. E. D. Rothblum and S. Solovay, 120–126. New York: New York University Press.

Wooley, S., and D. Garner. 1991. "Obesity Treatment: The High Cost of False Hope." *Journal of the American Dietetic Association* 91: 1248–1251.

PART II

DATA AND
METHODS

CHAPTER 12

PUBLICLY AVAILABLE DATA USEFUL FOR SOCIAL SCIENCE RESEARCH ON OBESITY

INAS RASHAD KELLY

INTRODUCTION

THIS chapter should prove useful to obesity researchers conducting empirical analyses using nationally representative, individual-level data that are publicly available. The goal is to facilitate empirical social research on obesity, and the chapter focuses on data from the United States. This overview is by no means exhaustive, and the most commonly used and easily accessible data sets are the focus of this chapter. Data sources with information on weight and height (both measured and self-reported) are highlighted, in addition to some information on caloric intake and physical activity, which are core lifestyle determinants of body weight.

Through *Healthy People*, the United States Department of Health and Human Services provides science-based, ten-year national objectives for promoting health and preventing disease. Two proposed objectives for *Healthy People* 2020 have not been modified from *Healthy People* 2010, which are to (1) reduce the proportion of children and adolescents who are overweight or obese (objective 19–3), and (2) reduce the proportion of adults who are obese (objective 19–2).[1] The need for more research on the determinants, the consequences, and the solutions for obesity is rising, and this chapter provides an overview of some useful data sets that can be used by obesity researchers in analyzing these topics. The sections that follow list cross-sectional and longitudinal data sources that are useful for research on obesity in adults, adolescents, children, and infants. Supplemental data sources that are not on the individual level but have a geographical area as the unit of observation, which are useful for merging with individual-level data sets, are suggested in the Discussion section below. The availability of the data, the years for which key variables of interest are available, and how researchers have already utilized these data in the context of obesity are summarized. Most of the surveys are ongoing, and so the years available pertain to those available at the time of this writing (late 2009). Summaries are listed in tables 12.1 and 12.2 for cross-sectional and longitudinal data sources, respectively.

Many surveys include self-reported values of weight and height rather than measured values, which are much more objective in nature. This may lead to self-report error, which tends to be non-random in nature and sometimes problematic, and, in this case, the underreporting of weight or overreporting of height may not be uncommon. Moreover, error due to rounding is problematic. Self-report error in this context will have a particular effect on classification of obese status, more so than affecting results of regression analyses (Spencer et al. 2002). One can correct for this type of error using data sets that collect information on both objective and subjective measures. Measured weight and height are available in all waves of the National Health and Nutrition Examination Surveys (NHANES), in addition to self-reported weight and height. As such, it is possible to exploit this information and use both objective and subjective anthropometric measures to correct for self-reported data in other surveys. The adjustment is done separately by age, gender, and race (Rashad 2008; Chou et al. 2004; Cawley 1999). A more thorough adjustment for BMI that distinguishes between fatness and fat-free mass, thus taking body composition into account, can be made using NHANES data (Burkhauser and Cawley 2008).

DATA SOURCES: CROSS-SECTIONAL

American Time Use Survey (ATUS)

The American Time Use Survey is conducted by the U.S. Census Bureau and sponsored by the Bureau of Labor Statistics (see http://www.bls.gov/tus/). ATUS data files,

---

1 See http://www.healthypeople.gov/ for more detail.

Table 12.1. Cross-Sectional Data Sources

Data source	Years of study	Years weight and height available	Self-reported or measured?	Age groups	Web site	Geographic identifier
ATUS	2003–2008	2006–2008	Self-reported	15+	http://www.bls.gov/tus	CBSA
BRFSS	1984–2008	All	Self-reported	Adults 18+	http://www.cdc.gov/brfss	County
NHANESI	1971–1975	All	Measured	1–74	http://www.cdc.gov/nchs/nhanes/nhanesi.htm	Region in public-use data, county in restricted use data
NHANESII	1976–1980	All	Measured	6mo–74	http://www.cdc.gov/nchs/nhanes/nhanesii.htm	Region in public-use data, county in restricted use data
NHANESIII	1988–1994	All	Measured	2mo+	http://www.cdc.gov/nchs/nhanes/nh3data.htm	Region in public-use data (also county for counties with populations >= 500,000), county in restricted use data
NHANES-Continuous	1999–2006	All	Measured	1–85	http://www.cdc.gov/nchs/nhanes/nhanes99_00.htm	National-level, zip code for restricted use data
NHESI	1959–1962	All	Measured	18–79	http://www.cdc.gov/nchs/nhanes/cyclei_iii.htm#Cycle1	Region in public-use data, county in restricted use data
NHESII	1963–1965	All	Measured	6–11	http://www.cdc.gov/nchs/nhanes/cyclei_iii.htm#Cycle2	Region in public-use data, county in restricted use data
NHESIII	1966–1970	All	Measured	12–17	http://www.cdc.gov/nchs/nhanes/cyclei_iii.htm#Cycle3	Region in public-use data, county in restricted use data
NHIS	1957–2009 (available starting 1963)	1976–2009	Self-reported	Children & Adults	http://www.cdc.gov/nchs/nhis.htm	Region in public-use data (SMSA is identified in data years 1969-84 if the sample person lived in one of the larger SMSAs), geocodes only through secure data
YRBSS	1991–2007 (biennially)	1999–2007	Self-reported	Adolescents Grades 9–12 (~12–18)	http://www.cdc.gov/HealthyYouth/yrbs/index.htm	National-level, state/district files available

Table 12.2. Longitudinal Data Sources

Data source	Years of study	Years weight and height available	Self-reported or measured?	Age groups	Web site	Geographic identifier
AddHealth	1994–2008 (4 waves: I grades 7–12 1994–1995, II 1996, III 2002–2003 ages 18–26, IV 2007–2008 ages 26–32)	Waves I, II, IV	Self-reported	Children/Adults	http://www.cpc.unc.edu/projects/addhealth	Region in public-use data, geocodes only through secure data facility
ECLS-B	2001–2007 (5 waves: 9mo, 2yr, preschool, K2006, K2007)	All	Measured	Infants/Children	http://nces.ed.gov/ecls/birth.asp	Zip code
ECLS-K	1998–2007 (7 waves: K (fall&spring), 1st (fall & spring), 3rd (spring), 5th (spring), 8th (spring))	All	Measured	Children	http://nces.ed.gov/ecls/kindergarten.asp	Zip code/Census block/tract/school lat/long for restricted-use data, Census region for public-use data
HRS	1992–2008 (biennially)	All	Self-reported (measured in 2004)	50+	http://hrsonline.isr.umich.edu/	Zip code & Census tract for restricted use data
MEPS	1996–2008	Children 1996–2008, Adults 17+ 2001–2008, BMI only, weight & height in 2000 (linked to NHIS starting 1996)	Self-reported	All	http://www.meps.ahrq.gov/mepsweb/	Region in public-use data, state/county/Census tract in restricted use data
NLSY79	1979–2006 (biennially starting 1994)	Height: 1981, 1982, 1983, 1985, 2006. Weight: 1981, 1982, 1985, 1986, 1988-1990, 1992-2006.	Self-reported	14–24	http://www.bls.gov/nls/nlsy79.htm	Region in public-use data, county for restricted data

	Waves	Height/weight measured	Reporting	Age	URL	Geographic identifiers
NLSY79-CYA	1986–2006 (biennially)	All	Child: measured or mother report, Young adult: self-reported	Children/Young Adults 15+	http://www.bls.gov/nls/nlsy79ch.htm	Region in public-use data, county for restricted data
NLSY97	1997–2007	All	Self-reported	Children/Adults 12+	http://www.bls.gov/nls/nlsy97.htm	Region in public-use data, county for restricted data
NLS-Mature Women	1967–2003 (1967–1969, 1971–1972, 1974, 1976–1977, 1979, 1981–1982, 1984, 1986–1987, 1989, 1992, 1995, 1997, 1999, 2001, 2003)	Height: 1992, 1997, 1999, 2001, 2003. Weight: 1992, 1995, 1997, 1999, 2001, 2003.	Self-reported	30–44	http://www.bls.gov/nls/nlsorig.htm	Region in public-use data, county for restricted data
NLS-Young Women	1968–2003 (1968–1973, 1975, 1977–1978, 1980, 1982–1983, 1985, 1987–1988, 1991, 1993, 1995, 1997, 1999, 2001, 2003)	Height: 1991. Weight: 1991, 1995.	Self-reported	14–24	http://www.bls.gov/nls/nlsorig.htm	Region in public-use data, county for restricted data
NLS-OlderMen	1966–1990 (1966–1969, 1971, 1973, 1975–1976, 1978, 1980–1981, 1983, 1990)	1973, 1990	Self-reported	45–59	http://www.bls.gov/nls/nlsorig.htm	Region in public-use data, county for restricted data
NLS-YoungMen	1966–1981 (1966–1971, 1973, 1975–1976, 1978, 1980–1981)	1973	Self-reported	14–24	http://www.bls.gov/nls/nlsorig.htm	Region in public-use data, county for restricted data
PSID	1968–2009, CDS: 1997, 2002–2003.	Main (head & wife): 1986, 1999–2009, CDS: 1997, 2002–2003.	Self-reported, CDS: measured	All	http://psidonline.isr.umich.edu	Region in public-use data, county for restricted data

collected from over 85,000 interviews conducted from 2003 to 2008, are used by researchers to study a broad range of issues. The survey provides nationally representative estimates of how, where, and with whom Americans spend their time.[2] Over the 2006–2008 survey period, the Economic Research Service sponsored the Eating and Health Module. The module contains questions on whether respondents ate or drank while engaged in other activities, such as driving or watching TV; self-reported height and weight; participation in the Food Stamp Program; children's consumption of meals obtained at school; grocery shopping and meal preparation; and household income. With recent increases in food stamp take-up (DeParle and Gebeloff 2009), it is possible to exploit this information in analyzing the food stamp program and obesity.

ATUS data files can be linked to data files from the Current Population Survey (CPS). Studies that have used this module in the obesity context include: Christian (2009), in his analysis of commuting to work on physical activity and BMI; and Hamermesh (2009), in his analysis of time use and obesity. Physical activity has been analyzed using the ATUS, by Christian (2009), Mullahy and Robert (2008); and Cawley and Liu (2007), among others.

Behavioral Risk Factor Surveillance System (BRFSS)

The Centers for Disease Control (CDC) conduct state-level analyses for overweight and obesity using the BRFSS (see http://www.cdc.gov/brfss/). As with the NHANES and National Health Examination Survey (NHES) data sets, while these sources are ideal for analyzing BMI, they are not as suitable for analyzing labor market outcomes, as family/household income is reported rather than individual income.

As the largest telephone-based health survey available, the Behavioral Risk Factor Surveillance System has tracked health conditions and risk behaviors for adults 18 years of age and older in the United States. The survey is conducted by state health departments in collaboration with the Centers for Disease Control.[3] While only 15 states participated in 1984, this number grew to 33 in 1987, to 45 in 1990, and to all 50 states plus the District of Columbia in 1996.[4] These data contain information on self-reported weight and height in each year, and county identifiers are publicly available from their web site. That is, it is possible to download county

---

2 Source: http://www.bls.gov/tus/overview.htm#1.
3 Source: http://www.cdc.gov/brfss/about.htm.
4 The following 15 states were in the BRFSS in 1984: Arizona, California, Idaho, Illinois, Indiana, Minnesota, Montana, North Carolina, Ohio, Rhode Island, South Carolina, Tennessee, Utah, West Virginia, and Wisconsin. In 1985, Connecticut, the District of Columbia, Florida, Georgia, Kentucky Missouri, New York, and North Dakota entered the survey. In 1986, Alabama, Hawaii, Massachusetts, and New Mexico entered. In 1987, Maine, Maryland, Nebraska, New Hampshire, South Dakota, Texas, and Washington entered. In 1988, Iowa, Michigan, and Oklahoma entered. In 1989, Oregon, Pennsylvania, and Vermont entered. In 1989, Colorado, Delaware, Louisiana, Mississippi, and Virginia entered. In 1991, Alaska, Arkansas, and New Jersey entered. In 1992, Kansas and Nevada entered. Wyoming entered in 1994. Rhode Island, which entered the survey in 1984, was not in it in 1994. The District of Columbia, which entered in 1985, was not in the survey in 1995.

identifiers without a data protection plan in this case. Also provided is information on a variety of personal characteristics, including gender, age, education, marital status, and family income. As such, it is not as useful for predicting wages or individual-level income, but family income has been used as a proxy (Rashad 2008). In addition, measures on general health, cholesterol, cardiovascular illness, and diabetes are included, as well as self-reported anthropometric measures such as weight and height.[5] A useful tool on the BRFSS web site is the "Question Archives" link on the "Questionnaires" page,[6] which allows one to view the years available for various areas of interest, including nutrition intake and physical activity (detailed until 2000).

The BRFSS has been used in numerous obesity studies, including but not limited to: Dave and Kaestner (2009) for physical activity and Medicare; Zhang and Rashad (2008) in analyzing obesity and time preference; Card et al. (2004), who use data from 1999–2002 in analyzing health behaviors (including smoking, exercise, and obesity) and Medicare eligibility; Chou et al. (2004) in their analysis of the determinants of adult obesity, with a focus on fast food prevalence and cigarette prices; and Ruhm (2000) in analyzing whether recessions are beneficial for health.

National Health and Nutrition Examination Surveys (NHANES)

The Centers for Disease Control (CDC) track obesity using the NHANES and NHES data. While these sources are ideal for analyzing the body mass index (BMI), calculated as weight in kilograms divided by height in meters squared, in addition to nutrition and physical activity, they are not as suitable for analyzing labor market outcomes, as family/household income is reported rather than individual income. Employment status, however, is available.

The National Health and Nutrition Examination Survey (see http://www.cdc. gov/nchs/nhanes.htm) is a program of studies designed to assess the health and nutritional status of adults and children in the United States. The survey combines interviews and physical examinations and has information on measured weight and height in all waves. NHANES is conducted by the National Center for Health Statistics (NCHS), a part of the Centers for Disease Control and Prevention (CDC). NHANES data start in 1971 and consist of a series of surveys focusing on different population groups or health topics. NHANES data include demographic, socioeconomic, dietary, and health-related information. The examination components consist of medical, dental, and physiological measurements, as well as laboratory tests administered by highly trained medical personnel.[7]

---

5 The height variable in the BRFSS prior to 1990 appears to contain some errors for a small portion of the sample.

6 See http://www.cdc.gov/brfss/questionnaires/questionnaires.htm.

7 Source: http://www.cdc.gov/nchs/nhanes/about_nhanes.htm.

The first National Health and Nutrition Examination Survey (NHANES I) was conducted from 1971 to 1975 and contains data for approximately 32,000 persons from one to 74 years of age. The second National Health and Nutrition Examination Survey (NHANES II) was conducted from 1976 to 1980 and contains information on 27,801 persons from 6 months to 74 years of age. The third National Health and Nutrition Examination Survey (NHANES III) was conducted from 1988 to 1994 and contains data for 33,994 individuals ages 2 months and older. In 1999, the survey became a continuous program with a focus on a variety of health and nutrition variables. Continuous NHANES (1999–2006) is an ongoing survey examining a nationally representative sample of about 5,000 persons each year, conducted in two-year increments.

While the NHANES I data set is not longitudinal in nature, a longitudinal component of the NHANES I is available through the NHANES I Epidemiologic Follow-up Study (NHEFS).[8] Measured weight and height are available in all waves, in addition to self-reported weight and height. As previously mentioned, it is therefore possible to exploit this information and use both objective and subjective anthropometric measures to correct for self-reported data in other surveys. Moreover, starting with NHANES III, waist circumference, useful in measuring the metabolic syndrome, is available. Indeed, the National Institutes of Health identify cutoff points for waist circumference of 35 inches for women or 40 inches for men as related to a variety of obesity-related illnesses (Janssen et al. 2002). Moreoever, information on waist-to-hip ratio and bioelectrical impedance analysis (BIA) are available and have been exploited by Burkhauser and Cawley (2008).

Obesity studies that have used NHANES data include: Burkhauser and Cawley (2008) in stressing body composition over BMI; Wada and Tekin (2010) in analyzing body composition; Rashad et al. (2006) in analyzing determinants of increased body weight, including access to fast food; Rashad (2006) in analyzing the effects of caloric intake and physical activity on BMI; Bhattacharya et al. (2004) in analyzing BMI and the school lunch program; and Cutler et al. (2003) in looking at the role of technological change in the obesity context.

National Health Examination Survey (NHES)

The National Health Examination Surveys (see http://www.cdc.gov/nchs/nhanes/cyclerrm.htm#ag) preceded NHANES and contain responses to detailed questionnaires for medical and developmental histories; results of medical, dental, and psychological examinations, and vision and hearing tests; anthropometric measurements; and laboratory tests. Cycle I (NHES I) was conducted on a nationwide probability sample of approximately 7,800 individuals 18–79 years of age between 1959 and 1962. Cycle II (NHES II) was conducted on a nationwide probability sample of 7,417 children 6–11 years of age between 1963 and 1965. The NHES II

---

8 Those surveyed include all individuals 25–74 years of age who completed a medical examination at NHANES I in 1971–1975. See http://www.cdc.gov/nchs/nhanes/nhefs/nhefs.htm for more detail.

contains information on birth weight. Cycle III (NHES III) was conducted on a nationwide probability sample of 7,514 youths 12–17 years of age between 1966 and 1970. Measured weight and height are included in all samples. Nearly one-third of the children examined in Cycle II were also examined in Cycle III.[9] The National Center for Health Statistics provides more information on this initial survey (NCHS 1965), which is used in tracking earlier trends in obesity.

National Health Interview Survey (NHIS)

The National Health Interview Survey (see http://www.cdc.gov/nchs/nhis.htm) has monitored the health of the nation since 1957. Data starting 1963 are available online. NHIS data on a broad range of health topics are collected through personal household interviews and conducted by the Census Bureau. Survey results allow for the tracking of health status and health care access. While the NHIS is conducted on the national level, a few NHIS State Data files have been constructed to allow for the production of direct state estimates.

Self-reported weight and height are available in the NHIS from 1976 to 2009 in the "person" file. As a result of concerns regarding the confidentiality of respondents, beginning in 1997 the NHIS public-use data file excluded individuals with heights below 59 inches and above 76 inches and weights below 99 pounds and above 285 pounds (Nelson et al. 2003). While the NHIS is not longitudinal in nature, a longitudinal component of the NHIS is available on CD-ROM for 1986–1994. Studies using the NHIS in the obesity context include: Bhattacharya and Packalen (2008) in measuring the ex ante moral hazard that may arise in this context from a positive innovation externality; Bhattacharya and Sood (2007) to measure the obesity externality in health insurance using the 1997 NHIS; Kaushal (2007) in her analysis of the effect of food stamps on obesity; Finkelstein et al. (2003), who used the 1996–1997 NHIS in measuring the economic costs of obesity; and Kenkel (2000), who used the 1990 NHIS to estimate possible moral hazard. His analysis suggested that people with private health insurance were more likely to engage in health-promoting behaviors, with the exception of obesity for men.

Youth Risk Behavior Surveillance System (YRBSS)

The Youth Risk Behavior Surveillance System (see http://www.cdc.gov/Healthy Youth/yrbs/index.htm) monitors health-risk behaviors and the prevalence of obesity and asthma among adolescents in grades 9–12. The YRBSS includes a national school-based survey conducted by the CDC and state, territorial, tribal, and local surveys conducted by state, territorial, and local education and health agencies and tribal governments. The data are available biennially, and self-reported weight and

---

9 The Cycle III Extended Data Tape (EDT) allows identification of sample persons examined in both surveys.

height are available starting 1999. Detailed information on overweight perception is available in all YRBSS years. The YRBSS includes a national school-based survey conducted by the Centers for Disease Control and Prevention (CDC) and state, territorial, tribal, and local surveys conducted by state, territorial, and local education and health agencies and tribal governments. The surveys are conducted biennially, usually during the spring semester. The national survey provides information on students in grades 9–12 in public and private schools across the United States.[10]

Studies that have used these data in the obesity context include Dave and Rashad (2009), in their analysis of the effect of overweight status and perception on suicidal behaviors, and other studies in the public health literature that analyze trends in overweight and obesity among children and adolescents over time, such as Eaton et al. (2008) and Sturm (2005).

Data Sources: Longitudinal

Early Childhood Longitudinal Surveys (ECLS)

The Early Childhood Longitudinal Study program (see http://www.nces.ed.gov/ecls/), conducted by the National Center for Education Statistics (NCES), includes three longitudinal studies that examine child development, school readiness, and early school experiences. The birth cohort of the ECLS-B is a sample of children born in 2001 and followed from birth through kindergarten entry. Micro-data for the ECLS-B are only available through a restricted-use data license agreement, although tables can be generated through the online Data Analysis System.[11] The Early Childhood Longitudinal Study Kindergarten Cohort of 1998–1999 (ECLS-K) is a sample of children followed from kindergarten through the eighth grade. The ECLS: 2011 kindergarten class of 2010–2011 cohort will follow a sample of children from kindergarten through the fifth grade.[12] ECLS data provide a wide range of information on student backgrounds and comprehensive information on demographic characteristics and parental background. Census region is available on public-use files.[13] For the ECLS, information on mother's education, a comprehensive SES measure, and birth weight are available. Moreover, the ECLS-B has self-reported information on the mother's prepregnancy weight and weight gain during pregnancy, in their 9-month parent questionnaire, and self-reported information on the resident father's weight and height, in their 9-month resident father questionnaire.

---

10 Source: http://www.cdc.gov/HealthyYouth/yrbs/brief.htm.

11 See http://nces.ed.gov/das/.

12 For more information on the latest cohort, see http://nces.ed.gov/ecls/kindergarten2010.asp.

13 Table 7-16 in the following document shows variables not on public-use files for the ECLS-K: http://nces.ed.gov/ecls/data/ECLSK_K8_Manual_part2.pdf.

Measured weight and height of the child are included in all waves. Studies that have used the ECLS in the obesity context include: Anderson and Whitaker (2009) to estimate obesity prevalence in preschool in the ECLS-B; Schanzenbach (2009) in analyzing the effect of school lunches on childhood obesity; and Datar and Sturm (2004) in looking at physical education and BMI in elementary school, among others.

Health and Retirement Study (HRS)

The Health and Retirement Study (see http://hrsonline.isr.umich.edu/) is an ongoing longitudinal study conducted by the Institute for Social Research at the University of Michigan, and is repeated biennially. Aside from self-reported weight and height, the HRS includes information on physical and mental health, insurance coverage, financial status, family support systems, labor market status, and retirement planning. Weight and height are measured in 2004. Prior to 1998, the HRS cohort included individuals born between 1931 and 1941, and a separate Study of Assets and Health Dynamics Among the Oldest Old (AHEAD) included individuals born before 1924. The original sample frames of the HRS and AHEAD studies comprised of 12,832 and 8,222 individuals, respectively. Since 1998, AHEAD respondents have been contacted as part of a joint data collection effort with the HRS, and the sample frame was also expanded by including cohorts born between 1924 and 1930 and those born between 1942 and 1947.

Starting in 2006, the HRS provided Biomarker Data through their Enhanced Face-to-Face Interviews, through funding from the National Institute on Aging and support from the Social Security Administration. The survey was conducted by the Institute for Social Research Survey Research Center at the University of Michigan. The physical measures and biomarkers component includes information on: waist circumference, which, as previously mentioned, is an important predictor of obesity-related diseases; height; weight; and measures of cardiovascular health. In addition, information on cholesterol and HbA1c levels, important in measuring blood sugar levels for people with diabetes, was gathered. More information can be found at http://hrsonline.isr.umich.edu/modules/meta/bio2006/desc/biomkr06dd.pdf.

Studies using the HRS in this context include: Dave and Kaestner (2009) in estimating moral hazard due to health insurance; and Weng et al. (2004) in finding an increased likelihood of obesity for both women and men with each additional child.

Medical Expenditure Panel Survey (MEPS)

The Medical Expenditure Panel Survey (see http://www.meps.ahrq.gov/mepsweb/), which began in 1996, is the primary data set used in calculating the health care costs of obesity. It is a set of large-scale surveys of families and individuals, their medical providers, and employers across the United States. MEPS collects data on the specific health services that Americans use, how frequently they use them, the cost of these services, and how they are paid for, as well as data on the cost, scope, and breadth of health insurance coverage. MEPS currently has two major components, the Household and Insurance Components. The Household Component provides data from individual households, their members, and their medical providers. The Insurance Component is a separate survey of employers that provides data on employer-based health insurance.

Self-reported weight and height are available starting in 2000 (available in the Household Component), with only BMI available (i.e., not weight and height separately) starting in 2001 in public-use versions. MEPS data files can be linked to data files pertaining to the prior year from the National Health Interview Survey (NHIS), as a subsample of NHIS respondents is chosen to be surveyed for MEPS in the following year starting in 1996. Studies that have used the MEPS data in the obesity context include previously mentioned studies that also use the NHIS: Bhattacharya and Packalen (2008); Bhattacharya and Sood (2007); and Finkelstein et al. (2003).

National Longitudinal Survey of Adolescent Health (Add Health)

The National Longitudinal Study of Adolescent Health (see http://www.cpc.unc. edu/projects/addhealth) is a longitudinal study of a nationally representative sample of adolescents in grades 7–12 in the United States during the 1994–1995 school year. The Add Health cohort has been followed into young adulthood with four in-home interviews, the most recent in 2008, when the sample was aged 24–32. Add Health combines longitudinal survey data on respondents' social, economic, psychological, and physical well-being, in addition to data on the family, neighborhood, community, school, friendships, peer groups, and romantic relationships. This allows for the analysis of the effect of behaviors in adolescence on adult outcomes in a panel framework. The fourth wave of interviews expanded the collection of biological data covered, allowing researchers to analyze health trajectories. Note that the public-use version contains only a subset of the full sample of respondents.

Self-reported weight and height are available in Waves I, II, and IV as part of the Adolescent In-Home Interview (Section 4: General Health and Diet). Studies using the Add Health in this context include: Sabia (2007), who analyzed the effect of body weight on academic performance; Gordon-Larsen et al. (2006) in looking at inequality in the built environment and physical activity and obesity; and Popkin and Udry (1998) in summarizing adolescent obesity in immigrants.

National Longitudinal Surveys of Youth (NLSY)

The National Longitudinal Surveys of Youth (see http://www.bls.gov/nls/) are a set of ongoing surveys designed to gather information at multiple points in time on the labor market activities and other significant life events. The 1979 cohort of the National Longitudinal Survey of Youth (NLSY79) is a nationally representative sample of 12,686 young men and women who were 14–22 years old when they were first surveyed in 1979. These individuals were interviewed annually through 1994 and are currently interviewed on a biennial basis. In 1986, a separate survey of all children born to NLSY79 female respondents began (the Child-Young Adult National Longitudinal Survey, or the NLS-CYA), with survey questions on assessment as well as additional demographic and development information collected from either the mother or child. For children aged 10 and older, information has been collected from the children biennially since 1988 on a variety of factors, including child-parent interaction, attitudes toward schooling, dating and friendship patterns, religious attendance, health, substance use, and home responsibilities. Out of 6,283 females in the NLSY79, 5,418 were interviewed in 1986, of which 2,922 were mothers. These mothers had 5,255 children in 1986, 4,971 of which were interviewed. In 2002, 7,467 children or young adults were interviewed. The 1997 cohort of the National Longitudinal Survey of Youth 1997 (NLSY97) is a survey of young men and women born in 1980–1984; respondents were ages 12–17 when first interviewed in 1997.[14] The NLS-CYA has information on the mother's prepregnancy weight and weight gain during pregnancy. Overweight perception is reported for young adults in the NLS-CYA in 2006 and regularly in the NLSY97, which also has information on parents' weight and height in 1997. In studies predicting BMI or obesity using the NLS-CYA or the NLSY97, mother's BMI may be used as a proxy for the genetic component of BMI.

Weight and height are available in several but not all years. This is not too problematic for height, which remains rather stable for young individuals after age 18. Self-reported weight is available in the NLSY79 in 1981, 1982, 1985, 1986, 1988–1990, and 1992–2006. Self-reported height is available in 1981, 1982, 1983, 1985, and 2006. For the NLS-CYA, measured (or reported by the mother) weight and height are available for children, while weight and height are self-reported for young adults. Self-reported weight and height are included in all years for the NLSY97 data set.

Obesity studies that have used the NLSY include but are not limited to: Chou et al. (2008) in analyzing the influence of fast food advertising on obesity in children; Wada and Tekin (2010) in their analysis of body composition; Smith et al. (2005) in the context of obesity and time preference; Zagorsky (2005) in analyzing the relationship between individual wealth and obesity; Baum and Ford (2004) in predicting wages; Cawley (2004) in predicting wages; Anderson et al. (2003) in analyzing maternal employment and childhood obesity; Cawley (1999) in analyzing food addiction; and Averett and Korenman (1996) in their analysis of the effect of body weight on wages.

National Longitudinal Survey Original Cohorts (NLS)

The original four National Longitudinal Survey cohorts of men and women (Mature and Young Women, Older and Young Men) were selected because their labor market decisions were of particular interest to policy makers at the time

---

14 Source: http://www.bls.gov/nls/overview.htm.

(see http://www.bls.gov/nls/). Female respondents continue to be interviewed on a biennial basis, and have been interviewed for over three decades. Both men's cohorts were discontinued in 1990 (for older men) and 1981 (for young men).

Interviews began in 1966 for both the NLS older men and the NLS young men. The older men consisted of a group of 5,020 men ages 45–59, while there were 5,225 young men, ages 14–24. Data collection focused on topics such as work and non-work experiences, retirement planning, health conditions, insurance coverage, job changes, retirement, and the ways in which respondents spent their leisure time. Although interviews with these cohorts ceased in 1981, information was collected in 1990 for older men from respondents and widows or other next-of-kin deceased sample members. Cause of death information was also collected from state vital records departments in 1990. For young men, data collection focused on education experiences, career choices, marital history, and work history.[15]

The NLS of mature women was a group of women in their thirties and early forties, who when surveyed provided interesting information on their varied roles as homemakers, mothers, and labor force participants. The NLS of young women was comprised of women in their teen and early twenties who were completing school, making initial career and job decisions, and starting families. Respondents in the mature and young women's cohorts continue to be interviewed on a biennial basis, and have been interviewed for over three decades. Interviews started in 1967 for the NLS mature women, a group of 5,083 women ages 20–44, and in 1968 for the NLS young women, a cohort of 5,159 women ages 14–24.[16]

While the original cohorts provide rich longitudinal data, self-reported weight and height are available in a limited number of years. See table 12.2 for available years.

Panel Study of Income Dynamics (PSID)

The Panel Study of Income Dynamics (see http://psidonline.isr.umich.edu/) was begun in 1968 and covers a representative sample of U.S. individuals (men, women, and children) and the family units in which they reside. By the end of 2003 survey, the PSID had collected information from over 65,000 individuals spanning as many as 36 years of their lives. Starting 1997, the surveys were conducted biennially.

Between 1968 and 1972, data collection took place through in-person interviews using paper and pencil questionnaires. Thereafter, most interviews were telephone interviews or, starting 1993, computer-assisted telephone interviews.[17]

Self-reported weight and height are included in the PSID in 1986, and 1999–2009 for the head of the household and the wife. The Child Development Supplement (CDS) of the Panel Study of Income Dynamics (PSID) includes measured weight and height, as well as time diaries of the child's activities. This was started in 1997

---

15 Source: http://www.bls.gov/nls/overview.htm.
16 Source: http://www.bls.gov/nls/overview.htm.
17 Source: http://psidonline.isr.umich.edu/Guide/Overview.html.

for children ages 0–12, who were followed over time. Interviews were in-person until age 18, after which they were telephone interviews for the Transition into Adulthood files (started in 2005 and repeated biennially).[18] The second interview, conducted in 2002–2003, re-interviewed children ages 5–18, and the third interview was conducted in 2007–2008 and re-interviewed children ages 10–19. CDS information can be linked to the main PSID, providing household information useful in analyzing a child's environment.

Studies using the PSID in this context include: Fertig et al. (2009), who explore mechanisms behind maternal employment and childhood obesity using the Child Development Supplement; and Conley and Glauber (2007), who look at gender, body mass, and SES. Burkhauser and Cawley (2008) apply the aforementioned correction for body composition using NHANES III to the PSID in order to show that while fatness is positively correlated with disability, results using fat-free mass yield a negative correlation.

Additional U.S. Data

Monitoring the Future (MTF)

Funded under grants from the National Institute on Drug Abuse, a part of the National Institutes of Health, MTF is an ongoing study of the behaviors, attitudes, and values of American secondary school students, college students, and young adults (see http://www.monitoringthefuture.org/). Questions on self-reported weight and height in the MTF are form-specific and not core-specific, so not all individuals respond to these questions. Each year, a total of approximately 50,000 8th, 10th, and 12th grade students are surveyed (12th graders since 1975, and 8th and 10th graders since 1991). In addition, annual follow-up questionnaires are mailed to a sample of each graduating class for a number of years after their initial participation. The MTF is publicly available at http://www.icpsr.umich.edu/SAMHDA/ (save for thorough geographic identifiers) and has been used by Powell et al. (2007) in analyzing the effect of food prices and food outlets on food consumption, BMI, and obesity among adolescents.

National Survey of Family Growth (NSFG)

Initially designed to be the national fertility survey of the United States, the NSFG focuses on factors such as contraception, infertility, sexual activity, and marriage (see http://www.cdc.gov/nchs/NSFG.htm). In the first five cycles of the survey

---

18 See http://psidonline.isr.umich.edu/CDS/.

(1973, 1976, 1982, 1988, and 1995), the NSFG was based on samples of women 15–44 years of age. In 2002, the survey was expanded to include a national sample of 4,928 men and 7,643 women. Data on behaviors that affect the risk of HIV and other sexually transmitted infections were included in 2002, and questions were added on fathers' involvement with children, and men's and women's attitudes toward marriage, children, and sexual activity. In June 2006, the NSFG began continuous interviewing. Self-reported weight and height are available in 2002 for both men and women. These data are publicly available online. The NSFG has been used by Vahratian (2008), who analyzed the prevalence of obesity in women of childbearing age, among others.

National Survey of Midlife Development in the United States (MIDUS)

A collaborative, interdisciplinary investigation of patterns, predictors, and consequences of midlife development in the areas of physical health, psychological well-being, and social responsibility, the MIDUS consists of four parts, the first with 7,108 respondents, which consist of a nationally representative random-digit-dial sample of non-institutionalized, English-speaking adults, ages 25–74, selected from working telephone banks in the coterminous United States (see http://www.icpsr. umich.edu/icpsrweb/ICPSR/studies/02760). Data on self-reported weight (current weight, weight one year prior to being surveyed, and weight at age 21) and height were collected in 1995–1996. Self-reported weight and height were also collected in a follow-up survey in 2004–2006, which also collected information on weight ten years prior to being surveyed. These data are publicly available from the ICPSR web site. Andreyeva et al. (2008) use the MIDUS data in their analysis of weight discrimination in the United States.

Non-U.S. Data

Non-U.S. individual-level, nationwide data sets that have been used in obesity studies include: the British Household Panel Survey (http://www.iser.essex.ac.uk/ survey/bhps), which measures height and weight in Wave 14 (2004–2005) (seventeen waves of data for the years 1991–2007 are currently available to researchers); the British National Child Development Study (http://www.esds.ac.uk/longitudinal/access/ncds/l33004.asp); the Canadian Community Health Survey (CCHS) (http://www.statcan.gc.ca/concepts/health-sante/index-eng.htm); and the Survey of Health, Aging and Retirement in Europe (SHARE) (http://www.share-project. org/), which is analogous to the HRS. These data sources have been used in the obesity context by Courbage and de Coulon (2004), Sargent and Blanchflower (1994), MacMinn et al. (2007), and Michaud et al. (2008), respectively.

DISCUSSION

This chapter has summarized several micro-data sources available for researchers in analyzing weight and height. With their focus on health, the NHANES data sets are useful in tracking not only objective measures of BMI but caloric intake, physical activity, and comprehensive results from blood tests. BRFSS and YRBSS data are excellent for comprehensive state-level analyses. In analyzing health insurance, the NHIS and MEPS data sources are invaluable. For older cohorts and the transition into Medicare, the HRS is becoming increasingly useful.

In this context, changes in BMI over time are particularly important, and so longitudinal data sources such as those mentioned in this chapter provide us with an opportunity to track the same individuals over time in looking at school policies (ECLS), long-term effects of birth weight (ECLS, NLSY-CYA), and labor market outcomes (NLS).

This chapter has focused on weight and height, which are relatively easily measured. However, we should be cautioned against a possible extreme focus on BMI, which is not always a good predictor of medical outcomes. For example, a recent study showed that obesity was a very poor gauge of high cholesterol in children (Lee et al. 2009). In adults, it has been shown that percent of body fat, or other measures of body composition, are far more accurate measures of adiposity than BMI (Burkhauser and Cawley 2008; Wada and Tekin 2010). Data sources that are useful in analyzing nutritional intake include the Continuing Survey of Food Intakes by Individuals (CSFII), the Consumer Expenditure Survey (CES), the Current Population Survey (CPS), and several data sets analyzing food stamp participation in detail.[19]

Supplemental data sources useful in merging with individual-level data include: detailed price data from the American Chamber of Commerce Researchers Association (ACCRA); outlet density and price data from Dun & Bradstreet; outlet and price data from County Business Patterns and the Census of Retail Trade; and data from the Bureau of Labor Statistics, Bureau of Economic Analysis, Census Bureau, United States Department of Agriculture, and Economic Research Service web sites. While it is usually straightforward to obtain data directly from the source's web site, the Inter-University Consortium for Political and Social Research (ICPSR) and National Bureau of Economic Research (NBER) are excellent sources for obtaining data (see http://www.icpsr.umich.edu/icpsrweb/ICPSR/index.jsp, and http://www.nber.org/data/, respectively).

The goal of this chapter has been to facilitate social science research related to obesity. Social science research related in this context is still a relatively new phenomenon, and the rich data sets mentioned may enable us to better understand trends and long-term relationships surrounding cognitive and labor market

---

19 See the ERS/USDA web site for a nice summary of national data sets useful in nutrition research: http://www.ers.usda.gov/Briefing/FoodNutritionAssistance/data/.

outcomes, in addition to the primary causes for the sharp increase we have seen in obesity rates since the 1970s, and perhaps why they have leveled off in recent years. More comprehensive measures are becoming available, and the importance of nutrition and physical activity has been highlighted, both by the medical community and the community at large.

ACKNOWLEDGEMENTS

The author would like to thank John Cawley for helpful comments and suggestions, and is grateful to Jennifer Tennant and Don Kelly for comments on earlier drafts. The author alone is responsible for any errors.

REFERENCES

Anderson, Patricia M., Kristin F. Butcher, and Philip B. Levine. 2003. "Maternal Employment and Overweight Children." *Journal of Health Economics* 22: 477–504.

Anderson Sarah E., and Robert C. Whitaker. 2009. "Prevalence of Obesity among US Preschool Children in Different Racial and Ethnic Groups." *Archives of Pediatrics and Adolescent Medicine* 163: 344–348.

Andreyeva, Tatiana, Rebecca M. Puhl, and Kelly D. Brownell. 2008." Changes in Perceived Weight Discrimination among Americans, 1995–1996 through 2004–2006." *Obesity* 16: 1129–1134.

Averett, Susan, and Sanders Korenman. 1996. "The Economic Reality of the Beauty Myth." *Journal of Human Resources* 31: 304–330.

Baum, Charles L., II, and William F. Ford. 2004. "The Wage Effects of Obesity: A Longitudinal Study." *Health Economics* 13: 885–899.

Bhattacharya, Jayanta, Janet Currie, and Steven Haider. 2004. "Breakfast of Champions? The School Breakfast Program and the Nutrition of Children and Families." *Journal of Human Resources* 41: 445–466.

Bhattacharya, Jayanta, and Mikko Packalen. 2008. "The Other Ex-Ante Moral Hazard in Health." NBER Working Paper No. 13863.

Bhattacharya, Jayanta, and Neeraj Sood. 2007. "Health Insurance and the Obesity Externality." *Advances in Health Economics and Health Services Research* 17: 279–318.

Bound, John, Charles Brown, and Nancy Mathiowetz. 2002. "Measurement Error in Survey Data." In *Handbook of Econometrics*, vol. 5, eds. James Heckman and Edward E. Leamer. 3705–3843. New York: Springer-Verlag.

Burkhauser, Richard, and John Cawley. 2008. "Beyond BMI: The Value of More Accurate Measures of Fatness and Obesity in Social Science Research." *Journal of Health Economics* 27: 519–529.

Card, David, Carlos Dobkin, and Nicole Maestas. 2004. "The Impact of Nearly Universal Insurance Coverage on Health Care Utilization and Health: Evidence from Medicare." NBER Working Paper No. 10365.

Cawley, John. 1999. "Rational Addiction, the Consumption of Calories, and Body Weight." Ph.D. dissertation. University of Chicago.

Cawley, John. 2004. "The Impact of Obesity on Wages." *Journal of Human Resources* 39: 451–474.

Cawley, John, and Feng Liu. 2007. "Maternal Employment and Childhood Obesity: A Search for Mechanisms in Time Use Data." NBER Working Paper No. 13600.

Chou, Shin-Yi, Michael Grossman, and Henry Saffer. 2004. "An Economic Analysis of Adult Obesity: Results from the Behavioral Risk Factor Surveillance System." *Journal of Health Economics* 23: 565–587.

Christian, Thomas J. 2009. "Effects of Commuting on Health Related Activities." Paper presented at the 2009 Eastern Economics Association meetings, February 27–March 1, in New York.

Conley, Dalton, and Rebecca Glauber. 2007. "Gender, Body Mass and Socioeconomic Status: New Evidence from the PSID." *Advances in Health Economics and Health Services Research* 17: 255–280.

Courbage, Christophe, and Augustin de Coulon. 2004. "Prevention and Private Health Insurance in the U.K." *Geneva Papers on Risk and Insurance* 29: 719–727.

Currie, Janet, and Enrico Moretti. 2007. "Biology as Destiny? Short and Long-Run Determinants of Intergenerational Transmission of Birth Weight." *Journal of Labor Economics* 25: 231–263.

Cutler, David M., Edward L. Glaeser, and Jesse M. Shapiro. 2003. "Why Have Americans Become More Obese?" *Journal of Economic Perspectives* 17: 93–118.

Danielzik, Sandra, Mareike Czerwinski-Mast, Kristina Langnäse, Britta Dilba, and Manfred J. Müller MJ. 2004. "Parental Overweight, Socioeconomic Status and High Birth Weight Are the Major Determinants of Overweight and Obesity in 5–7 Y-Old Children: Baseline Data of the Kiel Obesity Prevention Study (KOPS)." *International Journal of Obesity* 28: 1494–1502.

Datar, Ashlesha, and Roland Sturm. 2004. "Physical Education in Elementary School and Body Mass Index: Evidence from the Early Childhood Longitudinal Study." *American Journal of Public Health* 94: 1501–1506.

Dave, Dhaval, and Robert Kaestner. 2009. "Health Insurance and Ex Ante Moral Hazard: Evidence from Medicare." *International Journal of Health Care Finance and Economics* 9: 367–390.

Dave, Dhaval, and Inas Rashad. 2009. "Overweight Status, Self-Perception and Suicidal Behaviors among Adolescents." *Social Science and Medicine* 68: 1685–1691.

DeParle, Jason, and Robert Gebeloff. 2009. "Food Stamp Use Soars, and Stigma Fades." *New York Times*, November 29, p. A1.

Eaton, Danice K., Laura Kann, Steve Kinchen, Shari Shanklin, James Ross, Joseph Hawkins, William A. Harris, Richard Lowry, Tim McManus, David Chyen, Connie Lim, Nancy D. Brener, and Howell Wechsler. 2008. "Youth Risk Behavior Surveillance—United States, 2007." *MMWR Surveillance Summaries* 57:1–131.

Fertig, Angela, Gerhard Glomm, and Rusty Tchernis. 2009. "The Connection between Maternal Employment and Childhood Obesity: Inspecting the Mechanisms." *Review of Economics of the Household* 7: 227–255.

Finkelstein, Eric A., Ian C. Fiebelkorn, and Guijing Wang. 2003. "National Medical Spending Attributable to Overweight and Obesity: How Much, and Who's Paying?" *Health Affairs Web Exclusive* W3: 219–226.

Gordon-Larsen, Penny, Melissa C. Nelson, Phil Page, and Barry M. Popkin. 2006. "Inequality in the Built Environment Underlies Key Health Disparities in Physical Activity and Obesity." *Pediatrics* 117: 417–424.

Hamermesh, Daniel S. 2009. "Grazing, Goods and Girth: Determinants and Effects." NBER Working Paper No. 15277.

Janssen, Ian, Peter T. Katzmarzyk, and Robert Ross. 2002. Body mass index, waist circumference, and health risk. *Archives of Internal Medicine* 162: 2074–2079.

Joyce, Theodore. 1994. "Self-selection, Prenatal Care, and Birthweight among Blacks, Whites, and Hispanics in New York City." *Journal of Human Resources* 29: 762–794.

Kantarevic, Jasmin, and Stéphane Mechoulan. 2006. "Birth Order, Educational Attainment and Earnings: An Investigation using the PSID." *Journal of Human Resources* 41: 755–777.

Kaushal, Neeraj. 2007. "Do Food Stamps Cause Obesity? Evidence from Immigrant Experience." *Journal of Health Economics* 26: 968–991.

Kenkel, Donald S. 2000. "Prevention." In *Handbook of Health Economics,* vol. 1B, eds. Anthony J. Culyer and Joseph P. Newhouse. 1675–1720. Amsterdam: Elsevier.

Lee, Joyce M., Achamyeleh Gebremariam, Paula Card-Higginson, Jennifer L. Shaw, Joseph W. Thompson, and Matthew M. Davis. 2009. "Poor Performance of Body Mass Index as a Marker for Hypercholesterolemia in Children and Adolescents." *Archives of Pediatric and Adolescent Medicine* 163: 716–723.

Lee, Lung-fei, and Jungsywan H. Sepanski. 1995. "Estimation of Linear and Nonlinear Errors-In-Variables Models Using Validation Data." *Journal of the American Statistical Association* 90: 130–140.

MacMinn, William, James McIntosh, and Caroline Yung. 2007. "How Much Does Obesity Matter? Results from the 2001 Canadian Community Health Survey." *Advances in Health Economics and Health Services Research* 17: 333–364.

Michaud, Pierre-Carl, Arthur H.O. van Soest, and Tatiana Andreyeva. 2007. "Cross-country Variation in Obesity Patterns among Older Americans and Europeans." *Forum for Health Economics and Policy* 10: article 8.

Mullahy John, and Stephanie A. Robert. 2008. "No Time To Lose? Time Constraints and Physical Activity." NBER Working Paper No. 14513.

National Center for Health Statistics. 1965. "Plan and Initial Program of the Health Examination Survey." *Vital and Health Statistics* 1 4: 1–43.

Nelson, David E., Eve Powell-Griner, Machell Town, and Mary Grace Kovar. 2003. "A Comparison of National Estimates from the National Health Interview Survey and the Behavioral Risk Factor Surveillance System." *American Journal of Public Health* 93: 1335–1341.

Popkin, Barry M., and J. Richard Udry. 1998. "Adolescent Obesity Increases Significantly for Second and Third Generation U.S. Immigrants: The National Longitudinal Study of Adolescent Health." *Journal of Nutrition* 128: 701–706.

Powell, Lisa M., M. Christopher Auld, Frank J. Chaloupka, Patrick M. O'Malley, and Lloyd D. Johnston. 2007. "Access to Fast Food and Food Prices: Relationship with Fruit and Vegetable Consumption and Overweight among Adolescents." *Advances in Health Economics and Health Services Research* 17: 23–48.

Putnam, Robert D. 2000. *Bowling Alone: The Collapse and Revival of American Community.* New York: Simon and Schuster.

Rashad, Inas. 2008. "Height, Health, and Income in the U.S., 1984–2005." *Economics and Human Biology* 6: 108–126.

Rashad, Inas. 2006. "Structural Estimation of Caloric Intake, Exercise, Smoking, and Obesity." *Quarterly Review of Economics and Finance* 46: 268–283.

Rashad, Inas, Michael Grossman, and Shin-Yi Chou. 2006. "The Super Size of America: An Economic Estimation of Body Mass Index and Obesity in Adults." *Eastern Economic Journal* 32: 133–148.

Rose, Donald, and J. Nicholas Bodor. 2006. "Household Food Insecurity and Overweight Status in Young School Children: Results from the Early Childhood Longitudinal Study." *Pediatrics* 117: 464–473.

Royer, Heather N. 2009. "Separated at Girth: U.S. Twin Estimates of the Effects of Birth Weight." *American Economic Journal: Applied Economics* 1: 49–85.

Ruhm, Christopher J. 2000. "Are Recessions Good for Your Health?" *Quarterly Journal of Economics* 115: 617–650.

Sabia, Joseph J. 2007. "The Effect of Body Weight on Adolescent Academic Performance." *Southern Economic Journal* 73: 871–900.

Sargent, James D., and David G. Blanchflower. 1994. "Obesity and Stature in Adolescence and Earnings in Young Adulthood. Analysis of a British Birth Cohort." *Archives of Pediatric and Adolescent Medicine* 148: 681–687.

Schanzenbach, Diane Whitmore. 2009. "Do School Lunches Contribute to Childhood Obesity?" *Journal of Human Resources* 44: 684–709.

Smith, Patricia K., Barry Bogin, and David Bishai. 2005. "Are Time Preference and Body Mass Index Associated? Evidence from the National Longitudinal Survey of Youth." *Economics and Human Biology* 3: 259–270.

Spencer, Elizabeth A., Paul N. Appleby, Gwyneth K. Davey, and Timothy J Key. 2002. "Validity of Self-Reported Height and Weight in 4808 EPIC-Oxford Participants." *Public Health Nutrition* 54: 561–565.

Sturm, Roland. 2005. "Childhood Obesity—What We Can Learn from Existing Data on Societal Trends, Part 2." *Preventing Chronic Disease*. Available from: http://www.cdc.gov/pcd/issues/2005/apr/04_0039.htm.

Vahratian, Anjel. 2008. "Prevalence of Overweight and Obesity among Women of Childbearing Age: Results from the 2002 National Survey of Family Growth". *Maternal and Child Health Journal* 13: 268–273.

Wada, Roy, and Erdal Tekin. 2010. "Body Composition and Wages." *Economics and Human Biology* 8: 242–254.

Weng, Haoling H., Lori A. Bastian, Donald H. Taylor, Barry K. Moser, and Truls Ostbye. 2004. "Number of Children Associated with Obesity in Middle-Aged Women and Men: Results from the Health and Retirement Study." *Journal of Women's Health* 13: 85–91.

Zagorsky, Jay L. 2005. "Health and Wealth: The Late-20th Century Obesity Epidemic in the U.S." *Economics and Human Biology* 3: 296–313.

Zhang, Lei, and Inas Rashad. 2008. "Time Preference and Obesity: The Health Consequences of Discounting the Future." *Journal of Biosocial Science* 40: 97–113.

CHAPTER 13

THE COMPLEX SYSTEMS SCIENCE OF OBESITY

DIANE T. FINEGOOD

INTRODUCTION

CONCEPTUAL models of obesity have evolved over the last several decades from relatively simple models that frame obesity as just a result of energy imbalance (Garrow 1987), to physiological models which suggest that obesity is the result of aberrant homeostatic control (Bray 2004), through to social ecological models which suggest that the individual is acted on by external forces in the environment (Davison and Birch 2001; Kumanyika 2001). These external forces are often seen as nested layers or are lined up by their proximity to the individual from proximal (home, school, worksite) to more distal (community, national, and global). In general, these conceptual models of obesity frame the problem as either simple or complicated, but they do not convey the notion that obesity is complex.

More recently, the Foresight Programme of the Government Science Office in the United Kingdom produced a conceptual model that illustrates obesity as a complex problem arising from more than one hundred proximal and distal factors (see figure 13.1 and table 13.1). These factors are grouped into clusters at the level of the individual (engine, physiology, individual physical activity, food consumption, and individual psychology) and society (physical activity environment, social psychology, and food production). The variables in the map are interrelated through more than three hundred connections and more than one hundred feedback loops.

In the first part of this chapter the distinctions between simple, complicated, and complex problems will be delineated. The Foresight map will be used as a

Foresight
Obesity System Map

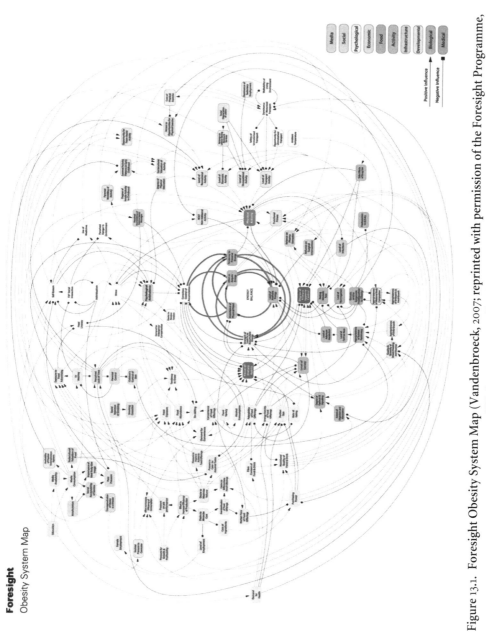

Figure 13.1. Foresight Obesity System Map (Vandenbroeck, 2007; reprinted with permission of the Foresight Programme, UK Government Office for Science).

Table 13.1. Variables in the Foresight Obesity System Map by Cluster (Vandenbroeck et al. 2007b)

Engine
- Conscious control of accumulation
- Effort to acquire energy
- Importance of physical need
- Level of available energy
- Strength of lock-in to accumulate energy
- Tendency to preserve energy

Physiology
- Appropriateness of child growth
- Appropriateness of embryonic and fetal growth
- Appropriateness of maternal body composition
- Appropriateness of nutrient partitioning
- Degree of optimal GI signaling
- Degree of primary appetite control by brain
- Extent of digestion and absorption
- Genetic and/or epigenetic predisposition to obesity
- Level of adipocyte metabolism
- Level of fat-free mass
- Level of infections
- Level of satiety
- Level of thermogenesis
- Predisposition to activity
- Quality and quantity of breast feeding
- Reliance on pharma remedies
- Reliance on surgical interventions
- Resting metabolic rate
- Side effects of drug use

Food Consumption
- Alcohol consumption
- Convenience of food offerings
- Demand for convenience
- De-skilling
- Energy-density of food offerings
- Fiber content of food and drink
- Food abundance
- Food exposure
- Food variety
- Force of dietary habits
- Nutritional quality of food and drink
- Palatability of food offerings
- Portion size
- Rate of eating
- Tendency to graze

Table 13.1 Cont'd

Food Production
- Cost of ingredients
- Demand for health
- Desire to differentiate food offerings
- Desire to maximize volume
- Desire to minimize cost
- Effort to increase efficiency of consumption
- Effort to increase efficiency of production
- Female employment
- Level of employment
- Level of female employment
- Market price of food offerings
- Pressure for growth and profitability
- Pressure on job performance
- Pressure to cater to acquired taste
- Pressure to improve access to food offerings
- Purchasing power
- Societal pressure to consume
- Standardization of food offerings

Individual Physical Activity
- Degree of innate activity in childhood
- Degree of physical education
- Functional fitness
- Learned activity patterns in early childhood
- Level of domestic activity
- Level of occupational activity
- Level of recreational activity
- Level of transport activity
- Non-volitional activity (NEAT)
- Parental modeling of activity
- Physical activity

Physical Activity Environment
- Accessibility to opportunities for physical exercise
- Ambient temperature
- Cost of physical exercise
- Dominance of motorized transport
- Dominance of sedentary employment
- Opportunity for team-based activity
- Opportunity for unmotorized transport
- Perceived danger in environment
- Reliance of labor-saving devices
- Safety of unmotorized transport
- Social depreciation of labor
- Sociocultural valuation of physical activity
- Walkability of living environment

(continued)

Table 13.1 Cont'd

Individual Psychology
• Demand for indulgence/compensation
• Desire to resolve tension
• F2F social interaction
• Food literacy
• Individualism
• Perceived inconsistency of science-based messages
• Psychological ambivalence
• Self-esteem
• Stress
• Use of medicines

Social Psychology
• Acculturation
• Availability of passive entertainment options
• Children's control of diet
• Conceptualization of obesity as a disease
• Education
• Exposure to food advertising
• Importance of ideal body-size image
• Media availability
• Media consumption
• Parental control
• Peer pressure
• Perceived lack of time
• Smoking cessation
• Social acceptability of fatness
• Social rejection of smoking
• Sociocultural valuation of food
• TV watching

heuristic tool to illustrate the various reasons why obesity can be viewed as an emergent property of a complex system. In the second half of the chapter, the implications of accepting obesity as complex will be considered, and solutions appropriate for complex problems will be introduced.

The Hallmarks of Obesity as a Complex Problem

There are a number of characteristics that distinguish complex systems from systems that are simple or merely complicated (see table 13.2). What follows is a consideration of each of these features with examples related to the challenges posed by obesity at both the individual and population levels.

Table 13.2 **Differences between Simple or Complicated and Complex Systems**

Simple or Complicated Systems	Complex Systems
Homogeneous	Heterogeneous
Linear	Nonlinear
Deterministic	Stochastic
Static	Dynamic (time dependent)
Independent	Interdependent
No feedback	Feedback
No adaptation or self-organization	Adaptation and self-organization
No connection between levels	Emergence

Homogeneous versus Heterogeneous

Homogeneous objects and systems are identical and have indistinguishable structural elements, whereas heterogeneous objects or systems have a large number of structural variations. At the level of the individual, heterogeneity is in part conferred by the large number of genes and chromosomal regions associated with the human obesity phenotype (Rankinen et al. 2006). Overfeeding studies in 12 pairs of young adult monozygotic twins demonstrated the powerful effects of genes on body weight and body fat distribution (Bouchard et al. 1990). The long-term response to overfeeding (1,000 kcal per day, 6 days a week for a period of 100 days) was an average weight gain of 8.1 kilograms, but the range was from 4.3 to 13.3 kilograms. This large range was due to the variance in weight gain between twin pairs. The variance between twin pairs was three-fold greater than the variance within twin pairs. Hence, differences in genetic makeup confer considerable heterogeneity to an individual's response to an obesogenic environment, while individuals with the same genotype have a more homogeneous response.

At the population level, the obesogenicity of the environment is also very heterogeneous. The Foresight map illustrates that a wide variety of factors affect food and physical activity environments (Vandenbroeck et al. 2007a). The importance of variables in clusters such as food production (e.g., "market price of food offerings" and "purchasing power") or the physical activity environment (e.g., "dominance of sedentary employment" and "dominance of motorised transport") will vary across populations and for each individual in a population. As such, the challenge posed for individuals and across a population will be very heterogeneous. The causes and consequences of the determinants of obesity vary considerably from person to person and from population to population, making single solutions or unified approaches of limited value.

Linear versus Nonlinear

A linear relationship between two elements in a system is a relationship with constant proportions. A nonlinear relationship is one in which the cause does not produce a proportional effect. For example, in a linear system, if a small push produces a small response, then twice the push results in twice the response. However, in a nonlinear system, if a small push produces a small response, it's possible that twice the push could lead to no response at all, or even a response in the opposite direction (Meadows 2008). A common misconception with respect to obesity is that weight loss or weight gain is a linear function of a daily energy imbalance. For example, if one is trying to lose weight and decreases his daily energy consumption by 500 kilocalories per day, he might lose one pound in one week. If the system were linear, then to lose two pounds a week he could decrease his intake by 1,000 kilocalories a day, and this loss would be the same whether he was at the beginning of losing 50 pounds or at the end of a 50-pound weight loss. Unfortunately, a variety of adaptations in energy expenditure, fuel selection, and various metabolic fluxes occur, making the body weight response nonlinear (Hall 2010; Leibel et al. 1995).

Deterministic versus Stochastic

In deterministic systems, the same result always occurs for a given set of inputs, whereas in a stochastic process an element of randomness leads to a degree of uncertainty about the outcome. In a deterministic system, it is possible to uniquely determine its past and future trajectories from its initial or present state (Rickles et al. 2007). Most theories of behavior change, such as social cognitive theory or the theory of planned behavior, have generally viewed behavior change as a function of cognitive factors such as knowledge, attitude, belief, efficacy, and intention (Baranowski et al. 2003). Change is conceptualized as a linear, deterministic process in which individuals weigh pros and cons, and when the benefits finally outweigh the costs, the decision to change behavior is made. Resnicow and Vaughan (2006) suggest that these models do not adequately account for the variance usually seen in studies based on the theories, nor do they account for the seemingly random quantum leaps in behavior that have been shown to occur. They argue that as a result of chaotic or quantum events, small changes in knowledge, attitude, or efficacy may dramatically alter motivation and behavioral outcomes. These authors suggest that the role of quantum processes in nutrition and physical activity behavior needs to be examined.

Although quantum behavior change has yet to be systematically studied with respect to weight loss, the potential importance of quantum or random events in both initiating and sustaining change is suggested by the finding that 77 percent of participants in the National Weight Control Registry report that a triggering event or incident preceded their successful weight loss (Klem et al. 1997)[1]. Although some of the reported triggering events may be considered predictable (e.g., medical or ongoing discontent), many participants reported that they "just decided to do it," a trigger that may not be possible to characterize as anything other than a random event. These data suggest that quantum or random events may be particularly important in sustained behavior change.

---

1 Participants in the registry must have lost at least 13.6 kg and kept it off for a minimum of 1 year to be eligible to register. In this report, the 629 women and 155 men lost an average of 30 kg and maintained a minimum 13.6 kg weight loss for 5 years.

Static versus Dynamic (Time Dependent)

Although it is unlikely that our genes have changed much over the last century and can thus be considered static variables, there is considerable evidence to demonstrate that many of the environmental variables that may be thought of as drivers of the obesity epidemic have changed over time. A quick scan of the obesity system map produces a whole host of variables that have changed over time and at different rates in different populations (see table 13.1). These variables include factors like the "dominance of motorized transport," "reliance on labor-saving devices and services," "degree of physical education," "portion sizes," "market price of food offerings," "media availability," "face-to-face social interactions," and "perceived danger in the environment." Hence the system giving rise to obesity is a complex mix of both static and dynamic variables. As George Bray once suggested in describing the interaction between these static and dynamic variables, "genetic background loads the gun, but the environment pulls the trigger" (Bray 2004).

Independent versus Interdependent

The reductionist paradigm under which most research is still conducted leads us to think of causal factors as being either independent of other factors or dependent on the variables that were observed or changed in the experimental setting. Rarely does the reductionist approach lead us to consider variables, components of a system, or even actors as interdependent. However, there are many interdependencies in intact systems where specific variables, subsystems, and actors interact with each other. In the Foresight map there are numerous pairs of variables that illustrate interdependence, such as the relationship between "appropriateness of maternal body composition" and "appropriateness of embryonic and fetal growth," or an individual's level of "physical activity" and "functional fitness."

Interdependencies also exist between subsystems. Although difficult to see clearly in the full Foresight system map, the interdependencies between clusters are more visible in a reduced version of the map where the thickness of the lines connecting the clusters reflects the number of linkages between variables in those clusters (see figure 13.2). This version of the map clearly illustrates the interdependence of whole subsystems and demonstrates that pushing on one part of the system may have unanticipated effects in other places. For example, changes in food production will have a significant impact on food consumption, but due to interdependencies may also have effects on physical activity environments and social psychology.

Feedback

In the simplest terms, feedback is a circular process of influence in which action has an effect on the actor or in which an action or event is part of a chain of cause and effect that forms a circuit or loop that "feeds back" on itself (Hamid 2009, p. 32). Feedback occurs in time-dependent systems. When described in the language of

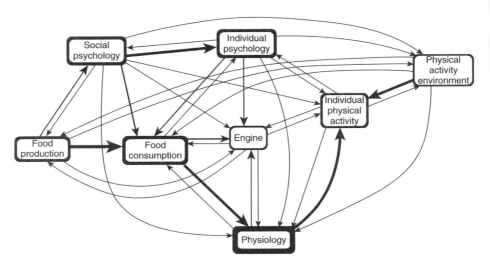

Figure 13.2. Reduced Foresight System Map (Finegood et al. 2010). The number of
individual connections between variables in each cluster is represented in the thickness
of the connecting lines, while the number of connections within a cluster is shown
as the cluster's border thickness.

system dynamics, a feedback loop is a closed chain of causal connections from a
stock, through a set of decisions, rules, physical laws, or actions that are dependent
on the level of the stock, and back again through a flow to change the stock (Meadows
2008, p. 27). In simple terms, body weight is a stock that is dependent (albeit in a
complex, nonlinear fashion) on the flow of energy into the body and the flow of
energy out of the body (i.e., energy expenditure). To lose weight, one must decrease
the flow of energy in and/or increase the flow of energy out. By weighing oneself,
one can assess the level of the stock and then make adjustments to the flow of energy
in or out in order to achieve a new level of the stock. So by measuring body
weight, a feedback loop is created that allows for decisions to be made with regard
to adjustments in energy intake and energy expenditure.

The Foresight map illustrates more than 100 feedback loops that include as few
as 2 to as many as 17 variables (see figure 13.1). These feedback loops are of two basic
types: stabilizing or balancing loops; and runaway or reinforcing loops. Balancing
feedback loops (also known as negative feedback loops) are equilibrating or goal-
seeking structures in systems and are both sources of stability and sources of resistance to change (Meadows 2008, p. 30). At the center of the Foresight map is the
individual with several dominant balancing feedback loops. The variable "importance of physical need" has a positive effect on both the "effort to acquire energy"
and the "tendency to preserve energy," which in turn both have a strong positive
effect on the "level of available energy." As the level of available energy grows, it in
turn feeds back to decrease the "importance of physical need." Although there is
currently an epidemic of obesity, these balancing or stabilizing feedback loops have
worked fairly well for thousands of years (Diamond 2003). The genes that control

these loops have evolved primarily in circumstances where food was not abundant in the environment and where considerable energy needed to be expended to obtain energy for consumption.

Unfortunately, in the last few decades a number of runaway reinforcing loops have grown in importance and now tend to dominate the obesity system map. Reinforcing feedback loops (also known as positive feedback loops) are self-enhancing and can lead to exponential growth (Meadows 2008, p. 32). Many reinforcing loops are present in the Foresight map. In some cases they illustrate a spiraling away from healthy food or physical activity behaviors, but in other cases they could be used to reinforce healthy behaviors. Consider the loop formed by the variables "demand for convenience," "convenience of food offerings," and "de-skilling". The more we purchase convenience foods, the more they are manufactured and sold, and the less we need to have skills to prepare food. As a result of this reinforcing loop, the availability of fast and convenience foods has risen over the last few decades, and the reduction in skills to prepare foods has reinforced the need for already prepared items. Another reinforcing loop on the map is the positive effect of "learned activity patterns in early childhood" on "sociocultural valuation of activity," which in turn has a positive effect on "learned activity patterns in early childhood." In this case, the reinforcement could go to reducing or improving support for engaging in physical activity. Likewise, the reinforcing loop created by "walkability of living environment" and "dominance of motorized transport" could either lead to more or less walkable environments. A decrease in the dominance of cars makes an environment more walkable, and vice versa. Unfortunately, many other factors push this loop into reinforcing the "dominance of motorized transport," such as "perceived lack of time," "perceived danger in the environment," and even "purchasing power."

Adaptation and Self-organization

An adaptive system (or a complex adaptive system) is a system that changes its behavior in response to its environment. The capacity of a system to make its own structure more complex is called self-organization (Meadows 2008, p. 79). Both adaptation and self-organization are a function of feedback loops. A system with many stabilizing and interconnecting loops will be fairly resilient to perturbations from the external environment, whereas systems with too many dominant reinforcing loops may be perturbed to runaway exponential growth that can result in collapse over time.

Since adaptation and self-organization are defined in terms of the relationship of the system with respect to its environment, it is necessary in considering examples relevant to obesity to define the system and its environment. The Foresight system map builders had the ambitious goal of illustrating "the sum of all the relevant factors and their interdependencies that determine the condition of obesity for an individual or a group of people" (Vandenbroeck et al. 2007). But even with this ambitious goal, there are many factors outside the boundaries of the system described in the Foresight map that push on this system. In this sense, the system map can be considered to have fuzzy boundaries, another characteristic of complex systems (Plsek and Greenhalgh 2001). Although food production is considered in the map, the impact of agricultural policies are not described; while physical activity environments are considered, land-use planning is not; and while media and advertising are considered important factors in the obesity system, government regulations on media and advertising are not included. Global, national, and municipal forces control the rules under which various parts of the system operate and create the perturbations to which the system as defined must adapt. With the boundaries of the obesity system delineated by the Foresight map, the problem of obesity can be said to emerge from the adaptive responses to the interaction between the system and policies (food, physical activity, and social environments) which shape the environment in which the system operates.

Social-ecological models of obesity suggest other ways in which the boundaries of the system can be drawn (Davison and Birch 2001). The boundaries could be drawn around the individual or the family, for example, making the environment the forces acting upon the individual or upon the family unit. In this way, many of the variables in the Foresight map would be considered part of the environment rather than the system. While this redrawing of the system and its environment does not alter the importance of the various factors, it does change the way in which the problem is framed, which may in turn alter perceptions about the solutions to the problem. We have been implicitly drawing the system boundaries around the individual for many years. We now recognize that many individuals have difficulty adapting to the obesogenic environments in which they live. While some individuals can adapt to an obesogenic environment and maintain a normal body weight, in others adaptation includes a significant increase in body weight and in some cases morbid obesity. Whether this is considered a failure of adaptation or simply a natural adaptation to the environment in which their system resides can certainly be debated, but drawing the system boundaries in this way tends to put the onus on the individual rather than the environment to adapt and change.

Defining the boundary of the system is relevant for describing the mechanisms of adaptation, but it may be even more important for the principle of self-organization, especially when self-organization is considered an avenue toward solutions. If the boundaries of the system are the individual, then the ability of the individual to self-organize, that is, make itself more complex in response to an obesogenic environment, may be limited. When we compare the systems defined by drawing the boundaries around the individual versus around the full Foresight map, the fraction of variables from the physiology cluster (dependent on an individual's genetic inheritance) is much larger. Since these variables are also relatively static, they cannot contribute to the adaptation by changing over time. As such, the ways in which the system can self-organize in response to an obesogenic environment are more limited than the ways in which the full system can adapt to changes in the policy environment. If the boundaries of the system are drawn as they are for the Foresight obesity map, then the ability of this system to self-organize and become more complex is vast. There are many actors who play a role in affecting the variables and feedback loops that currently exist, but the capacity of these actors to create new feedback loops is large.

Emergence

The last hallmark of complexity to be considered is *emergence*, a term that has been defined in many different ways. Some have defined emergence as "the arising of novel and coherent structures, patterns and properties during the process of self-organization in complex systems," while others have defined it as a subset of the many different types of synergies, specifically those in which constituent parts with different properties are modified, re-shaped, or transformed by their participation in the whole (Corning 2002). Bar-Yam (2004) suggests that what is important about emergence are not the details of the parts or the properties of the larger view, but rather the relationship between the two.

These definitions of emergence suggest that we can consider obesity an emergent property of the system described in the Foresight map. Although it may be difficult to get a sense of the relationship between the details of the system and the emergence of obesity by looking at the original system map, the impression that does arise is that the connections, interdependencies, and feedback loops are of particular importance in the development of obesity. If obesity resulted from more linear deterministic relationships between the variables in the map, a different picture would arise and a different set of solutions would be appropriate. Interestingly, by considering obesity as an emergent property of the reduced system map (see figure 13.2), a slightly more detailed picture of the important relationships between the subsystems and the whole emerges (Finegood et al. 2010). The reduced system map highlights the importance of relationships between food production and food consumption, between social psychology and individual psychology, and between food consumption and physiology as revealed by the thickness of the lines connecting these clusters. The thickness of the lines is proportional to the number of underlying connections and thus reflects the relative importance of influences of one cluster on another and the reciprocal effects (or lack thereof).

Summary

Like the definition of emergence, the definition of a complex system varies considerably in the literature. In its simplest form, a system can be described as a "set of entities with relationships between them" and a complex system as a system with some added characteristics such as nonlinearity, multiple elements, lack of predictability, interdependence and/or the ability to reduce the system clearly into its distinct parts (Plsek and Greenhalgh 2001; Resnicow and Vaughan 2006; Richardson 2005, Rickles et al. 2007). In the present chapter we have defined a complex system as a system with many if not all of the characteristics listed in table 13.2. In contrast, simple systems are usually small systems without any of these characteristics and complicated systems are larger, but still homogeneous, linear, deterministic, time independent, and so on.

Even without a detailed description of the hallmarks of complex systems, the Foresight obesity system map does an excellent job of conveying the notion that obesity is a complex problem. As illustrated, this complexity exists on many different levels and by many different mechanisms, any one of which by itself may make the problem seem intractable. But recognizing that obesity is a complex problem is a first critical step to understanding why it is such a challenging problem and why solutions appropriate for complex problems must be considered.

RESPONSES TO COMPLEX PROBLEMS

Common responses to complex problems include frustration, despair, disillusionment, or belief that a problem is beyond hope (Bar-Yam 2004; Plsek and Greenhalgh 2001). Complex problems tend to cause us to look for someone to blame, to focus on a simple solution, or to retreat altogether. Rittel and Webber (1973) suggest that the discontent of the public with "modern professionals," be they social workers, educators, public health officials, or city planners, exists because these professionals are still tackling problems by assuming they can analyze the relevant systems, identify the root cause of a problem, and then fix it. They point out that the most intractable problems are those of defining and locating problems (finding where in the complex causal networks the trouble really lies). Equally intractable is the problem of identifying the actions that might effectively narrow the gap between what is and what ought to be.

Rittel and Webber (1973, p.160) described complex social planning problems as "wicked" problems; "wicked" in the sense that they are ". . . 'malignant' (in contrast to 'benign') or 'vicious' (like a circle) or 'tricky' (like a leprechaun) or 'aggressive' (like a lion, in contrast to the docility of a lamb)." As a consequence of characteristics like heterogeneity, interdependence, feedback, and adaptation, they suggest that wicked social problems are challenging because they have no definitive formulation, no stopping rules, there is no ultimate test of a solution, and they do not have enumerable or an (exhaustively describable) set of potential solutions.

Despite the recognition more than 35 years ago that the reductionist approach to complex problems is likely to fail, many still persist in believing that we must rigorously apply the scientific method to problems in medicine and public health (Sterman 2006). Steeped in the scientific method is the belief that through a reductionist approach, including controlled experiments, testing of rival hypotheses and replication of results, we can ascertain causality. But as Wagner (1999) points out "causality can only be meaningfully defined for systems with linear interactions among their variables." Sterman (2006) suggests that policy resistance in public health and welfare results from this narrow reductionist worldview and arises because systems are complex, for example, constantly changing, nonlinear, history-dependent, self-organizing, adapting, evolving, and counterintuitive.

In recent years, the notion that complex problems cannot be tackled with the usual reductionist approach has started to take hold. Plsek and Greenhalgh (2001) suggest that this may be because our traditional ways of "getting our heads round the problem" are no longer appropriate. Although complex systems science originated in the physics literature, its application to social issues like education, psychology, and health has grown dramatically in the last decade (Hawe et al. 2009). In health, much of this application is with respect to health care systems, but there is a growing recognition that complex systems science might have something to offer in addressing public health issues like obesity and tobacco control (Best et al. 2003; Finegood 2006; Finegood et al. 2008, Leischow and Milstein 2006).

What is complex systems science? As already implied in this chapter, it is the study of many of the characteristics of complex systems, as well as a whole host of other topics including hierarchies, chaos, attractors, boundary conditions, scaling, power laws, phase transitions, criticality, fractals, control theory, small world phenomena, and network theory (Pslek and Greenhalgh 2001; Trochim et al. 2006). Systems science methods include a number of different computational modeling methods (e.g., systems dynamics, micro-simulation, agent-based), as well as a variety of more qualitative group engagement methods (e.g., group model building, concept mapping, systemic intervention). These methods are increasingly being used to better understand and solve complex public health challenges. The next section of this chapter will describe two new frameworks based on systems thinking for use in considering action to address complex problems like obesity (Finegood et al. 2008; Malhi 2009).

As suggested above, a rigid reductionist view of complex problems and careful adherence to the scientific method where control of a system is paramount contributes to our inability to tackle some of the current major public health challenges like obesity and chronic disease prevention. But as Trochim et al. (2006) point out, it is a misconception to think that systems science is a rejection of traditional scientific views like reductionism. Since systems are embedded within systems, the degree to which one is taking a holistic versus a reductionist view depends in part on where the boundaries of the system of interest are drawn. In some sense, systems thinking is the integration of reductionist perspectives. Many systems science modeling methods depend in part on data made available through controlling parts of a system to enable study of the interactions in smaller subsystems.

So why aren't we using systems science methods more to tackle problems like obesity? Like complex public health problems, public health practice is a complex and loosely coupled system of actors, including governmental entities at the international, regional, and local levels, many nongovernmental organizations such as foundations, advocacy and special interest groups, coalitions and partnerships, academic institutions, for-profit and not-for-profit organizations and even the public at large (Trochim et al. 2006). Review of the obesity system map suggests that the actors needed to address the obesity problem work in a large range of sectors including the food industry, media, marketing, transportation, urban planning, health care, public health, and education. Trochim et al. (2006) asked a group of people involved in systems approaches to public health for the specific challenges that need to be addressed to support systems thinking and modeling in public health work. Using a systems method called concept mapping, they identified roughly 100 specific challenges that fell into 8 clusters including the needs to: show potential of systems approaches, utilize system incentives, support dynamic and diverse networks, and expand cross-category funding. More will need to be done in public health if systems thinking is to become a common tool for analyzing and addressing public health problems.

Summary

Problems of the complexity of obesity are no longer tractable with traditional problem-solving approaches. Although seemingly overwhelming, it is not adequate to ignore the complexity and to only break the problem down into smaller pieces and subsystems, or to define the boundaries of the system around the individual and assume that the individual must adapt. An integrated holistic view of the challenge is required. Complex systems science offers new tools and techniques for tackling complex problems like obesity, but many barriers in the systems that support public health practice will need to be overcome if we are going to effectively tackle problems like obesity and some of the many other complex challenges of our times, including environmental degradation, terrorism, youth violence and social justice (Robinson 2010).

Solutions to Complex Problems

Recognition that a problem is complex is a first step to addressing the problem effectively. In this regard, the Foresight Programme's effort to produce an all-inclusive obesity system map is an important landmark in our efforts to address obesity. The map is an excellent heuristic tool to convey the notion of complexity, the importance of interdependencies and feedback loops, and the wide range of actors and sectors that need to be involved in addressing the problem. Some of the people involved in developing the Foresight obesity system map were concerned that the introduction of the map would lead to a sense of being overwhelmed and would result in a retreat from the problem. In our experience it has been a useful tool to establish the need for collaboration, cooperation, and building trust between sectors.

Unfortunately, the complexity of the map still makes it difficult to "get one's head around the problem." Likewise, the many dozens of summary reports making recommendations to address the problems of obesity and chronic disease prevention also make it somewhat difficult to grasp the full picture of what needs to be done (e.g., Barlow and Dietz 1998; Institute of Medicine 2009; Leitch 2007; Merrifield et al. 2007; Select Standing Committee 2006). This difficulty arises from the sheer number of recommendations, the fact that the recommendations vary from the highly specific to the more generic, and because they vary in their basis on everything from hard evidence, to "promising practices," to expert opinion and the opinion of the general public. With so many options for action and more recommended actions than we can afford to implement, how can we sort through these actions and decide what to do? We offer two frameworks based in systems thinking which may help us "get our heads around what to do" and move toward solutions appropriate for complex problems without worrying about whether there is adequate evidence of causality for the specific problem each action addresses (Finegood et al. 2010; Malhi et al. 2009).

Intervention Level Framework

In the early 1990s, Donella Meadows, a leading systems thinker working at the forefront of environmental and social analysis, articulated 12 leverage points or places to intervene in a complex system (see figure 13.3; Meadows 2008, pp. 147–165). She describes this list as "derived in a moment of frustration" that occurred during a meeting on the implications of global-trade regimes because, as often happens when people are tackling complex problems, their intuitions lead them to push "with all their might in the wrong direction" (Meadows 2008, p. 146).

At the top of Meadows's places to intervene is the highest level (most zoomed out) view of a system, the paradigm under which the system operates. The paradigm is linked to the deepest held beliefs that govern the actors in the system and, not surprisingly, is the hardest thing to change. Changing the paradigm, however, will have the greatest impact on the system in the future. To change the paradigm,

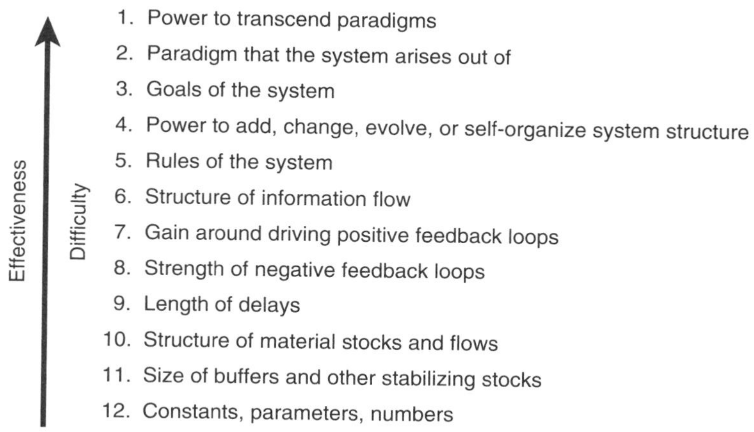

Effectiveness | Difficulty

1. Power to transcend paradigms
2. Paradigm that the system arises out of
3. Goals of the system
4. Power to add, change, evolve, or self-organize system structure
5. Rules of the system
6. Structure of information flow
7. Gain around driving positive feedback loops
8. Strength of negative feedback loops
9. Length of delays
10. Structure of material stocks and flows
11. Size of buffers and other stabilizing stocks
12. Constants, parameters, numbers

Figure 13.3. Meadows places to intervene in a complex system.

many things usually have to happen in the levels below this to support changing these deeply held beliefs. As one moves down the list of places to intervene, the goals of the system, its level of self–organization, and the rules by which the system operates become important tools in system change. While these are somewhat easier to change than the paradigm, they tend to be less effective in inducing system change. As Meadows (2008) points out, the true goals of a system are not necessarily what the actors say the goals are; rather, to deduce the true goals it is often necessary to observe the system in action.

The next set of "places to intervene" are system-level structures such as the structure of information flows, and the strength of the positive reinforcing and negative balancing loops. While in general these are somewhat less difficult places to intervene and sometimes less effective, if changes lead to a shift in the dominance of stabilizing and reinforcing loops they can be extraordinarily effective in shifting the whole system in a desirable (or undesirable) direction. Altering the delays in feedback loops is also a potentially useful strategy to changing their impact on the system. At the lowest level, the places to intervene are the structural elements of the various stocks and flows that make up the subsystems that together give rise to the system as a whole. Changes at this level can be helpful, but often their impact is more local and within a subsystem. Lots of changes are usually needed at this level to support and give rise to changes at higher levels.

Consider, for example, the case of tobacco cessation. Over the last 50 years or so, there has been a paradigm shift. Smokers were once considered "cool" and the social pressures to smoke were significant. Slowly, over time, the information flow about the hazards of smoking gave people working in public health some of the ammunition they needed to support subsystem change, including the banning of cigarette advertising and the increase in tobacco taxes. This reduced the various forms of social pressure to smoke and made it more difficult due to rising costs. New information about the hazards of secondhand smoke gave a larger number of people the power to demand new rules for smoke-free spaces, which in turn further reduced the social pressures to smoke and created a new social pressure to not smoke in the presence of others. This paradigm shift to stigmatization of the smoker might be considered a tipping point (Bayer 2008); the rate of tobacco consumption, which had reached a plateau, began to fall as the demand for smoke free spaces pushed smokers outside and away (see figure 13.4). Smokers went from being cool to being pariahs who were banished from workplaces, public spaces, and social networks if they wanted to engage in that unhealthy behavior (Christakis and Fowler 2008). Clearly, there were changes in many of these intervention levels, each of which supported subsequent changes at higher and lower intervention levels.

We sought to use Meadows's ideas in the development of a framework that could be applied to the problem of obesity and could provide insight into the various types of changes that will be needed to effectively reverse the obesity epidemic. Our initial experience suggested that 12 levels were too many to provide a useful framework for sorting actions to address obesity (Malhi 2009). Through an iterative process we settled on a 5-level framework that could be used reliably to

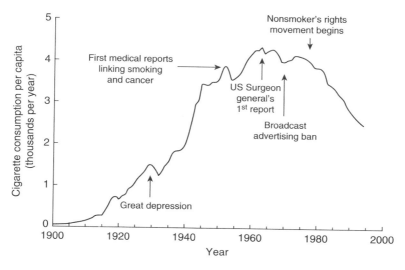

Figure 13.4. Tobacco consumption per capita in the United States, 1900–1994 (CDC 1994).

sort action statements. The 5 levels correspond roughly to the broader groups of Meadows' 12 levels described above: (1) paradigm, (2) goals, (3) system structure, (4) feedback loops and delays, and (5) structural elements (see table 13.1 in Malhi et al. 2009). The framework has been successfully applied to examine a series of papers prepared as pre-reading material for a conference on Food Systems and Public Health (Malhi et al. 2009; Story et al. 2009) and is currently being used to systematically sort actions from a large number of documents making recommendations to address obesity and chronic disease prevention (Johnston et al. 2010). This process is illustrated in table 13.3, which provides examples of the types of recommendations to address obesity that would be sorted into each of the levels of the framework.

Although the application of this Intervention Level Framework is still in its infancy, we have found it helpful in multiple ways. The framework streamlines consideration of the different levels of action required and helps to summarize a large number of action statements. It also enables the comparing of multiple agendas for the same system. In the food systems exercise, we found the framework helpful in surfacing places where the actions recommended to make food systems healthy, green, fair, and affordable were either compatible or incompatible (Malhi et al. 2009).

Since the framework helps us to "zoom out" on the problem and consider many actions together, it has provoked questions about what the distribution of effort and resources among the intervention levels needs to be to optimize efforts against obesity. Across the preliminary application of the framework to a number of different data sets about actions to address obesity or chronic disease prevention (Johnston et al. 2010; Malhi 2009), we see a distribution similar to that seen in the food systems example (see figure 13.5). The majority of ideas put forward are consistently at the level of structural elements, while the next most frequent area of

Table 13.3 Sample Actions According to the Intervention Level Framework for Obesity and Chronic Disease Prevention

Intervention Level	*Examples of Action Statements at That Level*
Paradigm	• Reframe obesity as a consequence of environmental inequities and not just the result of poor personal choices. • Develop a systems approach that recognizes the role that social conditions, politics, and economic forces play in prevention and treatment.
Goals	• Establish targets to achieve healthy weights for children through physical activity and healthy food choices. • Build trust across the multiple sectors that need to work to together to address obesity and chronic disease prevention. • Reduce inequities in the determinants of health that lead to inequities in health status. • Create a social expectation to emphasize prevention as more important than minimally extending life through expensive procedures.
System Structure	• Identify a lead department or agency for federal interdepartmental action on healthy weights for children. • Enable coalitions of health, environmental, labor, poverty, and public policy advocates to work together on common beneficial prevention projects. • Harmonize primary, secondary, and tertiary prevention program messages and policies across jurisdictions. • Implement the appropriate mix of individually-focused and environmentally-focused effort.
Feedback and Delays	• Assess effectiveness of self-regulation of marketing to children. • Establish legislative or regulatory action to enforce workplace standards for mothers who choose to breastfeed. • Conduct more research on natural policy and program experiments.
Structural Elements	• Establish a comprehensive public awareness campaign on healthy weights for children. • Implement a mandatory, standardized, simple, front of package labeling requirement on pre-packaged foods for easy identification of nutritional value. • Establish regulations to limit trans fat content in foods. • Expand funding available to local governments for safe walking and cycling programs.

suggestion is the structure of the system as a whole. Suggestions relevant to the paradigm and goals of the system are less frequent, and the least frequent suggestions for action are often regarding feedback loops and delays. Given the scales of difficulty and effectiveness that run parallel to the levels of the framework, the relatively infrequent consideration of feedback loops and delays appears to be a gap. We believe that this gap is due to the fact that we don't generally consider the importance of feedback loops or their potential value in a self-organizing system like obesity. New methods are likely required to assist stakeholders in thinking about the potential of creating new feedback loops as a means to shifting the dominance away from some of the more vexing reinforcing loops that have run unchecked and currently give rise to obesity.

Lastly, our preliminary examination of multiple sources of recommendations to address childhood obesity suggest that not all approaches to developing recommendations will provide the same distribution of action among the intervention levels (Johnston et al. 2010). It appears that for reports which rigorously adhere to making recommendations only where there is an adequate evidence base, nearly all of the recommendations fall into the structural element level. This is important to recognize, as solutions geared for this level are generally the least effective in creating complex system change, even though evidence-based actions are considered the gold standard for interventions by many decision makers. In contrast, reports and data sets where expert, stakeholder, or public opinion form a significant basis for recommendations, a distribution like that in figure 13.5 is much more likely to be found, though the gap in the feedback loop level still exists. Intuitively, it makes sense that when recommendations rigorously adhere to evidence derived from a reductionist paradigm, the evidence lies mostly at the level of subsystems and parts of subsystems. But as Trochim et al. (2006) point out, systems thinking is "familiar to us all" and we engage in systems thinking in our everyday lives. So when individuals (be they experts or lay people) make recommendations for action, they are more likely to be thinking about actions at multiple levels of a complex problem.

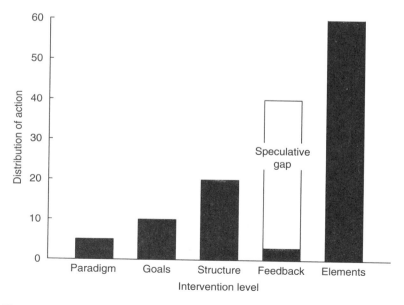

Figure 13.5. Common distribution of actions to address complex problems.

Making Things Work

One of today's leading systems thinkers, Yaneer Bar-Yam, published his approach to "making things work" in 2004. This book is an accumulation of his experience tackling a diverse set of complex problems in a diverse range of areas including health care, education, corporate management, the military, international development, ethnic violence, and terrorism. We recently distilled from this work a set of actions that make sense for complex problems in general and obesity in particular (see table 13.4; Finegood et al. 2010). The Intervention Level Framework described above provides a defined scaffolding for generating and sorting solutions to complex problems, while the following set of principles provides guidance against which specific actions can be tested as to their appropriateness for solving a complex problem.

Table 13.4 Solutions to Complex Problems

Consider that individuals matter
Match capacity to complexity
Set functional goals and directions for improvement
Distribute decision, action and authority
Form cooperative teams
Create competition
Consider feedback loops and delays
Assess effectiveness

Adapted from table 1 in Finegood et al. (2010), which is based on Bar-Yam (2004).

Individuals Matter

Although it may seem counterintuitive, in a system as large and complex as the obesity system, individuals do still matter. Given the heterogeneous nature of individuals and their environments, it is impossible to take individuals out of the solution equation. This does not mean that we should focus solely on the individual, as we have done for many years, or solely on the environment, as has tended to happen in recent years with the introduction of social ecological models. Given the heterogeneity in the relationship between individuals and their environment and the stochastic nature of behavior change, it is not surprising that population-level approaches to behavior change need to be comprehensive and multidimensional to be effective (Schooler et al. 1997). While one approach may be adequate for some, it will not be for others, so multiple approaches must be added together (Kahn et al. 2009). A systems approach suggests that it is not the details of the environment or of the individual that are important; rather it is the relationship between individuals and their environment that is important when looking for effective solutions (Brownell et al. 2010).

It is also helpful to remember that the individual at the center of the obesity system map is not the only individual who matters. There are individual actors all over the system in sectors as diverse as government, academia, and the private sector.

All of these individuals matter, and the relationship of each individual actor and each category of actor to their respective environments matter. As an example, there is considerable heterogeneity across sectors and companies that make up the environments for the actors who work in the food chain (Lang and Heasman 2004). Likewise, there is considerable heterogeneity across levels (e.g., national, regional, local) and mandate (e.g., transportation, health, agriculture) that make up the environments for the actors who work in government. While heterogeneity makes the system complex, it also affords considerable opportunity for self-organization and adaptation, especially if decision, action, and authority are distributed (see below).

Capacity and Complexity

As noted, it's not the specific details of individuals or their environments that matter, it is the relationship between individuals and their environments that matter because systems function best when the complexity of the tasks faced by individuals are matched to their capacity to handle their tasks. When the capacity of an individual to act is exceeded by the complexity of their task they are bound to fail, whereas when an individual's capacity to act is well matched to the complexity of their tasks they are more likely to succeed (Bar-Yam 2004). Heterogeneity in our genes and our environment means that there is a range in the complexity of the task of weight management across individuals and a range in individual's capacity to manage their food and physical activity behaviors. While most diet studies result in a "V-curve" of weight loss and weight regain, some people can lose large amounts of weight and keep it off for many years (Jeffrey et al. 2000; Klem et al. 1997). Factors like age, ethnicity, gender, education, and income can explain some of the differences in capacity of individuals and/or the complexity of their environments, but even in demographically homogenous populations there will be a range of body weights, suggesting that there is a range of capacity and complexity. A systems approach suggests that we need to learn how to measure variables like capacity and complexity, as well as create tools that help to match capacity and complexity, or increase capacity and decrease complexity.

Functional Goals

Goals that set targets for emergent properties such as the level of obesity or physical activity are not very helpful in guiding system change. Goals should set targets for system function and speak to changes at the level of system structure, feedback loops and delays, or structural elements. For instance, setting a goal to build trust between actors and across sectors addresses an important system function. Trust is system variable, and building trust allows actors to decrease the challenge of working in a complex environment. High trust allows for a better matching of capacity and complexity and a greater degree of self-organization (Solomon and Flores 2001). Functional goals at the level of structural elements, such as increasing the walkability of environments, increasing accessibility of public transportation, or increasing access to affordable fruits and vegetables, can be used to set clear targets for action, whereas goals like decreasing the prevalence of childhood obesity or reducing health inequities do not speak to the specific actions that need to be taken.

Distribute Decision, Action, and Authority

The Foresight map clearly illustrates that there is no particular hierarchy that controls activity within the obesity system. Without a clear hierarchy, a command and control approach to problem solving and innovation will not work (Bar-Yam 2004). To solve complex problems, it makes sense to distribute the authority to make decisions and take action to the actors in various parts of the actor network that support different subsystems (Greenhalgh et al. 2004). Care needs to be taken such that the distribution of decision making be to actors who have the ability to take action and not to create the condition that the complexity of an individual's task to make decisions exceeds his or her capacity to make it.

Form Cooperative Teams

The dominant notion conveyed by the Foresight map is that there are many interconnections and interdependencies in the system that give rise to obesity. As such, it is necessary to form teams across jurisdictions and sectors to tackle the interconnections that support the reinforcing feedback loops that drive the system in the wrong direction. Likewise, cooperative teams can look to strengthen balancing feedback loops or create new loops that will help to shift the system in the desired direction. Recent efforts to create "whole of government" approaches to addressing obesity and physical inactivity have been able to advance vertical and horizontal integration of efforts (Geneau et al. 2009). Many other cooperative efforts are needed both within and between sectors to address a variety of pressing problems (Yach 2008).

Create Competition

At face value it may seem that creating competition is the opposite of the previous suggestion to form cooperative teams, but teams will improve through adaptation and self-organization when they are involved in a competition that is structured to select the teams that are better at cooperation (Bar-Yam 2004). In business, cooperation between employees improves a company's performance, and competition between companies feeds back to ensure the selection of the most cooperative and helpful employees. In essence, cooperation at one level improves competition at the next level up. Competition also increases the complexity of the environment for other businesses, and that complexity in turn leads to either adaptation and growth, or failure. While this cycle of cooperation and competition has led to many consolidations (enforced cooperation) in the food value chain over the last few decades (Gereffi et al. 2009, Lang and Heasman 2004), the Foresight map suggests that "demand for health" is now one of the drivers of food production. As the importance of this variable grows, and the paradigm shifts from "value for money" to valuing health, the competition between organizations to deliver healthier options will grow, as will the need for cooperation between the public and private sectors (Yach 2008).

More thought needs to be given to new system-level goals and structures that create competitions to deliver healthier environments. This approach was used as part of efforts to promote health in British Columbia, Canada. The Ministry of Health created an incentive fund to jump-start cross-ministerial work. The Ministry was to spend $15 million over three years to support pilot projects proposed by other ministries. Eligible projects had to compete for funds and meet a number of criteria, including contribute to improving health and/or tackling a policy issue through a wellness lens; consist of "new" business; involve cost-sharing (money or in-kind contribution); and be sustainable. Thirty projects from ten ministries were funded, and according to government officials managing the program, the competition for incentive funds generated some projects that demonstrated real innovation (Geneau 2009).

Consider Feedback Loops and Delays

While it may seem counterintuitive to create more feedback loops in a system already dominated by feedback loops, the balance of positive and negative loops is important and tends to determine the direction in which the system is driven. As illustrated in the description of the intervention level framework, we don't tend to consider feedback loops or the impacts of their delays on loop function when we think about taking action to address obesity. However, feedback loops can be very powerful forces and can significantly shift the behavior of a system in the right or wrong direction (Meadows 2008).

Delays are also pervasive in complex systems, and they are strong determinants of system behavior (Meadows 2008). Delays in negative feedback loops can create oscillations and changing the length of a delay may or may not have a large effect on system behavior. Although delays are not explicitly illustrated in the Foresight map, a quick scan suggests that many exist. An increasing demand for healthy food offerings will not immediately change the food supply given the shifts in production and processing that need to take place. Improving the walkability of an environment might get some people out of their cars immediately, but it will take big shifts in walking behavior before the perceived dominance of motorized transport changes enough to further improve the walkability of an environment. More consideration needs to be given to understanding and using feedback loops and delays to address complex problems like obesity.

Assess Effectiveness

The assessment of effectiveness of actions taken to address obesity results in information that can be used in feedback loops. If we don't assess effectiveness, we don't learn from what we do, and as the old adage goes, history will likely repeat itself.

Unfortunately, our systems and support for research and evaluation are not well connected to the many policy and program interventions taking place in the public sector (Di Ruggerio et al. 2009; Green 2006). There are also many natural experiments in the private sector ranging from self-regulation to sales marketing that can and should be assessed to ensure transparency, accountability, and objective evaluation (Cameron et al. 2006; Sharma et al. 2010). Modest growth in research on natural experiments has taken place in recent years due to new research funding opportunities and new models for undertaking intervention research but we still have a long way to go. (Dietz 2006; Tremblay and Craig 2009).

CONCLUSIONS

Obesity clearly arises out of a complex system of interactions between many different variables at multiple levels, ranging from the genetics of individuals to policies that drive the composition of the food supply. These variables, and the interdependencies and feedback loops that exist between them, are controlled by many sectors and many different actors in the public and private sectors. Although it may seem overwhelming, by accepting obesity as a complex problem, methods and tools arising out of complex systems science can be applied to help elucidate important aspects of the system structure and suggest new ways of considering actions to effectively address the challenge.

Through application of an Intervention Level Framework, we can comprehend the many actions that are needed to address obesity at multiple levels of the system. Paradigm shifts are needed to make healthy food and physical activity behaviors the easy choice. To achieve these paradigm shifts, new functional goals and a better understanding of system-level variables will be needed. Supporting change at the level of the obesity system described by the Foresight Programme will require many actions to shift the dominance between feedback loops that reinforce the current paradigms and those that provide balance to food and physical activity environments. Lots of actions need to take place in the subsystems that give rise to food production, food consumption, physical activity, and social-cultural environments. New approaches, including ones that match the capacity of individuals to the challenge posed by their environments, set goals that create competitions to improve our environments and help to form cooperative teams across sectors are needed to address this most "wicked" of public health problems.

ACKNOWLEDGEMENTS

The author would like to thank the Canadian Institutes of Health Research (MT-10574) for financial support and Dr. Carrie Matteson, Lee Johnston, and Thomas D.N. Merth for their assistance with this manuscript.

REFERENCES

Baranowski, T., K.W. Cullen, T. Nicklas, D. Thompson, and J. Baranowski. 2003. "Are Current Health Behavioral Change Models Helpful in Guiding Prevention of Weight Gain Efforts?" *Obesity* 11: 23S-43S.

Barlow, S. E., and W.H. Dietz. 1998. "Obesity Evaluation and Treatment: Expert Committee Recommendations." *Pediatrics* 102: e29-e39.

Bar-Yam, Y. 2003. "Complexity Rising: From Human Beings to Human Civilization, a Complexity Profile." http://necsi.edu/projects/yaneer/EOLSSComplexityRising.pdf Accessed March 4, 2010.

Bar-Yam Y. 2004. *Making Things Work: Solving Complex Problems in a Complex World.* : NECSI–Knowledge Press.

Bayer, R. 2008. "Stigma and the Ethics Of Public Health: Not Can We but Should We." *Social Science and Medicine* 67(3): 463–472.

Best, A., G. Moor, B. Holmes, P. I. Clark, T. Bruce, S. Leischow, K. Buchholz, and J. Krajnak. 2003. "Health Promotion Dissemination and Systems Thinking: Towards an Integrative Model." *American Journal Health Behavior* 27 (Suppl 3): S206–16.

Bouchard, C., A. Tremblay, J. P. Després, A. Nadeau, P. J. Lupien, G. Thériault, J. Dussault, S. Moorjani, S. Pinault, G. Fournier 1990. "The Response To Long-Term Overfeeding In Identical Twins." *New England Journal of Medicine* 322(21): 1477–82.

Bray, G. A. 2004. "The Epidemic of Obesity and Changes in Food Intake: The Fluoride Hypothesis." *Physiology and Behavior* 82: 115–121.

Brownell, K. D., R. Kersh, D. S. Ludwig, R. C. Post, R. M. Puhl, M. B. Schwartz, and W. C. Willett. 2010. "Personal Responsibility and Obesity: A Constructive Approach to a Controversial Issue." *Health Affairs* 29(3): 379–387.

Cameron, R., A. Bauman, and A. Rose. 2006. "Innovations in Population Intervention Research: The Contributions of Canada on the Move." *Canadian Journal of Public Health* 97(Suppl1): S5–S9.

Centers for Disease Control. 1994. "Surveillance for Selected Tobacco-Use Behaviors— United States, 1900–1994." In *CDC Surveillance Summaries* (November 18). *Morbidity Mortality Weekly Report* 43(No. SS–3).

Christakis, N. A., and J. H. Fowler. 2008. "The Collective Dynamics of Smoking in a Large Social Network." *New England Journal of Medicine* 358: 2249–2258.

Corning, P.A. 2002. "The Re-emergence of "Emergence": A Venerable Concept in Search of a Theory." *Complexity* 7(6): 18–30.

Davison, K. K., and L. L. Birch. 2001. "Childhood Overweight: A Contextual Model and Recommendations for Future Research." *Obesity Reviews* 2(3): 159–71.

Diamond, J. 2003. "The Double Puzzle of Diabetes." *Nature* 423(6940): 599–602.

Dietz, W. H. 2006. "Canada on the Move: A Novel Effort to Increase Physical Activity among Canadians." *Canadian Journal of Public Health* 97(Suppl 1): S3-S4.

Di Ruggerio, E., A. Rose, K. Gaudreau. 2009. Canadian Institutes of Health Research Support for Population Health Intervention Research in Canada. *Canadian Journal of Public Health* 100(1): I15–I19.

Finegood, D. T. 2006. "Can We Improve Nutritional Health at an Affordable Price?" *Canadian Issues* Winter 2006 : 46–52.

Finegood, D. T., Ö. Karanfil, and C. L. Matteson. 2008. "Getting from Analysis to Action: Framing Obesity Research, Policy and Practice with a Solution-Oriented Complex Systems Lens." *Healthcare Papers* 9(1): 36–41.

Finegood, D. T., T. D. N. Merth, and H. Rutter. 2010. "Implications of the Foresight Obesity System Map for Solutions to Childhood Obesity." *Obesity* 18 (Suppl 1): S13–S16.

Garrow, J. S. 1987. "Energy Balance in Man: An Overview." *American Journal of Clinical Nutrition* 45: 1114–1119.

Geneau, R., G. Fraser, B. Legowski, and S. Stachenko. 2009. "Mobilizing Intersectoral Action to Promote Health: The Case of Actnow BC in British Columbia Canada." WHO Collaborating Centre on Chronic Non Communicable Disease Policy. http://www.phac-aspc.gc.ca/publicat/2009/ActNowBC/index-eng.php Accessed March 4, 2010.

Gereffi, G., J. Lee, and M. Christian. 2009. "US-based Food and Agricultural Value Chains and Their Relevance to Healthy Diets." *Journal of Hunger and Environmental Nutrition* 3(3–4): 357–374.

Green, L. W. 2006. "Public Health Asks of Systems Science: To Advance Our Evidence-Based Practice, Can You Help Us Get More Practice-Based Evidence?" *American Journal of Public Health* 96(3): 406–409.

Greenhalgh T., G. Robert, F. MacFarlane, P. Bate, and O. Kyriakidou. 2004. "Diffusion of Innovations in Service Organizations: Systematic Review and Recommendations." *The Milbank Quarterly*, 82(4): 581–629.

Hall, K. D. 2010. "Predicting Metabolic Adaptation, Body Weight Change, and Energy Intake in Humans." *American Journal of Physiology: Endocrinology and Metabolism* 298: E449–E466.

Hamid, T. K. A. 2009. *Thinking in Circles about Obesity. Applying Systems Thinking to Weight Management.* New York: Springer.

Hawe, P., L. Bond, and H. Butler. 2009. "Knowledge Theories Can Inform Evaluation Practice: What Can a Complexity Lens Add?" In *Knowledge Utilization, Diffusion, Implementation, Transfer, and Translation: Implications for Evaluation. New Directions for Evaluation*, eds. J. M. Ottoson and P. Hawe, 124: 89–100.

Institute of Medicine and National Research Council. 2009. *Local Government Actions to Prevent Childhood Obesity.* Washington, DC: The National Academies Press. http://www.nap.edu/catalog/12674.html Accessed January 5, 2010.

Jeffery, R. W., L. H. Epstein, G. T. Wilson, A. Drewnowski, A. J. Stunkard, and R. R. Wing. 2000. "Long-Term Maintenance of Weight Loss: Current Status." *Health Psychology* 19(1, Supp.): 5–16.

Johnston, L., C. L. Matteson, and D. T. Finegood. 2010. "Places to Intervene in the Complex Systems Giving Rise to Childhood Obesity–Stratification of Recommendations to Government with an Intervention Level Framework." Stockholm: International Congress on Obesity.

Khan L. K., K. Sobush, D. Keener, K. Goodman, A. Lowry, J. Kakietek, and S. Zaro. 2009. "Centers for Disease Control and Prevention. Recommended Community Strategies and Measurements to Prevent Obesity in the United States." *Morbidity Mortality Weekly Recommendation Report* 58(RR-7): 1–26. http://www.cdc.gov/mmwr/preview/mmwrhtml/rr5807a1.htm. Accessed March 4, 2010.

Klem, M. L., R. R. Wing, M. T. McGuire, H. M. Seagle, and J. O. Hill. 1997. "A Descriptive Study of Individuals Successful at Long-Term Maintenance of Substantial Weight Loss." *American Journal of Clinical Nutrition* 66: 239–246.

Kumanyika, S. 2001. "Minisymposium on Obesity: Overview and Some Strategic Considerations." *Annual Review of Public Health* 22: 293–308.

Lang, T., and M. Heasman. 2004. *Food Wars: The Global Battle for Mouths, Minds and Markets.* London: Earthscan.

Leibel, R. L., M. Rosenbaum, and J. Hirsch. 1995. "Changes in Energy Expenditure Resulting from Altered Body Weight." *New England Journal of Medicine* 332(10): 621–628.

Leischow, S. J., and B. Milstein. 2006. "Systems Thinking and Modeling for Public Health Practice." *American Journal of Public Health* 96: 403–405.

Leitch, K. K. 2007. *Reaching for the Top: A Report by the Advisor on Healthy Children and Youth.* Ottawa: Minister of Health. http://www.hc-sc.gc.ca/hl-vs/alt_formats/hpb-dgps/pdf/child-enfant/2007-advisor-conseillere/advisor-conseillere-eng.pdf Accessed December 15, 2009.

Malhi, L. 2009. "Places to Intervene in the Obesity System." BSc (Honours) Thesis, Simon Fraser University.

Malhi, L., Ö. Karanfil, T. Merth, M. Acheson, A. Palmer, and D. T. Finegood. 2009. "Places to Intervene to Make Complex Food Systems More Healthy, Green, Fair, and Affordable." *Journal of Hunger and Environmental Nutrition.* 4 (3–4): 466–476.

Meadows, D. H. 2008. *Thinking in Systems: A Primer,* ed. Diana Wright. White River Junction, VT: Chelsea Green Publishing.

Merrifield, R., et al. 2007. Canada. 39th Parliament. *Healthy Weights for Healthy Kids: Report of the Standing Committee on Health by Ottawa House of Commons.* http://www2.parl.gc.ca/HousePublications/Publication.aspx?Language=E&Mode=1&Parl=39&Ses=1&DocId=2795145&File=0 Accessed December 15, 2009.

Plsek, P. E., T. Greenhalgh. 2001. "The Challenge of Complexity in Health Care." *British Medical Journal* 323: 625–628.

Rankinen, T., A. Zuberi, Y. C. Chagnon, S. J. Weisnagel, G. Argyropoulos, B. Walts, L. Pérusse, and C. Bouchard. 2006. "The Human Obesity Gene Map: The 2005 Update." *Obesity* 14: 529–644.

Resnicow, K., and R. Vaughan. 2006. "A Chaotic View of Behaviour Change: A Quantum Leap for Health Promotion." *International Journal of Behavioral Nutrition and Physical Activity* 3:25–32.

Richardson, K. 2005. "The Hegemony of the Physical Sciences: An Exploration in Complexity Thinking." *Futures* 37: 615–653.

Rickles, D., P. Hawe, and A. Shiell. 2007. "A Simple Guide to Chaos and Complexity." *Journal of Epidemiology and Community Health* 61: 933–937.

Rittel, H., and M. Webber. 1973. "Dilemmas in a General Theory of Planning." In *Policy Sciences,* Vol. 4, 155–169. Amsterdam: Elsevier Scientific Publishing.

Robinson, T. N. 2010. "Save the World, Prevent Obesity: Piggybacking on Existing Social and Ideological Movements." *Obesity* 18 (Supp. 1), S17–S22.

Schooler, C., J. W. Farquhar, S. P. Fortmann, and J. A. Flora. 1997. "Synthesis of Findings and Issues from Community Prevention Trials." *Annals of Epidemiology* 7(7 Supp. 1): S54–S68.

Select Standing Committee on Health. British Columbia. Legislative Assembly. 2006. *A Strategy for Combating Childhood Obesity and Physical Inactivity in British Columbia.* The Legislative Assembly of British Columbia. http://qp.gov.bc.ca/CMT/38thparl/session-2/health/index.htm Accessed December 15, 2009.

Sharma, L. L., S. P. Teret, and K. D. Brownell. 2010. "The Food Industry and Self-Regulation: Standards to Promote Success and to Avoid Public Health Failures." *American Journal of Public Health* 100(2): 240–246.

Solomon, R. C., and F. Flores. 2001. *Building Trust in Business, Politics, Relationships, and Life.* Oxford: Oxford University Press.

Sterman J. 2006. "Learning from Evidence in a Complex World." *American Journal of Public Health* 96: 505–514.

Story, M., M. W. Hamm, and D. Wallinga. 2009. "Food Systems and Public Health: Linkages to Achieve Healthier Diets and Healthier Communities." *Journal of Hunger and Environmental Nutrition* 4: 219–224.

Tremblay, M. S., and C.L. Craig. 2009. "ParticipACTION: Overview and introduction of baseline research on the 'new' ParticipACTION". *International Journal of Behavioral Nutrition and Physical Activity* 6: 84–89.

Trochim, W. M., D. A. Cabrera, B. Milstein, R. S. Gallagher, and S. J. Leischow. 2006. "Practical Challenges of Systems Thinking and Modeling in Public Health." *American Journal of Public Health* 96: 538–546.

Vandenbroeck, I. P., J. Goossens, and M. Clemens. 2007a. *Foresight Tackling Obesities: Future Choices—Building the Obesity System Map.* Government Office for Science, UK Government's Foresight Programme, 2007. http://www.foresight.gov.uk/Obesity/12.pdf Accessed June 16, 2009.

Vandenbroeck, I. P., J. Goossens, and M. Clemens. 2007b. *Foresight Tackling Obesities: Future Choices—Obesity System Atlas.* Government Office for Science, UK Government's Foresight Programme, 2007. http://www.foresight.gov.uk/Obesity/11.pdf Accessed June 16, 2009.

Wagner, A. 1999. "Causality in Complex Systems." *Biology and Philosophy* 14: 83–101.

Yach, D. 2008. "The Role of Business in Addressing the Long-Term Implications of the Current Food Crisis." *Global Health* 5: 4.

CHAPTER 14

CHALLENGES FOR CAUSAL INFERENCE IN OBESITY RESEARCH

M. CHRISTOPHER AULD
AND PAUL GROOTENDORST

INTRODUCTION

OBESITY research is largely an observational science. Some research involves controlled experiments in which a possible contributor to body weight is randomized by the experimenter, but randomizing body weight directly is in principle impossible. Further, the causes of body weight are usually not subject to experimental manipulation: researchers cannot randomize genes, individual characteristics such as income or education or family background, nor contextual influences such as food prices or social norms. For these reasons, social science researchers typically attempt to infer the causes and consequences of body weight using observational data. In this chapter we briefly outline the empirical strategies that social scientists commonly use to make causal inferences in the absence of randomized experiments and then highlight particularly challenging issues in obesity research.

A Brief Overview of Causal Inference in Quantitative Social Science

To fix ideas for the discussion that follows, in this section we present a non-technical summary of several approaches to making causal inferences when the researcher only has observational data available, that is, data in which the researcher cannot control the values of the treatment of interest.[1] Suppose we are interested in estimating the causal effect of some *treatment* variable x on an *outcome* variable y. A univariate model for the outcome can be written,

$$y = \beta x + u, \tag{1}$$

where β denotes the causal effect of a one-unit change in x on y and u represents all causes of y other than x.[2] The research goal is to estimate β. If we were concerned with estimating the causes of overweight or obesity, then the outcome y might be the body mass index (BMI), the ratio of hip to waist circumference, or perhaps a measure of caloric expenditure or caloric intake or nutrition. The treatment x could be: some economic variable such as the relative price of healthy versus unhealthy food, or income, or the opportunity cost of engaging in leisure time physical activity; the features of ones physical environment, such as proximity to parks, or the ease with which one can walk or bike to work or a shop; the features of one's social environment, such as the physical activity and dietary habits of one's friends, or social norms concerning body weight; or a medical treatment, such as bariatric surgery. In studies that assess the consequences of overweight/obesity, the treatment is some measure of overweight/obesity, and the outcome y might be a health outcome, such as mortality, functional impairment, medical expenditures, or the presence of diabetes or some other chronic disease; or y might be a labour market outcome, such as employment or earnings; or y might be any of a number of other physical, mental, or social outcomes of interest to the researcher.

A linear least squares regression of y on x does not generally recover an unbiased estimate of the causal effect of x on y; that is, the linear regression estimator of β in equation (2) is not generally centered on the true causal effect of x on y. This problem persists even if the sample size is arbitrarily large. As the sample size increases without bound, the least squares estimator, denoted $\hat{\beta}$, converges to

$$\hat{\beta} \to \frac{\text{Cov}(x, y)}{V(x)} = \beta + \frac{\text{Cov}(x, u)}{V(x)} \tag{2}$$

---

1 See Pearl (2000) or Heckman (2005) for extensive discussions of causality and causal modeling.
2 Assume throughout that all variables are measured in deviations from sample means so that the constant term is zero.

where Cov denotes covariance and V variance.[3] The regression estimate does not recover the causal effect of x on y unless $\text{Cov}(x, u) = 0$. That is, if other causes of the outcome, u, are correlated with the treatment, x, then a regression of y on x yields an *inconsistent* estimate of the causal effect of x on y: even with an arbitrarily large number of observations, the estimated parameter will not recover the causal effect of interest. Other causes of y will be correlated with x if: (1) x is measured with error, or (2) y causes x ("reverse causality"), or (3) there are variables that do not appear in the model which affect both y and x ("unobserved heterogeneity" or "omitted variables" or "confounding"). Any of these problems, referred to in the econometrics literature as *endogeneity*, imply that correlations between the treatment and outcome do not reveal the causal effect of the treatment on the outcome.

Problems with Observational Data

Body weight outcomes are likely to be endogenous to other health and social outcomes. If the researcher is trying to explain body weight, so that y is a measure of weight and x is some possible cause of weight, we rarely have reason to believe that the cause in question is uncorrelated with other causes u. For example, if we find that schooling and body weight are negatively correlated, we cannot conclude that more education causes lower body weight because other factors (such as personality characteristics, cognitive ability, or family background) may cause both schooling and body weight. Or suppose that we find that the likelihood that an individual is obese (y) is higher the greater the density of fast food restaurants within five miles of her residence (x). It is possible that x exerts a causal impact on y. But it could also be that both fast food restaurants and obese individuals tend to locate in lower income areas. In other words, both x and y are associated with some other variable that may not be observable to the researcher. Further, it could be that x and y are mutually determined. It could be that density of fast food restaurants causally determines obesity prevalence, but that areas of higher obesity prevalence attract additional fast food restaurants, so that obesity "reverse" causes fast food outlet density.

Similarly, personal characteristics such as income, education, or the number of close friends who are obese are likely to be caused by the same unobservable characteristics that cause overweight or obesity. If we are attempting to determine a consequence of obesity, so that x is a measure of obesity and y is some other outcome, we could only claim that the correlation between x and y means x causes y if we can safely assume that all other causes of y are uncorrelated with body weight. Genetic, developmental, educational, social, economic, and contextual factors which that body weight x cannot be assumed to be uncorrelated with unobserved

---

3 Derivation of the estimator and its sampling properties can be found in any econometrics or regression analysis textbook, see for example Wooldridge (2001).

causes of body weight u. For example, evidence that adolescents who skip breakfast are more likely to be overweight does not imply that skipping breakfast causes overweight because many personality characteristics unobservable to the statistician (for example, poor eating habits in general) may affect both propensity to skip breakfast and body weight, or overweight may "reverse" cause increased propensity to skip breakfast.[4]

Randomized Controlled Trials

Note that if x can be controlled by the researcher, the researcher can randomize x with respect to all other causes of y and, therefore, make valid causal inferences. In obesity research, medical treatments for obesity can be randomized, but typically personal or social possible causes of body weight, such as income, education, smoking, peers, and food prices, are either costly or impossible to randomize through controlled experimentation. Some examples do exist. See Padwal et al. (2003) for a review of randomized trials on medical interventions for overweight and obesity. See Robinson (1999) for an example of a controlled experiment on a behavioral cause of obesity, television viewing. Since controlled experiments are frequently costly or infeasible, obesity researchers commonly use observational data to infer causation.

Covariate Adjustment

Researchers attempting to estimate causal effects with observational data often use *covariate adjustment* to address unobserved heterogeneity. One can include other variables in the model which make observational data look more like a controlled experiment in the sense that we can control for some common causes of both x and y. For example, controlling for education in a regression of body weight on income removes one possible common cause of both income and body weight. This approach rarely leads to models that have compelling causal interpretations because there will always be important causes of body weight and other outcomes which cannot be observed by the researcher. Moreover, covariate adjustment does not correct for other types of endogeneity, that is measurement error and reverse causality. Including more control variables in the regression, then, may mitigate but does not generally solve the problem. Typically covariate adjustment is performed through multivariate regression techniques, but closely related methods called matching estimators are becoming popular. Matching estimators, like regression estimators, fail to recover causal effects if there are unobserved causes of both the treatment and the outcome, but matching estimators impose fewer parametric assumptions than conventional regression estimators (Heckman et al. 1998).

---

4 See Rampersaud et al. (2005) for a summary of the literature on breakfast habits and, among other outcomes, body weight.

A special case of covariate adjustment called *regression discontinuity designs* allow the researcher to make causal inferences even in the presence of reverse causation or confounding by exploiting discontinuities in the causes of the treatment. For example, Schanzenbach (2009) estimates the causal effect of school lunches on children's body weight by, in effect, statistically comparing the body weight of children just below the income eligibility threshold to those just above—unobserved causes of both income and body weight should be smooth as income passes this point, but school lunch takeup is discontinuous at this point, allowing Schanzenbach to estimate the causal effect of interest.

Instrumental Variables

Instrumental variable (IV) methods can sometimes produce credible causal estimates in the absence of controlled experiments.[5] IV methods require *instruments*: variables that affect the outcome y *only* because they affect the value of the treatment x and for no other reason. Such instruments cause quasi–experimental variation in x, that is, part of the reason that x varies is because of variation in the instrument, and the researcher can isolate that variation and treat the problem as if a controlled experiment had taken place. For example, if a controlled experiment is conducted in which a randomly assigned treatment affects diet, and diet in turn affects weight, then the part of variation in weight across people attributable to experimental assignment can be used to infer the causal effect of weight on other outcomes. An example of IV methods in obesity research is Cawley (2004), who estimates the effect of body weight on wages. To do so, he exploits genetic variation in body weight by using the respondent's sibling's body weight as an instrument for respondent's body weight. Controlled experiments designed for other purposes are also sometimes analyzed using instrumental variables, for example, Bhattacharya et al. (2009) use the Rand Health Insurance Experiment to provide randomized variation in health insurance status. Similarly, Kling et al. (2007) use random assignment of neighborhood characteristics across families in the Moving to Opportunity study to estimate neighborhood effects on body weight.

If z is an instrumental variable, then as the sample grows in size $\hat{\beta}_{IV}$, the linear instrumental variable estimator of β, converges to

$$\hat{\beta}_{IV} \to \frac{\text{Cov}(z, y)}{\text{Cov}(z, x)} = \beta + \frac{\text{Cov}(z, u)}{\text{Cov}(z, x)}. \tag{3}$$

The IV estimator recovers a causal effect of x on y if, and only if, z causes y only through z's effect on x. In other words, all other causes of y besides x are uncorrelated with z: $\text{Cov}(z, u) = 0$. If that assumption fails and z and u covary, then the estimator may provide highly misleading estimates. As discussed further below in

---

5 See Auld (2006) or Grootendorst (2007) for lengthier and more technical discussions of IV methods in health research.

the context of obesity research, recent literature has highlighted serious difficulties with IV estimators when the instrumental variables either explain little of the variation in the treatment ($Cov(z, x)$ is close to zero) or are even slightly correlated with unobserved causes of the outcome, that is, z and u are even slightly correlated. Another recent strand of literature points out that the implicit assumption in equation (2) that all individuals experience the same effect on y of a given change in x (that is, that β does not vary across people) is not innocuous in this context. If causal effects vary across people, then IV estimates recover a weighted average of causal effects for people affected by changes in the instruments, where the weights in this weighted average are proportional to the responsiveness of an individual's treatment status to the instrument. Therefore, the researcher will recover different causal effects using different instruments, even when textbook conditions are satisfied, because different instruments affect the treatment status of different people.[6] The most important difficulty with IV methods, however, is that it is often difficult or impossible to find good instruments, a problem we return to later in this chapter.

Methods Exploiting Panel Data

Panel data—data that tracks individuals over time and give us multiple observations on a person's body weight and other outcomes—provides another approach to causal inference. If, in equation (2), we suppose that all other causes of y, u, is the sum of a component that does not vary over time and a component that does, then it is possible to remove the time-invariant component via a suitable transformation of the equation. Removal of the time-invariant portion of u eliminates a potential source of correlation between u and x. One transformation that removes the time-invariant, individual-specific unobserved component is the first difference. For example, if y is wages and x is body weight, the correlation between x and y reflects in part aspects of personality which affect both weight and outcomes in the labor market. With longitudinal data, we can ask whether *changes* in a subject's body weight over time are correlated with *changes* in her wages instead of just how levels of body weight are correlated with levels of wages. If personality is fixed over the sampling window for the population of interest, then personality does not affect these changes and, provided that changes in weight are not correlated with any unobservable time-varying determinants of wages, we can estimate causal effects. Various regression methods embody this intuition, including fixed effects regression, differenced models including difference-in-difference estimation, and long difference models.[7] Less frequently, panels may include a dimension other than time which gives multiple observations on the same cross-sectional unit; one can then employ variants of these methods. Examples include data on twins in which

---

6 See Imbens and Angrist (1994) or Heckman et al. (2006) for discussions of instrumental variables estimation when causal effects differ across units.
7 See Wooldridge (2001) for a review of panel methods.

differences between twins' outcomes are used analogously to differences across time to remove common genetic causes and data in which multiple members of the same family are observed such that family-specific factors can be statistically removed.[8]

Summarizing this section, social scientists studying obesity generally cannot conduct controlled experiments to make causal inferences. Methods that use observational data to make such inferences usually rely on some combination of: multivariate regression methods which hold observable confounders fixed, instrumental variable methods which infer causality from correlations between the outcome and variables which should only affect the outcome because they affect regressors of interest, or longitudinal data methods which difference out common causes of the treatment and the outcome. In the remainder of this chapter we discuss the use of these methods in obesity research, highlighting difficulties which make their use particularly challenging in the context of body weight.

Challenges to Causal Inference in Obesity Research

Measurement of Body Weight and Other Variables

One or more of the variables of interest, either the outcome y or an explanatory variable x, may be difficult to measure. Such difficulties often arise in empirical obesity research. Indeed, one need look no further than the concept of obesity itself. It is well–known that the standard measurement instrument, BMI, is a noisy measure of underlying obesity, for at least two reasons. First, BMI, height adjusted weight, fails to capture important dimensions of obesity. For instance, it does not distinguish fat mass from lean mass. Nor does it distinguish the location of fat mass, yet upper-body obesity is more strongly associated with metabolic disorders and cardiovascular disease than is lower-body obesity.[9] There is some evidence that the hip-to-waist ratio is a better measure of obesity than BMI (Yusuf et al. 2005), yet hip-to-waist measurements are generally unavailable in the survey data. Second, the inputs into the BMI formula, height and weight, are frequently misreported by survey respondents. This misreporting is not random. Instead, in some groups,

---

8 See Maes et al. (2005) for an example of an effort using twins data to determine the portion of body weight variability attributable to genetics. See Anderson et al. (2003) for an obesity research example of the use of family fixed effects.

9 See Burkhauser and Cawley (2008) for a discussion of BMI and other measures of body weight outcomes in social science research. See Ben-Noun et al. (2001); Willett et al. (1999) for evidence on fat distribution and health.

reported BMI tends to understate actual BMI and the degree of under-reporting increases with actual BMI (Cawley, 2000).

Obesity is not the only variable that is hard to measure accurately in this line of research. Other examples include the "built environment": how does one accurately measure the degree to which the layout of streets, sidewalks, and buildings promotes or hinders physical activity? Or consider food prices. The price that one pays for the same item varies considerably depending on where it is purchased (a local convenience store, say, or a warehouse type retail outlet such as Costco). It is also hard to model prices for the entire array of foods that are available (Powell and Chaloupka, 2009).

Measurement error adversely affects the properties of one's estimator, although the manner in which the estimator is affected depends on specifics. Measurement error in an *explanatory* variable renders conventional estimators of causal effects inconsistent. If x is measured with error in equation (2) and the error is random, the estimate of the causal effect of x on y will be biased towards zero, and we will tend to systematically find that the effect is smaller than it truly is.[10] Random measurement error in an *outcome* variable deflates the precision of one's estimator, which, unlike inconsistency, can be remedied by increasing one's sample size. If the measurement error in the outcome varies with the treatment x or other covariates in the model, then the estimator is generally inconsistent. Similarly, if a binary outcome (such as obese or not) is mismeasured, then the standard estimators (logit or probit) are also inconsistent (Kennedy 2008). Finally, panel methods relying on differencing or fixed effects exacerbate problems arising from measurement error. These methods use changes in body weight rather than levels of body weight, and changes in observed body weight may largely reflect noisy measurement. The statistical properties of panel estimators are often, therefore, poor when measurement error is present (Griliches and Hausman 1986).

How can one deal with the problems caused by measurement error? If the error occurs in a continuous outcome variable, such as BMI, one can follow Cawley (2000) and estimate the relationship between self-reported and actual BMI using data from a survey which contains information on both variables (such as the U.S. National Health and Nutrition Examination Survey) and, using this estimated relationship, replace self-reported with predicted actual BMI. If the measurement error occurs in an explanatory variable, then one can use an instrumental variables estimator, provided that one has access to either multiple independent measures of the problematic explanatory variable or other variables that are correlated with the problematic explanatory variable but not with unobserved causes of the dependent variable.

---

10 By "random" in this context we mean: the measurement error in x is statistically independent of the error term u.

DIFFICULTY EXPLAINING BODY WEIGHT
WITH OBSERVABLE CHARACTERISTICS
AND CONTEXTS

In multiple regression analyses, it is standard practice to report the coefficient of determination, R^2, which reflects the proportion of variation in the outcome variable explained by the model. The R^2 values reported in the obesity research literature are typically small, indicating that body weight is not highly correlated with observable demographic, economic, and contextual outcomes and thus model fits are usually poor.[11] Lack of a good fit does not mean the model is not useful, but it does pose problems for causal inference. When the analytic goal is to estimate determinants of body weight, these low correlations directly imply that the endeavor has not been highly successful, as by definition most of the variation in body weight has been left unexplained. When the goal of the analysis is to assess the consequences of body weight, the paucity of strong predictors of body weight undercuts efforts to use instrumental variables and similar techniques, as discussed in detail in the following subsection.

To illustrate the problem, in table 14.1 we display the R^2 statistics from selected recent studies using large survey datasets. In each study the dependent variable is BMI; the covariates differ across studies but all include detailed demographic information. The proportion of variation explained by observed characteristics is commonly less than 10% and ranges down to 1%. The proportion of variation explained is modestly high only in studies in which measures of parental (such as Chou et al. (2008)) or peer (Fletcher et al. (2009)) body weight outcomes are included as

Table 14.1. Coefficients of Determination from Selected BMI Regressions.

Study	R^2
Chou et al. (2004)	0.08
Rashad et al. (2006)	0.10–0.13
Chou et al. (2008)	0.15–0.24
Lakdawalla and Philipson (2009)	0.09–0.12
Bhattacharya et al. (2009)	0.01
Davis and Carpenter (2009)	0.10
Fletcher et al. (2009)	0.03
Zhao and Kaestner (2009)	0.13
Cawley et al. (2005)	0.03
Auld and Powell (2009)	0.05–0.07

---

11 In some studies, individual or regional fixed effects provide high goodness of fit, but this explanatory power merely means there is variation across people and places not attributable to observable characteristics. Goodness of fit can also be reasonable to good when detailed measures of food consumption and physical activity are included, but these proximate causes of body weight are themselves difficult to explain.

covariates, suggesting genetic or common household characteristics and sorting on friendship networks have good explanatory power.

To the best of our knowledge, the problem of poor fit in body weight models has been little-discussed in the primary literature, yet it is pervasive, reflects our difficulty in explaining the distribution of body weight, and leads to difficulties in determining the consequences of body weight when using observational data.

Finding Good Instruments

Instrumental variables estimators based on the intuition provided by equation (3) require the researcher to specify a causal model in which some variables z affect y only because they affect x. Such models are sometimes able to produce compelling estimates of causation from observational data. However, the major challenge in specifying such models is finding variables that have a strong effect on the problematic explanatory variable x and at the same time only affect the outcome y because they affect x.

If the instrumental variable z has a low correlation with x, the instrument is said to be *weak* and many difficult inference problems arise. In an influential paper, Bound et al. (1995) showed that fake instruments produced by a random number generator yielded estimates of the causal effect of schooling on wages similar to estimates produced by using quarter of birth as instruments, which are weak predictors of schooling.

If the instrumental variable z is correlated with x but also correlated with other causes of y, the instrument is said to be *invalid*. Put another way, the instrument is subject to the same problem as the problematic explanatory variable x—it is correlated with causes of y unobserved by the researcher. Equation (3) shows that the resulting estimator will not recover the true causal effect of interest no matter how large the sample, because $Cov(z, u) \neq 0$. This problem arises even when the instrument is not weak, but recent literature has emphasized that when an instrumental variables estimate is based on both weak and invalid instruments, the resulting estimates may be very misleading. The point estimate may be centered on a value even farther from the true value than the linear regression estimator; the sampling distribution of the estimator may be much more dispersed than the linear regression estimator, and the standard errors conventionally calculated for the instrumental variables estimate may not reflect the true sampling distribution (Stock et al. 2002).

These problems with instrumental variables strategies are severe in the context of obesity research. First consider attempting to estimate the causal effect of body weight, x, on some other outcome, y. The researcher needs to find at least one variable z which affects body weight but has no effect on y except through its effect on x. Further, the effect of the candidate instrument z on x must be substantial, not just statistically different from zero, to avoid a weak instrument problem. But as detailed in the preceding subsection of this chapter, obesity researchers have trouble finding variables that are strongly correlated with body weight, much less variables that can be credibly thought to affect body weight but not directly the outcome of interest.

Many seemingly promising instruments fail once scrutinized closely: for example, a researcher attempting to estimate the effect of child obesity on academic performance may consider parental education as instruments, reasoning that parental education is correlated with child obesity but does not directly affect child academic performance. However, parental education does not affect child academic performance *only* because of an effect on child body weight—the child's academic performance may be affected by genetic, parental inputs, and contextual factors that are all correlated with parental education even after holding child body weight fixed and that cannot all be observed by the researcher. So parental education is probably an invalid instrument. In light of these difficulties, attempts to use instrumental variables to estimate the causal effect of body weight on other outcomes are rare.[12]

These problems also arise when body weight is the outcome of interest, y, and researchers attempt to find instruments for suspected causes of body weight. To illustrate by example, social and medical scientists have both paid considerable attention to the association between income and body weight.[13] It is well-known that low income is associated with higher obesity rates, that is, that a regression of the form of equation (2) of obesity on household income produces a negative estimate of β. However, it is plausible that unobserved causes of body weight u are correlated with income and that body weight may "reverse" cause household income through its effects on labor market outcomes and marital outcomes. To solve these difficulties, researchers need to specify variables which are correlated with income but only affect body weight because they affect income, which rules out any number of personal or household characteristics, since these characteristics (for example, education) can be expected to affect both body weight and income. Schmeiser (2009) attempts to get around these issues by exploiting an experiment induced by changes in tax rates: he uses changes in the Earned Income Tax Credit as an instrumental variable for income of households affected by these changes, and finds that even though the correlation between income and BMI is negative, income appears to have a positive causal effect on BMI for women. Similarly, Cawley et al. (2009) use the Social Security "notch" to estimate the effect of income on body weight among the elderly. Another example of an instrumental variable estimate of a purported cause of body weight is Dunn (2008). Dunn is interested in estimating the effect of fast food outlet density on body weight, noting that the correlation between these outcomes does not recover a causal effect because fast food restaurants are not randomly assigned across regions. Dunn uses the number of interstate exits as an instrument for fast food outlets and finds that a 10 percent increase in fast food outlets causes BMI to rise by 0.33 units.

We close this section by briefly discussing use of genetic information as instruments to study the consequences of body weight. *Mendelian randomization*, random gene sequences that, for our purposes, affect phenotypic body weight outcomes, are promising instruments because they are randomized by nature and some gene

---

12 See Cawley (2004) for an example of such an attempt.
13 See McLaren in this volume.

sequences can be shown to be correlated with body weight outcomes. Examples include Ding et al. (2006) and Norton and Han (2008), who use genes regulating mood and (in the former case) liver enzymes to instrument for health behaviors including obesity in education and labor market outcome models. Like most other instrumenting strategies, though, the validity of the instruments may be questionable.[14] We require the gene used as the instrument, z, to affect the outcome of interest y *only* because z affects body weight x. Phenomena which invalidate that assumption include *linkage disequilibrium*, in which a given gene z may be correlated with genes not used in the analysis. If those genes not used in the analysis also affect y the instrumental variables estimate may be misleading. Or, a given gene may affect the outcome y both because it affects body weight and through other channels, a complication referred to as *pleiotropy*. To see how these problems affect inference, consider attempting to use "presence of a Y chromosome" as an instrument for body weight—the presence of that chromosome is randomized by nature, but it clearly affects any outcome of interest through many channels other than body weight.[15]

Dynamics

One's current body weight reflects the sum total of weight changes in previous years. Body weight and composition, in other words, is a "stock" that reflects the "flow" of caloric intake and expenditure in each year going back to birth. This complicates empirical research into the causes of obesity in several ways.

First, a model of individual obesity would need to consider, in addition to contemporaneous causal factors, those factors that operated in previous periods. But data on historical causal factors specific to each individual might not always be available. Even longitudinal data may be insufficient given that these data sets typically do not follow individuals for a long time.

Second, even if historical data on the causal determinants of obesity were available, it may be difficult to incorporate these into a parsimonious empirical model. Suppose, for instance, that one's weight loss/gain in a given year depends on just one contemporaneous variable: the relative price of "healthy" versus "unhealthy" food. If an analyst only had access to data on the current weight of a cross section of individuals, then she would need to model the effect of price in each of the previous years of life. In its most general form, the model would contain as many covariates as the number of years of age. Some restrictions would be required to make the empirical model tractable. If one were willing to assume that the impact of price on weight change was the same in each period, then one could simplify considerably; the model would have only one covariate, the sum total of previous prices. Similarly, if the only price variation was cross-sectional (i.e., individuals face different prices

---

14 See Didelez and Sheehan (2007); Nitsch et al. (2006); Smith and Ebrahim (2003) for discussions of the strengths and potential weaknesses of instrumentation through Mendelian randomization.

15 The Y-chromosone thought experiment is due to John Cawley.

but these prices do not vary over time), then individual weight must reflect its long-run steady state value. Or if the analyst had data on individuals' weight *changes*, and she was again willing to assume that the effect of price on weight change was time-invariant, then the model would again have just one covariate: current price.

In reality, of course, weight change is affected by numerous factors. Economics emphasizes that net caloric intake depends on the relative prices of the entire array of food and beverages available to the consumer, as well as the (implicit) price of physical activity and income. The consumer reacts to dozens of relative prices, and this makes it difficult to write down a reasonably parsimonious model. And, again, this exercise requires accurate measurements on a wide range of prices. The exclusion from the model of prices on some commodities leads to inconsistent estimates of the effects on weight change of prices that are included in the model, if these prices are correlated with the excluded prices. Consistent estimation also requires that prices be determined independently of the factors that determine obesity. And economic variables are only part of the story. Social interactions, for instance, are likely important as well.

An additional challenge in this line of research is that very small changes in behaviour can produce large changes in weight over time. Cutler et al. (2003) estimate that the accumulation of a net caloric increase of only 100 to 150 calories per day (about one can of Pepsi or three Oreo cookies a day) could explain the 10- to 12-pound increase in median weight observed in the United States in the past two decades. So while the magnitude of price change on weight gain is small in the short run, the long run effect can be large, only because the small impact accumulates over many periods. The difficulty for the analyst is that the data may not be sufficiently informative to precisely estimate the effects of price on weight change, if these effects are small in magnitude. There are a number of reasons for this. One is that one needs more data to distinguish a small effect than a large effect. Another reason is that the precision with which one can estimate the impact of a particular explanatory variable on the outcome (say soda prices on BMI) depends on how well the model fits the data. But, as we have already noted, models of weight outcomes typically don't fit the data well. Estimator precision also requires variation in the explanatory variable. But price variation may not be particularly large during the time period of study. A final reason is that weight gain/loss is often measured with less precision than weight itself. Technically, the variance of the change in weight is twice the variance of weight plus the covariance of the two weight measurements. These dynamic issues interact with the measurement error problem discussed above, since they imply that measurement errors may not be white noise but rather serially correlated within individuals, and such correlation leads to even more bias and inconsistency than white noise error (Griliches and Hausman 1986).

The discussion so far has focused on dynamic aspects of causal models of obesity. The same issues, however, can also apply to models of the consequences of obesity. Models of the health outcomes of obesity are a good case in point. The adverse sequelae of obesity—type 2 diabetes and heart disease, for instance—typically occur only after a long lag. This means that the analyst modeling the morbidity impact of obesity would need to record not only current obesity (and other risk factors), but obesity and other risks factors in previous years as well.

Given these difficulties, some analysts have attempted to identify causal effects using indirect approaches. As an example, Alston et al. (2008) questioned whether farm subsidies in the Unites States have caused that higher obesity rates by making fattening foods relatively cheap and plentiful. They note, for subsidies to have affected obesity, it must be the case that (1) farm subsidies have reduced the price of inputs used to making fattening foods, (2) these lower input prices have reduced the prices consumers pay for such foods, and (3) in response to lower prices, consumers have consumed more fattening food. They focus on each link in the causal chain and find that "the magnitude of the impact in each case is zero or small." They conclude that, contrary to some media reports, U.S. farm subsidies have had at best a very modest effect on obesity rates.

CONCLUSIONS

Causal inference in quantitative social science is challenging because controlled experiments are almost never available, and body weight is an outcome that cannot be experimentally manipulated. Body weight is an outcome of complex genetic, personality, demographic, and contextual influences, so that correlations between weight and most observable personal, family, or regional characteristics do not typically recover causation even after regression adjustment.

This chapter sketched common empirical strategies used to make estimate causal relations when treatments are not randomized with respect to outcomes and highlighted particularly difficult issues with their application in obesity research. In particular, (1) body weight is difficult to measure, in both conceptual and practical senses, (2) body weight is difficult to explain, making the search for identification through instrumental variables even more difficult than usual and undermining efforts to characterize the causes of body weight itself, (3) body weight is a stock that changes slowly over time, such that small influences on body weight over time may eventually cause large changes in weight but will be very difficult to detect statistically. These issues often arise in combination, making causal inference in this area particularly difficult.

ACKNOWLEDGEMENTS

Auld thanks the Alberta Heritage Foundation for Medical Research (AHFMR) for financial support. Grootendorst acknowledges financial support from the research program into the Social and Economic Dimensions of an Aging Population (SEDAP), based at McMaster University, and the Premier's

Research Excellence Award. Both authors acknowledge the excellent research assistance of Van Hai Nguyen.

REFERENCES

Alston, J., D. Sumner, and S. Vosti. 2008. "Farm Subsidies and Obesity in the United States: National Evidence and International Comparisons." *Food Policy* 33: 470–479.

Anderson, P., K. Butcher, and P. Levine. 2003. "Maternal Employment and Overweight Children." *Journal of Health Economics* 22: 477–504.

Auld, M. C. 2006. "Using Observational Data to Identify the Causal Effects of Health-Related Behavior." In *Elgar Companion to Health Economics*, ed. A. Jones, 36–45. Northampton, MA: Elgar.

Auld, M. C., and L. M. Powell. 2009. "Economics of Food Energy Density and Adolescent Body Weight." *Economica* 76 (304), 719–740.

Ben-Noun, L., E. Sohar, and A. Laor. 2001. "Neck Circumference as a Simple Screening Measure For Identifying Overweight and Obese Patients." *Obesity Research* 9(8): 470–477.

Bhattacharya, J., K. Bundorf, N. Pace, and N. Sood. 2009. "Does Health Insurance Make You Fat?" Working paper 15163, National Bureau of Economic Research.

Bound, J., D. Jaeger, and R. Baker. 1995. "Problems with Instrumental Variables Estimation When the Correlation between the Instruments and the Endogenous Explanatory Variable Is Weak." *Journal of the American Statistical Association* 90 (430): 443–450.

Burkhauser, R., and J. Cawley. 2008. "Beyond BMI: The Value of More Accurate Measures of Fatness and Obesity in Social Science Research." *Journal of Health Economics* 27(2): 519–529.

Cawley, J. 2000. "Body Weight and Women's Labor Market Outcomes." Working Paper 7841, National Bureau of Economic Research.

Cawley, J. 2004. "The Impact of Obesity on Wages." *Journal of Human Resources* 39(2): 451–474.

Cawley, J., C. Meyerhoefer, and D. Newhouse. 2005. "The Impact of State Physical Education Requirements on Youth Physical Activity and Overweight." Working Paper 11411, National Bureau of Economic Research.

Cawley, J., J. Moran, and K. Simon. 2010. "The Impact of Income on the Weight of Elderly Americans." *Health Economics.* 19(8): 979–993.

Chou, S., I. Rashad, and M. Grossman. 2008. "Fast-Food Restaurant Advertising on Television and Its influence on Childhood Obesity." *Journal of Law and Economics* 51(4): 599–618.

Chou, S.Y., M. Grossman, and H. Saffer. 2004. "An Economic Analysis of Adult Obesity: Results from the Behavioral Risk Factor Surveillance System." *Journal of Health Economics* 23: 565–587.

Cutler, D., E. Glaeser, and J. Shapiro. 2003. "Why Have Americans Become More Obese?" *Journal of Economic Perspectives* 17(3): 93–118.

Davis, B., and C. Carpenter. 2009. "Proximity of Fast-Food Restaurants to Schools and Adolescent Obesity." *American Journal of Public Health* 99(3): 505–510.

Didelez, V., and N. Sheehan. 2007. "Mendelian Randomization as an Instrumental Variable Approach to Causal Inference." *Statistical Methods in Medical Research* 16: 309–330.

Ding, W., S. Lehrer, J. N. Rosenquist, and J. Audrain-McGovern. 2006. "The Impact of Poor Health on Education: New Evidence Using Genetic Markers." Working Paper 12304, National Bureau of Economic Research.

Dunn, R. 2008. "Obesity And The Availability Of Fast-Food: An Instrumental Variables Approach." Working Paper, Texas A&M University.

Fletcher, J., D. Frisvold, and N. Tefft. 2009. "The Effects of Soft Drink Taxes on Child and Adolescent Consumption and Weight Outcomes." Working Paper 0908, Emory University.

Griliches, Z., and J. Hausman. 1986. "Errors in Variables in Panel Data." *Journal of Econometrics* 31: 93–118.

Grootendorst, P. 2007. "A Review of Instrumental Variables Estimation of Treatment Effects in the Applied Health Sciences." *Health Services and Outcomes Research Methodology* 7(3–4): 159–179.

Heckman, J. 2005. "The Scientific Model of Causality." *Sociological Methodology* 35(1): 1–98.

Heckman, J., H. Ichimura, and P. Todd. 1998. "Matching as an Econometric Evaluation Estimator." *Review of Economic Studies* 65: 261–294.

Heckman, J., S. Urzua, and E. Vytlacil. 2006. "Understanding Instrumental Variables in Models with Essential Heterogeneity." *Review of Economics and Statistics* 88(3): 389–432.

Imbens, G., and J. Angrist. 1994. "Identification and Estimation of Local Average Treatment Effects." *Econometrica* 62(2): 467–475.

Kennedy, P. 2008. *A Guide to Econometrics*, 6th ed. Malden, MA: Blackwell.

Kling, J., J. Liebman, and L. Katz. 2007. "Experimental Analysis of Neighbourhood Effects." *Econometrica* 75 (1), 83–119.

Lakdawalla, D., and T. Philipson. 2009. "The Growth of Obesity and Technological Change." *Economics and Human Biology* 7(3): 283–293.

Maes, H., M. Neale, and L. Eaves. 2005. Genetic and Environmental Factors in Relative Body Weight and Human Adiposity." *Behavior Genetics* 27(4): 325–351.

Nitsch, D., M. Molokhia, L. Smeeth, B. DeStavola, J. Whittaker, and D. Leon. 2006. "Limits to Causal Inference Based on Mendelian Randomization: A Comparison with Randomized Controlled Trials." *American Journal of Epidemiology* 163(5): 397–403.

Norton, E., and E. Han. 2008. "Genetic Information, Obesity, and Labor Market Outcomes." *Health Economics* 17(9): 1089–1104.

Padwal, R., S. Li, and D. Lau. 2003. "Long-term Pharmacotherapy for Overweight and Obesity: A Systematic Review and Meta-Analysis of Randomized Controlled Trials." *International Journal of Obesity* 27, 1437–1446.

Pearl, J. 2000. *Causality: Models, Reasoning, and Inference*. Cambridge: Cambridge University Press.

Powell, L., and F. Chaloupka. 2009. "Price, Availability, and Youth Obesity: Evidence from Bridging The Gap." *Preventing Chronic Disease* 6(3): A93.

Rampersaud, G., M. Pereira, B. Girard, J. Adams, and J. Metzi. 2005. "Breakfast Habits, Nutritional Status, Body Weight, and Academic Performance in Children and Adolescents." *Journal of the American Dietetic Association* 105(5): 743–760.

Rashad, I., M. Grossman, and S. Chou. 2006. "The Super Size of America: An Economic Estimation of Body Mass Index and Obesity in Adults." *Eastern Economic Journal* 32(1): 133–148.

Robinson, T. 1999. "Reducing Children's Television Viewing to Prevent Obesity." *Journal of the American Medical Association* 282: 1561–1567.

Schanzenbach, D. 2009. "Do School Lunches Contribute to Obesity?" *Journal of Human Resources* 44(3): 684–709.

Schmeiser, M. 2009. "Expanding Waistlines and Wallets: The Impact of Family Income on the BMI of Women and Men Eligible for the Earned Income Tax Credit." *Health Economics* 18(11): 1277–1294.

Smith, G., and S. Ebrahim. 2003. "'Mendelian Randomization': Can Genetic Epidemiology Contribute to Understanding Environmental Determinants of Disease?" *International Journal of Epidemiology* 32: 1–22.

Stock, J., J. Wright, and M. Yogo. 2002. "A Survey of Weak Instruments and Weak Identification in Generalized Method of Moments." *Journal of Business and Economic Statistics* 20(4): 518–528.

Willett, W., W. Dietz, and G. Colditz. 1999. "Guidelines for Healthy Weight." *New England Journal of Medicine* 341(6): 427–434.

Wooldridge, J. 2001. *Econometric Analysis of Cross Section and Panel Data.* Cambridge, MA: MIT Press.

Yusuf, S., S. Hawken, S. Ounpuu, L. Bautista, M. Franzosi, and P. Commerford. 2005. Obesity and the Risk of Myocardial Infarction in 27,000 Participants from 52 Countries: A Case-Control Study." Lancet 366(9497): 1640–1649.

Zhao, Z., and R. Kaestner. 2009. "Effects of Urban Sprawl on Obesity." Working Paper 15436, National Bureau of Economic Research.

PART III

THE CAUSES AND CORRELATES OF DIET, PHYSICAL ACTIVITY, AND OBESITY

CHAPTER 15

RACE, ETHNICITY, AND OBESITY

RENEE E. WALKER AND ICHIRO KAWACHI

INTRODUCTION

THE prevalence of obesity has increased dramatically over the last three decades among all segments of the U.S. population, that is, among children and adults, among men and women, and across all socio-economic strata and race/ethnic groups (Gordon-Larsen, Adair, and Popkin 2003; Ogden, Carroll, Curtin, McDowell, Tabak, and Flegal 2006). Estimates based on data from the 1999 to 2002 National Health and Nutrition Examination Survey (NHANES) suggest that during the past three decades obesity prevalence doubled among adults ages 20 years and older. During the same period, overweight prevalence among children and adolescents tripled (Flegal, Carroll, Ogden, and Johnson, 2002; Hedley, Ogden, Johnson, Carroll, Curtin and Flegal 2004; Ogden et al. 2006). At the same time, the overall upward trend in the prevalence of overweight and obesity across the population masks the dramatic disparities that exist between population subgroups. The aim of this chapter is twofold: to describe the obesity disparities between racial and ethnic groups in the U.S. population, and to summarize the evidence on the possible causes of these disparities. The patterns of obesity across racial and ethnic groups are complex and defy simple generalizations. As a stylized fact, racial and ethnic minorities—in particular, African Americans and Hispanic Americans—tend to be more overweight and obese compared to other ethnic groups (whites and Asian Americans). However, beyond that simple generalization, the patterns become much more complex when race/ethnicity is cross-classified by gender, age-group, and socioeconomic status (SES). For example, among adult women, there is a gradient between higher family incomes and lower prevalence of overweight among all race/ethnic groups. In contrast, among adult men, higher family incomes among black and Hispanic males tend to be associated with greater prevalence of over-weight (*Health United States, 1998 with Socioeconomic Status and Health Chartbook*). Chapter 16 in this Handbook by McLaren delves into more detail on the topic of socioeconomic disparities in overweight and obesity. In this chapter, we summarize what is known about the complex patterns of obesity by racial and ethnic status.

One of the overarching Healthy People 2010 objectives is to eliminate health disparities including disparities based on race/ethnicity, gender, and income (U.S. Department of Health and Human Services, December 2006). Enshrined in these set of objectives is the goal to reduce disparities in nutrition and overweight. Existing studies have focused on racial/ethnic disparities in overweight and obesity as well as SES disparities in overweight and obesity, citing higher prevalence among racial/ethnic minorities, in females compared to males, and among lower SES persons (Gordon-Larsen et al. 2003; Kumanyika, Obarzanek, Stettler, Bell, Field, Fortmann et al. 2008; Wang and Beydoun 2007). These trends offer insight into the evolving epidemic, however, few studies have been able to capture multiple dimensions of stratification, namely the intersection between race/ethnicity, gender, and SES.

To begin, we will dissect trends in obesity, thereby underscoring the need to explore racial/ethnic disparities in combination with gender and SES disparities in overweight and obesity among adults and children. Only by providing a comprehensive discussion of the patterns and trends can we begin to build a con-ceptual framework for understanding the causes and consequences of obesity and identifying pathways for reducing and eliminating these disparities. Our concep-tual framework for explaining the racial and ethnic disparities in obesity will focus on contextual and environmental factors—the so-called "obesogenic" environment—that racial and ethnic groups are differentially exposed to. Broadly speaking, these factors are rooted in differential exposures to the food environment (the energy intake side of the equation) and the physical activity environment (the energy expenditure side of the equation), as well as differences in cultural norms and practices.

Overweight versus Obesity

Overweight and obesity have been assessed using body mass index (BMI) a measure of relative weight to height (weight (kg)/height(m)^2). According to the World Health Organization, this measure is correlated with total body fat content and obesity-related consequences (Kumanyika et al. 2008; World Health Organization 2000). The National Heart, Lung, and Blood Institute defines overweight and obesity in adults as a BMI of 25 to 29.9 kg/m^2 and >30 kg/m^2, respectively (National Institutes of Health 1998).

For children and adolescents, different standards apply. The term "at risk of overweight" is the comparable term for overweight in adults. Similarly, "overweight" is used rather than "obesity" to refer to children and adolescents with a BMI at or above the sex-age-specific 95th percentile (Kumanyika et al. 2008; Wang and Beydoun 2007). These guidelines have been established by the 2000 Centers for Disease Control and Prevention Growth Charts for children between the ages of 2–19 years (Kuczmarski, Ogden, Grummer-Strawn, Flegal, Guo, Wei et al. 2000).

RACE/ETHNIC DISPARITIES IN OVERWEIGHT AND OBESITY: OVERALL PATTERNS AND TRENDS

Among adults, the National Health and Nutrition Examination Survey (NHANES) data have consistently revealed racial/ethnic differences in overweight and obesity prevalence (Gordon-Larsen et al. 2003; Kumanyika et al. 2008; Ogden et al. 2006; Wang and Beydoun 2007). Overall, non-Hispanic Blacks have the highest prevalence of obesity (BMI >30 kg/m^2) among all the race/ethnic groups. Data have also indicated a higher prevalence of obesity among Mexican Americans compared to non-Hispanic whites (Wang and Beydoun 2007). These disparities are accentuated when the data are stratified by gender, with black women having the highest rates of obesity (over 50 percent) of any race/ethnic group in the United States. Figures 15.1 and 15.2 illustrate racial/ethnic differences in overweight and obesity prevalence in 1999–2002 as well as projected 2010 estimates based on linear regression models for men and women, respectively.

Underscoring the complexity of the observed disparities, when we turn to prevalence of overweight (BMI of 25 to 29.9 kg/m^2), a different pattern emerges across race/ethnic groups compared to the pattern of obesity, Between 1999 and 2002, non-Hispanic black men had the lowest prevalence of overweight compared to white men and Hispanic men (even though they showed the highest prevalence of obesity compared to other groups). The 2010 projections are consistent with these overall patterns. By contrast among women, Hispanic women had the highest prevalence of overweight between 1999 and 2002.

RACE/ETHNICITY, INCOME AND OVERWEIGHT/OBESITY

An extensive literature demonstrates that in the overall U.S. population, lower income groups have the highest risk of obesity and overweight, particularly among

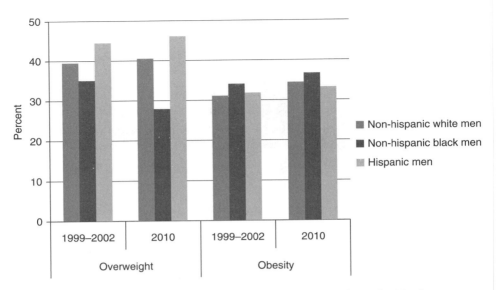

Figure 15.1. 1999–2002 Overweight and Obesity Prevalence for Men by
Race and Projected 2010 Estimates
(*Source:* Wang and Beydoun 2007).

women (Ogden et al. 2006; Robert and Reither 2004; Wang and Beydoun 2007;
Zhang and Wang 2004). Because blacks and Hispanics in the United States have
lower incomes compared with white Americans, it seems reasonable to postulate
that the observed racial and ethnic disparities in BMI can be explained by these
income differences. Stated another way, a large portion of the race/ethnic
disparities in overweight and obesity could be hypothesized to be attributable to the

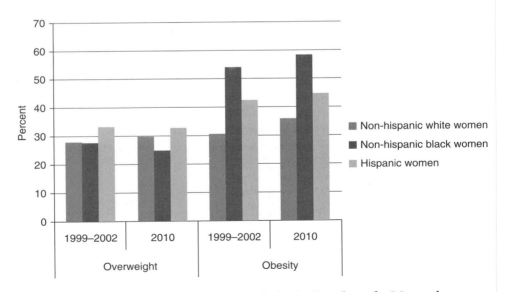

Figure 15.2. 1999–2002 Overweight and Obesity Prevalence for Women by
Race and Projected 2010 Estimates
(*Source:* Wang and Beydoun 2007).

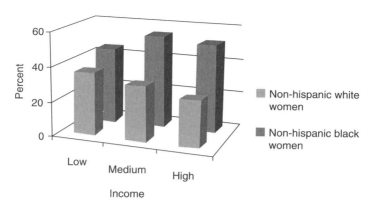

Figure 15.3. Prevalence of Obesity for Women by Race and Income, 1999–2000
(*Source*: Wang and Beydoun 2007).

known race/ethnic differences in socioeconomic status. In reality, however, the patterns are more complex. In particular, two caveats need to be borne in mind. First, when the prevalence of overweight within race/ethnic groups is stratified by income and gender, the same patterns are not replicated across groups. Among women, lower family incomes (particular poverty and near-poverty levels of income) are associated with higher prevalence of overweight. This income gradient holds across all race/ethnic groups, with poor Hispanic women exhibiting the highest prevalence of overweight in 2010 (figure 15.2). In contrast, when we turn to data on overweight among U.S. black males, the income gradient exhibits the opposite pattern, that is, a higher prevalence of overweight among middle or high income black men compared to poor or near-poor black men. Among white and Hispanic men there is an inverted U-shaped pattern, with the highest overweight prevalence among near-poor males, but the lowest prevalence among the poorest men. These complexities suggest that income differences are unlikely to completely account for race/ethnic differences in overweight—at least for U.S. males.

Gradients for obesity differ from those for overweight. Figures 15.3 and 15.4 illustrate the differences in obesity by race, gender and income during 1999–2000.

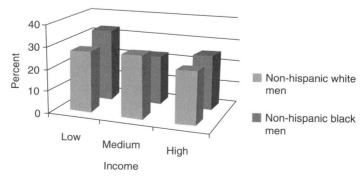

Figure 15.4. Prevalence of Obesity for Men by Race and Income, 1999–2000
(*Source*: Wang and Beydoun 2007).

Low-income white women are more likely than middle- or high-income white women to be obese (Wang and Beydoun 2007). By contrast, obesity among black women exhibits a modest inverted U-shaped pattern over income, with medium income black women showing the highest prevalence of obesity (approximately 55 percent). The pattern among white men indicates a similar prevalence of obesity among low- and medium-income men (28.3 percent and 27.7 percent, respectively), but a decline in prevalence among high income men, with nearly 24 percent of this group obese. Patterns for black men are the opposite of those observed for black women. For black men, the prevalence of obesity follows a modest U-shaped pattern, with low-income men having the highest prevalence of obesity (nearly 33 percent) and medium-income men having the lowest prevalence of obesity (22.6 percent). These differences suggest that in addition to racial/ethnic determinants of obesity, gender is a key factor associated with obesity prevalence.

A second source of complexity is that not all of the observed income disparities in overweight are likely to be causal. As we have mentioned, there is a strong nega-tive correlation between lower income and the prevalence of overweight among women of all race/ethnic groups, but the relationship is far less consistent among men—and in fact is of the opposite sign for black men. Whether these patterns reflect causation (that is, lower incomes are causally associated with increased risk of overweight) is debatable. Indeed, researchers have postulated that the association between income and overweight reflects reverse causation; that is, it is not lower incomes which cause people to become overweight, but rather, overweight which causes lower socio-economic mobility. In a siblings fixed effects analysis based on a follow-up sample of the Panel Study of Income Dynamics, Conley and Glauber (2006) found evidence for such reverse causation. Among women in that study, each 1 percent increase in BMI was associated with 0.6 percent lower family income, 1.1 percent lower spousal earnings, and 0.3 percent lower probability of being mar-ried during 15 years of follow-up (Conley and Glauber 2006). Interestingly, the same associations were not found among men, leading the authors to conclude that the well-established relationship between lower income and higher BMI reflects so-called "fat bias," that is, societal discrimination against overweight women leading to truncated success in the marriage market and labor market. Presumably, the same "fat bias" does not operate in American society against overweight males!

Children and Adolescents

The association of income with obesity for U.S. adolescents ages 12–17 years is sim-ilar to that for U.S. adults (see figure 15.5). For instance, among non-Hispanic white adolescents between 1988 and 1994, an income gradient was observed showing that adolescents from middle/high-income families were less likely to be overweight. For this group, approximately 19 percent of adolescents from poor families were overweight, compared to 7.2 percent of adolescents from middle/high-income families.

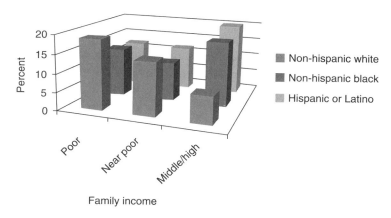

Figure 15.5. Average Percent Overweight among Adolescents by
Race and Income, 1988–1994
(*Source:* Pamuk et al. 1998).

This gradient was not observed among non-Hispanic black and Hispanic adolescents. There is a slight U-shaped pattern observed for black and Hispanic adolescents, indicating that adolescents from poor and high/middle-income families are more likely to be overweight compared to near-poor families. The greatest disparity was noted between near-poor and middle/high-income black and Hispanic adolescents. Approximately 10.7 percent of near poor blacks and 12 percent of near-poor Hispanics were overweight. But in middle/high-income families, the percent of overweight adolescents sharply increases to 17.5 percent of blacks and nearly 20 percent of Hispanics, respectively. In other words, middle/high-income Hispanic adolescents are nearly three times more likely than white adolescents to be overweight. These patterns underscore the importance of understanding the early life-course factors that contribute to overweight among racial/ethnic minority populations, particularly since health behaviors established in childhood tend to persist into adulthood.

Conceptual Framework for Racial/ Ethnic Disparities in Obesity

Overweight and obesity can be conceptualized as problems of energy imbalance. Energy imbalance is the consequence of too much energy intake relative to expenditure ("energy in") or too little energy expenditure relative to intake ("energy out"). The environmental and contextual factors that have received most attention in the literature include differences in the food environment ("energy in")—including the marketing of foods, portion sizes, snacking, the retail food environment (exposure to fast food outlets vs. supermarkets). On the energy-out side of the equation, attention has focused on features of the "built environment"—including neighborhood walkability, access to recreational physical activity resources, urban design, transport policies, and so on. While this framework is useful for explaining the general increase in obesity in American society over time, it is not relevant in every case for explaining the racial and ethnic disparities that we have described. For example, increased time pressure (due to the rise in dual earner couples) has been implicated as a major suspect in the consumption of extra calories in the form of prepared foods and snack foods (Cutler, Glaeser, and Shapiro 2003). However, no empirical analysis has implicated group differences in snacking patterns as the source of racial and ethnic disparities in obesity. Similarly, portion sizes of many foods have increased in tandem with the obesity epidemic (Nielsen and Popkin 2003), but we are not aware of evidence to suggest that racial/ethnic differences in portion sizes are to blame for the obesity disparities.

With these caveats, we summarize the evidence on six of the "leading suspects" in explaining the patterns of racial and ethnic disparities in overweight and obesity. They are: (1) overeating as a maladaptive coping strategy; (2) occupational segregation by race and sleep patterns; (3) cultural norms and practices; (4) disparities rooted in the residential environment; (5) targeting of television-based marketing of foods; and (6) acculturation (in the case of immigrant Hispanic Americans).

Overeating as a Coping Strategy

Ethnic minorities have higher prevalence of overweight and obesity, beginning in adolescence and continuing into adulthood. Social inequalities, including experiences of discrimination and the stresses associated with poverty, may set in motion unhealthy patterns of energy balance, including overconsumption of food as well as physical inactivity (Kumanyika et al. 2008). For example, Cozier et al. (2009) found that self-reported perceptions of racial discrimination were associated with increased weight gain among African Americans across all levels of BMI (Cozier, Wise, Palmer, and Rosenberg 2009). Similar findings have been reported by Gee and colleagues (2008), who found that reports of racial discrimination were positively associated with increased BMI and obesity in a nationally representative sample of Asian Americans (Gee, Ro, Gavin, and Takeuchi 2008). Studies have cited overeating as a coping strategy for stress in adults as well as a way for parents to ensure that their children can cope with the uncertainties associated with food insecurity (e.g., skipped meals) (Kumanyika 2008).

Beyond overeating as a compensatory mechanism for stress, a series of *structural* factors in American society are likely to explain racial/ethnic differences in overweight/obesity. There is no single "smoking gun" that completely accounts for the complex patterns of race/ethnic disparities in overweight/obesity, but instead, the patterns are likely to be explained by a cumulative and interacting set of factors that include occupational segregation and patterns of sleep, cultural influences over weight and body image perception, the residential built environment and local food environment (Wang and Beydoun 2007), television marketing and acculturation.

Occupational Segregation by Race/Ethnicity

The American labor force is racially segregated such that blacks and Hispanics are engaged in different types of occupations compared to white Americans. A generation ago, this meant that racial minorities were concentrated in manual work that involved physical activity on the job, which contributed to caloric expenditure during the work day, even in the absence of leisure-time physical activity. However, with the rise of the low-wage service sector in the U.S. economy, racial minorities now tend to be overrepresented in occupations that do not involve the same degree of physical activity. Racial/ethnic minorities are also more likely to be involved in occupations that involve shift work, such as cooks, cleaners, security personnel, drivers, shop clerks, and hospital workers (Chung-Bridges, Muntaner, Fleming, Lee, Arheart, LeBlanc et al. 2008; McKinnon, 2003). In turn, shift work—particularly, night shifts and rotating shift work—involves disrupted circadian rhythms that contribute to fewer hours of sleep as well as consumption of prepared foods. Sleep studies have consistently demonstrated that African Americans report fewer hours of sleep compared to white Americans (Fiorentino, Marler, Stepnowsky, Johnson, and Ancoli-Israel 2006; Mezick, Matthews, Hall, Strollo, Buysse, Kamarck et al. 2008), and in turn, sleep deprivation has been increasingly implicated as an important risk factor for overweight and obesity.

Weight and Body Image Perception

African Americans are more likely to be attracted to and accepting of larger body images than other racial/ethnic groups (Fitzgibbon, Blackman, and Avellone 2000; Gipson, Reese, Vieweg, Anum, Pandurangi, Olbrisch et al. 2005; Gross, Scott-Johnson, and Browne 2005; Katz, Gordon-Larsen, Bentley, Kelsey, Shields, and Ammerman 2004). For example, 60 percent of African American males attending a historically black university who, according to measured BMI, were either overweight or obese, inaccurately perceived their weight status as being within normal range (Gross et al. 2005). Interestingly, among men with inaccurate weight perception, 41 percent identified the desire to lose weight, 12 percent desired to maintain current weight, and 47 percent desired to gain weight (Gross et al. 2005). These results support findings from other research showing that overweight and obese Black males perceive themselves as normal weight (Cafri and Thompson, 2004; McCreary 2002; Paeratakul, White, Williamson, Ryan, and Bray 2002) and that overweight Black males perceived themselves as being more attractive than underweight males (McCreary and Sadava 2001). These findings underscore the importance of cultural and social norms, perceptions, and stereotypes of males being more attractive when they are perceived to be more stout (Gross et al. 2005). Similar findings have been reported among women, where studies suggest that non-Hispanic black women are less likely than non-Hispanic white women to perceive themselves as being overweight (Yancey, Simon, McCarthy, Lightstone, and Fielding 2006). In a study by Bish et al. (2005), survey data revealed racial/ethnic differences in attempts to lose weight, with fewer non-Hispanic black women reporting attempts to lose weight compared to non-Hispanic white women (Bish, Blanck, Serdula, Marcus, Kohl, and Khan 2005).

Built Environment and Supermarket Access

Increasing attention is being paid to the obesogenic influence of the residential environments in which people live, in part because of the major variations in the prevalence of overweight and obesity across neighborhoods within metropolitan areas. In the city of Boston, for example, there is a roughly twofold difference in the prevalence of overweight and obesity between the affluent (and predominantly white) Back Bay neighborhood compared to the less affluent (and predominantly African American) neighborhood of North Dorchester—a difference in prevalence of 31 percent versus 63 percent, respectively (Boston Health Commission data). Furthermore, multilevel analyses have repeatedly demonstrated that the between-neighborhood variations in overweight/obesity cannot be explained by compositional factors alone. In other words, the individual characteristics of residents cannot completely explain the BMI patterns of the neighborhoods in which they reside. There is something about certain neighborhoods that appears to increase the risk of overweight and obesity, controlling for the personal characteristics of residents. This is especially salient in American society where residential segregation—that is, the physical separation of people based on skin color or ethnic origin—is a fact of life. Residential racial segregation is associated with poorer health outcomes, decreased quality of life, and differential exposures to obesogenic environments by people of color (Litaker, Sudano, and Colabianchi 2004).

Broadly speaking, the two features of residential obesogenic environments that have received the most attention are the built environment and the local food environment. For example, on the built environment side, the lack of continuous sidewalks, inadequate parks and recreational facilities, poor street lighting, and high-speed traffic make it difficult for residents to be physically active (Burke, O'Campo, Salmon, and Walker 2009; Lopez and Hynes 2006). In a study involving every park and playground listed by Boston City, Cradock and colleagues trained a team of observers to carry out a systematic social observation of the safety of playground equipment. Playground safety was assessed using a 100-item safety checklist used by Boston city park inspectors. For example, failing grades were given to rusted playground slides that presented entrapment hazards for children, or swing sets where the children landed on concrete instead of soft woodchips of prescribed depth. The authors found that the higher the concentration of minority residents in Boston neighborhoods, the lower was the average safety rating of playgrounds in those neighborhoods (Cradock, Kawachi, Colditz, Hannon, Melly, Wiecha et al. 2005). In short, although we cannot directly infer causality from such findings, they provide tantalizing clues as to why parents living in minority neighborhoods might "rationally" keep their children away from exercising in local playgrounds. Racial and ethnic minority neighborhoods are also disproportionately affected by violence and crime—which serve as major deterrents to outdoor physical activity, especially for children, women, and the elderly.

On the local food environment side, supermarket access is a factor that is associated with obesity prevention. Supermarkets are believed to offer a larger variety of fresh and nutritious produce at a price that is more affordable than produce offered at smaller convenience stores (Chung and Myers 1999; Glanz, Sallis, Saelens, and Frank 2007). Furthermore, access to supermarkets has been shown to be associated with increased fruit and vegetable consumption and overall better diet and nutrition (Morland, Wing, and Diez Roux 2002a). Racial/ethnic disparities in the food environment have been extensively documented. For example, Morland et al. (2002b) found that predominantly white neighborhoods in the CARDIA study had four times as many supermarkets compared to predominantly African American neighborhoods (Morland, Wing, Roux, and Poole 2002b). Neighborhoods also differ in their number of unhealthy food sources, namely, fast food outlets. Here also, minority neighborhoods are at higher risk. In a study based in New Orleans, Block et al. (2004) reported that predominantly African American neighborhoods had a greater fast food density compared to predominantly white neighborhoods (Block, Scribner, and DeSalvo 2004).

As is the case with the built environment, access does not necessarily equate to utilization. In other words, just because a supermarket is located nearby does not mean that residents will exercise the option of purchasing fresh fruits and vegetables. Fast food franchises are also more likely to open for business in neighborhoods where the owners are betting that there is a demand for their product. In other words, a correlation between poor food environments and obesity among residents does not necessarily prove causality. As Drewnowski has argued (2007), the ability to maintain a healthy eating lifestyle often has less to do with exposure to local environmental conditions than it has to do with raw purchasing power and income. Thus, according to Drewnowski, healthy eating requires a secure level of income because the kinds of foods recommended by public health experts (e.g., fresh fruits and vegetables) can be 100- to 1,000-times more expensive per calorie delivered compared to energy-dense, processed foods that are high in sugar and fats (Drewnowski 2007). An unfortunate consequence is that low-income consumers often buy unhealthy foods, which are more affordable on a limited budget. The preference for the taste of these foods can also lead many consumers to overeat them, thereby contributing to the increased risk of obesity.

Television Marketing

The food system is the second largest advertiser in the American economy and the leading buyer of media slots for advertisements (Gallo 1999). Over the last two decades, food marketing and advertising has been repeatedly implicated in the rapid increases in obesity prevalence (Jeffrey and French 1998; Powell, Szczypka, and Chaloupka 2007; Story and French 2004). Previous studies have shown positive associations between television viewing and body weight in children (Dietz and

Gortmaker 1985; Shannon, Peacock, and Brown 1991) and in adults (Tucker and Bagwell 1991; Tucker and Friedman 1989). These studies report that men and women who report watching the most television are at increased risk of obesity compared to men and women who report watching the least amount of television. One speculation is that the increased exposure to food advertising resulted from the influx of and increased usage of home VCRs, DVD players, cable television (Salvaggio and Bryant 1989) and the Internet, which provides additional platforms for food messages to be distributed. The mechanisms whereby television viewing is associated with increased risk of obesity are manifold. First, increased television viewing may replace physical activity, resulting in a more sedentary lifestyle (Cleland, Schmidt, Dwyer, and Venn 2008). Second, increased television viewing is associated with increased energy intake through snacking while watching television (Robinson 2001; Tucker and Bagwell 1991; Tucker and Friedman 1989). Third, television viewing increases exposure to food advertising, which, among children, influences food preference, purchase requests and intake (Institute of Medicine 2006).

Food advertising is more common during prime time (8:00–11:00 P.M.) (Story and Faulkner 1990), TV shows targeted to African American viewers (Tirodkar and Jain 2003) and programs for children and adolescents (Story and French 2004). Prime time television is a highly sought after advertising bracket due to the potential for reaching the largest population of viewers. Story and Faulkner (1990) found that 60 percent of food references on the top 15 ranked prime time shows were for low nutrient beverages and sweets. In the same study, 35 percent of the commercials aired were food advertisements, with fast foods being advertised the most. Racial/ethnic differences in television viewing have been observed. African American households watch more television compared to the average American household (an estimated 75 hours compared to 52 hours per week). Furthermore, African Americans tend to watch shows with predominantly African American casts. Tirodkar and Jain (2003) reported that black prime time television (the top ranked situation comedies watched by a predominantly black audience) contained a greater number of food advertisements, featuring more candy and soda advertisements compared to general prime time shows. This exposure to food advertisements can lead to a preference for the low-nutrient products being advertised. Viewers' behaviors and food consumption patterns may be influenced by food references made by celebrities and on-screen characters. Additionally, the top ranked black prime time shows had a greater number of overweight characters compared to general prime time. The positive portrayal of overweight characters may lead black viewers to accept and even prefer larger body sizes without consideration of the health consequences associated with overweight and obesity (Tirodkar and Jain 2003).

Children and adolescents have been aggressively targeted by food advertising and marketing agencies due to their purchasing power, purchasing influence, and their role as future adult consumers (Story and French 2004). The ability of food advertisements to influence children is an effective strategy from a supplier perspective, but a force that public health professionals must contend with since health behaviors present in childhood are likely to persist into adulthood. Grade school children watch approximately 3.5 hours of television each day. Low-income and racial/ethnic minority children tend to watch more television (Story and French 2004). Black children watch 29 percent more daytime television programming and 35 percent more prime time programming compared to white children (Nielsen Media Research 2000). The increased viewing time of black children increases the number of food advertisements they are exposed to, potentially influencing their food preference, consumption, requests and overweight status. It is estimated that in 2002, children accounted for $330 billion of adult spending via requests primarily in the form of sweets, snacks, candy, sugary beverages, cereal, and fast foods (McNeal 1992, 1998; Schor 2004). Powell and colleagues (2007) reported that 36.4 percent of advertising viewed by children was for food, with cereal advertisements (27.6 percent of the advertisements) comprising the largest food category (Powell et al. 2007). While a causal link has yet to be determined for television viewing and obesity, sufficient evidence has been provided to support claims that television viewing decreases physical activity and snacking, while watching television increases energy intake, both of which are associated with increased risk for overweight and obesity.

Acculturation

Acculturation has been broadly defined as the modification of the culture of one group (or individual) that occurs as a result of continuous contact with another cultural group (Keefe 1980). Markers of acculturation commonly measured among U.S. Hispanic groups include, language preference, and duration of exposure to U.S. culture (Khan, Sobal, and Martorell 1997). Changes in dietary practices and obesity patterns have been observed as various Hispanic groups transition from a traditional diet to a more Americanized diet of increased total and saturated fat intake and less complex carbohydrates (Bermudez, Falcon, and Tucker 2000). Studies have examined diet and acculturation in Mexican Americans. These studies reported that Mexican American women born in the United States (and hence, more acculturated to the U.S.) had high fat diets with less fiber compared to women born in Mexico or less acculturated Mexican American women (Dixon, Sundquist, and Winkleby 2000; Winkleby, Albright, Howard-Pitney, Lin, and Fortmann 1994). The availability of affordable, energy-dense foods has been cited as a factor associated with increased weight gain observed during the acculturation process (Freimer, Echenberg, and Kretchmer 1983). Additional studies comparing acculturated and non-acculturated members of the same group have shown greater obesity prevalence among those who are more acculturated and who have adopted an Americanized diet and decreased physical activity. Consistent with these observations, Goel and colleagues (2004) have found that immigrant groups arriving in America are considerably leaner compared to U.S. -born individuals. However, after 10 or more years of residence in the United States, the average BMI of immigrant groups "catch up" with that of U.S.-born individuals, as does the prevalence of both overweight and obesity (Goel, McCarthy, Phillips, and Wee 2004). On average, after 10 years of residence in the United States, the average immigrant gains about 10 pounds in weight. Similarly, Sanchez-Vaznaugh et al. (2009) used data from the 2001 California Health Interview Survey to examine whether the SES patterning of BMI varied across the major U.S. racial/ethnic groups by gender and birthplace. The authors found that the effect of education (as a measure of SES) on BMI varied by country of origin. A clear education gradient in BMI (higher education, lower BMI) was found among all U.S.-born participants; however, among recent immigrants (Hispanic, Asian, or black), no consistent pattern was found between education and BMI (Sánchez-Vaznaugh, Kawachi, Subramanian, Sánchez, and Acevedo-Garcia 2009). On the other hand, no matter what the country of origin, with increasing duration of residence in the U.S., two patterns emerged among immigrants to the United States: (1) they progressively gained weight (even adjusting for age), and (2) a clear education gradient emerged that resembled the pattern among U.S.-born individuals. The bottom line here is that the pattern of racial/ethnic disparities is modified by processes of acculturation, and that a full description of these ethnic disparities necessitates the simultaneous consideration of race/ethnicity and SES, but also immigrant status.

Implications for Prevention

To address the alarming prevalence of overweight and obesity among racial/ethnic minorities, culturally appropriate and culturally sensitive approaches are needed that incorporate traditional foods and cultural practices that are familiar and preferred by members of a particular group. It is crucial to understand the interplay between perceptions of food, physical activity, and body image of African American women who experience disparate rates of obesity. For instance, African American women have identified lack of time, care-giving responsibilities, not enjoying exercising, and not wanting to sweat or mess their hair as barriers to physical activity (Carter-Nolan, Adams-Campbell, and Williams 1996). These barriers to physical activity highlighted by African American women—and the factors that contribute to even high-SES African American women having increased prevalence of obesity—warrant careful attention when designing health promotion efforts.

The design and implementation of effective weight reduction programs geared toward African American women have major implications for addressing the intergenerational transmission of overweight/obesity in this population, since a high proportion of African American households are headed by single mothers who are responsible for food purchasing and preparation for their children. Moreover, African American women tend to use food—as opposed to alcohol or nicotine—to cope with experiences of poverty, sexual abuse, violence, and racial discrimination (Hooks 1993). Among African Americans, larger body sizes also tend to be viewed favorably as an insurance against being victimized by domestic or street violence (Kumanyika, Whitt-Glover, Gary, Prewitt, Odoms-Young, Banks-Wallace et al. 2007).

In summary, the same broad principles of obesity prevention apply to racial/ethnic minorities as among the general population. First, interventions are likely to have more "bang for the buck" by targeting the producers of the obesity epidemic (e.g., television advertising, fast food producers) as opposed to targeting the consumers of their products and services. Second, interventions should pay more heed to curing the obesogenic environments in which individuals live and work, as opposed to attempts to influence or educate individuals to change their habits. Beyond these simple general principles (which incidentally have proved their effectiveness in the tobacco control movement), additional attention is merited in focusing on the *cultural* dimensions of the obesity epidemic, in particular, race/ethnic differences in desirable body image and the process of acculturation. We have already alluded to the absence of a single "smoking gun" that could explain the observed race/ethnic disparities in overweight and obesity. Just as there is no smoking gun, so there is no single "magic bullet" that would reverse the patterns and trends that we have described. The Healthy People 2010 objective of reducing racial and ethnic disparities in obesity is likely to succeed through a comprehensive set of strategies that address multiple points of intervention.

REFERENCES

Bermudez, O. I., Falcon, L. M., and Tucker, K. L. 2000. "Intake and Food Sources of Macronutrients among Older Hispanic Adults: Association with Ethnicity, Acculturation and Length of Residence in the United States." *Journal of the American Dietetic Association* 100: 665–673.

Bish, C. L., H. M. Blanck, M. K. Serdula, M. Marcus, H. W. Kohl, III, and L. K. Khan. 2005. "Diet and Physical Activity Behaviors among Americans Trying to Lose Weight: 2000 Behavioral Risk Factor Surveillance System." *Obesity Research* 13: 596–607.

Block, J. P., R. A. Scribner, and K. B. DeSalvo. 2004. "Fast Food, Race/Ethnicity, and Income." *American Journal of Preventive Medicine* 27(3): 211–217.

Burke, J., P. O'Campo, C. Salmon, and R. Walker. 2009. "Pathways Connecting Neighborhood Influences and Mental Well-Being: Socioeconomic Position and Gender Differences." *Social Science and Medicine* 68: 1294–1304.

Cafri, G., and J. K. Thompson. 2004. "Measuring Male Body Image: A Review of the Current Methodology." *Psychology of Men and Masculinity* 5: 18–29.

Carter-Nolan, P. L., L. L. Adams-Campbell, and J. Williams. 1996. "Recruitment Strategies for Black Women at Risk for Noninsulin-dependent Diabetes Mellitus into Exercise Protocols: A Qualitative Assessment." *Journal of the National Medical Association* 88(9): 558–562.

Chung-Bridges, K., C. Muntaner, L. E. Fleming, D. J. Lee, K. L. Arheart, W.G. LeBlanc, et al. 2008. "Occupational Segregation as a Determinant of US Worker Health." *American Journal of Industrial Medicine* 51: 555–567.

Chung, C., and S. L. Myers. 1999. "Do the Poor Pay More for Food? An Analysis of Grocery Store Availability and Food Price Disparities." *The Journal of Consumer Affairs* 33(2): 276–296.

Cleland, V. J., M. D. Schmidt, T. Dwyer, and A. J. Venn. 2008. "Television Viewing and Abdominal Obesity in Young Adults: Is the Association Mediated by Food and Beverage Consumption during Viewing Time or Reduced Leisue-Time Physical Activity?" *American Journal of Clinical Nutrition* 87: 1148–1155.

Conley, D., and R. Glauber. 2006. "Gender, Body Mass and Socioeconomic Status: New Evidence from the PSID." *Advances in Health Economics and Health Services Research* 17: 253–275.

Cozier, Y. C., L. A. Wise, J. R. Palmer, and L. Rosenberg. 2009. "Perceived Racism in Relation to Weight Change in the Black Women's Health Study." *Annals of Epidemiology* 19: 379–387.

Cradock, A. L., I. Kawachi, G. A. Colditz, C. Hannon, S. J. Melly, J. L. Wiecha, et al. 2005. "Playground Safety and Access in Boston Neighborhoods." *American Journal of Preventive Medicine* 28(4): 357–363.

Cutler, D. M., E. L. Glaeser, and J. M. Shapiro. 2003. "Why Have Americans Become More Obese?" *Journal of Economic Perspectives* 17(3): 93–118.

Dietz, W., and S. Gortmaker. 1985. "Do We Fatten Our Children at the Television Set? Obesity and Television Viewing in Children and Adolescents." *Pediatrics* 5: 807–812.

Dixon, L. B., J. Sundquist, J., and M. A. Winkleby. 2000. "Differences in Energy, Nutrient, and Food Intakes in a US Sample of Mexican-American Women and Men: Findings from the Third National Health and Nutrition Examination Survey, 1988–1994." *American Journal of Epidemiology* 152: 548–557.

Drewnowski, A. 2007. "The Real Contribution of Added Sugars and Fats to Obesity." *Epidemiologic Reviews* 29: 160–171.

Fiorentino, L., M. Marler, C. Stepnowsky, S. Johnson, and S. Ancoli-Israel. 2006. "Sleep in Older African Americans and Caucasians at Risk for Sleep-disordered Breathing." *Behavioral Sleep Medicine* 4: 164–178.

Fitzgibbon, M. L., L. R. Blackman, and M. E. Avellone. 2000. "The Relationship between Body Image Discrepancy and Body Mass Index across Ethnic Groups." *Obesity Research* 8: 582–589.

Flegal, K. M., M. D. Carroll, C. L. Ogden, and J. CL. Johnson. 2002. "Prevalence and Trends in Obesity among US Adults, 1999–2000." *Journal of the American Medical Association* 288: 1723–1727.

Freimer, N., D. Echenberg, N. Kretchmer. 1983. "Cultural Variation-Nutritional and Clinical Implications." *The Western Journal of Medicine* 139: 928–933.

Gallo, A. 1999. *Food Advertising in the United States. America's Eating Habits: Changes and Consequences.* Edited by USDA/Economic Research Service. Washington, DC, USDA: 173–180.

Gee, G. C., A. Ro, Gavin, and D. T. Takeuchi. 2008. "Disentangling the Effects of Racial and Weight Discrimination on Body Mass Index and Obesity among Asian Americans." *American Journal of Public Health* 98(3): 493–500.

Gipson, G. W., S. Reese, W. V. Vieweg, E. A. Anum, A. K. Pandurangi, M. E. Olbrisch, et al. 2005. "Body Image and Attitude toward Obesity in an Historically Black University." *Journal of the National Medical Association* 97: 225–236.

Glanz, K., J. F. Sallis, B. E. Saelens, and L. D. Frank. 2007. "Nutrition Environment Measures Survey in Stores (NEMS-S)." *American Journal of Preventive Medicine* 32(4): 282–289.

Goel, M. S., E. P. McCarthy, R. S. Phillips, and C. C. Wee. 2004. "Obesity Among US Immigrant Subgroups by Duration of Residence." *Journal of the American Medical Association* 292: 2860–2867.

Gordon-Larsen, P., L. S. Adair, and B. M. Popkin. 2003. "The Relationship of Ethnicity, Socioeconomic Factors, and Overweight in U.S. Adolescents." *Obesity Research* 11(1): 121–129.

Gross, S. M., P. E. Scott-Johnson, and D. C. Browne. 2005. "College-age, African-American Males' Misperceptions about Weight Status, Body Size, and Shape." *Ethnicity and Disease* 15: S5–34–S35–38.

Hedley, A. A., C. L. Ogden, C. L. Johnson, M. D. Carroll, L. R. Curtin, and K.M. Flegal. 2004. "Prevalence of Overweight and Obesity among US Children, Adolescents, and Adults, 1999–2002." *Journal of the American Medical Association* 291: 2847–2850.

Hooks, B. 1993. *Sisters of the Yam: Black Women and Self-Recovery*. Boston: South End Press.

Institute of Medicine. 2006. *Food Marketing to Children and Youth: Threat or Opportunity?* Washington, DC: National Academies Press.

Jeffrey, R. W., and S. A. French. 1998. "Epidemic Obesity in the United States: Are Fast Foods and Television Viewing Contributing?" *American Journal of Public Health* 88: 277–280.

Katz, M. L., P. Gordon-Larsen, M. E. Bentley, K. Kelsey, K. Shields, and A. Ammerman. 2004. "Does Skinny Mean Healthy?" Perceived Ideal, Current, and Healthy Body Sizes among African American Girls and Their Female Caregivers." *Ethnicity and Disease* 14: 533–541.

Keefe, S. E. 1980. "Acculturation and the Extended Family among Urban Mexican Americans." In *Acculturation Theory, Models and Some New Findings*, ed. A. M. Padilla, 85–110. Boulder, CO: Westview Press.

Khan, L. K., J. Sobal, and R. Martorell. 1997. "Acculturation, Socioeconomic Status, and Obesity in Mexican Americans, Cuban Americans, and Puerto Ricans." *International Journal of Obesity* 21: 91–96.

Kuczmarski, R., C. L. Ogden, L. Grummer-Strawn, K. M. Flegal, S. S. Guo, R. Wei, et al. 2000. "CDC Growth Charts: United States." *Advance Data* 314: 1–27.

Kumanyika, S. K. 2008. "Environmental Influences on Childhood Obesity: Ethnic and Cultural Influences in Context." *Physiology and Behavior* 94: 61–70.

Kumanyika, S. K., E. Obarzanek, N. Stettler, R. Bell, A. E. Field, S. P. Fortmann, et al. 2008. "Population-Based Prevention of Obesity: The Need for Comprehensive Promotion of Healthful Eating, Physical Activity, and Energy Balance: A Scientific Statement from the American Heart Association Council on Epidemiology and Prevention, Interdisciplinary Committee for Prevention (Formerly the Expert Panel on Population and Prevention Science)." *Circulation* 118: 428–464.

Kumanyika, S. K., M. C. Whitt-Glover, T. L. Gary, E. Prewitt, A. M. Odoms-Young, J. Banks-Wallace, et al. 2007. "Expanding the Obesity Research Paradigm to Reach African American Communities." *Preventing Chronic Disease: Public Health Research, Practice, and Policy* 4(4): A112.

Litaker, D. G., J. Sudano, and N. Colabianchi. 2004. "Understanding the Effects of Racial Residential Segregation on Health Status." *Journal of General Internal Medicine* 18 (Supplement 1): 180.

Lopez, R. P., and H. P. Hynes. 2006. "Obesity, Physical Activity, and the Urban Environment: Public Health Research Needs." *Environmental Health: A Global Access Science Source* 5: 25–34.

McCreary, D. R. 2002. "Gender and Age Difference in the Relationship between Body Mass Index and Perceived Weight: Exploring the Paradox." *International Journal of Men's Health* 1(1): 31–42.

McCreary, D. R., and S. W. Sadava. 2001. "Gender Differences in Relationships among Perceived Attractiveness, Life Satisfaction, and Health in Adults as a Function of Body Mass Index and Perceived Weight." *Psychology of Men and Masculinity* 2(2): 108–116.

McKinnon, J. 2003. *The Black Population in the United States: March 2002. Current Population Reports.* Washington, DC: U.S. Census Bureau, Series P20–541.

McNeal, J. U. 1992. "The Littlest Shoppers." *American Demographics* 14: 48–52.

McNeal, J. U. 1998. "Kids' Markets." *American Demographics* 20: 36–41.

Mezick, E. J., K. A. Matthews, M. Hall, P. J. Strollo, D. J. Buysse, T. W. Kamarck, et al. 2008. "Influence of Race and Socioeconomic Status on Sleep: Pittsburgh SleepSCORE Project." *Psychosomatic Medicine* 70, 410–416.

Morland, K., S. Wing, and A. V. Diez Roux. 2002a. "The Contextual Effect of the Local Food Environment on Residents' Diets: The Atherosclerosis Risk in Communities Study." *American Journal of Public Health* 92(11): 1761–1767.

Morland, K., S. Wing, A. D. Roux, and C. Poole. 2002b. "Neighborhood Characteristics Associated with the Location of Food Stores and Food Service Places." *American Journal of Preventive Medicine* 22(1): 23–29.

National Institutes of Health. 1998. "Clinical Guidelines on the Identification, Evaluation, and Treatment of Overweight and Obesity in Adults: The Evidence Report." *Obesity Research* 6(supp. 2): 51S–209S.

Nielsen Media Research. 2000. *2000 Report on Television.* New York: A. C. Nielsen.

Nielsen, S. J., and B. M. Popkin. 2003. "Patterns and Trends in Food Portion Sizes, 1977–1998." *Journal of the American Medical Association* 289:450-453.

Ogden, C. L., M. D. Carroll, L. R. Curtin, M. A. McDowell, C. J. Tabak, and K. M. Flegal. 2006. "Prevalence of Overweight and Obesity in the United States, 1999–2004." *Journal of the American Medical Association* 295(13): 1549–1555.

Paeratakul, S., M. A. White, D. A. Williamson, D. H. Ryan, and G. A. Bray. 2002. "Sex, Race/Ethnicity, Socioeconomic Status, and BMI in Relation to Self-Perception of Overweight." *Obesity Research* 10(5): 345–350.

Pamuk, E., D. Makuc, K. Heck, C. Reuben, and K. Lochner. Socioeconomic Status and Health Chartbook. Health, United States, 1998. Hyattsville, Maryland: National Center for Health Statistics. 1998.

Powell, L. M., G. Szczypka, and F. J. Chaloupka. 2007. "Exposure to Food Advertising on Television among US Children." *Archives of Pediatrics and Adolescent Medicine* 161: 553–560.

Robert, S. A., and E. N. Reither. 2004. "A Multilevel Analysis of Race, Community Disadvantage, and Body Mass Index among Adults in the US." *Social Science and Medicine* 59: 2421–2434.

Robinson, T. 2001. "Television Viewing and Childhood Obesity." *Pediatric Clinics of North America* 48: 1017–1025.

Salvaggio, J., and J. Bryant (eds.). 1989. *Media Use in the Information Age: Emerging Patterns of Adaptation and Consumer Use.* Hillsdale, NJ: Lawrence Erlbaum Associates.

Sánchez-Vaznaugh, E. V., I. Kawachi, S. V. Subramanian, B. N. Sánchez, and D. Acevedo-Garcia. 2009. "Do Socioeconomic Gradients in Body Mass Index Vary by Race/ Ethnicity, Gender, and Birthplace?" *American Journal of Epidemiology* 169(9): 1102–1112.

Schor, J. 2004. *Born to Buy: The Commercialized Child and the New Consumer Culture.* New York: Scribner.

Shannon, B., J. Peacock, and M. Brown. 1991. "Body Fatness, Television Viewing and Calorie-Intake of a Sample of Pennsylvania Sixth Grade Children." *Journal of Nutrition Education* 23: 262–268.

Story, M., and P. Faulkner. 1990. "The Prime Time Diet: A Content Analysis of Eating Behavior and Food Messages in Television Program Content and Commercials." *American Journal of Public Health* 80(6): 738–740.

Story, M., and S. French. 2004. "Food Advertising and Marketing Directed at Children and Adolescents in the US." *International Journal of Behavioral Nutrition and Physical Activity* 1: 3–19.

Tirodkar, M. A., and A. Jain. 2003. "Food Messages on African American Television Shows." *American Journal of Public Health* 93(3): 439–441.

Tucker, L., and M. Bagwell. 1991. "Television Viewing and Obesity in Adult Females." *American Journal of Public Health*, 81, 908–911.

Tucker, L., and G. Friedman. 1989. "Television Viewing and Obesity in Adult Males." *American Journal of Public Health* 79: 516–518.

U.S. Department of Health and Human Services. December 2006. *Healthy People 2010: Midcourse Review*. Washington, DC: U.S. Government Printing Office.

Wang, Y., and M. A. Beydoun. 2007. "The Obesity Epidemic in the United States-Gender, Age, Socioeconomic, Racial/Ethnic, and Geographic Characteristics: A Systematic Review and Meta-Regression Analysis." *Epidemiologic Reviews* 29: 6–28.

Winkleby, M. A., C. L. Albright, B. Howard-Pitney, J. Lin, and S. P. Fortmann. 1994. "Hispanic/white Differences in Dietary Fat Intake among Low Educated Adults and Children." *Prevetive Medicine* 23: 465–473.

World Health Organization. 2000. *Obesity: Preventing and Managing the Global Epidemic: Report of a WHO Consultation*. Geneva, Switzerland: World Health Organization (Technical report series non. 894).

Yancey, A. K., P. A. Simon, W. J. McCarthy, A. S. Lightstone, and J. E. Fielding. 2006. "Ethnic and Sex Variations in Overweight Self-Perception: Relationship to Sedentariness." *Obesity (Silver Spring)* 14: 980–988.

Zhang, Q., and Y. Wang. 2004. "Socioeconomic Inequality of Obesity in the United States: Do Gender, Age, and Ethnicity Matter?" *Social Science and Medicine* 58: 1171–1180.

CHAPTER 16

SOCIOECONOMIC STATUS AND OBESITY

LINDSAY McLAREN

INTRODUCTION

OBESITY (including body mass index [BMI] and other indicators of body size/adiposity) shows patterning by socioeconomic status (SES). The nature of the association varies by gender, geographic location, and aspect of SES. The socioeconomic patterning of obesity departs somewhat from the socioeconomic patterning of other health outcomes, thus providing unique insight into the more general issue of social inequalities in health. In this chapter, I will provide an overview of the association(s) between SES and obesity as informed by the significant number of cross-sectional and longitudinal studies available, followed by a discussion of mediators or mechanisms that may underlie the observed associations.

OBESITY AND SOCIOECONOMIC STATUS: THE NATURE OF ASSOCIATION(S)

In 1989, Sobal and Stunkard published the first major review of literature on the association between socioeconomic status and obesity. Based on an exhaustive search of the literature to date (primarily 1960s through mid-1980s inclusive), these authors located 144 pertinent studies that collectively pointed to a strong inverse association (higher SES, lower obesity) among women from developed societies, and a strong positive association (higher SES, higher obesity) among men, women, and children in developing societies. The relationship for men and children in developed societies was inconsistent.

McLaren (2007) updated and built on the earlier review, focusing on adults. Based on 333 studies containing 1,914 associations (association being the unit of analysis), McLaren (2007) observed a similar but more nuanced pattern of findings. For women in developed countries (defined based on the United Nations Development Program's Human Development Index), the majority of associations (63 percent) were inverse; a finding that was especially prominent for particular indicators of SES; namely, education (72 percent inverse), area-level indicators such as neighborhood deprivation (71 percent inverse), and occupation (68 percent inverse). For men in developed countries, the predominant association was non-significant/curvilinear (54 percent), followed by inverse (37 percent); associations with education were especially likely to be inverse (50 percent). Positive associations were unusual among men in developed countries (9 percent of associations), but they were overrepresented among associations with income (24 percent positive). For both men and women, there was a general pattern whereby as one moved from countries of high to medium to low development status, the proportion of positive associations increased (3 percent, 43 percent, 94 percent for women and 9 percent, 39 percent, 100 percent for men, respectively) and the proportion of inverse associations decreased (63 percent, 26 percent, and 0 percent for women and 37 percent, 6 percent, and 0 percent for men, respectively). This is consistent with Monteiro et al.'s (2004) observation that, among developing countries, as a country's GNP increases, the burden of obesity tends to shift toward those with lower SES within those countries, in a manner that manifests in women first. In medium and low HDI countries in McLaren's (2007) review, positive associations were most often based on income as an indicator of SES.

Shrewsbury and Wardle (2008) updated the work by Sobal and Stunkard (1989) for school-aged children (age 5–18) in developed countries. They identified 45 studies containing measured data on adiposity which showed that, in contrast to Sobal and Stunkard's results (in which there were approximately equal numbers of positive, inverse, and non-significant associations), associations in the newer review were predominantly inverse (42 percent), especially when parental education was used as the indicator of SES (75 percent inverse). No positive associations were detected. Unlike the patterns observed among studies of adults, there did not appear to be striking gender differences in the SES-obesity association among children: Shrewsbury and Wardle (2008) found that, of the studies that presented results stratified by gender, over half found the same association for boys and girls, and there was no difference in the percent of inverse associations for boys versus girls.

These reviews of predominantly cross-sectional studies have the advantage of being inclusive and thus having a sufficient number of studies or associations to draw some nuanced conclusions about the SES-obesity association by indicator of SES, or in the developing world from which fewer studies emanate. They have the disadvantage of providing no insight into temporality (e.g., does SES influences obesity, or vice versa) or causality. Two reviews were explicitly focused on longitudinal studies. Ball and Crawford (2005) examined the relationship between SES and weight change over time among adults from developed countries. The review was based on 70 distinct associations from methodologically strong studies (i.e., those that contained measured adiposity data, had a follow-up period of at least four years, and contained multivariate adjustment) of predominantly non-black samples. Among women, there was some indication of an inverse association between occupation and weight gain (89 percent of associations were inverse), and between education and weight gain (68 percent of associations were inverse), but not for income and weight gain (44 percent of associations were inverse). For men, there was some indication of an inverse association between occupation and weight gain (83 percent of associations were inverse), but only marginal support for an association between education and weight gain (50 percent inverse) and no support for an association between income and weight gain (17 percent inverse). Positive associations were rare. Collectively, Ball and Crawford's findings suggest that occupational status may influence later weight/obesity status in both men and women, and that the SES-obesity associations detected in cross-sectional studies cannot be explained by social selection alone.

Finally, Power and Parsons (2000; Parsons et al. 1999) conducted a comprehensive review of literature on childhood predictors of adult obesity and observed that, among the various risk factors examined (including nutrition and physical activity), socioeconomic status stood out as one of the most consistent predictors of adult obesity. Based on 12 studies that examined the influence of SES in childhood (i.e., parents' education, occupation, income, or a composite) on fatness in adulthood, with a study duration ranging from 10 to 55 years, the emergent pattern was that both men and women from lower socioeconomic origins had a greater risk of obesity in adulthood than those from higher socioeconomic origins. This inverse effect was observed in 4 of 5 associations among women, 8 of 9 associations among men, and 3 of 4 associations among combined male/female samples. The consistency of the inverse effect in both male and female samples departs somewhat from the conclusions of other reviews, which documented a more prominent inverse pattern in women.

Overall, the most consistent association observed, based on reviews to date, is that of an inverse relationship between SES and obesity among women in the developed world. In men from developed countries, inverse associations have also been observed, though not as consistently as in women, and for indicators other than income. Due to methodological differences between the reviews it is difficult to identify whether the strength or consistency of associations has changed over time, though Molarius et al. (2000) presented data suggesting that the inverse associations observed in developed countries may have, if anything, widened over time. Specifically, these authors present data on the relationship between education and obesity in 26 mostly highly developed countries from two surveys, ten years apart, and reported that in approximately two-thirds of the populations, the educational inequalities in obesity increased (widened) between the late 1970s/early 1980s and the late 1980s/early 1990s. In the developing world, the predominant association is positive, yet inverse associations appear to emerge as a country's GNP/development status increases (Monteiro et al. 2004; McLaren 2007). Among children in the developed world, a predominant inverse association for both boys and girls was observed in Shrewsbury and Wardle's (2008) review, which was not evident in Sobal and Stunkard's (1989) original paper.

THE SOCIAL DETERMINANTS OF WEIGHT: MATERIAL AND PSYCHOSOCIAL PATHWAYS

The prevalence of obesity has risen dramatically during the past two to three decades in parts of North America, the United Kingdom, Eastern Europe, the Middle East, the Pacific Islands, Australasia, and China (WHO 2003), with a particularly rapid increase in developing countries (Popkin 2002). Such a widespread increase clearly indicates the presence of large-scale and relatively non-discerning drivers, which have contributed to rising prevalence across social and demographic groups. However, because socioeconomic patterning remains and has perhaps intensified, consideration of the possible mechanisms underlying the patterns is an important issue that will constitute the focus of the remainder of this chapter. As a framework, I draw on the social determinants of health literature, which holds that social inequalities in health reflect inequalities in opportunities, resources, and constraints (Frohlich et al. 2006; Marmot and Wilkinson 2005; Raphael 2009). Inequalities thus have both material and psychosocial dimensions, both of which need to be considered to understand socioeconomic variation in obesity between and within countries. The following discussion will focus on adults.

Countries of Higher Development Status

Beginning with the most consistent finding of an inverse association between SES and obesity for women in the developed world, and, to a lesser extent, men in these countries, several studies have reported socioeconomic inequalities in diet, whereby persons of higher SES tend to have a healthier diet, characterized by greater consumption of fruit, vegetables, and lower-fat dairy, and lower consumption of dietary fats (Power 2005). To some extent, social inequalities in diet would reflect one's income and consequent ability to purchase healthier foods, which have been shown to be more expensive, on a cost-per-calorie basis, than less nutritious foods (Travers et al. 1997; Drewnowski and Specter 2004; Drewnowski and Darmon 2005). Research on gendered aspects of food and eating in families suggests that, despite some changes in gender roles over recent decades, women often remain responsible for food purchase and preparation (Jansson 1995; Kemmer 2000; McLaren et al. 2009); thus, these factors probably have some relevance to understanding why the social gradient in weight in developed countries is stronger/more consistent for women than men. Physical activity has likewise been associated with socioeconomic status, such that persons of lower socioeconomic status are less likely to engage in sufficient physical activity (especially leisure-time physical activity) to derive health benefits (Giles-Corti and Donovan 2002). Some studies have assessed whether diet, physical activity, and other health behaviors mediate the SES-obesity relationship, and have shown that diet (e.g., fruit/vegetable intake; eating out), physical activity, and smoking partially (but not fully) explain the SES-obesity association in both men and women (Kuhle and Veugelers 2008; Ball et al. 2003; Ward et al. 2007).

Continuing with mechanisms that have prominent material (e.g., income-based) dimensions, the literature on food insecurity presents a pertinent line of inquiry. Food insecurity, which is associated with low SES, refers to "the inability to acquire or consume an adequate diet quality or sufficient quantity of food in socially acceptable ways, or the uncertainty that one will be able to do so" (McIntyre 2004), thus conveying that food insecurity in rich countries does not necessarily mean insufficient intake, but rather reliance on poor quality, highly processed foods that are often calorie-dense and inexpensive. Reflecting these processes, several studies have observed the seemingly paradoxical association between food insecurity and obesity, particularly for women, in wealthy countries such as the United States (Dinour et al. 2007) and Finland (Sarlio-Lahteenkorva and Lahelma 2001); findings in Canada are more equivocal (Che and Chen 2001; Vozoris and Tarasuk 2003). One explanation put forth to explain the phenomenon is the "food stamp cycle" hypothesis (e.g., Townsend et al. 2001; Dinour et al. 2007), whereby an injection of new funds (e.g., from social assistance) and/or food stamps (in the U.S.) and therefore food at the beginning of the month to a food-depleted household could lead to overconsumption and hence weight gain. This association appears to be more consistent in women than in men, which, as noted above, may reflect gender roles and the division of household labor around food preparation for families, and which in turn is consistent with the inverse SES-obesity association being stronger among women than among men.

These explanations pertain most obviously to income as an indicator of SES, which, as we have seen, is neither the only nor the most consistent socioeconomic correlate of obesity in developed countries. Therefore consideration of psychosocial mechanisms is helpful, and for this I draw on Bourdieu's theory of *habitus* as a framework (Power 2005; Bourdieu 1984; Shilling 2005; Power 1999). Habitus, according to Bourdieu, refers to the embodiment of social structures in individuals, such that a person's body (including appearance, style, mannerisms, behaviors) is a social metaphor for his/her status. A person's status is comprised of various forms of capital, which may be economic, cultural, or social in nature. Forms of capital can furthermore take on symbolic value when they are recognized as having legitimacy or prestige in society; for example, a particular body size/shape, style of dress, or set of mannerisms may be socially valued in a way that is not necessarily in keeping with its economic dimensions. From this perspective, a thinner body, in line with its promotion as an ideal of physical beauty for women (Katzmarzyk and Davis 2001; Groesz et al. 2002), may be more zealously aspired to, as well as being more achievable, by women in higher socioeconomic strata, which in turn could contribute to the inverse SES-obesity relationship observed among women in the developed world. In support of this line of thinking is research showing that women of higher SES tend to show higher levels of an array of variables indicating concern with, and commitment to, managing one's weight, relative to women of lower SES, including: weight concern, restrictive dieting, body dissatisfaction, perceived over-weight (despite being lighter, on average), weight esteem, and perceived-ideal discrepancy (Jeffery and French 1996; Lynch et al. 2007; McLaren and Gauvin 2002; McLaren and Kuh 2004a; McLaren and Kuh 2004b; Paeratakul et al. 2002; Wardle and Griffith 2001; Wardle et al. 2000). For men, although similar processes may be at work, the dimensions of the valued body differ such that men may aspire to a larger body size as a symbol of physical dominance and prowess. This is apparent in studies of body image in children, which have shown that while girls often wish to be thinner, boys often wish to be larger and more muscular (McVey et al. 2005). The different dimensions of the valued body in men may also help explain why the inverse SES-obesity association is weaker/less consistent in men than in women: men may aspire to a different physical ideal.

Additional insight is gleaned from considering the other indicators of SES that showed an inverse association with obesity in the developed world in the McLaren (2007) review; for example, area-level indicators, which primarily included deprivation indices at the post code level. Based on the observation of significant disparities in obesity by economic and racial/ethnic minority status in the United States, Ford and Dzewaltowski (2008) reviewed research on the retail food environ-ment (i.e., the availability, accessibility, and pricing of foods associated with healthy eating behaviors) and its implications for these obesity disparities. Overall, their review supported the position that socioeconomically disadvantaged areas in the United States tend to have poor quality retail food environments (e.g., fewer chain groceries, higher costs of foods, more limited availability of fruits and vegetables), and that these environments may contribute to increased risk of obesity among those of limited personal finances. Opportunities for physical activity have also been found to be poorer in lower SES communities (Powell et al. 2006; Giles-Corti 2006). At the other end of the spectrum, living in an affluent area (neighborhood) has been associated with higher levels of body dissatisfaction among adult women, controlling for BMI (McLaren and Gauvin 2002; McLaren and Gauvin 2003); which may reflect a social environment in these areas that conveys heightened pressures to attain a thin body.

Looking to other SES indicators that have a consistent association with obesity, occupation (status/prestige) was inversely associated with obesity for women in developed countries, in both cross-sectional and longitudinal studies (McLaren 2007;

Ball and Crawford 2005). Occupation was inversely associated with obesity for men, too (McLaren 2007) but less often (in 39 percent of studies in the McLaren review). In line with research on stigma and discrimination associated with excess weight (Puhl and Brownell 2001), it is possible that persons—especially women—who are higher in the occupational hierarchy may internalize the symbolic value of a thin body and a healthy lifestyle (in line with their class) and at the same time face exposure to a workplace environment that promotes these values (McLaren and Godley 2009). For example, in a white-collar office environment with on-site exercise and shower facilities, one can easily imagine social norms surrounding practices such as going to the gym during lunch hour. McLaren and Godley (2009) observed that the association between occupational status and BMI for women was fairly linearly inverse (higher status job, lower BMI) while for men it was less straightforward, with men in certain higher status jobs (such as senior management) showing a higher BMI, but men in other higher status jobs (such as skilled administrative positions) showing a lower BMI than men in the reference occupations of elemental sales and service.

Education is the SES indicator that was used most frequently in studies of the socioeconomic patterning of obesity, and which shows the most consistent inverse relationship with obesity in both women and men (McLaren 2007). Several pathways to explain this association are plausible. One's educational attainment may have implications for the extent to which he or she is attuned to or influenced by health messages regarding diet and physical activity and the likelihood of acting on these messages. One's education may also imply expectations for personal achievement, whether in a general sense or specific to health, weight, and physical appearance (and thereby drive pursuit of achievement of a particular body size/shape). Previous work has identified education as the SES variable most strongly associated with body dissatisfaction in women (McLaren and Kuh 2004a), and thus an array of attributes favoring pursuit of thinness among highly educated women—for both health and appearance reasons—is plausible. Among men in developed countries, most associations were non-significant in the McLaren (2007) review, but an inverse association was most common when education was the indicator of SES (observed in 50 percent of associations), and it is likely that, to some extent, similar pathways are at work as in women.

The relation of income to obesity is less consistent than with other SES indicators (McLaren 2007; Ball and Crawford 2005), though there is some indication of a positive association in men (higher income; higher likelihood of obesity). For example, in the McLaren (2007) review, although there were few positive associations overall for men in developed societies, associations with income were overrepresented, with 24 percent being positive. In the Canadian literature, four studies have detected a positive income-obesity association for men (Tjepkema 2006; Kuhle and Veugelers 2008; McLaren and Godley 2009; Shields and Tjepkema 2006). Thus, income and education may work in opposite ways in men, with respect to body weight and obesity. As noted, higher education may prompt weight management through pathways related to health literacy and aspirations of achievement. Higher income, on the other hand, may promote a larger body size in line with the societal ideal for men. If a larger body size is desirable as a marker of dominance and physical authority, and with men being the traditional breadwinners in families, it is plausible that income and pursuit of physical dominance remain linked. The observation that associations between SES (especially education) and obesity are less consistent overall in men than in women may reflect that for men, contrary forces are at work: the link between weight and health, and related stigma associated with heavier weight on the one hand, and the valuation of a large body size as an indication of power and dominance on the other. McLaren et al. (2009) used time use data to examine a broad array of lifestyle behaviors by socioeconomic status (income and education) across a Canadian national sample of men and women, to explore implications for the socioeconomic patterning of obesity. We found that higher income men in Canada were more likely to spend time in paid work, commuting to/from paid work, and eating out, and less time sleeping than lower income men. This lifestyle profile is plausibly associated with higher body weight, through various social, behavioral, and biological pathways. In women, a similar pattern was observed with higher versus lower income; with one exception that higher income women were more likely than lower income women to spend time in personal care, which includes washing, dressing, grooming, and so on. This behavior could be a marker for vigilance about physical appearance, which protects against obesity to a greater extent than in men, in accordance with the differential associations observed (McLaren 2007).

A final line of inquiry pertinent to the SES-obesity relationship in the developed world is psychosocial stress. The stress response (i.e., activation of the hypothalamic-pituitary-adrenal [HPA] axis and the sympathetic nervous system) has been associated with the development of several risk factors for chronic disease, including abdominal obesity (Bjorntorp 2001). Neuroendocrine markers of chronic stress have been observed in persons living in circumstances characterized by social/economic deprivation and with limited power and control (Sapolsky 2004) and thus low SES constitutes a social stressor with plausible biological and bio-behavioral links to weight. Rosmond and Bjorntorp (2000) observed perturbed cortisol secretion in men of lower SES, and demonstrated that such neuroendocrine dysregulation constituted a viable mechanism linking socioeconomic status and visceral obesity. Daniel et al. (2006) extended this line of inquiry to women and showed that an inverse association between cortisol and BMI among a sample of blue-collar women was moderated by level of educational achievement, such that the magnitude of the BMI-cortisol association was smaller in women with more education. This raises the interesting possibility of a link between SES and obesity that is partially independent of health behaviors.

Countries of Medium and Lower Development Status

The various reviews, both older (Sobal and Stunkard 1989) and more recent (McLaren 2007), point to the predominance of positive associations (higher SES, higher obesity) within countries of low and, to a lesser degree, medium socioeconomic development. In the McLaren (2007) review, there was sufficient number of associations from countries of medium development status to explore whether different indicators of SES related differentially to obesity in these countries. Income was a key positive correlate of obesity for both men and women, and ownership of material possessions was a second key positive correlate for women. The relatively greater consistency observed with these economic/material indicators likely reflects the relatively more important role of the economic or material dimensions of class/status in the developing world, particularly in the poorest countries: where food is truly scarce, the ability to afford food determines whether weight gain or obesity is even possible. In addition, as pointed out by both Monteiro et al. (2004) and Sobal and Stunkard (1989), patterns of high energy expenditure among the poor and cultural values favoring a larger body size may also continue to contribute to the positive associations observed in lower-income countries. In studies of countries of medium development status in the McLaren (2007) review, it was observed that among women, for certain indicators of SES (i.e., area, education, occupation), the association with weight was more often inverse than positive. This was not observed for men, suggesting that the social patterning of obesity is perhaps in transition for women in these countries. This is consistent with the conclusion of Monteiro et al. (2004) that the shift of obesity toward persons with lower SES as a country's annual GNP increases occurs at an earlier stage of economic development for women than for men.

Thus, on the one hand, there exist large-scale factors contributing to dramatic increases in obesity worldwide, particularly in the developing world (WHO 2003; Popkin 2002); on the other hand, there are forces acting to shift the burden of obesity onto the poor within developing countries. The factors contributing to rising obesity rates worldwide, including societal and nutritional changes having to do with economic growth, modernization, and globalization of food markets (WHO 2003; Hawkes 2006; Hawkes 2005), are well illustrated by case studies of societies in developmental transition. Ruppel Shell (2002) provides a vivid account of the region of Kosrae, Micronesia, in which nearly 90 percent of adults are overweight. In tracing the roots of this remarkably high prevalence, she identifies a constellation of contributing factors relating to foreign dependence and influence, the global food trade, and massive associated social change, the effects of which are epitomized by the popularity and prestige associated with imported foods such as Spam™ and potato chips on an island where tropical fruit is plentiful and whose shores are one of the world's richest sources of tuna (Cassels 2006; Ruppel Shell 2002).

As Monteiro et al. (2004) point out, the burden of these changes within developing societies is not equal, raising the question of what is driving the disproportionate burden of obesity among the poor (those of lower SES) within countries of medium development or in transition. Hawkes (2006) points out that key processes related to globalization have had an enormous impact on food systems such that cheap foods are increasingly available in poorer countries, and even more so to the poor within a given country. This results in worsening inequalities in diet between the rich and poor, largely due to changes in the production and trade of agricultural goods, foreign direct investment in food processing and retailing, and global food advertising and promotion. Whereas higher-income groups (especially in poorer countries) tend to benefit from a more dynamic marketplace brought on by these global changes, lower-income groups are more likely to experience disproportionate negative impact, through economic and cultural convergence toward low-quality diets (e.g., inexpensive vegetable oils, trans fats), products which are heavily promoted and which become desirable, reflecting in part their earlier popularity among wealthier groups (Hawkes 2006).

Adding to this, there is evidence of global exportation of the thin ideal of beauty in the form of Western media images. In their work with ethnic Fijian schoolgirls, Becker et al. (2002, 2004) observed an increase in disordered eating attitudes and behaviors over the three years following introduction of Western television. Within this context of rapid social change in a culture that did not traditionally value thinness, girls' comments indicated a desire to emulate television characters. If the situation in higher-income countries is any indication, pursuit of thinness as an aesthetic ideal could well become an upper-class aspiration in the developing world, and potentially further exacerbate the inverse social gradient in weight that is currently prominent in the developed world—especially among women.

CONCLUSIONS

Concluding points are twofold. First, consistent socioeconomic patterning of obesity exists, and does not just reflect economic or material factors. This becomes evident when considering that different indicators of SES relate differently to obesity, particularly in men. Appropriate etiological and intervention frameworks are needed to embrace the social, cultural, and symbolic dimensions of the SES-obesity relationship. Second, given that socioeconomic patterning of weight persists and is perhaps widening, it is important that prevention initiatives incorporate evaluation not just of overall impact, but of differential impact by SES and other axes of social stratification.

REFERENCES

Ball, K., and D. Crawford. 2005. "Socioeconomic Status and Weight Change in Adults: A Review." *Social Science and Medicine* 60: 1987–2010.

Ball, K., G. D. Mishra, and D. Crawford. 2003. "Social Factors and Obesity: An Investigation of the Role of Health Behaviours." *International Journal of Obesity* 27: 394–403.

Becker, A. 2004. "Television, Disordered Eating, and Young Women in Fiji: Negotiating Body Image and Identity during Rapid Social Change." *Culture, Medicine and Psychiatry* 28: 533–559.

Becker, A., R. A. Burwell, S. E. Gilman, D. B. Herzog, and P. Hamburg. 2002. "Eating Behaviours and Attitudes Following Prolonged Exposure to Television among Ethnic Fijian Adolescent Girls." *British Journal of Psychiatry* 180: 509–514.

Bjorntorp, P. 2001. "Do Stress Reactions Cause Abdominal Obesity and Comorbidities?" *Obesity Reviews* 2: 73–86.

Bourdieu, P. 1984. *Distinction: A Social Critique of the Judgement of Taste.* London: Routledge.

Cassels, S. 2006. "Overweight in the Pacific: Links between Foreign Dependence, Global Food Trade, and Obesity in the Federated States of Micronesia." *Globalization and Health* 2: 10.

Che, J., and J. Chen. 2001. "Food Insecurity in Canadian Households." *Health Reports* 12: 11–22.

Daniel, M.D., D. S. Moore, S. Decker, L. Belton, B. DeVellis, A. Doolen, et al. 2006. "Associations among Education, Cortisol Rhythm, and BMI in Blue-Collar Women." *Obesity* 14: 327–335.

Dinour, L.M., D. Bergen, and M. C. Yeh. 2007. "The Food Insecurity–Obesity Paradox: A Review of the Literature and the Role Food Stamps May Play." *Journal of the American Dietetic Association* 107: 1952–1961.

Drewnowski, A., and N. Darmon. 2005. "The Economics of Obesity: Dietary Energy Density and Energy Cost." *American Journal of Clinical Nutrition* 82(Supp.): S265–S273.

Drewnowski, A., and S. E. Specter. 2004. "Poverty and Obesity: The Role of Energy Density and Energy Costs." *American Journal of Clinical Nutrition* 79: 6–16.

Ford, P. B., and D. A. Dzewaltowski. 2008. "Disparities in Obesity Prevalence Due to Variation in the Retail Food Environment: Three Testable Hypotheses." *Nutrition Reviews* 66: 216–228.

Frohlich, K. L., N. Ross, and C. Richmond. 2006. "Health Disparities in Canada Today: Some Evidence and a Theoretical Framework." *Health Policy* 79: 132–143.

Giles-Corti, B. 2006. "People or Places: What Should Be the Target?" *Journal of Science and Medicine in Sport* 9: 357–366.

Giles-Corti, B., and R. J. Donovan. 2002. "Socioeconomic Status Differences in Recreational Physical Activity Levels and Real and Perceived Access to a Supportive Physical Environment." *Preventive Medicine* 35: 601–611.

Groesz, L. M., M. P. Levine, and S. K. Murnen. 2002. "The Effect of Experimental Presentation of Thin Media Images on Body Satisfaction: A Meta-Analytic Review." *International Journal of Eating Disorders* 31: 1–16.

Hawkes, C. 2006. "Uneven Dietary Development: Linking the Policies and Processes of Globalization with the Nutrition Transition, Obesity and Diet-Related Chronic Diseases." *Globalization and Health* 2: 4.

Hawkes, C. 2005. "The Role of Foreign Direct Investment in the Nutrition Transition." *Public Health Nutrition* 8: 357–365.

Jansson, S. 1995. "Food Practices and Division of Domestic Labour–A Comparison between British and Swedish Households." *Sociological Review* 43: 462–477.

Jeffrey, R. W., and S. A. French. 1996. "Socioeconomic Status and Weight Control Practices among 20- to 45-Year Old Women." *American Journal of Public Health* 86: 1005–1010.

Katzmarzyk, P. T., and C. Davis. 2001. "Thinness and Body Shape Of Playboy Centerfolds from 1978 to 1998." *International Journal of Obesity* 25: 590–592.

Kemmer, D. 2000. "Tradition and Change in Domestic Roles and Food Preparation." *Sociology* 34: 323–333.

Kuhle, S., and P. J. Veugelers. 2008. "Why Does the Social Gradient in Health Not Apply to Overweight?" *Health Reports* 19: 7–15.

Lynch, E., K. Liu, B. Spring, A. Hankinson, G. S. Wei, and P. Greenland. 2007. "Association of Ethnicity and Socioeconomic Status with Judgments of Body Size: The Coronary Artery Risk Development in Young Adults (CARDIA) Study." *American Journal of Epidemiology* 165: 1055–1062.

Marmot, M., and R. Wilkinson, eds. 2005. *Social Determinants of Health*, 2nd ed. Oxford: Oxford University Press.

McIntyre, L. 2004. "Food Insecurity." In *Social Determinants of Health: Canadian Perspectives*, ed. D. Raphael, 173–185. Toronto: Canadian Scholars' Press.

McLaren, L. 2007. "Socioeconomic Status and Obesity." *Epidemiologic Reviews* 29: 29–48.

McLaren, L., and L. Gauvin. 2002. "Neighbourhood- vs. Individual-Level Correlates of Women's Body Dissatisfaction: Toward a Multilevel Understanding of the Role of Affluence." *Journal of Epidemiology and Community Health* 56: 193–199.

McLaren, L., and L. Gauvin. 2003. "Does the 'Average Size' of Women in the Neighbourhood Influence a Woman's Likelihood of Body Dissatisfaction?" *Health and Place* 9: 327–335.

McLaren, L., and J. Godley. 2009. "Social Class and Body Mass Index among Canadian Adults: A Focus on Occupational Prestige." *Obesity* 17: 290–299.

McLaren, L., J. Godley, and I. A. S. MacNairn. 2009. "Social Class, Gender, and Time Use: Implications for the Social Determinants of Body Weight?" *Health Reports* 20: 1–9.

McLaren, L., and D. Kuh. 2004. "Body Dissatisfaction in Midlife Women." *Journal of Women and Aging* 16: 35–54.

McLaren, L., and D. Kuh. 2004a. "Women's Body Dissatisfaction, Social Class, and Social Mobility." *Social Science and Medicine* 58: 1575–1584.

McVey, G., S. Tweed, and E. Blackmore. 2005. "Correlates of Weight Loss and Muscle-Gaining Behavior in 10- to 14-Year-Old Males and Females." *Preventive Medicine* 40: 1–9.

Molarius, A., J. C. Seidell, S. Sans, J. Tuomilehto, and K. Kuulasmaa. 2000. "Educational Level, Relative Body Weight, and Changes in Their Association over 10 Years: An International Perspective from the WHO MONICA Project." *American Journal of Public Health* 90: 1260–1268.

Monteiro, C. A., E. C. Moura, W. L. Conde, and B. M. Popkin. 2004. "Socioeconomic Status and Obesity in Adult Populations of Developing Countries: A Review." *Bulletin of the World Health Organization* 82: 940–946.

Paeratakul, S., M. A. White, D. A. Williamson, D. H. Ryan, and G. A. Bray. 2002. "Sex, Race/Ethnicity, Socioeconomic Status, and BMI in Relation to Self-Perception of Overweight." *Obesity Research* 10: 345–350.

Parsons, T., C. Power, S. Logan, and C. Summerbell. 1999. "Childhood Predictors of Adult Obesity: A Systematic Review." *International Journal of Obesity* 23(supp. 8): 1–107.

Popkin, B. M. 2002. "The Shift in Stages of the Nutrition Transition in the Developing World Differs from Past Experiences!" *Public Health Nutrition* 5: 205–214.

Powell, L. M., S. Slater, F. J. Chaloupka, and D. Harper. 2006. "Availability of Physical Activity-Related Facilities and Neighborhood Demographic and Socioeconomic Characteristics: A National Study." *American Journal of Public Health* 96: 1676–1680.

Power, E. M. 1999. "An Introduction to Pierre Bourdieu's Key Theoretical Concepts." *Journal for the Study of Food and Society* 3: 48–52.

Power, E. M. 2005. "Determinants of Healthy Eating among Low-Income Canadians." *Canadian Journal of Public Health* 96(Supp. 3): S37–S38.

Power, C., and T. Parsons. 2000. "Nutritional and Other Influences in Childhood as Predictors of Adult Obesity." *Proceedings of the Nutrition Society* 59: 267–272.

Puhle, R., and K. D. Brownell. 2001. "Bias, Discrimination, and Obesity." *Obesity Research* 9: 788–805.

Raphael, D., ed. 2009. *Social Determinants of Health: Canadian Perspectives* (2nd ed). Toronto: Canadian Scholars' Press.

Rosmond, R., and P. Bjorntorp. 2000. "Occupational Status, Cortisol Secretory Pattern, and Visceral Obesity in Middle-Aged Men." *Obesity Research* 8: 445–450.

Ruppel Shell, E. 2002. *The Hungry Gene: The Science of Fat and the Future of Thin*. New York: Atlantic Monthly Press.

Sapolsky, R. M. 2004. *Why Zebras Don't Get Ulcers: The Acclaimed Guide to Stress, Stress-related Diseases, and Coping* (3rd ed). New York: Owl Books.

Sarlio-Lahteenkorva, S., and E. Lahelma. 2001. "Food Insecurity Is Associated with Past and Present Economic Disadvantage and Body Mass Index." *Journal of Nutrition* 131: 2880–2884.

Shields, M., and M. Tjepkema. 2006. "Trends in Adult Obesity." *Health Reports* 17: 53–59.

Shilling, C. 2005. *The Body and Social Theory* (2nd ed). London: Sage Publications.

Shrewsbury, V., and J. Wardle. 2008. "Socioeconomic Status and Adiposity in Childhood: A Systematic Review of Cross-Sectional Studies 1990–2005." *Obesity* 16: 275–284.

Sobal, S., and A. J. Stunkard. 1989. "Socioeconomic Status and Obesity: A Review of the Literature." *Psychological Bulletin* 105: 260–275.

Tjepkema, M. 2006. "Adult Obesity." *Health Reports* 17: 9–25.

Townsend, M. S., J. Peerson, B. Love, C. Achterberg, and S. P. Murphy. 2001. "Food Insecurity Is Positively Related to Overweight in Women." *Journal of Nutrition* 131: 1738–1745.

Travers, K. D., A. Cogdon, W. McDonald, C. Wright, B. Anderson, and D. R. MacLean. 1997. "Availability and Cost of Heart Healthy Dietary Changes in Nova Scotia." *Journal of the Canadian Dietetic Association* 58: 176–183.

Vozoris, N., and V. Tarasuk. 2003. "Household Food Insufficiency Is Associated with Poorer Health." *Journal of Nutrition* 133: 120–126.

Ward, H., V. Tarasuk, and R. Mendelson. 2007. "Socioeconomic Patterns of Obesity in Canada: Modeling the Role of Health Behaviour." *Applied Physiology, Nutrition, and Metabolism* 32: 206–216.

Wardle, J., and J. Griffith. 2001. "Socioeconomic Status and Weight Control Practices in British Adults." *Journal of Epidemiology and Community Health* 55: 185–190.

Wardle, J., J. Griffith, F. Johnson, and L. Rapoport. 2000. "Intentional Weight Control and Food Choice Habits in a National Representative Sample of Adults in the UK." *International Journal of Obesity* 24: 534–540.

World Health Organization (WHO). 2003. *Global Strategy on Diet, Physical Activity, and Health. Obesity and Overweight Fact Sheet*. Available at: http://www.who.int/hpr/NPH/docs/gs_obesity.pdf.

CHAPTER 17

THE NUTRITION TRANSITION AND OBESITY

BARRY M. POPKIN

INTRODUCTION

THE concept of the nutrition transition is used in two different ways. One is as a theoretical construct similar to the demographic transition in which different sub-population groups across the globe have entered and left different stages of diet, activity and body composition since early hunter-gatherer societies. The second is focused on the rapid shift toward a world in which non-communicable diseases such as obesity are the dominant result of the way we eat, drink and move, and all the related consequences of this.

In this chapter, I list and describe the stages of the nutrition transition, then discuss changes in the way we are eating, drinking, and moving, and the subsequent increase in energy imbalance across the globe.

THE CONCEPT OF THE NUTRITION TRANSITION

Over the course of human existence, human diet and nutritional status have undergone a sequence of major shifts among characteristic states, defined as broad patterns of food use and corresponding nutrition-related disease. The concept of the nutrition transition focuses on large shifts in diet, especially its structure and overall composition. These dietary changes are reflected in nutritional outcomes, such as changes in average stature and body composition. Further, dietary changes are paralleled by major changes in health status, as well as by major demographic and socioeconomic changes. The concept of the nutrition transition places human diet in a broad historical perspective, with an emphasis on understanding the pace, magnitude, determinants, correlates, and results of dietary change across the centuries and millennia.

The nutrition transition has been manifested in five broad stages: (1) hunter-gatherers or collecting food, (2) famine, (3) receding famine, (4) noncommunicable disease, and (5) behavioral change. The major features of each stage are described below. These stages or patterns are not restricted to particular periods of human history. For convenience, the stages are outlined in past tense as historical developments; however, "earlier" stages are not restricted to the periods in which they first arose, but continue to characterize certain geographic and socioeconomic subpopulations.

Stage 1: Hunter-gatherers Collecting Food

Our knowledge of the initial stage of human diet and nutrition comes both from archaeological evidence and from study of extant hunter-gatherer groups in remote parts of the world. Although hunter-gatherer societies studied in the past century live in far more marginal environments than did their predecessors, their diets probably do not differ significantly.

From about 3 million to about 10 thousand years ago, all human subsistence was based on gathering, scavenging, and hunting; no food was produced. Hunting emerged as a significant component of subsistence only in the last million years (Gordon 1987); hunters progressed from small to large prey. The use or control of fire has been documented during this period for many locations.

The stage of collecting food was characterized by a diet about 50 percent to 80 percent from plants and 20 percent to 50 percent from animals (Eaton, Shostak, and Konner 1988; Jonsson et al. 2006; Cordain 2002; Cordain et al. 2002). In general, the diet was more varied than in agricultural societies (Truswell 1977; Truswell and Hansen 1976). Variety was ensured by seasonality and the need to combine hunting and gathering activities. Basic food sources were grass seeds, tree nuts, roots and tubers, fish, aquatic mammals, and herd ungulates. (Coastal dwellers received relatively more nutrition from fishing, and inland residents relatively more from hunting.)

Archaeological evidence indicates that early humans were relatively tall (comparable in height to well-nourished contemporary humans) and robust in skeleton and musculature (Eaton, Shostak, and Konner 1988; Schoeninger 1982). Early humans had short life spans, but evidently satisfactory nutritional status; infectious diseases were the major cause of illness and death.

Stage 2: Famine

The stage of famine accompanied the development of agriculture (often termed the "first agricultural revolution"), whereby humans first became able to produce food. Agriculture arose and became dominant at different times in different regions of the world; for example, by about 7000 B.C.E. in Southeast Asia and by about 500 B.C.E. in Mexico, when Tehuacan Valley agrarian-based economies were well established (Benz and Long 2000). The cause of the shift to agriculture is unclear; however, the most convincing explanation is a response to increased population density. Agricultural technology remained relatively simple until around 2000 B.C.E., becoming more complex in different regions at different times (Vargas 1990).

Compared with the diet of the hunter-gatherers, the early agriculturalists' diet was much less varied and was subject to larger fluctuations (including periodic famine) because of dependence on monocultures as food sources. The relative importance of plants, domesticated animals, or hunting as food sources differed among agricultural societies. In general, the onset of agriculture and animal husbandry was associated with a significant decline in the proportion of meat in the diet and an increase in plant foods (to up to 90 percent of the diet), especially cereal grains. For example, increases in strontium: calcium ratios in human bones from between 10 and 15 thousand years B.C.E. in the Middle East indicate a dietary shift from animal to plant food sources concurrent with the onset of agriculture (Schoeninger 1982). Alcohol consumption also increased. With the transition to the stage of famine, the diet generally became slightly lower in protein, higher in complex carbohydrates (providing 60 percent to 75 percent of energy), and lower in fat (10 percent to 15 percent of energy) (Trowell and Burkett 1981).

According to numerous studies of skeletal remains, these changes in diet were associated with nutritional stress and a reduction in stature, by an estimated average of 4 inches (Eaton and Konner 1985; Eaton, Shostak, and Konner 1988; Vargas 1990). The shift to agriculture resulted in the onset of a variety of deficiency diseases, all directly related to the reduction in dietary variety (Yudkin 1969).

Stage 3: Receding Famine

The stage of receding famine accompanied the Industrial Revolution and the second agricultural revolution, which began in eighteenth-century Western Europe with the application of modern technology to agriculture. Increasing human ability to control factors affecting seasonal and longer-term fluctuations in food supply made food available to fuel the labor force needed for the Industrial Revolution and the development of modern urban societies.

Technological changes such as the development of natural fertilizers and crop rotation systems increased agricultural productivity and the stability of the food supply, considerably reducing famine and resulting in large shifts in diet. An excess food supply allowed an increase in production of animals for food, which in turn provided animal manure for fertilizer. As the Industrial Revolution progressed, irrigation technology, transportation within and across national and regional borders, and other changes continued to reduce the effects of climatic fluctuations on agricultural production and local food supplies and to increase variety in the diet. This period also saw changes in food-processing technology with various nutritional repercussions.

Transition to the stage of receding famine was associated with dietary increases in animal protein, fat, sugar, vegetables, and fruits and decreases in fiber and starch (notably, less consumption of bread and potatoes). Increases in protein and fat consumption, together with changes in food-processing technology, led to increased stature and elimination of many nutritional deficiency diseases. However, newly introduced techniques for milling grain led to decline in fiber intake and short-term increases in certain deficiency diseases, such as pellagra and beriberi (which resulted from excessive milling of corn and rice, respectively).

Other features of the Industrial Revolution were increases in social inequality, clustering of the poor in slums and ghettoes, poor sanitation and impure water supplies, and development of a new set of infant nutrition problems related to early weaning from the breast. In the late nineteenth and early twentieth centuries, medical practitioners responded to infant nutrition problems by developing formulations for feeding infants, which stimulated the commercial infant formula sector (Wickes 1953a, 1953b, 1953c).

Many lower-income countries have achieved remarkable economic or social progress during the past century and continue to move through the stage of receding famine into the next dietary stage. There are regions and countries such as Haiti, parts of rural India, and rural sub-Saharan Asia, where the stage of receding famine is still found.

Stage 4: Non-communicable Disease

The stage of non-communicable disease began with rapid growth in animal husbandry, urbanization, and economic growth, which together formed the basis for a shift toward a diet substantially lower in nutrient density (i.e., less nutrients per calorie of food consumed) and higher in saturated fat and refined sugar. A diet high in total fat, cholesterol, sugar, and other refined carbohydrates and low in polyunsaturated fatty acids and fiber, often accompanying increasingly sedentary life, is characteristic of most high-income societies today, resulting in increased prevalence of obesity and the non-communicable diseases of Omran's final epidemiologic stage. Food balance studies in rural Wales well illustrate long-term dietary changes related to transition from the stage of receding famine to the stage of non-communicable disease (Hughes and Jones 1979).

Meat from modern domesticated animals is higher in calories and lower in protein than meat consumed in the stage of famine or the stage of collecting food; it contains much more fat in subcutaneous tissue and fascial planes and as marbling within the muscle. Furthermore, the fat in meat from earlier undomesticated animals was much more likely to be polyunsaturated. This recent change in fat content of meat explains some of the increase in fat-related non-communicable diseases, such as coronary heart disease; evidently, the human digestive system has not had time to evolve effective protection against adverse nutritional consequences of high animal fat intake.

Stage 5: Behavioral Change

A new dietary pattern appears to be emerging as a result of behavioral changes in diet that are apparently motivated by the desire to prevent non-communicable diseases and prolong health. It is only in selected subpopulation groups across the globe that we see such behavioral change. Whether these changes will constitute a large-scale transition in diet structure and body composition remains to be seen.

Public knowledge about the relationship between diet and disease—particularly cardiovascular disease, hypertension, osteoporosis, and selected cancers—has increased considerably. Related dietary changes have occurred mainly in certain higher-income countries, especially the United States. Increased consumption of low-fat products, reduced intake of higher-fat products, careful attention to cholesterol intake, and emerging concern about fiber intake are evidence of a potential new pattern in the nutrition transition. Several researchers have shown that such behavioral changes can extend the term of disability-free life (Manton and Soldo 1985). It is speculated that dietary change has been responsible for important decreases in coronary heart disease in several countries (Puska et al. 1998; Puska 2002).

Global Dynamics of Energy Imbalance

There is no clear consensus of the causes of the global shift over the past 20 years toward increased obesity. Elsewhere I have explored relative rates of change across the globe for adults and children. We have long-term comparable data for Brazil and the United States (Popkin, Conde et al. 2006). For example, studies of body composition and dietary pattern shifts indicate rates of change are accelerating in China. The rate of change in the prevalence of overweight plus obesity accelerated from less than 0.5 percent in the 1980–1990 period to 1.9 percent and 0.9 percent in the 1997–2000 period for men and women, respectively (Wang et al. 2007); data for 2004 and 2006 showed that these changes are still accelerating (Popkin 2008). In the dietary area, we have documented longitudinally that the income elasticity, or the proportion of food purchases with a 1 percent increase in income has accelerated at an increasing rate in the past 15 years (Du et al. 2004; Guo et al. 2000).

Evidence of the Role of Decreased Energy Expenditures in Low- and Middle-Income Countries

There is a surprising dearth of data on trends of overall energy expenditures. In my China Health and Nutrition Longitudinal Survey we have systematically collected these data on about 17,000 Chinese since 1991. In that study we have documented a large decline in overall physical activity and in its components. Key findings include:

- A significant and large reduction in overall METS (measured in metabolic equivalents—proxy for oxygen uptake and in reality energy expenditures) from work, home production, and transportation for men and women (Ng, Norton, and Popkin 2009)
- A significant effect of reductions in work both in terms of shifts in technology reducing work at the same occupation and a shifting pattern of occupations (Monda et al. 2007 Bell, Ge, and Popkin 2001)
- A significant effect of a shift from active to passive transport (Bell, Ge, and Popkin 2002)
- Some associations between home production technology that most likely is endogenous but also are time-saving assets (Monda et al. 2008)
- Reductions for women in the amount of time in home production (Monda et al. 2008).

Across the globe there is extensive documentation of the changes in leisure toward more passive leisure, personified by television viewing. Linked with that is greater inactivity.

Evidence of Shifts in the Structure of Diets but Minimal Documentation of Causal Relationships

Globally, our diets have greatly changed. Higher fiber foods are being replaced by processed versions. There is a universal shift toward increased caloric sweeteners in the diet (Popkin and Nielsen 2003; Duffey and Popkin 2008). At the same time, water appears to be increasingly replaced by sugar-sweetened beverages, juices, and other higher-calorie beverages. Edible oil intake has also increased greatly.

We have documented each of these changes and shown for China that the structure of the relationships has shifted over time such that increased income is associated with ever-increasing intakes (i.e., increasing income elasticities over time) of edible oils (Du et al. 2004).

The global shifts in the energy density of the diet are impossible to document with extant data. What we do know is that there is an increasing intake of animal source foods and edible vegetable oils. Elsewhere we have used food balance data and other individual intake dietary data to show that vegetable oil intake has accelerated with increasing income (Guo et al. 2000; Ng, Zhai, and Popkin 2008).

We have also shown that because of both major technological changes in vegetable oil extraction, plant breeding of higher oil content in these oilseeds, and changes in global tariffs and price controls, lower-income countries are increasingly able to consume greater amounts of these oils (Ng, Zhai, and Popkin 2008; Popkin and Drewnowski 1997).

Animal source food changes are equally dramatic, particularly in selected countries. In China, egg, poultry, beef, and pork consumption have increased rapidly, and milk intake has recently begun to rise. Today, the average Chinese adult consumes more than 1,300 kilocalories per day of pork, poultry, beef, mutton, fish, eggs, and dairy food (Popkin 2008; Du et al. 2004). As we have shown elsewhere, the structure of consumption shifts in China is such that for each additional increase in income, adults proportionally increase their intake of animal source foods.

Concurrent shifts are occurring in the use of caloric sweeteners. There are only a few countries with published studies of these trends of the exact foods where added caloric sweeteners are found; the United States and South Africa are two of these countries (Steyn, Myburgh, and Nel 2003; Duffey and Popkin 2008).

In the United States and Mexico we have documented very large increases in consumption of sugar-sweetened beverages (SSBs for more than half of the increase in added caloric sweeteners in the past several decades in the United States) (Duffey and Popkin 2007). In Mexico there was close to a doubling of all caloric beverages in the 1999–2006 period (Barquera et al. 2010; Barquera et al. 2008). This has led the Mexican government to attempt major policy shifts to reduce intake of these beverages (Rivera et al. 2008).

The studies on fiber intake and other changes toward processed foodstuffs are much more incomplete to date. Since the issue of reduced fiber intake in the Western diet was first discussed as a source of major health concerns, there have been few systematic studies of shifts in fiber intake throughout the world. There are, however, important historical case studies that document these shifts for selected population groups and countries. There is also documentation of specific shifts in diet from coarse grains to refined grains in a few countries (Popkin 1993; Popkin et al. 1993).

Similarly, studies on fruit and vegetable intake indicate declines in many countries and regions of the world, but again have not been systematically studied. There are also selected countries where fruit and vegetable intake remain very high (e.g., Spain, Greece, and South Korea).

DISCUSSION

Almost all countries in the world have a greater level of adult and child overweight and obesity today than they did a decade ago. And in some countries there is evidence of a speeding up of these changes; however, there is a limited number of countries with representative national surveys to allow us to examine shifts over time in BMI distribution. There are self-selected populations such as the women with children in many Demographic and Health (DHS) surveys that do provide a useful comparative picture (Mendez, Monteiro, and Popkin 2005).

The critical question is whether any countries are experiencing a leveling-off or even a reduction in obesity. In Brazil we have shown a significant decline only among women who are middle and high SES (Monteiro, Conde, and Popkin 2007). I know of no other country where adult women have experienced a reduction in obesity. I should add that in Brazil and all other countries there is no evidence of reduction in obesity among men. In the child obesity area, there is some limited data on selected populations to suggest a potential reduction or plateauing of obesity (Peneau et al. 2009; Sundblom et al. 2008).

The question is how do we address the rise in global obesity? There is limited evidence to explain the increase in caloric intake and more to explain the decline in energy expenditure. Most of the evidence on prevention and treatment of obesity indicates that dietary change is more successful. So we must be careful in utilizing the extant information on the causes of the decline in activity and shifts in dietary patterns as if there is symmetry in causes and policy changes for the future.

When we examine how trends in dietary intake have affected in a huge way the global shifts in energy balance, the data is far more limited. Aside from the shift to caloric beverages, there is little consensus on whether and how specific elements of diet affect weight dynamics. While it is not my role here to provide all the reasons for the concern with beverages rather than foods, the major reason is that there is no evidence that when we consume a caloric beverage, be it one based on fat, protein, or carbohydrates, that we reduce food intake (Mourao et al. 2007; Mattes 2006; DiMeglio and Mattes 2000). Except for a few industry-funded scholars and studies, there is unanimous consensus that there is very little or no reduction in food intake when more caloric beverages are consumed. In fact, the evidence is mounting that one of the more effective ways to cut caloric intake, particularly of refined carbohydrates, is to tax sugar added to water in any processed beverage (Brownell et al. 2009). Elsewhere many have reviewed the adverse effects of sugar sweetened beverages (SSBs) and other types of caloric beverages on increased energy intake, weight, and risks of diabetes and heart disease (Vartanian, Schwartz, and Brownell 2007; Malik, Schulze, and Hu 2006; Popkin, Armstrong et al. 2006).

Another major health concern is the increase in animal source foods. There are enormous environmental costs linked with animal source foods (Food and Agricultural Organization of the United Nations 2007; Popkin 2009). Also there are increased risks of heart disease and cancer and reduced survival rates linked with excessive animal food intake, particularly from beef and pork and processed meats (Sinha et al. 2009). However, there is no clear linkage of consumption of these products with obesity and energy balance.

Another issue raised by many is energy density (Rolls 2007). Rolls and others who follow her line of work have provided a strong case for the role of energy density. However, the question of the role of increased energy density on long-term energy imbalance is not settled. In fact, there is no consensus on this topic at all, so it is not possible to truly understand how the shift toward greater animal source foods and edible oils impacts weight gain.

Similarly, it is unclear how the increased intake of snacks affects overall energy intake (Popkin and Duffey Under Review). There is some evidence that snacking is linked to increased caloric intake and possibly increased energy imbalance but not enough to allow for strong conclusions. Some tantalizing new research shows that increased snacking does not affect subsequent food intake and hence is linked with increased energy imbalance among heavy individuals (Temple et al. 2009; Bray 2009).

From an energy expenditure perspective, there is extensive suggestive evidence that energy expenditures are decreasing across the lower- and middle-income world. China is one example of a country transitioning rapidly from an agrarian to a manufacturing and service economy and at the same time increasing access to labor-saving technology across both urban and rural sectors in market and home production and transportation. These reductions in energy expenditure are clearly relevant to the increased obesity in China and most likely many other countries. Elsewhere we have shown the large shifts in types of occupations toward more service sector jobs in urban areas (Popkin 1999). Generally we have found a significant reduction in energy expenditures at work due to both shifts in occupations toward the service sector and to increased access to modern energy expenditure–saving technology in urban areas.

So what do we do? As an economist and a person involved in program and policy research with a number of low- and middle-income countries, my belief is that we need major national initiatives. These include shifts in the structure of food prices based both on removal and shifting of subsidies and initiation of taxation. My own research in the United States, Mexico, and China gives me an empirical basis for stating that price changes can have a large effect (Duffey et al. 2010) Guo et al.; Ng, Zhai, and Popkin 2008; Barquera et al. 2008; Rivera et al. 2008). Other large scale changes in regulations regarding advertisement of SSBs and other types of foods for which a consensus might emerge about their unhealthfulness remain to be considered. In the tobacco control area, taxation and media regulation were clearly critical dimensions (Brownell and Warner 2009; Warner 2005). These same changes that are recommended to address obesity are among those seen by the cancer world as major prevention options (WCRF/AICR 2007; WCRF/AICR [World Cancer Research Fund/American Institute of Cancer Research] 2009).

The challenge for the globe is to do for obesity what was done for tobacco. The World Health Organization (WHO) in 2004 adopted a global strategy to address poor dietary and physical activity patterns that were causing global obesity (WHO 2004). Subsequently WHO has not taken a leadership role on this topic, but countries as diverse as Mexico, Brazil, France, and the United Kingdom have enacted major changes. We can only hope that this will stimulate other countries to do the same.

FURTHER READING

There are no clear concise scholarly books that pull together in a rigorous scientific way all of the components of research on the nutrition transition; my earlier edited book with Ben Caballero (Caballero and Popkin 2002) comes the closest. My recent popular book (Popkin 2008) describes the key issues in an easy-to-read, understandable manner.

REFERENCES

Barquera, S. F. Campirano, A. Bonvecchio, L. Hernández, J. A. Rivera, B. M. Popkin (2010) "Caloric beverage trends in Mexican children". *Nutrition Journal* 9: 47–56.

Barquera, S., L. Hernández-Barrera, M. L. Tolentino, J. Espinosa, J. Leroy, J. Rivera, and B. M. Popkin. 2008. "Energy from beverages is on the rise among Mexican adolescents and adults". *Journal of Nutrition* 138: 2456–2461.

Bell. A. C., K. Ge, and B. M. Popkin. 2001. "Weight Gain and Its Predictors in Chinese Adults." *International Journal of Obesity and Related Metabolic Disorders* 25(7): 1079–1086.

Bell. A. C., K. Ge, and B. M. Popkin. 2002. "The Road to Obesity or the Path to Prevention: Motorized Transportation and Obesity in China." *Obesity Research* 10(4): 277–283.

Benz, B. F., and A. Long. 2000. "Prehistoric Maize Evolution in the Tehuacan Valley." *Current Anthropology* 41(3): 459–465.

Bray, G. A. 2009. "Can We Reduce Snack Food Intake?" *American Journal of Clinical Nutrition* 90(2): 251–252.

Brownell, K., T. Farley, W. C. Willett, B. Popkin, F. J. Chaloupka, J. W. Thompson, and D. S. Ludwig. 2009. "The Public Health and Revenue Generating Benefits of Taxing Sugar Sweetened Beverages." *New England Journal of Medicine* 360(18): 1805–1808.

Brownell, K. D., and K. E. Warner. 2009. "The Perils of Ignoring History: Big Tobacco Played Dirty and Millions Died. How Similar Is Big Food?" *Milbank Quarterly* 87(1): 259–294.

Caballero, B., and B. M. Popkin, (eds.). (2002) *The Nutrition Transition: Diet and Disease in the Developing World.* London: Academic Press.

Cordain, L. 2002. *The Paleo Diet: Lose Weight and Get Healthy by Eating the Food You Were Designed to Eat.* Hoboken, NJ: Wiley.

Cordain, L., S. B. Eaton, J. B. Miller, N. Mann, and K. Hill. 2002. "The Paradoxical Nature of Hunter-Gatherer Diets: Meat-Based, Yet Non-Atherogenic." *European Journal of Clinical Nutrition* 56: S42–S52.

DiMeglio, D. P., and R. D. Mattes. 2000. "Liquid versus solid carbohydrate: effects on food intake and body weight." *International Journal of Obesity and Related Metabolic Disorders* 24(6): 794–800.

Du, S., T. A. Mroz, F. Zhai, and B. M. Popkin. 2004. "Rapid Income Growth Adversely Affects Diet Quality in China—Particularly for the Poor!" *Social Science and Medicine* 59(7): 1505–1515.

Duffey, K. J., P. Gordon-Larsen, J. M. Shikany, D. K. Guilkey, D. R. Jacobs, and B. M. Popkin (2010) Food price and diet and health outcomes: 20 years of The CARDIA Study. *Archives of Internal Medicine* 170:420–26. NIHMSID: NIHMS190425.

Duffey, K., C. E. Lewis, J. M. Shikany, D. K. Guilkey, D. R. Jacobs, and B. M. Popkin. Under review. "Increased Food Prices Are Associated with Changes in Diet, Weight, and HOMA Insulin Resistance over 20-Years of the CARDIA Study." Chapel Hill, NC.

Duffey, K., and B. M. Popkin. 2007. "Shifts in Patterns and Consumption of Beverages between 1965 and 2002." *Obesity* 15(11): 2739–2747.

Duffey, K. J., and B. M. Popkin. 2008. "High-fructose Corn Syrup: Is This What's for Dinner?" *American Journal of Clinical Nutrition* 88(6): 1722S–1732.

Eaton, S. B., and M. Konner. 1985. "Paleolithic Nutrition: A Consideration on Its Nature and Current Implications." *New England Journal of Medicine* 312: 283–289.

Eaton, S. B., M. Shostak, and M. Konner. 1988. *The Paleolithic Prescription: A Program of Diet and Exercise and a Design for Living*. New York: Harper & Row.

Food and Agricultural Organization of the United Nations. 2007. *Livestock's Long Shadow: Environmental Issues and Options*. Rome: Food and Agricultural Organization United Nations.

Gordon, K. D. 1987. "Evolutionary Perspectives on Human Diet." In *Nutritional Anthropology*, ed. F. Johnston. New York: Liss.

Guo, X. G., T. A. Mroz, B. M. Popkin, and F. Y. Zhai. 2000. "Structural Change in the Impact of Income on Food Consumption in China, 1989–1993." *Economic Development and Cultural Change* 48(4): 737–760.

Guo, X. G., B. M. Popkin, T. A. Mroz, and F. Zhai. 1999. "Food Price Policy Can Favorably Alter Macronutrient Intake in China." *Journal of Nutrition* 129(5): 994–1001.

Hughes, R. E., and E. Jones. 1979. "A Welsh Diet for Britain?" *British Medical Journal* 1(6171): 1145.

Jonsson, T., B. Ahren, G. Pacini, F. Sundler, N. Wierup, and S. Steen. 2006. "A Paleolithic Diet Confers Higher Insulin Sensitivity, Lower C-Reactive Protein and Lower Blood Pressure Than a Cereal-Based Diet in Domestic Pigs." *Nutrition and Metabolism (London)* 3: 39.

Malik, V. S., M. B. Schulze, and F. B. Hu. 2006. "Intake of Sugar-Sweetened Beverages and Weight Gain: A Systematic Review." *American Journal of Clinical Nutrition* 84(2): 274–288.

Manton, K. G., and B. J. Soldo. 1985. "Dynamics of Health Changes in the Oldest Old: New Perspectives and Evidence." *Milbank Memorial Fund Quaterly Health and Society* 63 (2): 206–285. .

Mattes, R. D. 2006. "Fluid Energy: Where's the Problem?" *Journal of the American Dietetic Association* 106 (12): 1956–1961.

Mendez, M. A., C. A. Monteiro, and B. M. Popkin. 2005. "Overweight Exceeds Underweight among Women in Most Developing Countries." *American Journal of Clinical Nutrition* 81(3): 714–721.

Monda, K. P. Gordon-Larsen, J. Stevens, and B.M. Popkin 2007. China's transition: The effect of rapid urbanization on adult occupational physical activity. *Social Science and Medicine* 64: 858–870

Monda, K. L., L. S. Adair, F. Zhai, and B. M. Popkin. 2008. "Longitudinal Relationships between Occupational and Domestic Physical Activity Patterns and Body Weight in China." *European Journal of Clinical Nutrition* 62: 1318–1325.

Monteiro, C. A., W. L. Conde, and B. M. Popkin. 2007. "Income-specific Trends in Obesity in Brazil: 1975–2003." *American Journal of Public Health* 97(10): 1808–1812.

Mourao, D. M., J. Bressan, W.W. Campbell, and R. D. Mattes. 2007. "Effects of Food Form on Appetite and Energy Intake in Lean and Obese Young Adults." *International Journal of Obesity (London)* 31(11): 1688–1695.

Ng, S. W., E. Norton, and B. M. Popkin. 2009. "Why Have Physical Activity Levels Declined among Chinese Adults? Findings from the 1991–2006 China Health and Nutrition Surveys." *Social Science and Medicine* 68(7): 1305–1314.

Ng, S. W., F. Zhai, and B. M. Popkin. 2008. "Impacts of China's Edible Oil Pricing Policy on Nutrition." *Social Science and Medicine* 66 (2): 414–426.

Peneau, S., B. Salanave, L. Maillard-Teyssier, M. F. Rolland-Cachera, A. C. Vergnaud, C. Mejean, S. Czernichow, S. Vol, J. Tichet, K. Castetbon, and S. Hercberg. 2009. "Prevalence of Overweight in 6- to 15-Year-Old Children in Central/Western France from 1996 to 2006: Trends Toward Stabilization." *International Journal of Obesity (London)* 33(4): 401–407.

Popkin, B., and A. Drewnowski. 1997. "Dietary Fats and the Nutrition Transition: New Trends in the Global Diet." *Nutrition Review* 55: 31–43.

Popkin, B. 1993. "Nutritional Patterns and Transitions." *Population and Development Review* 19(1): 138–157.

Popkin, B. M. 1999. "Urbanization, Lifestyle Changes and the Nutrition Transition." *World Development* 27: 1905–1916.

Popkin, B. M. Dec. 28, 2008. *The World Is Fat—The Fads, Trends, Policies, and Products That Are Fattening the Human Race.* New York: Avery-Penguin Press.

Popkin, B. M. 2008. "Will China's Nutrition Transition Overwhelm Its Health Care System and Slow Economic Growth?" *Health Affairs(Millwood)* 27(4): 1064–1076.

Popkin, B. M. 2009. "Reducing Meat Consumption Has Multiple Benefits for the World's Health." *Archives of Internal Medicine* 169 (6): 543–545.

Popkin, B. M., L. E. Armstrong, G. M. Bray, B. Caballero, B. Frei, and W. C. Willett. 2006. "A New Proposed Guidance System for Beverage Consumption in the United States." *American Journal of Clinical Nutrition* 83(3): 529–542.

Popkin, B. M., W. Conde, N. Hou, and C. A. Monteiro. 2006. "Is There a Lag Globally in Overweight Trends for Children as Compared to Adults?" *Obesity* 14: 1846–1853.

Popkin, B. M., and K. Duffey. Under review. "Does the Physiological Basis for Eating Exist Any More? Continuous Caloric Intake Is Becoming the Norm."

Popkin, B. M., and K.J. Duffey (2010) Does hunger and satiety drive eating anymore? Increasing eating occasions and decreasing time between eating occasions in the United States *American Journal of Clinical Nutrition* 91(5):1342–1347. PMC2854907.

Popkin, B. M., G. Keyou, F. Zhai, X. Guo, H. Ma, and N. Zohoori. 1993. "The Nutrition Transition in China: A Cross-Sectional Analysis." *European Journal of Clinical Nutrition* 47 (5): 333–346.

Popkin, B. M., and S. J. Nielsen. 2003. "The Sweetening of the World's Diet." *Obesity Research* 11(11): 1325–1332.

Puska, P. 2002. "Nutrition and Global Prevention on Non-Communicable Diseases." *Asia Pacifac Journal of Clinical nutrition* 11(Supp. 9): S755–758.

Puska, P., E. Vartiainen, J. Tuomilehto, V. Salomaa, and A. Nissinen. 1998. "Changes in Premature Deaths in Finland: Successful Long-Term Prevention of Cardiovascular Diseases." *Bulletin of the World Health Organization* 76(4): 419–425.

Rivera, J. A., O. Muñoz-Hernández, M. Rosas-Peralta, C. A. Aguilar-Salinas, B. M. Popkin, and W. C. Willett. 2008. "Consumo de bebidas para una vida saludable: Recomendaciones para la población [Beverage consumption for a healthy life: Recommendations for the Mexican population]." *Salud Publica Mexico* 50(2): 173–195.

Rolls, B. J. 2007. *The Volumetrics Eating Plan: Techniques and Recipes for Feeling Full on Fewer Calories*. New York: Harper Paperbacks.

Schoeninger, M. 1982. "Diet and the Evolution of Modern Human Form in the Middle East." *American Journal of Physical Anthropology* 58: 37–52.

Sinha, R., A. J. Cross, B. I. Graubard, M. F. Leitzmann, and A. Schatzkin. 2009. "Meat Intake and Mortality: A Prospective Study of over Half a Million People." *Archives of Internal Medicine* 169 (6): 562–571.

Steyn, N. P., N. G. Myburgh, and J. H. Nel. 2003. "Evidence to Support a Food-Based Dietary Guideline on Sugar Consumption in South Africa." *Bulletin of the World Health Organization* 81(8): 599–608.

Sundblom, E., M. Petzold, F. Rasmussen, E. Callmer, and L. Lissner. 2008. "Childhood Overweight and Obesity Prevalences Levelling Off in Stockholm but Socioeconomic Differences Persist." *International Journal of Obesity* 32(10): 1525–1530.

Temple, J. L., A. M. Bulkley, R. L. Badawy, N. Krause, S. McCann, and L. H. Epstein. 2009. "Differential Effects of Daily Snack Food Intake on the Reinforcing Value of Food in Obese and Nonobese Women." *American Journal of Clinical Nutrition* 90(2): 304–313.

Trowell, H. C., and D. P. Burkett. 1981. *Western Diseases: Their Emergence and Prevention*. Cambridge, MA: Harvard University Press.

Truswell, A. S. 1977. "Diet and Nutrition of Hunter-gatherers." In *Health and Diseases in Tribal Societies*, ed. Ciba Foundation Symposium 149. Amsterdam: Elsevier.

Truswell, A. S., and J. D. L. Hansen. 1976. "Medical Research among the!Kung." In *Kalahari Hunter-gatherers: Studies of the!Kung San and Their Neighbors*, eds. R. Lee and I. DeVore. Cambridge, MA: Harvard University Press.

Vargas, L. A. 1990. "Old and New Transitions and Nutrition in Mexico." In *Disease in Populations in Transition: Anthropological And Epidemiological Perspectives*, eds. A. Swedlund and G. Armelagos. New York: Bergin and Garvey.

Vartanian, L. R., M. B. Schwartz, and K. D. Brownell. 2007. "Effects of Soft Drink Consumption on Nutrition and Health: A Systematic Review and Meta-Analysis." *American Journal of Public Health* 97(4): 667–675.

Wang, H., S. Du, F. Zhai, and B. M. Popkin. 2007. "Trends in the Distribution of Body Mass Index among Chinese Adults, Aged 20–45 Years (1989–2000)." *International Journal of Obesity* 31: 272–278.

Warner, K. E. 2005. "Tobacco Policy in the United States: Lessons for the Obesity Epidemic." In *Policy Challenges in Modern Health Care*, eds. D. Mechanic, L. Rogut, D. Colby, and J. Knickman. New Brunswick, NJ: Rutgers University Press.

WCRF/AICR (World Cancer Research Fund/American Institute of Cancer Research). 2007. *Food, Nutrition, Physical Activity, and the Prevention of Cancer: A Global Perspective*, ed. AICR. Washington, DC: World Cancer Research Fund/American Institute for Cancer Research.

WCRF/AICR (World Cancer Research Fund/American Institute of Cancer Research). 2009. *Policy and Action for Cancer Prevention* London: World Cancer Research Fund/ American Institute of Cancer Research.

WHO. 2004. *Global Strategy on Diet, Physical Activity and Health, 57th World Health Assembly (WHA57.17)*. Geneva: World Health Organization.

Wickes, I. G. 1953a. "A History of Infant Feeding. II. Seventeenth and Eighteenth Centuries." *Archives of Disease in Children* 28(139): 232–240.

Wickes, I. G . 1953b. "A History of Infant Feeding. III. Eighteenth and Nineteenth Century Writers." *Archives of Disease in Children* 28(140): 332–340.

Wickes, I. G. 1953c. "A History of Infant Feeding. IV. Nineteenth Century Continued." *Archives of Disease in Children* 28(141): 416–422.

Yudkin, J. 1969. "Archaeology and the Nutritionist." In *The Domestication and Exploitation of Plants and Animals.* Chicago: Aldine.

CHAPTER 18

PEER EFFECTS AND OBESITY

JASON M. FLETCHER

INTRODUCTION

THE "obesity epidemic" has attracted the attention of researchers in each of the social sciences, both because of its rapid and largely unexpected increase in the past several decades as well as the many important individual and societal consequences of the increase. Various researchers have been interested in examining key determinants, consequences, and potential treatments and policy interventions of this important health condition (Cawley et al. 2007, Fletcher 2009, Dunn 2009; Cawley 2004, Finkelstein et al. 2009; Cawley and Rizzo 2007, Fletcher et al. 2010a, 2010b). Particularly in the economic literature, much of the initial research examining the determinants of obesity focused on the large decline in food prices over time and the increase in sedentary behaviors of individuals, both at work and during leisure activities (Lakdawalla and Philipson 2002; Chou et al. 2004; Cutler et al. 2003).

More recently, non-market factors, such as social norms and social pressure, have been of research interest. One reason for the increase in interest is the policy implications of the existence of peer effects in obesity. Specifically, peer effects often imply a "social multiplier" for interventions—if we can reduce the weight of one individual, the effect of the intervention may be multiplied through social networks. This type of social effect is called an "endogenous social effect" in the economics literature. The presence of such an effect could increase the potential benefits of intervention without increasing the costs. In contrast to these benefits, the presence of peer effects could also work to spread unhealthy behaviors (such as smoking) as well as reduce the effectiveness of individual-level interventions to affect behavioral change because of the difficulty of overcoming the countervailing influence of peers.

Understanding whether a social multiplier operates in determining obesity will also help to inform whether targeted (e.g., based on influential individuals within networks) or broad-based policy may be more effective. Also, peer effects imply that the composition of a person's neighborhood and/or school could have effects on his own obesity and other health behaviors; since many policies can reorganize peer groups, such as school tracking, busing, and residential zoning, there are a host of potentially important policy domains that could play a part in reducing obesity in the presence of peer effects. Peer effects that operate through the characteristics of peers (as opposed to the behaviors of peers) are labeled "exogenous social effects" or "contextual effects" (see Manski 1993).

There have been several recent advances in the literature that have further focused attention on whether social norms and peer effects help determine obesity. First, Burke and Heiland (2007) present a conceptual model that, while keeping a focus on food prices as a central force in the recent increase in obesity rates, highlights that social norms of "ideal weight" may have changed over time. In particular, they outline and simulate a model that allows for endogenous determination of social weight norms and models the dynamics of these norms over a 25-year period. Outside of the economics literature, a recent empirical advance by Christakis and Fowler (2007) shows evidence that obesity is "socially contagious"—that is, spread through social networks. While the research base that estimates peer effects on obesity is small, there is a growing interest in this question as well as increasing attention to the empirical issues of estimating peer effects using non-experimental data. This chapter will describe both the findings and challenges of this new literature.

BACKGROUND

Although the policy and health importance of peer effects is substantial, so too is the empirical difficulty of credibly estimating causal effects. There are (at least) four primary empirical issues that researchers face. Some are generic problems faced in many empirical settings, but others are somewhat specific to peer effects research.

First, researchers must define a relevant peer group. This step seems simple, but data limitations typically force researchers to define peers based on convenience rather than theory, which has created peer group definitions that range from state-based groups to nominated best friends and everything in between.[1] While there are

---

1 For example, Harding (2003) uses census tracts, Evans et al. (1992) use metropolitan level data, Case and Katz (1991) use city block level data, Fletcher (2010a) uses school grades, Fletcher (2010b) uses school classrooms, Mayer and Puller (2008) use "Facebook Friends," Sacerdote (2001) uses roommates to create relevant reference groups for the outcomes they examine.

several data sets that include friends and peers, the vast majority do not. Collecting additional data targeted at eliciting actual peer groups would be a worthwhile pursuit.

A second empirical difficulty is the endogeneity of peer groups. Does a person smoke because his friend smokes or did he choose his friend because his friend smokes? Because individuals typically have some choice over who they interact with (schoolmates, neighbors, friends, etc), separating peer selection from peer influence is a difficult empirical problem, and peer selection effects would typically inflate estimates of "peer effects". In addition, there appears to be a "relevance-endogeneity" trade-off between the first and second empirical difficulties. As the researcher broadens the definition of the social group (such as to the state level), the endogeneity of the peer group likely diminishes, but at the same time the relevance of the social group is weakened. In contrast, best friends are likely a relevant definition of a peer group but the endogeneity of best friend is magnified.

A third empirical difficulty in social network research is the potential for omitted variable bias through shared influences (called "contextual effects" in the literature). For example, smoking bans likely reduce tobacco use in all members of a school-based or community-based social group. These shared factors can lead to inflated estimates of "peer effects" if sufficient control variables are not included.

A fourth empirical difficulty is the reflection problem (Manski 1993), where the researcher may be unable to distinguish between whether Bill influences Ted or Ted influences Bill with typical data on these peers' health choices. Although it is not essential to disentangle these two influences in order to establish whether there is *any* social effect determining health behaviors, it can be useful to separate these effects in order to understand the importance of the initial causal effect in comparison to the feedback effects to further understand the processes of health behavior spillovers. While most researchers explicitly acknowledge each of these difficulties, they often take different approaches to attempt to overcome them.

While the interest in peer effects in obesity is relatively new, there is a two-decade history of examining peer effects in other health behaviors, which can provide some examples of the difficulty with this research topic as well as outline ways that other researchers have attempted to circumvent the empirical issues presented above. Typically, researchers have used neighborhood or school-based definitions of "peers" when examining health behaviors such as tobacco, alcohol, and drug use.

Case and Katz (1991) provide a seminal look at the effects of neighborhood peers on risky behaviors and other outcomes, though are unable to tackle many of the empirical issues outlined above. In particular, the authors acknowledge that they are unable to control for all environmental confounders and self-selection into neighborhoods. They are also unable to resolve the simultaneity bias (this issue was not fully discussed until Manski 1993). The authors find evidence of substantial correlations between own and neighborhood peer substance use, crime, and other behaviors.

Norton et al. (1998) further focus on schoolmate peer effects in alcohol and tobacco use of teenagers and use an instrumental variables strategy to address the endogeneity of peer groups.[2] While the focus on endogeneity was important, the instruments (such as neighborhood drug availability and safety) were potentially invalid[3] and there was little ability to control for the shared environment due to data limitations. The general approach of using schoolmates or grade-mates has been used by many subsequent studies (Gaviria and Raphael 2001; Powell et al. 2005), where the quality of the instruments was also uncertain; specifically, contextual effects are often assumed to not exist in order to use these variables as instruments.

Fletcher (2010a) suggests that this approach may be inappropriate and proposes a combined instrumental variables/fixed effects design with conceptually appealing diagnostic tests[4] to attempt to validate a preferred instrument set, although the validity of the instruments remains an open question. Specifically, Fletcher argues that the smoking status of individuals in grade-mates' households will increase the proportion of grade-mates who smoke (which can be empirically demonstrated), but the smoking status of individuals in the grade-mates' household does not directly affect respondent smoking once school-fixed effects are controlled (which is a maintained, untestable assumption). While Fletcher shows evidence that exposure to grade-mates from households who smoke is conditionally random within school, there are ways that the instrument could be invalid; for example, if mothers of grade-mates smoke, that could imply access to tobacco for the respondent.

As an alternative to an instrumental variable approach, Clark and Loheac (2007) use panel data and a lagged measure of peer behaviors combined with school-fixed effects in order to adjust for endogeneity, a large portion of the shared environment, and the reflection problem. The reflection problem is eliminated because current smoking decisions cannot affect past schoolmate smoking decisions. While school fixed effects reduce the issue of contextual effects, a maintained assumption is that, within schools, students choose friends randomly. A second weakness of this design is the need to assume a specific time structure in the individual decision-making and social influence processes (e.g., 1 day, 1 week, 1 month, 1 year, 2 years, etc.) (Manski 1995).[5]

An alternative to implementing a lag structure research design or an instrumental variables strategy is to focus on estimating contextual social effects instead of endogenous social effects. The most convincing work in this area uses random assignment of peers. For example, Kremer and Levy (2009) use data from a university that randomly assigns freshmen to shared dormitory rooms. This random assignment eliminates the concerns about the endogeneity of the peer group.

---

2 See also Evans et al. (1992).
3 In fact, the results suggested that the non-instrumented results were preferred and showed extremely large peer effect magnitudes.
4 See Lavy and Schlosser (2007) for original discussion and implementation and Bifulco et al. (in press) for application.
5 Manski (1995, p. 136) states, "Of course one cannot simply specify a dynamic model and claim that the problem of inference on social effects has been resolved. Dynamic analysis is meaningful only if one has reason to believe that the transmission of social effects follows the assumed temporal pattern."

Kremer and Levy show that a freshman who is randomly assigned a roommate who drank alcohol during high school has lower college performance than a student who is assigned a non-drinking roommate. The focus on the roommates' (predetermined) high school drinking behavior as the peer effect of interest also eliminates issues of simultaneity bias. Because not all data sets are able to leverage the random assignment of "friends," several studies attempt to leverage quasi-random variation in observational data. For example, Bifulco et al. (in press) use a cross-cohort, within-school design to link the outcomes of students to their (quasi-randomly assigned) classmates' characteristics. That is, the authors examine the "peer effects" of having a higher share of grade-mates with educated mothers or a higher share of grade-mates who are racial/ethnic minorities. This focus on contextual effects sidesteps the need for a solution to the reflection problem—because student smoking cannot affect grade-mate race—but some of the important policy issues tied to a social multiplier through endogenous peer effects cannot be evaluated directly.

RECENT RESEARCH EXAMINING
PEER EFFECTS IN OBESITY

Research focusing on peer effects in obesity faces the same empirical problems as those papers outlined above that examine smoking behaviors or other health choices. This section will outline the most visible work in this area, the proposed empirical solutions in the research, and follow-up research.

Christakis and Fowler (2007) received extensive media coverage for the finding that obesity was "socially contagious." Specifically, the chances of an individual becoming obese increased by over 50 percent when a friend became obese. The authors used the Framingham Heart Study data, which contains up to 32 years of longitudinal measures of BMI for individuals in one area of Massachusetts. To these data, the authors matched information from the original respondents' records, on which respondents were asked to list one person who would be able to contact them in case the survey team could not reach them directly at follow-up; this contact person is treated by Christakis and Fowler (2007) as a "friend." Thus, the first issue with this research is whether the contact person is truly a peer. This single measure of "friend" also makes it difficult to calculate broader measures of the social network—is a friend of a friend also my friend? Putting these issues aside, the authors estimate regressions using the following parsimonious empirical model:

$$health_{it} = \delta health_{jt} + \beta_1 health_{it-1} + \beta_2 health_{jt-1} + \beta_3 X_{it} + \varepsilon_{it} \tag{1}$$

where the health (obesity) of person i is linked to person j and δ is the coefficient of interest—the endogenous social effect or "social multiplier." A positive estimate on δ suggests that an intervention that reduces the chances of an individual becoming obese will also reduce the chances of obesity in his/her peer.

As discussed above, there are three additional empirical difficulties in attaining a causal peer effect estimate: (1) the endogeneity of the peer group (overweight individuals may choose overweight friends); (2) shared environmental influences (the opening of a fast food restaurant or gym) may affect the weights of all socially connected individuals; and (3) the issue of simultaneity—does Bill affect Ted or vice-versa? In order to overcome endogeneity, Christakis and Fowler (2007) assume that lagged health outcomes for the friend ($health_{jt-1}$) is a sufficient control.[6] That is, after controlling for lagged obese status of a friend, there is no additional issue of friendship selection. Unfortunately, to the extent that this control variable does not completely eliminate selection effects, the estimated coefficient of interest (δ) will likely be upwardly biased. The second issue is confounding due to shared influences. The authors did not explicitly control for shared environmental factors, but instead appealed to a comparison between mutual friends (who nominated each other) and non-mutual friends (where the nomination was not reciprocated), arguing that directionality of nominations should not matter if environmental confounding was the primary explanation. Finally, the authors did not discuss or attempt to overcome the empirical complications from the reflection problem. Unfortunately, each of the empirical issues (1–3) above would likely lead to upwardly biased estimates of peer effects; so, what proportion of the 50 percent estimated peer effect is due to bias and what proportion is an actual peer effect?

In order to begin to address these empirical concerns, Cohen-Cole and Fletcher (2008a) provided an examination focusing on one of the empirical issues in peer effects models—shared environmental factors that may upwardly bias the estimates. Because the Framingham data used by Christakis and Fowler have not been shared with outside researchers, Cohen-Cole and Fletcher were unable to provide a straightforward replication and extension of the obesity results. Instead, the authors used the National Longitudinal Study of Adolescent Health (Add Health), which includes national, longitudinal data on adolescents in the US over approximately seven years. While the Framingham study has a much longer time horizon and focuses on adults, the Add Health data contains data on actual "best friends" named by the respondent; this is arguably a more appropriate peer than the contact person listed in the Framingham data. Cohen-Cole and Fletcher first estimate equation (1) with the Add Health data in order to attempt to replicate the baseline findings of Christakis and Fowler (2007) that were based on the Framingham data. Interestingly, both papers, using different data of different age groups, arrive at point estimates for δ from equation (1) for the "peer effect" of BMI of 0.05, meaning that a one-unit increase in a friends' BMI over time is correlated with a 0.05 unit increase in own BMI. However, when Cohen-Cole and Fletcher controlled for shared environmental

---

6 The authors control for own-lagged health in order to control for aspects of the individual's genetic disposition or other time-invariant characteristics.

factors, such as school fixed effects, the coefficient fell by approximately 40 percent and was no longer statistically significant.

These findings by Cohen-Cole and Fletcher (2008a) cast some doubt of the Framingham claims of large "social contagion" of obesity and may show that results from the empirical model in (1) may be upwardly biased for the reasons outlined above. In a response, Fowler and Christakis (2008) pointed out that the Cohen-Cole and Fletcher (2008a) study used "static" friendship definitions rather than the dynamic definitions used in Christakis and Fowler.[7] This was a fair point, but as discussed in Cohen-Cole and Fletcher (2008c), the choice of using static versus dynamic friendship nominations in Add Health is far from straightforward due to various sample design issues. There were several additional points of disagreement in interpreting and replicating the results between research groups.[8]

In an attempt to further explore the potential upward bias in the Christakis/Fowler empirical model, Cohen-Cole and Fletcher (2008b) took an alternative approach. The authors asked the question: "Is the empirical model (1) so weak that it would produce estimates of peer effects in behaviors where the true peer effect should be zero?" That is, the authors conducted a falsification test of the empirical model by showing that estimating equation (1) with the Add Health data would also produce results suggesting "social contagion" in outcomes that are unlikely to be contagious: acne, headaches, and height. Indeed, the estimates for peer effects in these health behaviors were in some case larger than the Christakis/Fowler estimates of peer effects in obesity. The results of the falsification exercise strongly suggest that the model is too weak to distinguish between true social effects and the alternative hypotheses discussed above (e.g., endogeneity of friendships and exposure to shared environmental factors). As in previous work, Cohen-Cole and Fletcher (2008b) show that the magnitudes of the fictional social network effects are reduced and largely disappear once shared environmental influences are controlled.

Several other economists have used the Add Health data in order to examine the potential for peer effects in obesity outcomes in adolescents. Trogdon et al. (2008) use several empirical strategies to examine peer effects. They examine both grade-level peers, similar to the cross-cohort designs discussed above, as well as nominated friends. In order to control for shared environmental factors, the authors control for school fixed effects. In order to address friendship selection and simultaneity bias, the authors use an instrumental variables strategy, where friends' birth weight, friends' parents' weight, and other measures are used as instruments. The limitation with this approach is that it is unclear whether these variables are good

---

7 "Static" friends are determined at baseline and do not change (i.e., only the friendship nominations in the first wave of data are used to determine friendship links). "Dynamic" friendship definitions change over time based on the links found in each data wave. One might expect that using "static" friends will underestimate any peer effect, since some links that have dissolved over time are still classified as "friends." On the other hand, using dynamic friendship definitions may overestimate any peer effect, since the links are endogenously formed and dissolved over time.

8 See this author's web site for additional correspondence between Cohen-Cole/Fletcher and Christakis/Fowler: http://www.med.yale.edu/eph/faculty/labs/fletcher/homepage.html

instruments for friendship selection. It appears that the instruments were mainly employed to reduce the simultaneity issue, though they still need to be excludable from the equation determining own weight. In addition to controlling for shared environmental influences, the authors use school fixed effects to partially control for friendship selection. The implicit assumption with school fixed effects is that, within schools, friendships form randomly.

Like Trogdon et al. (2008), Renna et al. (2008) also use a single cross-section of the Add Health data to examine the correlations between own and friends' weight outcomes; however, these two papers use different subsamples and Renna et al. focus only on nominated friends. Renna et al. use school-level fixed effects to control for shared environmental factors and also attempt to reduce the simultaneity issue with an instrumental variables approach. The authors also use friends' parents' obesity status as instruments. In order to control for selection of friends, the authors include additional control variables and acknowledge that the estimates are likely biased upward. The authors find evidence for peer effects for both genders in the baseline models but only females in the IV models, though the point estimates are very similar. Overall, these papers are suggestive of peer effects but are unable to control for the empirical issues needed to make the evidence more conclusive.

CONCLUSION

The potential effect of peers on obesity has recently been the subject of several theoretical and empirical papers in economics and other disciplines. This question has been of interest both because of the desire to more fully understand principal determinants of obesity as well as because of the important policy implications of finding peer effects in obesity. In particular, peer effects could produce a social multiplier that allows the benefits of health interventions to be increased through social ties. Unfortunately, the empirical issues surrounding estimation of models of peer effects are considerable. Specifically, several empirical issues, such as peer selection, the shared environment, and joint decision making, if not properly controlled for in statistical models, would each tend to inflate any true causal effect of peers on weight outcomes. Therefore, because no current research in this area has adequately dealt with these empirical issues, the considerable evidence suggesting *correlations* in peer behaviors cannot yet be used to show that peers *cause* weight gain. This is an important area for future research—both in refining the definitions of peers as well as designing research that can focus on uncovering true peer effects, distinct from confounding influences. Only then can we potentially design and implement health interventions that may successfully leverage social ties to improve health.

REFERENCES

Bifulco, R., J. M. Fletcher, and S.L. Ross (2011). "The Effect of Classmate Characteristics on Individual Outcomes: Evidence from the Add Health." *American Economic Journal: Economic Policy* 3(1): 25–53.

Burke, M. A., and F. Heiland. (2007). "Social Dynamics of Obesity." *Economic Inquiry* 45(3): 571–591.

Case, A., and L. Katz. (1991). "The Company You Keep: The Effects of Family and Neighborhood on Disadvantaged Youth." NBER Working Paper 3705.

Cawley, John. (2004). "The Impact of Obesity on Wages." *Journal of Human Resources* 39(2): 451–474.

Cawley, John, and John A. Rizzo. (2007). "One Pill Makes You Smaller: The Demand for Anti-Obesity Drugs." *Advances in Health Economics and Health Services Research* 17: 149–183.

Cawley, John, Chad Meyerhoefer, and David Newhouse. (2007). "The Impact of State Physical Education Requirements on Youth Physical Activity and Overweight." *Health Economics* 16(12): 1287–1301.

Chou, Shin-Yi, Michael Grossman, and Henry Saffer. (2004). "An Economic Analysis of Adult Obesity: Results from the Behavioral Risk Factor Surveillance System." *Journal of Health Economics* 23(3): 565–587.

Clark, A., and Y. Loheac. (2007). "It Wasn't Me, It Was Them! Social Influence in Risky Behavior by Adolescents." *Journal of Health Economics* 26(4): 763–784.

Cohen-Cole, E., and J. M. Fletcher. (2008a). "Is Obesity Contagious? Social Networks vs. Environmental Factors in the Obesity Epidemic." *Journal of Health Economics* 27(5): 1382–1387.

Cohen-Cole, E., and J. M. Fletcher. (2008b). "Detecting Implausible Social Network Effects in Acne, Height, and Headaches: Longitudinal Analysis." *British Medical Journal* 337: a2533

Cohen-Cole, E., and J. M. Fletcher. (2008c). "Estimating Peer Effects in Health Outcomes: Replies and Corrections to Fowler and Christakis." SSRN Working Paper: http://papers.ssrn.com/sol3/papers.cfm?abstract_id=1262249

Cutler, D. M., E. L. Glaser, and J. M. Shapiro. (2003). "Why Have Americans Become More Obese?" *Journal of Economic Perspectives* 17(3): 93–118.

Dunn, Richard. (2009). "Obesity and the Availability Of Fast-Food: An Instrumental Variables Approach." Texas A&M University Working Paper.

Evans, W., W. Oates, and R. Schwab. (1992). "Measuring Peer Group Effects: A Study of Teenage Behavior." *Journal of Political Economy* 100: 966–991.

Finkelstein, Eric, Justin Trogdon, Joel Cohen, and William Dietz. (2009). "Annual Medical Spending Attributable to Obesity: Payer-and Service-Specific Estimates." *Health Affairs* 28(5): w822–w831.

Fletcher, J. M. (2009). "The Effect of Smoking Cessation on Weight Gain: Evidence Using Workplace Smoking Restrictions." Yale University Working Paper.

Fletcher, J. M. (2010a). "Social Interactions and Smoking: Evidence Using Multiple Student Cohorts, Instrumental Variables, and School Fixed Effects." *Health Economics* 19(4): 466–484.

Fletcher, J. M. (2010b). "Spillover Effects Of Inclusion Of Classmates With Emotional Problems On Test Scores In Early Elementary School." *Journal of Policy Analysis and Management* 2010 29(1): 69–83.

Fletcher, J. M., D. E. Frisvold, and N. Tefft. (2010a). "Can Soft Drink Taxes Reduce Population Weight?" *Contemporary Economic Policy* 28(1): 23–35.

Fletcher, J. M., D. E. Frisvold, and N. Tefft. (2010b). "The Effects of Soft Drink Taxation on Soft Drink Consumption and Weight for Children and Adolescents." *Journal of Public Economics*, 94 (11-12): 967–974.

Fowler, J. H., and N. A. Christakis. (2008). "Estimating Peer Effects on Health in Social Networks: A Response to Cohen-Cole and Fletcher; and Trogdon, Nonnemaker; Pais." *Journal of Health Economics* 27: 1400–1405.

Gaviria, A., and S. Raphael. (2001). "School-based Peer Effects and Juvenile Behavior." *Review of Economics and Statistics* 83(2): 257–268.

Halliday, T. J., and S. Kwak. (2009). "Weight Gain in Adolescents and Their Peers." *Economics and Human Biology* 7(2): 181–190.

Harding, D. J. (2003). "Counterfactual Models of Neighborhood Effects: The Effect of Neighborhood Poverty on Dropping Out and Teenage Pregnancy. *American Journal of Sociology* 109(3): 676–719.

Kremer, M., and D. M. Levy. (2008). "Peer Effects and Alcohol Use among College Students." *Journal of Economic Perspectives* 22 (3): 189–206.

Lakdawalla, D., and T. Philipson. (2002). "The Growth of Obesity and Technological Change: A Theoretical and Empirical Examination." NBER Working Paper 8946.

Lavy, V., and A. Schlosser. (2007). "Mechanisms and Impacts of Gender Peer Effects at School." NBER Working Paper 13292.

Manski, C. F. (1993). "Identification of Endogenous Social Effects: The Reflection Problem." *Review of Economic Studies* 60 (3): 531–542.

Mayer, A., and S. Puller. (2008). "The Old Boy (and Girl) Network: Social Network Formation on University Campuses." *Journal of Public Economics* 92: 329–347.

Norton, E. C., R. C. Lindrooth, and S. T. Ennett. (1998). "Controlling for the Endogeneity of Peer Substance Use on Adolescent Alcohol and Tobacco Use." *Health Economics* 7(5): 439–453.

Powell L., J. Taurus, and H. Ross. (2005). "The Importance of Peer Effects, Cigarette Prices, and Tobacco Control Policies for Youth Smoking Behavior." *Journal of Health Economics* 24: 950–968.

Renna, F., I. B. Grafova, and N. Thakur. (2008). "The Effect of Friends on Adolescent Body Weight." *Economics and Human Biology* 6: 377–387.

Sacerdote, B. (2001). "Peer Effects with Random Assignment: Results for Dartmouth Roommates." *Quarterly Journal of Economics* 116(2): 681–704.

Trogdon J., Nonnemaker J., and Pais J. (2008). "Peer Effects in Adolescent Overweight." *Journal of Health Economics* 27(5): 1388–1399.

CHAPTER 19

MATERNAL EMPLOYMENT

PATRICIA M. ANDERSON

CHILDHOOD obesity is a growing concern throughout the world, with the World Health Organization estimating that in 2007, 22 million children under the age of five were obese (World Health Organization 2008). Perhaps not surprisingly, studies of the determinants of obesity are manifold. In this chapter, I focus on the role of maternal employment. The first section discusses the theoretical reasons that one might expect there to be an impact of maternal employment patterns on children's obesity, and the second section reviews the growing empirical literature that estimates this impact. I then return to the theorized mechanisms for such an impact, reviewing what the empirical literature concludes about the role of each mechanism. Finally, I present some new empirical evidence on one potential mechanism.

WHY MATERNAL EMPLOYMENT MIGHT EFFECT CHILDREN'S OBESITY

Potential reasons that an increase in maternal labor supply might result in higher levels of obesity for children are myriad. For example, some medical professionals believe that one of the possible benefits of breast-feeding is that it is protective of obesity in later childhood (IOM 2005). Exactly how breast-feeding might be protective is unclear. One possibility is that breast milk contains a chemical or hormone that is itself protective. An alternative theory is that breast-fed babies learn more easily to regulate their intake according to their needs, since the mother does not get the same feedback about quantity consumed as she does when bottle-feeding. The idea, then, is that when bottle feeding, a mother may essentially force more formula on an infant than the child really desires, reducing the child's inherent inclination to balance intake with needs. A related theory is that since breast milk carries in it the flavors of the mother's diet, breast-fed children may be more receptive to a variety of foods later in life, and this acceptance of variety may imply a healthier later diet. Despite uncertainty over why (or as seen below, whether) breast-feeding might be protective of obesity, the Institutes of Medicine report on childhood obesity recommended that children be breast-fed exclusively for four to six months, and breast-fed with supplemental foods for up to one year as a preventive measure against obesity (IOM 2005). Working full-time while one's child is an infant, however, may make breast-feeding for this length of time difficult. In fact, Baker and Milligan (2007) find that, after a large change in maternity leave in Canada, mothers did breast-feed much more. Thus, if breast-feeding for one year really does reduce the probability of later obesity, then reduced breast-feeding by working mothers may be one mechanism by which increases in maternal labor supply could result in increases in childhood obesity.

Another potential mechanism to consider is the role of day care. As more children grow up in families with either two working parents or a single working mother, the time spent in non-parental care has increased. According to data from the Survey of Income and Program Participation (SIPP) reported by the U.S. Census Bureau on its web site, about 15 million children under the age of five spent time in non-parental care in the spring of 2005. Note that this number does not include children participating in early education programs, such as Head Start or private preschools. Depending on the quality of this non-parental care and of the forgone parental care, spending time in day care may have an impact on obesity. In low-quality day care (or self-care for slightly older children), more time may be spent watching television or videos and less time spent physically active. These same types of care may also result in an increase in unhealthy snacking, either through energy-dense foods being offered by the child-care provider, or obtained by the child in self-care. Note also that even in high-quality settings serving nutritious foods, there is the possibility that being fed on a rigid schedule may reduce a child's ability to self-regulate food intake with caloric needs (similar to the idea above for bottle-feeding versus breast-feeding).

While not directly providing evidence on physical activities and day care, studies have found that between 1981 and 1997 children's free time declined by 12 percent, a decline that is mainly attributed to more time spent in school and child care (Sturm 2005). Another potential impact of day care on activity is that it is very common for parents who drop their children off at day care on the way to work to continue this commuting pattern when the child becomes school-age. According to Sturm (2005), between 1977 and 2001, walking to school as a percentage of trips dropped from just over 20 percent to 12.5 percent, while Anderson and

Butcher (2006) note that in 2002, 53 percent of parents drove their children to school, and just 17 percent had children who walked and only 5 percent rode bikes.

Another theoretical reason for maternal employment having an effect on child obesity focuses not on what the children are doing with their time in non-parental care, but on what effect employment has on the use of the mother's non-working time. In the face of higher opportunity costs of time (i.e., the wages from market work), we would expect to see mothers substitute away from time-intensive methods of household production toward more goods-intensive methods. Thus, rather than spending many hours planning a menu, shopping, and preparing a home-cooked meal for dinner, there will likely be more reliance on convenience foods, prepared foods, and foods eaten away from home. This type of substitution may result in higher caloric intake for several reasons. First, time spent on meal planning may at least partially be thought of as time spent thinking about the nutritional needs of the family. When less time is spent considering these needs, worse choices may be made. Similarly, when less time is spent shopping, it is likely that less time is spent looking at nutritional labels, and again worse food choices may be made for the family. Finally, many convenience foods (especially meals from fast food restaurants) do not make it easy to determine their nutritional content, and they may have unrealistic portion sizes or otherwise encourage higher caloric intake than is optimal. In fact, Chou, Grossman, and Saffer (2004) report that increases in the density of fast food restaurants can explain an important fraction of the increasing trend in adult obesity, noting that reliance on such convenience foods has increased with increases in women's labor supply. However, Anderson and Matsa (2009) conclude that it is not the presence of fast food restaurants, per se, that increase obesity. Rather, they think that those most likely to eat at fast food restaurants are the same people most likely to consume more calories at home, and while overall caloric intake seems to be higher for restaurant meals, many people reduce calories at other meals to offset it.

Given these many theoretical reasons for increased maternal work time to influence children's weight, it is only natural that an empirical literature has emerged that investigates this relationship. The following section discusses this literature.

IS THERE A CAUSAL IMPACT OF PARENTAL EMPLOYMENT ON CHILDHOOD OBESITY?

Models of the prevalence of childhood obesity have occasionally included maternal employment as one of many explanatory variables (e.g., Wolf et al. 1994; Takahashi et al. 1999; Fredriks et al. 2000), sometimes finding significant effects. Typically, the focus of these studies was not directly on the role of maternal employment; any estimated employment effect was incidental to the model. In fact, these types of studies are best thought of as describing a correlation between maternal employment and childhood obesity, and thus should not be thought of as implying a causal relationship. We may be concerned that there are unobserved factors correlated with both obesity and maternal employment, making any observed relationship between employment and obesity entirely spurious. Anderson, Butcher, and Levine (2003) was the first paper to directly explore the relationship between maternal employment and childhood obesity, making a concerted effort to estimate a causal relationship. Using pre-adolescent children age 3 to 11 in the National Longitudinal Survey 1979 Mother-Child sample (NLSY), they establish that there is an observable relationship between the intensity of a mother's work over the child's life and the probability that the child is overweight. The main focus of the paper, though, is on determining whether this relationship is causal. Based on long-difference, sibling difference, and IV model estimates, they find that an additional 10 hours per week of work by a mother over the child's life causes about a 1 to 1.5 percentage point increase in the probability that her child is overweight. Interestingly, when they estimate separate models by subgroup, the largest impacts are seen for the higher socioeconomic status groups (greater than high school education, upper quartiles of income, whites). Based on these results, Anderson, Butcher and Levine hypothesize that time constraints may be the key mechanism behind the causal estimates, since time taken from higher SES mothers is more likely to be time that would have been spent planning and preparing home-cooked meals, supervising active play, and so on.

There are a few important things to note in interpreting these models. First, the models also include weeks worked over the child's lifetime, which is never statistically significant. Thus, the implication is that the estimates represent the impact of work intensity, not just the effect of working or not. Additionally, the models control for whether the child was breast-fed. Thus, if the only mechanism through which maternal employment affects obesity is via reduced breast-feeding, these models would find no impact. [1] Finally, they control for average family income over the child's life. Typically, when a mother works more, her family's income will be higher. In most developed countries, higher income implies better health and less obesity, so the overall impact of maternal employment may be positive for low-income groups (i.e., lower the probability of children's obesity). Conditional on income, however, the impact of work intensity will reflect the direct effect of changing time use.

Following Anderson, Butcher, and Levine, researchers set out to determine if similar causal impacts could be found for children in other countries, or for paternal labor supply, as well as looking at U.S. children of different ages, in different data sets, in different time periods or using different econometric techniques. Table 19.1 summarizes the many published and unpublished studies that focus on the role of maternal employment, and/or on use of child care, as well as several for

---

1 While the basic ordinary least squares (OLS) models do find a protective effect of breast-feeding, this effect disappears in the sibling difference models.

Table 19.1: **Summary of Studies of the Impact of Parental Employment on Childhood Obesity**

Study	Data	Results
Abdulai (2007)	Ghana IFPRI, 0–6 yr olds	Effects positive, but only significant for shop/factory/office workers
Anderson, Butcher and Levine (2003)	NLSY, 3–11 yr olds	10 hours more per week over child life increases obesity 1–1.5 percentage points; strongest results for higher SES children
Araneo (2008)	Fragile Families and Child Well-Being Study, 3 yr olds	Obesity probability higher with full-time employment, effect increases with education
Baker, Ballistreri and Van Hook (2007)	ECLS-K, 5th graders (focus on Hispanics)	For immigrants, maternal employment lowers BMI, especially for higher-income families. For natives, lowers BMI for low-income families, raises BMI for high-income families.
Burgess et. al (2004)	Britain's ALSPAC, 6–81 month olds	No maternal impact (incidental models)
Chia (2008)	Canada's NLSCY, 4–11 yr olds	10 hours more per week increases obesity 2.5 percentage points.
Classen and Hokayam (2005)	NLSY, 2–18 yr olds	No strong effect of maternal employment, some evidence for effect of >35 hours/wk
Courtemanche (2007)	NLSY, 3–17 yr olds	10 hours more per week increases obesity 0.8 to 1.6 percentage points
Fertig, Glomm and Tchernis (2009)	CDS of PSID, 3–17 yr olds	Positive impact of more hours, stronger for higher SES families
Fredriks et al. (2000)	Dutch children, 0–21 yrs old	BMI higher with employment dummy, employment hours (incidental models)
Gaina et al. (2009)	Japan's Toyama birth cohort, 12–13 yr olds	BMI higher with full-time mothers, more likely to be overweight, but not obese
Garcia, Labeaga and Ortega (2006)	Spain NHS 2–15 yr olds	Employment increases obesity 2.5 percentage points
Greve (2008)	Denmark's DALSC, 7.5 yr olds	Work hours reduce weight, effect only for those in formal care, no effect otherwise
Hawkins et al. (2008)	UK Millennium Cohort Study, 3 yr olds	More likely to be overweight for every 10 hours of weekly employment
Herbst and Tekin (2009)	ECLS-K, single mom kindergarteners	Higher BMI/overweight/obesity with relative care or center-based care vs. parent care
Lamerz et al. (2005)	Aachen, Germany children starting school	Full-time work overweight rates higher than for part-time work, but not significantly so
Liu, Hsaio and Chou (2005)	NLSY, 3–11 yr olds	FT work increases obesity 11.6%, BMI by 1.65

(continued)

Table 19.1 (Cont'd)

Study	Data	Results
Miller and Han (2008)	NLSY, 13–14 yr olds	BMI and overweight increase with years worked nonstandard schedules
Maher et al. (2007)	ECLS-K, kindergarteners	Family, friend and neighbor care more likely obese than parental care, except Latinos, where non-parental care may be protective of obesity
Mahler (2007)	German GSOEP, young adults	No paternal effect. Each year mother FT increases obesity .003 (base = 2.86)
Morrissey, Dunifon and Kalil (2009)	NICHD SECCYD, school-age children	Higher BMI with more years employment, initial impact, but no cumulative effect of working nonstandard schedules
Phipps, Lethbridge and Burton (2006)	Canada's NLSCY, 6–11 yr olds	No paternal effect. FT mother increases obesity to .32 vs. .24 for non-working
Reifsnider, Keller and Gallagher (2006)	Hispanic toddlers enrolled in WIC	No effect of employment on weight status (note just from one large southwestern city)
Ruhm (2008)	NLSY 10–11 yr olds	20 hours more increases obesity 1.6–4.5 percentage points, work after 3 most important, possibly not causal
Scholder (2007)	Britain's NCDS, 16 yr olds	Effects only for FT maternal work at age 7—a .055 percentage point obesity increase
Takahashi et al. (1999)	Japan's Toyama birth cohort, 3 yr olds	Full-time job significantly related to obesity
Wolf et al. (1994)	NY pupils, 2nd and 5th graders	Employment not related to overweight (incidental models)
Zhu (2007)	Australia's LSAC, 4–5 yr olds	1 hour increase in weekly work increases obesity .63 percentage points

which employment is incidentally part of a model. Below, I briefly discuss some of the follow-up studies to Anderson, Butcher, and Levine.

The majority of the studies focusing on American children find results broadly supportive of those in Anderson, Butcher and Levine (Araneo 2008; Courtemanche 2007; Fertig, Glomm, and Tchernis 2009; Liu, Hsaio and Chou 2005; Morrissey, Dunifon and Kalil 2009; Ruhm 2008). Note that while Ruhm estimates that an extra 20 hours of maternal work will increase the probability of obesity by 1.6 to 4.5 percentage points, and also finds bigger impacts for higher socioeconomic status families, he presents models in which future work hours are often significant, leading him to question whether the estimated effects should really be interpreted as causal. A few papers have looked not just at employment, per se, but at nonstandard work schedules. Morrissey, Dunifon, and Kalil (2009) and Miller and Han (2008) both find weight increases with non-standard work.

While Herbst and Tekin (2009) also find positive effects of maternal employment, when they include type of child care the effect of an indicator variable for employment is no longer significant. Instead, higher weights are limited to kindergartners who were previously in center-based care (especially) and those cared for by relatives. It is possible that being in these types of care are better proxies for a higher intensity of work than the simple employment indicator variable. Interestingly, when not limiting the data to single mothers, Maher et al. (2007) find that it is family, friend, and neighbor care that is significantly positively related to overweight, although for Latino children non-parental care was protective of obesity. When using older children from the same data set, but with a focus on Hispanics, Baker, Ballisteri and Van Hook (2007) similarly find that for immigrants, maternal employment results in lower BMI for children. When looking at children of natives, maternal employment is estimated to lower BMI for low-income families, but to increase it for higher-income families. The only US studies not finding significant effects of maternal employment are Classen and Hokayam (2005), Reifsnider, Keller, and Gallagher (2006), and Wolf et al. (1994). The latter of these is an incidental study, while Classen and Hokayam do find some evidence of an effect for full-time work, and Reifsnider, Keller, and Gallagher look at Hispanics only from just one Southwestern city.

It is not just studies from the United States, however, that largely seem to find effects of maternal employment. Studies from Canada (Chia 2008; Phipps, Lethbridge, and Burton 2006), Australia (Zhu 2007), the United Kingdom (Hawkins et al. 2008, Scholder 2007), Germany (Mahler 2007), the Netherlands (Fredriks et al. 2000), Spain (Garcia, Labeaga, and Ortega 2006), Japan (Gaina et al. 2009; Takahashi et al. 1994), and even Ghanna (Abdulai 2007) all find some effect of maternal employment. There are dissenting studies from the UK (Burgess et al., 2004) and from Germany (Lamerz et al. 2005) that find no significant effect. Additionally, a study from Denmark (Greve 2008) finds that maternal employment is protective, albeit only for children enrolled in formal care, which in Denmark is of very high quality.

WHY DOES MATERNAL EMPLOYMENT CAUSE INCREASED CHILDHOOD OBESITY?

In the previous section, we saw that there does appear to be an impact of maternal employment on childhood obesity, not just in the United States, but in many other countries as well. In general, effects seem stronger the greater the intensity of work, and in several cases the marginal effect is larger for children from higher socioeconomic status families, although the type of child care used also may play a role.

While we have learned a lot in recent years about the impact of parental employment on obesity, we know much less about the mechanisms behind this effect. Based on the theoretical possibilities outlined in the first section, however, there are some theoretical studies that we can consult to try to discern more about the explanations behind the findings in the previous section.

First, despite the IOM recommendations on breast-feeding, it appears very unlikely that the potential incompatibility of longer-term breast-feeding and intensive working hours is the driving mechanism. This conclusion is based mainly on a range of newer studies that are much less supportive of the idea that breast-feeding is protective of later obesity. Perhaps the most convincing of these is Kramer et al. (2009) which reports the results of a randomized trial in which breast-feeding incidence and length was successfully increased, but no reduction in obesity at age 6.5 was observed. In terms of children's behaviors being different in child care than in parental care, we saw some evidence of this possibility above, especially in terms of the protective role of high-quality care in Denmark. However, the U.S. results on type of care were a bit more mixed, making it difficult to draw strong conclusions. The consistency of the results on the impacts of more intensive working hours and non-standard shifts, though, does seem to indicate that it would be fruitful to look more closely at the changes in the mothers' behaviors.

Crepinsek and Burstein (2004), while not focused on children's obesity, do find that working mothers participate less in meal planning, shopping, and food preparation, and have more reliance on away from home food. Similarly, Ziol-Guest, DeLeire, and Kalil (2006) find that families with both parents employed spend more of their budget on food away from home (and less on vegetables, fruits, milk, and meat and beans), compared to married couples with a stay-at-home mom. Cawley and Liu (2007), using data from the 2003–2006 American Time Use Survey (ATUS), also find that employed women spend less time cooking and less time eating with their children, while being more likely to purchase prepared foods. Ben-Shalom (2009) confirms this ATUS finding of less time spent shopping for and preparing foods, and an increase in the purchase of prepared foods. However, he also uses the Continuing Survey of Food Intake by Individuals (CSFII) to find that the quality of food intake for family members falls (and obesity sometimes rises). Another impact of maternal employment on children's intake is found by Datar and Nicosia (2009), using data from the Early Childhood Longitudinal Study Kindergarten Cohort (ECLS-K). They find an increase in eating the school lunch and a decrease in eating school breakfast. School lunch has previously been found to increase obesity, while school breakfast appears protective (e.g. Schanzenbach 2009; Millimet, Tchernis and Husain, 2010).

In finding an increased reliance on prepared foods, Crepinsek and Burstein (2004) further focus separately on the prevalence of frozen entrees and carry-out foods, finding an effect only for the latter. In the context of the CSFII, they define carry-out as food from any restaurant or vending machine that is eaten at home. Thus, while in some ways it is a broader measure than just fast food, it is not entirely clear whether fast food eaten at the restaurant (or in the car!) is included as carry-out. Additionally, given the results on the effect of maternal employment that find stronger impacts of higher socioeconomic status groups, it would be informative to analyze the mechanisms across these groups as well. Crepinsek and Burstein are more interested in the poor than the better off, so present their estimates just for families under 130 percent of poverty, 130 to 185 percent, and over 185 percent. Significantly higher consumption of carry-out food was found among children of mothers who worked full-time relative to children of stay-at-home mothers, in both the lowest and highest income groups. They also present estimates separately for single mother families and those with multiple adults, but this is not necessarily a good indication of socioeconomic status. That said, children in multiple adult households with a full-time working mother consume significantly more carry out food than those with a stay-at-home mother. The same is not true of children in single-mother families.

Having seen that behavior changes by working mothers seems like a promising explanation, it is worth noting that a few studies look more at the children's behaviors. Fertig, Glomm, and Tchernis (2009) attempt to explore the mechanisms by which maternal employment may affect obesity using children's time diaries in the PSID, but without obtaining any very strong findings. Morrissey, Dunifon, and Kalil (2009), who use the NICHD's Study of Early Child Care and Youth Development, also look to see if maternal employment is correlated with children's time use and find no significant effects, ruling out important roles for TV and physical activity. Crepinsek and Burstein (2004) also found no impact of maternal employment on the amount of vigorous activity children get, although Cawley and Liu (2007) did find that the employed mothers themselves spent less time playing with their children. Finally, Parker (2007) finds that there is no impact of maternal employment on children's activity as measured by step counts. Thus, the evidence on maternal employment affecting children's activities appears quite weak.

Finally, a few non-US studies also have information about the potential mechanisms for maternal employment effecting children's obesity. Hawkins et al. (2009) looks at five-year-old children from the UK Millennium Cohort Study, finding that those with working mothers were more likely to drink sweetened beverages, use the TV or computer at least 2 hours per day, and to be driven to school. Additionally, having a mother who worked full-time reduced the amount of fruits and vegetables eaten. Gaina et al. (2009), focusing on junior high school children in Japan from the Toyama birth cohort study, finds children with full-time working mothers were more likely to snack (and to skip dinner), while those of part-time mothers ate larger meal portions. Overall, though, based on the existing evidence (which is admittedly mainly from the U.S.), it appears that the strongest case can be made for the idea that the time constraints imposed on working parents change their behaviors, especially in terms of food choices—that is, that working mothers substitute away from time-intensive meal production toward goods-intensive production. In the next section I expand upon the ideas in Crepinsek and Burstein (2004) to focus specifically on fast food consumption and maternal employment.

NEW EVIDENCE ON MATERNAL EMPLOYMENT AND FAST FOOD CONSUMPTION

In this section, I use food diary data from the third National Health and Nutrition Examination Study (NHANES III) that were collected in 1988–1994. The public-use version of these data do not link mothers and children in the same household, so I first identify "likely" mothers in a household as women age 25 to 55 who are either single and in a family with more than one person, or are married and in a family with more than two people. Based on the household identifier, I then match children in the survey with these likely mothers. [2] Because children are over-sampled in the NHANES, not all children can be matched to a mother. For the matched sample, I define a simple maternal employment indicator variable as equal to 1 if the likely mother indicated that she had worked in the past two weeks, and equal to zero otherwise. I then take the food diary data and limit it to foods eaten as part of dinner, since the time-constraint story mainly focuses on this meal (at least for school-age children). I then use the brand and fast food code variable to identify the presence of fast food in the meal, and I sum up the calories in that food.[3] To investigate the role of socioeconomic status, I consider not only the full sample, but also samples made up of only mothers with a high school degree or more, and only families with income of at least 280 percent of the poverty line.[4] Table 19.2 presents the means and standard deviations of the key variables for these three samples.

Looking at table 19.2, it is perhaps not surprising that the fraction of mothers who are employed increases across columns from left to right (full sample, high school graduates, income over 280 percent of the poverty line). Interestingly, mothers are less likely than children to have fast food for dinner, but when eating fast food the mothers consume more calories than their children. While the fraction of mothers consuming fast food and the resultant calorie count is lower in the high income sample than in the full sample or the high school plus sample, corresponding measures for the children are more stable across samples. Finally, while total calories at dinner for the mothers are lowest for the high income sample, for the children this is the sample that consumes the most dinner calories. While these summary statistics show some interesting facts, the real question is whether maternal employment affects what is eaten at dinner, and whether this effect is different across samples.

---

2 Note that for 88 percent of households, there is only one potential mother, so the match is automatic. Additional details on the matching process can be found in the Data Appendix of Anderson, Butcher, and Schanzenbach (2009).

3 I also used this code to identify all use of frozen foods and the calories from them. However, consistent with Crepinsek and Burstein (2004), there were no significant effects on frozen food, so I do not report those results here.

4 This approximates being in the top quartile of the income distribution.

Table 19.2. Means for NHANES III Samples

Variable	Full Sample	High School Graduate or Better Sample	280% Poverty Line or Better Sample
Mother is employed	0.646 (0.478)	0.687 (0.464)	0.742 (0.438)
Mother had fast food at dinner	0.072 (0.258)	0.075 (0.264)	0.064 (0.245)
Child had fast food at dinner	0.094 (0.292)	0.092 (0.290)	0.093 (0.290)
Calories from fast food for Mom	46.67 (190.41)	49.79 (198.18)	39.71 (173.51)
Calories if had fast food	648.06 (333.34)	647.68 (338.04)	567.65 (335.95)
Calories from fast food for child	58.12 (209.31)	56.73 (208.80)	56.29 (200.60)
Calories if had fast food	616.46 (347.14)	613.83 (360.69)	607.42 (316.25)
Total dinner calories for Mom	779.04 (428.97)	800.43 (443.07)	769.80 (434.15)
Total dinner calories for child	730.38 (450.32)	742.78 (451.70)	748.92 (459.21)
Observations	3,609	2,443	1,023

Note: Standard Deviations shown in parentheses. Full sample includes all children in the NHANES III who could be matched to a woman age 25–55 in their household.

Table 19.3 presents the results from simple regressions on an indicator variable for whether the mother was employed. Each coefficient (standard error) in the table is from a separate regression. The dependent variables are whether the individual reported having any fast food at dinner, the number of dinner calories that came from fast food, and the total number of dinner calories. Regressions are run separately for the mother and child, and each set of regressions is run for the full sample, the sample with education of high school or more, and the sample with income greater than 280 percent of the poverty line. Starting with the top panel, we see that overall there is a significantly positive 4 percentage point effect of maternal employment on the probability that the child had fast food at dinner.[5] While positive, the impact on the mother's own diet is much smaller, at 1.3 percentage points,

---

5 For the subgroups, it is never the case that the employment effect for that subgroup is significantly different at conventional levels from the effect for those not in the group.

Table 19.3. Effects of Maternal Employment

Had Fast Food at Dinner	Child	Mother	# Obs
Full sample	0.042*	0.013	3,609
	(0.020)	(0.020)	
High school graduate or beyond sample	0.046*	0.023	2,443
	(0.020)	(0.023)	
280% poverty line or greater sample	0.052	0.049*	1,023
	(0.034)	(0.024)	
Calories from fast food	Child	Mother	# Obs
Full sample	33.972*	6.796	3,609
	(13.736)	(15.173)	
High school graduate or beyond sample	35.623*	13.888	2,443
	(15.108)	(17.352)	
280% poverty line or greater sample	28.891	33.099*	1,023
	(26.274)	(13.786)	
Total calories at dinner	Child	Mother	# Obs
Full sample	74.820*	44.423	3,609
	(29.308)	(31.227)	
High school graduate or beyond sample	52.442	34.070	2,443
	(35.805)	(37.626)	
280% poverty line or greater sample	45.958	70.498	1,023
	(45.477)	(53.467)	

Notes: Each coefficient (standard error) comes from a separate regression. Standard errors are adjusted for heteroskedasticity and within-sample correlation. * indicates significance at the 5% level or better. The full sample includes all children in the NHANES III who could be matched to a woman age 25–55 in their household.

and not significantly different from zero. We see a similar pattern for the sample with education of high school or more. For the higher income sample, the point estimate for children is larger than the other samples, implying a 5.2 percentage point increase, but due to the small sample size, it is no longer significant at conventional levels. However, now the 5 percentage point impact on the mother's diet is not only much larger than for the other samples, but is also significantly different from zero.

Moving on to the second panel, we not surprisingly see a similar pattern for the effect of maternal employment on the amount of fast food calories consumed.[6] Finally, in the final panel, we see that while overall, children with a working mother consume more calories at dinner, there are no other significant effects, and the point

6 There is no significant effect of maternal employment on calories conditional on having eaten fast food, although for the highest-income mothers the effect is marginally significant at the 7.5% level. Thus, the main path through which maternal employment operates is by having fast food, not via what menu items are chosen at the restaurant.

estimates for the subgroups imply smaller impacts for the higher socioeconomic status children. [7] Focusing for now on the overall sample, it is worth asking whether these seemingly small caloric effects can be important contributors to the increase in childhood obesity. Cutler, Glaeser, and Shapiro (2003) estimate that the 10–15 percent increase in median adult BMI can be entirely explained by just 100–150 extra calories per day. If the dinners in the NHANES food diary are representative of all dinners, then we would expect that simply having a working mother will get children at least half way there, because it is predicted to increase just dinner calories by about 75.

Overall, then, while we see clear evidence of increased fast food consumption and a resultant increase in calories consumed (both from fast food and at dinner more generally), it is less clear whether higher socioeconomic status increases these impacts. The strongest evidence comes from the higher point estimates for having consumed fast food at dinner, which is significant for the higher education mothers, but not the children. However, the argument for fast food contributing more greatly to obesity for the children from better-off families is contradicted by the fact that the effect of maternal employment on total dinner calories is lower for these families, despite being more likely to consume fast food. Perhaps the mothers in these families are more likely to recognize that while eating fast food is a response to time constraints, they can still choose healthier menu items for their children.

SUMMARY AND CONCLUSIONS

This paper has reviewed the emerging literature on the effect of maternal employment on childhood obesity. The evidence appears fairly strong that more hours spent working by mothers (but not fathers) leads to a higher probability that a child is overweight. This result appears to not be confined to one country or data set, but can be found almost universally. Slightly less clear is the stability of the common finding that children from higher socioeconomic status families suffer more marginal harm from maternal employment. More questions remain as to the mechanisms behind the effect of increased maternal labor supply. There is fairly solid evidence that working mothers spend less time preparing meals and rely more on convenience foods. Here I add to the existing literature by showing that in the NHANES III, children with working mothers are 4 percentage points more likely than children whose mothers do not work to eat fast food; as a result they consume almost 75 more total calories at dinner. Given that Cutler, Glaeser, and Shapiro (2003) have estimated that just an extra 100–150 calories per day can explain the entire rightward shift in the adult BMI distribution, these extra calories are likely to be important determinants of the smaller shift in the child BMI distribution. However, I find no solid evidence in the food diary data that maternal employment has a

---

7 In fact for the high-school-or-more sample, compared to a non-high-school graduate sample the negative effect is marginally significant at the 7% level.

larger impact on children from higher socioeconomic backgrounds. In fact, the total extra calories consumed at dinner are closer to 50 than the 75 seen for the full sample. Thus, questions still remain regarding how much of childhood obesity is due to the interaction of maternal employment and socioeconomic status.

ACKNOWLEDGEMENTS

Early drafts of some sections of this chapter benefited from comments of participants at "The Effect of Parental Workforce Participation on Children" Workshop, University of Stavanger, Norway, June 17–18, 2008.

REFERENCES

Abdulai, Awadu. 2007. "Socio-economic Characteristics and Obesity in Underdeveloped Economies: Does Income Really Matter?" *Applied Economics* 42(2): 157–169.

Anderson, Patricia M., and Kristin F. Butcher. 2006. "Childhood Obesity: Trends and Potential Causes." *Future of Children* 16(1): 19–45.

Anderson, Patricia M., Kristin F. Butcher, and Philip B. Levine. 2003. "Maternal Employment and Childhood Overweight." *Journal of Health Economics* 22: 477–504.

Anderson, Patricia M., Kristin F. Butcher, and Diane Whitmore Schanzenbach. 2009. "Childhood Disadvantage and Obesity: Is Nurture Trumping Nature?" In *The Problems of Disadvantaged Youth*, ed. Jonathan Gruber, 149–180. Chicago: University of Chicago Press.

Araneo, Jackie. 2008. "The Effects of Maternal Employment on Childhood Obesity in the United States." Senior Thesis, Princeton University.

Baker, Elizabeth, Kelly Stamper Ballistreri, and Jennifer Van Hook. 2007. "Maternal Employment and Overweight among Hispanic Children of Immigrants and Children of Natives." *Journal of Immigrant Minority Health* 11(3): 158–167.

Baker, Michael, and Kevin Milligan. 2007. "Maternal Employment, Breastfeeding, and Health: Evidence from Maternity Leave Mandates." NBER Working Paper 13188.

Burgess, Simon, Carol Propper, John Rigg, and the ALSPAC Study Team. 2004. "The Impact of Low-Income on Child Health: Evidence from a Birth Cohort Study." CMPO Working Paper Series No. 04/098.

Cawley, John, and Feng Liu. 2007. "Maternal Employment and Childhood Obesity: A Search for Mechanisms in Time Use Data." NBER Working Paper 13600.

Chia, Yee Fei. 2008. "Maternal Labour Supply and Childhood Obesity and Canada: Evidence from the NLSCY." *Canadian Journal of Economics* 41(1): 217–244.

Chou, Shin-Yi, Michael Grossman, and Henry Saffer. 2004. "An Economic Analysis of Adult Obesity: Results from the Behavioral Risk Factor Surveillance System." *Journal of Health Economic*, 23(3): 565–587.

Classen, Timothy, and Charles Hokayem. 2005. "Childhood Influences on Youth Obesity." *Economics and Human Biology* 3: 165–187.

Courtemanche, Charles. 2007. "Working Yourself to Death? The Relationship between Work Hours and Obesity." Working paper, Washington University of St. Louis.

Crepinsek, Mary Kay, and Nancy R. Burstein. 2004. *Maternal Employment and Children's Nutrition:* Volume II: *Other Nutrition-Related Outcomes.* Washington, DC: Economic Research Service, U.S. Department of Agriculture. E-FAN-04- 006-2.

Cutler, David M., Edward L. Glaeser, and Jesse M. Shapiro. 2003. "Why Have Americans Become More Obese?" *Journal of Economic Perspectives* 17(3): 93–118.

Datar, Ashlesha, and Nancy Nicosia. 2009. "The Impact of Maternal Labor Supply on Children's School Meal Participation." Rand Working Paper WR-670.

Fertig, Angela, Gerhard Glomm, and Rusty Tchernis. 2009. "The Connection between Maternal Employment and Childhood Obesity: Inspecting the Mechanisms." *Review of Economics of the Household* 7(3): 227–255.

Fredriks, A. M., S van Buuren, J. M. Wit, and S. P. Verloove-Vanhorick. (2000). "Body Index Measurements in 1996–7 Compared with 1980." *Archives of Disease in Childhood* 82: 107–112.

Gaina, A., M. Sekine, T. Chandola, M. Marmot, and S. Kagamimori. 2009. "Mother Employment Status and Nutritional Patterns in Japanese Junior High Schoolchildren." *International Journal of Obesity* 33: 753–757.

Garcia, Emma, Jose M. Labeaga, and Carolina Ortega. 2006. "Maternal Employment and Childhood Obesity in Spain." Working paper, FEDEA, Madrid, Spain.

Greve, Jane. 2008. "New Results on the Effect of Mothers' Working Hours on Children's Overweight Status: Does the Quality of Childcare Matter?" The Danish National Centre for Social Research Working Paper 05: 2008.

Hawkins, S. Sherburne, T. J. Cole, C. Law, and The Millenium Cohort Study Child Health Group. 2008. "Maternal Employment and Early Childhood Overweight: Findings from the UK Millennium Cohort Study." *International Journal of Obesity* 32: 30–38.

Hawkins, S. Sherburne, T. J. Cole, C. Law, and The Millenium Cohort Study Child Health Group. 2009. "Examining the Relationship between Maternal Employment and Health Behaviors in 5-Year-Old British Children." *Journal of Epidemiology and Community Health* 63: 999–1004.

Herbst, Chris M., and Erdal Tekin. 2009. "Child Care Subsidies and Childhood Obesity." IZA Discussion Paper No. 4255.

Institute of Medicine. 2005. *Preventing Childhood Obesity: Health in the Balance.* Washington, DC: National Academies Press.

Kramer, Michael S., Lidia Matush, Irina Vanilovich, Robert W. Platt, Natalia Bogdanovich, Zinaida Sevkovskaya, Irina Dzikovich, Gyorgy Shisko, Jean-Paul Collet, Richard M. Martin, George Davey Smith, Matthew W. Gillman, Beverly Chalmers, Ellen Hodnett, and Stanley Shapiro. 2009. *The Journal of Nutrition* 139: 417S–421S.

Lamerz, A. J. Kuepper-Nybelen, C. Wehle, N. Bruning, G. Trost-Brinkhues, H. Brenner, J. Hebebrand, and B. Herpertz-Dahlmann. 2005. "Social Class, Parental Education, and Obesity Prevalence in a Study of Six-Year-Old Children in Germany." *International Journal of Obesity* 29: 373–380.

Liu, Echu, Cheng Hsiao, and Shin-Yi Chou. 2005. "Maternal Full-Time Employment and Childhood Obesity: Parametric and Semiparametric Estimation." Working paper, University of Southern California.

Maher, Erin J., Guanghui Li, Louise Carter, and Donna B. Johnson. 2007. "Child Care Participation and Obesity at the Start of Kindergarten." *Pediatrics* 122: 322–330.

Mahler, Philippe. 2007. "I'm Not Fat, Just Too Short for My Weight: Family Child Care and Obesity in Germany." Socioeconomic Institute University of Zurich Working Paper No. 0707.

Miller, Daniel P., and Wen-Jui Han. 2008. "Maternal Nonstandard Work Schedules and Adolescent Overweight." *American Journal of Public Health* 98(8): 1495–1502.

Millimet, Daniel L., Rusty Tchernis, and Muna Husain. 2010. "School Nutrition Programs and the Incidence of Childhood Obesity." *Journal of Human Resources* 45(3): 640–655.

Morrissey, Taryn, Rachel E. Dunifon, and Ariel Kalil. 2009. "Maternal Employment, Work Schedules, and Children's Body Mass Index." Paper presented at the Fall Research Conference of the Association for Public Policy Analysis and Management, November 5–7, in Washington, DC.

Parker, Michael Scott. 2007. "The Relationship between Maternal Employment and Children's Physical Activity." Master's Thesis, Brigham Young University.

Phipps, Shelley A., Lynn Lethbridge and Peter Burton. 2006. "Long-run Consequences of Parental Paid Work Hours for Child Overweight Status in Canada." *Social Science and Medicine* 62(4): 977–986.

Reifsnider, Elizabeth, Colleen S. Keller, and Martina Gallagher. 2006. "Factors Related to Overweight Status among Low-Income Hispanic Children." *Journal of Pediatric Nursing* 21(3): 186–196.

Ruhm, Christopher. 2008. "Maternal Employment and Adolescent Development." *Labour Economics* 15: 958–983.

Schanzenbach, Diane Whitmore. 2009. "Do School Lunches Contribute to Childhood Obesity?" *Journal of Human Resources* 44(3): 684–709.

Scholder, Stephanie von Hinke Kessler. 2007. "Maternal Employment and Overweight Children: Does Timing Matter?" CMPO Working Paper Series No. 07/180.

Sturm, Roland. 2005. "Childhood Obesity–What We Can Learn from Existing Data on Societal Trends, Part 1. *Preventing Chronic Disease: Public Health Research, Practice and Policy* 2(1): http://www.cdc.gov/pcd/issues/2005/apr/04_0038.htm.

Sturm, Roland. 2005. "Childhood Obesity–What We Can Learn from Existing Data on Societal Trends, Part 2. *Preventing Chronic Disease: Public Health Research, Practice and Policy* 2(1): http://www.cdc.gov/pcd/issues/2005/apr/04_0039.htm.

Takahashi, Eiko, Katsumi Yoshida, Hiroki Sugimori, Michiko Miyakawa, Takashi Izuno, Takashi Yamagami, and Sadanobu Kagamimori. 1999. "Influence Factors on the Development of Obesity in 3-Year-Old Children Based on the Toyama Study." *Preventive Medicine* 28: 293–296.

Wolf, Wendy S., Cathy C. Campbell, Edward A. Frongillo, Jr., Jere D. Haas, and Thomas A. Melnik. (1994). "Overweight Schoolchildren in New York State: Prevalence and Characteristics." *American Journal of Public Health* 84(5): 807–813.

World Health Organization. 2008. "Childhood Overweight and Obesity." Global Strategy on Diet, Physical Activity and Health. http://www.who.int/dietphysicalactivity/childhood/en/

Zhu, Anna. 2007. "The Effect of Maternal Employment on the Likelihood of a Child Being Overweight." University of New South Wales, School of Economics Discussion Paper 2007/17.

Ziol-Guest, Kathleen M., Thomas DeLeire, and Ariel Kalil. 2006. "The Allocation of Food Expenditure in Married- and Single-Parent Families." *Journal of Consumer Affairs* 40(2): 347–371.

CHAPTER 20

DEPRESSION AND OBESITY

ELLEN GRANBERG

THE association between depression and obesity has been a focus of inquiry among social scientists for close to 20 years, and as a result a large body of research is available for anyone interested in the topic. The "modern era" of study on this topic can arguably be dated to Friedman and Brownell's (1995) review "Psychological Correlates of Obesity: Moving to the Next Research Generation." Friedman and Brownell outlined the history of research in the area and called for greater attention on two topics: more prospective studies of the association between obesity and psychopathology; and greater attention to the groups most vulnerable to obesity-related psychological distress. That review sparked fifteen years of active research on the association between obesity and depression in general and on these two questions in particular. Given the size and scope of this literature, it is impossible to produce an exhaustive review; instead, this chapter is designed to focus on those two key questions: the association between obesity and depression, especially as seen in longitudinal assessments, and the role of moderating and mediating forces that indicate who will experience an association between obesity and depression and why.

Underlying all of this is an important but often ignored fact: although it appears that obesity and depression are related, most people who are obese are not depressed. Instead, the association is a relatively moderate one whose size and intensity likely fluctuates between individuals and groups and across individual biographies and community histories. The most interesting questions then involve the conditions under which it manifests and the forces that produce its ebbs and flows. The placement of this chapter in the section on correlates of obesity also underscores the extent to which the predominant direction of association between these two conditions remains unknown. In part this is because researchers who are interested in the effect of depression on obesity have worked largely independently from those interested in the effect of obesity on depression.

The earliest work on obesity and depression framed obesity as the dependent variable and attempted to identify clusters of psychological conditions that promoted disordered eating and weight gain (Friedman and Brownell 1995). This line of research provided few explanations for the development of obesity, and the attention of researchers evolved toward examining obesity as the cause, rather than the consequence, of psychological distress. More recently, with the development of high-quality longitudinal data sets and the refinement of epidemiological tools for assessing psychological distress, evidence has mounted suggesting that the association between obesity and depression operates in both directions and that each condition may contribute to the development of the other. I will discuss all three of these lines of argument: obesity as a contributor to depression, depression as a contributor to obesity, and depression and obesity as mutually reinforcing conditions. First, however, I briefly review broad patterns evident in associations between depression and obesity.

ASSOCIATIONS BETWEEN DEPRESSION AND OBESITY

Early research examining the association between obesity and depression often produced conflicting or non-significant associations (Friedman and Brownell 1995). However, over the past decade evidence has mounted that suggests that obesity and depression are at least moderately related. Among the most compelling research reports are those that employ epidemiologically valid measures of depression and objective measures of height and weight. Those analyses suggest that there is a relatively weak association between obesity and depression in the general population but that the association is considerably stronger among some sub-populations (e.g., women). Research focused on adolescents, for example, generally identify positive associations between body weight and depression that are stronger for girls than boys (BeLue, Francis, and Colaco 2009; Ge, Elder, Regnerus, and Cox 2001; Needham and Crosnoe 2005; Swallen, Reither, Haas, and Meier 2005). Studies using adult samples have reported similar patterns, for example, analysis using NHANES data reported that obesity was associated with past month depression in women but not men (Onyike, Crum, Lee, Lyketsos, and Eaton 2003) and a review of studies conducted between 1996 and 2003 reached the same conclusion (McElroy et al. 2004). Thus, over time, evidence has mounted for the existence of a moderate association between obesity and depression, particularly among women.

Socioeconomic status, degree of obesity, and race are three additional factors believed to moderate associations between obesity and depression. Some research shows that depression is more positively associated with obesity among higher-SES and better-educated populations (Faith, Matz, and Jorge 2002), a relationship that may reflect the greater degree of obesity stigma found among affluent classes. The association between obesity and depression is also stronger among groups for whom obesity is more severe (e.g., BMI of 35 and higher) (Onyike et al. 2003; Richardson et al. 2003).

Considerable attention has been given by American researchers to race as a moderator of the obesity-depression association. Specifically, it is often argued that Caucasians, particularly Caucasian females, are especially concerned about weight and consequently uniquely vulnerable to experiencing depression as the result of obesity (Siegel 2002). While many studies have documented this pattern, others have found no evidence of racial group interactions or have produced results suggesting that African Americans had stronger associations between obesity and depression than did European Americans (Grant et al. 1999; Sachs-Ericsson et al. 2007). It appears clear that racial groups differ in their orientation and concern about body size, but the resulting association with depression is not yet fully understood.

Finally, until recently the association between obesity and depression was also assumed to be an exclusively Western phenomenon. However, an increasing number of studies have identified the association in populations from other parts of the world (Li et al. 2007). One assessment pooled data from 13 cross-sectional general population surveys conducted as part of the World Mental Health Survey. That analysis also found a modest but significant association between obesity and depression in the general population with stronger associations reported for women and those with severe obesity (Scott et al. 2008). While this association appears to be increasing among non-Western, non-white groups, study results as a whole are still quite mixed and a relatively large number of studies using non-U.S. samples have failed to find an association (Kim and Kim 2001; Ozmen et al. 2007; Shin and Shin 2008; Wardle et al. 2006). Thus it remains unknown how widespread or robust the association is and what factors may be promoting its development. Far more work, especially using longitudinal samples, is required to assess the extent and pattern of this association in a greater variety of world populations.

Variations in Depression-Obesity Associations: The Role of Measurement

One-often cited explanation for the variety of results reported in both U.S. and non-U.S. studies is the considerable variation in sampling strategies and measurement techniques. In this review, I have not included results from clinical or treatment-seeking samples since depression and other forms of obesity-related distress can often be a motivation for entering a clinical treatment program.

However, even within community samples, the range, diversity, and representativeness of those samples vary widely. In characterizing the prevalence and distribution of obesity-depression associations in the population at large, I have relied primarily on analysis using data gathered from probability samples designed to be representative of the population of interest. However, when discussing evidence for prospective associations or pathways through which the association may occur, I have included other types of community-based samples.

Choices regarding the measurement of both obesity and depression are another potential source of bias and thus an important consideration when evaluating the evidence for an obesity-depression association. Calculation and classification of the body mass index (BMI) from respondents' height and weight data is the most common way to represent body size in this literature, with obesity generally termed to be a BMI of 30 or above. However, in most data sets used by social scientists, weight and height are self-reported. Data where measured height and weight is available tend to be drawn from smaller scale and less representative samples. Thus, social scientists interested in examining the association between obesity and depression can face a difficult choice between the validity of body size measures and the generalizability of their findings. The number of samples with measured height and weight is increasing, but its lack still represents a significant limitation to social scientific research on the obesity-depression link.

Measured BMI, which is preferable to self-reported BMI, is itself a relatively crude estimation of the degree to which an individual is actually "obese." The "gold standard" for assessing obesity requires the use of technologies such as Magnetic Resonance Imaging (MRI), Computed Tomography (CT), or Dual-Energy X-ray Absorptiometry (DEXA) (Sun et al. 2010). These techniques permit highly precise calculations of percent body fat and fat density, and thus highly valid estimates of obesity. However, they are also expensive, impose a fairly high subject burden, and can require complex interpretation methods. Perhaps because of these barriers, these technologies have only rarely been used to assess the association between obesity and depression. One study used DEXA to examine a convenience sample of children age 6–12 and found no evidence that depressive symptoms were associated with obesity across time (Tanofsky-Kraff et al. 2006). A second study, also using DEXA, assessed a sample of 979 women aged 20–93 and found that those with a lifetime history of depression had increased fat mass, percent body fat, and BMI (Williams 2008). These results and the known limitations of BMI as a measure of obesity, underscore the role that measurement choices may play in current understandings of the depression-obesity association. Data compiled using the most valid adiposity measures available will be important for fully specifying this association.

Like measures of body size, choices regarding the measure of depression can also vary considerably from study to study. These choices have been made more complex by disagreements over whether depression should be conceptualized as having a categorical or dimensional structure (Ruscio, Ruscio, and Keane 2002; Ruscio and Ruscio 2004). This debate reflects the two most common ways of conceptualizing depression: categorically, as a clinically significant episode of mental illness (e.g., major depressive disorder), or dimensionally, as a count of depressive symptoms. The former tends to be favored by medical researchers, the latter by social scientists. Clinical interviews that can result in a diagnosis of major depressive disorder (MDD) depressive illness have a very high degree of validity but are both time consuming and expensive and consequently are not always feasible, especially in very large community-based samples. In addition, among researchers focused on questions that are social rather than clinical, dichotomous diagnostic measures can obscure valuable variation in the ways individuals respond to social conditions or the role played by psychological distress in responding to life events (Mirowsky and Ross 2002). One recommended approach is to assess both dichotomous and continuous measures of depression (Horwitz 2002); however, in studies of obesity and depression such analyses are rare. In this review, papers using both dimensional and categorical analyses are included. In most cases, the results are consistent, but where conflicts occur, this is noted.

Causal Order: Does Obesity Cause Depression or Depression Cause Obesity?

Evidence for the presence of an association between obesity and depression immediately raises questions of the direction of causality. Does obesity cause depression? Or, are depressed people more likely to become obese? Several prospective studies have been published over the past 10 years and there are results suggesting support for both arguments, though, in general, the evidence for depression as a risk factor in the development of obesity is somewhat stronger than that for obesity as a cause of depression.

Evidence for obesity as a risk factor predicting elevated depression (or incidence of major depression) includes two prospective studies involving adolescents. The first used data from the National Longitudinal Survey of Adolescent Health and found that females who were obese during adolescence had more depressive symptoms in young adulthood than did their peers who were not obese during adolescence, an association that held after controlling for levels of depressive symptoms during adolescence (Merten, Wickrama, and Williams 2008). A community sample that followed adolescents over 20 years but measured depression as the incidence of major depressive disorder found a similar result (Anderson et al. 2007).

Prospective studies among adults have been more mixed but on balance suggest that obesity is associated with an increase in depressive symptoms over time and with increased incidence of major depressive disorder. A series of papers used Alameda County Study data to assess the prospective association between obesity and depression in a cohort of late middle-age adults (Roberts et al. 2000; Roberts et al. 2003). When obesity was defined as persons at the 85th percentile for weight, the results showed that obesity at age 50 was associated with elevated depressive symptoms at age 55 after controlling for both depressive symptoms at age 50 and other covariates. However, when obesity was measured as a BMI of 30 or higher, the association did not hold after controlling for BMI at age 50. Analysis of a sample of mothers followed from age 27 to age 59 found that being either overweight or obese at age 27 was associated with elevated risk for major depressive disorder at age 59 (Kasen, Cohen, Chen, and Must 2008). Such prospective data, though by no means conclusive, suggest that obesity may act as a risk factor in the development of depression over time, especially among women.

Studies assessing the prospective relationship between depression and subsequent obesity have also produced results suggesting that both a diagnosis of major depressive disorder or reports of elevated depressive symptoms predict an increased risk of obesity across time. In particular, depression during childhood and adolescence is associated with higher BMI and elevated risk of obesity by early to mid-adulthood (Liem, Sauer, Oldehinkel, and Stolk 2008). This direction of association appears to be less responsive to subgroup differences such as gender or class, though a few studies do suggest that girls are more vulnerable to depression-related weight gain than are boys (Anderson, Cohen, Naumova, and Must 2006; Goodwin et al. 2009). Importantly, however, the study which used the most valid measure of obesity (DEXA) found no prospective association for either boys or girls (Tanofsky-Kraft 2006), although the relatively small number of participants and convenience nature of the sample may also have influenced the strength of this association.

The analyses published thus far have not settled the question of causality but have provided evidence suggesting that weight is associated with depression across time and that depression may be an early warning indicator of obesity risk. To date, no studies have looked at associations between weight change and subsequent change in depressive symptoms (or vice versa), and these will be important for identifying whether something about obesity triggers elevated depressive symptoms or increases in depressive symptoms precedes weight gain.

Obesity as a Contributor to Depression: The Role of Mediating and Moderating Factors

As the previous discussion has shown, the question of causal ordering between obesity and depression is a relatively new and open question. Prior to about seven years ago, most of the social scientific research on obesity-depression framed depression as a result of obesity and focused on identifying "who will suffer and in what ways" (Friedman and Brownell 1995). As a result, a substantial body of literature developed, most of it cross-sectional, which has examined factors that are hypothesized as direct or indirect pathways through which obesity may influence depression. Three explanations have dominated work in this area: poor body image and appearance dissatisfaction, disrupted social relationships, and health problems. Each of these arguments will be reviewed briefly in this section.

Body Image as a Mediator of the Association between Obesity and Depression

The role of body image and body image dissatisfaction is an important element of the association between obesity and depression because it helps explain why some individuals may get depressed as the result of being obese while others do not. Several papers have explicitly examined the potential mediating effect of body image on the association between obesity and depression. One analysis, using a population-based sample of 2,500 youth found that among girls, pressure to be thin and body dissatisfaction accounted for a large proportion of the association between adiposity and depression (Chaiton et al. 2009). Similarly, a study of third-grade children found that BMI was associated with depressive symptoms until researchers controlled for concern about being overweight at which point BMI lost its significance. That same study also found that non-overweight girls who expressed concern about being overweight had higher depression scores than did girls who were overweight but who scored low on measures of overweight concern (Erickson, Robinson, Haydel, and Killen 2000). Results like these suggest that obesity is associated with depression, in part, because it promotes dissatisfaction with one's appearance and concern about weight.

Over the past 10 years, researchers from outside the United States have begun assessing the relative impact of actual body size and body size satisfaction on the link between obesity and depression. Research on samples from China, the Netherlands, and Portugal has produced results that are consistent with that based on American samples: much of the association between obesity and depression is attenuated by controlling for body or appearance satisfaction (de Sousa 2008; Li et al. 2007; ter Bogt et al. 2006). However, there have also been numerous exceptions to this emerging pattern. A sample of 2010 Turkish adolescents aged 15–18, for example, showed that depression was associated only with body dissatisfaction, not body size (Ozmen et al. 2007). Two samples of Korean children aged 10–13 also showed no association between body size or body satisfaction and depression (Kim and Park 2009; Park et al. 2009).

Taken as a group, these results suggest that one way in which obesity may act on depression is by increasing the likelihood that individuals will be dissatisfied with their appearance. This dissatisfaction, in turn, can elevate depressive symptoms. However, the associations are inconsistent, especially among studies conducted using non-U.S. samples. This raises the issue of moderating factors that may condition the circumstances under which either obesity or body dissatisfaction may be expected to be related to depression. Four moderating factors have generally been considered most important for understanding who is most at risk for depression resulting from obesity and poor body image: gender, class, age, and race. As was noted earlier, both longitudinal and cross-sectional research has shown that the link between obesity and depression is particularly strong among girls and that degraded body image is an important contributor to that link. High socioeconomic status may also amplify the role that body image plays in the association between obesity and depression (Smolak and Levine 2001). Age is also a potentially important moderator. The association between body size and body image and that between body image and depression appears to be strongest among women in their adolescent and young adult years and to diminish gradually as women get older. Thus, this mediating pathway may be most effective at explaining the obesity-depression association among young affluent women.

The fourth moderating factor, race, is more complex and thus will be the focus of greater attention. Evidence began mounting in the mid-1980s that, controlling for body size, black American women had more positive body images than white American women and consequently were less likely to experience obesity-related distress (Cash and Henry 1995; Hebl and Heatherton 1998). This has often led to the assumption that overweight African American women and girls are immune from white standards of slenderness and thus in little need of support when trying to cope with the emotional consequences of obesity and weight gain (Beauboeuf-Lafontant 2003). While there appears to be strong support for the idea that African American women and girls relate to and evaluate their bodies on a somewhat different basis than do Caucasian women, this should not be taken to mean they are unconcerned with weight or immune from the distressing effects of a either obesity or poor body image. Most important, when African American girls are compared with one another (rather than to whites), higher BMI is associated with higher rates of depressive symptoms (Granberg, Simons, Gibbons, and Melby 2008). This suggests that while African American girls may be less concerned about weight gain than their white counterparts, they are not immune from weight-based distress.

The relative advantage that African American women may experience with respect to body image has led to speculation that elements of African American culture and social experience confer some degree of immunity to the depressing effects of obesity. Factors such as ethnic identity and or family racial socialization have been offered as explanations for the relative advantage that African American women hold. To date, however, few studies have explicitly tested whether these factors buffer the association between body size and depression among African American women or what impact these factors may have on body image. The few studies that have examined the impact of ethnic identity or racial socialization on the association between obesity and depression have been mixed. On balance, the results published thus far suggest that such cultural socialization has more influence on self-esteem than on depression (Granberg, Simons, and Simons 2009; Granberg, Simons, Gibbons, and Melby 2008).

Scholarship in this area has also been critiqued for failing to account for potential racial group differences in the basis upon which body evaluations are made

(Roberts, Cash, Feingold, and Johnson 2006). For example, when the basis of the body image evaluation is centered on feelings about one's weight, black-white differences have declined over time because white women are reporting increased satisfaction with their bodies. However, when the measures of body satisfaction are focused on specific body parts, it is black women's advantage that has increased over time. Thus, before one can fully understand how racial group differences in body image may influence the association between obesity and depression, it is crucial that more research is done exploring how African American women understand and think about their bodies and what facets of African American life may influence those processes. Similarly, while considerable attention has been given to the experiences of African American and white women, young women (or men) in other racial or ethnic groups have received far less attention. Most studies that have made cross-race assessments beyond blacks and whites have been comparative in nature and thus tell us little about how individuals within those groups think about and relate to their own bodies.

Finally, the preponderance of cross-sectional studies in this area leaves open the question of how body dissatisfaction, depression, and obesity may be jointly associated and through which paths the causal order may flow. To date, no researchers have used population-level data to track the longitudinal relationship between weight change, change in body dissatisfaction, and change in levels of depressive symptoms or incidence of major depressive disorder. Study designs like these will be important for specifying the actual causal order among these constructs and for better outlining the conditions under which body dissatisfaction explains the association between obesity and depression.

Disrupted Social Interactions and the Association between Obesity and Depression

A second major pathway through which obesity may be related to depression is by disrupting personal and social relationships. This pathway can include experiences such as weight teasing, weight-based discrimination, and tension or criticism in intimate and personal relationships. Very few studies have explicitly examined disrupted personal relationships as a mediator of the association between obesity and depression though several have assessed indirect effects. Despite this relative paucity of empirical research, there are strong theoretical reasons to expect that disrupted social interactions are a mechanism through which the stigma directed at obese people can contribute to elevated depressive symptoms. Simple awareness of occupying a stigmatized social identity, however, is not generally enough to lead to psychological distress (Crocker and Major 1989; Link and Phelan 2001). Instead, stigma is most likely to contribute to depression when individuals perceive that a stigmatized characteristic contributes to poor treatment by others and limits their life chances. This argument would suggest that the pathway through which disrupted social interactions link obesity with depression may be moderated by the attributions individuals make regarding the influence of weight on their personal and social interactions.

Very few studies have explicitly examined any form of disrupted social relationship as a mediator of the association between obesity and depression. Those that exist have studied clinical rather than community-based samples (Puhl and Brownell 2006). However, some recent work has examined disrupted social relationships as a factor in obesity-related distress (though not depression). Carr and Friedman found that the quality of family relationships declined as BMI rose and that interpersonal strains attenuated the association between obesity and both negative and positive affect (Carr and Friedman 2006; Carr et al. 2007). Two papers have examined weight-based discrimination and its impact on psychological well-being in community samples and the results were mixed. Reports of discrimination mediated the association between obesity and self-acceptance in one mixed-gender community sample but were unrelated to depression in a sample of women only (Carr and Friedman 2005; Puhl and Brownell 2006).

Although research explicitly examining disrupted social relationships as mediators of the association between obesity and depression are rare, a number of papers have examined elements of this pathway. The results suggest that obesity and the stigma surrounding it can degrade the quality of personal and social relationships which may, in turn, promote depression. For example, obese youth are at elevated risk for victimization by peers (e.g., teasing, threats), which is, in turn, associated with increases in depressive symptoms (Adams and Bukowski 2008). In addition, there is some evidence that overweight children and adolescents react more strongly to weight teasing and other forms of peer victimization, which may also place them at elevated risk for depression (Adams and Bukowski 2008; Neumark-Sztainer et al. 2002). Overweight teenagers, even if not directly victimized, may be more likely to be marginalized within their social networks and find their opportunities for friendship formation limited (Crosnoe, Frank, and Mueller 2008). In each of these examples, the impact of obesity on depression would be indirect either because it makes distressing events more likely or because obese young people are more likely to experience negative social treatment in ways that could lead to psychological distress.

Physical Limitations and the Association between Obesity and Depression

The third pathway through which obesity may increase risk for depression is the psychological impact of obesity-related chronic illness and mobility problems. This is also an area in which middle-aged and older adults are at greater potential risk than are adolescents and young adults. Obesity is associated with lower health-related quality of life, higher rates of physical disability and chronic disease, and higher odds of difficulty with activities of daily living (ADL), each of which may, in turn, elevate depressive symptoms (Ferraro and Kelley-Moore 2003).

Declines in physical health during the last third of life are an important factor explaining the U-shaped association between age and depression and obesity may contribute to this (Mirowsky 1995; Mirowsky and Ross 1992; Turner and Lloyd 1999).

To date, very few studies have examined poor physical health as a pathway through which obesity may contribute to changes in depression in the latter half of life. Greater attention to this area is especially important because the number of obese elderly is increasing world-wide (Salihu, Bonnema, and Alio 2009; Zhao et al. 2009a; Zhao et al. 2009b). Given the strong associations between obesity and health and that between health and depression, it appears that obesity will become an increasingly relevant factor in the mental health status of older adults.

Most research linking obesity to psychosocial outcomes in older adults has focused on health-related quality of life and self-rated health rather than depression. Depression is typically included in these studies as a potential confounder or mediator rather than as the outcome of interest. Among those few studies that have directly examined physical health as an explanation for associations between obesity and depression, the results are inconclusive. Two studies used nationally representative health surveillance studies from the United States to assess how obesity co-morbidities may affect the association between obesity and depression and found that the primary association held after accounting for co-morbidities (Zhao et al. 2009a; Zhao et al. 2009b). An examination of physical stresses associated with obesity found that problems completing activities of daily life and high numbers of health symptoms attenuated the association between obesity and both positive and negative affect (Carr and Friedman 2006b).

Research in this area is too recent and unformed to warrant firm conclusions. However, there is a strong case to be made that physical illness, chronic pain, and functional limitations should contribute to the association between obesity and depression, particularly among those in the latter half of life. Greater attention to this area will also balance the plethora of studies that have examined the obesity-depression association among adolescents and young adults and will be increasingly important as the proportion of the population that is both elderly and obese continues to rise.

Summary Thoughts and Next Steps

Evidence has mounted suggesting that obesity and depression are, indeed, related and that at least some of the causal direction moves from obesity to depression; however, we still understand relatively little about why and in what ways obesity may contribute to depression. The work completed thus far suggests that among children, teenagers, and young adults, feelings of unattractiveness, poor body image, and weight dissatisfaction may link obesity and depression along a primarily meditational pathway. Some empirical evidence also suggests that obesity increases the risk of peer victimization and social marginalization, which may also contribute to depression in this age group. Among adults, there is evidence for the impact of disrupted social relationships on obesity-related depression. The potential that physical health problems and functional health limitations may also help explain the depression-obesity association has yet to be fully explored. Thus, while much has been learned over the past 10 years, there is still considerable work left to outline the conditions under which, and the pathways through which, obesity influences depression risk.

What is also largely missing from this literature is an effort to consider obesity-related depression within the context of psychosocial theories of depression etiology, for example those theories that conceptualize negative events and attributions regarding the controllability of negative events as triggers for the development of depressive symptoms (Abramson et al. 2002; Alloy, Abramson, Stafford, and Gibb 2006). Obesity itself as well as all of the major pathways hypothesized to link obesity with depression (body image disruptions, disrupted social interactions, and physical disruptions) could be conceptualized as negative events about which individuals can make attributions regarding controllability. Such attributions may exist as schemas against which individuals assess the trajectory and events of their lives and that are hypothesized to condition their individual vulnerability to depression. In this sense, it may not be obesity or events stemming from obesity that create risk for depression. Rather, it may be that obesity's impact on depression is conditioned both by events and by attributions about events.

Setting research on obesity and depression in a larger theoretical context will also allow a more generative approach to the topic. Currently, obesity is more often conceptualized as a unique social phenomenon to which unique attributions may be ascribed. This approach has yielded a large body of research, answered some important questions, and clearly illustrated the complexity of obesity as a psychosocial phenomenon. However, that very complexity also suggests it would benefit greatly from study that seats it within more general theories of the etiology and progression of depression across the life course.

DEPRESSION AS A CAUSE OF OBESITY

The vast majority of published research on depression-obesity associations operates from the perspective that obesity is a source of depression, especially among adolescents, young adults, and women. However, over the past decade, a series of prospective studies have also provided evidence that depression is a risk factor for the development of later obesity. At least ten studies have examined the prospective association between depression and subsequent obesity, and almost all found that prior depression was associated with elevated risk for obesity across time. The transition from childhood to young adulthood has been a particular focus, and one meta-analysis estimated that elevated depressive symptoms in childhood or adolescence would be associated with a 1.9- to 3.5-fold increase in the probability of overweight 1–15 years later (Liem, Sauer, Oldehinkel, and Stolk 2008).

Evidence that depressive episodes or elevated depressive symptoms are a risk factor for later obesity is also notable in that the interactions with gender and racial group membership, though present, are less pronounced than they are in analyses of obesity as a risk factor for depression. The latter analyses show that women are much more vulnerable than men to obesity-related depression while, in contrast, a considerable proportion of studies examining depression as a risk factor for obesity find no differences based on gender (Goodman and Whitaker 2002; Hasler, Lissek et al. 2005; Mamun et al. 2009; Pulkki-Raback et al. 2009) or find that both genders are affected but that women are affected differently from men (Hasler et al. 2005). (There are, of course, several studies that find men are unaffected by prospective associations between depression and obesity (Anderson, Cohen, Naumova, and Must 2006; Richardson et al. 2003; Rofey et al. 2009).) Taken as a group, however, the pattern suggests women are at higher risk than men for developing obesity in the wake of depression but that the gap between men and women is narrower than that found when obesity is examined as a risk factor for depression.

One study has examined the prospective association between depression and obesity across racial groups. Black and white women were compared using data from the NHLBI Growth and Health Study (Franko, Striegel-Moore, Thompson, Schreiber, and Daniels 2005). While black women were much more likely to be obese than were white women, there was no evidence of a race/depression interaction conditioning the association between depression and obesity across time. While only one study, this finding suggests that race may be a less influential moderator of depression as a risk factor for obesity than for obesity as a risk factor for depression.

The most obvious explanation for the association between depression and later obesity is a disruption in energy balance—increases in dietary intake, declines in physical activity, or both (Liem, Sauer, Oldehinkel, and Stolk 2008). Other frequently offered explanations draw on eating disorders, genetics or biochemical interactions to explain this association (Goodman and Whitaker 2002; Mamun et al. 2009). As work in this area develops, it will benefit greatly from psychological, sociological, and economic models that incorporate the impact of social environment, economic status, and stressful life events on these associations. For example, neighborhoods characterized by violence and disorder have been associated with both elevated depressive symptoms and increased risk for obesity (Cohen, Finch, Bower, and Sastry 2006) and some work suggests that depression may mediate the association between disordered communities and obesity (Wickrama, Wickrama, and Bryant 2006). Associations like these point to a role for physical and social context in explaining how depression may contribute to elevated risk for obesity.

The concentration of obesity among both African Americans and individuals of lower socioeconomic status is another arena that should be explored. There is a large literature on social conditions as "fundamental causes" of disease (Link and Phelan 1995). Racial segregation, for example, creates concentrated pockets of poverty and violence, poor quality municipal services, and limited access to fresh food and physical activity resources. Neighborhood violence and the threat of personal victimization are examples of chronic stressors, and chronic stress is a predictor of both MDD and elevated depressive symptoms (Simons et al. 2002). The association between perceived stress and weight gain has not yet been established but there is evidence that elevated stress is associated with greater increase in BMI among African American women (Fowler-Brown et al. 2009) and chronic stress has been suggested as one explanation for the prospective association between depression and obesity (Goodman and Whitaker 2002). Finally, it is increasingly clear that social environments condition the effect of genetics and biochemistry on human behavior (Guo, Roettger, and Cai 2008; Hart and Marmorstein 2009). Neighborhood and family environments are particularly likely to moderate the relationship between genetics and behavioral outcomes and social scientists are especially well qualified to explore these associations.

Research in this area is too nascent to offer predictions or prescriptives for the role played by social factors on the prospective link between depression and obesity. Previous research indicates that economic and racial inequality, residential segregation, neighborhood or family conditions, and differential exposure to personal stress, are factors with the potential to moderate some element of the path between depression and obesity. It is also likely that social factors operate as fundamental causes, simultaneously contributing to the development of both obesity and depression. What is striking is the degree to which social scientists are not yet active this discussion. While there is a strong likelihood that genetics and biochemistry play a direct role in explaining this association, the social patterning of obesity and depression is likely too strong for this to be the only explanation. For these reasons, it is important that social scientists engage in this debate from an early stage and bring their considerable insights to understanding this association.

Bi-causal Associations between Obesity and Depression

Given the availability of prospective evidence that obesity predicts later depression and depression predicts later obesity, it is not surprising that some have proposed a bi-directional causal relationship between the two. Among the most fully developed bi-causal explanations appeared in a review article by Markowitz, Friedman, and Arent (2008) and a response by Hrabosky and Thomas (2008). These two papers propose that depression and obesity act on each other through binge eating, perceived weight cycling, self-rated health, and problems with physiological responses to stress (e.g., hypothalamic-pituitary-adrenal dysregulation). In addition, the model proposes that obesity acts on depression through dieting and social stigma, while depression acts on obesity through lack of exercise, negative thoughts, and social isolation.

To date, few studies have explicitly examined whether the development of obesity and depression are reciprocally reinforced over time, and the results available to date have been mixed. One of the first analyses to identify a prospective association between depression and obesity among adolescents found that the association did not operate in reverse and baseline obesity did not predict later depression (Goodman and Whitaker 2002). A recent longitudinal assessment of a young and relatively healthy cohort found evidence of a small but significant longitudinal and reciprocal association between depression and metabolic syndrome among women (Pulkki-Raback et al. 2009). These early results, though mixed, suggest another important avenue for exploring the association between obesity and depression.

CONCLUSION

It has been 15 years since Friedman and Brownell (1995) published their seminal review "Psychological Correlates of Obesity: Moving to the Next Research Generation" in which they called for prospective assessments of the association between obesity and psychopathology and for greater attention on who suffers psychological distress as the result of weight and why. Research published since that time has largely focused on questions raised by their call. Today, dozens of prospective studies have assessed the association between obesity and depression and considerable progress has been made understanding both mediators and moderators of the depression-obesity link.

It is today clear that obesity and depression are linked, though to what degree and through what mechanisms remains the topic of much inquiry. Over the coming 15 years, prospective research is likely to garner even more attention, as will the possibility that these two conditions are mutually reinforcing. In addition, our understanding of the depression-obesity link would be enhanced, I would argue, with greater attention to three areas: the cross-sectional and longitudinal association between obesity and depression in non-Western countries; the role of physical health as a mediator of the obesity-depression link in older adults; and greater attention to understanding obesity-depression associations within the context of more general theories of depression.

Over the past 10 years, the association between depression and obesity has appeared in more nations, particularly non-Western nations. It is not yet known whether this is a new phenomenon or one that is only now being identified. In either case, the development of more cross-national comparisons, especially among nations of differing levels of industrial and economic development, will offer great opportunities to track obesity as both cause and consequence of psychological distress. The historic white, Western bias of obesity-depression research has included a bias toward studying the young and on those periods in life where obesity and depression threaten romantic opportunities and social relationships. Yet, the greatest threat stemming from obesity-depression links may be to the physical and emotional health of older adults. Obesity is rising rapidly in that population, bringing with it significant threats to health and functional mobility. Such problems are already known to contribute to increases in depression among older adults. When these adults are also obese, as increasing numbers are, there is the potential to create a "double jeopardy," increasing mental and physical suffering as well as the cost of caring for older adults.

Finally, most of the results published in the past decade have framed the obesity-depression link independently from major theories of either the etiology of depression or its consequences. To date, this has produced a wide-ranging literature with relatively few core explanatory principles upon which to build. In part, this is likely due to the fact that researchers interested in this question run the spectrum of social, medical, and behavioral sciences, and the creativity this engenders is itself of great benefit. Of equal benefit would be research that seats obesity within some of the major theories of depression and mental illness and that tests various theoretical explanations against one another. This could be the "fourth generation" of research on obesity and its psychosocial correlates and would provide more robust and generative answers to the question who suffers from obesity-related psychological distress and why.

REFERENCES

Abramson, Lyn Y., Lauren B. Alloy, Benjamin L. Hankin, Gerald J. Haeffel, Donal G. MacCoon, and Brandon E. Gibb. 2002. "Cognitive Vulnerability-Stress Models of Depression in a Self-Regulatory and Psychobiological Context." In *Handbook of Depression*, eds. I. H. Gotlin and C. L. Hammen, 268–294. New York: The Guilford Press.

Adams, Ryan E., and William M. Bukowski. 2008. "Peer Victimization as a Predictor of Depression and Body Mass Index in Obese and Non-obese Adolescents. " *Journal of Child Psychology and Psychiatry* 49: 858–866.

Alloy, Lauren B., Lyn Y. Abramson, Scott M. Safford, and Brandon E. Gibb. 2006. "The Cognitive Vulnerability to Depression (CVD) Project: Current Findings and Future Directions." in *Cognitive Vulnerability to Emotional Disorders*, eds. L. B. Alloy and J. H. Riskind, 33-62. Mahway, NJ: Lawrence Erlbaum Associates.

Anderson, Sarah E., Patricia Cohen, Elena N. Naumova, Paul F. Jacques, and Aviva Must. 2007. "Adolescent Obesity and Risk for Subsequent Major Depressive Disorder and Anxiety Disorder: Prospective Evidence." *Psychosomatic Medicine* 69: 740–747.

Anderson, Sarah E., Patricia Cohen, Elena Naumova, and Aviva Must. 2006. "Relationship of Childhood Behavior Disorders to Weight Gain from Childhood to Adulthood." *Ambulatory Pediatrics* 6: 297–301.

Beauboeuf-Lafontant, Tamara. 2003. "Strong and Large Black Women? Exploring Relationships between Deviant Womanhood and Weight." *Gender and Society* 17: 111–121.

BeLue, Rhonda, Lori Ann Francis, and Brendon Colaco. 2009. "Mental Health Problems and Overweight in a Nationally Representative Sample of Adolescents: Effects of Race and Ethnicity." *Pediatrics* 123: 697–702.

Carr, Deborah, and Michael A. Friedman. 2005. "Is Obesity Stigmatizing? Body Weight, Perceived Discrimination, and Psychological Well-Being inthe United States." *Journal of Health and Social Behavior* 46: 244–259.

Carr, Deborah, and Michael A. Friedman. 2006. "Body Weight and the Quality of Interpersonal Relationships." *Social Psychology Quarterly* 69: 127–149.

Carr, Deborah, Michael A. Friedman, and Karen Jaffe. 2007. "Understanding the Relation between Obesity and Positive and Negative Affect: The Role of Psychosocial Mechanisms." *Body Image* 4: 165–177.

Cash, Thomas F., and Patricia E. Henry. 1995. "Women's Body Images: The Results of a National Survey in the U.S.A." *Sex Roles* 33: 19–28.

Chaiton, M., C. Sabiston, J. O'Loughlin, J. J. McGrath, K. Maximova, and M. Lambert. 2009. "A Structural Equation Model Relating Adiposity, Psychosocial Indicators of Body Image and Depressive Symptoms among Adolescents." *International Journal of Obesity* 33: 588–596.

Cohen, Deborah A., Brian K. Finch, Aimee Bower, and Narayan Sastry. 2006. "Collective Efficacy and Obesity: The Potential Influence of Social Factors on Health." *Social Science and Medicine* 62: 769–778.

Crocker, Jennifer, and Brenda Major. 1989. "Social Stigma and Self-Esteem: The Self-Protective Properties of Stigma." *Psychological Review* 96: 608–630.

Crosnoe, Robert, Kenneth Frank, and Anna Strassmann Mueller. 2008. "Gender, Body Size and Social Relations in American High Schools." *Social Forces* 86: 1189–1216.

de Sousa, Pedro Miguel Lopes. 2008. "Body-Image and Obesity in Adolescence: A Comparative Study of Social-Demographic, Psychological, and Behavioral Aspects." *Spanish Journal of Psychology* 11: 551–563.

Erickson, Sarah J., Thomas N. Robinson, K. Farish Haydel, and Joel D. Killen. 2000. "Are Overweight Children Unhappy? Body Mass Index, Depressive Symptoms, and Overweight Concerns in Elementary School Children." *Archives of Pediatrics & Adolescent Medicine* 154: 931–935.

Faith, Myles S., Patty E. Matz, and Marie A. Jorge. 2002. "Obesity-Depression Associations in the Population." *Journal of Psychosomatic Research* 53: 935–942.

Ferraro, Kenneth F., and Jessica A. Kelley-Moore. 2003. "Cumulative Disadvantage and Health: Long-Term Consequences of Obesity." *American Sociological Review* 68: 707–729.

Fowler-Brown, Angela G., Gary G. Bennett, Melody S. Goodman, Christina C. Wee, Giselle M. Corbie-Smith, and Sherman A. James. 2009. "Psychosocial Stress and 13-year BMI Change among Blacks: The Pitt County Study." *Obesity* 17: 2106–2109.

Franko, Debra L, Ruth H. Striegel-Moore, Douglas Thompson, George B. Schreiber, and Stephen R. Daniels. 2005. "Does Adolescent Depression Predict Obesity in Black and White Young Adult Women?." *Psychological Medicine* 35: 1505–1513.

Friedman, Michael A., and Kelly D. Brownell. 1995. "Psychological Correlates of Obesity: Moving to the Next Research Generation." *Psychological Bulletin* 117: 3–20.

Ge, Xiaojia, Glen H. Elder, Jr., Mark Regnerus, and Christine Cox. 2001. "Pubertal Transitions, Perceptions of Being Overweight, and Adolescents' Psychological Maladjustment: Gender and Ethnic Differences." *Social Psychology Quarterly* 64: 363–375.

Goodman, Elizabeth, and Robert C. Whitaker. 2002. "A Prospective Study of the Role of Depression in the Development and Persistence of Adolescent Obesity." *Pediatrics* 110: 497–504.

Goodwin, R. D., A. Sourander, C. S. Duarte, S. Niemelä, P. Multimäki, G. Nikolakaros, H. Helenius, J. Piha, K. Kumpulainen, I. Moilanen, T. Tamminen, and F. Almqvist. 2009. "Do Mental Health Problems in Childhood Predict Chronic Physical Conditions among Males in Early Adulthood? Evidence from a Community-Based Prospective Study." *Psychological Medicine* 39: 301–311.

Granberg, Ellen M., Leslie G. Simons, and Ronald L. Simons. 2009. "Body Size and Social Self Image among Adolescent African American Girls." *Youth and Society* 41: 234–255.

Granberg, Ellen M., Ronald L. Simons, Frederick X. Gibbons, and Jan Nieuwsma Melby. 2008. "The Relationship between Body Size and Depressed Mood: Findings from a Sample of African American Middle School Girls." *Youth and Society* 39: 294–315.

Grant, Kathryn, Aoife Lyons, Dana Landis, Mi Hyon Cho, Maddalena Scudiero, Linda Reynolds, Julie Murphy, and Heather Bryant. 1999. "Gender, Body Image and Depressive Symptoms among Low-Income African American Adolescents." *Journal of Social Issues* 55: 299–316.

Guo, Guang, Michael E. Roettger, and Tianji Cai. 2008. "The Integration of Genetic Propensities into Social-Control Models of Delinquency and Violence among Male Youths." *American Sociological Review* 73: 543–568.

Hart, Daniel, and Naomi R. Marmorstein. 2009. "Neighborhoods and Genes and Everything in Between: Understanding Adolescent Aggression in Social and Biological Contexts." *Development and Psychopathology* 21: 961–973.

Hasler, Gregor, Shmuel Lissek, Vladeta Ajdacic, Gabriella Milos, Alex Gamma, Dominique Eich, Wulf Rössler, and Jules Angst. 2005. "Major Depression Predicts an Increase in Long-Term Body Weight Variability in Young Adults." *Obesity* 13: 1991–1998.

Hebl, Michelle R., and Todd F. Heatherton. 1998. "The Stigma of Obesity in Women: The Difference is Black and White." *Personality and Social Psychology Bulletin* 24: 417–430.

Horwitz, Allan V. 2002. "Outcomes in the Sociology of Mental Health and Illness: Where Have We Been and Where are We Going?" *Journal of Health and Social Behavior* 43: 143–151.

Hrabosky, Joshua I., and Jennifer J. Thomas. 2008. "Elucidating the Relationship between Obesity and Depression: Recommendations for Future Research." *Clinical Psychology-Science and Practice* 15: 28–34.

Kasen, S., P. Cohen, H. Chen, and A. Must. 2008. "Obesity and Psychopathology in Women: A Three Decade Prospective Study." *International Journal of Obesity* 32: 558–566.

Kim, Bong-Seog, and Mi Jung Park. 2009. "The Influence of Weight and Height Status on Psychological Problems of Elementary Schoolchildren through Child Behavior Checklist Analysis." *Yonsei Medical Journal* 50: 340–344.

Kim, Oksoo, and Kyeha Kim. 2001. "Body Weight, Self-Esteem, and Depression in Korean Female Adolescents." *Adolescence* 36: 315–322.

Li, Yan-Ping., Guan-Sheng Ma, Evert G. Schouten, Xiao-Qi Hu, Zhao-Hui Cui, Dong Wang, and Frans J. Kok. 2007. "Report on Childhood Obesity in China (5) Body Weight, Body Dissatisfaction, and Depression Symptoms of Chinese Children Aged 9–10 Years." *Biomedical and Environmental Sciences* 20: 11–18.

Liem, Eryn T., Pieter J.J. Sauer, Albertine J. Oldehinkel, and Ronald P. Stolk. 2008. "Association between Depressive Symptoms in Childhood and Adolescence and Overweight in Later Life: Review of the Recent Literature." *Archives of Pediatrics and Adolescent Medicine* 162: 981–988.

Link, Bruce G., and Jo Phelan. 1995. "Social Conditions as Fundamental Causes of Disease." *Journal of Health and Social Behavior* 36: 80–94.

Link, Bruce G., and Jo C. Phelan. 2001. "Conceptualizing Stigma." *Annual Review of Sociology* 27: 363–385.

Mamun, Abdullah A., Michael J. O'Callaghan, Susanna M. Cramb, Jake M. Najman, Gail M. Williams, and William Bor. 2009. "Childhood Behavioral Problems Predict Young Adults' BMI and Obesity: Evidence from a Birth Cohort Study." *Obesity* 17: 761–766.

Markowitz, Sarah, Michael A. Friedman, and Shawn M. Arent. 2008. "Understanding the Relation Between Obesity and Depression: Causal Mechanisms and Implications for Treatment." *Clinical Psychology: Science and Practice* 15: 1–20.

McElroy, Susan L., Renu Kotwal, Shishuka Malhotra, Erik B. Nelson, Paul E. Keck, and Charles B. Nemeroff. 2004. "Are Mood Disorders and Obesity Related? A Review for the Mental Health Professional." *Journal of Clinical Psychiatry* 65: 634–651.

Merten, Michael J., K. A. S. Wickrama, and Amanda L. Williams. 2008. "Adolescent Obesity and Young Adult Psychosocial Outcomes: Gender and Racial Differences." *Journal of Youth and Adolescence* 37: 1111–1122.

Mirowsky, John. 1995. "Age and the Sense of Control." *Social Psychology Quarterly* 58: 31–43.

Mirowsky, John, and Catherine E. Ross. 1992. "Age and Depression." *Journal of Health and Social Behavior* 33: 187–205.

Mirowsky, John, and Catherine E. Ross. 2002. "Measurement for a Human Science." *Journal of Health and Social Behavior* 43: 152–170.

Needham, Belinda L., and Robert Crosnoe. 2005. "Overweight Status and Depressive Symptoms during Adolescence." *Journal of Adolescent Health* 36:48–55.

Neumark-Sztainer, D., N. Falkner, M. Story, C. Perry, P. J. Hannan, and S. Mulert. 2002. "Weight-teasing among Adolescents: Correlations with Weight Status and Disordered Eating Behaviors." *International Journal of Obesity* 26: 123–131.

Onyike, Chiadi U., Rosa M. Crum, Hochang B. Lee, Constantine G. Lyketsos, and William W. Eaton. 2003. "Is Obesity Associated with Major Depression? Results from the Third National Health and Nutrition Examination Survey." *American Journal of Epidemiology* 158: 1139–1147.

Ozmen, Dilek, Erol Ozmen, Dilek Ergin, Aynur C. Cetinkaya, Nesrin Sen, Pinar E. Dundar, and E. Oryal Taskin. 2007. "The Association of Self-Esteem, Depression and Body Satisfaction with Obesity among Turkish Adolescents." *BMC Public Health* 7:80. Retrieved November 18, 2009, http://www.biomedcentral.com/1471-2458/7/80.

Park, Chul-Min, Moon-Doo Kim, Seong-Chul Hong, Yeol Kim, Mi-Youl Hyun, Young-Sook Kwak, Chang-In Lee, Min-Jeong Park, Yun-Hee Jang, Ji-Hyun Moon, Eun-Mi Seok, Young-Ja Song, and Hyeon Ju Kim. 2009. "Effects of Obesity and Obesity-Induced Stress on Depressive Symptoms in Korean Elementary School Children." *International Journal of Social Psychiatry* 55: 322–335.

Puhl, Rebecca M., and Kelly D. Brownell. 2006. "Confronting and Coping with Weight Stigma: An Investigation of Overweight and Obese Adults." *Obesity* 14: 1802–1815.

Pulkki-Raback, Laura, Marko Elovainio, Mika Kivimäki, Noora Mattsson, Olli T. Raitakari, Sampsa Puttonen, Jukka Marniemi, Jorma S. A. Viikari, and Liisa Keltikangas-Järvinen. 2009. "Depressive Symptoms and the Metabolic Syndrome in Childhood and Adulthood: A Prospective Cohort Study." *Health Psychology* 28: 108–116.

Richardson, Laura P., Robert Davis, Richie Poulton, Elizabeth McCauley, Terrie E. Moffitt, Avshalom Caspi, and Frederick Connell. 2003. "A Longitudinal Evaluation of Adolescent Depression and Adult Obesity." *Archives of Pediatrics and Adolescent Medicine* 157: 739–745.

Roberts, Alan, Thomas F. Cash, Alan Feingold, and Blair T. Johnson. 2006. "Are Black-White Differences in Females' Body Dissatisfaction Decreasing? A Meta-Analytic Review." *Journal of Consulting and Clinical Psychology* 74: 1121–1131.

Roberts, R. E., S. Deleger, W. J. Strawbridge, and G. A. Kaplan. 2003. "Prospective Association between Obesity and Depression: Evidence from the Alameda County Study." *International Journal of Obesity* 23: 514–521.

Roberts, Robert E., George A. Kaplan, Sarah J. Shema, William J. Strawjbridge. "Are the Obese at Greater Risk for Depression?" *American Journal of Epidemiology* 152: 163–170.

Rofey, Dana L., Rachel P. Kolko, Ana-Maria Iosif, Jennifer S. Silk, James E. Bost, Wentao Feng, Eva M. Szigethy, Robert B. Noll, Neal D. Ryan, and Ronald E. Dahl. 2009. "A Longitudinal Study of Childhood Depression and Anxiety in Relation to Weight Gain." *Child Psychiatry and Human Development* 40: 517–526.

Ruscio, Ayelet Meron, John Ruscio, and Terence M. Keane. 2002. "The Latent Structure of Posttraumatic Stress Disorder: A Taxometric Investigation of Reactions to Extreme Stress." *Journal of Abnormal Psychology* 111: 290–301.

Ruscio, John, and Ayelet Meron Ruscio. 2004. "Clarifying Boundary Issues in Psychopathology: The Role of Taxometrics in a Comprehensive Program of Structural Research." *Journal of Abnormal Psychology* 113: 24–38.

Sachs-Ericsson, Natalie, Andrea B. Burns, Kathryn H. Gordon, Lisa A. Eckel, Steven A. Wonderlich, Ross D. Crosby, and Dan G. Blazer. 2007. "Body Mass Index and Depressive Symptoms in Older Adults: The Moderating Roles of Race, Sex, and Socioeconomic Status." *American Journal of Geriatric Psychiatry* 15: 815–825.

Salihu, Hamisu M., Sarah M. Bonnema, and Amina P. Alio. 2009. "Obesity: What Is an Elderly Population Growing Into?" *Maturitas* 63: 7–12.

Scott, K. M., R. Bruffaerts, G. E. Simon, J. Alonso, M. Angermeyer, G. de Girolamo, K. Demyttenaere, I. Gasquet, J. M. Haro, E. Karam, R. C. Kessler, D. Levinson, M. E. Medina Mora, M. A. Oakley Browne, J. Ormel, J. P. Villa, H. Uda, and M. Von Korff. 2008. "Obesity and Mental Disorders in the General Population: Results from the World Mental Health Surveys." *International Journal of Obesity* 32: 192–200.

Shin, N. Y., and M. S. Shin. 2008. "Body Dissatisfaction, Self-Esteem, and Depression in Obese Korean Children." *Journal of Pediatrics* 152: 502–506.

Siegel, Judith M. 2002. "Body Image Change and Adolescent Depressive Symptoms." *Journal of Adolescent Research* 17: 27–41.

Simons, Ronald L., Velma Murry, Vonnie McLoyd, Kuei-Hsui Lin, Carolyn Cutrona, and Rand D. Conger. 2002. "Discrimination, Crime, Ethnic Identity, and Parenting as Correlates of Depressive Symptoms among African American Children: A Multilevel Analysis." *Development and Psychopathology* 14: 371–393.

Smolak, Linda, and Michael P. Levine. 2001. "Body Image in Children." In *Body Image, Eating Disorders, and Obesity in Youth: Assessment, Prevention, and Treatment*, eds. J. K. Thompson and L. Smolak, 41–66. Washington, D.C.: American Psychological Association.

Sun, Q., R. M. van Dam, D. Spiegelman, S. B. Heymsfield, W. C. Willett, F. B. Hu. 2010. "Comparison of Dual-Energy X-ray Absorptiometric and Anthropometric Measures of Adiposity in Relation to Adiposity-related Biologic Factors." *American Journal of Epidemiology* 172: 1442–1454.

Swallen, Karen C., Eric N. Reither, Steven A. Haas, and Ann M. Meier. 2005. "Overweight, Obesity, and Health-Related Quality of Life among Adolescents: The National Longitudinal Study of Adolescent Health." *Pediatrics* 115: 340–347.

Tanofsky-Kraff, Marian, Marc L. Cohen, Susan Z. Yanovski, Christopher Cox, Kelly R. Theim, Margaret Keil, James C. Reynolds, and Jack A. Yanovski. 2006. "A Prospective Study of Psychological Predictors of Body Fat Gain among Children at High Risk for Adult Obesity." *Pediatrics* 117: 1203–1209.

ter Bogt, Tom F. M., Saskia A. F. M. van Dorsselaer, Karin Monshouwer, Jacqueline E. E. Verdurmen, Rutger C. M. E. Engels, and Wilma A. M. Vollebergh. 2006. "Body Mass Index and Body Weight Perception as Risk Factors for Internalizing and Externalizing Problem Behavior among Adolescents." *Journal of Adolescent Health* 39: 27–34.

Turner, R. Jay, and Donald A. Lloyd. 1999. "The Stress Process and the Social Distribution of Depression." *Journal of Health and Social Behavior* 40: 374–404.

Wardle, J., N. H. Broderson, T. J. Cole, M. J. Jarvis, and D. R. Boniface. 2006. "Development of Adiposity in Adolescence: Five Year Longitudinal Study of an Ethnically and Socioeconomically Diverse Sample of Young People in Britain." *British Medical Journal* 332: 1130–1135.

Wickrama, K. A., Thulitha, K. A. S. Wickrama, and Chalandra M. Bryant. 2006. "Community Influences on Adolescent Obesity: Race/Ethnic Differences." *Journal of Youth and Adolescence* 35: 647–657.

Zhao, G., E. S. Ford, S. Dhingra, C. Li, T. W. Strine, and A. H. Mokdad. 2009a. "Depression and Anxiety among US Adults: Associations with Body Mass Index." *International Journal of Obesity* 33: 257–266.

Zhao, Guixiang X., Earl S. Ford, Chaoyang Li, Tara W. Strine, Satvinder Dhingra, Joyce T. Berry, and Ali H. Mokdad. 2009b. "Serious Psychological Distress and Its Associations with Body Mass Index: Findings from the 2007 Behavioral Risk Factor Surveillance System." *International Journal of Public Health* 54: S30–S36.

....

CHAPTER 21

FOOD MARKETING, TELEVISION, AND VIDEO GAMES

....

ELIZABETH A. VANDEWATER AND ELLEN A. WARTELLA

THE prevalence of obesity in American youth has reached alarming levels. The proportion of overweight children and adolescents, defined as a body mass index (BMI) exceeding the 95th percentile for age- and sex-based norms, has tripled in the past three decades (Ogden et al. 2002). The most recent U.S. estimates indicate that approximately 10 percent of 2–5 year-olds and 15 percent of 6–19 year-olds are overweight (Ogden et al. 2006). In fact, since the 1980s, the prevalence of childhood obesity has increased in almost all countries for which data are available (Wang and Lobstein 2006).

The rise of obesity among youth has placed an unprecedented burden on children's health. Obesity is strongly related to several chronic diseases, such as cardiovascular disease and diabetes (Must et al. 1999). Almost two-thirds (60 percent) of overweight children have at least one cardiovascular risk factor (e.g., hypertension, hyperlipidemia) (Freedman et al. 1999), and are at an increased risk of suffering comorbidities including type 2 diabetes, hypertension, dyslipidemia and hyperinsulinemia, fatty liver disease and orthopedic disorders (Lobstein 2005). Moreover, though overall prevalence rates are still low, the number of youth with some degree of glycemic abnormalities (precursors to type 2 diabetes mellitus) is on the rise, and closely parallels the trend in increasing weight status of youth globally (Bloomgarden 2004). Finally, obesity in childhood tends to persist in adulthood (Must et al. 1992; Must 1996). Overweight youth enter adulthood with a risk of obesity up to 17 times higher that of their normal weight peers (Hauner 2004). Thus, the striking increase in the prevalence of childhood obesity seen in the last three decades will dramatically affect public health expenses, programs and priorities well into the 21st century.

LINKING ELECTRONIC MEDIA USE
AND CHILDHOOD OBESITY

Fundamentally, overweight and obesity arise due to an imbalance of energy—the individual does not expend as much energy as he or she consumes. However, the reasons for this imbalance have proven to be complex and varied. Among them are reduced levels of physical activity for many children, shifting sociological factors that impact family eating patterns and habits, and the increased availability of calorically dense convenience foods with little nutritional value (Institute of Medicine 2005; Krishnamoorthy, Hart, and Jelalian 2006; Caroli et al. 2004; Stitt and Kunkel 2008).

However, the conviction that television viewing and video/computer game use, in particular, bear much of the responsibility for the increased prevalence of obesity in American youth is held by the lay public and scholars alike (Chen and Kennedy 2001; Dietz 2001; Dietz and Gortmaker 1985; Gortmaker et al. 1993). An expert panel convened by the American College of Sports Medicine stated unequivocally that "obesity is directly related to the number of hours spent watching television" (Bar-Or et al. 1998).

Moreover, this conviction has shaped prominent public health policies. Noting that high levels of viewing time and television in the bedroom have been linked (at least correlationally) with childhood weight status, the American Academy of Pediatrics (AAP) policy statement on prevention of pediatric obesity recommends that viewing time and video game play be limited to no more than two hours per day (American Academy of Pediatrics 2001). In its continuing series of *Healthy People* mission statements the US Department of Health and Human Services listed the reduction of television viewing as a means of promoting physical activity as a national health objective for the first time in *Healthy People 2010*.

It is certainly true that youth of all ages spend a fair proportion of their time using electronic media (3–5 hours a day watching television, for example), more time than in any other single free-time activity except for sleep (Huston, Wright, Marquis, and Green 1999; Wright et al. 2001). The Kaiser Foundation has surveyed the media use of youth between 8 and 18 years old in 1999, 2004, and 2009 (Kaiser Family Foundation 1999, 2005, 2009), as well as very young children between 6 months and 6 years of age in 2002 and 2005 (Kaiser Family Foundation 2003, 2006). These surveys confirm the general perception that children are growing up in media and technologically saturated environments. Ninety-nine percent of American households report television ownership, 97 percent VCR/DVD player ownership, 87 percent video game player ownership, and 93 percent computer ownership. Most families (roughly 75 percent) report multiple televisions in the household (an average of 3.8 televisions to be exact), with these televisions increasingly located in children's bedrooms. Roughly 71 percent of 8–18 year-olds, and 36 percent of very young children (6 months to 6 years old) have televisions in their bedrooms. Computer and video game use among children is also growing, with roughly 60 percent of youth ages 8–18 reporting that they use computers or play video games on a daily basis in 2009 (Kaiser Family Foundation 1999, 2005, 2009).

One popular hypothesis has been that screen-based media are related to obesity through displacement of physical activity. However, In a recent meta-analysis, Marshall, Biddle, Gorely, Cameron, and Murdey (2004) examined findings from 52 independent samples and report an average effect size (Pearson r) of $-.12$ for the relationship between television viewing and physical activity, and an effect size of $-.10$ for the relationship between video/computer game use and physical activity. Although these are in the predicted direction, their sizes are extremely small. Effects of this size would lead one to conclude that the relationship between media use and physical activity is not particularly meaningful. Indeed, the authors conclude that ". . . media-based inactivity may be unfairly implicated in recent epidemiologic trends of overweight and obesity among children and youth" (Marshall et al. 2004, p. 1238).

These findings have important implications for the notion that electronic media use has contributed to the obesity epidemic in U.S. youth via its impact on physical activity. Given the dire problem of overweight children in this country, it seems clear that American children are not active enough. The question at hand is whether electronic media use plays an important role in this lack of physical activity. Generally, the assumption has been that if children were not watching television, playing video games, or using the computer, they would be outside running up and down a soccer field. However, the overwhelming body of evidence indicates that this is not the case.

If screen-based media are not related to childhood obesity via the displacement of physical activity, the other possible mechanism linking the two is increased caloric consumption. Thus it is possible that the use of electronic media increased children's caloric intake, either through eating while viewing or in response to screen-based food advertising. The role of screen-based food advertising (whether via television or the computer) in children's caloric intake, nutritional knowledge, and eating habits has received increased attention of late (Institute of Medicine 2006), and this factor has continued to dominate the debate on the role of electronic media in childhood obesity rates. Many hold advertising responsible for childhood obesity because of its abundant promotion of energy-dense food, that is, products containing relative high proportions of fat, sugar, and salt (Hastings, Stead, and McDermott 2002; Schor 2005). Consequently, in many countries, consumer and health organizations are pleading for restrictive policies regarding food (and other) advertising directed at children (Gantz et al. 2007; Harris et al. 2009; Linn 2004).

TELEVISED FOOD ADVERTISING

After the automotive industry, the U.S. food industry is the second-largest advertiser in the American economy (McCall 2003). It is estimated that food marketers spend more than $10 billion annually to promote products specifically to children and youth (Institute of Medicine 2006; Palmer and Carpenter 2006). In the past decade in particular, U.S. children and adolescents have been increasingly targeted with intensive and aggressive forms of food advertising (Story and French 2004). For industry, the stakes are huge. It is estimated that children ages 14 and younger directly purchase $14 billion in goods annually, and influence another $190 billion in family purchases (McNeal 1998; Institute of Medicine 2006). When children begin to receive allowances and make spending decisions, roughly one-third of their spending is on candies, snacks, and beverages (Schor 2005).

Stitt and Kunkel (2008) note that the average amount of daily viewing by young children amounts to a cumulative exposure of more than 1,000 hours annually, which makes televised advertising one of the most effective vehicles to deliver food marketing messages to children (Palmer and Carpenter 2006; Stitt and Kunkel 2008; Kotz and Story 1994). Marketers are well aware of the ubiquitous nature of television viewing in children's lives, and televised advertising remains the preferred mode for reaching them (Rice 2001; Kunkel et al. 2004; Lauro 1999; Janz, Dawson, and Mahoney 2000; Institute of Medicine 2006). Over 75 percent of U.S. food manufacturers advertising budgets, and 95 percent of U.S. fast-food restaurant budgets are allocated to television (Gallo 1999). The proliferation of television channels due to the diffusion of cable television and direct broadcast satellite technologies has brought with it numerous channels with programming aimed at children such as Nickelodeon, Disney Channel, and Cartoon Network (Kunkel et al. 2004). The concentration of demographic collections of viewers brought about by such "niche" channels has made it easier for advertisers to target specific markets, including children (Batada and Wootan 2007).

Evidence suggests that food is one of the most frequently advertised products on television, accounting for approximately 50 percent of all commercials (Taras and Gage 1995; Byrd-Bredbenner 2002; Story, Neumark-Sztainer, and French 2002; Stitt and Kunkel 2008). The average child watches more than 40,000 television commercials per year, and commercial advertising has been found to account for as much as 16 percent of children's total viewing time (Taras and Gage 1995; Kunkel 2001). It has been estimated that children are exposed to an average of one food commercial for every five minutes of television viewing, and may see as many as three hours of food commercials every week (Gamble and Cotunga 1999). Recent analyses indicate that broadcast channels deliver more food advertising than cable channels, although the types of food marketed are highly similar (Stitt and Kunkel 2008). Perhaps even more importantly, it has been reported that foods were more commonly offered and consumed on children's shows, and that calorically dense, nutritionally poor foods were significantly more prevalent in youth-oriented programs than in adult-oriented programs (Greenberg et al. 2009).

The heavy food marketing directed at children, especially young children, seems to be driven largely by the desire to develop and build brand awareness, preference, and loyalty (Story and French 2004). Hite and Hite (1994) demonstrated that preschoolers rely heavily on "branding" for food preferences; young children reported that product samples bearing nationally advertised brand names/labels taste significantly better than the same products bearing store names/labels. This brand reliance was in fact most prominent among very young children. Children ages 2–3 chose brand names/labels 10 to 1 over store names/labels, while children ages 4–5 chose brand names 2 to 1 over store names/labels.

These findings have not gone unnoticed by marketers, who have been intensifying efforts to develop brand relationships with young consumers, particularly toddlers (Zollo 1999). Eighty percent of food items are branded (Harris et al. 2002), and marketers know young children can affect parental purchases through what is known in the business as the "nag factor" or "pester power" (McNeal 1998; Story and French 2004). Marketers also know that a child's first request for a product occurs at around 2 years of age, that 75 percent of the time this request occurs in a grocery store or supermarket, and that the most requested first in-store request is breakfast cereal (47 percent), followed by snacks and beverages (30 percent) and toys (21 percent) (McNeal 1998; Story and French 2004).

Most televised food advertising to children falls into one of five categories. These are known as the "Big 5" of food advertising and they include: (1) pre-sugared breakfast cereals, (2) soft drinks, (3) candy, (4) salty snack products, and (5) fast food and/or highly processed foods (Kotz and Story 1994). Not surprisingly, these foods also account for almost 50 percent of the U.S. food market share (Taras and Gage 1995; Kuribayashi, Roberts, and Johnson 2001). Kotz and Story (1994) constructed a "Saturday Morning Food Pyramid," based on food advertising to children in 1994. They found that 50 percent of advertised foods during children's television programs fell into the fats, oils and sweets food group, 5 percent into dairy, 2 percent into meat, poultry, fish, eggs, nuts and legumes, and 43 percent into bread, cereal, rice and pasta. Thus, sweets comprised the majority of the "Saturday Morning Pyramid," and vegetables and fruits were completely absent—the antithesis of the U.S. Department of Agriculture's Food Guide Pyramid at the time. A recent analysis of food advertising during children's programming in 2003 revealed that convenience foods, fast foods, and sweets (including candy and soft drinks) comprised 83 percent of advertised foods (Harrison and Marske 2005). These findings have been confirmed in more recent studies (Greenberg et al. 2009; Stitt and Kunkel 2008; Batada et al. 2008). Moreover, similar analyses examining the extent and content of food advertising to children in Spanish-language American television programs (Bell et al. 2009; Abbatangelo-Gray, Byrd-Bredbenner, and Austin 2008), in Australia (Chapman, Nicholas, and Supramaniam 2006), and in the United Kingdom and Canada (Adams et al. 2009) reveal highly similar patterns. There is little doubt that food advertising is a major form of advertising to children, and that the vast majority of food advertising to children is for foods of poor or questionable nutritional content.

FOOD ADVERTISING IN OTHER FORMS OF MEDIA

Although there is no sign that televised food advertising is decreasing, marketers concerned about the use of TiVo and other recording devices that can limit exposure to commercials have been expanding efforts to capture market share in other ways. Food marketers have also sought to capitalize on the popularity of video games and the Internet among youth. Product placement is a marketing strategy whereby products are placed in a setting outside of a typical advertisement (Institute of Medicine 2006). Typically, popular actors, programs and characters are seen using the product in the context of the story line. Product placement in movies has become commonplace since the character ET ate Reese's Pieces® candy and short-term national candy sales increased 66 percent (Institute of Medicine 2006). Though product placement is illegal in programs aimed at children, it is common in prime-time programming as well as in movies aimed at children and adolescents (Linn 2005; Institute of Medicine 2006).

Product placement has been more difficult to implement effectively in traditional console video games, because the placement must be part of the original programming and cannot be changed once the game is released (Institute of Medicine 2006)—though the industry is actively working to "fix" this problem (Webster and Bulik 2004). However, product placement on Internet-based games is easily incorporated and can be changed with product popularity. This has given rise to what is known as "advergames" or "advertainment" (Kretchmer 2004). Advergames are Internet-based games with a commercial message, either subtle or overt. Advergames can be found on product or brand web sites. Most (if not all) web sites for popular children's channels (Nick.com, Cartoonnetwork.com) or toy products (Lego.com, Hasbro.com) feature games incorporating characters and products, in order to build and extend brand loyalty (Calvert 2003; Kretchmer 2004). Increasingly, advergames can be found on web sites for foods marketed almost exclusively to children and adolescents (Moore 2006). The McDonalds, Kelloggs, General Mills, and Hostess Web sites all have games for children featuring their products. Though games on food and restaurant websites currently account for an extremely small percentage (less than 1 percent) of the combined Internet and television commercials for these companies (Institute of Medicine 2006), it seems likely that this share will increase in the next 5 to 10 years.

CHILDREN'S UNDERSTANDING
OF ADVERTISING

Part of the problem with all of this advertising is the plethora of evidence indicating that young children have difficulty making sense of commercials and commercial content. Under the age of 4, children have difficulty differentiating between programs and commercials (Kunkel 2004). Children under the age of 7 do not understand the persuasive intent of advertising—they are more likely to perceive ads simply as "information," provided by someone with their best interests at heart (Ward, Wackman, and Wartella 1977; Carruth et al. 2000). Even children between the ages of 7 and 11 have difficulty questioning commercial claims (John 1999). The matter is complicated by the fact that language providing important information about the product is often presented in ways that children cannot understand. For example, evidence shows that children under 7 do not understand the meaning of "part of a balanced breakfast," which is commonly (almost ubiquitously) used in sugared cereal advertisements (Palmer and McDowell 1981). As noted by Kunkel et al., "Rather than informing young viewers about the importance of a nutritious breakfast, this common disclaimer actually leaves many children with the misimpression that cereal alone is sufficient for a meal" (2004).

FEATURES OF ADVERTISING
TO CHILDREN

Market researchers and advertisers have spent a great deal of time and effort understanding how to best appeal to child audiences (John 1999). Formal features of advertising to children include music, quick-cut editing, sound effects and animation—all used because they capture children's attention (Huston and Wright 1989). Utilizing findings from educational research indicating that repetition is an effective educational strategy (especially for young children), television advertisers repeat ads more during children's programming than during adult programming (Kuribayashi, Roberts, and Johnson 2001). Marketers have also learned that products are most appealing when framed in terms of "fun" (Cantor 1981; Institute of Medicine 2006). The most common persuasive strategy employed in advertising to children is to associate the product with fun and happiness (Barcus 1980; Kunkel and Gantz 1992; Elliott 2008). Popular branded cartoon characters are frequently used in advertising directed to children because they aid children's recall and enhance children's product preference (Atkin and Block 1983; Lieber 1998; Kelly et al. 2008).

EFFECTS OF FOOD ADVERTISING
ON CHILDREN

There is little doubt that the diets of American children and adolescents are poor and do not meet national dietary goals (Cavadini, Siega-Riz, and Popkin 2000; Nicklas et al. 2001; Neumark-Sztainer et al. 2002). Moreover, U.S. food consumption data show a shift over the past few decades. Children and adolescents are eating more food away from home, drinking more soft drinks, and snacking more frequently (Jahns, Siega-Riz, and Popkin 2001; Gleason and Suitor 2001). In combination, American children now obtain over 50 percent of their calories from fat (32 percent) or added sugar (20 percent) (Gleason and Suitor 2001). But does this shift have anything to do with the heavy marketing of such foods to children?

There exist a fair number of studies examining the impact of advertising on children's food preferences, requests to parents for food products, and parental purchase of such products (Taras et al. 2000; Taras and Gage 1995; Taras et al. 1989; Borzekowski and Robinson 2001; McNeal 1998; Isler, Popper, and Ward 1987). Coon and Tucker (2002) recently reviewed this literature and came to the following conclusions: (1) evidence from experimental studies consistently show that exposure to advertised food products increases children's choice of and preference for such products; (2) exposure to televised food advertising increases children's requests to parents for the purchase of advertised items; and (3) purchase requests for specific brands or categories of food products reflect product advertising frequencies. Thus, there is a plethora of evidence that, from the perspective of marketers at least, food advertising works and it works well.

However, the critical question is whether televised food advertising actually increases children's *consumption* of advertised foods. Until recently, there was a great deal of evidence indicating that marketing increases children's preferences and requests for marketed foods, but relatively little evidence between marketing and the actual dietary *intake* of children and youth (Institute of Medicine 2006). A spate of recent studies have now largely filled this gap.

Studies have shown that television viewing in general is related to poor dietary intake (Barr-Anderson et al. 2009; Boynton-Jarrett et al. 2003). Boynton-Jarrett et al. (2003) found that television viewing was inversely associated with fruit and vegetable intake among adolescents. They hypothesize that this relationship is the result of replacement of fruits and vegetables in youth's diets by foods highly advertised on television. Barr-Anderson et al. (2009) found that television viewing among high school students was related to lower intakes of fruits, vegetables, whole-grain and calcium-rich foods, and higher intakes of trans fat, fried foods, fast foods, snack products, and sugar-sweetened beverages (which the authors note are the most commonly advertised) five years later.

However, studies examining total viewing time and diet cannot address the question of whether dietary intake is the result of marketing, or the popular notion that television viewing encourages "mindless" eating, resulting in greater caloric intake. A number of studies now exist which directly address this question (Buijzen, Schuurman, and Bomhof 2008; Harris, Bargh, and Brownell 2009).

Gorn and Goldberg (1982) conducted the now classic study examining the effect of exposure to televised snack food commercials on children's actual food consumption. Children ages 5–8 years old attending a summer camp viewed a 30-minute cartoon with roughly 5 minutes of embedded food advertising daily for two weeks. The kinds of advertising were varied to create four experimental conditions: (1) candy and Kool-Aid ads; (2) fruit and fruit juice ads; (3) public service ads for healthy foods; and (4) no ads (control). Each day after the television exposure, the children were offered a selection of fruits, juices, candy, or Kool-Aid to choose from for their snack. Children in the candy/Kool-Aid commercials condition chose candy as their snack more than children in the fruit ad conditions did, and also chose fruit and juice less than children in any other condition did.

Hitchings and Moynihan (1998) found that 9–11 year old children's recall of food advertisements was related to consumption of the advertised food as assessed by three-day food diaries. The researchers report correlations between children's knowledge of specific food advertisements and food consumption on the order of between .50 and .60. A more recent study (Halford et al. 2004) of recognition of food advertising and consumption of specific foods in response to advertising found that overweight and obese children recognized more ads and ate more of the food advertised following experimental exposures to food advertising compared to normal weight children. However, all children in this study, regardless of weight, ate more of the advertised food following exposure to televised advertising compared to controls.

Buijzen, Schuurman, and Bomhof (2008) examined the associations between children's exposure to food advertising and their consumption of advertised brands, advertised energy-dense food products, and food products overall among a sample of 234 Dutch children ages 4–12 years old. They found that exposure to food advertising was significantly and positively related to children's consumption of advertised brands and advertised energy-dense food products. The relation between children's consumption of food products overall and exposure to advertising was moderated by socioeconomic status (SES) and consumption-related family communication. The authors note that consumption of advertised brands and energy dense foods were associated with amount of advertising exposure, but not television time overall, suggesting that the caloric intake associated with viewing is the direct result of advertising, rather than simply increased eating while viewing (Buijzen, Schuurman, and Bomhof 2008).

Harris, Bargh, and Brownell (2009) found that elementary school-aged children exposed to advertising consumed 45 percent more snacks after exposure, compared to children who were not exposed. The authors note that the difference between the two groups of children amounted to an additional 94 kilocalories consumed daily, which would lead to a weight gain of almost 10 pounds per year. The authors also note that the lack of significant moderating effects of child characteristics suggests the considerable power of food advertising to consistently influence consumption across a highly diverse sample of children.

PROMOTING HEALTHY FOOD CHOICES: THE POTENTIAL OF PSAs

Overall, then, the existing literature indicates that children are susceptible to advertising, and that their food preferences, food choices, and food intake are shaped by their exposure to food advertising. In some sense, this should be no surprise, since it is tantamount to saying that children learn the things they are taught. If this is so, then we should be able to shape children's food behaviors in more desirable ways through advertising of healthy foods and food behaviors.

Various studies have demonstrated that children who were shown ads for healthy products or pro-nutritional PSAs chose more fruit and juice than those seeing ads for sugared products (Gorn and Goldberg 1982), ate fewer sugared foods in a post-viewing test (Galst and White 1976), and scored higher on nutritional knowledge tests (Sylvester, Achterberg, and Williams 1995). Recently, *Sesame Workshop*™ has been exploring the issue of whether the appeal of well-known *Sesame Street*® characters would increase children's preferences for fruits and vegetables. They found that placing a favorite Muppet character sticker on foods increased children's preferences for those foods, and that placing a character sticker on a healthier food (broccoli) could increase children's preference for that food over a less healthy choice (a chocolate bar). Though the children were choosing pictures of the foods rather than the foods themselves, these findings suggest that the simple placement of stickers depicting popular and well-known characters on healthier foods could play an important role in increasing the appeal of healthy foods (Cohen and Kotler 2005). Given evidence that it is easier to reinforce children's preferences for sweet and/or high-fat foods than for healthier foods (Birch 1992, 1999), these findings are promising.

SUMMARY AND CONCLUSIONS

There is little doubt that the diets of American children and adolescents do not meet national dietary goals (Cavadini, Siega-Riz, and Popkin 2000; Nicklas et al. 2001; Neumark-Sztainer et al. 2002). The question at hand is whether this is due in large part to food marketing. Taken as a whole, existing evidence implicates food advertising as a major mechanism linking television and other screen-media use with childhood obesity. A recent World Health Organization/Food and Agriculture Organization (WHO/FAO) report concluded that sufficient (albeit indirect) evidence exists that advertising of fast food restaurants and high-caloric, nutrient-poor food and beverages to children promotes obesity to suggest advertising as a "probable" causal factor in youth obesity (World Health Organization 2003). The even more recently released Institute of Medicine (IOM) report, *Food Marketing to Children and Youth: Threat or Opportunity?* (2006), came to a similar conclusion: Although evidence linking food advertising to childhood obesity is insufficient to support a call for a ban on all such advertising, enough evidence exists to support recommending approaches similar to those used to control cigarette and alcohol advertising to children (Institute of Medicine 2006).

Despite the conclusions of both the WHO and the IOM, it is important to note that the data connecting marketing to adiposity remains correlational. The IOM (2006) notes that though the data are consistent with the interpretation that marketing to children is at least partly causing weight problems, it is not possible to rule out every alternative explanation at this time. Even so, they argue that even a small causal relation translates into a very large health problem (IOM 2006). Using NHANES 2003–2004 data to conduct mathematical simulation models, Veerman et al. (2009) found that reducing televised food marketing exposure to zero would decrease the prevalence of obesity by roughly 2 percent. The authors conclude that their models indicate that from one in seven to one in three obese children in the United States might not have been obese in the absence of advertising for unhealthy food (Veerman et al. 2009).

In sum, existing evidence suggests that televised advertising for high-fat and sugared foods is one probable mechanism linking electronic media with childhood obesity. Yet, there are limitations to existing research. Though the research literature is growing, no meta-analysis examining the size of the relationship between food advertising and children's food preferences, food choices, food intake, or purchase requests has been undertaken, and prospective longitudinal studies are similarly absent (see however, the Institute of Medicine 2006 for the most comprehensive and recent review available at this time). There is a particular need for research focusing on key moderators of the relationship between advertising and caloric intake, as well as questions pertaining to food advertising and marketing exposure of ethnic minority children.

It seems likely that televised and other screen-based food marketing use is implicated in the childhood obesity epidemic in this country. If this is true, then it behooves public health scholars to understand the ways (and for whom) it is implicated—as well as the ways (and for whom) it is not. As a very real threat to public health, it is crucial to identify central contributing factors to the development of obesity, so that we may appropriately target prevention and intervention efforts. It seems safe to say that technology is here to stay, and is virtually guaranteed to play an ever-increasing role in young people's daily lives. Thus, a thorough understanding of the nature of its impact on health and well-being is a vital component of the public health agenda in the United States.

ACKNOWLEDGEMENTS

Funding for this research was provided by grant 1 R01 HD053652-01A1 from the National Institute of Child Health and Human Development, grant WTG 7236 from the William T. Grant Foundation, and the Children's Digital Media Center (funded by Grant BCS-0623856 from the National Science Foundation).

REFERENCES

Abbatangelo-Gray, Jodie, Carol Byrd-Bredbenner, and S. Bryn Austin. 2008. "Health and Nutrient Content Claims in Food Advertisements on Hispanic And Mainstream Prime-Time Television." *Journal of Nutrition Education and Behavior* 40(6): 348–354.

Adams, J., K. Hennessy-Priest, S. Ingimarsdóttir, J. Sheeshka, T. Ostbye, and M. White. 2009. "Food Advertising during Children's Television in Canada and the UK." *Archives of Disease in Childhood* 94(9): 658–662.

American Academy of Pediatrics. 2001. "Children, Adolescents, and Television." *Pediatrics* 107: 423–426.

Atkin, C., and M. Block. 1983. "Effectiveness of Celebrity Endorsers." *Journal of Advertising Research* 23: 57–61.

Barcus, F. E. 1980. "The Nature of Television Advertising to Children." In Edward L. Palmer (Ed.), *Children and the Faces of Television*: 273–285.

Bar-Or, O., J. Foreyt, C. Bouchard, K. D. Brownell, W. H. Dietz, E. Ravussin, A. D. Salbe, S. Schwenger, S. St. Jeor, and B. Torun. 1998. "Physical Activity, Genetic and Nutritional Considerations in Childhood Weight Management." *Medicine and Science in Sports and Excercise* 30: 2–10.

Barr-Anderson, Daheia J., Nicole I. Larson, Melissa C. Nelson, Dianne Neumark-Sztainer, and Mary Story. 2009. "Does Television Viewing Predict Dietary Intake Five Years Later in High School Students and Young Adults?" *The International Journal Of Behavioral Nutrition And Physical Activity* 6: 7–7.

Batada, Ameena, Maia Dock Seitz, Margo G. Wootan, and Mary Story. 2008. "Nine Out of 10 Food Advertisements Shown during Saturday Morning Children's Television Programming are for Foods High in Fat, Sodium, or Added Sugars, or Low in Nutrients." *Journal of the American Dietetic Association* 108(4): 673–678.

Batada, Ameena, and Margo G. Wootan. 2007. "Nickelodeon Markets Nutrition-Poor Foods to Children." *American Journal of Preventive Medicine* 33(1): 48–50.

Bell, Robert A., Diana Cassady, Jennifer Culp, and Rina Alcalay. 2009. "Frequency and Types of Foods Advertised on Saturday Morning and Weekday Afternoon English- and Spanish-Language American Television Programs." *Journal of Nutrition Education and Behavior* 41(6): 406–413.

Birch, L. L. 1992. "Children's Preferences for High-Fat Foods." *Nutrition Review* 50: 249–255.

Birch, L. L. 1999. "Development of Food Preferences." *Annual Review of Nutrition* 1999: 41–62.

Bloomgarden, Z. T. 2004. "Type 2 Diabetes in the Young: The Evolving Epidemic." *Diabetes Care* 27: 998–1010.

Borzekowski, D. L. G, and T. N. Robinson. 2001. "The 30 Second Effect: An Experiment Revealing the Impact of Television Commercials on Food Preferences of Preschoolers." *Journal of the American Dietetic Association* 101(1): 42–46.

Boynton-Jarrett, R., T. N. Thomas, K. E. Peterson, J. Wiecha, A. M. Sobol, and S. L. Gortmaker. 2003. "Impact of Television Viewing Patterns on Fruit and Vegetable Consumption." *Pediatrics* 112: 1321–1326.

Buijzen, Moniek, Joris Schuurman, and Elise Bomhof. 2008. "Associations between Children's Television Advertising Exposure and Their Food Consumption Patterns: A Household Diary-Survey Study." *Appetite* 50(2–3): 231–239.

Byrd-Bredbenner, C. 2002. "Saturday Morning Children's Television Advertising: A Longitudinal Content Analysis." *Family and Consumer Science Research* 30: 382–403.

Calvert, S. 2003. "Future Faces of Selling to Children." In *The Faces of Televisual Media*, eds. E. L. Palmer and B. M. Young. Mahwah, NJ: Lawrence Earlbaum Associates.

Cantor, J. 1981. "Modifying Children's Eating Habits through Television Ads: Effects of Humorous Appeals in a Field Setting." *Journal of Broadcasting* 25: 37–47.

Caroli, M., L. Argentieri, M. Cardone, and A. Masi. 2004. "Role of Television in Childhood Obesity Prevention." *International Journal of Obesity* 28: S104–S108.

Carruth, B. R., J. D. Skinner, J. D. Moran, and F. Coletta. 2000. "Preschoolers' Food Product Choices at a Simulated Point of Purchase and Mothers' Consumer Practices." *Journal of Nutrition Education* 32(3): 146–151.

Cavadini, C., A. M. Siega-Riz, and B. M. Popkin. 2000. "US Adolescent Food Intake Trends from 1965 to 1996." *The Western Journal of Medicine* 173: 378–383.

Chapman, K., P. Nicholas, and R. Supramaniam. 2006. "How Much Food Advertising Is There on Australian Television?" *Health Promotion International* 21: 172–180.

Chen, J. L., and C. M. Kennedy. 2001. "Televison Viewing and Children's Health." *Journal of Science and Pediatric Nursing* 6: 35–38.

Cohen, D. I., and J. A. Kotler. 2005. "Preschoolers' Perceptions of Healthy Food." In *Society for Research in Child Development*. Atlanta, Georgia.

Coon, K. A., and K. Tucker. 2002. "Television and Children's Consumption Patterns: A Review of the Literature." *Minerva Pediatrica* 54: 423–436.

Dietz, W. H. 2001. "The Obesity Epidemic in Young Children: Reduce Television Viewing and Promote Playing." *British Medical Journal* 322: 313–314.

Dietz, W. H., and S. L. Gortmaker. 1985. "Do We Fatten Our Children at the Television Set? Obesity and Television Viewing in Children and Adolescents." *Pediatrics* 75: 807–812.

Elliott, C. 2008. "Assessing 'Fun Foods': Nutritional Content and Analysis of Supermarket Foods Targeted at Children." *Obesity Reviews: An Official Journal of the International Association for the Study of Obesity* 9(4): 368–377.

Freedman, D. S., W. H. Dietz, S. R. Srinivasan, and G. S. Berenson. 1999. "The Relation of Overweight to Cardiovascular Risk Factors among Children and Adolescents: The Bogalusa Heart Study." *Pediatrics* 103: 1175–1182.

Gallo, A. E. 1999. "Food Advertising in the United States." In *America's Eating Habits: Changes and Consequences*. ed. E. Frazao. Washington, DC: Economic Research Service, United States Department of Agriculture.

Galst, J., and M. White. 1976. "The Unhealthy Persuader: The Reinforcing Value of Television and Children's Purchase Influence Attempts at the Supermarket." *Child Development* 47: 1089–1096.

Gamble, M., and N. Cotunga. 1999. "A Quarter Century of TV Food Advertising Targeted at Children." *American Journal of Health Behavior* 23: 261–267.

Gantz, W., N. Schwartz, J. R. Angelini, and V. Rideout. 2007. *Food for Thought: Television Food Advertising to Children in the United States*. Menlo Park: The Kaiser Family Foundation.

Gleason, P., and C. Suitor. 2001. *Children's Diets in the Mid 1990's: Dietary Intake and Its Relationship with School Meal Preparation*. Alexandria, VA: U.S. Dept. of Agriculture, Food and Nutrition Service.

Gleason, P., and C. Suitor. 2001. *Food for Thought: Children's Diets in the 1990s*. Princeton: Mathematica Policy Research.

Gorn, G. J., and M. E Goldberg. 1982. "Behavioral Evidence for the Effects of Televised Food Messages to Children." *Journal of Consumer Research* 9: 200–205.

Gortmaker, S. L., A. Must, J. M. Perrin, A. M. Sobol, and W. H. Dietz. 1993. "Social and Economic Consequences of Overweight in Adolescence and Young Adulthood." *The New England Journal of Medicine* 329(14): 1008–1012.

Greenberg, Bradley S., Sarah F. Rosaen, Tracy R. Worrell, Charles T. Salmon, and Julie E. Volkman. 2009. "A Portrait of Food and Drink in Commercial TV Series." *Health Communication* 24(4): 295–303.

Halford, J. C. G., J. Gillespie, V. Brown, E. E. Pontin, and H. Dowling. 2004. "Effect of Television Advertisements for Foods on Food Consumption in Children." *Appetite* 42: 221–225.

Harris, Jennifer L., John A. Bargh, and Kelly D. Brownell. 2009. "Priming Effects of Television Food Advertising on Eating Behavior." *Health Psychology: Official Journal of the Division of Health Psychology, American Psychological Association* 28(4): 404–413.

Harris, J. M., P. Kaufman, S. Martinez, and C. Price. 2002. *The US Food Marketing System, 2002*. Washington, DC: Economic Research Service, United States Department of Agriculture.

Harris, Jennifer L., Jennifer L. Pomeranz, Tim Lobstein, and Kelly D. Brownell. 2009. "A Crisis in the Marketplace: How Food Marketing Contributes to Childhood Obesity and What Can Be Done." *Annual Review of Public Health* 30(1): 211–225.

Harrison, K., and A.L. Marske. 2005. "Nutritional Content of Foods Advertised during the Television Programs Children Watch Most." *American Journal of Public Health* 95: 1568–1574.

Hastings, G., M. Stead, and L. McDermott. 2002. "From the Billboard to the School Canteen: How Food Promotion Influences Children." *Education Review* 17: 17–23.

Hauner, H. 2004. "Transfer into Adulthood." In *Obesity in Childhood and Adolescence*, eds. W. Kiess, C. Marcus and M. Wabitsch. Basel: Karger.

Hitchings, E., and P. J. Moynihan. 1998. "The Relationship between Television Food Advertisements Recalled and Actual Foods Consumed by Children." *Journal of Human Nutrition and Dietetics* 11: 511–517.

Hite, C. F., and R. E Hite. 1994. "Reliance on Brand by Young Children." *Journal of the Market Research Society* 37(2): 185–193.

Huston, A. C., and J. A. Wright. 1989. "Television Forms and Children." In *Public Communication and Behavior*, ed. G. Comstock. New York: Academic Press.

Huston, A. C., Wright, J. C., Marquis, J., & Green, S. B. (1999). How young children spend their time: Television and other activities. *Developmental Psychology*, 35, 912–925.

Institute of Medicine. 2005. *Preventing Childhood Obesity: Health in the Balance*. Washington, DC: National Academies Press.

Institute of Medicine. 2006. *Food Marketing to Children and Youth: Threat or Opportunity?* Washington, DC: National Academies Press.

Isler, L., H. T. Popper, and S. Ward. 1987. "Children's Purchase Requests and Parental Responses: Results from a Diary Study." *Journal of Advertising Research* 27: 28–39.

Jahns, L., A. M. Siega-Riz, and B. M. Popkin. 2001. "The Increasing Prevalence of Snacking among US Children from 1977 to 1996." *Journal of Pediatrics* 138: 493–498.

Janz, K. F., J. D. Dawson, and L. T. Mahoney. 2000. "Tracking Physical Fitness and Physical Activity from Childhood to Adolescence: The Muscatine Study." *Medicine and Science in Sports and Excercise* 32: 1250–1257.

John, D. R. 1999. "Consumer Socialization of Children: A Retrospective Look at Twenty-Five Years of Research." *Journal of Consumer Research* 26 (December): 183–213.

Kaiser Family Foundation. 1999. *Kids and Media @ the New Millennium*. Menlo Park, CA: Author.

Kaiser Family Foundation. 2003. *Zero to Six: Media Use in the Lives of Infants, Toddlers, and Preschoolers*. Menlo Park, CA: Author.

Kaiser Family Foundation. 2005. *Generation M: Media in the Lives of 8–18 Year Olds*. Menlo Park, CA: Author.

Kaiser Family Foundation. 2006. *The Media Family: Electronic Media in the Lives of Infants, Toddlers, Preschoolers and Their Parents*. Menlo Park, CA: Author.

Kaiser Family Foundation. 2009. *Generation M2: Media in the Lives of 8–18 Year Olds*. Menlo Park: Kaiser Family Foundation.

Kelly, Bridget, Libby Hattersley, Lesley King, and Victoria Flood. 2008. "Persuasive Food Marketing to Children: Use of Cartoons and Competitions in Australian Commercial Television Advertisements." *Health Promotion International* 23(4): 337–344.

Kotz, K., and M. Story. 1994. "Food Advertisements during Children's Saturday Morning Television Programming: Are They Consistent with Dietary Recommendations?" *Journal of the American Dietetic Association* 94(11): 1296–1301.

Kretchmer, S. B. 2004. "Advertainment: The Evolution of Product Placement as a Mass Media Marketing Strategy." *Journal of Promotion Management* 10: 37–54.

Krishnamoorthy, J. S., C. Hart, and E. Jelalian. 2006. "The Epidemic of Childhood Obesity: Review of Research and Implications for Public Policy." *SRCD Social Policy Report* 19: 2–17.

Kunkel, D. 2001. "Children and Television Advertising." In *The Handbook of Children and Media*, edited by D. G. Singer and J. L. Singer. Thousand Oaks, CA: Sage.

Kunkel, D., and W. Gantz. 1992. "Children's Television Advertising in the Multi-Channel Environment." *Journal of Communication* 42(3): 134–152.

Kunkel, D., B. L. Wilcox, J. Cantor, E. Palmer, S. Linn, and P. Dowrick. 2004. *Report of the APA Task Force on Advertising and Children*. Washington, D.C.: American Psychological Association.

Kuribayashi, A., M. C. Roberts, and R. J. Johnson. 2001. "Actual Nutritional Information of Products Advertised to Children and Adults on Saturday." *Children's Health Care* 30: 309–322.

Lauro, P. W. 1999. "Coaxing the Smile That Sells: Baby Wranglers in Demand in Marketing for Children." *New York Times*: C1.

Lieber, L. 1998. *Commercial and Character Slogan Recall by Children Aged 9 to 11 Years: Budweiser Frogs versus Bugs Bunny*. Berkeley, CA: Center on Alcohol Advertising.

Linn, S E. 2004. "Food Marketing to Children in the Context of a Marketing Maelstrom." *Journal of Public Health Policy* 25 (3–4): 367–378.

Lobstein, T., Baur, L., Uauy, R. 2005. "Obesity in Children and Young People: A Crisis in Public Health. Report to the World Health Organization by the International Obesity Task Force." *Obesity Reviews* 5 (Supp. 1): 5–104.

Marshall, S. J., S. J. H. Biddle, T. Gorley, N. Cameron, and I Murdey. 2004. "Relationships between Media Use, Body Fatness and Physical Activity in Children and Youth: A Meta-Analysis." *International Journal of Obesity* 28: 1238–1246.

McCall, K. L. 2003. *What's the Big Dif?: Differences between Marketing and Advertising.* Accessed October 3, 2005. Available from http://www.marketingprofs.com/preview. asp?file=/2/mccall5.asp.

McNeal, J. 1998. "Tapping the Three Kids' Markets." *American Demographics* 20(4): 37–41.

Moore, E. S. 2006. *It's Child's Play: Advergaming and the Online Marketing of Food to Children.* Menlo Park: The Kaiser Family Foundation.

Must, A. 1996. "Morbidity and Mortality Associated with Elevated Body Weight in Children and Adolescents." *American Society for Clinical Nutrition*: 63S, 445S–447S.

Must, A., P. F. Jacques, G. E. Dallal, C. J. Bajema, and W. H. Dietz. 1992. "Long-term Morbidity and Mortality of Overweight Adolescents: A Follow-Up of the Harvard Growth Study 1922 to 1935." *The New England Journal of Medicine* 327: 1350.

Must, A., J. Spadano, E. H. Coakley, A. E. Field, G. Colditz, and W. H. Dietz. 1999. "The Disease Burden Associated with Overweight and Obesity." *Journal of the American Medical Association* 282: 1523–1529.

Neumark-Sztainer, D., M. Story, P. J. Hannan, and J. Croll. 2002. "Overweight Status and Eating Patterns among Adolescents: Where Do Youths Stand in Comparison with the Healthy People 2010 Objectives?" *American Journal of Public Health* 92: 844–851.

Nicklas, T. A., A. Elkasabany, S.R. Srinivasan, and G. Berenson. 2001. "Trends in Nutrient Intake of 10-Year-Old Children over Two Decades (1973–1994): The Bogalusa Heart Study." *American Journal of Epidemiology* 153: 969–977.

Ogden, C. L., M. D. Carroll, L. R. Curtin, M. A. McDowell, C. J. Tabak, and K. M. Flegal. 2006. "Prevalence of Overweight and Obesity in the United States, 1999–2004." *Journal of the American Medical Association* 295: 1549–1555.

Ogden, C. L., K. Flegal, M. D. Carrol, and C. L. Johnson. 2002. "Prevalence and Trends in the Overweight among US Children and Adolescents, 1999–2000." *Journal of the American Medical Association* 288: 1728–1732.

Palmer, E., and C. Carpenter. 2006. "Food and Beverage Marketing to Children and Youth: Trends and Issues." *Media Psychology* 8: 165–190.

Palmer, E., and C. McDowell. 1981. "Children's Understanding of Nutritional Information Presented in Breakfast Cereal Commercials." *Journal of Broadcasting* 25: 295–301.

Rice, F. 2001. "Superstars of Spending: Marketers Clamor for Kids." *Advertising Age,* February 12, S1.

Schor, J. 2005. *Born to Buy: The Commercialized Child and the New Consumer Culture.* New York: Scribners.

Stitt, C., and D. Kunkel. 2008. "Food Advertising during Children's Television Programming pn Broadcast and Cable Channels." *Health Communication* 23(6): 573–584.

Story, M., and S. French. 2004. "Food Advertising and Marketing Directed at Children and Adolescents in the US." *International Journal of Behavioral Nutrition and Physical Activity* 1: 3–20.

Story, M., D. Neumark-Sztainer, and S. French. 2002. "Individual and Environmental Influences on Adolescent Eating Behaviors." *Journal of The American Dietetic Association* 102: S40–51.

Sylvester, G. P., C. Achterberg, and J. Williams. 1995. "Children's Television and Nutrition: Friends or Foes?" *Nutrition Today* 30: 6–14.

Taras, H. L., and M. Gage. 1995. "Advertised Foods on Children's Television." *Archives of Pediatric and Adolescent Medicine* 149: 649–652.

Taras, H. L., J. F. Sallis, T. L. Patterson, P. R. Nader, and J. A. Nelson. 1989. "Television's Influence on Children's Diet and Physical Inactivity." *Journal of Development and Behavioral Pediatrics* 10: 176–180.

Taras, H., M. Zive, P. Nader, C.C. Berry, T. Hoy, and C. Boyd. 2000. "Television Advertising and Classes of Food Products Consumed in a Paediatric Population." *International Journal of Advertising* 19: 487–493.

Veerman, J. L., E. F. Van Beeck, J. J. Barendregt, and J. P. Mackenbach. 2009. "By How Much Would Limiting TV Food Advertising Reduce Childhood Obesity?" *European Journal of Public Health* 19: 365–369.

Wang, Youfa, and Tim Lobstein. 2006. "Worldwide Trends in Childhood Overweight and Obesity." *International Journal of Pediatric Obesity: IJPO: An Official Journal of the International Association for the Study of Obesity* 1(1): 11–25.

Ward, S., D. Wackman, and E. Wartella. 1977. *How Children Learn to Buy: The Development of Consumer Information Processing Skills.* Beverly Hills, CA: Sage Publications.

Webster, N. C., and B. S. Bulik. 2004. "Now Down to Business: Counting Gamer Thumbs." *Advertising Age:* S6–S7.

Wright, J. C., Huston, A. C., Vandewater, E. A., Bickham, D. S., Scantlin, R., Kotler, J., et al. (2001). American children's use of electronic media in 1997: A national survey. *Journal of Applied Developmental Psychology,* 22, 31–47.

World Health Organization. 2003. Joint WHO/FAO Expert Consultation on Diet, Nutrition and the Prevention of Chronic Disease. Geneva: Author.

Zollo, P. 1999. *Wise Up to Teens: Insight into Marketing and Advertising to Teenagers,* 2nd ed. Ithaca, NY: New Strategist Publications.

CHAPTER 22

PORTION SIZE AND THE OBESITY EPIDEMIC

TANJA V. E. KRAL AND
BARBARA J. ROLLS

INTRODUCTION

THE estimated prevalence of overweight and obesity among U.S. adults has risen sharply in recent years, up from 47 percent in 1971–1980 to 66 percent in 2003–2004 (Ogden, Carroll, et al. 2006; Ogden, Yanovski, et al. 2007). Over the same period, portion sizes of many commercially available foods and beverages have increased. Population-based analyses as well as a number of controlled studies indicate that large portions of energy-dense foods are associated with increased energy intake in adults and children. The aim of this chapter is to review these findings and to consider whether portion size plays a role in the etiology of obesity. Strategies for getting portions back in synchrony with energy needs will be considered.

Since the 1970s, portion sizes of foods consumed both inside and outside the home have increased so that portion sizes of most current marketplace foods and beverages in the United States exceed those offered in the past (Nielsen and Popkin 2003; Smiciklas-Wright, Mitchell, et al. 2003). The largest excess (700%) over serving size standards specified by the U.S. Department of Agriculture has occurred for energy-dense foods such as cookies, muffins, salty snacks, and fast food items

(Young and Nestle 2002, 2007). One strategy that food marketers, such as fast food restaurants, have adopted to promote sales of their products is to extend their brands with larger portion sizes. For example, one fast food restaurant made available a multilayer hamburger that provides 1,410 calories, or about half the calories that a moderately active, adult male requires per day (Quilliam 2006). Cross-cultural studies show that many portions of commercially available foods and beverages in the U.S. exceed those available in Europe. For example, it is estimated that food portion sizes in restaurants and supermarkets and portions designated in cookbooks in France tend to be 25 percent smaller than those in the United States (Rozin 2005). Europeans should not, however, be complacent about the potential impact of portion size on intake because food portion sizes in Europe have been increasing significantly over the past decade (Matthiessen, Fagt, et al. 2003; Young and Nestle 2007).

Consumption habits have also changed. While the average American spent approximately $888 for food consumed away from home in 1988, this rose to $1,859 in 2008 (United States Department of Agriculture 2009). Sales strategies, such as value size pricing, used by many fast food establishments and family restaurants entice consumers to purchase large quantities of foods for only a small price increase. Such value pricing is problematic because a number of studies show that large portions can facilitate overconsumption of calories.

EXPERIMENTAL STUDIES ON THE EFFECTS OF PORTION SIZE ON INTAKE IN ADULTS

Portion Size and Different Types of Foods

In one of the first investigations to assess the effects of portion size on intake, men and women were served one of four portions (500, 625, 750, and 1000 g) of a pasta entrée once a week for four weeks (Rolls, Morris, et al. 2002). One group of participants received the pasta portions on a plate, and a second group was presented with a serving dish and was asked to determine the amount of food on their plates. Participants consumed 30 percent more energy when served the largest entrée portion compared to when served the smallest entrée portion; however, their response to portion size changes was not affected by the serving method. These data show that the portion size of an amorphous food (i.e., one with an undefined shape) can significantly influence energy intake in adults. Difficulties in estimating the portion size of amorphous foods may contribute to the increase in intake when large portions are served (see section "Possible Mechanisms Underlying Portion Size Effects" below).

While foods with an amorphous shape present the biggest challenge for determining appropriate portions (Yuhas, Bolland, et al. 1989), the portion size of foods that are served in clearly defined units such as sandwiches also influences intake. When served different sizes (6, 8, 10, or 12 inches) of sandwiches on different occasions, females consumed 12 percent more energy and males consumed 23 percent more energy with the 12-inch sandwich compared with the 8-inch sandwich (Rolls, Roe, et al. 2004a). Package or container size can also affect how much food is prepared and eaten. For example, when frying chicken, women poured 4.3 ounces of cooking oil from a 32-ounce bottle, but only 3.5 ounces from a 16-ounce bottle (Wansink 1996). Similarly, when women were provided with a 2-pound box of spaghetti and asked to take out enough pasta to make a dinner for two, they removed an average of 302 strands. However, when given a one-pound box, women removed only 234 strands. A more recent study (Rolls, Roe, et al. 2004b) showed that energy intake from a pre-packaged, mid-afternoon snack (i.e., potato chips) increased for both males and females when the package size of the snack increased (28, 42, 85, 128, or 170 g). Participants did not compensate for the greater snack intake, so that when served the largest snack package compared to the smallest, subjects consumed an additional 143 calories at snack and dinner combined. In another study conducted in a movie theater, patrons provided with 240 grams of popcorn ate 45 percent more than patrons given 120 grams (Wansink and Kim 2005).

Intake of beverages is also affected by the portion served. When different beverages (cola, diet cola, or water) were served in two portions (360 g/12 fl. oz. or 540 g/18 fl. oz.), increasing the portion size significantly increased beverage intake. When served the caloric beverage, women increased their energy intake from the beverage by 10 percent and men by 26 percent. The energy from the beverages added to that from the foods consumed during the meal. Hence, serving large portions of caloric beverages at a meal can significantly increase overall energy intake (Flood, Roe, et al. 2006).

A key question is whether, after a bout of consuming excess calories stimulated by large portions, compensatory mechanisms will limit subsequent intake. One study tested this by increasing the portion size of all foods and beverages (100 percent, 150 percent, or 200 percent of baseline amounts) served over two consecutive days (Rolls, Roe, et al. 2006a). Increasing portions by 50 percent increased participants' daily energy intake by 16 percent, and increasing portions by 100 percent increased intake by 26 percent. An even longer study showed that increasing portions of all available foods and beverages by 50 percent over 11 days resulted in a mean increase in daily energy intake of 423 calories (Rolls, Roe, et al. 2007). This increase in daily energy intake was sustained over the 11-day period leading to a cumulative increase in intake of 4,636 calories (see figure 22.1). Additionally, when employees of a medical facility were provided with free box lunches of the same foods, but different portion sizes (767 kcal vs. 1528 kcal) for two one-month periods, participants' energy intake at lunch and 24-hour energy intake were 332 kcal/day and 278 kcal/day higher in the large lunch than the small lunch periods, respectively. Participants did not compensate for the increased energy intake over the four

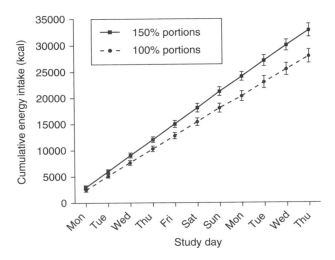

Figure 22.1. Mean cumulative energy intake for study participants served standard (100 percent) and large (150 percent) portions of all foods over 11 days. Serving larger portions significantly increased daily energy intake by an average of 423 kcal and the effect was sustained over the 11 days. Reproduced with permission from Obesity (2007;15:1535–1543), Nature Publishing Group.

weeks of exposure to the larger lunches (Jeffery, Rydell, et al. 2007). Thus the availability of large portions of food and beverages over a number of days is associated with a sustained increase in energy intake. Environmental cues related to portion size can override biological compensatory responses to excess energy consumption, supporting the possibility that large portions of energy-dense foods could play a role in the development of obesity.

Portion Size and Energy Density

Portion size affects intake across different types of foods and beverages, however, its effects on energy intake are most significant when consuming foods that are high in energy density. Energy density is the amount of energy provided in a particular weight of food (kcal/g). The main components of food that influence energy density are the fat content, which increases energy density, and the water content, which reduces it. While many studies (Bell, Castellanos, et al. 1998; Stubbs, Johnstone, et al. 1998; Rolls, Bell, et al. 1999; Bell and Rolls 2001) have examined the effects of energy density and portion size separately from each other, under free-living conditions the energy density and portion size of foods often vary simultaneously. Therefore, it is important to determine how these two factors interact with each other to affect energy intake. In a study by Kral and colleagues (Kral, Roe, et al. 2004), women were served breakfast, lunch, and dinner once a week for six weeks. The main entrée at lunch (pasta bake) was formulated in two versions that differed in energy density (1.25 or 1.75 kcal/g), each of which was served in three different portion sizes

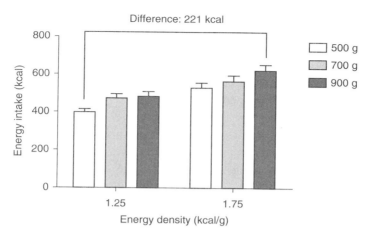

Figure 22.2. Mean energy intake at lunch when served an entrée that differed in energy density (1.25 or 1.75 kcal/g) and portion size (500, 700, or 900 g). Women consumed 56 percent more calories when served the largest portion of the higher-energy-dense entrée than when served the smallest portion of the lower-energy-dense entrée. Adapted from Kral et al. (Kral, Roe, et al. 2004); reproduced with permission from the *American Journal of Clinical Nutrition.*

(500, 700, or 900 g). In this study, increases in portion size and energy density resulted in independent and additive increases in energy intake. Women consumed 56 percent more energy (or 221 calories) when served the 900 g portion of the more energy-dense entrée compared to when served the 500 g portion of the less energy-dense entrée (see figure 22.2). The participants did not compensate for the additional energy by eating less at dinner, and they did not show any systematic differences in ratings of hunger and fullness across conditions.

These combined effects of portion size and energy density persist beyond a single meal. Another experiment was designed to determine whether decreases in portion size and energy density could be used strategically, either independently or in combination, to reduce energy intake over several days. Women were served the same two daily menus over a period of four weeks, but all foods were varied in portion size and energy density between a standard level (100 percent) and a reduced level (75 percent) (Rolls, Roe, et al. 2006b). A 25 percent decrease in portion size resulted in a 10 percent decrease in energy intake, and a 25 percent decrease in energy density resulted in a 24 percent decrease in energy intake. The effects of portion size and energy density were independent, and when combined, reduced daily energy intake by 32 percent, or by approximately 800 kcal each day. Despite this large difference in energy intake, participants reported no differences in how hungry or full they felt. These results indicate that changes in the portion size and energy density of foods do show potential to be used either independently or in combination to counter overconsumption without adversely affecting sensations of hunger and fullness.

Possible Mechanisms Underlying Portion Size Effects

The mechanisms by which portion size exerts its effects on intake are still poorly understood. Both visual cues (e.g., fill level of a dish) and cognitive factors (e.g., learning) are likely involved in estimating portion sizes and determining how much food to consume. Siegel suggested that people eat foods in units (1957). This was based on his finding that when different foods were proportioned into arbitrary units or servings, young men consumed whole units rather than intermediate amounts. Consumers appear to perceive food in units, or single entities that can guide their eating behavior (Geier, Rozin, et al. 2006). Also, consumption norms, such as culturally designated "appropriate" portions can influence food intake (Wansink 2004; Herman, Polivy, et al. 2005; Wansink, Painter, et al. 2005). Consumers' perceptions of standard or appropriate portion sizes are likely to be continually influenced by environmental cues stemming from the available foods. Food retailers, food packaging, and food labeling often set the standard for what consumers view as appropriate portion sizes.

Consumers not only have a distorted idea of appropriate portion sizes, but they also have difficulty estimating the size of portions and the calorie content. All of these factors could contribute to overconsumption when large portions are available (Lansky and Brownell 1982; Zegman 1984; Blake, Guthrie, et al. 1989; Howat, Mohan, et al. 1994; Ayala 2006). A study in young adults showed that only 34 percent of the portion size estimates and 22 percent of the calorie estimates for commonly consumed foods were within 25 percent of their actual amount (Schwartz and Byrd-Bredbenner 2006). Estimate accuracy depends on the shape and form of the food product and therefore is better for solid food than liquid or amorphous food (Yuhas, Bolland, et al. 1989). Visual illusions in which consumers tend to overestimate the length of a vertical line relative to a horizontal line with the same length can affect assessments of portion size (Piaget, Inhelder et al. 1960; van Ittersum and Wansink 2007). Children and adults perceive taller containers (e.g., glass, bottle) to hold more of a product (e.g., liquid) than shorter containers with larger diameters (Piaget 1969; Raghubir and Krishna 1999; Wansink and van Ittersum 2003; Wansink and van Ittersum 2005; Yang and Raghubir 2005). The shape of foods can also impact the visual perception of portion size. For example, study participants who were asked to serve an amount of thin or thick French fries that matched specific amounts of rice or French fries served a significantly smaller amount of thin compared to thick French fries (Wise, Arregui-Fresneda, et al. 2008).

Hence, difficulties in assessing food portions and acquired consumption norms may contribute to overeating when large portions of energy-dense foods are served, but more studies are needed to further examine these influences. More data are also needed to determine the extent to which individual characteristics such as differences in consumers' weight status may influence the accuracy of portion size estimates. One way to learn more about determinants of the influence of portion size on intake is to study children. It is likely that developmental factors and early experiences with foods play a role in shaping children's eating behavior and perception of portion sizes.

Portion Size, Energy Intake, and Weight Status in Children

Cross-sectional Studies

Given the high prevalence of overweight and obesity in children, it is important to isolate factors in their home food environments that promote excessive energy intake. Several cross-sectional studies examining the association between food portions and child body weight found that portion size was positively related to children's body weight. For example, Huang and colleagues (Huang, Howarth, et al. 2004) analyzed associations between eating behaviors and weight status of 3- to 19-year-old children and adolescents using data from the Continuing Surveys of Food Intakes by Individuals (CSFII). Results showed that meal portion size was positively related to the BMI-for-age percentile in boys 6 years and older and in girls 12 years and older. Another study used both cross-sectional and longitudinal samples of children to identify average quantities of commonly consumed foods (expressed as z-scores) and related those to children's body weight (McConahy, Smiciklas-Wright, et al. 2002). Results showed that average portion size z-scores were positively related to children's percentile body weight (expressed as BMI-for-age percentiles), indicating that children with greater body weights consumed larger food portions. Lastly, Lioret and colleagues (Lioret, Volatier, et al. 2009) obtained portion size estimates for foods from 23 food categories from 748 children between the ages of 3 and 11 years using 7-day food records. The results indicated that portion sizes of croissant-like pastries and other sweetened pastries were positively correlated with overweight in children ages 3 to 6 years.

Given the cross-sectional nature of these data, it cannot be determined if children in these studies attained their higher weight status as a result of being exposed to and consuming larger portions of food or if consuming larger portions of food is simply a reflection of these children's overall higher energy needs to maintain their higher body weight. More experimental and longer-term studies in children are needed to further establish if portion size effects on energy intake in children persist over a prolonged period of time, and if so, to determine the extent to which sustained increases in energy intake may affect the development of overweight and obesity in children.

Laboratory Studies with Children

A number of laboratory-based studies indicate that portion size can affect energy intake in children, although the effects have not been as consistent as those seen in adults. In the first study, 3- to 5-year-old children were served a small, medium, or large portion size of a lunch entrée (macaroni and cheese) (Rolls, Engell, et al. 2000). The findings showed that older children, but not younger children, consumed significantly more pasta when served the large portion compared to the small portion. These data suggested that children's responsiveness to environmental cues (such as the portion size of foods) started when they were about 5 years of age. Subsequent studies, however, showed that portion size effects were seen in children as young as 2 years of age. For example, Fisher (2007) assessed the effects of age on intake of age-appropriate (100 percent) compared to larger (200 percent) portions of an entrée among children 2–3, 5–6, and 8–9 years of age. Children in all age categories responded to the portion size manipulations. Their entrée intake was 29 percent greater and total energy intake was 13 percent greater when served the large compared to the small entrée portion. The data also showed that these increases in intake resulted from taking larger-sized bites. Although age-related differences in the response to portion size changes may be smaller than previously expected, results from another investigation (Fisher, Rolls, et al. 2003) with 3- to 6-year-old children indicated that older children showed larger increases in total energy intake when served a large portion size of a lunch entrée compared to younger children.

As was seen in adults, the effects of large portions on intake are sustained over multiple meals. In a recent study, 5-year-old children and their mothers were served 3 meals and a snack over a 24-hour period on two separate occasions (Fisher, Arreola, et al. 2007a). The portion size of the entrées (lunch, dinner, and breakfast) and an afternoon snack were varied (100 percent and 200 percent) while the size of the remaining foods and beverages remained constant. Doubling the portion size of the entrées and the snacks increased energy intake from those foods by 23 percent (180 calories) among children and by 21 percent (270 calories) among mothers. Total energy intake during the 24-hour period was 12 percent higher in children and 6 percent higher in mothers when served the large compared to the reference portions. While these data show that portion size effects are sustained in children across multiple meals to affect daily energy intake, it is not known whether compensatory behavior will be seen over a period longer than a day.

Portion Size and Energy Density

Under free-living conditions, children have access to foods that not only vary in portion size, but also differ in energy density. The energy density of foods has been identified as an important determinant of energy intake in preschool children. For example, when reducing the energy density of an entrée by 30 percent, 2- to 5-year-old children ingested 25 percent fewer calories (Leahy, Birch, et al. 2008a). It therefore is important to understand how both the portion size and the energy density of foods work together to influence children's energy intake. In a study with 5- and 6-year-old boys and girls, children were served two different energy densities (1.3 kcal/g vs. 1.8 kcal/g) of a pasta entrée, each of which was served in two portion sizes (250 g vs. 500 g) (Fisher, Liu, et al. 2007b). Children consumed 76 percent more energy from the entrée when served the larger portion size of the more energy-dense entrée, compared to when served the smaller portion size of the lower energy-dense entrée. The findings from this study showed that portion size and energy density added together to affect energy intake in children. Therefore, children may be particularly susceptible to overeating in environments where large portions of energy-dense foods are available.

Since both portion size and energy density influence children's intake, these food attributes could possibly be used positively to affect what and how much is eaten. This suggestion is supported by a study in which the energy density of a lunch entrée was decreased and the portion size was also decreased (Leahy, Birch, et al. 2008b). The energy density of a mixed pasta dish was varied by modifying the amount of vegetables in the entrée and by using cheeses with different fat content. Decreasing the energy density of the entrée by 25 percent significantly reduced children's energy intake from the entrée by 25 percent (63 calories) and total energy intake at lunch by 17 percent (61 calories) while increasing children's vegetable intake at lunch by half a serving of vegetables. Decreasing portion size of the entrée by 25 percent, however, did not significantly affect children's energy intake at lunch in this study. It is possible that the magnitude of the change in portion size (25 percent) in this study may not have been large enough to have affected children's intake. It is also conceivable that children's response to portion size changes may be food-specific. While the effects of portion size on children's intake have been variable, decreasing the energy density of foods has been shown to be a robust and effective strategy for moderating energy intake in children.

Although the data are not entirely consistent, they indicate that children as young as 2 years of age sometimes respond to portion size changes; however, the influence of large portions on children's eating becomes more consistent with increasing age. If susceptibility to large portion sizes is not firmly established in young children, strategies might be found that can diminish its development. One study showed that when 2- to 5-year-old children were allowed to serve themselves, they ate 25 percent less of a large main course, compared to when they were served the large portion by an adult (Orlet Fisher, Rolls, et al. 2003). Although more studies are needed, these data suggest that allowing children to serve themselves and to determine their own portions may help them to learn appropriate amounts to satisfy their hunger. It is also possible that the response to external cues such as portion size can be shaped by early experiences. This suggestion is supported by the finding that 4-year-old children who were taught to focus on satiety cues, indicated by the fullness of their stomachs, showed better self-regulation of energy intake than those who were rewarded for cleaning their plates (Birch, McPhee, et al. 1987). Thus, the response to portion size by children could be a learned behavior that leads to a shift away from internal hunger and satiety cues toward food cues in the external environment. Over time, individual child characteristics or home environmental factors such as parent feeding behaviors will play an important role in the development of children's eating behaviors or adherence to internal satiety cues.

Dietary Strategies to Moderate Portion Size Effects on Energy Intake

The studies reviewed above provide evidence that the portion size of foods is an important determinant of energy intake in both children and adults. In order for consumers to successfully counter the intake-promoting effects of portion size, it is crucial to develop sound dietary as well as food marketing strategies that can help consumers moderate their intake. Following is a list of examples of such strategies:

Promote Consumer Education and Awareness

- *Improve skills to estimate portion sizes in children and parents:* Parents create food environments that shape their children's early experiences with food and eating. Data from focus groups with mothers of 8- to 11-year-old children indicate that mothers often have limited knowledge about age-appropriate serving sizes for their children (Croker, Sweetman, et al. 2009). Some parents therefore may serve their children larger portions than are recommended. It is important that both parents and children acquire skills to identify age-appropriate portion sizes for foods consumed at home and away from home, especially for foods for which portion sizes are difficult to estimate (e.g., amorphous foods). Improving skills in children to identify age-appropriate food portions may be challenging in that children have difficulty assessing portion sizes because their perceptual abilities are still developing. Despite children's limited perceptual ability, a variety of tools exist that have proven helpful in teaching young children to estimate food portion sizes. For example, food photographs, food models, or interactive portion size assessment systems can increase the accuracy of portion size estimates in children (Foster, Matthews, et al. 2006, 2008; Foster, O'Keeffe, et al. 2008).
- *Improve skills among parents and caretakers surrounding child feeding practices:* Enhancing child feeding skills among parents and caretakers may play a crucial role in helping children meet, but not exceed, their daily energy requirements. Parent feeding strategies are particularly needed in environments where children are susceptible to overeating. For example, children who frequently eat while watching television or who frequent fast food restaurants reported a preference for larger portions of energy-dense foods, such as French fries and potato chips (Colapinto, Fitzgerald, et al. 2007). As mentioned previously, having children self-determine their own portions can help moderate their energy intake, especially when large food portions are available (Orlet Fisher, Rolls, et al. 2003). Parents should

ensure that they offer their children nutritious foods, and they should allow the children to determine how much to eat.

- *Improve skills to control portion sizes at restaurants*: Sixty-nine percent of Americans surveyed by the American Institute for Cancer Research said they finish entrées that they are served at a restaurant all or most of the time, regardless of the size (American Institute for Cancer Research 2009). Since portions often provide more energy than is needed and since the effects of overconsumption are not compensated for at subsequent meals, consumers need strategies to counter this trend. For example, they can share entrées or appetizers, order half-portions, if available, or save part of the entrée for another meal.

- *Train adults and children to adhere to satiety cues*: Food cues, such as portion size or ready availability, can override physiologic cues related to satiety. An experiment (Pudel and Oetting 1977) that was conducted in the late 1970s determined each participant's customary intake of soup over the course of three days. On the fourth day, they substituted a "trick bowl" that slowly refilled itself from a hidden reservoir as participants consumed soup from the bowl. The continual presence of soup in the bowl led participants to increase their intake. Hence, visual cues related to the filling of the bowl overrode participants' internal cues of satiety. It is possible that teaching people to be more aware of satiety signals could help to counter the effects of large portions. While research shows that children can be trained to recognize and respond to physiologic cues related to satiety (Birch, McPhee, et al. 1987), practical strategies need to be developed that can be used to teach both children and adults to respond to satiety.

- *Increase knowledge surrounding portion size and calorie intake:* Many consumers may not be aware of the relationship between portion size and calorie intake. Therefore, educating them on findings from recent studies is important. Learning how to read nutrition labels, how to distinguish between serving sizes and portion sizes, and how to relate this information to their daily energy needs may help consumers identify and select more adequate food portions.

Food Labels and Point-of-purchase Information

One environmental strategy that could help consumers to make more healthful food choices is to require clear nutrition information which lists calories per portion served on food labels or restaurant menus. Data indicate that consumers, such as fast food patrons (O'Dougherty, Harnack, et al. 2006), as well as representatives from food service providers (Vermeer, Steenhuis, et al. 2009) generally support clearer portion-size labeling and point-of-purchase nutrition information related to calories. While there is not yet agreement on the best way to convey information about portion size to consumers, there are some relevant data. For example, a study assessed the effects in dieters and non-dieters of providing nutrition information for a single serving as well as the entire package (dual-column labels) versus single-serving nutritional information only (single-column label) on intake of a snack food (Antonuk and Block 2006). Non-dieting participants, but not dieting participants, consumed significantly less of the snack when provided with the dual-column label compared to the single-column label. These data indicate that more comprehensive nutritional information, which includes information about the nutritional content of the entire package as well as that in a single serving, can help some consumers moderate their energy intake.

Pricing Strategies

Value size pricing, which involves structuring product prices such that the per unit cost (e.g., price per weight) is lowest for larger portion sizes, should be discouraged. Instead, a wider range of portion sizes should be made available to consumers, and attractive pricing strategies should be developed that offer the same value for money for small and large portions and thereby promote the purchase of smaller portions. When assessing the impact of proportional pricing (i.e., removing beneficial prices for large sizes) on customers' portion size selections in a fast food restaurant, a study showed that pricing strategies can help overweight and obese consumers select more appropriate portions of soft drinks and high-calorie snacks (Vermeer, Steenhuis, et al. 2009). Although food providers find value pricing is appealing to customers and helps to sell products they must be encouraged to increase the availability of a greater range of portion sizes and to develop initiatives to make smaller portions of energy-dense foods more appealing.

Package Size and Portion-controlled Packaging

Portion-controlled meals, such as frozen meals or liquid meal replacements, can help consumers control their energy intake. These meals provide consumers with a structured eating experience and can reduce exposure to environmental food cues such as portion size. They can also be used as a tool to teach consumers appropriate portion sizes (Heymsfield, van Mierlo, et al. 2003).

A recent trend in the marketing of foods, particularly snack foods, is "portion-controlled packaging" which provides consumers with smaller, individually portioned packages of foods. To date, data on the impact of this new packaging strategy on consumers' consumption patterns are conflicting. When providing participants with two different package sizes of snack foods (standard packages vs. 100-kcal packages) for two 7-day periods, participants, on average, consumed 187 fewer grams of snacks per week when receiving the portion-controlled 100-kcal snacks compared to the standard size packages (Stroebele, Ogden, et al. 2009). Another study (Raynor and Wing 2007), however, found that the amount of snack provided, but not the package unit size, significantly affected participants' energy intake. The effects of portion-controlled packaging may depend on characteristics of the study participants. For example, Scott and colleagues (Scott, Nowlis, et al. 2008) found that dietary restraint, or the tendency to consciously restrict food intake to control body weight, moderated the effect of portion-controlled packaging on intake. While unrestrained eaters consumed more food when presented with larger packages, restrained eaters ate at least as much (and sometimes more) food when presented with smaller packages. Hence, portion-controlled packaging may only be beneficial for a subset of consumers, while others may perceive the smaller, calorie-controlled packaging as a license to eat more, particularly individuals trying to restrain their intake (Coelho do Vale, Pieters, et al. 2008; Scott, Nowlis, et al. 2008). Further studies are needed to determine the extent to which portion-controlled packaging may help with weight control efforts.

Serve Larger Portions of Healthy Foods

The effects of portion size on intake can be used strategically to promote intake of healthy foods among children. For example, when doubling the portion size of fruit and vegetable side dishes at a meal while holding the main entrée constant, children significantly increased their fruit (Mathias, Rolls, et al. 2009; Kral, Kabay, et al. 2010) and vegetable (Mathias, Rolls, et al. 2009) intake at the meal. Therefore, parents and food service providers at schools and day care settings should be encouraged to serve larger portions of healthy, low-energy-dense foods, such as fruits and vegetables, in order to promote intake of these foods among children. Serving larger portions of healthy foods can also be used to moderate energy intake at meals in adults. For example, when served a large portion of a first-course, low-energy-dense salad, women lowered their energy intake at the subsequent meal by 12 percent (Rolls, Roe, et al. 2004c). Hence, consuming larger portions of healthy, low-energy-dense foods either during a meal or at the beginning of a meal can be an effective dietary strategy to increase consumption of those foods while displacing intake from more energy-dense main entrées.

Reduce Portion Size and Energy Density

Restaurant patrons often equate large portions with greater value for their money compared to smaller portions (Mills 1998; Grindy 1999). Therefore, simply reducing portion sizes of restaurant meals and commercially available foods could affect sales and may be opposed by both restaurant owners as well as customers (O'Dougherty, Harnack, et al. 2006; Condrasky, Ledikwe, et al. 2007; Vermeer, Steenhuis, et al. 2009). While reducing the portion size of energy-dense foods is an important goal, another effective strategy to help consumers reduce energy intake is to reduce the energy density of foods. If energy density were reduced, people could still consume their usual portions while consuming fewer calories. Since the effects of energy density and portion size combine to determine energy intake, it is possible that small imperceptible reductions in both portion size and energy density of commonly consumed foods would not affect their appeal or sales but would help consumers to moderate energy intake.

Improve Nutrition Knowledge of Restaurant Chefs

Executive chefs are primarily responsible for establishing portion sizes served in restaurants. A recent survey among 300 chefs indicated that 76 percent perceived the portions they served as "regular" size portions (Condrasky, Ledikwe, et al. 2007). When comparing the portions chefs indicated that they served to those recommended by the U.S. government, it was apparent that the restaurant portions often exceeded current recommendations. Therefore, improving chefs' nutrition knowledge about calories and portion size may be an important step for bringing restaurant portions more in line with consumers' energy needs.

SUMMARY AND CONCLUSION

Large portions of energy-dense foods can promote excess energy intake in children and adults. This effect is sustained over a number of days and hence potentially can increase body weight. On the other hand, the availability of large portions can promote consumption of foods with low energy density, such as fruits and vegetables. The increase in consumption of these foods can moderate feelings of hunger, displace the consumption of more energy-dense foods, and help with weight regulation in children and adults. Data from behavioral treatment studies in children and their parents, as well as obese women, indicate that modifying diets to incorporate more low-energy-dense foods, such as fruits and vegetables, significantly reduced body weight in all participants while controlling their hunger (Epstein, Gordy, et al. 2001; Ello-Martin, Roe, et al. 2007; Epstein, Paluch, et al. 2008). Therefore, portion size should be seen not only as a contributor to energy overconsumption, but also represents an environmental factor which can be strategically modified to help reduce the excess energy intake that leads to overweight and obesity.

ACKNOWLEDGMENTS

Barbara J. Rolls is supported by NIH grants R37DK039177, R01DK059853, and R01DK082580, and Tanja V.E. Kral is supported by NIH grant K01DK078601.

REFERENCES

American Institute for Cancer Research. "Drop Out of the Clean Plate Club." Accessed November 16, 2009. http://www.aicr.org/site/News2?page=NewsArticle&id=7718&news_iv_ctrl=0&abbr=pr_hf_.

Antonuk, B., and L. G. Block (2006). "The Effect of Single Serving versus Entire Package Nutritional Information on Consumption Norms and Actual Consumption of a Snack Food." *Journal of Nutrition Education and Behavior* 38: 365–370.

Ayala, G. X. (2006). "An Experimental Evaluation of a Group- Versus Computer-Based Intervention to Improve Food Portion Size Estimation Skills." *Health Education Research* 21: 133–145.

Bell, E. A., V. H. Castellanos, et al. (1998). "Energy Density of Foods Affects Energy Intake in Normal-Weight Women." *American Journal of Clinical Nutrition* 67: 412–420.

Bell, E. A., and B. J. Rolls (2001). "Energy Density of Foods Affects Energy Intake across Multiple Levels of Fat Content in Lean and Obese Women." *American Journal of Clinical Nutrition* 73: 1010–1018.

Birch, L. L., L. McPhee, et al. (1987). "'Clean Your Plate': Effects of Child Feeding Practices on the Conditioning of Meal Size." *Learning and Motivation* 18: 301–317.

Blake, A. J., Guthrie, H. A., and H. Smiciklas-Wright (1989). "Accuracy of Food Portion Estimation by Overweight and Normal-Weight Subjects." *Journal of the American Dietetic Association* 89: 962–964.

Coelho do Vale, R., Pieters, R., and M. Zeelenberg. (2008). "Flying under the Radar: Perverse Package Size Effects on Consumption Self-Regulation." *The Journal of Consumer Research* 35: 380–390.

Colapinto, C. K., A. Fitzgerald, et al. (2007). "Children's Preference for Large Portions: Prevalence, Determinants, And Consequences." *Journal of the American Dietetic Association* 107: 1183–1190.

Condrasky, M., J. H. Ledikwe, et al. (2007). "Chefs' Opinions of Restaurant Portion Sizes." *Obesity* 15: 2086–2094.

Croker, H., Sweetman, C., and L. Cooke. (2009). "Mothers' Views on Portion Sizes for Children." *Journal of Human Nutrition and Dietetics: The Official Journal of the British Dietetic Association* 22: 437–443.

Ello-Martin, J. A., L. S. Roe, et al. (2007). "Dietary Energy Density in the Treatment of Obesity: A Year-Long Trial Comparing 2 Weight-Loss Diets." *American Journal of Clinical Nutrition* 85: 1465–1477.

Epstein, L. H., C. C. Gordy, et al. (2001). "Increasing Fruit and Vegetable Intake and Decreasing Fat and Sugar Intake in Families at Risk for Childhood Obesity." *Obesity Research* 9: 171–178.

Epstein, L. H., R. A. Paluch, et al. (2008). "Increasing Healthy Eating vs. Reducing High Energy-Dense Foods to Treat Pediatric Obesity." *Obesity* 16: 318–326.

Fisher, J. O. (2007). "Effects of age on children's intake of large and self-selected food portions." *Obesity* 15: 403–412.

Fisher, J. O., Rolls, B. J., and L. L. Birch. (2003). "Children's Bite Size and Intake of an Entree Are Greater with Large Portions Than with Age-Appropriate or Self-Selected Portions." *American Journal of Clinical Nutrition* 77: 1164–1170.

Fisher, J. O., A. Arreola, et al. (2007a). "Portion Size Effects on Daily Energy Intake in Low-Income Hispanic and African American Children and Their Mothers." *American Journal of Clinical Nutrition* 86: 1709–1716.

Fisher, J. O., Y. Liu, et al. (2007b). "Effects of Portion Size and Energy Density on Young Children's Intake at a Meal." *American Journal of Clinical Nutrition* 86: 174–179.

Flood, J. E., Roe, L. S., and B. J. Rolls. (2006). "The Effect of Increased Beverage Portion Size on Energy Intake at a Meal." *Journal of the American Dietetic Association* 106: 1984–1990.

Foster, E., J. N. Matthews, et al. (2008). "Children's Estimates of Food Portion Size: The Development and Evaluation of Three Portion Size Assessment Tools for Use with Children." *British Journal of Nutrition* 99: 175–184.

Foster, E., M. O'Keeffe, et al. (2008). "Children's Estimates of Food Portion Size: The Effect of Timing of Dietary Interview on the Accuracy of Children's Portion Size Estimates." *British Journal of Nutrition* 99: 185–190.

Foster, E., J. N. Matthews, et al. (2006). "Accuracy of Estimates of Food Portion Size Using Food Photographs—The Importance of Using Age-Appropriate Tools." *Public Health and Nutrition* 9: 509–514.

Geier, A. B., Rozin, P., and G. Doros. (2006). "Unit Bias: A New Heuristic That Helps Explain the Effect of Portion Size on Food Intake." *Psychological Science: A Journal of the American Psychological Society* 17: 521–525.

Grindy, B. (1999). "Value Judgments." *Restaurants USA*, National Restaurant Association. Accessed December 15, 2005. http://www.restaurant.org/rusa/magArticle. cfm?ArticleID=241.

Herman, C. P., Polivy, J., and T. Leone. (2005). "The Psychology of Overeating." In *Food, Diet, and Obesity, ed*. D. Mela, 115–136. Cambridge: Woodhead Publishing.

Heymsfield, S. B., C. A. van Mierlo, et al. (2003). "Weight Management Using a Meal Replacement Strategy: Meta and Pooling Analysis from Six Studies." *International Journal of Obesity and Related Metabolic Disorders* 27: 537–549.

Howat, P. M., R. Mohan, et al. (1994). "Validity and Reliability of Reported Dietary Intake Data." *Journal of the American Dietetic Association* 94: 169–173.

Huang, T. T., N. C. Howarth, et al. (2004). "Energy Intake and Meal Portions: Associations with BMI Percentile in U.S. children." *Obesity Research* 12: 1875–1885.

Jeffery, R. W., S. Rydell, et al. (2007). "Effects of Portion Size on Chronic Energy Intake." *The International Journal of Behavioral Nutrition and Physical Activity* 4: 27.

Kral, T. V. E., A. C. Kabay, et al. (2010). "Effects of Doubling the Portion Size of Fruit and Vegetable Side Dishes on Children's Intake at a Meal." *Obesity* 18: 521–527.

Kral, T. V. E., Roe, L. S., and B. J. Rolls (2004). "Combined Effects of Energy Density and Portion Size on Energy Intake in Women." *American Journal of Clinical Nutrition* 79: 962–968.

Lansky, D., and K. D. Brownell. (1982). "Estimates of Food Quantity and Calories: Errors in Self-Report among Obese Patients." *American Journal of Clinical Nutrition* 35: 727–732.

Leahy, K., Birch, L. L., and B. J. Rolls (2008a). "Reducing the Energy Density of an Entrée Decreases Children's Energy Intake at Lunch" *Journal of the American Dietetic Association* 108: 41–48.

Leahy, K. E., L. L. Birch, et al. (2008b). "Reductions in Entree Energy Density Increase Children's Vegetable Intake and Reduce Energy Intake." *Obesity* 16: 1559–1565.

Lioret, S., J. L. Volatier, et al. (2009). "Is Food Portion Size a Risk Factor of Childhood Overweight?" *European Journal of Clinical Nutrition* 63: 382–391.

Mathias, K. C., B. J. Rolls, et al. (2009). "Does Serving Children Larger Portions of Fruit Affect Vegetable Intake?" Obesity 17: S90.

Matthiessen, J., S. Fagt, et al. (2003). "Size Makes a Difference." *Public Health Nutrition* 6: 65–72.

McConahy, K. L., H. Smiciklas-Wright, et al. (2002). "Food Portions Are Positively Related to Energy Intake and Body Weight in Early Childhood." *The Journal of Pediatrics* 140: 340–347.

Mills, S. (1998). "Healthy Portions." *Restaurants USA*, National Restaurant Association. Accessed December 15, 2009. http://www.restaurant.org/rusa/magArticle. cfm?ArticleID=295.

Nielsen, S. J., and B. M. Popkin (2003). "Patterns and Trends in Food Portion Sizes, 1977–1998." *Journal of the American Medical Association* 289: 450–453.

O'Dougherty, M., L. J. Harnack, et al. (2006). "Nutrition Labeling and Value Size Pricing at Fast-Food Restaurants: A Consumer Perspective." *American Journal of Health Promotion* 20(4): 247–250.

Ogden, C. L., M. D. Carroll, et al. (2006). "Prevalence of Overweight and Obesity in the United States, 1999–2004." *Journal of the American Medical Association* 295: 1549–1555.

Ogden, C. L., S. Z. Yanovski, et al. (2007). "The Epidemiology of Obesity." *Gastroenterology* 132: 2087–2102.

Orlet Fisher, J., Rolls, B. J., L. L. Birch. (2003). "Children's Bite Size and Intake of an Entree Are Greater with Large Portions Than with Age-Appropriate or Self-Selected Portions." *American Journal of Clinical Nutrition* 77: 1164–1170.

Piaget, J. (1969). *The Mechanisms of Perception.* London: Routledge Kegan Paul.

Piaget, J., Inhelder, B., and A. Szeminska. (1960). *The Child's Conception of Geometry.* New York: Harper Torchbooks.

Pudel, V. E., and M. Oetting. (1977). "Eating in the Laboratory: Behavioural Aspects of the Positive Energy Balance." *International Journal of Obesity* 1: 369–386.

Quilliam, E. T. (2006). "Mega, Monster or Misplaced? Do Portion Size Brand Extensions Meet Consumer Needs?" *Journal of Consumer Marketing* 23: 123–124.

Raghubir, P., and A. Krishna. (1999). "Vital Dimensions in Volume Perception: Can the Eye Fool the Stomach?" *Journal of Marketing Research* 36: 313–326.

Raynor, H. A., and R. R. Wing. (2007). "Package Unit Size and Amount Of Food: Do Both Influence Intake?" *Obesity* 15: 2311–2319.

Rolls, B. J., E. A. Bell, et al. (1999). "Energy Density but Not Fat Content of Foods Affected Energy Intake in Lean and Obese Women." *American Journal of Clinical Nutrition* 69: 863–871.

Rolls, B. J., Engell, D., and L. L. Birch. (2000). "Serving Portion Size Influences 5-Year-Old but Not 3-Year-Old Children's Food Intakes." *Journal of the American Dietetic Association* 100: 232–234.

Rolls, B. J., Morris, E. L., and L. S. Roe. (2002). "Portion Size of Food Affects Energy Intake in Normal-Weight and Overweight Men and Women." *American Journal of Clinical Nutrition* 76: 1207–1213.

Rolls, B. J., L. S. Roe, et al. (2004a). "Increasing the Portion Size of a Sandwich Increases Energy Intake." *Journal of the American Dietetic Association* 104: 367–372.

Rolls, B. J., L. S. Roe, et al. (2004b). "Increasing the Portion Size of a Packaged Snack Increases Energy Intake in Men And Women." *Appetite* 42: 63–69.

Rolls, B. J., Roe, L. S., and J. S. Meengs. (2004c). "Salad and Satiety: Energy Density and Portion Size of a First-Course Salad Affect Energy Intake at Lunch." *Journal of the American Dietetic Association* 104: 1570–1576.

Rolls, B. J., Roe, L. S., and J. S. Meengs. (2006a). "Larger Portion Sizes Lead to a Sustained Increase in Energy Intake over 2 Days." *Journal of the American Dietetic Association* 106: 543–549.

Rolls, B. J., Roe, L. S., J. S. Meengs. (2006b). "Reductions in Portion Size and Energy Density of Foods Are Additive and Lead to Sustained Decreases in Energy Intake." *American Journal of Clinical Nutrition* 83: 11–17.

Rolls, B. J., Roe, L. S., and J. S. Meengs. (2007). "The Effect of Large Portion Sizes on Energy Intake Is Sustained for 11 Days." *Obesity* 15: 1535–1543.

Rozin, P. (2005). "The Meaning of Food in Our Lives: A Cross-Cultural Perspective on Eating and Well-Being." *Journal of Nutrition Education and Behavior* 37: S107–S112.

Schwartz, J., and C. Byrd-Bredbenner. (2006). "The Ability of Young Adults to Estimate Portion Size and Calorie Content." *Topics in Clinical Nutrition* 21: 114–121.

Scott, M. L., S. M. Nowlis, et al. (2008). "The Effects of Reduced Food Size and Package Size on the Consumption Behavior of Restrained and Unrestrained Eaters." *The Journal of Consumer Research* 35: 391–405.

Siegel, P. S. (1957). "The Completion Compulsion in Human Eating." *Psychological Reports* 3: 15–16.

Smiciklas-Wright, H., D. C. Mitchell, et al. (2003). "Foods Commonly Eaten in the United States, 1989–1991 and 1994–1996: Are Portion Sizes Changing?" *Journal of the American Dietetic Association* 103: 41–47.

Stroebele, N., Ogden, L. G., and J. O. Hill. (2009). "Do Calorie-Controlled Portion Sizes of Snacks Reduce Energy Intake?" *Appetite* 52: 793–796.

Stubbs, R. J., A. M. Johnstone, et al. (1998). "Covert Manipulation of Energy Density of High Carbohydrate Diets in 'Pseudo Free-Living' Humans." *International Journal of Obesity and Related Metabolic Disorders* 22: 885–892.

United States Department of Agriculture. "Food CPI and Expenditures." Accessed November 24, 2009. http://www.ers.usda.gov/briefing/CPIFoodAndExpenditures/Data/Expenditures_tables/table13.htm.

van Ittersum, K., and B. Wansink. (2007). "Do Children Really Prefer Large Portions? Visual Illusions Bias Their Estimates and Intake." *Journal of the American Dietetic Association* 107: 1107–1110.

Vermeer, W. M., Steenhuis, I. H. M., and J. C. Seidell. (2009). "From the Point-of-Purchase Perspective: A Qualitative Study of the Feasibility of Interventions Aimed at Portion-Size." *Health Policy* 90: 73–80.

Wansink, B. (1996). "Can Package Size Accelerate Usage Volume?" *Journal of Marketing* 60: 1–14.

Wansink, B. (2004). "Environmental Factors That Increase the Food Intake and Consumption Volume of Unknowing Consumers." *Annual Review of Nutrition* 24: 455–479.

Wansink, B. and J. Kim. (2005). "Bad Popcorn in Big Buckets: Portion Size Can Influence Intake as Much as Taste." *Journal of Nutrition Education and Behavior* 37: 242–245.

Wansink, B., Painter, J. E., and J. North. (2005). "Bottomless Bowls: Why Visual Cues of Portion Size May Influence Intake." *Obesity Research* 13: 93–100.

Wansink, B., and K. Van Ittersum. (2003). "Bottom's Up! The Influence of Elongation on Pouring and Consumption Volume." *The Journal of Consumer Research* 30: 455–463.

Wansink, B., and K. van Ittersum. (2005). "Shape of Glass and Amount of Alcohol Poured: Comparative Study of Effect of Practice and Concentration." *British Medical Journal* 331: 1512–1514.

Wise, A., I. Arregui-Fresneda, et al. (2008). "Visual Perception of Portion Size. " *Ecology of Food and Nutrition* 47: 126–134.

Yang, S., and P. Raghubir (2005). "Can Bottles Speak Volumes? The Effect of Package Shape on How Much to Buy." *Journal of Retailing* 81: 269–282.

Young, L. R., and M. Nestle. (2002). "The Contribution of Expanding Portion Sizes to the US Obesity Epidemic." *American Journal of Public Health* 92: 246–249.

Young, L. R., and M. Nestle. (2007). "Portion Sizes and Obesity: Responses of Fast-Food Companies." *Journal of Public Health Policy* 28: 238–248.

Yuhas, J. A., Bolland, J. E., T. W. Bolland. (1989). "The Impact of Training, Food Type, Gender, and Container Size on the Estimation of Food Portion Sizes." *Journal of the American Dietetic Association* 89: 1473–1477.

Zegman, M. A. (1984). "Errors in Food Recording and Calorie Estimation: Clinical and Theoretical Implications for Obesity." *Addictive Behaviors* 9: 347–350.

CHAPTER 23

MINDLESS EATING: ENVIRONMENTAL CONTRIBUTORS TO OBESITY

BRIAN WANSINK

EVERYONE—every single one of us—eats how much we eat partially because of what is around us. We overeat not only because of hunger, but also because of family and friends, packages and plates, names and numbers, labels and lights, colors and candles, shapes and smells, distractions and distances, cupboards and containers. This list is almost as endless as it is invisible to us.

Most of us are largely unaware of what influences how much we eat. This is one of the ironies of food consumption research. Dozens of studies involving thousands of people show that people wrongly think that how much they eat is mainly determined by how hungry they are, how much they like the food, and what mood they are in (Wansink, Payne, and Chandon 2007). We all think we are too smart to be tricked by packages, lighting, or plates. This suggests that people may be influenced at a basic level of which they are not aware or which they do not monitor. Understanding these drivers of consumption volume has immediate implications for research, nutrition education, and consumer welfare (Meiselman 1992; Rozin and Tuorila 1993). This review aims to explain what environmental factors unknowingly influence consumption intake and why they do so.

When we examine how much one eats in the ecological context of the food environment, there are two common levels of analysis: macro-level and micro-level. At the macro-level, the focus is on government regulation, food industry incentives, school lunch programs, and advertising campaigns (Brownell and Horgren 2004). At the micro-level, the focus is on making a choice, such as between fresh fruit or a sweet snack.

Within this broad ecological context, there is an intermediate level that is often overlooked because it lies between the policy arena and personal choice. This intermediate level is the environment in which we live and work. It is a level that can influence food intake without involving the taste, texture, or quality of the food itself. That is, regardless of whether one is eating an apple or an apple pie, these environmental factors can often unknowingly drive intake. To avoid having to continually make caveats about different food categories, it is useful to differentiate those drivers that are independent of the food being examined from those that are more dependent.

We will use the term "eating environment" to refer to the ambient factors that are independent of food, such as atmosphere, the effort of obtaining food, the time of day, the social interactions that occur, and the distractions that may be taking place (Birch and Fisher 2000; Birch et al. 1987; Clendenen, Herman, and Polivy 1994; Pliner 1973). In contrast to the eating environment, the "food environment" refers to those factors that directly relate to the way that food is provided or presented, such as its salience, structure, package or portion size, whether it is stockpiled, and how it is served (Chandon and Wansink 2002; Rolls, Engell, and Birch 2000; Kahn and Wansink 2004). The specific features of a food, such as its taste, texture, nutritional value, and so forth, will not be directly examined here since they relate to the characteristics of a food category and not to the environment where they are eaten (eating environment) or presented (food environment).

Although many of the influences of the eating environment and the food environment have been identified and listed by some scholars (Stroebele and de Castro 2004), others have focused on identifying the domain of their influence, such as the kitchenscape, tablescape, platescape, and foodscape (Sobal and Wansink 2007). Perhaps a richer way to view the influence of these environments is by referring to *how* they influence our consumption. While the quantity of a food a person serves and eats is partly determined by personal norms (what they usually serve and eat), they can also be altered on any given occasion by the environmental cues around them. These cues can suggest an altered consumption norm, and can also interfere with our ability to monitor how much we have eaten. As figure 23.1 indicates, two of the principal ways in which these environments influence how much we consume is through (1) the consumption norms they suggest, and (2) the way they disrupt our intake monitoring ability.

Although the environmental factors outlined in figure 23.1 will be discussed individually, it is important to realize that they operate simultaneously. Consider the end-of-the-year weight gain that many experience over the holidays (Yanovski et al. 2000; Rosenthal et al. 1987). For most, this weight gain is a combined result of both the eating environment and the food environment. The holiday *eating environment* directly encourages overconsumption because it involves long parties

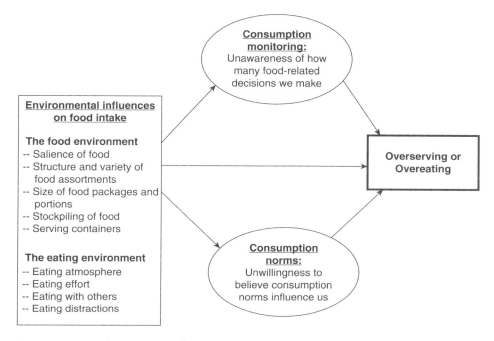

Figure 23.1. Environmental Influences on Overserving and Overeating (Modified from Wansink 2004, *Annual Review of Nutrition*).

(long eating durations), convenient leftovers (low eating effort), friends and relatives (eating with others), and a multitude of distractions. At the same time, the *food environment*—the salience, structure, size, shape, and stockpiles of food—simultaneously facilitates overconsumption.

After underscoring the ubiquitous impact that consumption norms and consumption monitoring have on behavior, this review describes the systematic influences of the eating environment and the food environment. For researchers, this review shows that redirecting our focus to the "whys" or to the processes behind consumption will raise the profile and impact of our research. For health professionals, this review underscores how small structural changes in personal environments can help reduce the unknowing overconsumption of food.

WHY DO ENVIRONMENTAL CUES MAKE US OVEREAT?

It has often been suggested that we overeat from larger portions because we have a tendency to "clean our plate" (Birch et al. 1987). While this may appear to *describe* why many people eat what they are served, it does not *explain* why they do so or why they may overserve themselves to begin with. Figure 23.1 suggests two reasons that portion size may have a ubiquitous, almost automatic influence on how much we eat: First, portion sizes create our consumption norms; second, we underestimate the calories in large portion sizes.

Environmental Cues Bias Consumption Norms

People can be very impressionable when it comes to how much they eat. There is a flexible range as to how much food an individual can eat (Herman and Polivy 1984), and one can often "make room for more" (Berry, Beatty, and Klesges 1985). For this reason, a person may be quite content eating 6–10 ounces of pasta for dinner without feeling overly hungry or overly full.

A key part of figure 23.1 is the role of *consumption norms* (Wansink 2004). For many individuals, determining how many ounces of pasta to serve themselves for dinner is a relatively low-involvement behavior which is a difficult nuisance to continually and accurately monitor. Sometimes people rely on consumption norms to help them determine how much they should consume. Food-related estimation and consumption behavior can be based on how much one normally buys or normally consumes. Yet consumption can also be unknowingly influenced by other norms or cues that are present in the environment. An important theme of this commentary is that larger packages in grocery stores, larger portions in restaurants, and larger kitchenware in homes all suggest a consumption norm that very subtly influences how much people believe is appropriate to eat.

In one series of studies that we are currently conducting, we ask people to serve the amount of four different foods (ice cream, popcorn, soup, and M&Ms) they thought would be appropriate, typical, reasonable, and normal to consume. However, we vary the size of the bowls (medium vs. large) we give them. Regardless of the food and regardless of the person, the larger the bowl people are given, the larger the consumption norm they believe is appropriate.

Large-size packages, large-size restaurant portions, and large-size dinnerware all have one thing in common—they suggest that it is appropriate, typical, reasonable, and normal to serve larger servings. These all implicitly influence our personal consumption norm for that situation.

Such norms suggest a consumption quantity (or a range) that is acceptable to consume. Large plates or packages may implicitly or at least perceptually suggest that it is more appropriate to eat more food than smaller plates or smaller packages would suggest. The use of consumption norms, as with normative benchmarks in other situations, may be relatively automatic and may often occur outside of conscious awareness (Schwarz 1996).

This is what makes these norms so powerful. Even when made aware of them, most people are unwilling to acknowledge they could be influenced by anything as seemingly harmless as the size of a package or plate. Even when shown that larger packages and plates lead them to serve an average of 31 percent more food than matched control groups, 98 percent of the diners in these field studies resolutely maintained that they were not influenced the size of package or plate they were given (Wansink and Sobal 2007); see table 23.1.

We Underestimate the Calories in Large Portions

The second key part of figure 23.1 is the role of *consumption monitoring*. When people pay close attention to what they eat, they tend to eat less. Unfortunately, large portion sizes can either bias people or confuse their estimate of how much they have eaten (van Ittersum and Wansink 2007).

Our ability to monitor our consumption can help reduce discrepancies between how much we eat and how much we *believe* we eat. Our environment can have an exaggerated influence on consumption because it can bias or confuse estimates of how much one has eaten, or even the number of times one thinks one is actively making a decision about starting or stopping an eating episode.

Not surprisingly, a major determinant of how much one eats is often whether one deliberately monitors or even pays attention to how much one eats (Polivy et al. 1986; Polivy and Herman 2002). In lieu of monitoring how much one is eating, people can use cues or rules of thumb (such as eating until a bowl is empty) to gauge the amount of food consumed.

Unfortunately, using such cues and rules of thumb can yield inaccurate estimates. In one study, unknowing diners were served tomato soup in bowls that were refilled through concealed tubing that ran through the table and into the bottom of the bowls. People eating from these "bottomless" bowls consumed 73 percent more soup than those eating from normal bowls, but estimated that they ate only 4.8 calories more (Wansink, Painter, and North 2005).

Our inability to monitor or estimate how many calories we eat becomes less accurate as portion sizes increase. It used to be believed that obese people were worse at underestimating the calories in their meals than people of normal weight (Lichtman, Pisarska, and Berman 1992). This was even believed to be a contributing cause of their obesity (Livingstone and Black 2003). Recent studies in the *Annals of Internal Medicine* have instead shown that this apparent bias is due to the size of the meals, not the size of people (Wansink and Chandon 2006). All people of all sizes—even registered nurses and dieticians—are equally inaccurate in their estimations of calories from large portions (Chandon and Wansink 2007). While it initially appears that heavier people are worse estimators of what they eat, a person of normal weight is just as inaccurate at estimating a 2,000-calorie lunch as a heavy-set person. It is just that obese people eat a lot more 2,000-calorie lunches.

With any large-sized portion of food, a lot of calories can be eaten before there is any noticeable sign that the supply has decreased. It does not matter how accurate or how diligent a person is at estimating calories; larger portions obscure any such changes until it is almost too late.

Table 23.1. Field Study Participants Deny the Influence Interventions Have on their Intake Behavior[1]

Sample and Context of Study	Intervention and Findings	"How much did you eat compared to what is typical for you?"				"In this study, you were in a group that was given [a larger container]. Those people in your group ate an average of 20–50 percent more than the others. Why do you think you might have eaten more?"[2]				
		Less	About the Same	More	Chi-Square	"I didn't eat more"	"I was hungry"	"The (intervention) influenced me"	Other	Chi-Square[4]
40 MBA students at a Super Bowl party in a bar in Champaign, IL (Wansink & Cheney 2005)	Those serving themselves Chex Mix from 4-liter bowls (n=19) served 53 percent more than those serving from 2-liter bowls	23 percent	57 percent	20 percent	10.55 (p<.01)	63 percent	31 percent	3 percent	3 percent	22.78 (p<.001)
98 adults preparing a spaghetti dinner for two in Hanover, NH (Wansink 1996)	Those given half-full 32-oz. boxes of spaghetti (n=51) prepared 29 percent more than those given full 16-oz. boxes.[3]	18 percent	73 percent	9 percent	70.36 (p<.001)	71 percent	27 percent	4 percent	8 percent	67.76 (p<.001)

Study	Intervention							
161 afternoon moviegoers in a Chicago suburb (Wansink & Park 2001)	Those given 240-gm buckets (n=82) ate 53 percent more than those given 120-gm buckets	19 percent	75 percent	6 percent	128.77 (p<.001)	15 percent	77 percent	5 percent	152.00 (p<.001)
158 evening moviegoers in Feasterville, PA (Wansink & Kim 2005)	Even when given stale, 14-day-old popcorn, those given 240-gm popcorn buckets (n=40) ate 34 percent more than those given 120-gm buckets of the same popcorn	14 percent	78 percent	8 percent	141.65 (p<.001)	12 percent	79 percent	2 percent	179.42 (p<.001)
Average across all studies (Weighted by the number of subjects per study)		19 percent	73 percent	**8 percent**	**331.26 (p<.001)**	52 percent	31 percent	2 percent	**203.97 (p<.001)**

[1] Answers are from those in the treatment group who received the intervention that resulted in greater consumption

[2] The specific intervention in the study was noted at this point. Here, the example of larger bowls was used.

[3] In this study, people poured spaghetti but did not actually consume it. Questions were modified to reflect pouring instead of eating

[4] The Chi-Square test was conservatively conducted excluding the "Other" response from the analysis. Including this resulting in all $Ps<.001$.

Are We Aware of the Consumption Norms That Have Led Us to Overeat?

People can be very impressionable when it comes to how much they eat (Herman and Polivy 1984). Someone can often "make room for more" (Berry, Beatty, and Klesges 1985; Lowe 1993) and be influenced by consumption norms around them (see figure 23.1). For many individuals, determining how much to eat or drink is a mundane and relatively low-involvement behavior that is a nuisance to continually monitor, so they instead rely on consumption norms to help them determine how much they should consume (Wansink and Cheney 2005). Many seemingly isolated influences on consumption—such as package size, variety, plate size, or the presence of others—may suggest how much is typical, appropriate, or reasonable to eat or drink.

As with normative benchmarks in other situations, they may often be relatively automatic and occur outside of conscious awareness. Indeed, when asked how many food-related decisions he or she makes in a particular day, the average person estimates between 15 and 30. In reality, a number of different studies have shown that the typical person makes between 200–300 food-related decisions a day (Wansink and Sobal 2007) (See figure 23.2.) Moreover, this appears to vary by BMI. Those who are obese (BMI > 30) make the most decisions, but estimate themselves as making the fewest.

Even when consumption norms do influence us, there is anecdotal evidence that people are generally either unaware of their influence or that they are unwilling to acknowledge it (Vartanian and Herman 2005). Past evidence of the presence or absence of this awareness has sometimes been suggested in the context of lab experiments (Nisbett and Wilson 1977). The problem with trying to generalize from such artificial contexts is that people are generally aware that some manipulation has occurred, and they may be reluctant to acknowledge any influence, primarily because of reactance. This phenomenon can best be observed in the context of controlled field studies conducted in natural environments (Meiselman 1992).

The basic organizing framework is that both the food environment and the eating environment directly contribute to consumption volume. Importantly, however, they also contribute to consumption volume *indirectly* through the mediated impact they have on consumption norms and on perceived consumption volume. For instance, while having dinner with a friend can have a direct impact on consumption (because of the longer duration of the meal), it can also have an indirect influence. This can be due to an individual following the consumption norms set by his friend or because his enjoyment distracts him from monitoring how much he consumes. Although these factors will be discussed individually, they often operate simultaneously. For instance, the holiday weight gain of .37 kg (Yanovski et al. 2000) is probably a combined result of consumption norms, food salience and availability, group sizes, and other factors.

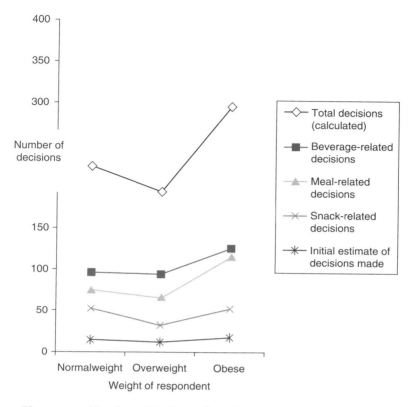

Figure 23.2. Number of Daily Food- and Beverage-related Decisions.

How the Food Environment
Encourages Mindless Eating

The allure of ice cream in the freezer is much stronger for most than the allure of broccoli in the refrigerator. Food intake can often be related to the perceived taste or cravings associated with foods (Polivy, Coleman, and Herman 2005; Wansink, Cheney, and Chan 2003), and such cravings can be different across gender and across age groups (Wansink, Cheney, and Chan 2003). One's liking for a food might increase chewing and swallowing rates (Bellisle and Le Magnen 1981) and is generally correlated with greater consumption (Bobroff and Kissileff 1986; Meiselman, King, and Weber 2003).

Despite this link between palatability and consumption, the availability of tasty, highly palatable foods is neither a necessary nor a sufficient cause for overconsumption (Mela and Rogers 1993). People can unknowingly overeat unfavorable foods as much as they do their favorites. This section examines the food-related environmental factors that influence consumption volume but which are unrelated to palatability. They can be characterized as the Five S's of the food environment because they refer to a food's (1) salience, (2) structure, and (3) size, and also (4) whether it is stockpiled and 5) how it is served.

Salient Food Promotes Salient Hunger

Simply seeing (or smelling) a food can stimulate unplanned consumption (Boon et al. 1998; Cornell, Rodin, and Weingarten 1989). For instance, when 30 chocolate kisses were placed on the desks of secretaries, those candies placed in clear jars were consumed 46 percent more quickly than those placed in opaque jars (Wansink, Painter, and Lee 2005). Similarly, people given sandwich quarters wrapped in transparent wrap were found to eat more than those who were given sandwiches in nontransparent wrap (Johnson 1974).

It had been believed that such increased intake of visible foods occurred because their salience served as a constant consumption reminder. While part of this may be cognitively based, part of it is also psychologically based. Simply seeing or smelling a favorable food can increase reported hunger (Bossert-Zaudig et al. 1991; Jansen and van den Hout 1991; Klajner et al. 1981; Staiger, Dawe, and McCarthy 2000) and can stimulate salivation (Hill, Magson, and Blundell 1984; Rogers and Hill 1989), which can be correlated with greater consumption (Nederkoorn and Jansen 2002). Recent physiological evidence suggests that the visibility of a tempting food can enhance actual hunger by increasing the release of dopamine, a neurotransmitter associated with pleasure and reward (Volkow et al. 2002). The impact of these cues can be particularly strong with unrestrained eaters (Jansen, Broekmate, and Heijmans 1992).

Although seeing or smelling a food can make it salient, salience can also be internally generated (Schachter 1971). For instance, one food-recall study suggested that eating bouts associated with internally generated salience may involve greater consumption volume than those associated with externally generated salience, such as the sight or smell of a food (Wansink 1994). Another study manipulated the salience of canned soup by asking people to write a detailed description of the last time they ate soup. Those who increased their consumption salience of soup in this way intended to consume 2.4 times as much canned soup over the next two weeks as did their counterparts in the control condition (Wansink and Deshpande 1994).

Structure and Perceived Variety Can Drive Consumption

Rolls and her colleagues have shown that if consumers are offered a plate with three different flavors of yogurt, they are likely to consume an average of 23 percent more yogurt than if offered only one flavor (Rolls et al. 1981). This basic notion that increasing the variety of a food can increase the consumption volume of that food (Miller et al. 2000; Rolls 1986) has been found across a wide range of ages (Rolls and McDermott 1991) and for both genders (Rolls et al. 1992; Rolls et al. 1998).

Recently, however, Kahn and Wansink (2004) have shown that simply increasing the *perceived variety* of an assortment can increase consumption. In one study they gave people an assortment of 300 chocolate-covered M&M candies that were presented in either seven or ten different colors. Although they were identically-tasting candies, people who had each been given a bowl with ten different colors ate 43 percent more (91 vs. 64 candies) over the course of hour than those who were given bowls with seven different colors. Further evidence of how perceived variety (versus actual variety) can influence consumption was shown when people were offered either organized or disorganized assortments of six flavors of jelly beans. Those offered the disorganized assortment rated the assortment as having more variety, and they ate 69 percent more jellybeans (22 vs. 13) than those offered the organized assortment (Kahn and Wansink 2004).

Even if the actual variety of the assortment is not increased, these studies suggest that simply changing the structure of an assortment (such as the organization, duplication, and symmetry) can increase how much is consumed. One reason this occurs is because increases in perceived variety make a person believe he or she will enjoy the assortment more. A second reason this occurs is because increasing the perceived variety can concurrently suggest an appropriate amount to consume (the consumption norm) in a particular situation (Kahn and Wansink 2004).

For researchers, it is important to know that perceptions of variety (Hoch, Bradlow, and Wansink 1999; Hoch, Bradlow, and Wansink 2002; van Herpen and Pieters 2002)–and not just actual variety–can influence consumption. For consumers, it is more important to know that they can physically adjust or design their immediate food environment in order to better control their intake.

The Size of Packages and Portions Suggest Consumption Norms

There is overwhelming evidence that the size of food packaging and portions has steadily increased over the past 30 years (Rolls 2003; Young and Nestle 2002). While this is a trend in much of the developed world, it is particularly prevalent in the United States and may help explain the greater obesity rate in the United States (Brownell and Horgen 2004; Nestle 2002). Rozin and his colleagues have shown that the size of packages and portions in restaurants, supermarkets, and even in recipes is much larger in the United States than in France, which is often considered to be a more food-centric country (Rozin et al. 2003).

In relating this to consumption, it is a well-supported fact that the size of a package can increase consumption (Wansink 1996), as can the size of portion servings in kitchens (Nisbett 1968; Rolls, Morris, and Roe 2002) and in restaurants (Edelman et al. 1986). What is notable is that package and portion size can even increase the consumption of unfavorable foods. For instance, when moviegoers in a Philadelphia suburb were given either medium-sized or large-sized containers of stale, 14-day-old popcorn, they still ate 38 percent more, despite the poor taste of the popcorn (Wansink and Kim 2005). It would appear that environmental cues may sometimes be as powerful—within limits—as the taste of food itself.

The impact of packages and portions on consumption is sizable. People will consume 18–25 percent more of meal-related foods (such as spaghetti) and 30–45 percent more of snack-related foods when the package sizes are twice as big as they would normally be (Wansink 1996). Such predictable increases in consumption occur even when the energy density of a food is altered, as Rolls and her colleagues demonstrated (Ello-Martin et al. 2004; Rolls et al. 2004). Something else clearly drives intake other than satiation; something is driving people to consume these foods past the point of satiation. In effect, the volume of food eaten tends to be a better indicator of how "full" one considers oneself than does the calorie density of the food (Rolls, Bell, and Waugh 2000; Rolls et al. 1998; Rolls, Morris, and Roe 2002.).

An important program of child development research by Birch and Fisher has shown that portion size first begins to influence children between three and five years of age (Birch et al. 1987; Rolls, Engell, and Birch 2000; Fisher, Rolls, and Birch 2003). This tendency to let portion size influence their consumption volume has been referred to as the "clean-your-plate" phenomenon or the completion principle (Siegel 1957) because of its possible developmental implications. Unfortunately, neither of these suggested mechanisms explains why large packages also increase the pouring of less-edible products such as shampoo, cooking oil, detergent, dog food, and plant food. Nor does it explain why large packages of M&Ms, chips, and spaghetti increase consumption in studies where even the smaller portions were too large to eat in one sitting (Folkes, Martin, and Gupta 1993; Wansink 1996). In both situations, people poured or consumed more even though there was no possibility of "cleaning one's plate."

The more general explanation of why large packages and portions increase consumption may be because they suggest larger consumption norms (recall figure 23.1). They implicitly suggest what might be construed as a "normal" or "appropriate" amount to consume. Even if one does not clean her plate or finish the contents of a package, the size of the food presented gives her liberty to consume past the point at which she might have stopped with a smaller, but still unconstrained, supply.

Stockpiled Food is Quickly Consumed

Having large stockpiles of food products at home (such as multi-unit packages purchased at wholesale club stores) can make those products more visible and salient than less plentiful ones. Not only do stockpiled products take up a great deal of pantry space, but they are often stored in salient locations until they are depleted to more manageable levels (Chandon and Wansink 2002). Because visibility and salience can stimulate consumption frequency, it is often alleged that bulk-buying or stockpiling causes overconsumption and may promote obesity.

To investigate this, Chandon and Wansink directly stockpiled peoples' homes with either large or moderate quantities of eight different foods. They then monitored each family's consumption of these foods for two weeks. It was found that when convenient, ready-to-eat foods were initially stockpiled, they were eaten at slightly twice the rate as non-stockpiled foods (an average of 112 percent faster) (Chandon and Wansink 2002). After the eighth day, however, the consumption of these stockpiled foods was similar to that of the less-stockpiled foods, even though plenty of both remained in stock. Part of this eventual decrease was due to "burn-out" or taste satiation (Inman 2001), but another factor was that the inventory level of these foods dropped to the point where they became much less visually salient (Wansink and Deshpande 1994).

To investigate the link between the visibility of stockpiled food and obesity, Terry and Beck (1985) compared food storage habits in homes of obese and non-obese families. Curiously, while their first study showed that stockpiled food tended to be visible in the homes of obese families, their second study showed the opposite. In general, however, recently stockpiled products tend to be visually salient, and this is one important reason that they are frequently consumed.

Serving Containers That are Wide or Large Create Consumption Illusions

Nearly 72 percent of a person's caloric intake is consumed using serving aids such as bowls, plates, glasses, or utensils (Wansink 2005). If a person decides to eat half a bowl of cereal, the size of the bowl can act as a perceptual cue that may influence how much they serve and subsequently consume. Even if these perceptual cues are inaccurate, they offer cognitive shortcuts that can allow serving behaviors to be made with minimal cognitive effort.

Consider drinking glasses and the vertical-horizontal illusion. Piaget and others have shown that when people observe a cylindrical object (such as a drinking glass), they tend to focus on its vertical dimension at the expense of its horizontal dimension (Krider, Raghubir, and Krishna 2001; Piaget 1969; Raghubir and Krishna 1999.). Even if the vertical dimension is identical to that of the horizontal dimension, people still tend to overestimate the height by 18–21 percent. This general principle explains why many people marvel at the height of the St. Louis Arch but not at its identical-size width.

In the context of drinking glasses, when people examine how much soda they have poured in their glass, there is a fundamental tendency to focus on the height of the liquid that has been poured and to downplay its width. To prove this, Wansink and van Ittersum conducted a study with teenagers at weight-loss camps (as well as a subsequent study with non-dieting adults) and showed that this basic visual bias caused teenagers to pour 88 percent more juice or soda into short, wide glasses than into tall, narrow glasses that held the same volume (and to subsequently consume more) (Wansink and van Ittersum 2003). These teenagers believed, however, that they poured half as much as much as they actually did. Similar support was found with veteran Philadelphia bartenders. When asked to pour 1.5 ounces of gin, whiskey, rum, and vodka into short, wide (tumbler) glasses, these bartenders poured 26 percent more than when pouring into tall, narrow (highball) glasses (Wansink and van Ittersum 2003).

What about the size of plates and bowls? The size-contrast illusion suggests that if we spoon 4 ounces of mashed potatoes onto a 12-inch plate and 4 ounces onto an 8-inch plate, we will underestimate the total amount spooned onto the larger plate because of its greater negative space, even though they contain the exact same amount (Wansink and van Ittersum 2010). That is, the size contrast between the potatoes and the plate is greater when the plate is 12 inches than when it is 8 inches. A study at an ice cream social showed similar results. People who were randomly given 24-ounce bowls dished out and consumed 15–38 percent more ice cream than those who were given 16-ounce bowls (Wansink, van Ittersum, and Painter 2006). The same appears to be true with spoon sizes. When cough medicine was given to health center patients, the size of the spoon they were given increased the dosage they poured by 41 percent over the recommended dosage level (Wansink and van Ittersum 2004). With plates and bowls and spoons, there is a basic tendency to use their size as an indication of how much should be served and consumed.

How the Eating Environment Stimulates Consumption

What causes the initiation and the cessation of eating? One study asked restrained dieters to maintain a consumption diary and to indicate what caused them to start and to stop eating (Tuomisto et al. 1998). Aside from hunger, people claimed they started eating because of the salience of food ("I saw the food"), the social aspects of eating ("I wanted to be with other people"), or simply because eating provided them with something to do ("I wanted something to do while watching TV or reading"). When asked why they stopped eating, some of them pointed to environmental cues (such as the time or the completion of the meal by others), which served as external signals that the meal should be over .Others stopped eating when they ran out of food, and still others stopped because their television program was finished or because they were at a stopping point in their reading.

These findings are consistent with other research (Rozin et al. 1998) that suggests people may have continued to eat had they been given more food, more time to eat, or more television to watch. These responses relating to consumption start and stop times illustrate four important consumption drivers in the eating environment: (1) eating atmospherics, (2) eating effort, (3) eating with others, and (4) eating distractions. These will each be investigated in turn.

Atmospherics Influence Eating Duration

Atmospherics refer to ambient characteristics—such as temperature, lighting, odor, and noise—that influence the immediate eating environment. Consider the direct physiological influence that temperature has on consumption. Ambient temperature leads people to consume more during prolonged cold temperatures than hot temperatures (Brobeck 1948). The basic process is a result of the body's need to regulate its core temperature by using food and liquid to either warm it or cool it. In prolonged cold temperatures, the body needs more energy to warm and maintain its core temperature (Westerterp-Platenga 1999), therefore more food is eaten. In prolonged hot temperatures, the body needs more liquid to cool and maintain its core temperature (Murray 1987), therefore more liquids are drunk.

While temperature has direct physiological influences on consumption, other atmospherics—such as lighting, odor, and noise—are similar to each other in that they have a much more indirect or mediated impact on consumption. These atmospherics are thought to influence consumption volume partly because they make it comfortable for a person to spend more time eating (see figure 23.3). The longer one eats, the more one consumes.

Lighting

Dimmed or soft lighting appears to influence consumption in two different ways: (1) by increasing eating duration, and (2) by increasing comfort and disinhibition. It has been widely reported that harsh or bright illumination decreases the amount of time consumers spend in a restaurant (Sommer 1969), while soft or warm lighting (including candlelight) generally causes people to linger and to enjoy an unplanned dessert or an extra drink (Lyman 1989; Ragneskog et al. 1996). Because people are less inhibited and less self-conscious when the lights are low, they are therefore likely to consume more than they otherwise would (Lavin and Lawless 1998).

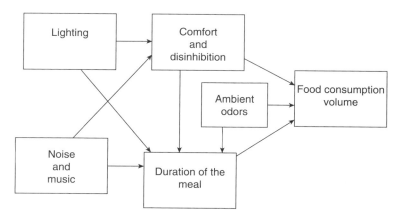

Figure 23.3. How Atmospherics Influence Food Consumption Volume.

Odor

Odor can influence food consumption through taste enhancement or through suppression (Rozin 1982; Stevenson, Prescott, and Boakes 1999). Unpleasant ambient odors are likely to shorten a meal and suppress food consumption. Yet the reverse is not necessarily true; it is not known whether favorable odors necessarily increase consumption volume. It has been found, for instance, that regardless of whether a person tastes a food or simply smells it, sensory-specific satiety can occur within a reasonably short period of time (Rolls and Rolls 1997). This suggests that while odors can have a depressing impact on consumption, they might not necessarily increase consumption other than by simply influencing one's choice of the food in the first place.

Noise and the Sound of Music

Soft music generally encourages a slower rate of eating, a longer meal duration, and a higher consumption of both food and drinks (Caldwell and Hibbert 2002). The more one enjoys the music, the more comfortable and disinhibited they feel, and the more likely they are to order a dessert or another drink (Milliman 1986). In contrast, when music (or ambient noise) is loud, fast, or discomforting, people tend to spend less time in a restaurant (North and Hargreaves 1996). In some cases, however, such an abbreviated meal can also lead people to quickly clean their plates and overeat without taking time to monitor the extent to which they are full (Lindman et al. 1986; Roballey, McGreevy, and Rongo 1985). Although more controlled field-work needs to be done in this area, it appears that both extremes (soft, comforting music as well as loud, irritating noise) increase consumption, but in different ways.

Increased Effort Decreases Consumption

Effort is related to the ease, access, or convenience with which a food can be consumed. It is one of the strongest influences on consumption (Levitsky 2002; Wansink 2004). The effort it takes to obtain food often explains which foods people prefer and how much they will consume (Wing and Jeffery 2001). Cafeteria studies showed that people ate more ice cream when the lid of an ice cream cooler was left open instead of closed (Meyers, Stunkard, and Coll 1980), that they consumed more milk when the milk machine was closer to the dining area (Lieux and Manning 1992), and that they imbibed more water when a water pitcher was sitting on their table than when it was farther away (Engell et al. 1996).

Scores of studies have investigated effort and animal feeding (such as pressing bars for food pellets), but surprisingly few have been conducted with people (Levitsky 2002). Notable exceptions showed that obese people were much more likely to eat almonds if they were shelled versus unshelled (Schachter and Friedman 1974), and they were more likely to use silverware instead of chopsticks (which require more effort) when compared to normal-weight patrons in Chinese restaurants (Schachter, Friedman, and Handler 1974). This same impact of effort has also been found with non-obese secretaries who were given chocolate candies that were either placed on their desks or two meters away from their desk. When they had to only reach for them on their desk, secretaries ate 5.6 more chocolates a day then when they had to stand up and walk two meters for them (Painter, Wansink, and Hieggelke 2002). These results help corroborate the initial findings regarding effort (Hearn et al. 1989), particularly when the foods are ready to eat (Chandon and Wansink 2002).

While these studies focused on physical effort, psychological effort may also play a role in consumption. Recent plate waste studies among U.S. soldiers indicate that once any component of a field ration is opened, it is generally completely consumed. Although the physical effort to open the small component packages in a field ration is minimal, there may be a psychological barrier that prevents a person from opening another individual item. Follow-up lab studies suggest that people tend to eat less when offered multiple small packages than when offered a large package of the same volume. Part of the reason is because these smaller packages provide discrete stopping points for consumption (Wansink 2004).

Socializing Influences Meal Duration and Consumption Norms

It has been well established that the presence of other people influences not only what is eaten, but also how much is eaten (see figure 23.4). Eating with familiar people can lead to an extended meal (Bell and Pliner 2003). In other cases, simply observing another's eating behavior—such as a role model (Birch and Fisher 2000), parent, friend, or stranger (de Castro 1994)—can provide a consumption norm that can also influence how much the observer eats. These effects can be dramatic. De Castro has shown that meals eaten with one other person were 33 percent larger

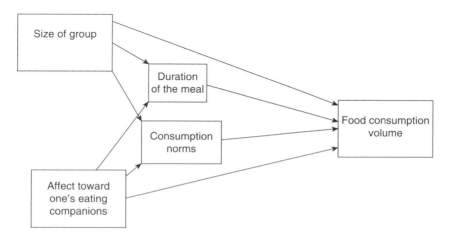

Figure 23.4. How Social Interactions Influence Food Consumption Volume.

than those eaten alone (de Castro 2000), and increases of 47 percent, 58 percent, 69 percent 70 percent, 72 percent and 96 percent have been associated with the presence of two, three, four, five, six, and seven or more people, respectively (de Castro and Brewer 1992).

Eating with familiar and friendly people also increase how much is eaten because they can help make a meal relaxing, enjoyable, and prolonged. These relaxing, enjoyable meals can reduce one's ability or motivation to monitor how much they consume. In contrast, eating with unfamiliar people can suppress food intake in situations where self-monitoring and self-awareness is high, such as during job interviews or first dates (Pliner and Chaiken 1990; Mori, Chaiken, and Pliner 1987; Stroebele and de Castro 2004).

Interestingly, as the number of eating companions increases, the average variability of how much is eaten may actually decrease (Clendennen, Herman and, Polivy 1994). For instance, people eating alone ate less than those eating in groups of two or four, but that this was driven by the amount of time they spent dining. What is most interesting about this study is that as the number of people in the group increased, the variance in how much they ate appears to have decreased. That is, a person eating alone was likely to eat either much more or much less (on average) than when eating with a larger group.

Indeed, simply viewing the behavior of others has been shown to have an implicit impact on consumption (Herman, Olmsted, and Polivy 1983; Polivy et al. 1979). Studies have shown that individuals will vary the amount of cookies they eat and the amount of water they drink (Engell et al. 1996) depending on how much others are consuming (Polivy et al. 1979). The impact of these external social cues can be particularly strong on obese individuals (Herman, Olmsted, and Polivy 1983).

DISTRACTIONS CAN INITIATE, OBSCURE, AND EXTEND CONSUMPTION

Distractions such as reading or watching television can initiate script-related food consumption that is uncorrelated with hunger, can obscure one's ability to monitor consumption, and can extend the duration of a meal.

It was noted earlier that a diary survey of obese people indicated that some had stopped eating simply because a television program was over or because they had finished reading a magazine (Tuomisto et al. 1998). Just as the completion of a television show or of a magazine article can lead one to terminate his dinner, a longer television show or a longer magazine article may prolong the duration of a meal past the point of satiation.

While part of the overconsumption associated with distractions such as television and magazines can be related to longer meals, another part of it is that distractions can obscure one's ability to accurately monitor how much has been eaten. One controlled study showed that people who ate lunch while listening to a detective story ate 15 percent more than those who ate their lunch in silence (Bellisle and Dalix 2001). Distractions such as television, reading, movies, and sporting events may simply redirect attention to the point where orosensory signals of satiation are ignored (Poothullil 2002). Consistent with this, another study showed that the key correlate of how much popcorn people ate in a Chicago movie theater was whether they claimed that they paid more attention to the movie or to how much they ate (Wansink and Park 2001). The more attention they paid to the movie, the more popcorn they ate.

In addition to the influence that these distractions have on meal duration and on monitoring consumption, they can also evoke consumption scripts which can initiate consumption because they lead people to associate the distraction with food. In fact, one's consumption during these events—be it a hot dog at a ballgame or popcorn during a movie—might simply be influenced by behaviorally ingrained eating scripts. That is, eating in these situations might be related more to habit than to hunger. Indeed, people in a two-week panel study were asked to indicate how hungry they were each time they ate a meal or snack. People who watched television while eating meals or snacks reported being less hungry than those who were not watching television when they ate (Stroebele and de Castro 2004).

All of these findings are consistent with the basic notion that people may elect to snack in these distracting environments because such eating is part of a habitual consumption script and not because they are necessarily hungry. Rozin showed that amnesiac patients who were told it was dinner time ate a second complete meal only 10 to 30 minutes after having eating a prior meal (Rozin et al. 1998). Even if they are not physically hungry, simply thinking it is time to have a meal or a snack is enough to cause some people to eat Weingarten 1984). Both children (Del Toro and Greenberg 1989; Dietz and Gortmaker 1985) and adults (Jeffery and French 1998; Tucker and Bagwell 1991; Tucker and Friedman 1989) tend to snack more when watching television, and they may do so even if they are not physically hungry. Although it is frequently found that television viewing, food intake, and obesity are related (Gortmaker, Dietz, and Cheung 1990; Klesges, Shelton, and Klesges 1993), these correlational studies are often confounded with factors such as a general lack of physical inactivity. Nevertheless, they do suggest an important relationship between distracted inactivity and consumption intake (Taras et al. 1989).

Yet this basic connection between distractibility and food intake may have an even more fundamental connection to obesity. Past work has indicated that obese people have a greater tendency to be distracted than non-obese people (Rodin 1974). In a media-rich, food-rich environment, people who are distraction-prone will not be able to accurately monitor their consumption and thus are likely to overeat. If obese people are more distraction-prone, they should tend to eat even more than normal weight people in identical, distracting circumstances, whether it involves a television program, a magazine, a newspaper, or a conversation.

CONCLUSION

In the past 30 years, reasonable advances have been made in "outcome-based" research regarding the environmental factors that influence intake. These studies have provided a convergent understanding along with important investigations into boundary conditions. The field of food consumption and intake is at a point, however, where the next evolutionary step needs to be in the direction of understanding the "whys" behind food intake. The focus needs to move beyond showing what we do to explain why we do what we do. This will entail more of a focus on developing and testing process-models and theories of consumption. Doing so will allow more productive integration across studies and an attempt to identify the more fundamental low-involvement drivers of consumption.

Two general mediators that appear to be promising starting points are the notions of consumption norms and consumption monitoring. As noted in figure 23.1, both of these are likely to be factors that at least partially mediate the impact of seemingly disparate concepts on consumption (such as package size, variety, and social influences).

The environment influences food-related decisions consistently throughout the day. There are two problems with this. First, we are not aware of how many decisions we make that are influenced by the environment. Second, we are not aware or we are unwilling to acknowledge that the environment has any impact on us at all. Although we make over 200 more food-related decisions a day than we think, many of these are "automatic" food choices wherein we unconsciously eat without considering what or how much food we select and consume (Rodin 1974). This is consistent with other psychological work that shows that people tend to have flawed self-assessments, leading to overconfidence (Dunning 2005). With food intake decisions, their overconfidence may lead to overconsumption and weight gain.

An important new area for environment and behavior research is to examine why environmental cues are so often discounted, and how the environment could better be altered to work for us rather than against us. Keeping a focus on the mechanisms or processes behind consumption—the "whys" behind it and the "hows" to influence it—will help the interdisciplinary topic of food consumption progress in ways that can raise its profile and its impact on academia, on health practitioners, and ultimately on consumer welfare. Table 23.2, adapted from Wansink (2004), lists environmental influences on food consumption, and how the environment can be altered to reduce food consumption.

Consumption occurs within a context wherein understanding fundamental behavior has immediate implications for consumer welfare. Yet simply knowing the relationship between environmental factors and consumption will not eliminate its biasing effects on consumers. People are often surprised at how much they consume, and this indicates that they may be influenced at a basic level of which they are not aware or which they do not monitor.

Table 23.2. How the Environmental Influences and Can Help Reduce
Consumption (Adapted from Wansink 2004)

How Environmental Factors Influence Consumption	How Environmental Changes Can Help Reduce Consumption
The Eating Environment	
Eating Atmospherics: Atmospherics Influence Eating Duration	• By having bread plates and entrees removed prior to completion, one can finish eating and still socially remain at the table • While soft music and candlelight can improve one's enjoyment of a meal, they have calorie intake consequences, and they can be enjoyed in lieu of a dessert.
Eating Effort: Increased Effort Decreases Consumption	• Repackaging foods in smaller containers increases subsequent opening effort and gives a person pause to reconsider • Tempting foods that are stored in less convenient locations (such as in the basement or in a top cupboard) can be "too much trouble" to obtain and unnecessarily consume • Leaving serving bowls and platters off the dinner table will decrease the amount consumed.
Eating with Others: Socializing Influences Meal Duration and Consumption Norms	• Pre-regulate consumption by deciding how much to eat prior to the meal instead of during the meal. • Ordering smaller quantities or having portions packaged "to go" before the meal is completed.
Eating Distractions: Distractions Initiate, Obscure, and Extend Consumption	• Let food regulate the activity, not vice versa. • Pre-allocating how much will be eaten prior to a distraction-related meal or snack (such as a television program) can help avoid "eating until it's over."
The Food Environment	
Salience of Food: Salient Food Promotes Salient Hunger	• Out of sight is out of mind. Tempting, less healthy foods should be stored out of sight. • Increase the consumption of healthy, low-energy-dense foods by making them more visible. Recall the popularity of fruit bowls in a less obese era.
Structure and Variety of Food Assortments: Perceived Variety Drives Consumption	• Decrease consumption in high variety environments (such as buffets, potlucks, or large dinners by putting the food into more organized patterns. Conversely, arranging food in less organized patterns may stimulate consumption of healthy foods in the cafeterias of retirement homes and hospitals. • Avoid multiple bowls of the same food (such as at parties, large dinners, or buffets) because they increase perceptions of variety and stimulate consumption
Size of Food Packages and Portions: Packages and Portion Size Suggest Consumption Norms	• Repackaging foods into smaller containers decreases consumption by suggesting smaller consumption norms • Pre-plating smaller portions onto plates and leaving the serving bowl off the dinner table will decrease consumption.

(continued)

Table 23.2. Cont'd

How Environmental Factors Influence Consumption	How Environmental Changes Can Help Reduce Consumption
The Food Environment (continued)	
Stockpiling of Food: Stockpiled Food is Quickly Consumed	• Reducing the visibility of stockpiled foods will reduce consumption frequency (out of sight out of mind) • Storing stockpiled foods out in a less accessible place or boxing it up will reduce its convenience and thus how frequently it is consumed.
Serving Containers: Serving Containers that are Wide or Large Create Consumption Illusions	• Replace short wide glasses with tall narrow ones • Use smaller bowls and plates to help reduce serving sizes and consumption

Our environment can unknowingly entice and contribute to our overconsumption of food. On the other hand, altering one's immediate environment to make it less conducive to overeating can help us lose weight in a way that does not require the discipline of dieting or the governance of another person.

We are at a point of economic and technological development when much of the incremental improvement in our life span—and especially in our quality of life—is likely to come from behavioral changes in our lifestyle. When it comes to contributing to the life span and quality of life in the next generations, well-intentioned marketers may be in a prime position to help lead the movement toward behavior change. Obesity is a good place to start.

REFERENCES

Baron, R. M., and D. A. Kenny. 1986. "The Moderator Mediator Variable Distinction in Social Psychological Research - Conceptual, Strategic, and Statistical Considerations." *Journal of Personality and Social Psychology* 51(6): 1173–1182.

Bell, R., and P. L. Pliner. 2003. "Time to Eat: The Relationship between the Number of People Eating and Meal Duration in Three Lunch Settings." *Appetite* 41(2): 215–218.

Bellisle, F., and A. M. Dalix. 2001. "Cognitive Restraint Can Be Offset by Distraction, Leading to Increased Meal Intake in Women." *American Journal of Clinical Nutrition* 74(2): 197–200.

Bellisle, F., and J. Le Magnen. 1981. "The Structure of Meals in Humans - Eating and Drinking Patterns in Lean and Obese Subjects." *Physiology and Behavior* 27(4): 649–658.

Berry, S. L., W. W. Beatty, and R. C. Klesges. 1985. "Sensory and Social Influences on Ice-Cream Consumption by Males and Females in a Laboratory Setting." *Appetite* 6(1): 41–45.

Birch, L. L., and J. O. Fisher. 2000. "Mothers' Child-Feeding Practices Influence Daughters' Eating and Weight." *American Journal of Clinical Nutrition* 71(5): 1054–1061.

Birch, L. L., L. McPhee, B. C. Shoba, L. Steinberg, and R. Krehbiel. 1987. "Clean up Your Plate - Effects of Child Feeding Practices on the Conditioning of Meal Size." *Learning and Motivation* 18(3): 301–317.

Bobroff, E. M., and H. R. Kissileff. 1986. "Effects of Changes in Palatability on Food-Intake and the Cumulative Food-Intake Curve in Man." *Appetite* 7(1): 85–96.

Boon, B., W. Stroebe, H. Schut, and A. Jansen. 1998. "Food for Thought: Cognitive Regulation of Food Intake." *British Journal of Health Psychology* 3: 27–40.

Bossert-Zaudig, S., R. Laessle, C. Meiller, H. Ellgring, and K. M. Pirke. 1991. "Hunger and Appetite During Visual Perception of Food in Eating Disorders." *European Psychiatry* 6(5): 237–242.

Brobeck, J. R. 1948. "Food Intake as a Mechanism of Temperature Regulation." *Yale Journal of Biology and Medicine* 20(6): 545–552.

Brownell, Kelly D., and Katherine Battle Horgen. 2004. *Food Fight : The Inside Story of the Food Industry, America's Obesity Crisis, and What We Can Do About It.* Chicago: Contemporary Books.

Caldwell, C., and S. A. Hibbert. 2002. "The Influence of Music Tempo and Musical Preference on Restaurant Patrons' Behavior." *Psychology and Marketing* 19(11): 895–917.

Chandon, P., and B. Wansink. 2002. "When Are Stockpiled Products Consumed Faster? A Convenience-Salience Framework of Postpurchase Consumption Incidence and Quantity." *Journal of Marketing Research* 39(3): 321–335.

Chandon, P., and B. Wansink. 2007. "Is Obesity Caused by Calorie Underestimation? A Psychophysical Model of Meal Size Estimation." *Journal of Marketing Research* 44(1): 84–99.

Clendenen, V. I., C. P. Herman, and J. Polivy. 1994. "Social Facilitation of Eating among Friends and Strangers." *Appetite* 23(1): 1–13.

Cornell, C. E., J. Rodin, and H. Weingarten. 1989. "Stimulus-Induced Eating When Satiated." *Physiology and Behavior* 45(4): 695–704.

de Castro, J. M. 2000. "Eating Behavior: Lessons from the Real World of Humans." *Nutrition* 16(10): 800–813.

de Castro, J. M. 1994. "Family and Friends Produce Greater Social Facilitation of Food-Intake Than Other Companions." *Physiology and Behavior* 56(3): 445–455.

de Castro, J. M., and E. M. Brewer. 1992. "The Amount Eaten in Meals by Humans Is a Power Function of the Number of People Present." *Physiology and Behavior* 51(1): 121–125.

De Toro, Wanda, Greenberg, Bradley, S. 1989. "Television Commercials and Food Orientations among Teenagers in Puerto-Rico." *Hispanic Journal of Behavioral Sciences* 11(2): 168–177.

Dietz, W. H., and S. L. Gortmaker. 1985. "Do We Fatten Our Children at the Television Set - Obesity and Television Viewing in Children and Adolescents." *Pediatrics* 75(5): 807–812.

Dunning, D. 2005. *Self-Insight: Roadblocks and Detours on the Path to Knowing Thyself, Essays in Social Psychology.* New York: Psychology Press.

Edelman, B., D. Engell, P. Bronstein, and E. Hirsch. 1986. "Environmental-Effects on the Intake of Overweight and Normal-Weight Men." *Appetite* 7(1): 71–83.

Ello-Martin, J. A., L. S. Roe, J. S. Meengs, D. E. Wall, and T. E. Robinson. 2004. "Increasing the Portion Size of a Packaged Snack Increases Energy Intake." *Learning and Motivation* 18(3): 301–317.

Engell, D., M. Kramer, T. Malafi, M. Salomon, and L. Lesher. 1996. "Effects of Effort and Social Modeling on Drinking in Humans." *Appetite* 26(2): 129–138.

Evans, G. W., and S.J. Lepore. 1987. "Moderating and Mediating Processing in Environment-Behavior Research." In *Advances in Environment, Behavior and Design*, eds. G. T. Moore and R. W. Marans. New York: Plenum.

Fisher, J. O., B. J. Rolls, and L. L. Birch. 2003. "Children's Bite Size and Intake of an Entree Are Greater with Large Portions Than with Age-Appropriate or Self-Selected Portions." *American Journal of Clinical Nutrition* 77(5): 1164–1170.

Folkes, V. S., I. M. Martin, and K. Gupta. 1993. "When to Say When: Effects of Supply on Usage." *Journal of Consumer Research* 20(3): 467–477.

French, S. A., M. Story, and R. W. Jeffery. 2001. "Environmental Influences on Eating and Physical Activity." *Annual Review of Public Health* 22: 309–335.

Furst, T., M. Connors, C. A. Bisogni, J. Sobal, and L. W. Falk. 1996. "Food Choice: A Conceptual Model of the Process." *Appetite* 26(3): 247–265.

Garg, N., B. Wansink, and J. J. Inman. 2007. "The Influence of Incidental Affect on Consumers' Food Intake." *Journal of Marketing* 71(1): 194–206.

Gortmaker, S. L., W. H. Dietz, and L. W. Y. Cheung. 1990. "Inactivity, Diet, and the Fattening of America." *Journal of the American Dietetic Association* 90(9): 1247ff.

Hannum, S. M., L. Carson, E. M. Evans, K. A. Canene, E. L. Petr, L. Bui, and J. W. Erdman. 2004. "Use of Portion-Controlled Entrees Enhances Weight Loss in Women." *Obesity Research* 12(3): 538–546.

Hearn, M.D., T. Baranowski, J. Baranowski, C. Doyle, M. Smith, L.S. Lin, and K. Resnicow. 1989. "Environmental Influences on Dietary Behavior among Children: Availability and Accessibility of Fruits and Vegetables." *Journal of Health Education* 29: 26–32.

Herman, C. P., M. P. Olmsted, and J. Polivy. 1983. "Obesity, Externality, and Susceptibility to Social-Influence - an Integrated Analysis." *Journal of Personality and Social Psychology* 45(4): 926–934.

Herman, C. P., and J. Polivy. 1984. "A Boundary Model for the Regulation of Eating." In *Research Publications: Association for Research in Nervous and Mental Diseases*, Vol. 62, *Eating and Its Disorders*, eds. A. J. Stunkard and E. Stellar, 141–156. New York: Raven Press.

Hill, A. J., L. D. Magson, and J. E. Blundell. 1984. "Hunger and Palatability - Tracking Ratings of Subjective Experience before, During and after the Consumption of Preferred and Less Preferred Food." *Appetite* 5(4): 361–371.

Hoch, S. J., E. T. Bradlow, and B. Wansink. 2002. "Rejoinder To 'The Variety of an Assortment: An Extension to the Attribute-Based Approach.'" *Marketing Science* 21(3): 342–346.

Hoch, S. J., E. T. Bradlow, and B. Wansink. 1999. "The Variety of an Assortment." *Marketing Science* 18(4): 527–546.

Inman, J. J. 2001. "The Role of Sensory-Specific Satiety in Attribute-Level Variety Seeking." *Journal of Consumer Research* 28(1): 105–120.

Jansen, A., J. Broekmate, and M. Heymans. 1992. "Cue-Exposure vs. Self-Control in the Treatment of Binge Eating: A Pilot-Study." *Behaviour Research and Therapy* 30(3): 235–241.

Jansen, A., and M. van den Hout. 1991. "On Being Led into Temptation: Counterregulation of Dieters after Smelling a Preload." *Addictive Behaviors* 16(5): 247–253.

Jeffery, R. W., and S. A. French. 1998. "Epidemic Obesity in the United States: Are Fast Foods and Television Viewing Contributing?" *American Journal of Public Health* 88(2): 277–280.

Johnson, W. G. 1974. "The Effects of Cue Prominence and Obesity on Effort to Obtain Food." In *Obese Humans and Rats*, eds. S. Schachter and J. Rodin. Potomac, MD: L. Erlbaum Associates.

Kahn, B. E., and B. Wansink. 2004. "The Influence of Assortment Structure on Perceived Variety and Consumption Quantities." *Journal of Consumer Research* 30(4): 519–533.

Klajner, F., C. P. Herman, J. Polivy, and R. Chhabra. 1981. "Human Obesity, Dieting, and Anticipatory Salivation to Food." *Physiologyand Behavior* 27(2): 195–198.

Klesges, R. C., M. L. Shelton, and L. M. Klesges. 1993. "Effects of Television on Metabolic-Rate - Potential Implications for Childhood Obesity." *Pediatrics* 91(2): 281–286.

Krider, R. E., P. Raghubir, and A. Krishna. 2001. "Pizzas: Pi or Square? Psychophysical Biases in Area Comparisons." *Marketing Science* 20(4): 405–425.

Lavin, J. G., and H. T. Lawless. 1998. "Effects of Color and Odor on Judgments of Sweetness among Children and Adults." *Food Quality and Preference* 9(4): 283–289.

Levitsky, D. A. 2002. "Putting Behavior Back into Feeding Behavior: A Tribute to George Collier." *Appetite* 38(2): 143–148.

Lichtman, S. W., K. Pisarska, E. R. Berman, M. Pestone, H. Dowling, E. Offenbacher, H. Weisel, S. Heshka, D. E. Matthews, and S. B. Heymsfield. 1992. "Discrepancy between Self-Reported and Actual Caloric-Intake and Exercise in Obese Subjects." *New England Journal of Medicine* 327(27): 1893–1898.

Lieux, E. M., and C. K. Manning. 1992. "Evening Meals Selected by College-Students: Impact of the Foodservice System." *Journal of the American Dietetic Association* 92(5): 560–566.

Lindman, R., B. Lindfors, E. Dahla, and H. Toivola. 1986. "Alcohol and Ambiance: Social and Environmental Determinants of Intake and Mood." *Alcohol and Alcoholism* 21(2): A40–A40.

Livingstone, M. B. E., and A. E. Black. 2003. "Markers of the Validity of Reported Energy Intake." *Journal of Nutrition* 133(3): 895S–920S.

Lowe, M. R. 1993. "The Effects of Dieting on Eating Behavior - a 3-Factor Model." *Psychological Bulletin* 114(1): 100–121.

Lyman, B. 1989. *A Psychology of Food : More Than a Matter of Taste*. New York: Van Nostrand Reinhold.

Meiselman, H. L. 1992. "Obstacles to Studying Real People Eating Real Meals in Real Situations: Response." *Appetite* 19(1): 84–86.

Meiselman, H. L., S. C. King, and A. J. Weber. 2003. "Relationship of Acceptability to Consumption in a Meal-Testing Environment, and the Use of Intake to Predict Product Acceptability in a Meal." *Appetite* 41(2): 203–204.

Mela, D. J., and P. J. Rogers. 1993. 'Snack Foods,' Overeating and Obesity: Relationships with Food Composition, Palatability, and Eating Behaviour." *British. Food Journal.* 95: 13–19.

Meyers, A. W., A. J. Stunkard, and M. Coll. 1980. "Food Accessibility and Food Choice - a Test of Schachter Externality Hypothesis." *Archives of General Psychiatry* 37(10): 1133–1135.

Miller, D. L., E. A. Bell, C. L. Pelkman, J. C. Peters, and B. J. Rolls. 2000. "Effects of Dietary Fat, Nutrition Labels, and Repeated Consumption on Sensory-Specific Satiety." *Physiology and Behavior* 71(1–2): 153–158.

Milliman, R. E. 1986. "The Influence of Background Music on the Behavior of Restaurant Patrons." *Journal of Consumer Research* 13(2): 286–289.

Mori, D., P. Pliner, and S. Chaiken. 1987. "Eating Lightly and the Self-Presentation of Femininity." *Journal of Personality and Social Psychology* 53(4): 693–702.

Murray, R. 1987. "The Effects of Consuming Carbohydrate-Electrolyte Beverages on Gastric-Emptying and Fluid Absorption During and Following Exercise." *Sports Medicine* 4(5): 322–351.

Nederkoorn, C., and A. Jansen. 2002. "Cue Reactivity and Regulation of Food Intake." *Eating Behavior* 3(1): 61–72.

Nestle, M. 2002. *Food Politics : How the Food Industry Influences Nutrition and Health*, California Studies in Food and Culture 3. Berkeley: University of California Press.

Neuendorf, K. A. 2002. *The Content Analysis Guidebook*. Thousand Oaks, CA: Sage Publications.

Nisbett, R. E. 1968. "Determinants of Food Intake in Obesity." *Science* 159(3820): 1254ff.

Nisbett, R. E., and T. D. Wilson. 1977. "Telling More Than We Can Know: Verbal Reports on Mental Processes." *Psychological Review* 84(3): 231–259.

North, A. C., and D. J. Hargreaves. 1996. "The Effects of Music on Responses to a Dining Area." *Journal of Environmental Psychology* 16(1): 55–64.

Oppenheimer, D. M. 2004. "Spontaneous Discounting of Availability in Frequency Judgment Tasks." *Psychological Science* 15(2): 100–105.

Painter, J. E., B. Wansink, and J. B. Hieggelke. 2002. "How Visibility and Convenience Influence Candy Consumption." *Appetite* 38(3): 237–238.

Pandelaere, M., and V. Hoorens. 2006. "The Effect of Category Focus at Encoding on Category Frequency Estimation Strategies." *Memory and Cognition* 34(1): 28–40.

Piaget, Jean. 1969. *The Mechanisms of Perception*. London: Routledge & Kegan Paul.

Pliner, P., and S. Chaiken. 1990. "Eating, Social Motives, and Self-Presentation in Women and Men." *Journal of Experimental Social Psychology* 26(3): 240–254.

Pliner, P. L. 1973. "Effects of Cue Salience on Behavior of Obese and Normal Subjects." *Journal of Abnormal Psychology* 82(2): 226–232.

Polivy, J., J. Coleman, and C. P. Herman. 2005. "The Effect of Deprivation on Food Cravings and Eating Behavior in Restrained and Unrestrained Eaters." *International Journal of Eating Disorders* 38(4): 301–309.

Polivy, J., and C. P. Herman. "Causes of Eating Disorders." 2002. *Annual Review of Psychology* 53: 187–213.

Polivy, J., C. P. Herman, R. Hackett, and I. Kuleshnyk. 1986. "The Effects of Self-Attention and Public Attention on Eating in Restrained and Unrestrained Subjects." *Journal of Personality and Social Psychology* 50(6): 1253–1260.

Polivy, J., C. P. Herman, J. C. Younger, and B. Erskine. 1979. "Effects of a Model on Eating Behavior: Induction of a Restrained Eating Style." *Journal of Personality* 47(1): 100–117.

Poothullil, J. M. 2002. "Role of Oral Sensory Signals in Determining Meal Size in Lean Women." *Nutrition* 18(6): 479–483.

Raghubir, P., and A. Krishna. 1999. "Vital Dimensions in Volume Perception: Can the Eye Fool the Stomach?" *Journal of Marketing Research* 36(3): 313–326.

Ragneskog, H., G. Brane, I. Karlsson, and M. Kihlgren. 1996. "Influence of Dinner Music on Food Intake and Symptoms Common in Dementia." *Scandinavian Journal of Caring Sciences* 10(1): 11–17.

Rappoport, L., G. R. Peters, R. Downey, T. McCann, and L. Huffcorzine. 1993. "Gender and Age-Differences in Food Cognition." *Appetite* 20(1): 33–52.

Roballey, T. C., C. McGreevy, R. R. Rongo, M. L. Schwantes, P. J. Steger, M. A. Wininger, and E. B. Gardner. 1985. "The Effect of Music on Eating Behavior." *Bulletin of the Psychonomic Society* 23(3): 221–222.

Rodin, J. 1974. "Effects of Distraction on the Performance of Obese and Normal Subjects." In *Obese Humans and Rats*, eds. S. Schachter and J. Rodin. Potomac, MD: L. Erlbaum Associates.

Rogers, P. J., and A. J. Hill. 1989. "Breakdown of Dietary Restraint Following Mere Exposure to Food Stimuli - Interrelationships between Restraint, Hunger, Salivation, and Food-Intake." *Addictive Behaviors* 14(4): 387–397.

Rolls, B. J. 1986. "Sensory-Specific Satiety." *Nutrition Reviews* 44(3): 93–101.

Rolls, B. J., A. E. Andersen, T. H. Moran, A. L. McNelis, H. C. Baier, and I. C. Fedoroff. 1992. "Food-Intake, Hunger, and Satiety after Preloads in Women with Eating Disorders." *American Journal of Clinical Nutrition* 55(6): 1093–1103.

Rolls, B. J., E. A. Bell, and B. A. Waugh. 2000. "Increasing the Volume of a Food by Incorporating Air Affects Satiety in Men." *American Journal of Clinical Nutrition* 72(2): 361–368.

Rolls, B. J., V. H. Castellanos, J. C. Halford, A. Kilara, D. Panyam, C. L. Pelkman, G. P. Smith, and M. L. Thorwart. 1998. "Volume of Food Consumed Affects Satiety in Men." *American Journal of Clinical Nutrition* 67(6): 1170–1177.

Rolls, B. J., D. Engell, and L. L. Birch. 2000. "Serving Portion Size Influences 5-Year-Old but Not 3-Year-Old Children's Food Intakes." *Journal of the American Dietetic Association* 100(2): 232–234.

Rolls, B. J., and T. M. McDermott. 1991. "Effects of Age on Sensory-Specific Satiety." *American Journal of Clinical Nutrition* 54(6): 988–996.

Rolls, B. J., E. L. Morris, and L. S. Roe. 2002. "Portion Size of Food Affects Energy Intake in Normal-Weight and Overweight Men and Women." *American Journal of Clinical Nutrition* 76(6): 1207–1213.

Rolls, B. J., L. S. Roe, T. V. E. Kral, J. S. Meengs, and D. E. Wall. 2004. "Increasing the Portion Size of a Packaged Snack Increases Energy Intake in Men and Women." *Appetite* 42(1): 63–69.

Rolls, B. J., E. A. Rowe, E. T. Rolls, B. Kingston, A. Megson, and R. Gunary. 1981. "Variety in a Meal Enhances Food-Intake in Man." *Physiology and Behavior* 26(2): 215–221.

Rolls, B. J. 2003. "The Supersizing of America: Portion Size and the Obesity Epidemic." *Nutrition Today* 38: 645–649.

Rolls, E. T., and J. H. Rolls. "1997. Olfactory Sensory-Specific Satiety in Humans." *Physiology and Behavior* 61(3): 461–473.

Rosenthal, N. E., M. Genhart, F. M. Jacobsen, R. G. Skwerer, and T. A. Wehr. 1987. "Disturbances of Appetite and Weight Regulation in Seasonal Affective-Disorder." *Annals of the New York Academy of Sciences* 499: 216–230.

Rozin, P. 1982. "Taste-Smell Confusions and the Duality of the Olfactory Sense." *Perception and Psychophysics* 31(4): 397–401.

Rozin, P., S. Dow, M. Moscovitch, and S. Rajaram. 1998. "What Causes Humans to Begin and End a Meal? A Role for Memory for What Has Been Eaten, as Evidenced by a Study of Multiple Meal Eating in Amnesic Patients." *Psychological Science* 9(5): 392–396.

Rozin, P., K. Kabnick, E. Pete, C. Fischler, and C. Shields. 2003. "The Ecology of Eating: Smaller Portion Sizes in France Than in the United States Help Explain the French Paradox." *Psychological Science* 14(5): 450–454.

Rozin, P., and H. Tuorila. 1993. "Simultaneous and Temporal Contextual Influences on Food Acceptance." *Food Quality and Preference* 4(1-2): 11–20.

Schachter, S. 1971. *Emotion, Obesity, and Crime.* New York: Academic.

Schachter, S., and L.N. Friedman. 1974. "The Effects of Work and Cue Prominence on Eating Behavior." In *Obese Humans and Rats*, eds. S. Schachter and J. Rodin. Potomac, MD: L. Erlbaum Associates.

Schachter, S., L. N. Freidman, and J. Handler. 1974. "Who Eats with Chopsticks?" In *Obese Humans and Rats*, eds. S. Schachter and J. Rodin. Potomac, MD: L. Erlbaum Associates.

Schwarz, N. 1996. *Cognition and Communication: Judgmental Biases, Research Methods, and the Logic of Conversation*, John M. Maceachran Memorial Lecture Series 1996. Mahwah, NJ: L. Erlbaum Associates.

Schwarz, N. 1998. "Warmer and More Social: Recent Developments in Cognitive Social Psychology." *Annual Review of Sociology* 24: 239–264.

Siegel, P. S. 1957. "The Completion Compulsion in Human Eating." *Psychological Reports* 3(1): 15–16.

Sobal, J., and B. Wansink. 2007. "Kitchenscapes, Tablescapes, Platescapes, and Foodscapes: Influences of Microscale Built Environments on Food Intake." *Environment and Behavior* 39(1): 124–142.

Sommer, R. 1969. *Personal Space: The Behavioral Basis of Design*. Englewood Cliffs, NJ: Prentice-Hall.

Staiger, P., S. Dawe, and R. McCarthy. 2000. "Responsivity to Food Cues in Bulimic Women and Controls." *Appetite* 35(1): 27–33.

Stevenson, R. J., J. Prescott, and R. A. Boakes. 1999. "Confusing Tastes and Smells: How Odours Can Influence the Perception of Sweet and Sour Tastes." *Chemical Senses* 24(6): 627–635.

Stroebele, N., and J. M. De Castro. 2004. "Effect of Ambience on Food Intake and Food Choice." *Nutrition* 20(9): 821–838.

Stroebele, N., and J. M. de Castro. 2004. "Television Viewing Is Associated with an Increase in Meal Frequency in Humans." *Appetite* 42(1): 111–113.

Sudman, S., and N. M. Bradburn. 1982. *Asking Questions*. 1st ed., Jossey-Bass Series in Social and Behavioral Sciences. San Francisco: Jossey-Bass.

Taras, H. L., J. F. Sallis, T. L. Patterson, P. R. Nader, and J. A. Nelson. 1989. "Televisions Influence on Children's Diet and Physical-Activity." *Journal of Developmental and Behavioral Pediatrics* 10(4): 176–180.

Terry, K., and S. Beck. 1985. "Eating Style and Food Storage Habits in the Home - Assessment of Obese and Nonobese Families." *Behavior Modification* 9(2): 242–261.

Tucker, L. A., and M. Bagwell. 1991. "Television Viewing and Obesity in Adult Females." *American Journal of Public Health* 81(7): 908–911.

Tucker, L. A., and G. M. Friedman. 1989. "Television Viewing and Obesity in Adult Males." *American Journal of Public Health* 79(4): 516–518.

Tuomisto, T., M. T. Tuomisto, M. Hetherington, and R. Lappalainen. 1998. "Reasons for Initiation and Cessation of Eating in Obese Men and Women and the Affective Consequences of Eating in Everyday Situations." *Appetite* 30(2): 211–222.

van Herpen, E., and R. Pieters. 2002. "The Variety of an Assortment: An Extension to the Attribute-Based Approach." *Marketing Science* 21(3): 331–341.

van Ittersum, K., and B. Wansink. 2007. "Do Children Really Prefer Large Portions? Visual Illusions Bias Their Estimates and Intake." *Journal of the American Dietetic Association* 107(7): 1107–1110.

Vartanian, Lenny R., C. Peter Herman, and Brian Wansink (2008), "Are We Aware of the External Factors That Influence Our Food Intake?" *Health Psychology*, 27:5, 533–538.

Volkow, N. D., G. J. Wang, J. S. Fowler, J. Logan, M. Jayne, D. Franceschi, C. Wong, S. J. Gatley, A. N. Gifford, Y. S. Ding, and N. Pappas. 2002. "'Nonhedonic' Food Motivation in Humans Involves Dopamine in the Dorsal Striatum and Methylphenidate Amplifies This Effect." *Synapse* 44(3): 175–180.

Wansink, B. 1994. "Antecedents and Mediators of Eating Bouts." *Family and Consumer Sciences Research Journal* 23(2): 166–182.

Wansink, B. 1996. "Can Package Size Accelerate Usage Volume?" *Journal of Marketing* 60(3): 1–14.

Wansink, B. 2004. "Environmental Factors That Increase the Food Intake and Consumption Volume of Unknowing Consumers." *Annual Review of Nutrition* 24: 455–479.

Wansink, B. 2005. *Marketing Nutrition: Soy, Functional Foods, Biotechnology, and Obesity*, The Food Series. Urbana: University of Illinois Press.

Wansink, B. 2006. *Mindless Eating : Why We Eat More Than We Think*. New York: Bantam Books.

Wansink, B., and P. Chandon. 2006. "Meal Size, Not Body Size, Explains Errors in Estimating the Calorie Content of Meals." *Annals of Internal Medicine* 145(5): 326–332.

Wansink, B., and M. M. Cheney. 2005. "Super Bowls: Serving Bowl Size and Food Consumption." *Jama-Journal of the American Medical Association* 293(14): 1727–1728.

Wansink, B., M. M. Cheney, and N. Chan. 2003. "Exploring Comfort Food Preferences across Age and Gender." *Physiology and Behavior* 79(4–5): 739–747.

Wansink, B., and Deshpande R. 1994. "'Out of Sight, Out of Mind': The Impact of Household Stockpiling on Usage Rates." *Marketing Letters*. 5: 91–100.

Wansink, B., and J. Kim. 2005. "Bad Popcorn in Big Buckets: Portion Size Can Influence Intake as Much as Taste." *Journal of Nutrition Education and Behavior* 37(5): 242–245.

Wansink, B., and J. Painter. 2005. "Proximity's Influence on Estimated and Actual Candy Consumption." *Obesity Research* 13: A204–A04.

Wansink, B., J. E. Painter, and J. North. 2005. "Bottomless Bowls: Why Visual Cues of Portion Size May Influence Intake." *Obesity Research* 13(1): 93–100.

Wansink, B., and S. B. Park. 2001. "At the Movies: How External Cues and Perceived Taste Impact Consumption Volume." *Food Quality and Preference* 12(1): 69–74.

Wansink, B., C. R. Payne, and P. Chandon. 2007. "Internal and External Cues of Meal Cessation: The French Paradox Redux?" *Obesity* 15(12): 2920–2924.

Wansink, B., and J. Sobal. 2007. "Mindless Eating: The 200 Daily Food Decisions We Overlook." *Environment and Behavior* 39(1): 106–123.

Wansink, B., and K. Van Ittersum. 2003. "Bottoms Up! The Influence of Elongation on Pouring and Consumption Volume." *Journal of Consumer Research* 30(3): 455–463.

Wansink, B., and K. van Ittersum. 2005. "Shape of Glass and Amount of Alcohol Poured: Comparative Study of Effect of Practice and Concentration." *British Medical Journal* 331(7531): 1512–1514.

Wansink, B., and K. Van Ittersum. 2010. "Illusive Consumption Behavior and the Delboeuf Illusion: Are the Eyes Really Bigger Than the Stomach?" Under review.

Wansink, B., K. van Ittersum, and J. E. Painter. 2006. "Ice Cream Illusions - Bowls, Spoons, and Self-Served Portion Sizes." *American Journal of Preventive Medicine* 31(3): 240–243.

Weber, Robert Philip. 1990. *Basic Content Analysis*. 2nd ed, Sage University Papers Series. Quantitative Applications in the Social Sciences No. 07–049. Newbury Park, CA: Sage Publications.

Weingarten, H. P. 1984. "Meal Initiation Controlled by Learned Cues - Basic Behavioral Properties." *Appetite* 5(2): 147–158.

Westerterp-Plantenga, M. S. 1999. "Effects of Extreme Environments on Food Intake in Human Subjects." *Proceedings of the Nutrition Society* 58(4): 791–798.

WHO. "Obesity: Preventing and Managing a Global Epidemic." Geneva: World Health Organization. 2009

Wing, R. R., and R. W. Jeffery. 2001. "Food Provision as a Strategy to Promote Weight Loss." *Obesity Research* 9: 271S–75S.

Yanovski, J. A., S. Z. Yanovski, K. N. Sovik, T. T. Nguyen, P. M. O'Neil, and N. G. Sebring. 2000. "A Prospective Study of Holiday Weight Gain." *New England Journal of Medicine* 342(12): 861–867.

Young, L. R., and M. Nestle. 2002. "The Contribution of Expanding Portion Sizes to the Us Obesity Epidemic." *American Journal of Public Health* 92(2): 246–249.

CHAPTER 24

FOOD ASSISTANCE
AND OBESITY

MICHELE VER PLOEG[1]

In the wake of the War on Poverty, the United States government implemented and expanded a number of programs designed to reduce hunger and improve nutrition among low-income and vulnerable populations. Since then, these programs have been expanded, so much so that over the course of a year, one in five Americans receives benefits from a U.S. Department of Agriculture (USDA) nutrition assistance program (USDA 2009a). Overall, about $60 billion per year is spent on food and nutrition assistance programs in the U.S., which comprises about 63 percent of the total USDA budget. The largest and most widely available of these programs are the Supplemental Nutrition Assistance Program (SNAP, formerly the Food Stamp Program), the National School Lunch and School Breakfast Programs (NSLP and SBP), and the Supplemental Nutrition Program for Women, Infants and Children (WIC). Each of these programs targets different subgroups of the population and emphasizes different nutritional and policy objectives. They share the common goal of addressing the food needs of Americans who otherwise would not be able to afford the food they need.

Increases in obesity rates in the United States have prompted a reexamination of the goals and policies of these programs. Some critics have wondered whether the programs had the unintentional consequence of providing too much food— leading participants to become overweight or obese. The healthfulness and nutritional quality of foods or meals provided through these programs have also been questioned. It has also been argued that the specific foods provided through some

---

1 The views expressed here are the author's and may not be attributed to the Economic Research Service or the United States Department of Agriculture.

of these programs should be reevaluated so that participants receive healthier foods. And while the promotion of healthy eating has always been a part of these programs, there are increasing calls to take more proactive steps to improve nutrition among participants by changing program rules to actively encourage the consumption of some foods, while discouraging the consumption of others.

This chapter reviews evidence of the relationship between food assistance programs and obesity. The focus is primarily on the largest U.S. food assistance programs, SNAP, the two school meals programs, and WIC, which are each reviewed in separate sections of this chapter. Each section begins with a short summary of the program and considers how the program rules and policies might be linked to obesity. Empirical evidence of the relationships between these programs and obesity is then reviewed. The chapter concludes with a discussion of changes to the programs' rules and practices that have been proposed or implemented in order to address obesity and poor nutrition.

Assessing causal relations between food assistance program participation and body weight is difficult because no experiments have been conducted that compare the body weight outcomes of some participants who are randomly assigned to receive program benefits with that of others who are assigned to a comparison program (or no program). Researchers must instead rely on non-experimental methods that try to determine what would have happened if recipients had not received program benefits or if an alternative program was implemented. But non-experimental methods may be subject to self-selection bias because not all those who are eligible for these programs choose to participate. Those who choose to participate may be different than those who choose not to participate in ways that are not observable and that may be correlated with body weight. For example, those with greater food needs relative to other needs may choose to enroll in a food assistance program. This self-selection may lead to biased estimates of the true effect of food assistance program participation on body weight if the selection is not controlled for in statistical models. In reviewing the evidence, distinctions are made between studies that account for these biases and those that do not. But in some cases, the literature is sparse and the best available studies are ones that have not accounted for selection bias.

The chapter focuses on the United States. While adult obesity rates in the United States are among the highest in the world, other developed and developing countries are battling this health problem as well. However, the United States is unique among the developed world in the scope and size of its food assistance policies. Food aid, either through the direct provision of commodities or through cash and in-kind transfers to poor families, is common among less-developed countries. In addition, some conditional cash transfer programs in less-developed countries are aimed at increasing food consumption (e.g., the PROGRESA program in Mexico and the Red de Proteccion Social (RPS) in Nicaragua). However, the primary health concerns in the populations targeted by these types of programs are underweight and stunting. Thus, there has yet been little attention paid to the impact of food assistance programs on obesity outside of the United States.

The Supplemental Nutrition Assistance Program (SNAP)

SNAP provides households with monthly Electronic Benefit Transfer (EBT) cards that can be used at participating food retailers to purchase food to be prepared at home. The program is an entitlement program available to all U.S. households that meet eligibility requirements for income, assets, work and immigration status. Eligibility and benefit levels are based on household size, household assets, and gross and net income. The average benefit level in 2008 was $227 for each household or $102 for each person. SNAP is the largest USDA food assistance program, serving a monthly average of 28.4 million people in 2008. Of these participants, 49 percent are children, 9 percent are elderly, and 42 percent are working-age adults (USDA 2009b).

How Might SNAP Be Linked to Body Weight?

The SNAP benefit can only be used to buy food. This could lead participants to spend more money on food (and presumably consume more) than they would if they were given cash. Increased consumption of food could lead to weight gain among some participants. This hypothesis is backed with empirical evidence on food spending from the food stamp cash-out experiments, where randomly assigned participants received an equal level of benefits as cash. For every dollar, food expenditures from food stamp benefits were $0.18 to $0.28 greater than food expenditures from cash (Fraker et al. 1995).

The implicit argument in this hypothesis is that participants use the food benefits to buy and consume more food. But participants could change the bundle of foods they buy, shifting spending to relatively more expensive foods that were previously out of reach (e.g., higher-quality cuts of meats or fresh fruits and vegetables instead of canned). Wilde et al. (2000) found that, compared with nonparticipants, SNAP participants consumed the same amount of fruits, vegetables, grains, and dairy, but more meat and added sugars and total fats.

A second hypothesis that has been offered to explain the association between SNAP participation and obesity is tied to the program's administrative practice that distributes SNAP benefits on a monthly basis. It has been argued that some participants may overconsume food right after the benefit is received and run out of food later in the month before the next month's benefit is received. This feast then famine pattern of consumption could lead to weight gain over time (Townsend et al. 2001). The "food stamp cycle hypothesis," as it has been called, has not been explicitly tested. However, descriptive analysis shows some participants' behaviors are consistent with the hypothesis (Townsend et al. 2001; Shapiro 2005; Wilde and Peterman 2006; Wilde and Ranney 2000).

Empirical Evidence on the Relationship between SNAP and Obesity

Evidence on the link between SNAP participation and body weight is mixed and depends on the age and sex of the group studied. For the majority of participants—children, non-elderly men, and the elderly—SNAP participation does not increase either BMI or the likelihood of being overweight or obese. Working age women, who make up 28 percent of SNAP participants, are the only group for which multiple studies find a link between participation and body weight.

Baum (2007), Gibson (2003) and Meyerhoefer and Pylypchuk (2008) each use longitudinal data and attempt to control for selection bias. Results from these three studies indicate that current SNAP participation increases the probability that a woman is obese by a range of 2 to 5 percentage points. Baum (2007), Kaushal (2007), and Jones and Frongillo (2006) examined the link between SNAP and BMI. Baum found that SNAP participation was associated with a 0.5-point increase in BMI for women. For women between 5'4" and 5'6" inches tall, this is about a 3-pound difference. Studying a specific subpopulation of the United States—foreign-born women—Kaushal found no link between SNAP and BMI (2007). Similarly, Jones and Frongillo (2006) focused specifically on women of different food security statuses and found no link between SNAP and BMI.

Long-term participation in SNAP may have a larger impact for women. Both Baum (2007) and Gibson (2003) find that the effects of long-term participation in SNAP on the probability of obesity are larger. The size of this effect varies from an increase in the likelihood of obesity by 10 percentage points for two or more years of participation (Baum 2007), to an increase of 4.5 percentage points for five years of participation (Gibson 2003).

None of the studies that examined the relationship between SNAP participation and men's body weight found a link between participation and BMI, overweight, or obesity (Ver Ploeg and Ralston 2008). Baum (2007) found some evidence that SNAP may be related to greater BMI for men, but not at a level that increases the likelihood of overweight or obesity. The increases in BMI could reflect an improvement in health among underweight men. Baum (2007) also found that long-term participation in SNAP was linked to increased BMI and the probability of obesity for men, although Gibson (2003) did not find such a link.

Most of the studies of the relationship between SNAP and children's body weight consider school-age children instead of preschool children, and most separately consider adolescents from preteens. None of the studies that consider adolescent children finds that SNAP participation is linked to BMI or the probability of overweight (see Ver Ploeg and Ralston 2008). Two studies of adolescents use either longitudinal data or instrumental variables to address selection bias (Gibson 2004; Hofferth and Curtin 2005). Neither finds a significant relationship between SNAP and obesity for adolescent children. For young school children, however, the results are mixed. Gibson found that an additional year of SNAP participation was positively linked to overweight among young girls, but negatively related to overweight among young boys (2004). Jones et al. (2003) found no relationship between SNAP participation and overweight for young boys. In contrast to Gibson (2004), however, the study found a negative effect of SNAP participation and overweight among young girls. Neither of these studies can explain why young boys and girls might be differentially affected by participation in the SNAP program. One possible explanation that was not explored in either paper is that there are differences in physical activity between young boys and young girls, especially among those who are low-income and more likely to be SNAP participants.

There are far fewer studies of the relationship between SNAP and body weight for elderly individuals. One descriptive study that did not account for selection bias found that SNAP participation increased the likelihood of obesity among women age 60–69, but not for women over 70 or men of either age group (Fox and Cole 2004). Another study found that SNAP participation had a protective effect against overweight among food-insecure elders (Kim and Frongillo 2007).

The differences in findings between men and women are not easily explained. Several factors may account for the inconsistency. Fox and Cole (2004) found that male SNAP participants consume fewer calories than higher-income male non-participants for most age groups, but that female SNAP participants consume more calories than higher income female non-participants. Differences in activity levels between low-income men and low-income women may possibly be a factor—if, for example, low-income men are more likely to have higher physical activity levels than otherwise similar low-income women and higher-income men. Chen et al. (2005) suggest that differences in caloric requirements between men and women may account for the differential effects, because SNAP benefit levels do not differ by the sex of a recipient. The implication of this is that SNAP benefit levels should be tied to the gender of the recipient. However, given equity concerns and the fact that the program is targeted to households, not individuals, such a policy is unlikely to receive much consideration.

National School Lunch Program and the School Breakfast Program

The National School Lunch Program (NSLP) and the School Breakfast Program (SBP) serve meals to children in schools. The NSLP serves lunch in public and non-profit private schools and residential child care institutions for free or at low cost to children each school day. School lunches must meet federal nutrition requirements for calories from fat and saturated fat, as well as recommended dietary allowances for protein, Vitamin A, Vitamin C, iron, calcium and calories. Aside from these requirements, the specific foods served and how they are prepared are at the discretion of local school food authorities.

The SBP generally operates in the same manner as the NSLP. School districts and independent schools can choose to participate in the SBP. Participating schools receive a cash subsidy from the USDA. In return, they must serve breakfasts that meet federal requirements and they must offer free or reduced-price breakfasts to eligible children.

Both programs offer free meals for students with income at or below 130 percent of federal poverty guidelines, reduced-price meals for students with income between 131 and 185 percent of federal poverty guidelines, and full-priced meals for all other students. In 2008, the NSLP served 15.4 million free, 3.1 million reduced-price, and 12.5 million full-priced meals in an average month. (See Ralston et al. 2008 for more background on the NSLP program.) The SBP program served 7.5 million free, 1.0 million reduced-price, and 2.1 million full-priced breakfasts in an average month in 2008.

How Might School Lunch and School Breakfast Affect Body Weight?

Some have worried that the foods served in school lunches and breakfasts are too high in fat, provide too many calories, and that the program could do a better job of promoting consumption of fruits, vegetables, and whole grains. The more energy-dense foods are hypothesized to contribute to increases in BMI and overweight among children who eat school meals.

Empirical Evidence of the Link between School Meals and Body Weight

Four studies have examined the relationship between NSLP participation and childhood overweight and obesity. Three find a positive effect of the NSLP program, while one does not find an effect.

Two studies use longitudinal data from the Early Childhood Longitudinal Study-Kindergarten cohort (ECLS-K) to examine the effect of NSLP participation on body weight later in the child's school career (at first grade, third grade, or fifth grade) (Schanzenbach 2005; Tchernis et al. 2008). Both of these studies, which use different techniques to account for selection bias, find that NSLP participation increases body weight or the likelihood of overweight or obesity. Schanzenbach (2005) found that children who ate school lunch were 2 percentage points more likely to be obese at the end of first grade than those who did not. Tchernis et al. (2008) find that when self-selection is not considered, there is no relationship between NSLP participation and body weight. But this study finds that selection into both the NSLP and SBP programs bias the average effect of NSLP participation downward—when selection is controlled, participation in the NSLP is positively related to BMI for children.

Hofferth and Curtin (2005) use two data sets and public school attendance as an instrumental variable to estimate the effect of NSLP participation on obesity and

BMI. They find that NSLP participation was positively linked to overweight and BMI. Finally, Gleason and Headley Dodd (2009) find no effect of NSLP participation and children's body weight. They use cross-sectional data from the School Nutrition Dietary Assessment Study (SNDA-III) to study how the frequency with which a student usually eats school lunch per week is associated with obesity. This study is not longitudinal, but it does include very rich measures of the school environment and parents' assessments of their child's physical activity and usual eating behaviors.

These studies suggest a positive link between NSLP and obesity and BMI, but the evidence is not universal. Differences in BMI between NSLP participants and non-participants could arise because of differences in total energy intake or differences in physical activity levels. A few studies have examined energy intake differences (Fox et al. 2004). Devaney et al. (1993) and Gleason and Suitor (2003) did not find a significant difference in energy intakes at lunch of NSLP participants and non-participants after adjusting for selection bias. Both studies found that similar levels of energy intake over a one-day period for NSLP participants and nonparticipants. In contrast, Schanzenbach (2005) found that school lunch eaters seem to eat about 40 more calories per day than students who do not eat school lunch and that all of these additional calories are consumed at lunch.

The role of physical activity in explaining any differences in BMI and obesity between participants and non-participants has not been fully explored. Gleason and Headley Dodd (2009) controlled for parental assessments of children's physical activity and found that these assessments were strong predictors of children's BMI. It is possible that the low-income segments of NSLP participants are less likely to be involved in extracurricular sports or recreational opportunities or may have home environments less conducive to outdoor play. As a result, they may engage in less physical activity than higher-income children.

In contrast to the NSLP, empirical evidence shows that participation in the SBP may have a protective effect on children's body weight. Gleason and Headley Dodd (2009) found that participation in the SBP is negatively correlated with a child's BMI and is not associated with the probability of overweight or obesity. This study found that a student who ate a school breakfast every day had an expected BMI that was 0.75 points lower than a student who never ate a school breakfast (or about 4 pounds for a student 5 feet tall). Tchernis et al. (2008) found a strong positive selection into SBP (participation in the program is correlated with trajectories in the child's weight). But once this selection was addressed, SBP participants had lower BMI relative to nonparticipants. Hofferth and Curtin (2005) found no association for SBP participation and body weight. Each of these studies also controlled for participation in the NSLP.

Corroborating this evidence are results from a study that used variation in the availability of SBP across schools and seasons, along with a difference-in-difference methodology to examine the relationship between SBP participation and children's dietary health outcomes (Bhattacharya et al. 2006). Results showed that SBP participation resulted in higher scores on the Healthy Eating Index—a measure of overall dietary quality—and reduced the percentage of calories from fat. SBP participation did not increase overall energy intake, nor did it increase the frequency of eating breakfast (children were not more likely to eat two breakfasts).

Gleason and Headley Dodd (2009) also found suggestive evidence that SBP participation could make students less likely to skip breakfast. Since eating breakfast is associated with lower BMI, the role of the SBP may be to provide a breakfast of any kind, not just one with specific nutritional qualities.

The Supplemental Nutrition Assistance Program for Women, Infants, and Children (WIC)

The WIC program provides vouchers for foods, nutrition education, and health referrals to pregnant and postpartum women, infants, and children up to age 4 years who have incomes below 185 percent of the federal poverty line or are adjunctively eligible through participation in Medicaid, SNAP, or the Temporary Assistance for Needy Families (TANF) program. Participants can use vouchers to purchase approved foods that contain specific nutrients (protein, calcium, iron, vitamin A, and vitamin C) that tend to be low in the diets of the populations served by the program. The foods that are approved vary according to the targeted population. The food voucher averages a retail value of $43.41 per month. WIC served 8.7 million women, infants, and children in 2008. For the first time since the program became nationally available, new food packages—or the lists of foods that can be purchased with the voucher—were implemented in states in 2009.

The WIC program has received less attention in terms of its role in obesity—probably because it covers only subsets of the population and provides foods with specific nutrients targeted to specific vulnerable populations. Some commentators criticized the old food packages for providing too many calories, even if those foods contain specific nutrients (Besharov 2002). A broader criticism of the program, but one that may have implications for obesity, is that the program unintentionally discourages breast-feeding among some postpartum women because it provides infant formula, a high-cost item for poor mothers. Breast-feeding may protect babies against becoming obese later in life (Arenz et al. 2004). Research shows that WIC participants have lower rates of exclusive breast-feeding for infants greater than four months old, but also that the infant formula provided through the program is important for women who do not exclusively breast-feed (Jacknowitz et al. 2007).

The few studies that directly examine the relationship between WIC participation and body weight all focus on children. One study that controlled for self-selection by using state variation in Medicaid eligibility limits for children

(Medicaid participation confers adjunctive eligibility for WIC) found that children who participated in the WIC program at age 4 had *lower* BMI and were less likely to be overweight (Bitler and Currie 2004). Two studies that did not account for selection bias found no association between WIC participation and weight status (CDC, 1996; Ver Ploeg et al. 2007). These results are consistent with a study that compared calories consumed from different foods for children who participate in WIC with those who do not (Oliveira and Chandran 2005). This study found that WIC participants consumed the same total number of calories as eligible non-participants. Further, WIC participants consumed more WIC-approved juice and cereal than non-participants at all income levels. These results suggest that the WIC foods substitute for other foods within food categories and that WIC does not lead to an overall increase in calories.

The effect of WIC participation on women's body weight has not been studied. This is likely due to the difficulty of studying the effect of current WIC participation on women's body weight given that the women who participate are either pregnant or within one year postpartum. It would be worthwhile to examine whether WIC participation is related to weight gain above recommended levels during pregnancy (either positively or negatively) or if postpartum women who receive WIC benefits have differential weight loss during the postpartum period. The nutrition education received as part of WIC participation may have longer-term effects on controlling body weight and healthier eating. Studying the longer-term relationship between WIC participation and body weight for women and children could also be informative.

The Effect of Multiple Program Participation on Body Weight

Many low-income families receive benefits from more than one food assistance program. For example, among children in low income households that received SNAP in 2004, 77 percent lived in a household where someone participated in the school meals programs and 34 percent lived in a household where someone participated in WIC (Todd et al. 2009). It is possible that the combined effects of participation in multiple food assistance programs on obesity are stronger than the effect of participation in any one program. Or, as seems to be the case with SBP and NSLP, there may be an interaction between the programs that plays a role in the body weight of participants.

Further, the benefits that some household members receive could have implications for the food consumption of other household members. For example, participation in the school meals programs by older children in the household could allow households to purchase more food for all household members. WIC foods targeted to one child in the household could be consumed by other children in the household.

Aside from the few studies that consider the effect of NSLP and SBP participation, no studies consider the joint effects of participating in multiple food assistance programs and body weight. Bhattacharya et al. (2006) consider the effects that participation in the SBP may have on the diets and dietary health of other household members, but they do not specifically examine body weight or obesity. New research on the effects of multiple food assistance program participation could further our understanding of the relationship between food assistance programs and body weight.

Food Assistance Programs as Obesity Combatants

Because U.S. food and nutrition assistance programs touch the lives of so many Americans, they have been considered as possible policy levers for combating obesity. This section discusses some of the policy changes that have been implemented or are being considered in order to reduce obesity and improve nutrition among program participants and low-income populations. Empirical findings about the potential success of different policy options will also be discussed.

SNAP Policy

SNAP benefits are targeted to households, not individuals, an important distinction when considering possible options for changing the SNAP program to address obesity. Results discussed above show that SNAP benefits may lead to weight gain among some participants but not others. A challenge for changing SNAP policy may be to address overconsumption of food for some household members while not adversely affecting food consumption, nutrition, or weight status of other household members.

One prominent critique of the SNAP program argues that food consumption could be reduced among program participants if the benefits were "cashed out," or given as cash instead of as a food benefit (Besharov 2002). No study has directly assessed whether higher marginal propensities to consume food out of food stamps cause participants to gain weight. Meyerhoefer and Pylypchuk (2008) provide an informal test, however. Using evidence from the cash-out experiments showing that only households with multiple adults had higher marginal propensities to consume food out of food stamps while single adult households did not (Breunig and Dasgupta 2005), Meyerhoefer and Pylypchuk conduct separate estimates of the effect of food stamp participation on the probability of obesity for women in single adult households and compare them with women in multiple adult households. If greater marginal propensities to consume food from food stamps are driving the weight gain among women, then we would expect that the effects of food stamp participation would be greater for women in multiple adult households. However, this test finds that the effect of food stamp participation on obesity is larger for women in single adult households than in multiple adult households. Thus, initial evidence does not support the idea that obesity is caused because food stamp benefits constrain participants to consume more food than they otherwise would.

The cash-out idea argues that participants should not be constrained to spend more on food than they otherwise would. Others have argued that some healthier foods are more expensive than less healthy foods and, as a result, participants should be given *greater* SNAP allotments so that they can afford healthier food options. A related idea is to issue a targeted benefit—a discount—to encourage purchases of healthy foods. The state of California has passed legislation to conduct a pilot program to give participants bonus benefits that can be spent only on fresh produce. Pilot programs with similar incentives will be funded through the new Healthy Incentive Pilot (HIP). Congress appropriated $20 million for projects to evaluate health and nutrition promotion in SNAP to determine if such incentives provided to recipients at the point of sale increase the purchase of fruits, vegetables, and other healthful foods (USDA 2009c). The flip side of this is to tax products that are overconsumed and less healthy.

While results from the HIP will eventually give a better idea of how successful these programs could be in promoting healthy eating and perhaps reducing obesity, cross-sectional analysis of consumer purchasing behaviors show that bonuses may need to be large in order to encourage a shift in healthier food choices.

An untargeted increase in food benefits may not have much of an impact on fruit, vegetable, cereal and bakery products, or dairy consumption given data on spending on these goods across the income spectrum. Spending on these food categories is fairly flat across income levels—an increase in fruit and vegetable spending occurs only in households with incomes above $70,000 annually (Frazao et al. 2007). For example, households with annual income of $15,000–$19,999 spend $4 more per month on average on fruits and vegetables than households with annual income of $10,000–$14,999. Given that such a difference in income between these groups (approximately $400 per month) induces a $4 increase in fruit and vegetables purchases, providing these lower-income households with an extra $100 in monthly income may increase spending on these goods by only $1 per month for the entire household (Frazao et al. 2007).

Consumer demand models of price sensitivity show estimates of the impact of a 10 percent discount in the price of fruits and vegetables. A 10 percent discount is estimated to increase the amount of fruits and vegetables purchased by 2.1 to 5.2 percent for fruits and 2.1 to 4.9 percent for vegetables (Dong and Lin, 2009). SNAP participants consume 0.96 cup of fruits and 1.43 cups of. Even using the higher estimates of price elasticities from a 10 percent discount would result in just over a cup of fruits and just over 1.5 cups of vegetables consumed by SNAP participants. The annual cost of a 10 percent discount on fruits and vegetables for low-income Americans would be about $310 million for fruits and $270 million for vegetables

(Dong and Lin, 2009). Such incentives to encourage healthier choices among SNAP participants and low-income households may increase consumption of those foods. It is not clear, however, whether increased consumption of those foods may affect obesity. The presumption is that increases in fruit and vegetable consumption will decrease consumption of less healthy foods so that total calories do not increase.

Restricting choices of foods that can be purchased with SNAP may be a more direct method of reducing consumption of less healthy foods. This has been proposed in at least one state—Minnesota unsuccessfully requested permission to prohibit the purchase of candy and soft drinks with SNAP benefits. Two factors make such restrictions difficult to implement effectively. First, most SNAP participants spend more money on food than their monthly SNAP allotment. For example, the average benefit for a family of 4 was $326 in fiscal year 2004, but the average low-income family of 4 spent $462 on food each month (Guthrie et al. 2007). The household could use their own money to purchase any foods restricted by SNAP. Another practical problem in implementing a restriction on what foods can be purchased with SNAP benefits come from defining what foods can be restricted. For example, in the Minnesota request, Hershey chocolate bars would not be allowed but Kit-Kat and Twix candies would because they contain flour (Guthrie et al. 2007). Food manufacturers would likely respond to any definition of a restricted product by developing new products that may be slightly different so that they are not restricted, but may not necessarily be any healthier. These complications could thwart the effectiveness of any restriction to the foods that can be purchased with SNAP benefits.

The SNAP program includes a component for nutrition education—the SNAP-Ed program. This program provides nutrition education to SNAP participants and eligible non-participants. The program is a federal-state partnership, with the USDA reimbursing states 50 percent of SNAP-Ed program costs. SNAP-Ed is operating in all 50 states with a federal budget of $247 million in 2006 (Guthrie and Variyam 2007). On average, the combination of state and federal funds resulted in SNAP-Ed spending of less than $20 per participant in 2006 (Guthrie and Variyam 2007). The educational components often include group classes, brochures and printed materials, and social marketing campaigns. Because the programs vary in content, size, and funding, there has been little systematic evaluation of whether the program has had an impact on nutrition. However, SNAP-Ed and its already existing infrastructure is one potential source of promoting healthier diets among low-income individuals.

School Meal Policies

The NSLP and SBP serve a large percentage of all children in the United States and provide a major part of total food consumption each day for participating children. Because of this, there are often calls to use the programs to address childhood obesity and improve overall nutrition.

Evidence suggests that SBP may have a protective effect against obesity among participants—seemingly because it provides a breakfast for many children who would not otherwise eat breakfast and would then over-consume calories throughout the rest of the day. If this is indeed the case, then expanding the SBP to other school districts may help reduce the number of children who skip breakfast and thus may protect against childhood obesity.

It may also be possible to modify the content of the foods available from both the NLSP and SBP to reduce the risk of overconsumption and greater BMI among participants. Content of school meals is primarily up to the discretion of local schools or the School Feeding Authorities (SFAs). However, to receive reimbursement for meals, SFAs are expected to meet USDA nutrition standards. The tie between nutrition standards and reimbursement rates could provide a policy lever for encouraging better meal content. A recent Institute of Medicine (IOM) report recommended a new set of school meal standards that would increase the amount of some foods served in school meals, such as fruits, vegetables, and whole grains (IOM 2009). This report estimated that the new standards would likely raise food costs and perhaps labor costs, which may mean that meal reimbursement rates would need to be raised. In addition to meeting nutritional standards, SFAs must also control costs while keeping revenues high by maintaining or increasing participation. Improving meal content, while keeping costs low and revenue high, is likely to pose a challenge to any change in standards. It has also been suggested that an additional school meal funding stream (outside of reimbursement) could be used as an effective tool to incentivize improvements in meals—so that local schools that meet some criteria for improving the content of meals within a budget could be rewarded with additional funding.

Another federal policy lever to improve school meals could be tied to the USDA commodity foods, which are foods directly given to school districts. This program could continue to improve and expand upon on-going efforts to provide healthier commodity foods to schools through the program's fruit and vegetable purchases and through reductions in the fat, sodium and sugar levels in commodities.

Almost all middle and high schools and a sizable proportion of elementary schools allow competitive foods to be sold in schools—through vending machines, snack bars, a la carte options, and school stores (Story 2009). There is evidence that such competitive food availability affects a child's food intake and increases BMI (Fox et al. 2009). Eliminating these foods, or discouraging the availability of low-nutrient, high-energy foods sold, could be effective in reducing total caloric intake and help control BMI (Fox et al. 2009). For the most part, the availability of competitive foods is the decision of local SFAs. However, the USDA can limit sales of foods in the cafeteria during mealtime if the food has only minimum nutritional value.

WIC Program Policy

A broad goal of the WIC program is to improve the nutrition and diets of low-income populations. The program includes a nutritional education component that could be used to specifically address overweight and obesity. In its report recommending changes to the WIC food package, the Institute of Medicine named the risk of obesity as a major new problem in the United States that spurred changes to the food package to promote healthy body weight for WIC participants (Institute of Medicine 2006). The new food packages that were adopted in states in 2009 omit some foods that were in the previous food packages, reduce the amounts of others, reduce the fat content of milk for women and children age 2 and older, and add new foods. New foods include whole grain bread and a $6–10 voucher for fruits and vegetables. These changes were made to encourage healthier eating overall, but specifically to encourage participants to substitute healthier for less healthy foods. The packages for postpartum women and infants were also changed to help encourage breast-feeding, which, if it is successful, could have future implications for childhood obesity since breast-feeding serves to protect babies against becoming obese later in life (Arenz et al. 2004).

CONCLUSIONS AND FUTURE RESEARCH

As the share of the U.S. population that is overweight and obese increases, food assistance programs in the U.S. are challenged to jointly address the problems of both under- and overnutrition. This review indicates some areas of concern where these programs may inadvertently be contributing to the problem of overweight and obesity. Specifically, current research shows that among adult women, those who participate in the SNAP program may have higher BMI and are more prone to obesity, although results for other gender and age groups show no effect of SNAP participation. Data on the NSLP program also show mixed results, with some studies showing a positive relationship between participation and BMI and overweight, while others find no effect. On the other hand, the SBP may have a protective effect on participants' body weights, while the WIC program is either not linked to BMI or overweight among children who participate or has a protective effect against overweight.

The programs, however, also represent opportunities for addressing the obesity problem. Several changes to the programs that are geared to improving diet and reducing the risk of obesity have recently been implemented or are being considered. The new WIC food package is a potential tool for reshaping part of the diets of low-income, nutritionally vulnerable groups by encouraging fruit and vegetable, whole grain, and other healthy food consumption. The new package is also designed to encourage breast-feeding, an outcome that could have longer-term implications for childhood obesity. For the SNAP program, evaluation of the Healthy Incentive Pilot program should give an indication of whether targeted bonuses to increase consumption of specific foods can effectively improve diet and reduce obesity.

Little work has been conducted to understand which program changes or new policies might be effective in addressing obesity among low-income individuals. Early indications show that the effects of proposed changes, such as an incentive to purchase more fruits and vegetables, may have an impact on diet—albeit, perhaps a small one. Less is known about how these changes may ultimately affect BMI and obesity. If coupled with other changes in public and private policy aimed at addressing obesity, these adjustments to food assistance programs could reinforce healthier diets and help reduce obesity among low-income and vulnerable populations.

REFERENCES

Arenz, S, R. Rückerl, B. Koletzko, and R. von Kries. 2004. "Breast-feeding and Childhood Obesity—A Systematic Review," *International Journal of Obesity* 28: 1247–1256.

Baum, C. (2007). "The Effects of Food Stamps on Obesity." Contractor and Cooperator Report No. 34. U.S. Department of Agriculture, Economic Research Service.

Besharov, D. J. (2002). "We're Feeding the Poor as if They're Starving." *Washington Post*, December 8.

Bhattacharya, J., J. Currie, S. Haider (2006). "Breakfast of Champions? The School Breakfast Program and the Nutrition of Children and Families." *Journal of Human Resources* 41(3): 445–466.

Bitler, M. P., and J. Currie. 2004. "Medicaid at Birth, WIC Take-up, and Children's Outcomes." Institute for Research on Poverty Discussion Paper no. 1286–1204. Madison, WI.

Breunig, R., and I. Dasgupta (2005). "Do Intra-Household Effects Generate the Food Stamp Cash-Out Puzzle?" *American Journal of Agricultural Economics* 87(3): 552–568.

Centers for Disease Control and Prevention. 1996. "Nutritional Status of Children Participating in the Special Supplemental Nutrition Program for Women, Infants, and Children—United States, 1988–1991." *Morbidity and Mortality Weekly Report* 45(3): 65–69.

Chen, Z., S. T.Yen, and D. B. Eastwood. 2005. "Effects of Food Stamp Participation on Body Weight and Obesity." *American Journal of Agricultural Economics* 87(5): 1167–1173.

Devaney, B. L., A. R. Gordon, and J. A. Burghardt. 1993. *The School Nutrition Dietary Assessment Study: Dietary Intakes of Program Participants and Nonparticipants*. Final report submitted to the USDA, Food and Nutrition Service. Princeton, NJ: Mathematica Policy Research.

D. Dong and B.H. Lin. 2009. *Fruit and Vegetable Consumption by Low-Income Americans: Would a Price Reduction Make a Difference?* Economic Research Report No. 70, Economic Research Service, U.S. Department of Agriculture.

Fox, M. K., and N. Cole, N. 2004. *Effects of Food Assistance and Nutrition Programs on Health*: Vol. 1: *Food Stamp Participants*. U.S. Department of Agriculture, Economic Research Service, E-FAN No. 040141. December.

Fox, M. K., W. Hamilton, and B. H. Lin. 2004. *Effects of Food Assistance and Nutrition Programs on Nutrition and Health*: Vol. 3, *Literature Review*. Economic Research Service, U.S. Department of Agriculture, Food Assistance and Nutrition Research Report No. 19–13. Washington, DC.

Fox, M. K., A. Hedley Dodd, A. Wilson, and P. M. Gleason. 2009. "Association between School Food Environment and Practices and Body Mass Index of US Public School Children." *Journal of the American Dietetic Association* 109*(2): S108–S117.

Fraker, T. M., A. P. Martini, and J. C. Ohls. 1995. "The Effect of Food Stamp Cash Out on Food Expenditures: An Assessment of the Findings from Four Demonstrations." *The Journal of Human Resources* 30(4): 633–649.

Frazao, E., M. Andrews, D. Smallwood, and M. Prell. 2007. "Food Spending Patterns of Low-Income Households: Will Increasing Purchasing Power Result in Healthier Food Choices?" Economic Information Bulletin No. 29–24. September, 2007.

Gibson, D. 2004. "Long-Term Food Stamp Program Participation Is Differentially Related to Overweight in Young Girls and Boys," *Journal of Nutrition* 134: 372–379.

Gibson, D. 2003. "Food Stamp Program Participation Is Positively Related to Obesity in Low Income Women," *Journal of Nutrition* 133: 2225–2231.

Gibson, D. 2001. "Food Stamp Program Participation and Health: Estimates from the NLSY97." In *Social Awakening: Adolescent Behavior as Adulthood Approaches,* ed. R. Michael. New York: Russell Sage Foundation.

Gleason, P. M., and A. Hedley Dodd. 2009. "School Breakfast Program but Not School Lunch Program Participation Is Associated with Lower Body Mass Index." *Journal of the American Dietetic Association* 109*(2): S118–S128.

Gleason, P. M., and C. W. Suitor. 2003. "Eating at School: How the National School Lunch Program Affects Children's Diets." *American Journal of Agricultural Economics* 85(4): 1047–1061.

Guthrie, J. F., E. Frazao, M. Andrews, and D. Smallwood. 2007. "Improving Food Choices: Can Food Stamps Do More?" Amber Waves, Economic Research Service, U.S. Department of Agriculture, April.

Guthrie, J. F., and J. N. Variyam. 2007. "Nutrition Information: Can It Improve the Diets of Low-Income Households?" Economic Information Bulletin No. 29–6. Economic Research Service, USDA, September.

Hofferth, S. L., and S. Curtin. 2005. "Poverty, Food Programs, and Childhood Obesity." *Journal of Policy Analysis and Management* 24(4): 703–726.

Institute of Medicine. 2009. *School Meals: Building Blocks for Healthy Children*, eds. V. A. Stallings, C. W. Suitor, and C. L. Taylor. Committee on Nutrition Standards for National School Lunch and Breakfast Programs. Washington, DC: The National Academies Press.

Institute of Medicine. 2006. *WIC Food Packages: Time for a Change*. Committee to Review the WIC Food Packages, Food and Nutrition Board. Washington, DC: The National Academies Press.

Jacknowitz, Alison, Daniel Novillo, and Laura Tiehen. 2007. "Special Supplemental Nutrition Program for Women, Infants, and Children and Infant Feeding Practices." *Pediatrics* 119(2): 281–289.

Jones, S. J,. and E. A. Frongillo. 2006. "The Modifying Effects of Food Stamp Program Participation on the Relation between Food Insecurity and Weight Change in Women." *Journal of Nutrition* 136: 1091–1094.

Jones, S. J., L. Jahns, B. A. Laraia, and B. Haughton. 2003. "Lower Risk of Overweight in School-Age Food Insecure Girls Who Participate in Food Assistance." *Archives of Pediatric and Adolescent Medicine* 157: 780–784.

Kaushal, N. 2007. "Do Food Stamps Cause Obesity? Evidence from Immigrant Experience." NBER Working Paper No. 12849. Cambridge, MA. January.

Kim, K., and E. A. Frongillo. 2007. "Participation in Food Assistance Programs Modifies the Relation of Food Insecurity with Weight and Depression in Elders." *Journal of Nutrition* 137: 1005–1010.

Leibtag, E. S., and P. R. Kaufman. 2003. "Exploring Food Purchase Behavior of Low-Income Households: How Do They Economize?" Agricultural Information Bulletin No. 747–70. Economic Research Service, U.S. Department of Agriculture, June.

Meyerhoefer, C., and Y. Pylypchuk. 2008. "Does Participation in the Food Stamp Program Affect the Prevalence of Obesity and Health Care Spending?" *American Journal of Agricultural Economics* 90(2): 287–305.

Oliveira, V., and R. Chandran. 2005. *Children's Consumption of WIC-Approved Foods*, Food Assistance and Nutrition Research Report No. 44, U.S. Department of Agriculture, Economic Research Service, February.

Ralston, K., C. Newman, A. Clauson, J. Guthrie, J. Buzby. 2008. "The National School Lunch Program: Background, Trends, and Issues." Economic Research Service, Economic Research Report No. July.

Schanzenbach, D. W. 2005. "Do School Lunches Contribute to Childhood Obesity?" Harris School Working Paper Series 05.13. University of Chicago: http://ideas.repec.org/p/har/wpaper/0513.html. Accessed November 13, 2009.

Shapiro, J. M, 2005. "Is There A Daily Discount Rate? Evidence from the Food Stamp Nutrition Cycle." *Journal of Public Economics* 89: 303–323.

Story, M. 2009. "The Third School Nutrition Dietary Assessment Study: Findings and Policy Implications for Improving the Health of US Children." *Journal of the American Dietetic Association* 109*(2): S7–S13.

Tchnernis, R., D. Millimet, and M. Hussain. 2008. "School Nutrition Programs and the Incidence of Childhood Obesity." Center for Applied Economic and Policy Research Working Paper #2007–14. Indiana University: http://ssrn.com/abstract=1005361. Accessed November 13, 2009.

Todd, J. E., C. Newman, and M. Ver Ploeg. 2009 "Changing Participation in Food Assistance Programs among Low-Income Children After Welfare Reform." Economic Research Report No. 92, Economic Research Service, USDA.

Townsend, M. S., J. Peerson, B. Love, and C. Achterberg, et al. 2001. "Food Insecurity Is Positively Related to Overweight in Women." *Journal of Nutrition* 131: 1738–1745.

U.S. Department of Agriculture. 2009a. "Leading the Fight Against Hunger: Federal Nutrition Assistance Programs." Food and Nutrition Service, USDA: http://www.fns.usda.gov/fns/40th/docs/leading.pdf. Accessed on November 13, 2009.

U.S. Department of Agriculture. 2009b. "Supplemental Nutrition Assistance Program: Frequently Asked Questions." Food and Nutrition Service, USDA: http://www.fns.usda.gov/snap/faqs.htm. Accessed on November 13, 2009.

U.S. Department of Agriculture. 2009c. "Healthy Incentives Pilot (HIP): Basic Facts." Food and Nutrition Service, USDA: http://www.fns.usda.gov/snap/HIP/qa-s.htm. Accessed on November 10, 2009.

Ver Ploeg, M., L. Mancino, B.H. Lin. 2007. "Food and Nutrition Assistance Programs and Obesity: 1976–2002." Economic Research Report No. ERR-48. Economic Research Service, U.S. Department of Agriculture.

Ver Ploeg, M., and K. Ralston. 2008. "Food Stamps and Obesity: What Do We Know?" U.S. Department of Agriculture, Economic Research Service, Economic Information Bulletin No. 34.

Wilde, P. E., P. E. McNamara, and C. K. Ranney. 2000. *The Effect on Dietary Quality of Participation in the Food Stamp and WIC Programs*. U.S. Department of Agriculture, Food and Rural Economics Division, Economic Research Service. Food Assistance and Nutrition Research Report Number 9.

Wilde, P. E., and J. N. Peterman. 2006. "Individual Weight Change Is Associated with Household Food Security Status." *Journal of Nutrition* 136: 1395–1400.

Wilde, P. E., and C. K. Ranney. 2000. "The Monthly Food Stamp Cycle: Shopping Frequency and Food Intake Decisions in an Endogenous Switching Regression Framework." *American Journal of Agricultural Economics* 82(1): 200–213.

CHAPTER 25

PHYSICAL ACTIVITY AND THE BUILT ENVIRONMENT

JAMES F. SALLIS,
MARC A. ADAMS, AND
DING DING

PHYSICAL inactivity is one of the leading underlying causes of death (Danaei et al. 2009). Physical activity reduces risk of developing obesity and is an effective strategy for maintenance of weight loss (Andersen 2003). Whether measured by self-report or objectively, the majority of adults and many youth are not meeting physical activity guidelines (Physical Activity Guidelines Advisory Committee 2008). Until recently, behavioral science research on physical activity etiology and intervention was based on conceptual models that emphasized the role of psychological and social factors primarily for recreational physical activity. This chapter describes a paradigm shift toward interdisciplinary research on environments with the goal of identifying promising built environmental and policy changes that could produce widespread and permanent changes in physical activity in multiple settings. The chapter summarizes the past, present, and future of research on built environments and physical activity.

PAST

Several significant trends laid the foundation for this vibrant and rapidly growing field of study. Experience with interventions designed to motivate and teach behavior change skills to individuals indicated important limitations of these approaches. Recruitment was difficult, so few people were affected; although physical activity often improved significantly, effect sizes were small; and virtually all studies showed poor maintenance (Marcus et al. 2006). One hypothesis for the latter limitations was that environments and policies outside the individual created powerful barriers to change; for example, lack of sidewalks, poorly maintained parks, and communities designed so that automobile travel was the only feasible option.

Psychosocial theories from behavioral science provided no guidance in understanding the role of environments, but the rediscovery of ecological models started the paradigm shift. Ecological models are based on the proposition that there are multiple levels of influence on behaviors, including individual and social levels, but also organizational, community, built environment, and policy (Sallis, Owen, and Fisher 2008). A second principle is that interventions that change all levels of influence should be most effective. An example would be building or renovating a park, motivating people to use it through marketing, and using activity programs to create a supportive social environment. Environmental and policy interventions are expected to have the most widespread and permanent influences, so they complement individual approaches. A third important principle is that environmental influences are specific to the type and purpose of behavior.

Behavior-specific models were developed that identified different built environment attributes as relevant to physical activity for recreation versus transportation purposes. Characteristics of recreation environments, such as parks, trails, and sidewalks, were expected to be related to recreational physical activity. The designs of communities and transportation infrastructure were expected to be related to walking and bicycling for transportation (Saelens et al. 2003). The literature has generally supported behavior-specific models (Gebel et al. 2007; Saelens and Handy 2008).

Interdisciplinary collaboration with non-traditional partners is another trend that has greatly facilitated built environment research on physical activity (Sallis et al. 2006). City and transportation planners brought concepts and measures of walkability, bikeability, and traffic calming. Walkable neighborhoods are designed so that residents can easily walk from their homes to places where they shop, work, play, and learn. Mixed land uses create proximity of destinations, and connected streets provide direct routes. By contrast, construction in the past 60 years in the United States and some other countries has been dominated by low-walkable suburbs, characterized by separation of uses, disconnected streets, and low residential density that make active travel difficult or impossible. Researchers from the leisure sciences and park and recreation fields brought expertise in park and trail design and measurement. Professionals from policy science, economics, law, geography, and others have contributed to interdisciplinary teams with powerful conceptual, measurement, and analytic tools that were not available in any single field (Sallis et al. 2006).

One area in which these collaborations produced rapid advances was in measurement of environments, which was a necessary development to allow the research to progress. Combining knowledge of environmental characteristics from city planning and leisure science, methods from geography, and rigorous measurement development and evaluation methods from behavioral sciences produced a variety of measures of neighborhood characteristics, transportation facilities, parks and trails, and schoolyards. Though some measures were self-reported, many others used direct observation methods and Geographic Information Systems (GIS) software, so the new research field could be built on objective data (Brownson et al. 2009). The first generation of these measures was limited by the number and complexity of variables collected, cost of collecting observational and GIS measures, and limited availability and questionable validity of some GIS data. These problems have not yet been solved. However, the measures allowed a wide range of environmental variables to be evaluated for their associations with physical activity for recreation and transportation purposes, as well as with measures of total physical activity, which are expected to be most related to health outcomes.

Environmental and policy research has inherent challenges. These include lack of control over the independent variables, making controlled studies difficult; the need to work with aggregate units, such as neighborhoods, parks, or schools; and related challenges in analyses. Thus, it was essential to have targeted funding to support researchers to work within these limitations. The Centers for Disease Control and Prevention (Active Community Environments program) and the National Institutes of Health (Obesity and the Built Environment initiative) provided early support for interdisciplinary research on built environments and physical activity, but the Robert Wood Johnson Foundation provided the most sustained and targeted early funding through the Active Living Research Program. The three goals of Active Living Research were to establish an evidence base of environmental and policy factors related to physical activity, build capacity of interdisciplinary teams to conduct this research, and use the results to stimulate and inform policy changes. The program funded the development of many new measures, supported interdisciplinary collaborations, documented a dramatic increase in publications on built environment and physical activity, and communicated results to practitioners and policy makers (Sallis, Linton et al. 2009).

The field of built environment—physical activity research advanced quickly because targeted funding allowed for the development of behavior-specific conceptual models, creation of interdisciplinary collaborations, and development of new environmental measures. At the turn of the twenty-first century, a recognizable field did not exist, but within 10 years, authoritative groups in the United States and other countries recommend environmental and policy changes as essential to meeting physical activity guidelines and obesity control goals (World Health Organization [WHO] 2004a; U.S. Department of Health and Human Services [USDHHS] 2001; Koplan, Liverman, and Kraak 2005).

PRESENT

Numerous studies have supported the association between the built environment and physical activity (Gebel, Bauman, and Petticrew 2007), and in the last decade the field has greatly accelerated (Sallis, Linton, et al. 2009). In this section, we summarize the current state of the literature on the relation of built environment to physical activity, organized by the environmental setting, domain of physical activity, and age group.

Recreation Environments and Recreational Physical Activity

Recreation environments are places where individuals participate in physical activity for recreation or health reasons and include parks, playgrounds, or recreational facilities that have amenities or provide opportunities for activity. A review of studies on parks, trails, and recreation amenities found that approximately 80 percent of studies showed some significant associations between parks/recreation variables and physical activity (Kaczynski and Henderson 2007).

Studies of Adults

Parks are one of the main settings for recreational physical activity (Bedimo-Rung, Mowen, and Cohen 2005). Distance or proximity is the most studied attribute of parks in relation to physical activity. Most studies found that proximity to parks was a significant correlate of park use and physical activity (Giles-Corti et al. 2005; Cohen et al. 2007), with one mile suggested as a reasonable recommended distance (Cohen et al. 2007). Park size, aesthetics, maintenance, and cleanliness may also be related to park use; however, few studies examined these attributes, making it difficult to summarize associations.

Physical activity in parks is often supported by facilities (e.g., trail, open field, pool, tennis court) and amenities (e.g., drinking fountain, bathroom, trash can), which provide opportunities for recreational physical activity. Kaczynski and colleagues (2008) found that the number of facilities and amenities in parks was positively associated with observed physical activity among adults in the parks, even after adjusting for distance, neighborhood safety and aesthetics.

Neighborhood streets are common locations for adults' recreational physical activity, such as walking or running. Evidence from multiple countries supports the association between neighborhood aesthetics and recreational walking (Carnegie et al. 2002; Cerin et al. 2006), recreational physical activity (Brownson et al. 2001; Velasquez, Holahan, and You 2009), and overweight/obesity (Ellaway, Macintyre, and Bonnefoy 2005). However, more evidence is needed to identify what exact aesthetic characteristics are important for streetscapes. Previous studies suggested factors such as maintenance (Boehmer et al. 2006), cleanliness (i.e., free from litter and graffiti) (Ellaway, Macintyre, and Bonnefoy 2005), and greenness (Sugiyama et al. 2008).

Studies of Youth

Children and adolescents are often active in public places such as parks, open spaces, and other recreational facilities such as school playgrounds, fields, and courts (Veitch et al. 2006; Grow et al. 2008; Timperio, Salmon, and Ball 2004). Several studies found that proximity to these places was associated with the frequency of using those facilities and with total physical activity (Cohen et al. 2006; Grow et al. 2008). Several studies indicated that design of parks (i.e., type of facilities present) and equipment are important. Areas equipped with facilities such as basketball courts, tennis courts, and fixed play equipment were associated with more active play and energy expenditure, compared to areas with no equipment (Floyd et al. 2008; Farley et al. 2008).

Children frequently play around the house, in the driveway, and in the streets or cul-de-sacs. Safety is an often-discussed concern about playing outside. Current research focuses on two aspects of safety: traffic-related and crime-related. No clear conclusions can be drawn from current studies because the results are mixed (Singh et al. 2008; Grow et al. 2008; Evenson et al. 2006; Carver et al. 2005; Spivock et al. 2008). One challenge in this area is measurement. Most studies used subjective measures for safety, which may differ from objectively measured safety. Future studies should incorporate objective measures such as traffic volume and crime data, in addition to perception.

Studies of Seniors

Older adults are likely to walk for recreation in local streets, parks, and other settings in the neighborhood. They may also participate in activity and fitness programs through senior centers, fitness clubs, and community recreational facilities (Berke et al. 2006). Due to lower functional ability and motor skills of older adults, it is reasonable to believe that their physical activity can be strongly facilitated or hindered by the built environment (Michael, Green, and Farquhar 2006).

Chad and colleagues (2005) found that leisure-time physical activity for elders was negatively correlated with the presence of hills and unattended dogs and positively correlated with biking or walking trails, street lights, and recreation facilities. Berke and colleagues found that elders who participated in structured and unstructured fitness programs lived significantly closer to facilities than those who did not participate (Berke et al. 2006). Li and colleagues also found that the number of recreational facilities and size of parks were significantly associated with walking in the neighborhood (Li et al. 2005).

Compared to other age groups, research on the older population is limited, despite rapidly increasing numbers of older adults. Current research has mostly focused on the proximity of recreational facilities, so the number of environmental variables investigated needs to be expanded.

Community Design and Active Transport

Active transportation is walking, bicycling, or skating to destinations, and it is usually called "non-motorized" transport in the transportation field. Active transport reduces driving, greenhouse gas emissions, air pollution, and traffic congestion. Research in urban planning and transportation has contributed to understanding community design and transportation behaviors (Handy et al. 2002). Individuals were more likely to walk or bike for transportation in areas with mixed land use, high street connectivity, and high residential density (Humpel, Owen, and Leslie 2002; Handy et al. 2002; Owen et al. 2004). Mixed land uses provide destinations near residences, and connected streets provide direct routes. These environmental attributes that support active transport are often used to define the "walkability" of a neighborhood, or the ability to walk to destinations (Saelens et al. 2003). Since the 1940s, most development in the United States has had disconnected streets with many cul-de-sacs and separation of uses required by zoning laws. This low-walkable design is often termed auto-dependent because active transport is not feasible.

Studies of Adults

A large literature has found that adults were more likely to walk or bike for transportation in neighborhoods with high walkability (Gebel, Bauman, and Petticrew 2007; Saelens and Handy 2008). Although the WHO (2004b) suggested 5 kilometers as a realistic distance for active transport for adults, the prevalence of active transportation for this distance is low, and it decreases significantly with distance from destinations (Badland, Schofield, and Garrett 2008).

For adults, worksites are a major destination for transport physical activity. Badland and colleagues (2008) found that individuals were more likely to walk or bike to work if the commute distance was shorter and the streets were better connected. Neighborhood facilities such as post offices, shopping malls, or shops provide destinations for active transport. McCormack and colleagues (2008) found a dose-response relation between the number of categories of destinations within 400 and 1,500 meters from home and the time individuals spent walking for transportation. Frank and colleagues (2004) found that land-use mix, intersection density, and residential density were positively associated with walking for transport and negatively associated with car time. The relation of walkability with active transport translated into 35 to 49 more minutes per week of total physical activity measured with accelerometers (Sallis, Saelens, et al. 2009). The substantial literature on community design and active transport led the Transportation Board and Institute of Medicine (Transportation Research Board and Institute of Medicine 2005) and the Task Force for Community Preventive Services to conclude that there is a consistent association between urban design, land use and physical activity (Heath et al. 2006).

Using public transit appears to contribute to overall physical activity. The average American public transit user spends 19 minutes walking to and from transit, which helps achieve recommended physical activity levels (Besser and Dannenberg 2005).

Proximity to a public transit stop (bus and rail) was related to more physical activity in an international study (Sallis, Bowles et al. 2009) and improved weight outcomes (Brown et al. 2009; Lovasi et al. 2009). Policies designed to increase public transit were associated with walking and meeting physical activity guidelines (USDHHS 2008; Aytur et al. 2008).

Studies of Youth

Compared to adults, youths usually commute to different types of destinations, such as schools and play areas. Active transport to school contributes significantly to children's total physical activity on weekdays (van Sluijs et al. 2009). However, in the last few decades, the percentage of youth who walk to school dramatically declined in many developed countries, while traveling by car increased (van der Ploeg et al. 2008; McDonald 2007).

Multiple factors are related to children and adolescents' active travel to school. Distance may be one of the most important determinants of walking or biking to school (McMillan 2007; Timperio et al. 2006). Almost half the US decline in walking to school between 1969 and 2001 was directly or indirectly related to the increased distance between home and school (McDonald 2007). Due to the suburban sprawl over the last 60 years, families live farther away from schools.

Several community design features may be related to youth active transport. Kerr and colleagues (2006) found that in higher-income neighborhoods, children were more likely to travel actively in more walkable neighborhoods, but walkability was less of a factor in lower-income neighborhoods. Additional studies indicated the importance of pedestrian infrastructure, such as sidewalks, traffic/pedestrian lights, and safe pedestrian crossings (Fulton et al. 2005; Grow et al. 2008; Hume et al. 2009; Carver, Timperio, and Crawford 2008).

Some community design features may be related to physical activity differently for youths and adults, street connectivity in particular. Most studies among adults have shown a positive association between street connectivity and physical activity, especially active transport (Gebel et al. 2007). However, some studies among youth have shown the opposite findings. Timperio and colleagues (2006) found that street connectivity was negatively associated with walking or biking to school. Norman and colleagues (2006) found that intersection density had an inverse association with total physical activity among adolescent girls. Carver and colleagues (2008) found that boys living on cul-de-sacs engaged in significantly more moderate-to-vigorous physical activity. Cul-de-sacs may provide low-traffic streets where children can safely play. Further studies needed to confirm these patterns of associations.

Studies of Seniors

A recent study examined multiple environmental attributes and their associations with transportation walking across different age groups (Shigematsu et al. 2009). A wide range of community design variables were related to walking for transport among younger adults. For the older age groups, only two measures of mixed use were significantly related to transportation walking, but the correlations were particularly strong (Shigematsu et al. 2009). Other studies confirmed the importance of proximity and diversity of destinations in neighborhoods for seniors (Michael et al. 2006; King et al. 2003).

Older adults are less comfortable driving, so it may be particularly important to design neighborhoods that support active transport among seniors. In a qualitative study, seniors reported resting places, traffic calming treatments, longer walk-signal times, and access to public transportation as important characteristics for a walkable neighborhood (Michael, Green, and Farquhar 2006).

CONCLUSION

There is a rapidly growing evidence base supporting the association between the built environment and physical activity, as documented in numerous reviews (Gebel, Bauman, and Petticrew 2007; Heath et al. 2006). Recreation environment attributes, including proximity, aesthetics, and quality of recreational facilities, were consistently associated with recreational physical activity. Community design, walkability, and access to public transit mainly contributed to transport physical activity. Some neighborhood attributes, such as sidewalks, may be related to both leisure-time physical activity and active transportation. Walkability has been related to active transport and total physical activity (Sallis, Bowles, et al. 2009; Frank et al. 2005) as well as overweight/obesity (Black and Macinko 2007; Papas et al. 2007). With few exceptions, built environment—physical activity associations have generalized across youth, adults, and older adults.

FUTURE

President Obama remarked in his 2009 address to a joint session of Congress on health care, "We did not come to fear the future. We came here to shape it." (Obama 2009). This section provides direction and a long-term view for research on the built environment.

Needed Conceptual Development

The complexity of physical environments is staggering, with many types of exposures and functions possible (Ball, Timperio, and Crawford 2006). It is likely impossible for a single study to measure all possible environmental exposures or to test the entire ecological model (Hovell, Wahlgren, and Adams 2009). Ecological models of health behavior are limited by a lack of specific hypotheses (Sallis, Owen, and Fisher 2008). Although recent physical activity models are more specific, future applications of ecological models must indicate the hypothesized strength of associations and interactions within and across levels of influence. For example, McCormack and colleagues (2008) conceptualized a within-level interaction regarding types of destinations in a neighborhood (e.g., transit stops, shops, convenience stores) for transport-related physical activity. They found that each additional type of destination was associated with approximately 9 minutes more walking every two weeks. Epstein and colleagues (2006) tested a between-level interaction for access to large parks and an intervention to reduce sedentary behaviors for youth. Youth in the intervention group living near large parks increased their MVPA by 39 minutes per day, compared to intervention participants with no nearby parks. Although specific interaction hypotheses will be difficult to conceptualize, the current results provide a good starting place.

Another conceptual priority is to explicate mediating pathways and moderating mechanisms of the association between the built environment and physical activity (Ball, Timperio, and Crawford 2006; Story et al. 2009). Experts have recommended research methods such as "natural experiments" to quasi-experimentally evaluate built environment and policy modifications (Story et al. 2009; Sallis, Story, and Lou 2009).

Examine Population-Specific Associations

Emerging evidence suggests that built environments may have differential effects on the activity behavior of various subgroups of people. As described above, disconnected streets may be negatively related to physical activity for adults, but positively related to children's activity (Davison and Lawson 2006; Norman et al. 2006). Some studies have found built environment associations for white but not black adults (Frank et al. 2009), while others found similar results for lower- and higher-income adults (Sallis, Saelens, et al. 2009). Research on older adults and people with disabilities is limited (Cunningham and Michael 2004; Spivock et al. 2008). It is important to understand how personal characteristics (e.g., age, gender, ethnicity, socioeconomic status, disability, activity level) interact with built environments to influence physical activity (Saelens et al. 2003). On the other hand, there are documented socioeconomic inequalities in access to parks (Gordon-Larsen et al. 2006; Abercrombie et al. 2008) and safety and maintenance of neighborhood environments (Zhu et al. 2008; Neckerman et al. 2009). Given these issues, research on disadvantaged populations should be a high priority. Ultimately, research will provide guidance about how to design environments to optimize their favorable influence on physical activity for all subgroups, with priority to be placed on vulnerable populations.

Measurement of Physical Activity

Advances in research on the built environment and physical activity will require improved measures, and there are roles for self-reports, direct observation, and electronic monitors. Self-reports can provide data on the purpose and context of physical activity and are being used for international prevalence studies (Guthold et al. 2008; Bauman et al. 2009). However, a better understanding of the validity of reported measures of physical activity is needed, especially for populations with limited education and for developing countries. Expanded use of direct observation methods can provide data on which subgroups of people are active in specific environmental settings, such as parks, school grounds, and bike paths (McKenzie et al. 2006). Routine use of electronic counters of pedestrians and bicyclists could provide data for research and ongoing assessment to use in transportation planning and policy.

Motion sensors, such as pedometers and accelerometers, are now being paired with global positioning systems (GPS) to objectively measure travel and recreational activities (Maddison and Mhurchu 2009). When motion sensors and GPS are integrated with geographic information systems (GIS) to produce detailed maps of where people are active in their communities, a clearer understanding of the influence of specific built environment attributes is likely to emerge. Technological advances in objective measures also create a need for theoretical approaches that conceptualize changes in physical activity as a dynamic process related to changing environmental exposures (Matthews, Moudon, and Daniel 2009). Individuals' physical activity may shift slowly as settings are modified over the years, or quickly as people are exposed to different environments throughout a day. Some environments may have a greater impact than others; traveling to work is a frequent behavior, so modifications to walkability or transportation systems might result in more overall activity. As measures of individuals' paths through space and time become available, a clearer account of how environments shape physical activity may be obtained.

Measurement of the Environment

Measures of the built environment include self-report surveys, direct observation audits, and analyses of publicly or privately developed spatial data in GIS (Brownson et al. 2009). Several self-report and direct observation tools are available (Giles-Corti et al. 2006; McKenzie et al. 2006; Saelens et al. 2003; Spittaels et al. 2009). A next step is to derive the most meaningful items or scales from the massive numbers of variables, so instruments can be simplified (Cerin et al. 2006). Further refinements should also ensure their relevance for specific populations (e.g., youth, low-income communities) and contexts (e.g., internationally) (Adams et al. 2009; Rosenberg et al. 2009).

A persistent question for built environment researchers is "How do we define neighborhood?" Sociologists have discussed this question since 1921 (Matthews 2008). Defining neighborhood by various distances from the home (e.g., 1 km or mile) assumes that residences are the most important environment for physical activity and that representations of environment are relatively static (Matthews, Moudon, and Daniel 2009). Are neighborhoods static, or do various travel modes produce different functional boundaries of a neighborhood? Are worksite neighborhoods important for understanding physical activity? The measurement of built environments may need to move from residential neighborhoods to other locations where individuals spend time, and may need to evolve from static places to dynamic exposure-based assessments of environment features. Dynamic representations of neighborhood could consider both the details of the environment (e.g. retail store hours) and individuals' travel habits to measure ongoing exposures of each individual. Advances in built environment measures should eventually allow more accurate assessment of spatial and temporal factors of exposure for each individual.

A better understanding of the details of environments is needed to make the results more useful for designers and policy makers. A "micro-scale" analysis (as opposed to macro-scale variables such as land use and street connectivity) may shed light on what amenities or qualities make certain locations more activity-friendly. A micro-scale analysis may include the quality and types of equipment available at parks, beaches, or recreational centers, width and condition of sidewalks, quality of crosswalks, types of facilities on different floors of a multistory building, whether a worksite has showers or safe bicycle storage, or posted speed of roadways. The collection of high quality micro-environment data in routine and systematic ways may require new research instruments that can be routinely used by city agencies, advocates, and community groups to evaluate their environments.

There is a need for accessible repositories of complete and accurate data sets of the built environment to improve the science. Secondary sources of GIS-based environmental information currently differ on types of data collected, completeness, recency, scale, and documentation. Secondary data on the environment can be difficult to discover or expensive to obtain, and primary data collection is laborious. Public repositories that maintain current and historical data of built environment features are needed to ensure equitable access and to track environmental modifications over time. Key environment variables, such as detailed land use categorizations, transportation and pedestrian networks, and bike and recreational facilities, should be routinely monitored. This could be the responsibility of local, state, or national governments, much as transportation departments collect traffic volume data. Current research can identify the most promising built environment variables relevant to physical activity that should be assessed routinely, and resulting databases could aid future research and application.

Research Designs

Early studies measured built-environment variables within a single city and detected small effect sizes. The range of built environment features for a city or country may be restricted (i.e., limited variance), leading to built environment—physical activity associations being underestimated. For example, the range of residential density and public transit use in major U.S. cities does not approach that of many European and Asian cities (Newman and Kenworthy 1991). International studies using similar measures of the built environment may be one method to overcome the limited range of urban form in each region or country. A study of eleven countries found that environmental form variables near homes (e.g., shops, sidewalks, transit stops, bicycle facilities, recreational facilities, residential density) differed greatly between countries, and rates of meeting physical activity guidelines doubled when all these environmental features were present (Sallis, Bowles, et al. 2009).

Designing Studies for Policy Impact

Many major engineering projects require an Environmental Impact Assessment to predict consequences such as their impact on flora and fauna, greenhouse gasses, and air quality. The purpose of these assessments is to quantify any detrimental effects of projects to the ecology of living organisms. Health impact assessments (HIA) of major projects on a community's physical activity and obesity are rare (Collins and Koplan 2009). HIA could be used to evaluate major building projects or policies for their estimated impact on community members' diet, physical activity and other health outcomes over the life of the project. Community members and city councils could use projections about a project's health consequences to decide whether a project's benefits outweigh potential side effects or to compare the effects of competing policies. Routine use of HIAs will require sustained political support and funding.

Conclusion

Ultimately, built environment research is part of a social process that uses evidence and political support for creating or changing environments to be "activity friendly." Current and future generations would benefit from population-wide policies and environments designed to increase rates of physical activity and prevent sedentary behavior and obesity. Because physical inactivity is a leading underlying cause of death in the United States (Danaei et al. 2009) and internationally (WHO 2004a), there is a strong need for robust built environment research to inform national and international policies to ensure that communities of the future are designed or redesigned to support physical activity for both transportation and recreation purposes.

REFERENCES

Abercrombie, L. C., J. F. Sallis, T. L. Conway, L. D. Frank, B. E. Saelens, and J. E. Chapman. 2008. "Income and Racial Disparities in Access to Public Parks and Private Recreation Facilities." *American Journal of Preventive Medicine* 34(1): 9–15.

Adams, M. A., S. Ryan, J. Kerr, J. F. Sallis, K. Patrick, L. Frank, and G. J. Norman. 2009. "Validation of the Neighborhood Environment Walkability Scale (NEWS) Items using Geographic Information Systems." *Journal of Physical Activity and Health* 6(S1): S113–S123.

Andersen, R. E. 2003. "Obesity: Etiology, Assessment, Treatment, and Prevention." . Champaign, IL: Human Kinetics.

Aytur, S. A., D. A. Rodriguez, K. R. Evenson, D. J. Catellier, and W. D. Rosamond. 2008. "The Sociodemographics of Land Use Planning: Relationships to Physical Activity, Accessibility, and Equity." *Health and Place* 14(3): 367–385.

Badland, H. M., G. M. Schofield, and N. Garrett. 2008. "Travel Behavior and Objectively Measured Urban Design Variables: Associations for Adults Traveling to Work." *Health Place* 14(1): 85–95.

Ball, K., A. F. Timperio, and D. A. Crawford. 2006. "Understanding Environmental Influences on Nutrition and Physical Activity Behaviors: Where Should We Look and What Should We Count?" *International Journal of Behavioral Nutrition Physical Activity* 3: 33.

Bauman, A., F. Bull, T. Chey, C. L. Craig, B. E. Ainsworth, J. F. Sallis, H. R. Bowles, M. Hagstromer, M. Sjostrom, M. Pratt, and the IPS Group. 2009. "The International Prevalence Study on Physical Activity: Results from 20 Countries." *International Journal of Behavioral Nutrition and Physical Activity* 6: 21.

Bedimo-Rung, A. L., A. J. Mowen, and D.A. Cohen. 2005. "The Significance of Parks to Physical Activity and Public Health." *American Journal Of Preventive Medicine* 28: 159–168.

Berke, E. M., R. T. Ackermann, E. H. Lin, P. H. Diehr, M. L. Maclejewski, B. Williams, M. B. Patrick, and J. P. LoGerto. 2006. "Distance as a Barrier to Using a Fitness-Program Benefit for Managed Medicare Enrollees." *Journal of Aging and Physical Activity* 14(3): 313–323.

Besser, L. M., and A. L. Dannenberg. 2005. "Walking to Public Transit: Steps to Help Meet Physical Activity Recommendations." *American Journal of Preventive Medicine* 29(4): 273–280.

Black, J. L., and J. Macinko. 2007. "Neighborhoods and Obesity." *Nutrition Reviews* 66: 2–20.

Boehmer, T. K., S. L. Lovegreen, D. Haire-Joshu, and R. C. Brownson. 2006. "What Constitutes an Obesogenic Environment in Rural Communities?" *American Journal of Health Promotion* 20(6): 411–421.

Brown, B. B., I. Yamada, K. R. Smith, C. D. Zick, L. Kowaleski-Jones, and J. X. Fan. 2009. "Mixed Land Use and Walkability: Variations in Land Use Measures and Relationships with BMI, Overweight, and Obesity." *Health and Place* 15(4): 1130–1141.

Brownson, R. C., E. A. Baker, R. A. Housemann, L. K. Brennan, and S. J. Bacak. 2001. "Environmental and Policy Determinants of Physical Activity in the United States." *American Journal of Public Health* 91(12): 1995–2003.

Brownson, R. C., C. M. Hoehner, K. Day, A. Forsyth, and J. F. Sallis. 2009. "Measuring the Built Environment for Physical Activity State of the Science." *American Journal of Preventive Medicine* 36(4): S99–S123.

Carnegie, M. A., A. Bauman, A. L. Marshall, M. Mohsin, V. Westley-Wise, and M. L. Booth. 2002. "Perceptions of the Physical Environment, Stage of Change for Physical Activity, and Walking among Australian Adults." *Research Quarterly for Exercise and Sport* 73(2): 146–155.

Carver, A., J. Salmon, K. Campbell, L. Baur, S. Garnett, and D. Crawford. 2005. "How Do Perceptions of Local Neighborhood Relate to Adolescents' Walking and Cycling?" *American Journal of Health Promotion* 20 (2): 139–147.

Carver, A., A. F. Timperio, and D. A. Crawford. 2008. "Neighborhood Road Environments and Physical Activity among Youth: The CLAN Study." *Journal of Urban Health-Bulletin of the New York Academy of Medicine* 85(4): 532–544.

Cerin, E., B. E. Saelens, J. F. Sallis, and L. D. Frank. 2006. "Neighborhood Environment Walkability Scale: Validity and Development of a Short Form." *Medicine and Science in Sports and Exercise* 38: 1682–1691.

Chad, K. E., B. A. Reeder, E. L. Harrison, N. L. Ashworth, S. M. Sheppard, S. L. Schultz, B. G. Bruner, K. L. Fisher, and J. A. Lawson. 2005. "Profile of Physical Activity Levels in Community-Dwelling Older Adults." ." *Medicine and Science in Sports and Exercise* 37(10): 1774–1784.

Cohen, D. A., J. S. Ashwood, M. M. Scott, A. Overton, K. R. Evenson, L. K. Staten, D. Porter, T. L. McKenzie, and D. Catellier. 2006. "Public Parks and Physical Activity among Adolescent Girls." *Pediatrics* 118(5): e1381–1389.

Cohen, D. A., T. L. McKenzie, A. Sehgal, S. Williamson, D. Golinelli, and N. Lurie. 2007. "Contribution of Public Parks to Physical Activity." *American Journal of Public Health* 97(3): 509–514.

Collins, J., and J. P. Koplan. 2009. "Health Impact Assessment: A Step Toward Health in All Policies." *Journal of the American Medical Association* 302(3): 315–317.

Cunningham, G. O., and Y. L. Michael. 2004. "Concepts Guiding the Study of the Impact of the Built Environment on Physical Activity for Older Adults: A Review of the Literature." *American Journal of Health Promotion* 18(6): 435–443.

Danaei, G., E. L. Ding, D. Mozaffarian, B. Taylor, J. Rehm, C. J. Murray, and M. Ezzati. 2009. "The Preventable Causes of Death in the United States: Comparative Risk Assessment of Dietary, Lifestyle, and Metabolic Risk Factors." *Public Library of Science (PLoS) Medicine* 6(4): e1000058.

Davison, K. K., and C. T. Lawson. 2006. "Do Attributes in the Physical Environment Influence Children's Physical Activity? A Review of the Literature." *International Journal of Behavioral Nutrition and Physical Activity* 3: 19.

Ellaway, A., S. Macintyre, and X. Bonnefoy. 2005. "Graffiti, Greenery, and Obesity in Adults: Secondary Analysis of European Cross Sectional Survey." *British Medical Journal* 331(7517): 611–612.

Epstein, L. H., S. Raja, S. S. Gold, R. A. Paluch, Y. Pak, and J. N. Roemmich. 2006. "Reducing Sedentary Behavior: The Relationship between Park Area and the Physical Activity of Youth." *Psychological Science* 17(8): 654–659.

Evenson, K. R., A. S. Birnbaum, A. L. Bedimo-Rung, J. F. Sallis, C. C. Voorhees, K. Ring, and J. P. Elder. 2006. "Girls' Perception of Physical Environmental Factors and Transportation: Reliability and Association with Physical Activity and Active Transport to School." *International Journal of Behavioral Nutrition and Physical Activity* 3:28. doi: 10.1186/1479–5868-3–28.

Farley, T. A., R. A. Meriwether, E. T. Baker, J. C. Rice, and L. S. Webber. 2008. "Where Do the Children Play? The Influence of Playground Equipment on Physical Activity of Children in Free Play." *Journal of Physical Activity and Health* 5(2): 319–331.

Floyd, M. F., J. O. Spengler, J. E. Maddock, P. H. Gobster, and L. J. Suau. 2008. "Park-based Physical Activity in Diverse Communities of Two U.S. Cities: An Observational Study." *American Journal of Preventive Medicine* 34(4): 299–305.

Frank, L. D., M. A. Andresen, and T. L. Schmid. 2004. "Obesity Relationships with Community Design, Physical Activity, and Time Spent in Cars." *American Journal of Preventive Medicine* 27(2): 87–96.

Frank, L. D., J. Kerr, B. E. Saelens, J. F. Sallis, K. Glanz, and J. Chapman. 2009. "Food Outlet Visits, Physical Activity and Body Weight: Variation by Gender and Race-Ethnicity." *British Journal of Sports Medicine* 43(2): 124–131.

Frank, L. D., T. L. Schmid, J. F. Sallis, J. Chapman, and B. E. Saelens. 2005. "Linking Objectively Measured Physical Activity with Objectively Measured Urban Form: Findings from SMARTRAQ." *American Journal of Preventive Medicine* 28(Suppl 2): 117–125.

Fulton, J. E., J. L. Shisler, M. M. Yore, and C. J. Caspersen. 2005. "Active Transportation to School: Findings from a National Survey." *Research Quarterly for Exercise and Sport* 76(3): 352–357.

Gebel, K., A. E. Bauman, and M. Petticrew. 2007. "The Physical Environment and Physical Activity: A Critical Appraisal of Review Articles." *American Journal of Preventive Medicine* 32(5): 361–369. e3.

Giles-Corti, B., M. H. Broomhall, M. Knuiman, C. Collins, K. Douglas, K. Ng, A. Lange, and R. J. Donovan. 2005. "Increasing Walking: How Important Is Distance to, Attractiveness, and Size of Public Open Space?" *American Journal of Preventive Medicine* 28(Supp. 2): 169–176.

Giles-Corti, B., A. Timperio, H. Cutt, T. J. Pikora, F. C. L. Bull, M. Knuiman, M. Bulsara, K. Van Niel, and T. Shilton. 2006. "Development of a Reliable Measure of Walking Within and Outside the Local Neighborhood: RESIDE's Neighborhood Physical Activity Questionnaire." *Preventive Medicine* 42(6): 455–459.

Gordon-Larsen, P., M. C. Nelson, P. Page, and B. M. Popkin. 2006. "Inequality in the Built Environment Underlies Key Health Disparities in Physical Activity and Obesity." *Pediatrics* 117(2): 417–424.

Grow, Helene Mollie, Brian E. Saelens, Jacqueline Kerr, Nefertiti H. Durant, Gregory J. Norman, and James F. Sallis. 2008. "Where Are Youth Active? Roles of Proximity, Active Transport, and Built Environment." *Medicine and Science in Sports and Exercise* 40(12): 2071–2079.

Guthold, R., T. Ono, K. L. Strong, S. Chatterji, and A. Morabia. 2008. "Worldwide Variability in Physical Inactivity: A 51-Country Survey." *American Journal of Preventive Medicine* 34(6): 486–494.

Handy, S. L., M. G. Boarnet, R. Ewing, and R. E. Killingsworth. 2002. "How the Built Environment Affects Physical Activity: Views from Urban Planning." *American Journal of Preventive Medicine* 23(2): 64–73.

Heath, G. W., R. C. Brownson, J. Kruger, R. Miles, K. Powell, and L. T. Ramsey. 2006. "The Effectiveness of Urban Design and Land Use and Transport Policies and Practices to Increase Physical Activity: A Systematic Review." *Journal of Physical Activity and Health* 3(S1): S55–S76.

Hovell, M. F., D. R. Wahlgren, and M. Adams. 2009. "The Logical and Empirical basis for the Behavioral Ecological Model." In *Emerging Theories and Models in Health Promotion Research and Practice: Strategies for Enhancing Public Health* (2nd ed.), eds. R. J. DiClemente, R. Crosby and M. Kegler. San Francisco: Jossey-Bass.

Hume, C., A. Timperio, J. Salmon, A. Carver, B. Giles-Corti, and D. Crawford. 2009. "Walking and Cycling to School: Predictors of Increases among Children and Adolescents. *American Journal of Preventive Medicine* 36(3): 195–200.

Humpel, N., N. Owen, and E. Leslie. 2002. "Environmental Factors Associated with Adults' Participation in Physical Activity: A Review." *American Journal of Preventive Medicine* 22(3): 188–199.

Kaczynski, A. T., and K. A. Henderson. 2007. "Envrionmental Correlates Of Physical Activity: A Review of Evidence about Parks and Recreation Amenities." *Leisure Sciences* 29: 316–354.

Kaczynski, A. T., L. R. Potwarka, and B. E. Saelens. 2008. "Association of Park Size, Distance, and Features with Physical Activity in Neighborhood Parks." *American Journal of Public Health* 98(8): 1451–1456.

Kerr, J., D. Rosenberg, J. F. Sallis, B. E. Saelens, L. D. Frank, and T. L. Conway. 2006. "Active Commuting to School: Associations with Environment and Parental Concerns." *Medicine and Science in Sports and Exercise* 38: 787–794

King, W. C., J. S. Brach, S. Belle, R. Killingsworth, M. Fenton, and A. M. Kriska. 2003. "The Relationship between Convenience of Destinations and Walking Levels in Older Women." *American Journal of Health Promotion* 18(1): 74–82.

Koplan, J. P., C. T. Liverman, and V. I. Kraak. 2005. *Preventing Childhood Obesity: Health in the Balance*. Washington, DC: National Academies Press.

Li, F., K. J. Fisher, R. C. Brownson, and M. Bosworth. 2005. "Multilevel Modelling of Built Environment Characteristics Related to Neighbourhood Walking Activity in Older Adults." *Journal of Epidemiology and Comunity Health* 59(7): 558–564.

Lovasi, G. S., K. M. Neckerman, J. W. Quinn, C. C. Weiss, and A. Rundle. 2009. "Effect of Individual or Neighborhood Disadvantage on the Association between Neighborhood Walkability and Body Mass Index." *American Journal of Public Health* 99(2): 279–284.

Maddison, R., and N. C. Mhurchu. 2009. "Global Positioning System: A New Opportunity in Physical Activity Measurement." *International Journal of Behavioral Nutrition and Physical Activity* 6:73. doi:10.1186/1479-5868-6-73.

Marcus, B. H., D. M. Williams, P. M. Dubbert, J. F. Sallis, A. C. King, A. K. Yancey, B. A. Franklin, D. Buchner, S. R. Daniels, and R. P. Claytor. 2006. "Physical Activity Intervention Studies: What We Know and What We Need to Know: A Scientific Statement from the American Heart Association Council on Nutrition, Physical Activity, and Metabolism (Subcommittee on Physical Activity); Council on Cardiovascular Disease in the Young; and the Interdisciplinary Working Group on Quality of Care and Outcomes Research." *Circulation* 114(24): 2739–2752.

Matthews, S. A. 2008. "The Salience of Neighborhood: Some Lessons from Sociology." *American Journal of Preventive Medicine* 34(3): 257–259.

Matthews, S. A., A. V. Moudon, and M. Daniel. 2009. "Work Group II: Using Geographic Information Systems for Enhancing Research Relevant to Policy on Diet, Physical Activity, and Weight." *American Journal of Preventive Medicine* 36(4): S171–S176.

McCormack, G. R., B. Giles-Corti, and M. Bulsara. 2008. "The Relationship between Destination Proximity, Destination Mix and Physical Activity Behaviors." *Preventive Medicine* 46(1): 33–40.

McDonald, N. C. 2007. "Active Transportation to School: Trends among U.S. Schoolchildren, 1969–2001." *American Journal of Preventive Medicine* 32(6): 509–516.

McKenzie, T., D. Cohen, A. Sehgal, S. Williamson, and D. Golinelli. 2006. "System for Observing Play and Recreation in Communities (SOPARC): Reliability and Feasibility Measures." *Journal of Physical Activity and Health* 3(Supp. 1): S206–S222.

McMillan, T. E. 2007. "The Relative Influence of Urban Form on a Child's Travel Mode to School." *Transportation Research Part A: Policy and Practice* 41(1): 69–79.

Michael, Y., T. Beard, D. Choi, S. Farquhar, and N. Carlson. 2006. "Measuring the Influence of Built Neighborhood Environments on Walking in Older Adults." *Journal of Aging and Physical Activity* 14(3): 302–312.

Michael, Y. L., M. K. Green, and S. A. Farquhar. 2006. "Neighborhood Design and Active Aging." *Health and Place* 12(4): 734–740.

Neckerman, K. M., G. S. Lovasi, S. Davies, M. Purciel, J. Quinn, E. Feder, N. Raghunath, B. Wasserman, and A. Rundle. 2009. "Disparities in Urban Neighborhood Conditions: Evidence from GIS Measures and Field Observation in New York City." *Journal of Public Health Policy* 30: S264–S285.

Newman, P. W. G., and J. R. Kenworthy. 1991. "Transport and Urban Form in 32 of the Worlds Principal Cities." *Transport Reviews* 11(3): 249–272.

Norman, G. J., S. K. Nutter, S. Ryan, J. F. Sallis, K. J. Calfas, and K. Patrick. 2006. "Community Design and Access to Recreational Facilities as Correlates of Adolescent Physical Activity and Body Mass Index." *Journal of Physical Activity and Health* 3(Supp. 2): S118–S128.

Obama, B. H. 2009. *Remarks by the President to a Joint Session of Congress on Health Care.* Washington, D.C: U.S. Capitol.

Owen, Neville, Nancy Humpel, Eva Leslie, Adrian Bauman, and James F. Sallis. 2004. "Understanding Environmental Influences on Walking; Review and Research Agenda." *American Journal of Preventive Medicine* 27(1): 67–76.

Papas, M. A., A. J. Alberg, R. Ewing, K. J. Helzlsouer, T. L. Gary, and A. C. Klassen. 2007. "The Built Environment and Obesity." *Epidemiologic Reviews* 29: 129–143.

Physical Activity Guidelines Advisory Committee. 2008. *Physical Activity Guidelines Advisory Committee Report.* Washington, DC, U.S. Department of Health and Human Services. http://www.health.gov/paguidelines/.

Rosenberg, Dori, Ding Ding, James F. Sallis, Jacqueline Kerr, Gregory J. Norman, Nefertiti Durant, Sion K. Harris, and Brian E. Saelens. 2009. "Neighborhood Environment Walkability Scale for Youth (NEWS-Y): Reliability and Relationship with Physical Activity." *Preventive Medicine* 49(2–3): 213–218.

Saelens, B. E., and S. L. Handy. 2008. "Built Environment Correlates of Walking: A Review." *Medicine and Science in Sports and Exercise* 40(7 Supp.): S550–566.

Saelens, B. E., J. F. Sallis, J. B. Black, and D. Chen. 2003. "Neighborhood-based Differences in Physical Activity: An Environment Scale Evaluation." *American Journal of Public Health* 93: 1552–1558.

Sallis, J. F., H. R. Bowles, A. Bauman, B. E. Ainsworth, F. C. Bull, C. L. Craig, M. Sjostrom, I. De Bourdeaudhuij, J. Lefevre, V. Matsudo, S. Matsudo, D. J. Macfarlane, L. F. Gomez, S. Inoue, N. Murase, V. Volbekiene, G. McLean, H. Carr, L. K. Heggebo, H. Tomten, and P. Bergman. 2009. "Neighborhood Environments and Physical Activity among Adults in 11 Countries." *American Journal of Preventive Medicine* 36(6): 484–490.

Sallis, J. F., R. B. Cervero, W. Ascher, K. A. Henderson, M. K. Kraft, and J. Kerr. 2006. "An Ecological Approach to Creating Active Living Communities." *Annual Review of Public Health* 27: 297–322.

Sallis, J. F., M. Story, and D. Lou. 2009. "Study Designs and Analytic Strategies for Environmental and Policy Research on Obesity, Physical Activity, and Diet: Recommendations from a Meeting of Experts." *American Journal of Preventive Medicine* 36(2): S72–S77.

Sallis, J. F., L. S. Linton, M. K. Kraft, C. L. Cutter, J. Kerr, J. Weitzel, A. Wilson, C. Spoon, I. D. Harrison, R. Cervero, K. Patrick, T. L. Schmid, and M. Pratt. 2009. "The Active Living Research Program: Six Years of Grantmaking." *American Journal of Preventive Medicine* 36(2 Supp.): S10–21.

Sallis, J. F., N. Owen, and E. B. Fisher. 2008. "Ecological Models of Health Behavior." In *Health Behavior and Health Education: Theory, Research, and Practice*, 4th ed., eds. K. Glanz, B. K. Rimer and K. Viswanath. San Francisco: Jossey-Bass.

Sallis, J. F., B. E. Saelens, L. D. Frank, T. L. Conway, D. J. Slymen, K. L. Cain, J. E. Chapman, and J. Kerr. 2009. "Neighborhood Built Environment and Income: Examining Multiple Health Outcomes." *Social Science and Medicine* 68(7): 1285–1293.

Shigematsu, R., J. F. Sallis, T. L. Conway, B. E. Saelens, L. D. Frank, K. L. Cain, J. E. Chapman, and A. C. King. 2009. "Age Differences in the Relation of Perceived Neighborhood Environment to Walking." *Medicine and Science in Sports and Exercise* 41(2): 314–321.

Singh, G. K., M. D. Kogan, P. C. Van Dyck, and M. Siahpush. 2008. "Racial/Ethnic, Socioeconomic, and Behavioral Determinants of Childhood and Adolescent Obesity in the United States: Analyzing Independent and Joint Associations." *Annals of Epidemiology* 18(9): 682–695.

Spittaels, H., C. Foster, J. M. Oppert, H. Rutter, P. Oja, M. Sjostrom, and B. I. De. 2009. "Assessment of Environmental Correlates of Physical Activity: Development of a European Questionnaire." *International Journal of Behavioral Nutrition and Physical Activity* 6: 39.

Spivock, M., L. Gauvin, M. Riva, and J. M. Brodeur. 2008. "Promoting Active Living among People with Physical Disabilities: Evidence for Neighborhood-Level Buoys." *American Journal of Preventive Medicine* 34(4): 291–298.

Story, M., B. Giles-Corti, A. L. Yaroch, S. Cummins, L. D. Frank, T. T. K. Huang, and L. B. Lewis. 2009. "Work Group IV: Future Directions for Measures of the Food and Physical Activity Environments." *American Journal of Preventive Medicine* 36(4): S182–S188.

Sugiyama, T., E. Leslie, B. Giles-Corti, and N. Owen. 2008. "Associations of Neighbourhood Greenness with Physical and Mental Health: Do Walking, Social Coherence and Local Social Interaction Explain the Relationships?" *Journal of Epidemiology and Community Health* 62(5): e9.

Timperio, A., J. Salmon, and K. Ball. 2004. "Evidence-based Strategies to Promote Physical Activity among Children, Adolescents and Young Adults: Review and Update." *Journal of Science and Medicine in Sport* 7(1 Supp.): 20–29.

Timperio, A., K. Ball, J. Salmon, R. Roberts, B. Giles-Corti, D. Simmons, L. A. Baur, and D. Crawford. 2006. "Personal, Family, Social, and Environmental Correlates of Active Commuting to School." *American Journal of Preventive Medicine* 30(1): 45–51.

Transportation Research Board and Institute of Medicine. 2005. *Does the Built Environment Influence Physical Activity? Examining the Evidence. Special Report 282. Washington, D.C.: Transportation Research Board.*

U.S. Department of Health and Human Services. 2001. *The Surgeon General's Call to Action to Prevent and Decrease Overweight and Obesity.* Rockville, MD: U.S. Department of Health and Human Services, Public Health Service.

United States Health and Human Services. 2008. "Physical Activity Guidelines for Americans." http://www.health.gov/PAGuidelines/pdf/paguide.pdf. Accessed Oct. 8, 2009.

van der Ploeg, H. P., D. Merom, G. Corpuz, and A. E. Bauman. 2008. "Trends in Australian Children Traveling to School 1971–2003: Burning Petrol or Carbohydrates?" *Preventive Medicine* 46(1): 60–62.

van Sluijs, E. M. F., V. A. Fearne, C. Mattocks, C. Riddoch, S. J. Griffin, and A. Ness. 2009. "The Contribution of Active Travel to Children's Physical Activity Levels: Cross-Sectional Results from the ALSPAC Study." *Preventive Medicine* 48(6): 519–524.

Veitch, J., S. Bagley, K. Ball, and J. Salmon. 2006. "Where Do Children Usually Play? A Qualitative Study of Parents' Perceptions of Influences on Children's Active Free-Play." *Health and Place* 12(4): 383–393.

Velasquez, K. S., C. K. Holahan, and X. You. 2009. "Relationship of Perceived Environmental Characteristics to Leisure-Time Physical Activity and Meeting Recommendations for Physical Activity in Texas." *Preventing Chronic Disease* 6(1): A24.

World Health Organization. 2004a. *Global Strategy on Diet, Physical Activity and Health.* Geneva: WHO.

World Health Organization. 2004b. *Tranport, Envrionment and Health* (No. 89). Regional Office for Europe of the World Health Organization, Austria.

Zhu, X., B. Arch, and C. Lee. 2008. "Personal, Social, and Environmental Correlates of Walking to School Behaviors: Case Study in Austin, Texas." *The Scientific World Journal* 8: 859–872.

CHAPTER 26

....

FOOD DESERTS

....

DIANNA SMITH AND
STEVEN CUMMINS

THE term "food desert" is a contested phrase often used in the social sciences to describe an urban residential area that has poorer access to foods that make up a healthy diet. This catch-all term usually encompasses a range of food access issues including physical access to shops and economic purchasing power, and has been applied to rural as well as urban settings. The broad concept has been present in the academic literature since the 1960s, but the current food desert terminology is thought to have originated in the West of Scotland in the early 1990s (Cummins and Macintyre 2002a). A recent systematic review of the food desert literature initially identified over 2,800 studies published between 1966 and 2007, giving an indication of the substantive history of this area of research (Beaulac et al. 2009).

This chapter considers the broad range of work in this area exploring the physical, social, and economic elements of food access and synthesizes findings from the extant international literature. Specifically, we look at how food deserts have been defined and operationalized and then consider the key concepts and debates surrounding around this term. A review of the evidence for the existence of food deserts follows, taking account of both observational and intervention studies. The chapter then explores the relationship between food access and health outcomes and summarizes the qualitative work on the experience of living in a "food desert" and how this affects food consumption patterns. A brief comment on future research needs concludes the chapter.

The publication of papers reporting the identification of "food deserts" in the early 1990s led to many contemporary studies that compared either the spatial distribution of store types or the cost of a basket of food items across neighborhoods with differing socioeconomic profiles. Much of the research that led to policies and interventions in the United Kingdom was underpinned by relatively meager evidence which appeared to make a plausible argument that more deprived areas of the country had poorer access to healthy and affordable food (Mooney 1990, Sooman 1995). However, later studies call for caution and demonstrate that food access is not necessarily worse in less wealthy areas. Some early and oft-cited research was sometimes misinterpreted to the extent that the existence of food deserts may well be a factoid rather than well-evidenced reality (Cummins and Macintyre 2002a).

The physical environment local to a person's home has largely been the focus of food access research in previous decades. However, as the prevalence of poor diet-related health increased in the developed world, researchers expanded the definition of environment to encompass aspects of a person's social network and the wider political and economic system in which a person resides. By extending the notion of food deserts to include the non-physical environment, existing and ongoing research can bridge several aspects of Egger and Swinburn's definitions of an obesogenic environment (Egger and Swinburn 1997). As we will show later in the chapter, the country of residence may have as much influence as the local neighborhood on differing levels of food access, particularly for disadvantaged populations.

TRADITIONAL DEFINITIONS

There are typically three components that define a food desert: food access, food affordability, and food availability. Access describes the physical proximity of a shop selling healthy food options, affordability relates to the cost of healthy food, and availability indicates the variety of healthy food choices (particularly fruit and vegetables) stocked in a shop or neighborhood.

In terms of physical access to healthy food, the Social Exclusion Unit in the United Kingdom defines a 500-meter boundary as the ideal parameter for good food access, based on the distance an average person could walk in 6–7 minutes (Furey et al. 2002). The notion of identifying areas that are relatively food accessible became salient after the major British food retailers began to withdraw from city centers to suburban and edge-of-town areas (Guy 1996; Clarke et al. 2002; Wrigley 1998; Wrigley 2002b). The result of this shifting pattern of food retail location was that some urban residents did not have grocery stores within a reasonable walking distance, placing people without vehicles or otherwise limited mobility at a relative disadvantage. The Low-Income Task Force began identifying areas where there was limited access to affordable healthy food as "food deserts," a popular term to describe the lack of retail food stores in the urban core (Wrigley 2002a).

The 500-meter boundary used in British research may be less useful in countries where more people have a private vehicle. In the United States, Australia, and Canada, where car ownership is greater, it may be more appropriate to consider a larger area as accessible under the assumption that more people in all socioeconomic groups have access to motorized transport (Smoyer-Tomic et al. 2006). However, the most disadvantaged groups who lack cars may have a more challenging journey to the larger stores as public transportation infrastructure may be poorer due to lower demand.

Physical access is often measured using Geographic Information Systems (GIS), with the option of either Euclidian (straight line) or road network distance as the preferred measure of assessing access. Even if people walk to the store, they will often use existing road networks so this option is a more realistic representation of distance traveled (Pearce et al. 2006). More advanced measures of food access may create an aggregate measure that considers local populations' likelihood of owning a car (and thus being able to travel farther), the size of store (larger stores provide better access) or the type of store that different social groups tend to shop in (Clarke et al. 2002; Smith 2007). These methods create a geographic surface of "access" that crosses administrative boundaries rather than simply drawing a circle around stores, or highlighting the administrative units which contain a store to identify areas with "good" access.

More recent research has found that physical food access may not always be lower in deprived areas, contrary to early reports in the United States and the United Kingdom. A detailed summary concludes that food deserts appear to be more common in North America, while UK and Australian cities show mixed results (Cummins et al. 2005; Turrell 2004; Winkler et al. 2006; Beaulac et al. 2009). However, there is still the suggestion that people in poorer areas could benefit from policies aimed at increasing food access for low-mobility groups, particularly their access to healthier alternatives to existing products (Cummins and Macintyre 1999).

In some cases, although physical access may not be difficult, residents may still perceive that there is a problem of poor access. This may be due to personal mobility restrictions or to the cost of food (Furey et al. 2002; Robinson 2001; Giskes et al. 2007). These studies emphasize the importance of qualitative research used in conjunction with quantitative methods to provide a more nuanced understanding of food access. Similarly, qualitative analysis suggests that access to private transport (either by owning a vehicle or through getting a ride to a shop from a friend or family member) is especially crucial in more rural areas, as would be expected due to a relative lack of public transportation options (Smith and Morton 2009).

Low-income neighborhoods may not only have fewer stores, they may have higher food prices (Furey et al. 2002; Drewnowski 2004; Chung and Myers 1999). Food desert theory suggests that food prices in low-income, inner-city areas tend to be higher compared to more affluent neighborhoods, placing poorer residents at a relative disadvantage due to geographic location. Price comparison research using "basket studies" has been one way to explore this hypothesis. Price data for a standard basket of food items can be collected in neighborhoods that vary by deprivation or income in order to compare prices between stores located in these areas. For example, one of the early studies of comparative food access looked at two simple baskets of food in London localities, one that contained recommended "healthy" items and a second that held foods for which reductions in consumption were recommended. Mooney (1990) then compared the prices and availability of these two baskets in affluent and deprived areas near Hampstead Heath. Although food was less expensive in the more deprived areas, there were fewer "healthy" foods available in the more deprived areas. A similar study in Glasgow found that food price and availability was only slightly different between more and less affluent areas, though food was again less expensive in more deprived areas (Cummins and Macintyre 2002b).

There are challenges in comparing the results of these pricing studies, particularly in defining a "basket" of food. Researchers have often created their own baskets of food, making it difficult to compare results from differing studies. However, in the United States, the Thrifty Food Plan Basket devised by the U.S. Department of Agriculture to allocate food stamps is frequently used as a basis for "healthy" food choices (Chung and Myers 1999; Drewnowski and Darmon 2005; Jetter and Cassady 2006).

Availability of healthy food, in particular fresh produce, often varies in relation to the type of stores rather than simply neighborhood characteristics. Smaller stores may be less able to carry a wide selection of fresh foods, as they will often spoil before purchase. Poor availability presents a challenge to local residents who demand fresh produce, particularly those in inner-city areas with limited mobility (Clarke et al. 2002; Furey et al. 2002; Morland et al. 2002b). A recent study in Scotland found that fruit and vegetable quality varied by store type, and that stores where food was not the main focus of the shop, produce quality was lower. These types of stores were more likely to be located in deprived urban areas (Cummins et al. 2009).

CONCEPTS

Studies of food access/deserts has shifted from the almost exclusive urban focus that characterized early studies to closer attention on rural areas (Cummins et al. 2009; Furey et al. 2002; Liese et al. 2007; Schafft 2009; Sharkey 2009; Smith et al. 2010; Wang 2009; Scarpello et al. 2009). In rural areas, typical measures of physical access may not always be useful as people will often have travel to farther due to lower population densities, have higher rates of car ownership, or may combine a shopping trip with another journey, such as one going home from work (Sharkey 2009). Use of a car is a major influence on the shopping behavior of rural residents (Scarpello et al. 2009).

Qualitative studies add richness and depth to the traditionally more quantitative research studies that may be somewhat removed from the day-to-day experience of a study population. While quantitative research is useful in measuring the phenomenon under investigation and predicting future changes, qualitative research reveals individual stories and experiences that otherwise may be overlooked. Individual interviews or focus groups can validate results from quantitative methods, or identify inconsistencies between the modeled results for food access and "real" experiences. For instance, even if there are many or large shops physically present in the local area, people may not shop there because of prohibitive costs compared to smaller discounters (Whelan et al. 2002).

Focus groups are useful for understanding food access, as they allow researchers to delve into the personal experiences of people with poor food access—for example, the coping mechanisms used by people who do not have immediate physical access to retail food stores. In the context of food access studies, discussions focus on topics such as physical and economic food access, as well as attitudes regarding food choices. Several recent studies use focus groups to learn about the realities of food access in deprived areas (Coveney and O'Dwyer 2009; Furey et al. 2002; Smith and Morton 2009; Whelan et al. 2002; Wilson et al. 2004; Wrigley et al. 2004).

In the United Kingdom, Sustain's community mapping project included several focus groups in Leicester, Coventry, and Brighton on the topic of food choices (Watson 2002). The results were collated and reported back to each community to ensure that their views were fairly represented. Many of the discussions centered on food purchasing and preparation, as well as the challenges of feeding a household on a limited budget. Several participants mentioned having to choose foods based on cost, children's preferences, and/or their own understanding of what comprises a healthy diet. This information is especially valuable as the debate about the existence and/or severity of "food deserts" continues, as such data can substantiate or disprove results from quantitative studies.

EFFECT OF FOOD ACCESS ON DIET

Many researchers conclude that where a person lives plays a part in his or her dietary choices (Fisher and Strogatz 1999; Furey et al. 2002; Horowitz 2004; Morland et al. 2002b). Within the United Kingdom, there are several studies that indicate that area of residence influences diet to some extent (White 2007; Wrigley et al. 2003).

For pregnant women, better proximity to supermarkets improved diet quality (Laraia et al. 2004), and in general, results from the United States indicate that shopping at supermarkets led to higher levels of fruit and vegetable consumption (Zenk et al. 2005). Poorer physical access to food retail for low-income groups may mean fewer shopping trips, which results in less consumption of milk and fresh fruit and vegetables (Wiig 2009).

In a smaller study, in which researchers collected data on individual body mass index (BMI) and where people shopped for food, those who shopped in more disadvantaged areas had a higher BMI (Inagami et al. 2006). A qualitative study of low-income women found that more disadvantaged households would undertake major shopping trips less frequently and suggested that the "top-up" shopping trips may be more common and take place more locally at convenience stores where healthy food selections are more limited (Wiig 2009).

However, not all research concludes that neighborhoods influence the diet of residents (Pearson et al. 2005; Turrell 2004; Wilson et al. 2004). One multilevel study based in Australia indicates that the area of residence does not have a substantial impact on diet over that of personal choice, although the researchers acknowledge this result is at odds with the results of studies based in the United States (Turrell 2004). The authors conclude that relative spatial socioeconomic differences are not sufficiently great in Brisbane to merit the same distinct patterns as those seen in other countries (Turrell 2004). Recent studies in the United Kingdom also show that area of residence may not always influence diet over the individual-level characteristics (Wilson et al. 2004; Pearson et al. 2005).

A direct causal link between neighborhood food access and residents' diets has been hypothesised in a study undertaken in Seacroft, Leeds, an area of formerly poor retail food access (Clarke et al. 2002). This study was the first to provide evidence that a retail intervention may improve the diets of local residents (Wrigley et al. 2003). In this study, a new Tesco opened in 2001, allowing the researchers to gather dietary data (via seven-day food diaries) before and after the store opening. The results showed a "positive but modest impact" on the fruit and vegetable consumption of neighbourhood residents near the new store (Wrigley et al. 2003). Additional focus groups from the Leeds study indicated that older residents who had switched to the new Tesco would spend money they had saved on transportation costs to buy fresh fruits and vegetables (Wrigley et al., 2004). However, this study has been criticized for not including a control group which suggests that evidence for causality may not be as strong as the authors suggest, and thus more confirmatory studies are required (Cummins et al. 2005).

Within the United States, research indicates that retail food access is an important factor in individual diet. A large-scale study (n = 10,623) incorporating four study areas used fruit and vegetable as well as fat consumption as a proxy for a healthy diet. The results demonstrate that proximity to a grocery store influences healthy dietary choices, showing a 32 percent increase in the fruit and vegetable consumption among black Americans with each additional grocery store in their home census tract (Morland et al. 2002a). Differing methodologies provide similar results, including a New York–based study comparing the shelf space allocated for low-fat milk in neighborhood stores with the type of milk found in residents' homes. The results show a direct relationship between the type of milk available in stores and that found in households (Fisher and Strogatz 1999).

Evidence for Links to Obesity

Several studies have been undertaken with the aim of identifying a relationship between food access and obesity in the local population. (Morland et al. 2006; Morland and Evenson 2009; Spence 2009). However, there is a lack of reliable causal studies to "prove" that food access (particularly healthy food access) leads to obesity and overweight (White 2007). One large-scale US study found that in areas with at least one supermarket or specialty food store, obesity was lower. Obesity prevalence was higher in areas where there was at least one independent shop, convenience store, or more than one fast food restaurant (Morland et al. 2006). Attempting to link food access to health outcomes, such as obesity, is a difficult challenge as local residents may move, so their access to various types of food can change over time. Longitudinal studies will be important in future research considering food access and overweight or obesity.

Commentators suggest that the prohibitively high cost of healthy food compared to more energy-dense options is inherently "obesogenic," and that obesity is directly linked to personal financial circumstances (Drewnowski 2009). Considering evidence from the United States, Drewnowski shows an inverse relationship between energy cost and energy intake, and shows that the gap between healthy (fruit and vegetables) and less healthy (fats and sweets) food costs is increasing, suggesting that the relatively high cost of "healthy" food may lead to negative health effects for people at an economic disadvantage.

To isolate one aspect of lifestyle and attribute it to the rise in obesity in more wealthy nations is difficult. Poor food access and the presence of food deserts certainly may contribute to ill health in some areas but the effects of food deserts are mediated by a number of factors.

Methodological Issues

One challenge in interpreting results from the international literature is the variability of methods used, as well as the indicators chosen to represent a healthy diet. In many cases, researchers define a healthy diet by measuring the purchase of fruit and vegetables among participants (Morland et al. 2002a; Thompson 1999; Wrigley et al. 2003). This is an easily quantifiable measure of a healthy diet, as higher levels of fruit and vegetable consumption help prevent certain types of cancers. While this proxy for a healthy diet is reasonable and largely utilized, a limiting factor is that it considers only one aspect of a person's diet. While some households have higher rates of fruit and vegetable consumption, these same households can still have a relatively poor diet in other areas, including higher fat, sodium, and sugar intake. One option to capture this amount of variation would be to include other aspects of the "foodscape," which is often the approach taken in "obesogenic" environment studies.

The geographical locations of research vary, but the majority of recent research has been undertaken in urban areas of the United States. While there are similarities between the United States and other nations, some major socioeconomic differences between the United States and other nations remain. These include access to private and public transportation, social and the spatial organization of land use, and differences in retail planning regulation, so that findings from one country cannot necessarily be translated from one country to another.

The definition of what constitutes a neighborhood or local area is another area of disagreement among researchers. Neighborhoods are more than a geographical area, defined by administrative boundaries; however, as yet, there is no consistent way of operationalizing an alternative approach in most research (Horowitz 2004; Morland et al. 2002a). Most U.S.-based studies use census tracts to define neighborhood boundaries; each tract containing approximately 4,500–6,000 residents. Unfortunately, this may not accurately capture retail food access for residents of that area, as it will not take into account stores in neighboring tracts that are patronized by residents "across the border"; this challenge has led to the development of "smoothed" measures of access which ignore administrative boundaries (Clarke et al. 2002; Smith 2007; Smoyer-Tomic et al. 2006).

Despite the shortcomings of current research methods, there remains sufficient evidence that where you live influences what you eat (Fisher and Strogatz 1999; Furey et al. 2002; Horowitz 2004; Thompson 1999; Wrigley et al. 2003; Larson et al. 2009; Bodor et al. 2008; Moore et al. 2008). As a link between food access and diet has been established, particularly in the United States, there is reasonable cause to extend such studies to examine the role of food access on the increasing prevalence of obesity.

REFERENCES

Beaulac, J., E., Kristjansson, and S. Cummins. 2009. "A Systematic Review of Food Deserts, 1966–2007." *Preventing Chjronic Disease* 6.

Bodor, J. N., D. Rose, T. A. Farley, C. Swalm, and S. K. Scott. 2008. "Neighbourhood Fruit and Vegetable Availability and Consumption: The Role of Small Food Stores in an Urban Environment." *Public Health Nutrition* 11: 413–420.

Chung, C., and S. L. Myers. 1999. "Do the Poor Pay More for Food? An Analysis of Grocery Store Availability and Food Price Disparities." *Journal of Consumer Affairs* 33: 276–296.

Clarke, G., H. Eyre, and C. Guy. 2002. "Deriving Indicators of Access to Food Retail Provision in British Cities: Studies of Cardiff, Leeds and Bradford." *Urban Studies* 39: 2041–2060.

Coveney, J., and L. A. O'Dwyer. 2009. "Effects of Mobility and Location on Food Access." *Health and Place* 15: 45–55.

Cummins, S., and S. Macintyre. 1999. "The Location of Food Stores in Urban Areas: A Case Study in Glasgow." *British Food Journal* 101: 545–553.

Cummins, S., and S. Macintyre. 2002a. "'Food Deserts'—Evidence and Assumption in Health Policy Making." *British Medical Journal* 325: 436–438.

Cummins, S., and S. Macintyre. 2002b. "A Systematic Study of an Urban Foodscape: The Price and Availability of Food in Greater Glasgow." *Urban Studies* 39: 2115–2130.

Cummins, S., D. M. Smith, M. Taylor, J. Dawson, D. Marshall, L. Sparks, and A. S. Anderson. 2009. "Variations in Fresh Fruit and Vegetable Quality by Store Type, Urban-Rural Setting and Neighbourhood Deprivation in Scotland." *Public Health Nutrition* 12: 2044–2050.

Cummins, S., M. Stafford, S. Macintyre, M. Marmot, and A. Ellaway. 2005. "Neighbourhood Environment and Its Association with Self Rated Health: Evidence from Scotland and England." *Journal of Epidemiology and Community Health* 59: 207–213.

Drewnowski, A. 2004. "Obesity and the Food Environment: Dietary Energy Density and Diet Costs." *American Journal of Preventive Medicine* 27: 154–162.

Drewnowski, A. 2009. "Obesity, Diets, and Social Inequalities." *Nutrition Reviews* 67: S36–S39.

Drewnowski, A., and N. Darmon. 2005. "Food Choices and Diet Costs: an Economic Analysis." *Journal of Nutrition* 135: 900–904.

Egger, G., and B. Swinburn. 1997. "An "Ecological' Approach to the Obesity Pandemic." *British Medical Journal* 315: 477–480.

Fisher, B. D. and D. S. Strogatz. 1999. "Community Measures of Low-Fat Milk Consumption: Comparing Store Shelves with Households." *American Journal of Public Health* 89: 235–237.

Furey, S., H. Farley, and C. Strugnell. 2002. "An Investigation into the Availability and Economic Accessibility of Food Items in Rural and Urban Areas of Northern Ireland." *International Journal of Consumer Studies* 26: 313–321.

Giskes, K., F. J. Van Lenthe, J. Brug, J. P. Mackenbach, and G. Turrell. 2007. "Socioeconomic Inequalities in Food Purchasing: The Contribution of Respondent-Perceived and Actual (Objectively Measured) Price and Availability of Foods." *Preventive Medicine* 45: 41–48.

Guy, C. 1996. "Corporate Strategies in Food Retailing and Their Local Impacts: A Case Study of Cardiff." *Environment and Planning A*, 28:1575–1602.

Horowitz, C. R., Kathryn A. Colson, Paul L. Herbert, and Kristie Lancaster. 2004. "Barriers to Buying Healthy Foods for People with Diabetes: Evidence of Environmental Disparities." *American Journal of Public Health* 94: 1549–1554.

Inagami, S., D. A. Cohen, B. K. Finch, and S. M. Asch. 2006. "You Are Where You Shop: Grocery Store Locations, Weight, and Neighborhoods." *American Journal of Preventive Medicine* 31: 10–17.

Jetter, K. M., and D. L. Cassady. 2006. "The Availability and Cost of Healthier Food Alternatives." *American Journal of Preventive Medicine* 30: 38–44.

Laraia, B. A., Anna Maria Siega-Riz, Jay S. Kaufman and S. J. Jones. 2004. "Proximity of Supermarkets Is Positively Associated with Diet Quality Index For Pregnancy." *Preventive Medicine* 39: 869–875.

Larson, N. I., M. T. Story, and M. C. Nelson. 2009. "Neighborhood Environments: Disparities in Access to Healthy Foods in the U.S." *American Journal of Preventive Medicine* 36: 74–81.

Liese, A. D., K. E. Weis, D. Pluto, E. Smith, and A. Lawson. 2007. "Food Store Types, Availability, and Cost of Foods in a Rural Environment." *Journal of the American Dietetic Association* 107: 1916–1923.

Mooney, C. 1990. "Cost and Availability of Healthy Food Choices in a London Health District." *Journal of Human Nutrition and Dietetics* 3: 111–120.

Moore, L. V., A. V. Diez Roux, J. A. Nettleton, and D. R. Jacobs, Jr. 2008. "Associations of the Local Food Environment with Diet Quality—A Comparison of Assessments based on Surveys and Geographic Information Systems: The Multi-Ethnic Study of Atherosclerosis." *American Journal of Epidemiology* 167: 917–924.

Morland, K., A. V. Diez Roux, and S. Wing. 2006. "Supermarkets, Other Food Stores, and Obesity: The Atherosclerosis Risk in Communities Study." *American Journal of Preventive Medicine* 30: 333–339.

Morland, K., S. Wing, and A. Diez-Roux. 2002a. "The Contextual Effect of the Local Food Environment on Residents' Diet: The Atherosclerosis Risk in Communities Study." *American Journal of Public Health* 92: 1761–1767.

Morland, K., S. Wing, A. Diez Roux, and C. Poole. 2002b. "Neighborhood Characteristics Associated with the Location of Food Stores and Food Service Places." *American Journal of Preventive Medicine* 22: 23–29.

Morland, K. B.,and K. R. Evenson. 2009. "Obesity Prevalence and the Local Food Environment." *Health and Place* 15: 491–495.

Pearce, J., K. Witten, and P. Bartie. 2006. "Neighbourhoods and Health: A GIS Approach to Measuring Community Resource Accessibility." *Journal of Epidemiology and Community Health* 60: 389–395.

Pearson, T., J. Russell, M. J. Campbell, and M. E. Barker. 2005. "Do 'Food Deserts' Influence Fruit and Vegetable Consumption?—A Cross-Sectional Study." *Appetite* 45: 195–197.

Robinson, N., M. Caraher, and T. Lang. 2001. "Access to Shops: The Views of Low-Income Shoppers." *Health Education Journal* 59: 121–136.

Scarpello, T., F. Poland, N, Lambert, and T. Wakeman. 2009. "A Qualitative Study of the Food-Related Experiences of Rural Village Shop Customers." *Journal of Human Nutrition and Dietetics* 22: 108–115.

Schafft, K. A. 2009. "Food Deserts and Overweight Schoolchildren: Evidence from Pennsylvania." *Rural Sociology* 74: 153–177.

Sharkey, J. R. 2009. "Measuring Potential Access to Food Stores and Food-Service Places in Rural Areas in the U.S." *American Journal of Preventive Medicine* 36: S151–S155.

Smith, C., and L. W. Morton. 2009. "Rural Food Deserts: Low-income Perspectives on Food Access in Minnesota and Iowa." *Journal of Nutrition Education and Behavior* 41: 176–187.

Smith, D. M. 2007. "Potential Health Implications of Retail Food Access." In *Geography*. Leeds: University of Leeds.

Smith, D. M., S. Cummins, M. Taylor, J. Dawson, D. Marshall, L. Sparks, and A. S. Anderson. 2010. "Neighbourhood Food Environment and Area Deprivation: Spatial Accessibility to Grocery Stores Selling Fresh Fruit and Vegetables in Urban and Rural Settings." *International Journal of Epidemiology* 39: 277–284.

Smoyer-Tomic, K. E., J. C. Spence, and C. Amrhein. 2006. "Food Deserts in the Prairies? Supermarket Accessibility and Neighborhood Need in Edmonton, Canada." *Professional Geographer* 58: 307–326.

Sooman, A., and S. Macintyre. 1995. "Health and Perceptions of the Local Environment in Socially Contrasting Neighborhoods in Glasgow." *Health and Place* 1:15–26.

Spence, J. C. 2009. "Relation between Local Food Environments and Obesity among Adults." *BMC Public Health* 9: 192.

Thompson, B., W. Demark-Wahnefried, G. Taylor, J. W. Mcclelland, G. Stables, S. Havas, Z. Feng, M. Topor, J. Heimendinger, K. Reynolds, and N. Cohen. 1999. "Baseline Fruit and Vegetable Intake among Adults in Seven 5-a-Day Study Centers Located in Diverse Geographic Areas." *Journal of the American Dietetic Association* 99: 1241–1248.

Turrell, G., T. Blakely, C. Patterson, and B. Oldenburg. 2004. "A Multilevel Analysis of Socioeconomic (Small Area) Differences in Household Food Purchasing Behaviour." *Journal of Epidemiology and Community Health* 58: 208–215.

Wang, J., M. Williams, E. Rush, N. Crook, N.G. Forouhi, and D. Simmons.2009. "Mapping the Availability and Accessibility of Healthy Food in Rural and Urban New Zealand – Te Wai o Rona: Diabetes Prevention Strategy." *Public Health Nutrition* 13:1049–1055.

Watson, A. 2002. *Hunger from the Inside*. London: Sustain.

Whelan, A., N. Wrigley, D. Warm, and E. Cannings. 2002. "Life in a 'Food Desert.'" *Urban Studies* 39: 2083–2100.

White, M. 2007. "Food Access and Obesity." *Obesity Reviews* 8: 99–107.

Wiig, K. 2009. "The Art of Grocery Shopping on a Food Stamp Budget: Factors Influencing the Food Choices of Low-Income Women as They Try to Make Ends Meet." *Public Health Nutrition* 12: 1726–1734.

Wilson, L. C., A. Alexander, and M. Lumbers. 2004. "Food Access and Dietary Variety among Older People." *International Journal of Retail Distribution and Management* 32: 109–122.

Winkler, E., G. Turrell, and C. Patterson. 2006. "Does Living in a Disadvantaged Area Entail Limited Opportunities to Purchase Fresh Fruit and Vegetables in Terms of Price, Availability, and Variety? Findings from the Brisbane Food Study." *Health and Place* 12: 741–748.

Wrigley, N. 1998. "How British Retailers Have Shaped Food Choice." In *The Nation's Diet: The Social Science of Food Choice*, ed. A. Murcott. Harlow: Addison Wesley Longman.

Wrigley, N. 2002a. "'Food Deserts' in British Cities: Policy Context and Research Priorities." *Urban Studies* 39: 2029–2040.

Wrigley, N., Daniel Warm, Barrie Margetts, and Amanda Whelan. 2002b. "Assessing the Impact of Improved Retail Access on Diet in a 'Food Desert': A Preliminary Report." *Urban Studies* 39: 2061–2082.

Wrigley, N., D. Warm, and B. Margetts. 2003. "Deprivation, Diet, and Food-Retail Access: Findings from the Leeds 'Food Deserts' Study." *Environment and Planning A*, 35: 151–188.

Wrigley, N., D. Warm, B. Margetts, and M. Lowe. 2004. "The Leeds 'Food Deserts' Intervention Study: What the Focus Groups Reveal." *International Journal of Retail Distribution and Management* 32: 123–136.

Zenk, S. N., A. J. Schulz, T. Hollis-Neely, R. T., Campbell, N. Holmes, G. Watkins, R. Nwankwo, and A. Odoms-Young. 2005. "Fruit and Vegetable Intake in African Americans: Income and Store Characteristics." *American Journal of Preventive Medicine* 29: 1–9.

CHAPTER 27

FOOD PRICES, INCOME, AND BODY WEIGHT

DARIUS LAKDAWALLA
AND YUHUI ZHENG

INTRODUCTION

THE recent rise in obesity has generated enormous popular interest and policy concern in developed countries, where it has become a major health problem. While obesity is most often conceived of as a problem of public health or personal attractiveness, it is very much an economic issue, of behavior in response to incentives. The stubbornness of obesity's rise owes itself in large part to several incentives promoting weight gain.

The most basic incentives are prices and income, both of which play an important role in the determination of food intake and body weight. While prices and income vary considerably across the population, they both display clear long-run trends. The relative price of food has declined consistently over time, while incomes have risen. The former trend tends to increase food intake and weight, while the latter trend has a variety of competing effects. Yet there appears to be little doubt that in developed countries, body weight has been rising consistently and continues to do so.

In this paper, we review and synthesize the evidence documenting the effects of food prices and income on body weight. We highlight areas in which the evidence is conclusive, and map out regions that are still lacking in solid evidence. There is a good deal of evidence that broad-based reductions in food prices raise body weight. However, results for price changes in specific food categories are more mixed; we discuss some possible reasons for this. Moreover, there is evidence that the effect of income on body weight is non-monotonic, and we discuss the theoretical basis of this empirical regularity.

THE ROLE OF FOOD PRICES

Theoretical Issues

From a theoretical point of view, the role of food prices is fairly clear. Decreases in the relative price of food will tend to increase food intake and thus body weight. However, the situation becomes more complex when we consider the many different kinds and types of food. For instance, decreases in the relative price of food compared to housing ought to lead to higher food intake. But what if this decline is triggered primarily by reductions in the price of leafy, green vegetables? And what if the declines in the price of these goods are much greater than corresponding declines in the price of sugary snacks?

The possibility of non-zero cross-price elasticities[1] creates a number of challenges for researchers. First and most simply, a reduction in the price of one type of food may be accompanied by relative increases in the prices of other types of food. Therefore, the net impact on body weight depends on whether the intake of one food rises by more than the intake of the other falls. This is not so much a problem of cross-price elasticities as one of the multidimensional nature of food.

The cross-price elasticity problem is thrown into sharpest relief when one thinks about the consumption of specific foods as a set of derived demands. Suppose, for instance, that an individual has a stable demand for calories, fat, sugars, vitamins, and so on. If true, there is a natural compensating mechanism that blunts the impact of food price changes on body weight and health. If the price of ice cream rises, the individual will naturally seek to fill her demand for fat through other types of foods. One can expect unambiguous effects on nutrient intake only when all fatty foods covary in price; however, this is extremely unlikely to be the case.

The general theme of compensating behavior recurs in the study of food price changes and body weight. There is no question that own-price elasticities[2] are negative, sometimes substantially so; it is less clear that price changes happen uniformly across broad enough food groups so as to effect changes in total nutrient intake.

---

1 A cross-price elasticity is the percentage change in quantity demanded of good A in response to a 1percent increase in the price of good B.
2 An own-price elasticity is the percentage change in quantity demanded of a good in response to a 1percent increase in the price of the same good.

The role of compensating behavior adds another layer of complexity atop the usual problems of simultaneity and identification.

CHALLENGES FOR IDENTIFICATION

Typically, researchers are interested in recovering the demand for food, and by extension, the demand for body weight. This requires identifying the impact of movement along the demand curve (how quantity demanded varies with price). The exogeneity of food prices is an important identification challenge faced by such an approach. Food prices might be higher in areas with higher demand for food, and during periods with higher demand for food. Both these examples would result in the classic form of simultaneity bias that exerts downward pressure on estimated coefficients; shifts in the demand curve become entangled with movements along it. Naturally, these biases presume that part of the observed variation in price is driven by demand. Pure supply-driven price variation results in clean identification using standard regression methods. Unfortunately, demand for food and body weight are unlikely to be homogeneous. Variation might occur due to differences in socioeconomic status, or the underlying demand for health.

The most common approach to identification is to control for area and time fixed-effects in panel data. This approach presumes fixed differences in demand across regions, or fixed aggregate differences in demand across time periods. This strategy is threatened by differing local time trends in demand. For instance, if demand is rising faster in southern states than northern states, then the differences between regions are not fixed over time; this invalidates the area fixed-effects approach. Moreover, the trends over time are not common across all areas; this invalidates the period fixed-effect approach. In principle, one could address these concerns by including local time trends within the empirical model, but this approach is sensitive to the specification used.

A more robust but much more difficult approach is to instrument for food prices. This requires identifying a factor that influences the supply of food, but not the demand for food. One seemingly natural candidate is the cost of transporting food across areas, but this candidate illustrates one of the difficulties with this approach: the cost of transporting food may be correlated with the cost of exercise (e.g., areas with extensive roads might attract populations more inclined to commute from outlying suburbs than to walk to work).

In spite of the difficulties, several instruments have been proposed in the literature. One candidate is the proximity of interstate highways, which is argued to affect the distribution of fast food and other restaurants (Anderson and Matsa 2007). The local average treatment effect in this case is specific to the impact of restaurants, although this in itself is an important policy question. This instrument has been shown to pass a variety of validity tests. The weakness is the relatively small size of the effect of interstate location on restaurant utilization. Alternatively, Lakdawalla and Philipson (2002) propose the use of relative food taxes as an instrument for the relative price of food. Specifically, this approach exploits differences across states in the decision to exempt food from sales taxation. Tax exemption lowers the relative price of food to consumers, compared to non-exempt states. The drawback to using this approach is the absence of significant changes over time in tax-exemption policies within states. As a result, relative taxes fail to vary much over time within a state. This precludes the use of state fixed-effects in combination with the instrument, and sacrifices the ability to test for the possibility that tax-exempt states have systematically different demands for food and body weight compared to non-exempt states.

A final approach, suitable for panel data, exploits dynamic panel data analysis methods. These models can partially address the simultaneity issue by controlling for lagged dependent variables. The identifying assumption here is that heterogeneity across individuals (or areas) is well captured by variation in the last period's weight or food intake. While this is a fairly easy solution to implement, it is only a partial solution to the problem of unobserved heterogeneity, because it does not address the deeper problem of identifying exogenous, supply-driven variation in prices. For this reason, an instrumental variable (or plausible fixed-effects) approach is required.

In sum, there are a number of possible approaches to identification, but all suffer from one or more key weaknesses. Nonetheless, the collage of evidence pieced together from different identification strategies can still be informative, as we will argue.

MEASUREMENT CHALLENGES

On top of the identification issues, the measurement of food prices is not straightforward. The first challenge is posed by the multidimensional nature of food. There are hundreds of food items that vary in taste, nutrition values, and energy density. It is not feasible to include the prices of each food item in an analysis. The common strategy is to construct a composite food price index that represents a group of food items. Such price indices include prices for all food items, prices for fast food, prices for full-service restaurants, and prices for food at home. But using such food indices assumes that the price effects on body weight are the same across different food items, which is not true for a number of reasons.

First, different food items might have different effects on weight. Even if lettuce and butter make up equal expenditure shares in a consumer's food basket, it is hard to argue that a fixed change in the price of lettuce has the same impact as a similarly sized change in the price of butter. One way to overcome this issue is to place more weight on foods that have larger impacts on body weight, by constructing an index of price per calorie. This approach implicitly places more weight on calorie-dense foods, for which a given change in intake should have a larger impact on body weight (Goldman, Lakdawalla, et al. 2009).

However, any approach to aggregation suffers from the need to make uniform assumptions about the composition of consumption. Individuals vary in their food intake, and this variation is systematically related to weight. If heavier people eat more calorically dense foods, any index approach will tend to understate the effect of a change in the price of such foods on the heavy, and overstate the effects on the light. An alternative approach is to split the index into components and avoid the problems associated with constructing an index. One way of implementing this approach is to include prices for a few key foods—for example, fruits and vegetables, milk, and meats. Forming price indices within these more homogeneous groups may pose less of a problem, since prices within these groups tend to co-vary, and the effects on weight may be similar. Various studies have implemented this by focusing on "high-calorie" versus "low-calorie foods," or "healthy" versus "unhealthy" food groups. (Sturm and Datar 2005; Gelbach, Klick, et al. 2007; Miljkovic, Nganje, et al. 2008; Sturm and Datar 2008; Powell 2009; Powell and Bao 2009; Powell and Chaloupka 2009) A key validity issue is whether or not these groups are in fact homogeneous in terms of price changes and effects on weight. In addition, omitted prices for other types of food might be correlated both with prices for the included food groups and with body weight.

The second issue is measurement error in food prices themselves. The most frequently used food price data is the American Chamber of Commerce Researchers Association (ACCRA) Cost of Living Index reports, which provide quarterly information on prices in approximately 300 U.S. cities (Lakdawalla and Philipson 2002; Chou, Grossman et al. 2004; Sturm and Datar 2005; Beydoun, Powell et al. 2008; Sturm and Datar 2008; Auld and Powell 2009; Goldman, Lakdawalla et al. 2009; Powell 2009; Powell and Bao 2009; Powell and Chaloupka 2009; Powell, Zhao, et al. 2009). Some studies used regional food prices provided by Bureau of Labor Statistics (Gelbach, Klick, et al. 2007). USDA provides prices for agricultural products at the state level (Miljkovic, Nganje, et al. 2008). Regardless of the source, measured prices almost always diverge from the prices that particular individuals face in their community. The result is downward bias in the estimated effects of food prices; this reinforces the typical simultaneity bias caused by poor identification.

A recent attempt to overcome the measurement issue is a USDA-sponsored project to link the National Health and Nutrition Examination Survey (NHANES) to local food prices. The idea is to link NHANES data at a disaggregated geographic level to supermarket scanner data on food prices in a local community.[3]

One advantage of the NHANES-USDA project is the availability of dietary recall data, laboratory measures of nutrient availability, and objective measures of body mass. This makes for an exceptionally rich database that allows researchers to

---

3 Description based on personal correspondence between an author (Darius Lakdawalla) and Professor Oral Capps, at Texas A&M University, in College Station, TX.

link prices to food intake, nutrient intake, and body weight. However, the limitations of the NHANES illustrate the inherent trade-offs of doing research on body weight and food prices. Due in part to the extremely burdensome nature of the survey, NHANES respondents are not followed longitudinally, nor are the samples as large as one finds in studies like the National Health Interview Survey (NHIS), which relies entirely on self-reported data on health-related variables.

EVALUATING THE EVIDENCE ON FOOD PRICES AND BODY WEIGHT

There is a substantial literature linking food prices and body weight. Here, we review 14 important examples drawn from this literature.

Effects in Children

We surveyed six studies examining the association between food prices and body weight among children and adolescents (Sturm and Datar 2005; Sturm and Datar 2008; Auld and Powell 2009; Powell 2009; Powell and Bao 2009; Powell and Chaloupka 2009). All of these studies relied on food price data from the same source: the ACCRA Cost of Living Index, discussed earlier. As a result, all are subject to the typical measurement concerns surrounding the ACCRA data, and indeed, all geographical food price data.

Apart from the similarity in the measurement of prices, however, these studies took a number of different empirical approaches. In particular, these studies run the gamut of fixed-effects, random effects, and repeated cross-section methods. A generic concern in the analysis of body weight data is unobserved heterogeneity across individuals in the propensity to gain weight. Unfortunately, all three approaches are imperfect solutions to the problem. Repeated cross-section methods impose the least general assumptions, by presuming that all individual-specific unobservables are uncorrelated with the model's variables of interest. The random effects method weakens these slightly, but imposes distributional assumptions on how the unobserved heterogeneity varies. The fixed-effect approach involves the most general assumption, by allowing each individual to have a unique and idiosyncratic level of weight; however, in most applications, the fixed-effects approaches used cannot cope with heterogeneity in the propensity to *gain* weight. This would amount to a fixed-effects model in first-differences of body weight.

Auld and Powell used repeated cross-sectional data of the Monitoring the Future Survey to examine how fast food price and price of fruits and vegetables are associated with adolescent BMI and overweight status (Auld and Powell 2009). While the repeated cross-sectional nature of the data limited them in some respects, the use of quantile regression methods was an important contribution to this literature. The study demonstrated that fast food price was negatively related to BMI and overweight status, while fruit and vegetable prices were positively related to BMI, but not statistically significantly associated with overweight status. The quantile regressions demonstrated that the effects were much larger in the top quintile of the conditional distribution of BMI. This latter effect suggests the most price-sensitivity in the portion of the distribution that policy makers often seek to target.

The fixed-effects studies relied on several different panel data sets. One study analyzed four waves of the National Longitudinal Survey of Youth (1997–2000) using individual fixed-effects models and found that among adolescents aged 12 to 17, price of fast food was negatively associated with BMI (elasticity of -0.078), while the relationship between price of food at home and BMI was statistically insignificant (Powell 2009). A second study analyzed two waves of the Child Development Supplement of the Panel Study of Income Dynamics (1997 and 2002–2003), using OLS and individual fixed-effects models. Price of fruits and vegetables was found to be positively correlated with higher BMI percentile in both OLS and fixed-effects estimations. Price of fast food, however, was not statistically significantly related to children's BMI (Powell and Chaloupka 2009). Finally, two studies used the Childhood Longitudinal Survey to examine the effects of prices for fruits and vegetables, and meats, on the change in child BMI. Fruit and vegetable prices were found to be positively associated with one-year, three-year or five-year BMI change among children while meat prices exhibited statistically insignificant effects (Sturm and Datar 2005; Sturm and Datar 2008).

Finally, the one study employing random effects found qualitatively similar results to an analogous fixed-effects study. Powell and Bao analyzed three waves of the child-mother merged files from the 1979 cohort of the National Longitudinal Survey of Youth (Powell and Bao 2009). Their findings resemble the earlier results of Powell and Chaloupka (2009).

Overall, the literature finds evidence that higher prices of fast food depress body weight, but higher prices for fruits and vegetables may have the opposite effect. There is also some evidence that price effects are most pronounced in the upper reaches of the BMI distribution. However, simultaneity is a problem in nearly all of these studies: if changes in body weight cause changes in food demand and prices, the estimates in this literature are not causal. Moreover, heterogeneity in the propensity to gain weight is also a concern.

Effects in Adults

We also surveyed seven studies examining food price effects for adults. Three of these attempted instrumental variables approaches to the simultaneity problem, while the remainder employed a mix of panel data and OLS approaches.

Chou, Grossman, et al. authored perhaps the earliest peer-reviewed study in this area (2004). They relied on repeated cross-sectional data from the 1984–1999 Behavioral Risk Factor Surveillance System, combined with ACCRA price data aggregated at the state level. They find that fast food prices, prices at full-service restaurants, and prices for food at home were all negatively related to adult BMI and obesity status, with price elasticities for BMI equal to −0.048, −0.021, and −0.039, respectively. The Chou et al. study allowed for fixed-effects at the geographic level, but individual fixed-effects were not possible with the data used.

Another study used the cross-sectional data of the Continuing Survey of Food Intakes by adults aged 20–65 and found that BMI was negatively associated with price of fruits and vegetables, but the effect of fast food prices on BMI was statistically insignificant. Neither price index was statistically significantly associated with obesity status (Beydoun, Powell, et al. 2008). This paper is largely in agreement, or at least fails to reject, the earlier work of Chou et al.

The last study in this vein investigated how the prices of three representative food items—sugar, potatoes, and milk—were related to BMI, using repeated cross-sectional data of the Behavioral Risk Factor Surveillance System (1991, 1997, and 2002). The authors found that the obesity status of adults was positively associated with the price of potatoes, but negatively associated with the prices of sugar and of milk (Miljkovic, Nganje, et al. 2008). While this study is somewhat hard to interpret, it represents a nice example of the difficulties associated with analyzing the prices of individual foods. Results may vary with the particular foods that are included *and* excluded. For example, what basket of foods does the price of potatoes most faithfully represent?

One study in this genre to use both individual fixed-effects and dynamic panel data methods is that of Goldman, Lakdawalla, and Zheng (2009). They apply dynamic panel data methods to panel data from the 1992–2004 Health and Retirement Study, linked to ACCRA price data (Goldman, Lakdawalla, et al. 2009). Moreover, Goldman et al. also constructed indices of price per calorie, using representative baskets of food consumption. They found that increases in price per calorie were negatively associated with BMI among Americans aged 50 and older (the sample frame of the Health and Retirement Study). Moreover, the effects differed over the time horizon studied: price elasticity was -0.06 in the short term, and -0.42 in the long term, where the long term spanned more than 30 years. This data set allowed for heterogeneity across individuals in their propensity to gain weight, but not for the endogeneity in food prices changes. Moreover, it is also limited to older adults.

At least three other studies used instrumental variables approaches to address the simultaneity problem in food prices and body weight. One recent study used the proximity of interstate highways as the instrument for effective food price at restaurants and found no causal relationship between restaurant price and obesity (Anderson and Matsa 2007). The validity argument presented in favor of this instrument is quite compelling, but the first-stage treatment effect is relatively modest. Proximity to interstate highways has a relatively small impact on restaurant patronage; it is thus hard to know whether restaurant availability has no effect, or whether the effects are not large enough to be detectable, given the size of the first-stage effect.

A second study used regional price of unleaded gasoline as the instrument for the regional relative price of healthy food (Gelbach, Klick, et al. 2007). Both BMI and obesity status were positively related to relative price of healthy food, with price elasticity of 0.01. This study is subject to concerns about validity, because gasoline prices might also affect the cost of transportation and of exercise.

Finally, Lakdawalla and Philipson (2002) used state-level relative food taxes as an instrument for the relative price of food and found a negative and large effect of relative food price on BMI (elasticity of -0.6) among young adults (Lakdawalla and Philipson 2002). However, the lack of time-series variation in the relative taxes imposed on food prevents the use of any fixed-effect design; as a result, this study is vulnerable to area-specific or individual-specific heterogeneity that persists in the local average treatment effect.

A final, somewhat unique, study estimated how the minimum wage affected adult BMI, using the repeated cross-sectional data of the Behavioral Risk Factor Surveillance System 1984–2006, and historical federal and state minimum wage data from the Bureau of Labor Statistics (Meltzer and Chen 2009). The authors hypothesized that minimum wage would be associated with body weight, since minimum wage labor is a major input into the production of restaurant food and fast food. The authors conclude that a $1 decrease in the real minimum wage is associated with a 0.06 increase in BMI. This study is both intriguing and compelling, but it is somewhat hard to translate into the context of the larger discussion about food prices, without further information about how much the minimum wage affects food prices.

The literature on adults somewhat clouds the issue of whether and to what extent changes in the price of restaurant food and fast food affect body weight. Anderson and Matsa (2007) is a well-conceived instrumental variables study arguing for no effect, but this may be due to a modest treatment effect. Most of the other studies in this literature seem to agree that high restaurant prices reduce body weight, although none has a design robust to the simultaneity issues that Anderson and Matsa emphasize.

However, most of the literature does seem to agree that broad-based increases in food prices tend to reduce body weight, as we would expect. The effects of prices for specific foods, however, remain much less certain. This is likely due to the intractable empirical problem of omitted variables, as it is fundamentally impossible to measure every dimension along which food prices vary.

Effects by Body Weight Status

One question that arises is whether or not the effects of prices vary across particular subpopulations. For example, Auld and Powell applied quantile regression methods to examine how food price effects vary across the body weight distribution (Auld and Powell 2009). Meltzer and Chen used similar methods to investigate how the effect of the minimum wage on body weight vary by weight distribution (Meltzer and Chen 2009). Both studies show that the effects, in terms of units of BMI, are larger at the upper tail of the BMI distribution. Since BMI is detrimental to health only when it is extremely low or high, such results would indicate that food price policies (either tax or subsidy) could be most effective among those who are obese.

However, identification issues remain to be addressed. While useful, both studies rely on cross-sectional methods. Using quantile regression in fixed-effects models or combining quantile regression with instrumental variable approach is both more robust and more challenging, as the corresponding methodologies are not well-developed yet.

Effects by Socioeconomic Status

An additional issue is whether the effects of food price on body weight vary by socioeconomic status. There are at least four studies that have attempted to address this question (Beydoun, Powell et al. 2008; Powell 2009; Powell and Bao 2009; Powell and Chaloupka 2009). One study (Beydoun, Powell, et al. 2008) conducted separate analyses for adults grouped by Poverty Income Ratio (PIR). The effects of the price of fruits and vegetables on BMI or obesity status were the largest among those near poor (PIR between 131 to 299), relative to those who were poor (PIR between 0 to 130) or non-poor (PIR 300 or more). However, it is unknown whether these effects were statistically different from each other.

The other three studies, examining food price effects among children or adolescents, stratified analyses by mother's education or family income level. It was found that the food price effects were greatest for the group with mother's education of high school or less, relative to the group with mother's education of some college and above (Powell 2009; Powell and Bao 2009). In addition, the low- or middle-income group was more price sensitive than the high-income group (Powell 2009; Powell and Bao 2009; Powell and Chaloupka 2009). However, again, there was no statistical test of whether the estimates from stratified analysis were different from each other. Nonetheless, taking the results at face value suggests that the poorest groups are most price-responsive.

INCOME AND BODY WEIGHT

Theoretical Issues

Theoretically, there are several channels of causality running from income to body weight. The first is the standard effect that operates on food as a normal good. Richer people have more to spend on food, and all other goods. By itself, this would imply that richer people are always heavier than poorer people.

The actual variation in body weight across income groups rarely matches this pattern; additional causal mechanisms are thus required. Another is the demand for health and attractiveness. Just like food, health and appearance are likely to be normal goods. It is interesting to ask how preferences for appearance are formed, but for our purposes, we can take as given the preference for a slender build, at least in Western countries. As a result, richer people might choose to purchase more attractiveness or health, in the form of weight-control or weight-reduction. Coupled with the pure income effects on food intake and weight, the result is a possibly non-monotonic relationship between income and weight, determined by the competing interaction between the demand for food, and the demands for health and appearance (Lakdawalla and Philipson 2009).

A final issue to consider is the manner in which income is earned. The arguments above fully summarize the impacts of unearned income on weight, but the effect of earned income reflects both the income itself, and the nature of the work that was done to earn the income. Earning income through participation in a sedentary job is likely to generate a positive relationship between income and weight, while participation in an active job will do the opposite (Lakdawalla and Philipson 2009).

These different effects help make sense of the differing relationships between income and weight within and between countries. Richer countries tend to be heavier than poorer countries, while richer women are often thinner than poorer women in developed countries. The nature of work will tend to vary more across countries than within countries. Therefore, richer countries might be more likely to engage in sedentary jobs than poorer countries: this may help explain the strength of the relationship between income and weight. On the other hand, it is less clear that a rich American executive has a systematically more sedentary job than a poor American retail clerk. Across these groups, the relevant underlying differences that may lead to differences in weight are the demand for food, and the competing demands for health and appearance (Lakdawalla and Philipson 2009).

Challenges for Identification

Adding to the theoretical complexity are the empirical challenges of identifying the causal impact of income on body weight. Clearly, there are a number of unobserved third factors that could influence both income and body weight: unobserved human capital, rate of time-preference, or baseline energy and metabolism. All these factors create problems of interpretation for simple correlations between income and weight.

While these issues are fairly well understood, there are few obvious candidates for valid identification strategies. As a result, identification of the causal impact of income on weight remains a somewhat open question. In the following discussion, we summarize what is known, given the limits of current methods, and attempt to draw some conclusions in light of the uncertainty.

The potentially non-monotonic income-weight effect imposes additional identification challenges. Conclusions could depend on the functional form of income: linear, log, quadratic, categorical, or splines.

Challenges for Measurement

The analysis of income and body weight faces fairly typical challenges that afflict many areas of economics. Self-reported income is subject to a variety of reporting errors both classical and non-classical, even in surveys that focus heavily on the accuracy of these measures (Moore, Stinson, et al. 2000).

In the particular context of body weight, this problem is exacerbated by the crudeness with which income tends to be elicited in health surveys like the NHIS, NHANES, and Behavioral Risk Factor Surveillance System (BRFSS). In NHIS and NHANES, two categorical family income variables are provided; one is the combined total family income based on separate questions on different sources of income, while the other is the poverty-to-income ratio (PIR). In both NHIS 2004 and NHANES 2003–2004, there were 11 family income levels, with the lowest level of 0–$4,999, and the highest of $75,000 or more. In addition, those who did not provide a specific income amount were asked whether their family income was more than $20,000. The poverty income ratio variable includes 14 levels, ranging from under 0.50 to 5.00 and over. In BRFSS 2004, one question was asked about annual household income from all sources, and the value items included 8 levels, with the lowest level of 0–$9,999, and the highest level of $75,000 and over.

There are some surveys, such as the Health and Retirement Study (HRS), specifically designed to measure income and wealth as accurately as possible, which also collect information on body weight. The HRS, for example, collects self-reported income on height and weight, although it will soon begin to collect objectively measured height and weight, further enhancing its value to this literature. Of course, it should be noted that the HRS samples the population over the age of 50 and thus prevents the analysis of effects on children and young adults, who could in principle exhibit quite a different level of responsiveness to income.

Evaluating the Evidence on Income and Body Weight

The evidence on income also encompasses both adults and children. The literature on children can be seen as part of the larger literature on how household income affects child health. The literature on adults, in contrast, has aligned itself more closely with the particularities of body weight.

Income and Child Weight

Using pooled data from the 1997–2002 Health Surveys of England, Currie, Shields, et al found that the log of family income was not statistically associated with measured obesity status for children in England (Currie, Shields, et al. 2007). In slight contrast, another study analyzed wave 2 (1996) and wave 3 (2001 to 2002) of the National Longitudinal Study of Adolescent Health, which surveyed a nationally representative sample of adolescents in the United States, and found that controlling for age, family poverty status was positively associated with becoming obese or staying obese from wave 2 to wave 3 among females. However, the effect was not present for males, and even the female effect disappeared once parental education, family structure, and neighborhood poverty measure were included as additional control variables (Lee, Harris, et al. 2009). Hofferth and Curtin (2005) examined how family income was associated with overweight status among children aged 6 to 11. Using the data of 1997 Panel Study of Income Dynamics Child Development Supplement, the authors found that relative to children of moderate household income (185% - < 300% poverty line), children of poor households (< 100% poverty line) were less likely to be overweight and had lower BMI. Childhood overweight status and BMI of near-poor households (100% - < 130% poverty line), households of working-class (130% - < 185% poverty line), and high-income households (300% or higher poverty line) were not statistically different from those of children from moderate-income households (Hofferth and Curtin 2005).

As a whole, the evidence suggests that income may not play an independent causal role in childhood weight, above and beyond the usual suite of socioeconomic characteristics. From the latter perspective, however, low socioeconomic status seems to be associated with less healthy body weight outcomes for children.

Income-Weight Patterns among Adult Populations

Several studies have found that income is negatively associated with body weight for women, but not for men. One example is Garcia Villar and Quintana-Domeque's work; this paper examined how the log of household income was associated with BMI and obesity status for Europeans, using European Community Household Panel, a survey based on a standardized questionnaire that involves annual interviewing of a representative panel of households and individuals in member states of the European Union during 1994–2001 (Garcia Villar and Quintana-Domeque 2009). OLS and Probit model results showed that log of household income was negatively associated with women's BMI or obesity status in six out of nine countries, and that the effects operated primarily through earned individual income. The associations between household income and men's BMI were not statistically significant for six out of the nine countries, positive for one country, and negative for the other two.

Another study on both U.S. and European data examined how various measures of energy intake and expenditure, as well as socioeconomic status, affect obesity rates in the United States and Europe, using cross-sectional data from the Survey of Health, Aging and Retirement in Europe, and the Health and Retirement Study in the United States (Michaud, van Soest, et al. 2007). The study found that controlling for wealth, income quintiles were negatively associated with obesity among females but the relationship for males was indefinite.

The differences across gender may point to a larger issue, identified by a number of other studies: the non-linearity of the body weight-income effect, as discussed earlier. Lakdawalla and Philipson (2009) examined how body weight varied with income quartiles in the United States, using National Health Interview Survey 1976–1994 (Lakdawalla and Philipson 2009). An inverted U-shaped BMI-income relationship was found among American males; individuals in the bottom and the top quartile of the income distribution had lower BMI than those in the 2nd quartile and average BMI peaked at the 3rd income quartile. Within females, however, the relationship was uniformly negative.

A number of other studies have focused on the non-linearities in the relationship between income and body weight. One finds a U-shaped relationship between household income and BMI or obesity status for male and female combined, using the Behavioral Risk Factor Surveillance System 1984–1999 (Chou, Grossman, et al. 2004). However, within the observed income range, the relationship was negative, with an income-BMI elasticity of -0.02. The pooling across genders, however, makes it hard to directly compare this result to other examples in the literature.

Another study that stratified by sex finds an inverted U-shaped relationship between BMI and income, for both males and females (Jolliffe 2007). This study employed three cross-sections of the National Health and Nutrition Examination Survey, 1999 to 2004. At lower income levels, there was a positive association between income and BMI, but at higher income levels the association turned negative. The study also pointed out that the association turns negative at a lower income threshold among women. This would make it more likely to observe the negative relationship among women, when estimating linear effects.

Finally, a study using the 2002 wave of Health and Retirement Study and the first wave of England Longitudinal Survey of Aging found that household income, measured in three categories, was negatively associated with obesity status in both the United States and England, with a steeper gradient for the United States (Banks, Marmot, et al. 2006).

A final strand of the literature examines the relationship between income and weight gain. Using the 1986 to 2002 data of the Behavioral Risk Factor Surveillance System, Truong and Sturm found no statistically significant association between relative income position and weight gain during the period of 1986 to 2002 (Truong and Sturm 2005). Another study, using the National Health and Nutrition Examination Surveys (1971–2002), found similar results (Chang and Lauderdale 2005). Both studies correlate a household's contemporaneous position in the income distribution, with body weight. This creates a difficulty of interpretation, since households can switch over from the low income to high income groups in the data. Contemporaneous income is clearly a noisy measure of permanent income; therefore, the finding of no effect may have more to do with measurement error than with the size of the underlying parameters.

These studies do not claim to identify causal effects (nor should they). All are focused on describing the patterns in body weight across income groups. The preponderance of evidence suggests that non-linearity is a frequent characteristic of this relationship, but that among women, the relationship is typically more negative. From a theoretical perspective, this would suggest that the demand for healthy body weight is a stronger force than the income effect on food consumption.

Causal Effects of Income

One of the very few studies to search for the causal impact of income on weight is Cawley, Moran et al (Cawley, Moran, et al. 2008), who exploit the "Social Security Benefit Notch" to examine the effects of Social Security income on body weight. Relative to birth cohorts born before 1915 or after 1917, Americans born from 1915 to 1917 received extra Social Security benefits due to a quirk in the benefit calculation formula. There is thus a discrete break in benefit amounts across cohorts, visible in the time series. The validity of the instrument seems quite plausible, although questions have been raised in other contexts about coincidental differences in health across these cohorts: the 1918 influenza pandemic has been argued to have affected the health of cohorts that were in utero at the time (Almond 2006). Nonetheless, this is likely to be a fairly indirect source of bias. Similar to the Anderson and Matsa paper, this is a reasonably compelling instrumental variable design (concerns about the 1918 influenza epidemic notwithstanding). The variation in retirement income due to the benefits notch was found to be statistically significantly related to total Social Security income, but had no statistically significant effect on measures of body weight.

The generalizability of this style of approach is unclear. The bump in Social Security income, or similar exogenous bumps in income transfer programs (e.g., the Earned Income Tax Credit) represent fairly small changes to permanent income. And, they typically target particular subpopulations—e.g., the elderly, or the poor—leaving open the question of whether and how the results generalize. It is also unclear whether the Social Security notch generates enough movement in *lifetime* income to generate an economically meaningful test of whether income matters.

CONCLUSIONS

There is a significant and growing literature on how food prices and income affect body weight. Nonetheless, all of it suffers from substantial empirical challenges of causal inference that have not yet been satisfactorily overcome. Regardless, the literature consistently finds that broad-based increases in food prices lead to lower body weight, as the simplest economic model would predict. It is much harder to identify the effects of changes in the prices of specific foods.

For income, it has been similarly difficult to recover causal effects. However, the literature has established with reasonable confidence the non-linearity of the relationship between income and body weight. This is a theoretical prediction of the competition between the demand for healthy body weight, which rises with income, and the demand for food, which also rises with income.

The future advance of this literature requires continued refinement in the measurement of body weight, food prices, and income, all of which suffer from serious inaccuracy. Moreover, methods of causal inference must improve, if we are to progress toward the estimation of causal parameters. While a variety of causal inference methods have been proposed, none has so far been demonstrated as compelling in both validity and power.

REFERENCES

Almond, D. 2006. "Is the 1918 Influenza Pandemic Over? Long-Term Effects of In Utero Influenza Exposure in the Post-1940 U.S. Population." *Journal of Political Economy* 114(4): 672–712.

Anderson, M., and D. Matsa 2007. "Are Restaurants Really Supersizing America?" Department of Agricultural and Resource Economics, University of California, Berkeley, Department of Agricultural and Resource Economics, Working Paper Series: 1056.

Auld, M. C., and L. M. Powell 2009. "Economics of Food Energy Density and Adolescent Body Weight." *Economica* 76: 719–740.

Banks, J., M. Marmot, et al. 2006. "Disease and Disadvantage in the United States and in England." *Journal of the American Medical Association* 295(17): 2037–2045.

Beydoun, M. A., L. M. Powell, et al. 2008. "The Association of Fast Food, Fruit and Vegetable Prices with Dietary Intakes among US Adults: Is There Modification by Family Income?" *Soc Science and Medicine* 66(11): 2218–2229.

Cawley, J., J. R. Moran, et al. 2008. "The Impact of Income on the Weight of Elderly Americans." National Bureau of Economic Research, NBER Working Papers: 14104.

Chang, V. W., and D. S. Lauderdale 2005. "Income Disparities in Body Mass Index and Obesity in the United States, 1971–2002." *Archives of Internal Medicine* 165(18): 2122–2128.

Chou, S.-Y., M. Grossman, et al. 2004. "An Economic Analysis of Adult Obesity: Results from the Behavioral Risk Factor Surveillance System." *Journal of Health Economics* 23(3): 565–587.

Currie, A., M. A. Shields, et al. 2007. "The Child Health/Family Income Gradient: Evidence from England." *Journal of Health Economics* 26(2): 213–232.

Garcia Villar, J., and C. Quintana-Domeque 2009. "Income and Body Mass Index in Europe." *Economics and Human Biology* 7(1): 73–83.

Gelbach, J. B., J. Klick, et al. 2007. "Cheap Donuts and Expensive Broccoli: The Effect of Relative Prices on Obesity." Florida State University College of Law.

Goldman, D., D. Lakdawalla, et al. 2009. "Food Prices and the Dynamics of Body Weight." National Bureau of Economic Research, NBER Working Papers: 15096.

Hofferth, S. L., and S. Curtin 2005. "Poverty, Food Programs, and Childhood Obesity." *Journal of Policy Analysis and Management* 24(4): 703–726.

Jolliffe, D. 2007. "The Income Gradient and Distribution-Sensitive Measures of Overweight in the U.S." National Poverty Center Working Paper Series #07–27.

Lakdawalla, D., and T. Philipson 2002. "The Growth of Obesity and Technological Change: A Theoretical and Empirical Examination." National Bureau of Economic Research, NBER Working Papers: 8946.

Lakdawalla, D. N., and T. J. Philipson 2009. "The Growth of Obesity and Technological Change." *Economics and Human Biology* 7(3): 283–293.

Lee, H., K. M. Harris, et al. (2009). "Life Course Perspectives on the Links between Poverty and Obesity during the Transition to Young Adulthood." *Population Research and Policy Review* 28(4): 505–532.

Meltzer, D. and Z. Chen 2009. "The Impact of Minimum Wage Rates on Body Weight in the United States." National Bureau of Economic Research, NBER Working Papers: 15485.

Michaud, P.-C., A. van Soest, et al. 2007. "Cross-Country Variation in Obesity Patterns among Older Americans and Europeans." McMaster University, Social and Economic Dimensions of an Aging Population Research Papers.

Miljkovic, D., W. Nganje, et al. 2008. "Economic Factors Affecting the Increase in Obesity in the United States: Differential Response to Price." *Food Policy* 33(1): 48–60.

Moore, J. C., L. L. Stinson, et al. 2000. "Income Measurement Error in Surveys: A Review." *Journal of Official Statistics* 16(4): 331–361.

Powell, L. M. 2009. "Fast Food Costs and Adolescent Body Mass Index: Evidence from Panel Data." *Journal of Health Economics* 28(5): 963–970.

Powell, L. M., and Y. Bao 2009. "Food Prices, Access to Food Outlets and Child Weight." *Economics and Human Biology* 7(1): 64–72.

Powell, L. M., and F. J. Chaloupka 2009. "Economic Contextual Factors and Child Body Mass Index." National Bureau of Economic Research, NBER Working Papers: 15046.

Powell, L. M., Z. Zhao, et al. 2009. "Food Prices and Fruit and Vegetable Consumption among Young American Adults." *Health Place* 15(4): 1064–1070.

Sturm, R., and A. Datar 2005. "Body Mass Index in Elementary School Children, Metropolitan Area Food Prices and Food Outlet Density." *Public Health* 119(12): 1059–1068.

Sturm, R., and A. Datar 2008. "Food Prices and Weight Gain during Elementary School: 5-Year Update." *Public Health* 122(11): 1140–1143.

Truong, K. D., and R. Sturm 2005. "Weight Gain Trends across Sociodemographic Groups in the United States." *American Journal of Public Health* 95(9): 1602–1606.

CHAPTER 28

AGRICULTURAL POLICY AND CHILDHOOD OBESITY

JOHN CAWLEY AND BARRETT KIRWAN

INTRODUCTION

THIS chapter examines the extent to which agricultural policies contribute to childhood obesity by: decreasing the prices of certain commodities, donating energy-dense commodities to school food programs, and advertising energy-dense commodities and fast food. Agricultural policy is multifaceted, and each component of it may have a different impact on childhood obesity. Some promote food consumption, for example through advertising or school food programs, whereas a few actually discourage food consumption, for example by restricting imports or acreage under production and thus keeping prices high. Agricultural policy is also dynamic; it changes, sometimes dramatically, approximately every five years when Congress passes a new Farm Bill. As a result, agricultural policy has complex, changing, and sometimes opposing effects on childhood obesity.

We approach the problem by analyzing the potential effects of each component of farm policy. First, we examine policies that directly affect production, such as agricultural subsidies (i.e., price supports, production subsidies, and farmland subsidies), acreage controls, tariffs on imported commodities, and agricultural extension research. We then examine policies aimed at stimulating the demand for food, such as commodity distribution programs and commodity promotion programs. We conclude by proposing reforms that would better align agricultural policy with health policy regarding childhood obesity.

AGRICULTURAL SUBSIDIES

Agricultural subsidies fall into three main categories: price supports, production subsidies, and farmland subsidies. Each has a different effect on food production, and thus on food prices and consumption. The subsequent sections explain the relevance of each of the three types of agricultural subsidies for childhood obesity.

Price Supports

Price supports were first instituted in 1933 as part of the New Deal to give "agriculture a fair share in the national income" (Nourse, Davis, and Black 1937, p. 20) and have survived in some form for over 75 years. Price supports are intended to decrease uncertainty by preventing prices from falling below the legislated amount and to raise farmer income by increasing the price of their crops. This has the unintended consequence of decreasing consumer demand for affected food.

Price supports create excess supply; to the extent that the legislated price exceeds that which would prevail in a free market, more of the crop is supplied, and less is demanded, than would occur in a free market. The government typically buys excess supply to prevent it from depressing the price.

During the 1980s, the U.S. government kept the prices of soybeans, barley, sorghum, wheat, rice, and corn high through price supports, and purchased any excess supply. These surpluses were stored until market prices rose above the price floor, at which point the government sold the surpluses on the open market. However, during the late 1980s this became a costly strategy because prices did not rise above the legislated price floor, which both prevented the government from selling past surpluses and obliged it to continue buying additional surpluses. The increasing stockpiles resulted in a dramatic increase in storage costs (Orden, Paarlberg, and Roe, 1999), causing policy makers to shift away from price supports (which required the purchase of excess supply) and toward production subsidies (which did not).

Production Subsidies

Production subsidies, or "direct payments," were first made by the U.S. government to farmers in 1973 and consist of a cash payment for each unit of the commodity produced. Congress, realizing that production subsidies gave farmers an incentive to increase their production, implemented supply controls but these were ineffective and government commodity purchases and storage costs continued to rise (Orden et al, 1999).

In part because of the skyrocketing storage costs associated with agricultural surpluses, a new farm bill was drafted in 1985 that reshaped agricultural policy. This bill transformed the production subsidy into a farmland-specific subsidy by tying payments to the number of acres farmed instead of the amount of the commodity produced. The bill also introduced a new kind of production subsidy, called loan deficiency payments (LDPs), that guarantees commodity prices without saddling the government with the burden of storing and reselling the commodity. Beginning in 1985 for cotton and rice, 1991 for soybeans and oilseeds, and 1993 for wheat and feed grains, farmers had the option to sell their commodity on the open market and if the price they received was less than the legislated support price, the government would pay farmers the difference. (The traditional price support continues to be offered as an alternative, but the vast majority of producers utilize the new policy.)

LDPs also resulted in increased production. In a free market, farmers would not intentionally grow crops to sell them at a price below the cost of production, but in the current system farmers can sell their crops for a price below the costs of production and then collect production subsidies from the government that raise the per-unit price to the supported level. As a result, total cropland acreage is 4 million acres greater than it would be in the absence of production subsidies (Westcott and Price 2001). The USDA estimates that in 2000 the system of production subsidies lowered the price of wheat by 2.8 percent, rice by 3.3 percent, corn by 5.0 percent, and soybeans by 10.5 percent, relative to what would prevail in a free market (Westcott et al. 2001). An extremely important consequence of this change in policy is that consumers switched from paying above-market prices to below-market prices for affected commodities. In other words, the unintended consequence of agricultural policy flipped from discouraging to encouraging food consumption.

Farmland Subsidies

In addition to receiving the price supports and production subsidies outlined above, farmers also receive subsidies tied to farmland. When the 1985 farm bill divorced direct payments from crop production and instead tied them to the number of acres on which the farmer grew the subsidized crop, it created incentives for farmers to shift their effort and land away from producing unsubsidized crops, such as most fruits and vegetables, toward producing subsidized crops such as corn. It is estimated that these direct payments have increased the number of acres under cultivation by 4.3 percent for wheat, 3.4 percent for corn, and 2.2 percent for soybeans; at the average yield per acre this implies a 4 percent reduction in commodity prices (Goodwin and Mishra 2006). Others have estimated that, because the newly added acres are likely to be less productive than average, the increase in acreage cultivated decreased the prices of grains and soybeans by 2 percent (Gardner 2002).

Currently, production subsidies account for 68 percent, farmland subsidies account for 27 percent, and traditional price supports account for 5 percent, of agricultural subsidies (authors' calculations based on Commodity Credit Corporation Budgetary Expenditures, various years).

Linking the Impact on Quantities and Prices to Childhood Obesity

This section links agricultural subsidies, through their impact on the prices of commodities, to changes in youth body mass index (BMI). No single study traces this entire chain from beginning to end; the best one can do is to estimate the total impact of agricultural policy on obesity by linking together estimates of each step from the best available studies.

Adding together the average estimates of the amount by which prices are lowered (5 percent from production subsidies and 3 percent from land subsidies) implies that together agricultural subsidies lower the prices of affected commodities by 8 percent. This is consistent with another estimate that *removing* subsidies would *raise* the prices of affected commodities by 7.3 percent (Alston 2007).

Consumers rarely purchase the raw agricultural commodities that are subsidized (for example, corn, wheat, and soybeans). Food processors purchase the agricultural commodities and transform them into the food products that consumers buy. Agricultural commodities are just one of many inputs into the production of food products (others include marketing and labor) so the cost of farm commodities typically represents a small percentage of food's retail price; for example, 20 percent for a one-pound bag of sugar, 10 percent for shortening, 10 percent for margarine, 20 percent for a one-pound jar of peanut butter, 4 percent for a one-pound loaf of bread, and 3 percent for a 16-ounce bottle of corn syrup (USDA 2009a). Overall, it is estimated that for each 1 percent decrease in the price of agricultural commodities, the price of food products falls by 0.27 percent. (Morrison and MacDonald 2003). This implies that agricultural subsidies, by reducing the price of commodities by 8 percent, lower the prices of consumer food products by 2.16 percent.

It is estimated that a 1 percent decrease in the price of food results in a 0.039 percent increase in adult body mass index (BMI) (Chou, Grossman, and Saffer 2004). Assuming that the relationship between food prices and BMI for children is the same as that for adults, agricultural subsidies raise youth BMI by 0.08 percent. For a youth who weighs 140 pounds (which is the mean weight of a 14-year-old boy, and between the mean weights of 17- and 18-year-old girls (Ogden, Fryar, Carroll, et al. 2004), this represents a modest 0.11 pound increase.

ACREAGE CONTROLS

Until 1995, price supports operated in combination with acreage controls; to qualify for price supports, farmers typically had to agree to reduce the number of acres on which they planted subsidized crops. These acreage controls reduced the supply, and increased the prices, of agricultural commodities.

As part of the shift away from price supports and toward production subsidies, acreage controls were terminated in 1995, bringing the previously set aside land back into cultivation and facilitating further increase in the production, and reduction in the prices, of affected commodities.

Today, two programs remain that attempt to limit cultivation of land. The first is that, in order to receive land-specific subsidies, farmers must agree not to grow fruits and vegetables on that land, either for market sale or personal use.

Second, in the Conservation Reserve Program (CRP), farmers agree to convert environmentally sensitive cropland to vegetative cover in exchange for an annual rental payment for a term of 10–15 years. This program, motivated by a desire to prevent erosion and otherwise protect the environment, removes 36 million acres (8 percent) of cropland from cultivation, which restricts the output, and therefore raises the prices, of agricultural commodities. However, the effect of the CRP on commodity prices is limited by the fact that farmers tend to enroll their least productive land (Wu 2000).

Tariffs on Imports of Agricultural Commodities

The United States imposes tariff-rate quotas on imports of certain agricultural commodities. These policies levy a reduced tariff on a certain quota of imports, and a higher tariff on all imports above the quota. Total imports are not capped; any amount can be imported if the importer is willing to pay the higher tariff. For example, a limited amount of imported sugar ("in quota") is subject to a lesser tariff of 0.625 cents per pound. An unlimited amount of sugar can be imported "over quota," but it is subject to a far higher tariff of 15.36 cents per pound of raw sugar and 16.21 cents per pound of refined sugar (USDA 2009b). As a result, the price of sugar in the United States is two to three times the world price (Beghin and Jensen 2008).

Tariff-rate quota programs also apply to anchovies, milk and cream, olives, mandarin oranges, tuna, and wheat gluten. As a result, the U.S. prices of these products are higher than the world price, reducing demand.

U.S. farm policy, by subsidizing the production of corn and restricting imports of sugar, has incentivized the substitution of high-fructose corn syrup (HFCS) for sugar, e.g., by the soft drink industry (Beghin and Jensen 2008). Some have argued that this shift contributes to increased food intake and obesity because fructose, unlike glucose, does not stimulate insulin secretion or leptin production, both of which regulate food intake (Bray, Nielsen, and Popkin, 2004). However, the American Medical Association has concluded that the composition of HFCS and other sweeteners is sufficiently similar that it is unlikely HFCS contributes more to obesity than other sweeteners (American Medical Association 2008). Moreover, while agricultural policy has incentivized the switch from sugar to HFCS, it has raised the price of sweetener overall, which discourages the use and consumption of sweetener (Beghin and Jensen 2008).

AGRICULTURAL EXTENSION RESEARCH

The agricultural policy with potentially the greatest impact on food prices and consumption is publicly funded agricultural research. Agricultural productivity in the US increased 150 percent between 1948 and 1991. During much of this time, public research expenditures grew 3–4 percent annually and accounted for half of all agricultural research spending. Although it is difficult to isolate the exact contribution of publicly funded research to productivity growth, the estimated return to public agricultural research is at least 35 percent (Fuglie, Ballenger, Day, et al. 1996).

The vast majority (70–80 percent) of publicly funded crop research focuses on increasing biological efficiency and crop protection; that is, yields (Huffman and Evenson 1992). In 1989, subsidized commodities received twice as many public research dollars as fruits and vegetables. Publicly funded agricultural research could be leveraged to achieve public health goals by allocating more research funding to nutritious, less-energy-dense commodities like fruits and vegetables.

COMMODITY DISTRIBUTION PROGRAMS

The U.S. Department of Agriculture distributes agricultural commodities through its Schools/Child Nutrition Commodities Program, which encompasses the National School Lunch Program, the Child and Adult Care Food Program, and the Summer Food Service Program. In each of these programs, the USDA provides cash and donates agricultural commodities. Some of the commodities are purchased on the open market and others represent excess supply purchased by the government as part of the remaining price support programs. In most cases, the commodities distributed through these programs are energy-dense, such as cheese, milk, beef, pork, shortening and oils, but fruits, vegetables, nuts, pasta, and rice are also distributed.

Table 28.1 describes the three major commodity distribution programs in terms of number of children participating and the pounds and dollar value of the commodities provided by the USDA. In 2008, the National School Lunch Program (NSLP) provided subsidized or free lunches to more than 30.5 million children each school day, which is roughly 60 percent of the total student population

Table 28.1. USDA Commodity Distribution Programs for Children

Program	Number of Children Participating Daily (millions)	Amount of Commodities Distributed Through Program by USDA in School Year 2009 (Millions of Pounds)	Value of Commodities Distributed Through Program by USDA in School Year 2009 ($ Millions)
National School Lunch Program (NSLP)	30.5	980	$972
Child and Adult Care Food Program (CACFP)	2.9	1.8	$2.2
Summer Food Service Program (SFSP)	2.0	1.5	$1.1

Sources: USDA (2010a, 2010b, 2010c, 2010d).

(USDA 2010a). In School Year 2009, the USDA provided 980 million pounds of commodities worth $972 million through the NSLP (USDA 2010b).

The Child and Adult Care Food Program (CACFP) subsidizes meals provided in day care centers for children and in nonresidential adult day care centers for the elderly. Each day, 2.9 million children and 86,000 adults consume meals subsidized by CACFP (USDA 2010c). In School Year 2009, the USDA provided 1.8 million pounds of commodities worth $2.2 million through the CACFP (USDA 2010c).

The Summer Food Service Program (SFSP) takes the place of NSLP when school is out during the summer. Almost 2 million children participated in 2005, receiving meals in school buildings or camps (USDA 2010d). In School Year 2009, the USDA provided 1.5 million pounds of commodities worth $1.1 million through the SFSP (USDA 2010b).

USDA regulations require that participating schools "accept and use, in as large quantities as may be efficiently utilized in their nonprofit school food service," the surplus commodities provided by USDA (Ralston, Newman, Clauson, et al. 2008, p. 17). The NSLP also mandates that milk be served with every meal.

Since 1996, meals provided in these programs are required to meet USDA Dietary Guidelines. However, two-thirds of schools serve lunches that exceed USDA guidelines for fat and saturated fat (Ralston et al. 2008).

The donation of millions of pounds of energy-dense foods to schools when the vast majority of school meals exceed healthy limits for fat has led the USDA to question whether its efforts to support agricultural producers are making children overweight (Ralston et al. 2008). Research confirms that children who consume the school lunch as opposed to a lunch brought from home face a significantly higher risk of obesity. Specifically, youths who eat the school lunch consume an extra 60 calories per day, with the result that, after two years of exposure to school lunches, children are 2 percentage points more likely (on a base of 9 percentage points) to be overweight than those who bring their lunch from home (Schanzenbach 2009).

We estimate the portion of this effect of school meals on childhood obesity that is due to the commodity donation program. We conservatively assume that the percentage of the overall effect of school lunches on obesity that is due to the commodity donation program is equal to the value of donated commodities as a percentage of total program benefits. In 2009–2010, schools participating in the NSLP receive 19.5 cents worth of donated commodities and $2.68 in cash for each free lunch (Ralston et al. 2008); thus the donated commodities represent 6.8 percent of all program benefits. (This is an underestimate, as donated commodities are likely responsible for a higher percentage of calories than they represent a percentage of market value, and schools also receive additional commodities that are in surplus, but we lack an estimate of their dollar value, so we exclude them from the estimate.) If 6.8 percent of the effect of school lunches on childhood obesity is due to donated commodities, then the USDA commodity distribution program is responsible for raising the risk of childhood overweight by 0.14 percentage points among children who consume school lunches.

COMMODITY PROMOTION ("CHECKOFF") PROGRAMS

Federal Farm Promotion Programs may also contribute to obesity. The U.S. government requires that producers of certain commodities contribute a specific amount of money for each unit they sell into a fund that is used for commodity-specific advertising and research. Such contributions are made at the time of sale, so these have become known as "checkoff" programs (meaning that at the time of sale, a box was checked to indicate that the contribution was made). The intention of this program is to increase consumer demand for the commodity. A list of current checkoff programs, and their most recent budgets, is listed in table 28.2 (Becker 2008). Note that the checkoff programs that spend the most on promotion are those for energy-dense products such as cheese, milk, beef, and pork, while the few programs that exist for fruits and vegetables have among the smallest budgets.

Checkoff funds are used to stimulate demand of the commodity in two ways: direct marketing to consumers of the generic commodity and research, development, and promotion of new products that use the commodity.

The advertising of generic commodities funded by checkoff dollars has included such memorable campaigns as: "Got Milk?," "Milk Moustache," "Ahh—The Power of Cheese," "The Incredible, Edible Egg," "Beef—It's What's For Dinner," and "Pork—The Other White Meat." These advertising campaigns can have dramatic effects. It is estimated that, between October 1995 and September 1996, generic

Table 28.2. Checkoff Programs and Most Recent Budgets

Agricultural Commodity	Budget (millions $)
Dairy products	281.2
Fluid milk	107.8
Soybeans	89.5
Beef	79.8
Pork	65.4
Haas avocados	24.2
Eggs	21.0
Sorghum	12–16 (projected)
Potatoes	10.7
Peanuts	5.7
Mangoes	3.9
Honey	3.8
Mushrooms	2.6
Lamb	2.3
Blueberries	1.9
Watermelons	1.6
Popcorn	0.6

Source: Becker (2008).

advertising funded by checkoff programs increased sales of milk by 1.4 billion pounds (5.9 percent) and cheese by 62.7 million pounds (2.8 percent) (Blisard 1999).

Checkoff funds are also used to increase sales of agricultural commodities by developing and promoting specific menu items for fast food chains. For example, the Dairy Checkoff has partnered with Pizza Hut on the Insider Pizza, which uses one pound of cheese per pizza, and with Domino's to launch a line of American Legend pizzas that use 40 percent more cheese than a regular Domino's pizza. The Pork Checkoff subsidized McDonald's development and promotion of the McRib and Breaded Pork sandwiches.

The collection of checkoff funds from producers is a form of a tax, which raises costs for producers and decreases the quantity supplied. On net, however, checkoff programs increase sales of commodities (Blisard 1999). Each checkoff program is required to evaluate its effectiveness, and these self-studies conclude that the programs are cost-beneficial for producers (Williams and Capps 2006).

Banning the use of checkoff funds to market fast food could reduce childhood obesity. It is estimated that a complete ban on television fast food advertising to children in the United States would reduce the prevalence of overweight by 18 percent among children aged 3–11 years and by 14 percent among youths aged 12–18 years (Chou, Rashad, and Grossman 2008). We assume that the percentage of the total impact of fast food advertising on obesity that is due to checkoff programs is equal to the percentage of all restaurant advertising spending that the checkoff budgets of dairy, pork, and beef represent. Restaurants spent $5.64 billion on advertising in 2008 (TNS Media Intelligence 2009), and the collective budgets of the dairy, pork, and beef checkoffs total $426.4 million. Assuming that 7.6 percent of all fast food marketing is due to checkoff programs, a ban on use of checkoff funds to promote fast food is estimated to reduce the prevalence of childhood overweight by 1.4 percent among children aged 3–11 years and by 1.1 percent among youths aged 12–18 years.

ENSURING CONSISTENCY BETWEEN AGRICULTURAL POLICY AND PUBLIC HEALTH

Agricultural policy and public health policy are formulated largely independently of each other. The goal of agricultural policy is to increase the average, and decrease the variance, of farmer income. The goal of public health policy is to maximize population health. Agricultural policy is stimulating the production of additional food at lower retail prices at the same time that public health policy is seeking to convince many Americans to decrease their calorie intake in order to prevent and reduce obesity. An even greater contradiction takes place within the USDA, which simultaneously recommends a healthy diet low in fat and encourages greater consumption of high-fat commodities (Wilde 2004).

Many economists, such as Milton Friedman, D. Gale Johnson, and Bruce Gardner, have recommended ending farm subsidies for reasons of efficiency. The link to childhood obesity is yet one more reason to end farm subsidies. We estimate that ending such subsidies would lower youth BMI by 0.08 percent, or a fraction of a pound.

We estimate that banning the use of checkoff funds to develop and market fast food could reduce the prevalence of overweight by 1.4 percent among those aged 3–11 years and by 1.1 percent among those aged 12–18 years. Reducing or eliminating checkoff programs may be among the most politically feasible reforms; producers have repeatedly sued to end checkoff programs, arguing that mandatory contributions to fund advertising is a violation of their First Amendment rights (Becker 2008).

We estimate that ending USDA donations of energy-dense commodities to school lunch programs would reduce the risk of childhood overweight by 0.14 percentage points among children who consume school lunches. The National School Lunch Program could be redesigned to maximize child health and nutrition instead of the incomes of a subset of agricultural producers. The National Academies' Institute of Medicine (IOM) independently reviewed and provided guidance on the WIC food package based on the nutritional needs of the program population (IOM 2006); likewise, the IOM could be asked to review and provide guidance on the foods provided through the NSLP.

Modifying agricultural policy to make it more consistent with public health will be challenging; Tillotson (2004) notes that: "No other business sector has equaled the agricultural interests' ongoing bipartisan political power in the U.S. Congress" (Tillotson 2004, p. 628). Despite the challenge, it should be a high priority to ensure that agricultural policy ceases to promote childhood obesity and is instead harmonized with public health policy.

ACKNOWLEDGEMENTS

We gratefully acknowledge financial support from an anonymous donor through J. P. Morgan Private Bank Global Philanthropic Services.

REFERENCES

Alston, J. M. 2007. "Benefits and Beneficiaries from U.S. Farm Subsidies." *AEI Agricultural Policy Series: The 2007 Farm Bill and Beyond.* Washington DC: American Enterprise Institute. http://www.aei.org/docLib/20070515_alstonSubsidiesfinal.pdf.

American Medical Association. 2008. "Report 3 of the Council on Science and Public Health (A-08). The Health Effects of High Fructose Corn Syrup: Executive Summary." http://www.ama-assn.org/ama1/pub/upload/mm/443/csaph3a08-summary.pdf.

Becker, G. S. 2008. "Federal Farm Promotion ('Checkoff') Programs." Washington, DC: Congressional Research Service Report.

Beghin, J. C., and H. H. Jensen. 2008. "Farm Policies and Added Sugars in US Diets." *Food Policy* 33: 480–488.

Blisard, N. 1999. "Advertising and What We Eat: The Case of Dairy Products.: In *America's Eating Habits: Changes and Consequences*, ed. E. Frazao. Agriculture Information Bulletin No (AIB750), May.

Bray, G. A., S. J. Nielsen, and B. M. Popkin. 2004. "Consumption of High-Fructose Corn Syrup in Beverages May Play a Role in the Epidemic of Obesity." *American Journal of Clinical Nutrition* 79(4): 537–543.

Chou, S.-Y., M. Grossman, and H. Saffer. 2004. "An Economic Analysis of Adult Obesity: Results from the Behavioral Risk Factor Surveillance System." *Journal of Health Economics.* 23: 565–587.

Chou, S.-Y., I. Rashad, and M. Grossman. 2008. "Fast-food Restaurant Advertising on Television and Its Influence on Childhood Obesity." *Journal of Law and Economics.* 51:599–618.

Commodity Credit Corporation Budgetary Expenditures. Various years. http://www.fsa.usda.gov/FSA/webapp?area=aboutandsubject=landingandtopic=bap-bu-cc.

Fuglie, K., N. Ballenger, K. Day, C. Klotz, M. Ollinger, J. Reilly, U. Vasavada, and J. Yee. 1996. "Agricultural Research and Development: Public and Private Investments under Alternative Markets and Institutions." USDA Agricultural Economic Report 735.

Gardner, B. 2002. "U.S. Agricultural Policies since 1995, with a Focus on Market Effects in Grains and Oilseeds." Working Paper 02–17, Department of Agricultural and Resource Economics, University of Maryland.

Goodwin, B. K., and A. K. Mishra. 2006. "Are 'Decoupled' Farm Payments Really Decoupled? An Empirical Evaluation." *American Journal of Agricultural Economics*. 88(1): 73–89.

Huffman, W. E., and R. E. Evenson. 1992. "Contributions of Public and Private Science and Technology to US Agricultural Productivity." *American Journal of Agricultural Economics*. 74(3): 751–756.

Institute of Medicine. 2006. *WIC Food Packages: Time for a Change*. Washington DC: National Academies Press.

Nourse, E., J. Davis, and J. Black. 1937. *Three Years of the Agricultural Adjustment Administration*. Washington, DC: Brookings Institution Press.

Ogden, C. L., C. D. Fryar, M. D. Carroll, and K. M. Flegal. 2004. "Mean Body Weight, Height, and Body Mass Index, United States 1960–2002." *Advance Data from Vital and Health Statistics*. 347: 1–17.

Orden, D., R. Paarlberg, and T. Roe. 1999. *Policy Reform in American Agriculture*. Chicago: University of Chicago Press.

Paul, C. J. M. and J. M. MacDonald. 2008. "Tracing the Effects of Agricultural Commodity Prices and Food Costs." *American Journal of Agricultural Economics*. 85(3): 633–646.

Ralston, K., C. Newman, A. Clauson, J. Guthrie, and J. Buzby. 2008. "The National School Lunch Program: Background, Trends, and Issues." ERR-61, U.S. Department of Agriculture, Economic Research Service, July.

Schanzenbach, D. W. 2009. "Do School Lunches Contribute to Childhood Obesity?: *Journal of Human Resources*. 44(3): 684–709.

Tillotson, J. E. 2004. "America's Obesity: Conflicting Public Policies, Industrial Economic Development, and Unintended Human Consequences." *Annual Review of Nutrition* 24: 617–643.

TNS Media Intelligence. 2009. "TNS Media Intelligence Reports U.S. Advertising Expenditures Declined 4.1 Percent in 2008." http://www.tns-mi.com/news/05042009.htm.

USDA. 2009a. "Price Spreads from Farm to Consumer: At-Home Foods by Commodity Group." http://www.ers.usda.gov/Data/FarmToConsumer/pricespreads.htm.

USDA. 2009b. "Sugar and Sweeteners: Policy." http://www.ers.usda.gov/Briefing/Sugar/Policy.htm#TRQ. Accessed December 29, 2009.

USDA. 2010a. "National School Lunch Program Fact Sheet." http://www.fns.usda.gov/CND/Lunch/AboutLunch/NSLPFactSheet.pdf.

USDA. 2010b. "Schools/CN Commodity Programs." http://www.fns.usda.gov/FDD/programs/schcnp/schcnp_faqs.htm.

USDA. 2010c. "Child and Adult Care Food Program." http://www.fns.usda.gov/cnd/Care/.

USDA. 2010d. "Summer Food Service Program." http://www.fns.usda.gov/cnd/summer/.

Westcott, P. C., and J. M. Price. 2001. "Analysis of the U.S. Commodity Loan Program with Marketing Loan Provisions." USDA Agricultural Economic Report 801.

Wilde, P. 2004. "Message under Revision: USDA Speaks about Beef, Pork, Cheese, and Obesity." Choices: The Magazine of Food, Farm and Resource Issues" 19(3): 47–51.

Williams, G. W., and O. Capps. 2006. "Measuring the Effectiveness of Checkoff Programs." *Choices: The Magazine of Food, Farm and Resource Issues* 21(2): 73–78.

Wu, J. 2000. "Slippage Effects of the Conservation Reserve Program." *American Journal of Agricultural Economics*. 82(4): 979–992.

PART IV

THE CONSEQUENCES OF OBESITY

CHAPTER 29

OBESITY AND MEDICAL COSTS

ERIC FINKELSTEIN AND HAE KYUNG YANG

THE prevalence of obesity in the United States has risen sharply, more than doubling in the past 25 years. This has lead to an increase in the medical expenditures on treating the many diseases that obesity promotes. In this chapter, we review the literature on the relationship between obesity and medical spending, including a discussion of both per capita and aggregate annual and lifetime medical costs attributable to obesity, and external costs funded by public sector health plans. We conclude with a discussion of the implications of these findings for setting health policy.

ANNUAL PER CAPITA COSTS

Quesenberry and colleagues (1998) estimate that moderately obese (BMI of 30 to 34.9) and severely obese (BMI of 35 or greater) individuals have 17 percent and 24 percent more physician visits, respectively, than individuals who are normal weight. Thompson and colleagues (2001) report that, on average, obese individuals have 48 percent more inpatient days per year. They also report that obese individuals have 1.8 times more pharmacy dispenses, including 6 times more dispenses for diabetes medications and 3.4 times more for cardiovascular medications.

Increased utilization resulting from a greater disease burden is expected to result in greater annual medical spending for obese persons. Several studies have reported per capita annual costs attributable to obesity, presumably resulting from an increase in both frequency and intensity of service. Sturm (2002) reports that obese adults incur annual medical costs that are 36 percent higher than costs for normal-weight adults. He estimates obesity is associated with a 35 percent increase in inpatient and outpatient spending and a 77 percent increase in spending on prescription drugs. In two related studies (Finkelstein et al. 2003, 2009), Finkelstein and colleagues report similar results; they report annual per capita increases due to obesity ranging between 36.5 and 41.5 percent. In their most recent analysis, they also report that obesity increases inpatient expenditures by 45.5 percent, non-inpatient expenditures by 26.9 percent, and prescription drug expenditures by 80.4 percent.

Sturm (2002) and Finkelstein and colleagues' studies (2003, 2009) reveal the large impact that obesity has on annual per capita medical expenditures for each type of service, and especially for prescription drugs. Other analyses further reveal that the largest per capita cost increases occur for those with body mass indices (BMIs) above 35. In an analysis focusing on the return on investment for bariatric surgery, Finkelstein and Brown (2008) show that obese individuals who are eligible for weight loss surgery (BMI above 35 with comorbidities or BMI above 40 without comorbidities) incur annual medical costs that are $1,680 greater than obese individuals who are not eligible for surgery. This is troubling, given that the prevalence of severe obesity has increased even faster than the prevalence of obesity over the past several decades (Flegal et al. 2002).

AGGREGATE ANNUAL COSTS OF OBESITY

Several studies have combined the per capita estimates with obesity prevalence data to quantify the total annual medical bill resulting from obesity. However, a brief review of obesity prevalence data reveals that these studies are quickly outdated. Between 1980 and 2002, obesity prevalence doubled in adults (Finkelstein et al. 2005). By 2006, 65 percent of adults were either overweight or obese, an increase from 46 percent in 1976–1980 and 56 percent in 1988–1994 (Finkelstein and Brown 2006). In the past decade alone, the rise in obesity prevalence, combined with a small increase in per capita costs, increased the aggregate cost attributable to obesity from $78.5 billion in 1998 to $147 billion in 2008 (Finkelstein et al. 2009).

Thorpe and colleagues (2004) report that the increase in obesity prevalence accounts for 12 percent of the growth in health care spending between 1987 and 2002. They also report that prescription drug spending is the largest driver for the cost increase. Obesity-attributable prescription drug costs may now be as high as $59 billion per year (Finkelstein et al. 2009), whereas inpatient and non-inpatient expenditures each total roughly $45 billion. In aggregate, largely due to increasing prevalence of obesity and severe obesity, Finkelstein and his colleagues (2009) estimate that obesity is now responsible for 9.1 percent of annual medical spending. This estimate is significantly higher than prior estimates, which ranged between 5.5 and 7 percent (Wolf and Colditz 1998, Thomson et al. 2001, Finkelstein et al. 2003, 2004).

LIFETIME MEDICAL COSTS

High annual medical costs attributable to obesity have been used to justify obesity prevention efforts. However, obesity also reduces life expectancy. Ironically, it is possible that the lifetime costs of obesity could be negative (suggesting that, over the life course, obese individuals might actually cost less). If true, this could diminish the financial motivation to address obesity.

Several studies have quantified the lifetime costs of obesity, taking into account differences in annual medical expenditures and differences in survival between obese and normal weight individuals. In the first study to consider both of these issues, Allison and colleagues (1999) estimate that the percentage of lifetime costs attributed to obesity is 4.32 percent, compared with an annual cost estimate of 5.7 prevailing at that time. Thompson and colleagues (1999) report that the lifetime cost of five obesity-related diseases—hypertension, hypercholesterolemia, type 2 diabetes, coronary heart disease, and stroke—ranges from $19,600 to $29,600, depending on the level of BMI.

In the most recent and most comprehensive analysis of the lifetime costs of obesity, Finkelstein and colleagues (2009) estimate lifetime costs separately by race and BMI class. BMI class is categorized as obese I (BMI of 30 to 34.9) and obese II/III (BMI of 35 or higher). They report that for 20-year-old obese I adults, lifetime costs range from $5,340 for black women to $21,550 for white women. For 20-year-old adults in the obese II/III class, black men have the lowest lifetime cost estimates of $14,580, while white women have the highest lifetime cost estimates of $29,460. Across studies, the lifetime cost estimates are consistently positive, revealing that successful obesity-prevention efforts have the potential to be both health improving and cost saving over time.

EXTERNAL COST

Externalities are often used by governments to justify legislation, taxation, and other forms of government interventions. An externality is an effect of a purchase or use decision by one set of parties on others who did not have a choice and whose interests were not taken into account. Secondhand smoke is a classic example of an externality. Because smokers impose health risks on non-smokers, governments have enacted anti-smoking bans in public places, cigarette taxes, and other strategies designed to minimize the damage causes by secondhand smoke. There is no clear secondhand smoke equivalent when it comes to obesity. Generally speaking, the health risks are borne entirely by the obese individual. However, obesity does impose significant health costs on publicly funded health plans, which many have deemed a financial externality.

Because many obese individuals are covered by Medicare, estimates reveal that the government finances roughly half the total annual medical costs attributable to obesity. As of 2004, the average taxpayer spends approximately $175 per year to finance obesity-related medical expenditures in these programs (Finkelstein et al. 2003, 2004). Current estimates reveal that annual Medicare and Medicaid spending would be 8.5 percent and 11.8 percent lower, respectively, in the absence of obesity (Finkelstein et al. 2009).

Medicare spending remains high even when differential mortality estimates are considered. Lakdawalla and colleagues (2005) and Daviglus and colleagues (2004) quantify the lifetime costs of obesity from Medicare's perspective. Daviglus and colleagues (2004) use Chicago Heart Association Detection Project in Industry data and study the impact of BMI in young adulthood and middle age on future Medicare expenditures. They report that obese men and women have significantly greater cumulative Medicare charges. Lakdawalla and colleagues (2005) report that Medicare will spend 34 percent more on obese individuals than individuals of normal weight, even after considering mortality differences.

Finkelstein and colleagues (2009) estimate that the cost of obesity I from the perspective of a 65 year old (the age at which most individuals become eligible for Medicare) range from $4,660 for black women to $19,270 for black men. For obese II/III, the estimates range from $7,590 for black women to $25,300 for white women. Although the causes of these differences are not clear, what is clear is that from both an annual and lifetime perspective, and even after taking into account differential survival probabilities by BMI, race, and gender, external costs attributed to obesity are positive for all race and gender groups.

POLICY IMPLICATIONS

As noted above, the high medical costs of obesity, be they annual, lifetime, or external, have all been used to justify government interventions aimed at preventing obesity. However, as a general rule, high annual and lifetime costs do not necessarily suggest a role for government. If anything, high costs are more likely to be indicative of high demand, suggesting that individuals are spending money on products or services of high value, such as treatments for obesity-related medical conditions. High external costs may provide the best case for government interventions to prevent obesity, but these costs should not be confused with traditional externalities such as pollution or secondhand smoke.

The reason that taxpayers finance the costs of obesity in Medicaid and Medicare is because we, as taxpayers and voters, opted to design and maintain the programs as entitlements. This means that, under their current designs, all people who qualify for the programs are given equal access. Regardless of whether someone is obese, smokes, or engages in other risky behaviors, he will pay the same Medicare premiums as everyone else who is eligible for the program and receives the same benefits.

If the high public sector costs of obesity are truly the motivation for government intervention, then there is an easy solution: government could remove the entitlement aspect of these programs and charge higher premiums for obese individuals or for others whose expected costs are greater than the average (Finkelstein and Zuckerman 2008). There is a precedent for this type of experience-rated approach for setting premiums. For example, smokers pay a higher fee to receive life insurance, and both smokers and obese individuals often pay a higher fee to receive health insurance in the individual (non-employment-based) market. Based on the results reported above, increasing premiums for obese individuals by roughly 35 to 40 percent would, on average, offset the external costs of obesity. Under this approach, obese individuals would have the option of paying the higher premium and maintaining their current weight, or they could attempt to lose weight and pay lower premiums. If the premiums are set correctly, the decision about whether to lose weight will not impact the bottom line of the health plans. On average, they will be paying out what they collect.

Whereas experience rating may work in some settings, particularly the private sector, as pointed out by Finkelstein and Zuckerman (2008), there are several reasons why this approach is problematic for publicly funded health plans. One reason is that it goes against the very nature of these programs as entitlements. What happens when an obese individual cannot afford the higher premium? For example, Medicaid is a safety net program and free for those who qualify. Who would cover the costs for those who cannot afford the premium? Would these individuals be refused coverage? We can drop the entitlement aspect of Medicare and Medicaid and charge experience-rated premiums, or we can keep these programs accessible for all who qualify. However, if we do the latter, then it is inappropriate to use the high costs of these programs as justification for government interventions aimed at reducing rates of obesity. For these costs are not truly external. After all, it is government intervention (i.e., creation of Medicare and Medicaid) that has made these high costs a "problem" in the first place.

Without changing the entitlement nature of these programs or cutting benefits, policy makers remain interested in reducing the resources spent treating obesity-related diseases. It is possible that some strategies could be a win-win for government and enrollees. For example, some Medicaid programs have begun offering coverage for Weight Watchers (Trapp 2007). There is not yet any evidence that this coverage will save money, but if it encourages weight loss and is cost effective, why not cover it? Another example might be for government to mandate or subsidize coverage for certain obesity treatments, wellness programs, or other interventions. It is possible that these interventions might save money in the long run, but due to concerns about the short time horizon of employers, few firms have the incentives to provide them on their own. If the government required every firm to provide the services or subsidized their costs, return on investment would be less of a concern, and this too could be a win-win situation, but only if the interventions are truly cost saving over time.

It is worth noting, however, that if the high total or external costs of obesity are the underlying justification for publicly funded obesity interventions, then, regardless of how effective an intervention is at reducing weight, unless it is cost-saving, it ultimately raises costs even more. Moreover, with the possible exception of bariatric surgery, few obesity interventions have proven to save money. However, saving money is not the only factor that policy makers consider when determining appropriate obesity prevention and treatment efforts.

REFERENCES

Allison, David B., Raffaella Zannolli, and K. M. Venkat Narayan. 1999. "The Direct Health Care Costs of Obesity in the United States." *American Journal of Public Health* 89: 1194–1199.

Daniel B. Garside, Renwei Wang, Alan R. Dyer, Philip Greenland, and Jeremiah Stamler. 2004. "Relation of Body Mass Index in Young Adulthood and Middle Age to Medicare Expenditures in Older Age." *Journal of the American Medical Association* 292: 2743–2749.

Finkelstein, Eric A., and Derek S. Brown. 2006. "Why Does the Private Sector Underinvest in Obesity Prevention and Treatment?" *North Carolina Medical Journal* 67(4): 310–312.

Finkelstein, Eric A., and Derek S. Brown. 2008. "Examining the Economics of Bariatric Surgery." *The American Journal of Managed Care* 14(9): 561–562.

Finkelstein, Eric A., Ian C. Fiebelkorn, and Guijing Wang. 2003. "National Medical Spending Attributable to Overweight and Obesity: How Much, and Who's Paying?" *Health Affairs* W3: 219–226.

Finkelstein, Eric A., Ian C. Fiebelkorn, and Guijing Wang. 2004. "State-level Estimates of Annual Medical Expenditures Attributable to Obesity." *Obesity Research* 12: 18–24.

Finkelstein, Eric A., Christopher J. Ruhm, and Katherine M. Kosa. 2005. "Economics Causes and Consequences of Obesity." *Annual Review of Public Health* 26: 239–257.

Finkelstein, Eric A., Justin G. Trogdon, Joel W. Cohen, and William Dietz. 2009. "Annual Medical Spending Attributable to Obesity: Payer And Service-Specific Estimates." *Health Affairs* 28(5): w822–w831.

Finkelstein, Eric A., and Laurie Zuckerman. 2008. *The Fattening of America*. Hoboken, NJ: John Wiley & Sons.

Flegal, Katherine M., Margaret D. Carroll, Cynthia, L. Ogden, and Clifford L. Johnson. 2002. "Prevalence and Trends in Obesity Among US Adults, 1999–2000." *Journal of the American Medical Association* 288(14): 1723–1727.

Lakdawalla, Darius N., Dana P. Goldman, and Baoping Shang. 2005. "The Health and Cost Consequences of Obesity among the Future Elderly." *Health Affairs* 24(Supp. 2): W5R30–W5R41.

Qusenberry, Charles P., Bette Caan, and Alice Jacobson. 1998. "Obesity, Health Services Use, and Health Care Costs among Members of a Health Maintenance Organization." *Archives of Internal Medicine* 158(5): 466–472.

Sturm, Roland. 2002. "The Effects of Obesity, Smoking, and Drinking on Medical Problems and Costs." *Health Affairs* 21(2): 242–253.

Thompson, David, Jonathan B. Brown, Gregory A. Nichols, Patricia J. Elmer, and Gerry Oster. 2001. "Body Mass Index and Future Healthcare Costs: A Retrospective Cohort Study." *Obesity Research* 9(3): 210–218.

Thompson, David, John Edelsberg, Graham A. Colditz, Amy P. Bird, and Gerry Oster. 1999. "Lifetime Health and Economic Consequences of Obesity." *Archives of Internal Medicine* 159: 2177–2183.

Thorpe, Kenneth E., Curtis S. Florence, David H. Howard, and Peter Joski. 2004. "The Impact of Obesity on Rising Medical Spending." *Health Affairs* W4: 480–486.

Trapp, Doug. 2007. "HMO offers Weight Watchers to West Virginia Medicaid Enrollees." *American Medical News* (February 19), http://www.ama-assn.org/amednews/2007/02/19/gvsd0219.htm. Accessed January 4, 2010.

Wolf, Anne M., and Graham A. Colditz. 1998. "Current Estimates of the Economic Cost of Obesity in the United States." *Obesity Research* 6(2): 97–106.

CHAPTER 30

OBESITY AND MORTALITY

NEIL K. MEHTA AND VIRGINIA W. CHANG

OBESITY is often considered a major cause of premature mortality in the United States, and its contribution is thought to rival that of cigarette smoking (Marshall 2004; U.S. Department of Health and Human Services 2001). Nevertheless, the magnitude of obesity's effect on mortality and its role relative to other causes has been a source considerable controversy. While evidence supporting the life-shortening effect of smoking is strong, the evidence for obesity is inconsistent and, in certain instances, contradictory. Debates surrounding the effect of obesity on mortality can be divided into uncertainty over estimates at two different levels of focus: the individual level and the population level. At the individual level, there are varied estimates of the relative risk of dying for overweight (25.0–29.9 kg/m^2) and obese ($\geq$ 30.0 kg/m^2) persons relative to normal weight persons (18.5–24.9 kg/m^2). At the population level, debates center on the number of annual deaths in the United States that should be attributed to a body mass index (BMI) $\geq$ 25.0 (Flegal et al. 2005; Mehta and Chang 2009; Mokdad et al. 2004) and on the extent to which rising BMI will affect U.S. life expectancy (Olshansky et al. 2005; Preston 2005; Stewart, Cutler, and Rosen 2009).

We begin at the population level and review recent studies on the number of excess deaths in the United States attributable to a BMI $\geq$ 25.0, because findings from these studies have been most central to ongoing controversies. The individual- and population-level perspectives, however, are closely tied because individual-level relative risks are a key input in the calculation of obesity's effect at the population level (e.g., the number of excess deaths attributable to obesity).

Indeed, we believe that divergent estimates at the population level are, in large part, explained by the use of divergent estimates at the individual level. As for variation in estimates at the individual level, we argue that it results from a variety of methodological differences across studies. Therefore, we next address selected methodological topics pertinent to estimating the relative risk of death for a high BMI (BMI ≥ 25.0) at the individual level. These topics include the age range of the study population and/or effect modification by age, the confounding role of smoking and preexisting illness, the confounding role of socioeconomic status (SES), and the period of the mortality follow-up. Most previous research uses BMI (weight [kg]/ height[m]^2) as a measure of weight status, so we focus on findings based on BMI. Nonetheless, alternative measures of weight status are receiving increasing attention, and we conclude with a discussion on the relevancy of these measures to current debates.

DIVERGENT ESTIMATES OF EXCESS DEATHS ATTRIBUTABLE TO OVERWEIGHT AND OBESITY

Estimates of excess deaths center on the concept of "attributable mortality," which refers to the fraction of deaths in a population that are avoided if a risk factor is eliminated from the population. Prior work on excess deaths associated with a high BMI in the United States have taken the same general approach. Studies first estimate relative risks for the overweight and obese using individual-level data ("derivation samples"). The reference category usually falls within the currently defined normal BMI range (18.5–24.9). The second step computes attributable mortality at the population level for a target year. Relative risks from the derivation sample(s) are combined with the prevalence of high BMI in the target year using one of a number of available approaches (Rockhill, Newman, and Weinberg 1998). This step produces the "attributable fraction" for high BMI. Excess deaths are then calculated by multiplying the attributable fraction with the number of total deaths in the target year.

In 2005, Flegal et al. (2005) published an article in the *Journal of the American Medical Association* that prompted a well-publicized and contentious debate over mortality attributable to high BMI. Flegal et al. (2005) estimated that a BMI ≥ 25.0 was responsible for approximately 25,800 adult U.S. deaths in 2000. This figure reflected both 112,000 excess deaths from obesity (BMI ≥ 30) and 86,000 fewer deaths from being overweight (25.0–29.9) (e.g., being overweight was protective). The estimates by Flegal et al. (2005), however, were considerably smaller than a previous and widely accepted figure by Mokdad et al. (2004, 2005), who estimated that approximately 350,000 U.S. deaths were attributable to a BMI ≥ 25.0 in 2000 (the authors did not present separate estimates for the overweight or obese). The Mokdad et al. (2004) estimate of 350,000 excess deaths placed high BMI second only to tobacco use (435,000 excess deaths) as a cause of avoidable mortality in 2000, while the Flegal et al. (2005) estimate suggested a considerably smaller role for high BMI.

The divergent estimates of Flegal et al. (2005) and Mokdad et al. (2004) were likely due to methodological differences between the studies. A first important difference is the treatment of covariates. Flegal et al. (2005) stratified the analysis by age (25–59, 60–69, 70+), among other factors. This approach allowed relative risks to vary within the individual subgroups, allowing for both confounding and effect modification. In contrast, the Mokdad et al. (2004) estimates were based on a method that only accounted for confounding, but not effect modification,[1] which could have introduced bias (Couzin 2005; Flegal, Graubard, and Williamson 2004). A second methodological difference was the period covered by the derivation samples. Flegal et al. (2005) estimated relative risks using nationally representative data from three National Health and Nutrition Examination Surveys (NHANES I–III), which together had a mortality follow-up covering 1971–2000. In contrast, Mokdad et al. (2004) combined six epidemiological cohorts with a mortality follow-up covering 1948–1992.[2] As we discuss below, relative risks for obesity may be declining over time. Therefore, to the extent that the relative risks are decreasing, estimates of attributable mortality based on earlier data will be higher.

More recently, Mehta and Chang (2009) investigated attributable mortality due to a high BMI using the Health and Retirement Study (HRS). One advantage of the HRS is that it covers a recent period rather than relying on more historical data to estimate relative risks. We estimated relative risks using data that spanned 1992–2004 and estimated attributable mortality in 1999, the average year of death among respondents in the study. Given that the treatment of age has contributed to the controversy, the HRS is also advantageous because it is designed for a birth cohort analysis along narrow age ranges (in contrast to the data used by Flegal et al. [2005] and Mokdad et al. [2004]). In our study, we investigated the 1931–1941 U.S. birth cohort, who were ages 50–61 when first interviewed in 1992.

The results from our study are shown in table 30.1. In addition to presenting mortality attributable to a BMI ≥ 25.0, table 30.1 also shows smoking-attributable mortality to compare the two risk factors. Attributable mortality is given as a percentage, reflecting the percent change in observed deaths that would be expected if the risk factor were eliminated. Negative percentages indicate underlying relative risks less than 1.0 and imply that deaths would increase if the risk category were eliminated. Table 30.1 reveals that class II/III obesity (BMI ≥ 35.0) was the only BMI category associated with significant and positive attributable mortality. Class II/III

---

1   Mokdad et al. (2004) relied on relative risks estimated from an earlier study by Allison et al. (1999). Relative risks in Allison et al. (1999) were derived by pooling ages 18 and older and treated age and other factors as confounders.

2   The derivation studies were the Alameda County Health Study, Framingham Heart Study, Tecumseh Community Health Study, Cancer Prevention Study I, Nurses' Health Study, and the NHANES I Epidemiological Followup Study.

Table 30.1. **Attributable Mortality (%) and 1999 Excess Deaths in U.S. Target Population for BMI Categories and Smoking, 1931-1941 HRS cohort; 1992–2004**

	Females (Total Deaths, 1999 = 140,808)		Males (Total Deaths, 1999 = 200,546)	
	Attributable Mortality, percent	No. Excess Deaths, 1999	Attributable Mortality, percent	No. Excess Deaths, 1999
Reference: Normal Weight (BMI of 18.5–24.9)				
Overweight (BMI 25.0–29.9)	−5.6 (−13.8, 2.5)	−7,933 (−19,392, 3,527)	−5.0 (−13.7, 3.7)	−10,023 (−27,486, 7,441)
Obese I (BMI 30.0–34.9)	−3.1 (−7.6, 1.5)	−4,308 (−10,739, 2,123)	0.1 (−3.7, 4.0)	224 (−7,475, 7,923)
Obese II/III (BMI 35.0+)	3.8* (0.1, 7.6)	5,416* (180, 10,652)	2.5* (0.5, 4.6)	5,034* (939, 9,128)
Reference: Never Smoker				
Former Smoker	13.2*** (7.1, 19.3)	18,583*** (9,990, 27,175)	18.1*** (11.2, 25.0)	36,286*** (22,518, 50,053)
Current Light Smoker	6.7*** (3.2, 10.3)	9,495** (4,459, 14,531)	7.8*** (5.1, 10.5)	15,582*** (10,179, 20,984)
Current Moderate Smoker	11.5*** (7.2, 15.8)	16,195*** (10,144, 22,246)	18.2*** (14.1, 22.3)	36,586*** (28,369, 44,802)
Current Heavy Smoker	3.9*** (1.6, 6.1)	5,467*** (2,301, 8,634)	5.8*** (3.4, 8.1)	11,571*** (6,824, 16,317)
Cigarette Smoking (total)	35.3*** (26.7, 43.9)	49,740*** (37,664, 61,817)	49.9*** (39.2, 60.6)	100,024*** (78,576, 121,471)

Note: Table adapted from Mehta and Chang (2009). Current smoking is measured by number of packs smoked per day: light (<1 pack), moderate (1 to <2 packs), and heavy (≥2 packs). Attributable mortality are based on relative risks, which are estimated from a model that includes categorical BMI, smoking status, education, income, wealth, race/ethnicity, marital status, and physical activity. Number of excess deaths are calculated in 1999, the mean year of death. The 1931–1941 birth cohort was ages 57–68 in 1999. 95 percent confidence intervals shown in parenthesis. Data reflect sampling weights.
$*p < .05; **p < .01; *** p < .001$

obesity was responsible for 3.8 percent (p < .05) and 2.5 percent (p < .01) of deaths among females and males, respectively (ref: BMI 18.5–24.9). This translated into 5,416 (of 140,808) and 5,034 (of 200,546) excess deaths among females and males, respectively. Overweight (25.0–29.9) and class I obesity (30.0–34.9), in contrast, were not associated with significant attributable mortality, and the negative estimates suggested a protective association (i.e., relative risks below 1.0). Smoking-attributable mortality was much higher than mortality due to a BMI ≥ 25.0. For example, approximately 35 percent (females) and 50 percent (males) of deaths would be avoided if smoking were eliminated (p < .001 for both values). This translated into approximately 50,000 and 100,000 excess deaths for females and males, respectively.

Our study analyzed middle-aged adults, but the findings are consistent with Flegal et al. (2005), who found that approximately 4 percent (both sexes) of deaths in 2000 would be avoided if class II/III obesity were eliminated (ages 25+). Flegal et al. (2005) also reported that the overweight (25.0–29.9) and class I obese (30.0–34.9) categories were not associated with significant and positive attributable mortality, which is consistent with our findings. Both studies thus imply a considerably smaller association of high BMI with population-level mortality compared to the earlier estimates by Mokdad et al. (2004), which suggested that a BMI ≥ 25.0 was responsible for approximately 15 percent of deaths in 2000.

As indicated, differences in the estimates of attributable mortality potentially arise from dissimilar methodologies (e.g., treatment of covariates, period covered by the derivation samples). Moreover, the controversy over the number of excess deaths raises important questions pertaining to the best method of estimating relative risks, regardless of whether studies are concerned with measuring population-level effects. In the next section, we provide a more in-depth discussion of four methodological issues that contribute to variations in prior estimates of relative risks.

SOURCES OF VARIATION IN RELATIVE RISKS

Effect Modification by Age

Age is considered an important modifier of the association between BMI and mortality. Prior studies based on large epidemiological cohorts have provided evidence that relative risks for the overweight and obese decline over the adult life course. In the Cancer Prevention Study II, a study of nearly one million adults ages 30+, Calle et al. (1999) found decreasing relative risks for the overweight and obese across three age-strata (30–64, 65–74, 75+) for both sexes. For example, a relative risk of 1.61 (p < .05) was reported for men with a BMI of 31.0–31.9 (ref: BMI 23.5–24.9). Among men ages 75+, the relative risk declined to 1.16 (p < .05). These findings were based on data covering 1982–1996 and were limited to never smokers and those without a history of disease (e.g., cancer, heart disease, stroke, respiratory disease). Similarly, in the earlier Cancer Prevention Study I (1960–1972), BMI categories above 25.0 were generally associated with relative risks that were significant and greater than 1.0 for adults younger than 75 years, but not for adults aged 75 and older (ref: BMI 19.0–21.9) (Stevens et al. 1998).

There have been numerous studies focusing on the association between BMI on mortality among older adults. Most of these findings were based on samples of individuals ages 65 and over. In a meta-analysis of 26 studies of adults ages 65 and over, Janssen and Mark (2007) found no excess risk of dying in the overweight category (relative to normal BMI). Obesity, however, was found to be associated with a relative risk of 1.10 (p < .05). Other studies on the elderly indicate that the overweight and class I obese categories were protective against mortality. For example, in a study using the nationally representative National Long Term Care Survey, Kulminski et al. (2008) reported that the relative risks for the overweight and class I obesity were 0.82 (p < .05) and 0.78 (p < .05), respectively (ref: BMI 22.0–24.9). These results were based on a sample of approximately 4,800 respondents followed during 1994–2003 and were adjusted for race, smoking, alcohol consumption, heart disease, and cancer. Similar estimates of relative risks for the overweight and class I obese groups were reported in an elderly sample of approximately 14,000 individuals followed for seven years beginning in 1982 from the Established Populations for Epidemiological Studies of the Elderly (Al Snih et al. 2007). This study was restricted to those who were not disabled and estimates were adjusted for smoking, education, race/ethnicity, health conditions, and other covariates.

Despite the large number of studies on the elderly, it is difficult to establish causal links between BMI and mortality in this population because of the high prevalence of co-morbidities (Manson et al. 2007). Additionally, changes in height and body mass composition complicate the measurement of weight status for this group (Gallagher et al. 1996; Janssen and Mark 2007), and we discuss these issues in more detail below. The influence of co-morbidities and compositional changes are presumably less problematic for studies measuring BMI when respondents are younger. Thus, studies that measure BMI when respondents are middle age and model mortality into late life can give a better sense of the BMI and mortality relationship at the older ages.

We took this approach with the HRS cohort described above (Mehta and Chang 2009). BMI was measured when respondents were between the ages of 50–61. We modeled mortality through age 73. Table 30.2 presents hazard ratios (same as relative risks) by sex (N = 9,278). The hazard ratios were adjusted for sociodemographic characteristics, SES, smoking, and physical activity. The overall pattern shown in table 30.1 indicated that being obese class II/III is significantly associated with excess mortality (ref: normal BMI 18.5–24.9). The hazard ratios for obese class II/III were 1.40 (women) and 1.62 (men). Importantly, the models show that the risks of mortality in the overweight and class I obese categories were not statistically different from that for the normal BMI category for either sex. Moreover, the point estimates indicate a moderately protective association. For women, the hazard ratios were 0.84 (overweight) and 0.83 (class I obese). For men, the hazard ratios were 0.90 (overweight) and 1.01 (class I obese). Overall, these findings show that the association between BMI and mortality was relatively flat across the normal, overweight, and class I obese categories, which collectively comprised more than 90 percent of the sample.

As indicated above, treatment of age has contributed to prior divergent estimates of excess deaths. The current evidence indicates that relative risks are higher for younger adults than older adults. Thus, age should be treated as an

Table 30.2. **Hazard Ratios Predicting Mortality from Any Cause by Sex in the 1931–1941 HRS Birth Cohort; 1992–2004**

BMI Categories	Females (N = 5,057)		Males (N = 4,221)	
	Distribution (%)	Hazard Ratio	Distribution (%)	Hazard Ratio
Normal (18.5–24.9)	40.0	1.00	29.4	1.00
Overweight (25.0–29.9)	33.8	0.84	49.3	0.90
		(0.66, 1.07)		(0.74, 1.08)
Obese I (30.0–34.9)	16.2	0.83	16.3	1.01
		(0.62, 1.10)		(0.79, 1.28)
Obese II/III (≥ 35.0)	8.2	1.40 *	4.5	1.62 **
		(1.02, 1.91)		(1.15, 2.27)

Note: Table adapted from Mehta and Chang (2009). Hazard ratios are based on a Cox proportional hazard regression, which models age at death. Respondents were ages 50–61 in 1992. Hazard ratios are adjusted for education, income, wealth, race/ethnicity, marital status, smoking status, and physical activity. 559 women and 742 men died during follow-up. 95 percent confidence intervals are shown in parenthesis. Data reflect HRS sample weights.
*$p < .05$; **$p < .01$; *** $p < .001$.

effect modifier. In addition, studies of middle- and older-age samples indicate that being overweight and, in certain instances, being class I obese, is associated with mortality risks that are the same or lower than that associated with being normal BMI. Given that more than half of American adults are overweight or class I obese (Ruhm 2007), accurate estimates of the association between BMI and mortality among the overweight and obese class I will have important implications for the population-level mortality effect of high BMI.

Smoking and Disease Confounding

Some have argued that previous studies underestimate the relative risks of high BMI because they include both smokers and individuals with preexisting diseases, even if adjustments are made for these characteristics (Hu 2008; Manson et al. 2007). Smokers have lower weight status than non-smokers and experience a higher mortality. Failure to fully account for this confounding, then, would spuriously reduce relative risks associated with high BMI. According to Hu (2008), adjustment for current smoking status is generally inadequate because it only partially captures variations in smoking intensity, smoking duration, and quitting patterns. In addition, preexisting diseases increase the risk of death and are also associated with weight loss (especially smoking-related illnesses such as cancer and respiratory disease). When individuals with preexisting illnesses are present, disease-induced weight loss would also depress the relative risk of the overweight and obese because of the higher proportion of sick individuals in lower weight classifications.

These critiques are supported by findings from large epidemiological cohort studies, which show that exclusion of smokers and those with preexisting conditions results in higher relative risks of being overweight or obese than would otherwise be the case if these subgroups are included in the analysis. In the National Institutes of Health-AARP Cohort of individuals ages 50–71 at baseline and followed during 1995–2005, Adams et al. (2006) showed that for men a BMI of 28.0–29.9 was associated with a relative risk of 1.0 when both smokers and non-smokers were combined and an adjustment for smoking status is included (ref: BMI 23.5–24.9). Restricting the sample to never smokers, however, resulted in a 20 percent increase in the relative risk for the same BMI group (RR = 1.20; p < .05). In the Cancer Prevention Study II, Calle et al. (1999) reported a stronger association of higher BMI with mortality among non-smokers compared to smokers, and those without a preexisting illness (including heart disease, cancer, and respiratory illnesses) compared to those with a preexisting illness.

Nonetheless, there is still conflicting evidence as to whether samples that include smokers and those with preexisting diseases produce significantly lower relative risks of high BMI compared to samples of healthy never smokers. For example, findings from the aforementioned studies by Flegal et al. (2005) and Mehta and Chang (2009), both of which adjusted for smoking status, were robust to the elimination of smokers and/or those with preexisting diseases from the sample. In a follow-up to their influential paper using NHANES I–III, Flegal et al. (2007) found that simultaneous exclusions of ever smokers and those with preexisting disease (cancer, cardiovascular disease) did not lead to higher estimates of attributable mortality for the overweight and only marginally increased estimates for obesity. Similarly, Mehta and Chang (2009) showed that the overweight and class I obese categories remain unassociated with excess mortality even after excluding those with a major illness (heart disease, stroke, respiratory illness, cancer) or ever smokers (ref: BMI 18.5–24.9).

Whether exclusionary approaches produce less biased estimates remains debated (Flegal et al. 2011). One limitation of exclusionary approaches is that a large fraction of deaths is eliminated. In the Cancer Prevention Study II, for example, a restriction to healthy non-smokers eliminates almost 90 percent of deaths. This loss may not be a desirable property for studies that are interested in producing nationally representative estimates for the U.S. population, which includes smokers and those with preexisting illnesses. Further research investigating the extent to which confounding by preexisting diseases and smoking occurs would be beneficial to current controversies.

Confounding by SES

Confounding by SES is less often considered in prior estimates of relative risks. Under-controlling for SES can lead to an overestimation of relative risks for high BMI, particularly among women. Among women, weight status is inversely associated with both education (Sanchez-Vaznaugh et al. 2009) and income (Chang and

Lauderdale 2005). Given the well-established relationship between SES and mortality, failure to adequately adjust for SES would lead to an over assignment of excess risk to the obese relative to the nonobese. Among men, the association between SES and BMI is more variable and appears to differ by race/ethnicity. Black and Mexican men display a positive BMI gradient across income in the NHANES (Chang and Lauderdale 2005), and black men show a positive gradient across both education and income in the Atherosclerosis Risk in Community Study (Mujahid et al. 2005). In contrast, weak associations between income and BMI have been shown among white and Asian men (Sanchez-Vaznaugh et al. 2009).

The extent to which incomplete adjustment for SES leads to biased estimates is difficult to ascertain because most papers do not present findings with and without adjustments for SES. In the HRS cohort, we showed that the inclusion of three SES dimensions (education, income, and wealth) reduces the excess risk for obese class II/III among women from 68 percent to 32 percent, a reduction of more than one-half (ref: BMI 18.5–24.9). Negligible changes were observed for the overweight and obese class I categories, suggesting that SES confounding is most relevant to the heaviest obese categories. While nationally representative samples possess substantial SES variation, analyses restricted to occupational cohorts could also be subject to residual SES confounding. In a response to a study by Hu et al. (2004) on BMI and mortality using the Nurses' Health Study (which did not adjust for SES), Lauderdale (2005) showed that the variation in family income among U.S. nurses is similar in magnitude to that of the U.S. population. Therefore, studies based on occupational cohorts should also address confounding by SES.

The most widely used SES measure in studies on obesity and mortality is education. However, attention to confounding by multiple SES dimensions is necessary. Income, for example, is shown to be associated with health and mortality end points net of education (e.g., Bond Huie et al. 2003; Braveman et al. 2005). Longitudinal research also suggests that income is a stronger predictor of disease progression and mortality after the onset of disability compared to education (Herd, Goesling, and House 2007). This finding has particular relevance for the obese, who are more likely to be disabled compared to the non-obese (Alley and Chang 2007). Hence, future research would benefit from a more careful consideration of confounding by SES across multiple dimensions.

Secular Trends

Secular changes in relative risks could also be a source of variation in prior studies, although current evidence is conflicting. Flegal et al. (2005) suggest that a decline in the magnitude of the obesity and mortality association has occurred since the 1970s. Specifically, the authors found that relative risks associated with obesity were higher in the earlier NHANES I (1971–1975) compared to the later NHANES II (1976–1980) and NAHNES III (1988–1994). In NHANES I, the relative risk for obese class I was approximately 1.5, but this declined to around 1.0 in NHANES III (ages 60–69). No trend was observed for the overweight category. In contrast, Calle,

Teras, and Thun (2005) reported no decline in the relative risk of being overweight or obese in the CPS II across three periods (1982–1991, 1992–1997, 1998–2002).

Despite the lack of conclusive evidence, other health-related trends lend support to the hypothesis that relative risks for the overweight or obese have experienced secular declines. Mortality from cardiovascular disease, a cause-of-death considered to be most closely linked with high BMI, was reduced by one-half between 1980 and 2000 (Ford et al. 2007), a period when levels of adult obesity increased. In addition, Gregg et al. (2005) found that cardiovascular risk factors have improved for overweight and obese persons since the early 1970s. Specifically, they found reductions in the prevalence of high blood pressure, total cholesterol, and smoking among those with a BMI ≥ 25.0. Absolute declines in these risk factors have occurred at all BMI levels, but the reductions in high cholesterol and high blood pressure were more pronounced among the overweight and obese (significant only for high cholesterol).

Although some health-related risk factors among the overweight and mildly obese could be declining, there is evidence of a parallel increase in disability among the obese (Alley and Chang 2007). Moreover, there is a disproportionate rise in diabetes in the obese relative to leaner individuals (Gregg et al. 2005). Given the changing health profile of the overweight and obese over time, estimates of the relative risks of mortality for the overweight and obese may be sensitive to the timing of mortality follow-up across studies, and studies examining different periods may produce different estimates. Hence, estimates based on studies using older data may not accurately reflect current or future conditions. To date, the direction and magnitude of secular trends in relative risks of the overweight and obese remains unclear.

ALTERNATIVE MEASURES OF WEIGHT STATUS

Due to the availability of height and weight measurements in survey data, most studies on obesity and mortality have relied on BMI as a measure of weight status. The notion that BMI is a proxy for underlying adiposity has been critiqued along a number of lines, most notably that BMI fails to distinguish between fat and lean body mass and that it does not account for fat distribution (Burkhauser and Cawley 2008; Koster et al. 2008; Strickler 2005). Among the elderly, BMI may be a particularly problematic measure because of the loss of lean body mass (termed "sarcopenic obesity"; Lewis et al. 2009). In addition, alternative anthropometric measures such as waist circumference and the waist-to-hip ratio are believed to be more accurate measures of visceral adiposity than BMI (Kalmijn et al. 1999; Price et al. 2006; Seidell and Visscher 2000; Snijder et al. 2006; Visscher et al. 2001). Nonetheless, the correlation between BMI and waist circumference is generally high and greater than 0.80 (e.g., Flegal and Graubard 2009; Dolan et al. 2007).

Recent studies on mortality have compared the predictive values of multiple measures of weight status, and the findings have been mixed. Manson et al. (1995) found that BMI was more strongly related to mortality compared to the waist-to-hip ratio over a 16-year period among women aged 30–55 (though the waist to hip ratio was a strong predictor of heart disease mortality). In a large study in Europe, Pischon et al. (2008) found that waist circumference and waist-to-hip ratio were both positively associated with mortality net of BMI in both sexes (ages 25–70 followed over an average of 10 years). High BMI was still significantly associated with higher mortality in models that included waist circumference or waist-to-hip ratio. In the NIH-AARP Study described above, Koster et al. (2008) also found that waist circumference is predictive of mortality net of BMI. For example, those in the fifth quintile of waist circumference had more than a 20 percent (p < .05) higher risk of dying compared to those in the second quintile net of BMI, education, smoking, and other covariates (ages 51–72). When the authors examined whether waist circumference was associated with mortality *within* BMI classifications, they found positive associations between waist circumference and mortality within the normal, overweight, and class I obese categories (waist circumference within the class II/II obese category was not examined). These findings suggest the need for further research into the comparative effects of multiple measures of weight status.

Conclusion

In sum, there are ongoing controversies surrounding the association of high BMI with mortality at both the individual and population levels. With respect to population-level attributable mortality, recent studies suggest that a high BMI is a small source of excess deaths in the United States, although this topic continues to be controversial. Since population-level indicators such as attributable mortality are based on individual-level relative risks, we devoted considerable attention to methodological issues that contribute to variations in estimates of relative risks in prior studies. Age appears to be an important modifier of the BMI and mortality association, and high BMI appears to have a more deleterious effect at younger ages. Moreover, studies based on the elderly may be biased due to the presence of a high level of co-morbidities and body compositional changes. In contrast, studies that measure BMI in middle age and model subsequent mortality may give a better sense of the effect of BMI on mortality for those over the age of 50. Prior research has also varied substantially with respect to the treatment of confounders. While the confounding roles of smoking and preexisting diseases have received much attention, future studies should more carefully address confounding by multiple dimensions of SES. Finally, one study suggests that the relative risks for the overweight and obese have declined since the 1970s, although this has not been confirmed in other studies. Moreover, there have been parallel changes in the health profile of the overweight and obese populations, some favorable and some unfavorable. The extent to which these trends have affected the BMI and mortality association is not known.

REFERENCES

Adams, K. F., A. Schatzkin, T. B. Harris, V. Kipnis, T. Mouw, R. Ballard-Barbash, A. Hollenbeck, and M. F. Leitzmann. 2006. "Overweight, Obesity, and Mortality in a Large Prospective Cohort of Persons 50 to 71 Years Old." *New England Journal of Medicine* 355(8): 763–778.

Al Snih, S., K. J. Ottenbacher, K. S. Markides, Y. F. Kuo, K. Eschbach, and J. S. Goodwin. 2007. "The Effect of Obesity on Disability vs. Mortality in Older Americans." *Archives of Internal Medicine* 167: 774–780.

Alley, D. E., and V. W. Chang. 2007. "The Changing Relationship of Obesity and Disability, 1988–2004." *Journal of the American Medical Association* 298(17): 2020–2027.

Allison, D. B., K. R. Fontaine, J. E. Manson, J. Stevens, and T. B. VanItallie. 1999. "Annual Deaths Attributable to Obesity in the United States." *Journal of the American Medical Association* 282(16): 1530–1538.

Bond Huie, S. A., P. M. Krueger, R. G. Rogers, and R. A. Hummer. 2003. "Wealth, Race, and Mortality." *Social Science Quarterly* 84(3): 667–684.

Braveman, P. A., C. Cubbin, S. Egerter, S. Chideya, K. S. Marchi, M. Metzler, and S. Posner. 2005. "Socioeconomic Status in Health Research: One Size Does Not Fit All." *Journal of the American Medical Association* 294(22): 2879–2888.

Burkhauser, R.V., and J. Cawley. 2008. "Beyond BMI: The Value of More Accurate Measures of Fatness and Obesity in Social Science Research." *Journal of Health Economics* 27 (2): 519–529.

Calle, E. E., L. R. Teras, and M .J. Thun. 2005. "Obesity and Mortality.' *New England Journal of Medicine* 353(20): 2197–2199.

Calle, E. E., M. J. Thun, J. M. Petrelli, C. Rodriguez, and C. W. Heath, Jr. 1999. "Body-mass Index and Mortality in a Prospective Cohort of U.S. Adults." *The New England Journal of Medicine* 341(15): 1097–1105.

Chang, V. W., and D. S. Lauderdale. 2005. "Income Disparities in Body Mass Index and Obesity in the United States, 1971–2002." *Archives of Internal Medicine* 165(18): 2122–2128.

Couzin, J. 2005. "A Heavyweight Battle over CDC's Obesity Forecasts." *Science* 308: 770–771.

Dolan, C. M., H. Kraemer, W. Browner, K. Ensrud, and J. L. Kelsey. 2007. "Associations between Body Composition, Anthropometry, and Mortality in Women Aged 65 Years and Older." *American Journal of Public Health* 97(5): 913–918.

Flegal, K. M., and B. I. Graubard. 2009. "Estimates of Excess Deaths Associated with Body Mass Index and Other Anthropometric Variables." *American Journal of Clinical Nutrition* 89(4): 1213–1219.

Flegal, K. M., B. I. Graubard, and D. F. Williamson. 2004. "Methods of Calculating Deaths Attributable to Obesity." *American Journal of Epidemiology* 160(4): 331–338.

Flegal, K. M., B. I. Graubard, D. F. Williamson, and R. S. Cooper. 2011. "Reverse Causation and illness-related Weight Loss in Observational Studies of Body Weight and Mortality." *American Journal of Epidemiology* 173(1): 1–9.

Flegal, K. M., B. I. Graubard, D. F. Williamson, and M. H. Gail. 2005. "Excess Deaths Associated with Underweight, Overweight, and Obesity." *Journal of the American Medical Association* 293(15): 1861–1867.

Flegal, K. M., B. I. Graubard, D. F. Williamson, and M. H. Gail. 2007. "Impact of Smoking and Preexisting Illness on Estimates of the Fractions of Deaths Associated with Underweight, Overweight, and Obesity in the US Population." *American Journal of Epidemiology* 166(8) (10/15): 975–982.

Ford, E. S., U. A. Ajani, J. B. Croft, J. A. Critchley, D. R. Labarthe, T. E. Kottke, W. H. Giles, and S. Capewell. 2007. "Explaining the Decrease in U.S. Deaths from Coronary Disease, 1980–2000." *The New England Journal of Medicine* 356(23): 2388–2398.

Gallagher, D., M. Visser, D. Sepulveda, R. N. Pierson, T. Harris, and S. B. Heymsfield. 1996. "How Useful Is Body Mass Index for Comparison of Body Fatness Across Age, Sex, and Ethnic Groups?" *American Journal of Epidemiology* 143: 228–239.

Gregg, E. W., Y. J. Cheng, B. L. Cadwell, G. Imperatore, D. E. Williams, K. M. Flegal, K. M. Venkat Narayan, and D. F. Williamson. 2005. "Secular Trends In Cardiovascular Disease Risk Factors According To Body Mass Index In US Adults." *Journal of the American Medical Association* 293(15): 1868–1874.

Herd, P., B. Goesling, and J. S. House. 2007. "Socioeconomic Position and Health: The Differential Effects of Education versus Income on the Onset Versus Progression of Health Problems." *Journal of Health and Social Behavior* 48(3): 223–238.

Hu, F. B. 2008. 'Obesity and Mortality." In *Obesity Epidemiology*, ed. Frank B. Hu, 216–233. New York: Oxford University Press.

Hu, F. B., W. C. Willett, T. Li, M. J. Stampfer, G. A. Colditz, and J. E. Manson. 2004. "Adiposity as Compared with Physical Activity in Predicting Mortality among Women." *New England Journal of Medicine* 351(26): 2694–2703.

Janssen, I., and A. E. Mark. 2007. "Elevated Body Mass Index and Mortality Risk in the Elderly." *Obesity Reviews* 8: 41–59.

Kalmijn, S., J. D. Curb, B. L. Rodriguez, K. Yano, and R. D. Abbott. 1999. "The Association of Body Weight and Anthropometry with Mortality in Elderly Men: The Honolulu Heart Program." *International Journal of Obesity and Related Metabolic Disorders* 23(4): 395–402.

Koster, A., M. F. Leitzmann, A. Schatzkin, T. Mouw, K. F. Adams, J. Th. M. van Eijk, A. R. Hollenbeck, and T. B. Harris. 2008. "Waist Circumference and Mortality." *American Journal of Epidemiology* 167(12): 1465–1475.

Kulminski, A. M., K. G. Arbeev, I. V. Kulminskaya, S. V. Ukraintseva, K. Land, I. Akushevich, and A. I. Yashin. 2008. "Body Mass Index and Nine-Year Mortality in Disabled and Nondisabled Older U.S. Individuals." *Journal of the American Geriatrics Society* 56(1): 105–110.

Lauderdale, D. S. 2005. "Letter to the Editor." *New England Journal of Medicine*: 352(13): 1381–1384.

Lewis, C. E., K. M. McTigue, L. E. Burke, P. Poirier, R. H. Eckel, B. V. Howard, D. B. Allison, S. Kumanyika, and F. X. Pi-Sunyer. 2009. "Mortality, Health Outcomes, and Body Mass Index in the Overweight Range: A Science Advisory from the American Heart Association." *Circulation* 119(25): 3263–3271.

Manson, J. E., S. S. Bassuk, F. B. Hu, M. J. Stampfer, G. A. Colditz, and W. C. Willett. 2007. "Estimating the Number of Deaths Due to Obesity: Can the Divergent Findings Be Reconciled?" *Journal of Womens Health* 16(2): 168–176.

Manson, J. E., W. C. Willett, M. J. Stampfer, G. A. Colditz, D. J. Hunter, S. E. Hankinson, C. H. Hennekens, and F. E. Speizer. 1995. "Body Weight and Mortality among Women." *New England Journal of Medicine* 333(11): 677–685.

Marshall, E. 2004. "Public Enemy Number One: Tobacco or Obesity?" *Science* 304: 804.

Mehta, N. K., and V. W. Chang. 2009. "Mortality Attributable to Obesity among Middle-Aged Adults in the United States." *Demography* 46(4): 851–872.

Mokdad, A. H., J. S. Marks, D. F. Stroup, and J. L. Gerberding. 2004." Actual Causes of Death in the United States, 2000." *Journal of the American Medical Association* 291(10): 1238–1245.

Mokdad, A. H., J. S. Marks, D. F. Stroup, and J. L. Gerberding. 2005. "Correction: Actual Causes of Death in the United States, 2000." *Journal of the American Medical Association* 293(3): 293–294.

Mujahid, M. S., A. V. Diez Roux, L. N. Borrell, and F. J. Nieto. 2005. "Cross-sectional and Longitudinal Associations of BMI with Socioeconomic Characteristics." *Obesity Research* 13(8): 1412–1421.

Olshansky, S. J., D. J. Passaro, R. C. Hershow, J. Layden, B. A. Carnes, J. Brody, L. Hayflick, R. N. Butler, D. B. Allison, and D. S. Ludwig. 2005. "A Potential Decline in Life Expectancy in the United States in the 21st Century." *New England Journal of Medicine* 352(11): 1138–1145.

Pischon, T., H. Boeing, K. Hoffmann, M. Bergmann, M. B. Schulze, K. Overvad, Y. T. van der Schouw, et al. 2008. "General and Abdominal Adiposity and Risk of Death in Europe." *New England Journal of Medicine* 359(20): 2105–2120.

Preston, S. H. 2005. "Deadweight? the Influence of Obesity on Longevity." *New England Journal of Medicine* 352(11): 1135–1137.

Price, G. M., R. Uauy, E. Breeze, C. J. Bulpitt, and A. E. Fletcher. 2006. "Weight, Shape, and Mortality Risk in Older Persons: Elevated Waist-Hip Ratio, Not High Body Mass Index, Is Associated with a Greater Risk of Death." *American Journal of Clinical Nutrition* 84(2): 449–460.

Rockhill, B., B. Newman, and C. Weinberg. 1998. "Use and Misuse of Population Attributable Fractions." *American Journal of Public Health* 88(1):15–19.

Ruhm, C. J. 2007. "Current and Future Prevalence of Obesity and Severe Obesity in the United States." *Forum for Health Economics and Policy* 10(2): 1–26.

Sanchez-Vaznaugh, E. V., I. Kawachi, S. V. Subramanian, B. N. Sanchez, and D. Acevedo-Garcia. 2009. "Do Socioeconomic Gradients in Body Mass Index Vary by Race/Ethnicity, Gender, and Birthplace?" *American Journal of Epidemiology* 169(9): 1102–1112.

Seidell, J. C., and T. L. Visscher. 2000. "Body Weight and Weight Change and Their Health Implications for the Elderly." *European Journal of Clinical Nutrition* 54 Supp. 3(06): S33–39.

Snijder, M. B., R. M. van Dam, M. Visser, and J. C. Seidell. 2006. "What Aspects of Body Fat Are Particularly Hazardous and How Do We Measure Them?" *International Journal of Epidemiology* 35(1): 83–92.

Stevens, J., J. Cai, E. R. Pamuk, D. F. Williamson, M. J. Thun, and J. L. Wood. 1998. "The Effect of Age on the Association between Body-Mass Index and Mortality." *New England Journal of Medicine* 338(1): 1–7.

Stewart, S. T., D. M. Cutler, and A. B. Rosen. 2009. "Forecasting the Effects of Obesity and Smoking on U.S. Life Expectancy." *New England Journal of Medicine* 361(23): 2252–2260.

Strickler, H. D., C. Hall, J. Wylie-Rosett, and T. Rohan. 2005. "Underweight, Overweight, Obesity, and Excess Deaths." *Journal of the American Medical Association* 294(5): 551.

U.S. Department of Health and Human Services. 2001. *The Surgeon General's Call to Action to Prevent and Decrease Overweight and Obesity.* Rockville, MD: U.S. Public Health Service, Office of the Surgeon General.

Visscher, T. L., J. C. Seidell, A. Molarius, D. van der Kuip, A. Hofman, and J. C. Witteman. 2001. "A comparison of body mass index, waist-hip ratio and waist circumference as predictors of all-cause mortality among the elderly: The Rotterdam study." *International Journal of Obesity and Related Metabolic Disorders* 25(11): 1730–1735.

CHAPTER 31

SCHOOLING AND HUMAN CAPITAL

KHOA TRUONG AND ROLAND STURM

INTRODUCTION

THE rise in childhood overweight in recent years has sparked numerous research studies that have examined the consequences of overweight at young ages on health and socioeconomic outcomes in adulthood. Educational achievement and obesity are correlated at the population level, which raises the question of whether obesity in early life could affect school outcomes and eventual educational achievement. Because children spend a significant amount of time in school daily, it is possible that the effects of being overweight are felt in various aspects of school life, including academic achievement, social skills, and attendance. There are multiple pathways through which obesity might affect educational achievement. Being overweight may lower self-esteem and body image and make it harder for children to concentrate or be attentive in class, thereby preventing them from learning in school. This psychosocial aspect has been emphasized in the literature, primarily in sociology and psychology. In addition, health problems associated with being overweight may increase sick days, leading to missed classes or tardiness, and subsequently affect school performance. Not all effects need to be negative, at least theoretically. If overweight children spend less time in physical activity and are less engaged in social activities, additional time spent studying might very well lead to better educational outcomes.

A completely different framework in economics frames education, health, and work experience in the terms of human capital. Individuals rationally invest in human capital (through education, training, health behaviors), but human capital also depreciates over time (through aging, lack of use, or knowledge becoming outdated). In the dominant neo-classical economic framework, schooling decisions are the optimal response to individual endowments and preferences; associations between education and obesity reflect omitted individual variables, in particular ability and time preferences (Becker 1964). Individuals who discount the future more heavily invest less in education and also less in their health, leading to a correlation between obesity and educational outcomes (Komlos et al. 2004). Human capital accumulated in the early years of life plays a particularly important role because of its contribution over the full life cycle. A key assumption that allows economists to identify their models and that drives conclusions is that individuals (and even children) have fixed preferences, rather than tastes and preferences that are malleable and to a large extent shaped by individual experiences and social environments.

A third stream in the literature has addressed the association between obesity and education, primarily considering obesity as an outcome determined by information and knowledge. This framework underlies many interventions and is more commonly found in clinical or public health journals.

In the U.S. population, obesity and educational outcomes are correlated, although the strength of the correlation differs across subgroups. Existing data cannot identify causal relationships without additional assumptions Depending on disciplinary predilection, different streams of the literature implicitly (and less often explicitly) impose different assumptions, which color conclusions and policy recommendations. Even if one tries to distinguish different possible explanations, auxiliary assumptions are needed that typically predispose findings to fit into one disciplinary framework. Economists tend to dismiss associations as selection effects (because individuals sort themselves according to their fixed preferences), while psychologists look for a confirmation of the shaping of preferences, and sociologists might see the working of environments. We suspect that researchers from different disciplines might even interpret identical numbers differently.

After presenting empirical data about the magnitudes of education and obesity, this chapter focuses on research that has by and large been interpreted as an effect of obesity on schooling experiences and academic performance. The key periods for those outcomes are childhood, adolescence, and young adulthood, in contrast to adverse health outcomes of obesity, which primarily appear in middle-aged adults.

EDUCATION AND OBESITY: WHAT DO THE DATA SAY?

When we look at trend data, *changes* in body mass index (BMI) appear to be very similar across all population groups, even though mean BMI or prevalence of obesity at any point are highest among groups with the lowest education. Figure 31.1 shows U.S. trends in mean BMI and figure 31.2 shows trends in the 80th percentile by educational status (we get similar results when stratifying by other variables, see Truong and Sturm 2005). At any time over the last 25 years, lower educational achievement is associated with higher BMI, but the average BMI increased steadily for all groups and the increases are fairly similar. It is not that the college-educated avoid obesity, they merely reach the level of other groups later. At the current rate, we estimate the time gap between those without a high school diploma and those

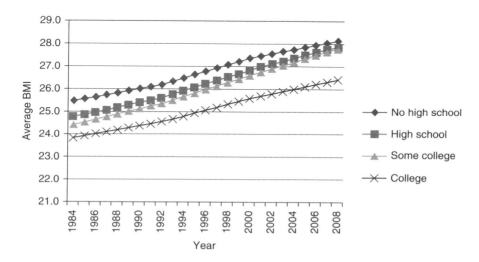

Figure 31.1. Trends in Average BMI by Education.
Source: BRFSS 1984–2008.

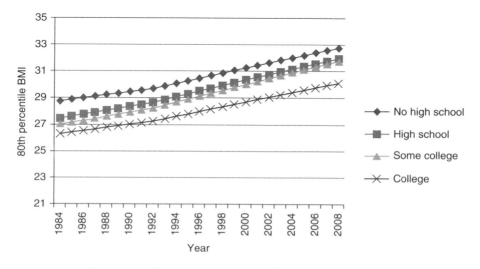

Figure 31.2. Trends in 80th Percentile BMI by Education.

with at least a college degree to be about 15 years. We consider the almost parallel increase in BMI across groups the most striking result, which suggests that if we want to prevent obesity, interventions need to affect the whole population and not just selected subgroups.

Of course, the trends are not exactly parallel, so there is another effect, although it appears secondary in importance. In particular, the gaps in mean BMI among those without a high school diploma, with a school diploma, and with some college degree became smaller in the recent years. In 2008, there was a gap of 0.22 BMI between those with and without a high school diploma and 0.12 BMI between those with high school diploma and with some college degree. Among heavier weight subpopulations, as represented by the 80th percentile BMI, similar patterns exist (figure 31.2).

Figures 31.1 and 31.2 are adjusted for several confounding changes over time, so the trends are not a consequence of population aging, immigration, or changes in data collection. We used the 1984–2008 Behavioral Risk Factor Surveillance System (BRFSS), which is the largest annual health interview survey worldwide, and our final data set contains approximately 3.9 million observations. The dependent variable was individual BMI (weight in kilograms divided by the square of height in meters) calculated from self-reported weight and height. The regression model included calendar year, education (no high school, high school, some-college, and college), race/ethnicity (non-Hispanic white; non-Hispanic black; Hispanic; other race), gender, marital status, employment status, age group (in five-year intervals), and state (to control for changing survey participation by states over time). To allow for nonlinear changes in weight gain over time, we used a linear spline with knots at 1992 and 2000. The regression model also included interaction terms between year and education, year and race, and year and gender to predict differential amounts of BMI gained over time across the groups.

The relatively similar increase in weight is surprising because many hypotheses have focused on the secondary phenomenon, namely either diverging or converging trends. Among those hypotheses are: decline in physical labor, which should have primarily increased BMI among lower educated males (widening gaps); weight gain due to increased female labor force participation, which would have increased BMI more among more educated women (narrowing gaps); and various hypotheses about racism and discrimination (widening gaps by race/ethnicity). One of the more widely discussed hypotheses concerns the economics of food supply and argues that individuals with more limited financial resources have to shift to more energy-dense foods, which in turn are more likely to encourage excessive energy intake (Drewnowski and Specter 2004). It is a very thoughtful theory with a clear prediction (widening disparities across income), but does not match the data (cross-sectionally, the results do not hold for men; longitudinally, weight gain across income groups is comparable after taking into account education). We only show graphs by education here, but generally there is little evidence for widening weight disparities across income, education, or race-ethnicity (the exception being African American women) over time (Truong and Sturm 2005).

The association between education and BMI or obesity can differ across population subgroups. Table 31.1 shows the descriptive statistics for 2008 stratified by race/ethnicity and separately for men and women age 30–65. For every subpopulation, those with a college degree are significantly less likely to be obese (at least based on self-reported height and weight). For women, there is a continuous gradient: the less education, the higher the obesity rate (or average BMI, not shown). For men, this is not true and obesity rates (and average BMI) are highest among those with some college (or at least with a high school degree), although there are no real differences among the three less-educated groups (anything less than a completed college degree). The only significant gap is between them and the group with a college degree (lowest obesity rates). Table 31.1 is also based on the BRFSS, but these are descriptive statistics with no additional adjustments for other variables.

A concern with studying obesity is measurement error, and it is well-known that self-reported height and weight tend to underestimate actual BMI, a bias that depends on actual BMI. For comparison, table 31.2 shows estimates parallel to those in table 31.1, but with objective height and weight measurements. We use the most recent national data that collects objective measures, the 2007–2008 NHANES. The limitation of NHANES is a much smaller sample size than BRFSS, too small to get precise estimates for obesity for subgroups. The usual rule of thumb is that to

Table 31.1. Obesity Rates (based on self-reported height and weight) by Education, Ethnicity, and Sex among Adults 30–65, U.S. 2008

	Less than High School	Completed High School	Some College	Completed College
Non-Hispanic White Male N=77,914	33.5	34.9	35.0	25.0**
Non-Hispanic White Female N=112,460	37.8**	30.8	28.5**	18.6**
Hispanic Male N=6,067	32.2	32.5	33.6	27.9**
Hispanic Female N=10,201	40.0**	34.7	31.5*	22.4**
African American Male N=6,627	32.7*	37.0	39.1	30.8**
African American Female N=13,732	51.5	49.2	46.8*	32.5**
Other Racial Groups Male N=4369	23.7*	29.7	31.1	10.5**
Other Racial Groups Female N=5,766	27.0	29.2	22.5**	9.7**

Source: BRFSS 2008, Obesity defined as measured BMI > 30, * statistically significant at P < 0.05, ** statistically significant at 0.01 from HS group (reference group).

Table 31.2. **Obesity Rates (objectively measured BMI over 30) by Education, Ethnicity, and Sex among Adults 30–65, U.S. 2007–2008**

	Less than High School	Completed High School	Some College	Completed College
Non-Hispanic White Male N=743	40.2	32.2	40.3	29.6
Non-Hispanic White Female N=730	47.2	38.6	39.6	22.6*
Hispanic (Mexican) Male N=297	31.2	36.3	51.5	36.8
Hispanic (Mexican) Female N-325	43.5	55.1	56.6	22.3*
African American Male N=335	21.8*	50.6	38.2	44.0
African American Female	53.7	51.3	54.4	43.4

Source: NHANES 2007–2008, Obesity defined as measured BMI > 30, * statistically significant at P < 0.01 from HS group (reference group).

describe a population characteristic with a precision of +/− 5 percentage points, a random sample of 400 is needed. But except for non-Hispanic whites, the sample across all four education groups is less than 400, so the precision is crude. For 30–65-year-old adults, the average BMI in NHANES (weighted to be nationally representative) is 29.0 and the obesity rate is 36.0 percent; using self-reported data in BRFSS, the average BMI is 28.0 and the obesity rate is 29.2 percent. Note that the difference of just 1 BMI unit on average increases obesity rates by 7 percentage points.

So far we have showed associations of educational status and obesity for adults. But if obesity were to affect education, then arguably the most relevant group would be children. Indeed, the association between obesity and school outcomes is quite strong and robust. Much more difficult, however, is to understand why it exists and what it means. Here is where disciplinary perspectives clash. Economists might be satisfied if the associations between obesity and test scores can be explained by other characteristics, such parental education, race/ethnicity, family income, or even neighborhoods. However, that only pushes the analysis back into the realm of other social sciences.

In table 31.3, we show the descriptive associations between school test scores and obesity status from kindergarten through fifth grade. We show standardized t-scores (raw test scores graded on a curve to be approximately normal). For every test, in every school year, in every subject (science was only tested in third and fifth grade), and for both boys and girls, the test scores of obese children (defined at BMI >= 95th percentile on the growth chart) are significantly worse than those of non-obese children, at p < 0.001 for every comparison. It does not really matter whether we stratify by obesity status in fifth grade (as in table 31.3)

Table 31.3. Obesity among Elementary School Students and Test Scores: Descriptive Statistics from ECLS-K

	Boys			Girls		
	Not Obese in 5th grade	Obese in 5th grade	Difference and p-value	Not-obese in 5th grade	Obese in 5th grade	Difference
Fall K Reading Scores	51.0	49.2	1.8 <0.001	52.7	49.9	2.8 <0.001
Spring K Reading Scores	51.1	49.4	1.67 <0.001	52.9	50.5	2.4 <0.001
Spring 1st grade Reading Scores	51.4	49.3	2.1 <0.001	52.8	50.5	2.3 <0.001
Spring 3rd grade Reading Score	51.3	49.3	2.0 <0.001	52.7	49.9	2.7 <0.001
Spring 5th grade Reading Score5	51.6	49.3	2.3 <0.001	52.4	50.1	2.3 <0.001
Fall K Math Scores	52.3	49.8	2.5 <0.001	52.0	49.3	2.7 <0.001
Spring K Math Scores	52.5	50.4	2.1 <0.001	51.9	49.4	2.5 <0.001
Spring 1st grade Math Scores	52.5	50.3	2.2 <0.001	51.5	49.0	2.5 <0.001
Spring 3rd grade Math Scores	53.0	50.8	2.2 <0.001	50.9	48.3	2.6 <0.001
Spring 5th grade Math Scores	53.3	50.9	2.4 <0.001	51.0	48.3	2.7 <0.001
Spring 3rd grade Science Scores	53.0	51.2	1.8 <0.001	50.7	48.2	2.5 <0.001
Spring 5th grade Science Scores	53.3	51.6	1.7 <0.001	50.8	48.4	2.4 <0.001

Source: ECLS-K, t-scores shown for all tests. Sample size for 6 grade math scores N=4511 for girls and N=4395 for boys, small changes in numbers for other years and tests depending on test participation.

or kindergarten or any other year; descriptively, these are very strong and robust associations.

In previous research, we have analyzed the data in various ways, considering mental health and behavior, adjusting for observed individual, family, and school characteristics, looking at change in scores or weight over time, and so on (Datar and Sturm 2004, 2006). There are many interesting results. For example, test scores of children who become obese over time are more similar to those that are obese at baseline than to children who never become obese, and usually (though there is an exception) becoming obese is associated with deteriorating test scores. However, without imposing additional assumptions that are untestable in the data, all results are open to a variety of interpretations. So what have others concluded?

PREVIOUS RESEARCH ON SCHOOL
OUTCOMES AND OBESITY

Taras and Potts-Datema (2005) summarized nine studies and all demonstrated significant associations between obesity and schooling outcomes. That study remains the best summary of existing research, although there have been additional studies since that we discuss below.

Three of the studies reviewed by Taras and Potts-Datema (2005) were very small and were cross-sectional with clinical or convenience samples. Schwimmer et al. (2003) compared 106 children and adolescents referred to an academic children's hospital because of obesity with normal weight children and adolescents, and found that the severely obese children miss more school days (and also have significantly lower health-related quality of life). Campos et al. (1996) compared intellectual characteristics of 65 obese children in Brazil (ages 8–13 years) to those of a control group from the same communities comprising 35 well-nourished, tall (> 95th percentile for height) children who had normal weights for their height. Children with normal height/weight ratios had a higher intelligence quotient (IQ), wider ranges of interests, and greater speed and dexterity. Li (1995) reported that more obese Chinese elementary school children had significantly lower performance IQ scores than the comparison group. Considering these three articles next to each other, one feels as if Schwimmer et al. (2003) firmly comes down on the "obesity causes bad outcomes," while the other two lean toward the "natural differences in ability and interests cause obesity and poor educational outcomes" camp. Both draw their conclusions from correlations in small selective samples.

At the next level of research designs are population studies with larger samples. Falkner et al. (2001) analyzed data from 4,742 male and 5,201 female public school students in the 7th, 9th, and 11th grades. For girls, obese (vs. normal weight) was associated with an odds ratio (OR) of 1.5 for being held back a grade and an OR of 2.1 for students considering themselves poor students. For boys, the odds ratios for obese versus normal-weight were 1.5 for considering themselves poor students, and 2.2 for expecting to quit school. Datar, Sturm, Magnabosco (2004) analyzed data from 11,000 children entering elementary school and there were already statistically significant associations between childhood overweight and test scores: overweight kindergartners and first graders scored lower than their non-overweight peers on standardized tests. Controlling for socioeconomic differences and other potential confounding factors (including parent-child interactions) weakened the association between overweight and test scores at baseline among boys and girls, and several became insignificant. An even larger population-based study in Finland had 60,252 adolescents and found that good school performance was inversely associated with being obese for both boys and girls (Mikkila et al. 2003). In Iceland, Kristjánsson et al. (2008) studied a population-based sample of 6,346 adolescents and found that lower BMI was predictive of higher academic achievement.

So cross-sectionally, there is strong evidence that obesity and school achievement are negatively related. However, it may be possible to "explain" some or even most of those associations with other variables (Datar, Sturm, Magnabosco 2004), although that does not necessarily shed any more light on underlying relationships or provide any guide for policy of what can or should be done so that all children have appropriate schooling experiences.

There have been efforts to strengthen the study design over cross-sectional comparisons. Longitudinal studies can provide at least temporal information on the relationship between two variables. One of the first studies (not reviewed in Taras and Potts-Datema 2005) followed a nationally representative sample of 10,039 randomly selected young people from adolescence and early adulthood for seven years (Gortmaker et al. 1993). Those above the 95th percentile of the BMI growth charts had significantly lower levels of schooling after seven years. In a longitudinal population-based study of 9,754 subjects born in 1966 in northern Finland, Laitinen et al. (2002) followed the cohort members at birth (year 1966) and at 1, 14, and 31 years of age. Data on BMI, work history, unemployment allowance, place of residence, family social class, school performance, marital status, and number of children were obtained. The authors found that obesity at age 14 was associated with a low school performance at age 16 and a low level of education persisting until at least age 31. The adverse social outcomes of adolescent obesity seemed to be stronger for women. A second birth cohort study is based on the National Child Development Study in the United Kingdom (Sargent and Blanchflower 1994). They found that men and women who had been obese at age 16 had significantly fewer years of schooling. Obese women (but not men) performed poorer on math and reading tests at ages 7, 11, and 16 when compared with their non-obese peers. Focusing on outcomes during elementary school, Datar and Sturm (2006) used the Early Childhood Longitudinal Study. Among girls, becoming overweight between kindergarten entry and end of third grade was significantly associated with reductions in test scores, and teacher ratings of social-behavioral outcomes and approaches to learning.

Economists are relative latecomers to obesity research, and this particular subfield is no exception. None of the papers reviewed by Taras and Potts (2005) would be considered economic analyses. Several recent studies by economists have tried to strengthen the analysis to deal with unobserved individual, household, peer, and community heterogeneities. Using data from the National Longitudinal Study of Adolescent Health, Sabia (2007) found consistent evidence across models of a significant negative effect of obesity on grades for white females aged 14–17, but results were much less convincing evidence for non-white females and males. Okunade et al. (2009) estimated the impact of BMI categories (obesity and overweight separately) on on-time high-school completion for U.S. adolescents. For females, but not for males, there was a negative and significant effect of obesity and overweight. The negative effects on females' academic attainment were among Asians, Caucasians, and Hispanics, but not among African Americans. Similar results are found in a study of adolescents in southern Italy (Barone et al. 2010). The authors found a strong and robust positive association between obesity and early school leaving with significant gender differences in the nature of this relationship. The most recent contribution reanalyzed the National Longitudinal Survey of Youth and concluded that after controlling for many variables (including self-reported health), overweight and obese teens have levels of attainment that are about the same as teens with average weight (Kaestner et al., unpublished).

SCHOOLING AND OBESITY: POTENTIAL CAUSAL PATHWAYS—OR SELECTION BIASES?

As children spend a significant amount of time in school, obesity could interfere with various aspects of school life, including academic achievement and socialization. Two plausible causal pathways that link obesity to lower rates of attendance, poor academic performance, and low test scores are the well-established health effect of obesity and psychosocial factors.

Increases in childhood obesity have been accompanied by a rise in type 2 diabetes among youth, as well as increased rates of cardiovascular problems (e.g., hypertension), hyperlipidemia, obstructive sleep apnea, asthma, orthopedic complications, non-alcoholic fatty liver disease, cancer, and lower measures of quality of life (Fletcher 2008; Friedlander et al. 2003; Taras and Potts-Datema 2005). There certainly is the potential for obesity-related health problems to cause increased sick days or difficulties in studying, resulting in poor schooling outcomes. However, for most children, even very severely obese children, most of these health consequences do not show up until adulthood. The signature medical complications of obesity, such as diabetes, are therefore unlikely to play a significant role at the population level to explain a meaningful fraction of the correlations in table 31.3. Some conditions that might occur more commonly among youth have been suggested in this context, such as sleeping disorders (e.g., sleep apnea) and orthopedic problems (Daniels 2008). While theoretically attractive, we could not find data that would allow an assessment of how relevant any medical condition could be empirically. Our best guess is that at best these would have subtle effects at the population level.

The pathway through which obesity could affect schooling and the one that has received the most attention in the literature is through stigma and social pressure, leading to lower self-esteem and resulting psychosocial outcomes (Strauss 2000; Erickson et al. 2000; Davison and Birch 2001; Strauss and Pollack 2003; French et al. 1995). Children with unhealthy weight are more likely to have low self-esteem and higher rates of anxiety disorders, depression, and other psychopathology (Kaplan and Wadden 1986; Zametkin et al. 2004; Vila et al. 2004; Mustillo et al. 2003). The problem with the stigma and discrimination argument is that this may have been very plausible when being overweight or obese was a rare situation. It is much less plausible when obesity has become more prevalent than what is labeled "normal" weight, that is, when obesity is becoming "normal." The argument might still apply to the extreme tail of the weight distribution, but it would fail to explain the results for large groups. In table 31.3, for example, the obese group is more than one-fifth of the sample. For specific clinical outcomes, such as depression, there is also the question about reverse causality or underlying factors. All of these pathways may contribute to the association of educational outcomes and obesity, but there are no estimates of relative magnitudes. Maybe even more fundamentally, there is no generally acceptable theoretical framework that would allow one to measure the sizes of these effects.

However, we suspect that these three pathways (medical conditions, stigmatization, psychological disorders) together would not account for all (not even most) of the correlations shown in table 31.3. That leaves us with the not too unsatisfying conclusion that most of the association between obesity and education is likely due to "other" pathways. Kristjánsson, Sigfúsdóttir, and Allegrante (2008) write "the precise pathways by which health behaviors and other potential exogenous factors influence academic achievement have yet to be illuminated in a coherent theoretical model." We do not attempt to solve that puzzle here and gladly leave that to future research.

ACKNOWLEDGEMENTS

This research was funded through NICHD grant HD057193.

REFERENCES

Barone A., and N. O'Higgins. 2010. "Fat and Out in Salerno and Province: Adolescent Obesity and Early School Leaving in Southern Italy." *Econ Hum Biol.* Mar;8(1):44–57. Epub 2009 Sep 15.

Becker, G. 1964. *Human Capital. A Theoretical and Empirical Analysis, with Special Reference to Education.* Chicago: University of Chicago Press.

Campos, A. L., D. M. Sigulem, D. E. Moraes, A. M. Escrivao, and M. Fisberg. 1996. "Intelligent Quotient of Obese Children and Adolescents by the Weschler Scale." *Revista de Saúde Pública* 30(1): 85–90. (Brazil)

Cawley, John. 2004. "The Impacts of Obesity on Wages." *Journal of Human Resources* 39:451–74.

Chang, V. W., and D. S. Lauderdale. 2005. Income Disparities in Body Mass Index and Obesity in the United States, 1971–2002. *Archives of Internal Medicine*165(18): 2122–2128.

Crosnoe, R., and C. Muller. 2004. "Body Mass Index, Academic Achievement, and School Context: Examining the Educational Experiences of Adolescents at Risk of Obesity." *Journal of Health & Social Behavior* 45(4): 393–407.

Daniels, D. Y. 2008. "Examining Attendance, Academic Performance, and Behavior in Obese Adolescents." *Journal of School Nursing* 24(6): 379–387.

Datar, A., and R. Sturm. 2006. "Childhood Overweight and Elementary School Outcomes." International *Journal of Obesity (London)* 30(9): 1449–1460.

Datar, A., R. Sturm, and J. L. Magnabosco. 2004. "Childhood Overweight and Academic Performance: National Study of Kindergartners and First-Graders." *Obesity Research* 12(1): 58–68.

Davison, K. K., and L. L. Birch. 2001. "Childhood Overweight: A Contextual Model and Recommendations for Future Research." *Obesity Review* 2: 159–171.

Dietz, W. H. 1998. "Health Consequences of Obesity in Youth: Childhood Predictors of Adult Disease." *Pediatrics* 101: 518–525.

Drewnowski, A., and S. E. Specter. 2004. "Poverty and Obesity: The Role of Energy Density and Energy Costs." *American Journal of Clinical Nutrition* 79(1): 6–16.

Erickson, S., T. Robinson, F. Haydel, and J. Killen. 2000. "Are Overweight Children Unhappy?" *Archives of Pediatrics & Adolescent Medicine* 154: 931–935.

Falkner, N. H., D. Neumark-Sztainer, M. Story, R. W. Jeffery, T. Beuhring, and M. D. Resnick. 2001. "Social, Educational, and Psychological Correlates of Weight Status in Adolescents." *Obesity Research* 9(1): 32–42.

Flegal, K. M., M. D. Carroll, C. L. Ogden, et al. 2002. "Prevalence and Trends in Obesity among US Adults, 1999–2000." *Journal of the American Medical Association* 288(14): 1723–1727.

Fletcher, J. M. 2008. "Adolescent Depression: Diagnosis, Treatment, and Educational Attainment." *Journal of Health Economics* 17: 1215–1235.

French, S. A., M. Story, and C. L. Perry. 1995. "Self-esteem and Obesity in Children and Adolescents: A Literature Review." *Obesity Research* 3: 479–490.

Friedlander, S. L., E. K. Larkin, C. L. Rosen, T. M. Palermo, and S. Redline. 2003. "Decreased Quality of Life Associated with Obesity in School-Aged Children." *Archives of Pediatrics & Adolescent Medicine.* 157(12): 1206–1211.

Gortmaker, S. L., A. Must, J. M. Perrin, A. M. Sobol, and W. H. Dietz. 1993. "Social and Economic Consequences of Overweight in Adolescence and Young Adulthood." *New England Journal of Medicine* 329(14): 1008–12.

Haskins, Katherine M., and H. Edward Ransford. 1999. "The Relationship between Weight and Career Payoffs Among Women." *Sociological Forum* 14(2): 295–318.

Janssen, I., W. M. Craig, W. F. Boyce, and W. Pickett. 2004. "Associations between Overweight and Obesity with Bullying Behaviors in School-Aged Children." *Pediatrics* 2004 113(5): 1187–94.

Kaestner, R., M. Grossman, and B. Yarnoff. 2009. "Effects of Weight on Adolescent Educational Attainment." Unpublished working paper, NBER, 2009.

Kaplan, K. M., and T. A. Wadden. 1986. "Childhood Obesity and Self-esteem." *Journal of Pediatrics* 109: 367–370.

Komlos, J., P. Smith, and B. Bogin. 2004. "Obesity and the Rate of Time Preference: Is There a Connection?" *Journal of Biosocial Science* 36: 209–219.

Kristjánsson, A. L., I. D. Sigfúsdóttir, and J. P. Allegrante. 2010. "Health Behavior and Academic Achievement among Adolescents: The Relative Contribution of Dietary Habits, Physical Activity, Body Mass Index, and Self-Esteem." *Health Education & Behavior.* Feb;37(1):51–64. Epub 2008 Jun 9.

Laitinen, J., C. Power, E. Ek, U. Sovio, and M. R. Jarvelin. 2002. "Unemployment and Obesity among Young Adults in a Northern Finland 1966 Birth Cohort." *International Journal of Obesity and Related Metabolic Disorders* 26(10): 1329–1338.

Li, X. 1995. "A Study of Intelligence and Personality in Children with Simple Obesity." *International Journal of Obesity and Related Metabolic Disorders* 19(5): 355–7.

Mikkila, V., M. Lahti-Koski, P. Pietinen, S. M. Virtanen, and M. Rimpela. 2003. "Associates of Obesity and Weight Dissatisfaction among Finnish Adolescents." *Public Health and Nutrition* 6(1): 49–56.

Mokdad, A. H., E. S. Ford, B. A. Bowman, W. H. Dietz, F. Vinicor, V. S. Bales, et al. 2003. "Prevalence of Obesity, Diabetes, and Obesity Related Health Risk Factors, 2001." *Journal of the American Medical Association* 289: 76–79.

Mo-suwan, L., L. Lebel, A. Puetpaiboon, and C. Junjana. 1999. "School Performance and Weight Status of Children and Young Adolescents in a Transitional Society in Thailand." *International Journal of Obesity and Related Metabolic Disorders* 23(3): 272–277.

Mustillo, S., C. Worthman, A. Erkanli, G. Keeler, A. Angold, and E. J. Costello. 2003. "Obesity and Psychiatric Disorder: Developmental Trajectories." *Pediatrics*111(4 pt. 1): 851–859.

Neufeld, N., L. Raffel, C. Landon, Y.-D. Chen, and C. Vadheim. 1998. "Early Presentation of Type 2 Diabetes in Mexican-American Youth." *Diabetes Care* 21:80–86.

Ogden, C. L., M. D. Carroll, L. R. Curtin, et al. 2006. "Prevalence of Overweight and Obesity in the United States, 1999–2004." *Journal of the American Medical Association* 295: 1549–1555.

Ogden, C. L., M. D. Carroll, and K. M. Flegal. 2008. "High Body Mass Index for Age among US Children and Adolescents, 2003–2006." *Journal of the American Medical Association* 299: 2401–2405.

Okunade, A., A. Hussey, and C. Karakus. 2009. "Overweight Adolescents and On-time High School Graduation: Racial and Gender Disparities." *Atlantic Economic Journal* 37(3): 225–242.

Renna, F., I. B. Grafova, and N. Thakur. 2008. "The Effect of Friends on Adolescent Body Weight." *Economics and Human Biology* 6: 377–87.

Sabia, Joseph J. 2007. "The Effect of Body Weight on Adolescent Academic Achievement." *Southern Economic Journal* 73(4): 871–900.

Sargent, J. D., and D. G. Blanchflower. 1994. "Obesity and Stature in Adolescence and Earnings in Young Adulthood: Analysis of a British Birth Cohort." *Archives of Pediatrics and Adolescent Medicine* 48(7): 681–87.

Schwimmer, J. B., T. M. Burwinkle, and J. W. Varni. 2003. "Health-related Quality of Life of Severely Obese Children and Adolescents." *Journal of the American Medical Association* 289(14): 1813–1819.

Strauss, R. S. 2000. "Childhood Obesity and Self-esteem." *Pediatrics* 105: e15.

Strauss, R. S., and H. A. Pollack. 2003. "Social Marginalization of Overweight Children." *Archives of Pediatrics and Adolescent Medicine* 157: 746–752.

Sturm, R. 2005a. "Childhood Obesity: What We Can Learn from Existing Data on Societal Trends, Part 1." *Preventing Chronic Disease.* Jan;2(1):A12. Epub 2004 Dec 15.

Sturm R. 2005b. "Childhood Obesity. What We Can Learn from Existing Data on Societal Trends, Part 2." *Prev Chronic Dis.* Apr;2(2):A20. Epub 2005 Mar 15.

Sturm, R. 2007. "Increases in Morbid Obesity in the USA: 2000–2005." *Public Health* 121(7): 492–496.

Sturm, R., and D. Cohen. 2004. "Suburban Sprawl and Physical, and Mental Health." *Public Health* 118(7): 488–496.

Taras, H., and W. Potts-Datema. 2005. "Obesity and Student Performance at School." *Journal of School Health* 75(8): 291–295.

Truong, K. D., and R. Sturm. 2005. "Weight Gain Trends across Sociodemographic Groups in the United States." *American Journal of Public Health* 95(9): 1602–1606.

Vila, G., E. Zipper, M. Dabbas, et al. 2004. "Mental Disorders in Obese Children and Adolescents." *Psychosomatic Medicine* 66(3): 387–394.

Yu, Z. B., S. P. Han, X. G. Cao, and X. R. Guo. 2010. "Intelligence in Relation to Obesity: A Systematic Review and Meta-Analysis." *Obesity Review* 23.

Zametkin, A. J., C. K. Zoon, H. W. Klein, and S. Munson. 2004. "Psychiatric Aspects of Child and Adolescent Obesity: A Review of the Past 10 Years." *Journal of the American Academy of Child & Adolescent Psychiatry* 43(2): 134–150.

....

CHAPTER 32

LABOR MARKET CONSEQUENCES: EMPLOYMENT, WAGES, DISABILITY, AND ABSENTEEISM

....

SUSAN L. AVERETT

INTRODUCTION

....

THE health costs related to obesity are often referred to as the direct costs of obesity. The purpose of the present chapter is to address the indirect costs of obesity, specifically the labor market consequences. Some of these costs are public costs in that there are externalities created that affect others, in addition to the obese; others are largely private—the costs are borne mostly by the obese themselves. In particular, this chapter is concerned with whether or not obesity *causes* adverse labor market outcomes. Previous studies have found a negative relationship between obesity and wages, but whether the inverse relationship is due to low wages causing obesity, obesity causing low wages, or a third factor causing both low wages and obesity is the important issue. Disentangling correlation from causation is essential for policy makers and employers alike. Less evidence exists for other labor market outcomes, such as disability, absenteeism, and employment but the same endogeneity concerns arise with these outcomes. As employers grapple with the increased health care costs of the obese and policy makers determine to what extent obesity is covered by disability insurance, the need to understand if obesity is the cause of adverse labor market outcomes becomes increasingly urgent.

Economics has contributed perspectives to the research question of whether or not the obese incur labor market penalties in at least two ways. First, economics provides a theoretical framework to analyze why obesity might result in adverse non-medical consequences such as lower wages. Second, because economics is particularly concerned with establishing causality, something that is important to policymakers, economists are often concerned about the identification of key parameters, and are willing to consider creative solutions to develop more plausibly consistent estimates.

Using these two general insights, economists have been willing to tackle a variety of outcomes potentially related to obesity, including wages, absenteeism, hiring, and occupation. However, the identification of the causal effect of obesity on labor market outcomes is challenging without a credible quasi-experiment or experimental data. That said, there does appear to be agreement among a wide array of credible studies using data from different countries that heavier women are penalized with lower wages, are less likely to be hired, and are more likely to be absent from work. The evidence for whether or not obese men face adverse labor market consequences is mixed.

In this chapter, I guide the reader through the research on obesity and labor market outcomes, with a particular emphasis on the econometric methods used to overcome the potential endogeneity of obesity. I commence with the early research on this topic, move to more sophisticated identification schemes (noting along the way the pros and cons of each method), review the evidence from other countries, and conclude with a discussion of the latest work in this area and my assessment of where we need to go from here.

A First Look at Wages and Obesity

Averett and Korenman (1996)

Sanders Korenman and I wrote one of the first papers on this topic.[1] Titled "The Economic Reality of the Beauty Myth," our work was initially motivated by a talk given at Lafayette College by feminist scholar Naomi Wolf, who wrote the

---

1 Other early studies include Register and Williams (1990), Loh (1993), Gortmaker et al. (1993), and Sargent and Blanchflower (1994).

book "The Beauty Myth" in which she notes, among other things, that there is tremendous social stigma to being overweight, particularly for women. The consequences of this stigma could perhaps manifest themselves in eating disorders that are thought to be prevalent among college women in particular. At the time of our research, the mid-1990s, there was also a growing awareness of the social stigma attached to obesity (e.g., Kolata et al. 1992). Yet, economists had had little to say on the issue of body weight in contemporary industrialized societies, although the medical literature had for decades warned of the medical costs of obesity. Wolf (2002) argues that women invest more in what can be termed the human capital of body image—for example, women know the number of calories in a muffin and are also more likely than men to know how many calories are burned in one hour of jogging. This raises the question of whether or not there are economic returns to thinness.[2]

To describe economic differentials by body weight, we used data from the National Longitudinal Survey of Youth 1979 cohort (NLSY79). The latest year available at the time of our research was 1988, when the respondents were 23 to 31 years old. To measure body weight we used the body mass index (hereafter BMI), defined as weight in kilometers divided by height squared where height is measured in meters. We used indicator variables for the clinical weight classifications underweight (BMI < 18.5), overweight (25 ≤ BMI < 30), and obese (BMI ≥ 30), where the excluded category is healthy weight (18.5 ≤ BMI < 25) and examined how these were related to four economic outcomes: log wages, income-to-needs ratio, probability of marriage, and, conditional on being married, spouse's earnings. The basic regression model is:

$$Y_i = \beta X_i + \varepsilon_i \tag{1}$$

Where Y is the outcome of interest described above, X is a vector of explanatory variables that includes the indicator variables for weight classification as well as other demographic and socioeconomic controls, and ε_i is the error term for observation i. If we assume that the error is a mean-zero, constant-variance random variable that is uncorrelated with the explanatory variables in X, we can use ordinary least squares (OLS) to estimate the effect of obesity on our economic outcomes.

However, there may be unobserved factors that affect wages and that are correlated with the explanatory variables in X, this is the endogeneity referred to earlier in this chapter. Such correlation would exist, for example, if unobserved variables such as an individual's discount rate and/or ability and motivation are correlated with both obesity and wages. This would be true if those with low motivation and/ or low ability were more likely to be obese and hence earn lower wages. If variables such as ability and motivation are unobserved, then they will be captured by the

---

2 A related line of research examines the economic returns to beauty. Interested readers should consult Hamermesh and Biddle (1994).

error term, the obesity variable and the error term will be correlated, and OLS estimates of the effect of obesity on wages will be biased. Reverse causality is also a potential source of endogeneity. It is possible that those with lower wages become obese in part because they cannot afford healthy food and therefore rely on calorie-dense fast foods. It is also possible that the obese, believing that their marriage market prospects are low, invest more heavily in labor market oriented human capital and thus have higher wages.

We dealt with this potential endogeneity bias in two ways. First, we used an early measure of the BMI, an average of the 1981 and 1982 BMI (1981 was the first time height and weight were asked of the NLSY79 respondents) rather than a contemporaneous measure. This is not a perfect strategy because the lagged BMI variable may still be correlated with the error term, and it is possible that the error term captures some omitted variable related to both past BMI and the contemporaneous labor market outcome of interest. However, for many of our respondents, this early BMI measure was taken before they had been in the labor market mitigating this concern somewhat.

As an additional experiment, we also estimated sibling fixed-effects models. Assuming that the error term can be divided into two parts, family specific unobserved heterogeneity, v_f, where f indexes families, and a white noise component ε_{it} we can rewrite equation (1) as:

$$Y_{if} = \beta X_{if} + v_f + \varepsilon_{if} \tag{2}$$

Subtracting family specific means from individual observations yields the sibling fixed-effects estimator:

$$Y_{if} - \bar{Y}_f = \beta(X_{if} - \bar{X}_f) + v_f - v_f + \varepsilon_{if} - \bar{\varepsilon}_f \tag{3}$$

thus v_f is differenced out of the model since it does not vary over time. By differencing out the family specific error term, v_f, the sibling fixed-effects estimator allows us control for unobserved family-specific factors such as the family environment that are constant over time.

We estimated models separately for men and women. Our OLS results using lagged BMI categories as our measure of obesity indicated that obese women suffer wage penalties in the neighborhood of 15 percent and this was robust to the addition of controls, including marital and child status. Controlling for sibling fixed-effects reduced the magnitude of the estimate and its precision but indicated the existence of an obesity wage penalty. The obesity penalty in terms of the income-to-needs was even larger. The association of obesity with the earnings of men is small, but there is still an 8 percent difference between the obese and healthy weight in the lagged BMI cross-section specification. Once again, as is the case for women, the sibling difference models confirm the signs of the coefficients but are of smaller magnitudes and are not as precisely estimated as the OLS models. The lack of precision in our sibling difference models is attributable in part to the relatively small sample of siblings (288 sister pairs and 570 brother pairs).

Racial Differences in the Obesity Penalty

There is a literature suggesting that there are cultural differences in norms pertaining to ideal body type (Furnham and Alibhai 1983). In particular, there may be a smaller social penalty attached to being overweight for black as compared to white women. Consistent with this hypothesis, black women are more likely to be above recommended body weight, but they are less likely to perceive themselves as overweight (Dawson 1988). We explored these racial differences and found that indeed the penalty to obesity is smaller for black women than white women. In related research (Averett and Korenman 1999), we investigated these racial differentials in obesity to see if the obesity wage penalty could be explained by differences in self-esteem. However, we found that differences in self-esteem (as measured by a series of questions asked of respondents in the NLSY79) could not account for race differences in the effects of obesity on socioeconomic status, although obese white women had lower self-esteem compared to their obese black counterparts.

Cawley (2003) also reports strong race and gender differences in the correlation between obesity and wages, and he explores four possible explanations for these differences: (1) there is voluntary sorting of the obese into jobs with better health benefits at the expense of lower wages, that differs by gender and race/ethnicity; (2) weight affects self-esteem or depression in a manner that varies by gender and race/ethnicity; (3) weight affects physical health and disability in a manner that varies by gender and race/ethnicity; (4) there is weight-based discrimination in employment that differs by gender and race/ethnicity. Using NLSY79 data for 1981–2000, he reports evidence consistent with hypothesis 3 regarding physical health and disability, but little evidence to support the other three hypotheses.

Mocan and Tekin (2009) revisit the question of whether self-esteem mediates the effect of obesity on wages. Using data from the National Longitudinal Survey of Adolescent Health (AddHealth) for 2001–2002 when respondents were aged 21 to 26 years they find that obesity is associated with lower self-esteem for women and black men. They conclude that obesity impacts the wages of white women in two ways: it lowers wages directly and also lowers them indirectly through self-esteem, although the magnitude of the latter effect is small.

Extending Early Work: The Endogeneity of Obesity in a Wage Equation

Other authors have since extended this literature in several ways, most with a particular focus on identifying the causal effect of obesity on the outcome of interest. Behrman and Rosenzweig (2001) examine the relationship between BMI and wages among monozygotic twins in the Minnesota Twins Registry. The drawback of their data is the relatively small sample size, but the advantage is that they can control completely for genetic factors that are associated with obesity. In their analysis, they find no significant effect of weight on wages in either an OLS cross-section model or in their twin fixed-effects specification. It is somewhat surprising that they found no effect of weight on wages in the cross section, and this raises the question of whether their sample size is too small or whether there is insufficient variation in weight to identify an effect in their sample.

Baum and Ford (2004) also use data from the NLSY79 from 1981 to 1998 extending earlier research in two ways. First, they include individual fixed-effects models and a hybrid individual and sibling fixed-effects model that allows the family heterogeneity component, v_f, to vary over time as well as across families, thus incorporating both individual and sibling fixed-effects. Their focus is solely on wages as an outcome. In addition to their various fixed-effects specifications, they also use OLS with a lagged value of BMI. Their findings indicate that the wage penalty for obesity for women and men ranges from 0.7 to 6.3 percent, depending upon the estimation method used and that the penalty is larger for women than for men. These estimates are smaller but overall consistent with the work of Averett and Korenman (1996).

Second, they also test several hypotheses for why the obese might earn lower wages: (1) Is the differential due to health limitations of the obese, which make them less productive? (2) Is the differential due to the obese being relatively more myopic? (3) Do employers pay the obese less due to expected higher health care costs? and (4) Is the obesity wage penalty due to customer discrimination? They find that the wage profile is flatter for the obese, suggesting perhaps myopic preferences (though this cannot be disentangled from employer discrimination) but no evidence for the other hypotheses.

Bhattacharya and Bundorf (2009) explore another reason that the obese earn lower wages. Labor market theory of employee benefits posits a trade-off between wages and employee benefits. The obese incur greater health care costs, and this is reflected in higher costs to the employer who provides the insurance. Therefore, it is plausible that the obese may have to accept lower wages (or be willing to trade wages) in order to receive employer-sponsored health insurance. This theoretically inverse relationship between benefits and wages is notoriously difficult to tease out empirically. Bhattacharya and Bundorf employ a differences-in-differences framework using data from the NLSY and from the Medical Expenditure Panel Survey (MEPS) to compare obese workers with and without health insurance to non-obese workers with and without health insurance. They conclude that obese workers with employer-sponsored health insurance pay for their higher expected medical expenditures through lower cash wages. Furthermore, their findings are strengthened by the fact that they find these types of wage offsets do not exist for obese workers with insurance coverage through an alternative employer. In addition, they report that there are no wage offsets for other types of fringe benefits whose cost to the employer is less likely to be affected by obesity, such as flexible hours, retirement benefits, or child care benefits. The authors also provide evidence on the level at which these wage offsets occur. The magnitude of the wage offset for employer-sponsored coverage varies by individual characteristics that affect expected medical expenditures, in this case obesity. This suggests that the wage offset for health insurance varies across individuals within a firm based on their health risk, assuming that obese workers are not highly concentrated within particular firms.

Cawley (2004) makes two important and lasting contributions to the literature on obesity related wage differentials that have had a tremendous impact on the research in this field going forward. First, weight and height are self-reported in the NLSY and may be biased as a result. To correct for this reporting error, Cawley predicts true height and weight in the NLSY, using information on the relationship between true and reported values obtained from Third National Health and Nutrition Examination Survey (see Burkhauser and Cawley 2006 for details of this procedure, which can be applied to similar U.S. data sets with self-reported height and weight). Second, to account for time-varying unobserved effects that the individual fixed-effects model cannot control for, Cawley used the econometric method of instrumental variables (IV). The BMI of a sibling, controlling for age and gender, is used as instrumental variables to explain the respondent's BMI, based on the assumption that the BMI of a sibling is strongly correlated with the respondent's BMI and that the sibling BMI does not affect the respondent's wage directly. Cawley estimates his models separately by gender and by race. A potential drawback with his instrument is that it requires information on a sibling—thus some observations have to be discarded if they do not have a sibling in the sample, raising sample-size issues as well as issues of external validity. However, this is also the case for the sibling fixed-effects model.

To facilitate comparisons with the extant literature, Cawley first uses an OLS model of log wages in levels and reports a remarkably similar coefficient on obesity for white females as compared to Averett and Korenman—about 12 percent (see Averett and Korenman 1996, table 7, column 8, and Cawley 2004, table 2, column 1). He also then employs a lagged weight value in his OLS specification and, commensurate with Averett and Korenman, the coefficient is smaller on the lagged weight than on the contemporaneous weight. However, as Cawley notes, the strategy of using lagged weight does not address the issue of time-invariant heterogeneity on both weight and wages. Thus, he turns to an individual fixed-effects model, which is used to eliminate time-invariant heterogeneity. While the previous literature took differences between siblings (Averett and Korenman 1996) or twins (Behrman and Rosenszweig 2001), he argues that individual-specific fixed-effects eliminates more variation due to unobserved non-genetic factors than does differences between either siblings or twins, arguing that shared family environments explain a negligible proportion of the variance in weight across siblings.

Although an individual fixed-effects strategy may improve on OLS with a lagged BMI, it relies on the unobserved factors being fixed over time and person specific. Yet unobservables influencing both weight and wages may well vary over time.

Instrumental variables (IV) is preferred to individual fixed-effects if a valid instrument can be found. To be a valid instrument, the BMI of a sibling must be strongly correlated with the BMI of the respondent. Siblings with the same parents are expected to share half their genes, so based on siblings' genetic variation in weight, this is easily satisfied and also can be easily tested through an F-test of the significance of the instrument in the first stage. Second, the weight of the sibling must be uncorrelated with the respondent's wage residual. Because his model is just identified, this cannot be tested empirically and thus must be argued on theoretical grounds. To bolster the case for his instrument, Cawley appeals to studies that have been unable to detect any effect of a common household environment on body weight. For example, adoption studies have consistently found that the correlation in BMI between a child and his/her biological parents is the same for adoptees and natural children, and these studies have been bolstered by studies of twins who have been reared apart—that is, there is no strong evidence of an effect of shared family environment on BMI. However, Cawley concedes that there exists the possibility that a substantial part of the genes responsible for obesity are also responsible for other factors that affect labor market outcomes, such as willingness to delay gratification (time discount rate) or other unobserved characteristics.

Using sibling weight as his instrument, Cawley finds that only for white females is the coefficient on weight significant. The magnitude is about 70 percent higher than his OLS estimate using the same sample and is roughly equal in magnitude to the difference associated with three years of education, or six years of work experience. This is an important finding, for not only does it confirm a wage penalty for obesity, it moves us closer to a causal interpretation of the impact of obesity on wages. Indeed, the use of a relative's BMI as an instrument has essentially become the norm in this literature (for those who have a dataset in which measurements of sibling height and weight are available).

Conley and Glauber (2007) add to the literature on U.S. obesity wage differentials by using a different data set, the Panel Survey of Income Dynamics (PSID) to address the issue of weight and wages. Their use of these data complements the earlier research because the PSID respondents are generally much older, allowing us to gain a sense of the longer-term impact of obesity on wages. This is particularly important because people tend to gain weight as they age. In addition to wages, they also examine occupational prestige, marriage, and income as outcomes. Following Cawley (2004) and Averett and Korenman (1996), they use OLS with a lagged measure of body weight, but they use a lag of 13 to 15 years rather than 7 years. Thus, they examine the effect of 1986 body mass on averaged 1999 to 2001 socioeconomic and 2001 marital status outcomes. They find that BMI is associated with a reduction in a woman's earnings and her family income as well as her likelihood of marriage, her spouse's occupational prestige, and her spouses' earnings.

They also argue that due to the older age of the PSID sample, splitting the sample into those above and below 35 years of age allows them to purge their estimates of bias due to endogenous body mass and socioeconomic outcome effects on the grounds that older individuals have stabilized socioeconomic status trajectories, so that any relation between body mass and socioeconomic status for the older cohort is more likely reflective of reverse causality. Thus, if body mass has more of an effect on younger respondents' outcomes, this provides evidence in support of more of a causal effect of body mass on outcomes rather than the reverse, and their results generally confirm this.

Han et al. (2008) estimate models of individual fixed-effects using the NLSY79 from 1982 to 1998 and allow the effect of BMI to vary by gender, age, and the type of interpersonal relationships required in each occupation. They find that the often-reported negative relationship between the BMI and wages is larger in occupations requiring interpersonal skills with presumably more social interactions and that the wage penalty for obesity increases as the respondents get older. Furthermore, there is a lower probability of employment among the obese and overweight for all race-gender subgroups except black women and men.

Norton and Han (2008) use data from the National Longitudinal Study of Adolescent Health (AddHealth) to examine the effect of obesity on wages. An important advantage of these data is that they contains genetic information for a subset of respondents. The authors argue that genetic information from specific genes that have been linked to obesity in the biomedical literature provides an ideal instrument for obesity because genes are a source of exogenous variation in obesity. They lagged BMI and instrumented BMI with genetic information and sibling BMI. They demonstrate that their genetic information coupled with sibling BMI is highly predictive of lagged BMI and the probability of being obese or overweight confirming these are good instruments. They also use additional genetic information as exogenous regressors in the wage models. In contrast to other studies, their preferred specification yields no effect of lagged obesity on wages or employment. However, their sample is relatively young (early to mid-twenties), so it is difficult to generalize these results or to compare them to those of others.

An additional strength of their research is that they are able to empirically test whether the sibling BMI instrument can legitimately be excluded from the wage equation. It is not possible to test directly whether the instruments are exogenous, though in an over-identified model it is possible to test the conditional validity of the additional instruments under other maintained assumptions. They find that lagged sibling BMI does pass the test of over-identifying restrictions, a particularly important finding because so many previous studies have used sibling BMI as the sole instrument (and thus have not been able to test the over-identification restriction because they have only one instrument and the model is just identified).

The studies reviewed above have all relied on data where the only measure of adiposity is BMI. Yet, recent research emphasizes that BMI is not the best measure for use in research on obesity, as it does not distinguish between fat and fat-free mass such as muscle and bone (Burkhauser and Cawley 2008; Larsson et al. 2006). Instead, Burkhauser and Cawley (2008) recommend using more accurate measures of fatness such as total body fat (TBF), percentage body fat, fat-free mass (FFM), and waist circumference in social research. In preliminary research,

Wada and Tekin (2010) circumvent this problem by estimating body fat and fat-free mass using data on bioelectrical impedance analysis (BIA) available in the NHANES III. They use the relationship between weight in pounds and body fat and fat-free mass in the NHANES to estimate body fat and fat-free mass in the NLSY79, and then estimate models of wages as a function of body composition in the NLSY79. Their results indicate that increased body fat is consistently associated with lower wages for both women and men.

In the United States, the evidence as to whether obesity affects wages is mixed, due to different data sets covering different time frames and different methods of dealing with endogeneity. A brief review of those methods and their potential drawbacks is in order.

The lagged BMI approach requires that the lagged BMI variable be uncorrelated with the error term yet, as noted, it is possible that the error term captures some omitted variable related to both past BMI and the contemporaneous labor market outcome of interest. Thus, this method is best if the lag can be measured before the individual enters the labor market so that reverse causality from an adverse labor market outcome does not influence BMI as in Norton and Han (2008).

Both individual and sibling fixed-effects models suffer from some potential drawbacks. In an individual fixed-effects model, the unobserved heterogeneity must be time invariant. The consistency of fixed-effects estimates of obesity on wages are still open to question because the differences may not be exogenous. Furthermore, the individual fixed-effects strategy involves a particular implicit trade-off between precision and consistency.

Sibling fixed-effects models have their own drawbacks. Even after differencing across siblings, we are still left with the variance in weight attributable to genes unshared by siblings and the variance in weight attributable to non-genetic factors unshared by siblings. To the extent that these factors are not captured by the regressors in our model, the coefficients on BMI will still be biased. For example, if parents treat children in the same family differently as a response to early academic potential that is related to wages, a sibling fixed-effects model would not capture this.

Cawley's use of the BMI of a biological sibling as an instrumental variable is appealing. Members of a biological family share some of their genes, which ensures a strong correlation between the endogenous variable and its instrument. In other words, the selected instrument is unlikely to be weak. The second condition requires that the BMI of a biological family member should be uncorrelated with the error term in the wage regression. This could fail to happen if there are unobserved factors that affect both the BMI of parents, siblings and children, and the wage residual. Cawley (2004) argues extensively that this is unlikely, quoting evidence from adoption studies, which suggests that the correlation of weight within families is due to genetic factors rather than to family environment. However, there is also evidence that obesity is negatively correlated with socioeconomic status for women in developed countries. Even if we subscribe to the view that the BMI of the biological family member is affected by family environment, Cawley's instrument remains valid if unobserved factors influence wages only via the variables in the vector X, that is, if the unobservables are sufficient to capture individual differences in ability and family background. Although Cawley was unable to empirically test the over-identifying restriction that sibling BMI could legitimately be excluded from the wage equation, Norton and Han (2008) are able to do this with their AddHealth data because they have access to a richer set of instruments. Their finding that sibling BMI passes the over-identifying restrictions test is reassuring. I also find this to be a plausible instrument because of the well-known correlation of individual ability and family background with educational outcomes, health, and occupational choice, which are controlled for in the models.

Norton and Han's successful use of a genetic identifier as an instrument for obesity makes a compelling case for using genetic information as an identification strategy in the social sciences. Their finding of no effect of BMI on wages is puzzling and may be an artifact of the more recent data that they use coupled with a younger cohort. More research is needed to sort this out since Averett and Korenman (1996), Conley and Glauber (2007), Baum and Ford (2004), and Han et al. (2008) all find some support for the hypothesis that obesity causes lower wages, whereas Behrman and Rosenzweig (2001) and Norton and Han (2008) do not find any evidence that obesity causes lower wages.

The area is ripe for more research. As Norton and Han (2008) note, theirs is the first to make use of genetic information, and future research will have to control for endogeneity of BMI in a way that accounts for both genetics and time-varying environmental factors that affect BMI.

EVIDENCE FROM OTHER COUNTRIES

In recent years, a number of papers have examined wage differentials due to obesity using data from several developed countries. Cawley (2007) questions whether there is a universal pattern across countries with respect to obesity and wages.

Garcia and Quintana-Domeque (2006) use data from nine European countries using the European Community Household Panel (ECHP), a standardized multipurpose annual longitudinal survey carried out in all 15 countries of the European Union between 1994 and 2001, to examine obesity related wage and employment differentials. They find an obesity wage penalty that is 2 to 10 percent for women but much lower for men. Their results must be interpreted as correlations, not causal, since they do not control for the endogeneity of obesity other than including a wide array of covariates.

Brunello and D'Hombres (2007) also use ECHP data to investigate the impact of body weight on wages in nine European countries. They instrument BMI with the BMI of a biological family member, a parent, child, or a sibling. Pooling the available data across countries and years, they find that a 10 percent increase in the average body mass index reduces the real earnings of males and females by 3.27 percent and 1.86 percent, respectively. Because European culture, society, and labor markets are fairly heterogeneous, they estimate separate regressions for northern and southern Europe and find that the negative impact of the body mass index on earnings is larger—and statistically significant—in the latter area.

Cawley et al. (2005) study the relationship between obesity and earnings in the United States and Germany, and use the weight of a child or of a parent as an instrument. They report a statistically significant and negative relationship between obesity and wages.

Atella et al. (2008) also use the ECHP and adopt a quantile regression approach to examine the impact of obesity at different points in the wage distribution. As we might expect, they find that OLS masks a significant amount of heterogeneity in the relationship between obesity and wages and they further argue that cultural, institutional, and environmental factors cannot explain the cross-country differences. Atella et al. test several alternative explanations related to the statistical association between wages and obesity. In particular, they examine whether it is due to losses in productivity, health problems, myopic behavior on the part of the obese, or provisions of health insurance by employers who discount higher health care costs for obese workers in the form of lower wages. When they control for these factors in their models, they cannot explain the lower wages of obese women with any of these hypotheses. They also attempt instrumental variables estimation but their instrument proves weak.

In contrast, the work of Kortt and Leigh (2009), which uses data from Australia and the BMI of a relative as an instrument, suggests that workers with higher BMI do not earn lower wages in Australia, even in the OLS models before controlling for endogeneity by instrumenting for BMI. The issue of whether different effects across countries are due to cultural differences and/or labor market institutions has been suggested by several researchers. Garcia and Quintana-Domeque (2006) note that we might expect less of a wage penalty for obesity in countries where unions and collective bargaining over wages are strong because they tend to compress the wage distribution. The presence of employer provided health insurance may work against the obese if employers pay them lower wages to make up for the higher health care costs they incur (Bhattacharya and Bundorf 2009). Greve (2008) notes that in some countries where the wage distribution is fairly compact, examining the employment effects rather than the wage effects of obesity makes more sense.

Garcia and Quintana-Domeque (2006) hypothesize that cultural norms for thin body types are inversely related to the obesity prevalence in a society; thus in societies with high obesity rates, we should expect to find low labor market penalties associated with obesity, and in countries where more social interaction occurs, a higher labor market penalty for obese persons would exist. They find some weak evidence to support this hypothesis for women. Fahr (2006) in preliminary research analyzes wage penalties associated with deviations from a social norm BMI. He regresses the log of wages on two dummy variables that account for the influence of deviations from an optimal BMI, where optimal is defined from a medical standpoint. He reports that a deviation of more than three index points in body mass in the upward direction is penalized with a 7 percent wage decline in Austria, Greece, and Spain, finding indirect support for Garcia and Quintana-Domeque's hypothesis.

Tao (2008) has a sample of female Taiwainese college graduates who graduated in June 2003 and were surveyed approximately one year after graduation. Tao argues that because self-confidence is also likely to be related to a person's appearance, these data are uniquely suited to this issue because all are surveyed at the entry level for their careers and therefore they do not have a labor market outcome to adversely affect their appearance—they are entering the labor market with a certain appearance. Although using a lagged BMI might well mitigate the reverse causality problem, it is still possible that a person's BMI might substantially change during the intervening years between the early BMI and the labor market outcome. Tao reports an optimal BMI in terms of earnings of 20.3—a number on the lower end of the recommended range.

Cawley, Han, and Norton (2009) examine the association between weight and labor market outcomes among legal immigrants to the United States from developing countries. The authors note that there exist striking differences between developed countries and developing countries in the sign of the correlation between weight and wages—it tends to be negative in developed countries and positive in developing countries. However, due to data limitations, they can only estimate correlations between body weight and the four labor market outcomes they study: employment, wages, white-collar occupation, and work limitations. The only significant association they find is that higher weight is associated with a lower probability of employment among women with a short duration of stay in the United States. Nevertheless, this study raises several questions worthy of further scrutiny.

The research using non-U.S. data provides more evidence that obesity exerts a negative and significant impact on wages, but the results are more mixed. This is an area where genetic information would also be useful, and further testing of hypotheses related to cultural and labor market differences across countries would enhance our understanding of the link between wages and obesity. In what follows, I turn attention to other labor market outcomes that may be adversely affected by obesity.

ABSENTEEISM

One of the less researched consequences of obesity is the cost of productivity losses at the workplace as measured by absenteeism. If obesity results in poor health, that may translate into increased absenteeism and lower productivity. Although some of the wage research mentioned earlier explored this in a preliminary way, the data that has good labor force information typically does not have as detailed information about health or vice versa (e.g., the NLSY79, the NHANES). Using data from the 2001–2002 National Health Interview Survey (NHIS), Finkelstein et al. (2005) found that the costs of obesity associated with absenteeism differ for males and females. Obese males miss approximately 2 more days of work per year due to illness or injury when compared with healthy recommended weight males. On the other hand, overweight females lost half a workday each year, while obese women lost several more.

Cawley et al. (2007) studied the costs of obesity associated with absenteeism across six different professions for males and females, using pooled 2000–2004 data from the Medical Expenditure Panel Survey (MEPS) to calculate the associations between obesity and the probability of any absenteeism, per-employee costs of obesity-related absenteeism, and the total U.S. costs of obesity-related absenteeism.

Results indicated that for women across all occupations, the morbidly obese are about 118 percent more likely, obese are 61 percent more likely, and the overweight are 32 percent more likely, than the healthy weight to miss work. Among men, the pattern varies by occupation. For male professional and sales workers, the risk of missing work increases with the degree of obesity from overweight to morbidly obese. For male managers, office workers, and equipment workers, being overweight or obese does not increase the risk of missing work, but morbidly obese men in these categories are at an increased risk of missing work.

Cawley et al. (2007) also provide estimates of the costs of obesity-related absenteeism per worker. Across all occupations, morbid obesity in women results in higher costs across all occupations, whereas obese women have higher job absenteeism costs in 4 of 6 professions. Across all occupations, absenteeism costs related with morbidly obese women average $238 per worker, whereas the absenteeism costs related to obese women averages $142 per worker. For men the costs are lower. Across all occupations, for morbidly obese men the cost is $198 per worker, and for obese men it is $70 per worker.

Overall, Cawley et al. (2007) estimate that the annual costs of obesity-related job absenteeism in the United States are 4.3 billion 2004 dollars (about 4.9 billion in 2009 dollars). Of these, about three-fourths are attributable to female workers. Among women, professionals have the highest obesity-associated costs of absenteeism (28 percent of all such costs), whereas among men, managers have the highest obesity-associated costs of absenteeism (37 percent of all such costs).

European data from the ECHP confirm that for women, the costs of absenteeism associated with obesity are statistically significant, although for men, obesity was not substantially correlated with higher absenteeism (Sanz-de-Galdeano 2007).

Related to absenteeism is the issue of employment disability. Cawley (2000) addresses this issue by estimating the effect of obesity on employment disability using an IV approach. He uses the BMI of a biological child aged six to nine years plus interactions of this with the child's age and gender as instruments in a sample of females who have borne children. Although he finds that heavier women are more likely to report an employment disability, the effect disappears when using the IV estimator. He attributes the observed correlation between body weight and disability to either reverse causality or unobservable factors causing both weight gain and employment disability. Job absenteeism and employment disability are potentially an important indirect cost of obesity that deserves more scrutiny in order to understand the true costs of the obesity epidemic.

OCCUPATION

A relatively small set of researchers have examined the potential discrimination that heavier individuals face in other ways in the workforce such as occupational attainment. Theoretically, one can expect obese and morbidly obese individuals to be at a substantially higher risk of being sick and/or having lower productivity (Cawley 2000). This should adversely affect not just their earnings, but also their ascent in their occupation. Morris (2006) investigates the impact of BMI on labor market occupational attainment in England. He measures wages in terms of mean hourly wages in each occupation, using data from a quarterly labor force survey and uses an IV estimator with two key instruments to estimate the effect of obesity on occupational attainment. The first instrument is the mean BMI of individuals living in the health authority in which the respondent lives. The second is the prevalence of obesity in the health authority in which the respondent lives. To be credible instruments, these variables must satisfy two conditions. First, they should be correlated with BMI conditional on other factors that affect occupational attainment. Area BMI measures provide a good summary of environmental influences on obesity. Second, the instruments should in fact not be correlated with the error term in the occupational attainment equation. To help ensure that this is the case, Morris includes a comprehensive set of individual and area level covariates measuring socioeconomic status and health, as well as a vector of regional dummy variables. Given these control variables, it is unlikely that area BMI measures are correlated with the unobserved area effects that impact individual occupational attainment. Morris notes of his use of more recent British data: "This is useful because as the prevalence of obesity increases over time the impact of BMI on labour market outcomes may change so that previous studies become out of date." (2006, p. 349). I return to this point in my conclusion.

Morris finds that, for males, BMI has a positive and significant direct effect on occupational attainment with an elasticity of 0.08, meaning that for every 10 percent increase in BMI, there is a corresponding 0.8 percent decline in mean occupation wage. In women, there is a direct negative impact of increased BMI on occupation attainment. However, the elasticity is lower; for every 10 percent increase in BMI, there is a corresponding 0.4 percent decline in mean occupation wage.

For the United States, Conley and Glauber (2007) using the Panel Study of Income Dynamics (PSID) also find lower occupational prestige for the obese, using lagged measure of obesity and sibling fixed-effects.

Ferreting out any occupation-specific penalty to being obese would help shed light on the potential source of discrimination against the obese. Customer discrimination models (e.g., Becker 1971) suggest that the obese should be less likely to be in a job where they work directly with customers. More research on this point is needed, although a recent audit study that I discuss in more detail below sheds some light on this issue (Rooth 2009).

EMPLOYMENT

Often the literature on the effects of obesity on wages tangentially discusses the effects on employment. For instance, Han et al. (2008) use the NLSY79 data to estimate the impact of BMI on logged wages and the probability of being employed. They find that, for women, being obese reduces the probability of being employed when compared with those women who are underweight or normal weight. This, however, was not the case for black women.

Sousa (2005), in preliminary research, finds a positive influence of weight on labor force participation in the case of males and an opposite influence in the case of females. Her work is noteworthy in that, to control for selection into obesity, she uses a propensity score matching (PSM) approach. This involves matching individuals on the basis of observable characteristics. PSM works best if there is substantial overlap in the characteristics of the treatment and control groups. It also requires the researcher to assume that the untreated (in this case those who are not obese) were untreated at random—an assumption that is perhaps not likely to hold in this case.

Several other studies have examined the effect of obesity on employment, including Tunceli et al. (2006), Lundborg et al. (2007), and Morris (2007). Using data from England, Morris (2007) examines employment and earnings using area-level variables as instruments (see his 2006 study described earlier under the heading of occupation differences). He finds negative effects of obesity on employment for men and women that disappear when he instruments for obesity using the area-level instruments.

A particularly policy-relevant example for the United States concerns women on public assistance. In 1996 the U.S. welfare system was restructured, making it mandatory that nearly all recipients work. Given that obesity is particularly prevalent among low-income women in the United States, examining barriers to employment among low-income obese women is a particularly important research question. Given the low skill level of these women, any obesity-related barriers to employment serve as an additional disadvantage for this group. Evidence from a unique panel data set of current and former welfare recipients indicates that obese white women have more trouble transitioning from welfare to work than do obese black women (Cawley and Danziger 2004) Specifically, heavier white women are less likely to be employed, and a 10 percent increase in weight from the mean reduces the probability of being employed by 12 percent. Similarly, a 10 percent increase in weight from the mean is associated with a 5.4 percent fewer hours worked that week.

While most of the literature focuses on the labor market success of prime aged working individuals, Lundborg et al. (2007) examine the impact of obesity on occupational attainment among those 50 years old or older using the Survey of Health, Aging and Retirement in Europe (SHARE). The survey, which follows the design of the U.S. Health Retirement Study, surveyed 22,000 Europeans over the age of 50 spanning 11 countries. Lundborg et al. report that obesity was associated with a significantly lower probability of being employed and that obese European women earned 10 percent less than their non-obese counterparts, but there was no detectable effect of obesity on hours worked. Given the compelling theoretical arguments made to support the existence of such a relationship, further research should examine the impact of obesity on productivity.

Greve (2008) examines the impact of obesity on the likelihood of being employed in Denmark. Examining employment rather than wages makes sense in Denmark because labor markets in the northern European welfare state economies are characterized by a compact wage distribution, and a considerable share of the labor force is employed in the public sector, with fixed wage structures. Thus, larger effects of obesity are expected on employment than on wages. OLS, individual fixed–effects, and instrumental variables are all used in an effort to isolate the causal effect of obesity on employment. Similar to Cawley (2004), Greve relies on the BMI of a relative (in this case whether or not the parent was prescribed medicine for obesity). Women are found to be penalized for obesity in employment more than men.

Johansson et al. (2009) examine Finnish data using more accurate measures of fatness than BMI. They report that all measurements of obesity are negatively associated with women's employment probability, while only fat mass is negatively associated with men's employment probability. Klarenback et al. (2006) examine obesity and workforce participation using Canadian Data. They find that obesity is associated with lower workforce participation, even after adding in controls for associated co-morbidities and controls for socioeconomic factors. However, neither of these studies attempt to control for the endogeneity of obesity.

THE GOLD STANDARD: EXPERIMENTAL EVIDENCE ON THE EFFECT OF OBESITY ON LABOR MARKET OUTCOMES

Until recently, there existed very little experimental evidence regarding obesity and economic outcomes and what did exist was not easy to generalize because the samples were too specialized. Yet, the gold standard for establishing causality is the random assignment experiment. Rooth (2009) is the first study of which I am aware that used an experimental framework, specifically an audit study, to ascertain whether or not employers discriminate against the obese when making hiring decisions. Audit studies measure discrimination directly with experimental fieldwork. Subtle discrimination can be hard to detect. Was a person rejected for a job because of the obesity or because they had a poor interview? Audit studies overcome this by presenting the subjects of their studies with two nearly identical candidates who differ in one only characteristic—in this case, obesity. Obesity was signalled by attaching a portrait photograph to the job application. A careful procedure was undertaken by the author to ensure that the photos pairs that were sent out differed only on their obesity—undergraduate students carefully rated photos for attractiveness, selecting pairs that were equally attractive. Seven pairs of photos (four male and three female) were used in the study. The authors acknowledge that this relatively small set of photo pairs may also limit the generalizability of their work.

Rooth (2009) collected data on all employment advertisements in selected occupations from January through August 2006; 1,970 applications were sent to 985 employers via e-mail, and photos were attached. Callbacks for job interviews were received via telephone (voicemail) and e-mail. Occupations were chosen such that there was a high demand for labor, so that callbacks did not occur simply because there was little demand. The range of occupations varied in skill requirement and the degree of customer contact needed. Rooth examined a total of seven occupations in two major cities in Sweden: Stockholm and Gothenburg.

The results indicate that obese men who applied for jobs as business sales assistants, restaurant workers, and shop sales assistants had significantly lower callback rates than their normal weight counterparts. Obese women were significantly less likely to be called back for preschool teacher positions, accountants, and restaurant workers.

Do these results reflect statistical discrimination? In other words, are employers acting on some belief, real or imagined, that the obese are less productive and then using that general belief to screen applicants? Evidence cited earlier in this chapter indicates the obese are more likely to be absent from work; employers may be aware of this and use obesity as a marker for absenteeism in applicants, even though a particular obese applicant may not have an absenteeism problem. This is the essence of statistical discrimination, using group characteristics to screen individuals for hiring or promotion or other decisions.

Another possibility for these results is customer discrimination. Rooth notes that in the occupations that require customer contact, such as sales, the difference in the callback rate is higher, suggesting some customer discrimination. The appearance penalty varies across occupations, suggesting that subjective dislike by employers is likely not the issue. If employer discrimination were responsible, then there would need to be an explanation for why the employers who discriminate are clustered in certain occupations.

One puzzling result is that restaurant work has the highest share of obese employees but is also the occupation with the highest degree of differential treatment by weight. It is somewhat paradoxical to find that the obese find themselves in this job category, where differential treatment toward them is the opposite from what occupational sorting theories would suggest. He argues that it must be that individuals sort themselves into this occupation prior to becoming overweight/obese and/or that the supply of obese applicants is sufficiently large so as to compensate for the differential treatment effect.

Conclusion

In this chapter I have reviewed a wide array of studies that have attempted to determine if there is a causal effect of obesity on labor market outcomes. As emphasized throughout, the associations between body size and labor market outcomes may reflect three possibilities: the first is that obesity does cause lower wages either because employers discriminate (as affirmed by Rooth 2009), or the obese are less productive, or that there is reverse causality; that is, low wages cause obesity perhaps because of a reliance on calorically dense but inexpensive foods, or that there is a third factor, for example rate of time preference, that causes both obesity and low wages.

Several empirical strategies have been used to disentangle causation from correlation in secondary data, with the most credible relying upon instrumental variables. This has been applied to European, Canadian, Australian, as well as U.S. data, and these data have yielded mixed evidence of a wage penalty to obesity. Recent experimental evidence from Sweden presents convincing evidence that the obese are less likely to be hired and that some of that might reflect customer discrimination.

There are several fruitful avenues for further research. First of all, the collection and interpretation of more genetic information merged with rich labor force data are an important avenue for future research. Identification of credibly exogenous variation in obesity is key to further testing whether obesity causes lower wages. It would be valuable for social science data sets to add more accurate measures of fatness than BMI. Finally, the audit study approach is fruitful and future studies should attempt to examine not only employment but also wage offers.

The finding that labor market penalties of obesity are concentrated among women deserves more scrutiny. Are women more sensitive to their appearance than men? Do employers statistically discriminate against heavy women? Given the findings with respect to absenteeism, employers may find the obese more costly to employ. Worksite weight loss programs may be "win-win," decreasing external costs of obesity to employers and helping workers lose weight.

More generally, has the labor market impact of obesity changed as the prevalence of obesity has risen? With two-thirds of Americans overweight or obese, we might well expect for the stigma associated with obesity to fall. In fact, as obesity becomes more prevalent, social norms about body weight may change. Some of the hiring differential may be related to higher health care costs, which is particularly relevant in the United States, where employers are a common source of health insurance. In contrast, in Europe most systems are sponsored by governments rather than employers.

In terms of public policy, the recent coincident rise in disability insurance rolls and obesity prevalence deserves further attention. Understanding the true effect of obesity on labor market outcomes may also be helpful in formulating better disability insurance policy with respect to obesity.

REFERENCES

Atella, V., N. Pace., D. Vuri. 2008. "Are Employers Discriminating with Respect to Weight? European Evidence using Quantile Regression." *Economics and Human Biology* 6: 305–329.

Averett, S., S. Korenman S. 1996. "The Economic Reality of the Beauty Myth." *Journal of Human Resources* 31: 304–330.

Averett, S., S. Korenman. 1999. "Black-white differences in social and economic consequences of obesity." *International Journal of Obesity,* 23: 166–73.

Baum, C., II, W. Ford. 2004. "The Wage Effects of Obesity: A Longitudinal Study." *Health Economics* 13: 885–899.

Becker, Gary S. 1971. *The Economics of Discrimination,* 2nd ed. Chicago: University of Chicago Press.

Behrman, J., and M. Rosenzweig. 2001. "The Returns to Increasing Body Weight." PIER, Working Paper 01–052.

Bhattacharya, J., and M. Kate Bundorf. 2009. "The Incidence of the Healthcare Costs of Obesity." *Journal of Health Economics* 28(3): 649–658.

Brunello, G., and B. d'Hombres. 2007. "Does Body Weight Affect Wages?: Evidence from Europe." *Economics and Human Biology* 5: 1–19.

Burkhauser, R. V, and J. Cawley. 2006. "Beyond BMI: The Value of More Accurate Measures of Fatness and Obesity in Social Science Research." NBER Working Paper 12291.

Burkhauser, R. V, and J. Cawley. 2008. "Beyond BMI: The Value of More Accurate Measures of Fatness and Obesity in Social Science Research." *Journal of Health Economics* 27: 519–529.

Cawley, J., and S. Danziger. 2000. "Obesity as a Barrier to Employment and Earnings for Current and Former Welfare Recipients." NBER Working Paper 10508 2000.

Cawley, J., M. M. Grabkal, and D. R. Lillard 2005. "A Comparison of the Relationships between Obesity and Earnings in the US and Germany." *Journal of Applied Social Science Studies* 125: 119–129.

Cawley, J. 2000. "Body Weight and Women's Labor Market Outcomes." NBER Working Paper 7841.

Cawley, J. 2003. "What Explains Race and Gender Differences in the Relationshiop between Obesity and Wages?" *Gender Issues* 21: 30–49.

Cawley, J. 2004. "The Impact of Obesity on Wages." *Journal of Human Resources* 39: 451–474.

Cawley, J. 2007. "The Labor Market Impact of Obesity." In *Obesity, Business, and Public Policy*, eds. Z. Acs and A. Lyles. Northampton: Edward Elgar.

Cawley, J., M. Grabka, and D. Lillard. 2005. "A Comparison of the Relationship between Obesity and Earnings in the U.S. and Germany." *Journal of Applied Social Science Studies (Schmollers Jahrbuch)* 125: 119–129.

Cawley J, Han E, Norton EC. 2009. "Obesity and labor market outcomes among legal immigrants to the United States from developing countries." Economics and Human Biology. 7(2):153–164.

Chou, S. Y., M. Grossman, and H. Saffer. 2004. "An Economic Analysis of Adult Obesity: Results from the Behavioral Risk Factor Surveillances System." *Journal of Health Economics* 23: 565–587.

Conley, D., and R. Glauber. 2005. "Gender, Body Mass and Economic Status." NBER Working Paper 11343.

Conley, D., and R. Glauber. 2007. "Gender, Body Mass, and Socioeconomic Status." In *Advances in Health Economics And Health Services Research*, eds. K. Bolin and J. Cawley, Vol. 17, *The Economics of Obesity*, 255–278. Amsterdam: Elsevier.

Costa-Font, J., and J. Gil. 2004. "Social Interactions and the Contemporaneous Determinants of Individuals' Weight." *Applied Economics* 36: 2253–2263.

Dawson, D. 1988. "Ethnic Differences in Female Overweight: Data from the 1985 National Health Interview Survey." *American Journal of Public Health* 78: 1326–1329.

Everett, M. 1990. "Let an Overweight Person Call on Your Best Customers? Fat Chance." *Sales and Marketing Management* 142: 66–70.

Fahr, R. 2006. "The Wage Effects of Social Norms: Evidence of Deviations from Peers' Body- Mass in Europe." IZA Discussion Paper.

Furnham, A., and F. Alibhai. 1983. "Cross-Cultural Differences in the Perception of Female Body Shapes." *Psychological Medicine* 13: 829–837.

Garcia I. Villar, Jaume and Quintana-Domeque, Climent. "Obesity, Employment and Wages in Europe." Advances in Health Economics and Health Services Research, Vol. 17, 2006. Available at SSRN: http://ssrn.com/abstract=940333.

Gortmaker, S., A. Must, J. Perrin, A. Sobol, and W. Dietz 1993. "Social and Economic Consequences of Overweight in Adolescence and Young Adulthood." *New England Journal of Medicine* 329: 1008–1012.

Greve, J. 2008. "Obesity and Labor Market Outcomes in Denmark." *Economics and Human Biology* 6: 350–362.

Hamermesh, D., and J. Biddle. 1994. "Beauty and the Labor Market." *American Economic Review* 84: 1174–1194.

d'Hombres, B., and G. Brunello. 2005. "Does Obesity Hurt Your Wages More in Dublin than in Madrid?" Evidence from the ECHP. IZA Discussion Paper No. 1704.

d'Hombres, B., and G. Brunello. 2007. "Does Body Weight Affect Wages? Evidence from Europe." *Economics and Human Biology* 5: 5–19.

Han, E., E. Norton, and S. Stearns. 2008. "Weight and Wages: Fat versus Lean Paychecks." *Health Economics* 18: 235–248.

Johansson, Edvard, Petri Bockerman, Urpo Kiiskinen, Markku Heliovaara. 2009. "Obesity and labour market success in Finland: The difference between having a high BMI and being fat" *Economics & Human Biology*, Volume 7, Issue 1, March 2009, Pages 36–45.

Kolata G., J. Brody, and E. Rosenthal. 1992. "Fat in America." *New York Times,* November 22–24. Vol. 142.

Kortt, M., and A. Leigh. 2009. "Does Size Matter in Australia?" *Economic Record,* Early View, July 2009.

Larsson I, Henning B, et al. 2006. "Optimized predictions of absolute and relative amounts of body fat from weight, height, other anthropometric predictions and age." *American Journal of Clinical Nutrition* 83:252–9.

Loh, E. 1993. "The Economic Effects of Physical Appearances.: *Social Science Quarterly* 74: 420–438.

Lundborg, P., K. Bolin, S. Höjgård, and B. Lindgren. 2007. "Obesity and Occupational Attainment among the 50+ of Europe." In *Advances in Health Economics and Health Services Research,* eds. K. Bolin and J. Cawley, Vol. 17, *The Economics of Obesity,* 221–254. Amsterdam: Elsevier.

Mocan, N., and E. Tekin. 2009. "Obesity, Self-Esteem and Wages." NBER Working Paper w15101. Forthcoming in Economic Aspects of Obesity, Michael Grossman and Naci Mocan (eds.), University of Chicago Press.

Morris. S. 2006. "Body Mass Index And Occupational Attainment." *Journal of Health Economics* 25: 347–364.

Morris, S. 2007. "The Impact of Obesity on Employment." *Labour Economics* 14: 413–433.

Norton, E., and E. Han. 2008. "Genetic Information, Obesity and Labor Market Outcomes." *Health Economics* 17: 1089–1104.

Pagán, J., Dávila, A. 1997. "Obesity, Occupational Attainment, and Earnings." *Social Science Quarterly* 8: 756–770.

Puhl, R. M., and K. D. Brownell. 2001. "Bias, Discrimination and obesity." *Obesity Research* 9: 788–805.

Register, C., and D. Williams. 1980 "Wage Effects of Obesity among Young Workers." *Social Science Quarterly* 71: 130–141.

Rooth, Dan-Olof. (2009). "Obesity, Attractiveness, and Differential Treatment in Hiring: A Field Experiment" *Journal of Human Resources* 44: 710–735.

Sanz-de-Galdeano, A., 2007. "An Economic Analysis of Obesity in Europe: Health, Medical Care and Absenteeism Costs". FEDEA Working Paper No. 2007–38.

Sargent, J., and D. Blanchflower. 1994. "Obesity and Stature in Adolescence and Earnings in Young Adulthood: Analysis of a British Birth Cohort." *Archives of Pediatrics and Adolescent Medicine* 148: 681–687.

Sarlio-Lahteenkorva, S., and E. Lahelma. 1999. "The Association of Body Mass Index with Social and Economic Disadvantage in Women And Men." *International Journal of Epidemiology* 28: 445–449.

Sousa, S. 2005. "Does Size Matter? A Propensity Score Approach to the Effect of BMI on Labour Market Outcomes." Paper presented at ESPE 2005, Paris.

Tao, Hung-Lin (2008). "Attractive Physical Appearance vs. Good Academic Characteristics: Which Generates More Earnings?" *Kyklos* 61(1): 114–133.

Tunceli, K. Li K, Williams LK. 2006. "Long-term effects of obesity on employment and work limitations among U.S. Adults 1986 to 1999. *Obesity* 14: 1637–46.

Wada, Roy, and Erdal Tekin. (2010) "Body Composition and Wages." *Economics and Human Biology, Volume 8, Issue 2, July 2010, Pages 242–254.

Wolf, Naomi. 2002. *The Beauty Myth: How Images of Beauty Are Used against Women.* New York: Harper Perennial.

CHAPTER 33

BIAS, STIGMA, AND DISCRIMINATION

REBECCA M. PUHL

INTRODUCTION

OBESE children and adults are vulnerable targets of stigma and discrimination because of their excess weight. Weight-based stigmatization, or "weight bias," occurs in many domains of daily living and poses significant and debilitating consequences for emotional well-being, social functioning, and physical health (Brownell et al. 2005). Weight-based stereotypes remain socially acceptable in North American culture, including widespread perceptions that obese persons are lazy, lacking in self-discipline, lacking in willpower, impulsive, incompetent, unmotivated, non-compliant, and sloppy (Puhl and Brownell 2001; Puhl and Heuer 2009, Roehling et al. 2008). These negative public attributions often lead to inequities in employment settings, disparities in health care, disadvantages in educational institutions, and damaged interpersonal relationships (Puhl and Heuer 2009). Recent estimates suggest that the prevalence of weight discrimination in the United States has increased by 66 percent over the past decade and is similar to rates of racial discrimination, particularly among women (Andreyeva, Puhl, and Brownell 2008; Puhl, Andreyeva, and Brownell 2008). Despite the increasing prevalence and documentation of this social problem, there has been little attention in research or public policy to reduce weight bias and improve public attitudes. Thus, thousands of obese children and adults are faced with stigma and must cope with the negative consequences of stigmatization on their own.

This chapter summarizes the evidence of weight bias in multiple settings and its negative impact on quality of life for those affected. With the majority of the

American population overweight, efforts are badly needed to address the social injustice of weight bias and to ensure that stigma is absent from public health interventions to address obesity.

Sources of Weight Bias

There is clear evidence of weight bias in diverse settings, including the workplace, health care facilities, educational institutions, and even in close interpersonal relationships with family members and friends. The mass media is also a significant source of weight bias, where negative stereotypes toward obese persons are pervasive in popular television shows, films, and news reporting. Taken together, these settings create an unwelcoming, and sometimes hostile, environment for obese children and adults. Each of these sources of weight bias is summarized below.

Employment Settings

Several decades of research demonstrate that weight bias is a persistent problem in the workplace (Larkin and Pines 1979; Roehling 1999; Roehling 2002; Rudolph et al. 2009). Findings from survey research, population-based studies, and experimental studies show that obese individuals face inequities in hiring, wages, promotions, and job termination, as well as negative attitudes from co-workers (Puhl and Heuer 2009; Roehling 2002; Rudolph et al. 2009).

Experimental research has been particularly important in demonstrating weight-based discrimination in employer hiring decisions. Participants in these studies are typically asked to evaluate the qualifications of a job applicant, whose body weight has been manipulated to appear overweight or non-overweight across experimental conditions (through written vignettes, photographs, videos, or morphed computer images). Across numerous studies, findings consistently indicate that overweight job applicants and employees are evaluated more negatively and have more negative employment outcomes compared to non-overweight applicants, even with identical qualifications, education, and credentials (Klassen, Jasper, and Harris 1993; Popovich et al. 1997; Pingitoire et al. 1994; Roehling, Roehling and Pichler 2007; Rudolph et al. 2009). Specifically, obese applicants receive fewer hiring recommendations, lower qualification/suitability ratings, lower salary assignments, more disciplinary decisions, worse placement decisions, and more negative personality ratings (Roehling, Roehling, and Pichler 2007; Rudolph et al. 2009. Findings additionally show that both overweight men and women are susceptible to these forms of weight discrimination in the workplace, and that obese applicants tend to be evaluated most negatively for jobs that require extensive public contact (Roehling, Roehling, and Odland 2008; Roehling, Roehling, and Pichler 2007). The extent of stigma in hiring decisions is especially pronounced in experimental research that manipulates both job qualifications and body weight, which demonstrates that obese applicants receive poorer evaluations even when they are more qualified for jobs than thinner applicants, who receive more favorable hiring recommendations (Sartore and Cunningham 2006).

Population-based studies have been informative in examining the wage penalty that exists for many obese employees. Research using the National Longitudinal Survey of Youth (NLSY) demonstrates a consistent obesity wage penalty, even after controlling for numerous socioeconomic, familial, and health variables (Baum and Ford 2004; Cawley 2004; Maranto and Stenoien 2000). Conservative estimates suggest that obese men face as much as a 3 percent wage penalty compared to thinner men, and obese women face a wage penalty of as much as 6 percent (Baum and Ford 2004). Other studies with large cohorts of adults have reported a 9 percent decrease in wages for white women who are 60+ pounds above average weight, and a 24 percent decrease in wages for obese women compared to thinner women (Cawley 2004). Similar penalties exist for African American obese women, who face as much as 14 percent lower wages compared to normal weight African American women. Among men, similar estimates suggest that morbidly obese white men earn almost 20 percent less than normal weight men, and morbidly obese African American men earn approximately 3 percent less than normal weight counterparts (Maranto and Stenoien 2000).

Self-reported experiences of obese employees support the findings of experimental and population-based studies. Obese employees frequently report differential treatment such as being denied promotions, not being hired, or wrongful termination because of their weight, as well as being the recipient of derogatory comments and negative attitudes from co-workers (Puhl and Brownell, 2006; Andreyeva, Puhl and Brownell 2008). Surveys from nationally representative samples such as the National Survey of Midlife Development in the United States (MIDUS) show significant discrepancies in perceptions of discrimination among obese and non-obese Americans. This research suggests that approximately one-quarter of obese adults and 30 percent of very obese adults have experienced job discrimination because of their weight (Carr and Friedman 2005). Compared to normal-weight adults, estimates indicate that overweight adults are 12 times more likely, obese adults are 37 times more likely, and severely obese persons are 100 times more likely to report employment discrimination (Roehling, Roehling, and Pichler 2008). Unfortunately, these experiences are not necessarily isolated events, as some findings suggest that almost 60 percent of those who report weight-based employment discrimination have had these experiences an average of four times throughout their career (Puhl, Andreyeva, and Brownell 2008).

Currently there is no federal legislation that prohibits weight discrimination in the workplace, and only one state (Michigan) protects obese individuals from weight discrimination. Unless body weight is added as a protected category in anti-discrimination statutes, obese employees who have been discriminated against have very few options and many challenges if they attempt to seek compensation in court (Pomeranz 2008).

Health Care Settings

Obese patients are vulnerable to negative attitudes and bias from health care providers. An accumulation of self-report studies and experimental research has demonstrated biased attitudes toward obese patients among a range of health care professionals, including physicians, nurses, psychologists, medical students, dietitians, and fitness professionals (Brown, 2006; Chambliss, Finley, and Blair 2004; Ferrante et al. 2009; Hebl and Xu 2001; Kristeller and Hoerr 1997; Price et al. 1987; Puhl, Wharton, and Heuer 2008; Teachman and Brownell 2001; Young and Powell 1985). Even health professionals who specialize in obesity are not immune to negative attitudes (Schwartz et al. 2003). Weight-based stereotypes that are commonly reported by health professionals include perceptions that obese patients are lazy, lacking in self-control, non-compliant, unsuccessful, unintelligent, and dishonest (Puhl and Heuer 2009). Recent research additionally shows that physicians report lower respect for their obese patients compared to thinner patients (Huizinga et al. 2009). It may be that inaccurate assumptions about the causes of obesity reinforce negative stereotypes among some providers, as research has demonstrated that some providers perceive that obesity can be prevented by self-control, that it is a patient's non-compliance which explains their failure to lose weight (rather than limitations of existing treatment approaches), and that obesity is caused by emotional problems (Bocquier et al. 2005; Campbell et al. 2000; Fogelman et al. 2002; Hebl and Xu 2001).

In addition to negative attitudes reported by health care providers, research reveals troubling findings about the quality of provider-patient interactions and weight management treatment practices with obese patients. Self-report studies of physicians and experimental research observing provider-patient interactions demonstrate that compared to thinner patients, providers spend less time in appointments with obese patients, engage in less discussion with obese patients, assign more negative symptoms to obese patients, are more reluctant to perform certain screenings with obese patients, provide less health education with obese patients, and intervene less with obese patients (Bertakis and Azari 2005; Hebl and Xu 2001; Hebl, Xu, and Mason 2003). Some research also indicates that patient BMI is positively associated with physician reports of disliking their job, having less patience, less desire to help the patient, and that seeing obese patients is a waste of their time (Hebl and Xu 2001).

Patient perceptions of health care experiences parallel these findings. Multiple self-report studies show that obese patients report negative attitudes and disrespectful treatment from providers, that they are upset by comments that providers make about their weight, that they believe they will not be taken seriously by their providers, and that they are reluctant to address weight concerns because of previous negative health care experiences (Anderson and Wadden 2004; Bertakis and Azari 2005; Brown et al. 2006). Unfortunately, these stigmatizing experiences are commonly reported among obese patients. In one study that examined experiences of weight stigma among over 2,400 overweight and obese women, it was found that 69 percent reported experiencing weight stigma from a doctor, and 52 percent reported that these experiences had occurred on multiple occasions (Puhl and Brownell 2006). Furthermore, when participants were provided with a list of over 20 possible sources of weight stigma, doctors were reported as the second most common source. Women frequently reported stigmatizing experiences from additional health professionals, including nurses (46 percent), dietitians (37 percent), and mental health professionals (21 percent) (Puhl and Brownell 2006). These findings are similar to research examining views of bariatric surgery candidates, where as many as 43 percent reported disrespectful treatment by medical professionals because of their weight and being very upset by comments that doctors have made about their weight (Anderson and Wadden 2004).

Efforts are needed to systematically improve health care experiences for overweight and obese patients, including provider education about weight bias and the complex etiology of obesity, training to help providers implement increased sensitivity in health care delivery, and broader efforts to challenge common weight-based stereotypes in the health care community.

Educational Settings

Although less research has examined weight bias in educational institutions compared to employment and health settings, accumulating evidence is documenting weight-based victimization and stigma toward obese students from peers and educators.

Several population-based and longitudinal studies have demonstrated lower educational attainment and achievement among obese students compared to thinner peers, even after adjustments for intelligence and parental socioeconomic status (Falkner et al. 2001; Gortmaker et al. 1993; Karnehed et al. 2006; Wardle et al. 2002). Recent research shows that weight-based teasing is significantly associated with poorer school performance, and may be an important mediator in the relationship between obesity and academic performance (Krukoswki et al. 2009). Indeed, studies repeatedly indicate that obese children are vulnerable to stigma at school, where they are ascribed numerous stereotypes by peers (e.g., as being lazy, mean, stupid, unclean, lacking in friends, undesirable playmates), are less likely to be nominated as friends, are excluded from peer activities, and are socially isolated (Latner and Stunkard 2003; Puhl and Latner 2007). Stigmatization starts as early as preschool and worsens throughout the educational career of obese students, and can take multiple forms, including verbal teasing, physical aggression, and relational victimization (Cramer and Steinwert, 1998; Greenleaf et al. 2006, Janssen et al. 2004; Kraig and Keel, 2001; Neumark-Sztainer et al. 1998; Wardle et al. 1995).

Recent estimates suggest that approximately one-third of overweight girls and one-quarter of overweight boys report weight-based victimization from peers, and among the heaviest youth, prevalence rates are as high as 63 percent (Neumark-Sztainer et al. 2002). Much more work is needed in this area to examine the ways in which weight-based teasing affects different indices of school functioning and achievement, as well as school absences among obese students.

Unfortunately, overweight and obese students are also vulnerable to bias from educators. Self-report studies have documented negatives attitudes among teachers including perceptions that obese persons are untidy, less likely to succeed, more emotional, and more likely to have family problems than thinner persons (Neumark-Sztainer et al, 1999). As with other sources of weight bias, negative attitudes from teachers appear to be quite common, with some retrospective research indicating that 32 percent of adult overweight women recalled experiencing weight stigma from an educator (Puhl and Brownell 2006).

Research has also demonstrated strong anti-fat attitudes among physical education teachers, who additionally report lower expectations for obese students across a variety of performance areas, including social, reasoning, physical, and cooperation skills compared to non-overweight students (Greenleaf and Weiller 2005; O'Brien, Hunter, and Banks 2006). As no research has examined the direct link between stigmatizing attitudes among educators and school performance of obese students, it will be important to assess whether biased attitudes from teachers result in differential treatment of obese students or impacts their school functioning and educational achievement in adverse ways.

Interpersonal Relationships

Increasing research has documented weight bias toward obese individuals from romantic partners, family members, and friends (Boyes and Latner 2009; Keery, Boutelle, van den Berg, and Thompson 2005). It appears that obese women are especially vulnerable to weight bias in interpersonal relationships, and that stigma may have a particularly negative impact on their romantic partnerships. For example, experimental research examining responses to personal advertisements placed by an overweight female showed that weight descriptors such as "obese," "overweight," or "fat" primed negative stereotypes about the target and less desire by respondents to date the target (Smith et al. 2007). Previous research has also demonstrated that men are more likely to respond to a personal advertisement in which a female target is identified as having a history of drug problems compared to one in which a woman is identified as obese (Sheets and Ajmere 2005). These findings support other studies which demonstrate that overweight women are perceived as less desirable dating partners compared to non-overweight peers, and are ranked as the least desirable sexual partner when compared to partners with various disabilities, including being in a wheelchair, missing an arm, with a mental illness, or described as having a history of sexually transmitted diseases (Chen and Brown 2005).

A consistent finding in these studies is that overweight women appeared to be more disadvantaged as dating partners compared to men, whose weight seems to be of less consequence in dating relationships. For example, men are more likely than women to evaluate an obese romantic partner as undesirable compared to a non-obese partner, and obese women (but not men) are perceived as being less sexually attractive, skilled, warm, and responsive (Regan 1996). In research examining the quality of romantic relationship among dating and married couples, heavier women report lower relationship satisfaction, are more likely to predict that their relationship will end, and are judged by their male partners to be low in attractiveness and a poor match to their partner's attractiveness ideals. In contrast, men's body mass index is not related to these aspects of relationship functioning (Sheets and Ajmere 2005).

Family members and friends can also be sources of harmful weight stigma. In a study that examined experiences of weight stigma among over 2,400 overweight and obese women, family members were the most frequent source of weight stigma, reported by 72 percent of participants (Puhl and Brownell 2006). When participants were asked about experiences of weight stigmatization from specific family members, they reported being stigmatized about their weight by mothers (53 percent), fathers (44 percent), sisters (37 percent), brothers (36 percent), sons (20 percent), and daughters (18 percent). Common forms of weight bias from family members included weight-based teasing, name calling, and inappropriate, pejorative comments. Friends were also common sources of weight bias, reported by 60 percent of participants, as were spouses (47 percent) (Puhl and Brownell 2006).

These findings support research with national data sets documenting that severely obese individuals report more relationship strain and less support from family members compared to thinner peers (Carr and Friedman 2006), and other research demonstrating a positive association between BMI and loneliness, even after controlling for age, gender, annual income, employment and marital status (Lauder et al. 2006). However, despite these findings, other studies have found no differences across BMI categories in self-reported quality of relationships with friends and spouses, and suggest that obese and non-obese persons report similar levels of social skills, social support, subjective well-being, size of social networks and socially based self-esteem (Sarlio-Lahteenkorva 2001; Miller et al. 1995). Thus, additional research is needed to understand the extent of weight bias in interpersonal relationships and its impact on relationship functioning, satisfaction, and emotional well-being.

Media

The media is a particularly pervasive source of weight-based stereotypes and stigmatization of obese individuals. In television and film, overweight characters appear much less frequently than thinner (and often underweight) characters who dominate central roles. When they are portrayed, overweight characters are often depicted in stereotypical roles, as the target of humor and ridicule, engaging in unhealthy eating behaviors, and rarely engaging in positive romantic and social relationships (Greenberg et al. 2003). Content analyses of prime-time television shows and popular films demonstrate that weight stigmatization and humor are often directed against overweight characters, and that the heavier a female character is, the more negative comments she receives from male characters (Himes and Thompson 2007).

Content analyses of children's media show a similar pattern. In children's cartoons, socially desirable traits are ascribed to thin characters, and undesirable traits are associated with overweight characters, who are often portrayed as being unattractive, unintelligent, unhappy, eating junk food, and engaging in physical aggression (Klein and Shiffman 2005). In children's television shows and videos, overweight characters are more likely to be portrayed as unattractive, unfriendly, evil, and having no friends compared to thinner characters, who are depicted as having desirable traits such as sociability, kindness, happiness, and success (Herbozo et al. 2004; Robinson et al. 2008). Exposure to these negative messages in the media may reinforce bias among youth, as some research has found that media exposure is significantly associated with stigmatizing attitudes toward obese youth, and that television viewing predicts and increases the likelihood of boys stereotyping overweight females (Harrison 2000; Latner et al. 2007).

News media may also reinforce weight-based stereotypes and stigma. A number of studies demonstrate that the news media often frame obesity in terms of personal responsibility and emphasizes individual-level causes and solutions for obesity (Kim and Willis 2007; Lawrence 2004). Although news coverage of obesity has increased substantially in recent years, the coverage of individual causes and solutions significantly outnumber other societal and environmental contributors to obesity (Kim and Willis 2007). As a result, the focus on personal responsibility overshadows other important causes of the obesity epidemic, and easily leads to blame of obese individuals and public perceptions that obesity is simply a matter of personal willpower, potentially reinforcing weight bias. Experimental research additionally suggests that photographs of obese persons that accompany news stories on obesity can lead to negative attitudes toward obese persons, even if the content of the news story itself is neutral (McClure, Puhl, and Heuer, in press).

Despite an increased understanding of the complex etiology of obesity within the scientific and public health communities, news coverage of obesity continues to emphasize solutions that remain within the individual, and rarely discusses the implications of these viewpoints on the quality of life for those affected by obesity. The emphasis on individual-level causes and solutions for obesity may also contribute to the plethora of news stories emerging which have reported that obese people are partially to blame for rising fuel prices, global warming, and causing weight gain in their friends, among other adverse outcomes (e.g., Sawer 2008). The role of these media reports (in addition to popular television shows and films) in shaping social norms and negative attitudes cannot be underestimated, and with such high levels of media consumption in North America, it is no surprise that stigmatization of obese persons occurs with such frequency.

CONSEQUENCES OF WEIGHT BIAS

Given the pervasiveness of weight bias in multiple domains of living, the impact of stigma is significant and far-reaching, with both short-term and potentially long-term consequences for well-being and quality of life. These consequences include adverse outcomes for emotional functioning, social well-being, physical health, and even public health efforts to address obesity.

Emotional Consequences

Not surprisingly, weight bias takes a considerable toll on emotional health. Among both clinical and non-clinical samples of obese adults and children, weight bias increases risk of depression, anxiety, low self-esteem, and body dissatisfaction. Importantly, these findings remain despite controlling for BMI and other variables like age, gender, obesity onset (Eisenberg et al. 2003; Friedman et al. 2005, 2008; Haines et al. 2006; Hayden-Wade et al. 2005). Thus, negative psychological consequences are associated with experiences of weight stigma rather than obesity or body weight per se. Recent research with a nationally representative sample of over 9,000 obese adults has additionally demonstrated that perceived weight discrimination is significantly associated with a current diagnosis of mood and anxiety disorders as well as utilization of mental health services, after controlling for sociodemographic characteristics and perceived stress (Hatzenbuehler, Keyes, and Hasin 2009).

Unfortunately, children appear to be especially vulnerable to the negative emotional consequences of weight stigma. Research indicates that overweight youth who are teased about their weight are two to three times more likely than overweight peers who are not teased to engage in suicidal thoughts and behaviors (Eisenberg, Neumark-Sztainer, and Story 2003). One study found that 51 percent of girls who reported weight-based teasing from peers and family members had suicidal thoughts, compared to 25 percent of those who had not been teased (Neumark-Sztainer et al. 2002). Among boys, 13 percent who reported weight-based teasing from family members reported attempting suicide compared to 4 percent who were not teased (Neumark-Sztainer et al. 2002). Other work suggests that body mass index and self-perceptions of being overweight are positively associated with suicidal ideation among white, Hispanic, and black youth (Eaton et al. 2005).

The impact of stigma on quality of life and the vulnerability of children to these consequences are of considerable concern. One study found that compared to non-obese children, obese youth displayed significantly lower health-related quality of life on multiple areas, including physical health, psychosocial health, emotional and social well-being, and school functioning (Schwimmer, Burwinkle, and Varni 2003). Findings of this study also indicated that obese children had quality of life scores comparable to children with cancer.

Physical Health Consequences

In recent years, there has been increasing attention to the negative impact of weight bias on physical health behaviors. This work shows that weight bias increases risk for unhealthy eating behaviors, avoidance of physical activity, and poorer outcomes in weight loss treatment, all of which may ultimately reinforce obesity and weight gain.

One of the most consistent findings is that individuals who are targets of weight bias are much more likely to engage in unhealthy eating patterns. Among children, several studies show that overweight youth who are teased about their weight are more likely to engage in binge-eating and unhealthy weight control behaviors compared to overweight peers who are not teased, even after controlling for variables like BMI and socioeconomic status (SES) (Ashmore et al. 2008; Haines et al. 2006; Neumark-Sztainer et al. 2002; Friedman, Ashmore and Applegate 2008). Prospective research additionally shows that weight-based teasing predicts binge-eating and extreme weight-control practices five years later, after controlling for variables like age, race, and SES (Haines et al. 2006). There are also a number of studies that have found positive correlations between weight-based teasing and bulimia and other eating disorder symptoms (Fairburn et al. 1998; Striegel-Moore et al. 2002; Thompson et al. 1995).

Among adults, the same pattern has emerged in both clinical and non-clinical samples, where those who report weight-based stigma engage in more frequent binge-eating behaviors, are more likely to be diagnosed with binge eating disorder, and are more likely to have maladaptive eating patterns and eating disorder symptoms (Grilo and Masheb 2005; Jackson, Grilo, and Masheb 2000). It may be that experiences of stigma lead to psychological distress, which in turn increases vulnerability of binge-eating patterns, or that individuals who internalize negative weight-based stigma are more vulnerable to binge-eating patterns (Puhl, Moss-Racusin, and Schwartz 2007). Stigma-induced psychological stress may also lead to maladaptive coping strategies that reinforce unhealthy eating behaviors. For example, in a sample of over 2,400 overweight and obese women, 79 percent reported that they coped with weight stigma on multiple occasions by eating more food, and 75 percent reported coping by refusing to diet (Puhl and Brownell 2006).

Although few studies have examined the impact of weight bias on physical activity behaviors, the same findings are emerging. Among overweight youth, weight-based teasing has been linked to lower levels of physical activity, negative attitudes about sports, and less participation in physical activity (Bauer et al. 2004; Faith et al. 2002; Storch et al. 2007). It may be that avoidance of physical activities and physical education classes is likely due to the amount of weight-based teasing that overweight students experience in these settings. Among adults, recent research shows that adults who report experiences of weight stigma are more likely to avoid exercise, and have less motivation for exercise, even after controlling for BMI and body dissatisfaction (Seacat and Mickelson 2009; Vartanian and Shaprow 2008).

A critical question to address is whether experiences of weight bias may affect weight loss treatment outcomes. This area of research remains in its infancy. Findings of one study showed that among overweight and obese women participating in a weight loss support organization, experiencing weight stigma did not predict adoption of weight loss strategies (Puhl et al. 2007). Other work found that weight stigmatization was related to greater caloric intake, higher program attrition, lower energy expenditure, less exercise, and less weight loss among treatment-seeking overweight and obese adults who participated in a behavioral weight loss program (Carels et al. 2009). Finally, one study showed that stigmatizing experiences (as well as higher initial BMI, low body dissatisfaction, and greater fear of fat) were related to weight loss among adults participating in a stringent behavior modification program (Latner et al. 2009). However, the authors cautiously interpret their findings because the treatment model required participants to lose a prescribed amount of weight each month or face dismissal from the program, which is not typical for the vast majority of weight loss treatment programs (Latner et al. 2009) The unusual treatment model and concurrent assessment of variables raise uncertainty about these findings. With so little research in this area, much more work is needed to assess the potential adverse impact of weight stigma on weight loss outcomes.

Finally, experiencing weight bias may have negative implications for health-seeking behaviors and health care utilization. A number of studies have consistently demonstrated that obese adults (especially women) are less likely to seek preventive health care services, such as mammograms, pelvic exams, and cancer screenings, even after controlling for variables such as education, lower income, lack of health insurance, and greater illness burden (Ostbye et al. 2005; Wee et al. 2000, 2004, 2005). It is possible that weight bias may play a contributing role in decisions to avoid or delay health care. In one study, 498 overweight and obese women (with health insurance and high access to health care) were surveyed about their perceived barriers to routine gynecological cancer screenings (Amy et al. 2006). Among the heaviest women, 68 percent reported delaying health care services because of their weight. When participants were asked why they delayed care, women reported disrespectful treatment and negative attitudes from providers, embarrassment about being weighed, receiving unsolicited advice to lose weight, and reporting that gowns, exam tables, and other medical equipment were too small to be functional for their body size. The percentage of women reporting these as barriers to health care increased with BMI (Amy et al. 2006).

Public Health Consequences

In the field of public health, there is a long-standing and broad recognition of the obstacles created by disease stigma, both for people who suffer from a stigmatized disease, and as barriers to effective treatment (Link and Phelan 2006). In the case of HIV/AIDS, the negative impact of stigma was so apparent that national health agendas identified stigma as a significant barrier in efforts to address the epidemic, and public health policies and national funding targeted reduction of HIV stigma and discrimination (Mann and Tarantola 1998). Despite numerous historical examples that stigma undermines public health, this principle has not been applied to the obesity epidemic, and the stigma of obesity has been primarily ignored in the context of public health (Puhl and Heuer 2010). This omission persists in the face of five decades of research documenting bias and discrimination against overweight and obese persons, and in spite of the significant increase in the prevalence of obesity during this time period.

Lack of attention to the stigma of obesity in public health efforts may be due, in part, to societal constructions of body weight that can affect societal reactions to obesity. There are widespread societal perceptions that obese individuals are at fault for their excess weight, and thus deserving of blame, which often reinforces stigmatization and disregard of stigma and its implications for health (Crandall 1994; Crandall and Reser 2005; Crandall and Schiffhauer 1998, Dejong 1980, 1993; Puhl, Schwartz and Brownell 2005). Although considerable scientific evidence has emerged to challenge these assumptions, demonstrating the complex etiology of obesity and the challenge of achieving significant long-term weight loss (see Puhl and Heuer 2010), societal perceptions that obesity is a simple matter of willpower or self-discipline persist.

As a result, national approaches to obesity primarily address individual behavior and nutrition education, reinforcing notions of personal responsibility as the primary cause of obesity (Brownell et al. 2010). In addition, prevention and intervention efforts often ignore weight stigma and its consequences for obese children and adults, and federal and state legislative initiatives related to obesity have largely avoided the broader societal and environmental conditions that have created obesity in the first place (Puhl and Heuer 2010). Certainly, more recent efforts are beginning to address environmental contributors to obesity (such as policies aimed at improving school foods, enacting menu labeling legislation, and taxing sugar-sweetened beverages), but much work remains to be done to ensure that obesity is addressed commensurate to its impact and that stigma receives legitimate recognition on the public health agenda. Without such recognition, it is likely that stigmatization of obese individuals will continue to pose serious risks to their emotional and physical health, generate health disparities, and interfere with effective obesity prevention efforts.

Conclusions

Weight bias is a significant social problem and has a detrimental impact on quality of life for those affected. Unfortunately, despite ample documentation of weight bias in the literature, the amount of research testing strategies to reduce weight bias pales in comparison. To date, the limited research assessing stigma reduction strategies in this area have employed different measures, intervention methods, samples, and have primarily relied on short-term assessment of attitude change, with little attention to whether interventions can affect behavioral changes. These limitations make it difficult to draw clear conclusions about what types of strategies might be most effective in reducing weight bias among different groups in the population. Thus, additional systematic research to identify effective stigma-reduction methods is critical to move this field forward.

As public health efforts continue to prioritize obesity prevention and treatment on the national agenda, it will be essential for efforts to address the adverse consequences of weight bias on the lives of overweight and obese persons, and to ensure that interventions include comprehensive strategies to address stigma and discrimination. This requires non-stigmatizing messages in obesity interventions, promotion of weight tolerance, policies that prohibit weight-based discrimination, stigma-reduction training for health professionals and educators, and evaluation of the impact of existing interventions on stigma. Larger-scale efforts are also needed to challenge existing societal assumptions about body weight and obesity that perpetuate stigma, and to consider legislative measures that can protect obese individuals from discrimination that is currently so normative in their daily lives.

REFERENCES

Amy, Nancy K., Annette Aalborg, Patricia Lyons, and L. Keranen. 2006. "Barriers to Routine Gynecological Cancer Screening for White and African-American Obese Women." *International Journal of Obesity* 30: 147–155.

Anderson, D. A., and Thomas A. Wadden. 2004. "Bariatric Surgery Patients' Views of their Physicians: Weight-Related Attitudes and Practices." *Obesity Research* 12: 1587–1595.

Andreyeva, Tatiana, Rebecca. M. Puhl, and Kelly D. Brownell. 2008. "Changes in Perceived Weight Discrimination among Americans: 1995–1996 through 2004–2006." *Obesity* 16: 1129–1134.

Ashmore, J. A., K. E. Friedman, S. K. Reichmann, and G. J. Musante. 2008. "Weight-based Stigmatization, Psychological Distress, and Binge Eating Behavior among Obese Treatment-Seeking Adults." *Eating Behaviors* 9: 203–209.

Bauer, K. W., Y. W. Yang, and S. B. Austin. 2004. "'How Can We Stay Healthy When You're Throwing All of This in Front of Us?' Findings From Focus Groups and Interviews in Middle Schools on Environmental Influences on Nutrition and Physical Activity." *Health Education and Behavior* 31: 34–46.

Baum, C. L., and W. F. Ford. 2004. "The Wage Effects Of Obesity: A Longitudinal Study." *Health Economics* 13: 885–899.

Berryman, D., G. Dubale, D. Manchester, and R. Mittelstaedt. 2006. "Dietetic Students Possess Negative Attitudes toward Obesity Similar to Nondietetic Students." *Journal of the American Dietetic Association* 106: 1678–1682.

Bertakis, K. D., and R. Azari. 2005. "The Impact of Obesity on Primary Care Visits." *Obesity Research* 13: 1615–1622.

Bocquier, A., P. Verger, A. Basdevant, et al. 2005. "Overweight and Obesity: Knowledge, Attitudes, and Practices of General Practitioners in France." *Obesity Research* 13: 787–795.

Boyes, A. D., and J. D. Latner. 2009. "Weight Stigma in Existing Romantic Relationships." *Journal of Sex and Marital Therapy* 35(4): 282–293.

Brown, I. 2006. "Nurses' Attitudes towards Adult Patients Who Are Obese: Literature Review." *Journal of Advanced Nursing* 53: 221–232.

Brownell, Kelly D., Rogan Kersh, David S. Ludwig, Robert C. Post, Rebecca M. Puhl, Marlene B. Schwartz, and Walter C. Willet. 2010. "Personal Responsibility and Obesity: A Constructive Approach to a Controversial Issue." *Health Affairs* 29: 379–387.

Brownell, Kelly D., Rebecca M. Puhl, Marlene B. Schwartz, and Leslie Rudd, eds. 2005. *Weight Bias: Nature, Consequences, and Remedies*. New York: The Guilford Press.

Campbell, K., H. Engel, A. Timperio, C. Cooper, D. Crawford. 2000. "Obesity Management: Australian General Practitioners' Attitudes and Practices." *Obesity Research* 8: 459–466.

Carels, Robert A., K. M. Young, C. B. Wott, J. Harper, A. Gumble, M. W. Oehlof, and A. M. Clayton. 2009. "Weight Bias and Weight Loss Treatment Outcomes in Treatment-Seeking Adults." *Annals of Behavioral Medicine* 37(3): 350–355.

Carr, Deborah, and Michael A. Friedman. 2005. "Is Obesity Stigmatizing? Body Weight, Perceived Discrimination, and Psychological Well-Being in the United States." *Journal of Health and Social Behavior* 46, 244–259.

Carr, Deborah, and Michael A. Friedman. 2006. "Body Weight and the Quality of Interpersonal Relationships." *Social Psychology Quarterly* 69: 127–149.

Cawley, John. 2004. "The Impact of Obesity on Wages." *The Journal of Human Resources* 39: 451–474.

Chambliss, Heather O., C. E. Finley, and Steven N. Blair. 2004. "Attitudes toward Obese Individuals among Exercise Science Students." *Medicine and Science in Sports and Exercise* 36(3): 468–474.

Chen, Eunice Y., and M. Brown. 2005. "Obesity Stigma in Sexual Relationships." *Obesity Research* 13: 1393–1397.

Cramer, P., and T. Steinwert. 1998. "Thin Is Good, Fat Is Bad: How Early Does It Begin?" *Journal of Applied Developmental Psychology* 19: 429–451.

Crandall, Christian S. 1994. "Prejudice against Fat People: Ideology and Self-interest." *Journal of Personality and Social Psychology* 66: 882–894.

Crandall, Christian S., and A. H. Reser. 2005. "Attributions and Weight-Based Prejudice." In *Weight Bias: Nature, Consequences, and Remedies*, eds. K. D. Brownell, R. M. Puhl, M. B. Schwartz, and L. Rudd. New York: Guilford Press.

Crandall, Christian S., and K. L. Schiffhauer. 1998. "Anti-fat Prejudice: Beliefs, Values, and American Culture." *Obesity Research* 6: 458–460.

DeJong, W. 1980. "The Stigma of Obesity: The Consequences of Naive Assumptions Concerning the Causes of Physical Deviance." *Journal of Health and Social Behavior* 21(1): 75–87.

DeJong, W. 1993. "Obesity as a Characterological Stigma: The Issue of Responsibility and Judgements of Task Performance." *Psychological Reports* 73: 963–970.

Eaton, D. K., R. Lowry, N. D. Brener, D. A. Galuska, and A. E. Crosby. 2005. "Associations of Body Mass Index and Perceived Weight with Suicide Ideation and Suicide Attempts among US High School Students." *Archives of Pediatric and Adolescent Medicine* 159: 513–519.

Eisenberg, M. E., D. Neumark-Sztainer, and M. Story. 2003. "Associations of Weight-Based Teasing and Emotional Well-Being among Adolescents." *Archives of Pediatric Adolescent Medicine* 157: 733–738.

Fairburn, C. G., H. A. Doll, S. L. Welch, P. J. Hay, B. A. Davies, and M. E. O'Connor. 1998. "Risk Factors for Binge Eating Disorder: A Community-Based, Case-Control Study." *Archives of General Psychiatry* 55: 425–432.

Faith, Myles S., M. A. Leone, T. S. Ayers, H. Moonseong, and A. Pietrobelli. 2002. "Weight Criticism during Physical Activity, Coping Skills, and Reported Physical Activity in Children." *Pediatrics* 110 (2 pt 1): e23.

Falkner, N. H., D. Neumark-Sztainer, M. Story, R. W. Jeffery, T. Beuhring, and M. D. Resnick. 2001. "Social, Educational, and Psychological Correlates of Weight Status in Adolescents." *Obesity Research* 9: 32–42.

Ferrante, J. M., A. K. Piasecki, P. A. Ohman-Strickland, and B. F. Crabtree. 2009. "Family Physicians' Practices and Attitudes Regarding Care of Extremely Obese Patients." *Obesity* 17: 1710–1716.

Fogelman, Y., S. Vinker, J. Lachter, et al. 2002. "Managing Obesity: A Survey of Attitudes and Practices among Israeli Primary Care Physicians." *International Journal of Obesity* 26: 1393–1397.

Friedman, Kelli E., J. A. Ashmore, and K. L. Applegate. 2008. "Recent Experiences of Weight-Based Stigmatization in a Weight Loss Surgery Population: Psychological and Behavioral Correlates." *Obesity* 16: S69–S74.

Friedman, Kelli E., S. K. Reichmann, P. R. Costanzo, A. Zelli, J. A. Ashmore, and G. J. Musante. 2005. "Weight Stigmatization and Ideological Beliefs: Relation to Psychological Functioning in Obese Adults." *Obesity Research* 13: 907–916.

Gortmaker, S. L., A. Must, J. M. Perrin, A. M. Sobol, and W. H. Dietz. 1993. "Social and Economic Consequences of Overweight in Adolescence and Young Adulthood." *New England Journal of Medicine* 399: 1008–1012.

Greenberg, B. S., M. Eastin, L. Hofshire, K. Lachlan, and K. D. Brownell. 2003. "The Portrayal of Overweight and Obese Persons in Commercial Television." *American Journal of Public Health* 93 (8): 1342–1348.

Greenleaf, C., H. O. Chambliss, D. J. Rhea, S. B. Martin, and J. R. Morrow. 2006. "Weight Stereotypes and Behavioral Intentions Toward Thin And Fat Peers among White And Hispanic Adolescents." *Journal of Adolescent Health* 39: 546–552.

Greenleaf, C., and K. Weiller. 2005. "Perceptions of Youth Obesity among Physical Educators." *Social Psychology of Education* 8: 407–423.

Griffiths, L. J., D. Wolke, A. S. Page, J. P. Horwood, and ALSPAC Study Team. 2006. "Obesity and Bullying: Different Effects for Boys and Girls." *Archives of Disease in Childhood* 91: 121–125.

Grilo, Carlos M., and Robin M. Masheb. 2005. "Correlates of Body Image Dissatisfaction in Treatment-Seeking Men and Women with Binge Eating Disorder." *International Journal of Eating Disorders* 38 (2): 162–166.

Grilo, C. M., D. E. Wilfley, K. D. Brownell, and J. Rodin. 1994. "Teasing, Body Image, and Self-Esteem in a Clinical Sample of Obese Women." *Addictive Behaviors* 19: 443–450.

Haines, Jessica, Diane Neumark-Sztainer, Marla E. Eisenberg, and P. J. Hannan. 2006. "Weight Teasing and Disordered Eating Behaviors in Adolescents: Longitudinal Findings from Project EAT (Eating Among Teens)." *Pediatrics* 117: 209–215.

Harrison, K. 2000. "Television Viewing, Fat Stereotyping, Body Shape Standards, and Eating Disorder Symptomatology in Grade School Children." *Communication Research* 27: 617–640.

Hatzenbuehler, Mark L., K. M. Keyes, and D. S. Hasin. 2009. "Associations between Perceived Weight Discrimination and the Prevalence of Psychiatric Disorders in the General Population." *Obesity* 17(11): 2033–2039.

Hayden-Wade, H. A., R. I. Stein, A. Ghaderi, B. E. Saelens, M. F. Zabinski, and D. E. Wilfey. 2005. "Prevalence, Characteristics, and Correlates of Teasing Experiences among Overweight Children vs. Non-Overweight Peers." *Obesity Research* 13: 1381–1392.

Hebl, Michelle R., and J. Xu. 2001. "Weighing the Care: Physicians' Reactions to the Size of a Patient." *International Journal of Obesity* 25: 1246–1252.

Hebl, M. R., J. Xu, and M. F. Mason. 2003. "Weighing the Care: Patients' Perceptions of Physician Care as a Function of Gender and Weight." *International Journal of Obesity* 27: 269–275.

Herbozo, S., S., Tantleff-Dunn, J. Gokee-Larose, and J. K. Thompson. 2004. "Beauty and Thinness Messages in Children's Media: A Content Analysis." *Eating Disorders* 12: 21–34.

Himes, S. M., and J. K. Thompson. 2007. "Fat Stigmatization in Television Shows and Movies: A Content Analysis." *Obesity* 15: 712–718.

Huizinga, Mary M., Lisa A. Cooper, Sara N. Bleich, Jeanne M. Clark, and Mary C. Beach. 2009. "Physician Respect for Patients with Obesity." *Journal of General Internal Medicine,* 24, 1236–9.

Jackson, T.D., Carlos M. Grilo, and Robin M. Masheb. 2000. "Teasing History, Onset of Obesity, Current Eating Disorder Psychopathology, Body Dissatisfaction, and Psychological Functioning in Binge Eating Disorder." *Obesity Research* 8: 451–458.

Janssen, I., W. M. Craig, W. F. Boyce, and W. Pickett. 2004. "Associations between Overweight and Obesity and Bullying Behaviors in School-Aged Children." *Pediatrics* 113: 1187–1193.

Karnehed, N., F. Rasmussen, T. Hemmingsson, and P. Tynelius. 2006. "Obesity and Attained Education: Cohort Study of More Than 700,000 Swedish Men." *Obesity* 14: 1421–1428.

Keery, H., K. Boutelle, P. van den Berg, and J. K. Thompson. 2005. "The Impact of Appearance-Related Teasing by Family Members." *Journal of Adolescent Health* 37: 120–127.

Kim, S.-H., and L. A. Willis. 2007. "Talking about Obesity: News Framing of Who Is Responsible for Causing and Fixing the Problem." *Journal of Health Communication* 12: 359–376.

Klassen, M. L., C. R. Jasper, and R. J. Harris. 1993. "The Role of Physical Appearance in Managerial Decisions." *Journal of Business Psychology* 8: 181–198.

Klein, H., and K. S. Shiffman. 2005. "Thin Is 'In' and Stout Is 'Out': What Animated Cartoons Tell Viewers about Body Weight." *Eating and Weight Disorders* 10: 107–116.

Kraig, K. A., and P. K. Keel. 2001. "Weight-based Stigmatization in Children." *International Journal of Obesity* 25: 1661–1666.

Kristeller, J. L., and R. A. Hoerr. 1997. "Physician Attitudes toward Managing Obesity: Differences among Six Specialty Groups." *Preventive Medicine* 26: 542–549.

Krukowski, Rebecca A., Delia. Smith West, Amanda Philyaw Perez, Z. Bursac, M. M. Phillips, and J. M. Raczynski. 2009. "Overweight Children, Weight-Based Teasing and Academic Performance." *International Journal of Pediatric Obesity* 4 (4): 274–280.

Larkin, J. C., and H. A. Pines. 1979. "No Fat Persons Need Apply: Experimental Studies of the Overweight Stereotype and Hiring Preference." *Sociology of Work and Occupations* 6: 312–327.

Latner, Janet D., J. K. Rosewall, and M. B. Simmonds. 2007. "Childhood Obesity Stigma: Association with Television, Videogame, and Magazine Exposure." *Body Image* 4: 147–155.

Latner, Janet D., and A. J. Stunkard. 2003. "Getting Worse: The Stigmatization of Obese Children." *Obesity Research* 11: 452–456.

Latner, Janet D., G. T. Wilson, M. L. Jackson, and A. J. Stunkard. 2009. "Greater History of Weight-Related Stigmatizing Experience Is Associated with Greater Weight Loss in Obesity Treatment." *Journal of Health Psychology* 24: 190–199.

Lauder, W., K. Mummery, M. Jones, and C. Caperchione. 2006. "A Comparison of Health Behaviors in Lonely and Non-Lonely Populations." *Psychology, Health and Medicine* 11: 233–245.

Lawrence, R. G. 2004. "Framing Obesity: The Evolution of News Discourse on a Public Health Issue." *The International Journal of Press/Politics* 9: 56–75.

Link, B. G., and J. C. Phelan. 2006. "Stigma and Its Public Health Implications." *Lancet* 367: 528–529.

Mann, J., and D. Tarantola. 1998. "Responding to HIV/AIDS: A Historical Perspective." *Health and Human Rights* 2: 5–8.

Maranto, C. L., and A. F. Stenoien. 2000. "Weight Discrimination: A Multidisciplinary Analysis." *Employee Responsibilities and Rights Journal* 12: 9–24.

McClure, Kimberly, Rebecca M. Puhl, and Chelsea Heuer. In press. "Obesity in the News: Do Photographic Images of Obese Persons Influence Anti-fat Attitudes?" *Journal of Health Communication*.

Miller, C. T., E. D. Rothblum, P. A. Brand, and D. Felicio. 1995. "Do Obese Women Have Poorer Social Relationships Than Nonobese Women? Reports by Self, Friends, and Co-Workers." *Journal of Personality* 63: 65–85.

Neumark-Sztainer, Diane, Mary Story, and L. Faibisch. 1998. "Perceived Stigmatization among Overweight African-American and Caucasian Adolescent Girls." *Journal of Adolescent Health* 23: 264–270.

Neumark-Sztainer, Diane, Mary Story, and T. Harris. 1999. "Beliefs and Attitudes about Obesity among Teachers and School Health Care Providers Working with Adolescents." *Journal of Nutrition Educucation* 31: 3–9.

Neumark-Sztainer, Diane, N. Falkner, Mary Story, C. Perry, P. J. Hannan, and S. Mulert. 2002. "Weight-teasing among Adolescents: Correlations with Weight Status and Disordered Eating Behaviors." *International Journal of Obesity* 26: 123–131.

O'Brien, Kerry S., J. A. Hunter, and M. Banks. 2006. "Implicit Anti-Fat Bias in Physical Educators: Physical Attributes, Ideology, and Socialization." *International Journal of Obesity* 31: 308–314.

Ostbye, T., D. H. Taylor, W. S. Yancy, and K. M. Krause. 2005. "Associations between Obesity and Receipt of Screening Mammography, Papanicolaou Tests, and Influenza Vaccination: Results from the Health and Retirement Study (HRS) and the Asset and Health Dynamics among the Oldest Old (AHEAD) Study." *American Journal of Public Health* 95: 1623–1630.

Pingitoire, R., R. Dugoni, S. Tindale, and B. Spring. 1994. "Bias against Overweight Job Applicants in a Simulated Employment Interview." *Journal of Applied Psychology* 79: 909–917.

Pomeranz, Jennifer L. 2008. "A Historical Analysis of Public Health, the Law, and Stigmatized Social Groups: The Need for Both Obesity and Weight Bias Legislation." *Obesity* 16: S93–S102.

Popovich, P. M., W. J. Everton, K. L. Campbell, et al. 1997. "Criteria Used to Judge Obese Persons in the Workplace." *Perceptual and Motor Skills* 85: 859–866.

Price, J. H., S. M. Desmond, R. A. Krol, F. F. Snyder, and J. K. O'Connell. 1987. "Family Practice Physicians' Beliefs, Attitudes, and Practices Regarding Obesity." *American Journal of Preventive Medicine* 3: 339–345.

Puhl, Rebecca M., Tatiana Andreyeva, and Kelly D. Brownell. 2008. "Perceptions of Weight Discrimination: Prevalence and Comparison to Race and Gender Discrimination in America." *International Journal of Obesity* 32: 992–1000.

Puhl, Rebecca M., and Kelly D. Brownell. 2001. "Bias, Discrimination, and Obesity." *Obesity Research* 9(12): 788–905.

Puhl, Rebecca M., and Kelly D. Brownell. 2006. "Confronting and Coping with Weight Stigma: An Investigation of Overweight and Obese Adults." *Obesity* 14(10): 1802–1815.

Puhl, Rebecca M., and Chelsea A. Heuer. 2009. "The Stigma of Obesity: A Review and Update." *Obesity* 17: 941–964.

Puhl, R. M., and Heuer, C.A. (2010). Obesity stigma: Important considerations for public health. *American Journal of Public Health,* 100, 1019–1028.

Puhl, Rebecca M., and Janet D. Latner. 2007. "Stigma, Obesity, and the Health of the Nation's Children." *Psychological Bulletin* 133: 557–580.

Puhl, Rebecca M., Corrine A. Moss-Racusin, and Marlene B. Schwartz. 2007. "Internalization of Weight Bias: Implications for Binge Eating and Emotional Well-Being." *Obesity* 15(1): 19–23.

Puhl, Rebecca M., Marlene B. Schwartz, and Kelly D. Brownell. 2005. "Impact of Perceived Consensus on Stereotypes about Obese People: A New Approach for Reducing Bias." *Health Psychology* 24: 517–525.

Regan, P. C. 1996. "Sexual Outcasts: The Perceived Impact of Body Weight and Gender on Sexuality." *Journal of Applied Social Psychology* 26: 1803–1815.

Robinson, T., M. Callister, and T. Jankoski. 2008. "Portrayal of Body Weight on Children's Television Sitcoms: A Content Analysis." *Body Image* 5: 141–151.

Roehling, Mark V. 1999. "Weight-Based Discrimination in Employment: Psychological and Legal Aspects." *Personnel Psychology* 52: 969–1017.

Roehling, Mark V. 2002. "Weight Discrimination in the American Workplace: Ethical Issues and Analysis." *Journal of Business Ethics* 40: 177–189.

Roehling, Mark V., P. V. Roehling, and L. M. Odland. 2008. "Investigating the Validity of Stereotypes about Overweight Employees: The Relationship between Body Weight and Normal Personality Traits." *Group and Organization Management* 33: 392–424.

Roehling, Mark V., P. V. Roehling, and S. Pichler. 2007. "The Relationship between Body Weight and Perceived Weight-Related Employment Discrimination: The Role of Sex and Race." *Journal of Vocational Behavior* 71: 300–318.

Rudolph, Cort W, Charles L, Wells, Marcus D. Weller, and Boris B. Baltes. 2009. "A Meta-Analysis of Empirical Studies of Weight-Based Bias in the Workplace." *Journal of Vocational Behavior* 74(1): 1–10.

Sarlio-Lahteenkorva, S. 2001. "Weight Loss and Quality of Life among Obese People." *Social Indicators Research* 54: 329–354.

Sartore, M. L., and G. B. Cunningham. 2006. "Weight Discrimination, Hiring Recommendations, Person-Job Fit and Attributions: Implications for the Fitness Industry." *Journal of Sport Management* 21: 172–193.

Sawer, Patrick. 2008. *Fat People Blamed for Global Warming* [Online article]. July 19. Available from http://www.telegraph.co.uk/news/1973230/Fat-people-blamed-for-global-warming.html.

Schwartz, Marlene B., Heather O. Chambliss, Kelly D. Brownell, S. N. Blair, and C. Billington. 2003. "Weight Bias among Health Professionals Specializing in Obesity." *Obesity Research* 11(9): 1033–1039.

Schwimmer, J.B., Burwinkle, T.M., and Varni, J.W. 2003 Health-Related Quality of Life of Severely Obese Children and Adolescents *Journal of the American Medical Association*, 289, 1813–1819.

Seacat, Jason D., and Kristin D. Mickelson. 2009. "Stereotype Threat and the Exercise/Dietary Health Intentions of Overweight Women." *Journal of Health Psychology* 14: 556–567.

Sheets, V, and K. Ajmere. 2005. "Are Romantic Partners a Source of College Students' Weight Concern?" *Eating Behaviors* 6: 1–9.

Smith, C. A., K. Schmoll, J. Konik, and S. Oberlander. 2007. "Carrying Weight for the World: Influence of Weight Descriptors on Judgments of Large-Sized Women." *Journal of Applied Social Psychology* 37: 989–1006.

Storch, E. A., V. A. Milsom, N. DeBraganza, A. B. Lewin, G. R. Geffken, and J. H. Silverstein. 2007. "Peer Victimization, Psychosocial Adjustment, and Physical Activity in Overweight and at-Risk-for-Overweight Youth." *Journal of Pediatric Psychology* 32: 80–89.

Striegel-Moore, Ruth H., F. A. Dohm, K. M. Pike, D. E. Wilfley, and C. G. Fairburn. 2002. "Abuse, Bullying, and Discrimination as Risk Factors for Binge Eating Disorder." *American Journal of Psychiatry* 159: 1902–1907.

Teachman, Bethany A., and Kelly D. Brownell. 2001. "Implicit Anti-Fat Bias among Health Professionals: Is Anyone Immune?" *International Journal of Obesity* 25: 1525–1531.

Thompson, J. K., M. D. Coovert, K. J. Richards, S. Johnson, and J. Cattarin, 1995. "Development of Body Image, Eating Disturbance, and General Psychological Functioning in Female Adolescents: Covariance Structure Modeling and Longitudinal Investigations." *International Journal of Eating Disorders* 18: 221–236.

Vartanian, Lenny R., and J. G. Shaprow. 2008. "Effects of Weight Stigma on Exercise Motivation and Behavior: A Preliminary Investigation among College-aged Females". *Journal of Health Psychology* 13: 131–138.

Wardle, J., C. Volz, and C. Golding, C. 1995. "Social Variation in Attitudes to Obesity in Children." *International Journal of Obesity* 19: 562–569.

Wardle, J., C. Volz, and M. J. Jarvis. 2002. "Sex Differences in the Association of Socioeconomic Status with Obesity." *American Journal of Public Health* 92: 1299–1304.

Wee, C. C., E. P. McCarthy, R. B. Davis, and R. S. Phillips. 2000. "Screening for Cervical and Breast Cancer: Is Obesity an Unrecognized Barrier to Preventive Care?" *Annals of Internal Medicine* 132: 699–704.

Wee, C. C., E. P. McCarthy, R. B. Davis, and R. S. Phillips. 2004. "Obesity and Breast Cancer Screening: The Influence of Race, Illness Burden, and Other Factors." *Journal of General Internal Medicine* 19: 324–331.

Wee, C. C., R. S. Phillips, and E. P. McCarthy. 2005. "BMI and Cervical Cancer Screening among White, African American, and Hispanic Women in the United States." *Obesity Research* 13: 1275–1280.

Young, L. M., and B. Powell. 1985. "The Effects of Obesity on the Clinical Judgements of Mental Health Professionals." *Journal of Health and Social Behavior* 26: 233–246.

CHAPTER 34

....

MEDICAL AND SOCIAL SCIENTIFIC DEBATES OVER BODY WEIGHT

....

ABIGAIL C. SAGUY AND PAUL CAMPOS

MOST of social research on obesity takes for granted the idea that having a body mass index (BMI) greater than 30 (the official cut-off for "obesity") or even 25 (the current cut-off for "overweight") is by definition medically pathological. If one additionally considers that over 65 percent of Americans aged 25–59 had a BMI greater than 25 in 1999–2002 (Flegal et al. 2005), it is easy to see why many people are alarmed. Consistent with this framing, social scientific research typically seeks the causes of "obesity" and/or "overweight," or searches for ways to prevent or reduce these alleged medical problems. Reflecting these patterns, chapters in this volume search for the causes of "obesity" or focus on prevention and treatment and policy making designed to reduce the incidence of "obesity" and/or "overweight." Here, in this section of the Handbook on "The Consequences of Obesity," is the place to consider, or reconsider, the medical and social consequences of higher body mass. We have been asked to specifically address skepticism—as expressed by both medical researchers and social scientists—about the underlying medical risks of obesity and overweight.

Note that the terms "obesity" and "overweight" are not neutral but themselves serve to frame higher body mass as a medical problem (Saguy and Riley 2005).

In other words, simply by using the terms "obesity" and "overweight" we, in effect, presume what we are supposed to be questioning: that higher body mass not only correlates with ill health and early mortality but causes such negative health outcomes. This vocabulary itself thus creates a seeming paradox of the healthy "overweight" or "obese" individual. Similarly, a "Handbook of Social Science of Homosexuality" would be expected to consider same-sex desire as a form of mental illness, while a "Handbook of Social Science of Gay and Lesbian Identity and Behavior" would be more likely to embrace diversity in sexual orientation. (The equivalent of gay and lesbian studies in relation to body size is fat studies [Rothblum and Solovay 2009; Rothblum this volume].)

Yet unbeknownst to many in the general public, and even to social scientists, the assumption that having a BMI over 30 or 25 is *in itself* or *necessarily* a medical problem is contested among medical researchers. This is a point that social scientists typically bracket (i.e., they set aside the question of whether the phenomenon is real) but sometimes address head-on. The majority ignores or dismisses the skepticism, insisting that obesity is a major medical and/or public health crisis, often relying on this assertion as a mandate for their research on the contributors or possible response to obesity (e.g., Christakis and Fowler 2007; Crossley 2004; Yancey, Leslie, and Abel 2006). Other research brackets medical debates over the health risks associated with higher body mass in order to focus on the social processes through which "obesity" or "fat" has been framed as a social problem (Saguy and Almeling 2008; Saguy and Riley 2005) or as a policy issue (Barry et al. 2009; Kersh and Morone 2002). Similarly, feminist research, which has offered trenchant critiques of how the fashion industry contributes to a "cult of thinness" (Bordo 1993; Hesse-Biber 1996; Wolf 1991), has been surprisingly silent about both the rationale for and social consequences of medical guidelines about "overweight" and "obesity." However, some social science has sought to debunk the "obesity myth," while investigating political, social, and/or economic factors contributing to public understandings of obesity as a public health crisis of epidemic proportions (Campos 2004; Campos et al. 2006; Glassner 2007).

Each of these approaches has its promises and pitfalls. Social science asserting that higher body mass is a health and/or economic liability contributes to public debate over "obesity" as a public health crisis, but may become largely obsolete if it turns out that no public health crisis ensues as a result of rising body mass in the U.S. population. Moreover, if treating higher body weight as medically pathological reinforces weight-based stigma, this work may ironically have negative social as well as medical implications (see Muennig 2008; Puhl this volume). Bracketing scientific debates over the health risks of higher body mass offers a way to sidestep medical controversy in order to ask interesting social scientific questions. The absence of direct engagement with medical debates, however, leaves readers to rely on other sources—often the news media (Carlsson 2000; Nelkin 1987)—for information about medical risk. Social science that enters the fray of medical debates over the health risks associated with higher body mass is likely to meet with resistance from medical researchers and social scientists alike, as it challenges deeply held assumptions that justify research careers. Yet, social science offers important analytical tools for interrogating and explaining the social construction of scientific expertise, as well as examining its social consequences.

This chapter is organized around these three separate but related goals: (1) critiquing medical assumptions that higher body mass is necessarily and in and of itself unhealthy, (2) explaining the social processes that contribute to scientific and popular understandings of obesity as a medical problem and public health crisis, and (3) examining the social implications of reinforcing and legitimizing such assumptions. While far from an exhaustive or representative survey of this research, this chapter seeks to provide readers with a useful guide to this line of inquiry and thus a fuller understanding of the range of social science of obesity, including work that would not refer to higher body weight in terms of obesity at all.[1]

INTERROGATING MEDICAL CLAIMS

Social scientists have played an important role in bringing attention to medical debates about the health risks associated with higher body mass and in offering their own methodological critiques of some the extant research (Campos 2004; Campos et al. 2006; Oliver 2005). It is uncontested that the number of Americans with a BMI of 30 or higher increased between 1976–1980 and 1988–1994 (Flegal et al. 1998) and again between 1988–1994 and 1999–2000 (Flegal et al. 2002). Yet, despite predictions that this trend would continue unabated, the most recent data shows that the number of people with a BMI of 30 or higher seems to have largely stabilized between 1999 and 2008 (Flegal et al. 2010).

The importance of these trends for population health, however, depends on the extent to which higher body mass causes increased mortality and/or morbidity. This is where there is significant scientific debate. Moreover, scientific and popular discussions of rates of overweight and obesity assume that "overweight" and "obesity" are "preventable" with simple lifestyle changes. For instance, a 2004 study estimating the number of annual deaths attributed to overweight and obesity claimed that these conditions would soon "overtake tobacco as the leading preventable cause of mortality" (Mokdad et al. 2004, p. 1242, emphasis added). Yet, the available research suggests that body size is, for most people, difficult if not impossible to change (Mann et al. 2007).

The claim that being overweight or (moderately) obese is associated with higher mortality rates is essential for treating overweight and obesity as medically pathological. While it is true that high (as well as low) statistical extremes of body mass

---

1 We focus on work that interrogates the medical framing of this issue. We do not discuss the field of fat studies, which tends to bracket medical questions, as this is discussed in chapter 11 of this volume.

are associated with higher rates of mortality, the vast majority of people categorized as overweight or obese do not face increased risk of mortality. Rather, analyses by senior researchers at the National Center for Health Statistics and Centers for Disease Control and Prevention have found that rates of mortality are statistically lower among those categorized as overweight but not obese (BMI equal to or > 25 but < 30), a category into which over one-third of the U.S. population fell in 1999–2002 (Flegal et al. 2005, p. 1863). In the NHANES III survey (1988–1994), rates of mortality were also lower in the obesity I category (BMI equal to or > 30 but < 35), compared to the "normal weight" category, into which another roughly 20 percent of the U.S. population fell in 1999–2002 (Flegal et al. 2005, p. 1863). In contrast, less than 15 percent of the U.S. population had a BMI equal to or greater than 35 in 1999–2002, a category that is associated with statistically significant increases in mortality (Flegal et al. 2005). (In 1999–2002, less than 2 percent of Americans aged 25–59 fell into the underweight category [BMI < 18.5], which is also associated with statistically significant increases in mortality [Flegal et al. 2005].)

Second, even granting an association between the highest BMI category and having increased rates of mortality and rates of certain illnesses (Flegal et al. 2008), the causal mechanisms between higher body mass and mortality and morbidity remain unclear (Campos et al. 2006). For instance, there is evidence that insulin resistance is a product of an underlying metabolic syndrome that also predisposes people to higher adiposity so that "obesity may be an early symptom of diabetes rather than its underlying cause" (Campos et al. 2006, p. 57; Neel, Weder, and Julius 1998). Moreover, prospective randomized studies showing that changes in exercise and nutrition can reduce blood pressure and improve insulin sensitivity and blood lipids independent of changes in body size (Appel et al. 1997; Fagard 1999, 2005; Kraus et al. 2002) suggest that nutrition and exercise may be better predictors of health than body weight per se (Campos et al. 2006). Given that poor nutrition and physical fitness are positively correlated with higher body mass and inadequately controlled for by most epidemiological studies, associations observed between body mass and mortality or morbidity may, in fact, be spurious, with nutrition and/or physical fitness as confounds driving the results (Blair and Church 2004; Wei et al. 1999).

Finally, not only do studies show that people can improve their health profiles without weight loss, but some studies have linked weight loss or weight cycling (weight loss followed by weight gain followed by weight loss) to negative health outcomes (Campos et al. 2006; Diaz, Mainous, and Everett 2005). Moreover, a large body of research shows that, even if weight loss were a desirable public health goal, weight loss diets overwhelmingly result in weight gain over the long term, as dieters end up regaining what they lost and then some (Mann et al. 2007). Finally, many weight loss methods, including diet drugs, weight loss surgery, and fad weight-loss diets, may have serious side effects. (Alvarez-Leite 2004; Campos et al. 2006; Fraser 1998; Kolata 1997; Morino et al. 2007). Together, this suggests that urging weight loss may not be the wisest public health strategy.

EXPLAINING THE SOCIAL CONSTRUCTION OF HIGHER BODY MASS AS PUBLIC HEALTH CRISIS

Once one starts to question the assumption that higher body weight is in and of itself and necessarily a medical and public health problem, a whole set of interesting social scientific questions emerge about why there is so much public concern about this issue. The question of interest thus shifts from "Why are we so fat and how can we become thinner?" to "How has fatness increasingly become defined as a medical and public health crisis?" The latter question speaks to broader questions about the social construction of expert and lay knowledge (Epstein 1996; Fleck 1979; Kuhn 1996; Shapin 1994) and of social problems (Best 2008; Gusfield 1981; Kitsuse and Spector 1973). This and other work lead us to ask about the economic, institutional, and cultural contributors to growing medical and public health concern about body weight. We address each of these, in turn, below.

There are many economic interests that stand to gain from greater public concern about body size. Most prominently, drug companies that sell weight-loss drugs or have patents pending for approval from the Food and Drug Administration (FDA) gain by having overweight and obesity defined as broadly as possible, as this expands their potential market share. The more urgent a problem overweight and obesity are perceived to be, the easier it is to claim that the review of weight-loss drugs should be expedited or that possible side effects are counterbalanced by the risks of higher body weight. Aware of this, Hoffman-La Roche (makers of the weight-loss drug Xenical) and Abbot Laboratories (makers of the weight-loss drug Meridia) provide much of the funding for the International Obesity Task Force (IOTF) (Bacon 2008), whose self-proclaimed mission is to "inform the world about the urgency of the problem [of soaring levels of obesity] and to persuade governments that the time to act is now" (International Association for the Study of Obesity 2009). The IOTF has been extremely successful in that mission. For instance, The World Health Organization (WHO) report that helped establish a BMI of 25 as the cutoff from overweight, a guideline that was subsequently adopted by National Institutes of Health (NIH) in 1998) was predominantly drafted by the IOTF (Bacon 2008; Oliver 2005).

One could counter that there are also economic interests that stand to gain by minimizing the seriousness of obesity as a health risk. For one, the food industry is a powerful economic interest seemingly aligned with weight gain, rather than weight loss. Indeed, the Center for Consumer Freedom, a food industry lobby, has publicized research showing that the risks of obesity have been overblown.[2]

Yet, while clearly intent on protecting its bottom line from accusations that its products contribute to illness, the food industry has not produced a counter-ideology

---

2 See http://www.consumerfreedom.com/advertisements_detail.cfm/ad/30.

that celebrates bigger bodies. On the contrary, advertisements for diet foods rein-force the idea that thinness should be a personal goal, while other food advertise-ments convey the same message, for instance, by exclusively featuring very thin models as consumers (Bordo 1993). In addition, diet foods represent a significant and especially profitable category of products within the food industry (Campos 2004). The industry most invested in creating positive and glamorous images of larger female bodies is probably plus-size fashion. However, while its cultural importance is growing, plus-size fashion still represents only a tiny segment of the fashion industry as a whole, which overwhelmingly caters to the slimmest women and emphasizes the desirability of slenderness.

There are also various institutional interests that stand to gain by drawing atten-tion to obesity as a social problem. For instance, government health agencies, includ-ing the CDC, have promoted the urgency of the "obesity epidemic," while lobbying for greater program funding and policy-setting authority (Campos et al. 2006; Oliver 2005). We may further expect that researchers who have spent years building aca-demic careers on the basis that obesity and/or overweight represent an important medical and/or public health problem would be committed to this initial assumption. And increases in the research money available for studying obesity, from private and public sources alike, is likely to fuel academic attention to this issue (Saguy 2006).

Nevertheless, some scholars are engaged in research that takes a skeptical view of the alleged obesity crisis. In addition to the work reviewed above, there is a grow-ing literature on the "obesity paradox," showing that, among patients with chronic conditions, those with a BMI equal to or greater than 30 have better outcomes than those with lower BMIs (Curtis et al. 2005; McAuley et al. 2009). Thus there are cracks in the dominant discourse; it is not monolithic. Because it has become such deeply entrenched conventional wisdom that higher body weight is a medical problem, evidence to the contrary has the advantage of being surprising and novel, qualities that are valued by scientific research.

The news media, which sells copy by dramatizing events, has further fanned the flames of obesity concern (Saguy and Almeling 2008). Compared to scientific stud-ies on which they reported, news reports are more likely to represent obesity as a public heath crisis and as an epidemic (Saguy and Almeling 2008). Such news reporting on obesity as a serious medical and public health concern has accorded legitimacy and gravitas to women's magazines' eternal obsession with body size as an aesthetic issue. Rather than trying to stigmatize a behavior that is widely glamor-ized, such as smoking or drinking, scientific and news reports of the health risks of higher body weight thus further taint a trait that is already stigmatized.

Finally, there is evidence that the obesity epidemic resonates on a symbolic level for many Americans, because it taps into underlying moral and societal con-cerns about personal responsibility (on the Right) and corporate greed and exploi-tation on the part of the food industry (on the Left) (Campos et al. 2006; Gard and Wright 2005; Oliver 2005; Saguy and Riley 2005). Comparative work suggests that the emphasis on personal responsibility is emphasized more in American public discourse, while the corporate critique is more likely to be articulated in socialist democracies such as France (Saguy, Elmen-Gruys, and Gong 2010). Because rising body weight is often attributed to increased eating out or reliance on prepared meals, this issue also serves as a lightning rod for anxieties about gender roles (Boero 2007; Campos et al. 2006; Saguy and Elmen-Gruys 2010). Finally, because higher body mass is inversely associated with higher socioeconomic status in the contemporary United States, especially for women (Sobal and Stunkard 1989), rising body mass may also evoke fears of downward mobility (for oneself and/or for one's children), as well as tapping into negative attitudes about the poor and people of color (Campos 2004; Campos et al. 2006; Saguy and Elmen-Gruys 2010).

SOCIAL IMPLICATIONS OF THE OBESITY FRAME

A third line of inquiry examines the social implications of framing higher body mass as a medical pathology. A long and established tradition of labeling theory in sociology and social psychology has established that the mere act of labeling a group of people as deviant can function as a self-fulfilling prophecy (Merton 1968), by which members of that group come to see themselves or be seen by others as deviant (Becker 1963). For instance, in a classic study, teachers were told at the start of a school year that specific students in the class had been identified as likely to make large academic strides during the school year. Sure enough, at the end of the year, these students had made more academic progress than the others. However, the initial prediction was made purely at random. Rather, it appears that because the teachers expected these particular students to do well, they were more likely to perceive and encourage academic success (Rosenthal and Jacobson 1968). Inversely, an ethnography of primary schools found that black boys are likely to be labeled as "bound for jail," a prophecy that shapes both teachers' evaluations and black boys' own self-concept (Ferguson 2000).

By extension, one might expect that the mere act of labeling people with a BMI over 25 or 30 as unhealthy could similarly function as a self-fulfilling prophecy, so that negative health consequences attributed to "overweight" or "obesity" would actually be the product of these labels themselves. Indeed, there is some evidence that this may indeed be the case. For instance, a 2008 study finds that weight-based stigma is an important factor contributing to medical conditions associated with "obesity" (Muennig 2008). This is the case for four related reasons. First, BMI is a strong predictor of serological biomarkers of stress. Second, "obesity" and stress are linked to the same diseases. Third, body norms appear to be strong determinants of morbidity and mortality among those categorized as obese, so that the two groups most affected by weight-related stigma in surveys—whites and women—are also the two groups most likely to suffer from excess mortality when they fall into the obese category. Finally, statistical models suggest that the desire to lose weight (i.e., discontent with current weight) is an important driver of weight-related morbidity, independent of BMI (Muennig 2008; see also Muennig, Jia, and Lubetkin 2008).

Research has shown that people are more likely to express anti-fat prejudice if they believe that being fat is something people bring upon themselves (Crandall 1994, 2000; Crandall and Eshleman 2003). However, we still know very little about the extent to which contemporary discussions of the "obesity epidemic" are contributing to anti-fat prejudice through this or other mechanisms. Research on news media reporting on overweight and obesity as a medical and public health problem overwhelmingly blames individual behavior for higher body weight, although there is also increasing discussion of social-structural factors over time (Lawrence 2004; Saguy and Almeling 2008). Given this, we might expect that exposure to such reporting would increase anti-fat prejudice and that, in contrast, exposure to "fat-positive" reporting would decrease anti-fat prejudice. Indeed, preliminary results of research being conducted by the first author and collaborators has found evidence that subjects who read a fat-positive news report are less likely to express anti-fat prejudice than subjects who read a control article or than subjects who read a news report linking overweight and obesity to early mortality. These sorts of questions merit further research.

CONCLUSION

The extent to which obesity and/or overweight represents a public health crisis is the topic of heated medical debate. While most social scientists choose to ignore, minimize, or bracket these debates, others are examining the evidence on both sides, searching for social, political and economic factors contributing to the emergence of obesity as a major social problem, and studying the social effects of framing higher body weight as a medical pathology. This is important work and there remain many avenues to explore. We hope this chapter provides a useful guide, as well as encouragement, for future work in this area.

ACKNOWLEDGEMENTS

The authors thank David Frederick for comments on this paper.

REFERENCES

Alvarez-Leite, Jacqueline I. 2004. "Nutrient Deficiencies Secondary to Bariatric Surgery." *Current Opinion in Clinical Nutrition and Metabolic Care* 7: 569–575.

Appel, Lawrence J., Thomaas J. Moore, Eva Obarzanek, William M. Vollmer, Laura
    P. Svetkey, Frank M. Sacks, George A. Bray, Thomas M. Vogt, Jeffrey A. Cutler,
    Marlene M. Windhauser, Pao-Hwa Lin, and Njeri Karanja. 1997. "A Clinical Trial
    of the Effects of Dietary Patterns on Blood Pressure." *The New England Journal of
    Medicine* 16: 1117–1124.
Bacon, Linda. 2008. *Health at Every Size: The Surprising Truth about Your Weight*. Dallas:
    BenBella Books.
Barry, Colleen L., Victoria L. Brescoll, Kelly D. Brownell, and Mark Schlesinger. 2009.
    "Obesity Metaphors: How Beliefs about the Causes of Obesity Affect Support for
    Public Policy." *Milbank Quarterly* 87: 7–47.
Becker, Howard. 1963. *Outsiders: Studies in the Sociology of Deviance*. New York: The Free
    Press.
Best, Joel. 2008. *Social Problems*. New York: Norton.
Blair, Steven N., and Tim S. Church. 2004. "The Fitness, Obesity, and Health Equation:
    Is Physical Activity the Common Denominator?" *Journal of the American Medical
    Association* 292: 1232–1234.
Boero, Natalie. 2007. "All the News That's Fat to Print: The American 'Obesity Epidemic'
    and the Media." *Qualitative Sociology* 30: 41–60.
Bordo, Susan. 1993. *Unbearable Weight: Feminism, Western Culture, and the Body*. Berkeley:
    University of California Press.
Campos, Paul. 2004. *The Obesity Myth*. New York: Gotham Books.
Campos, Paul, Abigail Saguy, Paul Ernsberger, Eric Oliver, and Glen Gaesser. 2006. "The
    Epidemiology of Overweight and Obesity: Public Health Crisis or Moral Panic?"
    International Journal of Epidemiology 35: 55–60.
Carlsson, Maria E. 2000. "Cancer Patients Seeking Information from Sources Outside the
    Health Care System." *Supportive Care in Cancer* 8: 453–457.
Christakis, Nicholas A., and James H. Fowler. 2007. "The Spread of Obesity in a Large
    Social Network over 32 Years." *The New England Journal of Medicine* 357: 370–379.
Crandall, Chris S. 1994. "Prejudice against Fat People: Ideology and Self-Interest." *Journal
    of Personality and Social Psychology* 66: 882–894.
Crandall, Chris S. 2000. "Ideology and Lay Theories of Stigma." In *The Social Psychology of
    Stigma*, eds. T. F. Heatherton, R. E. Kleck, M. R. Hebl, and J. G. Hull, 126–150.
    New York: Guilford Press.
Crandall, Chris S., and Amy Eshleman. 2003. "A Justification-Suppression Model of the
    Expression and Experience of Predudice." *Psychological Bulletin* 129: 414–446.
Crossley, Nick. 2004. "Fat Is a Sociological Issue: Obesity Rates in Late Modern,
    'Body-Conscious' Societies." *Social Theory and Health* 2: 222–253.
Curtis, Jeptha P., Jared G. Selter, Yongfei Wang, Saif S. Rathore, Ion S. Jovin, Farid
    Jadbabaie, Mikhail Kosiborod, Edward L. Portnay, Seth I. Sokol, Feras Bader, and
    Harlan M. Krumholz. 2005. "The Obesity Paradox." *Archives of Internal Medicine* 165:
    55–61.
Diaz, Vanessa A., Arch G. Mainous, and Charles J. Everett. 2005. "The Association between
    Weight Fluctuation and Mortality: Results from a Population-Based Cohort Study."
    Journal of Community Health 30: 1573–3610.
Epstein, Steven. 1996. *Impure Science: Aids*. Berkeley: University of California Press.
Fagard, Robert H. 1999. "Physical Activity in the Prevention and Treatment of
    Hypertension in the Obese." *Medicine and Science in Sports and Exercise* 31: S624.
Fagard, Robert H. 2005. "Effects of Exercise, Diet and Their Combination on Blood
    Pressure." *Journal of Human Hypertension* 19: S20–S24.

Ferguson, Ann Arnett. 2000. *Bad Boys: Public Schools in the Making of Black Masculinity*. Ann Arbor: University of Michigan Press.

Fleck, Ludwik. 1979. *The Genesis and Development of a Scientific Fact*. Chicago: University of Chicago Press.

Flegal, K. M., M. D. Carroll, R. J. Kuczmarski, and C. L. Johnson. 1998. "Overweight and Obesity in the United States: Prevalence and Trends, 1960–1994." *International Journal of Obesity* 22: 39–47.

Flegal, K. M., B. I. Graubard, D. F. Williamson, and M. H. Gail. 2005. "Excess Deaths Associated with Underweight, Overweight, and Obesity." *Journal of the American Medical Association* 293: 1861–1867.

Flegal, Katherine M., Margaret D. Carroll, Cynthia L. Ogden, and Lester R. Curtin. 2010. "Prevalence and Trends in Obesity among Us Adults, 1999–2008." *Journal of the American Medical Association* 303: 235–241.

Flegal, Katherine M., Margaret D. Carroll, Cynthia L. Ogden, and Clifford L. Johnson. 2002. "Prevalence and Trends in Obesity among US Adults, 1999–2000." *Journal of the American Medical Association* 288: 1723–1727.

Flegal, Katherine M., Barry I. Graubard, David F. Williamson, and Mitchell H. Gail. 2008. "Cause-Specific Excess Deaths Associated with Underweight, Overweight, and Obesity." *Journal of the American Medical Association* 298: 2028–2037.

Fraser, Laura. 1998. *Losing It: False Hopes and Fat Profits in the Diet Industry*. New York: Penguin Putnam.

Gard, Michael, and Jan Wright. 2005. *The Obesity Epidemic: Science, Morality, and Ideology*. New York: Routledge.

Glassner, Barry. 2007. *The Gospel of Food: Everything You Know About Food Is Wrong*. New York: Ecco.

Gusfield, Joseph R. 1981. *The Culture of Public Problems: Drinking-Driving and the Symbolic Order*. Chicago: University of Chicago Press.

Hesse-Biber, Sharlene. 1996. *Am I Thin Enough Yet?: The Cult of Thinness and the Commercialization of Identity*. New York: Oxford University Press.

International Association for the Study of Obesity. 2009. "What Is IOTF?", http://www.iotf.org/whatisiotf.asp.

Kersh, Rogan, and James Morone. 2002. "The Politics of Obesity: Seven Steps to Government Action." *Health Affairs* 21: 142–153.

Kitsuse, John L., and Malcolm Spector. 1973. "Toward a Sociology of Social Problems: Social Conditions, Value Judgments, and Social Problems." *Social Problems* 20: 407–419.

Kolata, Gina. 1997. "How Fen-Phen, a Diet 'Miracle,' Rose and Fell." *New York Times,* p. 1.

Kraus, William E., Joseph A. Houmard, Brian D. Duscha, Kenneth J. Knetzger, Michelle B. Wharton, Jennifer S. McCartney, Connie W. Bales, Sarah Henes, Gregory P. Samsa, James D. Otvos, Krishnaji R. Kulkarni, and Cris A. Slentz. 2002. "Effects of the Amount and Intensity of Exercise on Plasma Lipoproteins." *New England Journal of Medicine* 347: 1483–1492.

Kuhn, Thomas. 1996. *The Structure of Scientific Revolutions*. Chicago: University of Chicago Press.

Lawrence, Regina G. 2004. "Framing Obesity: The Evolution of News Discourse on a Public Health Issue." *Press/Politics* 9: 56–75.

Mann, Traci, A. Janet Tomiyama, Erika Westling, Ann-Marie Lew, Barbra Samuels, and Jason Chatman. 2007. "Medicare's Search for Effective Obesity Treatments: Diets Are Not the Answer." *American Psychologist* 62: 220–233.

McAuley, Paul, Jesse Pittsley, Jonathan Myers, Joshua Abella, and Victor F. Froelicher. 2009. "Fitness and Fatness as Mortality Predictors in Healthy Older Men: The Veterans Exercise Testing Study." *Journal of Gerontology: Medical Sciences* 64A: 695–699.

Merton, Robert. 1968. *Social Theory and Social Structure*. New York: Free Press.

Mokdad, Ali H., James S. Marks, Donna F. Stroup, and Julie L. Gerberding. 2004. "Actual Causes of Death in the United States, 2000." *Journal of the American Medical Association* 291: 1238–1245.

Morino, Mario, Mauro Toppino, Pietro Forestieri, Luigi Angrisani, Marco Ettore Allaix, and Nicola Scopinaro. 2007. "Mortality after Bariatric Surgery: Analysis of 13,871 Morbidly Obese Patients from a National Registry." *Annals of Surgery* 246: 1002–1007.

Muennig, Peter. 2008. "The Body Politic: The Relationship between Stigma and Obesity-Associated Disease." *BMC Public Health* 8:128.

Muennig, Peter, Haomiao Jia, and Erica Lubetkin. 2008. "I Think Therefore I Am: Perceived Ideal Weight as a Determinant of Health." *American Journal of Public Health* 98: 501–506.

Neel, James V., Alan B. Weder, and Stevo Julius. 1998. "Type II Diabetes, Essential Hypertension, and Obesity As 'Syndromes of Impaired Genetic Homeostasis': The "Thrifty Genotype" Hypothesis Enters the 21st Century." *Perspectives in Biology and Medicine* 42: 44–74.

Nelkin, Dorothy. 1987. *Selling Science: How the Press Covers Science and Technology*. New York: Freeman.

Oliver, J. Eric. 2005. *Fat Politics: The Real Story Behind America's Obesity Epidemic*. New York: Oxford University Press.

Rosenthal, Robert, and Lenore Jacobson. 1968. "Pygmalion in the Classroom." *The Urban Review* 3: 16–20.

Rothblum, Esther D., and Sondra Solovay. 2009. "The Fat Studies Reader." New York: New York University Press.

Saguy, Abigail. 2006. "Are Americans Too Fat? Conversation with Stanton Glantz." *Contexts* 5: 11–13.

Saguy, Abigail C., and Rene Almeling. 2008. "Fat in the Fire? Science, the News Media, and the 'Obesity Epidemic.'" *Sociological Forum* 23: 53–83.

Saguy, Abigail C., and Kjerstin Elmen-Gruys. 2010. "Morality and Health: News Media Constructions of Overweight and Eating Disorders." *Social Problems* 57:2, pp. 231–250.

Saguy, Abigail C., and Kevin W. Riley. 2005. "Weighing Both Sides: Morality, Mortality and Framing Contests over Obesity." *Journal of Health Politics, Policy, and Law* 30: 869–921.

Saguy, Abigail, Kjerstin Elmen-Gruys, and Shanna Gong. 2010. "Social Problem Construction and National Context: News Reporting on 'Overweight' and 'Obesity' in the U.S. And France." *Social Problems* 57:4, pp. 586–610.

Shapin, Steven. 1994. *The Social History of Truth: Civility and Science in Seventeenth-Century England*. Chicago: University of Chicago Press.

Sobal, Jeffery, and Albert J. Stunkard. 1989. "Socioeconomic Status and Obesity: A Review of the Literature." *Psychological Bulletin* 105: 260–275.

Wei, Ming, James B. Kampert, Carolyn E. Barlow, Milton Z. Nichaman, Larry W. Gibbons, Ralph S. Paffenbarger, Jr., and Steven N. Blair. 1999. "Relationship between Low Cardiorespiratory Fitness and Mortality in Normal-Weight, Overweight, and Obese Men." *Journal of the American Medical Association* 282: 1547–1553.

Wolf, Naomi. 1991. *The Beauty Myth: How Images of Beauty Are Used against Women.* New York: William Morrow.

Yancey, Antronette K., Joanne Leslie, and Emily K. Abel. 2006. "Obesity at the Crossroads: Feminist and Public Health Perspectives." *Signs: Journal of Women in Culture and Society* 31: 425–443.

PART V

SOCIAL SCIENCE INSIGHTS INTO PREVENTION, TREATMENT, AND POLICY

CHAPTER 35

....

THE IMPERATIVE OF CHANGING PUBLIC POLICY TO ADDRESS OBESITY

....

CHRISTINA A. ROBERTO AND
KELLY D. BROWNELL

Rates of obesity have risen dramatically in the United States during the last 30 years (Centers for Disease Control [CDC] 2009), and the prevalence of obesity continues to increase across the globe (World Health Organization 2009). Until recently, most resources have been allocated to treatment as a means of curbing obesity, despite relatively little progress in developing effective, safe, and affordable obesity treatments that could be used on a broad scale.

Adults entering traditional weight-loss programs face sobering statistics, notably an expectation of losing only 10 percent of their current body weight, with half of the weight loss being regained within one year and nearly all being regained within five years (U.S. National Institutes of Health Consensus 1993). Weight loss drugs like sibutramine and orlistat produce similarly modest results (Glazer 2001), while other obesity drugs have led to serious side effects (Connolly et al. 1997). Even future advances in medical and behavioral treatments will likely be accompanied by the common barriers of high costs and the need for long-term adherence to difficult diets or medications with side effects. Bariatric surgery, while effective, is costly and reserved for those in the highest weight categories (Strauss, Bradley, and Brolin 2001).

The disappointing results from available treatments show that the nation will not be able to treat its way toward lower prevalence, leaving a considerable strain on the health care system. Obesity is a primary risk factor for cardiovascular disease and cancers, two of the leading causes of death in industrialized nations (Must et al. 1999); it is also a risk factor for diabetes. Treating diabetes accounts for the greatest obesity-related health expense (Visscher and Seidell 2001). Finkelstein and colleagues (2009) estimated that costs of treating obesity-related diseases are at least $86 billion, but could be as high as $147 billion per year in 2008. They also estimated that an obese person spends $1,429 (42 percent) more on yearly medical expenses than an individual of normal weight. Furthermore, half of the health care costs are borne by taxpayers through the public health insurance programs Medicare and Medicaid, and these estimates do not capture the impact of obesity on disability, missed work days, reductions in productivity, and psychological distress (Kumanyika et al. 2002; Must et al. 1999).

WHO OR WHAT IS RESPONSIBLE FOR OBESITY?

For decades the nation has watched obesity rates spiral upward with little response. Even today, government resources devoted to obesity are less than what would be justified by prevalence and costs. There are many possible reasons, but one likely explanation pertains to attributions of responsibility (Brownell et al. 2010). Deeply embedded in the way in which the United States has addressed obesity is the concept that irresponsible personal choices create the problem, that personal rather than government or corporate responsibility is at fault, and at least until recently, that government's role might be minor efforts at education but little more.

The understanding of obesity as an issue of personal responsibility has led to weak government action, defaulting to industry to make self-regulatory pledges (Sharma, Teret, and Brownell 2010). There has been little government action against the bias, stigma, and discrimination directed at overweight individuals (Eisenberg et al. 2003; Keery et al. 2005; Libbey et al. 2008; Griffiths and Page 2008; Lunner et al. 2000; Shroff and Thompson 2004; Puhl and Brownell 2001; Puhl and Heuer 2009).

Twin, adoption, and animal studies show that an individual's weight is partially determined by genetics. Yet, the rise in obesity over the last 30 years has occurred among a genetically stable population in the midst of a rapidly changing food environment Also, there is no evidence that people are becoming less responsible with matters related to their health. The question is why, in the face of broad knowledge about the risks of obesity, general public awareness of the rudiments of nutrition (e.g., eating too much junk food is bad and eating fruits and vegetables is good), and strong desire in most people to be thin, is obesity such a problem. The answer, we believe, is clear—changing environmental food and activity conditions have overwhelmed biological mechanisms that regulate body weight.

There is abundant evidence that as the food and activity environment changes, population body weight changes with it. The comparison of weight and diabetes differences in Pima Indians living in Mexico versus Arizona is a prime example (Ravussin et al. 1994; Schulz et al. 2006). Substantial weight gain occurs in laboratory animals fed typical human diets of nutritionally poor foods (Sclafani 1989) and in migrant populations who move to industrialized nations like the United States (Misra and Ganda 2007). Taken together, this research identifies the environment as the major force underlying the obesity crisis.

ADOPTING A PUBLIC HEALTH MODEL, PREVENTION, AND POLICY

The greatest gains in public health over the last 100 years have come from social and environmental interventions that improved nutrition and sanitation, not from impressive but costly medical advances (Marmot 2005). The fact that the United States ranks first in health care spending but poorly on many measures of health may be explained by a lack of attention to the social and behavioral determinants of health and the focus on treatment over prevention (Schroeder 2007). More recently, however, the surge in media attention toward obesity (Kersh and Morone 2005), rising health care costs, and recognition that obesity is one of America's most important health problems (Schlesinger 2005) has set the stage for creative policy solutions. Indeed, public support has increased in favor of policies to address obesity (Oliver and Lee 2005), such as calorie labeling on restaurant menus, the removal of soft drinks and snack foods from schools, changes in food marketing practices, and one of the most controversial recommendations, taxing foods.

Support for such policies is consistent with countless examples of government policies designed to protect the health and safety of American citizens. These coexist with the nation's strong beliefs about individualism. Many states have laws requiring people to wear motorcycle helmets and seatbelts, parents must immunize their children, water is fluoridated, there are high taxes on cigarettes and alcohol, and so on. Such policies have far-reaching effects on public health and are highly cost-effective (White, Koplan, and Orenstein 1985; Beck and Shults 2009; Elder et al. 2010; Callinan et al. 2010.) Policy has a special role when there is an imbalance in the forces influencing people to make certain choices. In such cases, policy can play an important role in countering or reducing negative influences so that individuals can exercise their personal freedom and responsibility to make decisions consistent with their desired outcomes.

Before identifying the most promising policies, it is important to understand the specific factors in the food environment that are exercising undue influence on food choices. There are many contributors to obesity. To name a few, nutrient-poor and calorie-dense foods are less expensive and more widely available than healthier options; such foods are extensively marketed and easily accessible in communities and institutions such as schools; poor-nutrition foods are served in large portion sizes that encourage overconsumption (Vermeer, Steenhuis, and Seidell 2009; Wansink and Kim 2005); and consumers are unaware of the nutritional content of many of these foods (Burton et al. 2006).

While physical activity also plays an important role in weight regulation, studies examining the respective contributions of diet and physical activity have identified the food environment as the stronger driver in the obesity epidemic, suggesting that policies targeting increased food intake should be prioritized (Swinburn 2009).

The fact that there are multiple contributors to obesity is cited by the food industry when its particular interests are threatened by policy changes, exemplified by an OpEd by the CEO of Coca Cola in the *Wall Street Journal* opposing beverage taxes (Kent 2009). Our belief is that the multiple causes of obesity implies that many policy approaches are likely to be tried and, as with tobacco, it will be a combination of strategies that produces public health impact.

A key to developing concrete solutions is the conceptual framework used to identify targets for change. Traditionally, public health experts seek to identify specific environmental exposures causing negative health outcomes and then craft policies to reduce exposure. Policies can fall into one of the following six categories: (1) *restrict access* to the exposure; (2) create *incentive systems* for individuals and/or organizations that will *promote avoidance* of the exposure; (3) *reduce the promotion* of the exposure; (4) *inform the public* about the dangers of the exposure; (5) *change the environmental defaults* to assist people in choosing to avoid the exposure; (6) *mandate behaviors* that protect against the adverse effects of the exposure.

Examples of creative policy solutions in each of these six categories to reduce tobacco consumption can provide guidance for possible food policies. After tobacco was identified as a toxic exposure linked to lung cancer, a long battle with the industry ensued that ultimately led to a number of public health policies which have reduced tobacco consumption in the United States (Wisotzky et al. 2004). Examples include prohibiting the sale of tobacco products to minors to restrict access; increasing excise taxes on cigarettes to provide a disincentive to purchase tobacco; regulating the advertisement of tobacco products to reduce promotion; launching mass media and counter-advertising campaigns, as well as requiring warning labels on packaging to inform the public about tobacco's dangers; and smoke-free air laws to mandate behavior and change environmental defaults. All of these policies are designed to help people make healthy decisions when faced with a highly addictive substance that was once easily accessible and extensively marketed with no mention of its risks.

The goals of public health policies coupled with lessons from tobacco and other public health issues, along with knowledge of specific risk factors identified in the food environment have led to a variety of policy proposals. We will focus on several we believe to be most promising: (1) school food environments; (2) food access and cost; (3) sugared beverage consumption; (4) food marketing; (5) restaurant food nutrition content and portion size.

PUBLIC HEALTH POLICY SOLUTIONS

Change the School Food Environment

Students are faced with numerous food choice opportunities in a typical school day. Foods sold in vending machines, as à la carte items during lunch, and at school stores are termed "competitive foods" because they compete with foods sold as part of the National School Lunch Program, which adheres to basic nutritional standards. In addition, fund-raising events typically feature junk foods, as do classroom birthday and holiday celebrations. Beverage companies often partner with schools in ways that provide both sales and branding opportunities. Food is used as an academic incentive and open-campus policies frequently lead students to have lunch at nearby fast food restaurants. With the combination of a poor-nutrition environment in schools and children seen as a vulnerable population, it is no surprise that schools were the first front upon which the application of policy to obesity prevention took place.

In 2006 the Child Nutrition and WIC Reauthorization Act of 2004 mandated that school districts create wellness policies describing initiatives to improve nutrition and physical activity in schools. Many states and cities have also passed school-based legislation to improve the food environment (Boehmer et al. 2008). Research suggests that school policies may be most effective if they minimize access to unhealthy foods. For example, one study in schools found that limiting access to high-fat and high-sugar foods decreased consumption (Neumark-Sztainer et al. 2005). Others have found a positive association between lower body mass index among high school students and policies that limit access to unhealthy foods and prevent students from eating and drinking outside of designated mealtimes (Kubik, Lytle, and Story 2005). The presence of competitive foods in schools reduces consumption of vegetables, fruits, and milk during school lunches (Cullen and Zakeri 2004; Kubik et al. 2003), indicating that policies should restrict competitive foods in schools. Fortunately, schools that have implemented such policies have not seen cafeteria profits decrease as they feared; instead, more students have participated in the National School Lunch Program (Story, Kaphingst, and French 2006; Wharton, Long, and Schwartz 2008). It would also be useful for schools to develop sound nutritional standards for the foods that are permitted to be sold in school cafeterias, stores, vending machines and during fundraisers.

Additional research showing that earlier lunch periods predict higher à la carte sales (Probart et al. 2006) suggests the need for policies regarding the scheduling and duration of lunch. Other policies to consider are increasing the reimbursement rate for the National School Lunch Program to offset rising food costs (Rudd Center for Food Policy and Obesity 2009), implementing zoning laws that would restrict unhealthy food establishments from operating near schools, eliminating open-campus policies and restricting access to unhealthy foods during school celebrations.

Food Access and Cost

Access to healthy, affordable foods is a luxury not enjoyed by all. Individuals of lower socioeconomic status and those belonging to ethnic and racial minority groups have less access to healthy foods (Drewnowski 2009). Limited access to healthy foods has been linked to higher rates of obesity, diabetes, and other health problems (U.S. Department of Health and Human Services 2001). While wealthier neighborhoods enjoy full-service supermarkets, better restaurants, and fresher produce compared to lower-income neighborhoods, those living in poorer areas are exposed to more fast food restaurants and convenience stores (Andreyeva et al. 2008; Moore and Diez Roux 2006). There are positive associations between the presence of convenience stores and prevalence of overweight and obesity and negative associations between lack of access to nearby supermarkets and poor diet and high body mass index (BMI) (Moore et al. 2008; Powell et al. 2007). In contrast, the presence of supermarkets is associated with a lower prevalence of overweight and obesity (Morland et al. 2002). One Chicago study found that those living in poor neighborhoods had to travel over two miles to access the same number of supermarkets that were within a half-mile of wealthier areas (Alwitt and Donley 2005).

Not only do residents of poor neighborhoods have restricted access to healthy foods and ready access to calorie-rich, nutrient-poor food, but unhealthy foods also cost less (Drewnowski and Specter 2004). A United States Department of Agriculture (USDA) report concluded that food prices are higher in both central cities and rural areas, where poorer people tend to live (Kaufman et al. 1997). Research showing that decreasing the price of healthy foods is associated with an increase in the sales of those foods (French 2003; French, Jeffery, et al. 2001; French et al. 1997) suggests that policies should be aimed at lowering costs for healthy foods.

A number of policies can be considered for rectifying food access problems. Examples of policies include tax incentives for supermarkets to move to low-income neighborhoods, incentive programs to retrofit groceries with equipment that would enable fresher products to be sold, the establishment of farmers' markets where WIC and food stamps can be used to buy fresh fruits and vegetables, the development of easily accessible public transit connecting people to full-service supermarkets and the use of zoning laws to restrict access to unhealthy foods (Rudd Center for Food Policy and Obesity 2008).

Food Taxes

A policy gaining traction is a proposed tax on sugar-sweetened beverages (Brownell and Frieden 2009; Brownell et al. 2009). In the United States, per capita consumption between 1977 and 2002 doubled across all age groups (Duffey and Popkin 2007) and the research documenting a link between consumption of sugar-sweetened beverages and obesity, diabetes, and heart disease is strong and growing (Malik, Schulze, and Hu 2006; Vartanian, Schwartz, and Brownell 2007; Fung et al. 2009). The success of cigarette taxes in reducing cigarette purchases suggests that taxing sugar-sweetened beverages may be an effective means of reducing intake, which in turn could lead to reductions in obesity and therefore health care costs. A tax might also encourage companies to reformulate beverages to reduce sugar content. In addition, Brownell and colleagues (2009) note that a 1 cent per ounce tax on sugar-sweetened beverages would raise $14.9 billion in the first year nationally. These funds could then be earmarked for programs designed to promote good health.

Regulate Food Marketing to Children

Food advertising is pervasive (Harris et al. 2009). The average American child in the United Sates views 15 television food advertisements every day (Federal Trade Commission [U.S.] 2007), but food products are also promoted in schools (Government Accounts Office [U.S.] 2005), on the Internet (Montgomery and Chester 2009), and via product placements in movies, television shows, and video games, sponsorships of sports and entertainment events, cross-promotions with other products, and via in-store promotions (Center for Science in the Public Interest 2003; Montgomery and Chester 2009; Kenway 2001; Schor 2004).

The foods most heavily marketed toward children are nutrient-poor, calorie-dense foods (Government Accounts Office [U.S.] 2005; Montgomery and Chester 2009; Cowburn and Boxer 2007; Harris et al. 2009). In the U.S. 98 percent of the food advertisements seen by children while watching television and 89 percent seen by adolescents are marketing products high in fat, sugar, and/or sodium (Powell, Szczypka, and Chaloupka 2007). These advertisements increase children's preferences for the advertised foods, the number of requests made to parents for those foods (Hastings et al. 2003; Institute of Medicine 2006; Gunilla 2001; Office of Communications 2004; Story and French 2004), and consumption (Harris, Bargh, and Brownell 2009).

An example of industry targeting the worst products to children is the case of breakfast cereals. Table 35.1 shows a rank order list of cereals, with nutrition ratings ranging from the worst to the best nutrition ratings, with indications of which cereals are marketed most aggressively to children (Harris, Schwartz, and Brownell 2009).

Not only is the content of food marketing a serious concern, but the amount of marketing is stunning. One approach to counter the deluge of junk food

Table 35.1. Overall Rankings of Children's Cereals Based on Nutrition Score

Nutrition Score*	Cereal	Company	Heavy Child Marketing		
			Television Advertising	Advergaming Web Sites	Other Youth Web Sites
34	Reese's Puffs	General Mills	X	X	X
36	Corn Pops	Kellogg	X	X	X
36	Lucky Charms	General Mills	X	X	X
36	Golden Grahams	General Mills			
37	Cinnamon Toast Crunch	General Mills	X	X	X
37	Cap'n Crunch	Quaker		X	
38	Count Chocula	General Mills			
38	Trix	General Mills	X	X	X
38	Froot Loops	Kellogg	X	X	X
38	Smorz	Kellogg			
38	Fruity or Coca Pebbles	Post	X	X	X
39	Cocoa Puffs	General Mills	X	X	
40	Cookie Crisp	General Mills	X	X	
40	Apple Jacks	Kellogg	X	X	X
40	Cookie Crunch	Kellogg			
43	Frosted Flakes	Kellogg	X		X
44	Disney High School Musical	Kellogg			
44	Rice or Coca Krispies	Kellogg			
44	Mini-Swirlz	Kellogg			
44	Honey Nut Os	Cascadian Farm			
44	Honey Nut Cheerios	General Mills	X	X	X
44	Waffle Crisp	Post			
44	Chex	General Mills			
46	Honey Smacks	Kellogg			

Table 35.1. (Cont.d)

Nutrition Score*	Cereal	Company	Heavy Child Marketing		
			Television Advertising	Advergaming Web Sites	Other Youth Web Sites
46	Purely O's	Cascadian Farm			
46	Alpha Bits	Post			
46	Golden Crisp	Post			
46	Honeycomb	Post	X	X	X
48	Raisin Bran	Post			
50	Dora the Explorer	General Mills			
50	Cinnamon Crunch	Cascadian Farm			
51	Bunnies	Annie's			
51	EnviroKids Organic	Nature's Path			
51	Puffins	Barbara's Bakery			
52	Cheerios (except Honey Nut)	General Mills			
53	Kix	General Mills			
53	Life	Quaker			
54	Hannah Montana	Kellogg			
54	Clifford Crunch	Cascadian Farm			
56	Mighty Bites	Kashi			
56	Honey Sunshine	Kashi			
58	Organic Wild Puffs	Barbara's Bakery			
72	Mini-Wheats	Kellogg			

*The nutrition score is based on the nutrient profile system developed by Rayner and colleagues at Oxford University and used by the Food Standards Agency in the United Kingdom as the basis for determining which products can be marketed to children on television, and used in Australia as a basis for determining whether health claims can be made. Scores range from 0–100. A food scoring 62 or greater is defined as a healthy product.

advertising was the 1999 US National Cancer Institute's "5-a-day" informational media campaign which promoted the consumption of fruits and vegetables (U.S. Department of Agriculture 2008). Yet, the $1.1 million spent on that campaign was simply no contest for the $1.6 billion a year spent by the food industry to market to children and adolescents (Federal Trade Commission [U.S.] 2008). Therefore, one policy solution is to reign in the excessive advertising of nutritionally poor foods to children through regulating the types of foods that can be advertised to children.

Policies to limit food advertising to children have been instituted in some places outside the United States. In 1980 the province of Quebec banned the marketing of all food products to children under age 13, and Norway, Sweden, and the United Kingdom have also limited junk food advertising to children. Thorough evaluations of the impact of these policies have not been done.

Comprehensive bans on advertising are difficult to develop, given the range of ways in which foods are advertised, such as on the Internet and through videogames. There are questions of jurisdiction, the prime example being marketing through the Internet and satellite TV, where the source of the marketing may be outside the country wanting to regulate it. In addition, banning junk food advertising to children has met with opposition in the United States out of concern about limiting commercial speech. Yet, research suggests that removing television advertising for nutrient-poor, high-calorie foods and beverages in Australia was the most cost-effective means of reducing health care costs stemming from overweight and obesity (Magnus et al. 2009).

It would be useful to have a scientifically derived, agreed-upon nutrition standard to identify those "healthy" foods that could be marketed to children and those foods that should not be marketed. The United Kingdom, for example, has restrictions on the kinds of foods that can be advertised during children's television programming based on the Nutrient Profile Model scoring system developed by Rayner and colleagues (Lobstein and Davies 2008; Rayner, Scarborough, and Stockley 2004). Such nutrition guidelines could be expanded to regulation of health claims or foods to be sold in schools. In the United States, strengthening the Federal Trade Commission's authority so that it can better regulate the marketing of unhealthy foods to children could be very helpful.

Restaurant Food Nutrition Content and Portion Sizes

Americans spend nearly half of their food dollars on foods prepared outside the home (National Restaurant Association 2008). These foods tend to be high in calories and nutritionally poor (Lin 1996; Guthrie, Lin, and Frazao 2002). In addition, foods consumed outside the home are frequently served in oversized portions, which encourage overeating (Nielsen and Popkin 2003; Young and Nestle 2002; Diliberti et al. 2004; Rolls, Morris, and Roe 2002). Among adults, adolescents, and children, positive associations between consuming fast food and increased calorie and fat intake, as well as decreased consumption of fruits and vegetables, have been observed (Paeratakul et al. 2003; Zoumas-Morse et al. 2001; Bowman and Vinyard 2004; French, Story et al. 2001). Fast food consumption is also associated with being overweight (Pereira et al. 2005; Duffey et al. 2007; Jeffery et al. 2006) and with increased body fat (McCrory et al. 1999). Furthermore, people, including trained nutritionists, have great difficulty estimating the number of calories in restaurant meals (Burton et al. 2006; Backstrand et al. 1997). Currently, nutrition information provided via brochures, posters, and/or pamphlets in chain restaurants is inconsistently available (Wootan and Osborn 2006) and infrequently accessed (Roberto, Agnew, and Brownell 2009). Therefore, one approach to helping people make better decisions when dining out is menu labeling.

Menu labeling provides calorie information on restaurant menus and menu boards so that it is visible at the point of purchase. New York City was the first city to implement menu labeling legislation and was initially met with strong opposition from the restaurant industry, which twice unsuccessfully sued the city to stop the regulations. Menu-labeling legislation passed in several states and cities across the United States and was enacted nationally in 2010 as part of health care reform (Trust for America's Health 2009; Menu Education and Labeling Act 2009; Nutrition Labeling of Standard Menu Items at Chain Restaurants 2010).

Menu labeling has considerable public support. National and local polls have found that the majority of people support menu-labeling laws (Center for Science in the Public Interest 2009; Rudd Center for Food Policy and Obesity 2008) and a survey conducted after the passage of New York City's law found that 89 percent of individuals were in favor of the policy (Technomic Inc 2009). This may be because menu labeling is consistent with a long history of government intervention on behalf of informing the consumer. Nutrition information appears on packaged foods, clothing comes with labels, and cleaning products and prescription drugs bear labels of their ingredients (Pomeranz and Brownell 2008). In addition, menu labeling is a relatively inexpensive public health intervention. Since current menu labeling laws only apply to chain restaurants with 15–20 or more locations, the cost burden is small. Many of these restaurants have already determined the calorie content of their menus so would only have to add this information to the menus and menu boards.

Menu labeling is a policy that also addresses an inefficiency in the marketplace. In places without menu labeling, consumers lack information that sellers have (Variyam 2005). This is problematic because a consumer who desires a lower-calorie item, but is unaware of the actual nutrition content of the foods being sold, may make a choice that is inconsistent with his or her personal preference. This means that producers will not increase the supply of low-calorie items because they are seemingly not in demand. Such transactions are likely to occur given the counterintuitive caloric content of many restaurant foods (i.e., salads that are over 1,000 kilocalories). Menu labeling can therefore increase market efficiency. Given the lack of incentive for restaurants to reveal nutritional information because highly palatable foods are often more unhealthy (Drewnowski 1998), there is a clear need for menu labeling laws rather than a reliance on free market forces.

The aim of menu labeling is to inform consumers and, in doing so, to help them make healthier decisions and to encourage food companies to reformulate products, either through calorie reduction or portion control. Research on the positive impact of the Nutrition Labeling and Education Act (NLEA) of 1990 (Nutrition Labeling and Education Act of 1990) suggests that menu labeling has the potential to improve dietary choices (Drichoutis, Lazaridis, and Nayga 2006; Derby and Levy 2001; Abbott 1997; Hawkes 2004; Variyam and Cawley 2006; Shine 1997; Mojduszka and Caswell 2000). While initial studies on menu labeling have produced mixed results, more research is needed. An investigation of the impact of menu labeling among low-income individuals in New York City did not see a reduction in number of calories ordered by fast food restaurant patrons (Elbel et al. 2009). However, preliminary findings from a larger study, with a longer observation period conducted by the New York City Department of Health, saw a decrease in the number of calories ordered at some chain restaurants (Robert Wood Johnson Foundation 2010)). In a randomized, controlled trial of menu labeling, Roberto and colleagues (2010) randomized adults to receive one of three menus: a menu with calorie labels, a menu without calorie labels, or a menu with calorie labels and a label that read: "the average daily caloric intake for an adult is 2,000 calories." People then ordered and ate a dinner meal. Those who had calorie labels on their menus ordered and consumed fewer calories for dinner. However, people who received menus that only had calorie labels without any contextual information consumed more calories for snack later that evening than those who received menus without any calorie labels or menus with labels and the daily caloric intake statement. Therefore, when the number of calories people ate for dinner was combined with the number of calories they ate after dinner, those who had the daily caloric intake statement and calorie labels on their menus ate approximately 250 fewer calories than either of the other groups. These results highlight the importance of providing contextual information about daily caloric needs along with calorie labels on menus. Finally, a study examining the food choices parents make for their children found that parents who received calorie labels ordered approximately 102 calories fewer for their children than parents who did not receive calorie labels. The parents however, did not order fewer calories for themselves (Tandon et al. 2010).

Taken together, these findings suggest that menu labeling could promote healthier food choices when dining out. Indeed, a health impact analysis projected that 2.7 million pounds of annual weight gain in Los Angeles County could be prevented if 10 percent of chain restaurant customers reduced their intake by 100 calories per meal (Kuo et al. 2009) Additional research on food reformulations spurred by labeling policies such as trans fat labeling, the NLEA, and the alterations of health claim rules in the mid-1980s, also suggests that menu labeling could have a significant public health impact by encouraging restaurants to improve the nutrition content of their menu items (Roberto et al. 2009; Mathios and Ippolito 1999).

Policies that promote the disclosure of information and bring awareness to issues of health might also promote voluntary industry initiatives which change important environmental defaults. An example of the power of identifying "optimal defaults" is best illustrated in a study by Johnson and Goldstein (2003). They found that rates of organ donation in countries where being an organ donor was the default (individuals had to actively "opt out" if they did not want to be a donor) were considerably higher (an average of 97.6 percent) than in countries where individuals had to actively "opt in" to be an organ donor (an average of 15.2 percent). This suggests that the optimal default is to have individuals enrolled as organ donors, but anyone can make the personal decision to opt-out. To expand this concept to the food arena, we can examine a recent change made by Starbucks Coffee. Starbucks Coffee changed its default milk for espresso beverages in the United States and Canada from whole to 2 percent. Individuals can still request whole milk if they choose, but in the last year this new default has saved customers nearly 7 billion calories per year (Associated Press 2007; Starbucks Newsroom 2009). Identifying these types of small changes that come with little cost can have very far-reaching public health effects.

Conclusion

The nation (and increasingly the world) has a unique opportunity to improve public health by instituting policies to improve the food environment. The framing of obesity as an issue of personal responsibility leads to weak government policy built mainly on self-regulation by industry and calls for individuals to behave better. This approach has been tried, and has failed. Greater progress can be made through creative policy solutions that account for obesity as a product of environmental factors. These policies should be designed to enhance people's ability to exercise personal responsibility and reduce the forces that undermine it. Science should be used to guide the targets of specific policy interventions and to evaluate implemented policies.

There are some encouraging signs that the nation is moving in this direction. By far the largest funder of work on childhood obesity is the Robert Wood Johnson Foundation, which pledged a half billion dollars to reverse the rising prevalence of childhood obesity by 2015.

There are striking parallels between the nation's battle against tobacco and policies aimed at preventing obesity, and similarities in the ways companies in these two industries have responded to the specter of government action (Brownell and Warner 2009). Smoking has been banned in workplaces, restaurants, and bars, and New York City has banned the use of trans fats in restaurants. Cigarettes have been taxed with great success in reducing smoking and taxes on sugar-sweetened beverages are being considered. Tobacco advertisements were regulated, and regulations on food marketing aimed at children have been proposed. Warning labels appear on cigarettes, and menu labeling laws have been passed in several cities and states to inform restaurant customers of the caloric impact of their choices. Public health policies that target the school food environment, issues of access and cost of foods, sugar beverage consumption, food marketing and restaurant food nutrition content and portion size can have far-reaching effects in curbing the obesity epidemic and improving the world's diet and health in cost-effective ways.

There are many reasons for hope. Government has changed its focus from treatment to prevention and public health approaches are the dominant theme. This is also true for the largest funder of work on childhood obesity, the Robert Wood Johnson Foundation. Key presidential appointments after the 2008 election for agencies such as the FTC, FDA, HHS, CDC, and USDA signaled this same change in theme. The White House made obesity a priority beginning in 2009–2010 (Let's Move 2010), state attorneys general have become involved with the obesity issue, and state and local leaders around the nation are engaged with obesity prevention as never before. This, combined with increasing global attention to this issue, suggests that significant policy changes will be the future of addressing obesity.

REFERENCES

Abbott, Robert. 1997. "Food and Nutrition Information: A Study of Sources, Uses and Understanding." *British Food Journal* 99: 43–49.

Alwitt, Linda, and Thomas D. Donley. 2005. "Retail Stores In Poor Urban Neighborhoods." *Journal of Consumer Affairs* 31: 139–164.

Andreyeva, Tatiania, Daniel M. Blumenthal, Marlene B. Schwartz, Michael W. Long, and Kelly D. Brownell. 2008. "Availability and Prices of Foods across Stores and Neighborhoods: The Case of New Haven, Connecticut." *Health Affairs (Millwood)* 27 (5): 1381–1388.

Associated Press. 2007. "Starbucks Switching to Two Percent Milk." Available at: http://www.msnbc.msn.com/id/18964760/40118639

Backstrand, Jeffrey R, Margo G. Wootan, Lisa R. Young, and Jayne Hurley. 1997. *Fat Chance: A Survey of Dietitians' Knowledge of the Calories and Fat in Restaurant Meals.* Washington, DC: Center for Science in the Public Interest.

Beck, Laurie F., and Ruth A. Shults. 2009. "Seat Belt Use in States and Territories with Primary and Secondary Laws–United States, 2006." *Journal of Safety Research* 40: 469–472.

Boehmer, Tegan K., Douglas A. Luke, Debra L. Haire-Joshu, Hannalori S. Bates, and Ross C. Brownson. 2008. "Preventing Childhood Obesity Through State Policy: Predictors of Bill Enactment." *American Journal of Preventive Medicine* 34(4): 333–340.

Bowman, Shanthy A., and Bryan T. Vinyard. 2004. "Fast Food Consumption of U.S. Adults: Impact on Energy and Nutrient Intakes and Overweight Status." *Journal of the American College of Nutrition* 23(2): 163–168.

Brownell, Kelly D., Thomas Farley, Walter C. Willett, Barry M. Popkin, Frank J. Chaloupka, Joseph W. Thompson, and David S. Ludwig. 2009. "The Public Health and Economic Benefits of Taxing Sugar-Sweetened Beverages." *New England Journal of Medicine* 361: 1599–1605.

Brownell, Kelly D., and Thomas R. Frieden. 2009. "Ounces of Prevention—The Public
    Policy Case for Taxes on Sugared Beverages." *New England Journal of Medicine*
    360 (18): 1805–1808.
Brownell, Kelly D., Rogan Kersh, David S. Ludwig, Robert C. Post, Rebecca M. Puhl,
    Marlene B Schwartz, and Walter C Willett. 2010. "Personal Responsibility and
    Obesity: A Constructive Approach to a Controversial Issue." *Health Affairs*
    29: 379–387.
Brownell, Kelly D., and Kenneth E. Warner. 2009. "The Perils of Ignoring History:
    Big Tobacco Played Dirty and Millions Died. How Similar Is Big Food?" *Milbank
    Quarterly* 87(1): 259–94.
Burton, Scot, Elizabeth H. Creyer, Jeremy Kees, and Kyle Huggins. 2006. "Attacking the
    Obesity Epidemic: The Potential Health Benefits of Providing Nutrition Information
    in Restaurants." *American Journal of Public Health* 96: 1669–1675.
Callinan, Joanne E., Anna Clarke, Kirsten Doherty, and Cecily Kelleher. 2010. "Legislative
    Smoking Bans for Reducing Secondhand Smoke Exposure, Smoking Prevalence and
    Tobacco Consumption." *The Cochrane Library* 4: 1–128.
Center for Science in the Public Interest. 2003. *Pestering Parents: How Food Companies
    Market Obesity to Children.* Available at: http://www.cspinet.org/new/pdf/pages_
    from_pestering_parents_final_pt_1.pdf
Center for Science in the Public Interest. 2009. *Summary of Polls on Nutrition Labeling
    in Restaurants.* Available at: http://www.cspinet.org/new/pdf/census_menu_board_
    question.pdf
Connolly, Heidi . M., Jack. L. Crary, Michael. D. McGoon, Donald. D. Hensrud, Brooks. S.
    Edwards, William. D. Edwards, and Hartzell. V. Schaff. 1997. "Valvular Heart Disease
    Associated with Fenfluramine-Phentermine." *New England Journal of Medicine* 337
    (9): 581–588.
Cowburn, Gill, and Anna Boxer. 2007. "Magazines for Children and Young People and
    the Links to Internet Food Marketing: A Review of the Extent and Type of Food
    Advertising." *Public Health Nutrition* 10: 1024–1031.
Cullen, Karen. W., and Issa. Zakeri. 2004. "Fruits, Vegetables, Milk, and Sweetened
    Beverages Consumption and Access to a la Carte/Snack Bar Meals at School."
    American Journal of Public Health 94(3): 463–467.
Derby, Brenda M., and Alan S. Levy. 2001. "Do Food Labels Work? Gauging the
    Effectiveness of Food Labels Pre- and Post-NLEA." In *Handbook of Marketing and
    Society,* eds. P. B. a. G. Gundlach. Thousand Oaks, CA: Sage.
Diliberti, Nicole, Peter L. Bordi, Martha T. Conklin, Liane S. Roe, and Barbara J. Rolls.
    2004. "Increased Portion Size Leads to Increased Energy Intake in a Restaurant Meal."
    Obesity Research 12(3): 562–568.
Drewnowski, Adam. 1998. "Energy Density, Palatability, and Satiety: Implications for
    Weight Control." *Nutrition Reviews* 56: 347–353.
Drewnowski, Adam, and S. E. Specter. 2004. "Poverty and Obesity: The Role of Energy
    Density and Energy Costs." *American Journal of Clinical Nutrition* 79(1): 6–16.
Drewnowski, Adam. "Obesity, Diets, and Social Inequalities." 2009. *Nutrition Reviews*
    67: S36–S39.
Drichoutis, Andreas C., Panagiotis Lazaridis, and Rodolfo M. Nayga. 2006. "Consumers'
    Use of Nutritional Labels: A Review of Research Studies and Issues." *Academy of
    Marketing Science Review* 9: 1–22.
Duffey, Kiyah J., Penny Gordon-Larsen, David R. Jacobs, Jr., O. Dale Williams, and
    Barry M. Popkin. 2007. "Differential Associations of Fast Food and Restaurant Food

Consumption with 3-Y Change in Body Mass Index: The Coronary Artery Risk Development in Young Adults Study." *American Journal of Clinical Nutrition* 85(1): 201–208.

Duffey, Kiyah J., and Barry M. Popkin. 2007. "Shifts in Patterns and Consumption of Beverages between 1965 and 2002." *Obesity (Silver Spring)* 15(11): 2739–2747.

Eisenberg, Marla., Dianne Neumark-Sztainer, and Mary Story. 2003. Associations of Weight-Based Teasing and Emotional Well-being Among Adolescents. *Archives of Pediatrics and Adolescent Medicine* 157 (8): 733–738.

Elbel, Brian, Rogan Kersh, Victoria L. Brescoll, and L. Beth Dixon. 2009. "Calorie Labeling and Food Choices: A First Look at the Effects on Low-Income People in New York City." *Health Affairs (Millwood)* 28(6): w1110–1121.

Elder, Randy W., Briana Lawrence, Aneeqah Ferguson, Timothy S. Naimi, Robert D. Brewer, Sajal K. Chattopadhyay, Traci L. Toomey, Jonathan E. Fielding. 2010. "The Effectiveness of Tax Policy Interventions for Reducing Excessive Alcohol Consumption and Related Harms." *American Journal of Preventive Medicine* 38: 217–229.

Federal Trade Commission (U.S.). 2007. *Children's Exposure to TV Advertising in 1977 and 2004.* Bur. Econ. Staff Rep. Available at: http://www.ftc.gov/os/2007/06/cabecolor.pdf

Federal Trade Commission (U.S.). 2008. *Marketing Food to Children and Adolescents: A Review of Industry Expenditures, Activities and Self-regulation.* Available at: http://www.ftc.gov/os/2008/07/P064504foodmktingreport.pdf

Finkelstein, Eric A., Justin G. Trogdon, Joel W. Cohen, and William Dietz. 2009. "Annual Medical Spending Attributable to Obesity: Payer- and Service-Specific Estimates." *Health Affairs (Millwood)* 28 (5): w822–831.

French, Simone A. 2003. "Pricing Effects on Food Choices." *Journal of Nutrition* 133(3): 841S–843S.

French, Simone A., Robert W. Jeffery, Mary Story, Kyle K. Breitlow, Judith S. Baxter, Peter Hannan, and M. Patricia Snyder. 2001. "Pricing and Promotion Effects on Low-Fat Vending Snack Purchases: The CHIPS Study." *American Journal of Public Health* 91(1): 112–117.

French, Simone A., Mary Story, Dianne Neumark-Sztainer, Jayne A. Fulkerson, and Peter Hannan. 2001. "Fast Food Restaurant Use among Adolescents: Associations with Nutrient Intake, Food Choices and Behavioral and Psychosocial Variables." *International Journal of Obesity and Related Metabolic Disorders* 25(12): 1823–1833.

French, Simone. A., Robert W. Jeffery, Mary Story, Peter Hannan, and M. Patricia Snyder. 1997. "A Pricing Strategy to Promote Low-Fat Snack Choices Through Vending Machines." *American Journal of Public Health* 87(5): 849–851.

Fung, Teresa T., Vasanti. Malik, Kathryn M. Rexrode, JoAnn E. Manson, Walter C. Willett, and Frank B. Hu. 2009. "Sweetened Beverage Consumption and Risk of Coronary Heart Disease in Women." *American Journal of Clinical Nutrition* 89(4): 1037–1042.

Glazer, Gary. 2001. "Long-term Pharmacotherapy of Obesity 2000: A Review of Efficacy and Safety." *Archives of Internal Medicine* 161 (15): 1814–1824.

Government Accounting Office (U.S.). 2005. *School Meal Programs: Competitive Foods Are Widely Available and Generate Substantial Revenues for Schools.* Washington, DC: GAO.

Griffiths, Lucy J., and Angie S. Page. 2008. The Impact of Weight-related Victimization on Peer Relationships: The Female Adolescent Perspective. *Obesity* 16(S2): S39–S45.

Guthrie, Joanne F., Biing Hwan H. Lin, and Elizabeth Frazao. 2002. "Role of Food Prepared Away from Home in the American Diet, 1977–78 Versus 1994–96: Changes and Consequences." *Journal of Nutrition Education and Behavior* 34(3): 140–150.

Harris, Jennifer L., John A. Bargh, and Kelly D. Brownell. 2009. "Priming Effects of Television Food Advertising on Eating Behavior." *Health Psychology* 28(4): 404–413.

Harris, Jennifer L., Jennifer L. Pomeranz, Tim Lobstein, and Kelly D. Brownell. 2009. "A Crisis in the Marketplace: How Food Marketing Contributes to Childhood Obesity and What Can Be Done." *Annual Review of Public Health* 30: 211–225.

Harris, Jennifer L., Marlene B. Schwartz, and Kelly D. Brownell. 2009. *Cereal F.A.C.T.S. Food Advertising to Children and Teens Score*. Rudd Center for Food Policy and Obesity. Available at: http://www.cerealfacts.org.

Hastings, Gerard, Martine Stead, Laura McDermott, Alasdair Forsyth, Anne Marie MacKintosh, Mike Rayner, Christine Godfrey, Martin Caraher, and Kathryn Angus. 2003. *Review of Research on the Effects of Food Promotion to Children*. Glasgow, UK: Cent. Soc. Mark., University of Strathclyde.

Hawkes, Corinna. 2004. *Nutrition Labels and Health Claims: The Global Regulatory Environment*. Geneva: WHO.

Institute of Medicine. 2006. *Food Marketing to Children and Youth: Threat or Opportunity?*, ed. J. G. JM McGinnis and V. I. Kraak. Washington, DC: National Academic Press.

Jarlbro, Gunilla. 2001. *Children and Television Advertising. The Players, the Arguments, and the Research during the Period* 1994–2000. Stockholm, Sweden: Swedish Consumer Agency.

Jeffery, Robert W., Judy Baxter, Maureen McGuire, and Jennifer Linde. 2006. "Are Fast Food Restaurants an Environmental Risk Factor for Obesity?" *International Journal of Behavioral Nutrition and Physical Activity* 3: 2.

Johnson, Eric J., and Daniel Goldstein. 2003. "Medicine: Do Defaults Save Lives?" *Science* 302 (5649): 1338–1339.

Kaufman, Philip R., James M. MacDonald, Steve M. Lutz, and David M. Smallwood. 1997. *Do the Poor Pay More for Food? Item Selection and Price Differences Affect Low-Income Household Food Cost*. Washington, DC USDA Economic Research Service.

Keery, Helene, Kerri Boutelle, Patricia van den Berg, and J. Kevin Thompson. 2005. The impact of appearance-related teasing by family members. *Journal of Adolescent Health* 37: 120–127.

Kent, Muhtar. *October 7, 2009*. "Coke Didn't Make America Fat." *Wall Street Journal*. *Available at: http://online.wsj.com/article/SB10001424052748703298004574455464120581 696.html.*

Kenway, Jane, and Elizabeth Bullen. 2001. *Consuming Children: Education—Entertainment—Advertising*. Buckingham, UK: Open University Press.

Kersh, R., and J. A. Morone. 2005. "Obesity, Courts, and the New Politics of Public Health." *Journal of Health Politics, Policy and Law* 30(5): 839–68.

Kubik, Martha Y., Leslie A. Lytle, Peter J. Hannan, Cheryl L. Perry, and Mary Story. 2003. "The Association of the School Food Environment with Dietary Behaviors of Young Adolescents." *American Journal of Public Health* 93(7): 1168–1173.

Kubik, Martha. Y., Leslie. A. Lytle, and Mary Story. 2005. "Schoolwide Food Practices Are Associated with Body Mass Index in Middle School Students." *Archives of Pediatric and Adolescent Medicine* 159(12): 1111–1114.

Kumanyika, S., R. W. Jeffery, A. Morabia, C. Ritenbaugh, and V. J. Antipatis. 2002. "Obesity Prevention: The Case for Action." *Interntional Journal of Obesity and Related Metabolic Disorders* 26(3): 425–436.

Kuo, T., C. J. Jarosz, P. Simon, and J. E. Fielding. 2009. "Menu Labeling as a Potential Strategy for Combating the Obesity Epidemic: A Health Impact Assessment." *American Journal of Public Health* 99 (9): 1680–1686.

Let's Move. http://www.letsmove.gov/

Libbey, Heather P., Mary T. Story, Dianne Neumark-Sztainer, and Kerri N. 2008. Boutelle. Teasing, Disordered Eating Behaviors, and Psychological Morbidities Among Overweight Adolescents. *Obesity* 16(S2):S24–S29.

Lin, Biing Hwan. 1996. *Diets of America's Children: Influence of Dining Out, Household Characteristics, and Nutrition Knowledge*. Washington, DC.USDA Economic Research Service.

Lobstein, Tim, and S. Davies. 2008. "Defining and labelling 'healthy' and 'unhealthy' food." *Public Health Nutrition* 12: 331–340.

Lunner, Katarina, Elanor H. Werthem, J. Kevin Thompson, Susan J. Paxton, Fiona McDonald, and Klara S. Halvaarson. 2000. A cross-cultural Examination of Weight-related Teasing, Body Image, and Eating Disturbance in Swedish and Australian Samples. *International Journal of Eating Disorders* 28(4):430–435.

Magnus, Anne, Michele M. Haby, Rob Carter, and Boyd Swinburn. 2009. "The Cost-Effectiveness of Removing Television Advertising of High-Fat and/or High-Sugar Food and Beverages to Australian Children." *International Journal of Obesity (London)* 33 (10): 1094–1102.

Malik, Vasanti S., Matthias B. Schulze, and Frank B. Hu. 2006. "Intake of Sugar-Sweetened Beverages and Weight Gain: A Systematic Review." *American Journal of Clinical Nutrition* 84(2): 274–288.

Marmot, M. 2005. "Social Determinants of Health Inequalities." *Lancet* 365(9464): 1099–1104.

Mathios, Alan D., and Pauline M. Ippolito. 1999. "Health Claims in Food and Advertising and Labeling: Disseminating Nutrition Information to Consumers." *In America's Eating Habits: Changes and Consequences*, 189–212. USDA Economic Research Service.

McCrory, Megan. A., Paul. J. Fuss, Nicholas. P. Hays, Angela. G. Vinken, Andrew. S. Greenberg, and Susan. B. Roberts. 1999. "Overeating in America: Association between Restaurant Food Consumption and Body Fatness in Healthy Adult Men and Women Ages 19 to 80." *Obesity Research* 7(6): 564–571.

108th Congress. 2003-2004. *Menu Education and Labeling Act, H.R. 3444*. November 5, 2003.

Misra, Anoop, and Om P. Ganda. 2007. "Migration and Its Impact on Adiposity and Type 2 Diabetes." *Nutrition* 23 (9): 696–708.

Mojduszka, Eliza M., and Julie A. Caswell. 2000. "A Test of Nutritional Quality Signaling in Food Markets Prior to Implementation of Mandatory Labeling." *American Journal of Agricultural Economics* 82: 298–309.

Montgomery, Kathryn C., and Jeff Chester. 2009. "Interactive Food and Beverage Marketing: Targeting Children and Youth in the Digital Age." *Journal of Adolescent Health* 45(3): S18–S29.

Moore, Latetia V., and Ana V. Diez Roux. 2006. "Associations of Neighborhood Characteristics with the Location and Type of Food Stores." *American Journal of Public Health* 96(2): 325–331.

Moore, Latetia V., Ana V. Diez Roux, Jennifer A. Nettleton, and David R. Jacobs, Jr. 2008. "Associations of the Local Food Environment with Diet Quality—A Comparison of Assessments Based on Surveys and Geographic Information Systems: The Multi-Ethnic Study of Atherosclerosis." *American Journal of Epidemiology* 167(8): 917–924.

Morland, Kimberly, Steve Wing, Ana Diez Roux, and Charles Poole. 2002. "Neighborhood Characteristics Associated with the Location of Food Stores and Food Service Places." *American Journal of Preventive Medicine* 22(1): 23–29.

Must, Aviva, Jennifer Spadano, Eugenie H. Coakley, Alison E. Field, Graham Colditz, and William H. Dietz. 1999. "The Disease Burden Associated with Overweight And Obesity." *JAMA* 282 (16): 1523–1529.

National Restaurant Association. 2008. *Industry at a Glance.* Available at: http://www.restaurant.org/

Neumark-Sztainer, Dianne, Simone. A. French, Peter J. Hannan, Mary Story, and Jayne A. Fulkerson. 2005. "School Lunch and Snacking Patterns among High School Students: Associations with School Food Environment and Policies." *International Journal of Behavioral Nutrition and Physical Activity* 2(1): 14.

Nielsen, Samara J., and Barry M. Popkin. 2003. "Patterns and Trends in Food Portion Sizes, 1977–1998." *Journal of the American Medical Association* 289(4): 450–3.

Nutrition Labeling and Education Act of 1990. Pub L No. 101–535, 104 Stat 2353.

Nutrition Labeling of Standard Menu Items at Chain Restaurants. 2010. Sec 4205. HR 3590.

Office of Communications. 2004. "Childhood Obesity—Food Advertising in Context. Children's Food Choices, Parents' Understanding and Influence, and the Role of Food Promotion." London: 7.

Oliver, J. Eric, and Taeku Lee. 2005. "Public Opinion and the Politics of Obesity in America." *Journal of Health Politics, Policy and Law* 30 (5): 923–954.

Paeratakul, Sahasporn, Daphne P. Ferdinand, Catherine M. Champagne, Donna H. Ryan, and George A. Bray. 2003. "Fast-food Consumption among US Adults and Children: Dietary and Nutrient Intake Profile." *Journal of the American Dietetic Associations* 103(10): 1332–1338.

Pereira, Mark A., Alex I. Kartashov, Cara B. Ebbeling, Linda Van Horn, Martha L. Slattery, David R. Jacobs, Jr., and David S. Ludwig. 2005. "Fast-food Habits, Weight Gain, and Insulin Resistance (The CARDIA Study): 15-Year Prospective Analysis." *Lancet* 365(9453): 36–42.

Pomeranz, Jennifer L., and Kelly D. Brownell. 2008. "Legal and Public Health Considerations Affecting the Success, Reach, and Impact of Menu-Labeling Laws." *American Journal of Public Health* 98(9): 1578–1583.

Powell, Lisa M., M. Christopher. Auld, Frank J. Chaloupka, Patrick M. O'Malley, and Lloyd D. Johnston. 2007. "Associations between Access to Food Stores and Adolescent Body Mass Index." *American Journal of Preventive Medicine* 33(4 Supp.): S301–307.

Powell, L. M., G. Szczypka, and F. J. Chaloupka. 2007. "Exposure to Food Advertising on Television among US children." *Archives of Pediatric and Adolescent Medicine* 161 (6): 553–560.

Probart, Claudia, Elaine McDonnell, Terryl Hartman, J. Elaine Weirich, and Lisa Bailey-Davis. 2006. "Factors Associated with the Offering and Sale of Competitive Foods and School Lunch Participation." *Journal of the American Dietetic Association* 106 (2): 242–247.

Puhl, Rebecca M., and Kelly D. Brownell. 2001. "Bias, Discrimination, and Obesity." *Obesity Research* 9(12): 788–805.

Puhl, Rebecca M., and Chelsea A. Heuer. 2009. "The Stigma of Obesity: A Review and Update. "*Obesity (Silver Spring)* 17 (5): 941–964.

Ravussin, Eric, Mauro E. Valencia, Julian Esparza, Peter H. Bennett, and Leslie O. Schulz. 1994. "Effects of a Traditional Lifestyle on Obesity in Pima Indians." *Diabetes Care* 17(9): 1067–1074.

Rayner, Mike, Peter Scarborough, and Lynn Stockley. 2004. "Nutrient Profiles: Options for Definitions for Use in Relation to Food Promotion and Children's Diets."

British Heart Foundation Health Promotion Research Group, Department of Public Health, University of Oxford.

Robert Wood Johnson Foundation. 2010. "Report Suggests New York City Menu Labeling Law Is Effective at Promoting Health Changes." Robert Wood Johnson Foundation. Available at: http://www.rwjf.org/publichealth/digest.jsp?id=24564.

Roberto, Christina A., Henry Agnew, and Kelly D. Brownell. 2009. "An Observational Study of Consumers' Accessing of Nutrition Information in Chain Restaurants." *American Journal of Public Health* 99(5): 820–821.

Roberto, Christina A., Peter D. Larsen, Henry Agnew, Jenny Baik, and Kelly D. Brownell. 2010. "Evaluating the Impact of Menu Labeling on Food Choices and Intake." *American Journal of Public Health* 100(2): 312–318.

Roberto, Christina A., Marlene B. Schwartz, Kelly D. Brownell. 2009. "Rationale and Evidence for Menu-Labeling Legislation." *American Journal of Preventive Medicine* 37: 546–551.

Rolls, Barbara J., Erin L. Morris, and Liane S. Roe. 2002. "Portion Size of Food Affects Energy Intake in Normal-Weight and Overweight Men and Women." *American Journal of Clinical Nutrition* 76 (6): 1207–1213.

Rudd Center for Food Policy and Obesity. 2008. *Access to Healthy Foods in Low-Income Neighborhoods Opportunities for Public Policy.* New Haven, CT: Rudd Center for Food Policy and Obesity.

Rudd Center for Food Policy and Obesity. 2008. *Menu Labeling in Chain Restaurants: Opportunities for Public Policy.* New Haven, CT: Rudd Center for Food Policy and Obesity.

Rudd Center for Food Policy and Obesity. 2009. *School Wellness Policies.* New Haven, CT: Rudd Center for Food Policy and Obesity.

Schlesinger, Mark. 2005. "Weighting for Godot." *Journal of Health Politics, Policy and Law* 30(5): 785–801.

Schor, Juliet B. 2004. *Born to Buy: The Commercialized Child and the New Consumer Culture.* New York: Scribner.

Schroeder, Steve A. 2007. "Shattuck Lecture. We Can Do Better—Improving the Health of the American People." *New England Journal of Medicine* 357: 1221–1228.

Schroff, Hemal, and J. Kevin Thompson. 2004. Body Image and Eating Disturbance in India: Media and Interpersonal Influences. *International Journal of Eating Disorders* 35: 198–203.

Schulz, L. O., P. H. Bennett, E. Ravussin, J. R. Kidd, K. K. Kidd, J. Esparza, and M. E. Valencia. 2006. "Effects of Traditional and Western Environments on Prevalence of Type 2 Diabetes in Pima Indians in Mexico and the U.S." *Diabetes Care* 29(8): 1866–1871.

Sclafani, Anthony 1989. "Dietary-Induced Overeating." *Annals of the New York Academy of Sciences* 575: 281–291.

Sharma, Lisa L., Stephen P. Teret, and Kelly D. Brownell. 2010. "The Food Industry and Self-Regulation: Standards to Promote Success and to Avoid Public Health Failures." *American Journal of Public Health* 100(2): 240–246.

Shine, Angela, Seamus O'Reilly, Kathleen O'Sullivan 1997." Consumer Attitudes to Nutrition Labeling." *British Food Journal* 99: 290–296.

Starbucks Newsroom. *Starbucks Raises the Bar on Its Food to a Tastier Standard.* Starbucks 2009. Available from http://news.starbucks.com/article_display.cfm?article_id=238.

Story, Mary, and Simone French. 2004. "Food Advertising and Marketing Directed at Children and Adolescents in the US." *International Journal Behavioral Nutrition and Physical Activity* 1(1): 3.

Story, Mary, Karen M. Kaphingst, and Simone French. 2006. "The Role of Schools in Obesity Prevention." *Future Child* 16: 109–142.

Strauss, R. S., L. J. Bradley, and R. E. Brolin. 2001. "Gastric Bypass Surgery in Adolescents with Morbid Obesity." *Journal of Pediatrics* 138(4): 499–504.

Swinburn, Boyd A., Gary Sacks, Sing Kai Lo, Klaas R. Westerterp, Elaine C. Rush, Michael Rosenbaum, Amy Luke, Dale A. Schoeller, James P. DeLany, Nancy F. Butte and Eric Ravussin. 2009. "Estimating the Changes in Energy Flux That Characterize the Rise in Obesity Prevalence." *American Journal of Clinical Nutrition* 89: 1723–1728.

Tandon, Pooja S., Jeffrey Wright, Chuan Zhou, Cara B. Rogers, and Dimitri A. Christakis. 2010. "Nutrition Menu Labeling May Lead to Lower-Calorie Restaurant Meal Choices for Children." *Pediatrics* 125(2): 244–248.

Technomic Inc. 2009. *Executive Summary, Consumer Reaction to Calorie Disclosure on Menus/Menu Boards in New York City.* Available at: http://www.edhoman.com/public/files/HB783-3.pdf .

Trust for America's Health. 2009. *F as in FAT: How Obesity Policies Are Failing in America.* Robert Wood Johnson Foundation. Available at: http://healthyamericans.org/reports/obesity2009.

US Department of Agriculture. *Nutrition Education Home Page.* Food and Nutrition Service 2008. Available from http://www.fns.usda.gov/fns/nutrition.htm.

U.S. Department of Health and Human Services. 2001. *The Surgeon General's Call to Action to Prevent and Decrease Overweight and Obesity.* Rockville, MD: U.S. Department of Health and Human Services, Public Health Service, Office of the Surgeon General.

Variyam, Jayachandran. 2005. *Nutrition Labeling in the Food-away-from-home Sector: An Economic Assessment.* Washington, DC: Department of Agriculture.

Variyam, Jayachandran, and John Cawley. 2006. *Nutrition Labels and Obesity.* National Bureau of Economic Research. Available from http://www.nber.org/papers/w11956.

Vartanian, Lenny R., Marlene B. Schwartz, and Kelly D. Brownell. 2007. "Effects of Soft Drink Consumption on Nutrition and Health: A Systematic Review and Meta-Analysis." *American Journal of Public Health* 97(4): 667–75.

Vermeer, W. M., I. H. Steenhuis, and J. C. Seidell. 2009. "From the Point-of-Purchase Perspective: A Qualitative Study of the Feasibility of Interventions Aimed at Portion-Size." *Health Policy* 90(1): 73–80.

Visscher, Tommy L., and Jacob C. Seidell. 2001. "The Public Health Impact of Obesity." *Annual Review of Public Health* 22:355–75.

Wansink, Brian, and Junyong Kim. 2005. "Bad Popcorn in Big Buckets: Portion Size Can Influence Intake as Much as Taste." *Journal of Nutrition Education and Behavior* 37(5): 242–245.

Wharton, Christopher M., Michael Long, and Marlene B. Schwartz. 2008. "Changing Nutrition Standards in Schools: The Emerging Impact on School Revenue." *Journal of School Health* 78(5): 245–251.

White, Craig C., Jeffery P. Koplan and Walter A. Orenstein. "Benefits, Risks and Costs of Immunization for Measles, Mumps and Rubella." *American Journal of Public Health* 75: 739–744.

Wisotzky, Myra, Melissa Albuquerque, Terry F. Pechacek, and Barbara Z. Park. 2004. "The National Tobacco Control Program: Focusing on Policy to Broaden Impact." *Public Health Reports* 119(3): 303–310.

Wootan, Margo G., and Melissa Osborn. 2006. "Availability of Nutrition Information from Chain Restaurants in the United States." *American Journal of Preventive Medicine* 30(3): 266–268.

World Health Organization. Obesity and overweight. 2009. Available at: http://www.who.int/mediacentre/factsheets/fs311/en/index.html

Young, Lisa R., and Marian Nestle. 2002. "The Contribution of Expanding Portion Sizes to the US Obesity Epidemic." *American Journal of Public Health* 92(2): 246–249.

Zoumas-Morse, Christine, Cheryl L. Rock, Elisa J. Sobo, and Marian L. Neuhouser. 2001. "Children's Patterns of Macronutrient Intake and Associations with Restaurant and Home Eating." *Journal of the American Dietetic Association* 101(8): 923–925.

CHAPTER 36

ECONOMIC PERSPECTIVES ON OBESITY POLICY

TOMAS J. PHILIPSON AND RICHARD A. POSNER

INTRODUCTION

THE rise in obesity has generated enormous popular interest and policy concern in developed countries. But obesity (which we define broadly and loosely as weight significantly in excess of what the health care industry deems normal) is not only a public health issue—it is also an economic problem in several respects. First, it is, in major part at least, a function of two choices that people make: the number of calories to consume and the number to expend—the more the former number exceeds the latter, the more weight a person will gain. Consuming calories comes with costs and benefits, and likewise expending calories through exertion. Second, obesity has changed over time and differs across populations and, to the extent that it is a product of choice, explaining these changes and differences is a task for economics. The rate of the rise in obesity will also depend on biological factors that vary, within a range, across persons and time, but such factors *alone*, including genes, cannot explain the rise in obesity, because it has happened much too quickly to be explicable in evolutionary terms. Third, obesity may create social as well as private costs, and, if so, there is a question of whether the government should intervene to try to reduce obesity. Fourth, the answer to that question depends, to the economist, on the cost of alternative methods of public intervention and the benefits, in reducing the social costs of obesity, that each method can be expected to produce. A growing scholarly literature in economics and other social sciences addresses the growth in obesity. We shall discuss the positive and normative[1] analysis of obesity found in that literature.

From a positive perspective, the long run growth in obesity is most easily explained by changes in the price of consuming and expending calories. Agricultural innovation has greatly reduced the time and resources required to go from hungry to full. Human beings used to spend most of their time and energy on producing food. The switch from agricultural economies to ones based on manufacturing and later services was made possible by a dramatic gain in agricultural productivity that greatly reduced the cost of consuming calories. At the same time, technological changes in other forms of production, notably the movement from manual labor to automation, simultaneously raised incomes and increased the price of burning calories, as exercise was no longer a by-product of work, as it had been when work was mainly manual. The gym- and jogging revolution resulted from the reallocation of exercise from working time to leisure time. These economic changes explain the cross-sectional and time-series patterns of obesity better than do biological factors, addiction, and cultural changes, *none* of which alone can explain why Africans are less obese than Americans or why obesity has increased over time.

From a normative perspective, obesity may be a private health problem rather than a public one. The fact that a person is overweight in a medical sense does not necessarily imply that the person is overweight in the sense that he is failing to maximize his utility or that government intervention would make him better off.

Positive Aspects of the Growth in Obesity

Weight is clearly the outcome of diet and exercise, and both of these factors are needed to explain long-run weight trends in the United States. During the twentieth century, weights rose even when the total consumption of food did not, presumably due to a fall in caloric expenditure; the immediate postwar period witnessed substantial growth in weight and *declining* consumption of calories. This suggests that analysis of obesity must account not only for food consumption, but also for changes in the strenuousness of work and leisure, both at home and in the market, caused by economic development (Lakdawalla and Philipson 2002, 2007; and Lakdawalla, Philipson, and Bhattacharya 2005).

The neoclassical theory of obesity (Philipson and Posner 1999; Lakdawalla and Philipson 2002) stresses that technological change provides the best explanation of the time-series data. While food has gotten cheaper through technological change in agriculture, exercise has gotten more expensive, as work (at home and in

---

1 Positive statements concern objective statements of fact (i.e. "what is"). Normative statements concern subjective statements regarding values and beliefs (e.g. "what should be").

the market) has become less physically demanding through technologies that at the same time raise productivity and lower calorie spending. The theory also stresses the complementarities of calorie consumption and calorie expenditure. Cheaper food results in more eating, higher weight, *and* more exercise. Similarly, as the implicit price of exercise rises, there is less exercise, higher average weight, *and* less food consumption as people substitute toward other forms of weight control. The declining price of food and the rising price of exercise thus have offsetting impacts on food consumption, which is one interpretation of why the twentieth-century data show periods of both rising and falling food consumption in spite of continual increases in weight and falling food prices.

The neoclassical weight model also yields predictions about the relation between income and weight. Health, or "closeness" to one's preferred "ideal" weight, is likely to be a normal good, which implies a non-monotonic relationship between income and weight. For poor, underweight people, income growth leads to more food consumption and increased weight, while among well-off, overweight people, income growth might lead to weight loss as people may have increased resources to devote toward striving to attain their ideal weight. Thus, in rich countries, income raises weight among the poorest groups but lowers it throughout the upper half of the income distribution. In addition, while income has a non-monotonic effect on weight within countries, it has a strong positive effect across countries—a greater effect than can be accounted for by aggregation. The impact of technology on weight is essential to interpret this pattern. Across countries, more sedentary but more productive technologies are employed, causing both income and weight to rise.

Behavioral theories of obesity have been proposed (e.g., Cutler, Glaeser, and Shapiro 2003) following the initial work on rational addiction by Becker and Murphy (1988) and the more recent applications of this model to obesity by Cawley (1999). They can help us understand why people seek self-control or commitment devices (for example by joining a Weight Watchers group or undergoing bariatric surgery), but commitment issues *alone*, as initially discussed by Schelling (1978), do not explain well the cross-country and time-series evidence on obesity as they alone cannot account for why poorer countries are naturally less obese or what has changed recently in commitment incentives to generate the observed growth of weight.

Evidence related to the importance of technological change in driving weight change has been developed in several contexts. Lakdawalla and Philipson (2002, 2007) provide evidence that the strenuousness of work has very large effects on weight, while Cutler, Glaeser, and Shapiro (2003) emphasize the declining time cost of preparing food as a result of technological change in food processing. They also note that U.S. consumption of snack foods rose after their prices declined. But since obesity is a worldwide phenomenon, caution must be taken in generalizing from explanations tied to particular circumstances in the United States. Chou, Grossman, and Saffer (2004) analyze a wide variety of price effects and find that weight seems to rise with: lower relative prices of food at home, lower relative prices of fast food and full-service restaurants, the wider availability (and, hence, the lower full price) of such restaurants, lower relative prices of alcohol, and higher relative prices of smoking.[2] In addition, the percentage of income spent on food has steadily declined since the Great Depression (Putnam 2000). Lakdawalla and Philipson (2002) report that about half the growth in weight from the late 1970s to the late 1990s can be explained by the declining relative price of food. Lakdawalla, Philipson, and Bhattacharya (2005) report similar findings for food quality, as opposed to quantity: increases in the relative prices of certain types of foods seem to increase the prevalence of deficiencies in nutrients from those foods. For example, when orange juice is more expensive, vitamin C deficiency rises.

The social aspects of obesity may have a multiplier effect on the growth of obesity. When obesity is relatively rare, it is considered abnormal and repulsive, and this negative response helps to keep it in check. As obesity begins to rise, the negative image of obesity becomes less intense because obesity is now more common[3] (see also Levy 2002; Cohen-Cole and Fletcher 2008). Hence one cost of obesity declines, and this helps obesity continue to grow. At some point, however, the health effects of obesity become so serious that the reduction in the negative image of obesity is offset by health costs.

Childhood obesity has grown along with adult obesity, and indeed these are positively correlated because technological change in leisure (e.g., computers and television) has raised utility while lowering calorie expenditure. Kids are free to play outside if they wish, but they prefer to play inside on their computers. Cawley (2006) argues that parental control and bounded rationality are important factors in childhood obesity. They may be important factors, but that is nothing new and so cannot explain the growth in childhood obesity. Since children (after infancy) generally eat the same meals as their parents, food-related factors promoting adult obesity will work similarly with children. Cawley (2004) also discusses the effect of obesity on income (see also Hamermesh and Biddle 1994, Biddle and Hamermesh 1998; Averett and Korenman 1996; Baum and Ford 2004). To isolate that effect, he compares the wages of siblings of different weight. Surprisingly, he finds that the only effect is in reducing the wages of obese relative to normal white women.[4]

The rise in obesity in other developed countries has lagged the rise in the United States, and this leads Audretsch and DiOrio (2007) to argue that obesity is a negative outgrowth of today's American culture, with its emphasis on fast food and the rise of light service industries, and is bundled with other American practices and transferred to other countries through globalization. A more straightforward explanation, and one more consistent with economic analysis, is that, rather than imitating the United States, countries at a similar stage of development exhibit similar behaviors in their population because the same causal factors, such as rising income and automation, are at work.

Regarding the future of obesity, Acs, Cotton, and Stanton (2007) predict that half of the U.S. population will be obese by 2015, compared to about one-third at present.

---

2 Cawley, Markowitz, and Taurus (2004) focus more specifically on the effect of smoking on weight—they show that adolescents, particularly females, sometimes initiate smoking as a method of weight control.

3 For a discussion on weight as a signaling mechanism to potential mates, see Offer (2001).

4 However, Bhattacharya and Bundorf (2005) estimate that most of this wage differential can be explained by the higher health care premiums employers must pay for obese workers.

There is too much uncertainty about the demand for and supply of the factors that influence obesity to justify placing much weight on such a prediction, but the income or education effect on health will clearly be an important offsetting force to the further impact of technological change. The future of obesity depends on which of two effects on obesity that stem from income growth dominate: the more sedentary way the higher income is generated, or the larger demand for health that it induces.

NORMATIVE ASPECTS OF THE GROWTH IN OBESITY

Naturally, when obesity is regarded as a public health issue, government intervention to control it is recommended as soon as a substantial percentage of the population weighs more than is optimal for maximizing health. From an economic standpoint, the objective to maximize is not health but utility, of which good health is only one component. Rational persons constantly trade off health for competing goods, such as pleasure, income, and time. Interventions that consider such trade-offs unworthy of consideration are paternalistic. This is recognized in such areas as highway safety—no one proposes to shut down highways in order to reduce traffic deaths, or to force automobile manufacturers to equip their cars with engines that limit top speed to 25 miles per hour—but the principle that legitimizes trade-offs involving life and health is equally applicable to obesity. The point is not that governmental efforts to control obesity should be ruled out a priori, but that all relevant costs and benefits of such efforts should be considered.

This is particularly important in analyzing the claim that public intervention to control obesity is justified because of the higher average medical expenses of the obese on public health insurance, such as Medicare and Medicaid. [5] We are skeptical that such fiscal externalities are the true underlying concern of the public health community in promoting intervention. This is because other fiscal effects, such as higher mortality rates[6] of obese individuals (Garfinkel 1986) which reduce Social Security spending, are not considered. An exception is McCormick and Stone (2007) who argue that the medical expenses associated with obesity have been exaggerated because the cost savings resulting from the tendency of obese people to die earlier. However, standard analysis (Kuchler and Ballenger 2002; Finkelstein, Fielbelkorn, and Wang 2004; Finkelstein, Ruhm, and Kosa 2005; and Ostbye, Dement, and Krause 2007) focuses on health care alone. If fiscal externalities are the issue, a more extensive examination of whether obese individuals lower public spending, rather than raise it, seems warranted.

---

5 In the spirit of the early work by Keeler et al. (1989), Grossman and Rashad (2004) have argued that obesity externalities are created by public health insurance pools.

6 Sturm (2002); Joy, Pradhan, and Goldman (2006); and Pamuk et al. (1993) discuss the relationship between obesity and mortality.

Nor are insurance externalities a good argument for public intervention to reduce obesity. Rather, they are an argument for experience-rating health insurance, so that groups with above-average expected medical expenses pay higher insurance premiums (Bhattacharya and Sood 2005). There is no reason to single out obesity as a basis for higher insurance costs, since there are other equally or more risky "life style" choices that increase expected medical costs.

It is unclear whether obesity would create externalities if insurance were allowed to adjust. A more serious problem may be a combination of consumer ignorance with seller exploitation, based on people's addictive tendencies having biological roots; in the ancestral environment to which human beings were biologically adapted, a taste for high-caloric foods had great survival value.

Specific Actual and Proposed Interventions

The principal public interventions, actual or proposed, thus far are education, taxation, fast food regulation, and a little of everything on the model of the campaign against cigarette smoking.

Education

Education is the most frequently proposed and implemented public intervention to control obesity. It comes in several forms, including requirements for furnishing nutritional information on labels for food products, publicly financed advertising of the health consequences of obesity (similar to publicly financed advertising against smoking), nutrition or exercise education, and general education. The motivation for such interventions is the observation that obesity varies across socioeconomic, racial, and cultural groups (and even geographically), even though food is cheaper and work and leisure are more sedentary for everyone. But deficiencies in education and information cannot be the key to explaining the growth of obesity, since people have become much better informed about characteristics of food, including calories, as a result of food labels, diet advertising, and publicity about obesity. Incentives created by technological change have more than offset the increased understanding of caloric intake and expenditure. Thus, the effectiveness of labeling in combating obesity has not been confirmed in the empirical literature (see Aldrich 1999; Kim, Nayga, and Capps 2001; Variyam and Cawley 2006; Loureiro, Gracia, and Nayga 2006).

Still, particular subgroups in the population may be more ignorant than others about the health effects of obesity and about the foods that conduce to obesity. Of course there may be other factors; the feedback effect that we noted earlier may be especially important among groups, such as black and Hispanic women, where obesity is so common as to be normal, reducing social pressures to be thin.

Wilde (2006) discusses the ineffectuality of federal efforts to educate the public about a healthy diet. The government issues dietary guidelines that, if followed, would reduce obesity but, at the same time, through its commodity check-off program, it mandates promotional advertising for beef, pork, and other high-caloric foods. The result, Wilde argues, is to increase the demand for fad diets, which promise quick results enabling consumers to continue or soon resume eating their favorite foods but do not deliver.

Probably most of the obese population understands the mechanisms by which weight is gained and lost, and so additional nutritional education would have only a very limited effect. If we randomized our existing government programs for educating people about overweight and then measured weight five years later, it is unlikely that those who received the nutrition education would be thinner. (Kan and Tsai 2004 suggest otherwise)

More promising are programs of *general* education focused on increasing years of schooling for vulnerable populations (e.g., Variyam and Blaylock 1998). The problem is not that disadvantaged persons cannot read labels and are unaware that obesity is bad for their health, but that uneducated persons have less of an incentive to invest in their health because their longevity and their utility from living are below average.

Taxation

An excise tax on food would reduce consumption, although it would be regressive. A better form of obesity tax would be a nonlinear tax—a tax on *overconsumption* of food—rather than a flat tax on all sales of food. But such a tax would be extremely difficult to enforce; it would be the equivalent of taxing fat people. Elston et al. (2007) analyze four linear tax responses to obesity—a tax on all foods, a tax proportional to particular ingredients (such as sugar or butter), a tax applied to categories of foods, and a value-added tax on food producers. The last, which is the one they favor, would be proportioned to the difference between the price of the raw inputs and the selling price of the finished product, and thus would penalize heavily processed products. This is a feasible linear-tax response to obesity, although its effects would probably be quite limited. In principle the ingredient tax is attractive, but Elston et al. (2007) present a number of complicating factors (see also Kuchler et al. 2005). Probably any feasible tax response to obesity would cost more to enforce than it would be worth in reducing the social costs of obesity.

Fast Food Regulations

The shift of producing and preparing food from the home to the market (due to the increase in the market value of women's time), in particular to fast food preparation and carry-out, is often believed to be an important factor in the rise of obesity, though data are sparse. Chou, Rashad, and Grossman (2006) find a strong correlation between obesity and fast food establishments across regions. This strong correlation is puzzling, given that the vast majority of meals are still home-produced.[7]

Acs, Cotton, and Stanton (2007) proposed restricting access to vending machines and the location of fast food restaurants. These would be costly measures of uncertain efficacy, given substitution possibilities. Regulation of advertising may affect obesity growth more substantially. The food industry is the second largest advertiser in the United States (after the automotive industry) (Story and French 2004). In addition, 11 percent of food advertising geared to children is advertising for fast food and only 2 percent for foods low in sugar, fat, and salt, and almost no ads are directed at children for fruit or vegetables (Center for Science in the Public Interest 2003).

The Tobacco Precedent

Mercer et al. (2003) point out that federal, state, and local government have attempted with considerable success to curb tobacco consumption through a combination of mandatory warnings and other restrictions on labeling and advertising, media campaigns, stiff taxes, highly publicized lawsuits, and location restrictions that have culminated in the prohibition of smoking in most public places. Very little, in contrast, has been done to limit obesity, perhaps rightly so if obesity has fewer external costs than smoking. In any event, the tobacco model has only limited applicability to obesity. It is relatively easy not to begin smoking, so that over time campaigns designed to arouse public awareness of the dangers of smoking, and to increase the expense of the habit, as well as creating a non-monetary inconvenience cost resulting from the location restrictions, reduce the number of smokers, even if no current smokers are able to break their habit. Everyone has to begin eating, however, and having begun one is highly susceptible to becoming obese as a result of biological predisposition, poor information, and the asymmetry that gaining weight is easy but losing weight is hard. Stiff taxes on food, in contrast to stiff taxes on cigarettes, would be intolerable for persons of modest means, and ingredient, non-linear, and other superior forms of taxing calories are unlikely to be feasible and effective. Anderson (2007) argues that class action suits against the fast food industry can be effective in reining in obesity, but these actions are likely to fail for the same reason that most suits by smokers against cigarette companies have failed: juries see the illness resulting from voluntary consumption of dangerous products to be self-inflicted and hence not compensable.

Conclusion

Since economists started to analyze the incentives behind the growth in obesity about a decade ago, a substantial positive and normative literature has developed

---

7 Guthrie et al. (2002), on the basis of 1996 data, estimated that only 17 percent of total calories consumed by men aged 18 to 39, and 13 percent of the total calories consumed by women in that age group came from fast-food establishments.

on the topic. On a positive level, simple price changes seem to explain the overall patterns of change in diet and exercise and the resulting impact on weight. From a normative perspective, there has been little work addressing the possibility that obesity may be a private health problem rather than a public one. There needs to be greater recognition that a person who is overweight in a medical sense is not necessarily overweight in a Pareto sense.

ACKNOWLEDGEMENTS

We are thankful to Mary Peate for research assistance.

REFERENCES

Acs, Zoltan J., Ann Cotton, and Kenneth Stanton. 2007. "The Infrastructure of Obesity." In *Obesity, Business and Public Policy,* ed. Zoltan J. Acs and Alan Lyles. Northampton, MA: Edward Elgar.

Aldrich, Lorna, 1999. , *Consumer Use of Information—Implication for Food Policy.* U.S. Dept. of Agriculture, Economic Research Service (June 1999).

Anderson, Jose Felipe. 2007. "Perspectives on the Economic and Cultural Effects of Obesity Litigation: Lessons from Pelman v. McDonald's." In *Obesity, Business and Public Policy,* ed. Zoltan J. Acs and Alan Lyles. Northampton, MA: Edward Elgar.

Audretsch, David B., and Dawn DiOrio. 2007. "The Spread of Obesity." In *Obesity, Business and Public Policy,* ed. Zoltan J. Acs and Alan Lyles. Northampton, MA: Edward Elgar.

Averett, Susan, and Sanders Korenman. 1996. "The Economic Reality of the Beauty Myth." *Journal of Human* Resources 31(2): 304–330.

Baum, Charles L., II, and William F. Ford. 2004. "The Wage Effects of Obesity: A Longitudinal Study." *Health Economics* 13(9): 885–899.

Becker, Gary S., and Kevin M. Murphy. 1988. "A Theory of Rational Addiction." *Journal of Political Economy* 96(4): 675–700.

Bhattacharya, Jay, and M. Kate Bundorf. 2005. "The Incidence of the Healthcare Costs of Obesity." NBER Working Paper 11303.

Bhattacharya, Jay, and Neeraj Sood. 2005. "Health Insurance and the Obesity Externality." National Bureau of Economic Research Working Paper 11529.

Biddle, Jeff E., and Daniel S. Hamermesh. 1998. "Beauty, Productivity, and Discrimination: Lawyer's Looks and Lucre." *Journal of Labor Economics* 16(1): 172–201.

Cawley, John. 1999. "Obesity and Addiction." Unpublished.

Cawley, John. 2004. "The Impact of Obesity on Wages." *Journal of Human Resources* 39(2): 451–474.

Cawley, John. 2006. "Markets and Childhood Obesity Policy." *The Future of Children* 16(1): 69–88.

Cawley, John, Sarah Markowitz, and John Tauras. 2004. "Lighting Up and Slimming Down: The Effects of Body Weight and Cigarette Prices on Adolescent Smoking Initiation." *Journal of Health Economics* 23(2): 293–311.

Center for Science in the Public Interest. 2003. "Pestering Parents: How Food Companies Market Obesity to Children." http://www.cspinet.org/new/pdf/pages_from_ pestering_parents_final_pt_1.pdf.

Chou, Shin-Yi, Michael Grossman, and Inas Rashad. 2006. "Fast-Food Restaurant Advertising on Television and Its Influence on Childhood Obesity." National Bureau of Economic Research, Working Paper 11879 (Dec. 2006).

Chou, Shin-Yi, Michael Grossman, and Henry Saffer. 2004. "An Economic Analysis of Adult Obesity: Results From the Behavioral Risk Factor Surveillance System." *Journal of Health Economics* 23(3): 565–587.

Chow, Shin-Yi, Inas Rashad, and Michael Grossman. 2005. "Fast-Food Restaurant Advertising on Television and Its Influence on Childhool Obesity." National Bureau of Economic Research Working Paper 11879.

Cohen-Cole, Ethan & Fletcher, Jason M. 2008. "Is Obesity Contagious? Social Networks vs. Environmental Factors in the Obesity Epidemic." *Journal of Health Economics* 27(5): 1382–1387.

Cutler, David M., Edward L. Glaeser, and Jesse M. Shapiro. 2003. "Why Have Americans Become More Obese?" *Journal of Economic Perspectives* 17(3): 93–118.

Elston, Julie Anne, Kenneth Stanton, Levy, and Zoltan J. Acs. 2007. "Tax Solutions to the External Costs of Obesity." In *Obesity, Business and Public Policy*, ed. Zoltan J. Acs and Alan Lyles. Northampton, MA: Edward Elgar.

Finkelstein, Eric A., Ian C. Fiebelkorn, and Guijing Wang. 2004. "State-level Estimates of Annual Medical Expenditures Attributable to Obesity." *Obesity Research* 12(1): 18–24.

Finkelstein, Eric A., Christopher J. Ruhm, Katherine M. Kosa. 2005. "Economic Causes and Consequences of Obesity." *Annual Review of Public Health* 26: 239–257.

Flegal, Katherine. M., Margaret D. Carroll, R. J. Kuczmarski, and Clifford L. Johnson. 1998. "Overweight and Obesity in the United States: Prevalence and Trends, 1960–1994." *International Journal of Obesity* 22(1): 39–47.

Flegal, Katherine. M., Margaret D. Carroll, Cynthia L. Ogden, and Clifford L. Johnson. 2002. "Prevalence and Trends in Obesity among US Adults, 1999–2000." *Journal of the American Medical Association* 288(14): 1723–1727.

Garfinkel, Lawrence. 1986. "Overweight and Mortality." *Cancer* 58(8 Supplement): 1826–1829.

Grossman, Michael, and Inas Rashad. 2004. "The Economics of Obesity." *Public Interest* 156: 104–112.

Guthrie, Joanne F., Biing-Hwan Lin, and Elizabeth Frazao. 2002. "Role of Food Prepared Away from Home in the American Diet, 1977–78 versus 1994–96: Changes and Consequences." *Journal of Nutrition Education Behavior* 34(3): 140–150.

Hamermesh, Daniel S., and Jeff E. Biddle. 1994. "Beauty and the Labor Market." *American Economic Review* 84(5): 1174–1194.

Joy, Amy Block, Vijay Pradhan, and George Goldman. 2006. "Cost-Benefit Analysis Conducted for Nutrition Education in California." *California Agriculture* 60(4): 185–191.

Kan, Kamhon, and Wei-Der Tsai. 2004. "Obesity and Risk Knowledge." *Journal of Health Economics* 23(5): 907–934.

Keeler, Emmett B., Willard G. Manning, Joseph P. Newhouse, Elizabeth M. Sloss, and Jeffrey Wasserman. 1989. "The External Costs of a Sedentary Life-Style." *American Journal of Public Health* 79(8): 975–981.

Kim, Sung-Yong, Rodolfo M. Nayga, Jr., and Oral Capps, Jr. 2001."Food Label Use, Self-Selectivity, and Diet Quality." *Journal of Consumer Affairs* 35(2): 346–363.

Kuchler, Fred, and Nicole Ballenger. 2002. "Societal Costs of Obesity: How Can We Assess When Federal Interventions Will Pay?" *Food Review* 25(3): 33–37.

Kuchler, Fred, Elise Golan, Jayachandran N. Variyam, and Stephen R. Crutchfield. 2005. "Obesity Policy and the Law of Unintended Consequences." *Amber Waves* 3(3): 26–33.

Lakdawalla, Darius, and Tomas J. Philipson. 2002. "The Growth of Obesity and Technological Change." National Bureau of Economic Research Working Paper 8946.

Lakdawalla, Darius, and Tomas J. Philipson. 2007. "Labor Supply and Weight." *Journal of Human Resources* 42(1): 85–116.

Lakdawalla, Darius, Tomas J. Philipson, and Jay Bhattacharya. 2005. "Welfare-Enhancing Technological Change and the Growth of Obesity." *American Economic Review* 95(2): 253–257.

Levy, Amnon. 2002. "Rational Eating: Can It Lead to Overweightness or Underweightness?" *Journal of Health Economics* 21(5): 887–899.

Loureiro, Maria L., Azucena Gracia, and Rodolfo M. Nayga, Jr. 2006. "Do Consumers Value Nutritional Labels?" *European Review of Agricultural Economics* 33(2): 249–268.

McCormick, B., I. Stone, and Corporate Analytical Team. 2007. "Economic Costs of Obesity and the Case for Government Intervention." *Obesity Reviews* 8(Supp. 1): 161–164.

Mercer, S. L., L. W. Green, A. C. Rosenthal, C. G. Husten, L. K. Khan, and W. H.Dietz. 2003. "Possible Lessons from the Tobacco Experience for Obesity Control." *American Journal of Clinical Nutrition* 77(4): 1073–1082.

Offer, Avner. 2001. "Body Weight and Self-Control in the United States and Britain since the 1950s." *Social History of Medicine* 14(1): 79–106.

Ostbye, Truls, John M. Dement, and Katrina M. Krause. 2007. "Obesity and Workers' Compensation: Results from the Duke Health and Safety Surveillance System." *Archives of Internal Medicine* 167(8): 766–773.

Pamuk, Elsie R., David F. Williamson, Jennifer Madans, Mary K. Serdula, and Tim E. Byers. 1993. "Weight Loss and Subsequent Death in a Cohort of U.S. Adults." *Annals of Internal Medicine* 119(7 Part 2): 744–748.

Pamuk, Elsie R., David F. Williamson, Jennifer Madans, Mary K. Serdula, Joel C. Kleinman, and Tim E. Byersl. 1992. "Weight Loss and Mortality in a National Cohort of Adults, 1971–1987." *American Journal of Epidemiology* 136(6): 686–697.

Philipson, Tomas J., and Richard A. Posner. 1999. "The Long-Run Growth in Obesity as a Function of Technological Change." National Bureau of Economic Research Working Paper 7423.

Putnam, Judy J. 2000. "Major Trends in U.S. Food Supply: 1909–99." *Food Review* 23(1): 8–15.

Schelling, Thomas C. 1978. "Ergonomics, or the Art of Self-Management." *American Economic Review* 68(2): 290–294.

Story, Mary, and Simone French. 2004. "Food Advertising and Marketing Directed at Children and Adolescents in the US." *International Journal of Behavioral Nutrition and Physical Activity* 1(3). http://www.ijbnpa.org/info/about/

Sturm, Roland. 2002. "The Effects of Obesity, Smoking, and Drinking on Medical Problems and Costs. Obesity Outranks both Smoking and Drinking in its Deleterious Effects on Health and Health Costs." *Health Affairs* 21(2): 245–253.

Variyam Jayachandran N. 2005. "The Price Is Right: Economics and the Rise in Obesity." *Amber Waves* 3(1): 20–27.

Variyam Jayachandran N., and James Blaylock. 1998. "Unlocking the Mystery between Nutrition Knowledge and Diet Quality." *Food Review* 21(2): 21–28.

Variyam Jayachandran N., and John Cawley. 2006. "Nutrition Labels and Obesity." National Bureau of Economic Research Working Paper 11956.

Wilde, Park. 2006. "Federal Communication about Obesity in the Dietary Guidelines and Checkoff Programs." *Obesity* 14: 967–973.

LESSONS FOR OBESITY POLICY FROM THE TOBACCO WARS

FRANK J. CHALOUPKA

INTRODUCTION

THERE are many parallels between tobacco use and the behaviors that contribute to obesity. The diseases caused by tobacco use, physical inactivity, and unhealthy eating are the leading preventable causes of death in the United States, contributing significantly to various cancers, cardiovascular diseases, as well as separately to respiratory diseases and type 2 diabetes, among many others (Danaei et al. 2009). Together, they account for hundreds of thousands of premature deaths each year, and the disease and premature death they cause results in hundreds of billions of dollars in lost productivity. Hundreds of billions more are spent on health care to treat the diseases they cause, with significant fractions of these costs paid for through public health insurance programs (Finkelstein et al. 2009; Centers for Disease Control and Prevention [CDC] 2008).

Each has biological roots—the release of dopamine and other chemicals in the brain that create pleasure in response to nicotine in the case of tobacco; and the basic need for food, compounded by the evolutionary human trait of seeking out fatty foods (Pidoplichko et al. 1997; Campolongo et al. 2009). Each behavior tends to be firmly established before adulthood, with many of the consequences emerging years later (US Department of Health and Human Services [USDHHS] 1994;

Institute of Medicine [IOM] 2005). Tobacco use and obesity are both more common in the least-educated, lowest-income populations (Giovino et al. 2009; Zhang and Wang 2004).

At the same time, these behaviors are clearly shaped by a variety of environmental influences. The long history of tobacco in our society, sophisticated product designs, extensive marketing of tobacco products, and the ready availability of these products contribute significantly to uptake and their continued use (Brandt 2007). Similarly, the widespread availability and heavy marketing of low-priced, high-calorie foods and beverages with little or no nutritional content, coupled with environments that reduce opportunities for physical activity, are important determinants of unhealthy eating, inactivity, and obesity (Kirk et al. 2010). Historically, the low-income tobacco users who needed cessation services and products most had the least access to them (Giovino et al. 2009). Currently, the lowest-income populations face the most obesogenic environments, residing in food deserts where fresh fruits and vegetables and other healthier products are either unavailable or to be had at high prices and living in dangerous neighborhoods with few opportunities for affordable physical activity (Kirk et al. 2010).

For both tobacco use and obesity, there are large multinational industries with significant economic interests in continuing the consumption of their products (Brownell and Warner 2009). While there are clear differences between the two industries, there are several parallels. Both industries spend billions of dollars each year marketing their products through sophisticated advertising campaigns, price promotions, sponsorships, strategic product placement, and more. Their products have been engineered for mass appeal, and product innovations thought to be healthier often carry their own risks. Moreover, both industries spend considerable resources fighting policy interventions that they perceive as harmful to their profitability.

While tobacco use and obesity have much in common, there are also clear differences between the two. People need to eat to survive, but no one needs to consume tobacco products. There are myriad food and beverage products, and even those with little or no nutritional value can, when consumed in moderation, have no harmful effects on health, while the variety of tobacco products is more limited (but growing) and any use can be deleterious. Perhaps the greatest difference, however, is in the trends for the two. The recognition of the health consequences of tobacco use and the success of the resulting efforts to reduce tobacco use have been called one of the top ten achievements in public health of the twentieth century (CDC 1999). Per capita cigarette consumption in the United States peaked in the late 1970s and is now less than half that, adult smoking prevalence is just over 20 percent, down from 42.4 percent in 1965, and youth smoking rates are at historically low levels (Giovino et al. 2009). In contrast, rates of overweight and obesity are rising rapidly in the United States and obesity has emerged as one of the leading public health challenges of the early twenty-first century (USDHHS 2001). About one-third of adults are obese and almost one-third more are overweight, up sharply from rates a few decades ago (Wang et al. 2008). Nearly one-third of children and

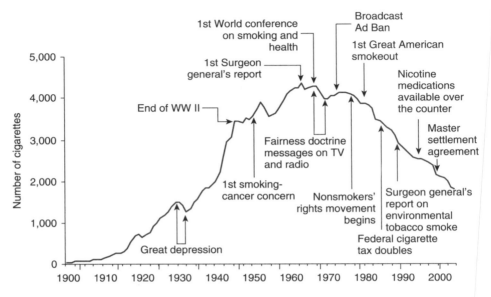

Figure 37.1. Evolution of Tobacco Control–Adult per Capita Cigarette Consumption.

adolescents are overweight or obese, with the obesity rate more than tripling over the past few decades (Ogden et al. 2008).

This chapter reviews the strategies that have been successful in causing the sharp declines in smoking and other tobacco product use observed over the past several decades and describes the potential for similar strategies to be effective in reversing the rise in obesity, using the World Health Organization's MPOWER package (WHO 2008) as an organizing framework. This is followed by a brief discussion of the industry's role in addressing tobacco use and obesity. As shown in figure 37.1, the clear lesson that emerges from the experiences of the "tobacco wars" is that coordinated efforts from the grassroots up and top-down lead to permanent policy, institutional, and social norm changes that generate lasting environmental and behavioral change.

The MPOWER Package: Effective Interventions for Reducing Tobacco Use and Implications for Obesity

In May 2003, the World Health Assembly unanimously adopted the Framework Convention on Tobacco Control (FCTC), the first treaty negotiated by the World Health Organization (WHO). The Convention entered into force in 2005, and currently, 168 countries representing the vast majority of the world's population are parties to the treaty. The FCTC is an evidence-based treaty that identifies a range actions for reducing the supply of and demand for tobacco products. Subsequently, WHO developed the MPOWER package, a technical assistance program for its member states that identifies the six most effective interventions for reducing tobacco use (WHO 2008). These include:

- Monitoring tobacco use and prevention policies
- Protecting people from tobacco smoke
- Offering help to quit tobacco use
- Warning about the dangers of tobacco
- Enforcing bans on tobacco advertising, promotion, and sponsorship, and
- Raising taxes on tobacco products.

These interventions were selected given the extensive evidence accumulated over the past 50 years, largely from high-income countries, about the impact of each in reducing tobacco use. The evidence for each and the potential for comparable interventions to curb obesity are briefly discussed in this section.

Monitor

The onset of the campaign to reduce tobacco use began with the accumulation of evidence linking cigarette smoking to lung cancer. The large-scale epidemiologic studies of the 1940s and 1950s led governments in the United States and other high-income countries to review this emerging evidence. In the United States, the result was the 1964 report of the Surgeon General that concluded that "cigarette smoking is a health hazard of sufficient importance in the United States to warrant appropriate remedial action" (U.S. Public Health Service 1964). The release of the 1964 Surgeon General's report was a catalytic event, itself leading to an immediate reduction in smoking, but perhaps more importantly, creating a strong impetus for governments to take action to reduce tobacco use and beginning the process of changing norms about tobacco use. Over the next few decades, the evidence continued to grow and strengthen, eventually linking tobacco use to a variety of cancers, respiratory diseases, cardiovascular diseases, and more. The most recent Surgeon General's review of this evidence concluded that "smoking harms nearly every organ of the body, causing many diseases and reducing the health of smokers in general" while also documenting the health benefits of smoking cessation (US Department of Health and Human Services [USDHHS] 2004).

Similarly, the evidence demonstrating the harmful effects of nonsmokers' exposure to tobacco smoke, first mentioned in the 1972 Surgeon General's report (U.S. Department of Health, Education and Welfare) grew and strengthened, so that by 2006, the Surgeon General concluded that "secondhand smoke causes premature death and disease in children and adults who do not smoke," linking this exposure to various cancers, respiratory diseases, cardiovascular diseases and more (USDHHS 2006). The evidence on the harmful effects of smoking on nonsmokers provided the spark that led to the creation of the nonsmokers' rights movement in the United States, driving policy change at all levels of government and spurring further changes in social norms about tobacco use.

The information provided by comprehensive surveillance systems that monitor tobacco use and its health and economic consequences, tobacco control policies and other interventions to reduce tobacco use, and the marketing practices and other actions of the tobacco industry has been critical for government and nongovernmental organizations. The information contained in tobacco-focused surveillance systems has been used to show how extensive tobacco use and its consequences are, what populations are most at risk, what factors are instrumental in promoting tobacco use, and what policies and other interventions are effective in reducing tobacco use and the death, disease, and economic costs that it causes (WHO 2008).

The availability of comparable data on diet, physical activity, and weight outcomes has been instrumental in bringing attention to the emerging obesity epidemic (USDHHS 2001). Data from the National Health and Nutrition Examination Surveys have clearly documented the rise in overweight and obesity in the United States since the early 1970s (e.g., Ogden et al. 2008), while the CDC's Behavioral Risk Factor Surveillance System data provide a dramatic illustration of the spread of obesity across the states (see figure 37.2) (CDC 2010). These and other epidemiological data have enabled researchers to link obesity to type 2 diabetes, hypertension, various cancers, and other health problems, as well as to show the considerable economic toll caused by obesity. In contrast, surveillance efforts that provide key data on the environmental factors that contribute to poor diets,

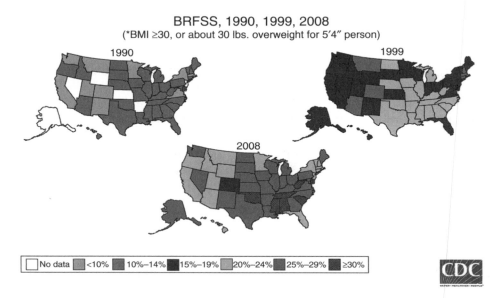

Figure 37.2. Obesity Ttrends among U.S. Adults.

physical inactivity, and obesity are in their infancy, as are similar monitoring systems for tracking local, state, and national policy and other interventions aimed at curbing obesity and its consequences (McKinnon et al. 2009). As these systems are further developed, they will enable the identification of effective policies and other interventions to promote healthier eating and increased activity and allow governments and other organizations to more effectively allocate resources to curbing obesity.

Protect

The emergence and spread of evidence concerning the health consequences for nonsmokers exposed to tobacco smoke helped stimulate the growth of the nonsmokers' rights movement in the United States and elsewhere (USDHHS 2006). The primary result of this effort has been the adoption and strengthening of policies limiting cigarette smoking in a wide variety of public places and private worksites. These policies first emerged in the mid-1970s, with early policies calling for separate smoking and nonsmoking sections in restaurants and/or allowing for designated smoking areas in workplaces and elsewhere (Eriksen and Chaloupka 2007). As evidence on the health consequences of exposure to tobacco smoke strengthened, so did the policies. The Surgeon General's conclusions in 2006 (USDHHS 2006) that "there is no risk-free level of exposure to secondhand smoke" and that "separating smokers from nonsmokers . . . cannot eliminate exposures of nonsmokers to secondhand smoke" has led an increasing number of national and subnational governments to adopt comprehensive bans on smoking in a wide variety of public places, restaurants, bars, and other venues. Currently, more than three-quarters of the U.S. population reside in a jurisdiction that prohibits all smoking in restaurants, bars, and/or worksites (Americans for Nonsmokers' Rights Foundation 2010).

These policies have been highly effective in protecting nonsmokers from exposure to tobacco smoke, while at the same time encouraging adult smokers to quit smoking and preventing youth from initiating smoking (International Agency for Research on Cancer [IARC] 2009). These reductions result, in part, from the strengthening of social norms against smoking that follows the adoption of these policies, as well as from limiting opportunities for smoking and raising the "costs" of smoking (e.g., the inconvenience of or discomfort associated with smoking outdoors). Comprehensive reviews of the research evidence on the impact of smoke-free workplace policies by the National Cancer Institute (2000), the Task Force on Community Preventive Services (2001, 2005) the Surgeon General (USDHHS 2006), and the International Agency for Research on Cancer (2009) find that these policies are effective in inducing some smokers to quit smoking and in reducing the number of cigarettes consumed by some smokers who continue to smoke. Likewise, among youth and young adults, these policies are associated with stronger perceptions of the risks from smoking and lower perceived smoking prevalence among adults.

There appear to be few parallels with respect to policies aimed at curbing obesity. Exposure to obese individuals—for example, a normal weight airline passenger seated next to an obese passenger—may cause some discomfort, but does not create the type of health risks caused by a nonsmoker's exposure to tobacco smoke. To the extent that there are externalities created by obesity, they are likely to be financial externalities, given the high costs of treating the chronic diseases caused by obesity (Brownell et al. 2009). Non-obese individuals share these costs through group health insurance policies that do not charge differential premiums to normal weight and obese individuals, as well as through publicly financed health insurance programs. The presence of financial externalities, however, would suggest different policies.

Instead, the lesson for obesity policy that emerges from the non-smokers' rights movement and resulting smoke-free air policies is the importance of grassroots efforts that change social norms and spur policy change (USDHHS 2006). While there were some state and national actions to restrict smoking in public places, much of the effort occurred at the local level in states like California and Massachusetts, with the support of advocacy and other nongovernmental organizations, including Americans for Nonsmokers' Rights, the Group Against Smoking Pollution, the American Lung Association, the American Heart Association, and the American Cancer Society. Many of the local smoke-free air policies that resulted from these efforts were stronger than those adopted at higher levels of government, and these local policies led the way for subsequent adoption, expansion, and strengthening of state policies.

Similar grassroots efforts around obesity prevention can stimulate local policy action and motivate policy change at higher levels while changing social norms around healthy eating and physical activity. This is perhaps most true currently with respect to efforts to change school environments, given the growing recognition of the consequences of ready availability and marketing of junk foods and sugar-sweetened beverages at schools, the limited availability of healthier options, and reductions in time for recess and physical education classes. Greater awareness has spurred local and state efforts to make healthy school environments the norm, with successful efforts in some jurisdictions leading Congress to require all school districts participating in the National School Lunch program or other child nutrition programs to adopt and implement a wellness policy by the start of the 2006–2007 school year. Among other things, these policies require goals for nutrition education and physical activity, guidelines for foods and beverages sold outside of school meal programs, and assurances that school meals meet the federal minimum nutrition standards. While current wellness policies vary widely in scope and strength, and average policies are weak overall—as most public place smoking restrictions were in the early days of the nonsmokers' rights movement—at least some districts have adopted strong, comprehensive policies that go well beyond the initial requirements (Chriqui et al. 2009). Initial experiences with these local wellness policies will almost certainly lead to a strengthening of the guidelines in the upcoming reauthorization of the law. As time passes, expecting the school environment to be healthy is likely to become the norm, much as expecting public places to be smoke-free is the norm in most of the country.

Offer Help to Change Behavior

Most tobacco users want to stop, but because of the addictive properties of nicotine, quitting tobacco use is difficult. For the typical user, it will take several tries before a successful quit, with many who eventually succeed requiring help (Lindson et al. 2010). This help may involve brief advice from a physician or other medical personnel, counseling received via the telephone through a quit line, face-to-face individualized or group counseling, pharmacotherapy, hypnosis, acupuncture, and/or other interventions (Fiore et al. 2008). Providing support to help quit tobacco use maximizes the impact of other tobacco-control interventions by increasing the success rates of those spurred to make a quit attempt by a smoke-free air policy, higher taxes, new information about the harmful effects of tobacco use, or other factors.

Incorporating cessation into the primary health care system has been a particularly successful and cost-effective intervention in the United States and other high-income countries (Fiore et al. 2008). A model program for this is the "five As": *asking* patients about their tobacco use, *advising* tobacco users to quit, *assessing* willingness to try to quit, *assisting* quit attempts with counseling and/or pharmacotherapy, and *arranging* follow-up (Fiore et al. 2008). Over time, the number of smokers who received advice to quit from a health professional has risen steadily, so that in recent years, nearly two-thirds of smokers report receiving advice to quit from a physician in the previous year and over one-third report receiving such advice from a dentist (Giovino et al. 2009). At the same time, publicly funded support for cessation has been widely expanded; the vast majority of states now provide coverage for cessation aids through their Medicaid programs, and all states provide telephone quit lines and web sites that offer counseling and other information on cessation (Giovino et al. 2009).

Similar interventions could prove successful for reducing obesity among youth and adults. Integrating advice and support for improving diets and increasing activity into the primary health care system is likely to be similarly cost-effective. The "five As" model could be adapted to include *assessing* patient weight status through BMI measurement, *advising* overweight and obese patients about the need to engage in healthier eating and increased physical activity, *assessing* patients' willingness to change their behavior, *assisting* behavior change through counseling and provision of information, and *arranging* follow-up visits to review progress in making these change. States could provide coverage through their Medicaid programs for behavioral counseling related to improving diets and weight outcomes, while employers could offer wellness programs that promote healthier eating and increased activity. As with support for tobacco cessation, this would increase the impact of other policy and environmental changes by providing support for those motivated by the intervention to change their behavior.

Warn about the Harms

Many tobacco users are unaware of the harmful effects of their tobacco use, both to themselves and to those around them, while some who are generally aware of the risks fail to internalize these (Slovic 2001). Still others, particularly young people, are unaware of how addictive tobacco products are, thinking that they will be able to quit when they want to, only to later come to regret their tobacco use and face a very difficult time quitting (Jha et al. 2000). Efforts to inform tobacco users about the risks they face from consuming tobacco products (including the risk of addiction) and the harm that their tobacco smoking causes to those around them have been highly effective in inducing current users to think about quitting and in preventing youth from taking up tobacco use. Particularly effective efforts include the release of new information on the harms caused by tobacco use (e.g., through the Surgeon General's and other reports), strong mandated warning labels on tobacco product packaging (especially the large, pictorial warnings that graphically depict the consequences of tobacco use), and mass-media counter-marketing and public education campaigns (Kenkel and Chen, 2000; National Cancer Institute [NCI] 2008; ITC Project 2009).

In addition to directly affecting tobacco use, these information-focused efforts are important in changing social norms about tobacco use and in building support for other tobacco control interventions. The graphic depiction of the harms caused by tobacco use offset the impact of tobacco company marketing efforts aimed at increasing the appeal of tobacco products and lead to reductions in tobacco use, while mass-media denormalization campaigns that highlight the deceptive practices of tobacco companies further reduce use (NCI 2008). Messages about the harmful effects of exposure to tobacco smoke on children, spouses, and other nonsmokers strengthen social norms against smoking in public places, increase compliance with smoke-free air policies, and motivate many families, including those of smokers, to make their homes smoke free (IARC 2009). Other messages inform current users about the health benefits of cessation and provide information on accessing quit lines and Internet sources that provide support to those who want to quit (NCI 2008).

Information-focused efforts to curb obesity are likely to have similarly positive effects. While it is unlikely that graphic warning labels showing the harmful effects of obesity will be added to high-fat, high-sugar, and/or otherwise unhealthy products in the foreseeable future, some early experiences with state and local policies that require provision of calorie and other information on menu boards and menus suggest that this information can lead to changes in fast food purchase behavior, although this early evidence is mixed (Larson and Story 2009; Elbel et al. 2009; Wisdom et al. 2010). School measurement and reporting to parents of student BMI can raise awareness of obesity and its consequences and lead to changes in diet and activity, particularly when coupled with information that supports behavior change (Nihiser et al. 2007). Public service advertising and other mass-media efforts to promote healthier eating and increase activity are promising, but have been under-utilized to date (Emery et al. 2007).

Enforce Limits on Marketing

Tobacco product advertising, price and other promotions, sponsorships, and other marketing practices increase tobacco use by encouraging greater use of tobacco products by reducing motivation to quit among continuing users, getting former users to restart, and attracting new users (NCI 2008). At the same time, pervasive marketing of tobacco products normalizes these products, while sophisticated advertising campaigns depict tobacco users as glamorous, worldly, athletic, adventurous, and healthful, misleading current and potential users about the harms caused by these products (NCI 2008). The effectiveness of tobacco company marketing in increasing tobacco use has led an increasing number of governments to adopt comprehensive bans on advertising, promotion, sponsorships, and related activities, with research evidence demonstrating that these comprehensive bans are effective in reducing tobacco use (Saffer and Chaloupka 2000; Blecher 2008).

In the United States, efforts to restrict tobacco company marketing practices are constrained by the constitutional protection of free speech. Since 1971, federal law has banned cigarette advertising on television and radio, with subsequent extensions banning broadcast advertising of other tobacco products. State and local governments have adopted relatively few limits on tobacco company marketing practices, with most of these addressing the placement or location of advertising (e.g., within a specified distance of schools or on public transit). The 1998 Master Settlement Agreement (MSA) between the states and major cigarette companies contained a variety of other restrictions, including: a ban on billboard, transit, and most other outdoor advertising; limits on tobacco company brand name sponsorships; prohibition of the use of cartoon characters in advertising and on packaging; a ban on the distribution of branded merchandise; restrictions on sponsorship and the targeting of minors. Despite these restrictions, cigarette company marketing expenditures have increased rapidly over the past few decades, with per pack marketing expenditures, adjusted for inflation, more than doubling in the years immediately following the MSA (Federal Trade Commission [FTC] 2009), resulting in higher cigarette consumption and increased youth smoking uptake (Keeler et al. 2004; Slater et al. 2007).

Food and beverage marketing in the United States is perhaps more pervasive than tobacco company marketing, with estimates suggesting that $10 billion was spent annually on advertising to children and youth alone in the mid-2000s (Institute of Medicine [IOM] 2006). While television advertising is their primary medium of marketing, food and beverage companies engage in a variety of other marketing practices, including product placement, character licensing, Internet marketing, and advergaming, as well as a range of efforts to market their products in schools (IOM 2006; Chriqui et al. 2009). Children and adolescents are particularly exposed to ads for fast foods, cereals, beverages, and sweets, and the vast majority of the food ads seen by youth are for products that are high in fat, sugar, and/or sodium (Powell et al., 2010) Powell et al. 2007). The weight of the evidence from existing research indicates that exposure to food and beverage marketing significantly affects children's and adolescents' diets and health outcomes (IOM 2006).

Efforts to restrict food and beverage advertising and other marketing practices in the United States face the same constitutional hurdles as past efforts to ban tobacco company marketing. As a result, existing efforts to reduce exposure to food and beverage marketing have focused on voluntary initiatives targeting children's exposure. Most prominent among these is the Council of Better Business Bureaus' Children's Food and Beverage Advertising Initiative (CFBAI). Under this Initiative, by 2009, 16 major U.S. companies had pledged not to engage in any televised advertising of foods or beverages on programs primarily directed to children under the age of 12 (4 of the 16 companies) or to engage in "better for you" advertising (the remaining 12 companies). While early data suggest that these pledges have led to some reductions in children's exposure to food and beverage advertising, particularly for sweets and sugar sweetened beverages (SSBs), there are several limits to how much improvement can be expected under the existing pledges (Powell et al. 2010). Strengthening these pledges by adopting more comprehensive definitions about what constitutes youth programming (e.g., by expanding it to cover adolescents and programs watched by large numbers of youth, in addition to those watched primarily by youth) and by setting evidence-based nutrition standards for what defines "better for you" products, while expanding the number of participating companies and extending the pledges to other marketing practices would almost certainly lead to significant reductions in youth exposure to unhealthy food and beverage marketing, leading to improved diets and better weight outcomes.

Raise Taxes

Governments have taxed tobacco products for many years. Historically, the primary motivation for such taxes was to generate revenue. Following the 1964 Surgeon General's report, however, a number of states increased their cigarette excise taxes at least in part motivated by the potential for higher taxes and prices to reduce cigarette smoking and its consequences. Over the past few decades, dozens of studies have clearly demonstrated that higher tobacco product tax and prices lead to significant reductions in tobacco use, particularly among youth and those with lower incomes (Chaloupka 2010). These include reductions resulting from current users quitting tobacco use and from preventing young people from taking up regular tobacco use.

In recent years, at least in part as the result of the evidence on the effectiveness of higher taxes in preventing youth smoking uptake and in reducing adult smoking, tobacco excise taxes have increased rapidly. Between 1990 and 2009, the federal excise tax on cigarettes rose from 16 cents per pack to just over $1.00, the average state cigarette excise taxes more than quadrupled, and a number of communities adopted significant additional excises. These tax increases, coupled with tobacco companies' pass through of costs from legal settlements (most notably the 1998 Master Settlement Agreement), led to a more than 125 percent increase in the

Figure 37.3. Cigarette Prices and Cigarette Sales, United States, 1970–2009.

inflation-adjusted price of cigarettes during this period. As shown in figure 37.3, these significant tax and price increases have played a significant role in the dramatic decline in cigarette smoking in the United States.

The success that governments have had in using higher tobacco product excise taxes to reduce tobacco use coupled with the growing evidence linking consumption of some foods/beverages to weight outcomes has sparked interest in using taxes as a tool for reducing overweight and obesity (e.g., Brownell and Frieden 2009; Brownell et al. 2009). While many states impose taxes on sugar-sweetened beverages (SSBs), candy, salty snacks, and other junk foods—typically by disfavoring these products under their sales tax systems—these taxes are small and have little impact on the relative prices of these products (Chriqui et al. 2008). Existing evidence indicates that these small taxes have little impact on adolescent and adult weight outcomes (Powell et al. 2009; Kim and Kawachi 2006).

Current proposals have focused on taxing SSBs, given the evidence that increased SSB consumption is associated with greater caloric intake, weight gain, obesity, and type 2 diabetes (Gortmaker et al. 2009; Vartanian et al. 2007), as well as the evidence showing that beverage consumption is responsive to changes in beverage prices (Andreyeva et al. 2010) and that changes in food and beverage prices can significantly affect weight outcomes, particularly among youths, lower-income populations, and individuals with higher BMI (Powell and Chaloupka 2009). Some current proposals call for SSB taxes of one or two cents per ounce, which would significantly increase the prices of these beverages. While no jurisdiction has imposed a tax of this magnitude yet, evidence from early adopters demonstrating that such a tax significantly reduces SSB consumption and improves weight outcomes could lead to a wave of SSB taxes in coming years, comparable to that seen for cigarettes and other tobacco products over the past two decades.

The Need for a Comprehensive Approach

While the interventions described above are effective individually, experiences with tobacco control clearly show that the coordinated implementation of the full set of interventions will be most effective in strengthening social norms against tobacco use, getting adult tobacco users to quit, and preventing young people from taking up tobacco use (CDC 2007). Public support for state tobacco tax increases, including among smokers, is greater when a portion of the new tax revenues are used to fund a comprehensive tobacco control program. Well-funded comprehensive state tobacco control programs include (CDC 2007):

- state and community interventions that include implementation of policies and programs that promote cessation, prevent initiation, and support tobacco-free norms;
- health communication interventions that include mass media public education campaigns that are informative about the consequences of tobacco use, strengthen tobacco-free norms, promote cessation, and prevent initiation;
- cessation interventions that include a range of policy, health system, and population-based approaches to encourage and support quitting among current tobacco users; and
- surveillance and evaluation that includes monitoring of tobacco-related attitudes, behaviors, and consequences and allows programs to assess the impact of their efforts.

States that have implemented comprehensive, well-funded tobacco control programs have seen larger reductions in tobacco use among youths and adults, as well as more rapid declines in lung cancer and heart disease deaths than in states without such programs (CDC 2007).

A similarly comprehensive approach to promoting healthy eating and increased physical activity through policy, environmental, and systems change would almost certainly have a greater impact in reducing obesity than would result from an uncoordinated series of efforts focused on more individual-level interventions. As with the longest-running state tobacco control programs, such a comprehensive effort could be funded by the considerable new revenues generated by an SSB tax.

THE ROLE OF THE INDUSTRY

As Judge Kessler ruled in the federal RICO case against the tobacco industry, the tobacco industry spent decades deceiving the public about the health consequences of tobacco use, including by denying the health consequences of tobacco use and exposure to tobacco smoke, denying that tobacco products are addictive while manipulating the nicotine content of these products in order to maintain addiction, marketing light and low-tar cigarettes as less harmful despite evidence showing that this was not the case, marketing their products to young people despite public statements to the contrary, and more (Kessler 2006). At the same time, tobacco companies actively worked against the adoption and implementation of policies and programs effective in reducing tobacco use. The net result of these actions was to keep many adults using their products who otherwise might have quit and to induce numerous young people to take up tobacco use, significantly adding to the public health and economic toll caused by tobacco use.

As Brownell and Warner (2009) describe:

> the tobacco industry had a playbook, a script, that emphasized personal responsibility, paying scientists who delivered research that instilled doubt, criticizing as "junk science" any research that found harms associated with smoking, making self-regulatory pledges, lobbying with massive resources to stifle government action, introducing "safer" products, and simultaneously manipulating and denying both the addictive nature of their product and their marketing to children.

As they note, the industry's public relations campaigns included statements about their commitment to public health and promises not to market their products to young people, which allowed them to get the benefit of the doubt for many years.

Brownell and Warner go on to draw a number of parallels between the tobacco industry's "playbook" and that of today's food and beverage industries. They note that food and beverage companies express similar concerns about the public health consequences of rising obesity rates, while at the same time challenge the science linking consumption of their products to obesity. They are reformulating their products in ways that make them appear healthier (e.g., by reducing fat or sugar content while adding vitamins and minerals), without evidence that these products are indeed "better for you." As described above, they adopt voluntary pledges to limit their advertising to children that do not include a variety of marketing efforts, do not extend to adolescents, and use similarly vague definitions of what constitutes products that are "better for you." They and a variety of front groups oppose policy interventions with the potential to have a significant impact (e.g., recent proposals for SSB taxes) while emphasizing the importance of individual responsibility.

At the same time, Brownell and Warner acknowledge that there are differences between the food and beverage industries' "playbook" and that of the tobacco industry, and that food and beverage companies are likely to have learned from the vilification of the tobacco industry brought on, at least in part, by the disclosure of internal company documents through litigation against the industry. Indeed, while tobacco-control practitioners, researchers, and advocates view the tobacco industry as the enemy in the tobacco wars, many working to curb obesity see the food and beverage industries as potential allies, although many others remain skeptical. One such alliance is that between the Alliance for a Healthier Generation (AHG), a partnership of the William J. Clinton Foundation and the American

Heart Association, and Coca-Cola, Pepsico, the Dr. Pepper Snapple Group, and the American Beverage Association that in May 2006 developed the Alliance School Beverage Guidelines aimed at reducing the availability of at least some SSBs in schools; a recently released report suggests that these guidelines have led to a significant reduction in the availability of beverages covered by the agreement in U.S. schools (American Beverage Association). In November 2006, the AHG worked with Kraft Foods, Mars, and a variety of other food and beverage companies to develop similar guidelines for competitive foods sold in schools. While promising, only time will tell whether the food and beverage industry is an ally or an enemy in the "war on obesity."

CONCLUSIONS

Considerable progress has been made in reducing tobacco use in the United States over the past several decades, beginning with the recognition of the harms that smoking causes both the smoker and nonsmokers exposed to tobacco smoke and accelerating with recognition of the effectiveness of comprehensive, policy-focused efforts that encourage current users to quit, prevent young people from taking up tobacco use, and build and strengthen social norms against tobacco. The experiences in the United States and other high-income countries were critical in developing the evidence base for the world's first public health treaty: the WHO's Framework Convention on Tobacco Control (FCTC), adopted unanimously by WHO member states in 2003, with 168 countries representing the vast majority of the world's population currently parties to the treaty. The FCTC calls for a variety of supply- and demand-side interventions to reduce tobacco use. To assist member states in implementing the treaty, the WHO has developed MPOWER, a technical assistance package that identifies six high priority, effective interventions for reducing tobacco use: monitoring tobacco use and prevention policies; protecting people from tobacco smoke; offering help to quit tobacco use; warning about the dangers of tobacco; enforcing bans on tobacco advertising, promotion, and sponsorship; and raising taxes on tobacco products.

A similar package of interventions, appropriately adapted to promote healthier eating and increased physical activity, would likely be highly effective in addressing the growing obesity epidemic the United States faces today. Similarly coordinated efforts from the grassroots up and top-down that lead to permanent policy, institutional, and social norm changes will generate lasting environmental and policy change that results in better diets, increased physical activity, and healthier weight outcomes.

ACKNOWLEDGEMENTS

The author gratefully acknowledges the Robert Wood Johnson Foundation for support for this work through its funding for the Bridging the Gap research program.

REFERENCES

American Beverage Association. 2010. *Alliance School Beverage Guidelines Final Progress Report*. Washington DC: American Beverage Association.

Americans for Nonsmokers' Rights Foundation. 2010. "Summary of 100% Smokefree State Laws and Population Protected by 100% U.S. Smokefree Laws." http://www.no-smoke.org/pdf/SummaryUSPopList.pdf.

Blecher, E. H. 2008. "The Impact of Tobacco Advertising Bans on Consumption in Developing Countries." *Journal of Health Economics* 27: 930–942.

Brandt, A. M. 2007. *The Cigarette Century: The Rise, Fall and Deadly Persistence of the Product That Defined America*. New York: Basic Books.

Brownell, K. D., T. Farley, W. C. Willett, B. Popkin, F. J. Chaloupka, et al. 2009. "The Public Health and Economic Benefits of Taxing Sugar-Sweetened Beverages." *New England Journal of Medicine* 361(16): 1599–1605.

Brownell, K. D., and T. R. Frieden. 2009. "Ounces of Prevention—The Public Policy Case for Taxes on Sugared Beverages." *New England Journal of Medicine* 360: 1805–1808.

Brownell, K. D., and K. E. Warner. 2009. "The Perils of Ignoring History: How Big Tobacco Played Dirty and Millions Died. How Similar Is Big Food?" *The Milbank Quarterly* 87(1): 259–294.

Campolongo, P., B. Roozendaal, V. Trezza, V. Cuomo, G. Astarita, et al. 2009. "Fat-Induced Satiety Factor Oleoylethanolamide Enhances Memory Consolidation." *Proceedings of the National Academy of Sciences USA* 106(19): 8027–8031.

Centers for Disease Control and Prevention. 1999. "Achievements in Public Health 1900–1999: Tobacco Use—United States, 1900–1999." *Morbidity and Mortality Weekly Reports* 48(43): 986–993.

Centers for Disease Control and Prevention. 2007. *Best Practices for Comprehensive Tobacco Control Programs – 2007*. Atlanta: U.S. Department of Health and Human Services, Public Health Service, Centers for Disease Control and Prevention, National Center for Chronic Disease Prevention and Health Promotion, Office on Smoking and Health.

Centers for Disease Control and Prevention. 2008. "Smoking-Attributable Mortality, Years of Potential Life Lost, and Productivity Losses—United States, 2000–2004." *Morbidity and Mortality Weekly Reports* 57(45): 1226–1228.

Centers for Disease Control and Prevention. 2010. *U.S. Obesity Trends: Trends by State, 1985–2008*. http://www.cdc.gov/obesity/data/trends.html#State.

Chaloupka, F. J. 2010. *Tobacco Control Lessons Learned: The Impact of State and Local Policy*. ImpacTeen Research Paper Number 38. Chicago: ImpacTeen, Health Policy Center, Institute for Health Research and Policy, University of Illinois at Chicago.

Chriqui, J. F., S. S. Eidson, H. Bates, S. Kowalczyk, and F. J. Chaloupka. 2008. "State Sales Tax Rates for Soft Drinks and Snacks Sold Through Grocery Stores and Vending Machines, 2007." *Journal of Public Health Policy* 29(2): 227–249.

Chriqui, J. F., L. Schneider, F. J. Chaloupka, K. Ide, and O. Pugach. 2009. *Local Wellness Policies: Assessing School District Strategies for Improving Children's Health, School Years 2006–07 and 2007–08*. Chicago: Bridging the Gap, Health Policy Center, Institute for Health Research and Policy, University of Illinois at Chicago.

Danaei, G., E. L. Ding, D. Mozaffarian, B. Taylor, and J. Rehm, et al. 2009 "The Preventable Causes of Death in the United States: Comparative Risk Assessment of Dietary, Lifestyle, and Metabolic Risk Factors." *PLoS Medicine* 6(4): e1000058. doi: 10.1371/journal. pmed. 1000058. http://www.plosmedicine.org/article/info%3Adoi%2F10.1371%2Fjournal.pmed.1000058

Elbel, B., R. Kersh, V. L. Brescoll, and L. B. Dixon. 2009. "Calorie Labeling and Food Choices: A First Look at the Effects on Low-Income People in New York City." *Health Affairs* 28(6): w1110–w1121.

Emery, S. L., G. Szczypka, L. M. Powell, and F. J. Chaloupka. 2007. "Public Health Obesity-Related TV Advertising: Lessons Learned from Tobacco." *American Journal of Preventive Medicine* 33(4, Supp.): s257–s263.

Eriksen, M., and F. J. Chaloupka. 2007. "The Economic Impact of Clean Indoor Air Laws." *Cancer* 57(6): 367–378.

Federal Trade Commission. 2009. *Cigarette Report for* 2006. Washington DC: Federal Trade Commission.

Finkelstein, E. A., J. G. Trogdon, J. W. Cohen, and W. Dietz. 2009. "Annual Medical Spending Attributable to Obesity: Payer- and Service-Specific Estimates." *Health Affairs* 18(5): w822–w831.

Fiore, M. C., C. R. Jaén, T. B. Baker, et al. 2008. *Treating Tobacco Use and Dependence: 2008 Update.* Clinical Practice Guideline. Rockville, MD: U.S. Department of Health and Human Services. Public Health Service.

Giovino, G. A., F. J. Chaloupka, A. M. Hartman, Joyce K. Gerlach, J. Chriqui, et al. 2009. *Cigarette Smoking Prevalence and Policies in the 50 States: An Era of Change—The Robert Wood Johnson Foundation ImpacTeen Tobacco Chartbook.* Buffalo NY: University of Buffalo, State University of New York.

Gortmaker, S., M. Long, and Y. C. Wang. 2009. *The Negative Impact of Sugar Sweetened Beverages on Children's Health: A Research Synthesis.* Minneapolis: Healthy Eating Research, School of Public Health, University of Minnesota.

Institute of Medicine. 2005. *Preventing Childhood Obesity: Health in the Balance.* Washington DC: The National Academies Press.

Institute of Medicine. 2006. *Food Marketing to Children and Youth: Threat or Opportunity?* Washington DC: The National Academies Press.

International Agency for Research on Cancer. 2009. *IARC Handbooks of Cancer Prevention, Tobacco Control,* Volume 13: *Evaluating the Effectiveness of Smoke-Free Policies.* Lyon, France: International Agency for Research on Cancer.

ITC Project. 2009. *FCTC Article 11—Tobacco Warning Labels: Evidence and Recommendations from the ITC Project.* Waterloo: University of Waterloo, International Tobacco Control Policy Evaluation Project.

Jha, P., P. Musgrove, F. J. Chaloupka, and A. Yurekli. 2000. "The Economic Rationale for Intervention in the Tobacco Market." In *Tobacco Control in Developing Countries,* eds. P. Jha and F. J. Chaloupka. Oxford: Oxford University Press.

Keeler, T. E., T. W. Hu, M. Ong, and H. Y. Sung. 2004. "The US National Tobacco Settlement: The Effects of Advertising and Price Changes on Cigarette Consumption." *Applied Economics* 36: 1623–1629.

Kenkel, D., and L. Chen. 2000. "Consumer Information and Tobacco Use.: In *Tobacco Control in Developing Countries,* eds. P. Jha and F. J. Chaloupka. Oxford: Oxford University Press.

Kessler, G. 2006. *Final Opinion, United States of America, et al., v. Philip Morris USA, Inc., et al.* Washington DC: United States District Court for the District of Columbia.

Kim, D., and I. Kawachi. 2006. "Food Taxation and Pricing Strategies to 'Thin Out' the Obesity Epidemic." *American Journal of Preventive Medicine* 30(5): 430–437.

Kirk, S., T. Penney, and T. McHugh. 2010. "Characterizing the Obesogenic Environment: The State of the Evidence with Directions for Future Research." *Obesity Reviews* 11(2): 109–117.

Larson, N., and M. Story 2009. *Menu Labeling: Does Providing Nutrition Information at the Point of Purchase Affect Consumer Behavior? A Research Synthesis*. Minneapolis: Healthy Eating Research, School of Public Health, University of Minnesota.

Lindson, N., P. Aveyard, and J. R. Hughes. 2010. "Reduction versus Abrupt Cessation in Smokers Who Want to Quit." *Cochrane Database of Systematic Reviews* 3(Art. No.: CD008033). http://mrw.interscience.wiley.com/cochrane/clsysrev/articles/CD008033/frame.html.

McKinnon, R. A., J. Reedy, S. L. Handy, and A. Brown Rodgers, eds. 2009 . "Measurement of the Food and Physical Activity Environments: Enhancing Research Relevant to Policy on Diet, Physical Activity, and Weight. *American Journal of Preventive Medicine* 36(4, Supplement 1): A1–A6, S81–S190.

National Cancer Institute. 2000. *Population Based Smoking Cessation: Proceedings of a Conference on What Works to Influence Cessation in the General Population*. Smoking and Tobacco Monograph 10. Bethesda, MD: U.S. Department of Health and Human Services, National Institutes of Health, National Cancer Institute.

National Cancer Institute. 2008. *The Role of the Media in Promoting and Reducing Tobacco Use: NCI Tobacco Control Monograph 19*. Bethesda, MD: U.S. Department of Health and Human Services, National Institutes of Health, National Cancer Institute.

Nihiser, A. J., S. M. Lee, H. Wechsler, M. McKenna, E. Odom, et al. 2007. "Body Mass Index Measurement in Schools." *Journal of School Health* 77: 651–671.

Ogden, C., M. Carroll, and K. Flegal. 2008. "High Body Mass Index for Age among US Children and Adolescents, 2003–2006." *Journal of the American Medical Association* 299: 2401–2405.

Pidoplichko, V. I., M. DeBiasi, J. T. Williams, and J. A. Dani. 1997. "Nicotine Activates and Desensitizes Midbrain Dopamine Neurons." *Nature* 390:401–404.

Powell, L. M., and F. J. Chaloupka. 2009. "Food prices and Obesity: Evidence and Policy Implications for Taxes and Subsidies." *The Milbank Quarterly* 87(1): 229–257.

Powell, L. M., J. F. Chriqui, and F. J. Chaloupka. 2009. "Associations between State-Level Soda Taxes and Adolescent Body Mass Index." *Journal of Adolescent Health* 45(3, Supp.): S57–S63.

Powell LM, Szczypka G, Chaloupka FJ (2010). "Trends in Exposure to Television Food Advertisements among Children and Adolescents in the U.S." *Archives of Pediatrics and Adolescent Medicine*. 164(9): 794–802.

Powell, L. M., G. Szczypka, F. J. Chaloupka,and C. L. Braunschweig. 2007. "Nutritional Content of Television Food Advertisements Seen by Children and Adolescents in the United States." *Pediatrics* 120: 576–583.

Saffer, H., and F. J. Chaloupka. 2000. "The Effect of Tobacco Advertising Bans on Tobacco Consumption." *Journal of Health Economics* 19(6): 1117–1137.

Slater, S., F. Chaloupka, M. A. Wakefield, L. D. Johnston, and P. M. O'Malley. 2007. "The Impact of Retail Cigarette Marketing Practices on Youth Smoking Uptake." *Archives of Pediatrics and Adolescent Medicine* 161: 440–445.

Slovic, P., ed. 2001. *Smoking: Risk, Perception, and Policy*. Thousand Oaks, CA: Sage Publications.

Task Force on Community Preventive Services. 2001. "The Guide to Community Preventive Services: Tobacco Use Prevention and Control." *American Journal of Preventive Medicine* 20(2S): 1–88.

Task Force on Community Preventive Services. 2005. *The Guide to Community Preventive Services: What Works to Promote Health?* New York: Oxford University Press.

Tauras, J. A. 2004. "Public Policy and Smoking Cessation among Young Adults in the United States." *Health Policy* 68(3): 321–332.

U.S. Department of Health and Human Services 1994. *Preventing Tobacco Use among Young People: A Report of the Surgeon General.* Atlanta, GA: U.S. Department of Health and Human Services, Public Health Service, Centers for Disease Control and Prevention, National Center for Chronic Disease Prevention and Health Promotion, Office on Smoking and Health.

U.S. Department of Health and Human Services. 2001. *The Surgeon General's Call to Action to Prevent and Decrease Overweight and Obesity.* Rockville, MD: U.S. Department of Health and Human Services, Public Health Service, Office of the Surgeon General.

U.S. Department of Health and Human Services. 2004. *The Health Consequences of Smoking: A Report of the Surgeon General.* Atlanta, GA: U.S. Department of Health and Human Services, Public Health Service, Centers for Disease Control and Prevention, National Center for Chronic Disease Prevention and Health Promotion, Office on Smoking and Health.

U.S. Department of Health and Human Services. 2006. *The Health Consequences of Involuntary Exposure to Tobacco Smoke: A Report of the Surgeon General.* Atlanta, GA: U.S. Department of Health and Human Services, Public Health Service, Centers for Disease Control and Prevention, National Center for Chronic Disease Prevention and Health Promotion, Office on Smoking and Health.

U.S. Department of Health, Education, and Welfare. 1972. *The Health Consequences of Smoking, A Report of the Surgeon General.* Washington, DC: U.S. Department of Health, Education and Welfare, Public Health Service, Health Services and Mental Health Administration.

U.S. Public Health Service. 1964. *Smoking and Health: A Report of the Advisory Committee to the Surgeon General.* Washington, DC: U.S. Public Health Service.

Vartanian, L. R., M. B. Schwartz, and K. D. Brownell. 2007. "Effects of Soft Drink Consumption on Nutrition and Health: A Systematic Review and Meta-Analysis." *American Journal of Public Health* 97(4): 667–675.

Wang, Y. M., A. Beydoun, L. Liang, B. Caballero, and S. K. Kumanyika. 2008. "Will All Americans Become Overweight or Obese? Estimating the Progression and Cost of the U.S. Obesity Epidemic." *Obesity* 16(10): 2323–2330.

Wisdom, J., J. S. Downs, and G. Loewenstein. 2010. "Promoting Health Choices: Information versus Convenience." *American Economic Journal: Applied Economics* 2(2): 164–178.

World Health Organization. 2008. *WHO Report on the Global Tobacco Epidemic, 2008: The MPOWER Package.* Geneva: World Health Organization.

Zhang, Q., and Y. Wang. 2004. "Trends in the Association between Obesity and Socioeconomic Status in U.S. Adults: 1971 to 2000." *Obesity Research* 12(10): 1622–1632.

CHAPTER 38

FOOD TAXES AND SUBSIDIES: EVIDENCE AND POLICIES FOR OBESITY PREVENTION

LISA M. POWELL AND JAMIE F. CHRIQUI

INTRODUCTION

FOOD taxes or subsidies are increasingly being proposed and assessed as potential policy instruments to address the obesity epidemic (Brownell et al. 2009a, 2009b; Powell and Chaloupka 2009). The idea behind such policies is to increase the relative price of consuming unhealthy energy-dense foods versus healthier, less-energy-dense foods in order to shift consumption patterns toward more healthful diets that would translate into lower weight. The marked increases in obesity observed over the past few decades have been related to changes in the relative costs of food and physical activity as a result of technological improvements such that individuals' behaviors have correspondingly shifted toward more energy intake and less activity (Lakdawalla and Philipson 2002; Philipson and Posner 2003). The declining real price of food and the relatively low cost and greater convenience of energy-dense foods, in particular, are hypothesized as key contributors to overweight based on substantial reductions in the cost of consuming a calorie (Cutler, Glaeser, and Shapiro 2003; Drewnowski and Darmon 2005; Bleich et al. 2008).

The extent to which tax and/or subsidy policy instruments can successfully shift consumption away from energy-dense unhealthy products toward more optimal less-dense healthful products and, in turn, improve weight outcomes depends on a number of factors. First, food consumption itself must be price sensitive. A number of controlled experimental studies have shown that reductions in prices have resulted in significant increases in healthy food purchases for fruits, vegetables, and low-fat items (Jeffery et al. 1994; French et al. 1997a, 1997b, 2001; Horgen and Brownell 2002; Epstein et al. 2006, 2007). However, for controlled field experiments, external validity may be low, and overall caloric intake may not change substantially if individuals compensate in uncontrolled environments. A vast literature has examined the price elasticity (percentage change in consumption resulting from a one percent change in price) of food and beverage demand. A recent literature review, including studies based on large survey data sets, shows that food consumption or expenditure is generally price sensitive with average price elasticities generally less than one: for example, -0.78 for soda; -0.35 for sweets/sugars; -0.77 for juice; -0.55 for fats/oils; -0.70 for fruit; -0.59 for vegetables; and, -0.81 for food away from home (Andreyeva et al. 2010).

Second, beyond the price sensitivity of demand, pricing interventions must reduce net calorie consumption in order for weight outcomes to improve. Even with significant price elasticities of demand, taxes, for example, may not translate into significant overall changes in diet or weight if individuals substitute toward alternate lower-priced energy-dense products. For total calories to fall, individuals must not substitute equally energy-dense non-taxed food items for taxed items, nor in the case of a subsidy should they increase overall total calories.

In this chapter, we begin with a brief description of the way in which food, beverage, and restaurant consumption products are currently taxed and subsidized in the United States. We then review the empirical evidence on the direct effect of food, beverage, and restaurant prices and taxes on individuals' weight outcomes to assess the potential effectiveness of using tax and subsidy pricing interventions to reduce obesity. Finally, we discuss important policy design considerations related to implementing pricing policy interventions aimed at obesity prevention.

TAXES AND SUBSIDIES IN THE UNITED STATES

Understanding the Current System of Taxation in the United States

Currently, in the United States, there is no federal tax on foods and beverages, as in other countries such as Canada and Australia (Caraher and Cowburn 2005; Leicester and Windmeijer 2004). Thus, any taxation of unhealthy foods and beverages such as candy and sugar-sweetened beverages is the responsibility of state and local governments. As a result, a patchwork system of taxation exists, whereby certain products are taxed in some but not all states and localities, and where the size of the taxes that do exist vary by state and locality (Jacobson and Brownell 2000; Chriqui et al. 2008).

Most food and beverage items are generally exempted from state sales taxes or are included in a general definition of food products that, when taxed, are taxed at a markedly lower rate than sales taxes applied to other goods and services. For example, according to our data compiled under the Robert Wood Johnson Foundation–supported Bridging the Gap Program, as of January 1, 2009, the average state (across the 50 states plus the District of Columbia) sales tax on food products generally was 1.02 percent; whereas, the average state sales tax on non-food items was 4.91 percent (see table 38.1). However, among states that actually impose sales taxes, the average rates are somewhat higher—only 14 states specifically tax food products generally (with an average sales tax rate of 3.69 percent) as compared to 46 states with a general sales tax (with an average rate of 5.45 percent).

The distinction between general and food sales taxes is important for understanding how unhealthy foods and beverages, such as fast food purchases, candy, and sodas, are currently taxed in the United States. For the most part, any foods or beverages purchased in a restaurant, including both fast food restaurants and full-service or sit-down establishments, follow the general state sales tax scheme. The few exceptions are in the District of Columbia, New Hampshire, and Vermont—each applies a restaurant-specific tax that is higher than the state's general sales tax. As of the beginning of 2009, the average state sales tax on restaurant (including fast food) sales was 5.21 percent across all states and was 5.66 percent in the 47 states with such a tax (table 38.1).

All other food and beverage products either are not taxed, are taxed as part of the definition of "food," or, depending on the item, are taxed at a higher rate than the general food tax but lower than the state sales tax (Chriqui et al. 2008). As table 38.1 illustrates, states currently tax items such as potato chips/pretzels and baked

Table 38.1. Average State Sales Taxes for Grocery Store Sales by Category of Tax/Taxable Item, 2009

Tax Category/Taxable Item	Mean Tax— All States (N=51; 50 states plus D.C.)	Mean Tax— States with a Tax	# of States with Tax
General sales tax	4.92 percent	5.45 percent	46
General food tax	1.02 percent	3.70 percent	14
Fast food restaurant	5.22 percent	5.66 percent	47
Soda	3.36 percent	5.20 percent	33
Candy	2.76 percent	4.85 percent	29
Chips/pretzels	1.02 percent	3.70 percent	14
Baked goods	1.02 percent	3.70 percent	14

Source: Bridging the Gap Program, Health Policy Center, Institute for Health Research and Policy, University of Illinois at Chicago based on data compiled by The MayaTech Corporation. All data reflect tax rates effective as of January 1, 2009.

goods at the same rate as food products generally (i.e., 1.02 percent). Taxes on candy and sodas, however, tend to be taxed at a higher rate than food products generally and, therefore, are considered "disfavored" relative to other food products (Chriqui et al. 2008; Stone et al. 2001). In fact, as of January 1, 2009, 33 states applied a sales tax to sodas sold through grocery stores, and 29 states applied such a tax to candy sales as compared to only 14 states that taxed food items generally. The average state sales tax for candy was 2.76 percent across all states and 4.85 percent in the 29 states that imposed such a tax. The sales tax on sodas was somewhat higher— 3.36 percent across all states and 5.20 percent in the 33 states with a soda sales tax. Notably, none of the revenues generated from these taxes is dedicated to obesity prevention efforts or programs.

Trends in Food and Beverage Taxation

With the exception of the general state sales tax and the tax on fast food restaurant items, state sales taxes on foods and sodas have declined or remained fairly stable between 1997 and 2009 (see figure 38.1). The largest percentage declines over this time period have been for chips/pretzels and baked goods. Specifically, the average general food tax across all states declined from 1.70 percent to 1.02 percent while the average sales tax on chips/pretzels and baked goods declined from 1.85 percent and 1.93 percent, respectively, to 1.02 percent (same as the food tax). The average state sales taxes on candy and sodas, however, declined by less than one-half of a percentage point over this time period—changing from 3.83 to 3.36 percent for soda and from 3.35 to 2.76 percent for candy (which was equivalent to a 12 percent and 17 percent decrease in the tax rates for these items, respectively). In contrast, the sales tax applied to fast food restaurant sales increased slightly from 4.99 percent in 1997 to 5.22 percent in 2009.

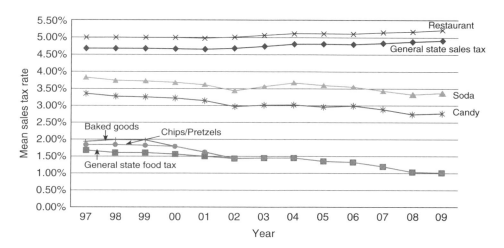

Figure 38.1. Mean State Sales Tax Rates on Food Products, Regular Soda, Restaurant
Sales, and Snacks, 1997–2009.
Source: Bridging the Gap Program, Health Policy Center, Institute for Health Research
and Policy, University of Illinois at Chicago based on data compiled by The MayaTech
Corporation. All Data reflect tax rates effective as of January 1 of each year and
include all 50 states and the district of Columbia.

Other Types of Taxes on Foods and Beverages

Besides sales taxes applicable to foods and beverages sold through grocery stores, a
number of states also impose a sales tax to items sold through vending machines. In
fact, in all cases, more states tax items through vending machines than through
grocery stores, and the tax rates are higher for vending sales than grocery sales
(Chriqui et al. 2008). For example, 29 states tax candy sold through grocery stores
at an average of 4.85 percent, but 37 states tax candy sold through vending machines
at an average of 5.14 percent. Similarly, while 33 states tax soda sold through grocery
stores at an average of 5.20 percent, 39 states tax soda sold through vending machines
at an average of 5.26 percent.

At the same time, in addition to sales taxes, seven states—Alabama, Arkansas,
Rhode Island, Tennessee, Virginia, Washington, and West Virginia—currently
impose other types of taxes or levy fees for the sale of soda (Chaloupka, Powell, and
Chriqui 2009; Chriqui et al. 2008). These additional taxes generally apply to bottles,
syrups, and/or powders/mixes and are targeted at various levels of the distribution
chain, including wholesalers, bottlers, manufacturers, and distributors; however,
none of the revenue generated from these additional taxes/fees is currently dedicated to obesity prevention programming. With the exception of the license fees
and taxes imposed on manufacturers, wholesalers, and/or retailers in Alabama
(Ala. Code §§ 40-12-65, -69, -70 [2010]), most of these additional taxes or levies
are based on volume of soda (typically in gallons) (Chriqui et al. 2008). For example, as of January 1, 2009, an excise tax is placed upon manufacturers, distributors,
wholesalers, and retailers in the amount of one cent per half liter or fraction of

soda placed in bottles. In Washington state, an excise tax of $1 per gallon of soda syrup is imposed upon wholesalers and retailers of soda syrup (Wash. Rev. Code Ann. § 82.64/020 (2010)). In Rhode Island, an excise tax of 4 cents per case of 24, 12-ounce soda cans is placed upon manufacturers (R.I. Gen. Laws § 44-44-3 (2010)).

Food and Beverage Subsidies Directed at Consumers in the United States

Food and/or beverage subsidies have not traditionally been targeted at consumers with the aim of shifting consumption patterns and preventing obesity. Rather, food in the United States is subsidized to help alleviate food insecurity for low-income individuals and families through a number of programs such as the Supplemental Nutrition Assistance Program (SNAP); the Women, Infant and Children (WIC) Nutrition Program; the Child and Adult Care Food Program; and the National School Lunch and Breakfast Programs. Subsidies directed at the consumer do not generally exist for specific food items, although some benefits such as WIC can only be used for certain foods and others are delivered through the provision of regulated foods such as school breakfasts and lunches. However, the USDA undertook a "Healthy Purchase" pilot program in California that targeted subsidies within the food stamp program such that for each dollar of food stamps spent on fresh produce, participants were subsidized a portion of the cost (Guthrie et al. 2007). Most recently, more permanent changes were made within the WIC program with the addition of monthly cash-value vouchers specifically for fruits and vegetables in the amount of $10 for fully breast-feeding women, $8 for non-breast-feeding women, and $6 for children (Oliveira and Frazao 2009). The scientific and nutrition communities also recently issued recommendations to improve the nutritional quality of USDA-subsidized school meals by including specific nutrient targets for calories, fats, cholesterol, protein, vitamins, and minerals; and recommending that school meals align with the 2005 Dietary Guidelines for Americans with the goal of increasing the amount of fruits, vegetables, and whole grains offered as part of the school meals (Institute of Medicine 2009b). Likewise, as part of the congressionally mandated wellness policy required of all school districts in the United States participating in the federal school meal programs (P.L. 108–265, Section 204), some districts have taken specific steps to require a minimum number of fruits and vegetables, whole grains, and skim/low-fat milk daily as part of the school meal offerings (Chriqui et al. 2009).

EMPIRICAL EVIDENCE ON PRICES AND WEIGHT OUTCOMES

We conducted a literature search in November 2009 to identify peer-reviewed articles published in English from 1990 through 2009. Studies were identified from the following data bases: Medline, PubMed, Econlit, and PAIS. Fifteen search combinations were used, which included the terms Obesity, Body Mass Index (BMI), and BMI, each in combination with the terms Price, Prices, Tax, Taxation, and Subsidy. Additional studies also were considered based on the authors' knowledge of the existing literature. The articles were reviewed by two individuals to assess their appropriateness for inclusion in our review, which was based on the criteria that the paper needed to provide published or in press original quantitative empirical evidence on the relationship between food prices (or taxes or subsidies) and body weight outcome measures using U.S. data. A total of 18 articles described in table 38.1 met our inclusion criteria and were reviewed as part of our evidence base on the potential effectiveness of using tax or subsidy pricing instruments to improve weight outcomes measured by BMI (weight in kilograms divided by height in meters squared) and obesity prevalence (BMI $\geq$ 30 for adults and defined by age- and gender-specific BMI $\geq$ 95th percentile for children).

Table 38.2 summarizes the 18 studies that examine the relationship between food, beverage, and restaurant prices or taxes and weight outcomes. Eleven of the studies are cross-sectional and seven use longitudinal estimation methods to control for unobserved individual-level heterogeneity. One study examines aggregate state-level obesity prevalence rates rather than individual-level weight outcomes. This literature is still not vast but there has been a proliferation of studies published or in press over the past year, doubling the available evidence reviewed just over a year ago (Powell and Chaloupka 2009). Note that the table reports price evidence for relevant products that are candidates for pricing policies, including fast food, sugar, soda, and high-calorie products as possible items for taxation and fruits and vegetables as candidates for subsidies. We do not report on price effects for items such as overall food at home price indices and full-service restaurant prices since such broad measures are not appropriate candidates for pricing policy interventions aimed at obesity prevention.

Empirical Evidence for Taxation

We begin by reporting on the evidence on the extent to which taxes on energy-dense high-calorie foods and/or beverages may translate into weight outcomes. As shown in Table 38.1, a number of studies, particularly those on adolescent weight, have examined the association between fast food prices and BMI and obesity. All of these studies used the American Chamber of Commerce Researchers' Association (ACCRA) price data as their source for fast food prices. The fast food price evidence available for adults is limited, based on cross-sectional models only, and the findings are mixed. Chou, Grossman, and Saffer (2004) undertook cross-sectional analyses using data from the Centers for Disease Control and Prevention's Behavioral Risk Factor Surveillance System (BRFSS) and found adult BMI to be statistically significantly negatively related to fast food restaurant prices (elasticity of -0.05) and obesity prevalence was found to be negatively but not statistically significantly related to fast food prices (elasticity of -0.65). In contrast, however, Beydoun,

Table 38.2. Evidence on Price Effects on Body Weight Outcomes

Author	Price/Tax Measure (Source)	Data Set	Population	Model	Outcome Measure	Evidence for Tax Effects: Fast Food Prices (FFP), Soft Drink Tax (SDT), Sugar Price (SP), or Price per Calories (PPC) (Direction (Elasticity[a]))	Evidence for Subsidy Effects: Fruit and Vegetable Prices (FVP) (Direction (Elasticity[a]))
Evidence for Adults:							
Chou, Grossman, and Saffer (2004)	Full-service restaurant prices, fast-food restaurant prices, and prices of food at home (ACCRA[2])	BRFSS[3], 1984–1999	Adults 18 years and older (*n*=1,111,074)	Cross-sectional	BMI[4] Obesity	**FFP:** - (0.05) FFP: - (0.65)	N/A N/A
Kim and Kawachi (2006)	State-level taxes on soft drinks and snacks	BRFSS[3], 1991–1998	State-level averages of adults	Cross-sectional	State-level obesity prevalence	N/A	N/A
Miljkovic and Nganje (2008)	Prices of sugar (National Agricultural Statistics Service, USDA[5])	BRFSS[3], 1991, 1997, and 2002	Adults 18 years and older (*n*=45,440)	Cross-sectional	Overweight Obesity	**SP:** - (0.20) **SP:** - (0.81)	N/A N/A

Study	Variables (data source)	Data and years	Sample	Design	Outcome		
Miljkovic, Nganje, and de Chastenet (2008)	Prices of sugar (National Agricultural Statistics Service, USDA[5])	BRFSS[3], 1991, 1997, and 2002	Adults 18 years and older (n=55,550)	Cross-sectional	Overweight	**SP:** -	N/A
					Obesity	**SP:** -	N/A
Beydoun, Powell, and Wang (2008)	Prices of fruits and vegetables and fast food (ACCRA[2])	CSFII[6], 1994–1996	Adults aged 20 to 65 (n=7331)	Cross-sectional	BMI[4]	FFP: +	**FVP:** -
					Obesity	FFP: +	FVP: +
Fletcher, Frisvold, and Tefft (2010)	Incremental soft drink tax rate and total soft drink tax rate (Web, Lexisnexis Academic Search, and States' Departments of Revenue web sites)	BRFSS[3] 1990–2006	Adults 18 years and older (n=2,709,422)	Pooled Cross-sectional	BMI[4]	**SDT:** -	N/A
					Obesity	**SDT:** -	N/A
					Overweight	**SDT:** -	N/A

(Continued)

Table 38.2. (Cont.)

Author	Price/Tax Measure (Source)	Data Set	Population	Model	Outcome Measure	Evidence for Tax Effects: Fast Food Prices (FFP), Soft Drink Tax (SDT), Sugar Price (SP), or Price per Calories (PPC) (Direction (Elasticity[a]))	Evidence for Subsidy Effects: Fruit and Vegetable Prices (FVP) (Direction (Elasticity[a]))
Goldman, Lakdawalla, and Zheng (in press)	Price per calorie, price of cigarettes, and price of gasoline (ACCRA[2])	HRS[7] 1992–2004	Adults born between 1931–1941 (n=9,733)	Longitudinal (FE[8])	BMI[4] and log(BMI[4])	PPC: - (0.06) short run PPC: - (0.42) long run	N/A
Powell and Han (in press)	Price of fruits and vegetables Price of fast food (ACCRA[2])	PSID[9] 1999, 2001, 2003, 2005	Adults 18–65 years old (n=6,045 men and 6,806 women)	Cross-sectional and Longitudinal (FE[8])	BMI[4]	FFP: -, men, CS[10] FFP: +, men, FE[8] FFP: -, women, CS[10] FFP: +, women, FE[8]	FVP: +, men CS[10] FVP:+, men FE[8] FVP: +, women CS[10] FVP: +0.02, women FE[8] FVP:+0.09, poor women FE[8] FVP:+0.03, women with children FE[8]

Evidence for Children and Adolescents:

Study	Measure	Data source	Design	Outcome	FFP	FVP
Sturm and Datar 2005	Price indices for meat, fruits and vegetables, dairy, and fast food (ACCRA[2])	ECLS-K[11], 1998–2002	Children K through 3rd grade (n=6,918)	Longitudinal	BMI[4]	FFP: not significant and not included in final model	FVP: - (0.05)
Powell et al. (2007)	Prices of fruits and vegetables and fast food (ACCRA[2])	MTFS[12], 1997–2003	Adolescents in 8th and 10th grade (n=72,854)	Cross-sectional	BMI[4] Overweight	FFP: - (0.04) FFP: - (0.59)	FVP: + FVP: +
Auld and Powell (2009)	Prices of fruits and vegetables and fast food (ACCRA[2])	MTFS[12], 1997–2003	Adolescents in 8th and 10th grade (n=73,041)	Cross-sectional	BMI[4]	FFP: - (0.03) FFP: - (0.10) male* FFP: - (0.11) female* *at the 90th quantile	FVP: + (0.03) FVP: + (0.05) male* FVP: + (0.06) female* * at the 95th quantile.
Chou, Rashad, and Grossman (2008)	Fast food, full service restaurant, and food at home price (Census of retail trade and ACCRA[2])	NLSY97[13] 1997–1999	Adolescent 12–18 years (n=14,852)	Cross-sectional Overweight	BMI[4]	FFP: - FFP: - female FFP: - male FFP: - whole sample, male, and female	N/A N/A

(Continued)

Table 38.2. (Cont.)

Author	Price/Tax Measure (Source)	Data Set	Population	Model	Outcome Measure	Evidence for Tax Effects: Fast Food Prices (FFP), Soft Drink Tax (SDT), Sugar Price (SP), or Price per Calories (PPC) (Direction (Elasticity))	Evidence for Subsidy Effects: Fruit and Vegetable Prices (FVP) (Direction (Elasticity))
Sturm and Datar (2008)	Price indices for meat, fruits and vegetables, dairy, and fast food (ACCRA[2])	ECLS-K[11], 1998–2004	Children K through 5th grade (n=4,557)	Longitudinal	BMI[4]	N/A	FVP: +, 3rd grade FVP: +, 5th grade
Powell (2009)	Fast food prices (ACCRA[2])	NLSY97[13] 1997–2000	Adolescents 12–17 years old in 1997 (n=11,900)	Cross-sectional, and longitudinal (RE[14], and FE[8])	BMI[4]	FFP: - (0.10), CS[10], RE[14], FFP: - (0.08), FE[8], FFP: - (0.08), FFP: - (0.13) mother low education, FE[8] FFP: - (0.31) middle income, FE[8]	N/A

Study	Measure (data source)	Population	Study design	Outcome	Results	
Powell and Bao (2009)	Fruit and vegetable and fast food prices (ACCRA[2])	NLSY79[15] 1998–2002	Children 6–18 years old (n=6,594)	Longitudinal (RE[14])	BMI[4]	FFP:- (0.67) FFP: - (0.26) low income FFP: - (0.13) mother low education	FVP: + (0.07) FVP: + (0.14) low income FVP: + (0.09) mother low education
Powell, Chriqui, and Chaloupka (2009)	Soda taxes (BTG[16])	Adolescents 13–19 years old (n=153,673)	Cross-sectional	BMI[4]	SDT: + SDT:-, at risk of overweight. Vending machine SDT:+ Vending machine SDT: - at risk of overweight	N/A
Powell and Chaloupka (in press)	Fast food and fruit and vegetable prices (ACCRA[2])	Children 2–18 years old (n=1,629)	Cross-sectional and Longitudinal (FE[8])	BMI[4]	FFP: - (0.16), CS[10] FFP: - (0.77) low income, CS[10] FFP: + (0.24), FE[8] FFP: - (0.21) low income, FE[8]	FVP: + (0.24), CS[10] FVP: + (0.27) low income, CS[10] FVP: + (0.25), FE[8] FVP: + (0.60), low income, FE[8]
Sturm et al. (2010)	State sales soda tax BTG[16]	Children (n=7,300)	Cross-sectional	BMI[4]	SDT: - SDT: -, at risk overweight SDT: - low income SDT: +, African American	N/A

(Continued)

Table 38.2. (Cont.)

Author	Price/Tax Measure (Source)	Data Set	Population	Model	Outcome Measure	Evidence for Tax Effects: Fast Food Prices (FFP), Soft Drink Tax (SDT), Sugar Price (SP), or Price per Calories (PPC) (Direction (Elasticity[1]))	Evidence for Subsidy Effects: Fruit and Vegetable Prices (FVP) (Direction (Elasticity[1]))
						SDT: − watches 9 or more hours of TV	

[1] All directions and elasticity are statistically significant when in bold. Elasticity measures provided when available. Results for selected sub samples noted.

2 American Chamber of Commerce Researchers Association
3 Behavior Risk Factor Surveillance System
4 Body Mass Index
5 United States Department of Agriculture
6 Continuing Survey of Food Intakes by Individuals
7 Health and Retirement Study
8 Longitudinal individual-level fixed effects
9 Panel Study of Income Dynamics
10 Cross-sectional model
11 Early Childhood Longitudinal Study- Kindergarten cohort
12 Monitoring the Future Survey
13 National Longitudinal Study of Youth 1997
14 Longitudinal individual-level random effects
15 National Longitudinal Study of Youth 1979
16 Bridging the Gap—Robert Wood Johnson Foundation–supported project, Health Policy Center, University of Illinois at Chicago
17 Child Development Supplement—Panel Study of Income Dynamics.

Powell, and Wang (2008), using older data from the 1994–1996 Continuing Survey of Food Intakes by Individuals (CSFII), did not find a statistically significant negative relationship between fast food prices and BMI or obesity prevalence.

Higher fast food prices have been related to lower BMI and obesity among adolescents in a number of studies. Estimating cross-sectional models using the 1997–1999 waves of the National Longitudinal Survey of Youth 1997 (NLSY97), Chou, Rashad, and Grossman (2008) found higher fast food prices to be significantly associated with lower youth BMI and in subsamples it was significant for female but not male youths; however, the negative association found with obesity prevalence was not statistically significant. Examining cross-sectional data from 1997 through 2003 from the University of Michigan's Monitoring the Future (MTF) study on 8th and 10th grade adolescents, Powell et al. (2007) found the price of fast food to be weakly statistically significantly related to lower BMI levels among youths (elasticity -0.04) and statistically significantly related to a lower probability of overweight (elasticity of -0.59). In a subsequent study using the MTF youth data, Auld and Powell (2009) used quantile regression analyses to assess the differential relationship between food prices and BMI across the BMI distribution. The BMI regression results showed that fast food prices were associated with BMI, but the effects were small: the fast food price elasticity for BMI was -0.03. The results from the quantile regressions showed that the fast food price effects at the higher quantiles were three to four times greater than across the distribution as a whole. For example, for male and female adolescents, the BMI fast food price elasticities were -0.10 and -0.11, respectively, at the 90th BMI quantile, suggesting that taxes would have larger effects for adolescents at risk of obesity.

Most recently, Powell (2009) found that estimates based on longitudinal individual-level fixed effects models confirmed previous cross-sectional findings that the price of fast food had a statistically significant effect on teen BMI. A one dollar increase in the price of fast food was estimated to reduce adolescent BMI by 0.65 units, corresponding to a fast food price elasticity of -0.08. Estimates from the individual-fixed effects model suggested that the cross-sectional model overestimated the price of fast food BMI effect by about 25 percent. This study found the weight of teens in low- to middle-socioeconomic-status families to be most sensitive to fast food prices. Teens with low-educated mothers (high school or less) were found to be more price elastic (BMI fast food price elasticity of -0.13) than those with mothers with college education. Estimates by income tertiles revealed significant price sensitivity for teens living in middle-income households with a BMI fast food price elasticity of -0.31.

In studies that included younger children, there was generally no evidence of significant fast food price effects on weight outcomes. Using a random-effects estimation model, Powell and Bao (2009) found that fast food prices were not statistically significantly related to BMI in the full sample of children aged 6–18 but were weakly negatively associated with BMI among adolescents with an estimated price elasticity of -0.12 (Powell and Bao 2009). Similarly, Sturm and Datar (2005) did not find any evidence that fast food prices were statistically significantly related to young children's weight outcomes. Powell and Chaloupka (in press) also found that fast food prices were not statistically significantly related to children's weight outcomes, in either the cross-sectional or longitudinal fixed effects models for the full sample. However, the cross-sectional results suggested that higher fast food prices were associated with lower BMI among low-income children (price elasticity of -0.77), but the estimated effect for the low-income sample from the longitudinal model was not statistically significant.

Two studies have focused on sugar prices and adult weight drawing on the BRFSS data merged with county-level price data obtained from the U.S. Department of Agriculture (USDA). Based on a rational addiction model, Miljkovic, Nganje, and de Chastenet (2008) found that individuals' weight was significantly negatively associated with the current price of sweet foods, but a future increase in the price of sweet foods was not associated with a current reduction in weight. In a subsequent study, Miljkovic and Nganje (2008) found that a one dollar increase in the current price of sugar was associated with a 0.20 and 0.33 percentage point reduction in the probability of overweight and obesity, respectively. Based on the summary statistics provided in the paper, the marginal effects correspond to a current price of sugar elasticity of -0.20 for overweight and -0.81 for obesity. In addition, statistically significant large associations were found between the historical price of sugar and overweight supporting the myopic model of addictive behavior. Overall, these results suggest that taxing high-sugar food items may have long-run significant effects on weight outcomes. Another recent study also suggests the potential for substantial long-run effects on BMI from taxes applied to high-calorie products. Drawing on data from the Health Retirement Survey (HRS), Goldman, Lakdawalla, and Zheng (in press) estimated the short-term (2 year) effect of the price of calories on body weight to be -0.063, but estimated that a permanent 10 percent increase in price per calorie would lead to a long-run (30 year) 4.2 percent reduction in BMI.

Finally, several studies have drawn on existing state-level food and beverage sales taxes to examine the tax sensitivity of weight, mostly with a focus on soda taxes. Overall, the results show that at the current tax levels there is minimal evidence of an effect on weight. A study using aggregated individual-level data at the state level from the BRFSS and state soda and snack sales taxes by Kim and Kawachi (2006) found no statistically significant differences in obesity prevalence between states without taxes and those with taxes or those with at least a 5 percent tax. They found weak statistical evidence that, compared to states with taxes, states that had repealed a specific soft drink or snack food tax were thirteen times more likely to have had a high relative increase in obesity prevalence (≥ 75 percentile in the relative increase). Using individual-level data from the 1990–2006 cross-sections of the BRFSS, Fletcher, Frisvold, and Tefft (2010) found statistically significant but very small associations between soda taxes and adult weight outcomes: a 1 percentage point increase in the state soft drink tax was associated with a 0.003 unit reduction in adult BMI and a 0.01 percentage point decrease in adult obesity prevalence.

Examining adolescents, Powell, Chriqui and Chaloupka (2009) found no statistically significant association between state-level soda taxes and adolescent

BMI based on analyses using the MTF cross-sectional data. However, they found a statistically significant but very small effect of state soda taxes applied to vending machines and adolescent BMI among teens at risk for overweight. Specifically, a one percentage point increase in the vending machine tax rate was associated with a 0.006 reduction in BMI among adolescents at risk of overweight. In a recent study focused on younger children drawn from the Early Childhood Longitudinal Study-Kindergarten (ECLS-K) cohort, Sturm et al. (2010) found that higher soda taxes were related to lower BMI change from 3rd to 5th grade, but this finding was not robust to alternative model specifications and it stemmed mainly from children already at risk for overweight. Among subpopulations, while they did find that higher soda taxes were significantly associated with lower soda consumption among children in lower-income families, African Americans, heavy television watchers, and heavier children, particularly those reporting soda availability at school, higher soda taxes were only statistically significantly associated with lower BMI gain among children already at risk for overweight, and the effect was very small. A one percentage point increase in the soda tax rate was associated with a -0.033 unit change in BMI among heavier children.

Empirical Evidence for Subsidies

In table 38.2, the last column reports on the results from the available evidence examining the relationship between fruit and vegetable prices and weight outcomes to highlight the extent to which fruit and vegetable subsidies may help to reduce obesity. The largest body of evidence to date, including the most consistent findings, is for children. All of the studies drew their fruit and vegetable price data from ACCRA, and a number of these studies used longitudinal individual-level data.

The evidence for adults is limited and mixed. Most recently, based on longitudinal data from the 1999–2005 waves of the Panel Study of Income Dynamics (PSID), Powell and Han (in press) found that higher fruit and vegetable prices were related to higher adult female BMI (elasticity of 0.03) but not statistically significantly related to male BMI. In particular, the effects of fruit and vegetable prices were found to be stronger among poor women (elasticity of 0.09) and women with children (elasticity of 0.04), suggesting that targeted subsidies would be most effective. However, Beydoun, Powell, and Wang (2008), who drew on cross-sectional data from the 1994–1996 CSFII, found that fruit and vegetable prices were not statistically significantly associated with obesity and were inversely associated with BMI.

Several of the studies that examined children and adolescents found statistically significant effects of fruit and vegetable prices on weight outcomes, particularly among those who were low-SES or at risk of overweight. Focusing on 8th and 10th grade youths from cross-sectional MTF data, Powell et al. (2007) found the price of fruits and vegetables was positively but not statistically significantly related to BMI or obesity among youths. Also using the MTF data, Auld and Powell (2009) found a very small association between fruit and vegetable prices (elasticity of 0.02) but using quantile regressions models found larger effects, albeit still quite small, among overweight teens: for example, the BMI fruit and vegetable price elasticities were 0.05 and 0.06, respectively, for male and female teens at the 95th BMI quantile.

Using longitudinal data on children from the ECLS-K and a random effects model, Sturm and Datar (2005) found that changes in child weight were positively related to the price of fruits and vegetables: an increase in the price of fruits and vegetables by one standard deviation raised BMI by 0.11 units by 3rd grade (equivalent to a BMI price elasticity of approximately 0.05). Examining a number of subpopulations, Sturm and Datar found that children in poverty and those at risk for overweight were roughly 50 percent and 39 percent, respectively, more price sensitive compared to their non-poor and not at risk counterparts. In an extended panel following the ECLS-K children until 5th grade, Sturm and Datar (2008) estimated that a one standard deviation increase in the price of fruits and vegetables increased children's BMI by 0.20 units by 5th grade suggesting a persistent and larger long-term effect of fruit and vegetable prices on children's weight outcomes. Powell and Bao (2009) also estimated a random effects model drawing on data from the 1998, 2000, and 2002 waves of the children of the NLSY79 and found that increasing the price of fruits and vegetables by one standard deviation increased BMI by 0.20 units. In terms of the price elasticity, a 10 percent reduction in the price of fruits and vegetables was associated with a 0.7 percent reduction in BMI. The estimated association between fruit and vegetable prices and BMI was stronger among low- versus high-socioeconomic-status children with estimated elasticities of 0.14 and 0.09 among low-income children and children with less educated mothers, respectively.

Powell and Chaloupka (in press) estimated an individual-level fixed-effects longitudinal model using data from the Child Development Supplement of the PSID and found that higher fruit and vegetable prices were statistically significantly related to a lower BMI percentile ranking among children, with larger effects for children in low-SES families. The fruit and vegetable price elasticity for BMI was estimated to be 0.25 for the full sample and 0.58 among low-income children. The results from this most recent study are consistent with the study findings based on individual-level random effects models that found children's BMI to be sensitive to the price of fruits and vegetables with greater effects for low-SES children.

PRICING POLICY DESIGN ISSUES
FOR OBESITY PREVENTION

A number of important issues require consideration in the design and implementation of pricing instruments, particularly in the area of taxation. As the evidence and data presented thus far indicate, the current approach to taxation of unhealthy foods and beverages in the United States is making a marginal impact, at best, on obesogenic behaviors and weight outcomes. Even still, governments at all levels are increasingly exploring the possibility of taxing unhealthy foods and beverages such as sodas (McKinley 2007; Congressional Budget Office 2008; New York State Division of Budget 2009; Patrick and Murray 2009), and the calls for increases in such taxes are mounting (Institute of Medicine 2009a; Brownell et al. 2009b; Brownell and Frieden 2009). Changes to food support programs such as SNAP and WIC also are being considered in the context of obesity prevention. However, before pursuing such policy levers in the fight to prevent obesity, a number of factors should be considered, including the size of the tax or subsidy intervention, the items to tax or subsidize, and the tax and subsidy design—each is discussed briefly below.

Size of the Tax or Subsidy

The size or amount of the tax depends heavily on the underlying purpose for the tax. In other words, is taxation being considered as a revenue generation source, as a funding stream for obesity prevention efforts, or to try to reduce individual consumption and BMI outcomes? The empirical evidence reviewed in this chapter found very small price elasticities for weight, suggesting that large taxes will be needed to have a marked effect on behavior and related weight outcomes. However, as indicated by the data presented earlier in this chapter, most of the taxes imposed to date have been small taxes. While these taxes have a marginal impact, at best, on individual-level behavior and BMI outcomes, they hold tremendous potential to raise revenue for cash-strapped governments, to raise revenue to offset medical costs, and to fund obesity prevention programs (Jacobson and Brownell 2000; Brownell and Frieden 2009; Brownell et al. 2009b). Indeed, the most recent estimates indicate that the annual economic burden of obesity has risen to 10 percent of all medical expenditures, or approximately $147 billion per year in 2008 (Finkelstein et al. 2009).

In terms of revenue potential, the Rudd Center for Food Policy and Obesity's Revenue Calculator for Soft Drink Taxes for 2010 indicates that a $0.01/ounce additional tax on regular, sugar-sweetened sodas could generate over $955 million in revenue for the state of California and over $210 million in revenue for New York City. In Mississippi, the state with the highest obesity rate in the country, such a tax could generate over $74 million in revenue for the state (Rudd Center for Food Policy and Obesity 2010). In recent years, proposals have emerged at the federal, state, and local levels of government related to the use of these taxes, particularly with regard to regular, sugar-sweetened sodas (Congressional Budget Office 2008; New York State Division of Budget 2009; Patrick and Murray 2009). While none of these recent proposals has passed, such proposals continue to emerge. For example, a bill was introduced in 2010 in the Mississippi state legislature that would have imposed a 2-cent-per-ounce excise tax on soft drinks, with the revenue generated dedicated to obesity prevention programs. They estimated that such a tax could have generated $200 million/year for the state ("Bill seeks . . ." 2010) (the bill later died in committee). Public support for such taxes is likely to be greater when the revenue is specifically designated to prevent obesity, particularly childhood obesity, rather than for general revenue generation purposes (Evans et al. 2005; Cawley 2008).

Finally, the size of subsidies that can be offered for healthful low-energy-dense foods or beverage products is largely constrained by available government funds. Revenue generated from taxes on energy-dense items also could be used to offset the cost of providing subsidies to products such as fruits and vegetables. The extent of such subsidies also would help to offset the regressive nature of food taxes.

What to Tax and or Subsidize?

One of the biggest challenges associated with taxing foods and beverages is "what to tax." Whereas the imposition of food taxes have been called for on the basis of nutrient content (i.e., fat taxes), it is generally recognized that from a legislative vantage it is easier to tax specific categories of food, in particular those with low nutritional value (Jacobson and Brownell 2000; Caraher and Cowburn 2005). Similarly, categories of food such as fruits and vegetables or low-fat milk, for example, are clearly more straightforward candidates for subsidies, rather than measuring the extent of nutrient content across multiple product categories.

Currently, the taxes applied to sodas and snack products, for example, are based largely on the category of food or on the definition of "food" as used by the given state or locality. In most cases, when a given item such as regular, sugar-sweetened soda or candy is taxed, it is because such items have been removed from the list of items that are otherwise exempt from the state sales tax and, therefore, become taxable items. However, even within products such as candy, debate surrounds the ingredients that comprise the end product and whether the end product should be taxed given that some of its ingredients are healthy. For example, "candy" is often a challenging item to consider for taxation purposes because many candy items contain milk or milk-based ingredients, flour, and other ingredients that would not be considered candy but, rather, "food." Regular, sugar-sweetened sodas, however, do not contain any items of nutritional value and have been shown to contribute to rising obesity rates and other chronic disease conditions (Wang et al. 2008; Bleich et al. 2009; Wang et al. 2009). Thus, sodas are an easier item to target for taxation purposes from an obesity-prevention standpoint than candy products.

Within product categories, the application of taxes to the broadest base possible is likely to be most successful for obesity prevention objectives because the inclusion of more products would help to limit substitution across products. For example, the application of a tax to a broader set of sugar-sweetened beverages as opposed to a narrow soda tax would limit substitution between soda and other sugared beverages, thereby increasing the likelihood of lowering total overall caloric intake and reducing related weight outcomes.

Policy Instrument Design

From a design perspective, the level of government and type of tax levied are important considerations. Currently, there is no federal tax (sale or excise) on foods and beverages. Thus, all such taxation, where it exists, occurs at the state and, to some extent, local levels of government. As noted earlier, this patchwork approach has led to tax variations both across and within states, by location of sale (e.g., grocery stores versus vending machines), and by product or item (e.g., sodas, potato chips, candy). For example, the state sales tax rate on regular, sugar-sweetened sodas sold in grocery stores ranges from 0 to 7 percent and in vending machines from 0 to 8 percent, exclusive of additional local sales taxes that apply in many counties and municipalities in the United States. Thus, the tax "burden" (albeit small) will vary, depending on the state within which and the location from which one purchases the given item. A federal tax, on the other hand, would apply to all consumers and not just consumers in a given state and/or locality. And, when combined with state/local taxes, federal taxes could have an additive impact on consumption behaviors and revenue generation. One estimate indicates that a 1-cent per ounce national tax on sugar-sweetened beverages would generate $14.9 billion in the first year alone, which could be used for revenue generation and obesity-prevention purposes (Brownell et al. 2009b). In fact, during the health care reform debates in Congress, one proposal emerged to impose a 3-cent excise tax per 12 ounces of sugar-sweetened beverages as a way to generate revenue to help offset the costs associated with health care reform. The Congressional Budget Office estimated that such an option would have generated an estimated $24 billion in revenue for the 2009–2013 period (Congressional Budget Office 2008).

In addition, a federal tax would be uniform across states and it would be universally applied across populations including those who make purchases using SNAP benefits. Food purchases under the SNAP are exempt from any state-level tax (7 CFR §272.1). Thus, if the objective of the tax policy is to alter food consumption behavior, then the imposition of or increases in state-level taxes cannot be expected to impact purchasing behaviors among low-income SNAP recipients. In terms of subsidies, a federal policy would help to ensure the most uniform and nationally comprehensive coverage to improve population health. The empirical evidence showed that subsidies targeted to low-SES populations had the potential for the greatest impact on weight outcomes. Thus, the delivery of targeted subsidies could be nationally operationalized through existing USDA food programs such as SNAP, WIC, and school meal programs.

A final important design issue, the form of taxation—whether sales, excise, privilege, and so on—must be considered. Several key arguments can be made in favor of an excise versus a sales tax, regardless of whether the tax is at the federal, state, or local level. First, excise taxes have the benefit of being incorporated into the shelf price of the given product (and, hence, are part of the visible price seen by consumers), whereas a sales tax is only applied at the point of purchase, after the decision to select and purchase the item has been made. With the few exceptions noted earlier in this chapter, most of the current taxes applied to unhealthy foods and beverages are sales taxes that are only applied at the point of purchase. Second, excise taxes would apply regardless of where the items were sold. That is, for example, the tax would apply whether sold in grocery stores, vending machines, convenience stores or any other venue. Third, excise taxes which are applied on a per unit measure are more effective in raising prices when volume discounts are given, compared to sales taxes that generally are applied as a percentage of price.

Conclusions

Evidence from empirical models that examine the effects of prices (or taxes) directly on weight outcomes help to assess whether changes in prices may translate to significant changes in BMI or obesity prevalence. The review of such study findings in this paper suggests that small tax- or subsidy-related price changes would not likely produce substantial changes in BMI or obesity prevalence. However, non-trivial pricing interventions may have measurable effects, particularly among low-SES populations and those most at risk for overweight, and such interventions may have larger impacts at the population level when applied widely. Among adults, some of the price evidence showed that higher prices of energy-dense foods (such as fast food, sugar and calorie dense items) were associated with lower weight outcomes. The potential effect of reducing adult weight through subsidies to healthy foods was limited to female adults, and the effect was greater for poor women and those with children. For adolescents, the empirical evidence supported changing relative prices by both taxing less healthy foods (such as fast food) and subsidizing fruits and vegetables, and the effects were found to be greater for those youths at risk of overweight. Among children, lower fruit and vegetable prices were consistently estimated to improve weight outcomes. In particular, the evidence suggested that fruit and vegetable subsidies would have the greatest effects among children from low-SES families. Also, a number of studies suggested that the price effects on weight were greater in the long run.

Whereas most of the empirical studies drew on price data, several recent studies linked state-level soda taxes to individual-level data. These studies found minimal evidence of a tax effect on weight, suggesting that the current soda tax rates are not large enough to generate sufficient changes in consumption that would translate into changes in weight outcomes. Further, given the narrow application of the tax on soda, even though it may reduce soda consumption itself, individuals may substitute to other non-taxed sugar-sweetened beverages (i.e., not all states tax all sugar-sweetened beverages equally), limiting the potential for the tax to translate into weight changes.

As governments consider moving forward with fiscal pricing policies aimed at obesity prevention, a number of important policy design issues will need to be addressed. As governments assess what products to tax or subsidize, they will be faced with issues of practicalities, minimizing adverse substitution behaviors, and undoubtedly industry backlash. The size of the tax will need to be determined based on balancing objectives related to changing behavior and generating revenue that can be used for a range of obesity prevention programs and to help offset the costs of obesity. States that already impose sales taxes on products such as soda and candy will be faced with decisions on whether to expand taxes that are already in place or whether to move to alternative forms of taxation such as excise taxes. Similarly, if subsidies are to be targeted to low-SES populations, a number of current federal food programs may be used as a vehicle for delivery. Finally, with respect to tax design, excise taxes were shown to potentially be a better tax design for obesity prevention given their visibility at the shelf, their application across different point of sale venues, and the fact that they will persist even when volume discounts are offered. As new taxes and or subsidies are implemented, researchers should continue to assess the extent to which such policies impact weight and other health outcomes.

ACKNOWLEDGEMENTS

This research was supported by the Robert Wood Johnson Foundation through the Bridging the Gap the ImpacTeen project and by award number R01HL096664 from the National Heart, Lung, and Blood Institute. The content is solely the responsibility of the authors and does not necessarily represent the official views of the National Heart, Lung, and Blood Institute or the National Institutes of Health. Research assistance from Ramona Krauss and Rebecca Schermbeck is gratefully acknowledged. We also are grateful to Shelby Eidson from The MayaTech Corporation for her work in compiling the state tax data.

REFERENCES

Andreyeva, T., M. Long, and K. D. Brownell. 2010. "The Impact of Food Prices on Consumption: A Systematic Review of Research on Price Elasticity of Demand for Food." *American Journal of Public Health* 100(2): 216–222.

Auld, M. C., and L. M. Powell. 2009. "Economics of Food Energy Density and Adolescent Body Weight." *Economica* 76: 719–740.

Beydoun, M. A., L. M. Powell, and Y. Wang., 2008. "The Association of Fast Food, Fruit and Vegetable Prices with Dietary Intakes among US Adults: Is There Modification by Family Income?" *Social Science and Medicine* 66: 2218–2229.

"Bill Seeks 'Sin' Tax on Soft Drinks." 2010. The Greenwood Commonwealth. Available at: http://gwcommonwealth.com/articles/2010/01/03/opinion/ editorials/01032010edit01.txt.

Bleich, S., D. Cutler, C. Murray, and A. Adams. 2008. "Why Is the Developed World Obese?" *Annual Review of Public Health* 29: 273–295.

Bleich, S. N., Y. C. Wang, Y. Wang, and S. L. Gortmaker. 2009. "Increasing Consumption of Sugar-Sweetened Beverages among US Adults: 1988–1994 to 1999–2004." *American Journal of Clinical Nutrition* 89: 372–381.

Brownell, K. D., T. Farley, W. C. Willett, B. M. Popkin, F. J. Chaloupka, J. W. Thompson, and D. S. Ludwig. 2009b. "The Public Health and Economic Benefits of Taxing Sugar-Sweetened Beverages.: *New England Journal of Medicine* 361: 1599–1605.

Brownell, K. D., and T. R. Frieden. 2009. "Ounces of Prevention—The Public Policy Case for Taxes on Sugared Beverages.: *New England Journal of Medicine* 18: 1805–1808.

Brownell, K. D., M. B. Schwartz, R. M. Puhl, K. E. Hendreson, and J. L. Harris. 2009a. "The Need for Bold Action to Prevent Adolescent Obesity." *Journal of Adolescent Health* 45: S8–S17.

Caraher, M., and G. Cowburn 2005. "Taxing Food: Implications for Public Health Nutrition." *Public Health Nutrition* 8: 1242–1249.

Cawley, J. 2008. "Contingent Valuation Analysis of Willingness to Pay to Reduce Childhood Obesity." *Economics of Human Biology* 6: 281–292.

Chaloupka, F. J., L. M. Powell, and J. F. Chriqui. 2009. *Sugar-Sweetened Beverage Taxes and Public Health*. Princeton, NJ: Robert Wood Johnson Foundation.

Chou, S.Y., M. Grossman, and H. Saffer. 2004. "An Economic Analysis of Adult Obesity: Results from the Behavioral Risk Factor Surveillance System." *Journal of Health Economics* 23: 565–587.

Chou, S. Y., I. Rashad, and M. Grossman. 2008. "Fast Food Restaurant Advertising on Television and Its Influence on Childhood Obesity." *The Journal of Law and Economics* 51: 599–618.

Chriqui, J. F., S. S. Eidson, H. Bates, S. Kowalczyk, and F. Chaloupka. 2008. "State Sales Tax Rates for Soft Drinks and Snacks Sold through Grocery Stores and Vending Machines, 2007.: *Journal of Public Health Policy* 29: 226–249.

Chriqui, J. F., L. Schneider, F. J. Chaloupka, K. Ide, and O. Pugach. 2009. *Local Wellness Policies: Assessing School District Strategies for Improving Children's Health. School Years* 2006–07 *and* 2007–08. Chicago: Bridging the Gap, Health Policy Center, Institute for Health Research and Policy, University of Illinois at Chicago. Available at: http://www.bridgingthegapresearch.org/client_files/pdfs/monograph.pdf.

Congressional Budget Office. 2008. *Budget Options*, Volume I: *Health Care*. Washington, DC: Congressional Budget Office.

Cutler, D. M., E. L. Glaeser, and J. M. Shapiro. 2003. "Why Have Americans Become More Obese?" *Journal of Economic Perspectives* 17: 93–118.

Drewnowski, A., and N. Darmon. 2005. "Food Choices and Diet Costs: An Economic Analysis." *Journal of Nutrition* 135: 900–904.

Epstein, L. H., K. K. Dearing, E. A. Handley, J. N, Roemmich, and R. A. Paluch. 2006. "Relationship of Mother and Child Food Purchases as a Function of Price: A Pilot Study." *Appetite* 47: 115–118.

Epstein, L. H., K. K. Dearing, R. A. Paluch, J. N. Roemmich, and D. Cho. 2007. "Price and Maternal Obesity Influence Purchasing of Low- and High-Energy-Dense Foods." *American Journal of Clinical Nutrition* 86: 914–922.

Evans, W. D., E. A. Finkelstein, D. B. Kamerow, and J. M. Renaud. 2005. "Public Perceptions of Childhood Obesity." *American Journal of Preventive Medicine* 28: 26–32.

Finkelstein, E. A., J. G. Trogdon, J. W. Cohen, and W. Dietz. 2009. "Annual Medical Spending Attributable To Obesity: Payer- and Service-Specific Estimates." *Health Affairs* 28: 822–831.

Fletcher, J. M., D. Frisvold, and N. Tefft. 2010. "Can Soft Drink Taxes Reduce Population Weight?" *Contemporary Economic Policy* 28(1): 23–35.

French, S. A., R. W. Jeffery, M. Story, K. K. Breitlow, J. S. Baxter, P. Hannan, and M. P. Snyder. 2001. "Pricing and Promotion Effects on Low-Fat Vending Snack Purchases: The CHIPS Study." *American Journal of Public Health* 91: 112–117.

French, S. A., R. W. Jeffery, M. Story, P. Hannan, and M. P. Snyder. 1997a. "A Pricing Strategy to Promote Low-Fat Snack Choices Through Vending Machines." *American Journal of Public Health* 87: 849–851.

French, S. A., M. Story, R. W. Jeffery, P. Snyder, M. Eisenberg, A. Sidebottom, and D. Murray. 1997b. "Pricing Strategy to Promote Fruit and Vegetable Purchase in High School Cafeterias." *Journal of the American Dietetic Association* 97: 1008–1010.

Goldman, D., D. Lakdawalla, and Y. Zheng. In Press. "Food Prices and the Dynamics of Body Weight." In *Economic Aspects of Obesity*, eds. M. Grossman and H. N. Mocan. Chicago: University of Chicago Press.

Guthrie, J., E. Frazão, M. Andrews, and D. Smallwood. 2007. "Improving Food Choices: Can Food Stamps Do More?" *Amber Waves* 5: 22–28.

Horgen, K. B., and K. D. Brownell. 2002. "Comparison of Price Change and Health Message Interventions in Promoting Healthy Food Choices." *Health Psychology* 21: 505–512.

Institute of Medicine. 2009a. *Local Government Actions to Prevent Childhood Obesity*. Washington, DC: The National Academies Press.

Institute of Medicine. 2009b. *School Meals: Building Blocks for Healthy Children*. Washington, DC: The National Academies Press.

Jacobson, M. F., and K. D. Brownell. 2000. "Small Taxes on Soft Drinks and Snack Foods to Promote Health." *American Journal of Public Health* 90: 854–857.

Jeffery, R. W., S. A. French, C. Raether, and J. E. Baxter. 1994. "An Environmental Intervention to Increase Fruit and Salad Purchases in a Cafeteria." *Preventive Medicine* 23: 788–792.

Kim, D., and I. Kawachi. 2006. "Food Taxation and Pricing Strategies to 'Thin Out' the Obesity Epidemic." *American Journal of Preventive Medicine* 30: 430–437.

Lakdawalla, D., and T. Philipson. 2002. *The Growth of Obesity and Technological Change: A Theoretical and Empirical Examination*. National Bureau of Economic Research Working Paper Series No. 8946.

Leicester, A., and F. Windmeijer. 2004. *The "Fat Tax": Economic Incentives to Reduce Obesity*. Briefing Note 49. London: Institute for Fiscal Studies.

McKinley, J., 2007. "San Francisco's Mayor Proposes Fee on Sales of Sugary Soft Drinks." *New York Times*. December 12.

Miljkovic, D., and W. Nganje. 2008. "Regional Obesity Determinants in the United States: A Model of Myopic Addictive Behavior in Food Consumption." *Agricultural Economics* 38: 375–384.

Miljkovic, D., W. Nganje, and H. de Chastenet. 2008. "Economic Factors Affecting the Increase in Obesity in the United States: Differential Response To Price." *Food Policy* 33: 48–60.

New York State Division of Budget. 2009. *2009–2010 Executive Budget–Briefing Book*. New York: State Division of the Budget.

Oliveira, V., and E. Frazao. 2009. *The WIC Program Background, Trends, and Economic Issues, 2009 Edition*. Economic Research Report No. 73. U.S. Department of Agriculture, Economic Research Service.

Patrick, D. L., and T. P. Murray. 2009. *FY2010 House 1 Budget Recommendation: Policy Brief.* http://www.mass.gov/bb/h1/fy10h1/exec10/hbudbrief19.htm.

Philipson, T. J., and R. A. Posner. 2003. "The Long-Run Growth in Obesity as a Function of Technological Change." *Perspectives in Biology and Medicine* 46: S87.

Powell, L. M. 2009. "Fast Food Costs and Adolescent Body Mass Index: Evidence from Panel Data." *Journal of Health Economics* 29: 963–970.

Powell, L. M., and Y. J. Bao. 2009. "Food Prices, Access to Food Outlets and Child Weight." *Economics and Human Biology* 7: 64–72.

Powell, L. M., C. M. Auld, F. J. Chaloupka, P. M. O'Malley, and L. D. Johnston. 2007. "Access to Fast Food and Food Prices: Relationship with Fruit and Vegetable Consumption and Overweight among Adolescents." *Advances in Health Economics and Health Services Research* 17: 23–48.

Powell, L. M., and F. J. Chaloupka. 2009. "Food Prices and Obesity: Evidence and Policy Implications for Taxes and Subsidies." *The Milbank Quarterly* 87: 229–257.

Powell, L. M., and F. J. Chaloupka. In Press. "Economic Contextual Factors and Child Body Mass Index." In *Economic Aspects of Obesity*, eds. M. Grossman and H. N. Mocan. Chicago: University of Chicago Press.

Powell, L. M., J. F. Chriqui, and F. J. Chaloupka. 2009. "Associations between State-level Soda Taxes and Adolescent Body Mass Index." *Journal of Adolescent Health* 45: S57–S63.

Powell, L. M., and E. Han. In Press. "Adult Obesity and the Price and Availability of Food in the United States." *American Journal of Agricultural Economics.*

Rudd Center for Food Policy and Obesity. 2010. *Revenue Calculator for Soft Drink Taxes.* Rudd Center for Food Policy and Obesity.

Stone, G. R., L. M. Seidman, and C. Sunstein. 2001. *Constitutional Law.* New York: Aspen.

Sturm, R., and A. Datar. 2005. "Body Mass Index in Elementary School Children, Metropolitan Area Food Prices and Food Outlet Density." *Public Health* 119: 1059–1068.

Sturm, R., and A. Datar. 2008. "Food Prices and Weight Gain during Elementary School: 5-Year Update." *Public Health* 122(11): 1140–1143.

Sturm, R., L. M. Powell, J. F. Chriqui, and F. J. Chaloupka. 2010. "State-level Soda Taxes, Soft Drink Consumption, and Body Mass Index: Results from the Early Childhood Longitudinal Study." *Health Affairs* 29: 1052–1058.

Wang, Y. C., D. S. Ludwig, K. Sonneville, and S. L. Gortmaker. 2009. "Impact of Change in Sweetened Caloric Beverage Consumption on Energy Intake among Children and Adolescents." *Archives of Pediatrics and Adolescent Medicine* 163: 336–343.

Wang, Y. C., S. N. Bleich, and S. L. Gortmaker. 2008. "Increasing Caloric Contribution from Sugar-Sweetened Beverages and 100 Percent Fruit Juices among US Children and Adolescents, 1988–2004." *Pediatrics* 121: e1604–e1614.

CHAPTER 39

SCHOOL-BASED INTERVENTIONS

TAMARA BROWN

INTRODUCTION

THIS chapter evaluates the evidence from systematic reviews of school-based interventions to prevent obesity in children through changes in diet and physical activity behaviors. Behavior change relating to diet and physical activity must form the foundation of any intervention to prevent children from becoming obese; however, behavior change interventions need to appreciate the interplay between the obesogenic environment and the child. Children are a vulnerable group, at high risk of developing obesity with various external influences of the obesogenic environment that are beyond their control.

The degree of relative social inequality and risk of obesity are inextricably linked (greater social inequality equals higher risk of obesity), and the obesity epidemic is contributing significantly to the wider socioeconomic inequalities in health (Law 2007). We currently do not know whether school-based interventions to prevent obesity will reduce or exacerbate inequalities in health. Long-term obesity prevention through school-based interventions can only occur as part of national and international strategies to tackle the underlying social, economic, and environmental determinants of health.

Behavior change interventions are probably the most challenging type of public health intervention yet could produce the greatest benefit to public health. Effective interventions to prevent obesity are needed for schoolchildren, who arguably have the greatest need for intervention. The school setting can be an ideal environment to implement an obesity prevention intervention because schools provide access to relatively large populations of children, including children from all socio-economic and ethnic backgrounds. School-based interventions enable continuous and intensive contact with children who spend a relatively large proportion of their waking hours at school, which includes time spent eating and playing. School-based interventions offer great potential for health improvement in terms of improved quality of life, increased life expectancy, and cost savings that could be directed toward other health care needs.

How Effective are School-Based Interventions to Prevent and Treat Obesity?

Guidance on the prevention and management of obesity in the United Kingdom, produced by the National Institute for Health and Clinical Excellence (NICE) is considered to be the most comprehensive review of obesity interventions produced in the United Kingdom to date and includes a review of the best available evidence of school-based interventions to prevent obesity (NICE 2006a, 2006b).

Many reviews have been published of interventions to prevent obesity in children, some of which focus specifically on school-based interventions (Dobbins 2001; Harris 2009; Katz 2005; Kropski 2008; Li 2008; Meininger 2000; Miccuci 2002; Resnicow and Robinson 1997; Sharma 2007; Shaya 2008; Story 1999).

The NICE review of school-based interventions to prevent obesity was recently updated in a comprehensive systematic review of school-based interventions to prevent childhood obesity (Brown and Summerbell 2009). The results of this review have been updated to include interventions published up to December 2009 to form the evidence base for this chapter.

Studies were included in the review if the design was a randomized controlled trial (RCT) or a controlled clinical trial, which focused on changing dietary intake and/or physical activity levels, was set in schools, and reported a weight outcome at least 12 weeks from the start of the intervention. Studies were excluded if they specifically targeted overweight or obese schoolchildren rather than the general school population.

Twenty of the 59 included studies were conducted in U.S. schools, and the remaining studies were based all over the world. The majority of interventions were based in primary schools, and about half of the interventions lasted less than one year. Many interventions published in the last two years were explicitly aimed at preventing obesity.

Previous reviews have highlighted that studies to prevent obesity in children have on the whole suffered from being under-powered, the lack of "upstream" environmental components (to help increase sustainability) and unit of analysis error regarding clustering by school or class. Authors of interventions published in the last two years appear to be addressing some of these issues and improving the methodology of the studies. Only 3 of the 21 interventions published in the last two years have been based in the United States, and there is also a trend for these interventions to be randomized, longer-term, in primary schools, and also in bigger populations of schoolchildren. Authors are increasingly accounting for cluster randomization and intracluster correlation in analyses of outcomes, which is an improvement.

SUMMARY OF MAIN RESULTS

School-based interventions that focus on physical activity or a combination of diet and physical activity can prevent excessive weight gain in schoolchildren. Thirty-six percent of interventions (21 of 59) were effective in significantly improving mean BMI, compared with control. Interventions that combined diet and physical activity had the greatest percentage of effective studies, closely followed by physical activity interventions. One of three interventions focusing on drinks, one of four diet interventions, 8 of 24 physical activity interventions, and 11 of 28 combined diet and physical activity interventions demonstrated significant and positive differences between intervention and control for BMI.

Despite amassing 59 controlled school-based interventions to prevent obesity, we currently do not know exactly what type of intervention is the most effective in preventing excessive weight gain in schoolchildren. It is unclear what elements of interventions, either separately or in combination, are consistently effective in preventing excessive weight gain in school-children. In addition we do not know how and why effectiveness varies according to age, gender, ethnicity, and socioeconomic status of schoolchildren.

Studies are only beginning to report information about process and contextual factors that will enable better understanding of how and why interventions work and don't work and about the sustainability of interventions.

WHAT WORKS? SCHOOL-BASED INTERVENTIONS THAT COMBINE DIET AND PHYSICAL ACTIVITY

Eleven out of 28 interventions that combined various diet and physical activity components were effective in preventing excessive weight gain in children.

Although the evidence base is not strong enough to provide conclusive results for exactly which interventions "work," the interventions described below provide a promising "direction of travel" and indicate what can "work".

A 6-month dietary education and sports intervention (including active recess, healthy kiosks, special activities, and parental involvement) in over 3,500 11-year-old children in five primary schools in Chile maintained baseline BMI in intervention boys while BMI in control boys increased (Kain 2004). This intervention resulted in a significant difference between groups at six months for boys only (non-significant difference in BMI at six months for girls).

An environmental, policy, and social marketing intervention in over 1,100 11- to 13-year-old children in 24 middle schools in the United States showed significant reduction in BMI in the intervention boys but not girls, compared with control over two school years (Sallis 2003).

"Planet Health" promoted physical activity, modification of dietary intake, and reduction of sedentary behaviors (with a strong emphasis on reducing TV viewing) in over 1,500 children aged 12 years in 10 secondary schools in the United States (Gortmaker 1999). The intervention significantly reduced the prevalence of obesity and increased remission of obesity in intervention girls compared with control girls over two school years. There was no significant difference in prevalence of obesity between intervention boys and control boys.

Another intervention combined environmental changes with personal computer-tailored feedback on BMI, with and without parental support, compared with control in nearly 3,000 13-year-olds in 15 middle schools in Belgium. The intervention included 4.7 hours extra physical education per week. In girls, BMI and BMI z-score increased significantly less in the intervention with parental support group compared with the control group or the intervention without parental support group. In boys, no significant positive intervention effects were found after two school years (Haerens 2006).

A diet and activity intervention that aimed to prevent cardiovascular disease (CVD) in schoolchildren in Crete by adapting the "Know Your Body" program showed significant improvements compared with control at three and six years for BMI and skin folds and at ten years by BMI z-score. (Kafatos 2007).

A 12-week diet and activity intervention to reduce risk of diabetes showed a significant improvement in percentage of body fat and BMI compared with control in 73 14-year-old adolescents in one New York public school. These adolescents were first or second generation migrants to the United States, mainly from the Dominican Republic, and 53 percent had a first- or second- degree relative with type 2 diabetes (Rosenbaum 2007).

The APPLE study of 460 8-year-old children from seven primary schools in the United States significantly reduced the rate of excessive weight gain in children at two years, although this may be limited to those not initially overweight. BMI z-score was significantly lower in intervention than in control children at one year and at two years, but the prevalence of overweight did not differ. A significant interaction existed between intervention group and overweight status, such that mean

BMI z-score was reduced in normal weight but not overweight intervention children relative to controls (Taylor 2007).

The WAY program was a physical activity and wellness program that was incorporated into the school curriculum. It included some family involvement in approximately 1,000 9 to 11-year-olds (grade 4–5) in 16 primary schools in the United States. At six months, there was a significant reduction in risk of developing overweight and a 2 percent reduction in overweight in the intervention group but not the control group. BMI was significantly improved in the intervention versus control children at 6 months (Spiegel and Foulk 2006).

A 14-week nutrition education and circuit training plus encouragement to reduce sedentary behaviors resulted in a significant difference in BMI in approximately 100 5- to 6-year-old children in four preschools in Israel. The BMI remained stable in the intervention children and increased by 0.3 kg/m^2 in the control children (Eliakim 2007).

A cluster randomized trial of a nutrition education and physical activity intervention produced a significant difference in mean BMI between intervention and control schools at three years. The intervention involved 2,425 8-year-old children in five primary schools in Beijing, China, and included parental involvement. Significantly more non-obese children became obese in the control schools than in the intervention schools, and among the children who were obese at baseline, significantly more remained obese in the control group compared with the intervention group at the end of the study (Jiang 2007).

An intervention that used the Theory of Planned Behavior to address barriers to physical activity, increase availability of fruit and vegetables, and engage parental support resulted in a significant reduction in BMI at one year. The intervention involved 646 10-year-old children in 26 primary schools in Greece (Angelopoulos 2009).

What Works? School-Based Interventions that Focus on Physical Activity

Eight of the 24 interventions that focused on physical activity were effective in preventing excessive weight gain in schoolchildren and are described in brief below. Some of the physical activity interventions were, however, not designed to prevent obesity but, for example, to increase fitness, and so a significant improvement in BMI might not be expected for such trials.

Increased physical activity in primary-school children may help to improve BMI, especially in girls and obese children (Lazaar 2007) and has also been shown to work in low-income ethnic minority schoolchildren (Stephens and Wentz 1998).

One intervention that used environmental change to increase physical activity showed significant improvement in BMI compared to control at four years; the effect was significant in adolescents who were normal weight at baseline. However, the benefit in adolescents who were overweight at baseline did not persist past the initial two years (Simon 2008).

An intervention that combined increase in physical activity with reduction in television viewing and lessons in fundamental movement skills resulted in significant difference in BMI compared to control at one year in 311 10-year-old schoolchildren from three local government schools in areas of low socioeconomic status in Melbourne, Australia (Salmon 2008).

Interventions to reduce sedentary behaviors such as watching television and videos and video game usage may help to reduce BMI in primary-school children (Robinson 1999).

Aerobic dance may reduce BMI in adolescent girls (Flores 1995) and aerobic exercise may reduce BMI in young girls (but not boys) (Mo-Suwan 1998). A physical activity intervention over two semesters, set in two primary schools and involving 753 children in China, showed significant benefit in terms of BMI for girls but not for boys (Liu 2008).

What Shows Potential to Work?

In the short term, simple interventions such as eating breakfast in schools may help to prevent excessive weight gain in adolescents (Ask 2006). Reducing the consumption of carbonated drinks in favor of water or diluted fruit juice may reduce the prevalence of obesity in primary-school children at least in the short term (James 2007).

An intervention that focused on increasing water consumption reduced the risk of overweight by 31 percent, although BMI z-scores did not significantly differ (Muckelbauer 2009). Another intervention that focused on decreasing sugar-sweetened drinks demonstrated significant improvement in BMI for overweight girls but not the overall intervention group compared with control (Sichieri 2009).

However, other combined diet and physical activity interventions which have included a component to increase consumption of water or decrease consumption of sugar-sweetened drinks have not always led to improvements in BMI.

Evaluating the Evidence

School-based interventions that focus on physical activity or a combination of diet and physical activity behaviors can prevent excessive weight gain in schoolchildren.

However, despite a dramatic increase in the popularity of school-based settings for interventions, just over one-third of the school-based interventions to prevent obesity were successful in terms of improving BMI compared to control.

Interventions to prevent obesity in schoolchildren include increasing fruit and vegetable intakes, increasing water consumption; reducing consumption of sugar-sweetened drinks; reducing the intake of foods high in sugar and fat; increasing physical activity and decreasing sedentary behaviors such as TV watching and computer use.

Results overall suggest that combined diet and physical activity school-based interventions may help prevent children becoming overweight in the long term. Physical activity interventions, particularly in girls in primary schools, may help to prevent these children from becoming overweight in the short term.

It is unclear what elements of interventions are consistently effective. Physical activity interventions appear more effective in girls than boys and more effective in primary schools than secondary schools. However, similar interventions were not tested across a range of ages, and effectiveness could be due to the type of interventions used in this age group rather than the age itself.

It is difficult to generalize about which interventions are effective and how the range and extent of intervention components influence effectiveness because results from the interventions are inconsistent and mainly short-term. The school-based studies were heterogeneous in terms of design, participants, intervention, and outcome measures; making it impossible to combine study findings using statistical methods.

Despite a lack of conclusive results in terms of weight, the majority of studies demonstrated significant improvement in diet and activity behaviors such as increasing fruit and vegetable intake, increasing water consumption, increasing active play and physical education in schools. However, the UK-based APPLES intervention that was underpinned by the "health promoting schools" philosophy was successful in changing the ethos of the schools and the attitudes of the children, but had little effect on children's behavior other than a modest increase in the consumption of vegetables (Sahota 2001).

There are various reasons why studies could show significant benefit in terms of behavior change but not BMI. Interventions may fail to show significant beneficial effect on weight because they are truly not effective or because methods of assessment and study design hamper evaluation of effectiveness. Some studies were not adequately powered to detect differences in BMI between groups, and some interventions were not of sufficient length or intensity to produce a significant change in BMI. Assessment of effectiveness can also be exacerbated by weaknesses in assessment measures.

There does not appear to be any clear pattern emerging from the data, in that both simple and complex interventions have demonstrated effectiveness. Simple interventions include interventions such as single component modifications to the curriculum, and complex interventions include interventions such as changes to the curriculum, school environment and school policy, and parental involvement.

Longer-term, more intensive and theory-driven interventions have not always produced better results. For example, Pathways was a culturally sensitive diet and physical activity intervention that included changes to the classroom curriculum and a family element. Pathways aimed to reduce percentage of body fat and involved over 1,700 American-Indian children in 41 schools in Arizona, New Mexico, and South Dakota over three years (Caballero 2003). The classroom curriculum was delivered successfully and the food service guidelines were implemented, with most schools achieving the minimum physical education sessions per week. Parents who attended the family events responded positively. The intervention was designed to be delivered by existing staff and was integrated into the school curriculum. Despite all these elements, this relatively large three year study did not significantly improve children's weight or BMI.

The Child and Adolescent Trial for Cardiovascular Health (CATCH) (Luepker 1996) was a school-based intervention in over 5,000 9-year-old children in 96 schools across four states in the United States, which lasted for three years and aimed at preventing CVD. CATCH included modifications to the school food service, physical education program and classroom curricula; included home-based elements and was underpinned by social cognitive theory. BMI did not significantly differ between groups at three years, despite beneficial changes in health behaviors such as reduction in intake of high-fat foods, high levels of participation, dose, fidelity, and compatibility.

Evidence shows that there can be significant weight gain prevention in children from interventions not conceptualized as obesity prevention interventions. The aim of interventions appears to influence weight outcomes; for example, systematic reviews which excluded studies that were not explicitly aimed at preventing excessive weight gain (i.e., the intervention focuses on improving healthy eating or physical activity but doesn't specifically mention aiming to prevent obesity) demonstrate a smaller percentage of effective interventions than reviews that do not exclude these studies (Doak 2009).

It is likely that the range and intensity of the components of an intervention, the duration of the intervention, along with the characteristics of the school setting and intervention providers, all influence effectiveness. The demographics of the schoolchildren in terms of age, gender, socioeconomic status, and ethnicity may all influence the effectiveness of an intervention as well as individual motivation to change behaviors.

GAPS IN THE EVIDENCE

It is unclear what elements of school-based interventions to prevent obesity are consistently effective. Evidence suggests that nutrition education alone is insufficient to prevent obesity in schoolchildren; the very limited evidence does not demonstrate effectiveness of diet-only interventions among schoolchildren.

Although some studies only recruited children from ethnic minorities, none of the other studies assessed weight according to ethnic minority status. Also, none of the studies assessed weight by socioeconomic status; however, the KOPS intervention has demonstrated a reduced cumulative four-year incidence of overweight only in children from families with high socioeconomic status (Plachta-Danielzik 2007).

Four interventions that combined diet and physical activity showed different and inconsistent effects for girls and boys aged 10 to 14 years, and it may be that girls and boys in this age group respond differently to different elements of these interventions (Gortmaker 1999; Haerens 2006; Kain 2004; Sallis 2003).

Process Evaluation

Limited information was provided within the study publications regarding process evaluations. Effectiveness can be influenced by how the intervention is provided, who provides it, and where it is provided. In addition to effectiveness, evidence is required about the appropriateness, implementation, feasibility, acceptability, and sustainability of school-based interventions.

The majority of the school-based interventions were partially provided by existing school staff who were trained by research staff, and evidence indicates that interventions may be better implemented if built into the curriculum (Gortmaker 1999; Kain 2004). Overall, the study authors reported that parents responded positively to diet and physical activity changes, but this did not necessarily lead to behavior change or change in BMI. There was a distinct lack of information reported on the level of parental engagement within the interventions.

Some specific examples of process indicators reported within the school-based interventions highlight the importance of issues about implementation, feasibility, and sustainability. A pilot study of 54 15-year-old adolescents in one secondary school in Norway aimed to evaluate if dietary habits and school performance improved by eating breakfast. Male adolescents who ate breakfast at school for four months reported a significant increase in school contentment as well as significant improvement in BMI compared to control (Ask 2006). However, teachers were not satisfied with the serving of breakfasts in classrooms, and the students missed the provision of free breakfast when it was stopped.

School nurses in one 12-week physical activity intervention experienced difficulty counseling some girls who lacked places, resources, and social support for engaging in physical activity. Some girls reported that their parents discouraged physical activity at home because of the noise and the low importance placed on being physically active as compared with doing homework or chores (Robbins 2006).

Other possible barriers reported to affect successful implementation of school-based interventions include lack of time and training of school staff; lack of equipment, administrative support, and finance; and conflicting interests of stakeholders.

The development of the "whole school approach" and "health promoting schools" recognizes the importance of these contextual factors to the success of health promotion interventions and yet very few interventions have, so far, incorporated such an approach (IUPHE 2008). Process and outcome data are equally important elements of interventions, and this is currently only just beginning to be reflected in the reporting of school-based interventions. The contextual factors of the school setting, the policy framework, and the views of stakeholders will all impact on any school-based intervention to prevent obesity and as such need to be assessed as crucial elements of an intervention and reported in detail. It is crucial that any intervention is developed and implemented with the engagement of school stakeholders (who are also facilitators of an intervention) and where the intervention is integrated into the school infrastructure, curricula, policy, and ethos and thus becomes potentially sustainable.

Findings from these latest interventions reflect the need to report both prevalence of overweight and BMI in order to produce a true picture of how an intervention is working. For example, one physical activity intervention (Vizcaino 2008) produced significant reduction in adiposity but not BMI. A school nutrition policy intervention reduced the incidence of overweight by 50 percent but did not reduce incidence or prevalence of obesity (Foster 2008).

Obesity prevention interventions aim to reduce the number of people becoming overweight and prevent the amount of overweight from increasing within those already overweight (i.e., mean BMI and prevalence of overweight). In order to evaluate the effectiveness of an obesity prevention strategy it is crucial to assess how change in prevalence and change in mean BMI have occurred. Ideally, information on changes in incidence and remission of overweight and obesity should also be reported.

These most recent school-based interventions show that effect may vary according to the aim of the intervention, age of the schoolchildren, baseline weight and gender, although only a minority of studies reported assessing such variables and we currently do not know how interventions could be targeted at such groups to improve effectiveness. Components of interventions may need to be targeted at different groups of schoolchildren and in different ways in order for the whole intervention to be effective.

CONCLUSION AND FUTURE DIRECTION

Disappointingly, despite 59 controlled school-based interventions, no clearer picture is evolving about what type of school-based intervention works best because the interventions are disparate. However, we can say that roughly about one-third of school-based interventions that focus on changing physical activity behaviors or a combination of diet and physical activity behaviors will be successful in preventing obesity. School-based settings clearly have an important role to play as part of national and international strategies to combat obesity.

The NICE review of school-based interventions has informed the Foresight report which informs an action plan to tackle obesity in the United Kingdom over the next 40 years (Brown 2007; Government Office for Science 2007). The Foresight report concluded:

> ... given the pressing need to tackle obesity, it is likely that interventions to prevent obesity will have to take place when the evidence is neither complete nor perfect. The need for policies is now moving faster than the speed that the evidence-base is being developed. The evidence base needs to develop alongside the delivery of novel interventions, informed by available evidence and strengthened by expert advice.

The conclusion of the Foresight report signals a move towards practice-based evidence, where strategies to prevent obesity may have to rely more on the potential of the "direction of travel" demonstrated within school-based interventions, rather than waiting for more definitive evidence from future interventions. The length of time needed to fill the evidence gaps is at odds with the need for urgent action. An increase in action (practice-based evidence) requires new methods of evaluation to synthesise different types of evidence. There are certain interventions that demonstrate effectiveness in terms of reduction in prevention of excessive weight gain and some that show potential through a "direction of travel." We can build upon and adapt these promising interventions while simultaneously improving methods of evaluating practice-based evidence. Both practice-based action and evidence of effectiveness from interventions need to develop simultaneously, although it remains unclear how both elements will be integrated. Do we take action on the best available evidence for large-scale implementation of school-based interventions, or do we wait and demonstrate strong evidence for efficacy first? Large-scale implementation of school-based interventions, with low efficacy but high reach, could produce significant benefit to the health of the population as a whole (Durant 2008).

Both prevention and treatment are necessary to manage obesity; the priority of any comprehensive strategy should be prevention of obesity through behavioral change, beginning in childhood. School-based interventions may be effective in preventing a population increase in prevalence of obesity only as part of a government strategy that includes environmental change and is coupled with targeted interventions to reduce the prevalence of obesity caused at least in part by social inequalities.

Multilevel, multicomponent interventions have the potential to demonstrate effectiveness: diet and physical activity interventions that involve the school in terms of individual behavior change, modifications to the school environment and policy, and also involve family and the wider community. "Shape Up Somerville" and "SWITCH" are examples of such community-based participatory research.

"Shape Up Somerville" demonstrated significant benefit to BMI z-score at eight months follow-up; however, "SWITCH" did not show such promising results with regard to BMI (Economos 2007; Gentile 2009).

In addition to effectiveness, public health decision makers require evidence of appropriateness, implementation, feasibility, acceptability, and sustainability of school-based interventions to prevent obesity. Combining quantitative and qualitative evidence can add context, provide corroboration and increase understanding, particularly with regard to complex public health interventions. Most studies failed to report effectiveness stratified by demographic characteristics or information about process and contextual factors.

More research is required into how and why study characteristics impact on effectiveness. Future evaluation of such effect modifiers will help towards producing optimal effective interventions that can be modified for vulnerable subgroups of schoolchildren.

In addition to effectiveness and process evaluation; the cost effectiveness of school-based interventions needs to be assessed. Very few studies have reported the cost effectiveness of school-based interventions; three published cost-effectiveness analyses of "CATCH," "Planet Health," and "FitKid" school-based interventions all demonstrated acceptable cost-effectiveness, in terms of weight loss and the avoided future costs of obesity-related disease in adulthood (Shelton Brown III 2007; Wang 2003; Wang 2008) The school setting can be cost-effective in that staff and facilities are already in place.

Recommendations for Researchers Carrying Out Primary Interventions in Obesity Research

Below are some recommendations for researchers carrying out school-based interventions to prevent obesity in children that were developed while reviewing the current evidence base and that aim to improve both the evidence base and the quality of reporting.

1. Systematic reviews of the best available evidence should be used to inform primary research. Primary studies should test interventions which show the greatest potential for health benefit (e.g., combined diet and physical activity interventions in schools) rather than interventions which evidence shows are unlikely to be effective (e.g., nutrition education alone). This will increase the likelihood of identifying an effective intervention and increase the evidence base.

2. Studies are needed which repeat interventions across the age range that have already shown potential for effectiveness in children, to evaluate

whether it is the nature of the intervention or the age of the child which influences the effect.

3. Many new policy interventions are community-based, and multilevel, multicomponent interventions are required that involve the school, family, and wider community. It would be interesting to evaluate how school-based elements of such interventions "fit" and interact within the wider community and the family.

4. Studies are required that are targeted and tailored for vulnerable groups of children at increased risk of obesity (e.g., children of minority ethnic groups, children from low-income families, and children with limiting disabilities).

5. Studies need to be sufficiently powered and of long enough duration to detect significant differences in outcome measures.

6. Study protocols should be registered to increase dissemination and reduce publication bias. Registration of protocols would also allow reviewers to assess whether outcomes that researchers aimed to measure were measured and reported (this is now recognized as an important element of quality assessment).

7. The aim of the study, details of the intervention, and the primary outcomes of interest should be explicitly stated and justified. The intervention and the outcomes measured should match the aim (e.g., do interventions that increase fruit intake or provide a healthy breakfast at school "fit" with an aim of preventing excessive obesity and is this best measured by behavior change and/or weight change?)

8. A detailed description of the intervention including range, intensity, who, when and how it was carried out should be reported.

9. Detailed reporting of demographic characteristics such as age, gender, socioeconomic status, and ethnicity is needed in order for reviewers to measure the impact of these variables on effectiveness and the impact of the intervention on health inequalities.

10. Change in mean BMI and prevalence of overweight should both be measured, as it is useful to assess how change in prevalence and mean BMI has occurred (e.g., is prevalence change due to weight loss in the overweight population or is reduction in mean BMI due to reduced incidence in the normal weight population?)

11. The number of participants assessed at each time point in each group and the mean and standard deviation change for each outcome needs to be reported in order for systematic reviewers to carry out meta-analyses where appropriate to do so.

12. Process data should be measured and reported, including data on appropriateness, implementation, feasibility, acceptability, sustainability and context.

13. Costs relating to carrying out the intervention should be measured and reported.

14. Methods of synthesizing quantitative and qualitative evidence should continue to be developed in order to improve analysis of the strength of the evidence of school-based interventions.

FURTHER READING

Doak, C. M., T. L. Visscher, C. M. Renders, and J. C. Seidell. 2006. "The Prevention of Overweight and Obesity in Children and Adolescents: A Review of Interventions and Programs." *Obesity Reviews* 7(1): 111–136.

Flynn, M. A. T., D. A. McNeil, B. Maloff, D. Mutasingwa, M. Wu, C. Ford, et al. 2006. "Reducing obesity and related chronic disease risk in children and youth: a synthesis of evidence with 'best practice' recommendations." *Obesity Reviews* 7(Supp. 1): 7–66.

Lobstein, T., L. Baur, and R. Uauy. 2004. "Obesity in Children and Young People: A Crisis in Public Health." *Obesity Reviews* 5(Supp. 1): 4–104.

Oude Luttikhuis, H., L. Baur, H. Jansen, V. A. Shrewsbury, C. O'Malley, R. P. Stolk, and C. D. Summerbell. 2009. "Interventions for Treating Obesity in Children." *Cochrane Database of Systematic Reviews* 1: Art. No. CD001872. DOI: 10.1002/14651858.CD001872. pub2.

Summerbell, C. D., E. Waters, L. D. Edmunds, S. Kelly, T. Brown, and K. J. Campbell. 2005. "Interventions for preventing obesity in children." *The Cochrane Database of Systematic Reviews* 3: Art. No. CD001871. DOI: 10.1002/14651858.CD001871.pub2.

REFERENCES

Angelopoulos, P. D., H. J. Milionis, E. Grammatikaki, G. Moschonis, and Y. Manios. 2009. "Changes in BMI and Blood Pressure after a School Based Intervention: The CHILDREN Study." *European Journal of Public Health* 19(3): 319–25.

Ask, A. S., S. Hernes, I. Aarek, G. Johannessen, and M. Haugen. 2006. "Changes in Dietary Pattern in 15-Year-Old Adolescents Following a 4 Month Dietary Intervention with School Breakfast—A Pilot Study." *Nutrition Journal* 5: 33.

Brown, T., S. Kelly, and C. Summerbell. 2007. "Prevention of Obesity: A Review of Interventions. Short Science Reviews. Foresight Tackling Obesities: Future Choices." *Obesity Reviews* 8(Supp. 1): 127–130.

Brown, T., and C. Summerbell. 2009. "Systematic Review of School-Based Interventions That Focus on Changing Dietary Intake and Physical Activity Levels to Prevent Childhood Obesity: An Update to the Obesity Guidance Produced by the National Institute for Health and Clinical Excellence." *Obesity Reviews* 10: 110–141.

Caballero, B., T. Clay, S. M. Davis, B. Ethelbah, B. H. Rock, T. Lohman, J. Norman, M. Story, E. J. Stone, L. Stephenson, and J. Stevens., Pathways Study Research Group. 2003. "Pathways: A School-Based, Randomized Controlled Trial for the Prevention of Obesity in American-Indian Schoolchildren." *American Journal of Clinical Nutrition* 78: 1030–1038.

Doak, C. M., C. D. Summerbell, and L. Lissner. 2009. "Prevention of Childhood Obesity: What Type of Evidence Should We Consider Relevant?" *Obesity Reviews*, published online Jan. 16, 2009, DOI: 10.1111/j. 1467–789X.2008.00550.x.

Dobbins, M., D. Lockett, I. Michel, J. Beyers, L. Feldman, J. Vohra, et al. 2001. *The Effectiveness of School-Based Interventions in Promoting Physical Activity and Fitness among Children and Youth: A Systematic Review.* Hamilton, Ontario: Effective Public Health Practice Project; Public Health Research, Education and Development Program.

Durant, N., M. L. Baskin, O. Thomas, and D, B, Allison. 2008. "School-based Obesity Treatment and Prevention Programs: All In All, Just Another Brick in the Wall?" *International Journal of Obesity* 32: 1747–1751; doi: 10.1038/ijo.2008.165.

Economos, C. D., R. H. Hyatt, J. P. Goldberg, A. Must, E. N. Naumova, J. C. Collins, and M. E. Nelson. 2007. "A Community Intervention Reduces BMI Z-Score in Children: Shape Up Somerville First Year Results." *Obesity* 15(5): 1325–1336.

Eisenberg, M. E., D. Neumark-Sztainer, and M. Story. 2003. "Associations of Weight-Based Teasing and Emotional Well-Being among Adolescents." *Archives of Pediatric and Adolescent Medicine* 157: 733–738.

Eliakim, A., D, Nemet, Y. Balakirski and Y. Epstein. 2007. "The Effects of Nutritional-Physical Activity School-Based Intervention on Fatness and Fitness in Preschool Children." *Journal of Pediatric Endocrinology & Metabolis: JPEM* 20: 711–718.

Fagot-Campagna, A., D. Pettitt, M. M. Engelgau, N. R. Burrows, L. S. Geiss, R. Valdez, et al. 2000. "Type 2 Diabetes among North American Children and Adolescents; An Epidemiological Review and a Public Health Perspective." *Journal of Pediatrics* 136: 664–672.

Flores R. 1995. "Dance for Health: Improving Fitness in African–American and Hispanic Adolescents." *Public Health Reports* 110: 189–193.

Foster, G. D., S. Sherman, K. E. Borradaile, K. M. Grundy, S. S. V. Veur, J. Nachmani, A. Karpyn, S. Kumanyika, and J. Shults. 2008. "A Policy Based School Intervention to Prevent Overweight and Obesity." *Pediatrics* 121: e794-e802. DOI: 10.1542/peds.2007–1365.

Gentile, D. A., G. Welk, J. C. Eisenmann, R. A. Reimer, D. A. Walsh, D. W. Russell, R. Callahan, M. Walsh, S. Strickland, and K. Fritz. 2009. "Evaluation of a Multiple Ecological Level Child Obesity Prevention Program: Switch® What You Do, View and Chew." BioMed Central *Medicine* 7:49 doi: 10.1186/1741–7015-7–49.

Gortmaker, S. L., K. Peterson, J. Wiecha, A. M. Sobol, S. Dixit, M. K. Fox, and N. Laird. 1999. "Reducing Obesity via a School-Based Interdisciplinary Intervention among Youth: Planet Health." *Archives of Pediatric and Adolescent Medicine* 153: 409–418.

Government Office for Science. 2007. *Tackling Obesity: Future Choices–Project Report.* London: Department for Innovation, Universities and Skills.

Haerens, L., B. Deforche, L. Maes, V. Stevens, G. Cardon, and I. De Bourdeaudhuij. 2006. "Body Mass Effects of a Physical Activity and Healthy Food Intervention in Middle Schools." *Obesity* 14: 847–854.

Harris, K. C., L. K Kuramoto, M. Schulzer, and J. E. Retallack. 2009. "Effect of School-Based Physical Activity Interventions on Body Mass Index in Children: A Meta-Analysis." *Canadian Medical Association Journal* 180(7): 719–726.

International Union for Health Promotion and Education (IUPHE). 2008. *Achieving Health Promoting Schools: Guidelines for Promoting Health in Schools.* France

James, J., P. Thomas, and D. Kerr. 2007. "Preventing Childhood Obesity: 2-Year Follow-Up Results from the Christchurch Obesity Prevention Program in Schools (CHOPPS)." *British Medical Journal* 335: 762.

Janssen, I., W. M. Craig, W. F. Boyce, and W. Pickett. 2004. "Associations between
    Overweight and Obesity with Bullying Behaviors in School-Aged Children." Pediatrics
    113: 1187–1194.
Jiang, J., X. Xia, T. Greiner, G. Wu, G. Lian, and U. Rosenqvist. 2007. "The Effects of a
    3-Year Obesity Intervention in Schoolchildren in Beijing." Child: Care, Health and
    Development 33(5): 641–646.
Kafatos, I., Y. Manios, J. Moschandreas, A. Kafatos, and Preventive Medicine and
    Nutrition Clinic University of Crete Research Team. 2007. "Health and Nutrition
    Education Program in Primary Schools of Crete: Changes in Blood Pressure over 10
    Years." European Journal of Clinical Nutrition 61: 837–845.
Kain, J., R. Uauy, C. Albala, F. Vio, R. Cerda, and B. Leyton. 2004. "Schoolbased Obesity
    Prevention in Chilean Primary School Children: Methodology and Evaluation of a
    Controlled Study." International Journal of Obesity 28: 483–493.
Katz, D. L., M. O'Connell, M. C. Yeh, H. Nawaz, V. Njike, L. M. Anderson, et al. 2005.
    "Public Health Strategies for Preventing and Controlling Overweight and Obesity
    in School and Worksite Settings: A Report on Recommendations of the Task Force
    on Community Preventive Services." Morbidity and Mortality Weekly Report
    (Recommended Report) 54: 1–12.
Kropski, J. A., P. H, Keckley, and G. L. Jensen. 2008. "School-based Obesity Prevention
    Programs: An Evidence-Based Review." Obesity 16: 1009–1018.
Law, C., C. Power, H. Graham, and D. Merrick. 2007. "Department of Health Public
    Health Research Consortium: Obesity and Health Inequalities." Obesity Reviews
    8 (Supp. 1): 19–22.
Lazaar, N., J. Aucouturier, S. Ratel, M. Rance, M. Meyer, and P. Duche. 2007.
    "Effect of Physical Activity Intervention on Body Composition in Young
    Children: Influence of Body Mass Index Status and Gender." Acta Paediatrica
    96: 1315–1320.
Li, M., S. Li, L. A, Baur, and R. R. Huxley. 2008. "A Systematic Review of School-Based
    Intervention Studies for the Prevention or Reduction of Excess Weight among
    Chinese Children And Adolescents." Obesity Reviews 9(6): 548–559.
Liu, A., X. Hu, G. Ma, Z. Cui, Y. Pan, S. Chang, W. Zhao, and C. Chen. 2008. "Evaluation
    of a Classroom-Based Physical Activity Promoting Program." Obesity Reviews
    9 (Supp. 1):130–134.
Luepker, R. V , C. L. Perry, S. M. McKinlay, P. R. Nader, G. S. Parcel, E. J. Stone,
    L. S. Webber, J. P. Elder, H. A. Feldman, and C. C. Johnson. 1996. "Outcomes of a
    Field Trial to Improve Children's Dietary Patterns and Physical Activity. The Child
    and Adolescent Trial for Cardiovascular Health. CATCH Collaborative Group."
    Journal of the American Medical Association 275: 768–776.
Meininger, J. C. 2000. "School-based Interventions for Primary Prevention of
    Cardiovascular Disease: Evidence of Effects for Minority Populations." Annual Review
    of Nursing Research18: 219–244.
Miccuci, S., H. Thomas, and J. Vohra. 2002. The Effectiveness of School-Based Strategies for
    the Primary Prevention of Obesity and for Promoting Physical Activity and/or Nutrition,
    The Major Modifiable Risk Factors for Type 2 Diabetes: A Review of Reviews. Hamilton,
    Ontario: Effective Public Health Practice Project; Public Health Research, Education
    and Development Program.
Morrison, J. A., B. A. Barton, F. M. Biro, S. R. Daniels, and D. L. Sprecher. 1999.
    "Overweight, Fat Patterning, and Cardiovascular Disease Risk Factors in Black and
    White Boys." Journal of Pediatrics 135(4): 451–457.

Morrison, J. A., D. L. Sprecher, B. A. Barton, M. A. Waclawiw, and S. R.Daniels. 1999. "Overweight, Fat Patterning, and Cardiovascular Disease Risk Factors in Black and White Girls: The National Heart, Lung, and Blood Institute Growth and Health Study." *Journal of Pediatrics* 135(4): 458–464.

Mo-suwan, L., S. Pongprapai, C. Junjana, and A. Puetpaiboon. 1998. "Effects of a Controlled Trial of a School-Based Exercise Program on the Obesity Indexes of Preschool Children." *American Journal of Clinical Nutrition* 68: 1006–1011.

Muckelbauer, Rebecca, Lars Libuda, Kerstin Clausen, Andre Michael Toschke, Thomas Reinehr, and Mathilde Kersting. 2009. "Promotion and Provision of Drinking Water in Schools for Overweight Prevention: Randomized, Controlled Cluster Trial." *Pediatrics* 123(4): e661–7.

National Institute for Health and Clinical Excellence (NICE). 2006a. *Obesity: Guidance on the Prevention, Identification, Assessment and Management of Overweight and Obesity in Adults and Children.* Clinical Guideline 43. National Institute for Health and Clinical Excellence.

National Institute for Health and Clinical Excellence (NICE). 2006b. *Obesity: The Prevention, Identification, Assessment and Management of Overweight and Obesity in Adults and Children.* Clinical Guideline CG43. Obesity: Full guideline, Section 3—Prevention: Evidence Statements and Reviews. National Institute for Health and Clinical Excellence.

NHS Information Centre. 2009. *Statistics on Obesity, Physical Activity and Diet.* England: The NHS Information Centre.

Parsons, T. J., C. Power, S. Logan, and C. D. Summerbell. 1999. "Childhood Predictors of Adult Obesity: A Systematic Review." *International Journal of Obesity and Related Metabolic Disorders: Journal of the International Association for the Study of Obesity* 23(Supp. 8): S1–S107.

Pinhas-Hamiel, O., L. M. Dolan, S. R. Daniels, D. Standiford, P. R. Khoury, and P. Zeitler P. 1996. "Increased Incidence Of Non-Insulin-Dependent Diabetes Mellitus Among Adolescents." *Journal of Pediatrics* 128(5): 608–615.

Plachta-Danielzik, S., S. Pust, I. Asbeck, M. Czerwinski-Mast, K. Langnäse, C. Fischer, A. Bosy-Westphal, P. Kriwy, and M. Müller. 2007. "Four-year Follow-Up of School-Based Intervention on Overweight Children: The KOPS Study." *Obesity* 15: 3159–3169.

Resnicow, K., and T. N. Robinson. 1997. "School-Based Cardiovascular Disease Prevention Studies: Review and Synthesis." *Annals of Epidemiology* S7: S14–S31.

Robbins, L. B., K. A. Gretebeck, A. S. Kazanis, and N. J. Pender. 2006. "Girls on the Move Program to Increase Physical Activity Participation." *Nursing Research* 55: 206–216.

Robinson, T. N. 1999. "Reducing Children's Television Viewing to Prevent Obesity: A Randomized Controlled Trial." *Journal of the American Medical Association* 282: 1561–1567.

Rosenbaum, M., C. Nonas, R. Weil, M. Horlick, I. Fennoy, I. Vargas, P. Kringas, El Camino Diabetes Prevention Group. 2007. "School-based Intervention Acutely Improves Insulin Sensitivity and Decreases Inflammatory Markers and Body Fatness in Junior High School Students." *Journal of Clinical Endocrinology & Metabolism* 92: 504–508.

Rosenbloom, A. L., J. R. Joe, R. S. Young, and W, E, Winter. 1999. "Emerging Epidemic of Type 2 Diabetes in Youth." *Diabetes Care* 22(2): 345–354.

Sahota, P., M. C. Rudolf, R. Dixey, A. J. Hill, J. H, Barth, and J. Cade J. 2001. "Randomized Controlled Trial of Primary School Based Intervention to Reduce Risk Factors for Obesity." *British Medical Journal* 323: 1029–1032.

Sallis, J. F., T. L. McKenzie, T. L. Conway, J. P. Elder, J. J. Prochaska, M. Brown, M. M. Zive, S. J. Marshall, and J. E. Alcaraz. 2003. "Environmental Interventions for Eating and Physical Activity: A Randomized Controlled Trial in Middle Schools." *American Journal of Preventive Medicine* 24: 209–217.

Salmon, J. K. Ball, C. Hume, M. Booth, and D. Crawford. 2008. "Outcomes of a Group-Randomized Trial to Prevent Excess Weight Gain, Reduce Screen Behaviors and Promote Physical Activity in 10-Year-Old Children: Switch-Play." *International Journal of Obesity* 32(4): 601–12.

Sharma, M. 2007. "International School-Based Interventions for Preventing Obesity in Children." *Obesity Reviews* 8: 155–167.

Shaya, F. T., D. Flores, C. M. Gbarayor, and J. Wang. 2008. "School-based Obesity Interventions: A Literature Review." *Journal of School Health* 78: 189–196.

Shelton Brown, H., III, A. Pérez, Y.-P. Li, D. M. Hoelscher, S. K. Kelder, and R. Rivera. 2007. "The Cost-Effectiveness of a School-Based Overweight Program." *International Journal of Behavioral Nutrition and Physical Activity* 4:47 doi: 10.1186/1479-5868-4-47.

Sichieri, Rosely, Paula Trotte, Ana. de Souza, Rita Adriana, and Gloria V. Veiga. 2009. "School Randomized Trial on Prevention of Excessive Weight Gain by Discouraging Students From Drinking Sodas." *Public Health Nutrition* 12(2): 197–202.

Simon, C., B. Schweitzer, M. Oujaa, A. Wagner, D. Arveiler, E. Triby, N. Copin, S. Blanc, and C. Platat. 2008. "Successful Overweight Prevention in Adolescents by Increasing Physical Activity: A 4-Year Randomized Controlled Intervention." [erratum appears in *International Journal of Obesity* 32(10): 1606]. *International Journal of Obesity* 32(10): 1489–1498.

Spiegel, S. A., and D. Foulk. 2006. "Reducing Overweight Through a Multidisciplinary School-Based Intervention." *Obesity* 14: 88–96.

Stephens, M. B., and S. W. Wentz. 1998. "Supplemental Fitness Activities and Fitness in Urban Elementary School Classrooms." *Family Medicine* 30: 220–223.

Story, M. 1999. "School-based Approaches for Preventing and Treating Obesity." International Journal of Obesity and Related Metabolic Disorders 23 (Supp. 2): S43–S51.

Taylor, R. W., K. A. McAuley, W. Barbezat, A. Strong, S. M. Williams, and J. Mann. 2007. "APPLE Project: Two-Y Findings of a Community-Based Obesity Prevention Program in Primary School-Age Children." *American Journal of Clinical Nutrition* 86: 735–742.

Vizcaino, V. Martinez, F. Salcedo Aguilar, R. Franquelo Gutierrez, M. Solera Martinez, M. Sanchez Lopez, S. Serrano Martinez, E. Lopez Garcia, and F. Rodriguez Artalejo. 2008. "Assessment of an After-School Physical Activity Program to Prevent Obesity among 9- to 10-Year-Old Children: A Cluster Randomized Trial." *International Journal of Obesity* 32(1): 12–22.

Wang, L. Y., B. Gutin, P. Barbeau, J. B. Moore, J. Hanes, Jr., M. H. Johnson, M. Cavnar, J. Thornburg, and Z. Yin. 2008. "Cost-effectiveness of a School-Based Obesity Prevention Program." *Journal of School Health* 78(12): 619–24.

Wang, L. Y., Q. Yang, R. Lowry, and H. Wechsler. 2003. "Economic Analysis of a School-based Obesity Prevention Program." *Obesity Research* 11: 1313–1324.

Whitlock, E. P., S. B. Williams, R. Gold, P. Smith, and S. Shipman. 2005. *Screening and Interventions for Childhood Overweight: Evidence Synthesis*. Report no. 36. Agency for Healthcare Research and Quality, U.S. Department of Health and Human Services.

CHAPTER 40

WORKPLACE OBESITY PREVENTION PROGRAMS

RON Z. GOETZEL, NIRANJANA KOWLESSAR, ENID CHUNG ROEMER, XIAOFEI PEI, MARYAM TABRIZI, RIVKA C. LISS-LEVINSON, DANIEL SAMOLY, AND JESSICA WADDELL

INTRODUCTION

OBESITY is described by Thorpe as the "fastest growing public health challenge the nation has ever faced" (2009, p. 2). In the United States, obesity rates have risen sharply over the past two decades, from 12 percent in 1989 to 27 percent in 2008 (Centers for Disease Control and Prevention [CDC] 2009). At the current pace, the proportion of U.S. adults classified as obese is expected to increase to 32 percent in 2013 and to 38 percent by 2018 (Thorpe 2009).

In addition to the health consequences of obesity, the financial toll is substantial. Finkelstein estimated that the United States spent about $75 billion on obesity-related disorders in 2003, half of which was privately financed (Finkelstein, Fiebelkorn, and Wang 2004). More recently, Finkelstein updated his figures, noting that obesity-related medical expenditures cost Americans $147 billion in 2008 (Finkelstein et al. 2009). Projecting prevalence and cost figures into the future, Thorpe expects U.S. medical spending for obesity alone to reach $344 billion by 2018, imposing a "tax" of $1,425 for every man, woman, and child (2009).

Today, about two out of three U.S. adults are either overweight or obese and are therefore placed at increased risk for developing obesity-related disorders, such as type 2 diabetes, cardiovascular disease, stroke, some forms of cancer, osteoarthritis, depression, gallbladder disease, and respiratory disorders (Must et al. 1999; National Heart Lung and Blood Institute 1998). These health problems lead to an estimated 280,000 to 325,000 premature deaths each year (Fontaine et al. 2003). In spite of an ambitious national health objective to reduce the prevalence of obesity among adults to less than 15 percent by 2010 (U.S. Department of Health and Human Services 2006), the situation is worsening rather than improving.

The causes of obesity are multifaceted. Physical inactivity and unhealthy eating behaviors have long been associated with obesity. Over the decades, there has been a shift toward a more obesogenic environment, characterized by a lack of physical activity and energy-dense, calorie-laden convenience foods (French, Story, and Jeffery 2001; Swinburn, Egger, and Raza 1999). Physical activity has seen a marked decline, largely as a consequence of the many mechanized labor-saving and entertainment devices that proliferate at work and home (Brownson, Boehmer, and Luke 2005; French, Story, and Jeffery 2001). Further, individuals and families pressured for time often rely on calorie-rich, heavily processed convenience foods and sugar-filled beverages ubiquitous on grocery shelves, in fast food restaurants, and vending machines, leading to poor nutrition (Putnam, Allshouse, and Kantor 2002; Nielsen, Siega-Riz, and Popkin 2002; French, Story, and Jeffery 2001; Kant 2000).

THE TOLL OF OBESITY ON EMPLOYERS

The public health problem of obesity imposes a significant burden on individuals and businesses alike. A large percentage of the U.S. population receives health insurance through an employer. Private health insurance premiums for U.S. businesses grew by an average of 5.0 percent annually from 1997 to 2000 and by 9.2 percent annually from 2000 to 2005 (Kaiser Family Foundation and Health Research and Educational Trust 2005). From 1999 to 2005, the average employer cost for health insurance rose from $1.60 to $2.59 per employee hour (Kaiser Family Foundation and Health Research and Educational Trust 2008). Consequently, many employers have dropped health insurance coverage for their workers because of the significant expense of providing that benefit. In 2007, 62.2 percent of employers offered health benefits to workers, a sharp decrease from the 68.4 percent who did so in 2000 (Fronstin 2008).

As the cost of health care continues to rise, many are left wondering how American society will pay for it. As Thorpe has illustrated, almost two-thirds of the growth in national health care spending over the past 20 years can be attributed to Americans' worsening lifestyle habits and, in particular, to the epidemic rise in obesity rates (Thorpe and Howard 2006). Over many years, poor lifestyle habits manifest themselves as chronic disease. Employees' poor health, often caused by modifiable risk factors, imposes an extra cost burden on employers, not only in additional health care spending, but also in productivity-related losses that include increased presenteeism (health-related performance deficits), absenteeism, short- and long-term disability, and safety incidents paid for, in part, by workers' compensation insurance (U.S. Department of Health and Human Services 2003). On-the-job impairment caused by poor health is estimated to account for 60 percent of total benefit-related costs for common health conditions such as diabetes, hypertension, and heart disease (Goetzel, Long, et al. 2004). Childress and Lindsay (2006) estimated that productivity losses related to personal and family health cost U.S. employers $226 billion in 2006, equivalent to $1,685 per employee per year.

Several researchers have focused their studies on employer costs specifically related to workers' obesity. For example, Finkelstein, Fiebelkorn, and Wang (2005) estimated medical and absenteeism expenditures for full-time obese employees to be in the range of nearly $400 to more than $2,000 per person per year. On a national scale, in 2003 the U.S. Department of Health and Human Services projected that obesity-related disorders would result in 39.3 million lost workdays, 239 million restricted activity days, and 62.7 million doctor office visits annually (U.S. Department of Health and Human Services 2003). Schulte et al., in their review of workplace literature, highlighted clear relationships between workers' obesity and consequent injury, asthma, musculoskeletal disorders, immune system response, neurotoxicity, stress, cardiovascular disease, and cancer (Schulte et al. 2007). Furthermore, Goetzel et al. calculated the annual excess costs of being overweight or obese to be 21 percent higher than for those not overweight. The analysis was conducted using a large, multi-employer database and controlled for demographics, job type, and medical plan, as well as for nine other modifiable risk factors (Goetzel, Anderson et al. 1998).

More recently, a study conducted by Goetzel et al. pooled self-reported health care utilization and productivity measures for over 10,000 workers in different professions across multiple employers in various regions of the country (Goetzel, Gibson et al. 2010). The researchers found that obese employees had 20 percent more doctor visits and 26 percent more emergency room visits than normal weight employees. In addition, compared to normal weight employees, presenteeism rates were 10 percent and 12 percent higher for overweight and obese employees, respectively. Overall, compared to normal weight employees, obese and overweight workers cost employers $644 and $201 more per employee per year, respectively.

In a separate study based on self-reported and biometric data for over 35,000 employees and spouses of a manufacturing company during 2001–2002, Wang, McDonald, Champagne, and Edington found that annual per-person health care spending rose in an almost linear fashion for overweight and obese participants (those with BMI ≥ 25), with a $120 (2004 US$) increase in medical spending per unit increase in BMI (Wang et al. 2004). Using a large medical and productivity database, Durden, Huse, Ben-Joseph, and Chu estimated excess costs for employees who are overweight, obese, and severely obese to be $147, $712, and $1,977, respectively (Durden et al. 2008). Other research examining medical claims data indicates that as BMI increases, so does health care utilization and associated expenditures (Goetzel et al. 2007; Pronk 2004; Heithoff et al. 1997). The implications of these studies examining the indirect costs of obesity are alarming, pointing to the conclusion that increases in obesity correlate with increases in employers' medical costs and related productivity losses.

Other research focused on productivity-related losses shows that obese employees take more sick leave than their non-obese counterparts and are twice as likely to experience high levels of absenteeism, defined as seven or more absences due to illness over a six-month period (Tucker 1998). Thompson and colleagues estimated that absenteeism related to obesity cost employers $2.4 billion in 1998 (Thompson et al. 1998). In a study of 341 employees of manufacturing firms in Kentucky, Gates et al. (2008) found that overweight and obese employees had higher rates of absenteeism and presenteeism. Moderately or extremely obese (BMI ≥ 35) employees experienced a 4.2 percent loss in productivity, which was monetized as $506 (in 2008 dollars) per employee per year (Gates et al. 2008). Using a national, population-based telephone survey, Ricci et al. (2005) determined that obese workers experienced greater losses in hours of productivity (absenteeism and presenteeism) than did overweight or normal-weight workers; however, overweight and normal-weight workers did not differ significantly in the amount of productivity lost. Finally, Cawley et al. estimated obesity-associated absenteeism costs to be approximately $4.3 billion annually in the United States (Cawley, Rizzo, and Haas 2007).

The Workplace as a Setting for Obesity Prevention Programs

According to the *Surgeon General's Call to Action to Prevent and Decrease Overweight and Obesity,* workplaces offer a unique opportunity to promote behavior change and the adoption of healthier lifestyles (U.S. Department of Health and Human Services 2001). In many ways, workplaces are to adults what schools are to children, since most working-age adults spend a substantial portion of their waking hours there (U.S. Department of Health and Human Services 2000). Nearly a quarter of the lives of working adults are spent at work (Ozminkowski et al. 1999, 2002), and many of the associated job-related pressures—long work hours, shift work, time demands, and job stress—negatively affect lifestyle and behavior patterns, including eating habits and activity levels, which, in turn, may lead to overweight and obesity (Knutsson and Akerstedt 1992; Geliebter et al. 2000; Niedhammer, Lert, and Marne 1996; Yamada et al. 2001; Di Lorenzo et al. 2003; Yamada, Ishikazi, and Tsuritani 2002).

Employers, unlike health plans, tend to have long-term relationships with their employees and thus have more reason to improve workers' health, since these improvements are likely to pay off in the end. Additionally, the duration of interventions can be longer, thus increasing the likelihood that healthy habits are adopted and workers accrue benefits from their behavior change. Workplace health promotion programs can also be combined with ongoing and mandatory practices such as those related to health surveillance, workplace occupational health and safety, and regulatory compliance. At the workplace, health and productivity goals can be set by management and tracked using available administrative data collection and reporting systems to which employers have ready access. In short, unlike other actors in the health care marketplace (e.g., hospitals, device manufacturers, insurers, pharmaceutical firms, and doctors), employers have a strong incentive for keeping their workers healthy and fit, because doing otherwise is likely to lead to increased health care utilization, decrements in on-the-job productivity, more safety incidents, and low morale.

Thus, a growing number of employers, led by large Fortune 100 companies, have in recent years introduced comprehensive, multicomponent worksite health promotion programs directed at improving the health and well-being of workers and, in some cases, their dependents. Further motivating their actions is the dramatic increase in overweight and obesity rates among working adults in the United States, which, in turn, has provided employers with sufficient impetus to design, implement, and evaluate risk-reduction programs that incorporate weight management and obesity prevention as core elements (U.S. Department of Health and Human Services 2006). Whereas these programs have traditionally targeted a variety of health risk factors such as smoking, stress, and motor vehicle safety, employers' attention has more recently directly turned to the problem of obesity, and has focused on addressing multiple obesity-related health risks, including poor diet, physical inactivity, high blood pressure, high blood glucose, and high lipid values (e.g., high cholesterol and triglyceride levels).

For employers at the forefront of this movement, the rationale for introducing interventions at the worksite is compelling. They realize that workplace programs can reach large segments of their population that normally would not be exposed to and engaged in organized health improvement efforts. Furthermore, in many cases, workplaces contain a concentrated group of people who usually live in close proximity to one another and share a common purpose. These employers can also leverage other advantages of the workplace, including built-in communication systems, social and organizational supports, and the ability to control certain policies, procedures, and practices. When these factors are managed carefully, organizational norms or culture can be established that promote certain behaviors and discourage others. Finally, financial or other types of incentives can be offered to increase participation in programs. All in all, many more health promotion interventions are possible in a closed system like the workplace, where greater influence on behavior and the environment is possible.

Workplace Health Promotion Programs: General Principles and Best Practices

Healthy People 2010 established goals for workplace health promotion, stating that 75 percent of all U.S. employers would provide comprehensive programs for their workers and that those programs would attain participation rates of 70 percent (U.S. Department of Health and Human Services 2000). The actual prevalence of workplace programs, as reported in the most recent survey on this topic, the *2004 National Worksite Health Promotion Survey*, was far lower than the goals set by the U.S. Office of Disease Prevention and Health Promotion (ODPHP). Specifically, in 2004, (Linnan et al. 2008), only 6.9 percent of all U.S. employers had in place comprehensive programs of sufficient intensity to achieve health improvements and cost savings.

Using *Healthy People* 2010 definitions, Linnan et al. (2008) tabulated the proportion of worksites that offered comprehensive programs that included the following five core elements: (1) health education, focused on skill development and lifestyle behavior change along with information dissemination and awareness building, preferably tailored to employees' interests and needs; (2) supportive social and physical environments, reflecting the organization's expectations regarding healthy behaviors, and implementing policies promoting healthy behaviors; (3) integration of the worksite program into the organization's benefits and human resources infrastructure; (4) linking related programs like employee assistance programs (EAPs) into worksite health promotion; and (5) screening programs followed by counseling, linked to medical care to ensure follow-up.

Complementary to the above core elements, researchers and practitioners have identified certain additional best or promising practices among employers. For example, Goetzel et al.'s (2001) review of common themes found in best performing programs identified the following six best practice elements: (1) organizational commitment; (2) incentives for employees to participate; (3) effective screening and triage; (4) state of the art theory- and evidence-based interventions; (5) effective implementation; and (6) ongoing program evaluation.

A subsequent initiative by Goetzel et al., in which a panel of experts was convened and asked to comment on what they believed constituted promising practices in the workplace, produced the following four broad themes: (1) employing features and incentives consistent with an organization's core mission, goals, operations, and administrative structures; (2) targeting the most important health care issues among the employee population; (3) achieving high rates of program engagement and participation in both the short and long term; and (4) evaluating programs based upon clear definitions of success, as reflected in scorecards and metrics agreed upon by relevant stakeholders (Goetzel et al. 2007).

In earlier studies, O'Donnell et al. identified the following 10 characteristics of sustainable programs: (1) linking of program to business objectives; (2) executive management support; (3) effective planning; (4) employee input when developing goals and objectives; (5) wide variety of program offerings; (6) effective targeting of high-risk individuals; (7) incentives to motivate employees to participate in the program, leading to high participation rates; (8) program accessibility; (9) effective communications; and (10) evaluation of effectiveness (O'Donnell, Bishop, and Kaplan 1997).

From these reviews, it becomes clear that many of the same themes recur in best and promising practices studies. In the wake of these reports, several health and wellness organizations have constructed tools that employers can use to determine whether their programs meet the standards of best or promising practices. These self-assessment scorecards were born out of a need by employers to keep up with the evolving science of worksite health promotion and compare their efforts against benchmarks. The tools include: the Health Enhancement Research Organization (HERO) Scorecard (Health Enhancement Research Organization), National Business Group on Health's (NBGH) Wellness Impact Scorecard (National Business Group on Health), and National Institute for Occupational Safety and Health (NIOSH) Essential Elements (NIOSH WorkLife Initiative). Although in their infancy, these self-assessment tools are helping define the key structural and process elements necessary to build and maintain successful worksite programs.

INDIVIDUAL-FOCUSED AND ENVIRONMENTAL INTERVENTIONS TO ADDRESS WORKPLACE OBESITY

Over time, employers have put in place many individual-oriented programs aimed at improving employees' health habits and reducing obesity rates. Strategies to improve individual nutrition and physical activity run the gamut from yearly health risk appraisals (HRAs), followed by behavioral counselling, to offering financial incentives to employees who lose weight (Volpp et al. 2008).

Other prominent examples of individual-oriented programs that promote weight management are those that use pedometers and online coaching. Two recent literature reviews have concluded that the workplace is an effective setting to encourage walking (Ogilvie et al. 2007; Dugdill et al. 2008). Additional evidence shows that worksite walking initiatives can lead to reductions in hypertension (Murphy et al. 2006), reductions in waist circumference (Chan, Ryan, and Tudor-Locke 2004), and improvements in well-being and productivity (Gilson, McKenna, and Cooke 2008). Online coaching is gaining popularity, as the Internet offers an efficient method for engaging large numbers of employees in health-promoting activities. Employees working in dispersed worksites may not have access to programs made available at larger sites; hence online coaching is an efficient means of reaching these employees cost-effectively (Herman et al. 2006; Sacks et al. 2009).

To motivate employee participation in individual-focused programs, employers are increasingly providing financial incentives as rewards for employees who participate. For example, Herman et al. (2006) reported that employees at IBM Corporation who were given a cash incentive in the form of a $150 rebate for participating in an online physical activity program showed higher rates of program participation and improved health status than those not offered the incentive. A systematic review that examined participation in worksite health promotion programs found that while, in general, participation levels tended to be below 50 percent, programs that provided incentives, offered multicomponent strategies, and focused on multiple behaviors, rather than solely on physical activity, achieved improved participation levels (Robroek et al. 2009).

Alongside individual change programs, employers are now beginning to change the workplace itself—its physical and social environment—as a way to encourage employees to lead healthier lifestyles. Historically, health promotion efforts focused on influencing individual employees' health behavior (Girgis, Sanson-Fisher, and Watson 1994; Harrison and Liska 1994). Affecting changes in corporate culture or the workplace environment, however, was not a main objective of such programs (Benedict and Arterburn 2008). O'Donnell (1989) was one of the first to challenge this paradigm, arguing that health behavior in the workplace can be influenced by environmental interventions to the same degree as it can be influenced by individuals' intrinsic motivation. O'Donnell reasoned that interaction with the workplace environment is critical to enabling and supporting sustained changes in employees' health behaviors. Researchers have increasingly embraced this perspective and designed studies targeting aspects of both the social and physical environments, particularly in the areas of physical activity and weight management (French, Story, and Jeffery 2001; Hill et al. 2003; Kremers et al. 2006; Swinburn, Egger, and Raza 1999).

Over the last 25 years, experts have concluded that interventions blending individual, educational, and environmental strategies produce greater effects than individual-based approaches alone (Sorensen et al. 1998; Eriksen and Gottlieb 1998; Erfurt and Holtyn 1991; Golaszewski, Barr, and Cochran 1998; Biener et al. 1999; Hennrikus and Jeffery 1996; McLeroy et al. 1988; DeJoy and Southern 1993; Stokols 1992; Glanz 1996). In a systematic review of 129 workplace health promotion interventions, Matson-Koffman et al. (2005) found that programs that also included policy and environmental components resulted in positive health outcomes. These interventions are founded on the notion of multilevel interactions between individuals and their physical and social environment, and the effect of these interactions on individual health behaviors (Golaszewski and Fisher 2002; Stokols 1992). Given this broader focus, it is not surprising that the federal government's *Healthy People 2010* references "comprehensive programs" in a discussion of worksite efforts to promote good health.

Sorensen and Barbeau's (2004) review of workplace interventions aimed at increasing fruit and vegetable consumption further underscored the conclusion that worksite interventions were most successful when grounded in a socio-ecological approach. Sorensen also suggested that program efficacy can be improved by involving employees in program planning and by addressing any barriers arising from employees' broader social contexts, such as their family members and their immediate circle of coworkers, in the design of the program.

Workplace environmental changes can be as minor and inexpensive as posting a reminder on the company vending machine to "eat healthy" or as major and costly as setting up a new exercise/workout facility as part of the company's physical plant. Less costly examples of environmental interventions include providing healthy eating options at lower cost in vending machines and on cafeteria menus, and encouraging walking groups or other physical activity during work hours. The prospect for effective environmental dietary interventions is supported by studies showing that reducing the price of healthy foods in vending machines increases sales of those foods (French et al. 2001), and interventions in which food labels are included in cafeterias produce decreases in fat consumption (Neuhouser, Kristal, and Patterson 1999; Sorensen et al. 1992). Other environmental interventions include increasing staircase access, creating marked walking trails, and installing bike racks on company grounds (Engbers et al. 2006). Such approaches do not require individuals to self-select into defined education programs, and have the potential to reach all employees with fewer resources for implementation and maintenance, thus potentially achieving long-lasting effects (Brownson, Haire-Joshu, and Luke 2006).

Preliminary evidence suggests that these types of physical environmental interventions are successful in increasing physical activity (Blamey, Mutrie, and Aitchison 1995; French, Story, and Jeffery 2001; Russell, Dzewaltowski, and Ryan 1999; Andersen et al. 1998; Brownell, Stunkard, and Albaum 1980) and altering dietary habits (French, Story, and Jeffery 2001; Biener et al. 1999; Holdsworth and Haslam 1998; French et al. 1997; Jeffery et al. 1994; Sorensen et al. 1992; Zifferblatt, Wilbur, and Pinsky 1980). For example, signs that prompt staircase use have been shown to significantly increase such use by 63 percent in a train station (Blamey, Mutrie, and Aitchison 1995; Brownell, Stunkard, and Albaum 1980), 113 percent in a shopping mall (Brownell, Stunkard, and Albaum 1980) and 5.5 percent in a library (Russell, Dzewaltowski, and Ryan 1999). Furthermore, an intervention to reduce the price of healthy foods in vending machines increased sales by 78 percent of those foods (French et al. 1997), and interventions to reduce the price of healthy foods in cafeterias produced similar results (Biener et al. 1999; French et al. 1997; Jeffery et al. 1994). In addition, interventions in which food labels were displayed in cafeterias produced a 5 percent decrease in caloric intake (Zifferblatt, Wilbur, and Pinsky 1980) and a 5 percent reduction in fat consumption (Sorensen et al. 1992). While many of these environmental and policy innovations have been offered at worksites, there is still sparse research on their individual and combined effects on such outcomes as improving the health of workers, reducing utilization of health care services, and increasing workers' productivity.

GAINING LEADERSHIP SUPPORT

A key social policy intervention involves achieving leadership support for workplace programs and aligning organizational and employee health objectives (Goetzel 1997; O'Donnell, Bishop, and Kaplan 1997; Goetzel, Guindon et al. 1998; Goetzel, Ozminkowski et al. 2001; Sorensen and Barbeau 2004). While leadership support is needed to institute and sustain individual-focused health promotion programs, higher levels of support may be required for programs that aim to make changes to the physical environment or introduce changes to operational and organizational policies related to worker health. Although management support has been widely discussed in the workplace health promotion literature, there have been surprisingly few attempts to describe or measure it.

Goetzel et al. (2007) and O'Donnell, Bishop, and Kaplan (1997) underscored the importance of visible upper-level management support to program success. Without management support, the financial and organizational resources necessary for program development and implementation may not be realized. Leadership support becomes increasingly important as programs seek to modify the workplace environment and mobilize social influence factors. For instance, physical changes to the workplace require leadership "sign-off" and financial backing, as does instituting incentive programs to reward employees for their healthy behavior and participation in intervention programs.

MEASURING THE PHYSICAL AND SOCIAL ENVIRONMENT SUPPORTING WORKPLACE INTERVENTIONS

Organizational support for workplace obesity prevention programs is critical for environmental interventions to be effective, implying that a set of measurement instruments needed to be developed to quantify the critical factors defining such support. A review of the literature uncovered several instruments designed to measure management commitment to worker safety, but few focused on health promotion initiatives, especially ones measuring work environments supportive of physical activity and healthy eating.

Of those that did focus on environmental supports for health promotion programs, two are noteworthy. One is the Heart Check, developed as part of New York State's Healthy Heart Program to measure organizational factors that support employer cardiovascular disease (CVD) risk-reduction efforts (Golaszewski and Fisher 2002). The assessment is a 226-item inventory that measures the following worksite features: organizational foundations, administrative supports, tobacco control, nutrition support, physical activity support, stress management, screening services, and company demographics. A longer 250-item Working Well tool is based on the Heart Check and is more comprehensive, measuring cancer and diabetes risk in addition to CVD risk and organizational structures supporting risk reduction (Golaszewski, Barr, and Pronk 2003). At the time of this writing, the CDC is engaged in updating, shortening, and improving the Heart/Stroke Check instrument to include 12 categories related to environmental, policy, and management support activities aimed at achieving heart disease and stroke prevention at the worksite (Personal communication, Dyann Matson-Koffman, CDC, Atlanta, GA).

Another instrument widely used to assess environmental supports for worksite health promotion is the 112-item Checklist of Health Promotion Environments at Worksites (CHEW) (Oldenburg et al. 2002). The tool was developed to evaluate a worksite's physical and "information distribution" environments within the context of the physical environment in the immediately surrounding community as they relate to physical activity, eating habits, alcohol consumption, and smoking. However, the CHEW does not include measures specific to social/administrative supports for health improvement efforts among workers (Flin et al. 2000; Hopkins 1995; Zohar 1980).

More recently, two new instruments were developed as a part of a National Heart, Lung, and Blood Institute (NHLBI) research initiative to study the impact of workplace environmental interventions to prevent obesity among workers (Pratt et al. 2007; Wilson et al. 2007). The first, called Leading by Example (LBE), was developed by Partnership for Prevention, and later adapted by a team of researchers from the University of Georgia, Emory University, and Thomson Reuters (Della et al. 2008). The original LBE provided a core of seven items directly related to management support, commitment, and engagement. New items were added in a modified LBE instrument to address topics such as health promotion goal setting and alignment, leadership training, communication, culture building, and financial and other supports for health promotion. The LBE composite score ranges from 1 to 5, where higher scores indicate greater organizational support for health improvement initiatives. The modified 13-item LBE can be used for diagnosing management issues and challenges, and tracking and evaluating management support of health promotion programs over time.

A second instrument, the Environmental Assessment Tool (EAT), is an adaptation of the CHEW instrument (DeJoy et al. 2008). It has several components. The physical activity component assesses on-site physical activity areas, stairways and elevators, hallways, parking lots, bicycle accessibility and use, showers and changing facilities, and signage and bulletin boards. The food choices and weight management component examines the workplace's cafeterias, vending machines, and food served at company meetings and events, as well as signage related to health promotion advice to workers. An organizational characteristics and support component includes questions about access to safe walkways and open space; presence of kitchenettes or refrigerators; work rules allowing employees access to on-site or off-site facilities; community resources that could support physical activity such as health clubs and parks; written policies; and ongoing health promotion programs related to physical activity, diet and nutrition, and weight management. EAT scores range from 0 to 100, depending on the presence of environmental supports encouraging healthy eating and physical activity, with higher scores denoting greater environmental support (DeJoy et al. 2008). Compared to the LBE tool, the EAT is considered a more objective measure of an organization's physical and support environment for promoting healthy lifestyles among workers (Wilson et al. 2007).

OUTCOMES: PROGRAM EFFECT ON BEHAVIORAL AND BIOMETRIC RISK FACTORS

Existing reviews of workplace health promotion programs suggest that the majority of these programs rely heavily on individual behavioral approaches of short duration and minimal intensity to increase physical activity or change dietary habits. These studies report variable amounts of weight loss and often fail to report maintenance data (Bull et al. 2003; Heaney and Goetzel 1998; Dishman et al. 1998; Hennrikus and Jeffery 1996; Wilson, Holman, and Hammock 1996).

In contrast, a review by Heaney and Goetzel (1998) found that comprehensive, multicomponent workplace programs, not those that just focus on obesity alone, are effective in changing health habits of workers. This review, along with a more systematic review concluded by the Community Guide Task Force in 2007, made significant headway in quantifying the effects of workplace programs (Soler et al. 2010).

The earlier review examined 47 peer-reviewed studies conducted over a 20-year period and found that worksite health promotion programs varied widely in their comprehensiveness, intensity, and duration. Consequently, the measurable impact of these programs was shown to be uneven because different intervention and evaluation methods were employed (Heaney and Goetzel 1998). Despite the variability in programs and study designs, the reviewers concluded that there was "indicative to acceptable" evidence supporting the effectiveness of multicomponent worksite health promotion programs in achieving long-term behavior change and risk reduction among workers. The most effective programs offered individualized risk-reduction counseling to the highest risk employees but did so within the context of broader health awareness programs and a healthy company culture. The authors noted that, based on the evidence, changing the behavior patterns of employees and reducing their health risks were achievable objectives in a workplace setting.

The more recent review by Soler et al. (2010) on behalf of Community Guide Task Force, released in 2007 and published in 2010, examined the literature on general workplace programs that include an assessment of health risks with feedback, delivered verbally or in writing, followed by health education or other health improvement interventions. Additional health promotion interventions include counseling and coaching of at-risk employees, invitations to group health education classes, and support sessions aimed at encouraging or assisting employees in their efforts to adopt healthy behaviors.

Specific findings from the review are summarized as follows. The Task Force found *strong* or *sufficient* evidence that worksite health promotion programs that employ an assessment plus feedback with targeted and tailored follow-up interventions reduced the following health risks among program participants: tobacco use (median reduction in prevalence of 1.5 to 2.3 percentage points), dietary fat consumption (median reduction in prevalence of 5.4 percentage points), seat belt use (median relative reduction in the proportion of employees who do *not* wear seat belts equaling 27.6 percent), high blood pressure (median reduction in prevalence of 4.5 percentage points), total serum cholesterol levels (median reduction in prevalence of 6.6 percentage points), high-risk drinkers (median reduction in prevalence of 2.0 percentage points), and the number of days absent from work because of illness or disability (median reduction of 1.2 days per employee per year). The review also found improvement in the percent of employees being physically active (median relative increase of 15.3 percentage points), and improvements in overall health and well-being and reduced health care use, especially hospital admissions and days of care. In contrast, there was insufficient evidence that these programs affected fruit and vegetable consumption, body composition (i.e., weight and BMI), and overall physical fitness.

While the more general review of worksite programs did not find an effect on overweight and obesity rates among workers, a more focused analysis of worksite obesity interventions conducted for the Centers for Disease Control (CDC) Community Guide Task Force found that worksite health promotion programs specifically aimed at improving nutrition, physical activity, or both resulted in modest weight loss of 2.8 pounds and 0.47 BMI reduction within 6 to 12 months of follow up. (Anderson et al. 2009)

RETURN-ON-INVESTMENT FROM WORKPLACE HEALTH PROMOTION PROGRAMS

In addition to attending to health outcomes, researchers in the field of workplace health promotion have devoted significant energy to studying financial results and the return-on-investment (ROI) from such programs. Over the past three decades, several studies addressed the question of whether worksite health promotion programs can be cost-neutral or cost-saving. Literature reviews that weighed the evidence from experimental and quasi-experimental studies have posited that such programs, when grounded in behavior change theory, utilizing tailored communications, and offering individualized counseling for high-risk individuals are likely to achieve cost savings and produce a positive ROI (Goetzel, Juday, and Ozminkowski 1999; U.S. Department of Health and Human Services 2003; Pelletier 1996).

The ROI research is largely based on evaluations of employer-sponsored health promotion programs, most often funded by the companies implementing the programs. Studies frequently cited with the strongest research designs and including large numbers of subjects are those performed at Johnson and Johnson (Bly, Jones, and Richardson 1986; Breslow et al. 1990), Citibank (Ozminkowski et al. 1999), Dupont (Bertera 1990), Bank of America (Leigh et al. 1992; Fries et al. 1993), Tenneco (Baun, Bernacki, and Tsai 1986), Duke University (Knight et al. 1994), the California Public Retirees System (Fries et al. 1994), Procter and Gamble (Goetzel, Jacobson et al. 1998), Highmark (Naydeck et al. 2008), and Chevron Corporation (Goetzel, Dunn et al. 1998). Even accounting for inconsistencies in design and results, most of these workplace studies produced positive financial results (Naydeck et al. 2008; Mills et al. 2007; Aldana 2001; Goetzel, Juday, and Ozminkowski 1999; Pelletier 1999; Chapman 2005; Baker et al. 2008).

In 2001, Aldana performed a comprehensive literature review of the financial impact of health promotion programming on health care costs, in which the rigor of the studies was rated on a scale of A (randomized trials) to E (expert opinion) (Aldana 2001). In the analysis, only 4 of 32 studies reviewed reported no effects on health care costs. However, these 4 studies were not A-rated, while several other studies reporting positive results applied experimental or rigorous quasi-experimental methods. The median savings-to-cost ratio reported for 7 studies in the review was $3.48 to $1.00. In a widely cited example of a rigorous ROI analysis, Citibank reported a savings of $8.9 million in medical expenditures attributable to its comprehensive health promotion program, as compared to a $1.9 million investment on the program, thus achieving an ROI of $4.56 to $1.00 (Ozminkowski et al. 1999).

In 2005, Chapman summarized results from 56 qualifying financial impact studies conducted over the past two decades and concluded that participants in workplace programs had 25–30 percent lower costs than non-participants considering medical or absenteeism expenditures (Chapman 2005). Most recently, Baicker et al. published a literature review in *Health Affairs* focused on cost savings garnered by worksite wellness programs (Baicker, Cutler, and Song 2010). In their meta-analysis, the investigators found the medical costs ROI to be $3.27 for every dollar spent and the absenteeism ROI to be $2.73 for every dollar spent. The authors concluded that "Although further exploration of the mechanisms at work and broader applicability of the findings is needed, this return on investment suggests that the wider adoption of such programs could prove beneficial for budgets and productivity as well as health outcomes" (Baicker, Cutler, and Song 2010, p. 1)

In sum, the above studies and reviews suggest that within closed systems, such as employer settings, where employers control program investments in health and tightly control intervention costs, workplace programs may not only be health-beneficial, but also cost-beneficial.

CASE STUDY: THE DOW CHEMICAL COMPANY

A case study of a large organization engaged in a comprehensive health promotion program targeting overweight and obesity is found at the Dow Chemical Company (Dow) (Goetzel, Baker et al. 2009; Goetzel, Roemer et al. 2010; Goetzel, Stapleton et al. 2004; Goetzel et al. 2005). A five-year study funded by the NHLBI concluded that implementing environmental health promotion interventions, in addition to individual-oriented programs, can produce small but significant impacts on weight loss. Goetzel and colleagues conducted studies examining the one- and two-year results from Dow's workplace environmental obesity prevention program (Goetzel, Baker et al. 2009; Goetzel, Roemer et al. 2010).

Dow's core health promotion program sought to improve employees' health behaviors through a combination of education and behavior change efforts that included dissemination of health education materials (newsletters, intranet messages, posters); health assessments followed by individual counseling; on-line behavior change programs; partial reimbursements for participating in weight management, tobacco cessation and diabetes education programs in the community; and preventive screening reimbursements (Goetzel, Baker et al. 2009).

Building upon these core elements, Dow introduced a series of evidence-based (Poole, Kumpfer, and Pett 2001; French, Story, and Jeffery 2001; Biener et al. 1999; Pescatello et al. 2001) environmental interventions at selected worksites. These interventions included providing labeling and healthy food choices in vending machines, cafeterias, and company-sponsored meetings; establishing marked walking paths at intervention sites; increasing targeted messages that encouraged healthy eating and physical activity; and developing an employee recognition program that focused on healthy lifestyles (Goetzel, Baker et al. 2009). Certain worksites also added more intensive environmental interventions that focused on fostering a healthy company culture along with increased leadership commitment to employee health. The intensive interventions included setting health-related site goals, training site leaders on health promotion topics, providing regular progress reports to senior leaders, and rewarding employees and managers for progress toward achieving health goals (Goetzel, Baker et al. 2009).

Analysis of behavioral and biometric HRA data for employee cohorts at intervention sites compared to controls showed a modest effect on weight, BMI, blood pressure, and total cholesterol. The more intense interventions produced better results than moderate sites compared to controls. Over the course of two years, employees at intervention sites maintained their weight while controls gained weight. These findings suggest that it may be worthwhile for companies to supplement individual-oriented health promotion interventions with relatively low-cost environmental interventions. While the effects are small in the near term, they can potentially translate to longer-term clinical gains, especially if comprehensive programs that include both environmental and individual components are sustained over time.

Barriers to Implementing Workplace Obesity Management Programs

Reading the above, one might conclude that employment-based health promotion and disease prevention programs offer obvious solutions, albeit partial, to growing employer-related health and cost problems related to obesity. In practice, however, there are multiple barriers and controversies that make implementation challenging. For one, not all employers realize the value of obesity prevention programs, in part, because most have not been exposed to the literature surrounding these programs. Further, while some employers may feel such programs have merit, they may not know how to design or implement them. They often lack the knowledge, expertise, and resources necessary for effective implementation.

Moreover, many employers remain unconvinced that such programs are capable of both improving health and generating cost savings along with a positive ROI. Additionally, many employers may feel that being actively engaged in improving their workers' health, and in particular a sensitive topic such as obesity, is not their business but rather the responsibility of the employee's health plan or employees themselves. They may also fear litigation by disgruntled workers or unions who would challenge such initiatives as overly intrusive into employees' personal lives. Employees, too, may resist the idea that a company can regulate their lives outside of work. Workers may argue that obesity has significant genetic components, that the work environment is obesogenic since it does not allow easy access to healthy foods and physical activity, or that these programs are ways that employers can cut back on benefits by imposing financial penalties on vulnerable populations unable to afford pricier healthy foods and who lack access to recreational facilities such as fitness centers.

Even employers who are convinced that health promotion programs are effective and necessary may lack the necessary financial resources to implement effective programs with sufficient dose to achieve health improvements and cost savings. This is especially relevant to small and mid-size employers that lack the financial wherewithal of larger employers that can hire in-house staff or vendors to conduct such programs. Research shows that small employers (those companies consisting of 75–299 employees) offer fewer policy and environmental supports for health promotion, compared to worksites with 300 or more employees (Brissette et al. 2008). Similar results were reported by Linnan et al. in their 2004 survey of workplace programs (Linnan et al. 2008).

Finally, although health improvement programs may be offered at the workplace, attempts at health improvement may not be supported by family members at home or in communities where the physical and social environments are obesogenic. For example, poor communities may lack food outlets containing fresh fruits and vegetables, and certain neighborhoods may be unsafe or lacking recreational facilities. These challenges raise the need for more comprehensive and integrated obesity prevention strategies that engage stakeholders in the community, such as schools, park districts, grocery stores and community advocacy groups to provide an environment conducive to healthy lifestyles.

RECOMMENDATIONS

This chapter was written immediately following the passage of the 2010 comprehensive health reform legislation sponsored by the Obama administration, and the full implications of this legislation are not yet known. Regardless, the following recommendations are offered to federal, state, and local policy makers as actions they can take to encourage increased adoption of evidence-based workplace health promotion and obesity management programs.

1. *Increase communication and dissemination activities directed at educating employers about the benefits of workplace health promotion.* A communications campaign would include broader dissemination of study results and translation of these findings into layperson language; convening high-level government-sponsored business meetings focused on workplace health promotion; preparing media kits and issuing press releases on successful programs; and supporting presentations at conferences frequented by business leaders.

2. *Increase funding for applied health promotion research set in "real-world" business settings.*

3. *Develop tools and resources to support employer efforts in health promotion.* Several tools and resources for workplace health promotion have already been developed with the support of government funding. These include the CDC's *Employer Guide for Preventing Cardiovascular Disease* (Matson-Koffman et al. 2005), the CDC/National Business Group on Health's *Employer Guide to Clinical Preventive Services* (National Business Group on Health), CDC's *LEAN Works! Employer Toolkit* (Centers for Disease Control and Prevention), and the New York City Department of Health and Mental Hygiene's *Wellness at Work Program* (Goetzel, Roemer, et al. 2009). Additional tools and resources are needed to enable employers to prepare business cases for health promotion programs, identify competent partners from the private and public sectors, and evaluate both health-related and financial outcomes from their programs.

4. *Pilot innovative health promotion programs at federal, state, and local departments and agencies.* It is ironic that most government agencies do not have evidence-based programs for their own employees and dependents. Some noteworthy exceptions can be found in King County, Washington, and a newly developed federal initiative managed by the Office of Personnel Management (OPM), based in Washington, DC (King County; Federal Occupational Health Service). These programs should be designed in consultation with scientists and industry experts and rigorously evaluated. In this way, they can function as experimental employer laboratories that inform policy decisions concerning successful program execution, allowing them to be emulated by other public and private organizations.

5. *Honor and reward America's healthiest organizations.* Government agencies at national, state, and local levels should recognize and reward innovative organizations that have successfully implemented health promotion programs. Current award programs include The Health Project C. Everett Koop National Health Award (The Health Project); Institute for Health and Productivity Management (IHPM); National Business Group on Health (NBGH) (National Business Group on Health); American College of Occupational and Environmental Medicine (ACOEM); and the Wellness Councils of America (WELCOA) National Awards. These and related efforts recognize organizations and leaders who have documented improved health and cost savings from workplace programs. To stay competitive and to attract top talent, other businesses would take notice of these awards and either adopt or enhance their own workplace programs.

6. *Create an employers' health promotion resource center.* A government-supported resource center would collect, develop, and disseminate objective, easy-to-use, and accessible workplace health promotion information and act as a clearinghouse for resources, tools, and expertise to support employer efforts. The information disseminated would be vetted by respected outside experts (similar to the work of the CDC

Community Guide Task Force) (Centers for Disease Control and Prevention) to ensure accuracy and objectivity.

7. *Establish a public-private technical advisory council.* While many large employers can afford to hire expert consultants to help them structure effective programs, smaller employers often cannot. A public-private technical advisory council would draw upon the expertise of private consultants and experts in government, who would support employers wishing to implement health promotion programs. The technical advisory council would help organizational leaders develop the business case for health promotion; structure needs assessments and baseline diagnostic studies; establish realistic goals for program outcomes; advise on the design of evidence-based interventions based on solid theoretical foundations; communicate learning from benchmarking studies and exemplary practices; support the transfer of knowledge and experience from large employers to small- and medium-sized organizations; and advise the government on systems for measuring and evaluating outcomes.

8. *Establish collective workplace health purchasing consortia for small employers.* Federal agencies would establish collective health promotion purchasing consortia, modeled after the concept of insurance exchanges such as the Massachusetts Connector Program. These consortia would define common health and business objectives for employers in a given community, achieve consensus on health promotion program designs, issue requests for proposals to vendors and health plans, and support the establishment of performance guarantees related to the success of these programs. The consortia would also require vendors to conduct rigorous, independent evaluations of the health and economic outcomes from their programs, with reasonable definitions of success and a timetable for reporting results. Making the results of such evaluations public would further enhance the credibility of public and private sector programs and weed out ineffective ones.

9. *Support establishment of health promotion program certification and accreditation programs.* Several established review and accreditation organizations, such as the National Committee for Quality Assurance (NCQA), the Utilization Review Accreditation Committee (URAC), and the Health Enhancement Research Organization (HERO), have introduced review processes focused on workplace health promotion vendors and health plans. Their goal is to objectively assess the quality of programs offered by these providers. Overall performance and the quality of workplace programs would improve as underperforming vendors and programs are eliminated because of their low grades. Further, having access to objective reviews of health promotion vendors and programs will help purchasers make more informed decisions about the value of these programs.

10. *Provide financial incentives to small employers that introduce workplace programs.* As part of health care reform legislation, a pilot program was

funded that would test offering tax credits to small employers implementing bona fide health promotion programs at the workplace. These tax credits would partially offset the cost of providing a qualified health promotion program.

CONCLUSIONS

There is little controversy about the health and cost consequences of obesity in our country and among employed populations. Obese employees have a greater need for medical care services, and there is growing evidence that they are less productive than their normal-weight counterparts, have increased absenteeism, disability, and safety incidents.

It is also clear that workplaces provide an under-utilized setting where health promotion and obesity management programs can be offered. Well-designed and evidence-based individual-oriented programs, supported by a healthy company culture, have been shown to positively influence employees' health and produce cost savings for companies. There are, of course, many challenges associated with implementing such programs including a lack of "know-how" among many employers, especially small businesses, on ways to run and maintain programs that follow best or promising practices.

Nonetheless, the combination of individual behavior change programs, supportive corporate cultures, environmental interventions, and effective leadership can together produce successful solutions to the current obesity pandemic faced by employers. This chapter has reviewed general principles and best practices in this area and has presented evidence for a positive ROI from interventions. What is needed now is a robust effort, supported by public and private sectors, to disseminate effective models to broader audiences and to conduct further research on what interventions work best, and where employers can achieve the best value for investments in workers' health.

ACKNOWLEDGEMENTS

No outside funding was provided for the preparation of this paper. The opinions expressed in this paper are the authors' and do not necessarily represent the opinions of Thomson Reuters and Emory University.

REFERENCES

Aldana, S. G. 2001. "Financial Impact of Health Promotion Programs: A Comprehensive Review of the Literature." *American Journal of Health Promotion* 15(5): 296–320.

Andersen, R. E., S. C. Fransckowiak, J. Snyder, S. J. Bartlett, and K. R. Fontaine. 1998. "Can Inexpensive Signs Encourage the Use of Stairs? Results of a Community Intervention." *Annuals of Internal Medicine* 129(5): 363–369.

Anderson, L. M., T. A. Quinn, K. Glanz, G. Ramirez, L. C. Kahwati, D. B. Johnson, L. R. Buchanan, W. R. Archer, S. Chattopadhyay, G. P. Kalra, and D. L. Katz. 2009. "The Effectiveness of Worksite Nutrition and Physical Activity Interventions for Controlling Employee Overweight and Obesity: A Systematic Review." *American Journal of Preventive Medicine* 37(4): 340–357.

Baicker, K., D. Cutler, and Z. Song. 2010. "Workplace Wellness Programs Can Generate Savings." *Health Affairs* 2: 1–8.

Baker, K. M., R. Z. Goetzel, X. Pei, A. J. Weiss, J. Bowen, M. J. Tabrizi, C. F. Nelson, R. D. Metz, K. R. Pelletier, and E. Thompson. 2008. "Using a Return-On-Investment Estimation Model to Evaluate Outcomes from an Obesity Management Worksite Health Promotion Program." *Journal of Occupational and Environmental Medicine* 50(9): 981–990.

Baun, W., E. Bernacki, and S. Tsai. 1986. "A Preliminary Investigation: Effects of a Corporate Fitness Program on Absenteeism and Health Care Costs." *Journal of Occupational Medicine* 28: 18–22.

Benedict, M. A., and D. Arterburn. 2008. "Worksite-based Weight Loss Programs: A Systematic Review of Recent Literature." *American Journal of Health Promotion* 22(6): 408–416.

Bertera, R. L. 1990. "The Effects of Workplace Health Promotion on Absenteeism and Employment Costs in a Large Industrial Population." *American Journal of Public Health* 80(9): 1101–1105.

Biener, L., K. Glanz, D. McLerran, G. Sorensen, B. Thompson, K. Basen-Engquist, L. Linnan, and J. Varnes. 1999. "Impact of the Working Well Trial on the Worksite Smoking and Nutrition Environment." *Health Education and Behavior* 26(4): 478–494.

Blamey, A., N. Mutrie, and T. Aitchison. 1995. "Health Promotion by Encouraged Use of Stairs." *British Medical Journal* 311: 289–290.

Bly, J. L., R. C. Jones, and J. E. Richardson. 1986. "Impact of Worksite Health Promotion on Health Care Costs and Utilization: Evaluation of Johnson & Johnson's Live for Life Program." *Journal of the American Medical Association* 256(23): 3235–3240.

Breslow, L., J. Fielding, A. A. Herrman, and C. S. Wilbur. 1990. "Worksite Health Promotion: Its Evolution and the Johnson & Johnson Experience." *Preventive Medicine* 19(1): 13–21.

Brissette, I., B. Fisher, D. A. Spicer, and L. King. 2008. "Worksite Characteristics and Environmental and Policy Supports for Cardiovascular Disease Prevention in New York State." *Preventing Chronic Disease* 5(2): A37.

Brownell, K. D., A. J. Stunkard, and J. M. Albaum. 1980. "Evaluation and Modification of Exercise Patterns in the Natural Environment." *The American Journal of Psychiatry* 137(12): 1540–1545.

Brownson, R. C., T. K. Boehmer, and D. A. Luke. 2005. "Declining Rates of Physical Activity in the United States: What Are the Contributors?" *Annual Review of Public Health* 26: 421–443.

Brownson, R. C., D. Haire-Joshu, and D. A. Luke. 2006. "Shaping the Context of Health: A Review of Environmental and Policy Approaches in the Prevention of Chronic Diseases." *Annual Review of Public Health* 27: 341–370.

Bull, S. S., C. Gillette, R. E. Glasgow, and Estabrooks. 2003. "Work Site Health Promotion Research: To What Extent Can We Generalize the Results and What

Is Needed to Translate Research into Practice?" *Health Education and Behavior* 30(5): 537–549.

Cawley, J., J. A. Rizzo, and K. Haas. 2007. "Occupation-specific Absenteeism Costs Associated with Obesity and Morbid Obesity." *Journal of Occupational and Environmental Medicine* 49(12): 1317–1324.

Centers for Disease Control and Prevention. *CDC's LEAN Works! A Workplace Obesity Prevention Program.* Available from http://cdc.gov/leanworks/.

Centers for Disease Control and Prevention. *Guide to Community Preventive Services, Worksite Programs to Control Overweight and Obesity.* Available from www. thecommunityguide.org/obesity/workprograms.html.

Centers for Disease Control and Prevention (CDC). *Behavioral Risk Factor Surveillance System Survey Data.* U.S. Department of Health and Human Services, Centers for Disease Control and Prevention, 2009. Available from http://www.cdc.gov/brfss/index.htm.

Chan, C. B., D. A. Ryan, and C. Tudor-Locke. 2004. "Health Benefits of a Pedometer-Based Physical Activity Intervention in Sedentary Workers." *Preventive Medicine* 39(6): 1215–1222.

Chapman, L. S. 2005. "Meta-evaluation of Worksite Health Promotion Economic Return Studies: 2005 Update." *American Journal of Health Promotion* 19(6): 1–11.

Childress, J. M., and G. M. Lindsay. 2006. "National Indications of Increasing Investment in Workplace Health Promotion Programs by Large- and Medium-Size Companies." *North Carolina Medical Journal* 67(6): 449–452.

DeJoy, D. M., and D. J. Southern. 1993. "An Integrative Perspective on Worksite Health Promotion." *Journal of Occupational and Environmental Medicine* 35(12): 1221–1230.

DeJoy, D. M., M. G. Wilson, R. Z. Goetzel, R. J. Ozminkowski, S. Wang, K. M. Baker, H. M. Bowen, and K. J. Tully. 2008. "Development of the Environmental Assessment Tool (EAT) to Measure Organizational Physical and Social Support for Worksite Obesity Prevention Programs." *Journal of Occupational and Environmental Medicine* 50(2): 126–137.

Della, L., D. M. DeJoy, R. Z Goetzel, R. J. Ozminkowski, and M. Wilson. 2008. "Assessing Management Support for Worksite Health Promotion: Psychometric Analysis of the Leading by Example Instrument." *American Journal of Health Promotion* 22(5): 359–367.

Di Lorenzo, L., G. De Pergola, C. Zocchetti, N. L'Abbate, A. Basso, N. Pannacciulli, M. Cignarelli, R. Giorgino, and L. Soleo. 2003. "Effect of Shift Work on Body Mass Index: Results of a Study Performed in 319 Glucose-Tolerant Men Working in a Southern Italian Industry." *International Journal of Obesity and Related Metabolic Disorders* 27: 1353–1358.

Dishman, R. K., B. Oldenburg, M. A. O'Neal, and R. J. Shepard. 1998. "Worksite Physical Activity Interventions." *American Journal of Preventive Medicine* 15(4): 344–361.

Dugdill, L., C. Brettle, S. Hulme, S. McCluskey, and A. F. Long. 2008. "Workplace Physical Activity Interventions: A Systematic Review." *International Journal of Workplace Health Management* 1(1): 20–40.

Durden, E. D., D. Huse, R. Ben-Joseph, and B. C. Chu. 2008. "Economic Costs of Obesity to Self-Insured Employers." *Journal of Occupational and Environmental Medicine* 50(9): 991–997.

Engbers, L. H., M. N. van Poppel, M. Chin A Paw, and W. van Mechelen. 2006. "The Effects of a Controlled Worksite Environmental Intervention on Determinants of

Dietary Behavior and Self-Reported Fruit, Vegetable and Fat Intake." *BMC Public Health* 6: 253.

Erfurt, J. C., and K. Holtyn. 1991. "Health Promotion in Small Business: What Works and What Doesn't Work." *Journal of Occupational Medicine* 33(1): 66–73.

Eriksen, M. P., and N. H. Gottlieb. 1998. "A Review of the Health Impact of Smoking Control at the Workplace." *American Journal of Health Promotion* 13(2): 83–104.

Federal Occupational Health Service. *FedStrive*. Available from http://www.foh.hhs.gov/ fedstrive/default.htm.

Finkelstein, E. A., I. C. Fiebelkorn, and G. Wang. 2004. "State-level Estimates of Annual Medical Expenditures Attributable to Obesity." *Obesity Research* 12(1): 18–24.

Finkelstein, E. A., I. C. Fiebelkorn, and G. Wang. 2005. "The Costs of Obesity among Full-Time Employees." *American Journal of Health Promotion* 20(1): 45–51.

Finkelstein, E. A., J. G. Trogdon, J. W. Cohen, and W. Dietz. 2009. "Annual Medical Spending Attributable to Obesity: Payer- and Service-Specific Estimates." *Health Affairs* 28(5): w822–w831.

Flin, R., K. Mearns, P. O'Connor, and R. Bryden. 2000. "Measuring Safety Climate: Identifying the Common Features." *Safety Science* 34: 177–192.

Fontaine, K. R., D. T. Redden, C. Wang, A O. Westfall, and D. B. Allison. 2003. "Years of Life Lost Due to Obesity." *Journal of the American Medical Association* Jan. 8 (289[2]): 187–193.

French, S. A., R. W. Jeffery, M. Story, K. K. Breitlow, J. S. Baxter, P. Hannan, and M. P. Snyder. 2001. "Pricing and Promotion Effects on Low-Fat Vending Snack Purchases: The CHIPS Study." *American Journal of Public Health* 91(1): 112–117.

French, S. A., M. Story, and R. W. Jeffery. 2001. "Environmental Influences on Eating and Physical Activity." *Annual Review of Public Health* 22: 309–335.

French, S. A., M. Story, R. W. Jeffery, P. Snyder, M. Eisenberg, A. Sidebottom, and D. Murray. 1997. "Pricing Strategy to Promote Fruit and Vegetable Purchase in High School Cafeterias." *Journal of the American Dietetic Association* 97(9): 1008–1010.

Fries, J. F., D. A. Bloch, H. Harrington, N. Richardson, and R. Beck. 1993. "Two-year Results of a Randomized Controlled Trial of a Health Promotion Program in a Retiree Population: The Bank of America Study." *The American Journal of Medicine* 94(5): 455–462.

Fries, J. F., H. Harrington, R. Edwards, L. A. Kent, and N. Richardson. 1994. "Randomized Controlled Trial of Cost Reductions from a Health Education Program: The California Public Employees' Retirement System (PERS) Study." *American Journal of Health Promotion* 8(3): 216–223.

Fronstin, P. 2008. "Sources of Health Insurance and Characteristics of the Uninsured: Analysis of the March 2008 Current Population Survey." *EBRI Issue Brief*.

Gates, D. M., P. Succop, B. J. Brehm, G. L. Gillespie, and B. D. Sommers. 2008. "Obesity and Presenteeism: The Impact of Body Mass Index on Workplace Productivity." *Journal of Occupational and Environmental Medicine* 50 (1): 39–45.

Geliebter, A., M. E. Gluck, M. Tanowitz, N. J. Aronoff, and G. K. Zammit. 2000. "Work-shift Period and Weight Change. *Nutrition* 16: 27–29.

Gilson, N., J. McKenna, and C. Cooke. 2008. "Experiences of Route and Task-Based Walking in a University Community: Qualitative Perspectives in a Randomized Control Trial." *Journal of Physical Activity and Health* 5(Supp. 1): S176–182.

Girgis, A., R. W. Sanson-Fisher, and A. Watson. 1994. "A Workplace Intervention for Increasing Outdoor Workers' Use of Solar Protection." *American Journal of Public Health* 84(1): 77–81.

Glanz, K. 1996. "Achieving Best Practices in Health Promotion: Future Directions." *Health Promotion Journal of Australia* 6(2): 25–28.

Goetzel, R., T. Gibson, M. E. Short, B. C. Chu, J. Waddell, J. Bowen, S. C. Lemon, I. D. Fernandez, R. J. Ozminkowski, M. G. Wilson, and D. M. DeJoy. 2010. "A Multi-Worksite Analysis of the Relationships among Body Mass Index, Medical Utilization, and Worker Productivity." *Journal of Occupational and Environmental Medicine: Supplement* 52(1): S52–S58.

Goetzel, R. Z., D. R. Anderson, R. W. Whitmer, R. J. Ozminkowski, R. L. Dunn, and J. Wasserman. 1998. "The Relationship between Modifiable Health Risks and Health Care Expenditures: An Analysis of the Multi-Employer HERO Health Risk and Cost Database." *Journal of Occupational and Environmental Medicine* 40(10): 843–854.

Goetzel, R. Z., K. M. Baker, M. E. Short, X. Pei, R. J. Ozminkowski, S. Wang, J. D. Bowen, E. C. Roemer, B. A. Craun, K. J. Tully, C. M. Baase, D. M. DeJoy, and M. G. Wilson. 2009. "First-year Results of an Obesity Prevention Program at The Dow Chemical Company." *Journal of Occupational and Environmental Medicine* 51(2): 125–138.

Goetzel, R. Z., R. L. Dunn, R. J. Ozminkowski, K. Satin, D. Whitehead, and K. Cahill. 1998. "Differences between Descriptive and Multivariate Estimates of the Impact of Chevron Corporation's Health Quest Program on Medical Expenditures." *Journal of Occupational and Environmental Medicine* 40(6): 538–545.

Goetzel, R. Z., A. Guindon, L. Humphries, P. Newton, J. Turshen, and R. Webb. 1998. *Health and Productivity Management: Consortium Benchmarking Study Best Practice Report*. Houston, TX: American Productivity and Quality Center International Benchmarking Clearinghouse.

Goetzel, R. Z., S. R. Long, R. J. Ozminkowski, K. Hawkins, S. Wang, and W. Lynch. 2004. "Health, Absence, Disability, and Presenteeism Cost Estimates of Certain Physical and Mental Health Conditions Affecting U.S. Employers." *Journal of Occupational and Environmental Medicine* 46(4): 398–412.

Goetzel, R. Z., R. J. Ozminkowski, C. M. Baase, and G. M. Billotti. 2005. "Estimating the Return-on-Investment from Changes in Employee Health Risks on the Dow Chemical Company's Health Care Costs." *Journal of Occupational and Environmental Medicine* 47(8): 759–768.

Goetzel, R. Z., D. Shechter, R. J. Ozminkowski, P. F. Marmet, and M. J Tabrizi. 2007. "Promising Practices in Employer Health and Productivity Management Efforts: Findings from a Benchmarking Study." *Journal of Occupational and Environmental Medicine* 49(2): 111–130.

Goetzel, R. Z., D. Stapleton, D. DeJoy, M. Wilson, and R.J. Ozminkowski. 2004. *Environmental Approaches to Obesity Management at the Dow Chemical Company*. National Heart Lung and Blood Institute RFA-HL-04–006, Sponsor Agreement ID: 1 R01 HL079546.

Goetzel, R. Z. 1997. "Wellness-essential Building Blocks For Successful Worksite Health Promotion Programs." *Managing Employee Health Benefits* 6: 89–94.

Goetzel, R. Z., A. M. Guindon, I. J. Turshen, and R. J. Ozminkowski. 2001. "Health and Productivity Management–Establishing Key Performance Measures, Benchmarks and Best Practices." *Journal of Occupational and Environmental Medicine* 43(1): 10–17.

Goetzel, R. Z., B. H. Jacobson, S. G. Aldana, K. Vardell, and L. Yee. 1998. "Health Care Costs of Worksite Health Promotion Participants and Non-Participants." *Journal of Occupational and Environmental Medicine* 40(4): 341–346.

Goetzel, R. Z., T. R. Juday, and R. J. Ozminkowski. 1999. "What's the ROI? A Systematic Review of Return on Investment (ROI) Studies of Corporate Health and Productivity Management Initiatives." *AWHP's Worksite Health* 6: 12–21.

Goetzel, R. Z., R. J. Ozminkowski, A .J. Asciutto, P. Chouinard, and M. Barrett. 2001. "Survey of Koop Award Winners: Life-Cycle Insights." *The Art of Health Promotion* 5 (2).

Goetzel, R. Z., E. C. Roemer, X. Pei, M. E. Short, M. J. Tabrizi, M. G. Wilson, D. M. DeJoy, B. A. Craun, K. J. Tully, and J. M. White. 2010. "Second-year Results of an Obesity Prevention Program at The Dow Chemical Company." *Journal of Occupational and Environmental Medicine* 52 (3): 291–302.

Goetzel, R. Z., E. C. Roemer, M. E. Short, X. Pei, M. J. Tabrizi, R. C. Liss-Levinson, D. K. Samoly, D. Luisi, K. Quitoni, T. Dumanovsky, L. D. Silver, and R. J. Ozminkowski. 2009. "Health Improvement from a Worksite Health Promotion Private-Public Partnership." *Journal of Occupational and Environmental Medicine* 51(3): 296–304.

Golaszewski, T., D. Barr, and S. Cochran. 1998. "An Organization-Based Intervention to Improve Support for Employee Heart Health." *American Journal of Health Promotion* 13(1): 26–35.

Golaszewski, T., D. Barr, and N. Pronk. 2003. "Development of Assessment Tools to Measure Organizational Support for Employee Health." *American Journal of Health Behavior* 27(1): 43–54.

Golaszewski, T., and B. Fisher. 2002. "Heart Check: The Development and Evolution of an Organizational Heart Health Assessment." *American Journal of Health Promotion* 17(2): 132–153.

Harrison, D. A., and L. Z. Liska. 1994. "Promoting Regular Exercise in Organizational Fitness Programs: Health-Related Differences in Motivational Building Blocks." *Personnel Psychology* 47(1): 47–71.

Health Enhancement Research Organization. *HERO Health Management Best Practice Scorecard.* Available from http://www.the-hero.org/scorecard.htm.

Heaney, C. G., and R. Z. Goetzel. 1998. "A Review of Health-Related Outcomes of Multi-Component Worksite Health Promotion Programs." *American Journal of Health Promotion* 11: 290–307.

Heithoff, K. A., B. J. Cuffel, S. Kennedy, and J. Peters. 1997. "The association between body mass and health care expenditures. *Clinical Therapy* 19(4): 811–820.

Hennrikus, D.J., and R.W. Jeffery. 1996. Worksite Intervention for Weight Control: A Review of Literature." *American Journal of Health Promotion* 10(6): 471–498.

Herman, C. W., S. Musich, C. Lu, S. Sill, J. M. Young, and D. W. Edington. 2006. "Effectiveness of an Incentive-Based Online Physical Activity Intervention on Employee Health Status." *Journal of Occupational and Environmental Medicine* 48(9): 889–895.

Hill, J. O., H. R. Wyatt, G. W. Reed, and J. C. Peters. 2003. "Obesity and the Environment: Where Do We Go from Here?" *Science* 299(5608): 853–855.

Holdsworth, M., and C. Haslam. 1998. "A Review of Point-of-Choice Nutrition Labelling Schemes in the Workplace, Public Eating Places and Universities." *Journal of Human Nutrition and Dietetics* 11(5): 423–445.

Hopkins, A. 1995. *Making Safety Work: Getting Management Commitment to Occupational Health and Safety.* St. Leonards, Australia: Allen & Unwin.

Jeffery, R. W., S. A. French, C. Raether, and J. E. Baxter. 1994. "An Environmental Intervention to Increase Fruit and Salad Purchases in a Cafeteria." *Preventive Medicine* 23(6): 788–792.

Kaiser Family Foundation and Health Research and Educational Trust. *Employer Health Insurance Costs and Worker Compensation* Available from http://www.kff.org/insurance/snapshot/chcm030808oth.cfm.

Kaiser Family Foundation and Health Research and Educational Trust. *Employer Health Benefits: 2005 Summary of Findings* 2005. Available from www.kff.org/insurance/7315/sections/upload/7316.pdf.

Kant, A. K. 2000. "Consumption of Energy-Dense, Nutrient-Poor Foods by Adult Americans: Nutritional and Health Implications. The Third National Health and Nutrition Examination Survey, 1988–1994." *American Journal of Clincial Nutrition* 72(4): 929–936.

King County. *Health Matters* [cited March 16, 2010]. Available from http://www.kingcounty.gov/employees/HealthMatters.aspx.

Knight, K. K., R. Z. Goetzel, J. E. Fielding, M. Eisen, G. W. Jackson, T. Y. Kahr, G. M. Kenny, S. W. Wade, and S. Duann. 1994. "An Evaluation of Duke University's LIVE FOR LIFE Health Promotion Program on Changes in Worker Absenteeism." *Journal of Occupational and Environmental Medicine* 36(5): 533–536.

Knutsson, A., and T. Akerstedt. 1992. "The Healthy-Worker Effect: Self Selection among Swedish Workers." *Work Stress* 6: 163–167.

Kremers, S. P. J., G. J. de Bruijn, T. L. S. Visscher, W. van Mechelen, N. K. de Vries, and J. Brug. 2006. "Environmental Influences on Energy Balance-Related Behaviors: A Dual-Process View." *International Journal of Behavioral Nutrition and Physical Activity* 3(1): 9.

Leigh, J. P., N. Richardson, R. Beck, C. Kerr, H. Harrington, C. L. Parcell, and J. F. Fries. 1992. "Randomized Controlled Study of a Retiree Health Promotion Program. The Bank of America Study." *Archives of Internal Medicine* 152(6): 1201–1206.

Linnan, L. A., M. Bowling, G. M. Lindsay, J. M. Childress, C. Blakey, S. Pronk, S. Wieker, and P. T. Royall. 2008. "Results of the 2004 National Worksite Health Promotion Survey." *American Journal of Public Health* 98(8): 1503–1509.

Matson-Koffman, D. M., J. N. Brownstein, J. A. Neiner, and M. L. Greaney. 2005. "A Site-Specific Literature Review of Policy and Environmental Interventions That Promote Physical Activity and Nutrition for Cardiovascular Health: What Works?" *American Jounal of Health Promotion* 19(3): 167–193.

McLeroy, K. R., D. Bibeau, A. Steckler, and K. Glanz. 1988. "An Ecological Perspective on Health Promotion Programs." *Health Education Quarterly* 15: 351–377.

Mills, P. R., R. C. Kessler, J. Cooper, and S. Sullivan. 2007. "Impact of a Health Promotion Program on Employee Health Risks and Work Productivity." *American Jounal of Health Promotion* 22(1): 45–53.

Murphy, M. H., E. M. Murtagh, C. A. Boreham, L. G. Hare, and A. M. Nevill. 2006. "The Effect of a Worksite Based Walking Programme on Cardiovascular Risk in Previously Sedentary Civil Servants." *BMC Public Health* 6: 136.

Must, A., J. Spadano, E.H. Coakley, A.E. Field, G. Colditz, and W.H. Dietz. 1999. "The Disease Burden Associated with Overweight And Obesity." *Journal of The American Medical Association* Oct. 27 (282[16]): 1523–1529.

National Business Group on Health. *An Employer's Guide to Preventive Services*. Available from http://www.businessgrouphealth.org/preventive/index.cfm.

National Business Group on Health. *National Business Group on Health Awards Programs*. Available from http://www.wbgh.org/about/awards.cfm.

National Business Group on Health. *WISCORE, Wellness Impact Scorecard*. Available from http://www.businessgrouphealth.org/scorecard_v2/index.cfm?event=logon.landing.

National Heart Lung and Blood Institute. 1998. "Clinical Guidelines on the Indentification, Evaluation, and Treatment of Overweight and Obesity in Adults: The Evidence Report." *Obesity Research* (Supp. 2): 51S–209S.

Naydeck, B. L., J. A. Pearson, R. J. Ozminkowski, B. T. Day, and R. Z. Goetzel. 2008. "The Impact of the Highmark Employee Wellness Programs on 4-Year Healthcare Costs." *Journal of Occupational and Environmental Medicine* 50(2): 146–156.

Neuhouser, M. L., A. R. Kristal, and R. E. Patterson. 1999. "Use of Food Nutrition Labels Is Associated with Lower Fat Intake." *Journal of the American Dietetic Association* 99(1): 45–53.

Niedhammer, I., F. Lert, and M. J. Marne. 1996. "Prevalence of Overweight and Weight Gain in Relation to Night Work in a Nurses' Cohort." *International Journal of Obesity and Related Metabolic Disorders* 20: 625–633.

Nielsen, S. J., A. M. Siega-Riz, and B. M. Popkin. 2002. "Trends in Energy Intake in U.S. between 1977 and 1996: Similar Shifts Seen across Age Groups." *Obesity Research* 10(5): 370–378.

NIOSH WorkLife Initiative. *Essential Elements of Effective Workplace Programs and Policies for Improving Worker Health and Wellbeing* [cited January 19, 2010]. Available from http://www.cdc.gov/niosh/worklife/essentials.html.

O'Donnell, M. P. 1989. "Definition of Health Promotion: Part III: Expanding the Definition." *American Journal of Health Promotion* 3(3): 5.

O'Donnell, M., C. Bishop, and K. Kaplan. 1997. "Benchmarking Best Practices in Workplace Health Promotion." *The Art of Health Promotion* 1(1): 1–8.

Ogilvie, D., C. E. Foster, H. Rothnie, N. Cavill, V. Hamilton, C. F. Fitzsimons, and N. Mutrie. 2007. "Interventions to Promote Walking: Systematic Review." *British Medical Journal* 334 (7605): 1204.

Oldenburg, B., J. F. Sallism, D. Harris, and N. Owen. 2002. "Checklist of Health Promotion Environments at Worksites (CHEW): Development and Measurement Characteristics." *American Journal of Health Promotion* 16(5): 288–299.

Ostbye, T., J. M. Dement, and K. M. Krause. 2007. "Obesity and Workers' Compensation: Results from the Duke Health and Safety Surveillance System." *Archives of Internal Medicine* 167(8): 766–773.

Ozminkowski, R. J., D. Ling, R. Z. Goetzel, J. A. Bruno, K. R. Rutter, F. Isaac, and S. Wang. 2002. "Long-term Impact of Johnson & Johnson's Health & Wellness Program on Health Care Utilization and Expenditures." *Journal of Occupational and Environmental Medicine* 44(1): 21–29.

Ozminkowski, R. J., R. L. Dunn, R. Z. Goetzel, R. I. Cantor, J. Murnane, and M. Harrison. 1999. "A Return on Investment Evaluation of the Citibank, N.A. Health Management Program." *American Journal of Health Promotion* 14(1): 31–43.

Pegus, C., T. L. Bazzarre, J. S. Brown, and J. Menzin. 2002. "Effect of the Heart At Work Program on Awareness of Risk Factors, Self-Efficacy, and Health Behaviors." *Journal of Occupational and Environmental Medicine* 44(3): 228–236.

Pelletier, K. R. 1999. "A Review and Analysis of the Clinical and Cost-Effectiveness Studies of Comprehensive Health Promotion and Disease Management Programs at the Worksite: 1995–1998 Update (IV)." *American Jounal of Health Promotion* 13(6): 333–345.

Pelletier, K. R. 1996. "A Review and Analysis of the Health and Cost-Effective Outcome Studies of Comprehensive Health Promotion and Disease Prevention Programs at the Worksite: 1993–1995 Update." *American Journal of Health Promotion* 10: 380–388.

Peregrin, T. 2005. "Weighing In on Corporate Wellness Programs and Their Impact on Obesity." *Journal of the American Dietetic Association* 105(8): 1192–1194.

Pescatello, L. S., D. Murphy, J. Vollono, E. Lynch, J. Bernene, and D. Costanzo. 2001. "The Cardiovascular Health Impact of an Incentive Worksite Health Promotion Program." *American Jounal of Health Promotion* 16(1): 16–20.

Plotnikoff, R. C., L. J. McCargar, P. M. Wilson, and C. A. Loucaides. 2005. "Efficacy of an E-mail Intervention for the Promotion of Physical Activity and Nutrition Behavior in the Workplace Context." *American Jounal of Health Promotion* 19(6): 422–429.

Poole, K., K. Kumpfer, and M. Pett. 2001. "The Impact of an Incentive-Based Worksite Health Promotion Program on Modifiable Health Risk Factors." *American Jounal of Health Promotion* 16(1): 21–26, ii.

Pratt, C. A., S. C. Lemon, I. D. Fernandez, R. Goetzel, S. A. Beresford, S. A. French, V. J. Stevens, T. M. Vogt, and L. S. Webber. 2007. "Design Characteristics of Worksite Environmental Interventions for Obesity Prevention." *Obesity* 15 (9).

Pronk, N., B. Martinson, R. C. Kessler, A. L. Beck, G. Simon, and P. Wang. 2004. "The Association between Work Performance and Physical Activity, Cardiorespiratory Fitness, and Obesity." *Journal of Occupational and Environmental Medicine* 56(1): 19–26.

Putnam, J., J. Allshouse, and L. S. Kantor. 2002. "U.S. per capita Food Supply Trends: More Calories, Refined Carbohydrates, and Fats." *Food Review* 25(3): 2–15.

Ricci, J. A., and E. Chee. 2005. "Lost Productive Time Associated with Excess Weight in the U.S. Workforce." *Journal of Occupational and Environmental Medicine* 47(12): 1227–1234.

Robroek, S. J., F .J. van Lenthe, P. van Empelen, and A. Burdorf. 2009. "Determinants of Participation in Worksite Health Promotion Programmes: A Systematic Review." *International Journal of Behavioral Nutrition and Physical Activity* 6(1): 26.

Russell, W. D., D. A. Dzewaltowski, and G. J. Ryan. 1999. "The Effectiveness of a Point-of-Decision Prompt in Deterring Sedentary Behavior." *American Jounal of Health Promotion* 13(5): 257–259, ii.

Sacks, N., H. Cabral, L. E. Kazis, K. M. Jarrett, D. Vetter, R. Richmond, and T. J. Moore. 2009. "A Web-Based Nutrition Program Reduces Health Care Costs in Employees with Cardiac Risk Factors: Before and After Cost Analysis." *Journal of Medical Internet Research* 11(4): e43.

Schulte, P. A., G. R. Wagner, A. Ostry, L. A. Blanciforti, R. G. Cutlip, K. M. Krajnak, M. Luster, A. E. Munson, J. P. O'Callaghan, C. G. Parks, P. P. Simeonova, and D. B. Miller. 2007. "Work, Obesity, and Occupational Safety and Health." *American Jounal of Health Promotion* 97(3): 428–436.

Soler, R. E., K. D. Leeks, S. Razi, D. P. Hopkins, M. Griffith, A. Aten, S. K. Chattopadhyay, S.C. Smith, N. Habarta, and R.Z. Goetzel. 2010. "A Systematic Review of Selected Interventions for Worksite Health Promotion: The Assessment of Health Risks with Feedback." *American Journal of Preventive Medicine* 38 (2): S237–S262.

Sorensen, G., and E. Barbeau. 2004. *Steps to a Healthier U.S. Workforce: Integrating Occupational Health and Safety and Worksite Health Promotion: State of the Science.* Rockville, MD: U.S. Department of Health and Human Services, Public Health Service, Centers for Disease Control, National Institute for Occupational Safety and Health.

Sorensen, G., D. M. Morris, M. K. Hunt, J. R. Hebert, D. R. Harris, A. Stoddard, and J. K. Ockene. 1992. "Work-site Nutrition Intervention and Employees' Dietary Habits: The Treatwell Program." *American Journal of Public Health* 82(6): 877–880.

Sorensen, G., A. Stoddard, M. K. Hunt, J. R. Hebert, J. K. Ockene, J. S. Avrunin, J. Himmelstein, and S. K. Hammond. 1998. "The Effects of a Health Promotion-Health Protection Intervention on Behavior Change: The Wellworks Study." *American Journal of Public Health* 88(11): 1685–1690.

Stokols, D. 1992. "Establishing and Maintaining Healthy Environments. Toward a Social Ecology Of Health Promotion." *American Journal of Psychology* 47(1): 6–22.

Swinburn, B., G. Egger, and F. Raza. 1999. "Dissecting Obesogenic Environments: The Development and Application of a Framework for Identifying and Prioritizing Environmental Interventions for obesity." *Preventive Medicine* 29(6 Pt 1): 563–570.

The Health Project. *C. Everett Koop National Health Awards.* Available from http://thehealthproject.com/.

Thompson, D., J. Edelsberg, K. L. Kinsey, and G. Oster. 1998. "Estimated Economic Costs of Obesity to U.S. Business." *American Journal of Health Promotion* 13 (2): 120–127.

Thorpe, K. *The Future Costs of Obesity: National and State Estimates of the Impact of Obesity on Direct Health Care Expenses* 2009. Available from http://www.fightchronicdisease.org/pdfs/CostofObesityReport-FINAL.pdf.

Thorpe, K. E., and D. H. Howard. 2006. "The Rise in Spending among Medicare Beneficiaries: The Role of Chronic Disease Prevalence and Changes in Treatment Intensity." *Health Affairs* 25(5): w378–w388.

Tucker, L., Friedman, G. 1998. "Obesity and Absenteeism: An Epidemiological Study of 10,825 Employed Adults." *American Journal of Health Promotion* 12(3): 202–207.

U.S. Department of Health and Human Services. 2000. *Healthy People 2010: With Understanding and Improving Health; Objectives for Improving Health.* U.S Government Printing Office.

U.S. Department of Health and Human Services. 2001. *The Surgeon General's Call to Action to Prevent and Decrease Overweight and Obesity.* Rockville, MD: U.S. Department of Health and Human Services, Public Health Service, Office of the Surgeon General.

U.S. Department of Health and Human Services. 2003. "Prevention Makes Common 'Cents.'" [cited May 22 2007]. Available from http://aspe.hhs.gov/health/prevention/prevention.pdf.

U.S. Department of Health and Human Services. 2006. *Overweight and Obesity: Introduction.* [cited December 19 2009]. Available from http://www.cdc.gov/nccdphp/dnpa/obesity/index.htm.

Volpp, K. G., L. K. John, A. B. Troxel, L. Norton, J. Fassbender, and G. Loewenstein. 2008. "Financial Incentive-Based Approaches for Weight Loss: A Randomized Trial." *Journal of the American Medical Association* 300(22): 2631–2637.

Wang, F., T. McDonald, L. J. Champagne, and D. W. Edington. 2004. "Relationship of Body Mass Index and Physical Activity to Health Care Costs among Employees." *Journal of Occupational and Environmental Medicine* 46(5): 428–436.

Wilson, M. G., R. Z. Goetzel, R . J. Ozminkowski, D. M. DeJoy, L. Della, E. Chung Roemer, J. Schneider, K. J. Tully, J. M. White, and C. M. Baase. 2007. "Using Formative Research to Develop Environmental and Ecological Interventions to Address Overweight and Obesity." *Obesity* 15(1): 37S–47S.

Wilson, M. G., P. B. Holman, and A. Hammock. 1996. "A Comprehensive Review of the Effects of Worksite Health Promotion on Health-Related Outcomes." *American Journal of Health Promotion* 10(6): 429–435.

Yamada, Y, M. Kameda, Y. Noborisaka, H. Suzuki, M. Honda, and S. Yamada. 2001. "Excessive Fatigue and Weight Gain among Cleanroom Workers after Changing from an 8-Hour to a 12-Hour shift." *Scandinavian Journal of Work, Environment and Health* 27: 318–326.

Yamada, Y., M. Ishikazi, and I. Tsuritani. 2002. "Prevention of Weight Gain and Obesity in Occupational Populations: A New Target of Health Promotion Services at Worksites." *Journal of Occupational Health* 44: 373–384.

Zifferblatt, S. M., C. S. Wilbur, and J. L. Pinsky. 1980. "A New Direction for Public Health Care: Changing Cafeteria Eating Habits." *Journal of the American Dietetic Association* 76(1): 15–20.

Zohar, D. 1980. "Safety Climate in Industrial Organizations: Theoretical and Applied Implications." *Journal of Applied Physiology* 65: 96–102.

CHAPTER 41

COMMUNITY INTERVENTIONS

CHRISTINA D. ECONOMOS
AND SARAH A. SLIWA

INTRODUCTION

INTERVENTIONS targeting human behavior through multiple actions at the community level have emerged as a promising means of promoting health and reducing risk behaviors at a population level (Merzel and D'Afflitti 2003; Chappell et al. 2006).

Reviews of childhood obesity prevention trials have identified successful interventions, but, ultimately, no one approach has emerged as a surefire solution (Doak et al. 2006, Flynn et al. 2006; Summerbell et al. 2005; Stice, Shaw and Marti 2006). Studies that did achieve an impact typically employed intensive approaches, which may be less sustainable, particularly those that rely heavily on in-school time and staff commitment to promote individual behavior change (Stice, Shaw, and Marti 2006; Flynn et al 2006).

Rather than focusing on changing the behavior of individuals, coordinated environmental and policy interventions aim to alter social norms and efficiently mobilize resources to influence the lives of many people (Economos et al. 2001; Robinson and Sirard 2005; Brownson, Haire-Joshu, and Luke 2006). Given the potential magnitude of their impact, environmental factors are central to prevention efforts (Hill and Peters 1998; French, Story, and Jeffery 2001; Doak et al. 2006; Butland et al. 2007). Within the field of obesity prevention, there is increasing support for employing multiple strategies across multiple settings, particularly to support health behaviors of children, who have less control of their environments than most adults (Huang et al. 2009; Ritchie et al. 2006; NCCOR 2009; Convergence 2009, Robert Wood Johnson Foundation 2008; Kettel Khan et al. 2009; Gittelsohn and Kumar 2007).

The recognition of social, cultural, and environmental factors influencing obesity has motivated a shift to community-level strategies for health promotion, with the understanding that change at this level will encourage and sustain individual level behavior change (Navarro et al. 2007; Institute of Medicine 2005). Communities hold diverse resources, ranging from the institutional (including worksites, places of worship, schools, service and information providers) to the interpersonal (including peer networks, coalitions and task forces) to community leaders and policy makers. Communities have their own history, social norms, traditions, and knowledge. These assets contribute points of leverage and resistance, intersections that spark strongly positive or negative reactions (Christens, Hanlin, and Speer 2007). Community-based interventions aim to purposefully and efficiently apply community assets to address an issue that the community would like to resolve.

Reflecting on his 30 years of work and research on community participation, Abraham Wandersman has identified four keys to success for intervening on a social problem: theory, implementation, evaluation, and resource/system support (2009). In our discussion of community interventions as an obesity prevention strategy, we will address these "keys" by identifying relevant theory and frameworks; reviewing several examples of implementation; exploring avenues for sustainability; and discussing methodological challenges for evaluation and analysis.

Defining Community

A community can be defined as " a group of people sharing a common interest—for example, culture, social, political, health, economic interests—but not necessarily a particular geographic association" (Macaulay et al. 1999). Within the field of community health, this broad definition gives way to two contentious sub-classifications of community: "communities of identity" and "communities of location" (Campbell and Murray 2004). Communities of identity can be drawn around ethnicity, religion, a shared illness, a common political concern etc., and are often addressed in community organizing efforts (Minkler, Wallerstein, and Wilson 2008). Communities of location have physical boundaries and can include towns, cities, distinct neighborhoods (e.g., Beacon Hill in Boston, the Mission in San Francisco), and even street blocks. A geographically delineated construct of community is often seen in the field of community development (Minkler, Wallerstein, and Wilson 2008) or urban planning.

The Centers for Disease Control situates "community" as a social entity that can be classified spatially on the basis of where persons live, work, learn, worship and play (e.g., homes, schools, parks, roads, and neighborhoods [Kettel Khan et al. 2009]). It is this definition that best fits community interventions as they are discussed in this chapter; culture and identity do play an in important role, but so do many of the institutions that operate in a spatially defined community—like politicians, city agencies, and school administrators.

Community Interventions

As communities encompass a broad spectrum of activities, it is important to distinguish between "community interventions" and interventions taking place in a community setting. The latter could include community-based treatment of obesity (e.g., a weight-loss clinic at a local health center) and programs run at the community institutions (e.g., an integration of health into church services). Other chapters in this section directly address school-based, faith-based, and worksite based interventions—all of which are examples of interventions focusing on key institutions within the community.

This chapter focuses on community interventions as a coordinated set of actions in community settings that involve more than one agency or institution. These actions can include, but are not limited to, social marketing, consciousness raising, coalition formation/strengthening, capacity building, policy changes, and stimulating environmental changes. Setting is just one component of a community intervention; the balance between researcher and community participation can be plotted on a continuum ranging from the scientist-anchored "community-placed" intervention to the community-driven approach (Kegler and Glanz 2008; Flodmark, Marcus, and Britton 2006). Community interventions may include efforts that utilize a participatory research approach.

Prevention

Obesity prevention efforts can be seen as approaches that address a "normal population, that is, participants should not be selected, but should represent a normal group such as a school, or the population within a given area" (Flodmark, Marcus, and Britton 2006). A traditional public health perspective identifies three types of prevention: primary, secondary and tertiary.

Primary prevention eschews the biological onset of diseases and conditions by preventing environmental exposures and/or providing education to decrease risk-taking behaviors. Primary obesity prevention efforts at the community setting often consist of health promotion programs targeting modifiable risk factors like physical activity and nutrition. Such programs include offerings from Parks and Recreation, community cooking classes, health education campaigns, and curricular tie-ins. Secondary prevention efforts aim to identify and detect an issue in its earliest stages, with the goal of slowing its progression—even reversing it. These efforts include BMI screening. Tertiary prevention is often referred to as disease management. The line between tertiary prevention and treatment is often blurred (Breslow 2002). Policy actions—like an employee wellness policy, or expansion of walking trails—may address multiple types of prevention.

Solutions to the obesity epidemic demand the achievement of a healthy weight, encompassing both weight maintenance and weight loss objectives. In the United States, where more than two-thirds of the adult population and one-third of the pediatric population is either overweight or obese, treatment cannot be ignored. In the interest of securing broad participation from all residents, community interventions seem better suited for primary and secondary prevention than for targeted treatment.

FRAMEWORKS FOR UNDERSTANDING COMMUNITY-BASED INTERVENTIONS

There is a tremendous amount to learn from existing community-level models that address community functioning and social systems (e.g., diffusion of innovations, community organization and community building, ecological frameworks, community coalition action theory, stage theory, and the community readiness model). Settings, rules, community norms, organizational policy, and opportunities for action, all influence behavior and comprise avenues for broad change in communities (Glanz, Rimer, and Viswanath 2008). Community-based interventions depend upon successful collaborative partnerships among people and organizations from multiple sectors to further their goals of improving the health of the community as a whole. These collaborations are likely to involve a variety of approaches from top-down (expert-led planning) to bottom up (community organizing), to policy advocacy and social planning (Roussos and Fawcett 2000). Although experts have called for the development of research frameworks to form community partnerships (Story et al. 2009), the existing theories of community organization and community building may prove applicable in the interim. Blended models that combine macro-level, policy focused approaches, with intrapersonal and interpersonal techniques of health education and health behavior may be useful in community-wide programming (Glanz, Rimer, and Viswanath 2008).

This represents a shift away from the theories that are typically utilized in health promotion interventions, which are focused on individual and small group behaviors, such as the health belief model, theory of planned behavior, social cognitive theory, and the transtheoretical model (Sallis et al. 2006). The stage concepts of the transtheoretical model have been adapted to understand community level behavior in the stage theory of organizational change (in Glanz 2008) and in models of community readiness (Plested, Edwards, and Jumper-Thurman 2006; Chilenski, Greenberg, and Feinberg 2007). For an in-depth review of theories of behavior change, refer to the fourth edition of the *Health Behavior and Health Education: Theory, Research, and Practice* manual (Glanz, Rimer, and Viswanath 2008), with particular attention to chapters 13–15, 20 (see Further Reading, below).

Ecological models are useful to studying physical activity and eating behaviors because these actions take place in multiple places (Sallis et al. 2006; Story et al. 2008). We eat in our homes, in our cars, out with our friends, at meetings for work, and in the movie theater. These actions are likely influenced by social norms and cultural expectations, by the zoning codes that shape retail environments and where foods are sold, by worksite policies about food procurement and/or foods served at meetings and, even further out, by national agricultural policies. Similarly, opportunities for physical activities are shaped by numerous factors at multiple points throughout the day (Sallis et al. 2006). By delineating the various settings that influence a behavior of interest, socioecological frameworks have contributed to a more holistic understanding of the determinants of obesity and have provided a practical tool for conceptualizing intervention activities (Swinburn, Egger, and Raza 1999; Sallis et al. 2006; Story et al. 2008; Brug, van Lenthe, and Kremers 2006). These approaches have been recommended for future research (Story et al. 2009).

ECOLOGICAL MODELS

Since Urie Brofenbrenner first proposed the ecological systems theory in the late 1970s, it has been adapted for use in public health by many researchers (Brofenbrenner 1979; McLeroy et al. 1988). Although some researchers have ascribed different names and characteristics to the levels of influence (Sallis et al. 2006), the underlying concept has remained intact: influences on human behavior can be outlined as nested factors.

- Micro-individual and interpersonal: e.g., genetics, individual preferences, knowledge, beliefs, attitudes, peer and family expectations, personality
- Meso-organizational/institutional: e.g., schools, worksites, places of worship
- Exo-community: e.g., the built environment, community norms, social networks
- Macro-intercultural (macro) factors: e.g., social norms, policy, mainstream media.

Ecological frameworks have been used to outline determinants of healthy eating and physical activity and have informed other tools, like the ANGELO framework (Analysis Grind for Environments Linked to Obesity) (Swinburn, Egger, and Raza 1999; Sallis et al. 2006; Story et al. 2008). These ecological models demonstrate that many risk regulators—opportunities and constraints for physical activity and healthy eating—operate at the community level. These regulators include neighborhood conditions (crime, safety, and traffic), food access and availability, the built environment, behavioral norms and expectations, and policies.

Work at the community level also responds to researchers' calls for multi-sectoral approaches—both indirect and direct—to changing physical activity patterns and food intake at the population level (Kumanyika et al. 2002).

Ecological models help illustrate multiple levels of influence and actors and agents involved at each level; however, they are not intended to explain the synergies between the layers. Simply adding more efforts to address more layers may not be effective. Reviews of the literature suggest an inverse relationship between the number of behaviors targeted in an intervention and the size of intervention effects for obesity (Stice, Shaw, and Marti 2006). This alludes to the challenges of designing and evaluating studies for multiple-behavior change strategies.

SYSTEMS APPROACH

Instead of conceptualizing an intervention as the sum of its activities and messages, the systems approach focuses on the dynamic properties of the context in which the intervention will be implemented. Interventions can be conceptualized on three dimensions (Hawe, Shiell, and Riley 2009): their constituent activity settings; the social networks that connect people and settings; and time.

Within this system, there are multiple actors—each of whom possesses a unique set of priorities—moving parts, operating pathways, all at different levels of scale that interact, often in nonlinear ways (e.g., with time-lags, through feedback loops), to produce multiple outcomes, none of which can be explained through a single mechanism (Hammond 2009). A systems approach may be an appropriate means of addressing multiple health behaviors, as is often the intention of lifestyle interventions. Co-variation occurs when "taking effective action on one behavior increases the odds of taking effective action on a second behavior" (Prochaska 2008). Co-variation is thought to occur with diet and exercise, but little is known about when it occurs, how, or with what types of interventions (Prochaska 2008). A systems perspective may help better understand the synergies between these behaviors. Although this approach is complex and potentially overwhelming, one clear benefit is the identification, leveraging, and concentration of resources (Wholey, Gregg, and Moscovice 2009). This can improve the efficiency of efforts.

Systems thinking has lead to an increased awareness of synergies of environmental factors relating to weight status and ecologic sustainability (Huang et al. 2009; Huang 2009; Sallis, Story, and Lou 2009). At the community level, responses to this synergy can be seen in partnership formation among environmentalists and bike and pedestrian safety advocates; or in demonstrating how increased the composting of discarded food can reduce demands on waste management and trash collectors.

In the United Kingdom, the government's Foresight program uses crosscutting literature reviews and techniques, including scenario planning, to inform government policy and strategies around chosen issues (see www.foresight.gov). The "Tackling Obesities: Future Choices" project involved food retailers, sports associations, local governments as well as ministers from Departments of Health, Culture, Media and Sport, and Children Schools and Families (King and Thomas 2007), in addition to scientists. The project resulted in the production of a report, and a systems graphic that illustrates the complex interrelationships of factors contributing to physical inactivity, excess caloric intake, and weight gain (Butland et al. 2007). A key conclusion of this systems-influenced report was that individuals hold less control over their weights than is commonly assumed, suggesting that societal changes may be needed.

SOCIAL CHANGE MODELS

Obesity may be a leading public health crisis today, but it is by no means the first public health issue to employ policy tools, social institutions, and cultural values in a multilevel campaign. Lessons learned from successful social change efforts— including movements around seat belt use, smoking cessation, breast-feeding rates, and recycling—can inform efforts to curb the spread of obesity (Economos et al. 2001).

These efforts are characterized by key features (Economos et al. 2001):

- Crisis recognition
- A science base rooted in research, data, and evidence
- Economics: identification of costs or financial benefits associated with this crisis
- "Sparkplugs"—leaders who advance their cause through knowledge, competence, skills, and personality traits (e.g., charisma)
- Advocacy efforts through integrated media and community coalition and grassroots organizing
- Mass communication through multiple outlets to disseminate science-based, consistent, positive messages
- Government involvement through local and state level action; with fiscal authority at the state level and implementation through local leadership
- Clearly targeted environmental and policy changes that promote healthy physical activity and eating behaviors
- A plan of action wherein multiple pieces work synergistically.

There is increased consensus around the need to apply social change strategies in communities to promote healthy lifestyle behaviors and address obesity at a population level (Hill and Peters 1998; French, Story, and Jeffery 2001; Kettel Khan et al. 2009; Campbell and Murray 2004; Institute of Medicine 2005; Glass and McAtee 2006).

COMMUNITY READINESS

Not all communities are at the point of crisis recognition. The construct of community readiness describes the ecological context and organizational system wherein community change efforts take place (Chilenski, Greenberg, and Feinberg 2007; Greenberg et al. 2007). The underlying idea is that communities differ in their readiness, or preexisting capacity, to address a given issue—like obesity prevention—and that interventionists need to "meet communities where they are at," employing different strategies for different readiness levels. The Community Readiness Model is a tool that can be used to assess and account for issues of readiness (Plested, Edwards, and Jumper-Thurman 2006; Edwards et al. 2000; Findholt 2007). The model helps to measure the process of community change and appreciate that this can be slow, especially during phases of relationship building, issue identification, and coalition formation.

PARTICIPATORY MODELS

In multiple social science disciplines, from anthropology to public health, investigators have responded to their frustrations with what they perceived to be an "us/them" dichotomy in research by embracing cooperative strategies and social engagement (Minkler 2000). These approaches include "mutual inquiry," "community-based action research," "participatory action research," "empowerment evaluation," and "community based participatory research." Despite some differences in their goals and theoretical underpinnings, these approaches build from the same fundamental values and principles (Minkler 2000); namely, an emphasis on community-driven priorities, the uniqueness of community dynamics and the need for a tailored approach; a focus on existing assets and strengths in the community ("asset-based"), and two-way education. These approaches are anchored by an understanding that communities have inherent problem-solving skills and expertise about the issues they face and, for these reasons, should be partners rather than subjects in research.

The Community Action Model is one of these approaches. It aims to address the social determinants of a health problem and involves a capacity-building approach (Hennessey, Lavery, et al. 2005). The first step of the process involves skills development and issue selection, followed by a needs assessment or "community diagnosis," analysis, information based action, and, ultimately, the maintenance and enforcement of action. The model applies to both actions and activities; wherein an action compels an achievable and sustainable environmental change and the activity is an educational intervention that precedes or accompanies an action (Hennessey Lavery et al. 2005). The community action model is similar to the community-based participatory research (CBPR) model, which explicitly denotes research partnerships between academic institutions and communities.

CBPR assumes that: (1) partnerships are reciprocal and foster co-learning, (2) research includes a commitment to building community capacity in research, (3) data benefits all partners, and (4) researchers hold long-term commitments to reducing health disparities (Wallerstein and Duran 2006). Ideally, the issues one addresses with the CBPR approach are those that have emerged as community-identified problems (Minkler 2005). The joint identification of a research question enables rigorous research and community action to grow in tandem.

Within a CBPR project, community partners are engaged in all aspects of the research—from shaping research goals and objectives to disseminating findings (Cashman et al. 2008; Horowitz et al. 2009). While researchers and academics typically possess skills pertaining to program methodology, evaluation, and grant-writing, it is the community that has the greatest knowledge of what strategies its members may be willing to embrace, what barriers and competing issues threaten to derail implementation, and what community beliefs and values may need to be addressed (Minkler 2005). High levels of community investment can bolster program credibility, achieve greater successes with recruitment and implementation, and cultivate a sense of ownership that can contribute to program sustainability.

Applying CBPR is not without its challenges. The process requires a high level of trust (Cashman et al. 2008), which can be vulnerable to history, power struggles, and grant mechanics. It is not uncommon for communities to harbor skepticism about the researchers' intentions, especially where previous "town-gown" interactions may not have been mutually beneficial. Often, researchers and community members come from different cultural, institutional, and socioeconomic backgrounds, which may lead to misreading of intentions (Wallerstein and Duran 2006). CBPR is typically funded through grants secured by academic institutions; however, this awarding of financial resources can aggravate a sense of skewed power dynamics. Ideally, researchers and community partners should negotiate the duration of the project (Macaulay et al. 1999); however, the grant cycles that support such efforts typically impose a time frame. The *true* time frame for change and the development of functioning partnerships may differ from the stated project length, which speaks to the value of follow-up evaluations (Roussos and Fawcett 2000). In spite of these complexities, and perhaps owing to them, community-university collaborations have yielded promising results.

Examples from the Literature

The successes and failures of earlier cardiovascular disease prevention and smoking cessation studies (e.g., the North Kerelia Project, Stanford Three Community Study,

Stanford Five-City Project, Minnesota and Pawtucket Heart Health Programs; see Further Reading below) informed the design of several community-based interventions that aimed to improve opportunities for physical activity and healthful eating (Prochaska 2008; Economos and Irish-Hauser 2007).

Pathways and Shape Up Somerville in the United States, Be Active Eat Well in Australia, and the Fleurbaix and Lavantie studies in France are among the few known research trials that have applied multiple intervention strategies at multiple levels with the goal of preventing undesirable weight gain in children. As a limited number of thoroughly evaluated studies have been set in the community, it may be premature to draw definitive conclusions (Flynn et al. 2006); however, these trials offer insights for intervention design and planning.

Pathways

The Pathways intervention was a three-year randomized controlled trial in seven Native American communities, across three states (Caballero et al. 2003; Davis et al. 1999). Pathways aimed to reduce body fat among children in third, fourth, and fifth grades by promoting behavioral change and a holistic view of health through a participatory approach (Caballero et al. 2003; Davis and Reid 1999). This school-based, multiple-component trial was pioneering in its consideration of cultural, theoretical, and operational viability in the study population as well as the need to operate at a large scale (1,704 participants in 41 schools in three different states) for a long duration (six years, including three years of feasibility testing). Pathways distinguished itself from traditional school-based approaches by enlisting the support of community and tribal leaders, in addition to parents. The intervention was developed through a collaboration of universities and American-Indian nations, schools, and families. To address individual, behavioral, and environmental factors, the intervention integrated constructs from the social learning theory with American-Indian customs and practices (Davis et al. 1999). For a review of the social learning theory, refer to the fourth edition of the *Health Behavior and Health Education: Theory, Research, and Practice* manual (Glanz, Rimer, and Viswanath 2008).

By changing the school food environment, Pathways successfully reduced the fat content and energy density of foods consumed; moreover, students in the intervention sites demonstrated significantly higher intentions to eat healthy foods than did the control schools (Snyder et al. 1999). Dietary intake measures showed significantly lower daily intakes of calories (1,892 vs. 2,157 kcal/d) and calories from fat in the intervention group compared to the control group. Ultimately, the main outcome of the study, change in percent body fat, was not significantly different between intervention and control schools (Caballero et al. 2003). For this reason, Pathways is cited as "ineffective" in literature reviews (Doak et al. 2006). In its commitment to formative research and the integration of theory, community involvement, and cultural appropriateness in its design, Pathways provided a valuable community research framework that would inform future efforts, like Shape Up Somerville.

Shape up Somerville

"Shape up Somerville (SUS): Eat Smart, Play Hard," (Economos et al. 2007) was a community-based participatory research (CBPR) intervention and one of the first studies to engage a host of environmental change strategies. Building on community awareness of its own childhood overweight problem, SUS targeted the before, during, and after-school environments to prevent a rise in excess weight gain among elementary school-aged children (grades 1–3). The three-year grant comprised one planning year and two intervention years (2002–2005).

SUS integrated environmental and policy change strategies within the school setting and provided reinforcing messages in homes and in the community. To reach families outside the schools, SUS targeted the broader community by attending and co-sponsoring community events, writing a monthly column in the local newspaper, creating an identifiable logo and launching an "SUS-approved" restaurant campaign. Professional development trainings for school personnel, project staff, and community partners, were central to building community capacity. Local champions, like the mayor, bolstered both credibility and visibility, which led to changes in city policy and the built environment. Relationship building on multiple levels enabled the initiative to offer a range of opportunities, throughout the day, for young children to consume healthy foods and increase caloric expenditure through physical activity.

After the first school year of intervention (8 months), BMI z-score decreased by -0.1005 (P = 0.001, 95 percent confidence interval -0.1151 to -0.0859) in Somerville, compared to children in two demographically similar comparison communities after controlling for baseline covariates (Economos et al. 2007). This corresponds to approximately one less pound of excess weight. In its application of an ecological framework to obesity prevention, the underlying assumption is that there is no stand-alone component: the model's strength lies in the collective approach and the cumulative impact of city-wide changes on behaviors. Since the close of the study period, the initiative has continued to grow (Economos and Curtatone 2010; Burke et al. 2009).

Be Active, Eat Well

Successful community-based interventions are being developed internationally. Evaluations of Be Active, Eat Well (BAEW), an Australian intervention program utilizing the socioecological model have demonstrated success in several areas (Sanigorski et al. 2008). BAEW was a multi-faceted, community capacity-building program, promoting physical activity and healthy eating for children (aged 4–12 years) in the Australian town of Colac. The study employed a quasi-experimental, longitudinal design and collected anthropometric data from four intervention preschools and six primary schools at baseline (2003) and follow-up (2006). A comparison sample included a stratified random sample of preschoolers and primary school children from a neighboring community.

The capacity-building objective took shape as "broad actions around governance, partnerships, coordination, training and resource allocation" (Sanigorski et al. 2008). The program was designed, planned, and implemented by key community organizations with technical support, training, and evaluation provided by academic researchers. BAEW was organized around ten objectives, five of which targeted evidence-based behavior changes wherein each objective was addressed through multiple strategies. For example, the objective "increase fruit and vegetable consumption" was met by the creation of a community garden, changes in school nutrition policies, menu changes in school canteens, and so on. At the close of the intervention period, children in Colac had significantly lower increases in body weight, waist, waist to height ratio, and BMI z-score than children from the comparison site (Sanigorski et al. 2008). Investigators also found that intervention did not increase health inequalities and stigma related to obesity nor did it seem to endorse undesirable weight-loss behaviors (Sanigorski et al. 2008).

Ville Santé III (FLVSIII) and EPODE

Fleurbaix and Laventie Ville Sante (FLVS) III was a quasi-experimental study involving two communities in northern France and two comparison communities. FLVS III is the third in a series of studies involving these four communities. From 1992–2005, FLVS I was a school-based nutrition education intervention targeting children ages 5 through 12. FLVS II (1997–2002) was a longitudinal epidemiological study following trends of overweight and monitoring the sustainability of program components from the completed FLVS I program. Although there had been no explicit mechanism for continuing the school-based components of FLVS I, the authors found that inputs were sustained (Romon et al. 2008). FLVS III (2002–2007) marked the expansion to a community-wide approach, which build upon the interest and awareness that FLVS I had piqued and that consecutive studies helped to sustain (Romon et al. 2008). FLVS III was a two-stage program, with a biological and behavioral screening phase (2003) followed by individualized counseling for individuals identified through screening (overweight, high blood pressure, sedentary behaviors, unhealthy eating habits, hyperlipiemia, and smoking) (Romon et al. 2008). In this regard, FLVSIII is more of a secondary and teritiary prevention program. However, messages about food consumption and physical activity behaviors were also disseminated to the general population in school settings, after-care settings, sports groups, and parent groups. Town councils promoted physical activity by starting a walk-to-school campaign, creating sports facilities, and hiring athletic staff to develop community programming. These actions and family activities designed by other stakeholders could reach non-targeted community residents (Romon et al. 2008).

Height, weight, and demographic data were collected from the intervention and comparison communities over multiple years. After an initial rise during the 2003 school year, the overweight prevalence was significantly lower in Fleurbaix and Laventie (8.8 percent) during the 2004 school year than in the comparison towns (17.8 percent, p < 0.0001) (Ramon et al. 2008). The study is not without its limitations, but it clearly demonstrates that the process of generating community awareness, building relationships, and moving to action around an issue can take years.

The FLVS study was scaled up in 2003 as part of EPODE (Together Let's Prevent Childhood Obesity) a community-based public health obesity prevention campaign that uses a multiple stakeholder approach to target families. In each EPODE community, a local official nominates a local project manager who coordinates activities and actions that are developed with input from a social marketing team and a national scientific advisory committee. The EPODE model is being implemented in more than 200 communities in France, and the framework is being applied in Belgium, Spain, and Greece (see http://www.epode-european-network.com/). Although numerous abstracts about EPODE have been published as part of conference proceedings, evaluation results have not appeared in peer-reviewed journals prior to program expansion. This seems to suggest that other criteria were considered when reviewing evidence to support replication. Evidence-based decision making will be discussed later in this chapter.

ONGOING INITIATIVES

Healthy Kids, Healthy Communities

The Robert Wood Johnson Foundation's Healthy Kids, Healthy Communities program aims to "help local community partnerships across the United States increase opportunities for physical activity and improve access to affordable healthy foods for children and families" by funding nearly 60 communities across the United States, with special consideration for proposals from states with the highest rates of overweight and obesity (Robert Wood Johnson Foundation 2008). The Healthy Kids, Healthy Communities project is a two-stage project wherein ten "model" communities received the first wave of funding, with the idea that these communities could serve as models to assist the second wave of communities with trouble-shooting and suggestions. It is expected that the experiences of these communities will yield valuable insights into the feasibility, cost, and effectiveness of community-based approaches.

SWITCH

The SWITCH study is a randomized community-, school-, and family-based intervention aimed at modifying key behaviors (physical activity, television viewing/screen time, and nutrition) related to childhood obesity in third through fifth graders in two midwestern cities (Eisenmann et al. 2008). Recognizing that community-based studies are a growing field, the research team has published an article about its conceptual framework, general approach, and process, to inform fellow practitioners about their approach to collaborative, interdisciplinary intervention design.

Shape Up Somerville Replications

Additionally, replication efforts of the Shape Up Somerville (SUS) model (Economos et al. 2007) are underway in two different research studies that explore the extent to which the Shape Up model can be implemented in other communities, and whether it can be successful with limited technical assistance from academic partners (see www.childreninbalance.org). The CHANGE Study was a collaborative effort between Tufts University, Save the Children, U.S. Programs, and four low-income rural communities located in the following regions: Central Valley (California), Mississippi River Delta, Appalachia (Kentucky), and South Carolina. The goal was to adapt the SUS model for underserved rural areas. Individual-level measures included BMI as well as dietary intake and physical activity behavior of elementary school-aged children.

The Balance Project looks to replicate SUS in three low-income, urban US communities in a two-year, randomized trial targeting first to third graders and their families. Six communities were selected from a Request for Application (RFA) process that considered demographics and levels of community readiness to participate in a comprehensive research trial, among other criteria. The three intervention sites received training (for teachers, program managers, and community leaders), tools, and funding. By choosing intervention and control communities at the same level of readiness to act on childhood obesity, the researchers are looking to determine what happens over a two-year period with and without an investment of resources and inputs. Data is being collected at the policy and environmental level only. Given the project's focus on the feasibility of replication, and the paths through which implementation efforts transpire, process data will be a critical component of the evaluation. Although the RFA aimed to choose demographically similar cities, each community is inherently unique. The heterogeneity that characterizes complex adaptive systems means that a given intervention may not enjoy equal success across all contexts or subgroups. These replication efforts explore issues of generalizability, fidelity, and cultural and situational appropriateness.

INTERVENTION PLANNING TOOLS

Community Needs Assessments and Community Mapping

Before planning an intervention, there needs to be an *objective* understanding of the status and scope of a problem in the community as well as a *subjective* understanding of how community members view and prioritize this issue. Shape Up Somerville and Pathways allocated time to formative research and planning (Caballero et al. 2003; Economos et al. 2007). Community needs assessments refer to actions taken to identify the health status, health problems, risk factors, facilitating factors, and resources in a community (Chappell et al. 2006). Secondary data from national surveys (e.g. Behavior Risk Factor Surveillance Survey [BRFSS]) or local level data (e.g., chart reviews, BMI surveillance data collected by school districts) can provide overviews of trends in resident demographics, health outcomes, and risk behaviors. Expanding a quantitatively based needs assessment to include qualitative data concerning residents' attitudes and opinions affords a more textured understanding of community capacity around "needs" or "problems." Soliciting input from community members furthers more than one objective: not only does this information contextualize quantitative data, but the process of engaging residents can help build relationships and gain support for future efforts.

Multilevel needs assessments are critical to planning integrative, community interventions (Levy et al. 2004). This involves an assessment of individual, family, community, and public policy influences, from which strengths and gaps can be identified. This data is analyzed for crosscutting themes that are used to propose intervention priorities (Levy et al. 2004). A thorough community assessment helps researchers understand what efforts a community can realistically take on and, hopefully, sustain.

Community assets assessments can be seen as an important complement to a needs assessment. Rather than focusing on deficits—asking "what do we need?", assets mapping focuses on existing resources—"what do we have?" Through this process, communities identify a broad range of resources that can support positive behaviors of interest. Assets can be built (e.g. schools, hospitals), economic (e.g. local businesses), social (e.g. citizen associations, relationships), natural (e.g. land), or service-based (e.g. non-profits). These can be identified through key-informant interviews, focus groups, walking tours, visioning, creative assessments, and mapping exercises (Sharpe, Greaney, and Royce 2000). Assets should then be ranked by the amount of control that community members have over them, in other words, the extent to which they are "internally focused" (Kretzmann and McKnight 1993). The mapping component can help visualize and situate disparities. To this end, Google Maps and Geographic Information Systems (GIS) can be valuable tools. Even with something as simple as paper maps and colored thumbtacks, community members can identify items of interest. For example, a blue thumbtack could be used to mark an intersection that feels unsafe and dangerous to cross. These hands-on techniques have been employed in community sessions for urban planning and development projects.

Rather than choosing between assessing needs or assets, practitioners may use a blended approach. For example, Baltimarket, also known as the Baltimore Virtual Supermarket Project enables community members to order groceries online using laptops at specific libraries, where they can pick up their groceries the following day. The project is a response to limited access to supermarkets and fresh produce in East and West Baltimore. The pinpointing of these locations speaks to the results of a needs assessment; whereas, the identification of free libraries as an accessible, and acceptable, community resource reflects an asset oriented approach.

Photovoice is a participatory photography method that literally focuses on community perspectives (see www.photovoice.org). Individuals from the community use photography to document assets and concerns pertaining to a designated topic. The photographs provide qualitative data but also an entry point into a guided discussion about environmental and social factors relating to an issue area (Lopez et al. 2005). The method has been used with adults and children alike.

A Health Impact Assessment is a systematic method that is gaining traction in the United States (Centers for Disease Control 2010). The World Health Organization describes a Health Impact Assessment (HIA) as a way of assessing the health impacts of policies, plans, and projects using a combination of techniques—quantitative, qualitative, and/or participatory—to inform decision makers about choices they face *before* they begin a project (World Health Organization 1999). Conducting an HIA involves the following steps: screening for relevant projects, scoping (i.e., what health effects should be considered?), assessing risks and benefits, developing recommendations to maximize positive/minimize adverse effects, communicating results, and evaluating (Centers for Disease Control 2010).

As researchers and practitioners have become more aware of environmental barriers to purchasing healthier foods and to engaging in physical activity, they have stimulated the development of several built environment and food environment assessment tools. These community audits can serve several research purposes. They can be used as an advocacy tool, to help structure a conversation about what's going on in the community; to present evidence of "what's missing" in a neighborhood (e.g., stores that sell quality produce; playgrounds with functioning lighting); or to help build coalitions. They can provide researchers with an understanding of community resources as they facilitate or discourage desired behaviors. Lastly, these audits can be used as part of impact evaluation efforts, to determine whether an intervention has succeeded in changing indicators of interest. Although there are an increasing number of environmental tools and assessment methods, there have been few validation studies and applications across diverse populations and settings (Story et al. 2009). When faced with inconsistencies regarding relationships between the built environment and health-related behaviors and outcomes,both measurement error and differential relationships across study populations may be plausible readings of results (Story et al. 2009).

RESEARCH METHODOLOGY AND CHALLENGES

Design and Evaluation

The randomized controlled trial (RCT) remains the gold standard for evaluating causal hypotheses in epidemiology and public health. Yet many of its applications are infeasible—politically, practically, and socially—to community interventions. Social factors like income inequality, racial discrimination, or civic engagement potentially influence an individual's ability to maintain a healthy weight; however, none of these can be randomly assigned (Glass and McAtee 2006). Even though researchers can randomize communities to receive an intervention, the concept of a "control" remains misleading. Communities can be matched on several observable characteristics—e.g., median household income, percentage of children eligible for free or reduced lunch, population size, density—but will likely differ in many unobservable ways that may be difficult to measure and even more challenging to control. Put simply: the manipulation of variables required by an RCT design is more often than not unrealistic and contrived within the systems that influence population health (Swinburn, Gill, and Kumanyika 2005; Sallis, Story, and Lou 2009). Sallis et al. (2009) conclude that "Investigators rarely are able to control environmental or policy factors, so RCT are impossible in most situations."

Evaluations of quasi-experiments and natural experiments, like the introduction of environmental or policy changes, are expected to contribute new insights into the relationship between environmental factors, physical activity, and/or eating behaviors and weight (Story et al. 2009). For these evaluations to be valuable, researchers must identify relevant factors to measure in food and activity environments and establish simple measures that are valid for different populations groups and settings and are sufficiently sensitive to detect change. Additionally, there is a lack of tools for assessing policy impact and implication, presenting a challenge for researchers pursuing research around the effectiveness of newly introduced policies. The implementation of multilevel community interventions demands the pooling of abilities, expertise, and resources of multiple stakeholders. Partnership development and coalition formation are seen as core components of a successful intervention strategy (Roussos and Fawcett 2000). Although theories of coalition functioning, in terms of developmental stages, can assist with planning efforts, tools for evaluating coalition effectiveness are lacking (Minkler, Wallerstein, and Wilson 2008; Granner and Sharpe 2004).

Our understanding of mechanisms underlying relationships among weight status, eating behaviors, physical activity, and the environment remains limited (Story et al. 2009; Hammond 2009). Systems science can be seen as a "third alternative to our past dependence on the either/or choices between inductive or deductive methods" (Green 2006). Computerized modeling, which allows for numerous combinations of variables under different conditions, like Agent Based Modeling (ABM), may help guide communities in discussions of choices, in the conceptualization of futures, and in exploring hypotheses (Green 2006; Schensul 2009; Hammond 2009). For models to aid in the development and identification of best practices in community-based interventions, they should capture multiple levels of analysis and incorporate heterogeneity among individuals while allowing for adaptation over time. It is hoped that these models may provide researchers and policy makers with a space to "play-out" different options and observe their impact—both intended and unintended—on system dynamics (Hammond 2009). (For a discussion of different simulation methods and modeling approaches, see Ross Hammond, "Complex Systems Modeling Research," 2009.)

Evidence for Decision Making

The complex factors underlying the obesity epidemic are also driving a debate about research priorities. Some researchers have proposed a shift away from the "problem-oriented research" that has supported causality-oriented studies toward a "solution-oriented research paradigm," that focuses on best practices and the identification of leverage points for behavior change (Glass and McAtee 2006; Robinson and Sirard 2005). Solution-oriented research prioritizes innovative, theory-based prevention strategies that are implemented and evaluated through experimental and quasi-experimental research, including community trials (Brug, van Lenthe, and Kremers 2006). It is hoped that these types of studies will generate more "practice-based evidence," which many see as more relevant than the clinical "evidence-based practice," which has its origins in a medical, treatment-centric model (Green 2006; Swinburn, Gill, and Kumanyika 2005). The concept of "evidence-based public health" (EBPH) has been proposed as an alternative (Brownson, Fielding, and Maylahn 2009; Satterfield et al. 2009).

Core tenets of evidence-based public health are (Brownson, Fielding, and Maylahn 2009):

- Making decisions using the best available peer-reviewed evidence (both quantitative and qualitative)
- Using data and information systems systematically
- Applying program-planning frameworks (that often have a foundation in behavioral science theory)
- Engaging the community in assessment and decision making
- Conducting sound evaluation
- Disseminating what is learned to key stakeholders and decision makers.

Note the overlap between EBPH and CBPR with regard to community engagement and dissemination of best practices. Evidence-based public health still places a premium on research-derived evidence that has been vetted through peer review. It still asks that scientists uphold a methodological rigor and that interventions build upon theoretical frameworks. Thorough evaluation is still expected. EBPH diverges from the normative evidence base by relaxing the focus on randomization, and by placing emphasis on community participation and the sharing of knowledge to decision makers and actors outside the scientific community. There are several domains of evidence that can contribute to decision making in EBPH, and they vary in their degree of objectivity—ranging from the systematic literature reviews (more objective), to public health surveillance data (fairly objective) to qualitative data (more subjective) to personal experience (most subjective) (Brownson, Fielding, and Maylahn 2009; Fielding and Briss 2006). Qualitative data provides context and insight into community members' experiences; whereas quantitative evidence is valued for its precision in addressing issues of effectiveness (Satterfield et al. 2009). Triangulation of data collection is seen as one means of avoiding bias inherent in any one type of methodology and can help "unpack" some of the complexity of analyzing data from different sources (Granner and Sharpe 2004; Brownson, Fielding and Maylahn 2009).

Within these information domains, there are three types of evidence. Type 1 evidence measures disease burden—disclosing the magnitude, severity, and preventability of risk factors (e.g., physical inactivity is an independent risk factor for the development of several types of chronic disease). This evidence tends to arise in clinical or closed community settings, like community health centers. Type I evidence encourages action but cannot articulate what needs to be done. Type 2 and Type 3 evidence are commonly found within social groups or at the community level. Type 2 evidence addresses the effectiveness of an intervention strategy (e.g., adults who joined a community Fitness Buddies program engaged in more minutes of physical activity per week than those who did not join) and can result in recommendations to implement an intervention, answering *what* needs to be done. Type 3 evidence yields information about *how* an effective intervention can be translated or adapted to generate evidence for decisions on how something should be implemented (e.g., understanding why some adults did not join the Fitness Buddies program; or following up to understand dropout rates and rationale behind it) (Brownson, Fielding and Maylahn 2009). For more information about categorizing interventions by level of scientific evidence, see Brownson, Fielding, and Maylahn (2009). For a practical framework to guide applying and summarizing different types of evidence for decision making, see *Bridging the Evidence Gap in Obesity Prevention: A Framework to Inform Decision Making* (Institute of Medicine 2010).

A "portfolio approach" to health promotion has been proposed, wherein concepts of financial planning are applied to public health decision making. Program and policy options are evaluated in terms of their health gains and non-health outcomes (i.e., potential population impact) compared to their risk, which is defined here as the expected efficacy (Swinburn, Gill, and Kumanyika 2005). Desirable portfolios include a mix of options from "low-risk" options with small to medium returns (e.g., interventions with small groups or individuals) to "high-risk" but potentially high returns strategies (e.g., a controversial policy approach—like broad endorsement of traffic calming measures to promote walking and cycling, at the risk of angering commuters).

As researchers continue to debate what types of outcomes and research methods constitute sufficient evidence, they must also consider the generalizability of any findings. Strategies that work in one community may not readily transfer to another location (Schensul 2009). Participatory research, qualitative data, economic cost-effectiveness evaluations, and modeling approaches are all examples of tools that can help communities determine feasibility and fit of proposed interventions (Fielding and Briss 2006).

The need for research to generate broad recommendations can chafe against the necessity of tailoring interventions to community needs. This points to the importance of process evaluation—the ongoing monitoring of *how* intervention components are being designed, implemented, responded to, and adapted, with attention to relationship development and community dynamics. In particular, there is an interest around the implementation of local/community-level policies (Sallis, Story, and Lou 2009). Process data can be collected for both formative and summative purposes. Information gleaned about the extent, fidelity, and quality of the intervention provides a valuable context for interpreting a program's impacts and broader outcomes (Helitzer et al. 1999). The field of ethnography offers techniques for detailing and tracking change through organizational and individual interactions and can help explain outcomes that are observable but not well foreseen (Schensul 2009). Having an analysis plan in place in advance of collecting data—including process data—is critical. Without the necessary staff, software, and salaries in place, data may spend far too much time sitting in a locked file cabinet.

ANALYSIS

Momentum around multilevel community interventions threatens to outpace the development of appropriate statistical methods. Environmental interventions targeting multiple settings often involve nested variables and demand multilevel or spatial statistics for analysis (Sallis, Story and Lou 2009). The confounding between neighborhood characteristics and self-selection among residents is also difficult to resolve (Sallis, Story, and Lou 2009).

The systems science approach helps to qualitatively identify feedback loops and synergistic relationships. These concepts are not equivalent to the interaction terms effects accounted for in multiple regression models or analysis of variance (ANOVA) (Green 2006). The computer modeling techniques discussed earlier in this chapter may be cost prohibitive for wide use at the community level.

SUMMARY

Communities have been identified as a promising setting for obesity prevention activities. At the community level, interventions can be sufficiently large in scale to achieve policy changes that influence many people, yet small enough to address local culture, attitudes, and values. Previous studies, including Be Active Eat Well, Shape Up Somerville, and Fleurbaix and Laventie Ville Sante (FLVS) III indicated that community interventions can lead to behavior change, and even statistically significant reductions in undesirable weight gain (Economos et al. 2007;

Sanigorski et al. 2008). Although community-based research is relatively new to the field of obesity research, other disciplines, including community psychology and anthropology, offer years of insights to build upon. Participatory approaches offer researchers a means of drawing upon community knowledge and capacity while applying skills that tend to be cultivated in academic communities.

As there are numerous factors—biologic, economic, cultural, psychosocial, environmental—influencing patterns of diet and physical activity, interventions must address multiple modifiable behaviors at multiple levels. Socioecological models and systems theory are just two approaches that can help researchers and practitioners conceptualize interventions. Calls for transdisciplinary approaches are further challenging traditional boundaries of discipline. If the field is to move toward working synergistically across disciplines and at multiple levels of influence, this shift needs to be accompanied by developments in statistical analysis, by the validation of tools for environmental assessments, and by developing guidelines for the types of evidence needed for decision-making.

FURTHER READING

Behavior Change

Glanz, Karen, Barbara Rimer, and K. Viswanath. 2008. *Health Behavior and Health Education: Theory, Research and Practice*, 4th edition. San Francisco: Jossey-Bass.

Community-based Interventions and Chronic-Disease Prevention

Finland: The North Karelia Project

- Vartiainen, E., et al. 2000. "Cardiovascular Risk Factor Changes in Finland, 1972–1997." *International Journal of Epidemiology* 29(1): 49–56.
- Pietinen P, et al. 1996. "Changes in Diet in Finland from 1972 to 1992: Impact on Coronary Heart Disease Risk." *Preventive Medicine* 25(3): 243–250.
- Pekka, P., P. Pirjo, and U. Ulla. 2002. "Influencing Public Nutrition for Non-Communicable Disease Prevention: From Community Intervention to National Programme—Experiences from Finland." *Public Health and Nutrition* 5(1A): 245–251.

United States

- Fortmann, S. P., P. T. Williams, S. B. Hulley, W. L. Haskell, and J. W. Farquhar. 1981. "Effect of Health Education on Dietary Behavior:

The Stanford Three Community Study." *American Journal of Clinical Nutrition* 34(10): 2030–2038.

- Farquhar, J. W., S. P. Fortmann, J. A. Flora, C. B. Taylor, W. L. Haskell, P. T. Williams, et al. 1990. "Effects of Communitywide Education on Cardiovascular Disease Risk Factors: The Stanford Five-City Project." *Journal of the American Medical Association* 264(3): 359–365.
- Carleton, R. A., T. M. Lasater, A. R. Assaf, H. A. Feldman, and S. McKinlay. 1995. "The Pawtucket Heart Health Program: Community Changes in Cardiovascular Risk Factors and Projected Disease Risk." *American Journal of Public Health* 85(6): 777–785.
- Mittelmark, M. B., R. V. Luepker, D. R. Jacobs, N, F. Bracht, R. W. Carlaw, R. S. Crow, et al. 1986. "Community-wide Prevention of Cardiovascular Disease: Education Strategies of the Minnesota Heart Health Program." *Preventive Medicine* 15(1): 1–17.
- COMMIT Research Group. 1991. "Community Intervention Trial for Smoking Cessation (COMMIT): Summary of Design and Intervention." *Journal of the National Cancer Institute* 83(22): 1620–1628.

Assessment Tools

Several organizations have come to serve as clearinghouses for assessment tools related to the built environment and food environments.

1. *Built environment—physical infrastructure in communities:*

    a. Active Living Research—Robert Wood Johnson Foundation: http://www.activelivingresearch.org/resourcesearch/toolsandmeasures
    b. National Cancer Institute—physical activity questionnaires: http://appliedresearch.cancer.gov/tools/paq/
    c. Environmental Protection Agency: Smart Growth Tools

2. *Healthy eating environments—food availability and quality:* National Cancer Institute, https://riskfactor.cancer.gov/mfe/instruments/

3. *Community resources and programs:*

    a. Community Healthy Living Index: Tools to Change Your Environment (CHLI) from Activate America/YMCA–CHLI is designed to assess programs, the physical environment, and policies related to healthy living across schools, afterschools, work sites, neighborhoods, and the community at large. The tool can be used to plan improvement strategies: http://www.ymca.net/communityhealthylivingindex.
    b. The Community Toolbox: offers guidance in community-building skills and offers toolkits outlining key tasks around sixteen core competencies. Topics include: agenda setting; community needs assessment; models for community change; facilitation adapting interventions; http://ctb.ku.edu/en/.

REFERENCES

Breslow, L. 2002. *Encyclopedia of Public Health.* New York: Macmillan Reference.

Bronfenbrenner, U. 1979. *The ecology of human development: Experiments by nature and design.* Cambridge, MA: Harvard University Press.

Brownson, R. C., J. E. Fielding, and C. M. Maylahn. 2009. "Evidence-based Public Health: A Fundamental Concept for Public Health Practice". *Annual Review of Public Health* 30: 175–201.

Brownson, R. C., D. Haire-Joshu, and D. A. Luke. 2006. "Shaping the Context of Health: A Review of Environmental and Policy Approaches in the Prevention of Chronic Diseases." *Annual Review of Public Health* 27: 341–370.

Brug, Johannes, Frank J. van Lenthe, and Stef P. J. Kremers. 2006. "Revisiting Kurt Lewin: How to Gain Insight into Environmental Correlates of Obesogenic Behaviors." *American Journal of Preventive Medicine* 31(6)(12): 525–529.

Burke, Noreen, M., Virginia R. Chomitz, Nicole A. Rioles, Stephen P. Winslow, Lisa B. Brukilacchio, and Jessie C. Baker. 2009. The Path to Active Living: Physical Activity Through Community Design in Somerville, Massachusetts. *American Journal of Preventive Medicine* 37 (6, Supplement 2)(12): S386–394.

Butland, B., S. Jebb, P. Kopelman, K. McPherson, S. Thomas, J. Mardell, and V. Parry. 2007. Tackling obesities: Future choices—Project report. (2nd). *Government Office of the Chief Scientist,* http://www.bis.gov.uk/foresight/our-work/projects/current-projects/tackling-obesities/reports-and-publications.

Caballero, B., T. Clay, S. M. Davis, B. Ethelbah, B. H. Rock, T. Lohman, J. Norman, M. Story, E. J. Stone, and L. Stephenson. 2003. "Pathways: A School-Based, Randomized Controlled Trial for the Prevention of Obesity in American Indian Schoolchildren." *American Journal of Clinical Nutrition* 78(5): 1030.

Campbell, C., and M. Murray. 2004. "Community Health Psychology: Promoting Analysis and Action for Social Change." *Journal of Health Psychology* 9(2): 187.

Cashman, Suzanne B., Sarah Adeky, Alex J. Allen III, Jason Corburn, Barbara A. Israel, Jaime Montano, Alvin Rafelito, et al. 2008. "The Power and the Promise: Working with Communities to Analyze Data, Interpret Findings, and Get to Outcomes." *American Journal of Public Health* 98(8) (August 1): 1407–1417.

Centers for Disease Control. 2010. Health Impact Asessment [cited 2/11 2010]. Available from http://www.cdc.gov/healthyplaces/hia.htm.

Chappell, Neena, Laura Funk, Arlene Carson, Patricia MacKenzie, and Richard Stanwick. 2006. "Multilevel Community Health Promotion: How Can We Make It Work?" *Community Development Journal* 41(3) (July 1): 352–366.

Chilenski, S. M., M. T. Greenberg, and M. E. Feinberg. 2007. "Community Readiness as a Multidimensional Construct." *Journal of Community Psychology* 35(3) (Apr): 347–365.

Christens, B. D., C. E. Hanlin, and P. W. Speer. 2007. "Getting the Social Organism Thinking: Strategy for Systems Change." *American Journal of Community Psychology* 39(3–4) (Jun): 229–238.

Convergence Partnership. 2009. [cited 11/21/2009]. Available from http://www.convergencepartnership.org/site/c.fhLOK6PELmF/b.3917533/k.BDC8/Home.htm.

Davis, Sally M., Scott B. Going, Deborah L. Helitzer, Nicolette I. Teufel, Patricia Snyder, Joel Gittelsohn, Lauve Metcalfe, et al. 1999. "Pathways: A Culturally Appropriate Obesity-Prevention Program for American Indian Schoolchildren." *American Journal of Clinical Nutrition* 69(4) (April 1): 796S–802.

Davis, Sally M., and Raymond Reid. 1999. "Practicing Participatory Research in American Indian Communities." *American Journal of Clinical Nutrition* 69(4) (April 1): 755S–759.

Doak, C. M., T. L. Visscher, C. M. Renders, and J. C. Seidell. 2006. "The Prevention of Overweight and Obesity in Children and Adolescents: A Review of Interventions and Programmes." *Obesity Reviews* 7(1): 111.

Economos, C. D., R. C. Brownson, M. A. DeAngelis, S. B. Foerster, C. T. Foreman, J. Gregson, S. K. Kumanyika, and R. R. Pate. 2001. "What Lessons Have Been Learned from Other Attempts to Guide Social Change?" *Nutrition Reviews* 59(3): 40–56.

Economos, C. D., and J. A. Curtatone. 2010. "Shaping up Somerville: A Community Initiative in Massachusetts." *Preventive Medicine* 50(Supp. 1) (Jan): S97–98.

Economos, C. D., R. R. Hyatt, J. P. Goldberg, A. Must, E. N. Naumova, J. J. Collins, and M. E. Nelson. 2007a. "A Community Intervention Reduces BMI Z-Score in Children: Shape Up Somerville First Year Results." *Obesity* 15(5) (May): 1325–1336.

Economos, C. D., and S. Irish-Hauser. 2007b. "Community Interventions: A Brief Overview and Their Application to the Obesity Epidemic." *Journal of Law Medicine and Ethics* 35(1) (Spr): 131ff.

Edwards, R. W., P. Jumper-Thurman, B. A. Plested, E. R. Oetting, and L. Swanson. 2000. "Community Readiness: Research to Practice." *Journal of Community Psychology* 28(3) (May): 291–307.

Eisenmann, J. C., D. A. Gentile, G. J. Welk, R. Callahan, S. Strickland, M. Walsh, and D. A. Walsh. 2008. "SWITCH: Rationale, Design, and Implementation of a Community, School, and Family-Based Intervention to Modify Behaviors Related to Childhood Obesity." *BMC Public Health* 8: 223 (Jun).

Fielding, Jonathan E., and Peter A. Briss. 2006. "Promoting Evidence-Based Public Health Policy: Can We Have Better Evidence and More Action?" *Health Affairs* 25(4) (July 1): 969–978.

Findholt, N. 2007. "Application of the Community Readiness Model for Childhood Obesity Prevention." *Public Health Nursing* 24(6) (Nov-Dec): 565–570.

Flodmark, C. E., C. Marcus, and M. Britton. 2006. "Interventions to Prevent Obesity in Children and Adolescents: A Systematic Literature Review." *International Journal of Obesity* 30(4): 579–589.

Flynn, M. A. T., D. A. McNeil, B. Maloff, D. Mutasingwa, M. Wu, C. Ford, and S. C. Tough. 2006. "Reducing Obesity and Related Chronic Disease Risk in Children and Youth: A Synthesis of Evidence with 'Best Practice' Recommendations." *Obesity Reviews* 7(s1): 7–66.

French, S. A., M. Story, and R. W. Jeffery. 2001. "Environmental Influences on Eating and Physical Activity." *Annual Review of Public Health* 22(1): 309–335.

Gittelsohn, J., and M. B. Kumar. 2007. "Preventing Childhood Obesity and Diabetes: Is It Time to Move Out of the School?" *Pediatric Diabetes* 8 (Dec): 55–69.

Glanz, Karen, Barbara K. Rimer, and K. Viswanath. 2008. *Health behavior and health education: Theory, research, and practice.* 4th ed. San Francisco, CA: Jossey-Bass.

Glass, Thomas A., and Matthew J. McAtee. 2006. "Behavioral Science at the Crossroads in Public Health: Extending Horizons, Envisioning The Future." *Social Science and Medicine* 62(7) (4): 1650–1671.

Granner, M. L., and P. A. Sharpe. 2004. "Evaluating Community Coalition Characteristics and Functioning: A Summary of Measurement Tools." *Health Education Research* 19(5) (October 1): 514–532.

Green, Lawrence W. 2006. "Public Health Asks of Systems Science: To Advance Our Evidence-Based Practice, Can You Help Us Get More Practice-Based Evidence?" *American Journal of Public Health* 96(3) (March 1): 406–409.

Greenberg, M. T., M. E. Feinberg, S. Meyer-Chilenski, R. L. Spoth, and C. Redmond. 2007. "Community and Team Member Factors That Influence the Early Phase Functioning of Community Prevention Teams: The PROSPER Project." *The Journal of Primary Prevention* 28(6): 485–504.

Hammond, R. A. 2009. "Complex Systems Modeling for Obesity Research." *Preventing Chronic Disease* 6(3) http://www.cdc.gov/pcd/issues/2009/Jul/09_0017.htm (accessed Nov. 29, 2009).

Hawe, P., A. Shiell, and T. Riley. 2009. "Theorizing Interventions as Events in Systems." *American Journal of Community Psychology* 43(3): 267–276.

Helitzer, Deborah L., Sally M. Davis, Joel Gittelsohn, Scott B. Going, David M. Murray, Patricia Snyder, and Allan B. Steckler. 1999. "Process Evaluation in a Multisite, Primary Obesity-Prevention Trial in American Indian Schoolchildren." *American Journal of Clinical Nutrition* 69(4) (April 1): 816S–824.

Hennessey Lavery, Susana, Mele Lau Smith, Alma Avila Esparza, Alyonik Hrushow, Melinda Moore, and Diane F. Reed. 2005. "The Community Action Model: A Community-Driven Model Designed to Address Disparities in Health." *American Journal of Public Health* 95(4) (April 1): 611–616.

Hill, James O., and John C. Peters. 1998. "Environmental Contributions to the Obesity Epidemic." *Science* 280(5368) (May 29): 1371–1374.

Horowitz, Carol R., Barbara L. Brenner, Susanne Lachapelle, Duna A. Amara, and Guedy Arniella. 2009. "Effective Recruitment of Minority Populations Through Community-Led Strategies." *American Journal of Preventive Medicine* 37(6, Supp. 1) (12): S195–200.

Huang, T. T., A. Drewnowski, S. K. Kumanyika, and T. A. Glass. 2009. "A Systems-Oriented Multilevel Framework for Addressing Obesity in the 21st Century." *Preventing Chronic Disease* 6(3) http://www.cdc.gov/pcd/issues/2009/jul/09_0013.htm. (accessed Nov. 2, 2009)

Huang, Terry T. -K. 2009. "Solution-oriented Research: Converging Efforts of Promoting Environmental Sustainability and Obesity Prevention." *American Journal of Preventive Medicine* 36(2, Supp. 1) (2): S60–62.

Institute of Medicine. 2005. In *Preventing Childhood Obesity: Health in the Balance*, 196-236. Washington, DC: The National Academies Press.

Institute of Medicine. 2010. Bridging the Evidence Gap in Obesity Prevention. A Framework to Inform Decision Making. Washington, D.C: The National Academies Press.

Kegler, M., and K. Glanz. 2008. "Perspectives on Group, Organization, and Community Interventions." In *Health Behavior and Health Education: Theory, Research, and Practice*, 4th ed., eds. Karen Glanz, Barbara K. Rimer and K. Viswanath, 552. San Francisco, CA: Jossey-Bass.

Kettel Khan, L., Sobush, K., Keener, D., Goodman, K., Lowry, A., Kakietek, J. and Zaro, S. 2009. "Recommended Community Strategies And Measurements to Prevent Obesity in the United States." In *Morbidity and Mortality Weekly Report (MMWR)* [database online] [cited 11/21/2009]. Available from http://www.cdc.gov/mmwr/preview/mmwrhtml/rr5807a1.htm.

Kretzmann J.P., J. McKnight. 1993. *Building Communities from the Inside Out: A Path Toward Finding and Mobilizing a Community's Assets*, First ed. 376. Evanston, IL: Northwestern University.

Kumanyika, S., R. W. Jeffery, A. Morabia, C. Ritenbaugh, and V. J. Antipatis. 2002. "Obesity Prevention: The Case for Action." *International Journal of Obesity* 26(3): 425, 425–436.

King, D. A., and S. M. Thomas. 2007. "Big Lessons for a Healthy Future." *Nature* 449(7164): 791–792.

Levy, Susan R., Emily E. Anderson, L. Michele Issel, Marilyn A. Willis, Barbara L. Dancy, Kristin M. Jacobson, Shirley G. Fleming, et al. 2004. "Using Multilevel, Multisource Needs Assessment Data for Planning Community Interventions." *Health Promotion Practice* 5(1) (January 1): 59–68.

Lopez, E., E. Eng, N. Robinson, and C. Wang. 2005. "Photovoice as a Community-based Participatory Research Method." In *Methods in Community-Based Participatory Research for Health*. ed. B.A Israel, E. Eng, A.J Schulz, E.A. Parker, 326–348. San Francisco, CA: Jossey-Bass.

Macaulay, A. C., L. E. Commanda, W. L. Freeman, N. Gibson, M. L. McCabe, C. M. Robbins, and P. L. Twohig. 1999. "Participatory Research Maximises Community and Lay Involvement." *British Medical Journal* 319(7212): 774–778.

McLeroy, Kenneth R., Daniel Bibeau, Allan Steckler, and Karen Glanz. 1988. "An Ecological Perspective on Health Promotion Programs." *Health Education and Behavior* 15(4) (January 1): 351–377.

Merzel, C., and J. D'Afflitti. 2003. "Reconsidering Community-Based Health Promotion: Promise, Performance, and Potential." *American Journal of Public Health* 93(4): 557–574.

Minkler M. 2000. "Using Participatory Action Research to Build Healthy Communities." *Public Health Reports* 115(2–3): 191–197.

Minkler, M. 2005. "Community-based Research Partnerships: Challenges and Opportunities." *Journal of Urban Health* 82(2 Supp): ii3–ii12.

Minkler, M., N. Wallerstein, and N. Wilson. 2008. "Health Behavior and Health Education: Theory, Research, and Practice." In *Improving Health Through Community Organization and Community Building*, 4th ed., eds. Karen Glanz, Barbara K. Rimer and K. Viswanath. 552. San Francisco, CA: Jossey-Bass.

Navarro, A. M., K. P. Voetsch, L. C. Liburd, H. W. Giles, and J. L. Collins. 2007. "Charting the Future of Community Health Promotion: Recommendations from the National Expert Panel on Community Health Promotion." *Preventing Chronic Disease* Jul 4(3)=. www.cdc.gov/pcd/issues/2007/jul/07_0013.htm (Accessed Oct. 13 2009).

NCCOR (National Collaborative on Childhood Obesity Research). 2009. [cited 11/21/2009]. Available from http://www.nccor.org/index.html.

Plested, B. A, R. W. Edwards, P. Jumper-Thurman. 2006. *Community Readiness: A Handbook for Successful Change*. Vol. 2008. Fort Collins, CO: Tri-Ethnic Center for Prevention Research.

Prochaska, J. O. 2008. "Multiple Health Behavior Research Represents the Future of Preventive Medicine." *Preventive Medicine* 46(3): 281–285.

Ritchie, L. D., P. B. Crawford, D. M. Hoelscher, and M. S. Sothern. 2006. "Position of the American Dietetic Association: Individual-, Family-, School-, and Community-Based Interventions for Pediatric Overweight." *Journal of the American Dietetic Association* 106(6): 925–945.

Robert Wood Johnson Foundation. 2008. *Healthy Kids, Healthy Communities: Call for Proposals*. Available from www.healthykidshealthycommunities.org (Accessed 11/20/2009).

Robinson, Thomas N., and John R. Sirard. 2005. "Preventing Childhood Obesity: A Solution-Oriented Research Paradigm." *American Journal of Preventive Medicine* 28(2, Supp. 2): 194–201.

Romon, M., A. Lommez, M. Tafflet, A. Basdevant, J. M. Oppert, J. L. Bresson, P. Ducimetiere, M. A. Charles, and J. M. Borys. 2008. "Downward Trends in the Prevalence of Childhood Overweight in the Setting of 12-Year School- and Community-Based Programmes." *Public Health Nutrition* 12(10): 1735–1742.

Roussos, S. T., and S. B. Fawcett. 2000. "A Review of Collaborative Partnerships as a Strategy for Improving Community Health." *Annual Review of Public Health* 21(1): 369–402.

Sallis, J. F., R. B. Cervero, W. Ascher, K. A. Henderson, M. K. Kraft, and J. Kerr. 2006. "An Ecological Approach to Creating Active Living Communities." *Annual Review of Public Health* 27: 297–322.

Sallis, J. F., M. Story, and D. Lou. 2009. "Study Designs and Analytic Strategies for Environmental and Policy Research on Obesity, Physical Activity, and Diet: Recommendations from a Meeting Of Experts." *American Journal of Preventive Medicine* 36(2) (Feb): S72–77.

Sanigorski, A. M., A. C. Bell, P. J. Kremer, R. Cuttler, and B. A. Swinburn. 2008. "Reducing Unhealthy Weight Gain in Children Through Community Capacity-Building: Results of a Quasi-Experimental Intervention Program, Be Active Eat Well." *International Journal of Obesity* 32(7) (Jul): 1060–1067.

Satterfield, J. M., B. Spring, R. C. Brownson, E. J. Mullen, R. P. Newhouse, B. B. Walker, and E. P. Whitlock. 2009. "Toward a Transdisciplinary Model of Evidence-Based Practice." *Milbank Quarterly* 87(2): 368–390.

Schensul, J. J. 2009. "Community, Culture and Sustainability in Multilevel Dynamic Systems Intervention Science." *American Journal of Community Psychology* 43(3): 241–256.

Sharpe, P. A., M. L. Greaney, P. R. Lee, and S. W. Royce. 2000. "Assets-Oriented Community Assessment." *Public Health Reports* 115(2–3): 205.

Snyder, Patricia, Jean Anliker, Leslie Cunningham-Sabo, Lori Beth Dixon, Jackie Altaha, Arlene Chamberlain, Sally Davis, Marguerite Evans, Joanne Hurley, and Judith L. Weber. 1999. "The Pathways Study: A Model for Lowering the Fat in School Meals." *American Journal of Clinical Nutrition* 69(4) (April 1): 810S–815.

Stice, E., H. Shaw, and C. N. Marti. 2006. "A Meta-Analytic Review of Obesity Prevention Programs for Children and Adolescents: The Skinny on Interventions That Work." *Psychological Bulletin* 132(5): 667.

Story, M., B. Giles-Corti, A. L. Yaroch, S. Cummins, L. D. Frank, T. T. K. Huang, and L. B. Lewis. 2009. "Work Group IV: Future Directions for Measures of the Food and Physical Activity Environments." *American Journal of Preventive Medicine* 36(4) (Apr): S182–188.

Story, M., K. M. Kaphingst, R. Robinson-O'Brien, and K. Glanz. 2008. "Creating Healthy Food and Eating Environments: Policy and Environmental Approaches." *Annual Review of Public Health* 29: 253ff.

Summerbell, C. D., E. Waters, L. D. Edmunds, S. Kelly, T. Brown, and K. J. Campbell. 2005. "Interventions for Preventing Obesity in Children." *Cochrane Database of Systematic Reviews* (Online) (3) (Jul 20): CD001871.

Swinburn, B., T. Gill, and S. Kumanyika. 2005. "Obesity Prevention: A Proposed Framework for Translating Evidence into Action." *Obesity Reviews* 6(1) (Feb): 23–33.

Swinburn, Boyd, Garry Egger, and Fezeela Raza. 1999. "Dissecting Obesogenic Environments: The Development and Application of a Framework for Identifying and Prioritizing Environmental Interventions for Obesity." *Preventive Medicine* 29(6) (12): 563–570.

Wallerstein, N. B., and B. Duran. 2006. "Using Community-Based Participatory Research to Address Health Disparities." *Health Promotion Practice* 7(3): 312.

Wandersman, A. 2009. "Four Keys to Success (Theory, Implementation, Evaluation, and Resource/System Support): High Hopes and Challenges in Participation." *American Journal of Community Psychology* 43(1): 3–21.

Wholey, D. R., W. Gregg, and I. Moscovice. 2009. "Public Health Systems: A Social Networks Perspective." *Health Services Research* 44(5p2): 1842–1862.

World Health Organization. 1999. "Health Impact Assessment: Main Concepts and Suggested Approach; The Gothenburg Consensus Paper." in *World Health Organization* [database online]. [cited 2/10 2010]. Available from http://www.euro.who.int/document/PAE/Gothenburgpaper.pdf.

CHAPTER 42

REGULATION OF FOOD ADVERTISING

PAULINE M. IPPOLITO

BACKGROUND

FOOD marketing is hypothesized to be among the many contributors to childhood obesity, and is a potential means of encouraging better food choices.[1] In this chapter, I will briefly describe the legal standards that govern food advertising in the United States and the policy approaches to food marketing developed under those legal standards.

LEGAL POLICY TOWARD ADVERTISING

The Federal Trade Commission (FTC) is the U.S. agency responsible for policing advertising at the federal level. The Commission's basic authority to regulate marketing derives from Section 5 of the FTC Act,[2] which broadly prohibits "unfair or deceptive acts or practices in . . . commerce."

---

1 See, for instance, the Institute of Medicine (2006) review of the literature related to children.
2 15 U.S.C § 45.

Deception

The Commission's 1983 Deception Statement laid out the basic approach to deception that governs today. The Commission "will find deception if there is a representation, omission, or practice that is likely to mislead the consumer acting reasonably in the circumstances, to the consumer's detriment."[3] When a representation targets a particular audience, the reasonableness is judged from the perspective of that audience; so, for instance, an advertisement directed to young men would be judged from the perspective of reasonable members of that audience.

Unfairness

The standard for unfairness articulated in 1980, and subsequently codified as a statutory definition,[4] is a balancing test. An act or practice is unfair if it causes or is likely to cause substantial consumer injury; the injury is not reasonably avoidable by consumers; and the injury is not offset by countervailing benefits to consumers or competition.[5]

The First Amendment and Commercial Speech

Of course, all challenges to advertising must reflect First Amendment commercial speech jurisprudence, which is premised on the value to consumers and competition of the free flow of truthful information. In 1977 the Supreme Court struck down a state of Virginia ban on price advertising for prescription drugs,[6] and a number of rulings since have expanded the protection accorded truthful commercial speech. In *Central Hudson Gas & Electric Corp. v. Public Service Commission*,[7] the Supreme Court articulated a four-part test for courts to apply in evaluating whether government restrictions on commercial speech are constitutional. First, if the commercial speech concerns unlawful activity or is misleading, it is not protected by the First Amendment. Second, if the commercial speech concerns lawful activity and is not misleading, the court will ask "whether the asserted governmental interest is substantial." Third, if it is substantial, the court "must determine whether the regulation directly advances the governmental interest asserted." Fourth, the court must determine "whether [the regulation] is not more extensive than is necessary to serve that interest."

To survive a First Amendment challenge, the government has the burden of proving that its restriction on commercial speech satisfies the *Central Hudson* test. For instance, in 1995, the Court struck down a federal prohibition on labeling the

---

3 Deception Policy Statement, appended to *Cliffdale Associates*, Inc. 103 F.T.C. 110, 176 (1984).
4 15 U.S.C. § 45(n).
5 Unfairness Policy Statement, appended to *International Harvester Co.*, 104 F.T.C. 949, 1070-76 (1984).
6 *Virginia Bd. Of Pharmacy*, 425 U.S.
7 477 U.S. 557 (1980).

alcohol content of beer,[8] despite the government's argument that it was designed to prevent "strength wars" among brewers, and that the ban would support the government's interest in the health, safety, and welfare of its citizens. Among other issues, the Court found that such a broad prohibition of truthful information was more extensive than necessary, and pointed to more targeted restrictions, such as limiting the alcohol content of beers, limiting marketing that emphasized high alcohol strength, or limiting the advertising ban to high alcohol beers.

More recently, the D.C. Circuit Court applied the *Central Hudson* test to commercial speech restrictions imposed by the Food and Drug Administration (FDA) on health claims on food labels. In *Pearson v. Shalala*,[9] manufacturers of dietary supplements challenged the FDA's refusal to approve the manufacturers' use of four health claims on the grounds that the claims were not supported by a level of science that met the agency's "significant scientific agreement" standard of evidence. The FDA, consistent with agency practice, refused to consider the manufacturers' argument that the use of disclaimers reflecting the state of the scientific support for the claims could prevent these four health claims from being misleading.[10] The government argued that some consumers potentially could be misled if the science behind the health claims did not meet the high level of certainty embodied in the agency's standard. The D.C. Circuit rejected the government's argument on the grounds that the First Amendment commercial speech doctrine embodies a "preference for disclosure over outright suppression" and the government had not shown that "disclosure would not suffice to cure misleadingness."[11]

Subsequent cases make clear that: (1) the government does not have a substantial interest in "preventing the dissemination of truthful commercial information in order to prevent members of the public from making bad decisions with the information;"[12] and (2) the government does have a substantial interest in restricting the dissemination of commercial speech that has the potential to mislead consumers, but the fit between the government restriction and its objective of stopping deceptive claims must be reasonable.[13]

---

8 *Rubin v. Coors Brewing Co.*, 514 U.S. 476 (1995).

9 164 F. 3d 650 (D.C. Cir. 1999), *reh'g en banc denied*, 172 F.3d 72 (D.C. Cir. 1999).

10 For instance, the agency might have distinguished between claims, such as "growing scientific evidence suggests," as opposed to "science proves," when there is a substantial body of scientific support for a diet-disease relationship but the evidence is not yet conclusive.

11 *Id.* at 658.

12 *Western States Med. Ctr.*, slip op. at 9 (rejecting argument that truthful and nonmisleading commercial speech for compounded drugs may be prohibited because it may cause consumers to purchase drugs they do not need); *Bates v. State Bar of Ariz.*, 433 U.S. 350, 375 (1977) ("We view as dubious any justification that is based on the benefits of public ignorance."); *Washington Legal Found. v. Friedman*, 13 F. Supp. 2d 51, 70 (D.D.C. 1998) ("To endeavor to support a restriction upon speech by alleging that the recipient needs to be shielded from that speech for his or her own protection, which is the gravamen of the FDA's claim here, is practically an engraved invitation to have the restriction struck.")

13 *See, e.g., Edenfield v. Fane,* 507 U.S. 761, 769 (1993) ("[T]here is no question that [the government's interest] in ensuring the accuracy of information in the marketplace is substantial.") See also, *Board of Trustees of the State of New York v. Fox*, 492 U.S. 469, 480 (1989). For a more extensive discussion of these issues, see Comments of the Staff of the Bureau of Economics, the Bureau of Consumer Protection,

As is clear from this brief review of the U.S. legal landscape, there are important limits on what government can do to restrict marketing, even in cases that deal with health-related issues. Nonetheless, marketing related to obesity has been an active area of government attention, using direct enforcement, where appropriate, and research, reports, and public attention in other cases. The remainder of this chapter illustrates these various approaches.

DECEPTIVE WEIGHT-LOSS CLAIMS

As the levels of overweight and obesity have risen in the American population, consumer interest in weight loss has created a large market for weight-loss products and services. Some of these are quite legitimate products, but some are not; and many are sold with deceptive claims about the efficacy and ease of achieving meaningful weight loss. These problematic products include nonprescription drugs, dietary supplements, creams, wraps, devices, and patches that often promise substantial weight loss without diet or exercise. Apparently, many consumers are willing to spend money to find an easy way to lose excess pounds.

As a legal matter, deceptive claims have no First Amendment protection, so direct enforcement against deceptive weight-loss products is a clear option, subject only to resource constraints. Between 1995 and 2005, the FTC brought over 100 cases challenging false or misleading claims in advertising for weight-loss products,[14] and enforcement has remained a priority since. But resources are a constraint, and deceptive weight-loss claims remained a concern despite significant enforcement. Many of the companies selling these products are not firms with strong reputations, and entry and exit in dietary supplements and some of these other products is relatively easy. From an economics perspective, these features make these markets more prone to deception and fraud, and the firms involved often have few assets, so fines have limited effect.[15]

In the early 2000s, the agency also examined other approaches to address the deceptive marketing of weight-loss products. In 2001, the staff collected a sample of 300 advertisements from major media to assess the content of weight-loss ads and found that nearly 40 percent of the ads had claims that were almost certainly false

---

and the Office of Policy Planning of the Federal Trade Commission Before the Department of Health and Human Services, Food and Drug Administration, *In the Matter of Request for Comment on First Amendment Issues*, September 13, 2002, available at http://www.ftc.gov/os/2002/09/fdatextversion.pdf.

14 See *2004 Weight-Loss Advertising Survey*, Staff Report, Federal Trade Commission, April 2005.

15 Sunk costs are traditionally viewed as limiting competition because they discourage entry. But sunk costs also can act as a bond to discipline deception and low quality choices by firms, because the firms have something to lose if challenged by legal authorities. As a result, markets with low sunk costs are more prone to fraud and deception; it is easy to enter, deceive, and then exit if challenged, with limited value in the firm for authorities to seize.

despite the heavy enforcement.[16] The staff also collected a sample of weight-loss ads from eight leading national magazines to match a sample collected in 1992. It showed that the number of weight-loss ads had doubled, and that the marketed products had shifted from primarily meal replacements to dietary supplements.[17]

The FTC decided to raise the public profile of the issue and to ask for the media's help in preventing facially false advertising claims. After convening a public workshop in November 2002 with relevant experts in weight loss, the agency developed a list of seven relatively common, facially false "red flag" claims, such as losing more than 2 pounds per week without reducing caloric intake or increasing exercise,[18] and publicly encouraged relevant media not to accept advertisements that contained the claims. A 2004 survey of advertising showed a marked decrease in the use of the "red flag" claims, but a continued growth in weight-loss advertising, including advertising with other potentially misleading claims.[19]

This example illustrates that legal authority alone is not sufficient to eliminate deceptive claims in markets prone to them. Consumer knowledge, resources, and effective remedies are also important to success.

FOOD ADVERTISING TO CHILDREN

Food advertising to children has been another focus of attention as childhood obesity has increased markedly since the early 1980s. Food marketing to children has come under scrutiny because children may be more susceptible to marketing and early eating habits may persist. At the behest of Congress, the Institute of Medicine (IOM 2006) reviewed the literature on food marketing to children and adolescents and found strong evidence that television advertising influences food and beverage requests and preferences of children 2–11 but found insufficient evidence for teens aged 12–18. With respect to consumption, the IOM concluded that there is strong evidence that television advertising influences the short-term consumption of children, but found insufficient evidence for teens. For usual dietary intake, or long-term food consumption, they found the evidence to be much weaker. Finally, the IOM found a strong statistical association between exposure to television advertising and adiposity in children and adolescents, but they could not make a finding of a causal relationship between the two.[20]

---

16 See *Deception in Weight-Loss Advertising Workshop*, Staff Report, Federal Trade Commission, December 2003.

17 See FTC (2005) at 7.

18 See id at 3.

19 Id at 5-7. For instance, 40 percent of the ads included testimonials from individuals who claimed to have lost at least 40 pounds.

20 Watching TV itself (as opposed to the ads) could lead to weight gain, encourage snacking, or be the entertainment of choice for overweight children; the available research is inadequate to disentangle whether there is a significant causal relationship between food ads themselves and children's weights.

From a legal point of view, most food advertising directed to children probably would not be seen as deceptive. An ad that says "this candy tastes great" is likely true; the concern usually expressed is that the ad encourages children to eat a food that adds calories that have a poor nutritional profile. As a result, even recognizing that children are a special audience, any broad effort to legally restrict advertising directed to children may have to be done under the FTC's unfairness authority and within the First Amendment limits for restricting truthful advertising.[21] This raises substantial issues for this direct enforcement-type approach.

"Kid-Vid" Rule Making

Moreover, the FTC has experience with broad efforts to restrict advertising to children. In 1978, the agency embarked on its ill-fated rule making to restrict the television advertising of highly sugared foods to children.[22] What came to be known as the "kid-vid" rule making was an attempt to craft a targeted rule that would limit advertising of highly sugared foods on children's programming—particularly to those too young to understand either the commercial nature of advertising or the health risks of excessive sugar consumption. At the time, dental cavities were a major health concern.

Three years and more than 60,000 pages of commentary later, the FTC staff recommended that the Commission terminate the rule making, which the Commission ultimately did.[23] The children's advertising proceeding was pivotal in the agency's history. While support was strong at the start of the rule making, the "kid-vid" proposal came to symbolize overreaching by the federal government. Congress allowed the agency's funding to lapse and ultimately passed a law prohibiting the FTC from adopting any rule in the children's advertising proceeding, or in any similar proceeding, based on its unfairness authority.[24] It was more than a decade before Congress was willing to reauthorize the agency.

Certainly, skilled lobbying may have played a role in this backlash, but the reaction was much broader. Even the *Washington Post*, normally a supporter of activist government at the time, editorialized that the proposal was "a preposterous intervention that would turn the FTC into a great national nanny." Further, it noted that "the proposal, in reality, is designed to protect children from the weakness of their parents—the parents from the wailing insistence of their children. That, traditionally, is one of the roles of a governess—if you can afford one. It is not the proper role of government."[25]

---

21 Note that as a legal matter this differs sharply from changes that could be made within public schools, because the government already has direct control over the foods made available to children in school lunches and vending machines.

22 FTC, Notice of Proposed Rulemaking, 43 Fed. Reg. 17,967 (Apr. 27, 1978). For a more extensive discussion of the FTC's children's advertising experience, see Beales (2004).

23 FTC Final Staff Report (1981).

24 FTC Improvements Act of 1980, Pub. L. No. 96-252, Sections 11(a)(1), 11(a)(3), 94 Stat. 374 (1980), codified in part at 15 U.S.C. § 57a(i).

25 Editorial, *The Washington Post* (Mar. 1, 1978), reprinted in Pertschuk (1984) at 69-70.

The issues underlying this backlash would be also relevant today, and First Amendment jurisprudence is stronger. Commercial-free television for children is more available today than in 1977, as are DVD and videotape programming. Parents who wish to limit their children's advertising exposure have options. Moreover, the kid-vid rulemaking illustrated the difficulty of developing evidence to support a remedy that targeted children's programs (and not general programming) in a way that would plausibly have a substantial effect on children's ad exposure, and ultimately, on their diets and weight. These are not trivial burdens. Certainly, the mix of food ads that children see today does not represent a well-balanced diet; but this was also true in 1977, when few children were obese. And where the case is strongest that children may not understand the selling intent of advertising—young children—parents are in direct control of purchases.

Self-regulation and Other Efforts

Given these difficult evidentiary issues, government has chosen initially to pursue a variety of other approaches. Whether food advertising is an important contributor to the growth of obesity or not, promotion of more healthful foods might play a positive role in educating parents and improving children's food choices. To this end, the FTC has joined with other government agencies to publicize the childhood weight issue, to encourage industry self-regulation, and to measure and report on marketing directed to children.[26]

In the United States, the Children's Advertising Review Unit of the Better Business Bureaus (BBB) has long had guides requiring advertising to children to be truthful, accurate, and developmentally appropriate. However, this self-regulation initiative never restricted the products that could be advertised to children. Partly as an outgrowth of the added attention and growing concern about children's obesity, in 2006 the BBB and leading food and beverage companies started a new initiative to change the mix of foods advertised to children.[27] Within broad guidelines established by the BBB, each firm publicly announced guidelines their company would follow in advertising to children. Among other things, these firm guidelines typically included nutritional criteria for "better for you" foods and a specification of the portion of total advertising on children's programming and in other venues that would be for these "better for you" foods. Over time, these criteria have evolved and compliance is monitored by the organization (BBB 2009).

The FTC has also initiated a series of studies to measure food marketing to children. Holt et al. (2007) provide detailed information on children's exposure to television advertising in 2004 and compare it to exposure estimates from 1977, developed during the kid-vid rulemaking. The study found that children in 2004

---

26 See http://www.ftc.gov/bcp/workshops/foodmarketingtokids/index.shtm for an index of these efforts and links to related reports.
27 See BBB (2009) for a more complete description of the Children's Food & Beverage Initiative.

were exposed to fewer paid advertisements and fewer minutes of advertising than in 1977. Children also were not exposed to more food advertising than in the past, though their ad exposure is more concentrated on children's programming. Also, the data do not indicate that children are seeing more ads for low-nutrition foods; in both years, advertised foods are concentrated in the snacking, breakfast, and restaurant product areas and do not constitute a balanced diet in either year.

Television is not the only media used to market to children, and many were concerned that a comparison of television ads missed important growth in marketing to children in newer media. To get a broader picture, the FTC used compulsory process orders to require 44 food and beverage firms to produce data on the broad scope of marketing directed to children during 2006. As reported in FTC (2008), television still constitutes nearly 50 percent of all marketing expenditures, but the firms use a variety of other media and methods for integrated marketing campaigns, including packaging, in-store marketing, event sponsorship, and in-school marketing. That said, the products marketed to children parallel those found in the television study, and new media (specifically child-oriented corporate web sites, Internet advertising, and other digital, word-of-mouth, and viral marketing) account for only approximately 5 percent of youth-directed food marketing expenditures, though this may be changing as firms experiment with the effectiveness of these new marketing outlets. The FTC is preparing to repeat this data request for 2009 data, along with a request for brand-level nutrition data. This should allow for a better assessment of whether the mix of foods marketed to children has changed in light of both the self-regulatory initiative and market pressures as parents and children learn more about the obesity issue.[28]

CALORIE-RELATED CLAIMS
IN ADVERTISING

Ideally, advertising enforcement should discourage deceptive calorie-related claims without stifling truthful, nonmisleading information. As in other markets, truthful, nonmisleading information about the caloric content of foods can benefit consumers and competition. Such information empowers consumers to make better-informed choices about the health consequences of the foods they eat. And as health consequences become more important to consumers, food marketers have stronger incentives to develop and market foods based on their nutritional attributes. These efforts, in turn, can provide consumers with still healthier products and more information about the health consequences of foods. An example of this beneficial cycle from the 1980s involved advertising and labeling describing the potential link

---

28 Fed. Reg. 48073 (Sept. 21, 2009).

between fiber in cereals and cancer risk. The information increased consumer awareness of the potential link between fiber and cancer, which increased demand for higher-fiber cereals, which, in turn, led manufacturers to expand the range of better-tasting, higher-fiber cereals available in the market.[29]

This deceptively simple goal of stopping deceptive claims without discouraging truthful claims raises difficult policy considerations that are common to many health-related issues. For instance, if consumers are sufficiently concerned about the caloric content of foods, producers of lower-calorie foods would have an incentive to point out situations where their foods would be desirable substitutes to reduce calorie intake. Like most advertising claims, short effective comparative calorie claims are not all the consumer needs to know in choosing foods, but they draw attention to calorie-reducing substitutions. Requiring longer claims may discourage firms from making comparative claims, and the reduced attention to truthful calorie differences means less competitive pressure to improve foods in that dimension. Whether a claim is sufficiently incomplete to be considered deceptive depends on consumer expectations and on other market conditions, and these factors are shaped by the information environment in which the claims are made. For instance, the availability of the Nutrition Facts Panel for most packaged foods provides a means of checking information that is not available in many other markets.

The inherent trade-off between the required length of the claims and the likelihood of their use is illustrated by the changes that followed the FDA's revised rules for comparative claims on labels implemented under the Nutrition Labeling and Education Act of 1990. Concerned that abbreviated claims were incomplete and potentially misleading, the labeling rules were changed to require that all comparative claims explicitly include the reference food, the standard serving amount, and the percentage and absolute level of the nutrient in both foods. So, for instance, under the revised rules a baked potato chip label that used to say "85 percent less fat, 27 percent fewer calories" would become (italicized phrases could be placed on the back label):[30]

> Reduced fat and fewer calories than our Classic Potato Chips. Fat reduced by 85 percent, *from 10 grams per ounce to 1.5 grams per ounce.* Calories reduced by 27 percent, *from 150 calories per ounce to 110 calories per ounce.*

While not technically binding on advertisers, most advertisers are reluctant to make claims in ads that are not permitted on labels. In a sample of over 11,000 magazine advertisements covering the years 1977 to 1997, comparative claims fell for 7 of 8 nutrients measured following the addition of these claim requirements.[31] For instance, in 1990 more than 10 percent of ads had comparative calorie claims, but after the rule change, less than 3 percent of ads had such claims. Absolute calorie

---

29 See Ippolito and Mathios (1989, 1990).
30 If sodium were also reduced by more than 25 percent, the claim would be even more unwieldy; in this case the sodium was reduced by 17 percent, and thus, could not be reported.
31 See Ippolito and Pappalardo (2002) at 107.

claims also fell after the revised label rules were implemented, but only modestly, suggesting that the added requirements for comparative claims selectively discouraged their use.

Finally, consumers are more likely to pay attention to a food characteristic, such as calories, if they believe that it is important. It is well established that excess calories lead to excess weight or obesity, and that excess weight is related to increased risk of a variety of diseases. For instance, the Surgeon General's 2001 report on obesity finds that being overweight or obese increases the risk of coronary heart disease, type 2 diabetes, some cancers, osteoarthritis, asthma, and sleep apnea, among other diseases.

Current FDA labeling rules do not allow firms to discuss the health reasons to be concerned with calories. FDA's normal process for approving a health claim is to respond to a petition from a firm. But in the case of calories, individual firms face a substantial free-rider problem in submitting such a petition; the legal costs would be borne by the petitioning firm alone, but the claim would be available to all firms once approved, and lower calorie claims could be made for many foods. As the FDA has recognized (FDA 2004), an alternative is for the FDA on its own initiative to establish permissible claims relating calorie reductions to the health effects of excess weight. The FDA has recently initiated a new round of consumer research to explore potential changes to nutrition labeling,[32] with a particular focus on calorie issues, so change may be forthcoming. Research on consumer use of information and firm incentives to use particular classes of claims would be useful in helping to guide policy toward obesity-related claims.

CONCLUSION

Food advertising can be a powerful means of spreading information on calories and their role in promoting excess weight. Advertising can also point out ways in which consumers can make changes that cut calories from their diets, and in doing so, put competitive pressure on firms to improve their products.

But advertising can also mislead consumers, for instance, through deceptive claims about ineffective weight loss products, or misleading food comparisons or other claims. And food advertising to children is a particular concern. The challenge for enforcement and policy is to preserve the potential power of marketing to spread health-related information and create competitive pressure for product improvement, while effectively deterring deception.

---

32 Fed. Reg., 59553, November 18, 2009.

ACKNOWLEDGEMENTS

The author is Deputy Director, Bureau of Economics, Federal Trade Commission. The views expressed in this chapter are the author's and do not necessarily represent the views of the Federal Trade Commission.

REFERENCES

Beales, J. Howard, 2004. "Advertising to Kids and the FTC: A Regulatory Retrospective That Advises the Present." *George Mason Law Review* 12: 873.

Better Business Bureaus. 2009. *The Children's Food & Beverage Advertising Initiative in Action*, October 2009.

Federal Trade Commission. 2005. *2004 Weight-Loss Advertising Survey*. Staff Report, April 2005.

Federal Trade Commission. 2006. *Perspectives on Marketing, Self-Regulation, and Childhood Obesity*. A Report on a Joint Workshop of the Federal Trade Commission and the Department of Health and Human Services, Washington, DC, April 2006.

Federal Trade Commission. 2008. *Marketing Food to Children and Adolescents: A Review of Industry Expenditures, Activities, and Self-Regulation*. Federal Trade Commission Report to Congress, July 2008.

Food and Drug Administration (FDA). 2004. *Calories Count, Report of the Working Group on Obesity*, February 2004.

Holt, Debra J., Pauline M. Ippolito, Debra M. Desrochers, and Christopher R. Kelley, 2007. *Children's Exposure to TV Advertising in 1977 and 2004*. Bureau of Economics Staff Report, Federal Trade Commission, June 2007.

Institute of Medicine of the National Academies. 2006. *Food Marketing to Children and Youth: Threat or Opportunity?* Washington, DC: IOM.

Ippolito, Pauline M., and Alan D. Mathios, 1989. *Health Claims in Advertising and Labeling: A Study of the Cereal Market*. Bureau of Economics Staff Report, Federal Trade Commission, Washington, DC, August 1989.

Ippolito, Pauline M., and Alan D. Mathios, 1990. "Information, Advertising, and Health Choices: A Study of the Cereal Market." *RAND Journal of Economics* 21(Autumn). 459–480.

Pertschuk, Michael, 1984. *Revolt against Regulation: The Rise and Pause of the Consumer Movement*. Berkeley: University of California Press.

Surgeon General. 2001. *The Surgeon General's Call to Action to Prevent and Decrease Overweight and Obesity*. Washington, DC: Department of Health and Human Services.

CHAPTER 43

UNINTENDED CONSEQUENCES OF OBESITY PREVENTION MESSAGES

SAHARA BYRNE AND JEFF NIEDERDEPPE

INTRODUCTION

SUCCESSFUL efforts to prevent childhood and adult obesity will require intervention strategies that influence (1) individual decisions about diet and exercise and (2) broader societal factors like social conditions, physical environments, and economic circumstances (Kumanyika et al. 2008). These interventions will likely involve the development and dissemination of targeted messages designed to promote behavior change, mobilize community action and/or increase support for specific obesity prevention policies. Communication scholars have long studied the effects of persuasive messages with the goal of identifying specific strategies and tactics that maximize the likelihood of attitude or behavior change (O'Keefe 2002). Public communication campaigns utilizing these principles have, on average, been successful at increasing healthy behaviors among targeted populations (Noar 2006). At the same time, there are many examples of well-funded campaigns that have failed to meet their objective or, worse, produced outcomes directly opposite from their original persuasive goal (Byrne and Hart 2009). Campaigns focused on one outcome can also have unintended consequences for another outcome (Guttman and Salmon 2004). For instance, behavior change campaigns could undermine community mobilization efforts or support for societal-level policies by emphasizing individual responsibility for health and/or stigmatizing unhealthy individuals (MacLean et al. 2009). There are many ways that messages designed to prevent disease can lead to unintended consequences that undermine their broader impact on public health (Cho and Salmon 2007).

This chapter reviews theory and research about possible unintended consequences of obesity prevention messages. We begin by outlining a variety of intended and unintended consequences that could occur in response to an obesity prevention message. We continue with a discussion of what is known about mental processes that can occur in response to such a message. Next, we review examples of research on specific unintended consequences of messages designed to promote active living and healthy eating among children, caregivers, and adults. We also review research about unintended consequences of messages related to support for public policies to prevent obesity. We conclude with a series of recommendations about how to avoid unintended consequences in messages designed to prevent childhood and adult obesity.

Strategic and "Potentially Strategic" Messages

Many communication scholars examine the process and effects of exposure to messages. Of primary interest to readers of this volume are messages created with the specific goal of preventing or reducing rates of obesity. Communication scholars classify messages as "strategic" if they target specific populations with specific goals such as preventing obesity, encouraging a more active lifestyle, or promoting healthy eating. Strategic messages are broadly defined as communication efforts created with a clear, well-defined intent, often aiming to change opinions, attitudes and/or behaviors of a specific population (Piotrow and Kincaid 2001). Public service announcements, curriculum interventions, and advertisements are included in this category. Strategic message campaigns address many topics including, but not limited to, health. For example, campaigns have been designed with the intention of increasing voter turnout and lowering aggression (McGuire 1986).

This chapter discusses unintended outcomes of exposure to "strategic" messages, and also describes studies of messages that may not have been created with the intention of reducing obesity yet still possess that potential. For example, a journalist reporting a news story about soda taxes may not directly intend to motivate viewers to support a change in school policy. However, lessons learned from studies that gauge responses to this type of message would be informative for strategic campaigns designed to increase support for such a policy. Furthermore, public health advocates can shape the volume and content of news coverage using strategic media advocacy (Wallack and Dorfman 2001). Therefore, this chapter will also review research on other types of "potentially strategic" messages that may result in consequences that run counter to the mission of preventing obesity such as celebrity health news stories, election campaigns, and media coverage of obesity-related research and policy debates.

DEFINING THE OUTCOMES

Messages with the potential to reduce or prevent obesity can result in one or more of three possible outcomes: intended effects, null effects, or unintended effects.

Intended effects: Many efforts to persuade individuals to live healthier lives are quite effective. By effective, we mean that a message reached its objective(s). There are many examples of effective campaigns (Hornik 2002; Snyder et al. 2004). While we focus on unintended consequences here, we do so with the knowledge that such effects are not necessarily the norm.

Null effects: One would hope that strategic efforts to encourage individuals to live healthier lives would be effective, but this is not always the case. These efforts can result in no measureable or observable effects on targeted objectives. While it is not the goal of this chapter to present a detailed review of message strategies that do not achieve their goals, it is important to realize that null effects, while not always published, can and do happen (Snyder et al. 2004).

Unintended effects: Of primary interest here is to promote scholarly aware-ness of, and direct empirical attention toward, the emergence of unintended consequences under the philosophy that pro-social or health messages should "first do no harm" (O'Dea 2005, p. 259). Strategic messages can produce *unintended* consequences, defined as any effect that was not intended in the first place. Cho and Salmon (2007) outlined 11 potential unintended consequences of health messages. One of the most disheartening and potentially harmful unintended consequences is what is known as a "boomerang effect." While messages can result in many types of effects that are not intended, a boomerang effect is a specific type of unintended effect that is defined as the *opposite* of the intended effect (Byrne and Hart 2009; Hovland, Janis, and Kelly 1953). For example, if the intent of an environmental appeal is to *increase* household energy conservation, a boo-merang effect would be a *decrease* in household energy conservation (Schultz et al. 2007).

MECHANISMS THAT EXPLAIN HOW
UNINTENDED EFFECTS OCCUR

The fields of communication, persuasion, public health, psychology, and education offer various theories to explain unintended consequences of messages. Byrne and Hart (2009) detailed many of these explanations and grouped them into two general categories: (1) *intended* construct activation and (2) *unintended* construct activation. This "construct activation" perspective holds that some message recipients are susceptible to greater risks than simply not being persuaded.

Intended Construct Activation

Intended construct activation involves an individual taking away the content of the message as intended, but not complying with it (Byrne and Hart 2009). The process of intended construct activation is perhaps best illustrated through a hypothetical example.

Messages strategically designed to lower obesity most likely contain elements that are placed in the message with the intent to change beliefs, attitudes, or behaviors about exercise and nutrition, community action, and/or obesity-related policy. Ideally, these elements would be constructed in ways that build on existing theory and research. Take, for example, a public service announcement (PSA) placed during children's television programming created with the intention of persuading schoolchildren that healthy foods are better for you than unhealthy foods. Assume that this belief was targeted with the ultimate goal of changing behavior—prompting kids to select healthy foods over unhealthy ones at lunch in the school cafeteria. To achieve this desired effect, suppose the ad contrasted a testimonial from one child who chose fruits and vegetables at lunch and obtained a high grade on a test with another child who chose potato chips and earned a low grade on the same exam. Some explicit information in these testimonials—that choosing healthy food during lunch leads to good grades and choosing unhealthy food leads to bad grades—exemplifies *intended elements* in the message that would be expected to motivate kids to act in a healthy manner.

For the sake of argument, let's assume the message was successful in generating substantial attention among viewers and was clearly understood by children in the audience. Even though individuals may attend to and process the message as intended, they can still resist its content. For example, psychological reactance may occur if kids who view the PSA perceive that their freedom to eat unhealthy foods is under threat ("*Don't tell me what to do!*") and work to restore that freedom by eating more bad foods than they would have, had they not been exposed to that message (Brehm 1966; Brehm and Brehm 1981). Additionally, kids who are told repeatedly *not* to engage in a behavior, like choosing unhealthy food during lunch, may have difficulty complying because the idea of unhealthy food could become "hyper-accessible" in their minds (*"I don't want to, but I just can't stop thinking about those potato chips!"*) (Monteith, Sherman, and Devine 1998; Wegner 1994). Finally, if a child is overly fearful of receiving bad grades and does not perceive himself as having enough willpower to make healthy lunch choices, s/he may work to reduce this fear by convincing him- or herself that s/he in fact is not the target of the message (*"That only happens to younger kids."*) (Witte 1994).

Unintended Construct Activation

Unintended construct activation occurs when viewers attend to and process harmful or unintended elements in a message at the expense of those elements that were designed to promote the intended effect (Byrne and Hart 2009). Ideally, messages to prevent obesity would only contain elements that were universally interpreted by target audiences as intended—even at the risk of participants resisting those ideas. However, messages also contain many elements that have the potential to run directly counter to the specific goal. These elements often exist for the purposes of narrative structure, to aid comprehension, to gain attention of viewers, or to increase viewers' identification with the issue. If these elements are more powerful than the intended elements, receivers may process a message in a way that leads to an effect that was not intended. As with intended construct activation, researchers can identify parts of messages that are likely to result in unintended consequences by applying existing theory and drawing on research (Byrne and Hart 2009).

To illustrate the process of unintended construct activation, again consider the cafeteria-choice PSA. Depending on how the message is executed, a variety of unintended messages could be conveyed. For instance, children exposed to the PSA could develop an unintended social norm, such as stigmatizing kids who eat unhealthy food as being stupid or lacking willpower (Cialdini 2003). Portrayals of bad foods may also generate a new awareness of those foods, encouraging kids who had did not know they were available to try them, through a process of ambiguity reduction (*"Wow, I've never had caramel-flavored potato chips before!"*) (Bushman and Stack 1996). Additionally, if children believe that smart kids are less popular, depictions of eating healthy may be associated with negative consequences and eating unhealthy with positive consequences (*"Don't choose fruits and vegetables—that's not what the cool kids do!"*)–an idea explained through observational learning (Bandura 1986). Similarly, if the viewer identifies with the unhealthy child, or finds the unhealthy child more attractive, he or she may be inclined to model that child's behavior. Finally, portrayals of unhealthy food may simply prime, or make more accessible, thoughts related to those foods in the mind of the viewer. If the viewer has had positive associations with those foods in the past, the priming effect could override the intended effect (*"I had forgotten how much I enjoy potato chips!"*) (Berkowitz and Rogers 1986).

Selecting unintended elements of a message can become a particular problem if those elements are easier to process than elements associated with the goal of the message, or if those elements are more intrinsically motivating (Byrne and Hart 2009; Byrne, Linz, and Potter 2009; Petty and Cacioppo 1986).

OUTCOMES OF STRATEGIC COMMUNICATION AIMING TO INCREASE HEALTHY BEHAVIORAL DECISIONS

Having discussed the basic psychological mechanisms that underlie at least some types of unintended consequences, we move now to a selective review of research examining unintended consequences of obesity prevention messages. Empirical evaluations of strategic messages intended to reduce obesity by changing diet and exercise behavior are relatively rare (Hornik and Kelly 2007). Therefore, we also cover some specific examples of similar efforts that have "gone wrong" in the broader health communication context and discuss how the outcome of these efforts might apply to obesity prevention.

Individuals may feel threatened. A large literature exists on the evaluation of campaigns with the intent to prevent or reduce excessive alcohol intake, drug abuse, and cigarette smoking. Scholars and practitioners of anti-obesity messages are encouraged to take a close look at outcomes of these studies. For example, Grandpre et al. (2003) manipulated two anti-smoking ads to reflect either an explicit demand that teens not smoke versus a message that emphasized their freedom of choice. They found that adolescents in the 10th grade who viewed anti-smoking messages were more likely to say that they would try a cigarette soon if they heard an explicit message telling them not to smoke than they would have been if they had heard a message emphasizing personal choice. When members of a target audience perceive that a valued freedom is under direct threat, such as the freedom to drink soda or eat French fries, viewers may reject the public health message. In Grandpre et al. (2003) the explicit message strategy may have been overly demanding, causing viewers to reject the message. In turn, they are likely to have worked to restore their freedom to smoke, therefore increasing their intentions to smoke. Another study demonstrated that some college students, especially males who drink often, consumed more alcohol directly after observing a message telling them to abstain from drinking. In contrast, a comparison group who heard a less restrictive message to drink "in moderation" did not exhibit this effect (Bensley and Wu 1991). Combined, these studies suggest that messages targeting teens and young adults may be at particular risk of experiencing reactance in response to obesity prevention messages. An overly explicit or demanding message is unlikely to be an effective strategy for a target population developmentally prone to resisting directive messages (Byrne and Hart 2009; Miller et al. 2007; Ringhold 2002).

Individuals can be attracted to things that they are told are harmful. There is also evidence that campaigns can activate unintended constructs in the mind of viewers, resulting in undesirable consequences (Byrne and Hart 2009; Byrne, Linz, and Potter 2009). Communicative efforts to curtail unhealthy dietary behaviors by labeling them as harmful use may inadvertently activate positive attitudes toward those behaviors. For instance, Bushman (1998) tested the effects of warning labels specifically designed to help people avoid fatty foods. He found that warning consumers that a product contained more fat made that product more desirable. The attraction to things that are explicitly labeled as harmful is robust in that it transfers to many other contexts. Bushman and Cantor (2003) conducted a meta-analysis of 18 reports (from 70 independent samples) that examined the effects of entertainment program ratings (movies and TV shows) on attraction to particular types of content. Overall, restrictive ratings tended to make programs more attractive to viewers. While considerable evidence attests that children, particularly boys, are drawn to restrictive ratings and advisories, young adults are not immune to the attractiveness of ratings. College students reported greater interest in seeing films labeled as containing harmful violent content, compared to when they were not labeled, or simply described as violent (Bushman and Stack 1996).

This "forbidden fruit" effect has also been found in other health-related contexts. For example, Rosenbaum and Hanson (1998) concluded that suburban children who participated in project D.A.R.E. (Drug Awareness and Resistance Education) used drugs significantly more through high school than all urban participants and the suburban control group. Similarly, Hornik et al. (2008) found evidence that the more some young people were exposed to the National Youth Anti-Drug Media Campaign (NYADMC), a national campaign aimed at enabling America's youth to reject illegal drugs, the less they reported intentions to avoid marijuana use. By portraying drugs as addictive and a huge national problem, some viewers may instead hear that drugs are fun, feel good, and everyone is using them—that's what makes them addictive. The lesson to take away from these studies is that campaigns portraying food or exercise as unhealthy might instead, or also, be portraying these activities as desirable.

Individuals may think that something is more common and, therefore, more attractive. Campaigns may also cultivate undesirable social norms about diet and exercise that run counter to the intention of the messages. So-called "social norms" campaigns adopt a specific communicative strategy that attempts to reduce anti-social behavior by changing misconceptions about the prevalence of such behaviors (Cialdini 2003). These campaigns can also backfire. For instance, a nationwide study of 118 colleges revealed that many formal attempts to reduce alcohol consumption through social norms campaigns resulted in an *increase* of alcohol consumption (Wechsler et al. 2003). These efforts may result in increased awareness of the behavior which, in turn, increases its prevalence. For example, if a campaign indicates that 60 percent of the population is overweight or obese, viewers might take solace in the fact that it is normal to be overweight.

Some scholars and stakeholders have directly implicated the mass media, particularly advertising for unhealthy foods, as a causal agent in the rise in obesity (Kunkel et al. 2004). In response, media literacy interventions have been developed in an effort to teach critical thinking skills that combat the effects of heavy exposure to ads for unhealthy foods and portrayals of unrealistic body types. Several of these efforts have resulted in an increased appeal of unhealthy foods and negative body image, the very things targeted for change (Austin et al. 2005; Choma, Foster, and Radford 2007). Children under the age of 8 are particularly at risk of selecting visual elements of an intervention, which may convey unintended messages, over the critical content of such interventions (Kunkel et al. 2004). For example, junk food ads used as examples during a media literacy lesson may be noticed and emphasized over the very elements in the lesson designed to combat the effects of the ads. Direct evidence of this processing problem has been found in other health-related contexts (Byrne 2009; Byrne, Linz, and Potter 2009). It is perhaps this logic that led advocacy groups to fight against the animated super-star named SHREK, famous for endorsing unhealthy products and a sedentary lifestyle, from being used as a animated anti-obesity advocate and educator (Meltz 2007). Certainly, strong evidence exists that interventions designed to mitigate the effects of junk food ads may actually increase awareness and interest in such products.

Individuals may (not) respond emotionally. Messages intending to evoke emotions are often utilized to induce persuasion (Nabi, Moyer-Guse, and Byrne 2007). If used improperly, these messages could have counterproductive effects. For example, Fishbein et al. (2002) examined the effectiveness of 30 anti-drug public service announcements. The authors concluded that humorous messages have a high likelihood of producing a boomerang effect, perhaps because they undermine the seriousness of drug use as a social or health issue. Patterns of unintended consequences have also been found in reaction to strategic messages utilizing fear and/or guilt appeals (see Leventhal 1971; Witte 1994). Fear tactics have backfired in efforts aiming to increase self-administered routine breast cancer exams (Kline 1995; Kline and Mattson 2000), interventions to promote healthy body image (Schwartz, Thomas, Bohan, and Vartanian 2007) and safe sex campaigns (Priester 2002). Similarly, strategic campaigns designed to evoke feelings of guilt are sometimes rejected because audiences feel manipulated by the advertisement and develop anger toward the message and its source (Cotte, Coulter, and Moore 2005). Therefore, messages intending to evoke the fear of becoming obese or developing heart disease, or aim to encourage guilty feelings associated with unhealthy foods or a lack of physical activity, may be met with considerable efforts to reduce such emotions and rejection of the message (Keller and Lehmann 2008).

Exposure to messages about health, especially when related to mortality, can also create unnecessary worry and confusion (Guttman, Kegler and McLeroy 1996). Certain types of individuals, like those who are particularly oriented to disease prevention, may be particularly susceptible to overreacting (Abrams, Mills, and

Bulger 1999; Keller and Lehmann 2008). Individuals in this state of anxiety who have the financial means to do so may make unnecessary demands on the medical system, leaving those most in need of help with fewer resources (Guttman, Kegler, and McLeroy 1996; Guttman and Salmon 2004). For example, because obesity is related to mortality, people who are overweight may desire to be screened for heart disease and cancer even if screening is not logical or consistent with clinical recommendations. People may also view messages targeted at one at-risk population, determine that they are not part of that population, and either discontinue feeling concerned when in fact they are susceptible or even feel neglected for consideration (Guttman, and Salmon 2004).

Individuals may adopt alternative unhealthy behaviors. In situations where viewers *are* persuaded to make healthier food choices and engage in an active lifestyle, another concern is that potential unhealthy behaviors will be replaced by alternative unhealthy behaviors (Hornik and Kelly 2007, p. 7). In response to this concern, the American Heart Association sponsored a conference, in October 2006, with the goal of reducing trans fat in American food products without increasing the use of saturated fat as a replacement (Eckel et al. 2007). In fact, while Americans are increasingly reporting purchasing foods labeled with "zero trans fat," awareness of the replacement oils, such as saturated fats, remains quite low (Eckel et al. 2009). The concern is that individuals are replacing a potentially harmful product with one that is only slightly less harmful.

Individuals may become confused or disillusioned. Audiences live in a world saturated with mixed messages. Driving down the freeway in Los Angeles, one finds side-by-side billboards advertising both fast food restaurants and miracle diets. Viewers are frequently exposed to messages defining one or more harmful aspect of food , be it trans fat, polyunsaturated fat, carbohydrates, or calories. These messages can confuse and tire audiences, especially those that are less skilled at filtering (Potter 2004; Niederdeppe and Levy 2007). Hornik and Kelly (2006) that argue that messages intending to promote healthy lifestyles, like changes in diet, have a particular struggle against prevalent counter-messages. A recent study, in fact, concluded that Americans who are frequently exposed to local TV news are more likely than those with less exposure to believe that "everything causes cancer" and that "there are so many recommendations about preventing cancer, it's hard to know which ones to follow" (Niederdeppe, Fowler, Goldstein and Pribble 2010). People who hold these beliefs are less likely than those who do not hold them to exercise regularly and eat a diet rich in fruits and vegetables (Niederdeppe and Levy 2007).

Individuals may stigmatize targeted groups. Obese people have long suffered from being stigmatized as possessing little self-control and prone to make unhealthy life choices in general (Saguy and Riley 2005). This situation is exacerbated by an onslaught of messages that focus on personal lifestyle choices as the solution to the problem, when in fact many genetic and environmental factors contribute (Guttman, Kegler and McLeroy 1996; MacLean et al. 2009). Additionally, if a communication campaign singles out a particular segment of a population as particularly susceptible to obesity or its consequences, stigmatization of that group could occur (Guttman and Salmon 2004; Solomons 2005). For example, school-based weight-loss programs may stigmatize, or at least draw attention to, over-weight children (McLeroy et al. 1995). Likewise, some suggest that race-based targeting of strategic health messages can encourage the development of negative stereotypes about the targeted group (Hornik and Ramirez, 2006).

UNINTENDED EFFECTS OF MESSAGES TARGETING COMMUNITY MOBILIZATION AND POLICY SUPPORT

There is also research, albeit less of it, suggesting that messages designed to mobilize community action and/or increase support for public health policy can produce unintended consequences. Much of this work focuses on the dissemination of, and response to, news stories about policies to improve health. Lessons learned from this work have direct implications for strategic efforts to prevent obesity via community empowerment or policy change.

Mobilizing the opposition. Media advocacy involves the strategic use of mass media and community organizing to advance health policy (Wallack and Dorfman 2001). Specifically, it is an attempt to generate news coverage about a health issue and offer frames for that coverage which emphasize policy solutions. Many contend that obesity prevention efforts, in order to succeed, will require changes in societal factors like the marketing of low-cost unhealthy foods, agricultural policies, and lack of resources for healthy food and exercise in many neighborhoods (Sallis et al. 2006; Story et al. 2008). Changes in these factors will most likely require legislative action at local, state, and/or national levels. Thus media advocacy is likely to be used in strategic obesity prevention efforts.

While a limited evidence base suggests that media advocacy *can* contribute to success in policy goals (see Wallack and Dorfman, 2001), Harwood et al. (2005) offer a cautionary tale of the strategy's potential for unintended consequences. The authors studied news coverage and policy activity related to underage drinking in Louisiana between 1994 and 2003. They examined the relationship between (1) the volume and content of news stories related to the topic in two Louisiana newspa-pers and (2) state legislative activity related to bans on minors in bars, alcohol taxes, keg registration, and zero tolerance laws. The authors reported two main findings. First, news media attention increased after a statewide underage drinking coalition was created in 1997, suggesting that this coverage was a product of strategic media advocacy efforts. Second, high volume of policy-related news stories tended to correlate with *failure* to pass legislation. The vast majority of policies passed during the observation period occurred during periods of little or no media coverage.

The authors suggested that media coverage may have mobilized opposition to the issue by drawing attention to it and reduced the likelihood of successful political compromise. Smith et al. (2008) offered a similar explanation as to why they found that a greater volume of news coverage about secondhand smoke was associated with lower levels of public support for clean indoor air laws in the United States.

It is worth noting that neither study directly measured community or political mobilization, and both were limited by either a small number of policies for statistical analysis (Harwood et al. 2005) or limitations of cross-sectional data (Smith et al. 2008). Nevertheless, the patterns observed in these studies illustrate one possible outcome of media advocacy for obesity prevention: mobilizing the opposition (for further reading, see Cho and Salmon 2007, p. 307, and their discussion of "system activation"). In the case of obesity prevention, several proposed policies enjoy very limited public support, and few less so than a junk-food tax (Barry et al. 2009). Tax policy is a highly political topic in the United States. When policies have the potential to affect the bottom line of a large and powerful industry, they are likely to catalyze substantial opposition. The limitations of advocating for such a policy were on full display when New York's governor, David Patterson, proposed an 18 percent tax on carbonated sodas in 2009. He abandoned the proposal a few months later amid substantial public outcry and industry opposition.

Decreasing policy support among particular groups: Gollust et al. (2009) studied responses to messages about an issue of direct relevance to obesity prevention: type II diabetes. The authors randomly assigned a diverse sample of respondents to one of four messages, designed to resemble a news article, emphasizing one of the following: (1) genetic factors as a cause of diabetes, (2) lifestyle choices (e.g., diet and exercise) as a cause, (3) neighborhood conditions (e.g., lack of access to healthy foods and safe or convenient places for exercise) as a cause, or (4) no mention of causes (control group). Respondents were then asked to indicate their level of support for a series of seven policies designed to reduce rates of type II diabetes, including school bans on fast food concessions, financial incentives for groceries to relocate in underserved neighborhoods, and junk food taxes. Response to the randomized messages differed dramatically as a function of political partisanship. Democrats exposed to the neighborhood conditions message had higher levels of support for policy interventions relative to the control group. Republicans exposed to the neighborhood conditions message, on the other hand, had *lower* levels of support for the policies relative to the control group. The authors concluded that a dominant ideology of personal responsibility, held strongly by many Republicans, may result in antagonistic response to messages emphasizing factors outside of the individual.

This pattern of results illustrates the possibility of boomerang effects in response to at least some types of messages explicitly designed to raise awareness of societal causes of obesity (Byrne and Hart 2009). Several obesity prevention initiatives, such as the Active Living Research (www.activelivingresearch.org/) and

Healthy Eating Research (www.healthyeatingresearch.org/) programs initiated by the Robert Wood Johnson Foundation, as well as major grant programs from the National Institutes of Health, aim to support research on the role of social conditions, physical environments, and economic circumstances on childhood obesity. While there is no doubt that this work is of major importance for obesity prevention, Gollust et al.'s (2009) work suggests that simply accumulating and disseminating scientific evidence about the role of societal factors in shaping obesity may, among some groups, undermine public support for obesity-reducing policies. Furthermore, news coverage of research about causes of obesity raises the possibility of another unintended consequence.

Diverting attention from more important issues: Saguy and Almeling (2008) examined the correspondence between the content of (1) scientific studies about obesity and (2) news media coverage of those studies. The authors analyzed the content of a sample of scientific articles published in the *Journal of the American Medical Association*, press releases about those articles, and news coverage about the research reported therein. They distinguished between three causes of obesity: (1) individual decisions (e.g., diet and exercise), (2) societal factors (e.g., food advertising and restaurant portions), or (3) genetic predispositions. They also examined four possible solutions to obesity: (1) individual behavior change, (2) policy change, (3) weight-loss drugs, and (4) weight-loss surgery. Overall, Saguy and Almeling (2008) concluded that news coverage emphasized individual causes of obesity more than the original scientific articles on which they were based (see Kim and Willis 2007; Lawrence 2004).

This study illustrates a third possible unintended consequence of strategic efforts to reduce obesity: diverting attention from more important issues (for further reading, see the discussion of "opportunity cost" by Cho and Salmon 2007, p. 304). In the case of obesity news coverage, Saguy and Almeling's (2008) results suggest that strategic efforts to publish and promote research that directly implicates societal causes of obesity and suggests broader policy solutions for obesity prevention can still translate into news coverage that emphasizes individual causes. This, in turn, could divert attention away from the broader, structural, and economic issues that contribute to obesity. In the context of tobacco-related media advocacy, Niederdeppe et al. (2007) suggest that intense efforts to generate news coverage and policy action for a relatively ineffective policy strategy may divert political will and attention away from policies with stronger evidence for efficacy, such as clean indoor air laws or excise tax increases (Levy, Chaloupka and Gitchell 2004). Niederdeppe et al. explored the relationship between program-related news coverage, the passage of tobacco product placement ordinances (requiring retailers to place tobacco products behind the counter), and youth smoking rates. Overall, they concluded that media advocacy efforts appeared successful in promoting policy change, but the policy itself did not contribute to reduce rates of youth smoking. Unfortunately, the ultimate outcomes of strategic efforts to promote public health may fall short of what could have been accomplished through other means.

STRATEGIES TO MINIMIZE
UNINTENDED CONSEQUENCES OF OBESITY
PREVENTION MESSAGES

This chapter describes theory and evidence suggesting that unintended conse-quences may result from strategic efforts to prevent obesity. While some of the accumulated evidence on message design strategies takes the potential for undesir-able effects into account (Fishbein et al. 2002; Salmon and Murray-Johnson 2001), more often message designers are concerned with the possibility of the message simply not achieving their objective (Witte et al. 2001). There is a considerable amount of work in the persuasion literature on how to design messages that over-come resistance to persuasion and, to a lesser extent, prevent unintended effects (e.g., Guttman and Salmon 2004; MacLean et al. 2009; Witte, Meyer, Martell 2001). We argue that neglecting to consider unintended consequences in the planning stages of an intervention is a mistake. The challenge is to be aware of the potential emergence of such effects and to make efforts to avoid their manifestation.

At first glance, the sheer number of possible unintended consequences may appear overwhelming and discouraging. Our goals were twofold: (1) to raise aware-ness of these consequences and, using this knowledge, (2) to minimize the likeli-hood that they occur. In service of the latter goal, this final section offers strategies to prevent or overcome such effects.

A first step in preventing an unintended consequence is to clearly identify and understand the target audience, as well as any other populations that may be exposed to the message. This step in designing any persuasive message or interven-tion is nearly universally accepted (Atkin 2002; Fishbein and Yzer 2003; Rice and Atkin 2001; Stiff and Mongeau 2003; Witte et al. 2001). This goal can be accom-plished by identifying both the target audience and secondary or unintended audi-ences, and using a variety of methods to profile their attitudes, behaviors, and demographics (see Atkin and Freimuth 2001, for more details on formative evalua-tion methods).

A second step is to clearly outline the specific intention of the message. Identifying the intended effect is the step that allows the communicator to pinpoint potential unintended or harmful effects. For example, research has shown that spe-cific populations prefer to consume highly sweetened soda to diet soda (Binkley and Golub 2007). Therefore, the intention of a message may be to increase the like-lihood that individuals within the target population will choose to drink non-sug-ar-sweetened beverages when thirsty.

The third step is to identify potential unintended consequences using theory and previous research. One might start with the boomerang effect—the opposite of the intended effect. Several persuasion theories describe conditions under which boomerang effects are most likely (Byrne and Hart 2009). For instance, the extended parallel process model (EPPM) predicts that boomerang effects are likely to occur when a message emphasizes a major threat to health and well-being but provides little information about how to reduce or minimize that threat (Witte 1994). Considering this and other relevant theoretical perspectives in message design is likely to minimize the possibility of unforeseen consequences. Likewise, it is always good practice to systematically examine previous efforts to achieve similar persuasive objectives.

A fourth step is to develop strategies that encourage the audience to devote substantial cognitive resources toward processing the intended elements of the message. If the message must contain some unintended elements, be sure to engage the audience in such a way that the intended elements are selected and processed by the viewer and are more likely to override the harmful ideas. For example, one could encourage viewers to apply the intended elements to their own lives by asking directed questions or completing an interactive campaign component (Byrne, 2009).

The fifth and final step in designing a strategic message is to pre-test the message on a small subset of the target population and possible secondary populations to look for unintended effects. A list of potential effects generated in step three can be directly tested on a small subset of members of the relevant populations. In this stage, it is of primary importance to use methods that permit the researcher to identify whether unintended consequences arise as a result of intended construct activation (understanding the message but rejecting it) or unintended construct activation (paying attention or responding to non-central elements of the message). Randomized experiments and thought-listing techniques can aid the researcher in identifying which constructs are activated (e.g., Cacioppo, von Hippel and Ernst, 1997). This knowledge will be essential to devise strategies for modifying the message to reduce the likelihood of unintended effects.

REFERENCES

Abrams, David B., Sherry Mills, and David Bulger. 1999. "Challenges and Future Directions for Tailored Communications Research." *Annals of Behavioral Medicine* 21(4): 299–306.

Atkin, Charles K. 2002. "Promising Strategies for Media Health Campaigns." In *Mass Media and Drug Prevention,* eds. W. D. Crano and M. Burgoon, 35–64. Mahwah, NJ: Earlbaum.

Atkin, Charles K., and Vicki S. Freimuth. 2001. "Formative Evaluation Research in Campaign Design." In *Public Communication Campaigns* (3rd ed.), eds. Ronald E. Rice and Charles K. Atkin, 125–145. Thousand Oaks, CA: Sage Publications.

Austin, Erica Weintraub, Bruce E. Pinkleton, Stacey J. T. Hust, and Marilyn Cohen. 2005. "Evaluation of an American Legacy Foundation Washington State Department of Health Media Literacy Pilot Study." *Health Communication* 18: 75–95.

Bandura, Albert. 1986. *Social Foundations of Thought and Action: A Social Cognitive Theory.* Englewood Cliffs, NJ: Prentice Hall.

Barry, Colleen L., Victoria L. Brescoll, Kelly D. Brownell, and Mark Schlesinger. 2009. "Obesity Metaphors: How Beliefs about the Causes of Obesity Affect Support for Public Policy." *The Milbank Quarterly* 87: 7–47.

Bensley, Lillian S., and Rui Wu. 1991. "The Role of Psychological Reactance in Drinking Following Alcohol Prevention Messages." *Journal of Applied Social Psychology* 21: 1111–1124.

Berkowitz, Leonard, and Karen Heimer Rogers. 1986. "A Priming Effect Analysis of Media Influences." In *Perspectives on Media Effects*, eds. J. Bryant and D. Zillman, 57–81. Mahwah, NJ: Erlbaum.

Binkley, James, and Alla Gollub. 2007. "Grocery Purchase Patterns of Diet Soda Buyers and Regular Soda Buyers." *Appetite* 29: 561–571.

Brehm, Jack. 1966. *A Theory of Psychological Reactance*. New York: Academic Press.

Brehm, Sharon S., and Jack W. Brehm. 1981. *Psychological Reactance: A Theory of Freedom and Control*. San Diego, CA: Academic Press.

Brock, Timothy C. 1968. "Implications of Commodity Theory for Value Change." In *Psychological Foundations of Attitudes*, eds. A. G. Greenwald, T. C. Brock, and T. M. Ostrom, 243–275. New York: Academic Press.

Bushman, Brad J. 1998. "Effects of Warning and Information Labels on Consumption of Full-Fat, Reduced-Fat, and No-Fat Products." *Journal of Applied Psychology* 83: 97–101.

Bushman, Brad J., and Joanne Cantor. 2003. "Media Ratings for Violence and Sex: Implications for Policymakers and Parents." *American Psychologist* 58: 130–141.

Bushman, Brad J., and Angela. D. Stack. 1996. "Forbidden Fruit versus Tainted Fruit: Effects of Warnings Labels on Attraction to Television Violence." *Journal of Experimental Psychology: Applied* 2: 207–226.

Byrne, Sahara. 2009. "Media Literacy Interventions: What Makes Them Boom or Boomerang?" *Communication Education* 58: 1–14.

Byrne, Sahara, and P. Sol Hart. 2009. "The 'Boomerang' Effect: A Synthesis of Findings and a Preliminary Theoretical Framework." In *Communication Yearbook* 33, ed. Christina Beck, 3–37. Mahwah, NJ: Lawrence Erlbaum.

Byrne, Sahara, Daniel Linz, and W. James Potter. 2009. "A Test of Competing Cognitive Explanations for the Boomerang Effect in Response to the Deliberate Disruption of Media-Induced Aggression." *Media Psychology* 12: 227–248.

Cacioppo, John T., William von Hippel, and John M. Ernst. 1997. "Mapping Cognitive Structures and Processes Through Verbal Content: The Thought-Listing Technique." *Journal of Consulting and Clinical Psychology* 65: 928–940.

Cho, Hyunyi, and Charles T. Salmon. 2007. "Unintended Effects of Health Communication Campaigns." *Journal of Communication* 57: 293–317.

Choma, Becky L., Mindi D. Foster, and Eileen Radford. 2007. "Use of Objectification Theory to Examine the Effects of a Media Literacy Intervention on Women." *Sex Roles* 56: 581–590.

Cialdini, Robert B. 2003. "Crafting Normative Messages to Protect the Environment." *Current Directions in Psychological Research* 12: 105–109.

Cotte, June, Robin A. Coulter, and Melissa Moore. 2005. "Enhancing or Disrupting Guilt: The Role of Ad Credibility and Perceived Manipulative Intent." *Journal of Business Research* 58: 361–368.

Eckel, Robert H., Susan Borra, Alice H. Lichtenstein, and Shirley Y. Yin-Piazza. 2007. "Understanding the Complexity of Trans Fatty Acid Reduction in the American Diet." *Circulation* 115: 2231–2246.

Eckel, Robert H., Penny Kris-Etherton, Alice H. Lichtenstein, Judith Wylie-Rosett, Allison Groom, Kimberly F. Stitzel, and Shirley Yin-Piazza. 2009. "Americans' Awareness, Knowledge, and Behaviors Regarding Fats: 2006–2007." *Journal of the American Dietetic Association* 109: 288–296.

Fishbein, Martin, Kathleen Hall-Jamison, Eric Zimmer, Ina von Haeften, and Robin Nabi. 2002. "Avoiding the Boomerang: Testing the Relative Effectiveness of Antidrug Public Service Announcements before a National Campaign." *American Journal of Public Health* 92: 238–245.

Fishbein, Martin, and Marco C. Yzer. 2003. "Using Theory to Design Effective Health Behavior Interventions." *Communication Theory* 13: 164–183.

Fromkin, Howard. L., and Timothy C. Brock. 1973. "Erotic Materials: A Commodity Theory Analysis of the Enhanced Desirability That May Accompany Their Unavailability." *Journal of Applied Social Psychology* 3: 219–231.

Gollust, Sarah E., Paula M. Lantz, and Peter A. Ubel. 2009. "The Polarizing Effect of News Media Messages about the Social Determinants of Health." *American Journal of Public Health* 99: 2160–2167.

Grandpre, Joseph, Eusebio M. Alvaro, Michael Burgoon, Claude H. Miller, and John R. Hall. 2003. "Adolescent Reactance and Anti-Smoking Campaigns: A Theoretical Approach." *Health Communication* 15: 349–366.

Guttman, Nurit, Michelle Kegler, and Kenneth R. McLeroy. 1996. "Health Promotion Paradoxes, Antinomies and Conundrums." *Health Education Research* 11: i–xiii.

Guttman, Nurit, and Charles T. Salmon. 2004. "Guilt, Fear, Stigma and Knowledge Gaps: Ethical Issues in Public Health Communication Interventions." *Bioethics* 18: 531–552

Harwood, Eileen M., Jean C. Witson, David P. Fan, and Alexander C. Wagenaar. 2005. "Media Advocacy and Underage Drinking Policies: A Study of Louisiana News Media from 1994 through 2003." *Health Promotion Practice* 6: 246–257.

Hornik, Robert C., ed. 2002. *Public Health Communication: Evidence for Behavior Change.* Mahwah, NJ: Lawrence Erlbaum.

Hornik, Robert, and Bridget Kelly. 2007. "Communication and Diet: An Overview of Experience and Principles." *Journal of Nutrition Education and Behavior* 39: S5–S12.

Hornik, Robert, Lela Jacobsohn, Robert Orwin, Andrea Piesse, and Graham Kalton. 2008. "Effects of the National Youth Anti-Drug Media Campaign on Youths." *American Journal of Public Health* 98: 2229–2236.

Hornik, Robert, and Susana Ramirez. 2006. "Racial/Ethnic Disparities and Segmentation in Communication Campaigns." *American Behavioral Scientist* 49: 868–884.

Hovland, Carl Iver, Irving L. Janis, and Harold H. Kelly. 1953. *Communication and Persuasion: Psychological Studies of Opinion Change.* New Haven, CT: Yale University Press.

Keller, Punam Anand, and Donald R. Lehmann. 2008. "Designing Effective Health Communications: A Meta-Analysis." *Journal of Public Policy and Marketing* 27: 117–130.

Kim, Sei-Hill, and L. Anne Willis. 2007. "Talking about Obesity: News Framing of Who Is Responsible for Causing and Fixing The Problem." *Journal of Health Communication* 12: 359–376.

Kline, Kimberly Nicole. 1995, November. *Applying Witte's Extended Parallel Process Model to Pamphlets Urging Women to Engage in BSE. Where Are the Efficacy Messages?* Paper presented at the annual meeting of the Speech Communication Association, San Antonio, TX.

Kline, Kimberly Nicole, and Marifran Mattson. 2000. "Breast Self-Examination Pamphlets: A Content Analysis Grounded in Fear Appeal Research." *Health Communication* 12: 1–21.

Kumanyika, Shiriki K., Eva Obarzanek, Nicholas Stettler, Ronny Bell, Alison E. Field, Stephen P. Fortmann, Barry A. Franklin, Matthew W. Gillman, Cora E. Lewis, Walker

C. Poston, June Stevens, and Yuling Hong. 2008. "Population-based Prevention Of Obesity: The Need for Comprehensive Promotion of Healthful Eating, Physical Activity, and Energy Balance: A Scientific Statement from the American Heart Association Council on Epidemiology and Prevention, Interdisciplinary Committee for Prevention (Formerly the Expert Panel on Population and Prevention Science)." *Circulation* 118: 428–464.

Kunkel, Dale, Brian L. Wilcox, Joanne Cantor, Edward Palmer, Susan Linn, and Peter Dowrick. 2004. "Psychological Issues in the Increasing Commercialization of Childhood." *Report of the APA Task Force on Advertising and Children*, 1–35. Available at http://www.apa.org/releases/childrenads/pdf#search=%22FTC%20report%201978&20advertising%22.

Lawrence, Regina G. 2004. "Framing Obesity: The Evolution of News Discourse on a Public Health Issue." *The Harvard International Journal of Press/Politics* 9: 56–75.

Leventhal, Howard. 1971. "Fear Appeals in Persuasion: The Differentiation of a Motivational Construct." *American Journal of Public Health* 61: 1208–1224.

Levy, David T., Frank Chaloupka, and Joseph Gitchell. 2004. "The Effects of Tobacco Control Policies on Smoking Rates: A Tobacco Control Scorecard." *Journal of Public Health Management and Practice* 10: 338–353.

MacLean, Lynne, Nancy Edwards, Michael Garrard, Nicki Sims-Jones, Kathryn Clinton, and Lisa Ashley. 2009. "Obesity, Stigma and Public Health Planning." *Health Promotion International* 24: 88–93.

McGuire, William J. (1986). "The Myth of Massive Media Impact: Savaging and Salvagings." In *Public Communication and Behavior*, ed. George Comstock, Vol. 1, 173–257. New York: Academic Press.

McLeroy, Kenneth . R., Noreen M. Clark, Bruge G. Simons-Morton, Jean Forster, Cathleen M. Connell, David Altman, and Marc A. Zimmerman. 1995. "Creating Capacity: Establishing a Health Education Research Agenda for Special Populations." *Health Education Quarterly* 22: 390–405.

Meltz, Barbara F. 2007 (May 07). "Fighting Obesity, But Fronting for Junk Food." *The Boston Globe*. Retrieved on Jan. 10, 2010, from: http://www.boston.com/news/globe/living/articles/2007/05/21/fighting_obesity_but_fronting_for_junk_food/.

Miller, Claude H., Lindsay T. Lane, Leslie M. Deatrick, Alice M. Young, and Kimberly A. Potts. 2007. "Psychological Reactance and Promotional Health Messages: The Effects of Controlling Language, Lexical Concreteness, and the Restoration Of Freedom." *Human Communication Research* 33: 219–240.

Monteith, Margo J., Jeffrey W. Sherman, and Patricia G. Devine. 1998. "Suppression as a Stereotype Control Strategy." *Personality and Social Psychology Review* 2: 63–82.

Nabi, Robin, Emily Moyer-Gusé, and Sahara Byrne. 2007. "All Joking Aside: A Serious Investigation into the Persuasive Effects of Funny Social Issue Messages." *Communication Monographs* 74: 29–54.

Niederdeppe, Jeff, Matthew C. Farrelly, and Dana Wenter. 2007. "Media Advocacy, Tobacco Control Policy Change, and Teen Smoking in Florida." *Tobacco Control* 16: 47–52.

Niederdeppe, J., Erika Franklin Fowler, Kenneth Goldstein, and James Pribble. 2010. "Does Local Television News Coverage Cultivate Fatalistic Beliefs about Cancer Prevention?" *Journal of Communication* 60: 182–205.

Niederdeppe, Jeff, and Andrea Gurmankin Levy. 2007. "Fatalistic Beliefs about Cancer Prevention and Three Prevention Behaviors." *Cancer Epidemiology, Biomarkers, and Prevention* 16: 998–1003.

Noar, Seth M. 2006. "A 10-year Retrospective of Research in Health Mass Media Campaigns: Where Do We Go from Here?" *Journal of Health Communication* 11: 21–42.

O'Dea, Jennifer A. 2005. "Prevention of Child Obesity: 'First, Do No Harm.'" *Health Education Research* 20: 259–265.

O'Keefe, Daniel J. 2002. *Persuasion: Theory and Research* (2nd ed.). Thousand Oaks, CA: Sage Publications.

Petty, Richard E., and Cacioppo, John T. 1986. *Communication and Persuasion: Central and Peripheral Routes to Attitude Change.* New York: Springer-Verlag.

Piotrow, Phyllis Tilson, and D. Lawrence Kincaid. 2001. "Strategic Communication for International Health Programs." In *Public Communication Campaigns* (3rd ed.), ed. Ronald E. Rice and Charles K. Atkin, 249–267. Thousand Oaks, CA: Sage Publications.

Potter, W. James. 2004. *Theory of Media Literacy: A Cognitive Approach.* Thousand Oaks, CA: Sage Publications.

Preister, Joseph R. 2002. "Sex, Drugs and Attitudinal Ambivalence: How Feelings of Evaluative Tension Influence Alcohol Use and Safe Sex Behaviors." In *Mass Media and Drug Prevention,* eds. W. D. Crano and M. Burgoon, 145–162. Mahwah, NJ: Erlbaum.

Rice, Ronald E., and Charles K. Atkin. 2001. *Public Communication Campaigns* (2nd ed.). Thousand Oaks, CA: Sage Publications

Ringhold, Debra Jones. 2002. "Boomerang Effects in Response to Public Health Interventions: Some Unintended Consequences in the Alcoholic Beverage Market." *Journal of Consumer Policy* 25: 27–63.

Rogers, Ronald W. 1983. "Cognitive and Physiological Processes in Fear Appeals and Attitude Change: A Revised Theory of Protection Motivation." In *Social Psychophysiology: A Sourcebook,* eds. J. T. Cacioppo and R. E. Petty, 153–176. New York: Guilford Press.

Rosenbaum, Dennis. P., and Gordon S. Hanson. 1998. *Assessing the Effects of School-Based Drug Education: A Six-Year Multi-Level Analysis of Project D.A.R.E.* Retrieved March 9, 2006, from http://www.drugsense.org/tfy/uic.htm.

Saguy, Abigail, and Rebe Almeling. 2008. "Fat in the Fire? Science, the News Media and the Obesity Epidemic." *Sociological Forum* 23: 53–83.

Saguy, Abigail C. and Kevin W. Riley. 2005. "Weighing Both Sides: Morality, Mortality, and Framing Contests over Obesity." *Journal of Health Politics, Policy and Law* 30: 869–923.

Sallis, James F., Robert B. Cervero, William Ascher, Karla A. Henderson, M. Katherine Kraft, and Jacqueline Kerr. 2006. "An Ecological Approach to Creating Active Living Communities." *Annual Review of Public Health* 27: 297–322.

Salmon, Charles T and Murray-Johnson, Lisa. 2001. "Campaign Effectiveness: Some Critical Distinctions." In *Public Communication Campaigns* (3rd ed.), eds. Ronald Rice and Charles Atkin, 55. Newbury Park, CA: Sage Publications.

Schultz, P. Wesley, Jessica M. Nolan, Robert B. Cialdini, Noah J. Goldstein, and Vladas Griskevicius. 2007. "Constructive, Deconstructive, and Reconstructive Power of Social Norms." *Psychological Science* 18: 429–434.

Schwartz, Marlene B., Jennifer J. Thomas, Kristin M. Bohan, and Lenny R. Vartanian,. 2007. "Intended and Unintended Effects of an Eating Disorder Education Program: Impact of Presenter Identity." *International Journal of Eating Disorders* 40: 187–192.

Smith, Katherine Clegg, Catherine Siebel, Luu Pham, Juhee Cho, Rachel Friedman
    Singer, Frank Joseph Chaloupka, Michael Griswold, and Melanie Wakefield. 2008.
    "News on Tobacco and Public Attitudes Toward Smokefree Air Policies in the
    United States." *Health Policy* 86: 42–52.
Snyder, Leslie B., Mark A. Hamilton, Elizabeth W. Mitchell, James Kiwanuka-Tondo,
    Fran Fleming-Milici, and Dwayne Proctor. 2004. "A Meta-Analysis of the Effect of
    Mediated Health Communication Campaigns on Behavior Change in the United
    States." *Journal of Health Communication* 9(Supp. 1): 71–96.
Solomons, Noel W. 2005. "Programme and Policy Issues Related to Promoting Positive
    Early Nutritional Influences to Prevent Obesity, Diabetes and Cardiovascular Disease
    in Later Life: A Developing Countries View." *Maternal and Child Nutrition* 1: 204–215.
Stiff, James Brian, and Paul A. Mongeau. 2003. *Persuasive Communication*. New York:
    Guilford.
Story, Mary, Karen M. Kaphingst, Ramona Robinson-O'Brien, and Karen Glanz. 2008.
    "Creating Healthy Food and Eating Environments: Policy and Environmental
    Approaches." *Annual Review of Public Health* 29: 253–272.
Wallack, Larry, and Lori Dorfman. 2001. "Putting Policy into Health Communication: The
    Role of Media Advocacy." In *Public Communication Campaigns* (3rd ed.), eds. Ronald
    E. Rice and Charles K. Atkin, 389–401. Thousand Oaks, CA: Sage Publications.
Wechsler, Henry, Toben F. Nelson, Jae Eun Lee, Mark Seibring, Catherine Lewis, and
    Richard P. Keeling. 2003. "Perception and Reality: A National Evaluation of Social
    Norms Marketing Interventions to Reduce College Students' Heavy Alcohol Use."
    Quarterly Journal of Studies on Alcohol 64: 484–494.
Wegner, Daniel M. 1994. "Ironic Processes of Mental Control." *Psychological Review* 101:
    34–52.
Witte, Kim. 1994. "Fear Control and Danger Control: A Test of the Extended Parallel
    Process Model (EPPM)." *Communication Monographs* 61: 113–134.
Witte, Kim, Gary Mcyer, and Dennis Martell. 2001. *Effective Health Risk Messages:
    A Step-By-Step Guide*. Thousand Oaks, CA: Sage Publications.

CHAPTER 44

BEHAVIORAL TREATMENT OF OBESITY

LASHANDA R. JONES-CORNEILLE, REBECCA M. STACK, AND THOMAS A. WADDEN

THE rapidly growing number of overweight and obese Americans is cause for alarm. Two-thirds of the U.S. population (66 percent) is either overweight (body mass index [BMI] = 25.0–29.9 kg/m²) or obese (BMI ≥ 30 kg/m²) (Ogden et al. 2006), and many of these individuals suffer from weight-related comorbidities such as hypertension, hyperlipidemia, and type 2 diabetes (Must et al. 1999). On a more positive note, recent studies have demonstrated that losses as small as 5–10 percent of initial weight can improve these health complications (Blackburn 1995; Knowler et al. 2002). Behavioral treatment consistently induces losses of this size.

This chapter describes the behavioral treatment of obesity, including its short- and long-term results and approaches to improve long-term weight management. It also examines obesity outcomes and treatment recommendations for ethnic minority populations. The terms "behavioral treatment," "lifestyle modification," and "behavioral weight control" are often used interchangeably, as they will be in this chapter (Wadden, McGuckin, Rothman, and Sargent 2003). Lifestyle modification includes three principal components: diet, physical activity, and behavior therapy.

The latter term, as applied to weight control, refers to a set of principles and techniques to help patients adopt new diet and exercise habits that can be sustained long-term to promote health.

PRINCIPLES AND CHARACTERISTICS OF BEHAVIORAL TREATMENT

The goal of behavioral treatment, as applied to obesity, is to improve habits with respect to eating, activity, and thinking that contribute to a patient's weight. This treatment approach recognizes that body weight is affected by a multitude of factors, including genetic, metabolic, and hormonal influences (Wadden and Butryn 2003; Spiegelman and Flier 2001; Hebebrand, Sommerlad, Geller, Gorg, and Hinney 2001) that may predispose some persons to weight gain and establish the range of attainable weights that an individual can achieve (Keesey 1986). Behavioral treatment helps overweight individuals develop a set of skills (e.g., low-fat diet, physically-active lifestyle, realistic cognitive style) to regulate weight at the lower end of their weight range, even though some patients may remain obese after treatment (Wadden and Butryn 2003).

Principles

The principle of classical conditioning is fundamental to behavioral treatment. It asserts that stimuli repeatedly presented before or simultaneously with a given behavior will subsequently become associated with that behavior (Wing 1998). The more often two events are paired together, the stronger the association between them becomes. Eventually the presence of one will automatically trigger the desire for the other. For instance, after repeatedly snacking while watching television, simply turning on the television may trigger cravings for a snack, regardless of actual hunger. The goal of behavioral treatment is to help patients identify and extinguish cues (i.e., antecedent events) that trigger maladaptive behaviors such as overeating or physical inactivity. Although eating can be triggered by a single cue, typically several events linked together lead to overeating or inactivity, as illustrated in the behavior chain in figure 44.1 (Brownell 2004).

In addition to targeting eating and exercise behaviors themselves, behavioral treatment examines the antecedents and consequences of these behaviors (Wing 1998, 2002). Once antecedents of problem behaviors (e.g., overeating) are identified, steps are taken to control or modify those events. For example, thoughts and images are internal cues that serve as antecedents to behaviors (Beck 1976). Thus, how people think about a situation determines how they feel and what they do in response to those feelings. To illustrate, a person who overeats at a party and then

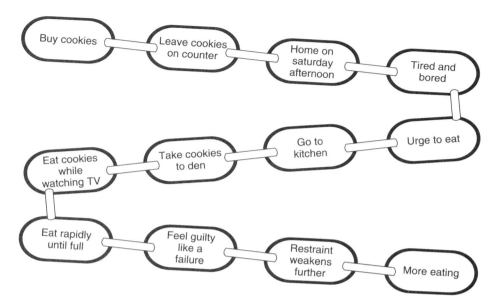

Figure 44.1. A behavior chain. The figure presents an example of a behavior chain, illustrating how one behavior, linked to another, can contribute to an overeating episode. What appears to be an unexpected dietary lapse can be traced to a whole series of small decisions and behaviors. The behavior chain also reveals where the individual can intervene in the future to prevent unwanted eating. Thus, the individual might avoid bringing cookies into the house or at least store them out of sight to reduce impulse eating. Reprinted with permission from Brownell 2004.

tells himself that he has blown his diet (antecedent) may proceed to eat triple the original amount (consequence) because of feelings of disgust and despair (Brownell 2004). Cognitive therapy is used in behavioral treatment to teach a patient to correct maladaptive thinking so these thoughts do not lead to overeating or inactivity (Foster 2002; Wadden and Foster 2000). In the above example, the person might be encouraged to think of overeating as a momentary slip that can be corrected during the next meal by reducing calorie intake or by increasing exercise to expend the extra calories.

Consequences determine whether behaviors are repeated (Foster 2002; Skinner 1938). Behaviors, such as eating favorite foods, that are reinforcing (i.e., provide positive consequences) are likely to be repeated (Foster 2002). Those that yield negative effects, such as exercising to exhaustion, are unlikely to be practiced regularly (Foster 2002; Skinner 1938). For example, if a sedentary person begins a weight-management program by trying to run 4 miles a day, s/he is likely to experience soreness and other discomfort that may lead to abandonment of exercise all together. If the person had begun by walking 10 minutes per day, s/he might have experienced more positive consequences (i.e., a sense of accomplishment) and been motivated to continue exercising.

Characteristics

Behavioral treatment has three distinctive characteristics (Wadden and Foster 2000). First, it is goal-oriented. Goals are specified in clear and measurable terms. This is true whether the goal is increasing physical activity by 10 minutes per day, reducing calorie intake by 3,500 kcal/wk, or rehearsing at least one positive self-statement per day.

Second, treatment is process-oriented (Wadden and Foster 2000). In addition to helping people decide what they want to accomplish, it helps them identify how to do so. Patients identify the specific behavior they wish to adopt and then identify exactly when, where, how, and with whom they will practice the new behavior. In cases in which adopting the new behavior proves difficult, attention is devoted to examining new strategies or to problem-solving barriers. This skill-building philosophy views weight management as a set of skills to be learned rather than as willpower to be enhanced.

Third, behavioral treatment advocates small successive changes rather than large abrupt ones (Wadden and Foster 2000). This is based on the learning principle of *shaping,* which advocates making small incremental steps toward the achievement of complex goals. Making small changes provides patients successful experiences on which to build, rather than attempting drastic changes, which are difficult to maintain.

COMPONENTS AND STRUCTURE OF BEHAVIORAL TREATMENT

Forty years of research on the behavioral treatment of obesity have yielded a comprehensive approach that encompasses several components, including self-monitoring, stimulus control, problem solving, cognitive restructuring, and relapse prevention (Wadden, Crerand, and Brock 2005). These techniques have been summarized in several manuals, including the LEARN Program for Weight Management (Brownell 2004). Given the availability of such manuals and reviews of the literature (Wing 1998, 2002; Wadden et al. 2005a), this section will review only three components of behavioral treatment: self-monitoring, cognitive restructuring, and stimulus control.

Self-Monitoring

Self-monitoring (i.e., recording one's behavior) is perhaps the most important component of behavioral weight loss treatment (Brownell 2004; Wing 2002). Patients are taught to keep detailed records of their food intake, physical activity, and weight throughout treatment. Record keeping focuses on accuracy and thoroughness (i.e., noting everything that is consumed) rather than spelling or grammar.

In the initial weeks, patients record daily the types, amounts, and caloric value of foods eaten. Equipped with this information, they then work to reduce hidden sources of fat and sugar in their diet and, thus, decrease their energy intake by approximately 500–1,000 kcal/d. Calorie reduction of this amount should result in a weight loss of 0.5 to 1.0 kg per week. Self-monitoring records often reveal patterns of which patients were previously unaware, such as consuming excess calories from high-sugar sodas or juices.

Record keeping is increased over time to include information about times, places, and feelings associated with eating. The records also yield targets for intervention, as suggested by the behavior chain in figure 44.1 (Brownell 2004). Patterns are examined to determine the precipitants of inappropriate eating and to plan interventions. Several studies have demonstrated that self-monitoring is associated with successful long-term weight control (Sbrocco, Nedegaard, Stone, and Lewis 1999; Latner et al. 2000; Foster, Wadden, Phelan, Sarwer, and Sanderson 2001; Wadden et al. 2005b). We note that record keeping decreases, but does not eliminate, patients' tendencies to underestimate their caloric intake, often by as much as 40 percent to 50 percent per day (Lichtman et al. 1992; Prentice, Black, Coward, and Cole 1996).

Cognitive Restructuring

Cognitive restructuring teaches patients to modify irrational thoughts that frequently undermine weight control efforts (Wing 1998; Brownell 2004). Thoughts typically fall into one of three categories: (1) the impossibility of successful weight control (in view of previous failed attempts); (2) unrealistic eating and weight loss goals; and (3) self-criticism in response to overeating or gaining weight (Brownell 2004; Wadden et al. 2005a). Patients are taught to recognize their negative thoughts (through self-monitoring) and then challenge and correct them with more rational, reality-based thoughts (Brownell 2004). A common cognitive distortion involves catastrophizing, as captured by the statement, "I'm already 10 minutes late for my exercise class, I may as well skip exercising today." A more rational response would be, "I'm only a few minutes late. If I hurry, I might be able to warm up and then catch the last half of class." Cognitive restructuring is vital to helping patients maintain newly developed eating and activity habits in the face of chronic stressors and life events.

Stimulus Control

Stimulus control techniques help patients manage cues associated with overeating or eating in the absence of hunger (Wing 1998; Brownell 2004). Patients are taught to control stimuli by avoiding high-risk venues such as fast food restaurants, all-you-can-eat buffets, convenience stores, and certain aisles of the grocery store. Reducing exposure to problem foods is likely to reduce their consumption. Shopping from a list also aids this effort. Other strategies, such as not keeping high-fat foods in the home, storing tempting items out of sight, serving modest portion sizes, keeping serving dishes off the table, and clearing plates immediately after eating (to decrease nibbling on leftovers), may help to reduce inappropriate eating (Brownell 2004). All of these interventions support the importance of controlling the food environment and overeating cues. They illustrate the belief of "out of sight, out of mind, out of mouth." Despite their commonsense appeal, there have been no specific studies of stimulus control techniques. These techniques only have been tested as part of the larger behavioral package.

STRUCTURE OF TREATMENT

Behavioral treatment typically is provided weekly for an initial period of 16 to 26 weeks (Wing 2002; Wadden et al. 2005a). This time-limited approach provides a clear starting and finishing point that helps patients pace their efforts. In hospital- and university-based clinics, therapy often is provided to groups of 10 to 20 individuals (during 60- to 90-minute sessions) by registered dietitians, behavioral psychologists, or related health professionals. Group sessions provide a combination of social support and a dose of healthy competition. A well-controlled study found that group treatment induced a larger initial weight loss (approximately 2 kg) than did individual treatment (Renjilian et al. 2001). This held true even for patients who indicated that they preferred individual treatment but were randomly assigned to receive group care (Renjilian et al. 2001). These individuals lost more weight than people who preferred and received individual treatment. Group treatment also is more cost-effective than individual care (Renjilian et al. 2001).

Treatment sessions are conducted using a structured curriculum, as provided by the LEARN program (Brownell 2004) or the Diabetes Prevention Program (Knowler et al. 2002). At each session, the practitioner reviews patients' completed food and activity records, helps them generate strategies to cope with problems identified, and introduces new behavioral strategies for weight loss. Lecturing is held to a minimum in favor of participants asking questions or discussing their progress in completing assignments. Visits conclude with discussion of behavioral assignments for the coming week.

OUTCOMES OF BEHAVIORAL TREATMENT OF OBESITY

Behavior therapy was introduced in the treatment of obesity in 1967. Stuart treated eight overweight women who lost an average of 17 kg over 12 months

Table 44.1. **Summary of Behavior Therapy for Obesity**

	1974	1985–1987	1991–1995	1996–2002 *
Number of studies	15	13	5	9
Sample size	53.1	71.6	30.2	28.0
Initial weight (kg)	73.4	87.2	94.9	92.2
Length of treatment (wk)	8.4	15.6	22.2	31.4
Weight loss (kg)	3.8	8.4	8.5	10.7
Loss per week (kg)	0.5	0.5	0.4	0.4
Attrition (percent)	11.4	13.8	18.5	21.2
Length of follow-up (wk)	15.1	48.3	47.7	41.8
Loss at follow-up (kg)	4.0	5.3	5.9	7.2

All studies sampled were published in the following four journals: *Addictive Behaviors, Behavior Therapy, Behavior Research and Therapy, and Journal of Consulting and Clinical Psychology.* All values, except for number of studies, are weighted means; thus, studies with larger sample sizes had a greater impact on mean values than did studies with smaller sample sizes. Table reprinted from Wadden and Butryn 2003.

*Studies included in 1996–2002 sample are found in Sbrocco et al. 1999; Meyers, Graves, Whelan, and Barclay 1996; Perri, Martin, Leermakers, Sears, and Notelovitz 1997; Wadden et al. 1997; Fuller, Perri, Leermakers, and Guyer 1998; Harvey-Berino 1998; Wing and Jeffery 1999; Perri et al. 2001; Ramirez and Rosen 2001; Wadden and Butryn 2003.

of treatment. Stuart's report spawned hundreds of subsequent studies. Table 44.1 summarizes the results of behavioral treatment from 1974 to 2002, as determined from randomized controlled trials published in four journals: *Addictive Behaviors, Behavior Research and Therapy, Behavior Therapy*, and *Journal of Consulting and Clinical Psychology*. Only studies representative of standard behavioral treatment are included in the table (Sbrocco et al. 1999; Meyers, Graves, Whelan, and Barclay 1996; Perri, Martin, Leermakers, Sears, and Notelovitz 1997; Wadden et al. 1997; Fuller, Perri, Leermakers, and Guyer 1998; Harvey-Berino 1998; Wing and Jeffery 1999; Perri et al. 2001; Ramirez and Rosen 2001; Wadden and Butryn 2003). All interventions prescribed a diet that provided at least 900 kcal/d.

Examination of early (i.e., 1974) and more recent (1996–2002) studies shows that weight losses have increased almost threefold over the past 40 years as treatment duration has increased by the same amount (Sbrocco et al. 1999; Meyers et al. 1996; Perri et al. 1997; Wadden et al. 1997; Fuller et al. 1998; Harvey-Berino 1998; Wing and Jeffery 1999; Perri et al. 2001; Ramirez and Rosen 2001; Wadden and Butryn 2003). Studies conducted between 1996 and 2002 show that patients treated with a comprehensive group behavioral approach lose approximately 10.7 kg (about 10 percent of initial weight) in 30 weeks of treatment. In addition, about 80 percent of patients who begin treatment complete it (Sbrocco et al. 1999; Meyers et al. 1996; Perri et al. 1997; Wadden et al. 1997; Fuller et al. 1998; Harvey-Berino 1998; Wing and Jeffery 1999; Perri et al. 2001; Ramirez and Rosen 2001; Wadden and Butryn 2003). Thus, behavior therapy yields very favorable results as judged by the criteria for success (i.e., a 5–10 percent reduction in initial weight) proposed by the World Health Organization (WHO 1998; Wadden, Brownell, and Foster 2002).

Improving Short-Term Results of Behavioral Treatment

Women in behavioral weight loss programs usually are prescribed a 1,200 to 1,500 kcal/d diet of conventional foods and men a diet of 1,500 to 1,800 kcal/d. Dietary recommendations are based on the Food Guide Pyramid and limit fat to no more than 30 percent of total calories (with no more than 10 percent from saturated fat) (Wadden et al. 2005a). Patients, however, are encouraged to eat foods they like (including sweets and salty foods) to avoid feeling deprived. Calorie counting is critical to this approach; it allows patients to eat desired foods, provided the selections fall within the daily calorie allotment.

Although behavioral treatment recommends modest and flexible dietary changes that can be maintained long-term, the behavioral approach can be used with a variety of dietary interventions. This section briefly describes the use of more structured or restrictive diets that have been used to induce larger initial weight losses (i.e., greater than 10 percent of initial weight).

Very Low Calorie Diets

Early studies examined the use of very low calorie diets (VLCD) that provided 400 to 800 kcal/d. These diets induced losses nearly twice as large as those produced by 1,200–1,500 kcal/d diets consisting of conventional foods. However, a recent meta-analysis revealed that there were no long-term (1 year or more) differences in weight loss between patients treated by the two approaches because of greater regain observed in those treated by a VLCD (Gilden Tsai and Wadden 2006). This shortcoming, combined with the high expense of VLCDs, has resulted in the decreased use of this approach.

Meal Replacements

VLCDs have been replaced by 1,000–1,500 kcal/d diets that combine two servings or more of a liquid meal replacement with a meal of conventional foods. A study by Ditschuneit et al. found that patients who replaced two meals and two snacks a day with a liquid supplement (e.g., SlimFast) lost 8 percent of initial weight during 3 months of treatment, compared with a loss of only 1.5 percent for patients who were prescribed the same number of calories (i.e., 1,200–1,500 kcal) but who consumed a self-selected diet of conventional foods (1999). Patients who continued to replace one meal and one snack per day maintained a loss of 11 percent at 27 months and 8 percent at 51 months (Flechtner-Mors, Ditschuneit, Johnson, Suchard, and Adler 2000).

Meal replacements provide patients a fixed amount of food with a known calorie content. Obese individuals typically underestimate their calorie intake by 40 percent to 50 percent when consuming a diet of conventional foods (Lichtman et al. 1992) because of difficulty in estimating portion size, macronutrient composition, and calorie content. Meal replacements help patients meet their calorie goals. They also simplify food choices, require little preparation, and allow dieters to avoid contact with problem foods. This may increase patients' adherence to their targeted calorie goals.

Portion-Controlled Diets

Portion-controlled servings of conventional foods also improve the induction of weight loss. Patients in one study, for example, who were prescribed a diet of 1,000 kcal/d and were provided foods for five breakfasts and dinners per week lost significantly more weight at 6 and 18 months than did people who were prescribed the same number of calories but consumed a diet of self-selected foods (Jeffery, Wing, Thorson, and Burton 1993). Further, a study by Wing et al. demonstrated that the provision of structured meal plans resulted in larger weight losses than did behavioral treatment without meal plans (1996). Weight losses were similar regardless of whether foods for structured meal plans were provided to participants or they were required to purchase them. Thus, specifying the foods and amounts patients should eat eliminates guesswork and improves weight loss outcomes.

IMPROVING LONG-TERM RESULTS OF BEHAVIORAL TREATMENT

Weight regain remains an inevitable challenge for all weight loss interventions. As shown in table 44.1, patients treated by behavior therapy for 20–30 weeks typically regain about 30 percent-35 percent of their lost weight in the year following treatment. Weight regain slows after the first year, but by five years, 50 percent or more of patients are likely to have returned to their baseline weight (Perri and Corsica 2002). These results illustrate the need for long-term treatment to prevent weight regain. Perri and Corsica have studied several weight management strategies that include continued patient-provider contact, relapse prevention training, social support, and exercise (2002). Long-term patient-provider contact can be achieved in several ways, including on-site visits, telephone, Internet, and e-mail contact.

LONG-TERM ON-SITE TREATMENT

Numerous studies have shown the benefits of patients continuing to attend weight maintenance sessions after completing the initial phase of weight loss (Perri and Corsica 2002; Perri et al. 1988). These sessions provide patients the social support and motivation needed to continue to practice weight control skills. Perri and colleagues, for example, found that individuals who attended every-other-week group maintenance sessions for the year following weight reduction maintained 13.0 kg of their 13.2 kg end-of-treatment weight loss, whereas those who did not receive such therapy maintained only 5.7 kg of a 10.8 kg loss (1988). In reviewing 13 studies on this topic, Perri and Corsica found that patients who received long-term treatment, which averaged 41 sessions over 54 weeks, maintained 10.3 kg of their initial 10.7 kg weight loss (2002). Figure 44.2 illustrates the difference in weight loss produced by standard and long-term treatment, as determined from three randomized trials (Perri et al. 1986; Perri et al. 1988; Perri et al. 2001) in which all participants received behavioral weight control for the first 20 weeks. Thereafter, half the patients continued to have every-other-week treatment for one year, while the other half received no further care.

The figure shows a clear limitation of long-term behavioral treatment in that it appears only to delay rather than to prevent weight regain. Patients maintain their

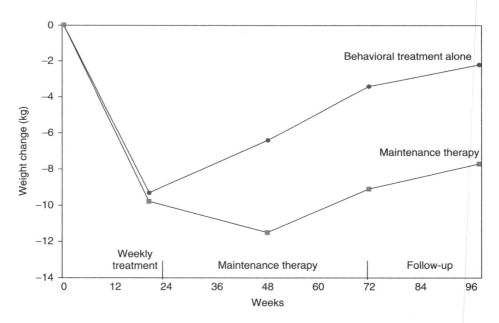

Figure 44.2. Long-term results of standard behavioral treatment with or without bi-weekly maintenance therapy. Data are taken from references Perri et al. 2001; Perri et al. 1988; Perri et al. 1986.
Note: Data for week 96 are available for Perri and colleagues' studies only (1986, 1988).

full end-of-treatment weight loss as long as they participate in bi-weekly maintenance sessions. In fact, they lose additional weight during the first 6 months of extended treatment but regain the additional loss during the second 6 months of therapy. Weight gain continues with the termination of maintenance therapy. The optimal frequency of maintenance therapy is not known. Patients, however, eventually tire of attending sessions twice monthly (and 50 percent may drop out) (Wadden, Foster, and Letizia 1994; Wing 1998), but monthly visits do not appear to be sufficient to maintain full end-of-treatment weight loss (Jeffery et al. 1993).

Telephone and Mail Contact

Long-term contact also may be provided by telephone or mail, which may be more convenient than on-site visits. Perri and colleagues (1984) found that participants who received mail and phone contact for 24 weeks following 15 weeks of on-site treatment maintained significantly greater losses (9.2 kg at the end of treatment and 10.3 kg one year after treatment concluded) than did those who received no further contact (8.5 kg at the end of treatment and 2.9 kg one year later). Although phone contact can be an effective tool for maintaining lost weight, maintaining the same contact person is an important component of its effectiveness. When scheduling phone calls, the same therapist optimally should contact the patient on each occasion. A study in which patients were contacted by staff members unknown to them failed to produce weight maintenance results superior to those of a no-contact group (Wing, Jeffery, Hellerstedt, and Burton 1996).

INTERNET AND E-MAIL

Recent studies indicate that the Internet and e-mail can be used to provide both short- and long-term behavioral treatment. A study by Tate and colleagues (2001) assigned participants to one of two 6-month weight loss programs delivered over the Internet: (1) an education intervention that provided online resources for weight control; or (2) a behavior therapy intervention that provided Internet resources in addition to 24 weekly lessons conducted by e-mail, weekly submission of self-monitoring food diaries, and an online bulletin board. The behavior therapy participants lost significantly more weight at 6 months than participants in the education group (4.1 kg vs. 1.6 kg, respectively). Tate and colleagues replicated (2003) these results in a one-year study that revealed greater weight losses for those in the Internet plus behavioral counseling group than those in the Internet only group (4.4 kg vs. 2.0 kg, respectively).

Several studies have examined the use of the Internet as a means of facilitating weight maintenance. Harvey-Berino and colleagues (2004) randomly assigned patients to one of three 22-week maintenance programs: (1) an on-site therapist-led program; 2) an Internet therapist-led program; or (3) a control condition.

There were no significant differences among the three maintenance groups in total weight loss (7.6 kg vs. 5.5 kg vs. 5.1 kg, respectively). However, participants in the on-site program were more satisfied with their treatment and attended more sessions than those in the Internet program. A more recent study by Wing et al. investigated weight maintenance in patients who had lost a mean of 19.3 kg in the previous two years (2006). Patients were assigned to one of three groups: (1) a control group that received quarterly newsletters; (2) a group that received face-to-face behavioral counseling; or (3) a group that received Internet-based weight loss education. The face-to-face group regained significantly less weight than both the Internet and control groups (2.5 kg vs. 4.7 kg vs. 4.9 kg, respectively).

Internet-delivered interventions, for both the induction and maintenance of weight loss, currently are not as effective as traditional face-to-face behavioral interventions. Nonetheless, Internet-based programs do induce clinically significant weight losses and potentially could be provided to the millions of overweight and obese individuals who do not have access to behavioral weight control, as delivered at academic medical centers. Further research is likely to improve upon these initial very promising findings.

EXERCISE

Increased physical activity is the single best predictor of weight loss maintenance (Wadden 1995). Numerous studies have shown that persons who continue to exercise regularly, after losing weight, are more likely to keep the weight off than are individuals who lapse in their physical activity (Wadden et al. 1997, 2003; Blair and Leermakers 2002). Additional studies have revealed the importance of high levels of activity, as demonstrated in a recent randomized trial by Jeffery et al. (2003).

Patients in a high-activity group were instructed to expend 2,500 kcal/wk, while those in a low-activity group were prescribed a goal of 1,000 kcal/wk. As shown in figure 44.3, weight losses of the two treatment conditions did not differ significantly at the end of 6 months, during which participants attended weekly group meetings. Participants in the high-activity group, however, maintained their losses significantly better at both the 12- and 18-month follow-up assessments than did patients in the low-activity group. Jakicic and colleagues (1999) similarly found that obese individuals who exercised 200 or more minutes per week maintained significantly greater weight losses at 18 months than persons who exercised less than 150 minutes per week.

Long- versus Short-bout Activity

Jakicic et al. (1995) have investigated the effects of prescribing exercise in multiple short bouts rather than a single long bout to improve exercise adherence and

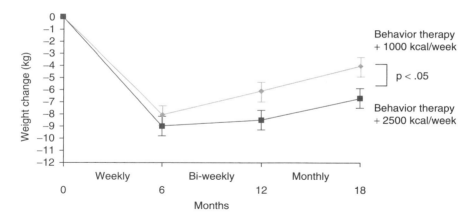

Figure 44.3. Short and long-term weight losses for participants assigned to
low-intensity exercise (i.e., 1,000 kcal/week) or high intensity exercise
(i.e., 2,500 kcal/week). Data are taken from Jeffery et al. 2003.

weight loss. Results revealed a trend in favor of multiple short bouts of activity. Participants who completed 40 minutes of daily activity in 10-minute bouts exercised more days per week (87.3 vs. 69.1 days over 20 weeks) and lost more weight than those who completed their exercise sessions in one 40-minute bout (8.9 kg vs. 6.4 kg, respectively). These results, however, were not replicated in an 18-month follow-up study (1999). Nonetheless, the finding that multiple short bouts of activity are as effective as one long bout should facilitate patients' efforts to increase their activity. They do not need to set aside a 30- to 60-minute block of time in which to "exercise." Several brief walks during the day are equally effective for weight loss and maintenance.

Programmed vs. Lifestyle Activity

Individuals can increase their energy expenditure in two ways: programmed and lifestyle activity. Programmed activity (e.g., jogging, biking, aerobics) is planned and completed in a discrete period of time (i.e., 30–60 min intervals), usually at a relatively high level of intensity (i.e., 60–80 percent of maximum heart rate). Lifestyle activity, by contrast, involves increasing energy expenditure while completing everyday tasks. Examples include parking farther away from an entrance, taking the stairs instead of the elevator, and walking or biking to work rather than driving. Andersen and colleagues (2002) compared the effects of programmed and lifestyle activity in women. Results revealed that both types of activity, when combined with a 1,200 kcal/d diet, produced a weight loss of approximately 8 kg in 16 weeks. Participants in the lifestyle activity group tended to maintain their weight losses better than those in the programmed-exercise group, although the difference was not statistically significant. These results were promising. Future studies are needed to determine if these results are replicable in men and in larger samples of individuals.

OUTCOMES OF BEHAVIORAL OBESITY
TREATMENT IN ETHNIC MINORITIES

The weight-loss studies summarized in this chapter focused primarily on Caucasian participants. However, ethnic minorities, particular African American women, have higher rates of obesity and its associated health complications (Ogden et al. 2006; Lethbridge-Cejku, Schiller, and Bernadel 2004). When treated with the same interventions as their Caucasian counterparts, ethnic minorities typically have suboptimal outcomes. Minority participants tend to begin treatment at a heavier weight, lose less weight, and have higher rates of attrition than their majority counterparts (Kumanyika, Obarzanek, Stevens, Hebert, and Whelton 1991; Bronner and Boyington 2002). Most ethnic comparisons have been limited to African American versus Caucasian samples. Table 44.2 summarizes the results of several such studies and shows that African Americans generally lost less weight at the end of treatment and regained more than did Caucasians.

Potential Factors Related to Differences in Treatment Outcomes

Disparities in obesity outcomes are not well understood but have been attributed to several possible factors. These include biological, socioeconomical, and psychosocial influences. For instance, investigators have suggested that ethnic differences in the presence of a "thrifty gene" could account for variations in body fat composition and weight loss. This hypothesis asserts that some minority groups (Native Americans, Africans, Pacific Islanders, and Hispanics) possess a gene variant that allows for fat/energy storage and conservation during times of food scarcity (Neel 1999). Several studies have identified ethnic differences in weight-related genotypes (i.e., genotype is the GNB3 825T) (Naber, Erbel, and Siffert 2003), but more research is needed.

Another hypothesis has proposed that ethnic differences in metabolic rate may account for some of the variance in obesity prevalence rates. Foster et al. (1997) and Jakicic and Wing (1998) both found that obese African American females had lower resting metabolic rates (RMR) than did obese Caucasian females. A low RMR may contribute to weight gain, as well as impair efforts to lose weight (Foster, Wadden, Swain, Anderson, and Vogt 1999).

Other studies have demonstrated a link between socioeconomic status (SES) and obesity (see chapter 16 by McLaren in this volume). Obesity is more common among those of low SES, and the majority of those who fall into lower income levels tend to be ethnic minorities (Swinburn and Egger 2004). Further, many low SES communities lack supermarkets or neighborhood physical fitness facilities, but have a ubiquitous supply of fast food restaurants and convenience stores that

Table 44.2. **Ethnic Comparison of Weight Loss Outcomes in Controlled Trials**

Study	Number of Subjects	Baseline Weight (kg)	Short-term Weight Loss† Weeks 22–26	Long-term Weight Loss Months 12–18	Long-term Weight Loss Months 36
Darga et al. (1994)					
African Americans	125	112	−13.3**		
Whites	705	110	−18.8		
Yanovski et al. (1994)					
African Americans	12	104 to 114	13.7%**		
Whites	26	104 to 114	21.4%		
Wing and Anglin (1996)					
African Americans	16	106.4	12.5	7.1*	
Whites	59	106.9	15.6	13.9	
Foster et al. (1999)					
African Americans	24	97.8	13.4*		
Whites	85	95.1	16.4		
Stevens et al. (2001)					
African Americans	101	84.1 to 98.9	2.3*	.02*	+.07
Whites	442	84.1 to 98.9	4.9	2.5	.04
Kumanyika et al. (2002)					
African Americans	164	89.1	2.7**		2.0**
Whites	421	86.9	5.9		4.9
Weisner et al. (2002)					
African Americans	23	78.2	12.6		
Whites	23	79.1	13.1		

† Unless otherwise noted, weight losses are in kg.
* Difference between African American and Whites significant at $p < .05$.
** Difference between African American and Whites significant at $p < .01$
Table adapted from Kumanyika, 2003.

offer unhealthy food selections (Robert and Reither 2004). For example, affluent neighborhoods have four times the number of supermarkets, which provide ample fresh fruit and vegetables, than do impoverished communities (Morland, Wing, and Diez-Roux 2002). Kumanyika (2004) has asserted that those with the "least latitude in personal choices have the greatest lifestyle constraints." Thus, limited resources in an environment plagued by inexpensive, unhealthy foods or unsafe environments in which to exercise make it difficult for many low SES, ethnic families to practice appropriate weight control behaviors.

Research also has suggested that ethnic differences in body image may contribute to excess weight in some minorities. African Americans, for example, appear to be more comfortable with a larger body size and participate in fewer weight-restraining practices than do Caucasians (Gluck and Geliebter 2002; Jackson and McGill 1996; Klesges, DeBon, and Meyers 1996). Although African Americans' preferences for a larger body size may protect them against the development of poor body-esteem and eating disorders, these preferences also may promote cultural norms that increase risk for overweight and obesity (Celio, Zabinski, and Wilfley 2002).

Further research clearly is needed to determine the contribution of SES, cultural norms, and other factors to obesity in ethnic minorities. Several researchers have suggested culture-specific recommendations to improve weight management in these individuals.

Suggestions to Improve Treatment Outcomes in Ethnic Minority Populations

Kumanyika has summarized the recommendations of the National Heart Lung and Blood Institute (NHLBI) for adapting weight-loss programs to diverse populations (1997, 1998, 2002). She has cautioned that the standardization of treatment for ethnic minorities is difficult because of within-group variability and the vast overlap of subcultures within the larger society. A full discussion of these issues is provided by other sources, and, thus, they are only briefly addressed in this chapter.

Recommendations for tailoring treatments to diverse populations include consideration of the setting, method, and manner of treatment delivery. Programs should provide a setting that is familiar and accessible to participants, such as community, recreation, or religious centers. The immediate environment should be socially comfortable and communal. Program materials must be adapted to the language, reading level, communication style, knowledge base, and experiences of participants. Content and examples should reflect cultural norms and values of the population of study.

Interventions also need to anticipate barriers to adhering to treatment. For example, weight-loss protocols that include liquid meal replacements should be prepared to offer alternative treatments, as many African Americans are lactose intolerant (Kiple and Himmelsteib King 1982). Programs should strive to include staff and treatment providers who are culturally competent and self-aware. This competence and self-awareness will translate into the development and delivery of treatment that takes in account the unique factors related to weight loss in ethnic minority populations. Research is needed to assess the benefits of culturally tailored interventions as compared with traditional behavioral weight control.

SUMMARY AND CONCLUSIONS

This chapter has shown that behavioral treatment is effective in inducing weight loss and improving health-related complications of obesity. Further research is now needed to make this treatment more accessible to the millions of Americans who require it and to tailor treatment to the needs of ethnic minorities. Ultimately, far greater effort and resources must be devoted to preventing obesity in both children and adults. Treatment alone is no match for the epidemic of obesity that threatens the United States and other nations.

ACKNOWLEDGEMENTS

....

Preparation of this chapter was supported, in part, by National Institutes of Health grants U01-DK57135 and DK065018.

REFERENCES

....

Andersen, R. E., S. C. Franckowiak, S. J. Bartlett, and K. R. Fontaine. 2002. "Physiologic Changes after Diet Combined with Structured Aerobic Exercise or Lifestyle Activity." *Metabolism* 51: 1528–1533.

Beck, A. T. 1976. *Cognitive Therapy and the Emotional Disorder*. New York: International Universities Press.

Blackburn, G. L. 1995. "Effect of Degree of Weight Loss on Health Benefits." *Obesity Research* 3: 211S–216S.

Blair, S. N., and E. A. Leermakers. 2002. "Exercise and Weight Management." In *Handbook of Obesity Treatment*, eds. T. Wadden and A. Stunkard, 283–300. New York: Guilford Press.

Bronner, Y., and J. E. Boyington. 2002. "Developing Weight Loss Interventions for African-American Women: Elements of Successful Models." *Journal of the National Medical Association* 94: 224–235.

Brownell, K. D. 2004. *The LEARN Program for Weight Management*. 10th ed. Dallas: American Health Publishing.

Celio, A. A., M. F. Zabinski, and D. E. Wilfley. 2002. "African American Body Images."*In Body Image: A Handbook of Theory, Research, and Clinical Practice*. eds. T. F. Cash and T. Pruzinsky, 234–242. New York: Guilford Press.

Darga, L. L., J. H. Holden, S. M. Olson, and C. P. Lucas. 1994. "Comparison of Cardiovascular Risk Factors in Obese Blacks and Whites." *Obesity Research* 2: 239–245.

Ditschuneit, H. H., M. Flechtner-Mors, T. D. Johnson, and G. Adler. 1999. "Metabolic and Weight-Loss Effects of a Long-Term Dietary Intervention in Obese Patients." *American Journal of Clinical Nutrition* 69: 198–204.

Flechtner-Mors, M., H. H. Ditschuneit, T. D. Johnson, M. A. Suchard, and G. Adler. 2000. "Metabolic and Weight Loss Effects of Long-Term Dietary Intervention in Obese Patients: Four-Year Results." *Obesity Research* 8: 399–402.

Foster, G. D. 2002. "Goals and Strategies to Improve Behavior-Change Effectiveness." In *Evaluation and Management of Obesity*, eds. D. Bessesen and R. Kushner, 29–32. Philadelphia: Hanley & Belfus.

Foster, G. D., T. A. Wadden, S. Phelan, D. B. Sarwer, and R. S. Sanderson. 2001. "Obese Patients' Perceptions of Treatment Outcomes and the Factors That Influence Them." *Archives of Internal Medicine* 161: 2133–2139.

Foster, G. D., T. A. Wadden, R. M. Swain, D. A. Anderson, and R. A. Vogt. 1999. "Changes in Resting Energy Expenditure after Weight Loss in Obese African American and White Women." *American Journal of Clinical Nutrition* 69: 13–17.

Foster, G. D., T. A. Wadden, and R. A. Vogt. 1997. "Resting Energy Expenditure in Obese African American and Caucasian Women." *Obesity Research* 5: 1–8.

Fuller, P. R., M. G. Perri, E. A. Leermakers, and L. K. Guyer. 1998. "Effects of a Personalized System of Skill Acquisition and an Educational Program in the Treatment of Obesity." *Addictive Behaviors* 23(1): 97–100.

Gilden Tsai, A., and T. A. Wadden. 2006. "The Evolution of Very-Low-Calorie Diets: An Update and Meta-Analysis." *Obesity* 14: 1283–1293.

Gluck, M. E., and A. Geliebter. 2002. "Racial/ethnic Differences in Body Image and Eating Behaviors." *Eating Behaviors* 3: 143–151.

Harvey-Berino, J. 1998. "Changing Health Behavior via Telecommunications Technology: Using Interactive Television to Treat Obesity." *Behavior Therapy* 29: 505–519.

Harvey-Berino, J., S. Pintauro, P. Buzzell, and E. C. Gold. 2004. "Effect of Internet Support on the Long-Term Maintenance of Weight Loss." *Obesity Research* 12: 320–329.

Hebebrand, J., C. Sommerlad, F. Geller, T. Gorg, and A. Hinney. 2001. "The Genetics of Obesity: Practical Implications." *International Journal of Obesity and Related Metabolic Disorders* 25(Supp. 1): S10–18.

Jackson, L. A., and O. D. McGill. 1996. "Body Type Preferences and Body Characteristics Associated with Attractive and Unattractive Bodies by African Americans and Anglo Americans." *Sex Roles* 35: 295–307.

Jakicic, J. M., and R. R. Wing. 1998. "Differences in Resting Energy Expenditure in African-American vs Caucasian Overweight Females." *International Journal of Obesity and Related Metabolic Disorders*: 22: 236–242.

Jakicic, J. M., R. R. Wing, B. A. Butler, and R. J. Robertson. 1995. "Prescribing Exercise in Multiple Short Bouts versus One Continuous Bout: Effects on Adherence, Cardiorespiratory Fitness, and Weight Loss in Overweight Women." *International Journal of Obesity and Related Metabolic Disorders* 19: 893–901.

Jakicic, J. M., C. Winters, W. Lang, and R. R. Wing. 1999. "Effects of Intermittent Exercise and Use of Home Exercise Equipment on Adherence, Weight Loss, and Fitness in Overweight Women: A Randomized Trial." *Journal of the American Medical Association* 282: 1554–1560.

Jeffery, R. W., R. R. Wing, C. Thorson, and L. R. Burton. 1993. "Strengthening Behavioral Interventions for Weight Loss: A Randomized Trial of Food Provision and Monetary Incentives." *Journal of Consulting and Clinical Psychology* 61: 1038–1045.

Jeffery, R. W., R. R. Wing, N., E., Sherwood, and D. F. Tate. 2003. "Physical Activity and Weight Loss: Does Prescribing Higher Physical Activity Goals Improve Outcome?" *American Journal of Clinical Nutrition* 78: 684–689.

Keesey, R. E. 1986. "A Set-Point Theory of Obesity." In. *Handbook of Eating Disorders: Physiology, Psychology, and Treatment of Obesity, Anorexia, and Bulimia*, eds. K. D. Brownell and J. P. Foreyt, 63–87. New York: Basic Books.

Kiple, K., and V. Himmelsteib King. 1982. *Another Dimension to the Black Diaspora: Diet, Disease, and Racism*. New York: Cambridge University Press.

Klesges, R. C., M. DeBon, and A. Meyers. 1996. "Obesity in African American women: Epidemiology, Determinants, and Treatment Issues." In *Body Image, Eating Disorders, and Obesity: An Integrative Guide for Assessment and Treatment*, ed. J. K. Thompson, 461–477. Washington, DC: American Psychological Association.

Knowler, W. C., E. Barrett-Connor, S. E. Fowler, et al. 2002. "Reduction in the Incidence of Type 2 Diabetes with Lifestyle Intervention or Metformin." *New England Journal of Medicine* 346: 393–403.

Kumanyika, S. 2004. "Restyling Our Lives to Reduce Cardiovascular Disease Risk: What Will It Take?" *Ethnicty and Disease* 14: 185–188.

Kumanyika, S. K. 1998. "Cultural Differences as Influences on Approaches to Obesity Treatment." In *Handbook of Obesity: Clinical Applications*, 2nd ed., eds. G. A. Bray and C. Bouchard, 45–67. New York: Marcel Dekker.

Kumanyika, S. K. 2002. "Obesity Treatment in Minorities." In *Handbook of Obesity Treatment*, eds. T. Wadden and A. Stunkard, 416–448. New York: Guilford Press.

Kumanyika, S. K., M. A. Espeland, J. L. Bahnson, et al. 2002. "Ethnic Comparison of Weight Loss in the Trial of Nonpharmacologic Interventions in the Elderly." *Obesity Research* 10: 96–106.

Kumanyika, S. K., C. B. Morssink. 1997. "Cultural Appropriateness of Weight Management Programs." In *Overweight and Weight Management*, ed. S. Dalton, 69–106. Baltimore, MD: Aspen.

Kumanyika, S. K., E. Obarzanek, V. J. Stevens, P. R. Hebert, and P. K. Whelton. 1991. "Weight-loss Experience of Black and White Participants in NHLBI-Sponsored Clinical Trials." *American Journal of Clinical Nutrition* 53: 1631S–1638S.

Latner, J. D., Stunkard, A. J., Wilson, G. T., Jackson, M. L., Zelitch, D. S., and E. Labouvie. 2000. "Effective Long-Term Treatment of Obesity: A Continuing Care Model." *International Journal of Obesity and Related Metabolic Disorders* 24: 893–898.

Lethbridge-Cejku, M., J. S. Schiller, and L. Bernadel L. 2004. "Summary Health Statistics for U.S. Adults: National Health Interview Survey, 2002." *Vital Health Statistics* 10: 1–151.

Lichtman, S. W., K. Pisarska, E. R. Berman, et al. 1992. "Discrepancy between Self-Reported and Actual Caloric Intake and Exercise in Obese Subjects." *New England Journal of Medicine* 327: 1893–1898.

Meyers, A. W., T. J. Graves, J. P. Whelan, and D. R. Barclay. 1996. "An Evaluation of a Television-Delivered Behavioral Weight Loss Program: Are the Ratings Acceptable?" *Journal of Consulting and Clinical Psychology* 64(1): 172–178.

Morland, K., S. Wing, and A. Diez-Roux. 2002. "The Contextual Effect of the Local Food Environment on Residents' Diets: The Atherosclerosis Risk in Communities Study." *American Journal of Public Health* 92: 1761–1767.

Must, A., M. S. Spadano, E. H. Coakley, A. E. Field, G. Colditz, and W. H. Dietz. 1999. "The Disease Burden Associated with Overweight and Obesity. *Journal of the American Medical Association* 282: 1523–1529.

Naber, C. K., R. Erbel, and W. Siffert. 2003. "The G Protein β3 Subunit Gene (GNB3) 825T Allele: A Thrifty Genotype." *Current Genomics*, 4: 337–342.

Neel, J. V. 1999. "The 'Thrifty Genotype' in 1998." *Nutrition Reviews* 57: S2–9.

Ogden, C. L., M. D. Carroll, L. R. Curtin, M. A. McDowell, C. J. Tabak, and K. M. Flegal. 2006. "Prevalence of Overweight and Obesity in the United States, 1999–2004." *Journal of the American Medical Association* 295: 1549–1555.

Perri, M. G., R. M. Shapiro, W. W. Ludwig, C. T. Twentyman, and W. G. McAdoo. 1984. "Maintenance Strategies for the Treatment of Obesity: An Evaluation of Relapse Prevention Training and Posttreatment Contact by Mail and Telephone." *Journal of Consulting and Clinical Psychology* 52: 404–413.

Perri, M. G., and J. A. Corsica. 2002. "Improving Maintenance of Weight Lost in Behavioral Treatment of Obesity." In *Handbook of Obesity treatment* Wadden T, Stunkard A, editors. (pp 357–79). New York: Guilford Press.

Perri, M. G., A. D. Martin, E. A. Leermakers, S. F. Sears, and M. Notelovitz. 1997. "Effects of Group- versus Home-Based Exercise in the Treatment of Obesity." *Journal of Consulting and Clinical Psychology* 65(2): 278–285.

Perri, M. G., W. G. McAdoo, D. A. McAllister, J. B. Lauer, and D. Z. Yancey. 1986. "Enhancing the Efficacy of Behavior Therapy for Obesity: Effects of Aerobic Exercise and a Multicomponent Maintenance Program." *Journal of Consulting and Clinical Psychology* 54: 670–675.

Perri, M. G., D. A. McAllister, J. J. Gange, R. C. Jordan, G. McAdoo, and A. M. Nezu. 1988. "Effects of Four Maintenance Programs on the Long-Term Management of Obesity." *Journal of Consulting and Clinical Psychology* 56: 529–534.

Perri, M. G., A. M. Nezu, W. F. McKelvey, R. L. Shermer, D. A. Renjilian, and B. J. Viegener. 2001. "Relapse Prevention Training and Problem-Solving Therapy in the Long-Term Management of Obesity." *Journal of Consulting and Clinical Psychology* 69: 722–726.

Prentice, A. M., A. E. Black, W. A. Coward, and T. J. Cole. 1996. "Energy Expenditure in Overweight and Obese Adults in Affluent Societies: An Analysis of 319 Doubly-Labeled Water Measurements." *European Journal of Clinical Nutrition* 50: 93–97.

Ramirez, E. M., and J. C. Rosen. 2001. "A Comparison of Weight Control and Weight Control Plus Body Image Therapy for Obese Men and Women." *Journal of Consulting and Clinical Psychology* 69: 440–446.

Renjilian, D. A., M. G. Perri, A. M. Nezu, W. F. McKelvey, R. L. Shermer, and S. D. Anton. 2001. "Individual versus Group Therapy for Obesity: Effects of Matching Participants to Their Treatment Preferences." *Journal of Consulting and Clinical Psychology* 69: 717–721.

Robert, S. A., and E. N. Reither. 2004. "A Multilevel Analysis of Race, Community Disadvantage, and Body Mass Index among Adults in the US." *Social Science and Medicine* 59: 2421–2434.

Sbrocco, T., R. C. Nedegaard, J. M. Stone, and E. L. Lewis. 1999. "Behavioral Choice Treatment Promotes Continuing Weight Loss: Preliminary Results of a Cognitive-Behavioral Decision-Based Treatment for Obesity." *Journal of Consulting and Clinical Psychology* 67: 260–266.

Skinner, B. F. 1938. *The Behavior of Organisms: An Experimental Analysis.* New York: Appleton-Century-Crofts.

Spiegelman, B. M., and J. S. Flier. 2001. "Obesity and the Regulation of Energy Balance." *Cell* 104: 531–543.

Stevens, V. J., E. Obarzanek, N, R. Cook, et al. 2001. "Long-term Weight Loss and Changes in Blood Pressure: Results of the Trials of Hypertension Prevention, Phase II." *Annals of Internal Medicine* 134: 1–11.

Swinburn, B., and G. Egger. 2004. "The Runaway Weight Gain Train: Too Many Accelerators, Not Enough Brakes." *British Medical Journal* 329: 736–739.

Tate, D. F., E. H. Jackvony, and R. R. Wing. 2003. "Effects of Internet Behavioral Counseling on Weight Loss in Adults at Risk for Type 2 Diabetes: A Randomized Trial." *Journal of the American Medical Association* 289: 1833–1836.

Tate, D. F., R. R. Wing, and R. A. Winett. 2001. "Using Internet Technology to Deliver a Behavioral Weight Loss Program." *Journal of the American Medical Association* 285: 1172–1177.

Wadden, T. A. 1995. "Characteristics of Successful Weight Loss Maintainers." In *Obesity Treatment: Establishing Goals, Improving Outcomes, and Reviewing the Research Agenda*, eds. D. B. Allison and F. X. Pi-Sunyer, 103–111. New York: Plenum Press.

Wadden, T. A., R. I. Berkowitz, R. A. Vogt, S. N. Steen, A. J. Stunkard, and G. D. Foster. 1997. "Lifestyle Modification in the Pharmacologic Treatment of Obesity: A Pilot Investigation of a Potential Primary Care Approach." *Obesity Research* 5: 218–226.

Wadden, T. A., R. I. Berkowitz, L. G. Womble, et al. 2005b. "Randomized Trial of Lifestyle Modification and Pharmacotherapy for Obesity." *New England Journal of Medicine* 353(20): 2111–2120.

Wadden, T. A., K. D. Brownell, and G. D. Foster. 2002. "Obesity: Responding to the Global Epidemic." *Journal of Consulting and Clinical Psychology* 70: 510–525.

Wadden, T. A., and M. L. Butryn. 2003. "Behavioral Treatment of Obesity." *Endocrinology Metabolism Clinics of North America* 32: 981–1003.

Wadden, T. A., C. E. Crerand, and J. Brock. 2005a. "Behavioral Treatment of Obesity." In *Obesity: A Guide for Mental Health Professionals,* eds. T. Wadden, A. Stunkard, and R. Berkowitz, 141–150. Philadelphia: Saunders.

Wadden, T. A., and G. D. Foster. 2000. "Behavioral Treatment of Obesity." *Medical Clinics of North America* 84: 441–461.

Wadden, T. A., G. D. Foster, and K. A. Letizia. 1994. "One-year Behavioral Treatment of Obesity: Comparison of Moderate and Severe Caloric Restriction and the Effects of Weight Maintenance Therapy." *Journal of Consulting and Clinical Psychology* 62: 165–171.

Wadden, T. A., B. G. McGuckin, R. A. Rothman, and S. L. Sargent. 2003. "Lifestyle Modification in the Management of Obesity." *Journal of Gastrointestinal Surgery* 7: 452–463.

Wadden, T. A., R. A. Vogt, R. E. Andersen, et al. 1997. "Exercise in the Treatment of Obesity: Effects of Four Interventions on Body Composition, Resting Energy Expenditure, Appetite, and Mood." *Journal of Consulting and Clinical Psychology* 65: 269–277.

Weinsier, R. L., G. R. Hunter, Y. Schutz, P. A. Zuckerman, and B. E. Darnell. 2002. "Physical Activity in Free-Living, Overweight White and Black Women: Divergent Responses by Race to Diet-Induced Weight Loss." *American Journal of Clinical Nutrition* 76: 736–742.

Wing, R. R. 2002. "Behavioral Weight Control." In *Handbook of Obesity Treatment,* eds. T. Wadden and A. Stunkard, 855–873. New York: Guilford Press.

Wing, R. R. 2004. "Behavioral Approaches to the Treatment of Obesity." In *Handbook of Obesity,* eds. G. Bray, C. Bouchard, W. James, 147–167. New York: Marcel Dekker.

Wing, R. R., and R. W. Jeffery. 1999. "Benefits of Recruiting Participants with Friends and Increasing Social Support for Weight Loss and Maintenance." *Journal of Consulting and Clinical Psychology* 67: 132–138.

Wing, R. R., and K. Anglin. 1996. "Effectiveness of a Behavioral Weight Control Program for Blacks and Whites with NIDDM." *Diabetes Care* 19: 409–413.

Wing, R. R., R. W. Jeffery, L. R. Burton, C. Thorson, K. S. Nissinoff, and J. E. Baxter. 1996. "Food Provision vs Structured Meal Plans in the Behavioral Treatment of Obesity." *International Journal of Obesity and Related Metabolic Disorders* 20: 56–62.

Wing, R. R., R. W. Jeffery, W. L. Hellerstedt, and L. R. Burton. 1996. "Effect of Frequent Phone Contacts and Optional Food Provision on Maintenance of Weight Loss." *Annals of Behavioral Medicine* 8: 172–176.

Wing, R. R., D. F. Tate, A. A. Gorin, H. A. Raynor, and J. L. Fava. 2006. "A Self-Regulation Program For Maintenance Of Weight Loss." *New England Journal of Medicine* 355: 1563–1571.

World Health Organization. 1998. *Obesity: Preventing and Managing the Global Epidemic.* Geneva: World Health Organization.

Yanovski, S. Z., J. F. Gormally, M. S. Leser, H. E. Gwirtsman, and J. A. Yanovski. 1994. "Binge Eating Disorder Affects Outcome of Comprehensive Very-Low-Calorie Diet Treatment." *Obesity Research* 2: 205–212.

CHAPTER 45

....

ANTI-OBESITY DRUGS AND BARIATRIC SURGERY

....

WILLIAM ENCINOSA, DONGYI (TONY) DU, AND DIDEM BERNARD

INTRODUCTION

....

DESPITE the magnitude of the obesity epidemic, only two effective medical treatments for obesity have emerged: bariatric surgery and bariatric pharmacotherapy. As one of the fastest-growing surgeries in the late 1990s and early 2000s, bariatric surgery involves restricting the size of the stomach and bypassing part of the intestines to reduce the absorption of food. Bariatric pharmacotherapy involves long-term prescription weight-loss medications that either reduce the absorption of fat or suppress the appetite. Because dietary therapy, behavioral therapy, and exercise do not always result in sufficient weight loss for obese patients, these two bariatric treatments are their only alternatives.

The clinical guidelines for undergoing these two bariatric treatments have remained stable over time, since 1991 for surgery and since 1998 for drugs, when the National Institutes of Health set up the following guidelines (National Institutes of Health 1998). For obese patients with a body mass index (BMI) ≥ 30, bariatric pharmacotherapy is recommended as a weight-loss treatment. Bariatric pharmaco-therapy is also recommended for a BMI ≥ 27 when the patient also has one or more risk factors (e.g., hypertension, dyslipidemia, chronic heart disease, type 2 diabetes, and sleep apnea). In contrast, bariatric surgery is recommended for a BMI ≥ 40 (morbidly obese). However, bariatric surgery is also recommended for a BMI ≥ 35 with serious medical conditions (e.g., severe sleep apnea, Pickwickian syn-drome, obesity-related cardiomyopathy, or diabetes mellitus). In 2009, these guide-lines were empirically validated as being appropriate by Yermilov et al. (2009). In addition, this research recommended lowering the guidelines, approving surgery for non-elderly adult patients with a BMI of 32–35 only for the most severe category of diabetes (Hgb A1c > 9 and on maximal medical therapy). Surgery is recom-mended for only a small subgroup of adolescents: those at least age 15 with a BMI of 50 or higher (Inge et al. 2004).

Many patients are potentially eligible for bariatric treatments under these guidelines. Encinosa et al. (2005) estimated that there were at least 11.5 million adults eligible for bariatric surgery in 2002. Adjusting for multiple surgeries per patient, they estimated that there were a total of 70,124 adult bariatric patients in 2002. Thus, of the 11.5 million adults clinically eligible for the surgery, only 0.6 percent received the surgery in 2002. Encinosa et al. (2005) also estimated that in 2002 there were 63.3 million adults in the United States who were clinically eli-gible for bariatric medications. However, less than 2.4 percent of those clinically eligible were using prescription weight-loss medications. But, at the same time, many people who do not meet the guidelines do in fact use anti-obesity drugs. Cawley and Rizzo (2007) found that 34 percent of those using prescription weight-loss medications were not clinically eligible.

ANTI-OBESITY DRUGS

There are two main types of prescription drugs approved by the U.S. Food and Drug Administration (FDA) for treating obesity: appetite suppressants, which reduce the appetite or increase satiety, and lipase inhibitors, which block fat absorp-tion in the intestines. A third class of drugs increases energy expenditure, such as the asthma medicine ephedrine. The fourth class of drugs inhibits intestinal alpha-glucosidase enzyme to decrease carbohydrate absorption, such as acarbose. The latter two classes of drugs and several other drugs are often used off-label[1] for weight loss, including antidepressants (such as fluoxetine, sertraline, and bupropion), anti-diabetes drugs (such as metformin, acarbose, and miglitol), and antiepileptic drugs (such as topiramate and zonisamide). The first drug approved by the Food

---

1 Off-label use refers to the practice of prescribing pharmaceuticals for an indication other than those for which the FDA has approved the drug.

and Drug Administration (FDA) for the treatment of obesity was an appetite suppressant amphetamine, desoxyephedrine, in 1947. By 1973, the FDA had approved eight appetite suppressants for the treatment of obesity. These were approved for short-term use (12 weeks). Amphetamines are no longer approved for weight loss because of their potential for abuse. Similarly, in November of 2000, the FDA requested that phenylpropanolamine (PPA), the only approved over-the-counter appetite suppressant, be removed voluntarily from the market because of safety concerns about an association with hemorrhagic stroke among women. Thus, by 2002 there were five short-term drugs approved for anti-obesity: phentermine, benzphetamine, phendimetrazine, diethylpropion, and mazindol (voluntarily withdrawn from sale by manufactures). Overall, these short-term appetite suppressants show an efficacy of 2 to 10 kilograms in weight loss compared to placebo (for a review of efficacy, see Yanovski and Yanovski 2002).

The potential long-term benefits of anti-obesity drugs came to the forefront with the nine publications by Weintraub et al. in 1992 on the continued use of fenfluramine and phentermine over three and a half years. By 1997, two long-term appetite suppressants were approved by the FDA, dexfenfluramine (Redux®) and sibutramine (Meridia®). At its peak in 1997, 2.5 million Americans were taking anti-obesity medications, a fourfold increase over the prior two years (Stafford and Radley, 2003). However, dexfenfluramine was removed from the market in 1997 due to safety concerns, including associations with valvular heart disease and pulmonary hypertension. In 1999, the long-term lipase inhibitor orlistat (Xenical®) was approved. At its launch, orlistat, a drug that blocks about one-third of ingested fat, was the third most heavily advertised drug in 1999, with $76 million spent on its direct-to-consumer advertising (Bymark and Waite 2001). In 2007, orlistat was approved as an over-the-counter drug. A recent meta-analysis of the two long-term anti-obesity drugs, sibutramine and orlistat, found that they result in a net weight loss of less than 10 pounds (over the placebo weight loss) at one year, but this amount may still be clinically significant in reducing diabetes and high blood pressure (Shekelle 2004; Yanovski and Yanovski 2002).

The effectiveness of these long-term drugs is often compromised, since many patients do not actually adhere to them for the long term. While orlistat and sibutramine are recommended for long term use up to two years, Encinosa et al. (2005) showed that in 2002 the average number of days of medication supplied per patient per year was 110 days for orlistat, 102 days for sibutramine. This suggests that the discomfort of side effects may reduce adherence. In a 104-week clinical trial, 12.9 percent of patients on orlistat dropped out of the study due to adverse events (such as diarrhea) and treatment failure (Hauptman et al. 2000). In contrast, Encinosa et al. (2005) also showed that the average number of days of medication supplied per patient per year was longer for the short-term appetite suppressants, 111 days. Overall, the average total supply of drugs per year per patient was 118 days, reflecting the fact that 10 percent of patients took multiple weight-loss medications. Among the users, 45 percent used orlistat, 30 percent used sibutramine, and 35 percent used short-term appetite suppressants (10 percent used multiple drugs).

Close to 71 percent of the short-term appetite suppressants prescriptions were for phentermine. In 2002, there were an annualized 1.2 million office visits for phentermine prescriptions (Stafford and Radley 2003). Overall, the industry reported that total U.S. sales for bariatric medications in 2002 were $362 million (Datamonitor 2004).

BARIATRIC SURGERY

The first bariatric surgery was performed in 1954, by A. J. Kremen. This procedure was then called intestinal (jejunoileal) bypass. The upper and lower regions of the small intestine were cut and joined together to bypass the middle section to reduce food absorption. However, many patients developed complications such as dehydration, diarrhea, electrolyte imbalance, and irreversible hepatic cirrhosis. Thus, such intestinal bypasses were abandoned until safer methods evolved. The first step in this direction was developed in 1966 by Dr. Edward E. Mason of the University of Iowa. He created a pouch across the upper stomach and then combined it with a bypass of a portion of the small intestine (gastric bypass). The small stomach pouch reduced the intake of food and the bypassing of part of the intestines reduced the absorption of food. Later, surgical staplers were used by Gomez in 1981 and Mason in 1982 to create the small pouch. There were complications in the initial procedure, and elastic bands were used later instead of staples. Additional innovations resulted in the Roux-en-Y[2] gastric bypass, which involved restricting the upper stomach into a 30-milliliter pouch and creating an outlet to the biliopancreatic intestine. The next main advancement was the introduction of laparoscopy to bariatric bypass surgery in 1994. Laparoscopic gastric bypass is performed through five small abdominal incisions, with the abdomen insufflated with carbon dioxide gas to create a space to work within via a small video camera. In contrast, open gastric bypass is performed through a large incision in the abdominal wall. By reducing the size of the surgical incision and the trauma associated with the operative exposure, laparoscopy reduces the rate of infection and complication and allows the patient to recover more quickly, saving costs in the long run.

Bariatric surgery procedures can be categorized by: (1) procedure type (banding, gastric bypass, etc.), (2) whether the procedure was performed laparoscopically, and (3) more specific surgical details such as the length of the Roux limb or whether the band was adjustable or non-adjustable. Using nationally representative data, Zhao and Encinosa (2007) report that between 1998 and 2004, the total number of bariatric surgeries in the United States increased ninefold, from 13,386 to 121,055. Total national inpatient hospital costs for bariatric surgeries increased by

---

2 The name of Roux-en-Y surgery comes from the surgeon Cesar Roux, who first described it, and the fact that after the surgery the attached bowel segments resemble a letter Y.

more than eight times, from $147 million in 1998 to $1.26 billion in 2004 (in 2004 dollars). Encinosa et al. (2009) reported that in 2006, 2.9 percent of bariatric surgeries were banding (without bypass) and open (non-laparoscopic), 8.5 percent were laparoscopic banding, 26.1 percent were open bypass, and 62.5 percent were laparoscopic bypass. Overall, 71 percent were laparoscopic and 11 percent were banding without bypass.

Bariatric Surgery Efficacy

Research shows that there is significant weight loss under bariatric surgery. In one of the first main observational studies of bariatric surgery, the Swedish Obese Subjects (SOS) study, middle-aged adults with a BMI of about 41 were assessed in two groups: those who voluntarily underwent bariatric surgery (most treated with vertical banded gastroplasty), and a group of matched controls treated medically (Sjostrom et al. 2004). At eight years follow-up, among 251 surgically treated patients, the average weight loss was 20 kilograms (or 16 percent of body weight), whereas among 232 medically treated patients, the average weight did not change. Patients treated with RYGB (Roux-en-Y gastric bypass) lost more weight than those treated with vertical banded gastroplasty or banding procedures. Although the SOS study was not randomized, and thus the treatment group may have been more suitable candidates for the surgery than the control group, the magnitude of observed differences provides strong evidence that surgical treatment is superior to medical treatment. A strength of the study was the long follow-up period, documenting sustained weight loss and improved health up to ten years after treatment.

There are three meta-analyses of the impact of bariatric surgery on weight loss (Shekelle et al. 2004; Maggard et al. 2005; Buchwald et al. 2004). In the Buchwald et al. (2004) meta-analysis, the percentage of excess weight loss was 47.5 percent under gastric banding, 68.2 percent under gastroplasty, 61.6 percent under gastric bypass, and 70.1 percent under bilopancreatic diversion or duodenal switch bypass. In the Shekelle et al. (2004) meta-analysis, the weight loss reported in surgical studies is an order of magnitude greater than weight loss reported in pharmaceutical or diet studies of obesity (weight losses of 20–40 kg at one or two years in surgical studies, versus 2–5 kg in pharmaceutical studies). Note that direct comparisons across these studies cannot be made due to difference in patient populations: surgical studies enrolled only patients who are severely obese, whereas the average BMI in the medical weight-loss studies is about 33. Furthermore, surgery leads to sustained weight loss (i.e., at 24 months or later), whereas medical weight-loss therapies do not report data beyond 12 months or report regain of most initial weight loss beyond 12 months. To summarize, surgical treatment results in greater weight loss than does medical treatment in morbidly obese individuals (BMI $\geq$ 40), resulting in 20–30 kilograms of weight loss, maintained up to eight years.

Maggard et al. (2005) reviewed two Randomized Controlled Trials comparing RYGB and VBG (vertical banded gastroplasty), which included 231 patients in total; pooled weight loss outcomes for both procedures were substantial (at least 30 kg at

36 months for both) and favored RYGB at both 12 and 36 months (8–9 kg more weight loss from RYGB). Pooled results from both RCTs and case studies, reporting data on approximately 2,000 patients for each procedure, show that RYGB patients reported about 10 kilograms more weight loss than patients treated with VBG, at both 12 and 36 months. Both RCT data and observational data demonstrate clearly that RYGB results in greater weight loss than vertical banded gastroplasty. All three procedures, RYGB, VBG, and laparoscopic adjustable band procedures, report substantial long-term weight loss.

Several studies have found that bariatric surgery also decreases long-term mortality after the operation. The SOS study found that surgical patients had a 23.7 percent reduction in mortality during a mean follow-up of 10.9 years (Sjostrom et al. 2007). Another retrospective cohort study involving 7,925 patients who underwent gastric bypass and matched controls found that, mortality was reduced by 40 percent in the patients who underwent gastric bypass during a mean follow-up of 7.1 years. Cause-specific mortality in the surgery group decreased by 56 percent for coronary artery disease, by 92 percent for diabetes, and by 60 percent for cancer (Adams et al. 2007). Christou et al. (2004) found that that gastric bypass patients had an 89 percent reduced relative risk of death. Another study by Flum and Dellinger (2004) found that 3 percent of gastric bypass patients younger than 40 died within 13.6 years, compared to 13.8 percent of obese patients who did not have bariatric surgery.

Bariatric surgery is also recommended to help control the morbidities associated with excess weight. The SOS study results showed that obesity surgery is superior to medical therapy in reducing or preventing the co-morbidities of obesity. At 24 months after surgery, among 845 surgically treated patients and 845 matched controls, the incidence of hypertension, diabetes, and lipid abnormalities was markedly lower in the surgically treated patients (adjusted odds ratios of 0.02 to 0.38, depending on condition). At ten years of follow-up, the effect of surgery on the reduction in diabetes risk was still substantial, while the effect of surgery on reduction in risk for hypertension did not persist (Sjostrom et al. 2004). The SOS study also showed that surgery reduces sleep apnea, symptoms of dyspnea, and chest pain, and improves quality of life. The study assessed health-related quality of life in four domains: health perception, mental well-being/mood disorders, psychosocial functioning, and self-assessment of eating behavior. Differences between the surgical patients and the control patients were substantial in all domains: in general, one-half to one-third of an effect size. Patients who lost a greater amount of weight had greater improvements in quality of life.

There are two reviews of studies on the impact of bariatric surgery on four obesity co-morbidities (diabetes, hyperlipidemia, hypertension, and obstructive sleep apnea) (Maggard et al. 2005; Buchwald et al. 2004). Among 21 case studies reviewed in Maggard et al. (2005), the proportion of patients with pre-operative diabetes who showed improvement or resolution of diabetes after surgery ranged from 69 percent to 100 percent, with a median reported value of 100 percent. Among 18 case studies reporting on hypertension, 25 percent to 100 percent of patients showed improvement or resolution of hypertension, with a median reported improvement of 88 percent. Among 14 studies reporting on improvement or resolution of sleep apnea, the range of improvement was 95 percent to 100 percent, with a median of 100 percent. Among 10 studies reporting on hyperlipidemia, 60 percent to 100 percent of patients showed improvement or resolution of hyperlipidemia following surgery. In addition, improvements in cardiac dysfunction, gastroesophageal reflux, pseudotumor cerebri, polycystic ovary syndrome, complications of pregnancy, stress urinary incontinence, degenerative joint disease, non-alchoholic steatohepatitis, severe venous stasis disease, and overall quality of life have been reported in some case series of obesity surgery (Maggard et al. 2005). In the Buchwald et al. (2004) meta-analysis, similar results were found. Diabetes was completely resolved in 76.8 percent of the patients. Hyperlipidemia was improved in 70 percent of the patients, while hypertension was resolved in 61.7 percent of the patients.

Bariatric Surgery Safety

Despite the effectiveness of bariatric surgery in reducing weight, the primary concern with bariatric surgery is its high complication rate given that it is an elective procedure. While it has long been known that obese patients have a higher rate of complication in almost all surgeries (Mason, Renquist, and Jiang 1992), in the early 2000s several state Medicaid agencies were alarmed by the high rate of complications seen in the bariatric surgeries among the Medicaid population. They were debating whether to drop or restrict coverage until outcomes improved. At the same time, Medicare was debating whether to expand coverage for bariatric surgery for the treatment of obesity in light of these safety concerns. Until then, Medicare covered the surgery only for co-morbidities associated with obesity, such as diabetes. These safety concerns in the Centers for Medicaid and Medicare Services (CMS) resulted in two actions. First, CMS's new bariatric surgery coverage rules in 2006 included the requirement that CMS-insured patients undergo bariatric procedures in hospitals with a Center of Excellence (COE) designated by either the American College of Surgeons or the American Society for Metabolic and Bariatric Surgery. Both organizations issued identical guidelines, which required COEs to perform at least 125 bariatric surgeries a year and to keep a registry of outcomes data. Second, the Agency for Healthcare Research and Quality (AHRQ) hosted an expert meeting on bariatric surgery safety in 2004, and subsequently published a meta-analysis from the AHRQ-funded Southern California-RAND Evidenced-Based Practice Center (EPC).

The EPC examined 128 studies of bariatric complications published prior to July 2003 (Shekelle et al. 2004; Maggard et al. 2005). Overall, the EPC found a general complication rate between 10 percent and 20 percent in the literature. However, most of these complication rates were in-hospital complication rates for the initial surgery. Moreover, most of these studies were not population-based studies; almost all of the studies reviewed by the EPC were case studies of a small number of patients from selected surgery centers or selected physicians. Small case studies may be biased, as they are typically studies of experienced physicians with low complication rates. Population-based studies include all patients from all doctors in the population. As a result, population-based studies will generally have higher complication rates than case studies.

One population-based study funded by AHRQ subsequent to the AHRQ expert meeting was Encinosa et al. (2006). They used insurance claims for 2,522 bariatric surgeries at 308 hospitals across the United States, among a population of 5.6 million non-elderly people covered by large employers in 2001–2002, to examine 12 major complications that the EPC found specific to bariatric surgery: anastomosis complications, marginal ulcer, abdominal hernia, dumping syndrome (severe vomiting and diarrhea), hemorrhage, wound dehiscence (bursting open along the sutures), infection, DVT/PE (deep vein thrombosis and pulmonary embolism), respiratory failure, pneumonia, post-operative AMI, and post-operative stroke. They found that the complication rate during the initial surgery hospitalization was 22 percent, on the high end of the 10–20 percent range found by the EPC. Such large rates of complications are usually found in population-based studies. For example, one population-based study of all 4,685 bariatric surgeries in Pennsylvania in 2001 found a respiratory complication rate of 7.7 percent (Courcoulas et al. 2003). This is similar to the combined 180-day rate for respiratory failure and pneumonia, 7.13 percent, found in Encinosa et al. (2006). Another population-based study of all bariatric surgeries in California in 2000 found a respiratory complication rate of 5.5 percent (Liu et al. 2003). In comparison, the EPC reports a respiratory complication rate (including pneumonia) of only 2.4 percent among 26 case studies. The average number of patients in these case studies was 205. Thus, bariatric surgery case studies might not be representative of the general population undergoing bariatric surgery.

In addition, some studies may find a much lower rate of complication, simply because they focused on a smaller subset of bariatric complications. For example, the population-based study by Livingston (2004) found an in-hospital complication rate of 10 percent. However, Livingston only examined a limited subset of complications with ICD-9 codes of 996.x to 999.x. This ignores many common codes for anastomosis complications, infections, hernias, and marginal ulcers. Similarly, the Longitudinal Assessment of Bariatric Surgery (LAB 2009) from 2005 to 2007 found a low 30-day complication rate of 4.3 percent since it used a very small subset of complications.

Moreover, reporting only the inpatient complication rate is often misleading. Many complications such as infections, hernias, and dumping do not appear until after the patient has left the hospital. Encinosa et al. (2006) found that the complication rate increased from an inpatient rate of 22 percent to 32 percent over 30 days, and to 40 percent over the 180 days following surgery. In fact, 10.8 percent of the patients without 30-day complications developed a complication between 30 days and 180 days. Overall, 18.2 percent of the patients had some type of post-operative visit to the hospital with a complication (via re-admission, outpatient hospital visit, or ER visit) within 180 days. They also found that the rate of re-admission with

44 post-operative conditions increased further by 64.5 percent between 30 days and 180 days after surgery, from 6.50 percent to 10.68 percent. Beyond 180 days, re-admissions are likely to increase further. In California, Zingmond et al. (2005) found a one-year re-admission rate of 19.3 percent from 1995 to 2004 for Roux-en-Y bypass. Similarly, Flum et al. (2005) found that the death rate following bariatric surgery among Medicare patients increased from 2.2 percent after 30 days to 4.6 percent after one year.

Many 180-day complications are predicted by the number of pre-surgery co-morbidities. Cawley et al. (2007) estimated that an additional pre-surgery co-morbidity is associated with a 27.5 percent higher likelihood of dumping syndrome, 24.5 percent higher likelihood of anastomosis, and 23.5 percent higher probability of sepsis in the first 180 days after surgery.

While complication rates are high for bariatric surgery, they have improved over time. Using nationally representative data, Zhao and Encinosa (2007) found that the national inpatient death rate associated with bariatric surgery declined 78.7 percent, from 0.89 percent in 1998 to 0.19 percent in 2004. Encinosa et al. (2009) found that the risk adjusted 180-day complication rates between 2001 and 2006 declined 21 percent, from 41.7 percent to 32.8 percent. The risk-adjusted infection rate had the largest decline, 54 percent. Most of the improvement in the overall complication rate was in the initial hospital stay, where the risk-adjusted inpatient complication rate declined 37 percent from 23.6 percent to 14.8 percent. Risk-adjusted rates of re-admissions with complications also declined 31 percent, from 9.8 percent to 6.8 percent. Risk-adjusted hospital days declined from 6 to 3.7 days.

This improvement was despite the fact that patients with a higher severity case mix were operated on in 2006 compared to 2001. First, the age of the average surgi-cal patient increased, with a greater proportion being near-elderly (44 percent versus 28 percent). Second, the average number of patients with two or more co-morbidities (besides obesity) increased more than threefold, from 6 percent to 20 percent.

What led to these improvements? Encinosa et al. (2009) found that increased use of laparoscopy was responsible for the improvements in complications and costs. Between 2001 and 2006, the use of laparoscopy, which increased from 9 percent to 71 percent, reduced the odds ratio of having a complication by 30 per-cent. The study further shows that this improvement was not due simply to physi-cians selecting healthier patients for laparoscopic surgery. However, not all improvements were due to laparoscopy. The reduction in re-admissions was due to the increased use of gastric banding. Using the larger HCUP National Inpatient Sample (NIS), the study also found that banding has 31 percent lower odds of having a complication than bypass. Improvements in complication rates and readmission rates over 2001–2006 were shown to be associated with increases in hospital volume.

Did any improvements result from CMS's 2006 introduction of the require-ment that bariatric Centers of Excellence (COE) perform at least 125 surgeries a year? Livingston (2009) does not find any impact of COE designation in the 2005

National Inpatient Sample. However, he finds a volume effect. Hospitals with fewer than 125 bariatric cases have a 10 percent higher likelihood of complication. This may be an underestimation, since his definition of complications is narrow (Clinical Classification Software Code 238, complications of the procedure) and ignores many common codes for anastomosis complications, infections, hernias, and marginal ulcers. In contrast, using the full set of 12 bariatric complications, Encinosa et al. (2009) finds a stronger volume effect in a longer panel of the National Inpatient Sample from 2001 to 2006. Hospitals with less than 159 cases had 43 percent higher odds of a complication.

AFFORDABILITY OF BARIATRIC TREATMENTS

Because of safety concerns, bariatric treatments are not widely covered by insurance. Encinosa et al. (2005) found that in a 2002 employer sample, out of the 5.1 million people with drug coverage, about 4 million had bariatric drug coverage. Average annual weight-loss medication expenditures for those with such drug insurance were $304 per patient (conditional upon use), of which patients paid 26 percent and health plans paid 74 percent on average. This annual total payment per person increased with age, from $192 per person for age 8–17 to $361 for age 55–64. While only 22 percent of the users were men, men spent on average more on the drugs than women ($327 versus $297). This is due to the fact that men used these drugs longer than women (122 days versus 117 days per year) and that a greater proportion of men than women used the most expensive drug, orlistat (44 percent versus 36 percent).

Thus, with coverage, bariatric drugs are relatively inexpensive. However, bariatric surgery is much more expensive and coverage is much more limited. For example, Blue Cross and Blue Shield of Florida and Nebraska in 2004 discontinued coverage for bariatric surgery due to high demand and high costs (Stein 2004). The state of Arkansas, where the rate of morbid obesity is significantly higher than the national average (25 percent compared to 5 percent), eliminated bariatric coverage from its self-funded employee benefit plan in 2003. Similarly, the nation's largest employer, the Wal-Mart Corporation, in 2003 excluded coverage for bariatric surgery (Alt 2003). Overall, only about one-half of all large employers cover bariatric surgery, according to a 2003 William Mercer National Survey of Employer-Sponsored Health Plans (Haberkorn 2004). As a result, bariatric surgery is the single most frequently appealed medical-surgical procedure in the United States (Hall 2003).

Based on a 3 percent sample of those Americans with employer insurance between 2001 and 2006, Encinosa et al. (2009) observed a shift away from patients being covered by fee-for-service and point-of-service HMOs and more covered by PPOs and capitated HMOs. They also found a demographic shift away from the East and Central to the West and South. These two shifts were likely due to changes in insurance coverage policies toward bariatric surgery, since the distribution of regional location did not change for the overall pool of covered lives between the periods, and since the overall enrollment in capitated HMOs actually declined from 23 percent to 11.4 percent in the overall pool of covered lives.

For patients with employer coverage, the average payments for bariatric surgery and its 180-day follow-up care per patient were $31,000 in 2001 and $27,600 in 2006 (in 2006 dollars), as reported by Encinosa et al. (2009). Between 2001 and 2006, the increased use of laparoscopy (from 9 percent to 71 percent) reduced payments by 12 percent. But, most of the reduction in payments in 2006 was due to banding (a 20 percent reduction). The 30 percent increase in hospital volume over 2001–2006 had no impact on payments. Thus, the decline in payments for bariatric surgery was due to a move to less intensive, less costly forms of the surgery (laparoscopy and banding).

Patients with insurance coverage for bariatric surgery on average paid only 3 percent of the costs through co-payments and deductibles (Encinosa et al. 2005). However, for the uninsured, having to pay the full costs of $20,000 to $30,000 does indeed limit access. In fact, Zhao and Encinosa (2007) found that in 2004 the uninsured accounted for only 3 percent of all the bariatric surgeries in the United States. While the high rate of complications and the readmissions contribute to the high costs of bariatric surgery, this has declined over time. Encinosa et al. (2009) found that the hospital payments for patients with complications declined from $41,807 to $38,175 from 2001 to 2006. The total hospital payments for those with the most expensive outcome, re-admissions, also declined substantially, from $80,001 to $69,960. Hospital payments for those patients without any readmissions also dropped, from $26,578 to $23,115.

Thus, further reductions in complications and readmissions will make bariatric surgery more affordable for insurers to cover. Even at current costs, bariatric surgery has been found cost-effective; the cost savings from reduced co-morbidities exceed the initial costs of the surgery. Sampalis et al. (2004) found that the initial costs of the surgery can be amortized over 3.5 years. Similarly, Cremieux et al. (2008) estimated that downstream cost savings associated with bariatric surgery can offset the initial costs in 2 to 4 years. Finkelstein and Brown (2005, 2008) find that a longer period of five or more years is required for a return on investment for employers who pay for the surgery. The average age of a bariatric surgery patient with health insurance coverage through an employer is 44 years, so it is cost-effective for employers to cover bariatric surgery without the fear that patients will have transitioned to Medicare before the cost savings associated with reduced obesity-related co-morbidities can be captured by the employer. Similarly, bariatric medications have been shown to be cost-effective (see, for example, Ara and Brennan 2007).

Conclusion

Bariatric surgery results in much more weight loss and reduction in co-morbidities (e.g., diabetes) and mortality than bariatric medications. However, the costs of bariatric surgery, the lack of insurance coverage of the surgery, and safety issues are barriers to many obese patients potentially eligible for the surgery. Indeed, costs and insurance barriers should not be an issue, since the cost-savings from reduced diabetes and other co-morbidities has been shown to make the surgery cost-effective over a three- to five-year period. Thus, the major barrier appears to be safety issues. Even though the death rate for bariatric surgery has declined to very low levels (0.1 percent, and only 6 in a 1,000 complications results in death), complication rates remain over 30 percent (Encinosa et al. (2009)). Reducing complications and re-admissions would further reduce costs substantially. Such safety improvements will likely come from future innovations that make the surgery less invasive (as was the case with laparoscopy). Future research should examine the safety and cost-effectiveness of gastric-balloons and other endoscopically-placed gastric devices that require no surgery. Moreover, many of these less invasive techniques are being performed at outpatient centers. This shift from inpatient to outpatient is another factor that will lower the costs of bariatric surgery.

The potential move to endoscopically placed gastric devices is based on research that shows that many of the benefits of gastric bypass, such as immediate mitigation of diabetes, is due to a change in gut peptide release, not due to a reduction in food intake (Vetter et al. 2009). Such beneficial peptide action may be accomplished not just by endoscopically placed gastric devices, but also by future bariatric drugs. On the horizon, there are 22 new drugs in development at Phase II and above, and 18 are in early stage development in the pharmaceutical pipeline (Scrip 2008). Some of the new drugs in the pipeline are targeting the biology and chemistry of obesity. For example, some drug studies are evaluating different formulations of leptin and leptin-replacement therapy during low-calorie dieting, because severe, early-onset obesity has been associated with an inability to produce functional leptin protein in some children (Yanovski and Yanovski 2002). Other medications that are currently in clinical trials to determine their ability to induce weight loss include ciliary neurotrophic factor, a neuroactive cytokine that exerts its effects through a receptor whose mode of signal transduction is similar to that of the leptin receptor; a peptide analogue of the human growth hormone fragment; and agonists of the b3-adrenergic and cholecystokinin-A receptors (Yanovski and Yanovski 2002). Some of the other new drugs in the pipeline, such as rimonabant (Acomplia®), block a pathway in the brain that produces the craving for food. In recent trials of rimonabant, 44 percent of subjects lost more than 10 percent of body weight at one year compared with 10 percent of subjects taking placebo (Korner and Aronne 2004). However, in 2009 rimonabant was denied approval in Europe and the U.S. until safety concerns are resolved. Other new drugs block the hormone ghrelin, which is sent from the stomach to the brain to create an appetite (Bays and Dujovne 2002). Some drugs instead stimulate beta 3 receptors to increase fat-burning within the body (Vansal 2004). These new medications will likely increase the demand for bariatric pharmacotherapy.

REFERENCES

Adams, T. D., R. E. Gress, S. C. Smith, et al. 2007. "Long-term Mortality after Gastric Bypass Surgery." *New England Journal of Medicine* 357: 753–761.

Alt., S. 2003. "Bariatric Surgery May Become a Self-Pay Service." *Health Care Strategic Management* 21 (December 12): 1.

Ara, R., and A. Brennan. 2007. "The Cost-Effectiveness of Sibutramine in Non-Diabetic Obese Patients: Evidence from Four Western Countries." *Obesity Reviews* 8: 363–371.

Bays, H., and C. Dujovne. 2002. "Anti-obesity Drug Development." *Expert Opinion on Investigational Drugs* 11(9): 1189–1204.

Bray, George A., and Frank L. Greenway. 2007. "Pharmacological Treatment of the Overweight Patient." *Pharmacological Reviews.* 59(2): 151–184.

Buchwald, H., Y. Avidor, E. Braunwald, et al. 2004. "Bariatric Surgery: A Systematic Review and Meta-Analysis." *Journal of the American Medical Association* 292: 1724–1737.

Bymark, Lori, and Kevin Waite. 2001. *Prescription Drug Use and Expenditures in California: Key Trends and Drivers.* California Healthcare Foundation. Oakland, CA.

Cawley, John, and John A. Rizzo. 2007. "One Pill Makes You Smaller: The Demand for Anti-Obesity Drugs." *The Economics of Obesity: Advances in Health Economics and Health Services Research* 17: 149–183.

Cawley, John, Matthew J. Sweeney, Marina Kurian, Susan Beane, and the New York State Bariatric Surgery Workgroup. 2007. "Predicting Complications after Bariatric Surgery Using Obesity-Related Comorbidities." *Obesity Surgery* 17(11): 1451–1456.

Christou, N., J. Sampalis, M. Liberman, et al. 2004. "Surgery Decreases Long-Term Mortality, Morbidity, and Health Care Use in Morbidly Obese Patients." *Annals of Surgery* 240(3): 416–424.

Courcoulas, A., M. Schuchert, G. Gatti, J. Luketich. 2003. "The Relationship of Surgeon and Hospital Volume to Outcome after Gastric Bypass Surgery in Pennsylvania: A 3-Year Summary." *Surgery* 134(4): 613–623.

Cremieux. P. 2008. "A Study on the Economic Impact of Bariatric Surgery." *American Journal of Managed Care* 14(9): 589–596.

Datamonitor. 2004. *Commercial and Pipeline Perspectives: Obesity.* Datamonitor: London, UK.

Encinosa W., D. Bernard, C. Chen, and C. Steiner. 2006. "Healthcare Utilization and Outcomes after Bariatric Surgery." *Medical Care* 44(8): 706–712.

Encinosa W., D. Bernard, C. Steiner, and C. Chen. 2005. "Use and Costs of Bariatric Surgery and Prescription Weight Loss Medications." *Health Affairs* 24(4): 1039–1046.

Encinosa, W., Didem Bernard, Dongyi Du, and Claudia Steiner. 2009. "Recent Improvements in Bariatric Surgery Outcomes." *Medical Care* 47(5): 531–535.

Finkelstein, E. A., and D. S. Brown. 2005. "A Cost-benefit Simulation Model of Coverage for Bariatric Surgery among Full-time Employees." *American Journal of Managed Care* 11: 641–646.

Finkelstein, E.A., and D.S. Brown. 2008. "Return on Investment for Bariatric Surgery." *American Journal of Managed Care* 14(9): 561–562.

Flum, D., and E. Dellinger. 2004. "Impact of Gastric Bypass Operation on Survival: A Population-Based Analysis." *Journal of the American College of Surgeons* 199: 543–551.

Flum, D., et al. 2005. "Early Mortality among Medicare Beneficiaries Undergoing Bariatric Surgical Procedures." *Journal of the American Medical Association* 294: 1903–1908.

Haberkorn, J. 2004. "Obesity's New Status Will Not Affect Insurers." *Washington Times.* July 16, 2004.

Hall, M. 2003. "State Regulation of Medical Necessity: The Case of Weight-Reduction Surgery." *Duke Law Journal* 53(600): 101–127.

Hauptman, J., et al. 2000. "Orlistat in the Long-Term Treatment of Obesity in Primary Care Settings." *Archive of Family Medicine* 9: 160–167.

Inge, T., et al. 2004. "Bariatric Surgery for Severely Overweight Adolescents: Concerns and Recommendations." *Pediatrics* 114(1): 217–223.

Korner, J., and L. Aronne. 2004. "Pharmacological Approaches to Weight Reduction: Therapeutic Targets." *Journal of Endocrinology and Metabolism* 89(6): 2616–2621.

Liu, J., et al. 2003. "Characterizing the Performance and Outcomes of Obesity Surgery in California." *The American Surgeon* 69(10): 823–828.

Livingston, E. H. 2004. "Procedure Incidence and In-Hospital Complication Rates of Bariatric Surgery in the United States." *The American Journal of Surgery* 188: 105–110.

Livingston, E. H. 2009. "Bariatric Surgery Outcomes at Designated Centers of Excellence vs Nondesignated Programs." *Archives of Surgery* 144: 319–325.

Maggard, M., et al. 2005. "Meta-analysis: Surgical Treatment of Obesity." *Annals of Internal Medicine* 142(7): 547–559.

Mason, E. E., K. E. Renquist, and D. Jiang. 1992. "Perioperative Risks and Safety of Surgery for Severe Obesity." *American Journal of Clinical Nutrition* 55: 573S–576S.

McKay, B. 2004. "Blue Cross of North Carolina to Cover Cost of Treating Obesity." *Wall Street Journal*, October 13, p. D17.

Mehrotra, C., et al. 2004. "Weight Loss Surgeries: Assessing Complications." Centers for Disease Control and Prevention. Presentation at the Safety Issues in Bariatric Surgery: Expert Panel Meeting, Agency for Healthcare Research and Quality, Rockville, MD, October.

National Institutes of Health. 1998. *Clinical Guidelines on the Identification, Evaluation, and Treatment of Overweight and Obesity in Adults.* Department of Health and Human Services: Bethesda, MD. http://www.nhlbi.nih.gov/guidelines/obesity/sum_clin.htm (accessed November 24, 2009).

Sampalis, J. S., M. Liberman, S. Auger, and N. V. Christou. 2004. "The Impact of Weight Reduction Surgery on Health-Care Costs in Morbidly Obese Patients." *Obesity Surgery* 14: 939–947.

Scrip Drug Market Developments. August 8, 2008. *Informa Healthcare: New York.* http://www.taylorwessing.com/uploads/tx_siruplawyermanagement/scrip_rehmann_morgan.pdf (accessed December 2, 2009).

Shekelle P., S. Morton, M. Maglione, et al. 2004. *Pharmacological and Surgical Treatment of Obesity.* Evidence Report/Technical Assessment No. 103. (Prepared by the Southern California-RAND Evidenced-Based Practice Center, Santa Monica, CA, under contract Number 290–02-0003.) AHRQ Publication No. 04-E028–2, Rockville, MD: Agency for Healthcare Research and Quality.

Sjöström, L., Lindroos A, Peltonen M. et al. 2004. "Life style, Diabetes, and Cardiovascular Risk Factors 10 Years after Bariatric Surgery." *New England Journal of Medicine* 351: 2683–2693.

Sjöström, L., K. Narbro, CD Sjöström, et al. 2007. "Effects of Bariatric Surgery on Mortality in Swedish Obese Subjects." *New England Journal of Medicine* 357: 741–752.

Stafford, R. S., and D. C. Radley. 2003. "National Trends in Antiobesity Medication Use." *Archives of Internal Medicine* 163: 1046–1050.

Stein, R. 2004. "As Obesity Surgeries Soar, So Do Safety, Cost Concerns." *Washington Post.* April 11, 2004.

The Longitudinal Assessment of Bariatric Surgery (LABS) Consortium. 2009. "Perioperative Safety in the Longitudinal Assessment of Bariatric Surgery." *New England Journal of Medicine* 361: 445–454.

Vansal, S. 2004. "Beta-3 Receptor Agonists and Other Potential Anti-Obesity Agents." *American Journal of Pharmaceutical Education* 68(3) Article 69: 1–10.

Vetter, M. L., S. Cardillo, M. R. Rickels, and M. Iqbal. 2009. "Narrative Review: Effect of Bariatric Surgery on Type 2 Diabetes Mellitus." *Annals of Internal Medicine* 150: 94–103.

Weintraub, M. 1992. "Long-term Weight Control: The National Heart, Lung, and Blood Institute Funded Multimodal Intervention Study." *Clin Pharmacol Ther* 51: 581–585. [Erratum, *Clinical Pharmacology and Therapeutics* 52: 323].

Weintraub, M. 1992. "Long-term Weight Control Study: Conclusions." *Clinical Pharmacology and Therapeutics* 51: 642–646.

Weintraub, M., P. R. Sundaresan, and C. Cox. 1992. "Long-term Weight Control Study. VI. Individual Participant Response Patterns." *Clinical Pharmacology and Therapeutics* 51: 619–633.

Weintraub, M., P. R. Sundaresan, M. Madan, et al. 1992. "Long-term Weight Control Study. I (Weeks 0 to 34). The Enhancement of Behavior Modification, Caloric Restriction, and Exercise by Fenfluramine Plus Phentermine versus Placebo." *Clinical Pharmacology and Therapeutics* 51: 586–594.

Weintraub, M., P. R. Sundaresan, B. Schuster. 1992. "Long-term Weight Control Study. VII (Weeks 0 to 210). Serum Lipid Changes." *Clinical Pharmacology and Therapeutics* 51: 634–641.

Weintraub, M., P. R. Sundaresan, B. Schuster, et al. 1992. "Long-term Weight Control Study. II (Weeks 34 to 104). An Open-Label Study of Continuous Fenfluramine Plus Phentermine Versus Targeted Intermittent Medication as Adjuncts to Behavior Modification, Caloric Restriction, and Exercise." *Clinical Pharmacology and Therapeutics* 51: 595–601.

Weintraub, M., P. R. Sundaresan, B. Schuster, et al. 1992. "Long-term Weight Control Study. IV (Weeks 156 to 190). The Second Double-Blind Phase." *Clinical Pharmacology and Therapeutics* 51: 608–614.

Weintraub, M., P. R. Sundaresan, B. Schuster, M. Averbuch, E C. Stein, and L. Byrne. 1992. "Long-term Weight Control Study. V (Weeks 190 to 210). Followup of Participants after Cessation of Medication." *Clinical Pharmacology and Therapeutics* 51: 615–618.

Weintraub, M., P. R. Sundaresan, B. Schuster, M. Moscucci, and E. C. Stein. 1992. "Long-term Weight Control Study. III (Weeks 104 to 156). An Open-Label Study of Dose Adjustment of Fenfluramine and Phentermine." *Clinical Pharmacology and Therapeutics* 51: 602–607.

Yanovski, S., and J. Yanovski. 2002. "Drug Therapy: Obesity." *New England Journal of Medicine* 746(8): 591–602.

Yermilov, Irina, Marcia L. McGory, Paul W. Shekelle, Clifford Y. Ko, and Melinda
   A. Maggard. 2009. "Appropriateness Criteria for Bariatric Surgery: Beyond the
   NIH Guidelines." *Obesity* 17(8): 1521–1527.
Zhao, Y. (Social and Scientific Systems, Inc.), and Encinosa, W. (AHRQ). 2007. *Bariatric
   Surgery Utilization and Outcomes in 1998 and 2004.* Statistical Brief #23. Agency for
   Healthcare Research and Quality, Rockville, MD http://www.hcup-us.ahrq.gov/
   reports/statbriefs/sb23.pdf (accessed November 24, 2009).
Zingmond, D., M. McGory, and C. Ko. 2005. "Hospitalization before and after Gastric
   Bypass Surgery." *Journal of the American Medical Association* 294: 1918–1924.

CHAPTER 46

CORRELATES OF SUCCESSFUL MAINTENANCE OF WEIGHT LOSS

VICTORIA A. CATENACCI, PAUL
S. MacLEAN, LORRAINE G.
OGDEN, SARIT POLSKY,
HOLLY R. WYATT, AND
JAMES O. HILL

INTRODUCTION

SUCCESSFUL obesity treatment involves both producing negative energy balance to create weight loss and subsequently achieving a state of energy balance that maintains the new lower body weight over the long term. While weight loss can be achieved with many different strategies, maintenance of weight loss has been much more elusive. Success in weight loss maintenance is dependent on how success is defined. Research has found that following intentional weight loss, most people regain much of their lost weight over the subsequent three to five years. (McGuire, Wing, et al. 1999; Field, Wing, et al. 2001; Weiss, Galuska, et al. 2007) In this chapter we will explore reasons why weight loss maintenance is difficult and examine what we know about factors that contribute to successful weight loss maintenance.

Weight Loss versus Weight Loss Maintenance

It helps to view weight loss and weight loss maintenance as separate processes, each with different overall objectives. Weight loss is the result of a temporary period of negative energy balance, whereas weight loss maintenance requires achieving and sustaining energy balance at a new, lower body weight. Typically weight loss is produced by "going on a diet" which results in a reduction in total energy intake, and negative energy balance. Weight loss can also be produced by increasing physical activity when energy intake is held constant (Ross, Dagnone, et al. 2000; Ross, Janssen, et al. 2004), but the amount of physical activity required for substantial weight loss is very high and may not be feasible for many obese individuals. Thus, most experts recommend that weight loss be achieved with a combination of energy intake restriction and increased physical activity (1998; Seagle, Strain, et al. 2009). Adding moderate amounts of physical activity to food restriction results in only slightly (and often non-significantly) greater weight loss (Wing 1999; Catenacci and Wyatt 2007). This is because the degree of negative energy balance produced by moderate physical activity is small in relationship to the large degree of negative energy balance produced by food restriction. However, increasing physical activity during weight loss is important because it seems to help minimize loss of lean body mass (Ballor and Keesey 1991; Ross, Pedwell, et al. 1995; Ross, Rissanen, et al. 1996) and because it helps prepare the person for weight loss maintenance.

The Transition between Weight Loss and Weight Loss Maintenance

The transition between weight loss and weight loss maintenance is imprecise. In an ideal situation, weight loss maintenance would commence when the goal weight has been reached. In reality, many people who undergo weight loss never reach their goal weight. Weight loss maintenance could begin when the person feels that they have lost all of the weight they want; however, many people would then delay weight loss maintenance in the hopes of losing more weight. An alternative approach is to use a specific time frame for weight loss. Most research suggests that regardless of method used, most weight loss will occur within three to six months of beginning a weight loss program (Jeffery, Drewnowski et al. 2000; Mann, Tomiyama et al. 2007; Sarwer, von Sydow Green et al. 2009). In our programs, we use a six-month time frame for weight loss. Participants know up front that they have six months to lose all of the weight that they can, and then they will enter weight loss maintenance, regardless of amount of weight lost. Participants are told that once they demonstrate success in weight loss maintenance, it is possible to go back and lose more weight.

Regardless of when weight loss maintenance begins, it is a long-term, not a time-limited process. Many dieters erroneously believe that after weight loss, energy intake and expenditure can return to pre-weight loss levels. This is not the case, because an individuals' total energy expenditure decreases with weight loss. Thus, if energy intake and physical activity return to pre-weight loss levels, positive energy balance (and thus weight regain) will occur. Energy expenditure declines with weight loss for several reasons. First, resting metabolic rate (RMR) declines in pro-portion to the amount of lean body mass lost. (Ballor and Poehlman 1995). Second, the thermic effect of food (the energy cost of processing food for use and storage) declines due to a lower total energy intake. Finally, the energy expended in physical activity declines due to the lower costs of moving a smaller body mass (Goldsmith, Joanisse, et al.). Thus, while the goal during weight loss is to produce some degree of negative energy balance, the challenge is even greater with weight loss maintenance—to precisely match energy intake and energy expenditure over the long-term, but at a new, lower body weight.

The Energy Gap for Weight Loss Maintenance

We have called the difference between energy expenditure before and after weight loss "the energy gap for weight loss maintenance" (Hill, Peters, et al. 2009) and have developed ways to estimate this value. Closing the energy gap is a critical concept in weight loss maintenance. In order to achieve energy balance at a new lower body weight, this energy gap must be closed, with decreased food intake, increased physical activity, or a combination of both (see figure 46.1). In general, energy expenditure can be expected to decline by about 8–10 kilocalories per pound of weight lost such that a 10 percent pound weight loss can result in an energy gap of 200–400 kilocalories depending on initial weight.

The energy gap for weight loss maintenance provides an estimate of the degree of behavior change required to maintain a given weight loss. For example, let's assume that Mrs. Jones has lost 40 pounds, and that her energy gap for weight loss maintenance is 400 kilocalories per day. This means that her total energy expenditure has declined by 400 kilocalories per day from pre-weight loss levels. To maintain this weight loss, she would have to change her behavior by 400 kilocalories per day from her pre-weight loss state in order to close her energy gap. This could be achieved by eating 400 kilocalories less each day, increasing physical activity by 400 kilocalories per day or any combination of eating less and increasing physical activity equal to

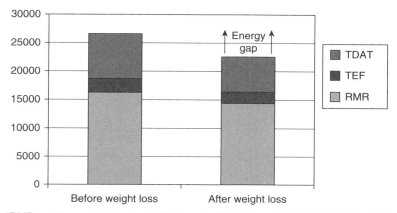

*RMR, resting metabolic rate: TEF, thermic effect of food, TDAT, total daily activity thermogenesis. This figure illustrates the decline in energy expenditure that occurs with weight loss and the resulting "energy gap" between the pre and post weight loss state. In this example, an average height 200 pound middle aged woman has lost approximately 40 pounds. All components of TDEE (RMR, TEF and TDAT) decline, creating an energy gap of approximately by approximately 400 kilocalories.

Figure 46.1.

400 kilocalories per day. Because the drop in energy expenditure is proportional to the amount of weight loss, the more weight lost, the greater the degree of behavioral change required for weight loss maintenance. With very large amounts of weight loss, the energy gap for weight loss maintenance could be several hundred kilocalories per day. The energy gap for weight loss maintenance allows us to tailor behavioral strategies for weight loss maintenance to the individual. Rather than just tell people to eat less and exercise more, we can now give them a much more precise behavioral prescription for weight loss maintenance.

WHY IS IT HARD TO MAINTAIN WEIGHT LOSS?

Experts debate the extent to which weight regain is a problem in biology or behavior. Do most people fail because they cannot maintain the necessary eating and physical activity patterns, or do they fail because their own biology is working against them to promote weight regain? Is it a little of both? Or are they essentially the same thing? We will examine what we know about the reduced-obese state.

Many aspects of biology change after an obese individual loses weight, and it is difficult to assess what impact each change has on weight maintenance. Beyond a decline in energy expenditure, insulin sensitivity and glucose tolerance improve, circulating metabolites (glucoses, triglycerides, and free fatty acids) generally decline, metabolic regulation in a number of key tissues (liver, muscle, adipose tissue) becomes more responsive, the postprandial response of a number of hormones and cytokines changes, a key adipose tissue hormone, leptin, is dramatically reduced, and markers of oxidative stress, inflammation, and other aspects of metabolic disease dissipate or are reduced (Friedman 2002; Aronne and Isoldi 2007; Doucet and Cameron 2007; McGill, Haffner, et al. 2009). At first glance, these changes all appear to be beneficial to health. Why would they have a negative impact on weight loss maintenance? To address this apparent conundrum, we have to separate how these aspects of biology affect health from how they affect body weight regulation.

Our understanding of the biological system of body weight control has dramatically improved over the last few decades, primarily because of research in animals. This system is very complex, but in basic terms, it is a feedback loop between the brain and peripheral tissues, whereby the brain sends out signals to adjust energy balance and nutrient metabolism, while peripheral signals reflecting nutrient availability and energy stores are sent back to the brain. When energy is in short supply (fasting, food restriction, starvation, dieting, etc.) the peripheral signals adjust the neural control centers of the brain in a manner that increases hunger, reduces satiety, and increases the metabolic efficiency of movement and basic processes in tissues that are required for proper function (MacLean, Higgins et al. 2006).

The result is that energy intake increases to levels that are well beyond the level to which energy expenditure is suppressed (positive energy imbalance), and the excess energy repletes energy stores and resolves the issues with nutrient availability. The periphery then signals the brain that the there are adequate nutrients, and the animal returns to eating in relation to its energy requirements (energy balance). Overfeeding generally elicits an opposite response from the periphery and an opposite consequence on energy balance (a negative energy imbalance occurs) (Morrison 2008). It seems simple and relatively intuitive, but many parts of the brain receive both short- and long-term peripheral signals that can be neural, endocrine, or nutrient in nature. However, from day to day, the opposing responses to overfeeding and underfeeding prevent uncontested, limitless weight gain, as well as uncontrolled wasting away. A homeostatic "steady state" is established that keeps an animal relatively weight stable, under a given set of environmental conditions.

This "steady state" weight, however, is not unchangeable for a given animal. If one changes the environmental conditions (diet composition, level of physical activity, amount of stress, etc.), the "steady state" weight will often shift in one direction or the other. Moreover, with the right genetic disposition (obesity-prone) and environmental conditions (a diet high in saturated fat and simple sugars and low levels of physical activity), weight can gradually drift upward, such that the animal becomes obese. For reasons that are not entirely clear, this type of drift has a persistent impact on the "steady state" weight; that is, returning the animal to the original diet or activity regimens does not return it to its original weight. In order to return to its original weight, the animal's food intake has to be proactively restricted—it has to go on a diet.

As with humans, placing obese animals on an energy-restricted diet to return them to their original weight leads to the cascade of aforementioned biological changes that are consistent with an improvement in overall metabolic health (MacLean, Higgins, et al. 2006). From a metabolic health perspective, they look much like lean animals at a similar weight. However, the reduced-obese animal is fundamentally different from an animal that never became obese in the first place in that its biological drive to eat is much higher than its expenditure requirements (MacLean, Higgins, et al. 2004). In contrast, the "never-obese" animal eats roughly what it expends (MacLean, Higgins, et al. 2004). Its "steady state" weight has been established, while the reduced-obese animal appears to be constantly hungry and subjected to a biological drive to regain the lost weight. Animal studies clearly show that this biological drive to overeat does not dissipate over time, but becomes stronger the longer the animal stays weight reduced (MacLean, Higgins et al. 2004). Even more challenging is that all of the peripheral adaptations that reflect improved metabolic health collectively work to promote rapid, energetically efficient storage of the food when the animal eventually overeats (MacLean, Higgins, et al. 2006; Jackman, Steig, et al. 2008). The weight comes back faster than when it was originally gained.

There is little evidence to suggest that the response to weight reduction in an obese human is any different from obese non-human primates, horses, dogs, cats, rats, mice, and a number of other mammals. Even fruit flies and nematodes have the same general response to energy restriction. While studies have shown that hunger increases after weight loss in humans, one only has to ask someone who is dieting by restricting their calories what makes it difficult to stay on their diet. The answer, more often than not, is that s/he is hungry all of the time. While there are nuances of homeostatic body weight regulation that differentiate humans from other animals, the overall outcome is the same—consuming more than what is expended. The discrepancy between appetite and expenditure requirements eventually brings the weight back, if the individual is allowed to eat what he or she wants. It would be surprising if humans differ substantially from the rest of the animal kingdom in a biological response that is so closely tied to survival. However, there are two important characteristics of body weight regulation unique to humans, which may give some hope to those attempting to lose weight.

First, our biology is generally not the only, or even the most prominent factor, affecting energy balance on a day-to-day basis. While biology likely emerges to play a more influential role after weight loss, studies have consistently shown that a normal healthy human is not driven to eat more or less by the biological signals known to control food intake in a normal healthy animal housed in a research setting. Instead, humans are greatly influenced by their environment: the regularly scheduled meals, their social interactions and pressures, and the type and amount of food that is readily available (Levitsky 2005). These environmental cues are far more influential on food intake in most humans from day to day. In a similar fashion, other environmental cues, requirements, and opportunities have a sub-stantial influence on the level of physical activity. Our environmental pressures are overlaid upon the biological feedback system and often override it. Most experts believe that the obesogenic environmental pressures that have emerged in our soci-ety over the past several decades are fundamentally responsible for the current obe-sity epidemic, and the biological response to counter these persistent pressures has been too weak to prevent the gradual accumulation of weight (Zheng, Lenard, et al. 2009). "Steady state" weights have slowly risen, resulting in new "steady state" con-ditions at obese, rather than lean body masses. The new biological system is now primed to emerge and exhibit a much stronger influence after a dramatic weight loss occurs from calorie-restricted dieting. If the environmental cues and perhaps genetic factors that promoted the development of obesity remain the same, the individual now must face these daily cues and their intrinsic genetic predisposition to obesity, while challenged with a biological drive that generates persistent hunger and an insatiable desire to overeat. The odds are stacked in favor of weight regain for both biological and environmental reasons.

The hope for successful long-term weight loss maintenance comes with the second aspect of body weight regulation that is unique to humans. Unlike other animals, we are conscious of our weight, and we can recognize the biological and environmental pressures for what they are. We can change our environment and social influences in a manner that would make it easier to ignore hunger pains, counter the insatiable desire to overeat, and increase our levels of physical activity. Recent evidence in rodent models of weight regain suggests that our behavior may even be able to lessen the biological responses to weight loss to help us maintain weight (MacLean, Higgins, et al. 2009). We have the ability to close the energy gap and give ourselves a better chance to succeed. In the following section, we'll review some of the strategies that are used to facilitate this success.

What Is Required to Succeed in Long-Term Weight Loss Maintenance?

Maintaining a reduced body weight is a long-term process that involves matching energy intake and energy expenditure following weight loss. Currently, there appear to be several forces that oppose maintaining reduced body weight. In addition to metabolic factors predisposing to weight regain and the challenge of maintaining the behavioral changes needed to sustain weight loss, individuals trying to maintain weight loss are faced with powerful environmental pressures to overeat and be sed-entary. The collective effects of these environmental, social, and biological forces promote overfeeding and physical inactivity. Most people do not have the tools, knowledge, or support system to counter these forces effectively. It is likely that a combination of approaches will be needed to counter the forces promoting weight regain, including dietary restraint, physical activity, self-monitoring strategies, social support, recognition of and countering strategies to avert failure, addressing the individual's environment, and perhaps pharmacotherapy. We will discuss these strategies in the following section; however it is important to recognize that the collection of strategies that may work for one person may not work for another. It may take some trial and error for someone to find the right plan or combination of strategies that will lead to successful weight loss maintenance for that individual.

ADDRESSING BIOLOGICAL FACTORS THAT PROMOTE WEIGHT REGAIN

As demonstrated with the rodent model of obesity, we have identified several biological processes in the reduced-obese state that promote weight regain (including an increased drive to eat) as well as a number of peripheral adaptations that result in an enhanced metabolic efficiency and promote rapid weight regain when the animal does overeat. If these exist for humans, it suggests that maintaining a weight reduction will require reducing or overcoming these biological tendencies toward weight regain. It is possible that medications could be developed to specifically address and reduce the biological factors promoting weight regain in the reduced-obese. While it certainly makes sense to focus drug development on "correcting" the "abnormal" physiological state of the reduced obese, it will be years before drugs such as these are identified, tested, and approved for use. Recent studies suggest that regular physical activity might be able to "attenuate" or "correct" the biologic drive to eat and several of the other metabolic changes that occur in the reduced obese state. MacLean and colleagues used a rodent model of the reduced obese state to assess the effects of a regular bout of treadmill exercise on the metabolic adaptations that occur with weight loss (MacLean, Higgins, et al. 2009). During weight maintenance, regular exercise reduced the biological drive to eat so that it came closer to matching the suppressed level of energy expenditure. Compared with sedentary rats, relapsed exercising rats exhibited a lower 24-hour oxidation of carbohydrates, fewer adipocytes in abdominal fat pads, and peripheral signals that overestimated their adiposity. Thus, regimented exercise altered several metabolic adaptations to weight reduction in a manner that would attenuate the propensity to regain lost weight.

If the biological drives toward weight regain are not reduced, then a reduced-obese individual may have to work harder to maintain a reduced body weight than someone at the same weight who has never been obese. Studies assessing levels of physical activity in reduced-obese individuals suggest that this may in fact be the case. When objectively measured physical activity levels were compared between a group of weight-loss maintainers and a group of always-normal weight controls of a similar BMI, significantly higher average levels of physical activity were found in the weight-loss maintainers (Phelan, Roberts, et al. 2007). Data from our research group using activity monitors to objectively measure physical activity also suggest that physical activity levels of reduced-obese individuals are higher than those of either obese individuals or weight-matched individuals who have never been obese (Catenacci, Ogden et al. 2010 Thus, it appears that a weight reduced individual may need to perform more activity to maintain his or her BMI than a never-obese individual of a similar BMI. Given the strong biologic drive to eat that has been observed in weight-reduced animals, it may also require more cognitive effort for a weight-reduced human to maintain an energy-restricted diet, although this has not been specifically studied.

Addressing Behavior: Lessons from the National Weight Control Registry

Because energy expenditure declines with weight loss, some permanent behavior change is necessary in order to keep the weight off. This means that lifelong changes in eating and physical activity behavior are essential for success. Much of what we have learned about successful weight loss maintenance comes from studies of the National Weight Control Registry (NWCR). The NWCR was founded in 1994 by James Hill and Rena Wing to identify individuals who have succeeded in long-term weight loss maintenance and to determine if we could identify common strategies used for weight loss and maintenance of weight loss (Klem, Wing, et al. 1997). To join the NWCR an individual must have maintained a weight loss of at least 30 pounds (13.6 kg) for at least one year. At present the average weight loss of the more than 6,000 participants is over 66 pounds (30 kg). The average length of time the weight loss has been maintained is about 6 years (Klem, Wing, et al. 1997).

The major intent of the NWCR research is to identify characteristics of successful weight-loss maintainers (Hill, Wyatt, et al. 2005). This is not a prevalence study, and these individuals do not constitute a random sample of those who have attempted weight loss. We recognize that the weight losses achieved in NWCR participants may be much greater than weight losses achieved by most people who attempt weight loss. However, we believe that there is value in learning from those who have been the most successful, and the NWCR represents the largest group of successful weight-loss maintainers that has ever been studied.

There are certainly other limitations to the NWCR. Individuals self-identify as eligible for the NWCR, and we only have retrospective self-reported information about them before weight loss. We ask that they provide some documentation, such as physician-measured weight or pre-post pictures, but we do not vigorously evaluate this documentation for all participants. However, in a subgroup of NWCR participants, we did contact their physicians or weight-loss counselors and found extremely high correlation between the participants' self-reported weights and the verified weights. Additionally, most of the information about NWCR members is derived from questionnaires that are mailed to participants; this type of self-reported information has been shown to underestimate energy intake and overestimate physical activity. In over 20 publications, we have described NWCR participants and the behaviors associated with their success in weight loss maintenance (Klem, Wing, et al. 1997; Klem, Wing, et al. 1998; McGuire, Wing, et al. 1998; Shick, Wing, et al. 1998; McGuire, Wing, et al. 1999; Wyatt, Grunwald, et al. 1999; Klem, Wing, et al. 2000a; Klem, Wing et al. 2000b; Wing and Hill 2001; Wyatt, Grunwald, et al. 2002; Phelan, Hill, et al. 2003; Gorin, Phelan, et al. 2004a; Gorin, Phelan, et al. 2004b; Hill, Wyatt, et al. 2005; Raynor, Jeffery, et al. 2005; Wing and Phelan 2005; Phelan, Wyatt, et al. 2006; Raynor, Phelan, et al. 2006; Phelan, Wyatt, et al. 2007; Catenacci, Ogden, et al. 2008; Bond, Phelan, et al. 2009).

Based on the registry, it appears that successful weight-loss maintainers use many different approaches for weight loss. Some lost weight on their own and others used some type of help or support from commercial programs, their physicians, or dieticians. NWCR participants used a variety of dietary approaches for their weight loss. Some restricted particular types of food (88 percent), some just limited amounts of food eaten (44 percent), and some counted calories (44 percent). Most (90 percent) used both diet and physical activity in combination to achieve their weight loss (Wing and Hill 2001). Despite the lack of similarity in how the weight was lost, there was substantial commonality in strategies used for weight loss maintenance.

Physical Activity

Physical activity levels of NWCR participants are assessed yearly using the Paffenbarger self-report scale (Paffenbarger, Wing, et al. 1978). Most NWCR participants report that they engage in high levels of physical activity, averaging over 2,600 kilocalories per week (Catenacci, Ogden, et al. 2008). This level of physical activity would be accomplished by walking 27 miles per week or almost 4 miles a day, and would probably take 60–90 minutes per day to complete. Walking is the most popular type of physical activity (Catenacci, Ogden, et al. 2008). One-quarter of registry members report walking as their only form of activity, and another 50 percent report walking plus another activity. Other commonly reported activities are resistance training, cycling, cardio-machines, running, and aerobics (Catenacci, Ogden et al. 2008).

Other studies have confirmed that high levels of physical activity are needed to maintain weight loss. Jakicic and colleagues compared the weight losses at 6, 12, and 18 months of women who report < 150 minutes of activity, 150–200 minutes, or > 200 minutes at each of these time points (Jakicic, Marcus, et al. 2003). Women who reported > 200 minutes per week of activity had significantly better weight loss and less weight regain over time. At month 18, women who reported > 200 minutes per week of activity maintained a weight loss of over 12 kilograms, compared to approximately 8 kilograms in those reporting 150–200 minutes and 2 kilograms in those reporting < 150 minutes per   week. Fogelholm and Kukkonen-Harjula reviewed 13 non-randomized weight reduction studies with a prospective follow-up of > 1 year and found that the results were quite consistent: 12 of 13 studies found that a large amount of physical activity at follow-up was associated with less weight regain after weight reduction (Fogelholm and Kukkonen-Harjula 2000).

Within the NWCR, there also appears to be a significant relationship between the level of physical activity reported on registry entry and the amount of weight loss maintained. Subjects in the highest quartile of activity were maintaining an approximately 9 pound greater weight loss than those in the lowest quartile of activity, even after adjustment for age and gender (Catenacci, Ogden et al. 2008). Taken together, these data suggest there may be a dose-response relationship between physical activity and weight loss maintenance. However, it should be noted that though the average level of physical activity is quite high, there is considerable individual variability in amount of activity reported by NWCR members as reflected in the high standard deviation in physical activity level (2,621 ± 2,252 kcals per week). Approximately 25 percent of NWCR participants appear to be able to maintain a significant weight loss with relatively low levels of physical activity (< 1,000 kcals per week), while over one-third of participants report extremely high levels of activity (>3,000 kcals per week). Thus, individual specific factors such as dietary caloric intake, amount of weight lost, age, gender, and genetic factors may significantly impact the amount of activity needed for weight loss maintenance.

Although we do not have information on how these individuals find time for this high degree of physical activity, we do know that they spend much less time watching television than the average American (Raynor, Phelan et al. 2006). Within the NWCR, 36 percent report watching < 5 hours per week of TV and 62 percent report < 10 hours of TV per week. Only 12 percent report watching TV ≥ 21 hours per week. These data contrast with the national average of 28 hours of TV viewing per week by American adults.

Dietary Intake

Each year, the National Weight Control Registry members complete a food frequency questionnaire describing their current intake. NWCR members report consuming a low-calorie, moderate-fat diet to maintain their weight losses. While registry members report consuming an average of 1,379 kilocalories per day (Klem, Wing, et al. 1997), we know that self-report underestimates actual energy intake, so that actual intake is probably much higher.

The percent of total energy intake from dietary fat reported by NWCR members has increased over the past few years. In the early years of the registry (1995), participants reported consuming only 24 percent of their calories from fat on average; more recently (2003) this has increased to 29 percent (Phelan, Wyatt, et al. 2006). However, this still represents a moderate fat diet. Moreover, 21 percent of current enrollees report consuming a diet with < 20 percent fat and over 78 percent report a diet with < 35 percent kilocalories from fat. The slight increase in dietary fat intake appears to reflect national trends and popularity of low-carbohydrate diets.

NWCR participants eat an average of 4.7 times per day: breakfast, lunch, dinner, and 1–2 snacks. Of particular interest is that they report consuming breakfast on 6.3 of the 7 days in the week (Wyatt, Grunwald, et al. 2002); 78 percent report that they eat breakfast every day. Eating breakfast may reduce hunger later in the day, help promote higher levels of physical activity or just serve as a marker of a low-calorie, low-fat eating style. NWCR participants eat in restaurants on average 2.5 times per week but visit fast food restaurants on average only 0.77 times per week.

Interestingly, NWCR participants report a lack of variety in the types of foods consumed. Some prior research has suggested that total energy intake increases with the variety of choices offered. We hypothesized that NWCR participants might have reduced variety in food groups such as snack foods and desserts. However, we found that they had reduced variety in all food groups (Raynor, Jeffery, et al. 2005). It is possible that this reduced variety may help them maintain a low calorie intake long-term.

Vigilance

We have consistently found that NWCR participants continue to be vigilant about their body weight, exercise, and diet, even those who lost their weight many years ago. NWCR participants weigh themselves regularly with 38 percent reporting that they weigh themselves at least once a day and 75 percent reporting that they weigh themselves at least weekly (Klem, Wing, et al. 1997). Many NWCR participants report that they periodically keep diet and physical activity diaries. Scores on the Three-Factor dietary restraint scale (Stunkard and Messick 1985), which measures conscious control over eating and body weight, are high in registry members, approximating the levels seen at the end of a behavioral weight loss trial.

Predictors of Weight Regain in NWCR Participants

We have reported that NWCR members are experiencing weight gain over time (McGuire, Wing, et al. 1999; Gorin, Phelan, et al. 2004; Phelan, Wyatt, et al. 2006; Raynor, Phelan, et al. 2006) just like the rest of the population. Not unexpectedly, weight gain is associated with increases in percent of calories from fat, decreases in physical activity, and increases in TV viewing time (Phelan, Wyatt, et al. 2006; Raynor, Phelan, et al. 2006). Interestingly, the effect of TV on weight gain is independent of the effect of diet and physical activity, suggesting that all three contribute to weight gain. Weight gain is also more likely in NWCR participants who are not consistent with their diet strategy (i.e., those who occasionally take a break from their routine) (Gorin, Phelan, et al. 2004). Those participants who reduce self-monitoring and those with decreases in dietary restraint are more likely to show weight gain (McGuire, Wing, et al. 1999).

We have also found that the longer weight loss is maintained, the lower the risk for weight regain. In particular, the risk of weight regain seems to be reduced in those who have maintained their weight loss for at least 3–5 years (McGuire, Wing, et al. 1999). This may offer some hope that getting through the first few years can pay off in long-term success. Individuals whose weight loss was initially triggered by a medical event also have lower risk of regain (Gorin, Phelan, et al. 2004)

Strategies for Filling the Energy Gap and Achieving Success in Weight Loss Maintenance

Does it matter how the energy gap for weight loss maintenance is filled? While any combination of eating less and increasing physical activity could theoretically work to "fill" the energy gap for weight loss maintenance, some strategies may be more effective than others. While many individuals try to maintain weight loss with dietary restriction—ignoring hunger and environmental pressures to overeat—this strategy alone is rarely effective. We believe that increasing physical activity may be a critical component of a successful weight maintenance program. We base this on several key concepts.

First, food restriction is not a viable long-term strategy for weight loss maintenance. Human biology evolved to promote food intake, and there appear to be multiple redundant systems to promote eating. While caloric restriction is effective for weight loss, it appears ineffective as a sole strategy for long-term weight loss maintenance (Wadden 1993; Mann, Tomiyama et al. 2007). While it is possible to reduce food intake by small amounts over the short term, we believe that long-term reductions of 200 kilocalories per day and greater from pre-weight loss levels are difficult for most people. The difficulty in maintaining reductions in energy intake is, we believe, a common reason for failure in weight loss maintenance. For example, in our previous scenario, Mrs. Jones can probably close her energy gap of 400 kilocalories per day completely with food restriction for some period of time. However, weight loss maintenance is a long-term process, and few people can sustain this degree of restricted intake over time. People begin to overeat due to a number of biological, behavioral, and environmental reasons, and regain their lost weight. Research suggests that people who rely exclusively on reducing energy intake to maintain their weight loss are more likely to fail than those who increase their physical activity levels. In the National Weight Control Registry, less than 10 percent of participants report that they use only food restriction to maintain their reduced body weight (Klem, Wing, et al. 1997). Put simply, increasing physical activity can allow someone to be able to eat enough to satisfy hunger while maintaining energy balance at their new, lower body weight.

Second, it is possible that the level at which energy balance is achieved may affect the ease of achieving energy balance. There may be a level or threshold of physical activity (or energy expenditure) below which maintenance of energy balance is more difficult. This is an idea suggested several decades ago by Jean Mayer and colleagues, who studied a male population of mill workers in West Bengal, India (Mayer, Roy, et al. 1956). They observed that energy intake was better matched to energy expenditure when people were performing moderate to high levels of physical activity. The matching was less precise when people were sedentary. Thus, high levels of energy expenditure may create an environment in which body weight regulation systems function optimally to match energy intake to expenditure. For example, a person might find it easier to achieve energy balance by eating and expending 3,000 kilocalories per day than by eating and expending 2,000 kilocalories per day. Although theoretically, energy balance could be achieved at either level, Mayer and colleagues suggest that at higher levels of energy expenditure, intake and expenditure are tightly coupled (Mayer, Roy, et al. 1956). At lower levels of energy throughput, the physiological adjustments for intake and expenditure may be less accurate and matching would not occur as easily or as often.

In fact, there is evidence from animal studies to suggest that exercise may play a role in appetite regulation during weight loss maintenance. MacLean and colleagues have shown that regular treadmill exercise attenuated weight regain in a rodent model of the reduced obese state (MacLean, Higgins et al. 2009). A very interesting finding in this study was that, during the relapse that occurs when weight-reduced rats are allowed unlimited access to food, the exercising rats appeared to eat less than the sedentary rats. These results suggest that during weight maintenance, regular exercise reduced the biological drive to eat. Recent studies in humans also suggest that exercise may in fact "fine tune" the physiological mechanisms that regulate energy intake. Habitual exercisers have also been reported to demonstrate increased accuracy of short-term regulation of food intake in compensation for covert preload manipulation (Long, Hart, et al. 2002). In another study, a 6 week exercise intervention improved the accuracy of short-term regulation of food intake in compensation for covert preload manipulation (Martins, Truby, et al. 2007). The impact of exercise on regulation of energy intake may in part be mediated by effects on hormones that regulate hunger and satiety. For example, a 2007 study found that an acute exercise bout significantly increased postprandial plasma levels of the satiety hormones polypeptide YY (PYY), glucagon-like peptide–1(GLP-1) and pancreatic polypeptide (PP) (Martins, Morgan, et al. 2007), suggesting that acute exercise, of moderate intensity, temporarily decreased hunger sensations and was able to produce a short-term negative energy balance. Based on these and other studies Martins and colleagues have proposed that the critical role of exercise in weight loss maintenance may be, in fact, attributable to an improved appetite regulation (Martins, Morgan, et al. 2008). At present, the available human data in this area are confined to normal weight population, and studies are needed in reduced-obese individuals for these hypotheses to be tested. However, these findings suggest that exercise may facilitate maintenance of weight loss by impacting both sides of the energy balance equation.

OTHER CORRELATES OF SUCCESSFUL
WEIGHT LOSS MAINTENANCE

Extended Contact with Participants

The longer individuals remain in treatment, the longer they maintain the prescribed behavior changes, and consequently the longer they maintain their weight loss (Perri and Foreyt 2003). However, face-to-face meetings are costly, and even successful participants seem to get tired of continuing to attend meetings over the long term. Several groups have investigated use of the telephone and the internet to replace face-to-face meetings for weight loss maintenance.

Wing and colleagues randomized subjects who had completed a 6-month behavioral weight control program and had lost > 4.0 kilograms to a 12-month phone-maintenance program and to a control group. Participants in the phone-maintenance condition received weekly calls to inquire about adherence to self-monitoring and body weight (Wing, Jeffery, et al. 1996). The hypothesis was that these calls would serve as a prompt to participants to continue to adhere to these aspects of the protocol. Weekly phone calls were completed with high frequency (76 percent completion rate); call completion and self-reported adherence to daily monitoring were negatively associated with weight regain (r = –0.52 to –0.59, p < .01). However, weight regain did not differ significantly in the phone maintenance group as compared to controls (+ 3.9 kg versus + 5.6 kg, p = .28). In contrast, telephone calls made by the client's therapists, which included counseling and advice did improve maintenance. Such calls, however, may be just as expensive (or more expensive) than seeing participants in face-to-face meetings. Adding alternative technologies to increase contact with patients, either via e-mail or web-based mechanisms, may provide additional opportunities to promote successful weight maintenance (Tate, Jackvony, et al. 2006; Wing, Tate, et al. 2007).

Ongoing clinical trials may provide further information regarding how to facilitate successful weight loss maintenance. The Weight Loss Maintenance Trial is a large, four-year NIH funded trial being conducted at the Pennington Institute in Louisiana, focusing on prevention of weight regain after weight loss. The aim of this study is to determine the effects of two innovative behavioral interventions, each designed to maintain frequent contact with participants during the weight maintenance phase, as compared to a usual-care control group. If the interventions are effective, they would provide evidence-based paradigms to provide long-term support to aid in long term maintenance of weight loss.

Relapse Prevention or Problem Solving Skills

Marlatt and Gordon have suggested that an important aspect of behavior change programs is to teach participants how to deal with brief behavioral lapses to keep them from becoming sustained relapses (Marlatt and Gordon 1985). They argue that lapses are inevitable, and that it is the reaction to these lapses (rather than the lapse per se), that leads to relapse. Following the suggestions of Marlatt and Gordon, many programs now include "relapse prevention training," which includes both learning to anticipate and avoid lapses, and learning how to deal with lapses if they do occur.

Two studies have tested relapse prevention training as part of maintenance intervention. Perri, Shapiro, and Ludwig found that using relapse prevention training as one component of a multi-component program, which also included ongoing therapist contact, was effective in improving maintenance of weight loss (Perri, Shapiro, et al. 1984). They speculated that teaching relapse prevention training during the maintenance phase, and using the telephone contacts to help participants actually learn to apply these strategies when they experienced lapses, may have made this an effective combination. This combination of relapse prevention training and post-treatment contact was also shown to be effective by Baum, Clark, and Sandler (Baum, Clark, et al. 1991).

However, a more recent study (Perri, McKelvey, et al. 2001) found that teaching participants the skills related to relapse prevention was not as effective as a problem-solving approach. Participants in this trial received a standard 5-month behavioral program and then either (1) no further contact; (2) bi-weekly meetings with training in relapse prevention; or (3) bi-weekly meetings with problem solving. In the problem-solving group, the therapist led the group in applying a problem solving approach to a specific problem identified by one of the group members. Weight loss from baseline to month 17 averaged 10.8 kilograms in the problem solving condition, 5.8 kilograms in relapse prevention, and 4.1 kilograms in those given no further contact. The problem-solving intervention also significantly improved maintenance of weight loss while the relapse-prevention program did not. In interpreting these findings, the authors suggest that the relapse-prevention program was a more didactic program and may not have allowed as much opportunity for individualization (Perri, McKelvey, et al. 2001). In contrast, in the problem-solving condition, participants spent each session dealing with a problem that a group member recently encountered. Thus, this study suggests that the mode of delivery, as well as the content of the intervention may influence the outcome.

Social Support

One study has been conducted to specifically evaluate peer support as a maintenance strategy (Perri, Lauer, et al. 1987). After completion of a standard behavioral program, participants in the peer support condition were taught to run their own peer-support meetings. Space was provided and meetings were held bi-weekly for 7 months. This intervention did not significantly improve maintenance compared to a no-contact control.

In contrast, Wing and Jeffery found that a peer-based manipulation facilitated weight loss maintenance (Wing and Jeffery 1999). In this study, participants were allowed to choose whether to enter a program by themselves or with three friends or family members. Thus, this part of the study was not randomized. However, within each of these groups, half of the subjects were randomized to receive a social support intervention, which included inter-group competitions and intra-group cohesiveness activities, and half did not receive this intervention. Both recruitment strategy and social support manipulation affected the maintenance of weight loss from the end of the 4-month program to a follow-up at month 10. Only 24 percent of participants who were recruited alone and received a standard behavioral program without the social support manipulation maintained their weight loss in full. In contrast, 66 percent of those who were recruited with friends and received the social support intervention maintained their weight loss in full.

Multi-component Behavioral Approaches to Weight Loss Maintenance

In almost all of the trials described above, even the most successful groups experience some weight regain over the 12-month follow-up interval. One of the few examples of a program that led to no weight regain was a multi-component program that was designed to evaluate the effect of four maintenance programs on the long-term management of obesity (Perri, McAllister et al. 1988). Participants who were assigned to receive post-treatment contact (bi-weekly group sessions over the full year), plus social influence (monetary group incentives, active participant involvement, and training in peer support strategies), plus aerobic exercise (with exercise goals gradually increasing to 180 minutes/week) maintained 99 percent of their initial weight loss at the 18-month follow-up. Although this appeared most effective, the only statistically significant effect was that all four groups that received ongoing therapist contact had better maintenance of weight loss than the group receiving no ongoing contact. This finding highlights the importance of ongoing contact for the maintenance of weight loss, but suggests that adding a variety of other strategies may be useful in maintaining weight loss long-term.

Pharmacologic Approach to Weight Loss Maintenance

Long-term use of weight-loss medications provides another option for weight maintenance, and may augment behavioral approaches (Bray 2008; Sarwer, von Sydow Green et al. 2009). Two weight loss medications, sibutramine (Meridia; Abbott Laboratories, North Chicago, Illinois) and orlistat (Xenical; Roche

Laboratories, Burlington, North Carolina), have been studied in long-term (one to four year) randomized controlled trials. Orlistat, a pancreatic lipase inhibitor, inhibits the absorption of dietary fat by approximately 30 percent. Sibutramine is a centrally acting agent that enhances satiety and thermogenesis by inhibiting the re-uptake of serotonin and norepinephrine. Despite their distinct mechanisms of action, these medications have been shown to produce approximately equivalent weight losses of 7–10 percent of initial body weight after one year of treatment when combined with lifestyle modification (Rucker, Padwal, et al. 2007; Bray 2008).

Several clinical studies have evaluated the effect of these medications in sustaining a weight loss long term by either 1) continuing pharmacotherapy after a drug induced weight loss (Torgerson, Hauptman et al. 2004) or 2) a randomized placebo controlled evaluation of continuing pharmacotherapy after a drug induced weight loss (Sjostrom, Rissanen, et al. 1998; Apfelbaum, Vague, et al. 1999; Davidson, Hauptman, et al. 1999; Hill, Hauptman, et al. 1999; James, Astrup, et al. 2000; Mathus-Vliegen 2005). Both orlistat and sibutramine have been shown to facilitate the maintenance of weight loss over 1–4 years. For example, Hill and colleagues (Hill, Hauptman, et al. 1999) found that a significantly greater number of participants who received orlistat 120 mg TID regained less than or equal to 25 percent of their body weight during the one-year maintenance phase compared to that of the placebo group. The majority of these studies all evaluated the effect of continuing a medication that had been initially used as a weight-loss therapy during a subsequent specified (12–18 month) maintenance phase. In addition, all except one of these trials provide data for less than two years of continued use of the study drug. The one trial that extended beyond this time frame (the Xendos study) evaluated the efficacy of orlistat in addition to lifestyle modification for the prevention of diabetes in an obese population (BMI $\geq$ 30) and found that compared with lifestyle changes alone, orlistat plus lifestyle changes produced greater weight loss (5.8 vs. 3.0 kg with placebo; p < 0.001) and resulted in a greater reduction in the incidence of type 2 diabetes over four years (Torgerson, Hauptman, et al. 2004). Whether these medications are effective in maintaining weight loss induced by other means, and whether these medications will remain effective in maintaining a weight loss beyond 4 years remains to be studied.

Of note, in October 2010 the FDA requested that the manufacturer of sibutramine voluntarily withdraw this drug from the United States market due to concerns that this drug may pose unnecessary cardiovascular risks to patients. The FDA's recommendation was based on data from the Sibutramine Cardiovascular Outcomes Trial (SCOUT) (James, Caterson et al. 2010) which enrolled 10,744 overweight or obese subjects, 55 years of age or older, with cardiovascular disease, type 2 diabetes mellitus, or both to assess the cardiovascular consequences of weight management with and without sibutramine in subjects at high risk for cardiovascular events. The primary end point was the time from randomization to the first occurrence of a primary outcome event (nonfatal myocardial infarction, nonfatal stroke, resuscitation after cardiac arrest, or cardiovascular death) and the mean duration of treatment was 3.4 years. The risk of a primary outcome event was 11.4%

in the sibutramine group as compared with 10.0% in the placebo group (hazard ratio, 1.16; 95% confidence interval [CI], 1.03 to 1.31; P=0.02). Abbott has agreed to stop marketing of sibutramine (Meridia) in the United States, thus at present there is only one medication (orlistat) currently approved by the FDA for long-term use in treatment of obesity.

Phentermine (Lonamin; Medeva Pharmaceuticals, Rochester, NY and Adipex-P; Gate Pharmaceuticals, North Wales, PA) is an appetite suppressant that inhibits reuptake of norepinephrine (Bray 2008). There are no long-term studies of phentermine. Short-term studies have found that phentermine produces at least a 5% placebo-subtracted weight loss (Bray 2008). The FDA has approved use of phentermine for weight loss for 12 weeks, however a number of experts advocate its use for weight loss maintenance for patients who demonstrate a good response (Kaplan 2010). Therefore, many medical professionals prescribe phentermine off-label for weight loss maintenance.

Addressing the Environment

It is now clear that our environment discourages eating and physical activity patterns consistent with successful weight loss maintenance (Hill and Peters 1998). The environmental influences on eating and physical activity patterns can be so powerful that it may be difficult for most people to "swim upstream" against the drive toward positive energy imbalance. Effective obesity treatment programs are likely going to have to address the environment. Unfortunately, we know far less than we need to about how to do this. Approaches could consist of helping participants learn to manage better within the current environment or helping them change their own environments for diet and physical activity. Unfortunately, research is just beginning to investigate the ways in which environmental modifications can be made on an individual or a societal level.

SUMMARY

The lack of prolonged success in behavioral therapy for weight loss is well recognized. While successful weight loss maintenance is possible, it is rare. Individuals attempting to maintain weight loss face biological, behavioural, and environmental barriers. Successful weight loss maintenance requires closing the energy gap between the pre- and post-weight loss state. To achieve energy balance at a new, lower body weight, individuals must eat fewer or burn more calories (or some combination of the two) for the rest of their lives. The people who succeed may be those who can maintain vigilance in food and physical activity habits despite pressures against maintenance of these behaviors. Physical activity may be a key component of weight loss maintenance not only because it serves to increase energy expenditure, but also because of a potential beneficial impact on appetite and energy balance regulation. Further investigation of innovative strategies to promote long-term adherence to an energy-restricted diet and increased physical activity will likely be beneficial in assisting with weight maintenance. Increasing success in weight loss maintenance may also require figuring out how to lessen these biological pressures toward weight regain, perhaps with pharmacologic therapy, as well as strategies to promote environmental changes conducive to maintenance of a normal body weight.

REFERENCES

Apfelbaum, M., P. Vague, et al. 1999. "Long-term Maintenance of Weight Loss after a Very-Low-Calorie Diet: A Randomized Blinded Trial of the Efficacy and Tolerability of Sibutramine." *American Journal of Medicine* 106(2): 179–184.

Aronne, L. J., and K. K. Isoldi. 2007. "Overweight and Obesity: Key Components of Cardiometabolic Risk." *Clinical Cornerstone* 8(3): 29–37.

Ballor, D. L., and R. E. Keesey. 1991. "A Meta-Analysis of the Factors Affecting Exercise-Induced Changes in Body Mass, Fat Mass and Fat-Free Mass in Males and Females." *International Journal of Obesity* 15(11): 717–726.

Ballor, D. L. and E. T. Poehlman. 1995. "A Meta-Analysis of the Effects of Exercise and/or Dietary Restriction on Resting Metabolic Rate." *European Journal of Applied Physiology and Occupational Physiology* 71(6): 535–542.

Baum, J. G., H. B. Clark, et al. 1991. "Preventing Relapse in Obesity Through Posttreatment Maintenance Systems: Comparing the Relative Efficacy of Two Levels of Therapist Support." *Journal of Behavioral Medicine* 14(3): 287–302.

Bond, D. S., S. Phelan, et al. 2009. "Weight-loss Maintenance in Successful Weight Losers: Surgical vs Non-Surgical Methods." *International Journal of Obesity (London)* 33(1): 173–180.

Bray, G. A. 2008. "Medications for Weight Reduction." *Endocrinology and Metabolism Clinics of North America* 37(4): 923–942.

Catenacci V.A., G.K.,Grunwald J.P.Ingebrigtsen, et al. 2010. "Physical Activity Patterns Using Accelerometry in the National Weight Control Registry". *Obesity (Silver Spring)*. 2010 Oct 28. [Epub ahead of print]

Catenacci, V. A., L. G. Ogden, et al. 2008. "Physical Activity Patterns in the National Weight Control Registry." *Obesity (Silver Spring)* 16(1): 153–161.

Catenacci, V. A. and H. R. Wyatt. 2007. "The Role of Physical Activity in Producing and Maintaining Weight Loss." *Nature Clinical Practice Endocrinology & Metabolism* 3(7): 518–529.

Davidson, M. H., J. Hauptman, et al. 1999. "Weight Control and Risk Factor Reduction in Obese Subjects Treated for 2 Years with Orlistat: A Randomized Controlled Trial." *Journal of the American Medical Association* 281(3): 235–242.

Doucet, E., and J. Cameron. 2007. "Appetite Control after Weight Loss: What Is the Role of Bloodborne Peptides?" *Applied Physiology, Nutrition, and Metabolism* 32(3): 523–532.

Field, A. E., R. R. Wing, et al. 2001. "Relationship of a Large Weight Loss to Long-Term Weight Change among Young and Middle-Aged US Women." *International Journal of Obesity and Related Metabolic Disorders* 25(8): 1113–1121.

Fogelholm, M. and K. Kukkonen-Harjula. 2000. "Does Physical Activity Prevent Weight Gain—A Systematic Review." *Obesity Review* 1(2): 95–111.

Friedman, J. M. 2002. "The Function of Leptin in Nutrition, Weight, and Physiology." *Nutrition Reviews* 60(10 Pt 2): S1–14; discussion S68–84, 85–87.

Goldsmith, R., D. R. Joanisse, et al. 2010 "Effects of Experimental Weight Perturbation on Skeletal Muscle Work Efficiency, Fuel Utilization, and Biochemistry in Human Subjects." *American Journal of Physiology Regulatory, Integrative, and Comparative Physiology* 298(1): R79–88.

Gorin, A. A., S. Phelan, et al. 2004a. "Medical Triggers Are Associated with Better Short and Long-Term Weight Loss Outcomes." *Preventive Medicine* 39: 612–616.

Gorin, A. A., S. Phelan, et al. 2004b. "Promoting Long-Term Weight Control: Does Dietary Consistency Matter?" *International Journal of Obesity* 28: 278–281.

Hill, J. O., J. Hauptman, et al. 1999. "Orlistat, a Lipase Inhibitor, for Weight Maintenance after Conventional Dieting: A 1-Y Study." *American Journal of Clinical Nutrition* 69(6): 1108–1116.

Hill, J. O., and J. C. Peters. 1998. "Environmental Contributions to the Obesity Epidemic." *Science* 280(5368): 1371–1374.

Hill, J. O., J. C. Peters, et al. 2009. "Using the Energy Gap to Address Obesity: A Commentary." *Journal of the American Dietetic Association* 109(11): 1848–1853.

Hill, J. O., H. Wyatt, et al. 2005. "The National Weight Control Registry: Is It Useful in Helping Deal with Our Obesity Epidemic?" *Journal of Nutrition Eduation and Behavior* 37(4): 206–210.

Jackman, M. R., A. Steig, et al. 2008. "Weight Regain after Sustained Weight Reduction Is Accompanied by Suppressed Oxidation of Dietary Fat and Adipocyte Hyperplasia." *American Journal of Physiology Regulatory, Integrative, and Comparative Physiology* 294(4): R1117–1129.

Jakicic, J., B. H. Marcus, et al. 2003. "Effect of Exercise Dose and Intensity on Weight Loss in Overweight, Sedentary Women: A Randomized Trial." *Journal of the American Medical Association* 290: 1323–1330.

James, W. P., A. Astrup, et al. 2000. "Effect of Sibutramine on Weight Maintenance after Weight Loss: A Randomised Trial. STORM Study Group. Sibutramine Trial of Obesity Reduction and Maintenance." *Lancet* 356(9248): 2119–2125.

James W.P., I.D. Caterson , et al. 2010 "Effect of Sibutramine on Cardiovascular Outcomes in Overweight and Obese Adults" *New England Journal of Medicine* 363(10):905–17

Jeffery, R. W., A. Drewnowski, et al. 2000. "Long-term Maintenance of Weight Loss: Current Status." *Health Psychology* 19(1 Suppl): 5–16.

Kaplan LM 2010. "Pharmacologic Therapies for Obesity." *Gastroenterology Clinics of North America* 39(1): 69–79.

Klem, M. L., R. R. Wing, et al. 1997. "A Descriptive Study of Individuals Successful at Long-Term Maintenance of Substantial Weight Loss." *American Journal of Clinical Nutrition* 66(2): 239–246.

Klem, M. L., R. R. Wing, et al. 1998. "Psychological Symptoms in Individuals Successful at Long-Term Maintenance of Weight Loss." *Health Psychology* 17(4): 336–345.

Klem, M. L., R. R. Wing, et al. 2000a "A Case-Control Study of Successful Maintenance of a Substantial Weight Loss: Individuals Who Lost Weight Through Surgery Versus Those Who Lost Weight Through Non-Surgical Means." *International Journal of Obesity and Related Metabolic Disorders* 24(5): 573–579.

Klem, M. L., R. R. Wing, et al. 2000b. "Does Weight Loss Maintenance Become Easier over Time?" *Obesity Research* 8(6): 438–444.

Levitsky, D. A. 2005. "The Non-Regulation of Food Intake in Humans: Hope for Reversing the Epidemic of Obesity." *Physiology & Behavior* 86(5): 623–632.

Long, S. J., K. Hart, et al. 2002. "The Ability of Habitual Exercise to Influence Appetite and Food Intake in Response to High- and Low-Energy Preloads in Man." *British Journal of Nutrition* 87(5): 517–523.

MacLean, P. S., J. A. Higgins, et al.2004. "Enhanced Metabolic Efficiency Contributes to Weight Regain after Weight Loss in Obesity-Prone Rats." *American Journal of Physiology Regulatory, Integrative, and Comparative Physiology* 287(6): R1306–1315.

MacLean, P. S., J. A. Higgins, et al. 2006. "Peripheral Metabolic Responses to Prolonged Weight Reduction That Promote Rapid, Efficient Regain in Obesity-Prone Rats." *American Journal of Physiology Regulatory, Integrative, and Comparative Physiology* 290(6): R1577–1588.

MacLean, P. S., J. A. Higgins, et al. 2009. "Regular Exercise Attenuates the Metabolic Drive to Regain Weight after Long-Term Weight Loss." *American Journal of Physiology Regulatory, Integrative, and Comparative Physiology* 297(3): R793–802.

Mann, T., A. J. Tomiyama, et al. 2007. "Medicare's Search for Effective Obesity Treatments: Diets Are Not the Answer." *American Psychologist* 62(3): 220–233.

Marlatt, G. A., and J. R. Gordon. 1985. *Relapse Prevention: Maintenance Strategies in Addictive Behavior Change.* New York: Guilford.

Martins, C., L. M. Morgan, et al. 2007. "Effects of Exercise on Gut Peptides, Energy Intake and Appetite." *Journal of Endocrinology* 193(2): 251–258.

Martins, C., L. Morgan, et al. 2008. "A Review of the Effects of Exercise on Appetite Regulation: An Obesity Perspective." *International Journal of Obesity (London)* 32(9): 1337–1347.

Martins, C., H. Truby, et al. 2007. "Short-term Appetite Control in Response to a 6-Week Exercise Programme in Sedentary Volunteers." *British Journal of Nutrition* 98(4): 834–842.

Mathus-Vliegen, E. M. 2005. "Long-term Maintenance of Weight Loss with Sibutramine in a GP Setting Following a Specialist Guided Very-Low-Calorie Diet: A Double-Blind, Placebo-Controlled, Parallel Group Study." *European Journal of Clinical Nutrition* 59 (Supp. 1): S31–38; discussion S39.

Mayer, J., P. Roy, et al. 1956. "Relation between Caloric Intake, Body Weight, and Physical Work: Studies in an Industrial Male Population in West Bengal." *American Journal of Clinical Nutrition* 4(2): 169–175.

McGill, J. B., S. Haffner, et al. 2009. "Progress and Controversies: Treating Obesity and Insulin Resistance in the Context of Hypertension." *Journal of Clinical Hypertension (Greenwich)* 11(1): 36–41.

McGuire, M. T., R. R. Wing, et al. 1998. "Long-term Maintenance of Weight Loss: Do People Who Lose Weight Through Various Weight Loss Methods Use Different Behaviors to Maintain Their Weight?" *Int J Obes Relat Metab Disord* 22(6): 572–577.

McGuire, M. T., R. R. Wing, et al. 1999. "The Prevalence of Weight Loss Maintenance among American Aadults." *International Journal of Obesity and Related Metabolic Disorders* 23(12): 1314–1319.

McGuire, M. T., R. R. Wing, et al. 1999. "What Predicts Weight Regain in a Group of Successful Weight Losers?" *Journal of Consulting and Clinical Psychology* 67(2): 177–185.

Morrison, C. D. 2008. "Leptin Resistance and the Response to Positive Energy Balance." *Physiology & Behavior* 94(5): 660–663.

National Institute of Health (NIH). 1998. "Clinical Guidelines on the Identification, Evaluation, and Treatment of Overweight and Obesity in Adults—The Evidence Report. National Institutes of Health." *Obesity Research* 6(Supp. 2): 51S–209S. http://www.nhlbi. nih.gov/guidelines/obesity/ob_gdlns.pdf

Paffenbarger, R. S., Jr., A. L. Wing, et al. 1978. "Physical Activity as an Index of Heart Attack Risk in College Alumni." *American Journal of Epidemiology* 108(3): 161–175.

Perri, M. G., J. P. Foreyt. 2003. *Preventing Weight Regain after Weight Loss*. In: Bray, G., Bouchard, C., editors. Handbook of Obesity. New York: Marcel Dekker. p. 185–199.

Perri, M. G., J. B. Lauer, et al. 1987. "Effects of Peer Support and Therapist Contact on Long-Term Weight Loss." *Journal of Consulting and Clinical Psychology* 55(4): 615–617.

Perri, M. G., D. A. McAllister, et al. 1988. "Effects of Four Maintenance Programs on the Long-Term Management of Obesity." *Journal of Consulting and Clinical Psychology* 56(4): 529–534.

Perri, M. G., W. F. McKelvey, et al. 2001. "Relapse Prevention Training and Problem-Solving Therapy in the Long-Term Management of Obesity." *Journal of Consulting and Clinical Psychology* 69(4): 722–726.

Perri, M. G., R. M. Shapiro, et al. 1984. "Maintenance Strategies for the Treatment of Obesity: An Evaluation of Relapse Prevention Training and Post-Treatment Contact by Telephone and Mail." *Journal of Consulting and Clinical Psychology* 52: 404–413.

Phelan, S., J. O. Hill, et al. 2003. "Recovery from Relapse among Successful Weight Maintainers." *American Journal of Clinical Nutrition* 78(6): 1079–1084.

Phelan, S., M. Roberts, et al. 2007. "Empirical Evaluation of Physical Activity Recommendations for Weight Control In Women." *Medicine & Science in Sports & Exercise* 39(10): 1832–1836.

Phelan, S., H. Wyatt, et al. 2007. "Three-year Weight Change in Successful Weight Losers Who Lost Weight on a Low-Carbohydrate Diet." *Obesity (Silver Spring)* 15(10): 2470–2477.

Phelan, S., H. R. Wyatt, et al. 2006. "Are the Eating and Exercise Habits of Successful Weight Losers Changing?" *Obesity (Silver Spring)* 14(4): 710–716.

Raynor, H. A., R. W. Jeffery, et al. 2005. "Amount of Food Group Variety Consumed in the Diet and Long-Term Weight Loss Maintenance." *Obesity Research* 13(5): 883–890.

Raynor, D. A., S. Phelan, et al. 2006. "Television Viewing and Long-Term Weight Maintenance: Results from the National Weight Control Registry." *Obesity* 14: 1816–1824.

Ross, R., D. Dagnone, et al. 2000. "Reduction in Obesity and Related Comorbid Conditions after Diet-Induced Weight Loss or Exercise-Induced Weight Loss in Men: A Randomized, Controlled Trial." *Annals of Internal Medicine* 133(2): 92–103.

Ross, R., I. Janssen, et al. 2004. "Exercise-induced Reduction in Obesity and Insulin Resistance in Women: A Randomized Controlled Trial." *Obesity Research* 12(5): 789–798.

Ross, R., H. Pedwell, et al. 1995. "Effects of Energy Restriction and Exercise on Skeletal Muscle and Adipose Tissue in Women as Measured by Magnetic Resonance Imaging." *American Journal of Clinical Nutrition* 61(6): 1179–1185.

Ross, R., J. Rissanen, et al. 1996. "Influence of Diet and Exercise on Skeletal Muscle and Visceral Adipose Tissue in Men." *Journal of Applied Physiology* 81(6): 2445–2455.

Rucker, D., R. Padwal, et al. 2007. "Long term Pharmacotherapy for Obesity and Overweight: Updated Meta-Analysis." *British Medical Journal* 335(7631): 1194–1199.

Sarwer, D. B., A. von Sydow Green, et al. 2009. "Behavior Therapy for Obesity: Where Are We Now?" *Current Opinion Endocrinology Diabetes and Obesity* 16(5): 347–352.

Seagle, H. M., G. W. Strain, et al. 2009. "Position of the American Dietetic Association: Weight Management." *Journal of the American Dietetic Association* 109(2): 330–346.

Shick, S. M., R. R. Wing, et al. 1998. "Persons Successful at Long-Term Weight Loss and Maintenance Continue to Consume a Low-Energy, Low-Fat Diet." *Journal of the American Dietetic Association* 98(4): 408–413.

Sjostrom, L., A. Rissanen, et al. 1998. "Randomised Placebo-Controlled Trial of Orlistat for Weight Loss and Prevention of Weight Regain in Obese Patients. European Multicentre Orlistat Study Group." *Lancet* 352(9123): 167–172.

Stunkard, A. J., and S. Messick. 1985. "The Three-Factor Eating Questionnaire to Measure Dietary Restraint, Disinhibition and Hunger." *Journal of Psychosomatic Research* 29: 71–83.

Tate, D. F., E. H. Jackvony, et al. 2006. "A Randomized Trial Comparing Human E-Mail Counseling, Computer-Automated Tailored Counseling, and No Counseling in an Internet Weight Loss Program." *Archives of Internal Medicine* 166(15): 1620–1625.

Torgerson, J. S., J. Hauptman, et al. 2004. "XENical in the Prevention of Diabetes in Obese Subjects (XENDOS) Study: A Randomized Study of Orlistat as an Adjunct to Lifestyle Changes for the Prevention of Type 2 Diabetes in Obese Patients." *Diabetes Care* 27(1): 155–161.

Wadden, T. A. 1993. "Treatment of Obesity by Moderate and Severe Caloric Restriction. Results of Clinical Research Trials." *Annals of Internal Medicine* 119(7 Pt 2): 688–693.

Weiss, E. C., D. A. Galuska, et al. 2007. "Weight Regain in U.S. Adults Who Experienced Substantial Weight Loss, 1999–2002." *American Journal of Preventive Medicine* 33(1): 34–40.

Wing, R. R. 1999. "Physical Activity in the Treatment of the Adulthood Overweight and Obesity: Current Evidence and Research Issues." *Medicine & Science in Sports & Exercise* 31(11 Supp.): S547–552.

Wing, R. and J. O. Hill. 2001. "Successful Weight Loss Maintenance." *Annual Review of Nutrition* 21: 323–341.

Wing, R. and R. Jeffery. 1999. "Benefits of Recruiting Participants with Friends and Increasing Social Support for Weight Loss And Maintenance." *Journal of Consulting and Clinical Psychology* 67(1): 132–138.

Wing, R. R., R. W. Jeffery, et al. 1996. "Effect of Frequent Phone Contacts and Optional Food Provision on Maintenance of Weight Loss." *Annals of Behavioral Medicine* 18: 172–176.

Wing, R. R., and S. Phelan. 2005. "Long-term weight loss maintenance." *American Journal of Clinical Nutrition* 82(1 Supp.): 222S–225S.

Wing, R. R., D. F. Tate, et al. 2007. "STOP Regain: Are There Negative Effects of Daily Weighing?" *Journal of Consulting and Clinical Psychology* 75(4): 652–656.

Wyatt, H. R., G. K. Grunwald, et al. 1999. "Resting Energy Expenditure in Reduced-Obese Subjects in the National Weight Control Registry." *American Journal of Clinical Nutrition* 69(6): 1189–1193.

Wyatt, H. R., G. K. Grunwald, et al. 2002. "Long-Term Weight Loss and Breakfast in Subjects in the National Weight Control Registry." *Obesity Research* 10(2): 78–82.

Zheng, H., N. R. Lenard, et al. 2009. "Appetite Control and Energy Balance Regulation in the Modern World: Reward-Driven Brain Overrides Repletion Signals." *International Journal of Obesity (London)* 33 (Supp. 2): S8–13.

CHAPTER 47

COST-EFFECTIVENESS OF ANTI-OBESITY INTERVENTIONS

LARISSA ROUX

Currently, the U.S. federal government allocates $6.5 trillion for education, health care, pensions, welfare, protection, and defense. Within health care, a staggering annual investment of $1.1 trillion is needed to keep pace with acute and chronic illness of every description, to promote the health of populations, and to sustain the research programs that will define the health of future generations (U.S. Health Care Budget 2010). In this world of finite resources and unsustainable growth of health care expenditures, how do we know where action is most urgently needed, and what action to prioritize?

By showing us a glimpse of the magnitude of some of our worst problems, *cost of illness* studies have given us a good start. For example, it is estimated that Americans spend $147 billion on the direct costs of overweight and obesity each year (Finkelstein et al. 2009). Obesity trends suggest that the rate of obesity across U.S. adults is leveling off; however, costs will remain astronomical unless effective obesity control polices continue to be implemented (Flegal et al. 2010). On the basis of data such as these, obesity is universally acknowledged as a problem that continues to need intensified action. But intensified action is also needed to confront other pressing issues in health, including cardiovascular disease, road traffic crashes, and diabetes (see table 47.1). With so many important health priorities and a myriad of possible solutions, choosing wisely and finding good value for investment is more important than ever.

Table 47.1. **Cost of Illness of Common Conditions and Cost Effectiveness of Associated Interventions**

Condition	Cost of illness	Intervention	Cost effectiveness
Cardiovascular Disease	$503 billion (*Heart Disease and Stroke Prevention: Adressing the Nation's Leading Killers* 2010)	Coronary heart disease risk reduction counseling	$74,000/QALY (Salkeld et al. 1997)
Road traffic crashes	$230 billion (*Motor Vehicle Safety* 2009)	Adding driver-side airbags	$24,000/QALY (Graham et al. 1997)
Diabetes	$174 billion (Economic costs of diabetes in the U.S. In 2007 2008)	Targeted screening for Type 2 diabetes	$34,000/QALY (Hoerger et al. 2004)
Obesity	$147 billion (Finkelstein et al. 2009)	Physical activity promotion	$14,000–$68,000/ QALY (Roux et al. 2008)

Cost of illness studies, which attach a dollar figure to the burden of illness, do not provide information about what conditions are treatable, what interventions work, or how much these interventions cost, and therefore cannot, on their own, inform decisions or prioritize action. To inform policy development, a more "rigorous evaluation of the impact of different options" is needed (Orszag 2007; Vanlare, Conway, and Sox 2010). This more rigorous approach, known as *comparative effectiveness research* (CER) has recently gained prominence in deliberations of health policy and health care reform, and with $1.1 billion allocated to CER from the 2009 American Recovery and Reinvestment Act stimulus package, it will likely play a pivotal role in U.S. health care in the years ahead (Iglehart 2009; Mushlin and Ghomrawi 2010).

Cost effectiveness analysis (CEA) is perhaps the most comprehensive and action-oriented form of CER. CEA provides a powerful tool for researchers to integrate the best cost and effectiveness data in a systematic determination of which interventions provide the best value for money (see figure 47.1). Equally importantly,

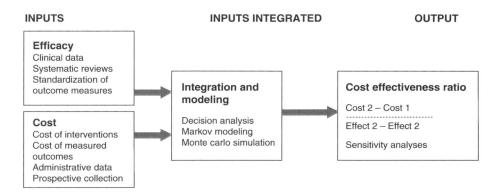

Figure 47.1. **Cost effectiveness Analysis as a Means of Integrating and Modeling Data.**

CEA methods identify gaps in our knowledge of both intervention costs and effectiveness, and highlight future priorities for policy-relevant research. This chapter highlights key methodologic features of CEA, explores its potential to inform policy and direct future research, and summarizes the current state of the CEA literature in obesity.

CEA provides a means to integrate and model the best available data in confronting issues of resource scarcity, incomplete knowledge about the efficacy and cost of interventions, and important competing priorities in health care. The comparative performance of alternate interventions is summarized by a cost effectiveness ratio, which is defined as the additional cost of a specific intervention divided by its additional clinical benefit, compared with a relevant alternative.

DESIGNING A COST EFFECTIVENESS ANALYSIS TO ADDRESS AN EPIDEMIC: THE CASE STUDY OF PHYSICAL ACTIVITY PROMOTION

Analyses that compare alternate courses of action in terms of costs and consequences are referred to in general as *economic evaluations* (EEs). All forms of EE seek to "identify, measure, value and compare" the costs and consequences of competing alternatives (Critical Assessment of Economic Evaluation 1997). Studies that compare competing interventions by relating their consequences and costs to a single common effect (for example, change in BMI or years of life saved) are referred to as *cost effectiveness analyses* (CEAs). The relationship between cost and consequence can be explored in various ways, particularly because consequences of interventions are often complex and far-reaching. *Cost benefit analyses* integrate and convert consequences into dollar figures, while *cost utility analyses* (CUAs) report and compare consequences in terms of their value or *utility* to individuals or society. CUAs refine CEAs by taking into account quality of life as an additional measured benefit. In the case of a CUA, the relative value of different health states is often measured by the *quality adjusted* life year (QALY), which simultaneously captures gains from reduced morbidity and reduced mortality and combines them into a single benefit measure (Weinstein 1977). Alternatives to the QALY include the disability-adjusted-life-year (DALY) (Murray 1994); however, the QALY has been most highly adopted in economic evaluations.

QALYs measure the effect of an intervention on both quality and length of life, and therefore more completely reflect the value of an intervention. The lower line represents the trajectory of quality of life with no intervention. The upper line represents improved quality of life in the presence of an intervention.

In many ways, obesity and the modern epidemics of chronic diseases, with their complex determinants, their significant and diverse downstream consequences, and their incompletely characterized interventions, are well suited to the systematic approaches of CEA. Successful obesity prevention, for example, will require broad and sustained investment in effective measures to address deeply entrenched behaviors, lifestyles, and socioeconomic conditions. CEAs have the potential to guide this investment, or at least to identify the deficits in our understanding of costs and consequences that must be addressed before critical decisions on resource allocation can be made.

CEAs begin by carefully *defining the research question* of interest and specifying the outcomes to be compared. For the obesity epidemic, a pressing issue has been whether community-based physical activity (PA) promotion efforts are effective enough in improving health to justify investment of scarce resources. In 2002, the Centers for Disease Control and Prevention and the Robert Wood Johnson Foundation assembled a team of health economists, epidemiologists, prevention gurus, physical activity researchers, and health policy experts (Project MOVE) to launch an economic evaluation of community-based PA promotion programs (Roux et al. 2008). From the outset, this was a large-scale project that aimed to use the highest-quality data available to define the value for money of established community-based PA promotion efforts. Once the question was defined, the group decided on a cost-utility analysis approach as its *research strategy*, and committed to measuring QALYs as a PA promotion outcome measure. Next, the group had to *specify the interventions* that were to be analyzed. Fortunately, an exhaustive review of PA promotion strategies had just been completed and published in the Guide to Community Preventive Services (Kahn et al. 2002). The most promising of these strategies

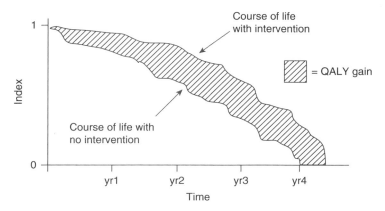

Figure 47.2. Measuring the Value of Health States for Cost Utility Analyses:
The Quality-Adjusted Life Year (Stephens 2001)
Note: QALYs measure the effect of an intervention on both quality and length of life, and therefore, more completely reflect the value of an intervention. The lower line represents the trajectory of quality of life with no intervention. The upper line represents improved quality of life in the presence of intervention.

provided the focus for Project MOVE. In the design phase of the study, prior to determining all of the inputs to be collected, it was imperative for the group to decide who the study results were intended to inform, or the *target audience,* and what *perspective* the analysis should take. Given that public health policy leaders and health departments would serve as the anticipated audience, the societal perspective, which considers all the costs and consequences regardless of who accrues them, was thought to be most appropriate. The study assumed that the interventions would be in place for one year (*time frame*), but that they would have long-term measurable health effects. Participants' lifetimes were therefore used as the baseline analytic *time horizon.* The group then set out to *define the costs and outcome measures* for these interventions and carefully compiled these from the published literature and from administrative and actuarial data. These included common lifetime outcomes related to physical inactivity such as coronary artery disease, type 2 diabetes, and various types of cancer. Attaching value, or utility, to each of these health states was a large undertaking and required the use of national survey data. Costs and effects of the evaluated Community Guide PA promotion interventions were *compared to the alternative* of no intervention, which was felt to be the status quo in most North American communities. Having addressed all of these steps allowed the base and sensitivity analyses to be performed and for the results to be interpreted. Table 47.2 presents the fundamental steps of setting up a CEA, using Project MOVE as an example.

These data, and this research framework are useful inputs for a *decision analysis* (DA). DA is a modeling technique that provides a systematic, explicit, and quantitative

Table 47.2. **Fundamental Steps of CEA, Using Project MOVE as an Example**

Steps in cost effectiveness analyses	Project MOVE example
Define the research question	Is physical activity promotion a worthwhile investment?
Select a research strategy	Cost-utility analysis
Select the interventions	Community Guide for Preventive Services recommendations
Consider the target audience	Health departments, policy leaders
Select the analytic perspective	Societal
Specify the intervention time frame	One year
Determine the analytic time horizon	10, 20, 30, and 40 years (lifetime)
Quantify the costs to be included	Direct medical and non-medical costs and opportunity costs of interventions Annualized disease-specific costs
Quantify the outcome measures	Intervention effect size and quality of life across PA levels PA level-specific relative risks for disease and disease incidence Disease-specific mortality and quality of life
Consider the comparator	No PA intervention (natural history)

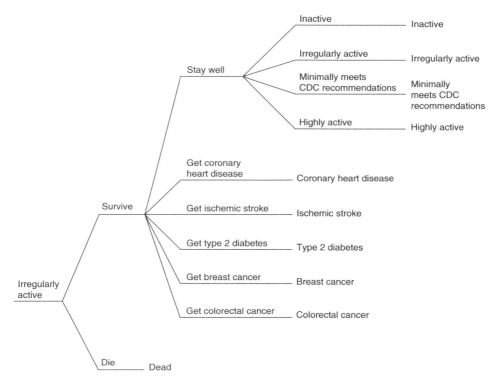

Figure 47.3. Some Branches Stemming from Any Given Intervention in the
Project MOVE Decision Tree.

framework for decision- making under uncertainty (Goldie 2003). Project MOVE
used a DA model structure to illustrate the competing interventions and to portray
the downstream probabilities of the various health consequences of implementation of these interventions (branches) across the modeled lifespan (see figure 47.3).
Assumptions made during the decision analysis can be tested in *sensitivity analyses*,
in which uncertain parameters of the model are varied across their plausible ranges
in multiple model runs. The more stable the results are through sensitivity analysis
testing, the more robust the results of the DA are thought to be.

   This study found that all of the evaluated physical activity interventions, applied
to the adult US population, offered good value for money. All interventions examined appeared to reduce disease incidence and improve quality of life at costs that
are comparable to many well-accepted public health strategies. Cost effectiveness
ratios ranged between $14,000 and $69,000 per QALY gained, relative to no intervention. Reductions in disease incidence ranged from 5 cases per 100,000 people
for colon cancer to nearly 500 cases per 100,000 people for coronary heart disease.
Estimated cost effectiveness was most influenced by intervention cost and effect
size. However, varying parameter estimates across a wide range in multiple
sensitivity analyses still resulted in cost effectiveness ratios below widely accepted
thresholds for public health value.

The findings of this analysis have several important implications for research and public health practice. First, the results from this study support using any of the evaluated interventions as part of public health efforts to promote physical activity. Second, this study helps to demonstrate that it is possible to carry out complex prevention modeling of community-based interventions using decision-modeling approaches that are often focused on clinical analyses. Third, the modeling approach used is a useful adjunct to the rigorous evidence-based review carried out by the task force of the Guide to Community Preventive Services to identify recommended interventions for the Community Guide. Last, applied in context with information on program reach, effectiveness, feasibility, and community priorities and resources, such a cost effectiveness analysis can also be a powerful decision-making tool for public health practitioners and advocates.

State of the Art: Cost Effectiveness Analyses in Obesity

Until recently, gaps in cost and effectiveness data in the obesity literature and great variability in study designs and end points posed significant methodological challenges for economic evaluations in obesity. However, the accumulation of increasingly higher-quality and more standardized cost and efficacy data and the use of more innovative and ambitious CEA designs have created new opportunities for economic evaluations in obesity and promise to inform innovative obesity policy in the years ahead.

Obesity Prevention

In a recent Cochrane Review of obesity-prevention strategies for children, Summerbell and colleagues assessed the effectiveness of interventions designed to prevent obesity in childhood through diet, physical activity, and/or lifestyle and social support. The majority of studies were short-term. Studies that focused on combining dietary and physical activity approaches did not significantly improve body mass index (BMI), but some studies that focused on dietary or physical activity approaches showed a small but positive impact on BMI status. Nearly all studies included resulted in some improvement in diet or physical activity. The review, which provided a comprehensive baseline of intervention effectiveness for future CEAs, noted that appropriateness of development, design, duration, and intensity of interventions to prevent obesity in childhood needed to be reconsidered alongside comprehensive reporting of the intervention scope and process (Summerbell et al. 2005). In another systematic review focusing on obesity prevention in children under five, Bond and colleagues found no controlled trials or cost effectiveness studies of obesity in children under five in the published literature between 1990 and 2009. The authors concluded that well-designed clinical trials of weight management schemes for preschool children with long-term follow-up and careful assessment of costs are urgently needed (Bond et al. 2009).

The cost effectiveness of Planet Health, a school-based intervention designed to reduce obesity in middle-school aged children in Massachusetts, was assessed. Using standard cost effectiveness methods and a societal perspective, a cost effectiveness ratio, or the ratio of net intervention costs to the total number of QALYs saved, was obtained. Under base-case assumptions, at an intervention cost of $33,677 or $14 per student per year, the program would prevent an estimated 1.9 percent of the female students from becoming overweight adults. These findings translated to a cost of $4,305 per QALY saved. The authors concluded that school-based prevention programs of this type were likely to be cost effective uses of public funds and warranted careful consideration by policy makers and program planners (Wang et al. 2003).

In Australia, Assessing Cost-Effectiveness (ACE) investigators used CEA methods in a thoughtful and systematic approach to informing policy directed at preventing unhealthy weight gain in Australian children and adolescents. Part of their analysis focused on modeling the impact of a school-based physical activity (PA) program, the Walking School Bus (WSB), on changes in BMI and subsequently on DALYs (Moodie, Haby, et al. 2009). The study found that the cost of the WSB program was $AUD 760,000 per DALY saved—an amount that was not considered to be highly cost-effective. Before making policy recommendations based on these findings, the ACE group subjected this cost-effectiveness estimate to a second stage of analysis, which considered factors such as strength of evidence, equity, feasibility, and sustainability to more fully assess the attractiveness of the program.

As part of the ACE project, Moodie and colleagues also assessed the cost effectiveness (from the societal perspective) of the Active After-School Communities (AASC) program, in Australia (Moodie, Carter, et al. 2009). The intervention was modeled for a one-year time frame for Australian primary school children. DALY benefits and cost-offsets (consequent savings from reductions in obesity-related diseases) were tracked until the cohort reached the age of 100 years or death. For one year, the intervention cost $AUD 40.3 million, and resulted in an incremental saving of 450 DALYs. The resultant cost-offsets were $AUD 3.7 million, producing a net cost-per-DALY saved of $AUD 82,000. Although the program had intuitive appeal, it was not cost-effective under base-case modeling assumptions. To improve its cost-effectiveness credentials as an obesity prevention measure, it was concluded that a reduction in costs needed to be coupled with increases in the number of participating children and the amount of physical activity undertaken.

Another innovative Australian study provided a glimpse into the potential for advertising legislation to impact societal health. Magnus and colleagues modeled the effects of a ban on television advertising of energy-dense, nutrient-poor foods (Magnus et al. 2009). The analysis considered changes in BMI and associated future health care costs. The study suggested that banning such advertising had an incremental cost-effectiveness ratio of $AUD 3.70 per DALY. Acknowledging limitations in available evidence, the authors concluded that "restricting TV food advertising to children would be one of the most cost-effective population-based interventions available to governments today."

Muller and colleagues summarized our knowledge of CEAs of physical activity promotion for healthy adults in a recent systematic review (Muller-Riemenschneider 2009). The review involved a comprehensive search of electronic databases and identified relevant literature published until June 2008. Out of 6,543 identified publications, 8 studies investigating 11 intervention strategies met the inclusion criteria. There was substantial heterogeneity in study quality, intervention strategies, and intervention effects. There was evidence that current physical activity intervention strategies can be a cost-effective means of resource allocation, but, despite the growing literature on physical activity promotion, appropriate cost-effectiveness analyses were rare and the generalizability of presented findings was limited.

Treatment of Obesity

Diet

Caloric restriction is central to most weight loss efforts. Few cost-effectiveness analyses have focused on evaluating the modest effects of diet alone. Tsai compared the cost-effectiveness of low-carbohydrate diets to standard diets for weight loss. The patient population included 129 severely obese subjects (average BMI = 42.9) from a randomized trial; participants had a high prevalence of diabetes or metabolic syndrome. Within-trial costs, QALYs, and the incremental cost-effectiveness ratio (CER) for the two study groups were compared. The low-carbohydrate diet was not found to be more cost-effective for weight loss than the standard diet in the patient population studied. This study, despite its negative result, generated an intriguing hypothesis and identified the need for more CEAs to better assess the cost-effectiveness of dietary therapies for weight loss (Tsai et al. 2005).

Physical Activity

Physical activity is a fundamental aspect of obesity control and is often integrated into more comprehensive interventions that include measures to transition to lifestyles that emphasize healthy eating and active living. A holistic approach that recognizes the complex determinants of obesity has intuitive appeal and has shown promise in early CEAs. For example, we conducted an evaluation of outpatient weight loss strategies in overweight and obese adult US women. Evaluated interventions included routine primary care and varying combinations of diet, physical activity, behavior modification, and/or pharmacotherapy. Efficacy data were obtained from clinical trials, population-based surveys, and other published literature, while information on costs and quality of life required primary collection. This study found that a three-component intervention of diet, physical activity, and behavior modification cost $12,600 per QALY gained, compared with routine care, and suggested that comprehensive care of obesity compared favorably with other established health care interventions. These results were found to be somewhat dependent on our measurement of obesity-related quality of life and the probabilities of weight-loss maintenance, which highlighted the need for accurate measurements of these phenomena in future studies (Roux et al. 2006).

Pharmacological Management of Obesity

The three most studied oral anti-obesity pharmacological agents to date, including orlistat (an agent that prevents fat absorption), sibutramine (a centrally acting appetite suppressant), and rimonabant (an oral anorectic), have all been found to be modestly effective at inducing weight loss and in reducing obesity-associated comorbidities. A number of economic evaluations of these agents have been conducted recently, mostly in Europe, and the findings from several of these studies are reviewed by Encinosa in chapter 45 of this volume.

In 2005, several important studies emerged. Hertzman conducted an incremental cost-effectiveness analysis using a Monte Carlo simulation model to determine the cost effectiveness of two one-year weight management programs, one based on the use of orlistat and diet modification in orlistat responders, and the other based on diet only, from the perspective of the Swedish health care system. Efficacy data were obtained from pooled clinical trials, intervention cost data were measured, and the incidence of type 2 diabetes was costed for each treatment arm. The therapeutic approach consisting of the combination of orlistat and dietary modification was found to be most cost effective, with an incremental cost-effectiveness ratio similar to many other well-accepted health care treatment options, at just over 13,000 Euros per QALY (Hertzman 2005). In this same year, the cost utility of orlistat treatment was further examined and subjected to criteria set by the National Institute for Clinical Excellence (NICE) and the European Agency for the Evaluation of Medicinal Products (EMEA) by Foxcroft. Data collected on nearly 1,400 obese individuals from three large European Phase III trials were included in the analysis. Using both sets of criteria, the cost utility of 24,400 pounds per QALY (NICE) and 19,000 pounds per QALY (EMEA) both supported the continued use of orlistat (Foxcroft 2005). In Sweden and Switzerland, as a means to rationalize reimbursement of orlistat in these countries, a study published by Ruof and colleagues used a Markov approach, an 11-year time horizon, and pooled data from seven clinical trials, to determine the cost effectiveness of orlistat in the treatment of overweight and obese type 2 diabetic patients. With resultant CEA ratios of 14,000 Euro/QALY and 16,000 Euro/QALY in Sweden and Switzerland, respectively, the findings supported the utilization and reimbursement of orlistat for those who responded to it in this population (Ruof et al. 2005).

Similar studies assessed the clinical and economic benefits of weight management with sibutramine. In 2006, in Germany, Brennan and colleagues published a study that compared the cost effectiveness of sibutramine in combination with diet and lifestyle advice to that of diet and lifestyle advice alone in otherwise well obese patients. Using clinical trial data on 1,000 patients treated with sibutramine for one year, the estimated cost utility of 13,700 Euros per QALY gained was well within the acceptable range for being cost effective (Brennan et al. 2006).

In 2008, a study conducted by Hampp examined the cost-effectiveness of a third drug available for weight loss in Europe, rimonabant. Using pooled data from three clinical trials and a third party payer's perspective, the incremental cost-utility for the use of rimonobant with lifestyle modification in various treatment scenarios was assessed. With incremental cost-effectiveness ratios of nearly $53,000 per QALY gained compared to no treatment, and almost $72,000 per QALY gained compared to placebo, rimonobant appeared to be somewhat effective, but at considerable cost (Hampp, Hartzema, and Kauf 2008). During this same year, a very important systematic review was published by Neovius and colleagues, which considered the cost-effectiveness of all 3 pharmacological anti-obesity agents; orlistat, sibutramine, and rimonabant. While published economic evaluations demonstrated that each treatment was within the range of what is thought to be cost-effective, many critical data gaps and methodologic limitations were highlighted, which are still challenges to date (Neovius and Narbro 2008). They concluded that uncertainties remain about weight loss sustainability, how best to extrapolate transient weight loss to long-term outcomes, and the utility gains associated with weight loss. Furthermore, they noted that most analyses were conducted by the pharmaceutical industries, that head-to-head comparisons of competing pharmacologic treatments for obesity were not available, and that very little is known about attrition from these studies. Such insights from a rapidly evolving body of literature and the research that stems from it are invaluable in making iterative quality improvements to cost-effectiveness models. As of 2009, it has been found that the benefits of rimonabant no longer outweigh its risks and its approval has been officially withdrawn (Wathion 2009). The cost-effectiveness of orlistat and sibutramine continue to be studied.

In the Netherlands, van Baal and colleagues in 2008 studied the incremental cost-effectiveness of a low-calorie diet with or without one year of orlistat therapy relative to a no intervention alternative. Change in BMI was used as the primary proximal endpoint. The diet-only intervention resulted in an incremental cost effectiveness ratio of 17,900 Euros per QALY gained relative to no intervention, while the diet and orlistat intervention cost an additional 58,800 Euros per QALY gained compared to diet alone, implying that diet alone is the most cost-effective (van Baal et al. 2008). The results were found to be most sensitive to BMI-associated quality of life estimates.

Surgery

Although diet, physical activity, behavior modification, and pharmacotherapy are considered first-line treatments for overweight and obesity, non-surgical therapy for severe obesity has shown limited success. Weight loss surgery (bariatric surgery) with adjunct non-surgical therapies generally results in greater weight loss than non-surgical treatments alone, and leads to improvements in quality of life and a reduction in obesity-related comorbidities. There are a number of surgical procedures available to treat severe obesity, each with advantages as well as risk and side effect profiles that need be carefully weighed. Bariatric surgery procedures are discussed in detail in chapter 45 by Encinosa in this volume.

A number of studies have shown that, in carefully selected subjects, surgery for the treatment of obesity is money well spent. This finding is persistent across a variety of study populations, operative techniques, and research methodologies.

In 2006, Ackroyd and colleagues estimated the cost-effectiveness of adjustable gastric banding (AGB) and gastric bypass (GBP) relative to conventional care, in obese patients (BMI $\geq$ 35 kg/m) with type 2 diabetes, in Germany, France, and the United Kingdom, from a payer's perspective. At five years, not only were both surgical procedures clinically effective, but they were cost saving in Germany and France, and cost effective in the United Kingdom, relative to conventional treatment (Ackroyd et al. 2006). This study was recently replicated by applying the same model, under similar conditions, to three more European countries, Austria, Italy, and Spain, by Anselmino and colleagues in 2009. Strikingly similar estimates of cost effectiveness were obtained. In Austria and Italy, both AGB and GBP were found to be cost saving at five years, and cost-effective in Spain, assuming a willingness-to-pay of 30,000 Euros per QALY gained. From a payer's perspective, in each country, these operations showed good value for money (Anselmino et al. 2009).

A 2006 study published by van Mastrigt and colleagues, examined the cost-effectiveness of vertical-banded gastroplasty and laparoscopic banding. At one year following surgery, the costs and quality of life associated with the two procedures were found to be equal. The authors concluded that the selection of surgical procedure could be based therefore on efficacy and safety considerations, rather than on cost-effectiveness (van Mastrigt et al. 2006).

In 2009, a systematic review carried out by Picot and colleagues considered the clinical and cost effectiveness of bariatric surgery. Although the studies they reviewed differed in methodological quality, bariatric (or metabolic) surgery was found to be both clinically effective and cost-effective compared to non-surgical therapy, in patients with severe obesity or moderate obesity with concomitant co-morbidities. Patient quality of life, late complications requiring reoperation, duration of co-morbidity remission, and impact of surgeon experience on outcome were identified as critical data gaps in need of further research (Picot et al. 2009).

CONCLUSIONS: GAPS, PRIORITIES, AND POLICY

CEA studies grapple with numerous methodological challenges. The creation of models that aim to completely describe the course of obesity and the effects of interventions immediately identifies critical data gaps. For instance, if an intervention is successful in reducing BMI, what is the likelihood that this reduction will be sustained over time? In the absence of good probability data, the ACE Obesity model and other models have assumed that BMI reductions were sustained. This assumption can be tested in sensitivity analyses, where imprecise estimates are varied to see what effect they have on the ultimate cost-effectiveness ratios. Greater attention must also be given to the value we attach to post-intervention health states, as these values are critical in determining the outcome of interventions. For example, can health state utilities be reliably assigned to BMI? Are these utilities even comparable across socioeconomic or geographic groups? These fundamental assumptions need further study in order to increase the credibility and generalizability of economic evaluations.

Although data gaps may influence the accuracy of our CEA estimates, they also point the way to research priorities—as data accumulate, CEAs will become more and more refined. This continuous evolution of CEAs in response to new data means that many CEAs may be out of date before they are published! It also means that CEAs are continuously getting better and perhaps more useful. As data accumulate, obesity models must balance considerations of completeness and parsimony: inclusion of more data may allow us to model reality more closely, but we run the risk of distorting our estimates if data quality is poor. Furthermore, as models increase in complexity, their efficacy and cost inputs are less likely to be understood by a single investigator. This means that these studies will become increasingly multidisciplinary, a phenomenon that, while adding sophistication, makes accurate modeling highly dependent on close cooperation and communication.

Cost-effectiveness research is at a critical moment in its history. As data gaps are filled and methodological challenges are addressed by increasingly sophisticated techniques and increasingly diverse research teams, the rigor and scope of CEAs will expand. This expansion comes at a time when increases in health budgets are becoming unsustainable. As we continue to make important strides in finding solutions to battle our global obesity epidemic, CEAs will help policy makers prioritize public health decisions in both high and low resource settings.

REFERENCES

Ackroyd, R., J. Mouiel, J. M. Chevallier, and F. Daoud. 2006. "Cost-effectiveness and Budget Impact of Obesity Surgery in Patients with Type-2 Diabetes in Three European Countries." *Obesity Surgery* 16 (11): 1488–1503.

Anselmino, M., T. Bammer, J. M. Fernandez Cebrian, F. Daoud, G. Romagnoli, and A. Torres. 2009. "Cost-effectiveness and Budget Impact of Obesity Surgery in Patients with Type 2 Diabetes in Three European countries (II)." *Obesity Surgery* 19 (11): 1542–1549.

Bond, M., K. Wyatt, J. Lloyd, K. Welch, and R. Taylor. 2009. "Systematic Review of the Effectiveness and Cost-Effectiveness of Weight Management Schemes for the Under Fives: A Short Report." *Health Technology Assessment* 13 (61): 1–75, iii.

Brennan, A., R. Ara, R. Sterz, B. Matiba, and R. Bergemann. 2006. "Assessment of Clinical and Economic Benefits of Weight Management with Sibutramine in General Practice in Germany." *European Journal of Health Economics* 7 (4): 276–284.

Centers for Disease Control and Prevention. 2009. "Motor Vehicle Safety." *from* http://www.cdc.gov/MotorVehicleSafety/index.html.

Centers for Disease Control and Prevention, National Center for Chronic Disease Prevention and Health Promotion. 2010. "Heart Disease and Stroke Prevention: Addressing the Nation's Leading Killers." from http://wwwtest.cdc.gov/chronicdisease/resources/publications/aag/pdf/2010/dhdsp.pdf.

Dall, T., Mann, S. E., Zhang, Y., Martin, J., Chen, Y. 2008. "Economic Costs of Diabetes in the U.S. in 2007." *Diabetes Care* 31(3): 596–615.

Drummond, M. F., M. J. Sculpher, G.W. Torrance, B.J. O'Brien, and G. L. Stoddart. 1997. *Methods for the Economic Evaluation of Health Care Programmes.* New York: Oxford Medical Publications.

Finkelstein, E. A., J. G. Trogdon, J. W. Cohen, and W. Dietz. 2009. "Annual Medical Spending Attributable to Obesity: Payer- and Service-Specific Estimates." *Health Affairs (Millwood)* 28 (5): w822–831.

Flegal, K. M., M. D. Carroll, C. L. Ogden, and L. R. Curtin. 2010. "Prevalence and Trends in Obesity among US Adults, 1999–2008." *Journal of the American Medical Association* 303 (3): 235–241.

Foxcroft, D. R. 2005. "Orlistat for the Treatment of Obesity: Cost Utility Model." *Obesity Review* 6 (4): 323–328.

Goldie, S. J., and P. S. Corso. 2003. "Decision Analysis." In *Prevention Effectiveness: A Guide to Decision Analysis and Economic Evaluation*, eds. A. C. Haddix, S. M. Teutsch, and P. S. Corso. New York: Oxford University Press.

Graham, J. D., K. M. Thompson, S. J. Goldie, M. Segui-Gomez, and M. C. Weinstein. 1997. "The Cost-Effectiveness of Air Bags by Seating Position." *Journal of the American Medical Association* 278 (17): 1418–1425.

Hampp, C., A. G. Hartzema, and T. L. Kauf. 2008. "Cost-utility Analysis of Rimonabant in the Treatment of Obesity." *Value Health* 11 (3): 389–399.

Hertzman, P. 2005. "The Cost Effectiveness of Orlistat in a 1-Year Weight-Management Programme for Treating Overweight and Obese Patients in Sweden: A Treatment Responder Approach." *Pharmacoeconomics* 23 (10): 1007–1020.

Hoerger, T. J., R. Harris, K. A. Hicks, K. Donahue, S. Sorensen, and M. Engelgau. 2004. "Screening for Type 2 Diabetes Mellitus: A Cost-Effectiveness Analysis." *Annals of Internal Medicine* 140 (9): 689–699.

Iglehart, J. K. 2009. "Prioritizing Comparative-Effectiveness Research—IOM Recommendations." *New England Journal of Medicine* 361 (4): 325–328.

Kahn, E. B., L. T. Ramsey, R. C. Brownson, G. W. Heath, E. H. Howze, K. E. Powell, E. J. Stone, M. W. Rajab, and P. Corso. 2002. "The Effectiveness of Interventions to Increase Physical Activity: A Systematic Review." *American Journal of Preventive Medicine* 22 (4 Supp.): 73–107.

Magnus, A., M. M. Haby, R. Carter, and B. Swinburn. 2009. "The Cost-Effectiveness of Removing Television Advertising of High-Fat and/or High-Sugar Food and Beverages to Australian Children." *International Journal of Obesity (London)* 33 (10): 1094–1102.

Moodie, M. L., R. C. Carter, B. A. Swinburn, and M. M. Haby. 2009. "The Cost-effectiveness of Australia's Active After-school Communities Program." *Obesity,* 18 (8): 1585–92.

Moodie, M., M. Haby, L. Galvin, B. Swinburn, and R. Carter. 2009. "Cost-effectiveness of Active Transport for Primary School Children: Walking School Bus Program." *International Journal of Behavioral Nutrition and Physical Activity* 6: 63.

Muller-Riemenschneider, F. 2009. "Cost-effectiveness of Interventions Promoting Physical Activity." *British Journal of Sports Medicine* 43 (1): 70–76.

Murray, C. J . L. 1994. "Quantifying the Burden of Disease: The Technical Basis for Disability-Adjusted Life Years." *Bulletin of the World Health Organization* 77: 429–445.

Mushlin, A. I., and H. Ghomrawi. 2010. "Health Care Reform and the Need for Comparative-Effectiveness Research." *New England Journal of Medicine* 362 (3): e6(1)–e6(3).

Neovius, M., and K. Narbro. 2008. "Cost-effectiveness of Pharmacological Anti-Obesity Treatments: A Systematic Review." *International Journal of Obesity*, 32 (12): 1752–1763.

Orszag, P. R. 2007. *Research on the Comparative Effectiveness of Medical Treatments*, Congress of the United States, Congressional Budget Office.

Picot, J., J. Jones, J. L. Colquitt, E. Gospodarevskaya, E. Loveman, L. Baxter, and A. J. Clegg. 2009. "The Clinical Effectiveness and Cost-Effectiveness of Bariatric (Weight Loss) Surgery for Obesity: A Systematic Review and Economic Evaluation." *Health Technology Assessment*, 13 (41): 1–190, 215–357, iii–iv.

Roux, L., K. M. Kuntz, C. Donaldson, and S. J. Goldie. 2006. "Economic Evaluation of Weight Loss Interventions in Overweight and Obese Women." *Obesity,* 14 (6): 1093–106.

Roux, L., M. Pratt, T. O. Tengs, M. M. Yore, T. L. Yanagawa, J. Van Den Bos, C. Rutt, R. C. Brownson, K. E. Powell, G. Heath, H. W. Kohl, III, S. Teutsch, J. Cawley, I. M. Lee, L. West, and D. M. Buchner. 2008. "Cost Effectiveness of Community-Based Physical Activity Interventions." *American Journal of Preventive Medicine,* 35 (6): 578–588.

Ruof, J., A. Golay, C. Berne, C. Collin, J. Lentz, and A. Maetzel. 2005. "Orlistat in Responding Obese Type 2 Diabetic Patients: Meta-Analysis Findings and Cost-Effectiveness as Rationales for Reimbursement in Sweden and Switzerland." *International Journal of Obesity,* 29 (5): 517–523.

Salkeld, G., P. Phongsavan, B. Oldenburg, M. Johannesson, P. Convery, P. Graham-Clarke, S. Walker, and J. Shaw. 1997. "The Cost-Effectiveness of a Cardiovascular Risk Reduction Program in General Practice." *Health Policy* 41 (2): 105–19.

Stephens, M. 2010. *Pharmacoeconomic Research: Getting the Biggest Bang for the Buck* [cited February 20 2010]. Available from http://www.ukmi.nhs.uk/Research/pharma_res.asp.

Summerbell, C. D., E. Waters, L. D. Edmunds, S. Kelly, T. Brown, and K. J. Campbell. 2005. "Interventions for Preventing Obesity in Children." *Cochrane Database of Systematic Reviews* (3): CD001871.

Tsai, A. G., H. A. Glick, D. Shera, L. Stern, and F. F. Samaha. 2005. "Cost-effectiveness of a Low-Carbohydrate Diet and a Standard Diet in Severe Obesity." *Obesity Research* 13 (10): 1834–40.

"U.S. Health Care Budget." 2010. Available at: http://www.usgovernmentspending.com/health_care_budget_2010_1.html Accessed June 3, 2010.

van Baal, P. H., M. van den Berg, R. T. Hoogenveen, S. M. Vijgen, and P. M. Engelfriet. 2008. "Cost-effectiveness of a Low-Calorie Diet and Orlistat for Obese Persons: Modeling Long-Term Health Gains Through Prevention of Obesity-Related Chronic Diseases." *Value in Health* 11 (7): 1033–1040.

van Mastrigt, G. A., F. M. van Dielen, J. L. Severens, G. B. Voss, and J. W. Greve. 2006. "One-year Cost-Effectiveness of Surgical Treatment of Morbid Obesity: Vertical Banded Gastroplasty versus Lap-Band." *Obesity Surgery* 16 (1): 75–84.

Vanlare, J. M., P. H. Conway, and H. C. Sox. 2010. "Five Next Steps for a New National Program for Comparative-Effectiveness Research." *New England Journal of Medicine.* Vol. 362, 11, 2010, p. 970.

Wang, L. Y., Q. Yang, R. Lowry, and H. Wechsler. 2003. "Economic Analysis of a School-based Obesity Prevention Program." *Obesity Research* 11(11): 1313–1324.

Wathion, N. 2009. *Public Statement on Rimonabant: Withdrawal of the Marketing Authorisation in the European Union.* London: European Medicines Agency.

Weinstein, M. C. and W. B. Stason. 1977. "Foundations of Cost-Effectiveness Analysis for Health and Medical Practice." *New England Journal of Medicine* 296: 716–721.

Cited Authors Index

Index Note: Institutional authors are listed in the subject index.

SUBJECT INDEX

"5-a-day" campaign, 596
2004 National Worksite Health Promotion Survey, 688

AAP (American Academy of Pediatrics), 351
absenteeism, 127, 128, 543–545, 685, 686, 696–697
abuse, domestic, 90, 180, 270
academic scores, 127–128
ACCRA (American Chamber of Commerce Researchers Association), 467, 468–470, 645
Acomplia® (rimonabant), 803, 841, 842
Active Living Research Program, 435, 762
activity, physical. *See* physical activity
Add Health (National Longitudinal Survey of Adolescent Health), 15, 39, 308–310, 333, 525, 539
advertising. *See* community interventions; food advertising
African Americans
  behavioral treatment outcomes, 784–786
  children and youth, 263, 268–269
  depression among, 336–337, 341–342
  employment, 535, 546, 555
  historical changes in BMI, 50–51, 54–56
  medical costs, lifetime, 497, 498
  mothers, 178, 270
  overeating as coping strategy, 264, 270
  physical activity barriers, 270
  psychosocial stress, 283, 342
  rates of obesity, 17, 40–41, 259, 261–262
  residential patterns, 110
  self-perception, 265–266, 268, 336–337, 785
  sleep deprivation, 265
  television targeted to, 268
  weight as protection, 270
  welfare reform and, 546–547
  women, 17, 40, 44
  See also race and ethnicity
age. *See* age cohorts; children and youth; demography; senior citizens
age cohorts
  adolescent, 198–199
  birth, 38, 196–197, 525
  child, 199
  life course analysis in, 111–112
  mature, 199–200
  senior citizens, 197, 509

Agency for Healthcare Research and Quality (AHRQ), 798, 799
age-period-cohort analyses, 44
agricultural policy
  acreage controls, 483–484
  childhood obesity and, 480–481, 483
  commodity promotion, 487–489, 615
  farmland subsidies, 482–483
  fast food chains and, 488
  Federal Farm Promotion programs, 487–488
  food assistance programs and, 485–487
  food prices and, 482, 483
  high-fructose corn syrup, 484–485
  loan deficiency payments, 482
  price supports, 481
  production subsidies, 481–482
  public policy goals, 489–490
  rates of obesity, effect on, 250
  tariffs on imports, 484–485
  See also food prices; politics; public policy
AHEAD (Study of Assets and Health Dynamics Among the Oldest Old), 197
AHG (Alliance for a Healthier Generation), 633
AHRQ (Agency for Healthcare Research and Quality), 798–799
AICR (American Institute of Cancer Research), 297
alcohol use, 307, 757, 758, 761–762
Alliance for a Healthier Generation (AHG), 633
AMA (American Medical Association), 484–485
American Academy of Pediatrics (AAP), 351
American Beverage Association, 634
American Chamber of Commerce Researchers Association (ACCRA), 467, 468–470, 645
American Heart Association, 760
American Indians, 69, 589, 672, 722
American Institute of Cancer Research (AICR), 297, 377
American Medical Association (AMA), 484–485
American Time Use Survey (ATUS), 188, 192
Americans for Nonsmoker's Rights Foundatoin, 625
amphetamines. *See* drugs, anti-obesity
Analysis Grind for Environments Linked to Obesity (ANGELO), 717
ANGELO (Analysis Grind for Environments Linked to Obesity), 717
animal foods. *See* meat consumption